D1452186

INTERNATIONAL LAW FOR THE ENVIRONMENT

■ ■ ■

Edith Brown Weiss
Francis Cabell Brown Professor of International Law
Georgetown Law, Georgetown University

Daniel Barstow Magraw
Professional Lecturer and Senior Fellow
Foreign Policy Institute, School of Advanced International Studies,
Johns Hopkins University

Stephen C. McCaffrey
Distinguished Professor of Law
University of the Pacific, McGeorge School of Law

Stephanie Tai
Associate Professor
University of Wisconsin Law School

A. Dan Tarlock
Distinguished Professor of Law
IIT Chicago-Kent College of Law

AMERICAN CASEBOOK SERIES®

American Casebook Series is a trademark registered in the U.S. Patent and Trademark Office.

© 2016 LEG, Inc. d/b/a West Academic
    444 Cedar Street, Suite 700
    St. Paul, MN 55101
    1-877-888-1330

West, West Academic Publishing, and West Academic are trademarks of West Publishing Corporation, used under license.

Printed in the United States of America

ISBN: 978-0-314-28827-1

To our students, past, present and future, and to all dedicated stewards, past, present and future, of our fragile planetary home

PREFACE

We live on a vulnerable and fragile planet. Our actions now have profound effects on our environment, locally, nationally, and internationally. They affect the integrity and resilience of our environment and of human society. At the same time, several billion people still live on less than a few dollars per day. International environmental law offers a critical path to protect the environment and at the same to promote environmental justice.

This course book is designed to introduce students to the growing body of international environmental law and to enable them to use it effectively, whether as lawyers for specific clients or as policy-makers. The book is designed both to provide an overview and to communicate the nuances of specific problems. Ultimately it should prepare students to be able to identify international environmental problems, to analyze their legal dimensions and to assist in devising and implementing effective solutions.

International environmental law first emerged as a discrete field of law after the 1972 United Nations Conference on the Human Environment held in Stockholm, Sweden. At that time, environmental law had only recently emerged as a new field of domestic public law in North America and Europe as well as in a few other industrialized countries. The United States, for example, passed its National Environmental Policy Act only in 1969, and the U.S. Environmental Protection Agency was established in 1970.

Both domestic and international environmental law have faced common problems such as the need to quickly mitigate the public health and ecosystem impacts of the over-use of air, water and soil as waste sinks and the stresses on ecosystems from the exploitation of natural resources. Both legal systems have had to deal with the realization that identifying and mitigating these adverse public health and other impacts requires regulating in the face of uncertainty, the modification of long-established and fiercely defended behaviors, and ultimately the development of a new philosophical and legal balance between conserving natural systems, ensuring use of them for human economic and social development, and promoting environmental justice

Since 1972, well over 1000 international environmental legal instruments have been negotiated at the global, regional and bilateral levels. These deal with an enormous variety of environmental problems, including: transboundary air and water pollution, notification and assistance in the case of natural and human-made environmental disasters, such as from nuclear or chemical accidents; loss of biological diversity, including interference with bird and animal migration patterns; protection of world natural and cultural heritages; allocation of international rivers and lakes and of ground water; contamination of food by hazardous chemicals; control of marine pollution; depletion of the stratospheric ozone layer; and climate change. These problems and their solutions are often inter-related. In addition, important principles and rules of international law have developed regarding environmental protection.

At the national level, since 1972 States and sub-national governmental bodies have greatly developed environmental law. Virtually all countries, including developing countries, have enacted environmental laws. These laws deal with a wide array of environmental threats, including some that are not addressed at the international level such as noise pollution.

The link between international environmental law and domestic environmental law is essential. The sharp distinctions between international and domestic law and between public and private international law have become blurred, as evidenced by national environmental laws that seek to address transboundary problems or private sector transnational standards that address international environmental problems. The course book recognizes these trends. It focuses on the links between international and domestic law by asking how specific agreements are implemented domestically and by identifying how developments in domestic environmental law influence the development of international environmental law and vice versa.

In studying international environmental law, it is important to note that while States are central actors, many other actors are important: intergovernmental organizations, nongovernmental organizations, business organizations, communities and ad hoc coalitions, and individuals. The public has an essential interest in the environment, including the international environment. The roles of these other actors are considered in the coursebook, including in the context of the overall governance of international environmental institutions.

International environmental law has features distinct from domestic environmental law. States make international agreements. There is no overarching sovereign authority at the international level to make, adjudicate and enforce laws in the same sense that there is at the domestic level. International environmental law consists not only of binding agreements, customary rules, and general principles, but also increasingly of non-binding or "soft law", and even of voluntary commitments. There is a relative paucity of authoritative judicial interpretations of these rules. We have endeavored to present the existing international "precedents," including those of the International Court of Justice, but we have equally stressed the increasing incorporation of customary and treaty law into national judicial decisions and legislation and the use by national courts of general principles of international environmental law to decide domestic cases.

On the institutional level, international environmental law also has some distinct features. There are a variety of international institutions concerned either fully or in part with international environmental law. Moreover, international agreements are often accompanied by the establishment of secretariats and the holding of regular meetings of State Parties, through which States address treaty issues, implementation, and compliance. The resulting treaty regime functions as a mini international institution. Chapters 18 and 19 provide a basic but comprehensive overview of the international legal system and relevant international institutions. These chapters should be especially useful for students who have not studied international law.

In other ways, international and domestic environmental laws and institutions are similar. The development of the field of environmental law (like human rights) historically has been strongly influenced by the involvement of civil society, including both individuals and non-governmental organizations. This continues to be the case, at all levels (global, regional, national and sub-national). Environmental protection also is profoundly influenced by the activities and external and internal policies of business enterprises of many types (e.g., agricultural, industrial, and pharmaceutical), including transnational ones. The involvement of non-State actors such as these affects the identification of international environmental problems, policy- and law-making regarding such problems, implementation of and compliance with international environmental law, and the settlement of disputes involving it.

The subject of environmental law is context-rich. The legal regimes are informed by natural sciences, social sciences and basic philosophical principles, and they have a distinct political history. We have tried to strike a balance between overburdening students with too much detail and providing enough background to understand the law. This field is also unusual in the degree to which it must constantly evolve to deal with uncertainty, with changes in scientific understanding, and with new factual circumstances. The theme of risk assessment and risk management runs throughout the book.

Certainly, international environmental laws, like domestic environmental laws, are often inadequate and not sufficiently complied with or enforced, although they are followed better than often alleged. International environmental law, like domestic environmental law, and indeed all laws, depends on a country's political will and its capacity, one or both of which may be lacking. At the same time, stresses on the environment are increasing due, for example, to: increasing demands for water, consumer goods and living space from the world's growing population; unsustainable use of resources such as groundwater; expanding and changing agricultural and industrial production; and new activities with potential environmental risks, such as nanotechnology and the genetic engineering of plants designed to grow in saltier or drier conditions. It is not surprising, therefore, that most environmental indicators—including those relating to air and water pollution, loss of biological diversity, presence of hazardous chemicals, and climate change—are worsening at the global scale. The rule of law in the field of the environment, or what UNEP has designated as environmental rule of law, whether nationally or internationally, is thus profoundly important and unusually rich and complicated. This book is intended to enable students to address the many legal issues involved in it.

The book is divided into four parts. The first consists of Chapters 1–6 and deals with basic concepts in the field of international environmental law. Chapters 1–3 introduce the students to the environmental threats facing our fragile planet in the Anthropocene Epoch, the philosophical framework that we use to address these problems, and the difficulties of making rational, scientifically robust and economically responsible decisions. Chapters 4–5 address the basic principles of international environmental law and place in context the problems of implementing, monitoring, and complying with international agreements (Chapters 18 and 19 in part IV discuss basic aspects of the international legal system as it pertains to environmental protection, including governance issues). Chapter 6 covers environmental disasters and emergencies.

The second part of the book treats specific environmental problems. Chapters 7–13 examine the various post-Stockholm Conference media- or source-specific legal regimes. Chapter 7 sets forth the agreements that govern regional transboundary air and water pollution; Chapter 8 examines the agreements on the control of stratospheric ozone depletion. Chapter 9 tackles the "great white whale" of global climate change (or "disruption" as some prefer). Chapter 10 covers the efforts to manage the risks associated with hazardous substances and wastes, including their movement across national borders. Chapter 11 is an introduction to the protection of marine and polar environments, and Chapter 12 chronicles important treaty and judicial developments in the use of fresh waters and the protection of aquatic ecosystems. Chapter 13 continues this theme with a comprehensive examination of the international agreements that focus on the conservation of biological diversity. The final chapter in Part II, Chapter 14, considers how food and agriculture impact and are impacted by efforts to protect the environment. While this relationship has been significant for the past 10,000 years, it will become even more so with the need to feed an additional two billion people in coming decades.

The third part of the book, Chapters 15–17, examines the integration of environmental considerations into other areas of international law and the influence of those areas on the development of international environmental law. Chapter 15 details the remarkable integration of environmental law and human rights law. Chapter16 analyzes the thus-far less successful interaction of environmental law with international trade law, and Chapter 17 addresses the critical issue of financing for sustainable development.

The fourth and final part of the book consists of two chapters that underlie the whole field. Chapter 18 deals with the institutions that international environmental law has spawned, as well as with the important governance issues associated with international environmental protection. Chapter 19 provides an overview of the international legal system, including dispute settlement. Both may be used as supplements to analysis in earlier parts of the course book, and the materials on governance as a stand-alone segment.

This book tries to cover the international environmental issues that are likely to define much of the international landscape in coming decades. It features a strong focus on implementation of and compliance with international environmental law through national laws and policies and other actions. It contains practice problems and exercises so that students can think about how these international legal questions play out in actual practice.

We welcome you to the fascinating, intriguingly complex, and challenging area of international environmental law. We hope that we have struck the right balance between our deep collective commitment to, and passion for, this field of law, which is vital to the future of our species and our planet, on the one hand, and asking the hard questions that must be addressed if the field is to maintain its legitimacy and increase its effectiveness, on the other. We look forward to learning with you in the years to come.

EDITH BROWN WEISS
DANIEL MAGRAW
STEPHEN C. MCCAFFREY
STEPHANIE TAI
A. DAN TARLOCK

August, 2015

ACKNOWLEDGMENTS

Many people have been involved in the preparation of these materials over many years. It is virtually impossible for us to thank properly all of those who have contributed in one way or another. We do wish to extend special thanks to the following:

Professor Brown-Weiss thanks research assistants Maria Choi, Brian Greenert, Sturti Kokalena, Lydia Siobodian, Kiran Sahdov, and Satoko Sawada; Professor Weiss also thanks Betsy Kuhn, her faculty assistant, as do all the authors; Professor Mcgraw thanks research assistant Andrea Martinez; Professor Tai thanks research assistants James Bonar-Bridges and Samantha Wagner; and Professor Tarlock thanks research assistant Greg Sussman and Nicole Lechuga, his Faculty Assistant.

We also gratefully acknowledge the permission granted by the authors, publishers, and organizations to reprint portions of the following copyrighted materials:

Adede, Andronico O., Overview of Legal & Technical Aspects of Nuclear Accident Pollution, International Law & Pollution (D. Magraw, ed.) (1991), 129–132, 136–138. Reprinted with permission of the University of Pennsylvania Press.

Bernasconi-Osterwalder, Nathalie, Daniel Magraw, Maria Julia Oliva, Marcos Orellana & Elisabeth Tuerk, Environment and Trade: A Guide to WTO Jurisprudence, pp. 206–207, (2006). Reprinted by permission.

Bilder, Richard, Controlling Great Lakes Pollution: A Study in United States–Canadian Environmental Protection, 70 Michigan Law Review, pp. 473–475 (1972), Reprinted by Permission.

Benedick, Richard, Ozone Diplomacy Chapter 2 excerpts (1991), Reprinted with Permission Harvard University Press.

Bernasconi-Osterwalder, Nathalie and Daniel Magraw, Maria Julia Oliva, Marcos Orellana & Elisabeth Tuerk, Environment and Trade: A Guide to WTO Jurisprudence, pp. 206–207 (2006). Reprinted by permission.

Birnie, Patricia and Alan Boyle, International Law and the Environment (pp. 136–137, 160–163, 303–304) (2009) (3rd ed 2009). Reprinted with permission of Oxford University Press.

Boyd, David R, The Environmental Rights Revolution: A Global Study of Constitutions, Human Rights, and the Environment 8–9, 47, 4–56, 52–53, 66–68, 290–291 (2010), Reprinted with permission of the

Publisher from The Environmental Rights Revolution by David Boyd©
University of British Columbia Press 2011. All rights reserved.

Breidenich, Clare, Daniel Magraw, Anne Rowley, and James Rubin,
Current Development: The Kyoto Protocol to the United Nations
Framework Convention on Climate Change, 92 American Journal of
International Law 317 (1998). © The American Society of International
Law. Reprinted with permission.

Brown Weiss, Edith and M.P.A. Kindall. Emissions Trading and
Climate Change (mimeo 1992). Reprinted with the permission of the
authors.

Brown Weiss, Edith, Environmental Disasters in International Law,
Anuario Juridico Interamerican, 1986, 141. Reprinted with permission of
the Organization of American States.

Brown Weiss, Edith, The Changing Structure of International Law,
Georgetown University Law Center, May 23, 1996, reprinted in
Georgetown Law—Res Ipsa Loquitur 52 (Spring 1997). Reprinted with
permission of the author.

Brown Weiss, Edith, In Fairness to Future Generations:
International Law, Common Patrimony and Intergenerational Equity,
204–205, 219–223 (1989). Reprinted by the permission of Transnational
and United Nations University Press.

Brown Weiss, Edith, Strengthening National Compliance with
International Environmental Agreements, Environmental Policy and
Law, vol. 27, No. 4 (1997), p. 297. This article first appeared in
Environmental Policy and Law, vol. 27, No. 4 (1997), at p. 297. Reprinted
with permission of IOS Press.

Brown Weiss, Edith and Charles Weiss, Jr., Transnational Norms of
Environmental Behavior and the Spread of the Industrial Ecology Ethic
(1997). Reprinted with the permission of the authors.

Brown Weiss, Edith, The Planetary Trust Conservation and
Intergenerational Equity, 11 Ecology Law Quarterly 495 (1984).
Reprinted by permission of author

Brown Weiss, Edith, Rule of Law for Nature in a Kaleidoscopic
World, adapted from Rule of Law for Nature: New Dimensions and Ideas
in Environmental Law, Christina Voight ed. (2013), reprinted with by
permission of author.

Brown Weiss, Edith, Voluntary Commitments as Emerging
Instruments in International Environmental Law, 44 Environmental Law
& Policy pp 205–207 (2014). Reprinted with permission of IOS Press.

Brown Weiss, Edith, The Five International Treaties: A Living
History, Chapter 2 in Engaging Countries Strengthening Compliance

with International Environmental Accords (Edith Brown Weiss & Harold K. Jacobson eds., MIT Press, 1998)

Caldwell, Lynton, International Environmental Policy (first edition). © 1984 Duke University Press. Reprinted by permission.

Charney, Jonathan I., Third State Remedies for Environmental Damage to the World's Common Spaces, International Responsibility for Environmental Harm 149, 175–177 (Francesco Francioni & Tullio Scovazzi eds., 1991). Reprinted by permission.

Climate Changes Sciences: An Analysis of Some Key Questions, pp. 1–5 (2001). Reprinted with Permission from The Missouri River Ecosystem Recovery © 2002 by the National Academy of Sciences, Courtesy of the National Academies Press, Washington D.C.

Colborn, Theo, Dianne Dumanoski, and John Peterson Myers, To the Ends of the Earth from Our Stolen Future 91–104 (1996). Copyright © 1996 by Theo Colborn, Dianne Dumanoski, Dr. John Peterson Myers. Used by permission of Dutton, a division of Penguin Putnam, Inc.

Committee on Science, Engineering and Public Policy, National Academy of Sciences, National Academy of Engineering, Institute of Medicine, Policy Implications of Greenhouse Warming. Reprinted with permission. Copyright © 1991 by the National Academy of Sciences. Courtesy of the National Academy Press, Washington, D.C.

Conservation International, The Debt for Nature Exchange: A Tool for International Conservation, pp. 11, 17–19, 23–30, 37–40 (September 1989). Reprinted by permission.

Cross, Frank, Valves Attributable to Natural Resources, 42 Vanderbilt Law Revie, pp. 269–341 (1989), reprinted with permission Vanderbilt Law Review.

Anthony D'Amato & Sudhir K Chopra, Whales: Their Emerging Right to Life, 85 American Journal of International Law 21 (1991). Reproduced by permission. © The American Society of International Law.

D'Arge, Ralph and Kneese, Alan, State Liability for International Environmental Degradation, 20 Natural Resources Journal 427 (1990), Reprinted with permission.

Desai, BH; Oli, KP; Yang Yangping; Chettri, N; Sharma, E, Implementation of the Convention on Biological Diversity: A Retrospective analysis in the Hindu Kush-Himalayan countries. (Kathmandu: ICIMOD 2011). Reprinted by permission.

Easterbrook, Gregg, A Moment on Earth, 1995. Used by permission of Viking Penguin, a division of Penguin Putnam Inc.

Enders, Alice & Porqes, Amerlia, Why an International Agreement on the Ozone Layer Was Possible, The Greening of World Trade (K. Anderson & R. Blackhurst eds. 1991), Reprinted by permission.

Farber, Daniel, Uncertainty, 99 Georgetown Law Journal, pp 907–909, 914–915 (2015). Reprinted by permission of the author.

Federeci, Valery, Genetically Modified Food and Informed Consumer Choice: Comparing U.S. and E.U. Labeling Laws, 35 Brooklyn Journal International Law, 533–535, 337–38, 340–41, 341–46, (2010), Reprinted with permission.

Final Report of the World Commission on Dams, Dams and Development: A New Framework for Decision-Making, pp. 45–48 & 206 (2000). Reprinted with the Permission of the United Nations Environment Programme.

Foley, Jonathan A, Can We Feed the World and Sustain the Planet, Scientific American 62–63 (November 2011). Reprinted with permission.

Frosch, Robert A., Adapting Technology for a Sustainable Worlds, 37 Environment 16 (1995). Reprinted by permission of Heldref Publications.

Fuller, Kathryn S., & Williamson, Douglas F., Debt-for-Nature Swaps, A New Means of Funding Conservation in Developing Nations. Reprinted with permission from the International Environment Reporter, Vol. 11, No. 5, pp. 301, 302–303 (May 11, 1988). © by the Bureau of National Affairs, Inc.

Gaines, Sanford, Taking Responsibility for Transboundary Environmental Effects, Hastings International & Comparative Law Review Vol. 14 No. 4, pp. 801, 802–807, (1991). © 1991 by University of California, Hastings College of the Law. Reprinted with permission from Hastings Comparative Law Review Vol. 14, No. 4, pp. 801, 802–807.

Gleick, James, Chaos: Making a New Science. © 1987. Reprinted by permission of James Gleick.

Gonzalez, Carmen, The Global Food System and Human Rights, 26 Natural Resources and Environment, pp. 7–8 (2012). © 2012. Published in Natural Resources & Environment, Winter 2012, by the American Bar Association. Reproduced with permission. All rights reserved. This information or any portion thereof may not be copied or disseminated in any form or by any means or stored in an electronic database or retrieval system without the express written consent of the American Bar Association or the copyright holder.

Handl, Gunther, Internationalization of Hazard Management in Recipient Countries: Accident Preparedness and Response in Transferring Hazardous Technologies and Substances: The International

Legal Challenge, 106–107, 111–117 (G. Handl and R. Lutz eds. 1999), Reprinted by permission.

Handl, Giinther, Human Rights and Protection of the Environment: A Mildly "Revisionist" View, Human Rights, Sustainable Development and the Environment 117, pp. 120–122 (A. Cancado Trinidade ed., 1992). Reprinted by permission.

Hardin, Garrett, The Tragedy of the Commons, 162 Science 1243, pp 1244–1245 (1968), Reprinted by permission.

Heppes, John B. and Eric J. McFadden, The Convention on International Trade in Endangered Species of Wild Flora and Fauna: Improving the Prospects for Preserving our Biological Heritage, 5 Boston University International Law Journal 229 (1987). Reprinted by permission.

Institute of Medicine, Environmental Decisions in the Face of Uncertainty, pp 3–5, 82–83, Reprinted with permission National Academies Press.

Ives, Mike, In Developing World, A Push to Bring E-Waste Out of Shadows, Yale Environment 360 (2014).

Joyner, Christopher C., The Legal Regime for the Arctic Ocean, pp. 202–204 (2009). Reprinted by permission.

Karl, Thomas R. and Kevin E Trenberg, Modern Global Climate Change, 302 Science, 1721–1722 (2003). Reprinted with permission.

Keane, David, The Environmental Causes and Consequences of Migration: A Search for Meaning or "Environmental Refugees," 16 Georgetown International Environmental Law Review 209, pp. 210–219 (2004). Reprinted by permission.

Kessler, Rebecca, The Minamata Convention on Mercury: A First Step Toward Protecting Future Generations, 121 Environmental Health Perspectives A306–08 (Oct. 2013).

Klitgard, Robert, Tropical Gangsters, 8–12, 207 (1991). © 1990 by Basic Books, Inc. Reprinted by Permission of Basic Books, a subsidiary of Persens Books Group, LLC.

Kneese, Allen V., Economics and the Environment: A Materials Balance Approach, (1970). Reprinted with the Permission of Resources for the Future.

Kummer, Katharina, International Management of Hazardous Wastes (1995). Reprinted by permission of Oxford University Press.

Lallas, Peter and Steve Wolfson, International Cooperation to Address Risks from Pesticides and Hazardous Chemicals (mimeo 1997). Reprinted with the permission of the authors.

Lallas, Peter, and Andreas Ziegler, International Economics, Trade and the Environment, in International Occupational and Environmental Medicine (Jessica Herzstein et al., eds., Mosby, 1988). Reprinted with the permission of the authors.

Lammers, Johan, The European Approach to Acid Rain, International Law & Practice, pp. 265, 267–282 (Daniel McGraw ed. 1991), Reprinted with permission.

Lyster, Simon, International Wildlife Law: An Analysis of International Treaties concerned with the Conservation of Wildlife, 1985. © Grotius Publications Ltd 1985. Reprinted with permission from Cambridge University Press.

Magraw, Daniel B., The Bhopal Disaster: Structuring a Solution, 57 University of Colorado Law Review 835, 815, 838, 840–847 (1986). Reprinted with permission of University of Colorado Law Review, Inc.

Magraw, Daniel B., International Law and Park Protection: A Global Responsibility from Our Common Lands, David J. Simon, ed. (1988). © 1988 National Parks and Conservation Association. Reproduced by permission of Island Press, Washington, D.C.

Magraw, Daniel B. NAFTA and the Environment—Substance and Process, Section of International Law and Practice, American Bar Association (1995). Reprinted by permission from the American Bar Association © 1995.

Magraw, Daniel Barstow, Environmental Protection and Role of Law, 44 Environmental Policy & Law 205–207 (2014), Reprinted by permission of author.

Magraw, Daniel, Defending the National Parks, in Our Common Lands (David J. Simonad 1983), reprinted by permission of author.

Magraw, Daniel, NAFTA and the Environment: Substance and Process, pp. 12–19 (1995), reprinted by permission of author.

Mare Nostrum Project: Bridging the Legal Institutional Gap in Mediterranean Coastline Management, Reprinted with permission.

Matthews, Jessica Tuchman, Redefining Security, 68 For. Aff. 162 (1989). © 1989 by the Council on Foreign Relations, Inc. Reprinted by permission of Foreign Affairs.

McCaffrey, Stephen, Crimes Against the Environment, 1 International Criminal Law 541, 541–561 (M. Cherif Bassoiuni, ed.) (1986). Reprinted with permission of Transnational Publishers, Inc.

McCaffrey, Stephen, The Human Right to Water, in Edith Brown Weiss et al., eds., Fresh Water and International Economic Law, 93, 109–11, (2005). Oxford University Press. Reprinted by permission.

McCaffrey, Stephen, Water, Politics, and International Law, Water in Crisis, p. 96 (Peter Gleick ed. 1993), Reprinted by permission.

Millennium Ecosystem Assessment, Living Beyond Our Means: Natural Assets and Human Well-Being pp. 5–6. (2005) Reprinted with the permission of the World Resources Institute.

Nanda, Ved & Bailey, Bruce, Nature and Scope of Problem, Transferring Hazardous Waste Technologies and Substances, pp. 3–7, 7–11, 16–19 (G. Hamal & R. Lutz eds 1989), reprinted with permission.

Narula, The Global Land Rush: Markets, Rights, and the Politics of Food, 49 Standford Journal International Law, 101–16, 117–19, 120–24, 126–32 (2013), Reprinted by permission.

Nash, Jennifer and John Ehrenfeld, Code Green, 8 Environment 16 (1996). Reprinted by permission of Heldref Publications.

National Research Council, The Impact of Genetically Engineered Crops on Farm Sustainability in the United States (2010). Reprinted with permission from the National Academies Press.

National Research Council, The Missouri River Ecosystem Recovery, pp. 107–110 (2002). Reprinted with Permission from The National Academies Press.

Norton, Bryan, Environmental Ethics and the Rights of Future Generations, 4 Environmental Ethics 322 (1982). Reprinted with permission of Bryan Norton and Environmental Ethics, Department of Philosophy and Religion, University of Georgia, Athens, GA 30602.

Passmore, John, Man's Responsibility to Nature: Ecological Problems and Western Tradition (1974). Reproduced with permission of Duckworth General Publishers.

Pejan, Ramin, The Right to Water: The Road to Justiciability, 36 George Washington Int'l Law Review 1181, 1183–92 (2004). Reprinted by permission.

Pisillio-Mazzeschi, Ricardo, Forms of International Responsibility for Environmental Harm (Francesco Francioni & Tullio Scovazzi, eds.) (1991) pp. 15, 16–17, 29, 34–35. Reprinted with permission of Kluwer Academic Publishers.

Rafferty, Brian P., The Door Opens Slightly, 16 Georgetown Int'l Envtl. L. Rev., 281, 283, 287, 294–96 (2004). Reprinted with permission of the publisher, Georgetown International Environmental Law Review © 2004.

Sachs, Jeffrey D., The End of Poverty: Economic Possibilities for Our Time, 2005. © Jeffrey D. Sachs, 2005. Reprinted with permission from The Penguin Press.

Sagoff, Mark, On Preserving the Natural Environment, 84 Yale Law Journal 205 (1974). Reprinted by permission of the Yale Law Journal Company and Fred B. Rotharn & Company from the Yale Law Journal, Vol. 84, pp. 205–267 and Mark Sagoff.

Sagoff, Mark, Economic Theory and Environmental Law, 79 Michigan Law Review, pp. 146–1419 (1981), Reprinted with permission.

Sand, Peter, Lessons Learned in Global Environmental Governance (pp. 30–34) (1990). Reprinted with permission of World Resources Institute.

Shelton, Dinah, Human Rights, Environmental Rights, and the Right to Environment, 28 Stanford Journal of International Law 103, pp. 105–07, 112–13, 116, 122–24, 133 (1991). Reprinted with the permission of the Stanford Journal of International Law. © 1991 by the Board of Trustees of the Leland Stanford Junior University.

Shelton, Dinah, Developing Substantive Environmental Rights, 1 Journal of Human Rights and the Environment 95–96 (2010). Reprinted with Permission Elgar Press.

Sielen, Alan, Sea Changes? Ocean Dumping and International Regulation, 1 Georgetown International Environmental Law Review 2 (1998), Reprinted with Permission.

Silvertown, Jonathan, Demons in Eden: The Paradox of Plant Diversity, pp. 123–127, (2005). Reprinted with the permission of University of Chicago Press.

Sohn, Louis B., The New International Law: Protection of the Rights of Individuals Rather than State, 32 American University Law Review 1, pp. 17–21 (1982). Reprinted by permission.

Sohn, Louis B., The Stockholm Declaration on the Human Environment, 14 Harvard International Law Journal 423, 496–502 (1973). Reprinted with permission of Harvard International Law Journal.

Speth, James Gustave, Red Sky at Morning: America and the Crisis of the Global Environment, 2005, Copyright D 2005 by James Gustave Speth. Reprinted with Permission from Yale University Press.

Stiglitz, Joseph E., Globalization and its Discontents, Excerpts from pp. 3–20, 241 (2002). © 2002 by Joseph Stiglitz. Reprinted by permission of W.W. Norton & Company, Inc.

Stone, Christopher D., Should Trees Have Standing?—Toward Legal Rights for Natural Objects, 45 S. Cal L. Rev. 450 (1972). Reprinted by permission.

Tarlock, A. Dan, The Non-Discrimination Principle in United States and International Law, Annales de la facultéde Droit, Economie et

Administration de Metz No. 7637 (2007), Reprinted by Permission of Author.

United Nations Environment Programme, Poverty and the Environment. © United Nations Environment Programme, 1995. Reprinted with permission.

Weisskopf, Michael, The Washington Post, April 4, 1991, section A, page 25. © Washington Post. Reprinted with permission of The Washington Post.

Williams, Angela, Turning the Tide: Recognizing Climate Refugees in International Law, 30 Law & Policy 502 (2008). Reprinted with permission John Wiley and Sons.

World Commission on Environment and Development, Our Common Future, 1987. Reprinted with permission of Oxford University Press.

World Resources Institute, Millennium Ecosystem Assessment: Ecosystems and Human Well-being, Synthesis 40, 61 (2005). Reprinted by permission.

SUMMARY OF CONTENTS

TABLE OF CONTENTS

TABLE OF CASES

The principal cases are in bold type.

INTERNATIONAL LAW
FOR THE
ENVIRONMENT

CHAPTER 1

THE NATURE OF INTERNATIONAL ENVIRONMENTAL PROBLEMS

. . .

We are in a new geological epoch, the Anthropocene, in which humans have become a major force affecting the global environment. This means that for the first time we have the ability to profoundly change not only our local environments but the global environment, and not only for ourselves, but for future generations. We run the risk of reaching what natural scientists refer to as a "tipping point," in which we cause unparalleled changes in the global environment, with potentially devastating consequences to life as we know it today.

"Climate Change has brought into sharp focus the capability of contemporary human civilization to influence the environment at the scale of the Earth as a single, evolving planetary system. . . . But climate change is only the tip of the iceberg. In addition to the carbon cycle, humans are (i) significantly altering several other biogeochemical, or element cycles, such as nitrogen, phosphorus and sulphur, that are fundamental to life on the Earth; (ii) strongly modifying the terrestrial water cycle by intercepting river flow from uplands to the sea and through land-cover change, altering the water vapour flow from the land to the atmosphere; and (iii) likely driving the sixth major extinction event in Earth history. Taken together, these trends are strong evidence that human kind, our own species, has become so large and active that it now rivals some of the great forces of Nature in its impact on the functioning of the Earth system. . . . The concept of the Anthropocene . . . was introduced to capture the quantitative shift in the relationship between humans and the global environment. The term Anthropocene suggests: (i) that the Earth is now moving out of its current geological epoch, called the Holocene and (ii) that human activity is large responsible for this exit from the Holocene." Will Steffen, Jacques Grinevald, Paul Crutzen & John McNeill, *The Anthropocene: Conceptual and Historical Perspectives*, Philosophical Transactions of The Royal Society 369, 842 (2011).

Crutzen, who identified the Anthropocene, put the beginning of the new epoch near the end of the 18th century with the industrial revolution and James Watt's invention of the steam engine in 1784. Data now indicate that there has been a great acceleration since 1945/1950 in our impact on Earth, and that our impact continues to accelerate. Will Steffen, Wendy Broadgate, Lisa Deutsch, Owen Gaffney & Cornelia

1

Ludwig, *The Trajectory of the Anthropocene: The Great Acceleration"*, The Anthropocene Review 1–18 (2015). This means that more than ever we need to address our stewardship of planet Earth.

To understand international environmental law, it is necessary to consider the general and specific contexts in which international environmental problems occur. The materials in this chapter are intended to convey a sense of the richness of the interconnections in the environment and of the complexity of the issues pertaining to them. The first excerpts are classic works on the interdependence of the various elements of the environment. These are followed by excerpts on important factors affecting environmental sustainability and brief explorations of basic concepts. The next section presents the development of international environmental law and the challenges posed by the emergence of the Anthropocene epoch and a kaleidoscopic political, economic, and social world. We reference the United Nations 1972 Stockholm Declaration on the Human Environment and the 1992 Rio Declaration on Environment and Development to consider the extent to which these instruments reflect some of these complexities. The final section on the commons raises the basic conceptual issues related to how to manage a commons and provides the underlying framework for much of international environmental law.

A. INTERCONNECTEDNESS

1. THE EARTH: A FRAGILE, INTERDEPENDENT WHOLE

OUR COMMON FUTURE
World Commission on Environment and Development [The "Brundtland Commission"]
1 (1987)

In the middle of the 20th century, we saw our planet from space for the first time. Historians may eventually find that this vision had a greater impact on thought than did the Copernican revolution of the 16th century, which upset the human self-image by revealing that the Earth is not the center of the universe. From space, we see a small and fragile ball dominated not by human activity and edifice but by a pattern of clouds, oceans, greenery, and soils. Humanity's inability to fit its doings into that pattern is changing planetary systems, fundamentally. Many such changes are accompanied by life-threatening hazards. This new reality, from which there is no escape, must be recognized—and managed.

Fortunately, this new reality coincides with more positive developments new to this century. We can move information and goods faster around the globe than ever before; we can produce more food and more goods with less investment of resources; our technology and science give us at least the potential to look deeper into and better understand natural systems. From space, we can see and study the Earth as an organism whose health depends on the health of all its parts. . . .

INTERNATIONAL ENVIRONMENTAL POLICY—EMERGENCE AND DIMENSIONS
Lynton Caldwell
9 (1984)

Humanity lives in two realities. The abiding reality is that of the earth—the planet—independent of man and his works; the other reality—the transient reality—is that of the world, which is a creation of the human mind. The earth and its biosphere form a grand synthesis of complex interactive systems within systems, organic and inorganic, animate and inanimate. The world is the way humanity understands and has organized its occupancy of the earth: an expression of imagination and purpose materialized through exploration, invention, labor, and violence. Oceans, islands, species and ecosystems are integral parts of the earth, but the world is not integrated—its cultures and their values do not comprise a unity. All living men may be of one species, but their values are diverse. Physically, men belong to the earth, yet intellectually they may transcend it—a dangerous liberty when dissociated from regard for the necessities of life on earth.

———————

One of the concepts used to understand the importance of nature and the relationship between nature and human society is that of "ecosystem services." Ecosystem services are the benefits that humans receive from nature and that we would have to pay for if we had to provide them for ourselves, if indeed we could do so.

An appreciation of the extent of ecosystem services has led to a growing understanding that nature and natural systems are, in fact, the infrastructure of human society. Indeed, they constitute the human life-support system. *See* World Charter for Nature, UNGA Res. 37/7 (1982) (recognizing the centrality of the natural system).

The excerpt immediately following provides a typology of ecosystem services. Before reading it, we recommend you make a list of the ecosystem services you can identify on your own. Revisit the list after reading the excerpt. Did you identify any services that are not on the list? How close were you to identifying the full range of services provided by the environment? How close would a typical policymaker come? Note that many items on the list are sufficiently broad to cover many more specific ecosystem services. Where does the role of stratospheric ozone in protecting life from ultraviolet radiation appear on the list?

MILLENNIUM ECOSYSTEM ASSESSMENT
UNEP, World Resources Institute, Ecosystems and Human Well-Being
Synthesis 40 (2005)

ECOSYSTEM SERVICES

Ecosystem services are the benefits people obtain from ecosystems. These include provisioning, regulating, and cultural services that directly affect people and the supporting services needed to maintain other services. Many of the services listed here are highly interlinked. Primary production, photosynthesis, nutrient cycling, and water cycling, for example, all involve different aspects of the same biological processes.

PROVISIONING SERVICES

These are the products obtained from ecosystems, including:

Food. This includes the vast range of food products derived from plants, animals, and microbes.

Fiber. Materials included here are wood, jute, cotton, hemp, silk, and wool.

Fuel. Wood, dung, and other biological materials serve as sources of energy.

Genetic resources. This includes the genes and genetic information used for animal and plant breeding and biotechnology.

Biochemicals, natural medicines, and pharmaceuticals. Many medicines, biocides, food additives such as alginates, and biological materials are derived from ecosystems.

Ornamental resources. Animal and plant products, such as skins, shells, and flowers, are used as ornaments, and whole plants are used for landscaping and ornaments.

Fresh water. People obtain fresh water from ecosystems and thus the supply of fresh water can be considered a provisioning service. Fresh water in rivers is also a source of energy. Because water is required for other life to exist, however, it could also be considered a supporting service.

REGULATING SERVICES

These are the benefits obtained from the regulation of ecosystem processes, including:

Air quality regulation. Ecosystems both contribute chemicals to and extract chemicals from the atmosphere, influencing many aspects of air quality.

Climate regulation. Ecosystems influence climate both locally and globally. At a local scale, for example, changes in land cover can affect both temperature and precipitation. At the global scale, ecosystems play an important role in climate by either sequestering or emitting greenhouse gases.

Water regulation. The timing and magnitude of runoff, flooding, and aquifer recharge can be strongly influenced by changes in land cover, including, in particular, alterations that change the water storage potential of the system, such as the conversion of wetlands or the replacement of forests with croplands or croplands with urban areas.

Erosion regulation. Vegetative cover plays an important role in soil retention and the prevention of landslides.

Water purification and waste treatment. Ecosystems can be a source of impurities (for instance, in fresh water) but also can help filter out and decompose organic wastes introduced into inland waters and coastal and marine ecosystems and can assimilate and detoxify compounds through soil and subsoil processes.

Disease regulation. Changes in ecosystems can directly change the abundance of human pathogens, such as cholera, and can alter the abundance of disease vectors, such as mosquitoes.

Pest regulation. Ecosystem changes affect the prevalence of crop and livestock pests and diseases.

Pollination. Ecosystem changes affect the distribution, abundance, and effectiveness of pollinators.

Natural hazard regulation. The presence of coastal ecosystems such as mangroves and coral reefs [and barrier islands—Eds.] can reduce the damage caused by hurricanes or large waves.

CULTURAL SERVICES

These are the nonmaterial benefits people obtain from ecosystems through spiritual enrichment, cognitive development, reflection, recreation, and aesthetic experiences, including:

Cultural diversity. The diversity of ecosystems is one factor influencing the diversity of cultures.

Spiritual and religious values. Many religions attach spiritual and religious values to ecosystems or their components.

Knowledge systems (traditional and formal). Ecosystems influence the types of knowledge systems developed by different cultures.

Educational values. Ecosystems and their components and processes provide the basis for both formal and informal education in many societies.

Inspiration. Ecosystems provide a rich source of inspiration for art, folklore, national symbols, architecture, and advertising.

Aesthetic values. Many people find beauty or aesthetic value in various aspects of ecosystems, as reflected in the support for parks, scenic drives, and the selection of housing locations.

Social relations. Ecosystems influence the types of social relations that are established in particular cultures. Fishing societies, for example, differ in many respects in their social relations from nomadic herding or agricultural societies.

Sense of place. Many people value the "sense of place" that is associated with recognized features of their environment, including aspects of the ecosystem.

Cultural heritage values. Many societies place high value on the maintenance of either historically important landscapes ("cultural landscapes") or culturally significant species.

Recreation and ecotourism. People often choose where to spend their leisure time based in part on the characteristics of the natural or cultivated landscapes in a particular area.

SUPPORTING SERVICES

Supporting services are those that are necessary for the production of all other ecosystem services. They differ from provisioning, regulating, and cultural services in that their impacts on people are often indirect or occur over a very long time, whereas changes in the other categories have relatively direct and short-term impacts on people. (Some services, like erosion regulation, can be categorized as both a supporting and a regulating service, depending on the time scale and immediacy of their impact on people).

These services include:

Soil Formation. Because many provisioning services depend on soil fertility, the rate of soil formation influences human well-being in many ways.

Photosynthesis. Photosynthesis produces oxygen necessary for most living organisms.

Primary production. The assimilation or accumulation of energy and nutrients by organisms.

Nutrient cycling. Approximately 20 nutrients essential for life, including nitrogen and phosphorus, cycle through ecosystems and are maintained at different concentrations in different parts of ecosystems.

Water cycling. Water cycles through ecosystems and is essential for living organisms.

A MOMENT ON THE EARTH
Gregg Easterbrook
49–51 (1995)

THE MAGNITUDE OF NATURAL TIME

The cosmos is thought to be eight to 20 billion years old; Earth and its companion sun 4.5 billion years old; simple microbial life 3.8 million years old; complex microorganisms perhaps 2.8 billion years old; animal life perhaps 600 million years old; mammalian life about 200 million years old. Given time in such vastness, researchers are prone to describing as "recent" events that occurred within the last few hundred million years. Recently, the land mass called North America was located at the South Pole. Recently, life was already very old.

By contrast, the world of intellect is in childhood. The lineage of genus Homo stretches perhaps 30,000 centuries into the past; toolmaking humankind may be 8,000 centuries old; Homo sapiens, the creatures that look like us, appeared around 350 centuries ago; civilization, defined by agriculture, is thought to have begun perhaps 80 centuries ago; technology may be said to have begun around 50 centuries ago, with Egyptian pyramids and sailing vessels; the human attempt to take over Earth's ecosphere began about two centuries ago, with the industrial era.

NOTES AND QUESTIONS

1. *Geologic time.* Can humans appreciate geologic time? Is the time span (billions of years) comprehensible to a species whose longest-lived members live barely more than a century? Disposal of nuclear waste is said to require at least 100,000 years. Is that period understandable to humans?

2. *Generations.* As noted, the period of human civilization has lasted approximately 320 generations, whereas the chambered nautilus has existed in essentially the same form for 120 million generations, and whales five million. Do you think humans will last five million generations? 1000 generations?

3. *Recovery over time.* Do the facts that nature exists over spans of time beyond human experience, that species persist over very long periods, and that the biosphere has demonstrated a remarkable resiliency in spite of massive cataclysms such as meteor impacts, rises and falls of seas, ice ages, and periodic mass extinctions mean that what humans do to our environment

does not matter—either in the short run or long run? How does the emergence of the Anthropocene epoch, in which humans have become a major force of change for the environment, affect your assessment of the resiliency of the Earth?

4.   *Reality or arrogance: the web of life.* Some have argued that the notion that humans can affect planet Earth as a whole is the height of arrogance. Many others point to the inherent interconnectedness of the biosphere, to the fact that humans are part of that biosphere and to the undeniable effect that human activity is having on the biosphere as evidence that the concept of the Anthropocene is not arrogant but rather reflects reality.

One of the most oft-quoted aphorisms about the environment concerns the image of the web of life:

> This we know: the earth does not belong to man, man belongs to the earth. All things are connected like the blood that unites us all. Man did not weave the web of life, he is merely a strand in it. Whatever he does to the web, he does to himself.

This quotation has been attributed to Chief Seattle of the Duwamish and Squamish tribes in the area around Puget Sound, Washington, in 1855, but that is controversial; it may have originated in Hollywood. *See generally* Paul S. Wilson, *What Chief Seattle Said*, 22 Envtl. L. 1451(1992); Rudolf Kaiser, *A Fifth Gospel, Almost, Chief Seattle's Speech(es): American Origins and European Reception, in* Indians and Europe: An Interdisciplinary Collection of Essays 505, at 519–20 (Christian Feest, ed.,1987). Regardless of whether Chief Seattle uttered these exact words, the image of the web beautifully and powerfully captures the notion of interdependence and humans' relation to it in at least three ways.

First, the image of the web conveys the critical message of the interdependence of all forms of life on the earth. Because of this interdependence, actions in one part of the web can affect other parts. Consider, for example, the unexpected (though logical) relationship between replacing indigenous trees with non-indigenous palm trees on Palmyra Atoll in the Pacific and the off-shore population of manta rays: as the non-indigenous trees replaced indigenous trees, fewer seabirds roosted in the trees, reducing the amount of guano under the trees, which reduced the amount of guano that washed into the lagoon, which in turn reduced the number of plankton in the water that fed on the nutrients in the dissolved guano; this ultimately led to a decrease in the number of manta rays off-shore because they feed on plankton. *See Non-Native Trees Lead to Fewer Manta Rays*, by LiveScience Staff, May 18, 2012, http://www.livescience.com/ 20437-native-trees-lead-manta-rays.html. For another example of a surprising interdependence—in this case a trophic cascade (i.e., a series of effects stemming from a change at the top of a food chain)—between the introduction of wolves into Yellowstone National Park and the shape of the river there, *see* www.youtube.com/embed/ysa5OBhXz-Q?feature=player_

embedded. An appreciation of the ubiquity of phenomena such as these is essential to an understanding of environmental problems and equips us to evaluate policy and legal responses to those problems.

Second, the image of the web emphasizes that humans and society are part of that set of relationships. Regardless of whether one takes an anthropocentric view of environmental issues, it is clear that human welfare is affected by the health of nonhuman aspects of the web, and vice versa. In fact, human society depends on nature. In addition, in the Anthropocene epoch, humans are affecting nature in serious ways and on a global scale.

Third, the image reminds us that we are dealing with the conditions that make life possible and define its quality. International environmental law involves human, plant and animal health and the well-being of entire ecosystems, as well as the allocation of natural resources and the more aesthetic but nevertheless important issues such as preservation of, and access to, natural and cultural sites. The health aspect of international environmental law is often not fully understood or appreciated, a fact that may lead to more resistance to "environmental" initiatives than would otherwise arise.

5.   *Optimism or only pessimism?* Is there room for optimism in dealing with the long term future? Might increased scientific understanding and improved technology enable future generations to deal with environmental problems as they come up? Could our political institutions and our laws keep up to let this happen?

A NOTE ON MODELS IN ENVIRONMENTAL SCIENCE
Charles Weiss
(2015)

How are we to understand the complexity of the world that surrounds us? Scientists often try to explain the workings of the natural world by building models, usually but not always using mathematical tools. A model incorporates assumptions about the most important scientific laws and principles needed to explain a particular phenomenon or set of phenomena.

You can think of a model as analogous to a vending machine. In go scientific principles, assumptions and data, and out comes one or more predicted results, which may or may not agree with observation. A model is no better than the assumptions that underlie it, and its predictions can be no better than the data that are fed into it. In some situations, even small variations in input data—changes well within the error in practical measurements—lead to quite different results, a phenomenon explored in "chaos" theory.

Models are tested by how well they agree with actual data on the phenomena they are supposed to explain. If a model fails to do this, scientists reexamine their assumptions to see whether some important influence has been poorly represented or left out of the model, or whether the input data is defective in a way that affects the result of the calculation. A good model not only explains existing data, but also makes testable predictions that go beyond the assumptions and data that were fed into it.

The reliance of scientists on models leads to a number of difficulties. Scientific understanding of the forces at play in a particular situation—say the dynamics of a particular population of fish or of an endangered species—may be incomplete. The data to be fed into the model may be inaccurate or difficult to obtain, or may be insufficient to establish long-term trends. In some cases, it may be necessary to use proxies for the data one would really like to have—for example, fish landings instead of population counts of actual fish.

Finally, the phenomena being modeled may be too complicated for even the most powerful computers, so that important inputs must be approximated (in the jargon, "parameterized") and the calculations repeated with different versions of these approximations in hopes that the most important results will be consistent from calculation to calculation.

This means that scientific models are inevitably an imperfect representation of objective reality, a fact that introduces uncertainty and engenders risk in whatever policy recommendations emerge from its conclusions. The question is whether a given model is a sufficient representation of the actual situation as to be an adequate basis for practical purposes. In some situations, there may be sufficient uncertainty for both sides of a controversy to claim support from the same or similar models. Conversely, in some situations, the actual uncertainty may be very small but exaggerated by interested parties.

CHAOS: MAKING A NEW SCIENCE
James Gleick
34, 7–8, 23, 59–64 (1987)

Where chaos begins, classical science stops. For as long as the world has had physicists inquiring into the laws of nature, it has suffered a special ignorance about disorder in the atmosphere, in the turbulent sea, in the fluctuations of wildlife populations, in the oscillations of the heart and the brain. The irregular side of nature, the discontinuous and erratic side—these have been puzzles to science, or worse, monstrosities.

But in the 1970s a few scientists in the United States and Europe began to find a way through disorder. They were mathematicians, physicists, biologists, chemists, all seeking connections between different kinds of irregularity. Physiologists found a surprising order in the chaos that develops in the human heart, the prime cause of sudden, unexplained death. Ecologists explored the rise and fall of gypsy moth populations. Economists dug out old stock price data and tried a new kind of analysis. The insights that emerged led directly into the natural world—the shapes of clouds, the paths of lightning, the microscopic intertwining of blood vessels, the galactic clustering of stars.

The simplest systems are now seen to create extraordinarily difficult problems of predictability. Yet order arises spontaneously in those systems—chaos and order together. Only a new kind of science could begin to cross the great gulf between knowledge of what one thing does— one water molecule, one cell of heart tissue, one neuron—and what millions of them do.

Watch two bits of foam flowing side by side at the bottom of a waterfall. What can you guess about how close they were at the top? Nothing. . . . The modern study of chaos began with the creeping realization in the 1960s that quite simple mathematical equations could model systems every bit as violent as a waterfall. Tiny differences in input could quickly become overwhelming differences in output. . . . In weather, for example, this translates into what is only half-jokingly known as the Butterfly Effect—the notion that a butterfly stirring the air today in Peking can transform storm systems next month in New York.

. . .

In science as in life, it is well known that a chain of events can have a point of crisis that could magnify small changes. But chaos meant that such points were everywhere. They were pervasive. In systems like the weather, sensitive dependence on initial conditions was an inescapable consequence of the way small scales intertwined with large. . . .

Ravenous fish and tasty plankton. Rain forests dripping with nameless reptiles, birds gliding under canopies of leaves, insects buzzing like electrons in an accelerator. Frost belts where voles and lemmings flourish and diminish with tidy four-year periodicity in the face of nature's bloody combat. The world makes a messy laboratory for ecologists, a cauldron of five million interacting species. Or is it fifty million? Ecologists do not actually know.

Mathematically inclined biologists of the twentieth century built a discipline, ecology, that stripped away the noise and color of real life and treated populations as dynamical systems. Ecologists used the elementary tools of mathematical physics to describe life's ebbs and flows. Single species multiplying in a place where food is limited, several species competing for existence, epidemics spreading through host populations— all could be isolated, if not in laboratories then certainly in the minds of biological theorists.

In the emergence of chaos as a new science in the 1970s, ecologists were destined to play a special role. They used mathematical models, but they always knew that the models were thin approximations of the seething real world. . . .

. . . To describe a population changing each year, a biologist uses a formalism that a high school student can follow easily. Suppose next year's population of gypsy moths will depend entirely on this year's population. You could imagine a table listing all the specific possibilities—31,000 gypsy moths this year means 35,000 next year, and so forth. Or you could capture the relationship between all the numbers for this year and all the numbers for next year as a rule—a function. . . .

In a simple model like this one, following a population through time is a matter of taking a starting figure and applying the same function again and again. . . . The whole history of the population becomes available through this process of functional iteration—a feedback loop, each year's output serving as the next year's input. Feedback can get out of hand, as it does when sound from a loudspeaker feeds back through a microphone and is rapidly amplified to an unbearable shriek. Or feedback can produce stability, as a thermostat does in regulating the temperature of a house: any temperature above a fixed point leads to cooling, and any temperature below it leads to heating.

Many different types of functions are possible. A naive approach to population biology might suggest a function that increases the population by a certain percentage each year. That would be a linear function. . . .

Ecologists realized generations ago that they would have to do better. An ecologist imagining real fish in a real pond had to find a function that matched the crude realities of life—for example, the reality of hunger, or competition. When the fish proliferate, they start to run out of food. A small fish population will grow rapidly. An overly large fish population will dwindle. . . .

. . . Anyway, if the population kept bouncing back and forth, ecologists assumed that it was oscillating around some underlying equilibrium. The equilibrium was the important thing. It did not occur to the ecologists that there might be no equilibrium.

NOTES AND QUESTIONS

1. *Interrelationships and interdependence.* What interrelationships in nature are identified in the foregoing excerpts? What relationships between nature and human activity? What relationships between specific international environmental issues, or between possible solutions to those problems?

In terms of ecological interdependence, is it accurate to say that aspects of the biosphere (i.e., the layer of land, water, and atmosphere that supports life) are increasingly interdependent or that humans have become increasingly aware of that interdependence or that anthropogenic (i.e., human generated) activity is increasingly affecting the details of that interdependence? What does interdependence imply for coexistence or cooperation among States?

2.   *Feedback and self-correction.* What sorts of feedback, reinforcement, and self-correcting mechanisms and effects are evident in the foregoing excerpts?

3.   *Feedback, self-correction, and logic.* Does the presence of feedback loops and reinforcement or self-correction effects make linear logic unsuitable and require the adoption of a new ecologic that takes account of these phenomena?

4.   *Uncertainty.* Chaos Theory, as described in the excerpt by James Gleick, has implications for our ability to predict the behavior and fate of species and ecosystems. Indeed, uncertainty is a fundamental reality for those involved in protecting human health and the environment. Domestic environmental regulators, for example, seldom if ever know all the facts they would like to know in order to make a regulatory decision. Scientific and other uncertainties and ways in which the international legal system can take account of these uncertainties are addressed throughout this book.

5.   *Health.* What is the relationship between the environment and human health? Does it matter whether a particular issue (e.g., air pollution) is described as a health problem or an environmental one?

6.   *Infrastructure.* What does it mean to say that the environment is the true infrastructure of society? What implications does that have for policymaking?

2.   SOME ESSENTIAL DEFINITIONS

The following concepts are essential to understanding international environmental issues and thus international environmental law. You will encounter them in various parts of this book.

FEEDBACK LOOP

A feedback loop is when a change in a parameter (A) causes a change in another parameter (B), which in turn affects the likelihood of the first parameter (A) occurring. There are both positive and negative feedback loops. A positive feedback loop is one in which the second perturbation (B) makes it more likely that the initial perturbation (A) will occur, therefore exacerbating the change. A negative feedback loop is one where the second perturbation (B) leads to a decrease in the likelihood of the first perturbation (A) occurring. Note that in this context, the terms "positive and "negative" do not connote anything about whether the effect of the feedback loop is desirable.

Feedback loops have the potential to affect environmental conditions significantly. Feedback loops can be either positive or negative. For example, with respect to climate change, warming (A) causes an increase in evaporation of water and thus an increase in water vapor in the atmosphere (B). Because water vapor is a greenhouse gas, its increased presence in the atmosphere makes additional warming (A) more likely—a positive feedback loop. Conversely, the increased water vapor in the atmosphere also creates clouds (B). Because clouds reflect sunlight back into space, this decreases the likelihood of additional warming (A)—a negative feedback loop. *See* Intergovernmental Panel on Climate Change, Climate Change 2013: The Physical Science Basis (Thomas Stocker et al., eds., 2013), *available at* http://www.ipcc.ch/pdf/assessment-report/ar5/wg1/WG1AR5_ALL_FINAL.pdf; Ben Booth, Climate Feedbacks, Met Office, September 27, 2013, *available at* http://www.metoffice.gov.uk/climate-change/guide/science/explained/feedbacks.

LIFE CYCLE ASSESSMENT

Life cycle assessment (or analysis) takes into account the entire range of effects (e.g., costs and benefits) stemming from the lifetime of an activity or product. Life cycle assessment is a "cradle-to-grave" approach in which the analysis takes everything into account from the very beginning of the activity—e.g., research or gathering raw materials—through production, transport and consumption to the point when all materials have been recycled or disposed of. Life cycle assessment enables an accurate understanding of the environmental impacts of a particular activity or product. *See* U.S. Envt'l Protection Agency, Life Cycle Assessment, *available at* http://www.epa.gov/nrmrl/std/lca/lca.html; British Columbia Climate Action Tool Kit, Life Cycle Analysis, *available at* http://www.toolkit.bc.ca/tool/life-cycle-analysis.

TIPPING POINT

A tipping point is that point at which one stable equilibria changes abruptly to another stable equilibria. For example, with respect to climate change, it is a hypothesized critical threshold of climate at a regional or global level at which one stable state is altered to another stable state, such as if the Gulf Stream were to cease. There are reversible and irreversible tipping points. A reversible tipping point returns to the original stable state in a gradual or abrupt manner. An irreversible tipping point is one that does not return to the original state and would only do so, if at all, with a significant change. *See* Intergovernmental Panel on Climate Change, Climate Change 2013: The Physical Science Basis 1463 (Thomas Stocker et al., eds., 2013), *available at* http://www.ipcc.ch/pdf/assessment-report/ar5/wg1/WG1AR5_ALL_FINAL.pdf; Timothy M. Lenton, Earth System Tipping Points, *available at* http://yosemite.epa.gov/ee/epa/eerm.nsf/vwAN/EE-0564-112.pdf/$file/EE-0564-112.pdf.

EXTERNALITY

An externality is a consequence, such as an economic cost or benefit, of an action that the actor does not experience. There are positive and negative externalities. The OECD refers to externalities as "uncompensated environmental effects of production and consumption that affect consumer utility and enterprise cost outside the market mechanism."[1] Note that in this context (unlike for feedback loops), the terms "negative" and "positive" connote that the externality is harmful or beneficial, respectively.

An example of a negative externality is pollution. For example, if a pulp mill causes water and air pollution outside the premises of the mill, in the absence of government regulation there will be no cost to the pulp mill owner even though the environment and local community may be harmed and thus bear costs. If the pulp mill owner were charged the full cost of the pollution, there would not be a negative externality. An example of a positive externality is when a downstream farmer benefits from fertilizer-containing run-off from an upstream farm.

B. HUMAN ENVIRONMENT AND SUSTAINABILITY

1. POPULATION

> In many parts of the world, the population is growing at rates that cannot be sustained by available environmental resources, at rates that are outstripping any reasonable expectations of improvements in housing, health care, food security, or energy supplies.

World Commission on Environment and Development
(The "Brundtland Commission"), Our Common Future 9 (1987)

> If we lift our gaze from the frightening daily headlines ... we shall see that economic life in the United States and the rest of the world has been getting better rather than worse during recent centuries and decades. There is, moreover, no persuasive reason to believe that these trends will not continue indefinitely.... [A]dditional children have positive long-run effects on the standard of living.

Julian Simon (1990)

Human population growth is often raised either as a problem in itself or as a factor significantly affecting international environmental issues. As the two quotations above indicate, however, opinions differ greatly (and passionately) regarding the effect of increases in human population. Population data from 2004 to 2012 indicates that the world's population has continued to grow, and projections to the year 2050 indicate this will continue. In 2004, the world's population stood at approximately 6.5 billion and in 2012, at approximately 7.2 billion. Population is projected

---

[1] *See* OECD, Glossary of Statistical Terms, Environmental Externalities (last updated March 4, 2003), *available at* http://stats.oecd.org/glossary/detail.asp?ID=824.

to reach approximately 10.9 billion. U.N. Dept. of Econ. And Soc. Affairs, Population Division, World Population Prospects: The 2012 Revision, *available at* http://esa.un.org/wpp/. The vast majority of the growth will occur in developing or advanced developing countries for the foreseeable future. Notably, projections for China indicate population stabilization by 2050 just slightly below the figure for 2012 of 1.385 billion. It is predicted that India will have the world's largest population well before 2050.

Despite early attention by the environmental community and others to the population issue, it is not at the front of the environmental agenda as of the beginning of 2015.

NOTES AND QUESTIONS

1. *Population and the Rio Declaration.* The only reference to population in the Rio Declaration—the statement of principles on environment and development adopted at the 1992 UN Conference on Environment and Development (UNCED)—is in Principle 8: "To achieve sustainable development and a higher quality of life for all people, States should reduce and eliminate unsustainable patterns of production and consumption and promote appropriate demographic policies." What guidance does this provide?

2. *Population growth and economic growth.* Economic structures in most countries are based on growth. Can economies remain or become stable or strong if the national population is declining? What are some of the effects of fewer people in a society? If you were a government leader, under what circumstances would you be concerned about a stable population size? A declining population? Or population growth?

3. *Population and climate change.* How might the evidence of greenhouse gas buildup in the atmosphere leading to climate change affect one's approach to population growth? Should limits on greenhouse gas emissions be based on per capita emissions or on per country emissions of the same gasses?

4. *Cornucopians vs. Malthusians.* Julian Simon, determined to prove his "Cornucopian" theory, offered to bet anyone $1,000 that commodity prices would decrease over a ten-year period. Paul Ehrlich, a leader of modern Malthusian theory, accepted the offer. Ehrlich chose five metals (chrome, copper, nickel, tin, and tungsten) that he believed would increase in price over ten years, due to increased pressure from growing populations. The bet was in the form of a futures contract. Simon "bought" quantities of each metal for $200 each and in 1990 would sell these to Ehrlich at 1980 prices. Thus if the combined 1990 price of these metals was higher than $1,000, Simon would pay Ehrlich the difference; if the quantities were worth less than $1,000, Ehrlich would pay the difference.

In 1990, Ehrlich wrote Simon a check for $576.07 to pay off the bet. Does this add credibility to Simon's population theory? Would he assert that it shows that natural resources are not really "scarce" and that we are not running out of them? Does it detract from the Malthusian theory of more mouths, less food? What about other implications of population growth?

2.   SOCIAL AND CULTURAL CONTEXT

The relationship between the environment and the cultural and social aspects of society is to some extent intuitively obvious: one would expect that a society will reflect the ecological conditions in which that society exists—e.g., that diet, hunting practices, and living arrangements in hunter-gatherer societies will bear a relationship to the abundance and migration patterns of game, to the agricultural potential of a particular locale, and to the weather patterns of that locale. The relationship is also complicated, however, not only because it involves human psychology and because different effects may offset each other but also because modern humans have developed means of coping with limitations that otherwise would be placed on us by our environments (e.g., heating and air conditioning systems, pesticides, agricultural irrigation, and synthetic materials). In addition, decisions made in one geographic location now often affect living conditions at other, distant locations (e.g., a decision to test nuclear weapons in a specific locale or to build a dam on an international river), and individuals' and groups' aspirations and expectations are now influenced by global communications.

We should note that very few people today live in complete harmony with their environment. They have been conditioned to enjoy abundance or to strive to enjoy abundance. There is some movement back toward living more in harmony with the environment and to consuming less, but it is still small in scale.

NOTES AND QUESTIONS

1.   *Relationship between environment and social conditions.* What effect does culture have on the environment of a group? To what extent do changes in the physical environment affect the culture that exists with it? We will encounter this issue, for example, in law related to the rights of indigenous peoples.

2.   *Culture's effect on attitudes.* In what ways does your culture affect your attitudes or behavior toward protecting health and the environment?

3.   *Religious backgrounds.* Do you think persons with Buddhist, Christian, Hindu, Islamic, Jewish, other religious traditions and atheistic backgrounds are likely to have the same reactions or approaches to environmental protection or sustainable development?

3. ECONOMIC CONTEXT: POVERTY AND ECONOMIC DISPARITIES

Vast numbers of people in the world—more than 2.2 billion in 2011, according to World Bank figures—live in poverty (i.e., they live on less than $2.00 per day), with over one billion of those people living in a state of extreme poverty (also referred to as "absolute poverty"), i.e., less than $1.25 per day.

As a result of the international agenda and purely domestic pressures and policies, the need to improve the living conditions of poor people is viewed as an imperative and can put what are often perceived as irresistible pressures on policymakers, e.g., pressure to choose short-term gains in employment or to exploit natural resources over more sustainable policies.

At the same time, massive economic disparities exist among countries and regions. These disparities are typically linked to other social and environmental differences, such as literacy, access to safe drinking water, access to healthcare facilities, and access to open spaces, as well as historical experiences such as colonialization. These disparities affect the policies adopted by developing countries. The disparities also strongly influence the political setting in which discussions of international environmental issues occur. There are also, of course, significant disparities in income and wealth distribution within countries—both developed and developing.

The following excerpt indicates the extent of the disparities in per capita income between countries and explores some questions about the relationship between poverty and the environment.

THE END OF POVERTY, ECONOMIC POSSIBILITIES FOR OUR TIME

Jeffrey D. Sachs
24–31 (2005)

The move from universal poverty to varying degrees of prosperity has happened rapidly in the span of human history. Two hundred years ago the idea that we could potentially achieve the end of extreme poverty would have been unimaginable. Just about everybody was poor, with the exception of a very small minority of rulers and large landowners. Life was as difficult in much of Europe as it was in India or China. Our great-great-grandparents were, with very few exceptions, most likely poor and living on a farm. One leading economic historian, Angus Maddison, puts the average income per person in Western Europe in 1820 at around 90 percent of the average income of Africa today. Life expectancy in Western Europe and Japan as of 1800 was about forty years.

A few centuries ago, vast divides in wealth and poverty around the world did not exist. China, India, Europe and Japan all had similar income levels at the time of European discoveries of the sea routes to Asia, Africa, and the Americas. Marco Polo marveled at the sumptuous wonders of China, not at its poverty. Cortes and his conquistadors expressed astonishment at the riches of Tenochtitlan, the capital of the Aztecs. The early Portuguese explorers were impressed with the well-ordered towns of West Africa.

THE NOVELTY OF MODERN ECONOMIC GROWTH

If we are to understand why a vast gap between rich and poor exists today, we must return to the very recent period of human history when this divide emerged. The past two centuries, since around 1800, constitute a unique era in economic history, a period the great economic historian Simon Kuznets famously termed the period of modern economic growth. Before then, indeed for thousands of years, there had been virtually no sustained economic growth in the world, and only gradual increases in the human population. The world population had risen gradually from around 230 million people at the start of the first millennium in A.D. 1, to perhaps 270 million by A.D. 1000, and 900 million people by A.D. 1800. Real living standards were even slower to change. According to Maddison, there was no discernible rise in living standards on a global scale during the first millennium, and perhaps a 50 percent increase in per capita income in the eight-hundred-year period from A.D. 1000 to A.D. 1800.

In the period of modern economic growth, however, both population and per capita income came unstuck, soaring at rates never before seen or even imagined. . . . [T]he global population rose more than sixfold in just two centuries, reaching an astounding 6.1 billion people at the start of the third millennium, with plenty of momentum for rapid population growth still ahead. The world's average per capita income rose even faster . . . increasing by around nine times between 1820 and 2000. In today's rich countries, the economic growth was even more astounding. The U.S. per capita income increased almost twenty-five-fold during this period, and Western Europe's increased fifteen-fold. Total worldwide food production more than kept up with the booming world population (though large numbers of chronically hungry people remain until today). Vastly improved farm yields were achieved primarily on the basis of technological advances. If we combine increases in world population and world output per person, we find that total economic activity in the world (the gross world product, or GWP) rose an astounding forty-nine times during the past 180 years.

The gulf between today's rich and poor countries is therefore a new phenomenon, a yawning gap that opened during the period of modern economic growth. As of 1820, the biggest gap between the rich and poor—

specifically, between the world's leading economy of the day, the United Kingdom, and the world's poorest region, Africa—was a ratio of four to one in per capita income (even after adjusting for differences in purchasing power). By 1998, the gap between the richest economy, the United States, and the poorest region, Africa, had widened to twenty to one. Since all parts of the world had a roughly comparable starting point in 1820 (all very poor by current standards), today's vast inequalities reflect the fact that some parts of the world achieved modern economic growth while others did not. Today's vast income inequalities illuminate two centuries of highly uneven patterns of economic growth.

NOTES AND QUESTIONS

1. *Economic disparities and environmental cooperation.* How do economic disparities between countries and regions complicate environmental cooperation efforts? Are poorer countries likely to face the same threats to health and environment as richer countries face? Are they likely to prioritize dealing with environmental threats in the same way? Is public participation regarding environmental issues likely to be the same in the two sets of countries? Will these differences affect the likelihood that poor and rich countries will be able to reach agreement on an international regime to address a particular environmental problem? Consider the following quotation from Our Common Future 17 (1987): "Two conditions must be satisfied before international economic exchanges can become beneficial for all involved. The sustainability of ecosystems on which the global economy depends must be guaranteed. And the economic partners must be satisfied that the basis of exchange is equitable. For many developing countries, neither condition is met."

2. *Participation of poor countries in environmental protection efforts.* Is a poorer country likely to be able to commit the same resources to an international environmental cooperation effort as a richer one? Is the poorer country likely to have the capacity to comply with international legal obligations to the same extent as a richer country? Will these differences affect the effectiveness of international environmental regimes? Will they affect the substantive content of those regimes? During negotiations of the Basel Convention on International Transport of Hazardous Waste, many developing countries sought an outright ban on international trade in hazardous waste, rather than the prior informed consent regime eventually adopted, arguing that they do not have the capacity to administer a prior informed consent approach.

3. *Indigenous Peoples.* How do indigenous peoples fit into the developmental picture?

4. *Health and environmental tradeoffs.* What tradeoffs would a policymaker in a developing country face with respect to investments in human health and the environment?

5.   *Patterns of production and consumption.* Agenda 21 in 1992 and subsequent international instruments stated that unsustainable patterns of production and consumption, especially among developed countries, are the primary cause of the degradation of the global environment. A commonly asked question is what the world would be like if every person in China and India (which together account for about 40 percent of the world's population) had the same access to automobiles as do people in Japan, the United States, and Europe. The prospect of negotiating or overseeing a decline in the standard of living is anathema to political leaders. Does the path to sustainable patterns of consumption and production necessarily lead in that direction? What role might technology play?

6.   *Private capital flow.* One of the most important economic phenomena of the 1990s was that the international flow of private investment capital came to vastly exceed that of public assistance—both multilateral and bilateral. One of the great challenges is thus how to ensure that those investments are socially and environmentally responsible. It also emphasizes the need for international finance institutions and bilateral assistance agencies to consider the impact of private investment. These issues are discussed in Chapter 17.

4.   POLITICAL CONTEXT

The political context in which international environmental protection efforts occur can be viewed at several levels—e.g., local, national, regional, global—and considering the roles of various players—e.g., various levels of government, individuals, non-governmental organizations, business entities, international finance institutions, and other regional and global international organizations. There is a sharp disconnect between the inclination of governments to address short-term issues that produce immediate results and the longer term focus that is needed for many environmental issues. Moreover, as Lynton Keith Caldwell noted several decades ago, "[e]nvironmental issues are numerous and disparate; but public attention is drawn to immediate, comprehensible concerns more readily publicized than are the larger, more complex developments of which they are manifestations. It is easier to attract public attention to the effects of acid rain, the plight of fur seals, or pollution from pesticides than to the more fundamental problems of biogeochemical cycles or species-habitat relationships." Lynton Keith Caldwell, INTERNATIONAL ENVIRONMENTAL POLICY 14–15 (1984)

The following excerpts provide some insights into significant elements of the political context.

REDEFINING SECURITY

Jessica Tuchman Mathews
68 For. Aff. 162 (1989)

The 1990s will demand a redefinition of what constitutes national security. In the 1970s the concept was expanded to include international economics as it became clear that the U.S. economy was no longer the independent force it had once been, but was powerfully affected by economic policies in dozens of other countries. Global developments now suggest the need for another analogous, broadening definition of national security to include resource, environmental and demographic issues.

The assumptions and institutions that have governed international relations in the postwar era are a poor fit with these new realities. Environmental strains that transcend national borders are already beginning to break down the sacred boundaries of national sovereignty, previously rendered porous by the information and communication revolutions and the instantaneous global movement of financial capital. The once sharp dividing line between foreign and domestic policy is blurred, forcing governments to grapple in international forums with issues that were contentious enough in the domestic arena. . . .

Environmental decline occasionally leads directly to conflict, especially when scarce water resources must be shared. Generally, however, its impact on nations' security is felt in the downward pull on economic performance and, therefore, on political stability. The underlying cause of turmoil is often ignored; instead governments address the poverty and instability that are its results. . . .

On the political front, the need for a new diplomacy and for new institutions and regulatory regimes to cope with the world's growing environmental interdependence is . . . compelling. Put bluntly, our accepted definition of the limits of national sovereignty as coinciding with national borders is obsolete. The government of Bangladesh, no matter how hard it tries, cannot prevent tragic floods, such as it suffered [in 1988]. Preventing them requires active cooperation from Nepal and India. The government of Canada cannot protect its water resources from acid rain without collaboration with the United States. Eighteen diverse nations share the heavily polluted Mediterranean Sea. Even the Caribbean Islands, as physically isolated as they are, find themselves affected by others' resource management policies as locusts, inadvertently bred through generations of exposure to [be impervious to] pesticides and now strong enough to fly all the way from Africa, infest their shores.

The majority of environmental problems demand regional solutions [and] encroach upon what we now think of as prerogatives of national governments. This is because the phenomena themselves are defined by the limits of watershed, ecosystem, or atmospheric transport, not by national borders. Indeed, the costs and benefits of alternative policies cannot often be accurately judged without considering the region rather than the nation.

THE CHANGING STRUCTURE OF INTERNATIONAL LAW

Edith Brown Weiss
Georgetown University Law Center, May 23, 1996, reprinted in
Georgetown Law—Res Ipso Loquitur 52 (Spring 1997)

The Peace of Westphalia that ended the Thirty Years War three hundred and fifty years ago established a new international order based on sovereign, independent, territorially defined States, each striving to maintain political independence and territorial integrity. . . .

The international system is rapidly changing and with it the structure of international law. Two changes have profound implications for the structure of international law: the simultaneous push toward integration and fragmentation; and the rise of thousands of organizations and millions of individuals as relevant actors.

. . . [O]ur world is becoming both more integrated and more fragmented. Evidence of global integration abounds: regional trading units, global communication networks such as the worldwide web, international regimes covering issues ranging from banking and trade, to human rights, environmental protection, and arms control. The information revolution, the spread of financial markets, the penetration of industries across borders, the rapid technological advances, the global environmental problems and other economic interdependencies compel greater integration. Future problems will require global cooperation to address them effectively.

At the same time nationalism, ethnicity, and the need for personal affiliations and satisfaction push toward fragmentation and decentralization. Less than 10 percent of the more than 185 states are homogeneous ethnically. Only about 50 percent of the states have one ethnic group that accounts for three-quarters of the population. Scholars write of the rise of "tribalism" and the revealed need for community bonds. States are relinquishing elements of sovereignty to transnational networks of nonstate actors; the sense of community (with intense loyalty and identification) that served to bind together the citizens of the state is not being extended to the networks. . . .

The emerging system has many new international actors other than states. The 1995/96 edition of the Yearbook of International Organizations records 5,668 intergovernmental organizations and 36,054 nongovernmental organizations, for a total of 41,722 international organizations. There are other relevant actors in addition: multinational corporations, ethnic minorities, subunits of national governments, local nongovernmental organizations, illicit actors such as transnational drug cartels or terrorist networks, and ad hoc transnational associations of individuals. These new transnational elites are interested in particular outcomes, and may have extensive resources at their disposal. They are bound together in complex ways that change frequently. Most are part of the integrative pulse that is sweeping the globe.

. . . [Political scientists have suggested] that two-level games, internationally and domestically, are being played in all international negotiations and in the implementing and compliance theater that ensues after agreements go into effect. Robert Putnam offered in 1988 a theory of two-level games in which a state is engaged in separate games at the international and the national level, each influencing the other. "At the national level, domestic groups pursue their interests by pressuring the government to adopt favorable policies, and politicians seek power by constructing coalitions among those groups. At the international level, national governments seek to maximize their own ability to satisfy domestic pressures, while minimizing the adverse consequences of foreign developments. Neither of the two games can be ignored by central decision-makers, so long as their countries remain interdependent, yet sovereign."[2] Those who have been involved in international negotiations, whether over trade, environment, military security, or energy, have experienced this first hand. . . .

Traditionally states have been accountable to each other as sovereign independent states for assuring compliance with international law. This is still true. But the communications revolution has made governance more transparent and hence public involvement greater. . . .

[A]ccountability for the many nonstate actors has yet to emerge. Many are constructive in their influence; others not. Their sheer number poses congestion problems.

In a very important sense, participation by nonstate actors in the international legal system greatly enhances accountability, because it can give a voice to citizens who would otherwise be unrepresented, ensure that actions taken meet local needs, counter effects of high-level governmental corruption, and therefore produce outcomes that maximize human welfare efficiently. Information technology can assist because it makes information readily accessible to groups and individuals across the world and empowers them. It makes governments and international organizations more transparent. . . .

Two problems arise: how to structure constructively NGO [nongovernmental organization] and private sector participation in international governmental and international organization deliberations and how to ensure that the transnational norms developed largely outside of governments are responsive to public needs and concerns.

---

[2] Robert D. Putnam, *Diplomacy and Domestic Politics: The Logic of Two-Level Games*, 42 Intl. Org. 427, 434 (1988).

Particularly in international environmental law, nonstate actors are now prominent participants, either formally or informally, in international negotiations, conferences of parties, and other meetings. Some are membership-based and accountable to their members, while others are loosely accountable to their funders, who may be dispersed. While the UN ECOSOC still determines accreditation to intergovernmental meetings, the sheer number of NGOs suggests that the system needs to be reconsidered to ensure effective representation. Moreover, it is time to consider additional processes that legitimate NGO participation in the international legal system.

On the other hand, nongovernmental organizations also need to be held accountable for their actions. Spurious information, unrelenting pressures for special interest pleading outside the intergovernmental forum, unlimited demands for transparency, and similar concerns mean that pressures are building for at least an informal code of conduct. Leading nongovernmental organizations, who have contributed so much to developing and implementing international law in fields such as human rights and environment, may find it in their best self-interest to take the lead in initiating this. . . .

RED SKY AT MORNING
James Gustave Speth
132-33 (2004)

[Market failure and policy and political failure] taken together reflect our badly flawed political economy. Basically, our economic system does not work when it comes to protecting environmental resources, and, second, the political system does not work when it comes to correcting the economic system.

NOTES AND QUESTIONS

1.   *Prospects for cooperation.* What do the excerpts above suggest about the prospects and mechanisms for dealing with international environmental problems? Even during the height of the Cold War, the United States and the USSR often cooperated on environmental issues. *See* Magraw & Vinogradov, *Environmental Law*, in Beyond Confrontation: International Law for the Post-Cold War Era (L.F. Damrosch, G.M. Danilenko & R. Mullerson eds., 1995).

2.   *Developing countries and climate change.* Do small island developing countries, such as Vanuatu, have the same interests in climate change as landlocked developing countries like Bolivia or highly advanced developing countries like China?

3.   *Roles of various players.* What obstacles exist to the potential roles of individuals, non-governmental organizations, and various levels of government envisioned in the following excerpt from Gary Lawrence, Will

Habitat II Matter to the Members of the Organization for Economic Cooperation and Development? 14–15 (1996):

> [S]ome of the forces now at work which will affect public expectations on the legitimate role of national governments [are:]
>
> - Globalization of information, business and finance suggests that Ned Beatty's chilling line in the movie "Network"—"there are no nations . . . there are only corporations"—is true. If it were true, would the public think this better or worse?
>
> - Numerous examples of alternative ways of living, many of them make-believe, blanket the globe through movies, television and advertising, changing ideas of what constitutes a "normal" or "good" life. What will it mean to be German, Norwegian, Japanese or Australian if one's wants and desires are shaped by the same sources?
>
> - Changes from homogeneous to multi-cultural populations who bring expectations that differ from traditional expectations, thereby increasing complexity and diversity of interests within communities, making it much more difficult to develop national solutions which will work.
>
> Coupled with these trends toward homogenization of norms, values and expectations is an increased desire for individual identity. People will be looking for ways to demonstrate that they are part of a community, whether it is a community of place or community of interest. The most important factor will be that the community is small enough so that the individual can get some sense that his or her life matters and that his or her fate is somewhat within the individual's control . . .

4. *A New Economic System to Protect the Environment?* Do we need a new economic system to protect the environment? James Gustave Speth, the former Executive Director of the United Nations Development Programme, argues that "[t]here is a paradox at the heart of our economic system. The imperatives of today's economy are sharply at odds with those of the environment. Yet the environment is the very basis of the economy and of human well-being." James Gustave Speth, *From Crisis to Sustainability,* A Pivotal Moment: Population, Justice and the Environmental Challenge 329 (L.Mazur, ed. 2010). How could we make environment a central factor in our economy?

5. SUSTAINABLE DEVELOPMENT

Policymakers have not found it easy to deal with the relationship between environmental protection and other aspects of human behavior. As the foregoing materials indicate, the protection of health and the environment is inextricably related to economic activity and social conditions. But what precisely are those relationships, and how is a policymaker to approach dealing with them?

Sustainable development was officially recognized as the paradigm for improving the quality of life at the 1992 U.N. Conference on Environment and Development (UNCED, or the Earth Summit), in Rio de Janeiro, Brazil. The first publicly visible use of the term "sustainable development" was most probably in 1980 when it appeared in the World Conservation Strategy (WCS), a document prepared by the International Union for Conservation of Nature and Natural Resources (IUCN). The WCS defined sustainable development as "the integration of conservation and development to ensure that modifications to the planet do indeed secure the survival and well-being of all people." The WCS examined the contribution of living resource conservation to human survival and sustainable development, identified the priority conservation issues and main requirements for dealing with them, and proposed ways for effectively achieving the Strategy's aim.

The term "sustainable development" was further popularized and refined in 1987 by the World Commission on Environment and Development (WCED) (also known as the "Brundtland Commission"), an independent body created by the United Nations General Assembly. Its report, Our Common Future (1987), brought the term "sustainable development" to the forefront of international discourse and policymaking. The Brundtland Commission's discussion of sustainable development emphasized global interdependence, the need to consider future generations, the need to meet the needs of the world's poor, and the need to protect the environment at least to a significant degree.

Some have argued that the term sustainable development is oxymoronic (how can development, as change, be sustainable), or so general as to be meaningless. Commentators have responded that the former argument fails because it is the gains made by sustainable development that should be sustainable, not necessarily the process of change. Regarding the latter argument, many have pointed out that the concept of sustainable development needs to be general, to be able both to encompass a global phenomenon and to accommodate local economic and environmental conditions, cultures, values, etc.

One view is that sustainable development may best be viewed as a process rather than as a static end-point—a process that is not necessarily the same for all countries but that is founded on informed public input from all and the use of integrating tools such as sustainable development impact analysis, cost-internalization techniques, sustainability indicators, and natural resource accounting.

It is clear that there is no officially agreed-upon definition of sustainable development. The Brundtland Commission's definition, set forth in the following excerpt from Our Common Future 8–9, 43 (1987) (emphasis added), is the most repeated and generally subscribed to:

> Humanity has the ability to make development sustainable—to ensure that it meets the needs of the present without compromising the ability of future generations to meet their own needs. The concept of sustainable development does imply limits—not absolute limits but limitations imposed by the present state of technology and social organization on environmental resources and by the ability of the biosphere to absorb the effects of human activities. But technology and social organization can be both managed and improved to make way for a new era of economic growth. The commission believes that widespread poverty is no longer inevitable. Poverty is not only an evil in itself, but sustainable development requires meeting the basic needs of all and extending to all the opportunity to fulfill their aspirations for a better life. A world in which poverty is endemic will always be prone to ecological and other catastrophes.

> Meeting essential needs requires not only a new era of economic growth for nations in which the majority are poor, but an assurance that those poor get their fair share of the resources required to sustain that growth. Such equity would be aided by political systems that secure effective citizen participation in decision making and by greater democracy in international decision making.

> Sustainable global development requires that those who are more affluent adopt lifestyles within the planet's ecological means—in their use of energy, for example. Further, rapidly growing populations can increase the pressure on resources and slow any rise in living standards, thus sustainable development can only be pursued if population size and growth are in harmony with the changing productive potential of the ecosystem.

> Yet in the end, sustainable development is not a fixed state of harmony, but rather a process of change in which the exploitation of resources, the direction of investments, the orientation of technological development, and institutional change are made consistent with future as well as present needs. We do not pretend that the process is easy or straightforward. Painful choices have to be made. Thus, in the final analysis, sustainable development must rest on political will. . . .

> *Sustainable development is development that meets the needs of the present without compromising the ability of future*

generations to meet their own needs. It contains within it two key concepts:

- *the concept of "needs," in particular the essential needs of the world's poor, to which overriding priority should be given; and*

- *the idea of limitations imposed by the state of technology and social organization on the environment's ability to meet present and future needs.*

———————

Some developing countries have made an ongoing effort to place "sustained economic growth" as an equally important goal with sustainable development, or even to have it replace sustainable development. That effort came to a head at the 1995 World Summit for Social Development. The process of negotiating this issue revealed that high-level politicians from developing countries readily acknowledged the need to integrate social, economic, and environmental considerations. The result was a clear reaffirmation of sustainable development as the paradigm and, for the first time in a United Nations instrument, an explicit linkage of economic development, social development, and environmental protection. Paragraph 6 of the Copenhagen Declaration on Social Development makes this clear:

> We are deeply convinced that economic development, social development and environmental protection are interdependent and mutually reinforcing components of sustainable development, which is the framework for our efforts to achieve a higher quality of life, for all people. . . .

In 2000, the United Nations General Assembly adopted eight Millennium Development Goals (commonly referred to as "MDGs") and 15 related targets to be achieved by 2015. *See* UN Millennium Goals and Beyond 2015, *available at* http://www.un.org/millenniumgoals/. The MDGs are: (1) Eradicate extreme poverty and hunger; (2) Achieve universal primary education; (3) Promote gender equality and empower women; (4) Reduce child mortality; (5) Improve maternal health; (6) Combat HIV/AIDS, malaria, and other diseases; (7) Ensure environmental sustainability; and (8) Develop a global partnership for development. The MDGs have been instrumental in shaping international dialogue and setting international priorities. They were reaffirmed at the 2002 World Summit on Sustainable Development (WSSD) in Johannesburg and in the 2005 World Summit Outcome adopted by the United Nations General Assembly. The MDGs include obvious elements of sustainable development and are viewed by some as providing needed clarity to the concept.

The United Nations General Assembly adopted a new set of Sustainable Development Goals in September 2015, in a process that is described briefly in Chapter 18. A number of the 17 SDGs and 169 associated targets relate to environmental protection. *See* Transforming Our World: The 2030 Agenda for Sustainable Development, UN. Doc A/69/L.85 (Aug. 11, 2015). Those aspects relating to rule of law are also directly relevant to both domestic and international environmental law.

NOTES AND QUESTIONS

1.   *Sustainable development and the Global South.* Does sustainable development reflect an adequate understanding of the interrelationship among economic, social, and environmental issues? Would a focus on sustained economic growth be a return to the pure growth strategy or the trickle down strategy of the past?

2.   *Is the concept useful?* Does the concept of sustainable development actually provide detailed guidance? If not, is the concept nevertheless useful? If sustainable development is not the appropriate paradigm, what should the over-arching model be? Can there be one? If there is not one, can a successful international dialogue occur?

3.   *Sustainable development in case law.* In the decision of the International Court of Justice in the *Gabčíkovo-Nagymaros* case (Hungary/Slovakia), Sept. 25, 1997, extracted later in this book, then-Vice President Weeramantry devoted an entire section of his separate opinion to "The Concept of Sustainable Development." He stated that while the Court "referred to it as a concept . . . I consider it to be more than a mere concept, but as a principle with normative value. . . ." He also wrote that "the principle of sustainable development . . . , in my view, . . . is an integral part of modern international law. It is clearly of the utmost importance, both in this case and more generally." See the discussion in Chapter 4.

4.   *Implementation of sustainable development.* It is sometimes said that sustainable development is essentially an approach that requires consideration of various components (economic, social, environmental) and of the interests not only of the present generation but also of future generations and that also requires both transparency and meaningful public participation. What tools are useful in carrying out such an approach? Some that might be considered include environmental impact assessments, sustainability impact assessments, cost-benefit analyses (including environmental degradation and impact on ecosystem services), natural resource accounting, corporate responsibility mechanisms (voluntary and involuntary), partnerships between government and various elements of the private sector and civil society, education, and transparency and public participation. Can you think of others?

5.   *Gender.* MDG 3 is to "Promote gender equality and empower women." In many societies, women have traditionally had a different relation to nature than have men, women are subject to different environmental

stresses than men, and women have somewhat different susceptibilities to those stresses. Regarding the first aspect of this, consider the following excerpt from Women and the Environment 11 (2004), a UNEP publication:

> The world is unique for every human being, but, in general, women's lives vary greatly from those of men because of patterns of socialization related to gender. In terms of the environment, women around the world play different roles: in managing plants and animals in forests, drylands, wetlands and agriculture; in collecting water, fuel and fodder for domestic use and income generation; and in overseeing land and water resources. . . . Women's extensive experience makes them an invaluable source of knowledge and expertise on environmental management.

Draft SDG 5 of 2015 also addresses gender equality by committing to "Achieve gender equality and empower all women and girls." Targets for the goal include elimination of all forms of discrimination and violence against women and girls, as well as equal rights to economic resources and full participation and equal opportunity for leadership.

6.   ETHICAL CONTEXT

Many would argue that the environmental problems we face today demand a new ethical approach and that we have a moral obligation to protect the environment for ourselves and for future generations. Consider the following excerpt.

ENCYCLICAL LETTER LAUDATO SI' OF THE HOLY FATHER FRANCIS ON CARE FOR OUR COMMON HOME
Released May 24, 2015

Part IV, The Principle of the Common Good, Chapter 3, paragraph 156: Human ecology is inseparable from the notion of the common good, a central and unifying principle of social ethics. The common good is "the sum of those conditions of social life which allow social groups and their individual members relatively thorough and ready access to their own fulfilment."

Part I, Chapter 1 paragraph 23: The climate is a common good, belonging to all and meant for all. At the global level it is a complex system linked to many of the essential conditions for human life.

Chapter 6, paragraph 202: Many things have to change course, but it is we human beings above all who need to change. We lack an awareness of our common origin, of our mutual belonging, and of a future to be shared with everyone. This basic awareness would enable the development of new convictions, attitudes and forms of life. A great cultural, spiritual and educational challenge stands before us, and it will demand that we set out on the long path of renewal.

NOTES AND QUESTIONS

1. *The principle of the Common Good.* Does this provide a basis for legal obligations toward ensuring the sustainability of our environment?

2. *The Common Concern of Humankind.* States have described both climate change and biodiversity as "a common concern of humankind" in the UN Framework Convention on Climate Change and the Convention on Biological Diversity, respectively. Might this reflect an ethical basis such as that in the Common Good?

3. *Role for Ethics.* What role do you see for ethics in addressing international environmental problems? Consider also the materials in Chapter 2 regarding the philosophical framework.

C. DEVELOPMENT OF INTERNATIONAL ENVIRONMENTAL LAW IN THE ANTHROPOCENE

Both domestic and international environmental law were developed mainly in the latter half of the twentieth century during the early emergency of the Anthropocene Epoch. The law rested on several fundamental assumptions. First, the problems were scientific and thus in good part technocratic. Thus, one could expect a significant level of consensus across the planet. Second, environmental issues could be addressed within existing structures, so that property rights, for example, were left in place. Third, individuals in developed countries could continue their life styles and those in the developing world could aspire to those life styles. A few voices argued that more radical changes would be needed in governance, the legal system, and in the range of options open to individuals and to governments. But advocates of a deeper philosophical and political response were marginalized. As you study the legal regime that emerged since the 1970s, you should ask yourself if the international agreements, nonbinding instruments, international institutions and other structures are capable of addressing the magnitude of the problems that face us in the accelerating Anthropocene. If not, what might we need? There are no simple answers to these questions, but they need to be carefully considered and addressed.

RULE OF LAW FOR NATURE IN A KALEIDOSCOPIC WORLD
Edith Brown Weiss
Adapted from Rule of Law for Nature: New Dimensions and Ideas in Environmental Law
(Christina Voigt ed, 2013) (Most footnotes deleted)

"Now I truly believe that we in this generation must come to terms with nature, and I think we're challenged, as mankind has never been challenged before, to prove our maturity and our mastery, not of nature but of ourselves." [Rachel Carson, *Silent Spring*, 1962]

We stand at a critical juncture in conserving our human environment and protecting nature. Scientists warn that while we have been living in the stable Holocene Epoch, we may be entering a new geological epoch— the Anthropocene—in which humans have become the central force affecting the planet. We are challenged as never before to work together to sustain the integrity and robustness of the environment and at the same time to ensure that everyone can benefit from it. Law has an important role, for it embodies our values and shapes our behavior. It obligates us to engage in certain practices and to refrain from others.

The special challenge confronting the rule of law and the protection of nature is that we are living now in a kaleidoscopic world, in which not only States but transnational networks, corporations, nongovernmental organizations, *ad hoc* coalitions, and increasingly individuals shape and implement the rule of law for nature. At the same time, our environmental problems have become more complex and systemic.

In order to understand our ability to use international environmental law to address the problems, it is useful to analyze its evolution over the last four decades. We shall find that the field has flourished and expanded, but at the same time that much more needs to be done. And the path ahead is far from clear.

1. The Path to Today[2]

Our concern for the environment is ancient and embedded in various religious and cultural traditions. But the emergence of international and national environmental law is recent—less than five decades ago. In 1970, when environmental law began to flourish, States were concerned with environmental issues within their country and to a lesser extent with transboundary pollution and protection of specific fauna and flora.

In 1972, States gathered for the first international conference on the environment: the Stockholm Conference on the Human Environment. The insertion of "human" before environment in the title of the Stockholm Declaration on the Human Environment reflected an important recognition that the issues were not just about conserving nature for nature's sake, but also about humans in relation to the environment. The world was quite different in 1972. States were still the central and largely unchallenged actors, and there were many fewer than today. The United Nations had only 132 member countries. An international intergovernmental organization dedicated to the environment did not yet exist. The United Nations Environment Programme was established only after the 1972 Stockholm Conference on the Human Environment. In 1972, few multilateral environmental agreements existed, and these were concerned mainly with sustainable use of specific living resources and

---

    2   For more detail, see E. Brown Weiss, 'The Evolution of International Environmental Law', 54 *Japanese Yearbook of International Law* 1–28 (2011).

with transboundary pollution problems. We did not yet have agreements on globally common resources, such as the high-level ozone layer, or on the complex problem of climate change, or on natural resources within national borders of concern to the international community, such as biodiversity and deserts.

At the national level, most countries did not yet have environmental legislation. In the United States, the 1969 National Environmental Policy Act was the first major piece of national environmental legislation, which required environmental impact statements for major federal activities significantly affecting the environment. The United States established its national environmental agency, the Environmental Protection Agency, only in 1970. Businesses did not have councils or networks that were concerned with environmental issues, and there were still relatively few non-governmental organizations focused on environment, especially outside North America and Europe.

In 1972, a central issue was the perceived conflict between economic development and environmental protection. Developing countries feared that a focus on environmental protection would be at the expense of economic development. A path-breaking meeting of governmental and non-governmental experts from developed and developing countries, which met in Founex, Switzerland developed a conceptual framework for reconciling economic development and environmental protection. This was essential to the success of the Stockholm Conference and laid the foundation for States to confirm sustainable development as the guiding normative framework in Rio de Janeiro twenty years later.

Since the Stockholm Conference, States have concluded hundreds of new international legal instruments concerned with environment or with important provisions related to environment. Some are formal binding agreements, while many others are legally nonbinding instruments, or what is sometimes referred to as "soft law." Already in 1999, there were more than 1100 such international legal instruments, and the numbers have climbed dramatically since then.[6] The agreements and other instruments have expanded from focusing on individual species (whales, fur seals, and migratory birds) to protecting ecosystems and marine areas, from focusing on transboundary air and water pollution to depletion of the high-level ozone layer, and from single-focused problems, such as pollution by heavy metals or persistent organic pollutants, to the enormously complex systemic issues related to climate change.

International legal principles related to the environment have also developed during the last four decades. Principle 21 of the 1972 Stockholm Declaration on the Human Environment and a number of

---

[6] E. Brown Weiss, D.B. Magraw & P.C. Szasz, *International Environmental Law, Basic Instruments and References* (Transnational, 1992, 1999), Vol I (1992), Vol. II (1999) (Volume I provides a list of 900 such international legal instruments).

principles in the 1992 Rio Declaration on Environment and Development have become part of international law or are in the process of becoming so. In 1996, the International Court of Justice recognized the essence of Principle 21 of the Stockholm Declaration on the Human Environment as part of the corpus of international law, According to the Court, "the general obligation of States to ensure that activities within their jurisdiction and control respect the environment of other States or of areas beyond national control is now part of the corpus of international law relating to the environment."[7] In the later *Pulp Mills Case*, the Court pronounced the requirement for an environmental impact assessment for activities having a significant adverse transboundary impact, especially on a shared resource, to be a general rule of international law.

At the national level, every country now has at least one environmental statute or regulation, usually at least several. These cover air pollution, water pollution, waste disposal, hazardous chemicals, forests, water, biodiversity, wetlands, and desertification, among other topics. In 2012, the United Nations Environment Programme (UNEP) established a new program on the Rule of Law and the Environment, to increase respect for environmental laws at the national and subnational level and to address them effectively in judicial and auditing proceedings.

Within the last fifteen years, States have become less concerned with negotiating new binding international agreements and much more concerned with implementing and complying with them. UNEP adopted Guidelines on Compliance with and Enforcement of Multilateral Environmental Agreements and published a manual on the subject. States have increasingly established Implementation and/or Compliance Committees within multilateral environmental agreements to address issues of noncompliance by member States. Market mechanisms have also been incorporated into the design and implementation of certain multilateral environmental agreements, such as the Kyoto Protocol [on climate change].

The actors who participate in developing, implementing, and interpreting international environmental law have expanded far beyond States to include international organizations, multilateral development banks, nongovernmental organizations, private sector business councils, industry associations, civil society, and most importantly, individuals. . . .

One of the most significant developments in the last two decades is that international environmental law has been increasingly joined with other areas of international law. The latter include international trade, international investment, economic development, human rights and national security. Protection of the environment is no longer viewed in isolation from other issues. This has important implications for the rule of

---

[7]   Legality of the Threat or Use of Nuclear Weapons, *Advisory Opinion, I.C.J. Reports 1996,* 226; Gabčíkovo-Nagymaros Project (*Hungary/Slovakia*), Judgment, *I.C.J. Reports 1997,* 7.

law and nature, because it brings relevant bodies of law to bear on the issue and provides a voice for protecting nature in deliberations in other fora.

Finally, and essentially, environmental protection and thereby protection of nature are now seen as including issues of justice, for poor communities may suffer most from environmental degradation and the failure to implement sustainable development. This is especially relevant, since more than 1 billion people live in extreme poverty, and 2.2 billion people [updated figures] live on less than $2.00 per day. That is less than the cost of an espresso or a cup of tea in many countries. While sustainable development is most in the interest of poor people, their voices are the most likely to be overlooked in the process of development, or in responding to environmental challenges. The current emphasis in international environmental law on transparency, access to information, public participation, and access to remedies could help to give a voice to poor communities and to poor people, and to ensure that sustainable economic development responds to local needs and cultural traditions.

These are the encouraging developments in the last forty years. Quite remarkably, we have witnessed the emergence and rapid growth of a new field of international law. Governments at all levels, industries, nongovernmental organizations, transnational groups, and civil society more generally have become engaged in the issues. We may view this as a glass half-full, as one filled with accomplishment and promise, but with still much to do. Or we may look to the onset of the Anthropocene epoch and the increasingly grave environmental problems facing our planet and conclude that the glass is half-empty, and that it is not clear we can fill the glass. In this view, there is serious doubt about whether we have the capacity and requisite intent to protect nature in the future and to ensure sustainable development for all people. We are at a critical juncture in international environmental law, in which we will need to forge new paths to address global environmental problems and to advance the rule of law for nature.

2.   Path to the Future

The path to the future is enormously challenging, especially in the face of two developments.

The Anthropocene

We may be leaving the Holocene epoch, in which nature held sway, and entering the Anthropocene epoch, in which humans are the major force shaping the planet in profound ways.

Since the end of the Pleistocene geological epoch, about 11,500 to 12,000 years ago, we have been living in the geological epoch known as the Holocene. In geological time, this is considered a warm period, between glacial periods. In 2000, Nobel Laureate Paul Crutzen and

Eugene Stoermer observed that human activities have now assumed a central role in shaping the planet and suggested that accordingly we have now entered a new geological epoch called the Anthropocene. . . . Humans are now a force of nature shaping the planet on a geological scale and at a far faster rate than traditional geological speed.

There are many examples of our dramatic effects. One engineering project alone, the Syncrude mine in the Athabasca tar sands in Alberta, Canada, will move 30 billion tons of earth, which is twice the amount of sediment that flows down all the rivers of the world in one year. The sediment in river flows is also shrinking. Over the last 40 to 50 years, 50,000 large dams have reduced sediment flow in rivers by 20%. Deltas, where many people live, are eroding faster than they can be replenished. Ninety per cent of the world's fauna and flora lies in ecosystems significantly affected by human activity. The extinction rate of species has been accelerating and is far higher than during other geological periods, of which biologists have long been warning us. The impacts from human activities will only increase, as our population is expected to reach 10 billion by 2100.

One of the most disturbing developments is that scientists have begun to warn that both the carbon cycle and the nitrogen cycle are accelerating, the latter by 150%. Moreover, within the last decade, hydrologists have uncovered evidence that the hydrological cycle is speeding up, with potentially devastating impacts from more frequent and intense severe storms, floods, and droughts. We are interrupting the natural processes of our planet, refashioning them and, most importantly, accelerating them.

The Anthropocene epoch sharply strengthens the fundamental message that all of us share a global environment, that we are for the foreseeable future locked into the same atmosphere and biosphere, and that what we do in one place, either individually or cumulatively, can significantly affect the local and global resilience and integrity of our planet. The scale and rapidity of change make action urgent. We could invoke the analogy of a ship that has a big hole in it, which is expanding rapidly. Something needs to be done to ensure that the ship stays afloat. UNEP's 5th edition of its Global Environmental Outlook concludes that Earth's systems are being pushed to the limit and warns that "several critical thresholds are approaching or have been exceeded, beyond which abrupt and non-linear changes to the life-support functions of the planet could occur. This has significant implications for human well-being now and in the future." The emergence of the Anthropocene epoch raises issues of intergenerational equity as never before, for what we do today will have enormous impacts on the welfare of future generations. The global impact of our activities and the rapid pace of change make actions urgent but also complicated in new and as yet not well-understood ways.

The Kaleidoscopic World

We are now living in what may be termed a kaleidoscopic world, in which information technology is transforming the ways in which individuals, ad hoc coalitions, nongovernmental organizations, transnational networks, business associations, and other groups participate in governance at global, national and local levels. Governments and the increasing array of international intergovernmental organizations are critical players, but the system is much more chaotic, and less hierarchical than before.

Opposite movements exist in the international system: both toward greater integration and toward greater fragmentation. According to the 2015 Yearbook of International Organizations, there are now over 30,000 active intergovernmental and international nongovernmental organizations, and if special international organizations and inactive ones are included, over 67,000 [updated figures]. At the same time, fragmentation has increased within countries and across countries. Since 1648, we have lived, at least in the West, in a world dominated by sovereign, theoretically equally independent States. It has been a hierarchical system, in which States reach agreements among themselves and are responsible for those activities that take place within their borders or jurisdiction. In recent decades, scholars have written about transnational actors, networks, and other groupings, which have also become significant international actors. These are not States but are still formal groupings.

We are now entering a new stage, in which informal groups, *ad hoc* coalitions, and individuals are becoming important actors in influencing the development and implementation of international and domestic environmental law, and in carrying out (or not carrying out) obligations to conserve the environment. States remain central, but the context in which they operate is in flux. This world context may be called the kaleidoscopic world. It is a world in which change occurs rapidly, in which communication is rapid, and in which shifting informal groups, *ad hoc* coalitions and increasingly individuals are significant actors. Most importantly we are living in a period in which there are rapid and often unforeseen changes with widespread effects.

Information technology is transforming the participation of peoples globally in political, economic, and social life. The technology makes possible ever shifting *ad hoc* coalitions and informal groups and a myriad of individual initiatives. Information technology and social networking let people collaborate across time and place through Facebook, YouTube, blogs, Twitter, and their analogs in various countries. As of March 2015, Tumblr alone hosted more than 226 million blogs. On WordPress, 409 million people view more than 17 billion pages each month, in 120 different languages. Tens of thousands of WordPress sites are created every day. Twitter reported 288 million users in March 2015, with the vast majority of UN member countries having a presence on Twitter [updated figures]. Mobile phones are now widely used to communicate across borders and to help organize coalitions, which can lead to direct action within and across countries. While many poor people do not have direct access yet to mobile phones, their rate of access is sharply increasing, especially in Africa, Asia and Latin America. The explosive developments in information and communication technology mean that groups and especially individuals can increasingly participate in the development, interpretation, and implementation of international law generally, and of environmental law at all levels. This may be characterized as "bottom-up empowerment."

. . .

The kaleidoscopic world is characterized by rapid change and bottom-up empowerment. It is dynamic and in many ways informal. Unlike a real kaleidoscope, no one entity controls the interactions of the many actors in the kaleidoscope. Here a word of caution is necessary, for at the same time that bottom-up empowerment is occurring, top-down control is becoming vastly easier through information technology. Certain governments or other powerful actors, even illicit ones, may soon be able to monitor nearly all communications and through crowd sourcing all meetings, which would give them unprecedented power. This could threaten, or even triumph over, democracy and the rule of law, and make it much harder for all actors, especially non-State actors, to respond flexibly and effectively to environmental challenges.

With this caveat, the kaleidoscopic world may provide an important key to dealing effectively with the global crises of the Anthropocene. Bottom-up empowerment of non-State actors through easy access to information and communications technology can provide fast, flexible, powerful ways to target specific environmental problems directly. It minimizes blockages and administrative costs. However, the very aspects of the kaleidoscopic world that could allow it to respond rapidly and effectively may at the same time undermine its ability to address problems on a more integrated and larger scale efficiently. States and communities within States may be faced with multiple standards and requirements, with multiple demands for accountability, and with little co-ordination or mutual recognition between them.

. . .

The kaleidoscopic world is in many ways democratic in the sense that there are many fewer barriers to participation. It also implicitly carries a certain degree of anarchy within it. . . .

In a kaleidoscopic world, many of the actions we need to take to sustain the integrity and robustness of our environment will be voluntary in nature. The effectiveness of these for managing complex environmental problems depends upon shared values and shared concerns about common problems. . . . In this context, shared values will be the glue that keeps everything together, and makes possible the necessary widespread and sustained cooperation. . . .

NOTES AND QUESTIONS

1. What makes environmental degradation, natural resource use, or risk creation issues of international concern, which international environmental law might address? Consider the following:

    a. A chemical company regulated by State A spills toxic wastes into a transboundary river which forces a city in State B to cease withdrawing water from the river.

    b. An oil tanker 40 miles off-shore from State A breaks apart due to the failure of flag State B to correct design defects in the ship and the oil spill forces the closure of a world famous beach for the summer season.

    c. An industry in State A negotiates a private contract with a company in State B, which has no legislation regulating hazardous waste disposal, to deposit barrels of hazardous wastes on the latter company's land in State B.

    d. State A has a huge rain forest which has served as a global carbon sink, but State A's national development plan contemplates converting 40% of the forest to beef and corn production.

    e. Arid State A buys 10,000 acres on a river in State B, which has more water than State A has, to grow fruits and vegetables for the citizens of State A, and the water diversions prevent subsistent farming in State B.

    f. Novel genes from genetically engineered corn being grown in State A are incorporated into the genes of corn in State B making that corn unfit for use in ceremonies that are essential to the culture of indigenous people in State B.

    g. The World Bank finances an industrial project in State A that damages a fragile ecosystem there.

    h. State A finances a lead mine within its own territory that causes sickness and death to nearby residents within its own territory.

    i. Virtually all countries of the world face the need to deal with a particular environmental problem within their respective borders.

2. *The 1972 Stockholm Declaration on the Human Environment and the 1992 Rio Declaration on Environment and Development.* These two short

texts are foundational instruments for international environmental law and policy. The Stockholm Declaration was agreed to in 1972 at the watershed UN Stockholm Conference on the Human Environment, which in many ways inaugurated the modern international environmental movement. The Rio Declaration was adopted at the 1992 UN Conference on Environment and Development (referred to as UNCED, or the Earth Summit), at which the international community adopted sustainable development as the framework for improving the quality of life for all. Both Declarations were negotiated by governments with input from civil society. The full texts of both Declarations are *available at* www.unep.org. They will often be referred to later in this book, and it is useful to read them both in their entirety at this point. Note that the principles often use the term "shall", which in international parlance normally connotes a legally binding norm; but the Declarations were considered nonbinding statements when they were adopted. However, Principle 21 of the Stockholm Declaration and some principles in the Rio Declaration are now accepted as customary international law, and hence binding.

At this point in the course, we would like you to consider the question: To what extent do these instruments reflect the interdependencies, complexities and concepts set forth in the excerpts in this chapter? For example, do the instruments call for taking into account the interests of future generations? Do they contain provisions about transboundary harm? As mentioned earlier in this chapter, Rio Principle 8 refers to "appropriate demographic policies"; the earlier Stockholm Declaration's Principle 16 refers to "[d]emographic policies which are without prejudice to basic human rights." Is there a difference between these two principles? Rio Principles 16 and 18 refer respectively to taking a precautionary approach in light of scientific uncertainty and to conducting environmental impact assessment. How does the Stockholm Declaration deal with uncertainty? Do the instruments have provisions relating to poverty? The interests of developing countries? Pollution control? Natural resource protection? International cooperation? Economic activity, including international trade? Culture? The interconnectedness of nature?

3.   *A kaleidoscopic world.* How will a kaleidoscopic world affect the development and implementation of international environmental law?

D. THE COMMONS

The traditional definition of a commons is an area to which access cannot be prevented. It is thus shared in common. The high-level ozone layer is a commons. The term has been employed more broadly to areas such as the high seas and a shared ground water aquifer. Commons can occur at many different geographical scales. One might argue that for some purposes our planet constitutes a global commons.

1. NATURAL RESOURCES PROTECTION

The first excerpt, the Tragedy of the Commons, is a classic article by population biologist Garrett Hardin. The title has emerged as the principal metaphor for a wide range of environmental problems from cross-border pollution to the loss of biodiversity and global climate change. Hardin both explains why the lack of restraint in the use of resources can lead to their degradation, and provides a justification for government intervention to prevent such degradation. He also provides the basis for exploring other alternatives. An excerpt from Elinor Ostrom, a political scientist who was awarded a Nobel Prize in Economics, follows the Hardin piece. Ostrom's research shows that the management of commons is possible and occurs in many places but under well-defined circumtances.

THE TRAGEDY OF THE COMMONS
Garrett Hardin
162 Science 1243, 1244–1245 (1968)

The tragedy of the commons developed in this way. Picture a pasture open to all. It is to be expected that each herdsman will try to keep as many cattle as possible on the commons. Such an arrangement may work reasonably satisfactorily for centuries because tribal wars, poaching, and disease keep the numbers of both man and beast well below the carrying capacity of the land. Finally, however, comes the day of reckoning, that is, the day when the long-desired goal of social stability becomes a reality. At this point, the inherent logic of the commons remorselessly generates tragedy.

As a rational being, each herdsman seeks to maximize his gain. Explicitly or implicitly, more or less consciously, he asks, "What is the utility to me of adding one more animal to my herd?" This utility has one negative and one positive component.

1. The positive component is a function of the increment of one animal. Since the herdsman receives all the proceeds from the sale of the additional animal, the positive utility is nearly +1.

2. The negative component is a function of the additional overgrazing created by one more animal. Since, however, the effects of overgrazing are shared by all the herdsmen, the negative utility for any particular decision-making herdsman is only a fraction of –1.

Adding together the component partial utilities, the rational herdsman concludes that the only sensible course for him to pursue is to add another animal to his herd. And another; and another. But this is the conclusion reached by each and every rational herdsman sharing a commons. Therein is the tragedy. Each man is locked into a system that compels him to increase his herd without limit—in a world that is limited. Ruin is the destination toward which all men rush, each pursuing his own best interest in a society that believes in the freedom of the commons. Freedom in a commons brings ruin to all.

GOVERNING THE COMMONS
Elinor Ostrom
1 (1990)

Hardly a week goes by without a major news story about the threatened destruction of a valuable natural resource. In June of 1989, for example, a *New York Times* article focused on the problem of overfishing in the Georges Bank about 150 miles off the New England coast. Catches of cod, flounder, and haddock are now only a quarter of what they were during the 1960s. Everyone knows that the basic problem is overfishing; however, those concerned cannot agree how to solve the problem. Congressional representatives recommend new national legislation, even though the legislation already on the books has been enforced only erratically. Representatives of the fishers argue that the fishing grounds would not be in such bad shape if the federal government had refrained from its sporadic attempts to regulate the fishery in the past. The issue in this case—and many others—is how best to limit the use of natural resources so as to ensure their long-term economic viability. Advocates of central regulation or of privatization, and of regulation by those involved have pressed their policy prescriptions in a variety of different arenas.

Similar situations occur on diverse scales ranging from small neighborhoods to the entire planet. The issues of how best to govern natural resources used by many individuals in common are no more settled in academia than in the world of politics. Some scholarly articles about the "tragedy of the commons" recommend that "the state" control most natural resources to prevent their destruction; others recommend that privatizing those resources will resolve the problem. What one can observe in the world, however, is that neither the state nor the market is uniformly successful in enabling individuals to sustain long-term, productive use of natural resource systems. Further, communities of individuals have relied on institutions resembling neither the state nor the market to govern some resource systems with reasonable degrees of success over long periods of time.

For a discussion of English philopher John Locke's principle that a person may take as much from the commons as he wants provided that there is enough left for others and there is no waste, see James Nickel & Daniel Magraw, *Philosophy of International Environmental Law*, in The

Philosophy of International Law (S. Benson & J. Tasioulas, eds., 2010). For an analysis which identifies commons at multiple geographical levels and discusses the governance structures needed to deal with them, see, Burns H. Weston & David Bollier, Green Governance (2013).

2. POLLUTION

In a reverse way, the tragedy of the commons reappears in problems of pollution. Here it is not a question of taking something out of the commons, but of putting something in—sewage, or chemical, radioactive, and other wastes into water; noxious and dangerous fumes into the air; and distracting and unpleasant advertising signs into the line of sight. The calculations of utility are much the same as before. The rational person finds that his share of the cost of the wastes he discharges into the commons is less than the cost of purifying his wastes before releasing them. Since this is true for everyone, we are locked into a system of "fouling our own nest," so long as we behave only as independent, rational, free-enterprisers.

The tragedy of the commons as a food basket may be averted, at least in part, by private property, or something formally like it. But the air and waters surrounding us cannot readily be fenced, and so the tragedy of the commons as a cesspool must be prevented by different means, such as coercive laws or taxing devices that make it cheaper for the polluter to treat his pollutants than to discharge them untreated. We have not progressed as far with the solution of this problem as we have with the first. Indeed, our particular concept of private property, which deters us from exhausting the positive resources of the earth, favors pollution. The owner of a factory on the bank of a stream—whose property extends to the middle of the stream—often has difficulty seeing why it is not his natural right to muddy the waters flowing past his door. The law, often behind the times, requires elaborate stitching and fitting to adapt it to this newly perceived aspect of the commons.

3. HOW TO LEGISLATE TEMPERANCE?

Analysis of the pollution problem as a function of population density uncovers a not generally recognized principle of morality, namely: the morality of an act is a function of the state of the system at the time it is performed. A hundred and fifty years ago a plainsman could kill an American bison, cut out only the tongue for his dinner, and discard the rest of the animal. He was not in any important sense being wasteful. Today, with only a few thousand bison left, we would be appalled at such behavior.

NOTES AND QUESTIONS

1. *A game theory explanation.* The classic prisoner's dilemma case illuminates the tragedy of the commons. In the prisoner's dilemma, there are two prisoners who, during a private interrogation, must decide whether to confess to a moderate crime or to accuse the other prisoner of a serious crime. The accuser goes free unless the other prisoner has also accused him or her of a serious crime, in which case both receive a much heavier sentence than if they had confessed to a moderate crime in common. If you were a prisoner who would never see the other person again after this event, what would you choose? Would it make a difference if you played this game and knew that the two of you would encounter the same situation together at least 20 times? Would it make a difference if you could communicate with the other prisoner before making your choice? If there were 20 other prisoners instead of two? Does it change your opinion to know that real prisoners in this situation rarely confess or implicate their partner? *See* Brian Forst & Judith Lucianovic, *The Prisoner's Dilemma: Theory and Reality*, 5 J. Crim. Justice 55–64 (1977).

2. *Some hard questions.* In the tragedy of the commons, the goal is to move from a situation in which countries are increasingly worse off to one in which they use the commons on a sustainable basis and make modest gains. What are the different kinds of approaches that a community can take to manage a commons on a sustainable basis? What does each require? What are the limitations of each? What are the transaction costs? Is government regulation always necessary?

3. *What implications for managing the commons?* What do you see as the major impediments to making international environmental law effective in addressing problems of a commons, whether regional or global, or even local? Do differences between countries, e.g., access to information or level of understanding of the implications, matter?

4. *What might be helpful?* What role do you see for governments? For non-governmental organizations? For business enterprises and the private sector? For international intergovernmental organizations or multilateral development and financial institutions?

5. How could we implement an ethical principle such as the Common Good in the context of the commons? What implications would that have for environmental rule of law?

CONCLUDING QUESTIONS

Can you think of examples from your daily life of the interdependence and interconnectedness of the various elements and systems of the environment? Has the material in this chapter caused you to think differently about law and governance in the field of environment generally, and in the internationally shared environment, in particular? If so, how?

CHAPTER 2

THE PHILOSOPHICAL FRAMEWORK: SUSTAINABILITY, INTERGENERATIONAL EQUITY, AND THE HUMAN RELATIONSHIP WITH NATURE

• • •

Climate change is inherently intergenerational. What we do today affects not only our children, grandchildren, and great grandchildren, but generations beyond. For the first time, all peoples have to confront questions of fairness to future generations as well as to people living today.

Two philosophical dimensions underpin the content of international environmental law: our relationship to future generations and our relationship to nature. The positions that we hold on these two relations are embodied in international legal principles, agreements, and nonbinding legal instruments. Understanding our approaches to these two dimensions will help us articulate what legal measures we want to have in place. A third dimension is environmental justice—our responsibilities to those who are economically impoverished, which is fundamental to national and international environmental law and addressed elsewhere in specific contexts in the course book.

Many problems in addition to climate change raise profound questions about our obligations to future generations and the rights they have. These include destruction of the high-level ozone layer, disposal of nuclear wastes, loss of biological diversity, degradation of productive soils, toxic contamination of lakes and the marine environment, loss of tropical forests, and depletion of nonrechargeable ground water aquifers. Similarly, concern for whales, with their special intelligence, and other animal species and for flora raise concerns about our relationship with and obligations to them. In both cases, what obligations do we have toward future generations or toward other species? What does international law have to say about these questions?

47

A. THE INTERGENERATIONAL DIMENSION

1. INTERGENERATIONAL ENVIRONMENTAL ISSUES

The following article sets out the author's view that any generation must address three problems of fairness among generations: depletion of resources resulting in the loss of options or diversity in resources, degradation in the quality of the environment and its resources, and discriminatory access to resources among generations and within the present generation.

IN FAIRNESS TO FUTURE GENERATIONS: INTERNATIONAL LAW, COMMON PATRIMONY AND INTERGENERATIONAL EQUITY

Edith Brown Weiss
Ch. 1 (Transnational & UNU 1989)

As we develop and use the natural and cultural resources of our planet, we will face problems in allocating the wealth from these resources between members of the present generation and those of future generations. Since future generations are not represented in the processes for making decisions today, potential trade-offs between the preferences of present and future generations are usually ignored. Thus, the present generation may benefit from these resources at the expense of future generations.

Development and use of our natural and cultural resources raise three kinds of equity problems between generations: depletion of resources for future generations, degradation in quality of resources for future generations, and discriminatory access to use and benefit from the resources received from past generations.

A. DEPLETION OF RESOURCES

At least three kinds of actions by the present generation may deplete resources and thereby conflict with the interest of future generations: (1) consumption of higher quality resources, leading to higher real prices of resources for future generations; (2) consumption of resources not yet identified as valuable by the present generation or prior to discovery of their best use; and (3) exhaustion of resources, resulting in the narrowing of the range of available natural resources. The effects of these actions, particularly of the last two, may be effectively irreversible. . . .

Some economists would object to the possibility of a rise in real prices of natural resources on the grounds that there is infinite substitution of resources and unlimited capacity of improvement in extraction technology. If a rise in real prices occurs, they would contend that it may be due to higher labor costs or costs of other factors in the production process. But this is optimistic. Countries may not be able to find alternative energy supplies at the same real price as they have paid for oil or coal, or they may not find equally cheap alternatives for the products derived from particular species of plants and animals. . . .

The second problem of equity among generations arises because natural resources are often exploited in ignorance of their potential economic importance, which may deplete potentially valuable resources. History offers many examples. Companies flared the natural gas which was a byproduct of extracting oil, because the cost of delivery exceeded the price that it could command at that time. . . . Unless we proceed cautiously, we will discard natural resources that future generations would have wanted to pay us handsomely to retain.

The third problem arises from the exhaustion of resources, which leads to a narrowing of the diversity of the resource base that we pass to future generations and, in some cases, eliminates resources that people depend upon. To the extent that we consume all or nearly all known quantities of an existing natural resource, we reduce the natural resource options available to future generations. This reduces the economic soundness of the natural resource base for future generations, because we lose important options for developing new beneficial products. For example, through the rapid extinction of species, we can lose important options for developing new food crops and new medicines. . . .

Reducing the diversity of known reserves of nonrenewable resources raises several problems for future generations. It forecloses applications for the resources that the present generation has not yet appreciated, but which could be very valuable for future generations. Substitutes may be found, but the price of developing them may be substantially higher. It also reduces the range of nonrenewable resources available to tackle any given problem, which may lead to inferior solutions or to more costly ones, particularly for those communities that were once rich in the nonrenewable resource.

[A similar analysis applies to cultural resources, particularly the knowledge that we have acquired about how natural and social systems work.]

B. DEGRADATION IN ENVIRONMENTAL QUALITY

In this century we have seen increasing degradation of the quality of the global natural environment, particularly air, water, and soils, caused by pollution and, in some cases, exhaustion of resources. From an ecological perspective, waste products are an integral part of our system. We can produce fewer, recycle them, or dispose of them in land, air, fresh waters, or marine areas, and now conceivably in outer space or under the seabed. We cannot ignore them.

Problems of intergenerational equity relating to degradation of quality arise from the following uses: (1) disposal of wastes that trigger damaging, costly and essentially irreversible changes in the quality of the environment; (2) actions that reduce the variety of uses to which any given resource can be put; (3) uses that so degrade the quality of the environment that they lead to depletion of specific resources in it; and (4) actions that degrade the environmental services which natural resources otherwise provide. In many instances the focus of concern is the risk that our actions will have these effects in the future; in other instances the problems are already apparent. . .

At the global level, it is predicted that the increasing concentrations of greenhouse gases, such as carbon dioxide and methane, will lead in the first half of the next century to a rise in global mean temperature "which is greater than any in man's history." This will profoundly affect global climate patterns, with effects on ecosystems, agriculture, water resources and ocean levels. Activities contributing to these changes may occur several generations before their full effects are felt. Similarly, emissions of chlorofluorocarbons lead to the depletion of the global ozone layer, which can seriously damage human health and plant activity. . . . The disposal of nuclear wastes in permanent geologic sites on land or in other areas can also lead to irreversible changes in the quality of the immediate environment since the hazards of nuclear radiation continue for thousands of years . . .

The loss of natural environmental services caused by mismanaging natural resources raises another intergenerational problem of degraded environmental quality. For example, tropical forests may be so mismanaged that the fragile soils are unable to sustain productive growth, including sustainable agriculture. Clear-cutting of forested slopes can cause soil erosion and degradation of the watershed, with resulting siltation of rivers, lakes and dams downstream, loss of wildlife, and changes in climate.

C. DISCRIMINATORY ACCESS AND USE OF RESOURCES

As beneficiaries of a planetary trust, each generation has an equitable right to use and benefit from the planetary resources. The two previous sections identified actions which the present generation might take to benefit itself at the expense of future generations. This section identifies factors that prevent the present generation from fully using and benefiting from the legacy.

There are three problems of equity regarding access to and use of the legacy: (1) the needs of future generations, which foreclose the present generation from consuming all of the fruits of the natural and cultural resources of its ancestors; (2) the severe impoverishment of some communities, which prevents them from being able to share equitably in the planetary legacy; and (3) actions by members of the present generation that prevent other members from enjoying the fruits of the legacy.

The first problem of access and use arises if the present generation is viewed as having no right to exploit and use the natural and cultural resources of the planet, because they must be conserved for future generations. This is the preservationist argument. Taken to its extreme, it deprives the present generation of its legitimate claim to use and benefit from the earth's natural resources and the cultural resources of our species. This position can also easily become an apology for failing to assist those currently in economic need. . . . Preserving all resources for future generations . . . would exacerbate the inequities in poverty and wealth that would be passed on unchanged to future generations.

The second problem of equitable access is an intragenerational problem, which is related to the first. It is theoretically based on the relationship which all members of the present generation have as beneficiaries of the natural and cultural resources of the planet. Although all members have an equitable right of access to and use of these resources, many are effectively unable to realize this right because of the great economic disparities in the world community. . . . Members of the present generation may also prevent other members of their generation from enjoying natural and cultural resources when their activities cause environmental or other damage to them. . . . The problems are particularly acute when parties dispose of their pollutants and waste in global commons, such as the oceans, where the benefits of externalizing the cost are reaped by a few and the costs ultimately borne by many. Such examples raise problems of equitable access and use among members of the present generation, and in such instances as toxic contamination, also among generations.

The three problems of intergenerational equity—depletion of resources for future generations, degradation in quality of resources and [discriminatory] access to the benefits from and use of the resources—are interrelated. . . . While it is important to recognize these interconnections, the problems need to be addressed separately if we are to develop effective principles of equity among generations.

NOTES AND QUESTIONS

1. Do all environmental issues raise questions of intergenerational equity? Can you think of specific environmental situations that do raise intergenerational concerns? Do the categories suggested in the article above cover them?

2. What intergenerational issues do you see in the protection of cultural resources?

2. THEORETICAL PERSPECTIVES

Conceptually there are several approaches to intergenerational issues. The first is a preservationist approach, in which the present generation saves all resources for future generations. People can use resources so long as they do not deplete them in any way. This approach has deep roots in the natural flow theory in English water law and in efforts to preserve such unique places as the Grand Canyon. If carried to the extreme, it would promote the status quo over any change. While the approach is consistent with a subsistence economy, it is not consistent with an industrial economy.

At the opposite end of the spectrum is the opulent approach, in which the present generation consumes all that it wants today and generates as much wealth as it can, in the belief that maximizing consumption today is the best way to maximize wealth for future generations or that future generations will be much better off than we are, so that there is no need for us to sacrifice on their behalf. This approach ignores long-term degradations, such as irreversible losses of species diversity and non-renewable resources.

Still another approach is to view the earth as an investment, with each generation living off the interest on the capital.

Consider the following excerpt in the context of these three perspectives:

INTERGENERATIONAL EQUITY: TOWARD AN INTERNATIONAL LEGAL FRAMEWORK

Edith Brown Weiss
Global Accord 332–353 (Nazli Choucri ed., 1993)

Sustainable development rests on a commitment to equity with future generations. Sustainability . . . is possible if we look at the earth and its resources not only as an investment opportunity but as a trust, passed to us by our ancestors, to be enjoyed and passed on to our descendants for their use. Such a "planetary trust" conveys to us both rights and responsibilities. Most important, it implies that future generations, too, have rights, although these rights have meaning only if we, the living, respect them and if this respect transcends the differences among states, religions, and cultures. The notion that each generation holds the earth as a steward or in trust for its descendants strikes a deep chord with men and women of all cultures, religions, and nationalities. . . .

There are two relationships that must shape any theory of intergenerational equity: our relationship to other generations of our own species and our relationship to the natural system of which we are a part. . . . The theory of intergenerational equity stipulates that all generations have an equal place in relation to the natural system. There is no basis for preferring the present generation over future generations in their use of the planet. This assumption finds deep roots in international law. The preamble to the Universal Declaration of Human Rights begins, "Whereas recognition of the inherent dignity and of the equal and inalienable rights of all members of the human family is the foundation of freedom, justice and peace in the world." The reference to all members of the human family has a temporal dimension that brings all generations within its scope. The reference to equal and inalienable rights affirms the basic equality of such generations in the human family.

. . . The anchor of a legal framework is thus the notion of equality as the norm connecting sequential generations in their use and care of the environment. The corollary is the concept of partnership between humans and nature and between sequences of humans born. . . . In this partnership no generation knows beforehand when it will be the living generation, how many members it will have, or even how many generations there will ultimately be. It is useful, then, to take the perspective of a generation that is placed somewhere along the spectrum of time, but does not know in advance where it will be located. (*See* John Rawls, Theory of Justice (1971).) Such a generation would want to inherit the earth in a condition at least as good as the condition it has been in for any previous generation and to have as much access to it as previous generations have had. This requires each generation to pass the planet on in no worse condition than in which it received it and to provide equitable access to its resources and benefits. Each generation is thus both a trustee for the planet with obligations to care for it and a beneficiary with rights to use it.

One of the questions that always arises in any discussion of intergenerational equity is how we can afford to address equity to future generations when there are widespread inequities today.

The author of the reading above comments as follows:

While intergenerational equity may be viewed as in conflict with achieving intragenerational equity, the two are consistent and in fact must go together. Members of the present generation have an intragenerational right of equitable access to use and benefit from the planet's resources, which derives from the underlying equality which all generations have with each other in relation to their use of the natural system. Moreover, even the most selfish members of the present generation who care only about their own descendants must, as they extend their time horizon further, increasingly care about the general environment that their descendants will inherit. Since no one country or group of countries alone has the power to ensure a healthy environment, all must cooperate to ensure a robust planet in the future. This means meeting the basic needs of the poor so that they will have both the desire and ability to fulfill their intergenerational obligations to conserve the planet.

Id. at 336.

The article below questions how much a generation must do for future generations. Note the difference which arises from whether happiness or justice is the standard for our actions. Note that the arguments put forward in this classic article have not changed.

MAN'S RESPONSIBILITY FOR NATURE: ECOLOGICAL PROBLEMS AND WESTERN TRADITION

John Passmore
75–77, 86–87 (1974)

So the conservationist programme confronts us with a fundamental moral issue: ought we to pay any attention to the needs of posterity? To answer this question affirmatively is to make two assumptions: first, that posterity will suffer unless we do so; secondly that if it will suffer, it is our duty so to act as to prevent or mitigate its sufferings. Both assumptions can be, and have been, denied. To accept them does not, of course, do anything to solve the problem of conservation, but to reject them is to deny that there is any such problem, to deny that our society would be a better one—morally better—if it were to halt the rate at which it is at present exhausting its resources. . . .

To begin with the assumption that posterity will suffer unless we alter our ways, it is still often suggested that, on the contrary, posterity can safely be left to look after itself, provided only that science and technology continue to flourish. This optimistic interpretation of the situation comes especially from economists and from nuclear physicists. So Norman McRae, writing in the *Economist*, happily informs us that with the aid of the new sensors carried by satellites, which are now available to geologists, vastly increased reserves of fossil fuels and minerals will soon be available for man's use. And nuclear fusion . . . should," he continues, "give to mankind a virtually unlimited source of industrial power, with the oceans serving as a boundless reservoir of fuel—even for a world population far larger and many times richer than today's." If there is a problem, in his view, it lies only in the disposal of wastes—a pollution rather than a conservation problem . . .

Very many scientists, of course, take the opposite view, especially if they are biologists. Expert committees set up by such scientific bodies as the American National Academy of Sciences have, in fact, been prepared to commit themselves to definite estimates of the dates at which this resource or that will be exhausted. . . . The possibility that substitutes will be discovered introduces a note of uncertainty into the whole discussion, an uncertainty which cannot be simply set aside as irrelevant to our moral and political decisions about conservation, which it inevitably and properly influences. . . . Any adequate extrapolation would also have to extrapolate technological advances. But by the nature of the case—although technologists have a bad habit of trying to persuade us otherwise—we cannot be at all certain when and whether those advances will take place, or what form they will assume . . .

The uncertainties, however, remain. We can be confident that someday our society will run out of resources, but we do not know when it will do so or what resources it will continue to demand. The Premier of Queensland recently swept aside the protests of conservationists by arguing that Queensland's oil and coal resources should be fully utilized now, since posterity may have no need for them. This is not a wholly irrational attitude. One can readily see the force of an argument which would run thus: we are entitled, given the uncertainty of the future, wholly to ignore the interests of posterity, a posterity whose very existence is hypothetical—granted the possibility of a nuclear disaster— and whose needs, except for such fundamentals as air and water, we cannot possibly anticipate.

A somewhat different line of argument—which takes justice rather than happiness as its starting point—has been put forward by John Rawls. He does not so much as mention the saving of natural resources. (How rare it is for moral philosophers to pay any attention to the world around them!) But he has a good deal to say about the general concept of saving for posterity; that we ought to save for posterity, he in general argues, is a consequence of the fact that we ought to act justly, to posterity as to our contemporaries. The utilitarian principle of impartiality, taken literally, demands too much from us; we cannot reasonably be expected to share our resources between ourselves and the whole of posterity. . . . Exactly to what degree we should save for posterity, it is not possible, he admits, accurately to determine. But about the general character of what we ought to do he has no doubts. "Each generation," he writes, "must not only preserve the gains of culture and civilisation, and maintain intact those just institutions that have been established, but it must also put aside in each period of time a suitable amount of real capital accumulation." The "capital accumulation" may take various forms—investment in learning and education as well as in machinery, factories, and agriculture . . .

Each generation, Rawls is suggesting, should decide what it ought to save for posterity by answering in particular terms a general question: what is reasonable for a society to expect, at the stage of development it has reached, from its predecessor? If it then acts upon the answer at which it arrives, each generation will be better off than its predecessor but no generation will be called upon to make an exceptional sacrifice. . . . Yet if the conservationists are right it is precisely such a heroic sacrifice we are now called upon to make, a sacrifice far beyond-anything our ancestors had to make. And this transforms the situation.

Not everyone agrees that future generations have rights that obligate individuals in the present generation to act in a prescribed manner. The following is an example of the reasoning behind the idea that future generations do not have rights.

ENVIRONMENTAL ETHICS AND THE RIGHTS OF FUTURE GENERATIONS

Bryan Norton
4 Envtl. Ethics 19, 322–324 (1982)

We can now return to the main question, is there a concept of the rights of future generations according to which individuals currently have rights that impose obligations on present individuals? Can one base an ethic of environmental preservation on this? Criticisms of such rights are based on two separable grounds—their futurity and their referential ambiguity. The futurity objection, offered by Richard De George, is as follows: "Future generations by definition do not exist now. They cannot now, therefore, be the present bearer or subject of anything, including rights." But this futurity objection is unconvincing. One can respond that future people have hypothetical rights in the present. These are the rights they will have when they in fact exist . . .

[Another] line of attack concentrates rather on the concept of future personhood which, I believe is necessarily incoherent in the context of environmental preservation. This incoherence can be introduced by "Parfit's Paradox." Parfit describes two social policies, which he calls High Consumption and Low Consumption.

If we choose High rather than Low Consumption, the standard of living will be higher over the next century. This effect implies another. The people who will live more than a century from now would be different on the two policies. Given the effects of two such policies on the details of our lives, different marriages would increasingly be made. More simply, even in the same marriages, the children would increasingly be conceived at different times. As we have seen, this would in fact be enough to make them different children . . .

Return next to the moral questions. If we choose High Consumption, the quality of life will be lower more than a century from now. But the particular people who will then live would never have existed if instead we have chosen Low Consumption. Is our choice of High Consumption worse for these people? Only if it is against their interest to have been born. Even if this makes sense, we can suppose that it would not go as far as this. We can conclude that, if we choose High Consumption, our choice will be worse for no one.

This argument may appear to have an air of sleight of hand about it. Indeed, its being dubbed a "paradox" suggests that it is a minor conceptual anomaly, rather than a cogent, substantive point. Nevertheless, the argument deserves serious consideration.

Three consequences follow from Parfit's argument:

(1) No one is harmed by a policy of High Consumption.

(2) No future person's rights are infringed by a policy of High Consumption.

(3) Rights of future generations are an inadequate basis for an environmental ethic.

Consequence (1) is Parfit's conclusion. Consequence (2) follows from (1) together with the principle that rights must be possessed by some actual individual. If rights must be possessed by some individual and if no harm has occurred to any individual, then no rights have been infringed upon by a policy of depletion. If (2) is true, (3) seems to follow. High consumption is precisely what an ethic of environmental protection is intended to forbid. If an environmental ethic cannot rule out such a policy by invoking infringements of rights, it is surely inadequate.

[Norton favors general obligations based in multi-generational community.]

For discussion of the moral dimensions of intergenerational equity, see Brett M. Frischmann, *Some Thoughts on Shortsightedness and Intergenerational Equity*, 36 Loy. U. Chi. L.J. 457 (2005).

The historic Encyclical Letter of Pope Francis on Care for Our Common Home includes an important section on "Justice Between the Generations." The Pope relates concern for future generations to the notion of the common good and invokes a moral obligation to care for the environment that we leave to future generations.

ENCYCLICAL LETTER LAUDATO SI' OF THE HOLY FATHER FRANCIS ON CARE FOR OUR COMMON HOME
Released May 24, 2015

Paragraph 159: The notion of the common good also extends to future generations. . . . We can no longer speak of sustainable development apart from intergenerational solidarity. Once we start to think about the kind of world we are leaving to future generations, we look at things differently; we realize that the world is a gift which we have freely received and must share with others. . . . Intergenerational solidarity is not optional, but rather a basic question of justice, since the world we have received also belongs to those who will follow us.

Paragraph 161: Doomsday predictions can no longer be met with irony or disdain. We may well be leaving to coming generations debris, desolation and filth. The pace of consumption, waste and environmental change has so stretched the planet's capacity that our contemporary lifestyle, unsustainable as it is, can only precipitate catastrophes, such as those which even now periodically occur in different areas of the world. The effects of the present imbalance can only be reduced by our decisive action, here and now. We need to reflect on our accountability before those who will have to endure the dire consequences.

NOTES AND QUESTIONS

1.   Why should we care about future generations? As the saying goes, what have future generations ever done for us? Where does a moral obligation come from?

Sociologists would agree that we innately act in ways calculated to promote the survival and reproduction of our genes. Others would say that caring about future generations represents a primordial social value, necessary for maintaining human communities. Only when a community is fighting a losing battle for survival does it no longer care for its children. *See* Colin Turnbull, The Mountain People (1972) for a description of the desperate plight of the Ik tribe in Kenya and Uganda.

Still others contend that there is a basic psychological need in all of us to transcend the self, which is expressed through the creation of books, artistic works, institutions, music, and other things that may last beyond our lifetime. Kenneth Boulding has written, "the most satisfactory individual identity is that which identifies not only with a community in space but also with a community extending over time from the past into the future. . . . There is a great deal of historical evidence to suggest that a society which loses its positive image of the future loses also its capacity to deal with present problems and soon falls apart." Kenneth Boulding, *The Economics of the Coming Spaceship Earth*, in The Environmental Handbook 99–100 (G. de Bell ed., 1970). *See also* Edith Brown Weiss, In Fairness to Future Generations: International Law, Common Patrimony and Intergenerational Equity, ch. 2, (1989).

2.   What assumption should we make about intergenerational equity?

• Should we preserve the planet intact? If so, doesn't this thwart economic growth and ignore poverty?

• Alternatively, should we consume as much as we can today to generate more wealth to pass to future generations in the form of capital investments, technology, knowledge, and infrastructure? Are significant environmental costs then ignored?

- Should we promote equality among generations in their access to and use of the environment? Are we trustees/custodians of the environment?

- How would John Rawls' Theory of Justice apply to our care and use of the natural system?

3.   How could the interests of future generations be represented in our legal system?

4.   Do future generations have rights in relation to the natural system?

5.   What is the difference between having a right and relying only on an obligation? How are rights and obligations related? How are the two terms—"rights" and "obligations"—relevant to the way one generation handles the earth's resources? What are the implications for intragenerational equity?

Consider the following:

> Planetary rights and obligations coexist in each generation. In the intergenerational dimension, the generations to which the obligations are owed are future generations. Thus, the rights of future generations are linked to the obligations of the present generation. In the intragenerational context, planetary obligations and rights exist between members of the present generation. . . . Thus, intergenerational obligations to conserve the planet flow from the present generation who has the right to use and enjoy the planetary legacy.
>
> . . . Can intergenerational obligations exist without rights? While rights are always connected to obligations, the reverse is not always true.

Edith Brown Weiss, *Our Rights and Obligations to Future Generations for the Environment*, in AGORA: What Obligation Does Our Generation Owe to the Next? An Approach to Global Environmental Responsibility, 84 Am. J. Intl. L. 198 202–203 (1990).

6.   What would be our corresponding obligations toward future generations if we accepted the proposition that they had rights?

7.   The United Nations Report of the UN Secretary-General, Intergenerational Solidarity and the Needs of Future Generations, UNGAA A 68/322 (August 15, 2013) provides a very useful review of the issues and the principle of intergenerational equity. Importantly, the UN Report addresses a number of proposals for the United Nations to institutionalize representation of the interests of future generations.

With the rise of the Anthropocene Epoch, there has been growing concern about future generations and the implementation of intergenerational equity. Key developments include the 2015 Encyclical

Letter of Pope Francis (excerpted above), the 1997 UNESCO Declaration, the U.N. Secretary-General's Report in 2013, judicial references in international and national court decisions, institutional innovations at the national and subnational levels, and calls for a United Nations High Commissioner for Future Generations.

UNESCO DECLARATION ON THE RESPONSIBILITIES OF THE PRESENT GENERATIONS TOWARDS FUTURE GENERATIONS

UNESCO General Conference, 29th Sess, 12 November 1997

[The UNESCO Declaration resulted in part from the efforts of Jacques-Yves Cousteau, the President of the Cousteau Society, who circulated a petition among people in many countries that gathered more than several hundred thousand signatures. The key provisions of the Declaration are as follows:]

Article 1
Needs and Interests of Future Generations

The present generations have the responsibility of ensuring that the need and interests of present and future generations are fully safeguarded.

Article 4
Preservation of Life on Earth

The present generations have the responsibility to bequeath to future generations an Earth which will not one day be irreversibly damaged by human activity. Each generation inheriting the Earth temporarily should take care to use natural resources reasonably and ensure that life is not prejudiced by harmful modifications of the ecosystems and that scientific and technological progress in all fields does not harm life on Earth.

Article 5
Protection of the Environment

1.   In order to ensure that future generations benefit from the richness of the Earth's ecosystems, the present generations should strive for sustainable development and preserve living conditions, particularly the quality and integrity of the environment.

2.   The present generations should ensure that future generations are not exposed to pollution which may endanger their health or their existence itself.

3.   The present generations should preserve for future generations natural resources necessary for sustaining human life and for its development.

4. The present generations should take into account possible consequences for future generations of major projects before these are carried out.

NOTES AND QUESTIONS

1. What status does the Declaration have in international law?

2. What problems do you foresee in implementing the Declaration?

3. What legal difference does UNESCO's Declaration on the Responsibilities of the Present Generations Toward Future Generations create when it refers only to responsibilities of the present generations and not to the rights of future generations?

3. JUDICIAL APPLICATION OF INTERGENERATIONAL EQUITY

a. International Court of Justice

In the maritime boundary delimitation case of *Denmark v. Norway* before the International Court of Justice, 1993 I.C.J. 38, Judge Weeramantry issued a concurring opinion in which he discusses the role of equity. He notes that a broader perspective on equity comes from traditional legal systems such as the African, the Pacific, and the Amerindian, "which contained a deeply ingrained respect for the earth, the atmosphere, the lakes and the seas, which the evolving law of the sea can consider with profit. . . . Respect for these elemental constituents of the inheritance of succeeding generations, dictated rules and attitudes based upon a concept of an equitable sharing which was both horizontal in regard to the present generation and vertical for the benefit of generations yet to come." Judge Weeramantry then cites *In Fairness to Future Generations* (excerpted above) for the proposition that principles of intergenerational equity "can build upon the increasing use by the International Court of Justice of equitable principles to achieve a result that the Court views as fair and just."

In the 1995 *Nuclear Test Case (New Zealand v. France)*, 1995 I.C.J. 288, New Zealand argued that France's proposed underground nuclear tests constituted a violation of international law and that it was "unlawful for France to conduct such nuclear tests before it has undertaken an Environmental Impact Assessment according to accepted international standards." Formally the case arose as a request to examine the proposed nuclear tests in accordance with the ICJ's 1974 Judgment in the Nuclear Test Cases involving atmospheric nuclear tests by France. In that case, the Court decided that the issue was moot because of declarations by France that it would not carry out further atmospheric nuclear tests but noted in paragraph 63 of the Judgment that "if the basis of this Judgment were to be affected, the Applicant could request an examination of the situation in accordance with the provisions of the Statute."

The 1995 Judgment of the Court declined to accept the request since underground rather than atmospheric tests were now involved. Order of September 22, 1995. Two of the dissenting opinions discussed the importance of intergenerational equity to the dispute. Judge Weeramantry wrote as follows:

The Concept of Intergenerational Rights

The case before the Court raises, as no case ever before the Court has done, the principle of intergenerational equity—an important and rapidly developing principle of contemporary environmental law.

Having regard to the information before us that the half life of a radioactive by-product of nuclear tests can extend to over 20,000 years, this is an important aspect that an international tribunal cannot fail to notice. In a matter of which it is duly seized, this Court must regard itself as a trustee of those rights in the sense that a domestic court is a trustee of the interests of an infant unable to speak for itself. If this Court is charged with administering international law, and if this principle is building itself into the corpus of international law, or has already done so, this principle is one which must inevitably be a concern of this Court. The consideration involved is too serious to be dismissed as lacking in importance merely because there is no precedent on which it rests.

New Zealand's complaint that its rights are affected does not relate only to the rights of people presently in existence. The rights of the people of New Zealand include the rights of unborn posterity. Those are rights which a nation is entitled, and indeed obliged, to protect. In considering whether New Zealand has made out a prima facie case of damage to its interests sufficient to bring the processes of this Court into operation in terms of paragraph 63, this is therefore an important aspect not to be ignored.

In the words of an important recent work on this question:

The starting proposition is that each generation is both a custodian and a user of our common natural and cultural patrimony. As custodians of this planet, we have certain moral obligations to future generations which we can transform into legally enforceable norms.[11]

---

[11] *See* E. Brown Weiss, In Fairness to Future Generations: International Law, Common Patrimony, and Intergenerational Equity (1989).

On July 8, 1996, the International Court of Justice handed down its *Advisory Opinion on The Legality of the Threat or Use of Nuclear Weapons.* 35 I.L.M. 801 (1996). The opinion responded to the request from the United Nations General Assembly in December 1994. The Court concluded it could not conclude definitively: whether the threat or use of nuclear weapons would be lawful or unlawful in an extreme circumstance of self-defense, in which the very survival of a state would be a stake." In its opinion, the court explicitly referred to the interests of future generations: "it is imperative for the court to take account of the unique characteristics of nuclear weapons, and in particular . . . their ability to cause damage to generations to come." (para. 36).

In his dissenting opinion, Judge Weeramantry discussed the damage to future generations and wrote:

> This Court, as the principal judicial organ of the United Nations, empowered to state and apply international law with an authority matched by no other tribunal must, in its jurisprudence, pay due recognition to the rights of future generations. If there is any tribunal that can recognize and protect their interests under the law, it is this court.
>
> It is to be noted in this context that the rights of future generations have passed the stage when they were merely an embryonic right struggling for recognition. They have woven themselves into international law through major treaties, through juristic opinion and through general principles of law recognized by civilized nations. [at 17.]

NOTES AND QUESTIONS

1.   On June 26, 1992, the International Court of Justice decided that it had jurisdiction to hear the dispute between Nauru and Australia, *Case Concerning Certain Phosphate Lands in Nauru*, 1992 I.C.J. 240 (jurisdictional issues). Nauru argued that it suffered large-scale environmental damage as a result of Australia's violation of its rights under the United Nations Trusteeship and under general principles of international law. Article 5 of the Trusteeship Agreement referred to the well-being of both "present and future interests" of Nauru's inhabitants. The case was subsequently settled before the Court decided the merits of the case. Do you think a principle of intergenerational equity could have been applicable in this case? What difference would it make?

2.   Hungary and the Slovak Republic agreed to have the International Court of Justice decide a dispute over the flow of the Danube River. Among other items Hungary alleged that the Slovak Republic had diverted the waters of the Danube River and thereby deprived Hungary of groundwater and made Hungarian land near the Danube arid. Are there any intergenerational issues that you see in this dispute? While the Court did not

decide the case on intergenerational issues, Judge Weeramantry, in a separate opinion, affirmed the principle of intergenerational rights and further identified a principle of trusteeship of earth's resources.

3.   The 2013 Report of the UN Secretary-General, "Intergenerational Solidarity and the Needs of Future Generations" sets forth the "fundamental principle of intergenerational equity," and notes the three parts to it described earlier: conservation of options, conservation of quality, and conservation of access. UNGA A/68/322, August 15, 2013.

b.   National Courts

An increasing number of judicial cases have invoked intergenerational equity. In the first case below, standing was granted to children as representative of future generations. In many other cases, the principle has been used in deciding substantive outcomes for the case. The selected judicial cases below represent only some of the relevant case law at the domestic level. They are intended to illustrate how intergenerational equity has been used and to suggest ways that it could be invoked in the future.

One may distinguish two categories of use. The first is procedural, such as to give standing to representatives of future generations or to toll a statute of limitations for a violation that involves significant harm to future generations. The second is substantive, namely, that given actions threaten the well-being of future generations.

i.   *Supreme Court of the Philippines*

On August 9, 1993, the Supreme Court of the Republic of the Philippines granted standing to a group of children as representative of themselves and of future generations to bring a case against the Environment and Natural Resources Department to seek cancellation of existing timber license agreements and to ban the approval of new ones.

The Supreme Court said:

> [w]e find no difficulty in ruling that they can, for themselves, for others of their generation and for the succeeding generations, file a class suit. Their personality to sue in behalf of the succeeding generations can only be based on the concept of intergenerational responsibility insofar as the right to a balanced and healthful ecology is concerned. Such a right, as hereinafter expounded, considers the "rhythm and harmony of nature." Nature means the created world in its entirety. Such rhythm and harmony indispensably include, inter alia, the judicious disposition, utilization, management, renewal and conservation of the country's forest, mineral, land, waters, fisheries, wildlife, off-shore areas and other natural resources to the end that their exploration, development and utilization be

> equitably accessible to the present as well as future generations. Needless to say, every generation has a responsibility to the next to preserve that rhythm and harmony for the full enjoyment of a balanced and healthful ecology. Put a little differently, the minors' assertion of their right to a sound environment constitutes, at the same time, the performance of their obligation to ensure the protection of that right for generations to come.

The Supreme Court found the right to a balanced and healthful ecology in the Constitution of the Philippines. *Minors Oposa v. Secretary of the Department of the Environment and Natural Resources,* 33 I.L.M. 173 (1994). For analysis of the case, *see* Ted Allen, *The Philippine Children's Case Recognizing Legal Standing for Future Generations*, 6 Geo. Intl. Envtl. L. Rev. 713 (1994). For a discussion about the practical effect that the Supreme Court's decision has had in the Philippines, *see* Dante B. Gatmaytan, *The Illusion of Intergenerational Equity: Oposa v. Factoran as Pyrrhic Victory*, 15 Geo. Intl. Envtl. L. Rev. 457 (2003) and Ma. Socorro Z. Manguiat & Vincente Paolo B. Yu III, *Maximizing the Value of Oposa v. Factoran*, 15 Geo. Intl. Envtl. L. Rev. 487 (2003). Professor Gatmaytan posits that *Oposa* adds little to Philippine jurisprudence or to environmental protection. He points out that the *Oposa* decision did not have a real impact on government protection of the environment because after the case was remanded, the children petitioners failed to pursue their claim. Furthermore, standing has always been viewed in a liberal manner in the Philippines, and the Supreme Court's recognition of standing to sue for generations of the future was merely *obiter dictum*. In a response to Professor Gatmaytan's article, Manguiat and Yu note that, despite the modest practical effect of the *Oposa* decision, the Philippine Supreme Court's recognition of intergenerational equity in terms of standing is an important step for expanding the doctrine of standing and construing the right to a balanced and healthful ecology. They argue that linking children petitioners with future generations can be viewed as an interpretation of the right to a balanced and healthful ecology as it relates to future generations. Thus, the intergenerational aspects of the *Oposa* decision are more than just *obiter dictum* and constitute a genuine advance in national law, which could promote similar progress in international law.

ii. High Court of Brazil. S.T.J. REsp No. 1.120.117/AC (2d Panel), 19 October 2009

In a case involving illegal logging in the Amazonia State of Acre, the indigenous people raised the issue of the statute of limitations for environmental claims. The Panel of the Court unanimously held that the right to compensation for environmental damage does not lapse and that hence there is no statute of limitations. As Nicholas Bryner described the case, "the Court was particularly concerned with how, under a statute of limitations, past or present inaction would bind future owners of a common asset. Given that 'environmental assets [belong] not only to current but also future generation,' the Court asked: 'How could the current generation assure its right to pollute, to the detriment of generations yet unborn?' As the Court reasons, eliminating a time limit on collective claims is in keeping with the principle of intergenerational equity in environmental law." Nicholas S. Bryner, *Brazil's Green Court*, 29 Pace Envt'l L. Rev. 470,525 (2012).

NOTES AND QUESTIONS

1.   Do you agree with the Supreme Court of the Philippines that children can represent the interests of those generations yet unborn?

2.   What consequences do you foresee in granting standing to representatives of future generations?

3.   Critics of deforestation and other such actions have often argued that the economic instruments that we have to consider future costs and benefits inherently discriminate in favor of exploiting resources in the present.

4.   Should a statute of limitations always be tolled in cases involving reparations for environmental damage? What criteria would you suggest?

iii. The Supreme Court of India

At least five decisions of the Supreme Court of India use the principle of intergenerational equity. Supreme Court decisions are binding on all lower courts including High Courts of states (highest appellate courts in each state).

In *Vellore Citizens Welfare Forum v. Union of India,* the Supreme Court recognized the principle of sustainable development. In *Vellore*, directions were sought against tanneries and other industries in the State of Tamil Nadu from discharging untreated effluents into agricultural land, waterways and other open areas. The *Vellore* court stated:

"We have no hesitation in holding that Sustainable Development as a balancing concept between ecology and development has been accepted as a part of the Customary International Law though its salient features have yet to be finalized by the International Law Jurists." *Vellore Citizens Welfare Forum v. Union of India*, (1996) 5 S.C.C. 647, 658 (India).

In *Intellectuals Forum, Tirupathi v. State of Andhra Pradesh and Others*, the public interest litigation pertained to the preservation of two historical water tanks [reservoirs] in the Tirupathi region. The petitioners argued that the municipal authorities had failed to conserve these tanks and instead used the tank beds as lands for construction and commercial use despite the region being prone to periodic droughts. Citing the development of the principle of intergenerational equity in international law, the Court held that:

> "As Professor Weiss puts it, 'conservation, however, always takes a back seat in times of economic stress.' It is now an accepted social principle that all human beings have a fundamental right to a healthy environment, commensurate with their well being, coupled with a corresponding duty of ensuring that resources are conserved and preserved in such a way that present as well as the future generations are aware of them equally." *Intellectuals Forum, Tirupathi v. State of Andhra Pradesh and Others*, (2006) 3 S.C.C. 549.

In *State of Himachal Pradesh and Others v. Ganesh Wood Products and Others*, a writ petition was filed against the Himachal Pradesh state government to prohibit the establishment of any new manufacturing units that required residue from cut trees, on the basis that excessive felling of trees had adversely impacted the environment in the region. Agreeing with this petition, the Supreme Court set aside the establishment of any new units that would undertake the cutting of the trees in the state. The Court held that the decision of the government to grant new licenses for manufacturing unit violated the National Forest Policy and the State Forest Policy. According to Justice Reddy:

> ". . . it is contrary to public interest involved in preserving forest wealth, maintenance of environment and ecology and considerations of sustainable growth and intergenerational equity. After all, the present generation has no right to deplete all the existing forests and leave nothing for the next and future generations." *State of Himachal Pradesh and Others v. Ganesh Wood Products and Others*, (1995) 6 S.C.C. 363.

In 2014, in response to a writ petition to regulate the large scale mining of iron ore in the state of Goa, the Supreme Court invoked Article 21 of the Indian Constitution and intergenerational equity to require all mining leases in the future to deposit 10% of the sale proceeds into a new Goa Iron Ore Permanent Fund for sustainable development and intergenerational equity. The Court stated that damage caused by the mining cannot be rectified by regulation and monitoring alone, and gave the state authorities six months to come up with a comprehensive plan for the new Fund. *Goa Foundation v. Union of India* (2014) 6 SCC 590. *See also Samaj Parivartana Samudaya v. State of Karnataka* (2013) 8 SCC 154 (setting limits on amount of minerals that could be mined); Intergenerational Equity, A Note on behalf of the Goa Foundation, submitted to the Supreme Court in the 2014 Goa Foundation case.

iv. High Court of Kenya

The High Court of Kenya (the country's second highest court), in *Waweru v Republic of Kenya* (2006), applied the principle of intergenerational equity to a case of water pollution. The case was brought by 23 property owners from the Kiserian Township, who had erected buildings on their plots with septic tanks for waste disposal. However, after receiving complaints that waste was being discharged into the river, which could affect the riverbed, the local Public Health Officer investigated and found that most of the 102 property owners in the area were discharging overflow waste from their septic tanks into open channels along the road that led to the Kiserian River. The Court ordered the local authorities to construct sewerage treatment works and required the property owners to comply with the health requirements concerning the disposal of wastewater and sewage, despite petitioners' claims that the cost would be prohibitive.

The Court ended its decision with a lengthy consideration of the role of intragenerational and intergenerational equity. The court quoted at length Edith Brown Weiss *In Fairness to Future Generations*, excerpted above, and stated:

> [T]he need to formulate and maintain ecologically sustainable development that does not interfere with the sustenance, viability and the quality of the water table and the quality of the river waters . . . [also gives] rise to the equally important principle of intergenerational equity because the water table and the rivers courses affected are held in trust by the present generation for future generations. Yes, the intergenerational equity obligates the present generation to ensure that health, diversity and productivity of natural resources are maintained or enhanced for the benefit of future generations. We observe that water tables and clean rivers are for this and future generations.

Waweru v. Republic of Kenya, (2006) eKLR. The opinion ended with an exhortation to fight for environmental justice, for as the court passionately noted, "This generation can never have the excuse of lacking in inspiration."

v. Australia and New Zealand

Numerous judicial decisions from Australia and New Zealand have recognized the principle of intergenerational equity, several of which are discussed here. Australia has recognized the principle of intergenerational equity as a principle of "ecological sustainability" in any development project through various statutes at the federal and state levels. For example, in the Environment Protection and Biodiversity Conservation Act, 1999, sustainable development is defined to include the principle of intergenerational equity. Prior to this Act, in *Northcompass*

Inc. v. Hornsby Shire Council [1996] NSWLEC 213 (Aug 26, 1996), the Land and Environment Court of New South Wales held that the Hornsby Shire Council could establish a bioremediation facility as an ecologically sustainable facility that takes green wastes away from diminishing landfills because such a project would adhere to the principle of intergenerational equity. However, the court added that in order to do so, it must comply with the precautionary principle of complying with environmental impact assessments in accordance with current laws and state policies.

Later, in *BGP Properties Pty Ltd v. Lake Macquarie City Council* [2004] NSWLEC 399 (Aug 12, 2004), the same court rejected an appeal from the appellant corporation against the city council's refusal to approve a project that involved subdividing certain plots in a residential zone for industrial use and storage. The Court held that according to the Environmental Planning and Assessment Act, the Protection of the Environment Administration Act, 1991 (New South Wales) and the Inter-Governmental Agreement on the Environment, also endorsed by the local governments, the "ecologically sustainable development strategy" involved applying proper principles of protecting the environment by authorities and that included the principle of intergenerational equity.

In New Zealand, the purpose of the Resource Management Act, 1991 (RMA) includes 'sustainable management,' which involves *"sustaining the potential of natural and physical resources (excluding minerals) to meet the reasonably foreseeable needs of future generations.* Section 5(2)(a) of the Resource Management Act 1991. There have been a limited number of judicial decisions that directly discuss intergenerational equity. In *Villages of NZ (Mt. Wellington Limited v. Auckland City Council* [A023/09], the Environment Court allowed the development of a sports field because it would meet the recreational needs of future generations without compromising the provisions of the RMA.

In *NZ Recreational Fishing Council v. Sanford Limited* [2009] NZSC 54, the Supreme Court applied the principle of conserving natural resources for future generations within the framework of sustainable management as in the RMA to commercial and recreational fishing:

vi. South America

Brazil's Constitution of 1988 includes a right to environment. Article 225 provides that "[a]ll have the right to an ecologically balanced environment, which is an asset of common use and essential to a healthy quality of life, and both the Government and the community shall have the duty to defend and preserve it for present and future generations." Under Article 129, the Prosecutors' functions include bringing civil actions to protect "the environment and other diffuse and collective interests." Between 2007 and 2011, the High Court handed down five decisions that emphasized the constitutional duty to protect the environment for future generations. The High Court has been a world leader in recognizing obligations to future generations. In a case involving the protection of mangrove swamps in Brazil, the High Court noted that there is a legal duty to preserve the threatened ecosystem and equated the deprivation of its public use and use by future generations to the theft of chattel under criminal law. *S.T.J. REsp No. 650.728 (2d Panel)*, Relator: Min. Herman Benjamin, 2.12.2009.

In Chile, communities living near the Huasco river basin in the Atacama region of Chile filed suit against a subsidiary of Canada-based Barrick Gold and the Chilean Environmental Agency on the grounds that the Pascua Lama mining project had begun mining operations without complying with the Environmental Assessment Resolution of maintaining the region's water sources. The Pascua Lama case moved up to the Supreme Court of Chile in 2013 where the Court ordered that the project be halted until all works aimed at protecting water resources were completed. The Court based its reasoning on a broader view of environmental rights by acknowledging that the impact from the mining operations would not only affect the present community but also future generations.

Further reading: For analysis of the incorporation of intergenerational equity into Canadian judicial cases and legislation, see Jerry V. DeMarco, *Law of Future Generations: The Theory of Intergenerational Equity in Canadian Environmental Law*, 15 (1) J. Envt'l L. and Practice 1 (2004). For Brazil, see D. Ramos, Jr., Meio Ambiente E Conceito Juridico de Futuras Geracões (Juruá Editora Juvevê.2012).

4. PARLIAMENTARY IMPLEMENTATION

An increasing number of countries are making special institutional provisions for protecting the interests of future generations and promoting sustainable development. This section highlights some of the major developments.

In March 2015, the National Assembly of Wales passed ground-breaking legislation, which puts future generations and sustainable development at the center. The bill, entitled Well-Being of Future Generations, establishes measures for implementing sustainable development and, most notably, established the position of "The Future Generations Commissioner for Wales," to which Peter Davies, a teacher and businessman, was appointed as the first Commissioner. The Commissioner's functions include providing advice and assistance on the issues, encouraging best practices, undertaking needed research, reviewing the extent to which a public body is "safeguarding the ability of future generations to meet their needs," and preparing and publishing regular reports on the extent to which the legislation's objectives are being met.

In Finland, the Committee for the Future, established in 1993, is a permanent parliamentary committee. It is made up of 17 members of Parliament, along with a state employee serving as a specialist. The committee chooses topics to focus on, submits reports on the future and analyzes policies of other parliamentary committees that affect the future. It also responds to requests from other committees to review other measures for their impacts on the future. The Committee proposed an ombudsman for future generations in its May 2014 report.

In 2007, an order of the Hungarian Parliament established an Ombudsman for Future Generations. In 2011, the Hungarian Government recognized the need to protect natural resources at the constitutional level by stating in the Fundamental Law that: *"agricultural land, forests and drinking water supplies, biodiversity, in particular native plant and animal species and cultural assets are part of the nation's common heritage,"* and named the *"State and every person to be obliged to protect, sustain and preserve them for future generations."* [Article P, Preservation of Natural Resources, Hungarian Fundamental Law, Amendment 2011]. The Parliament then created the Office of the Commissioner for Fundamental Rights and turned the Ombudsman position into a Deputy Commissioner position under this broader rubric. The duties of the Deputy-Commissioner include monitoring the enforcement of the interests of future generations, regularly informing the Commissioner for Fundamental Rights on his/her experience regarding the enforcement of the interests of future generations or minorities living in Hungary, drawing the Commissioner's attention to the danger of infringing on the rights of a larger group of persons, participating in the inquiries of the Commissioner for Fundamental Rights, proposing that the Commissioner institute proceedings ex officio and proposing that the Commissioner turn to the Constitutional Court on any matter that may affect future generations.

In 2001, the Knesset, Israel's parliamentary body, passed a law creating a Commission on Future Generations with a Knesset Commissioner for Future Generations. (The person appointed as the Commissioner was formerly a judge.) The Knesset Law 1994 (Amendment No. 14), 5761–2001. The Commissioner for Future Generations was to assess bills that have "particular relevance for future generations," and to advise Members of the Knesset and present recommendations on issues particularly relevant for future generations. The original bill defined "particular relevance for future generations" as referring to an issue "which may have significant consequences for future generations, in the realms of the environment, natural resources, science, development, education, health, the economy, demography, planning and construction, quality of life, technology, justice and any matter which has been determined by the Knesset Constitution, Law and Justice Committee to have significant consequences for future generations." In December 2010, the Knesset Plenum approved a bill dissolving the Commission, allegedly for political reasons. In 2014, a new bill for a new form of Commission was tabled in the Israeli Parliament. *See* Shlomo Shahom, *The Knesset, the Israeli Parliament: Presentation on the Commission for Future Generations*, presented at Office of the Commissioner for Human Rights, *Model Institutions for a Sustainable Future: A Comparative Constitutional Perspective*, April 24–26, 2014 in Budapest, Hungary, at 12.

In December 2009, the German Bundestag established the Parliamentary Advisory Council on Sustainable Development as an advisory body through a joint motion that stressed "the necessity against the background of the challenges posed by globalization, for the Bundestag to make clear its commitment to sustainable development." The Council is to serve as the advocate of long-term responsibility in the political process, structure policy for future generations, and to support the work of the bodies created by the Federal Government. *See* Joint Motion, 17/245, December 16, 2009. The Council is comprised of 22 full members and 22 substitute members, and presents a report of its efforts once every two years.

5. OTHER NATIONAL GOVERNMENT INITIATIVES FOR IMPLEMENTING INTERGENERATIONAL EQUITY

With the persuasion of the late Jacques Yves Cousteau, France established a Commission for Future Generations. However, after deliberations regarding nuclear issues, the Commission was abandoned. More recently, the French Government has established the Inter-ministerial Committee for Sustainable Development which submits reports on policies that affect future generations. In 2003, the Government published the National Sustainable Development Strategy which is updated every year. In 2010, the Inter-ministerial Committee for Sustainable Development published a National Sustainable Development Strategy for the years 2010–2013.

In April 2014, the Hungarian Office of the Commissioner for Fundamental Rights organized a conference on Model Institutions for a Sustainable Future: A Comparative Constitutional Perspective at the Parliament in Budapest Hungary. The Conference was aimed at creating a closer network among different national institutions mentioned in the UN Report on Intergenerational Solidarity (2013) to promote and protect the needs of future generations. The goal of the Conference was to link theoretical perspectives to actual implementation of the principle of intergenerational equity. At the end of the Conference, a memorandum was signed by all the Conference participants, which supported establishing institutions in countries to protect and promote the interests of future generations. The participants agreed to have the network meet on an annual basis to exchange experiences, identify problems, and advance their work.

6. REGIONAL AND INTERNATIONAL IMPLEMENTATION

In 2003, 26 different members of the European Union, from different political parties, signed a motion for a resolution in the Council of Europe Parliamentary Assembly to establish a Committee for Future Generations within the Assembly to issue opinions and guidelines on any matters that affect future generations. *See* Parliamentary Assembly, EU Council, Doc. 9668, January 22, 2003. There has not been further discussion on the motion. In September 2013, the United Nations Secretary-General released a report that discusses options at the international level for considering the interests of future generations. These include a new High Commissioner for Future Generations, a proposal that many nongovernmental organizations championed at the Rio+20 Conference in June 2013, or a Special Envoy of the UN Secretary-General for Future Generations. *See* UN Report on Intergenerational Solidarity and the Needs for Future Generations of the Secretary-General, UNGA, A/68/322, 15 August 2013.

NOTES AND QUESTIONS

1. What problems do you foresee in creating effective parliamentary bodies to consider the interests of future generations? If you were a Commissioner for Future Generations, how would you go about assessing the implications of a proposed bill for future generations? What legal provisions would you regard as essential?

2. There is a broader question. How do you keep the mandate of commissions for future generations reasonably limited? Doesn't almost everything affect future generations if treated broadly enough? Could a commission use its position to propose big tax cuts on the grounds that the supposedly resulting economic growth would benefit future generations and provide money with which to protect the environment for future generations?

3. What legal issues and problems do you foresee in having an Ombudsman for Future Generations intervene in judicial proceedings to represent the interests of future generations? How would you ensure that the interests of impoverished people today are protected?

B. RELATIONSHIP OF HUMANS TO THE NATURAL SYSTEM

1. FLORA

SHOULD TREES HAVE STANDING?—TOWARD LEGAL RIGHTS FOR NATURAL OBJECTS

Christopher D. Stone
45 S. Cal. L. Rev. 450 (1972sd)

INTRODUCTION: THE UNTHINKABLE

In *Descent of Man*, Darwin observes that the history of man's moral development has been a continual extension in the objects of his "social instincts and sympathies." Originally each man had regard only for himself and those of a very narrow circle about him; later, he came to regard more and more "not only the welfare, but the happiness of all his fellowmen"; then "his sympathies became more tender and widely diffused, extending to men of all races, to the imbecile, maimed, and other useless members of society, and finally to the lower animals . . . "

History of the law suggests a parallel development. Perhaps there never was a pure Hobbesian state of nature, in which no "rights" existed except in the vacant sense of each man's "right to self-defense." But it is not unlikely that so far as the earliest "families" (including extended kinship groups and clans) were concerned, everyone outside the family was suspect, alien, rightless. And even within the family, persons we presently regard as the natural holders of at least some rights had none. Take, for example, children. . . .

Nor is it only matter in human form that has come to be recognized as the possessor of rights. The world of the lawyer is peopled with inanimate right-holders: trusts, corporations, joint ventures, municipalities, Subchapter R partnerships, and nation-states, to mention just a few. Ships, still referred to by courts in the feminine gender, have long had an independent jural life, often with striking consequences. We have become so accustomed to the idea of a corporation having "its" own rights, and being a "person" and "citizen" for so many statutory and constitutional purposes, that we forget how jarring the notion was to early jurists. . . .

The fact is, that each time there is a movement to confer rights onto some new "entity," the proposal is bound to sound odd or frightening or laughable. This is partly because until the rightless thing receives its rights, we cannot see it as anything but a *thing* for the use of "us"—those who are holding rights at the time. . . . There is something of a seamless web involved: there will be resistance to giving the thing "rights" until it can be seen and valued for itself; yet it is hard to see it and value it for itself until we can bring ourselves to give it "rights"—which is almost inevitably going to sound inconceivable to a large group of people.

The reason for this little discourse on the unthinkable [is that] I am quite seriously proposing that we give legal rights to forests, oceans, rivers and other so-called "natural objects" in the environment—indeed, to the natural environment as a whole.

TOWARD HAVING STANDING IN ITS OWN RIGHT

It is not inevitable, nor is it wise, that natural objects should have no rights to seek redress in their own behalf. It is no answer to say that streams and forests cannot have standing because streams and forests cannot speak. Corporations cannot speak either; nor can states, estates, infants, incompetents, municipalities or universities. Lawyers speak for them, as they customarily do for the ordinary citizen with legal problems. One ought, I think, to handle the legal problems of natural objects as one does the problems of legal incompetents—human beings, who have become vegetable. If a human being shows signs of becoming senile and has affairs that he is de jure incompetent to manage, those concerned with his well being make such a showing to the court, and someone is designated by the court with the authority to manage the incompetent's affairs. The guardian (or "conservator" or "committee"—the terminology varies) then represents the incompetent in his legal affairs. Courts make similar appointments when a corporation has become "incompetent"— they appoint a trustee in bankruptcy or reorganization to oversee its affairs and speak for it in court when that becomes necessary.

On a parity of reasoning, we should have a system in which, when a friend of natural object perceives it to be endangered, he can apply to a court for the creation of a guardianship. Perhaps we already have the machinery to do so. California law, for example, defines an incompetent as "any person, whether insane or not, who by reason of old age, disease, weakness of mind, or other cause, is unable, unassisted, properly to manage and take care of himself or his property, and by reason thereof likely to be deceived or imposed upon by artful or designing persons." Of course, to urge a court that an endangered river is "a person" under this provision will call for lawyers as bold and imaginative as those who convinced the Supreme Court that a railroad corporation was a "person" under the fourteenth amendment, a constitutional provision theretofore generally thought of as designed to secure the rights of freedom.

SIERRA CLUB V. MORTON, SECRETARY OF THE INTERIOR
Prior History: Certiorari to the United States Court of Appeals for the Ninth Circuit
405 U.S. 727 (1971)

SYLLABUS

No. 70–34 Argued November 17, 1971—Decided April 19, 1972. Petitioner, a membership corporation with "a special interest in the conservation and sound maintenance of the national parks, game refuges, and forests of the country," brought this suit for a declaratory judgment and an injunction restraining federal officials from approving an extensive skiing development in the Mineral King Valley in the Sequoia National Forest. Petitioner relies on § 10 of the Administrative Procedure Act, which accords judicial review to a "person suffering legal wrong because of agency action, or [who is] adversely affected or aggrieved by agency action with the meaning of a relevant statute." On the theory that this was a "public" action involving questions as to the use of natural resources, petitioner did not allege that the challenged development would affect the club or its members in their activities or that they used Mineral King, but maintained that the project would adversely change the area's aesthetics and ecology. The District Court granted a preliminary injunction. The Court of Appeals reversed, holding that the club lacked standing, and had not shown irreparable injury. Held: a person has standing to seek judicial review under the Administrative Procedure Act only if he can show that he himself has suffered or will suffer injury, whether economic or otherwise. In this case, where petitioner asserted no individualized harm to itself or its members, it lacked standing to maintain the action. Pp. 4–14, 433 F.2d 24 affirmed.

STEWART, J., delivered the opinion of the Court in which BURGER, C.J., and WHITE and MARSHALL J.J., joined.

MR. JUSTICE DOUGLAS, dissenting.

I share the views of my Brother, BLACKMUN and would reverse the judgment below.

The critical question of "standing" would be simplified and also put neatly in focus if we fashioned a federal rule that allowed environmental issues to be litigated before federal agencies or federal courts in the name of the inanimate object about to be despoiled, defaced, or invaded by roads and bulldozers and where injury is the subject of public outrage. Contemporary public concern for protecting nature's ecological equilibrium should lead to the conferral of standing upon environmental objects to sue for their own preservation. See Stone, *Should Trees Have Standing? Toward Legal Rights for Natural Objects*, 45 S. Cal. L. Rev. 450 (1972). This suit would therefore be more properly labeled as *Mineral King v. Morton*.

Inanimate objects are sometimes parties in litigation. A ship has a legal personality, a fiction found useful for maritime purposes. The corporation soul—a creature of ecclesiastical law—is an acceptable adversary and large fortunes ride on its cases. The ordinary corporation is a "person" for purposes of the adjudicatory processes, whether it represents proprietary, spiritual, aesthetic, or charitable cases.

So it should be as respects valleys, alpine meadows, rivers, lakes, estuaries, beaches, ridges, groves of trees, swampland, or even air that feels the destructive pressures of modern technology and modern life. The river, for example, is the living symbol of all the life it sustains or nourishes—fish, aquatic insects, water ouzels, otter, deer, elk, bear, and all other animals, including man, who are dependent on it or who enjoy it for its sight, its sound, or its life. The river as plaintiff speaks for the ecological unit of life that is part of it. Those people who have a meaningful relation to that body of water—whether it be a fisherman, a canoeist, a zoologist, or a logger—must be able to speak for the values which the river represents and which are threatened with destruction. . . .

The voice of the inanimate object, therefore, should not be stilled. That does not mean that the judiciary takes over the managerial functions from the federal agency. It merely means that before these priceless bits of Americana (such as a valley, an alpine meadow, a river, or a lake) are forever lost or are so transformed as to be reduced to the eventual rubble of our urban environment, the voice of the existing beneficiaries of these environmental wonders should be heard.

Perhaps they will not win. Perhaps the bulldozers of "progress" will plow under all the aesthetic wonders of this beautiful land. That is not the present question. The sole question is who has standing to be heard? . . .

Ecology reflects the land ethic; and Aldo Leopold wrote in A Sand County Almanac 204 (1949), "The land ethic simply enlarges the boundaries of the community to include soils, waters, plants, and animals, or collectively, the land."

That, as I see it, is the issue of "standing" in the present case and controversy.

————————

The idea of rights for natural objects is highly controversial. The following article criticizes the ideas previously expounded.

ON PRESERVING THE NATURAL ENVIRONMENT

Mark Sagoff
84 Yale L.J. 205, 221–222 (1974)

What is wrong with this suggestion? [That natural objects have rights.] We have already seen that it is a little vague as it stands. But suppose it were put into effect. Even then we would have no rationale for preserving the natural environment. When only human interests are considered, as Stone admits, there is no "utilitarian" argument against development. [Humans have] learned to enjoy plastic forests and artificial parks. Man has chosen to live in manufactured habitats ever since he came down from the trees; there is no reason to think his trend away from nature will change today. But what about the interests of animals and other natural things? There is every reason to suppose that these interests differ very little from those of man. This conclusion follows from the example with which Stone himself defends the thesis that "natural objects can communicate their wants (needs) to us, and in ways that are not terribly ambiguous." Stone explains: "The lawn tells me that it wants water by a certain dryness of the blades and soil—immediately obvious to the touch—the appearance of bald spots, yellowing, and a lack of springiness after being walked on." Notice that nature is unlikely to take care of Stone's lawn. He has to water it with a hose, and this is a step toward an artificial, not a natural environment. Now consider how trees choke one another and gasp for air, water, and light. How much happier they would be planted in neat rows, as the timber companies would have them, and saved from their struggle for life! Consider animals. Many animals already inhabit our houses; no one can maintain that pets, rodents, and vermin would do as well in the wild. And wild animals often show their preference for the sanctuary of a domestic environment.... The salmon might prefer the aquarium or the fish tank, where it can lay its eggs quietly, without making the arduous journey upstream. There is no reason to think that the interests of animals must differ from ours. Nature is a war of each against all, as Hobbes said, and man and beast alike prefer the safety and comfort of an artificial environment.

The interests of nonliving things are a little harder but perhaps not impossible to imagine. Let us suppose, for the sake of argument, that resorts, factories, and electric plants are not among the objects which have to be represented in court. That leaves us with rivers, mountains, lakes and other natural things. Environmentalists always assume that the interests of these objects are *opposed* to development. How do they know this? Why wouldn't Mineral King want to host a ski resort, after doing nothing for a billion years? In another few millennia it will be back to original condition just the same. The Sequoia National Forests tells the developer that it wants a ski lift by a certain declivity of its hills and snowiness during the winter—immediately obvious to the sight—and that it needs a four lane highway by the appearance of certain valley passages and obvious scenic turnouts on the mountainsides.... Finally, it is reasonable to think that Old Man River might like to do something for a change, like make electricity, and not just keep on rolling along. It is an incredible optimism which assumes the guardians appointed to represent nature would take an environmentalist position. These guardians would be chosen by the government, in other words by the lobbies, and thus nature could enter suits on the side of development.... Can we rule out a priori the possibility that since man is the most dangerous animal, a rigorous cost-benefit analysis equitable to all nature would send him back to the caves? This is a real possibility—if objects of nature are always the victims, and never beneficiaries of development.

NOTES AND QUESTIONS

1.   What is our relationship to the natural system? Does the human species have a right to exploit it without limit for its own benefit? Is there equality between the human species and other species? What does it mean to say, as human ecologists do, that the human species is part of the natural system? What legal constraints does this imply?

2.   Should we give standing to trees, rivers, and plants? How do we know the interests of these objects? Would a redwood tree prefer to remain alive in the Redwood National Park or be made into a table and put in the Oval Office in the White House? What is the value of giving standing to trees? Couldn't you accomplish the same goal by liberalizing current judicial standing requirements?

3.   What legal approaches can be used to ensure that natural objects are not always the "victims of development"? What approaches could be used to reconcile development with conservation of the environment? How does the Planetary Trust model of our relationship to the environment address development?

2. FAUNA

As already noted, there is a subtle difference between having rights and being owed an obligation. In the context of the environment, some scholars argue that a sense of moral obligation to protect the animals is not sufficient.

The following passage argues that whales must have a legal status to adequately protect their lives.

WHALES: THEIR EMERGING RIGHT TO LIFE

Anthony D'Amato Sudhir K Chopra
Reproduced with permission from 85 AJ.I.L. 21 (1991)
© The American Society of International Law

The middle four stages of the legal progression that we traced in part II—from   (2) regulation,   to   (3) conservation,   to   (4) protection,   to

(5) preservation—might be thought to serve whales well enough for all practical and legal purposes. What need is there to move to the sixth, entitlement, stage? Specifically, what particular value is added by ascribing rights to whales, as distinct from recognizing a duty of nations and individuals toward whales?

We contend, first, that it is intelligible to regard whales as rights holders and, second, that viewing the rights in this way makes a difference. On both these points, we employ the pioneering analysis of Christopher Stone.

History has seen a widening of the circle of rights holders. When infanticide was freely practiced, infants had no rights; now of course their right to life is protected in nearly all countries by the law against murder. Convicted felons used to be stripped of all rights; now they have certain basic protections (e.g., equal medical care). The laws of most countries have seen a gradual progression in ascribing rights to aliens, married women, mentally enfeebled and racial minorities. Rights have also been extended to inanimate, intangible entities: trusts, corporations, joint ventures, partnerships and municipalities. Professor Stone has suggested the important differences that would accrue if we ascribed rights to natural objects in the environment. The first is what we might call the aspect of generality: that having rights is a generalized legal competence, whereas being the beneficiary of the obligations of others breaks down into a series of specialized, specific rules.

Second, the idea of having "rights" includes a notion of moral rights that can inform existing law or even push it in a certain direction. Take, for example, a battered wife suing her husband in the nineteenth century. Courts routinely dismissed such cases on the ground that they had no jurisdiction over what happened in the home, and in any event a wife had an adequate remedy under the laws of divorce. But at some point, courts changed their approach and began recognizing tort claims by wives against their husbands. . . . What happened is that the court accepted the powerful moral claim of right and recognized it as somehow subsisting in the common law all along, even though legal precedent was to the contrary. We say that the court "articulated" the preexisting right, much as we argue that an international court could articulate an entitlement of whales arising from the customary law practice of their preservation.

Third, the burden of proof in litigation and negotiation can turn on which party is a rights claimant. Courts may be predisposed to giving a far more "liberal" construction of applicable rules to a party that claims to be asserting rights than to one that claims to be a third-party beneficiary of asserted rights. Even the rules regarding burden of proof, Professor Stone suspects, would be more liberally interpreted in favor of a rights claimant.

Fourth, the development of a jurisprudence regarding whales is more likely if whales are perceived by courts as rights holders, just as a jurisprudence of corporate law has developed as a result of viewing corporations as legal entities entitled to sue and be sued and even to be prosecuted for corporate crime.

Finally, standing is facilitated for rights holders. Standing may be a lesser problem in American law than in the law of many other countries because of the separation-of-powers tradition of contesting many forms of governmental action in the courts. Yet even in U.S. courts when the protection of whales arises, the need to assert harm to one's own interests, as opposed to the interests of whales, may exert a subtle negative influence upon the petitioners. In *Japan Whaling Association v. American Cetacean Society*, although the Supreme Court found (in a footnote) that the American Cetacean Society, Greenpeace, Friends of the Earth and other environmental organizations had "alleged a sufficient 'injury in fact' in that the whale watching and studying of their members will be adversely affected by continued whale harvesting," the Court ultimately held against those organizations on the merits. For these reasons, and similar ones that could be adduced, the extension of legal rights to whales would have significant legal consequence. To move from "preservation" to "entitlement" is not just a way of talking. Rather, it acknowledges the creation of a new subject of international law.

A "right" may be legal or moral or both. The attempt to draw a sharp distinction between legal and moral rights often flounders on two grounds. First, as H.L.A. Hart has demonstrated, moral considerations influence the content of law over time. Second, there may be a deeper connection between law and morality than positivists such as Professor Hart are willing to admit. Although this connection may not be a "necessary" one in the substantive sense of Cicero or in the procedural sense of Lon Fuller, it exists in the claim of legitimacy that the law makes—a claim that surpasses that which can be enforced and spills over into the realm of that which is morally persuasive. For these general reasons, we have not attempted in this article to draw lines between the moral and the legal in our discussion of the emerging rights of whales. Although we have indicated when we are primarily talking about moral rights and when we are primarily talking about legal rights, the considerable degree of overlap between the two, we submit, reflects the way a norm develops over time.

On March 31, 2014, the International Court of Justice delivered its judgment in the Whaling in the Antarctic case [*Australia v. Japan with New Zealand as Intervening*]. The Court declared that Japan must halt its current program of conducting scientific research on whales in the region. Australia filed proceedings against Japan in the ICJ on the grounds that Japan violated its obligations under the 1946 International Convention for the Regulation of Whaling, (ICRW) as well as other international obligations to preserve the marine environment. Article VIII of the ICRW permits 'taking of whales for purposes of scientific research'. Australia alleged that Japan's program was not a scientific research program within the meaning of Article VIII of the ICRW and had breached certain obligations under the schedule to the ICRW relating to respecting the catch limits for the killing of whales and preserving certain species of whales. The ICJ examined Japan's program in light of the preamble of the ICRW that recognizes "the interest of the nations of the world in safeguarding for future generations the great natural resources represented by the whale stocks." It concluded that "the special permits granted by Japan for the killing, taking and treating of whales in connection with JARPA II are not 'for purposes of scientific research' pursuant to Article VIII, paragraph 1, of the Convention." The Court ordered Japan to revoke any extant authorization, permit or license to kill, take or treat whales in relation to JARPA II, and refrain from granting any further permits under Article VIII of the Convention. This case is discussed further in Chapter 13.

NOTES AND QUESTIONS

1.   What rights do animals have? Who represents them? Should a representative of whales be allowed to enforce the provision of the International Whaling Convention? If we do not give standing to animals, won't the protection of their interests be subordinate to economic and political considerations which may have little to do with a need to protect the whales?

2.   One author has argued that it makes a difference whether nonhumans are treated "as though they have rights" or treated so as not to violate the rights they actually possess. Richard A. Watson, *Self-Consciousness and the Rights of Nonhuman Animals and Nature*, in The Animal Rights/Environmental Ethics Debate: The Environmental Perspective, 1–35, 12 (Eugene C. Hargrove ed., 1992).

3.   Could there be a conflict between intergenerational rights and animal rights? Don't we regularly conduct animal research to sustain the present and future quality of human life and the robustness of the natural environment? An Australian Senate Report stated, "Experiments are . . . conducted on wildlife to obtain more effective and humane methods of controlling them with less detrimental effects on non-target species. Within this area of research specific projects may present difficult decisions . . . such as research using traps to check on the contents of dingos' stomachs and LD50 tests to examine the effect of 1080 baiting on non-target species." Report by the Senate Select Committee on Animal Welfare, Animal Experimentation 130 (1989). How could we reconcile rights of future generations and those of individual animals?

4.   What about the culling of wildlife, which we do for many reasons, e.g. to prevent overpopulations and to favor certain species over others. Does this practice violate animal rights or does it promote intergenerational interests? Is there a conflict?

5.   Do certain animals within species sometimes acquire special rights? For example, in July 2015, a U.S. wildlife hunter allegedly paid $50,000 to hunt and kill a lion. He killed the lion "Cecil", who had acquired a special revered status among lions in Hwange National Park in Zimbabwe, the country's largest game reserve. Cecil was 13 years old and distinguishable by his distinctive dark mane and his size. He was apparently killed in an area outside Hwange National Park. His killing generated worldwide attention and protest. The Zimbabwe government has been seeking to arrest the hunter and to have him extradited from the U.S. to Zimbabwe.

6.   *The WTO EC—Seal Products Decision.* The European Union adopted a regime for seal products, which generally prohibits the import and marketing of seal products, with certain exceptions for hunts conducted by indigenous communities or for purposes of managing marine resources. The WTO Appellate Body found that the regulations could come within the General Agreement on Tariffs and Trade (GATT) Article XX(a) exception as "necessary to protect public morals," though it did not meet the tests in the chapeau for Article XX. EC—Measures Prohibiting the Importation and Marketing of Seal Products, WTO Appellate Body Decision, adopted 18 June 2014. Why would seals be entitled to protection as a matter of public morals? Do seals have special rights? See Chapter 16 for analysis of environment and trade.

CHAPTER 3

RISK, ECONOMICS AND UNCERTAINTY

■ ■ ■

This chapter describes two disciplines that have influenced international environmental law: risk analysis and economics. The discipline of risk analysis has played a major role in shaping both domestic and international environmental law. Risk analysis involves the process of assessing and understanding the risks posed by particular environmental problems. Such analyses often involve both natural and physical sciences (evaluating, for example, the types of risk, degrees of risk, and distributions of risk) and social sciences (evaluating, for example, the ways in which particular human activities exacerbate or mitigate risks or are affected by risks). Such analyses can provide guidance to, or justifications for, legal choices by characterizing the risks posed by particular conditions or choices. However, their estimates are often uncertain in ways that challenge decision makers who desire more finality and certitude out of science.

The discipline of economics has also shaped domestic and international environmental law. Economic analysis has helped to provide powerful justifications for legal principles which constrain private and public behavior that causes environmental damage, as well to inform the choice of the regulatory and market-based instruments to cope with cross-border, regional, and global environmental problems. All the major international environmental problems—e.g., pollution prevention and abatement, the management of commons and shared resources, the well-being of future generations, the measurement of environmentally sustainable development and the valuation of environmental damage—raise the issue of how many resources society should allocate to address these problems and how these resources should be deployed. Although economic analyses are often presented in concrete dollar-value terms, they, too, contain uncertainties that are often glossed over even by economists themselves, and only recently have experts begun thinking more deliberately about how to incorporate this understanding into legal processes and decisions.

A. THE THEORETICAL BASIS OF THE POLLUTER PAYS PRINCIPLE: EXTERNALITY THEORY

Who is to blame for the tragedy of the commons? An influential early article placed the blame solely on the Judeo-Christian tradition, Lynn

White, *The Historical Roots of Our Ecological Crisis*, 155 Science 1203 (1967). The Australian philosopher John Passmore, Man's Responsibility for Nature: Ecological Problems and Western Traditions (1974), placed the blame more on the Greco-Christian thought. *See also* J. Donald Hughes, Pan's Travail: Environmental Problems of the Ancient Greeks and Romans (1994). Another early classic, Barry Commonor, The Closing Circle (1967), blamed modern technology.

Our more immediate concern is with the two principal competing theories of the reasons for commons degradation, each with different legal consequences. In A Sand County Almanac (1949), which is the source of much of modern environmental ethics throughout the world, wildlife ecologist Aldo Leopold argued that the Abrahamic concept of private property must give way to a land ethic based on "love, respect, and admiration for land, and a high regard for its value." By "value" Leopold meant "something far broader than mere economic value; I mean value in the philosophic sense." *Id.* at 223. Leopold hoped that humans would internalize a collaborative, stewardship ethic, but lawyers influenced by this seminal work drew the conclusion that regulation was necessary to limit private choice, especially after an economist pointed out the high costs of organizing effective collective action to address problems such as environmental degradation. Mancur Olson, The Logic of Collective Action (1965). In the international area, the favored policy instrument was the creation of legal duties through international agreements to be followed by effective domestic command and control systems.

Many, though not all, economists do not share Leopold's distaste for property rights because they believe that exchanges and markets are the best way to improve human welfare over time. Thus, most economists draw the opposite conclusion from Leopold and argue that the tragedy of the commons is not caused by the institution of private property but by the opposite: the lack of clearly assigned property rights in common resources. From this perspective, environmental degradation is simply a symptom of market failure, which should presumptively be corrected. As the following excerpt illustrates, economists took a largely theoretical concept, external costs, which was a minor aspect of welfare economics, and made it the organizing concept of environmental economics. Although this material is from the 1970s, the ideas presented still remain in use today.

ECONOMICS AND THE ENVIRONMENT: A MATERIALS BALANCE APPROACH

Allen V. Kneese, Robert U. Ayres & Ralph C. D'Arge
2–6 (1970)

EXTERNALITIES AND ECONOMIC THEORY

Economic theory has long recognized in a limited way the existence of "common property" problems and resource misallocations associated with them. It was early appreciated that when property rights to a valuable resource could not be parceled out in such a way that one participant's activities in the use of that resource would leave the others unaffected, except through market exchange, unregulated private exchange would lead to inefficiencies. These inefficiencies were of two types: those associated with "externalities" and those associated with "user costs." The former term refers to certain broader costs (or benefits) of individual action which are not taken into account in deciding to take that action. For instance, the individual crude petroleum producer, pumping from a common pool, has no market incentive to take account of the increased cast imposed on others because of reduced gas pressure resulting from his own pumping. Also, because he cannot be sure that a unit of petroleum he does not exploit now will be available for his later use, acting individually he has no reason to conserve petroleum for later and possibly higher value use. Thus he has no incentive to take account of his user cost. The only limit to his current exploitation is current cost—not the opportunity cost of future returns. Consequently the resource will be exploited at an excessively rapid rate in the absence of some sort of collective action. While these problems were recognized with respect to such resources as petroleum, fisheries, and groundwater, and there was rather sophisticated theorizing with respect to them, still private property and exchange have been regarded as the keystones of an efficient allocation of resources.

To quote the famous welfare economist Pigou:

When it was urged above, that in certain industries a wrong amount of resources is being invested because the value of the marginal social net product there differs from the value of the marginal private net product, it was tacitly assumed that in the main body of industries these two values are equal. . . .

It is the main thesis of this book that at least one class of externalities—those associated with the disposal of residuals [e.g., waste—Eds.] resulting from modern consumption and production activities—must be viewed quite differently. In reality they are a normal, indeed inevitable, part of these processes. Their economic significance tends to increase as economic development proceeds, and the ability of the natural environment to receive and assimilate them is an important natural resource of rapidly increasing value. We suggest below that the common failure to recognize these facts in economic theory may result from viewing the production and consumption processes in a manner which is somewhat at variance with the fundamental physical law of conservation of mass.

Modern welfare economics concludes that if (1) preference orderings of consumers and production functions of producers are independent and their shapes appropriately constrained, (2) consumers maximize utility subject to given income and price parameters, and (3) producers maximize profits subject to these price parameters, then a set of prices exists such that no individual can become better off without making some other individual worse off. For a given distribution of income this is an efficient state. Given certain further assumptions concerning the structure of markets, this "Pareto optimum" can be achieved via a pricing mechanism and voluntary decentralized exchange.

If the capacity of the environment to assimilate residuals is scarce, the decentralized voluntary exchange process cannot be free of uncompensated technological external diseconomies unless (1) all inputs are fully converted into outputs, with no unwanted material and energy residuals along the way, and all final outputs are utterly destroyed in the process of consumption, or (2) property rights are so arranged that all relevant environmental attributes are in private ownership and these rights are exchanged in competitive markets. Neither of these conditions can be expected to hold in an actual economy, and they do not. Nature does not permit the destruction of matter except by annihilation with antimatter, and the means of disposal of unwanted residuals which maximizes the internal return of decentralized decision units is by discharge into the environment . . .

NOTES AND QUESTIONS

1.   *From theory to liability?* The fundamental insight of economics is that pollution is a sign of market failure and thus external cost which should be internalized. However, does it follow that "polluters" are always responsible for waste discharges and other behavior that degrades the environment? One of the foundational principles of international environmental law, derived from externality theory, is the "polluter pays principle." *See, e.g.*, Phillipe Sands, Principles of International Environmental Law 213–217 (1994). The principle originated in concern over trade-distortion of pollution-control subsidies in the 1972 OCED Council Recommendation on Guiding Principles Concerning the International Aspects of Environmental Policies, 14 I.L.M. 236 (1972), which stated that the cost of pollution control measures "should be reflected in the costs and goods and services which cause pollution in production and/or consumption." The evolution of the principle is discussed in more detail in Chapter 7, p. 387. The principle has been widely interpreted to mean that polluters should pay these external costs of production. It is also invoked to argue that State industrial

subsidies which encourage pollution both violate the principle and goal of environmentally sustainable development. The polluter pays principle has been widely adopted in international instruments, EU directives and other contexts. *See, e.g.*, Directive on Environmental Liability, Directive 2004/35/CE, Official Journal L. 143, 30/04/2004, p. 56. Domestic courts have relied on it as a justification for laws which impose compliance and clean up duties on polluters. In upholding the power of Quebec to issue an order requiring an oil company to assess the extent of contamination of formerly owned land, the Supreme Court of Canada wrote:

> Section 31.42 EQA, which was enacted in 1990 (S.Q. 1990, c. 26, s. 4), applies what is called the polluter-pay principle, which has now been incorporated into Quebec's environmental legislation. In fact, that principle has become firmly entrenched in Environmental law in Canada. It is found in almost all federal and provincial environmental legislation. . . . That principle is also recognized at the international level. One of the best examples of that recognition is found in the sixteenth principle of Rio Declaration on Environment and Development, UN Doc. A/Conf. 151/5/Rev. 1 (1992).[1]
>
> To encourage sustainable development, that principle assigns polluters the responsibility for remedying contamination for which they are responsible and imposes on them the direct and immediate costs of pollution. At the same time, polluters are asked to pay more attention to the need to protect ecosystems in the course of their economic activities. [Imperial Oil Ltd. v. Quebec 2003 S.C.C. 58]

2. *Polluter pays and property rights.* The polluter pays principle raises a host of complex operational problems. First, it seems to assume that the right to use commons as waste sinks has been partially reassigned from "polluters" to the public. This reassignment has only occasionally been explicitly acknowledged, although the cumulative impact of domestic and international law effectively does this. One example of an explicit acknowledgment is an early U.S. Clean Water Act case. The issue was whether pulp and paper dischargers should receive credit for discharging wastes into the ocean, which has a high assimilative capacity. In holding that all dischargers had to comply with the technology-forcing standards of the Act, the U.S. Court of Appeals for the D.C. Circuit wrote, "[m]ore fundamentally, the new approach implemented changing views as to the relative rights of the public and industrial polluters. Hitherto, the right of the polluter was pre-eminent, unless the damage caused by the pollution could be proven. Henceforth, the right of the public to a clean environment would be pre-eminent . . ." Weyerhaeuser Co. v. Costle, 590 F.2d 1011 (D.C. Cir. 1978).

---

[1] "National authorities should endeavor to promote the internationalization of environmental costs and use economic instruments, taking into account the approach that the polluter should, in principle, bear the costs of pollution, with regard to the public interest and without distorting international trade and investment." [Eds.]

Second, is such a reassignment a necessary condition to implement the polluter pays principle? Ronald Coase argued that it was not. His famous article, *The Problem of Social Cost*, 3 J. Law and Econ. 1 (1960), posited that absent transaction costs, the parties would reach an efficient allocation of resources through bargaining, regardless of the initial assignment of property rights. In contrast, the Austrian School of Economics posits that the assignment or reassignment of property rights is a necessary condition to resolve pollution conflicts. Roy E. Cordato, The Polluter Pays Principle: A Proper Guide for Environmental Policy (2001). Given the diverse nature of the international community and the resulting high transaction costs, one can ask if the Coase theorem has any relevance for international environmental law.

Third, is a discharger always a polluter? Take the case of vehicles with low mileage per unit of gasoline and discharge pollutants into the atmosphere. Who is a polluter? The vehicle manufacturer, the State which allows the use of the vehicle with low fuel efficiency standards or the person who purchases and uses the vehicle?

3. *Flawed theory or done in by self-interest?* Do you agree with the following? "A more fundamental problem with the broader use of the polluter pays' principle is that it does not indicate who is a polluter, and cannot as such determine liability." Patricia Birnie & Alan Boyle, International Law & the Environment 94 (2d ed. 2002). Nonetheless, externality theory is often invoked to justify strict liability. The basic argument is that fault-based liability, e.g., negligence, often induces firms and other polluters to pollute and risk the cost of damage liability, including administrative fines, while strict liability often requires firms to install technology to produce the efficient amount of a product or good. A. Mitchell Polinsky, An Introduction to Law and Economics 107–110 (2003). Does the principle also require the victims of pollution to take any steps to mitigate the damage? Polinsky argues that efficiency requires that strict liability for polluters be complemented by a contributory negligence defense. *Id.* at 111.

Economic theory aside, one of the reasons governments have been reluctant to embrace the polluter pays principle is the political problem of hurting industry. The principle not only requires the installation of pollution control technology but also the elimination of subsidies to producers. At any given price, a subsidy makes production more profitable for the producer since costs are lowered. This, therefore, distorts the results of a cost-benefit analysis and may cause less environmentally desirable options to be chosen. What does this imply for assistance to developing countries to achieve environmental standards set by the industrialized countries? What about European Union assistance in the form of economic subsidies to certain member countries to allow them to comply with community requirements? Should economic subsidies be treated as legal requirements?

1. SHOULD STATES PAY?

The next article explores the relevance of externality theory for the fundamental norm of international environmental law, State responsibility for transboundary and global commons damage. Although the material is from the 1980s, it summarizes some of the relevant concepts in use today.

STATE LIABILITY FOR INTERNATIONAL ENVIRONMENTAL DEGRADATION: AN ECONOMIC PERSPECTIVE
Ralph C. D'Arge & Allen V. Kneese
20 Nat. Res. J. 427 (1980)

INTRODUCTION

State responsibility and liability are not clearly defined with respect to environmental degradation. But a limited number of cases and declarations by international tribunals do point in a definable direction. In the famous Trail Smelter Case, the tribunal declared: "A State owes at all times a duty to protect other states against injurious acts by individuals from within its jurisdiction." The Organization for Economic Cooperation and Development (OECD) adopted the "polluter pays" principle (PP) in 1972, which states that the waste discharger must pay for any ameliorating measures which are caused to be undertaken. This principle does not apply to any residual damages which may remain. However, the German government has recently issued an interpretation which requires payment of an effluent charge which presumably, in some manner, is meant to reflect remaining damages within German territory. The Stockholm Declarations could also be interpreted as placing responsibility upon those undertaking the actions which result in environmental degradation, although the emphasis is upon "common action" among states. The tendency then is to interpret state responsibility as requiring that states within whose boundaries harmful actions occur must pay or cause to be paid the cost of ameliorating those actions and, possibly, must pay for the remaining damages as well.

In this paper, we shall define and analyze four major principles of assigning state responsibility and discuss the economic meaning of those principles. The first principle is that each state is responsible for all waste discharge control costs internally and externally but is not responsible for compensation of remaining damages following installation of the agreed-upon controls. This is a variant of the OECD principle cited above in that we apply it, as an area of major concern, to transfrontier pollution problems; application of the principle to such problems was explicitly excluded by OECD member nations. The second major principle is the full costing principle (FC), which requires the state responsible for waste discharge to pay compensation for remaining damages as well as control costs. The third principle is the "victim pays" principle (VP), which requires the affected state to compensate the affecting state (or internal parties creating harmful residuals) for all costs of control and to absorb all residual damages after controls are implemented. The fourth principle, in its simplest form, requires the establishment of an internal or international autonomous agency to regulate the joint use of common property resources by individual or multiple states. In the international case, the various states would give powers to the agency to regulate waste discharges into the commonly shared environment. For lack of a better description, we term this principle of responsibility the common property resources institution principle (CPRI).

DIRECT TECHNOLOGICAL EXTERNALITIES

THE BILATERAL CASE

The current implied legal doctrine that each country must pay for transnational pollution by ceasing activities that cause it may for various reasons (including the difficulty of estimating damages, especially internationally) be adopted as the best practical type of polluter pays principle, but it can be shown to be inefficient in many instances. Let us suppose that agriculture in Arizona is very much more productive than downstream in Mexico and that the only way to reduce salt content downstream is to take land out of cultivation upstream. Then the current legal doctrine offers the following choice: let the Mexicans continue to suffer uncompensated losses or take more productive land out upstream and replace it with less productive land downstream. Other considerations aside, a PP principle with compensatory flexibility would be more efficient, since agricultural production across both countries could be maintained at a higher level and the parties involved could share the gain through compensation arrangements to the betterment of both.

Under certain simplified conditions, it can be shown that the VP and PP principles applied to transnational pollution problems both produce Pareto efficiency in the short run and the long run if consumers and factors of production are immobile internationally. The only difference between the two is in the international distribution of income. This result might lead one to favor the VP principle for the simple reason that it can be implemented without international enforcement machinery which in the past has proved so intractable. The damaged party has an incentive both to get information and to bargain with the sovereignty within which the offending activity is taking place. The principle also has the advantage that the willingness of the affected sovereignty to pay for reduction provides a quantitative estimate of the damage loss, which might otherwise be very hard to calculate. But aside from the fact that most people would probably consider the arrangement quite inequitable, it has another basic flaw. If the VP principle is applicable, the externality-generating country may threaten (by giving high estimates of future loads) to discharge materials as an incidental aspect of the production of other goods simply to obtain compensation for not doing so. One may hypothesize that polluting material could be produced at low cost Thus, if the VP principle were to be applied, an aspect of state responsibility would have to be structured to remove the incentives underlying "pollution for profit." Of course, under the PP or FC principles, the injured country could also exaggerate its losses, but it is not in the superior position which would permit it to exact retribution if its demands are not met. Thus, there seem to be significant preliminary grounds for preferring the FC or PP principles for both efficiency and equity reasons.

Before turning to the multilateral case, we should point out that the theoretical symmetry among the PP, FC, and VP principles indicated above is dependent upon the assumption (usually made in the classical international trade literature) that resources are immobile internationally. If this is not the case, capital or labor movements will cause the outcomes of the principles to differ.

THE MULTILATERAL CASE

With multi-country environmental problems, assessment of the efficiency of the previously stated principles in allocating global resources is much less clear than in the bilateral case just analyzed. As an example, consider one upstream country with waste discharges affecting two downstream countries. With the FC principle, there is the problem of arriving at an agreement between the downstream countries about which is damaged the most and which should consequently be compensated the most. The PP principle contains similar problems in that there must be joint agreement on acceptable levels of upstream control. Finally, the VP principle is fraught with so-called "free-rider" problems in that, if one country provides a substantial amount of the necessary controls, the second downstream country receives reduced damages at no cost. If, in general, there are more receptor countries than emitters, then it will be more difficult, in terms of coordination, for a solution to emerge under the VP principle than under the FC principle. This result follows because the agreement on compensation requires a greater number of sovereignties arranging to make a payment, which inherently seems more difficult to negotiate than those same sovereignties agreeing to receive a payment.

SUMMARY

The various principles of state responsibility have substantially different impacts on the global efficiency of resources unless there are no transfers of resources among nations. With no transfers or movements, the various principles lend to affect only the distribution of wealth among nations. In terms of allocative efficiency, the "best" principle would be one of converting all [common property resources] to internationally operated and regulated resources. But such a conversion may imply substantial changes in wealth and therefore may be unacceptable. The principle with the most desirable efficiency properties would appear to be a modified FC principle where the emitter country's government taxed internal firms according to receptor country damages but did not provide compensation to the receptor country.

NOTE AND QUESTIONS

Is the polluter pays principle described by Kneese and d'Arge a liability standard? Do you agree with Kneese and d'Arge's characterization? Compare it with the OECD principle described on page 91. Kneese and d'Arge identify a victim pays principle. Does it ever make economic sense for the victim to pay the polluter to install a filter to control the emission of pollutants? What would the full costs to the victim be in this case? The Federal Republic of Germany helped the former State of Czechoslovakia to install air pollution control technology on a factory near the border. Could this make economic sense? Should a developed country that is a victim of pollution from a neighboring developed country pay for the installation of control technology by the polluter? If not, why not? If the victim State is a developed country and the host State a developing, does your answer change? Why?

2. EXTERNALITY THEORY IN PRACTICE

It is not always easy to apply externality theory to concrete liability problems. One must first make the heroic assumption that the externality or pollution damage can be monetized or at least mitigated (if in-kind mitigation is a possibility). But even if it can, the question becomes, should all damage be eliminated? Put differently, the term "pollution" is neither self-defining nor a pure scientific concept. As anyone who has ever hand-washed a sweater knows, most of the water can be removed by wringing the sweater two or three times. Thereafter, progressively more energy must be expended to remove incrementally smaller amounts of water. The same typically holds for pollution damages. Research shows that the cost of removing the last two or three percentage points of damage equals the cost of removing the first 97 percent. Peter Rogers, America's Water: Federal Roles and Responsibilities 141–142 (1993). Thus, to most economists, it is clear that not all pollution need or should be eliminated. Welfare economics teaches that the discharges which should be curtailed are those beyond the point where the marginal private benefit exceeds the marginal social cost.

The following excerpt presents an early and still widely used scheme of total pollution cost minimization that tries to determine the optimal amount of pollution.

COUNCIL ON ENVIRONMENTAL QUALITY, ENVIRONMENTAL QUALITY: THE FOURTH ANNUAL REPORT OF THE COUNCIL ON ENVIRONMENTAL QUALITY
74–76 (1973)

[There are] four categories of costs that must be examined and balanced in environmental decisionmaking. Damage costs are those costs which directly result from a polluting activity, for example, illness and property damage stemming from air pollution. Avoidance costs are those that people incur in order to avoid or reduce damage costs, for example, the cost of driving farther to find an unpolluted beach. Transaction costs represent the resources consumed in making and enforcing policies and regulations, such as the costs of monitoring air pollution. Abatement costs are those associated with reducing the amount of environmental degradation, such as the cost of sewage treatment plants. Damage, avoidance, and transactional costs are discussed in this section, abatement costs in the next section.

DAMAGE COSTS

Our present high level of environmental concern grew from a recognition that pollution was damaging man and nature. The damages occur when a pollutant is not stopped at its source or successfully avoided after it has been released. Damage costs include damage to health, to vegetation, and to materials; the costs of repairing such damages; the destruction of ecosystems; and the loss of aesthetic, recreational, and other environmental amenities.

Many damage costs represent a loss of tangible resources—the medical care required to treat pollution-caused illness, for example, and the cost of cleaning clothes or painting houses more often. These are the costs most often estimated and reported as pollution damage costs, and they are usually measured in terms of the market-place value of the resources destroyed or consumed.

In addition to these tangible costs, there are various intangible damage costs—the anxiety created by congestion, risks to health and safety, the aesthetic blight of a strip development, the unpleasantness of foul odors, and the annoyance of excessive noise. Often called psychic costs, they embrace the range of annoyance and other psychological costs associated with environmental degradation beyond the value of any physical resources damaged. Often they are matters of preference, and their importance is not usually measured accurately by the marketplace. The fact that these psychic costs do not consume tangible resources does not make them less important. A human want that does not directly consume a tangible resource is no less important than one that does.

Many types of environmental damage will create both tangible and intangible costs. By damaging health, air pollution affects tangible resources by causing lost production and by consuming equipment, supplies, and the time of highly skilled manpower required to restore good health. The illness, as well as the threatened loss of income security, may also arouse anxiety and fear in the individual and his family and friends. These are some of the psychic costs of air pollution-costs that are rarely included in damage estimates.

Although probably comprising a significant portion of total damage costs, psychic costs, unfortunately, cannot be accurately quantified. Further, they change over time. Opinion surveys indicate that the degree of concern about such problems as air and water pollution has increased substantially in less than a decade. . . . In the past, people were less aware of the extent and dangers of environmental degradation and had less interest in the amenities offered by a clean environment. Even as we improve our environment, the psychic costs may be higher than before because of this heightened concern.

AVOIDANCE COSTS

Often ignored in environmental analyses, the most common method of reducing damages costs in the past was simply to avoid the pollution. One way to do this is to erect a barrier between people and pollution-building a fence to hide an ugly landscape or installing a window unit which hums to mask street noises. Coating low-voltage electrical contacts for electronic devices with gold, platinum, and other precious metals to avoid the effects of air pollution cost over $20 million in 1968, and the devices are often kept in specially air-conditioned rooms at an additional estimated annual cost of $25 million.

A second way of avoiding pollution is to move away from it. If a nearby lake becomes polluted, forcing people to drive farther to swim, the extra travel costs are avoidance costs. The damages caused by aircraft noise can be reduced by moving residential and other incompatible land uses away from airports, as is being done in Los Angeles. A study of eight other airports indicates that this kind of operation would cost between $1.3 billion and $1.6 billion per airport.

Avoidance costs are often ignored because they are generally very hard to estimate. In most cases an action is taken for several reasons, only one of which is to avoid pollution. It is difficult to know what value to assign to each reason. . . .

B. THE PROBLEM OF UNCERTAINTY

Both risk analysis and economic analysis can be powerful analytical tools for rational decisionmaking, but the scientific, social, and economic information necessary to make an informed decision is generally not available or can only be made available at great cost sometime in the future. Environmental regulation must confront the problem that decisions must be made under varying degrees of uncertainty, on both scientific and economic fronts. International environmental law requires, more than most areas of law, a detailed scientific understanding of the biosphere or aspects of it. Some of the complexities and interrelationships are evident from the materials in Chapter 1. While our knowledge of the global environmental system and its associated local systems has been rapidly growing, it is still far from complete. Our understanding is constantly changing as we acquire new knowledge about the environment. Moreover, the environment itself is dynamic, as evident from changes wrought by climate change. We often realize that what we thought we knew was actually not true or that newly discovered knowledge changes our ideas about our old knowledge, leading us to a different understanding of the environment as a system or of the efficacy of various approaches to environmental protection. Indeed, it is rare that we can be nearly one hundred percent sure of anything. From both scientific and economic perspectives, there is always an element of uncertainty. This is also true with respect to the social impacts associated with environmental problems, which are not dealt with specifically in this chapter for brevity's sake. Chapter 15 considers the human rights aspects of environmental protection.

This element of uncertainty in both risk and economic analysis can present a quandary for legal systems. The constraints of the scientific method seldom allow science to provide the definitive answers that policy-makers want. Science seeks knowledge through a careful, iterative process of experimentation and validation, and scientists thus are often most comfortable giving answers as ranges of probability rather than a single bottom line figure or in linear causal relationships. Similarly, economic analysis typically involves using models that also contain various uncertainties, despite the disciplinary instinct towards presenting results as concrete, "certain," figures. Policy experts are only recently beginning to incorporate this understanding of economic uncertainties into their recommendations.

The following sections contain excerpts from the U.S. Institute of Medicine Report on Environmental Decisions in the Face of Uncertainty, which discusses uncertainty in the context of the Environmental Protection Agency (EPA), one of the federal bodies engaged in environmental protection in the United States. The report provides an introduction to the kinds of uncertainties involved in scientific/risk analysis and economic analysis, as well as an overview of tools used to incorporate uncertainty into legal decisionmaking.

1. SCIENTIFIC UNCERTAINTY

INSTITUTE OF MEDICINE, ENVIRONMENTAL DECISIONS IN THE FACE OF UNCERTAINTY

3–5 (2013)

All EPA decisions involve uncertainty, but the type of uncertainty can vary widely from one decision to another. For an analysis of uncertainty to be useful or productive and for decision makers to determine when to invest resources to reduce the uncertainty, a first and critical step is identifying the types of key uncertainties that contribute to a particular decision problem. The types of uncertainty also, in part, determine the best approaches for analyzing and communicating uncertainty. In this report, the committee classifies the various types of uncertainty into three categories: (1) statistical variability and heterogeneity (also called aleatory or exogenous uncertainty), (2) model and parameter uncertainty (also called epistemic uncertainty), and (3) deep uncertainty (uncertainty about the fundamental processes or assumptions underlying a risk assessment).

Variability and heterogeneity refer to the natural variations in the environment, exposure paths, and susceptibility of subpopulations. They are inherent characteristics of a system under study, cannot be controlled by decision makers, and cannot be reduced by collecting more information. Empirical estimates of variability and heterogeneity can, however, be better understood through research in order to refine such estimates. Variability can often be quantified with standard statistical techniques, although it may be necessary to collect additional data.

Model and parameter uncertainty include uncertainty due to the limited scientific knowledge about the nature of the models that link the causes and effects of environmental risks with risk-reduction actions as well as uncertainty about the specific parameters of the models. There may be various disagreements about the model, such as which model is most appropriate for the application at hand, which variables should be included in the model, the model's functional form (that is, whether the relationship being modeled is linear, exponential, or some other form), and how generalizable the findings based on data collected in another context are to the problem at hand (for example, the generalizability of findings based on experiments on animals to human populations). In theory, model and parameter uncertainty can be reduced by additional research.

Deep uncertainty is uncertainty that is not likely to be reduced by additional research within the time period in which a decision must be made. Typically, deep uncertainty is present when underlying environmental processes are not understood, when there is fundamental disagreement among scientists about the nature of the environmental processes, and when methods are not available to characterize the processes (such as the measurement and evaluation of chemical mixtures). When deep uncertainty is present, it is unclear how those disagreements can be resolved. In situations characterized by deep uncertainty, the probabilities associated with various regulatory options and associated utilities may not be known. Neither the collection and analysis of data nor expert elicitation to assess uncertainty is likely to be productive when key parties to a decision do not agree on the system model, prior probabilities, or the cost function. The task instead is to make decisions despite the presence of deep uncertainty using the available science and judgment, to communicate how those decisions were made, and to revisit those decisions when more information is available.

2.   ECONOMIC UNCERTAINTY

INSTITUTE OF MEDICINE, ENVIRONMENTAL DECISIONS IN THE FACE OF UNCERTAINTY
82–83 (2013)

Uncertainty in economic analyses can stem from determining what costs and benefits should be included in the analyses, in the estimates of the costs and benefits themselves, and in adjusting the costs and benefits to reflect that they will occur in the future (that is, discounting).

The outcome of an economic analysis can vary greatly depending on the boundaries of that analysis, that is, on what is included in the analysis. Analyses can include mental health care costs and other health care costs, costs from lost employment, and a variety of other costs, such as the costs from the increased domestic violence that results from lost employment. In its guidelines, EPA (2010) considers social cost—which is described as the "total burden a regulation will impose on the economy" and "the sum of all opportunity costs incurred as a result of the regulation"—to be the most comprehensive and appropriate measure of cost for a CBA [benefit-cost analysis, also referred to in the report as BCA]. "Opportunity costs consist of the value lost to society of all the goods and services that will not be produced and consumed if firms comply with the regulation and reallocate resources away from production activities and toward pollution abatement." Social cost is narrower than the "total cost," which is considered in a number of regulatory impact analyses and includes costs beyond the social costs.

At the time of an economic analysis, the mean estimated values of anticipated benefits and costs and the corresponding net benefit or the benefit-cost ratio might indicate that a project is worth undertaking or that a rule is worth adopting, but after implementation the actual benefits and costs seen in retrospect can differ considerably from the estimated mean values because of uncertainties at the time of the analysis. For example, if there is an unanticipated increase in energy prices after a decision, the actual cost of a decision could exceed the anticipated cost, and what was thought to be a project of positive net benefit may turn out to have a substantial negative net benefit. That uncertainty, however, is rarely detailed in a BCA or CEA [cost-effectiveness analysis], let alone in the rationale for the decisions that use the BCA or CEA (NRC, 2002a).

[The report then discusses uncertainties in cost analysis, including compliance costs and costs imposed economy-wide; uncertainties in benefits analysis, including establishing baseline values, marginal effects of policies and rules, valuing endpoints, and discounting (which is addressed in part D of this Chapter, below).]

3. APPROACHES FOR INCORPORATING UNCERTAINTY INTO DECISIONMAKING

Both international and environmental policies and laws must take uncertainty into account. A number of legal/policy approaches have been used to try to address the problems of scientific and economic uncertainty (or at least incorporate the understanding of its existence). The following sections outline a few of these approaches. For further discussion, *see* Jorge E. Vinuales, *Legal Techniques for Dealing with Scientific Uncertainty in Environmental Law*, 43 Vand. J. Transnat'l L. 437 (2010).

a. Precautionary Approach

The gap between the identification of a potential risk and the degree of scientific proof that it is likely to materialize is often great. One strategy is simply to continue to study and monitor the risk, but many argue that this is unacceptable because it means that no risk will ever be addressed. To close the gap, many scholars and diplomats argue that there is a precautionary principle emerging in international law to provide a norm to determine whether actions are justified to address a given risk under conditions of uncertainty, or at least to authorize action in the face of uncertainty. Some argue it is not a principle, but rather an "approach." It is clear that precaution appears in a number of international declarations (e.g., the Rio Declaration on Environment and Development) and even in some international agreements (e.g., the Cartagena Biosafety Protocol). *See generally* D. Magraw & L. Hawke, *Sustainable Development*, in International Environmental Law 611–38 (D. Bodansky, J. Brunnee & E. Hay, eds., 2007).

The precautionary "principle" or "approach" is a method of dealing with threatened environmental harm in the face of scientific uncertainty. It emphasizes risks more than benefits and, unlike more utilitarian approaches, doesn't incorporate the idea that the prospect of greater benefits might justify assuming greater risks. Moreover, by focusing on avoidance of overall risk, this approach also does not expressly weigh who bears the costs of taking precautions and who loses the prospective benefits from the activity being considered for precaution. The following materials are presented to allow you to explore this concept.

RIO DECLARATION ON ENVIRONMENT AND DEVELOPMENT, PRINCIPLE 15

Adopted by the United Nationals Conference on Environment and Development, June 14, 1992 U.N. Doc. A/CONF.151/5/Rev.1, June 13, 1992, reprinted in 31 I.L.M. 874 (1992)

Principle 15

In order to protect the environment, the precautionary approach shall be widely applied by States according to their capabilities. Where there are threats of serious or irreversible damage, lack of full scientific certainty shall not be used as a reason for postponing cost-effective measures to prevent environmental degradation.

UNCERTAINTY

Daniel Farber
99 GEO. L.J. 901, 914–15 (2015)

THE PRECAUTIONARY PRINCIPLE

The European Union and other nations are less wedded to quantitative risk assessment than the United States. They are therefore more willing to take seriously hazards that cannot be quantified via the precautionary principle. We will first discuss the principle and a partial analog found at one time in U.S. law and then turn to debates about the validity of the precautionary principle.

. . .

In contrast to the United States' reliance on conventional risk assessment, the European Union has favored an approach that more forthrightly addresses uncertainty: the precautionary principle. Indeed, the precautionary principle's influence is much broader than just the European Union: "The precautionary principle is nothing short of ascendant on the international stage, so much so that many categorize it as constituting customary international law." In its most general sense, the precautionary principle advises that lack of certainty is not a justification for inaction in the face of possible risks; more precise statements of the principle focus on situations involving nonquantifiable harms, irreversible harm, or catastrophic harm. This principle has been explained on the basis of risk aversion or skepticism about the environment's ability to tolerate damage. The implication of the precautionary principle is that it is better to overregulate than underregulate new technologies—but this can actually result in more harm to public health or welfare under some circumstances.

The precautionary principle is endorsed in numerous international environmental statements and treaties. The precautionary principle appears as part of the Rio Declaration an Environment and Development. Principle 15 of the Declaration states that "to protect the environment, the precautionary approach shall be widely applied by States according to their capabilities," and that given "threats of serious or irreversible damage, lack of scientific certainty shall not be used as a reason for postponing cost-effective measures to prevent environmental degradation."

The precautionary principle also appears in international conventions on ozone, global climate, and biodiversity. It has also been adopted by Germany as a guide to environmental policy and has been invoked by courts in Canada, Pakistan, and India. The precautionary principle served as the basis for the European Union's effort to regulate the use of genetically modified organisms in foods, with concerns about the possible adverse effects as dominant rather than concerns about the balance between possible costs and benefits.

CAN THERE BE SCIENCE-BASED PRECAUTION?

Charles Weiss

2006 Environ. Res. Lett. 1 (2006)

The idea of precaution can be expanded in such a way as to help the decision maker to structure a policy discussion, and to provide at least a rough measure of uncertainty and of attitude toward risk. Reduced to its essentials, precaution is an attitude toward risk: an inclination to accept financial, political or social costs today (including the loss of possible benefits), in order to avoid or mitigate future dangers in situations in which the scientific evidence for these dangers is uncertain. The 'strong' version of precaution—as expressed, for example, in the Wingspread Principle—constitutes a willingness to accept substantial costs, even at a very low level of such proof.

Insistence on 'good science' is also a statement of an attitude toward risk—in this case, a willingness to trust that the danger in question will not turn out to be real, or that methods will be developed to deal with it in the future, so as to put off costs until the reality of the danger is proven to a very high standard. As the size of the putative danger increases, everyone's willingness to accept costs will increase, until at the extreme (say an asteroid striking the Earth) even the technological optimist would be willing to accept substantial costs at a high level of uncertainty. Conversely, people are likely to be willing to accept additional risks if the possible benefits are very large.

In any particular situation, proponents and opponents of precautionary measures may actually agree on the danger, but disagree on its associated uncertainty. Alternatively, they may agree on both the danger and the uncertainty, but hold differing attitudes toward risk and hence disagree on what should be done to avoid or mitigate that danger. The policy debate on a particular danger should thus be divided into three parts: the science underlying the danger, the uncertainty surrounding that science—i.e., the degree of certainty that the danger will come to pass—and the costs that would be justified to avert or mitigate this uncertain danger.

NOTES AND QUESTIONS

1.   *A "principle" or an "approach"?* Although entitled a "principle," the text of Principle 15 refers only to a precautionary "approach." Is there a normative difference in your view? Some countries, notably the United States, insisted on the use of the term "approach" rather than "principle" at Rio. Does this suggest they thought there was a distinction that would have normative consequences?

2.   *Cost-effective measures.* Principle 15 requires only that "cost-effective" measures be taken. What does this mean in the field of environmental protection? Must the threatened harm to the environment be monetized in order to make the calculation as to whether the preventative measures are "cost-effective"? If so, how does cost effectiveness depend on whether we are risk-neutral or risk-averse? How is cost effectiveness measured in cases where the threatened damage is "serious or irreversible"? Does the manner in which the term "environment" is defined—narrowly or broadly—affect the calculus? How do uncertainties in economic analyses factor in?

3.   *Full scientific certainty.* Does Principle 15 offer any guidance as to how close to "full" scientific certainty our knowledge must be before preventative measures are taken? In other words, if there is a 50 percent probability of harm, must preventative measures be taken? 75 percent? 90 percent? And, is there ever "full" scientific uncertainty?

4.   *Additional questions.* What should be the balance between the risks avoided and benefits foregone? Might the level of certainty desired in a given situation depend on how large the benefits might be if the dangers do not come to pass? Should there be an obligation to continue research and monitoring to add new underswtanding? How could such a requirement work?

b.   Information Production

Information-production requirements are also useful for incorporating understandings of uncertainty into legal and policy decision making, by forcing institutions to evaluate (and sometimes reevaluate) the effects of proposed actions. One instrument for assessing risk is the environmental impact statement (EIS) or environmental impact assessment (EIA), which requires an evaluation of the likely environmental effects of proposed actions and, in the United States, the discussion of alternative courses of actions and their effect on the environment and related social impacts. The United States National Environmental Policy Act of 1969 set forth the now famous requirement of an environmental impact statement (EIS) for all major federal actions that significantly affect the environment. 42 U.S.C. 4332 (1988). Under this statute, federal projects must "identify and develop methods and procedures, . . . which will insure that presently unquantified environmental amenities and values may be given appropriate consideration in decisionmaking along with economic and technical considerations." The goal is to ensure that environmental effects are considered throughout the decisionmaking process and that the concerned public be able to participate in this process. However, ironically, the United States Supreme Court has held that risks such as "severe psychological health damage to persons living in the vicinity of a leaking nuclear power plant," e.g., fear of future injury, do not need to be assessed because "a risk of an accident is not an effect on the physical environment. A risk is, by definition, unrealized in the physical environment." Metropolitan Edison Co. v. People Against Nuclear Energy, 460 U.S. 766 (1983). See pages 213–216, Chapter 4 for a discussion of possible international legal duties to conduct environmental impact assessments.

NOTE AND QUESTIONS

The timing of information production. Information production can take time. And because of the nature of environmental problems, uncertainty can never be entirely eliminated. Thus calls for additional information can often be used strategically in order to delay action. *See, e.g.,* Naomi Oreskes & Eric M. Conway, Merchants of Doubt (2010). What is an appropriate balance between seeking more information and engaging in action? Can you think of tests for determining that appropriate balance?

c. Adaptive Management

Risk assessment techniques often assume that once a regulatory decision, such as a standard or management object, is established, it will remain unchanged for a long period of time. This static theory of decisionmaking has been strongly criticized because it has no feedback mechanism to incorporate new information that may resolve earlier uncertainties. For the management of natural resources, the concept of adaptive management has been developed, as described in the following excerpt. As you read this excerpt, keep in mind that adaptive management may carry a political risk, since managers will have to admit mistakes and explain changes of policy to the public in light of any new information and understanding developed through the process of adaptive management.

NATIONAL RESEARCH COUNCIL, THE MISSOURI RIVER ECOSYSTEM: EXPLORING THE PROSPECTS FOR RECOVERY
107–110 (2002)

Adaptive management is an approach to natural resources management that promotes carefully designed management actions, assessment of these actions' impacts, and subsequent policy adjustments. An adaptive management strategy explores ways to couple natural and social systems in mutually beneficial ways. It seeks to maintain or restore ecosystem resilience, which is defined as the capacity of key ecosystem structures and processes to persist and adapt over time in the face of natural and anthropogenic challenges. Adaptive management was initially conceived as a way to overcome limitations of static environmental assessment and management and it encompasses efforts to improve understanding of how culture, policy, and social systems are interwoven and affect ecosystems from local to global scales. The premises that underpin adaptive management are theoretically and practically appealing:

> Most principles of decision-making under uncertainty are simply common sense. We must consider a variety of plausible hypotheses about the world; consider a variety of possible strategies; favor actions that are robust to uncertainties; hedge; favor actions that are informative; probe and experiment; monitor results; update assessments and modify policy accordingly; and favor actions that are reversible.

Adaptive management recognizes that ecological and social systems are not static, but that they evolve in ways that are often unpredictable over both time and space. In addition to flux in natural systems, adaptive management assumes that human systems change and intervene, and thus induce subsequent ecological adjustments. These interactions then contribute to or detract from ecological stability and resilience.

Adaptive management seeks to narrow differences among stakeholders by encouraging them to implement something new that will allow people to live with and profit from natural ecosystem variability at socially-acceptable levels of risk.

Adaptive management is characterized by the following components and assumptions:

It maintains and restores some degree of ecosystem resilience. . . .

It explicitly recognizes and seeks to profit from uncertainty. . . .

It promotes interdisciplinary collaboration and inquiry. . . .

It uses models to support decisions and collaboration. . . .

. . . This modeling generally includes these steps:

- Bound the problem. Policy domains, key variables, time horizons, spatial area, and spatial resolution are identified and defined.

- Model invalidation. There is always something in the real world that an abstract model will fail to mimic properly.

- Modeling should therefore explore the limits of credibility.

- Simplification and compression. Adaptive management modeling should encapsulate understanding in clear and insightful ways.

- Develop policy alternatives. The goal is to explore the full range of options based on diverse perspectives, not create a perfect policy solution.

- Evaluate policy performance with a broad range of stakeholders. This step seeks to understand how alternative composite scenarios might perform under meaningful characterizations of management systems.

It seeks meaningful representation of a wide array of interest groups. . . .

It uses ecosystem monitoring to evaluate impacts of management actions. . . .

[.]

NOTE AND QUESTION

A reality test. As you consider the materials in the rest of this book, consider how international environmental law of all types allow for uncertainty and changes in knowledge and understanding. Do the various norms or instruments do that by expressing norms in a manner that allows flexibility in interpretation, by establishing mechanisms for adjusting the content of norms, or by changing the legal threshold for modifying normative content and institutions?

d. Changing the Standard of Proof or Reversing the Burden of Proof

Environmental law has sometimes dealt with uncertainty by liberalizing traditional standards of proof for regulation. One of the leading United States judges who pioneered this project has written that negligence law is simply inadequate to deal with these emergent problems and opportunities. He points out that environmental pollutants are often impossible to trace to their source. Their health effects are uncertain, and their harms may not show up for years or even generations. Such uncertainty makes a finding of negligence liability unlikely, inappropriate and therefore ineffective in protecting society. Moreover, a case-by-case approach cannot match the scale of impact from pollution. David L. Bazelon, *Science and Uncertainty: A Jurist's View*, 5 Harv. Envtl. L. Rev. 209, 211 (1981).

In many instances countries have explicitly or implicitly substituted proof of some level of risk for proof that an activity has caused or is likely to cause damage in the immediate future. In the process, we now distinguish between identifying and assessing a risk and doing something about the risk, that is, managing the risk. Is this distinction an artificial one?

In other instances, countries have reversed the normal standard of proof regarding risk. For example, the United States and other countries prohibit the import of drugs that have not previously been imported unless the importer proves that the drug is safe. This requirement prevented the import of thalidomide for use by pregnant women, thus sparing the United States from the birth defects cause by thalidomide in some European countries. Especially because this approach interferes with international trade, an important question is, when is this permissible? It is known that drugs can pose health risks, for example; what about other types of substances intended for consumer use?

C. RISK ANALYSIS

1. RISK ANALYSIS AND INTERNATIONAL ENVIRONMENTAL LAW

Is international risk analysis useful for understanding the development of international environmental law? International environmental processes typically involve an explicit inquiry into whether a particular potential problem is "international." An example is an inquiry into whether the manufacture and use of nano-materials (i.e., materials on the scale of a billionth of a meter) warrants being addressed by the international community.

One can view this as a separate step, or one can view international risk assessment as the international processes for determining whether a risk exists that merits action by the international community, and international risk management as those actions the international community takes to minimize or to respond to the risk.

2. RISK ASSESSMENT AND ITS BLIND SPOTS

UNCERTAINTY
Daniel Farber
99 GEO. L.J. 901, 907–09 (2015)

1. The Basics

A quick, albeit superficial, introduction to the standard economic approach to probabilistic events may be helpful for some readers. The standard approach to risk analysis is based on expected utility theory. Application of expected utility theory can be extremely complex, particularly given the difficulty of determining the probability of various outcomes. Because we are largely concerned with situations in which the theory breaks down, however, knowledge of the details is not necessary for present purposes.

We begin with the idea of the expected outcome. The probability that a tossed coin will come up heads is 0.5. Suppose that you can win $10 if the coin comes up heads but lose $5 if it comes up tails. The question is whether to take the bet. If you repeated a bet of this kind many times, on average you would expect to win $10 half the time and lose $5 half the time. So the expected return is [(0.5 x 10) – (0.5 x 5)] = $2.50. (Imagine doing a hundred coin tosses—you would expect to win $10 fifty times and lose $5 the other fifty, for a net gain of $250 or on average $2.50 every time you toss the coin.) Thus, if you played this game often enough, on average you would expect to win $2.50 each time. This amount is the expected value of the bet. Although cost—benefit analysis can be complex because of the difficulty of determining the probabilities and measuring costs and benefits, conceptually it is fundamentally as simple as deciding what to bet on this coin toss. In this case, an individual should be willing to put down any amount up to $2.49 on this bet—provided that the individual is neither attracted nor repelled by the lack of certainty about the outcome.

Understanding attitudes about risk requires an additional concept: utility maximization. We used the term expected utility earlier, and the concept of utility requires a small revision in the analysis. People are often risk averse—that is, they prefer not to gamble. For instance, they may prefer a certainty of losing $1000 in the form of paying an insurance premium rather than take a 1% chance of losing $90,000. Yet, if you do the arithmetic, you will see that in expected value terms, the premium costs more than the expected value of the insurance (1 x 1000 = 1000 > 0.01 x 90,000 = 900). Economists explain this by saying that the utility of an additional dollar declines as wealth rises. This seems intuitively right—a homeless person would presumably care far more than a billionaire about the loss of a dollar. Thus, in the preceding example, the homeless person might not be willing to take the bet, even though the expected payoff is $2.50, because the risk of losing the stakes outweighs the possibility of gain. The billionaire, however, would be quite willing to accept the risk of losing because the stakes are inconsequential from her point of view.

The existence of insurance can be explained on the basis of utility and risk aversion. Because of declining marginal utility, the dollars in the premium are less "valuable" than the dollars the policyholder would lose from an uninsured loss. Thus, paying a premium for insurance is justified even if the expected value of the insurance is a bit lower than the premium. The upshot is that what people (individually and as a society) care about is not the expected dollar value of a loss but its expected utility value.

In practice, of course, risk analysis is much more complex than these simple examples. Finding the correct probabilities is rarely as easy as it is with coin tosses. Partly because of risk aversion, it is important to know the probabilities associated with the full range of possible harms, not just the most likely level of harm. In other words, we should not consider merely the "typical" California earthquake or the "typical" Gulf Coast hurricane. (Indeed, in those settings, the term "typical" may actually be misleading, as we will see.) Rather, we should account for the entire "distribution" of potential disasters (though we sometimes may lack sufficient knowledge of that distribution). This difficulty turns out to be critically important, as we will see later.

2. Risk Analysis's Blind Spot

Risk analysis requires that risks be quantified. Not all risks can be readily quantified, and a focus on conventional risk analysis can lead to disregard of nonquantifiable risks. This can bias decision making and mislead the public about the possible consequences. A policy of ignoring all nonquantifiable harms is literally a recipe for disaster—consider the chance of a hijacked airplane being crashed into a building pre-2001 or the chance of a market meltdown pre-2009. Neither risk was quantifiable, and ignoring the risks led to catastrophic outcomes.

Placing this blind spot into context helps to clarify the flaws in conventional risk analysis. The Nuclear Regulatory Commission (NRC) has been a prime offender in ignoring uncertainties to reach desired results. Apparently in the belief that a problem is not significant unless it can be precisely quantified, the NRC refuses to discuss the possibility of terrorist attacks on nuclear facilities in its environmental impact statements (EIS) because the risk cannot be quantified.

3.   RISK ASSESSMENT AND RISK MANAGEMENT

Risk assessment is used to determine the magnitude and likelihood of the risk and to clarify the assumptions and uncertainties involved. While assessments may help in determining what actions would not be overly restrictive or themselves harmful to either the environment or the economy, risk management is the tool used to choose the means used to reduce risks. The "management decision may involve economic, social, and political considerations and is subject to the constraints of particular statutes, which differ in the way they allow risk to be considered." Risk management helps to minimize the economic impact of risk reduction policies.

Milton Russell and Martin Gruber recognize that assessment methods may either over- or underestimate risks. Milton Russell & Martin Gruber, *Risk Assessment in Environmental Policymaking*, 236 Science 4799 (1987). Nevertheless, they say these types of problems are not necessarily inherent to the process of risk assessment itself. They can be alleviated by better information and communication. More important than the shortcomings, say the authors, are the effects risk assessment and risk management have on the community:

> They confront people with the fact that they are inevitably, as a consequence of their membership in an industrial society, exposed to risks. Public officials are understandably uncomfortable with bearing such news and most people are not comfortable with receiving it. Recent studies suggest, however, that communicating risk has become important to policy-makers at the national level.

> Confronting risk in this way also raises disturbing questions about what kind of society we want to have and about the distribution of risk among different areas and social sectors. Such questions are as vexing ethically and as politically sensitive as the more familiar ones about the distribution of income and opportunities among our people. Much of the heat generated by the risk assessment policies described here derives from the association, perhaps barely sensed by most, between such policies and the profound issues that arise from our conflicting desires for prosperity, justice, equity, and environmental quality. *Id.*

NOTES AND QUESTIONS

1.   *Risk and technology.* Debates often take a static view of risk; that is, they fail to include future reductions in risk made possible by initially risky technology. Similarly, they often fail to include reductions in risks in some areas that are made possible by increases in risks in other areas, as well as increases in risk resulting from other changes. For a discussion of some of

these issues, *see* Peter Huber, *Safety and the Second Best: The Hazards of Public Risk Management in the Courts*, 85 Colum. L. Rev. 277 (1985).

2. *Who takes the risk?* Who should decide to accept certain risks and prevent others? Why should a majority, which may be risk-accepting, be able to impose those risks on a minority that is risk-averse? Conversely, why should a majority that is risk-averse be able to deny the minority the benefits of potentially risky activities? Richard Abel, for example, has argued that "Each person ought to be able to control the risk to which he or she is exposed . . . no one ought to be subjected to a risk whose nature or level is determined by another." Richard Abel, *A Socialist Approach to Risk*, 41 Mary. L. Rev. 695, 702 (1982). However, is there any way around the fact that some people (be they scientists, bureaucrats, or a majority of voters) are going to decide to impose risks that others are unwilling to accept? Does this help to explain the growing phenomenon of NIMBY (Not In My Back Yard)? On these issues, *see* Daniel J. Fiorino, *Environmental Risk and Democratic Process: A Critical Review*, 14 Colum. J. Envtl. L. 501 (1989). How would this analysis apply to the transboundary shipment of hazardous and nuclear wastes for disposal and storage?

3. *Familiar risks.* The scientific approach to risk management emphasizes quantitative mortality rates. Social psychology research has found other principles that people use. Thus David Farber has argued that:

> People find two other factors important to assessing risk. One is the unfamiliarity of the risk. Familiar risks are given less weight than those involving mysterious technology or esoteric scientific knowledge. The other major factor is voluntariness. The most dramatic example is cigarette smoking, which poses the most serious health risk of any known toxic substance. Cigarettes kill approximately 350,000 people per year. Nevertheless, because smoking at least appears voluntary, most people think government intervention is much less warranted than for hazardous waste sites or drinking water contamination. The result is that we spend vast sums of money dealing with relatively minute health hazards, but very little on controlling cigarettes. Yet cutting smoking in half would save more lives than every environmental statute ever passed.

Daniel A. Farber, *Risk Regulation in Perspective: Reserve Mining Revisited*, 21 Envtl. L. 1321, 1338–1339 (1991).

For other findings, *see* Roger G. Noll & James E. Krier, *Some Implications of Cognitive Psychology for Risk Regulation*, 19 J. Legal Stud. 747 (1990).

4. *Risk and poverty.* Developing countries, especially those with a high birthrate, often face exacerbated risk levels. For example, the notorious Union Carbide plant explosion in Bhopal, India killed more people than if it had been in a less populated area. For a short treatment of various views of the risks posed by population growth, *see* Ronald G. Ridkeer, *Population*

Issues, in Global Development and the Environment 7–14 (Joel Darmstadter ed., 1992). Similarly, financial problems along with lower levels of training among the workforce may make probabilities of harm greater for threats which are easily controlled by technologies widely available in a wealthier economy. The risks from an industrial accident, for instance, could be much greater in a country that relied upon technical experts to arrive from distant countries to minimize immediate damage than in one where the experts lived within a short distance and could be on hand in case of problems. What effects should these factors have in the formulation and implementation of international legal principles that address risk? *See also* Roger Kasperson et al., *The Social Amplification of Risk: A Conceptual Framework*, 8 Risk Analysis 177 (1988) (discussing impact of culture on risk perception).

D. ECONOMIC ANALYSIS

1. COST-BENEFIT ANALYSIS

a. Theory and Historic Practice

In a world of constrained resources, choices, private and public, other than those made on purely moral grounds, must make some effort to compare the benefits of an expenditure with its costs and to calculate the opportunity costs of the expenditure—the returns from alternative expenditures. For private consumers, available assets perform this function. For private investment, the market, assuming no significant imperfections, will signal whether the choice was efficient. Public expenditures have historically stood on a different footing. Governments have the ability to raise revenues through taxes and other charges, and the only constraint on the choices of expenditures is political accountability. No legal principle that requires governments to allocate resources efficiently. Thus, governments can make decisions on distributional—i.e., regional politics—considerations and focus on the performance of the expenditure rather than its efficiency. In the 1930s, this practice attracted the criticism of economists as many countries were beginning to invest in large-scale multiple-purpose water resources projects. To discipline public spending, economists developed the technique of formal cost-benefit analysis, also referred to as "benefit-cost analysis". *See* Roland N. McKean, Efficiency in Government with Emphasis on Water Resources Development 3–21 (1958).

Cost-benefit analysis is often loosely used to describe any effort to compare the costs and benefits of an activity, but there are generally three accepted uses of the term. As you read more about cost-benefit analysis, recall the economic uncertainties introduced earlier.

BENEFIT-COST ANALYSIS IN NATURAL RESOURCES DECISIONMAKING: AN ECONOMIC AND LEGAL OVERVIEW

Deborah Lee Williams
4 Nat. Resources L. 761, 766–767 (1979)

1. Informal benefit-cost analysis: an analysis which compares in a systematic manner the benefits and costs of alternative projects, but which does not quantify or monetize all the benefits and costs. This analysis often uses a large amount of qualitative description.

2. Quantitative benefit-cost analysis: an analysis which compares quantified, but not necessarily monetized, benefits and costs of alternative projects. Quantification involves measuring all benefits and costs in terms of measurable units such as square miles, gallons and decibels.

3. Monetized (or formal) benefit-cost analysis: an analysis which defines all benefits and costs in terms of their dollar value.

Virtually all economic writings have focused on monetized benefit-cost analysis. . . .

To do this [benefit-cost analysis] relies upon the theory of consumer sovereignty. Any benefit, under this theory, can be measured by how much a consumer would be willing to pay for the good, service, or opportunity. A cost is the minimum amount a consumer would be willing to accept to forego the good, service, or opportunity. The preferences of all persons affected by the project in question are included in the calculations on a one dollar, one vote basis.

———————

Cost-benefit analysis has played a major role in the worldwide environmental movement for two related reasons. First, it has been used to criticize the logic of large public works with adverse environmental and social consequences. Second, it is an essential technique to promote the environmentally sustainable use of resources because it can spotlight subsidies which promote the environmentally unsustainable use and development of resources.

The following excerpts illustrate the power of these two uses of cost-benefit analysis.

WORLD COMMISSION ON DAMS, DAMS AND DEVELOPMENT: A NEW FRAMEWORK FOR DECISION-MAKING
46–48 and 206 (2000)

FINANCIAL AND ECONOMIC PROFITABILITY

Since the 1930s in the industrial countries and from the 1970s in developing countries, financial and economic profitability have become an important, if not the dominant, decision criteria in water projects. Consequently, approval of many large dam projects was contingent upon estimates of their predicted profitability. The measures typically used to assess profitability are the financial internal rate of return (FIRR) and economic internal rate of return (EIRR) as determined through cost-benefit analyses. The FIRR tells the project owner if the project is profitable, while the EIRR is intended to tell society if the project improves the overall economic welfare (or well-being) of the nation. Under-performance relative to targets does not necessarily imply that a project is unprofitable in economic terms, as the rate of return of a project may fall short of its target but still exceed the opportunity cost of capital to the economy.

Typically, an EIRR of over 10% is judged acceptable in the context of a developing economy. On this basis, irrigation dam projects in the WCD Knowledge Base have all too often failed to deliver on promised financial and economic profitability—even when defined narrowly in terms of direct project costs and benefits.

Given the lack of evaluation studies on large dams for irrigation purposes, the WCD compiled financial and economic performance data from a series of project appraisal, completion, and audit reports on large dam projects funded by the World Bank and ADB [Asian Development Bank]. The average EIRR at appraisal for the 14 irrigation dams was slightly above 15%, and at evaluation it was 10.5%, a significant shortfall in economic performance for the group. Whereas 12 projects had expected returns of over 12% at appraisal, this number had fallen to five by evaluation. In four cases, the EIRR at evaluation fell below the cut-off rate of 10%.

The results extracted from the ADB and World Bank reports are of course based only on evaluation studies undertaken at completion of the implementation phase or just a few years after commissioning. They incorporate the effects of cost overruns and initial operating results, but are not long-term or comprehensive in nature. They typically only consider the direct project costs and benefits of the project and do not account for the social and environmental impacts associated with the dam or agricultural production. In the case of the Columbia Basin Project, even a cursory analysis of the long-term performance data available from the WCD Case Study which shows that the large cost overruns and lower-than-expected delivery of benefits raise questions about the economics of the project.

In post-evaluation studies of irrigation and rural development projects by the World Bank and the ADB, half the projects were judged as unprofitable in economic terms, that is having EIRRs of less than 10%. More than three-quarters of the projects returned less than expected at appraisal. In fact, the average of the EIRRs for the World Bank irrigation projects was 17.7% at appraisal. At completion, this dropped to 14.8%, and at the time of impact evaluation—typically six to eight years after completion—the EIRRs had fallen to 9.3%. This rather strong downward trend indicates that many irrigation projects—not just large dams projects—suffer from a tendency to overstate project returns at the outset, also referred to as "appraisal optimism."

COST RECOVERY

Public agencies have not always attempted to recover costs associated with public infrastructure projects. Where the services provided by large dams are valued as consumption goods or productive inputs, the absence of cost recovery by the sponsoring agency is often equivalent to a subsidy in the sense that the large dam project provides a benefit for which no fees are paid. A lack of cost recovery is not just a matter of subsidy, however. Provision of free services and subsidised inputs often leads to misallocation of resources and inefficient production. Further, it may lead to perverse behaviour as people direct their efforts to obtaining such subsidies (rent-seeking behaviour) rather than productive activities.

Both the findings of the WCD Global Review and the implications of the normative framework summarised in this chapter demonstrate that the traditional "balance sheet" approach of assessing costs and benefits of a project is an inadequate tool for effective development planning and decision-making. The case of dams clearly illustrates that development choices made on the basis of such trade-offs neither capture the complexity of considerations involved, nor can they adequately reflect the values societies attach to different options in the broader context of sustainable development.

---

b. Some Hard Questions

It is an understatement to say that cost-benefit analysis is controversial. In general, there are two basic categories of criticism, technical and philosophical. The first assumes the validity of the idea that scarce resources should be allocated efficiently, but question whether this is possible for political and cost reasons, as well as the difficulties posted by uncertainties in risk assessments and economic analyses. Among the criticisms of the first category is that benefits are often overstated or double-counted. The purpose of formal cost-benefit analysis has historically been to ensure that the expenditure of public monies produces net efficiency gains. Economists distinguish between primary and secondary benefits. Primary benefits are the immediate value of the goods and services produced by an expenditure, such as irrigation deliveries from a dam. Secondary benefits are the ripple or multiplier effects such as increased employment and softer benefits such as healthy rural communities. Secondary benefits are often inflated and many of the claims do not represent a net gain to society but simply reflect the redistribution of income within an area. This has been the case, as the World Commission on Dams found, in many irrigation projects and is frequently the result of studies measuring the effects of public investment in sports facilities.

The most trenchant technical problem is information assembly. To do true cost-benefit analysis, a great deal of accurate information must be assembled, and even then, uncertainties may remain in terms of model choice and estimates. Modern economics recognizes that information is often a scare, costly resource. One solution to the information problem is to substitute cost-effectiveness for cost-benefit analysis. Cost-effectiveness seeks "to achieve the greatest possible health benefits for the amount of resources expended, [and] cost-effective resource allocation would give the highest priority to actions that achieve the greatest health benefit per dollar drawn from the resource pool. Given a fixed resource pool, a cost-effective scheme sets priorities so as to achieve as much in total environmental protection as possible, usually but not necessarily in terms of reducing risk." John S. Appelgate, *Worst Things First: Risk, Information, and Regulatory Structure in Toxic Substances Control*, 9 Yale J. on Reg. 217, 295–296 (1992).

Philosophical criticisms arise when cost-benefit analysis is used to judge the value of present environmental regulations with high immediate costs and uncertain future benefits. On the whole, environmentalists have been willing to use cost-benefit analysis to challenge public works projects and spotlight subsidies but have bridled at the use of cost-benefit analysis to evaluate the use of risk assessment and management to question precautionary health and safety programs. The objections include the difficulty or impossibility of measuring benefits and costs (e.g., of saving or extinguishing a species), the inevitable monetization of the value of life and health, and the necessity to discount future benefits. In addition, many regulatory programs trade one risk for another, such as immediate health gains for the reduction of the risk of serious future illness such as cancer.

Critics argue that different types of environmental harms and benefits cannot simply be traded off and that the uncertainties about the benefits over time prevent a meaningful comparison of benefits and costs. For introductions to the topic *see* David Driesen, *The Societal Cost of Environmental Regulation: Beyond Administrative Cost-Benefit Analysis*, 24 Ecology L.Q. 545 (1997); Lisa Heinzerling, *Regulatory Costs of Mythic Proportions*, 107 Yale L.J. 1981 (1998); Lisa Heinzerling, *Environmental Law and the Present Future*, 87 Geo. L. Rev. 2025 (1999); Frank Ackerman and Lisa Heinzerling, Priceless: On Knowing the Price of Everything and the Value of Nothing (2004). Other critics have observed that prior estimates of costs have also been demonstrated, post-hoc, to be inflated. *See* Sidney A. Shapiro & Robert L. Glicksman, Risk Regulation at Risk: Restoring a Pragmatic Approach at 107 tbl.6.1 (2003).

Discounting is a particularly thorny problem philosophical problem. The basic theory is that people inevitably prefer a bird in hand to one in the bush: e.g., dollar today is worth more than a dollar in a year. Thus, it we are to maximize efficiency we should maximize the present value of consumption over time. To do this, all investments in the future must be discounted. There are two major discounting standards.

THE PLANETARY TRUST: CONSERVATION AND INTERGENERATIONAL EQUITY
Edith Brown Weiss
11 Ecol. L.Q. 495, 516–519 (1984)

Economists use the discount method to decide whether or not a natural resource should be exploited at a given time. The discount rate is defined as the opportunity cost of capital—the rate of return that could be earned by investing money in alternative investments of the same risk. A potential investor takes the current money value of the natural resource and applies the formula for compound interest, using the discount rate as the interest rate, to calculate the value that the investment would achieve by some future date if it were invested in an alternative opportunity. The investor compares this value to the value the natural resource is anticipated to have achieved by the same future date if it is reserved for development. To determine this anticipated value, the investor estimates the return from the future sales of the resource, less the costs of extraction, to yield a net price.

At the point of equilibrium, when the net price is expected to increase at the same rate as the value of the alternative investment (that is, at the compound interest rate), the investor is, in theory, indifferent to holding or extracting the resource. If the net price rise exceeds that yielded by the compounded rate of interest, the investor will hold the resource for later development; if the net price rises more slowly than that rate, he will choose to extract it and thus exhaust it sooner.

From the point of view of public policy, the private discount rate can be used to determine the wisdom of exploiting or holding natural resources only if we assume that each individual unit, acting separately, inherently works in the best interests of the whole, extended over time. Hotelling, Pigou, Solow, and others challenge this assumption, pointing out that the long-term interests of society may not be identical to the interests of individuals.

If the private discount rate derived from the market is too high natural resources will be exploited too soon. There are several reasons to suspect that private discount rates are too high. Individuals may discount for some risks, such as wealth transfers, that society as a whole does not share. Equally important, private time preferences may favor the present generation at the expense of future generations, because future generations cannot bid in the market place.

To allow quantitative analysis of the gap between societal preferences and the individual's interest, economists have developed the conceptual tool of social discount rate. The social discount rate is usually lower than the private discount rate. Thus, even if the anticipated increase in value of resources held in the ground is not so high as to encourage private investors to forego immediate development, public decisionmakers may determine, by applying a lower social discount rate, that preservation is warranted. In effect, the choice of a social discount rate is a policy decision about the intertemporal distribution of income.

The major problem with using social discount rates to make investment or policy decisions is that the decisions rendered are still likely to favor the present generation over future ones. Traditionally, the discount rate has been applied over a period of ten years or, sometimes, twenty years. Some agricultural investments, such as forestry, however, require thirty to fifty years or more to reach maturity for commercial harvest. Hardwoods, like white oak, may require 200 years to reach maturity. Moreover, in analyzing certain investments, like nuclear power plants, economists often ignore substantial long-term costs by discounting them, in effect, to zero; but they may not be zero. Thus, while the discount rate may be a suitable tool for analyzing the relative merits of short-term investments, it is not particularly useful for taking account of posterity.

One can further argue that economics is a useful framework for decision making but it is not the sole legitimate one. *See* E.F. Schumacher, Small Is Beautiful 40–51 (1973). For example, Robert Nelson, Economics as Religion: From Samuelson to Chicago and Beyond (2001) argues that the veneration of the market, which lies behind case for cost-benefit analysis, is an effort to develop a secular religion rather the development of a predictive science as modern economics claims. *See also* Mark Sagoff, Price, Principle, and the Environment (2004).

NOTE AND QUESTIONS

How do you decide? Do you make decisions based on cost-benefit analysis? Do you consider trust, personal relationships, group affiliations, or charitable elements in making decisions?

c.   The Problem of Soft Benefits

i.   *What Are They?*

A major environmental criticisms of the use cost-benefit analysis is that the benefits of alternative options such as less intensive development and the conservation and restoration of ecosystem services are ignored because these values cannot be easily monetized. The ability to reduce decision criteria to a common denominator can be defended as an important step in promoting democratic values because it leads to a consensus about measures that in fact enhance the welfare of society as a whole. E.J. Mishan, Cost Benefit Analysis (1976). Modern environmental economics has rejected the narrow calculus of traditional cost-benefit analysis and posited that the total economic value (TEV) of a resource must be measured in deciding among alternative use and management options.

The basis of TEV is John Krutilla, *Conservation Reconsidered*, 57 Am. Econ. Rev. 787 (1967). Krutilla argued that natural areas should be the most important resources in the future because there is no technological substitute for them. And, they had a value even though no market existed to purchase them because people "place a value on the mere existence of resources, such as species, even though they do not intend to consume or own them." Ecologists contributed the idea that nature was a great service provider and classified ecosystem components by the services that they provide to humanity beyond wonder and visual delight. *See* Harold A. Mooney & Paul R. Ehrlich, *Ecosystem Services: A Fragmentary History*, in Nature's Services: Societal Dependence on Natural Systems 11 (Gretchen Daily ed., 1997). An influential article published in 1997, Robert Costanza et al., *The Value of the World's Ecosystem Services and Natural Capital*, 387 Nature 253 (May 15, 1997), put the ecosystem value of 17 ecosystem services at between $16–44 trillion per year at that time:

> We estimated that at the current margin, ecosystems provide at least US$33 trillion dollars worth of services annually. The majority of the value of services we could identify is currently outside the market system, in services such as gas regulation (US$1.3 trillion yr-1), disturbance regulation (US$1.8 trillion yr-1), waste treatment (US$2.3 trillion yr-1) and nutrient cycling (US$17 trillion yr-1). About 63% of the estimated value is contributed by marine systems (US$20.9 trillion yr-1). Most of

this comes from coastal systems (US$10.6 trillion yr-1). About 38% of the estimated value comes from terrestrial systems, mainly from forests (US$4.7 trillion yr-1) and wetlands (US$4.9 trillion yr-1). . . .

A distinguished ecologist, Stuart L. Pimm, commenting on the study above, notes:

> Market prices are the easier objects of study, recorded abundantly in units (currencies) with known, if varying, calibrations. Values are more slippery, being likely to vary widely from person to person and from generation to generation. Prices, moreover, reflect incremental (or "marginal") costs. Diamonds trade for a higher price than does fresh water. Yet the value of all fresh water is infinite: we could not survive without it. For ecologists, prices are woefully incomplete measures of nature's value that poorly prefigure the consequences of humanity's exponential growth. For economists, the challenge is how to assess an ecosystem's non-market values and predict their future trends.

Stuart L. Pimm, *The Value of Everything*, Nature (May 15, 1997), at 231.

The most comprehensive assessment of the state of ecosystem services and their value to humanity, Millennium Ecosystem Assessment, Living Beyond Our Means: Natural Assets and Human Well-Being 2–3 (2005) (also excerpted in Chapter 1) provides a summary of what is involved with assessing the value of ecosystem services. Consider the following excerpt.

ECOSYSTEMS AND THEIR SERVICES
UNEP, World Resources Institute, Ecosystems and Human Well-Being
Synthesis 40 (2005)

An ecosystem is a dynamic complex of plant, animal, and microorganism communities and the nonliving environment interacting as a functional unit. Humans are an integral part of ecosystems. Ecosystems provide a variety of benefits to people, including provisioning, regulating, cultural, and supporting services. Provisioning services are the products people obtain from ecosystems, such as food, fuel, fiber, fresh water, and genetic resources. Regulating services are the benefits people obtain from the regulation of ecosystem processes, including air quality maintenance, climate regulation, erosion control, regulation of human diseases, and water purification. Cultural services are the nonmaterial benefits people obtain from ecosystems through spiritual enrichment, cognitive development, reflection, recreation, and aesthetic experiences. Supporting services are those that are necessary for the production of all other ecosystem services, such as primary production, production of oxygen, and soil formation.

Biodiversity and ecosystems are closely related concepts. Biodiversity is the variability among living organisms from all sources, including terrestrial, marine, and other aquatic ecosystems and the ecological complexes of which they are part. It includes diversity within and between species and diversity of ecosystems. Diversity is a structural feature of ecosystems, and the variability among ecosystems is an element of biodiversity. Products of biodiversity include many of the services produced by ecosystems (such as food and genetic resources), and changes in biodiversity can influence all the other services they provide. In addition to the important role of biodiversity in providing ecosystem services, the diversity of living species has intrinsic value independent of any human concern.

The concept of an ecosystem provides a valuable framework for analyzing and acting on the linkages between people and the environment. For that reason, the "ecosystem approach" has been endorsed by the Convention on Biological Diversity, and the [Millenium Assessment] conceptual framework is entirely consistent with this approach. The [Convention on Biological Diversity] states that the ecosystem approach is a strategy for the integrated management of land, water, and living resources that promotes conservation and sustainable use in an equitable way. This approach recognizes that humans, with their cultural diversity, are an integral component of many ecosystems.

In order to implement the ecosystem approach, decisionmakers need to understand the multiple effects on an ecosystem of any management or policy change. By way of analogy, decisionmakers would not make a decision about financial policy in a country without examining the condition of the economic system, since information on the economy of a single sector such as manufacturing would be insufficient. The same need to examine the consequences of changes for multiple sectors applies to ecosystems. For instance, subsidies for fertilizer use may increase food production, but sound decisions also require information on whether the potential reduction in the harvests of downstream fisheries as a result of water quality degradation from the fertilizer runoff might outweigh those benefits.

. . .

People seek multiple services from ecosystems and thus perceive the condition of given ecosystems in relation to their ability to provide the services desired. Various methods can be used to assess the ability of ecosystems to deliver particular services. With those answers in hand, stakeholders have the information they need to decide on a mix of services best meeting their needs. The [Millenium Assessment] considers criteria and methods to provide an integrated view of the condition of ecosystems. The condition of each category of ecosystem services is evaluated in somewhat different ways, although in general a full assessment of any service requires considerations of stocks, flows, and resilience of the service.

---

ii. Valuation of Non-Market Values

How should we value these ecosystem services? An economist typically would answer that valuation should be based on willingness to pay. The following provide some insight into the concepts that economists have developed and their reception in United States courts.

VALUES ATTRIBUTABLE TO NATURAL RESOURCES
Frank B. Cross
42 Vanderbilt L. Rev. 269–341 (1989)

The first difficulty in valuation is determining the meaning of value itself and then determining which value characteristics of natural resources should be compensable. A useful approach recognizes at least three analytically distinct types of natural resource value that could be compensable: use value, existence value, and intrinsic value. Use value recognizes that natural resources only have value to humans when the resources are used for practical human ends, such as for fishing or hunting. Use value seeks to measure the monetary importance of the loss of these human uses. Existence value acknowledges that the presence of natural resources, even unused, may have value to humans. For example, some people may want to preserve the availability of resources for future generations. Intrinsic value recognizes that natural resources may have value independent of humans, based on their status as natural creatures or objects.

Use value is more precise and less speculative than other types of resource value because it isolates the extent to which people put their money where their mouth[s are]. Use value measures actual behavior, rather than attitudes and therefore is a more certain means of ascertaining damages. Complete reliance on use value has some shortcomings however. Greater public use of recreation sites actually may diminish the recognized public value of those facilities. Most significantly, use value ignores the reality that natural resources may have value beyond their use by humans. Surely a fish is worth something even if a fisherman never catches it.

Emphasis on market value for natural resources strikes many people as exalting economics above other socially held values. In the context of natural resources, unthinking reliance on economic principles would recommend selling the Grand Canyon to the highest bidder for commercial development, if that sale would yield the most profit. Not long ago, Milton Friedman proposed closing the national parks in which the commercial value of lumber or minerals exceeded the value of recreational use. The democratic process has rejected this result unequivocally.

Natural resources may possess intertemporal value. If society values these resources today, future generations almost certainly will value the preservation of these resources. This generation may regret the extinction of the passenger pigeon because of the actions of past generations and should consider the consequences that our acts may have for people living in the future.

However, there is no good behavioral test for existence value. Because the concept is demonstrated attitudinally, and not behaviorally, an economist may question how strongly the value is truly held. For skeptics, the absence of a behavioral test of existence value renders the concept impossible to measure accurately. Existence has other troublesome aspects. Under the existence value and use value paradigms, nature's only value is its value to human beings. The human-based or anthropocentric valuation can prescribe undue environmental destruction. The occasional practice of "planting" plastic artificial trees in place of real trees provides an example. Humanity might someday be persuaded to prefer plastic trees to growing trees. Should this occur, existence value would recognize no harm in replacing all of nature with man-made objects. Intuitively, this result seems wrong. Nature surely must have some value even when humans fail to recognize it.

Some ecologists contend that man must recognize his fiduciary obligation to other species of life. According to modern "deep ecologists," all living things have inherent value and have moral significance independent of their use by human beings, or even of human existence. Perhaps only recognition of intrinsic value can protect mankind from a future of forests comprised of plastic trees. For these ecologists, relying on economics is "technocratic" and the root of environmental degradation; monetary natural resource damages contribute to the problem rather than the solution. These people refuse to place a monetary value on nature. [However,] their refusal leaves the law only two options: economically valuing natural resources at zero or infinity. The former alternative inevitably creates an incentive to destroy the resources; the latter is transparently unworkable. Valuing natural resources at infinity also reflects a lack of understanding of nature. As Darwin proved, destruction of some elements of nature is itself natural. When a snake eats a mouse, it is fulfilling nature, not destroying it. Humans themselves are part of nature and should not be hesitant to destroy some other parts of nature when necessary. The desire to protect nature may be best understood as an effort to prevent unnecessary damage.

METHODS FOR MONETIZING DAMAGE TO NATURAL RESOURCES

The four leading procedures for valuing natural resource damage are: (a) restoration and replacement costs, (b) market valuation, (c) behavioral use valuation, and (d) contingent valuation.

When natural resources are damaged, one obvious policy option is to restore or replace them. When restoration is effective, the remedy at least partially can cure the injuries to use value (by providing repaired resources for recreational use), existence value (by restoring to existence of any destroyed resources), and intrinsic value (by reproducing intrinsically valuable natural resources). If a State were to select this option, then the correct measure of natural resource damages would be the cost of their restoration or replacement.

However, ecologists dispute the practicality of restoration. Because wildlife systematics and ecology is a complex science, government may be unable to reproduce preexisting environmental conditions. The greatest objection to restoration is probably the enormous cost that the process sometimes entails.

A readily available and appealing approach to valuing natural resources uses existing free market value as the measure of damages. For at least some natural resources, a court can determine value by consulting a price list. For example, commercial hatcheries provide an established price for certain species of fish. Even if no market exists for a resource, a court can measure damages by the reduction in land value from the loss of the resource. Market valuation is easy to measure and promotes economic efficiency.

For some naturalists, particularly those who find some intrinsic value in nature, complete reliance on market valuation is illegitimate or even immoral. A remarkable example illustrates this point well. Certain rare butterflies lived only in isolated corners of Africa. Reportedly, unscrupulous collectors would collect a few specimens and then burn the surrounding grassland to destroy as many others of the species as possible, thereby enhancing the uncommonness of their own collection and increasing their value. This natural response to market incentives obviously is contrary to the goals of applicable environmental legislation and illustrative of the shortcomings of market valuation. Senator Max Baucus of Montana, a critic of market valuation, has observed that it "is inconceivable that any reasonable person would suggest measuring the [value of the] Grand Canyon or Yellowstone Park on the basis of a land appraisal." Economists seeking to overcome the shortcomings of market valuation of public goods have developed new methods for valuing natural resources based on human behavior, including travel cost studies and hedonic valuation. Travel cost valuation is based on the intuitive assumption that the value of a site to visitors is reflected in the expense they incur to visit the site. Hedonic valuation measures the extent to which the value of a nonmarketed commodity, such as a pristine environment, is captured directly in the price of marketed commodities, such as land. The best example of hedonic price valuation measures the value of air quality changes by linking high levels of pollution to lowered housing prices or wage rates.

Contingent valuation simplifies the process of valuing natural resources by asking people directly what monetary value they place on identified resources. Contingent valuation is controversial. Empirical studies suggest that people's expressed attitudes do not accurately predict their actual behavior.

2. ALTERNATIVES TO COST-BENEFIT ANALYSIS

ECONOMIC THEORY AND ENVIRONMENTAL LAW
Mark Sagoff
79 Mich. L. Rev. 1393, 1410–1419 (1981)

Economic methods cannot supply the information necessary to justify public policy. Economics can measure the intensity with which we hold our beliefs; it cannot evaluate those beliefs on their merits. Yet such evaluation is essential to political decision making. This is my greatest single criticism of cost benefit analysis. The many problems involved in applying the concept of shadow pricing are secondary, because the concept itself rests on a mistake.

To recognize this mistake, we must first understand what it is that economists attempt to measure. If they measure consumer interests, market data are appropriate and relevant. The pricing mechanism can suggest when resources used to satisfy certain wants might he more efficiently employed to satisfy others. When economists approach issues that concern us as citizens, however, they do not, as they should, abandon the pricing mechanism. They believe that they can account for citizen-preferences as well as consumer-preferences by determining their dollar value. They do this, for example, by asking citizens what they would pay for a certain level of environmental protection. But this attempt to measure the convictions or values of citizens by pricing them as market externalities confuses what the individual wants as an individual and what he or she, as a citizen, believes is best for the community.

This confusion involves what logicians call a category-mistake. One makes category-mistake by treating facts or concepts as if they belong to one logical type or category, when they actually belong to another. Several examples are illustrative. It is logically correct to predicate whiteness of snow or even of coal. (It may not be true, but it is intelligible.) To say that the square root of four is white, however, makes no sense because it is impossible meaningfully to predicate color of a number. When two concepts are in different categories, one cannot measure the first by methods that are appropriate only to the second.

Private and public preferences also belong to different logical categories. Public "preferences" do not involve desires or wants, but opinions or beliefs. They state what a person believes is best or right for the community or group as a whole. These opinions or beliefs may be true or false, and we may meaningfully ask the individual for the reasons that he or she holds them. But an economist who asks how much citizens would pay for opinions that they advocate through political association commits a category-mistake. The economist asks of objective beliefs a question that is appropriate only to subjective wants.

When an environmentalist argues that we ought to preserve wilderness areas because of their cultural importance and symbolic meaning, he or she states a conviction and not a desire. When an economist asserts that we ought to attain efficient levels of pollution, he or she, too states a belief. But beliefs are to be supported by arguments, not by money. One cannot establish the validity of these beliefs by pricing them, nor can that mechanism measure their importance to society as a whole. One can judge how strongly people hold their beliefs by asking how much they would pay to see them implemented, but that is not how we make policy decisions. Those who think that Creationism should be taught in the public schools, for example, are able to raise a lot of money. But the amount of money that partisans raise does not demonstrate the merit of their position. A person who wants his or her child taught a particular doctrine is free to pay for that; willingness to pay may correctly measure the strength of that desire. When a person advocates a policy as being right or, appropriate for society as a whole, however, the intensity of the desire is no longer relevant. Rather, advocates must present arguments that convince the public or its representatives to adapt a policy. Political decision makers judge ideas on their merits, and made decisions based on what is good for us all. These policymakers may consider economic factors, but they should not use the economic method to evaluate competing beliefs.

The distinction between public and private interests is indispensable to the study of political philosophy. "To abolish the distinction," as one commentator has written, "is to make a shambles of political science by treating things that are different as if they were alike." Markets are the appropriate arena for the competition of private interests. This competition may best be understood and regulated in terms of individual willingness to pay. When one advocates not a special or private interest of all, however, the framework of debate completely changes. Public discussion must then be carried on in public terms. . . . What matters is whether the argument that he or she offers is sound. . . . This is not to say that economic data are irrelevant in public decision making. It is to argue that the satisfaction of revealed preferences is only one goal among others that policymakers must take into account.

The blurring of the distinction between public and private interest—and therefore, between the competition of preferences and the contradiction of ideas—produces results that we should do well to avoid. First, the policymaker, employing the willingness-to-pay criterion, attempts to remain neutral among contending positions. As a result, the analyst must grant equal credibility to every position, no matter how bizarre or preposterous. . . .

Second, the willingness-to-pay approach to public policy removes the basis of legitimacy from the political process. I do not mean merely that it crushes the "cherished illusion" that policy comes from the minds of elected officials in Congress rather than from the computer of economists in the back room. I refer, rather, to the fact that cost-benefit approaches deal only with values of preferences already extant in society. A political process—a process of debate and compromise—is supposed to be creative. The ability of the political process to change values and to rise above self-interest is crucial to its legitimacy. Political leaders are supposed to educate and elevate public opinion; they are not supposed merely to gratify preexisting desires.

A third likely consequence in public policy may be the most disastrous. Economic analysis limits conflict to those parties who have something at stake for which they are willing to pay. This approach would prevent the socialization of conflict that is crucial to the functioning of a democracy. Consider an example. Suppose a corporation proposes and an environmentalist group opposes the building of a shopping center in a rural area just outside of town. An economist might make a recommendation based upon prices assigned to the various wants or preferences of relevant interest groups. This would effectively limit conflict to the immediate parties. The genius of democracy, however, is to let the conflict spread to a larger audience. The institutions of democratic government—legislatures, agencies, parties, courts, and the press—depend and thrive on the potential for conflicts of this kind to widen beyond their original bounds. This happens when one side—usually the side that otherwise would be defeated—finds a public issue (e.g., a "snail darter") and moves the conflict into the press, the legislature, and the courts. The shopping center may then never be built because it takes so long to work through the resulting political process.

This might seem grossly inefficient to economists, and perhaps it is, but it is what democratic government is all about. An alternative—technocracy—quarantines or localizes conflict so that it may be resolved by the application of some mechanical rule or decision procedure. Cost-benefit approaches to public policy, if taken to their extreme, would do this, and thus they would make useless the institutions of democratic government. Cost-benefit analysis localizes conflict among affected individuals and prevents it from breaking open into the public realm. This suggests that the reason that industry favors economic to public policy is not necessarily the obvious one, namely, that cost-benefit analysis is sensitive to the costs of regulation. The deeper reason may be that cost-benefit analysis defines a framework for conflict that keeps the public qua public and the citizen qua citizen out.

Once we recognize the logical difference between wants and beliefs, it becomes clear that cost-benefit analysis can measure only the former. To conduct such an analysis, the economist asks how much we would pay for certain policies. How much would you pay to save Lange's metalmark? How much would you pay to preserve the quality of the air in the Southwest? Our responses indicate only the degree to which we care about the issues. If the analyst prices these views by willingness-to-pay criteria, or makes any similar economic trade-off, he tests neither the validity of the views nor the reasons for them, but only the intensity with which they are held. Economic efficiency is usually defined in terms of the maximum satisfaction of the wants or preferences of individuals in the order that those individuals rank them. A market in which competition is perfect, in theory, achieves this kind of efficiency. . . .

If we were to pursue efficiency as our goal in environmental policy, I believe that we would quickly turn all of our natural beauty into commercial blight. This is what happens when self fueling and irreversible consumer markets have their way. To forestall this result by "pricing" beliefs, values, and ideals as if they were consumer benefits, I have argued, is to commit a category-mistake. Cost-benefit analysis, at that point, disintegrates into storytelling; it becomes a bad exercise in ad hoc justification.

The environmental legislation of the last twenty years has consistently indicated our preference for national policies that respond to concerns other than economic efficiency. This legislation rejects markets as the indicator of the national will. There is nothing in this legislation or in the public debate on environmental protection that remotely suggests that most people regard pollution as a problem only because pollution is inefficient. Rather, we regard it as a problem because it is efficient. The "gospel of efficiency" is now as anachronistic as is the Lochner decision that is its most typical expression. . . .

NOTE AND QUESTIONS

How would Mark Sagoff's analysis apply to the problem of valuing ecosystem services? Sagoff has been a consistent critic of the entire idea of non-use value as a justification for environmental protection because it confuses political and personal values. *See, e.g.*, Mark Sagoff, Price, Principle, and the Environment (2004). His basic argument is that either ecosystem services will be perpetually available or if they do become scare, technology will provide substitutes. Thus, the case for nature preservation remains exclusively ethical, religious, or aesthetic. Mark Sagoff, *Locke Was Right: Nature Has Little Economic Value*, 25 Philosophy & Public Policy Quarterly 2 (Summer 2005). If one assumes that Sagoff is correct, does it follow that there is no role for economic analysis in environmental decision-making? Environmental protection is ultimately a good because it costs to produce it and there are opportunity costs in the form of foregone alternatives. Are opportunity costs relevant in political and moral discourse? Price, Principle, and the Environment, *supra*, at 198–200, endorses the use of economics to identify alternative institutional arrangements such as markets, to measure environmental progress, and to measure the costs of environmental protection, including the transaction costs.

E. CASE STUDY: GENETICALLY MODIFIED CROPS

All uncertainty is not equal. Below are two brief introductions to one international environmental issue fraught with uncertainty: genetically modified organisms (GMOs, also referred to as genetically engineered organisms or GE organisms). GMOs may have effects on food safety, food security, the environment, the seed industry, and food producers, among other things. *See* Chapter 14 for a discussion of genetic modification/engineering. The first excerpt provides the findings of the National Academies of Science in a 2010 report regarding environmental and economic effects. The second excerpt provides the approach used by the European Food Safety Authority (EFSA), the European Union risk assessment body for food and feed safety, for developing risk assessments related to the safety of GMOs to humans, animals and the environment.

As you read these excerpts, ask yourself what is the level of currently identified risk? Is this lack of clearly identified risk sufficient to trigger precautionary responses? Anne Ingeborg and Terje Traavik, *Genetically Modified (GM) Crops: Precautionary Science and Conflicts of Interest*, 16 J. Agriculture & Food Ethics #27 (2003), argue that the "obvious lack of data and insufficient information concerning ecological effects" trigger the precautionary principle. Why? Is there a threshold of confidence about the nature of the risk and its likelihood of it materializing? Or is fear of the unknown a sufficient basis for a precautionary response?

Consider also the critique that the risk assessment of GMOs may obscure significant equity issues. For example, Robert Paarlsberg has criticized how European concerns with the safety of GMOs have led to European States avoiding risks that are likely minimal, while African States lose out on benefits that are potentially significant. *See* Robert Paarlsberg, Starved for Science (2009).

THE IMPACT OF GENETICALLY ENGINEERED CROPS ON FARM SUSTAINABILITY IN THE UNITED STATES

National Research Council, National Academies of Science

(2010)

KEY FINDINGS

... In general, the committee finds that genetic-engineering technology has produced substantial net environmental and economic benefits to U.S. farmers compared with non-GE crops in conventional agriculture. However, the benefits have not been universal; some may decline over time; and the potential benefits and risks associated with the future development of the technology are likely to become more numerous as it is applied to a greater variety of crops. The social effects of agricultural biotechnology have largely been unexplored, in part because of an absence of support for research on them.

Environmental Effects

Generally, GE crops have had fewer adverse effects on the environment than non-GE crops produced conventionally. The use of pesticides with toxicity to nontarget organisms or with greater persistence in soil and waterways has typically been lower in GE fields than in non-GE, nonorganic fields. However, farmer practices may be reducing the utility of some GE traits as pest-management tools and increasing the likelihood of a return to more environmentally damaging practices. [The excerpt describes some positive environmental effects. These include the substitution of the herbicide glyphosate for more toxic herbicides, although the reliance on glyphosate has also been reducing its effectiveness; the complementation of GE crops with conservation tillage practices that reduce the adverse effects of tillage on soil and water quality; and reduction of insecticide use. The committee also found that at the time, emergence of insect resistance and gene flow has been minimal, although it recognized that changing conditions of GE crop production could lead to additional resistance or gene flow.]

Economic Effects

The rapid adoption of GE crops since their commercialization indicates that the benefits to adopting farmers are substantial and generally outweigh additional technology fees for these seeds and other associated costs. The economic benefits and costs associated with GE crops extend beyond farmers who use the technology and will change with continuing adoption in the United States and abroad as new products emerge. [The excerpt describes two positive effects, including lower cost of production for farmers and increased worker safety for farm workers. However, the committee also observed uncertainties in some elements of its economic analysis, described below.]

Studies suggest that the adoption of GE crops that confer productivity increases ultimately puts downward pressure on the market prices of the crops. However, early adopters benefit from higher yields or lower production costs more than nonadopters even with lower prices. The gains tend to dissipate as the number of adopters increases, holding technological progress constant. Thus, as the first adopters, U.S. farmers have generally benefited economically from the fact that GE crops were developed and commercialized in the United States before they were planted by farmers in other countries. The extent to which GE-crop adoption in developing countries will influence productivity and prices, and therefore U.S. farm incomes, is not completely understood. There is a paucity of studies of the economic effects of genetic-engineering technology in recent years even though adoption has increased globally.

. . .

To the extent that economic effects of GE-crop plantings on non-GE producers are understood, the results are mixed. By and large, these effects have not received adequate research. Decisions made by adopters of GE crops can affect the input prices and options for both farmers who use feed and food products made with GE ingredients and farmers who have chosen not to grow GE seed or do not have the option available. Favorable and unfavorable externalities are not limited to the cost and availability of inputs. To the extent that genetic-engineering technology successfully reduces pest pressure on a field and regionally, farmers of fields in the agricultural landscape planted with non-GE crops may benefit via lower pest-control costs associated with reductions in pest populations. However, nonadopters of genetic-engineering technology also could suffer from the development of weeds and insects that have acquired pesticide resistance in fields within the region planted to GE crops. When that happens, farmers might have to resort to managing the resistant pests with additional, potentially more toxic or more expensive forms of control, even though their practices may not have led to the evolution of resistance.

Social Effects

The use of GE crops, like the adoption of other technologies at the farm level, is a dynamic process that both affects and is affected by the social networks that farmers have with each other, with other actors in the commodity chain, and with the broader community in which farm households reside. However, the social effects of GE-crop adoption have been largely overlooked. [The excerpt suggests a number of uncertainties and data gaps with respect to the social effects of the use of GE crops. These include how evolving market structures affect access to non-GE seed, as well as how increasing market concentration of seed suppliers affects overall yield benefits, crop genetic diversity, seed prices, and farmers' planting decisions and options.]

RISK ASSESSMENT OF GENETICALLY MODIFIED ORGANISMS (GMOs)

European Food Safety Authority, *available at* http://www.efsa.europa.eu/en/efsajournal/
doc/as1008.pdf
(2012)

INTRODUCTION

EFSA [the European Food Safety Authority]'s remit in the risk assessment of GMOs is very broad encompassing genetically modified (GM) plants, microorganisms and animals and assessing their safety for humans, animals and the environment. Within this remit, the main focus of EFSA's GMO Panel and GMO Unit lies in the evaluation of the scientific risk assessment of new applications for market authorisation of GMOs, and in the development of corresponding guidance for the applicants.

. . .

In the following, the main milestones in GMO risk assessment are highlighted by discussing some of the guidance documents (GD) that have been developed by the GMO Panel, and are used in the evaluation of risk assessments provided by the applicants for market authorisation of their products.

EFSA GUIDANCE DOCUMENTS MARK MILESTONES IN GMO RISK ASSESSMENT

1. Specific guidance on selection of comparators for GM plants

The selection of appropriate comparators is central to the comparative approach in the risk assessment of GMOs. The identification and production of such comparators is becoming increasingly challenging due to the increasing complexity of breeding schemes and the GM plants themselves, e.g., those developed by combining (stacking) events through conventional breeding, or those in which compositional changes are targeted. [The excerpt describes a number of recent EFSA guidances on the selection of comparators, with a comprehensive safety/nutritional assessment where none are available.]

2. Guidance for food/feed risk assessment of GM plants

. . .

The updated food/feed GD . . . outlines the principles of the risk assessment of GM plants and derived food and feed, providing a detailed description of the comparative approach and definitions of the different steps and objectives of the risk assessment process. Reference is made to internationally agreed protocols for the toxicological assessment of newly expressed proteins and other new constituents, and of natural compounds the levels of which may have been altered through the genetic modification. Furthermore, attention has been paid to the testing of whole GM food/feed, which may be considered on a case-by-case basis, and approaches for allergenicity assessment of food/feed derived from GM plants have been further updated. . . . [The excerpt also describes areas of special attention, such as the design and the statistical analysis of field experiments, and guidance for the minimum replication of trials necessary to produce relevant data.]

3.   Guidance on environmental risk assessment of GM plants

Assessment of the environmental effects of cultivation of GM plants has remained controversial for the entire ten years of EFSA's existence. Two working groups of the Panel have updated guidance for environmental risk assessment (ERA) in 2008. The focus was on four areas: potential effects on non-target organisms (NTOs); new criteria for design and analysis of field trials; characterization of different relevant receiving environments within the European Union (EU) where GM plants may have environmental effects; techniques to assess potential long-term effects. The work on NTOs resulted in a stand-alone scientific opinion . . . adopted simultaneously with the new guidance in October 2010. . . . [The excerpt describes the analytical requirements used to evaluate the possible effects of GM plants on non-target organisms.]

4.   EFSA's involvement in post market environmental monitoring

Since 2007, EFSA has been asked to play an increasing role in recommendations for risk management for GM plants. For example, in 2011 EFSA assumed responsibility for the assessment of yearly reports on the post-market environmental monitoring (PMEM) for all cultivated GM plants, designed to detect and limit possible adverse environmental effects, including those that are long-term. In 2011, the GMO Panel issued the new GD on PMEM. . . . The PMEM GD made recommendations for both, general surveillance to detect unanticipated adverse effects, as well as case-specific monitoring when the ERA identifies a particular potential risk or uncertainty that can be mitigated during cultivation. [The excerpt describes various updated tools used for such monitoring, including the design and analysis of farmer questionnaires, recommendations on the use of existing biodiversity monitoring networks and proposals for the establishment of reporting centres at the Member State level.]

5.   Guidance on GM microorganisms

The guidance on the risk assessment of genetically modified microorganisms was updated in 2011 (EFSA Panel on Genetically Modified Organisms (GMO), 2011c) based on the feedback and experience gained with the 2006 version (EFSA, 2006b). Another motivation for the update was a recent change in the legislation, as e.g. food enzymes became regulated products that require pre-market safety evaluation. Previously the main focus of the GMO Panel had been in genetically modified microorganisms used to produce feed additives. . . . The aim was to simplify and clarify the guidance, but at the same time provide more details where felt necessary. As the guidance covers a range of products besides enzymes, a major effort was made to develop sensible and realistic categories to reflect the extent of data needed to provide a reasonable evidence for safety. . . .

6. Guidance for non-food/feed risk assessment

EFSA's mission also includes products other than food and feed relating to genetically modified organisms as defined by Directive 2001/18/EC, which excludes medicinal products for human and veterinary use. Applications would include e.g. plants used for the production of non-food enzymes or biofuels. As the safety evaluation has somewhat distinct character from that for food and feed, a scientific opinion was developed in 2009 on guidance for the risk assessment of genetically modified plants used for non-food or non-feed purposes (EFSA, 2009). . . .

NOTES AND QUESTIONS

1. *Do we know what we are doing?* Genetic engineering entails modifying the genetic structure of an organism, and possibly the germ line of that organism's species. Genetic engineering may also modify the expression of an organism's genes through epigenetic effects. Several techniques are being used to accomplish genetic engineering as this casebook goes to press, including transferring genetic material from one organism to another or, increasingly, editing the genetic material of a single organism; and new techniques are constantly being developed. An important question is what uncertainties are involved in changing genetic or epigenetic structures, in testing for the effects of such changes and in prescribing risk-management methodologies, including in the context of constantly changing technology. The excerpts above are intended to provide insights into uncertainty in this context. For further exploration into genetically engineered organisms, see the website of the U.S. National Academy of Sciences, which has produced many research reports regarding genetically engineered organisms over the past two decades. http://www.nas.edu.

2. *Approaches to managing uncertainty.* Consider the approaches to managing uncertainty addressed in section B.3 above. How would these play out in the context of GMOs?

F. RISK ASSESSMENT OF STACKING AND GENE DRIVES

As mentioned in Chapter 14, genetic modification techniques include (as of August 2015) gene editing technologies that allow relatively simple and highly precise editing of a genome. The simplest of these technologies is known as the clustered, regularly interspaced palindromic repeats (CRISPR)/Cas9 nuclease system. This system utilizes a defense mechanism that some bacteria use against viruses. These bacteria use CRISPRs to create small bits of ribose nucleic acid (RNA) that bind to deoxyribonucleic acid (DNA) in a virus that has a complementary sequence. A protein called Cas9 recognizes the complex made when the CRISPR RNA and the virus DNA bind and cuts it at exactly that point (Cas9 has been described as a molecular scissors), thus preventing the bacteria from being infected.

Scientists have learned to design CRISPR/Cas9 systems to guide Cas9 to the specific location on a chromosome that is sought to be modified and to insert foreign genetic material into the chromosome once the Cas9 has cleaved it. Alternatively, DNA can be removed from the chromosome. In either event, a genetic trait is modified.

CRISPR/Cas9 can be used on a wide variety of organisms, including plants and animals (even primates). Moreover, it can be used to make more than one genetic change at a time, thus either "stacking" more than one novel trait into the genome or achieving one trait via more than one genetic change (also referred to as "stacking"). Other genetic modification techniques also allow stacking, but not as easily. Scientists have created crops, for example, that contain both multiple Bt genes (Bacillus thuringia, or Bt, is a naturally occurring pesticide) aimed at a single target pest and multiple Bt genes aimed at different pests. Such stacking, which is becoming more commonplace as this book goes to print, considerably complicates attempts to prevent weeds from becoming resistant to Bt because it is not clear what type of refuges are necessary around the modified crops, and thus makes safety evaluations more difficult.

A new type of risk has also been created using CRISPR. Scientists have known that the system could be used to edit the germ-line of species, so that any change would be passed on to future offspring, but this was subject to the usual rules of inheritability and evolution. Moreover, many scientists were reluctant to pursue this to its logical end for ethical reasons. In 2015, scientists proved the feasility of a CRISPR technology referred to as "gene drive" (or "gene pusher"), which can cause a genetic modification to be passed on to offspring in such a manner that for a sexually reproducing organism with a short reproductive cycle, the modification can spread throughout the entire population of that species in that location, regardless of whether there is any advantage from an evolutionary point of view. This is achieved because the CRISPR technology is used in such a way that once one chromosome is changed, the change is automatically replicated in the other chromosome in that organism. The offspring of that organism thus will have not one chromosome with the modification, but both chromosomes once the automatic replication occurs.

The organism used for the experiment was a mosquito. *See* Valentino M. Gantz & Ethan Bier, *The Mutagenic Chain Reaction: A method for Converting Heterozygous to Homozygous Mutations*, Science Express (March 15, 2015), *available at* http://www.Scieencemag.org. For a description of this technology in layperson's terms, *see*: *The Age of the Red Pen*, The Economist (August 22, 2015), *available at* http://www.economist. com/news/briefing/21661799-it-now-easy-edit-genomes-plants-animals-and-humans-age-red-pen; and The Most Selfish Gene, The Economist (August 22, 2015) *available at* http://www.economist.com/news/briefing/ 21661801-giving-bits-dna-power-edit-themselves-intriguing-and-worrying-possibility.

To recapitulate, the use of gene drive technology in one organism could result in that organism's entire species being modified even if there is no evolutionary advantage, and indeed even if there is an evolutionary disadvantage. Because species inter-relate in many, often unpredictable, ways in nature, it is probable that there would be many effects on the surrounding ecosystem and that these effects would be incalculable. Human society has not faced this type of risk before.

Similar concerns, though, were raised with recombinant DNA in the late 1970s and early 1980s. Scientists held a conference at Asilomar in California to reach agreement among themselves on the nature of the risk and ways to address it. The scientific community could initiate a similar approach here, but another Asilomar Conference would need to involve more actors than just those in the scientific community. And there is no guarantee that this approach could effectively address the problems. Gene drive technology is highly controverial as this book goes to print.

NOTES AND QUESTIONS

1. How would you evaluate the risk of a proposed use of gene drive techonology? Given the myriad inter-relationships in nature, is it realistic to think that the impacts on an ecosystem of the use of gene drives are predictable?

2. How would you regulate gene drive technology? Should there be another Asilomar or high level meeting among scientists and others to develop guidelines? Should or can there be binding international regulations? Or would you leave control of it to the free market and conscience?

G. RISK ASSESSMENT AND CLIMATE CHANGE

Climate change involves significant uncertainties in causation, extent and effects, as is evident from Chapter 9, which complicate policy- and law-making. Consider the following excerpt regarding climate change effects in the members of the Association of Southeast Asian Nations (ASEAN).

ASEAN DISASTER RISK MANAGEMENT INITIATIVE, SYNTHESIS REPORT ON TEN ASEAN COUNTRIES DISASTER RISKS ASSESSMENT
98 (December 2010)

ASEAN is one of the most vulnerable regions of the world to climate change. Climate change is likely to affect all aspects and sectors adversely, from national and economic security to human health, food production, infrastructure, water availability, and ecosystems and biodiversity. Several studies on ASEAN predict an increase in temperature from 1°C to 1.8°C per century. Precipitation patterns are also changing with a general decrease in mean annual rainfall and number of rainy days. The number of extreme weather events is increasing, and sea levels are rising at a rate of 1–3 mm per year (ADB, 2009). Climate change is expected to be a major contributor to extreme temperature, floods, droughts, intensity of tropical cyclones, and higher sea levels. Based on recent studies, climate change is expected to manifest itself in terms of:

- Rise in temperature (studies show that the global average temperatures are likely to rise by between 0.5°C and 1.7°C by the 2050s)

- Variation in precipitation (largest changes are anticipated in the equatorial regions and Southeast Asia)

- Extreme weather events, such as tropical cyclones (these are likely to become increasingly frequent and intense, involving heavy rainfall, high winds and storm surges)

- Rise in sea levels (these are expected to rise with severe implications for coastal areas and low-lying islands in particular)

These climatic changes are likely to influence people's vulnerability adversely affecting livelihoods and in turn contribute to poverty. Vulnerability to these hazards is also increasing, due to continuing poverty and social vulnerability, poorly planned urbanization, environmental degradation, and population growth. Climatic variability has both a short term and long-term impact: it can increase the vulnerability of society causing sudden loss of income and assets, sometimes on a periodic basis or otherwise in the long term, on a gradual basis. Many international summits calling attention to these issues have been taking place at international, regional and national levels (Bali conference, 2007; Oslo policy forum meeting, 2008, Copenhagen climate change conference, 2009). The 'mainstreaming' of climate risk management and [Disaster Risk Reduction] into development policy and planning is a key priority for the international community. Adaptation strategies need to ensure that they are environmentally sensitive in order to address the potential impact of climate change both in the short and long terms.

Water Resources

ASEAN has extensive natural inland water systems, which play a vital role in the economic development of the member countries. The temperature increase may enhance the rate of evapotranspiration, which in turn affects the quantity and quality of water available for agricultural and industrial production as well as human consumption. ASEAN is already facing water stress and many areas in the region are depending upon limited groundwater and rainfall collection. Under this situation, climate change may worsen the water shortage due to extreme events like drought. Moreover, sea level rise may result in salt-water intrusions into available freshwater resources.

Projected maximum and minimum monthly flows in major river basins in ASEAN suggest increased flood risk during the wet season and increased water shortages during the dry season by the end of the century. It has been projected that areas under severe water stress in ASEAN may affect millions of people and influence the region's attainment of sustainable development. Hydropower, urban water supply and agriculture are among the sectors that may face serious impacts due to a reduction in flow of snow-fed rivers, coupled with increases in peak flows and sediment yields. It is estimated that water stress would be more evident on drier river basins with low seasonal flows.

Agriculture

Agriculture, a major economic sector throughout ASEAN, is expected to be affected by climate change in several ways. Temperature and rainfall are the primary key factors affecting agriculture in this region. Climate change through heat stress, water stress (drought), climate-associated pests and diseases, flooding, and typhoons, constitutes a significant challenge to ASEAN's status as a major producer of grain and industrial crops (such as rice, maize, soybean, rubber, oil palms, coconut).

The increased frequency and intensity of extreme events have already resulted in considerable economic damage to agricultural production in ASEAN. The region, in recent years, has experienced many strong tropical cyclones that have affected agricultural production significantly. Moreover, during the El Niño period, agricultural crops become vulnerable to pest attacks and diseases. Several studies have predicted a possible decline in agricultural production potential in ASEAN due to climate change. In a study conducted by the International Rice Research Institute, it was found that rice production could decrease by 10 per cent for every 1°C increase in growing season minimum temperature. Another study, conducted by the Office of Natural Resources & Environmental Policy and Planning, shows that corn productivity may decrease by 5–44 per cent depending on the location of production in the ASEAN region. Cline predicts that crop yields in Asia could decline by about 7 per cent with CO_2 fertilization and 19 per cent without CO_2 fertilization towards the end of this century.

If these negative impacts on the region's agricultural production continue, with the increasing population of ASEAN, it is very likely that millions of people in the region will be unable to produce or purchase sufficient food.

Coastal and Marine Resources

The coastline of ASEAN region is highly vulnerable [from] the effects of climate change due to increased coastal hazards to large tidal variations or tropical cyclones (UNCCD, 2009). As the majority of population of the region lives in proximity to low-lying coastal areas, the effects of climate change on coastal areas and marine resources are of high importance.

Coral bleaching is the most commonly reported impact of climate change on marine resources. Wetland International estimates that the 1997–1998 El Niño damaged about 18 per cent of the coral ecosystems in the region.

Sea-level rise and increases in sea-surface temperature are the most probable major climate change-related stresses on coastal ecosystem. Rising sea level causes saltwater intrusions into both coastal freshwater and groundwater resources increasing the water shortage. Moreover, with many of the mangrove forests converted into aquaculture and other related activities, coastal areas are increasingly exposed to tidal waves and coastal erosion increasing their overall vulnerability.

According to Wassmann et al. and the Stern Report, by 2100 rising sea levels are predicted to severely affect millions of people in ASEAN. Among these . . . Indonesia, Philippines, Thailand, and Vietnam are most vulnerable to the impact of sea level rise.

NOTES AND QUESTIONS

1. *Comparing risk assessment and the precautionary principle.* Under the risk assessment/risk management approach used frequently in the United States, what risk management measures might be warranted given this risk assessment? Would this differ using a precautionary approach?

2. *Soft benefits/costs.* Are there soft benefits/costs (as discussed in subpart D.1.c.i above) left out of this assessment? If so, what might those be?

3.   *Other values.* How should non cost-benefit factors weigh into this assessment? For example, what about any obligation we might have to future generations? What about equity issues of richer States being the larger generators of CO_2 and poorer States bearing more of the brunt of climate change impacts?

CHAPTER 4

BASIC PRINCIPLES OF INTERNATIONAL ENVIRONMENTAL LAW

■ ■ ■

A. INTRODUCTION

International Environmental Law is a branch of International Law. Therefore, to understand how International Environmental Law operates a general understanding of how the international legal system functions is necessary. Chapter 19 contains an Introduction to International Law and Dispute Settlement for those who have not taken the course in Public International Law. But for present purposes a brief overview of the sources of international law may be useful and is therefore given in the following paragraphs.

Article 38 of the Statute of the International Court of Justice, which "forms an integral part of the [United Nations] Charter" (U.N. Charter, Article 92), provides in relevant part as follows:

1. The Court, whose function is to decide in accordance with international law such disputes as are submitted to it, shall apply:

   a. international conventions, whether general or particular, establishing rules expressly recognized by the contesting states;

   b. international custom, as evidence of a general practice accepted as law;

   c. the general principles of law recognized by civilized nations;

   d. subject to the provisions of Article 59,[1] judicial decisions and the teachings of the most highly qualified publicists of the various nations, as subsidiary means for the determination of rules of law. . . .

This provision was drafted in the mid-1940s and, like the rest of the Statute, is based on the Statute of its predecessor, the Permanent Court

---

[1] Article 59 provides: "The decision of the Court has no binding force except between the parties and in respect of that particular case." The authoritative value of the ICJ's judgments is therefore more like that of Civil Law courts than those in Common Law countries.

of International Justice, adopted by the Assembly of the League of Nations in 1921. In some respects, therefore, it has a somewhat antiquated feel and is outdated. In addition, when the ICJ Statute was adopted in 1945, customary international law constituted the great bulk of the international normative order. That is much less true today, with multilateral treaties having supplanted and added to large areas of customary international law, so much so that they may to some extent be thought of as international legislation. This is true in particular in the field of the environment. However, customary international law continues to be of critical importance with respect to some basic norms (such as those prohibiting the causing of transboundary harm and requiring transboundary environmental impact assessments) and for the interpretation of treaties and filling gaps in their coverage.

Although Article 38 is addressed to the ICJ, it is generally taken as reflecting an authoritative, though by now incomplete, catalogue of the sources of international law that are applicable in the relations between states. Boiled down to their essence, the sources listed in sub-paragraphs **a** through **c** are: treaties; customary international law; and principles of domestic law generally recognized in the domestic legal systems of States. Treaties and customary international law are addressed briefly below. As to the source listed in sub-paragraph **c**, it will suffice for present purposes to note two points. First, in this context, "civilized nations" means States that have organized legal systems. And second, it bears emphasis that these are not general principles of international law. They are rather common elements of all, or virtually all, domestic legal systems. (See Restatement 3rd of the Restatement of Foreign Relations Law of the United States, § 102, Reporters' Note 7.) They consist for the most part of fundamental principles that are universally recognized, principles relating to the administration of justice, and other internal law principles that fill gaps in international law.

While the sources are not thought to be listed hierarchically, in practice they would generally be given priority in the order listed, with the exception of those norms of customary international law (such as the prohibition of slavery) that are *jus cogens* or peremptory norms that cannot be changed by treaty. Sub-paragraph **d** refers to forms of evidence of customary international law, which consist of relevant judicial and arbitral decisions, usually from international tribunals, and the writings of scholars or organizations of high repute. In possible contrast to sub-paragraph **d**, many international tribunals are treating prior decisions of international courts and arbitral tribunals as more than mere evidence, possibly to ensure stability, predictability and coherency. In addition, it is now generally recognized that there is a body of international administrative law including the rules of inter-governmental organizations. These have not yet proven to be of significance for environmental protection, with the exception of those rules relating to transparency and participation of civil society. Only a few words will be said at this point about treaties and customary international law, or "custom," which are treated more fully in Chapter 19.

Treaties are international agreements between States, States and international organizations, or different international organizations (always assuming that the organization in question has treaty-making capacity under its constituent instrument). They are governed by the 1969 Vienna Convention on the Law of Treaties, most of whose important provisions have been held by the ICJ to reflect codifications of customary international law. These provisions are therefore binding on all states, whether or not they are parties to the Vienna Convention. The cornerstone of the law of treaties is *pacta sunt servanda*, the customary international law principle, embodied in Article 26 of the Vienna Convention, that treaties are binding on the parties and must be performed in good faith. The law of treaties parallels in many respects domestic contract law, but unlike private contracts treaties are very difficult to terminate unilaterally. *See, e.g., Gabčíkovo-Nagymaros Project* (Hungary/Slovakia), 1997 I.C.J. Rep. 7, considered in Chapter 12.

Customary international law is formed by the practice of States that is engaged in out of sense of legal obligation to do so. At some point, such practice is said to "crystallize," or harden, into a binding legal norm. The reader will have noticed the circularity of this definition—i.e., how can a practice be thought to be required by a legal obligation before it has crystallized into a binding norm of customary international law? Be this as it may, the International Court has left no doubt that both elements— the "material," objective or factual element of practice, and the "psychological," subjective or mental element, sometimes referred to as the *opinio juris*—are required for the formation of customary international law. See, e.g., the *North Sea Continental Shelf Cases*, 1969 I.C.J. Rep. 3. Customary international law can be universal, regional or even bilateral, depending on the character of the practice that created it. Within the respective geographic scope, it is binding on all States except those that have been "persistent objectors," i.e., have publicly and persistently objected to the rule as it was being formed. After the rule has crystallized, however, no amount of objection, persistent or otherwise, can release a State from being bound by it.

This chapter will assume some basic knowledge of the international legal system, from either a separate course or a perusal of Chapter 19. From those sources it should be clear that International Law is fundamentally a decentralized system, in the sense that unlike domestic legal systems there is no central government with a president, a legislature, and a system of courts with compulsory jurisdiction. Of course, the international community is organized to some extent through the United Nations, whose Security Council can exercise some "legislative" and "enforcement" powers in the field of international peace and security. But while the maintenance of peace is a central value of the international community, there are many other areas of great importance in international life that are not governed by a similar structure. Protection and preservation of the environment is one of them. This chapter will seek to assist the reader in developing a working understanding of the normative structure of international environmental law. By "normative structure" we mean a structure, or system, of standards of conduct (norms) that countries expect each other to abide by. As we will see, these standards may be binding or non-binding. They may be enforceable or, more often, not enforceable, at least in the way that laws are enforceable on the domestic level. Yet countries generally comply with these standards. One of our tasks is to try to understand why this is the case. In the following chapter we will examine whether in the international system accountability and compliance can be achieved even without enforcement systems.

The chapter is organized as follows: The chapter begins with a problem that is intended to provide factual context within which to consider the issues examined in the chapter (Part B). The problem is followed by an introductory discussion covering hard and soft law, and commitments that are legally binding and non-binding (Part C). The chapter then moves to a survey of the substantive and procedural principles of international environmental law governing the conduct of states in the field (Part D).

B. THE PROBLEM: THE TRAIL SMELTER AND INTERNATIONAL REGULATION OF TRANSBOUNDARY POLLUTION

Figure 1. The Trail Smelter

In the 1920s and 1930s, the Consolidated Mining and Smelting Company of Canada, Ltd. (known as COMINCO since the 1960s) operated a large zinc and lead smelter at Trail, British Columbia, Canada (the smelter is still operating as of this writing). The smelter is located on the Columbia River just north of the international boundary, about seven miles as the crow flies, or about 11 miles along the course of the river. The smelting process produced sulfur dioxide, which was discharged into the air through tall stacks. Certain atmospheric conditions prevailing from time to time carried these fumes down the Columbia River valley into the United States, to Washington State, where they caused damage to private farms and timber lands.

In 1928 the United States and Canadian governments referred the problem to the International Joint Commission (IJC), established by the two countries under the 1909 Boundary Waters Treaty, for an investigation and report. In 1931 the IJC submitted its report in which it found that the smelter had caused damage in the amount of $350,000 and made certain recommendations. The unacceptability of these recommendations to the United States led to negotiations that resulted in a convention signed on April 15, 1935, in which the parties agreed to submit the matter to an arbitral tribunal.

1.   Assume you are a lawyer for Canada. What arguments will you make before the tribunal?

2.   Assume you are a lawyer for the United States. What arguments will you make before the tribunal?

3.   Assume you are a lawyer for the Trail Smelter (COMINCO). What should your strategy be?

4.   Assume you are a non-governmental organization (NGO) in the US state of Washington. What approach would you take to this case?

————————

As you go through the materials in this chapter, consider whether and to what extent Canada could be held internationally responsible for the harmful effects of the Trail Smelter.

C. THE "BINDINGNESS" OF ENVIRONMENTAL NORMS AND COMMITMENTS

In this section we consider a set of questions that relates to international law as a whole, but is of particular interest with regard to international environmental law because of the way that field has developed: Are there different types of norms, some of which are legally binding while others are not, or are less so? If so, what would be the utility of norms that were not legally binding? Can non-legally binding norms take on a binding or quasi-binding character, or even ripen into fully-legally binding norms? Bear these questions in mind as we go through the material in this section.

1. HARD AND SOFT LAW

In the international community's ever-developing efforts to regulate international environmental problems, a distinction is often drawn between "hard" and "soft" norms of international law. "Hard" law is generally legally binding on its subjects (the principal subjects being States, or countries) while "soft" law is not. Indeed, the expression "soft law" may seem oxymoronic: how can something be "law" if it is "soft," or non-binding? Part of the answer is that even non-binding instruments or provisions can have normative—i.e., behavior-influencing—effect. They can also give rise to expectations of compliance, and function as precursors to the acceptance of binding norms, or to the development of such norms.

The most common examples of hard law in the international field are treaties and customary, or general, international law. However, while treaties are binding on the parties to them, they may contain provisions of both an obligatory ("States shall . . .") and a hortatory ("States should . . .") nature. The latter is an example of soft law, even though it is a provision contained in a "hard-law" instrument. For example, the 1992 United Nations Framework Convention on Climate Change (UNFCCC), the subject of Chaper 9, contains the following provision:

> "The Parties should protect the climate system for the benefit of present and future generations of humankind, on the basis of equity and in accordance with their common but differentiated responsibilities and respective capabilities. . . ."[2]

The UNFCCC is a treaty, and hence a binding, hard-law instrument, yet the above provision (among others) contains the hortatory term "should," indicating that it is not intended to be binding (or is it?). Conversely, soft-law instruments, such as U.N. General Assembly resolutions or declarations adopted at international conferences, may contain hard-law language. For example, the 1992 Rio Declaration on Environment and Development provides in Principle 19:

> "States shall provide prior and timely notification and relevant information to potentially affected States on activities that may have a significant adverse transboundary environmental effect and shall consult with those States at an early stage and in good faith."[3]

The word "shall" is normally taken to connote a binding, or hard, obligation. Yet as an instrument adopted at an international conference by the participating States, the Rio Declaration was not intended to be binding and thus is itself non-binding.

NOTES AND QUESTIONS

1. *Why can't countries make up their minds?* Why would a non-binding instrument contain provisions couched in binding terms? Why would governments do this? On the other hand, why would a binding instrument contain provisions couched in non-binding terms? Why would governments do this? Wouldn't either of these techniques be confusing to the Parties? Why might it be worth including non-binding wording in a treaty despite the potential for confusion?

2. *Binding law in non-binding instruments.* There is a feature of certain non-binding instruments, principally U.N. General Assembly

---

[2] United Nations Framework Convention on Climate Change, Article 3(1), Rio de Janeiro, 9 May 1992, U.N. Doc. A/CONF.151/26, reprinted in 31 I.L.M. 849 (1992).

[3] Adopted by the United Nations Conference on Environment and Development, June 14, 1992, U.N. Doc. A/CONF.151/5/Rev.1, June 13, 1993, reprinted in 31 I.L.M. 874 (1992).

resolutions, that should be noted: Such instruments, though they are themselves non-binding (though an exception of sorts may exist for a unanimously adopted resolution that states it expresses international law), may reflect existing customary international law. Perhaps the *locus classicus*, or leading case, on this phenomenon is the *Texaco v. Libya* arbitration, in which the sole arbitrator found that a General Assembly resolution "confirm[ed]" a rule of customary international law.[4]

2. LEGALLY BINDING, NON-LEGALLY BINDING AND VOLUNTARY COMMITMENTS

VOLUNTARY COMMITMENTS AS EMERGING INSTRUMENTS IN INTERNATIONAL ENVIRONMENTAL LAW

Edith Brown Weiss
44 Environmental Policy and Law 83 (April 2014)

Nonbinding Legal Instruments.

Nonbinding legal instruments, or what is frequently referred to as "soft" law, have always had a significant place in international environmental law. Already in 1992, a list compiled of binding agreements and nonbinding legal instruments concerned with environment included almost 900 items.[15] Nonbinding legal instruments take many forms: declarations, charters, codes of conduct, resolutions, decisions of international intergovernmental organizations, and guidelines. They set forth norms that States and other actors are expected to respect, even though they are not required to do so. In the past, they have frequently been a first step toward the later negotiation of binding agreements. For example, the UNEP London Guidelines for the Exchange of Information and Chemicals in International Trade, 1987 and amended in 1989, and the UN FAO International Code of Conduct on the Distribution and Use of Pesticides, 1985, laid the basis for a subsequent binding agreement: the Rotterdam Convention for the Application of Prior Informed Consent Procedure for Certain Hazardous Chemicals and Pesticides in International Trade.[16]

States negotiate nonbinding legal instruments for many reasons. Sometimes they believe it would not be possible to reach a binding agreement on specific legal obligations, or to convince their Congress or Parliament to ratify such an agreement. Such instruments may also be useful in addressing new problems quickly. They may provide greater

---

[4] Texas Overseas Petroleum Co. v. Libyan Arab Republic, award of 19 Jan. 1977, para. 87, 17 I.L.M. 1 (1978).

[15] Edith Brown Weiss, Paul Szasz, Daniel Magraw, INTERNATIONAL ENVIRONMENTAL LAW: BASIC INSTRUMENTS AND REFERENCES (Transnational, 1992).

[16] Convention for the Application of Prior Informed Consent Procedure for Certain Hazardous Chemicals and Pesticides in International Trade, 11 September 1998, UNEP/FAO/PIC/INC.5/3, Appendix I; 2244 UNTS 337.

flexibility, so that States may alter strategies to address the problem more easily. The transaction costs of negotiating such instruments are usually considerably less. Especially as diverse new environmental problems have arisen, which may affect millions of people globally, nonbinding legal instruments can send an important signal about how States and all of the actors are expected to behave and can foster shared values.[17]

There is considerable literature on the relationship between so-called "hard" and "soft" law, much of which suggests that the latter cannot replace the former and indeed that "soft" law needs support in "hard" law or a "hard" law framework to be effective. To highlight a few more recent works, Shaffer and Pollack provide an overview of the literature on both forms of law and conclude that most scholars view "soft" law as second best and useful when "hard" law is not available. They suggest that States deliberately use "soft law" to undermine and change "hard law" rules.[18] Guzman and Meyer reject some previous explanations regarding the choice of "soft" law, such as that nonbinding instruments are necessarily easier to reach, and offer their own theories as to why States may indeed choose "soft" law over "hard" law.[19] Brummer argues that in the global financial sector "soft" law is endemic and necessary.[20] Two earlier ASIL [American Society of International Law] sponsored studies on "soft" law looked across the spectrum of international law to focus on specific cases of nonbinding legal instruments and analyze the reasons for using them, compliance with them, and their impacts. The studies generally support the analysis offered earlier as to the reasons for using them and suggest that compliance with them may be as favorable under certain conditions as with binding agreements.[21]

The development of international law in the Arctic illustrates the linkages between such so called "soft" law and "hard" law, namely that nonbinding legal instruments can be effective and may lead to the negotiation of binding instruments. When concern arose about the Arctic, [considered in Chapter 11] the Arctic States signed the Arctic Environmental Protection Strategy in 1991, and subsequently adopted the 1993 Nuuk Declaration on Environment and Development in the

---

[17] Edith Brown Weiss, INTERNATIONAL COMPLIANCE WITH NONBINDING ACCORDS, ASIL Studies in Transnational Law No. 29 (ASIL, 1997).

[18] Gregory Schaffer and Mark Pollack, *Hard v. Soft Law: Alternatives, Complements, and Antagonists in International Governance,* 94 Minnesota L.Rev. 706 (2010).

[19] Andrew Guzman and Timothy Meter, *International Soft Law,* 2 JOURNAL OF LEGAL ANALYSIS 171 (2010).

[20] Christopher Brummer, Soft Law and the Global Financial System: Rule Making in the 21st Century (Cambridge U Press, 2012).

[21] Dinah Shelton (ed.), Commitment and Compliance: Role of Nonbinding Norms in the International Legal System (Oxford, 2003); Edith Brown Weiss (ed), International Compliance with Nonbinding Accords, ASIL Studies in Transnational Law No. 29 (ASIL, 1997).

Arctic.[22] Although there were loud calls for a binding agreement at that time, the resulting instrument was nonbinding. In 1996, the seven Arctic States meeting in Ottawa signed a Declaration establishing the Arctic Council.[23] Again, a nonbinding instrument established a formal intergovernmental institution. In both cases, the form enabled States to reach agreement and to move forward flexibly to address new challenges in the region.

The Arctic Council created working groups to address various issues: the Conservation of Arctic Flora and Fauna, Protection of the Arctic Marine Environment, Sustainable Development Working Group, the Arctic Monitoring and Assessment Program, the Arctic Contaminants Action Program and the Emergency Prevention, Preparedness and Response working group. Each group created special environmental protection programs, such as the Circumpolar Protected Area Network. Working groups have also created nonbinding legal instruments, such as the Arctic Oil and Gas Exploration Guidelines, guidelines on ship operations in the Arctic, and the Alta Declaration on environmental impact assessment in the Arctic.[24] For the first time, on 15 May 2013, the Arctic countries signed a new binding agreement: the Agreement on Arctic Marine Oil Spill Preparedness and Response.[25]

The Arctic example is especially useful because States operating under nonbinding legal instruments have developed and continue to initiate a plethora of new activities to address new challenges to the Arctic. Yet, they operate within a fragmented field of binding legal agreements that pertain to the Arctic: the United Nations Convention on the Law of the Sea,[26] the International Convention for the Prevention for the Pollution from Ships,[27] and the Polar Bear Treaty[28]. Five of the Arctic States—Canada, Denmark, Norway, The Russian Federation and the United States—met in 2008 and adopted the Ilulissat Declaration, which

---

[22] Nuuk Declaration on Environment and Development in the Arctic, 16 September 1993, reprinted in 4 YEARBOOK INTERNATIONAL ENVIRONMENTAL LAW 687 (1993); Arctic Environmental Protection Strategy, 14 June 1991, reprinted in 30 INTERNATIONAL LEGAL MATERIALS 1624 (1991).

[23] Ottawa Declaration on the Establishment of the Arctic Council, 19 September 1996, reprinted in 15 INTERNATIONAL LEGAL MATERIALS 1382 (1996).

[24] http://www.arctic-council.org. The recent Kiruna Declaration established a Task Force to " 'to develop arrangements on actions to achieve enhanced black carbon and methane emission reductions in the Arctic." Kiruna Declaration, 15 May 2003, http://www.arctic-council.org.

[25] Agreement on Arctic Marine Oil Spill Preparedness and Response, 15 May 2013, http://www.arctic-council.org. The agreement provides for provisional application pending the receipt of necessary documents from member States to become party.

[26] United Nations Convention on the Law of the Sea, 10 December 1982, 1833 UNTS 3, reprinted in 21 ILM 1261 (1982).

[27] International Convention for the Prevention of Pollution of the Sea by Oil, 12 May 1943, TIAS 4900.

[28] Oslo Agreement on the Conservation of Polar Bears, 15 November 1973, 27 UST 3918, TIAS 8409.

committed the countries to the existing international legal framework, particularly to provisions of the Law of the Sea Convention, and explicitly noted that they "see no need to develop a new comprehensive international legal regime to govern the Arctic Ocean."[29] This contrasts with Antarctica, where a comprehensive overall agreement governs the area[30] and preceded the development of nonbinding legal instruments to address various facets of Antarctic problems.

INTERNATIONAL LAW COMMISSION, GUIDING PRINCIPLES APPLICABLE TO UNILATERAL DECLARATIONS OF STATES CAPABLE OF CREATING LEGAL OBLIGATIONS
2006 Y.B. Int'l L. Comm'n, vol. 2, pt. 2, p. 160

1.   Declarations publicly made and manifesting the will to be bound may have the effect of creating legal obligations. When the conditions for this are met, the binding character of such declarations is based on good faith; States concerned may then take them into consideration and rely on them; such States are entitled to require that such obligations be respected;

. . .

3.   To determine the legal effects of such declarations, it is necessary to take account of their content, of all the factual circumstances in which they were made, and of the reactions to which they gave rise;

4.   A unilateral declaration binds the State internationally only if it is made by an authority vested with the power to do so. By virtue of their functions, heads of State, heads of Government and ministers for foreign affairs are competent to formulate such declarations. Other persons representing the State in specified areas may be authorized to bind it, through their declarations, in areas falling within their competence;

5.   Unilateral declarations may be formulated orally or in writing;

6.   Unilateral declarations may be addressed to the international community as a whole, to one or several States or to other entities;

7.   A unilateral declaration entails obligations for the formulating State only if it is stated in clear and specific terms. In the case of doubt as to the scope of the obligations resulting from such a declaration, such obligations must be interpreted in a restrictive manner. In interpreting the content of such obligations, weight shall be given first and foremost to

---

[29] The Ilulissat Declaration, 28 May 2008. (Meeting of representatives of the five coastal States bordering the Arctic Ocean, in Ilulissat, Greenland).

[30] Antarctic Treaty, 1 December 1959, 402 UNTS 71, TIAS 4780.

the text of the declaration, together with the context and the circumstances in which it was formulated;

. . .

10. A unilateral declaration that has created legal obligations for the State making the declaration cannot be revoked arbitrarily. In assessing whether a revocation would be arbitrary, consideration should be given to:

(i) any specific terms of the declaration relating to revocation;

(ii) the extent to which those to whom the obligations are owed have relied on such obligations;

(iii) the extent to which there has been a fundamental change in the circumstances.

NOTES AND QUESTIONS

1. *There's an "International Law Commission?"* The International Law Commission, or ILC, is a subsidiary body of the U.N. General Assembly, established by the Assembly in 1947 to "promot[e] . . . the progressive development of international law and its codification." ILC Statute, Article 1, U.N. Doc. A/CN.4/4/Rev.2 (1982). At that point in history, in the immediate post-World War II years, international law still consisted for the most part of customary international law. The job of the Commission, therefore, was to try to write down these customary, and by definition unwritten, norms (codification), as well as to propose draft treaties on "subjects which have not yet been regulated by international law or in regard to which the law has not yet been sufficiently developed in the practice of States" (progressive development). ILC Statute, *supra*, Article 15. The great "codification conventions"—principally the 1961 Vienna Convention on Diplomatic Relations, and the 1969 Vienna Convention on the Law of Treaties—were products of ILC work, as were the four 1958 Geneva Conventions on the Law of the Sea, which formed the basis of the 1982 U.N. Convention on the Law of the Sea. The Commission also prepares sets of draft principles or guidelines, some examples of which are set forth in this chapter.

2. *Many shades of gray?* Black and white the "Guiding Principles" are not. Why all the equivocation? The answer owes much to the complexity of this issue. As the ILC notes in the preamble to its draft guiding principles, "behaviours capable of legally binding States may take the form of formal declarations or mere informal conduct including, in certain situations, silence, on which other States may reasonably rely. . . ." Guiding Principles, preamble, 2006 ILC Yearbook, vol. 2, pt. 2, at 161. And even in the case of formal declarations, factors such as the intent to be bound are key, but are not always dispositive alone: "in practice, it is often difficult to establish whether the legal effects stemming from the unilateral behavior of a State are the consequence of the intent that it has expressed or depend on the

expectations that its conduct has raised among other subjects of international law." *Id.*, at 162. Because of these complexities, the ILC decided to focus on unilateral *declarations* rather than all unilateral acts of States, which had been the original topic studied by the Commission. *Id.*, at 159, para. 161.

3. *I won't hit Johnnie anymore. Really, I won't.* In the *Nuclear Tests Cases*, New Zealand v. France, Australia v. France, the International Court of Justice ruled, by a vote of 9 to 6, that the claims of applicant States no longer had any object because unilateral public declarations by French officials that France's program of atmospheric nuclear testing in the South Pacific had ended gave rise to a legal obligation binding on France. 1974 ICJ Rep. 457. Why should we take States at their word? Should we always, or only under certain circumstances?

D. GENERAL PRINCIPLES OF INTERNATIONAL ENVIRONMENTAL LAW

The general principles reviewed here concern what are sometimes called "primary" rules of international law, i.e., rules governing the conduct of States. For example, a principal obligation of this kind in the field of the environment is the duty not to cause transboundary environmental harm, as we will see below. There are also, logically, "secondary" rules, which are those concerning the consequences of breaching a primary obligation. The latter will be dealt with in the following chapter, but for now a brief overview may be helpful to contextualize the primary obligations surveyed in the present chapter.

When a State breaches an international obligation, whether derived from a treaty, customary international law or some other source, it is required by international law to cease the violation if it is a continuing one and is said to have a new set of obligations which fall within the general obligation to make "reparation." Reparation consists, first and foremost, of the obligation of "restitution," i.e., to restore the situation created by the breach to the status quo ante insofar as possible. Secondly, to the extent that restoration is not possible, the breaching State is obliged to provide compensation to the injured State. And thirdly, there is an obligation to provide "satisfaction" for any moral or other type of injury for which the injured State is not made whole through the provision of restitution or compensation. Satisfaction may take a number of forms, such as apologies, punishing minor officials, and in some cases the payment of exemplary, or punitive, damages. Bear these principles in mind as you go through the following materials.

Legal obligations are often divided into those that are substantive and those that are procedural. While obligations sometimes display characteristics of both substantive and procedural norms or otherwise defy easy categorization, we will follow that taxonomy here for organizational purposes.

1. SUBSTANTIVE NORMS

a. The Obligation Not to Cause Transboundary Environmental Harm

TRAIL SMELTER ARBITRATION

(United States v. Canada)

Ad Hoc International Arbitral Tribunal, 1941 3 U.N. Rep. Intl. Arb. Awards 1911, 1938
(1941), reprinted in 35 Am. J. Int'l L. 684 (1941)

[The facts are as stated in the Problem.]

... The duty imposed upon the Tribunal by the Convention[5] was to "finally decide" the following questions:

(1) Whether damage caused by the Trail Smelter in the State of Washington has occurred since the first day of January, 1932, and, if so, what indemnity should be paid therefor?

(2) In the event of the answer to the first part of the preceding question being in the affirmative, whether the Trail Smelter should be required to refrain from causing damage in the State of Washington in the future and, if so, to what extent?

(3) In the light of the answer to the preceding question, what measures or regime, if any, should be adopted or maintained by the Trail Smelter?

(4) What indemnity or compensation, if any, should be paid on account of any decision or decisions rendered by the Tribunal pursuant to the next two preceding questions?

[Article IV of the Convention provided as follows as to the applicable law: "The Tribunal shall apply the law and practice followed in dealing with cognate questions in the United States of America as well as International Law and Practice, and shall give consideration to the desire of the High Contracting Parties to reach a solution just to all parties concerned."]

On April 16, 1938, the Tribunal reported its "final decision" on Question No. 1, as well as its temporary decisions on Questions No. 2 and No. 3, and provided for a temporary regime thereunder. The decision

---

[5] This was the treaty by which the two States submitted the dispute to arbitration. Convention for the Final Settlement of the Difficulties Arising through Complaints of Damage Done in the State of Washington by Fumes Discharged from the Smelter of the Consolidated Mining and Smelting Company, British Columbia, April 15, 1935, 49 Stat. 3245 (1935), T.S. No. 893, 162 L.N.T.S. 74. (Editors' footnote.)

reported on April 16, 1938, will be referred to hereinafter as the "previous decision." Concerning Question No. 1, in the statement presented by the Agent for the Government of the United States, claims for damages of $1,849,156.16 with interest of $250,855.01—total $2,100,011.17—were presented, divided into seven categories, in respect of (a) cleared land and improvements; (b) of uncleared land and improvements; (c) live stock; (d) property in the town of Northport; (e) wrong done the United States in violation of sovereignty, measured by cost of investigation from January 1, 1932, to June 30, 1936; (f) interest on $350,000 accepted in satisfaction of damage to January 1, 1932, but not paid on that date; (g) business enterprises. The area claimed to be damaged contained "more than 140,000 acres," including the town of Northport.

The Tribunal disallowed the claims of the United States with reference to items (c), (d), (e), (f) and (g) but allowed them, in part, with respect to the remaining items (a) and (b).

In conclusion . . . , the Tribunal answered Question No. 1 as follows:

Damage caused by the Trail Smelter in the State of Washington has occurred since the first day of January, 1932, and up to October 1, 1937, and the indemnity to be paid therefor is seventy-eight thousand dollars ($78,000), and is to be complete and final indemnity and compensation for all damage which occurred between such dates. Interest at the rate of six per centum per year will be allowed on the above sum of seventy-eight thousand dollars ($78,000) from the date of the filing of this report and decision until date of payment. This decision is not subject to alteration or modification by the Tribunal hereafter. The fact of existence of damage, if any, occurring after October 1, 1937, and the indemnity to be paid therefor, if any, the Tribunal will determine in its final decision.

Answering Questions No. 2 and No. 3, the Tribunal decided that, until a final decision should be made, the Trail Smelter should be subject to a temporary regime (described more in detail in Part Four of the present decision) and a trial period was established to a date not later than October 1, 1940, in order to enable the Tribunal to establish a permanent regime based on a "more adequate and intensive study," . . .

II

In 1896, a smelter was started under American auspices near the locality known as Trail, B.C. In 1906, the Consolidated Mining and Smelting Company of Canada, Limited, . . . acquired the smelter plant at Trail as it then existed. Since that time, the Canadian company, without interruption, has operated the Smelter, and from time to time has greatly added to the plant until it has become one of the best and largest equipped smelting plants on the American continent. In 1925 and 1927, two stacks of the plant were erected to 409 feet in height and the Smelter greatly increased its daily smelting of zinc and lead ores. This increased production resulted in more sulphur dioxide fumes and higher concentrations being emitted into the air. In 1916, about 5,000 tons of sulphur per month were emitted; in 1924, about 4,700 tons; in 1926, about 9,000 tons—an amount which rose near to 10,000 tons per month in 1930. In other words, about 300–350 tons of sulphur were being emitted daily in 1930. (It is to be noted that one ton of sulphur is substantially the equivalent of two tons of sulphur dioxide or SO_2.)

From 1925, at least, to 1937, damage occurred in the State of Washington, resulting from the sulphur dioxide emitted from the Trail Smelter as stated in the previous decision. . . .

Since the Tribunal has, in its previous decision, answered Question No. 1 with respect to the period from the first day of January, 1932, to the first day of October, 1937, it now answers Question No. 1 with respect to the period from the first day of October 1937, to the first day of October, 1940, as follows: (1) No damage caused by the Trail Smelter in the State of Washington has occurred since the first day of October, 1937 and prior to the first day of October, 1940, and hence no indemnity shall be paid therefor.

PART THREE

The second question under Article III of the Convention is as follows:

In the event of the answer to the first part of the preceding question being in the affirmative, whether the Trail Smelter should be required to refrain from causing damage in the State of Washington in the future and, if so, to what extent?

Damage has occurred since January 1, 1932, as fully set forth in the previous decision. To that extent, the first part of the preceding question has thus been answered in the affirmative.

[T]he report of the International Joint Commission . . . contained a definition of the word "damage" excluding "occasional damage that may be caused by SO_2 fumes being carried across the international boundary in air pockets or by reason of unusual atmospheric conditions," as far, at least, as the duty of the Smelter to reduce the presence of that gas in the air was concerned.

The correspondence between the two Governments during the interval between that report and the conclusion of the Convention shows that the problem thus raised was what parties had primarily in mind in drafting Question No. 2. Whilst Canada wished for the adoption of the report, the United States stated that it could not acquiesce in the proposal to limit consideration of damage to damage as defined in the report. . . . The view was expressed that "so long as fumigations occur in the State of Washington with such frequency, duration and intensity as to cause injury," the conditions afforded "grounds of complaint on the part of the United States, regardless of the remedial works . . . and regardless of the effect of those works." . . .

The first problem which arises is whether the question should be answered on the basis of the law followed in the United States or on the basis of international law. The Tribunal, however, finds that this problem need not be solved here as the law followed in the United States in dealing with the quasi-sovereign rights of the States of the Union, in the matter of air pollution, whilst more definite, is in conformity with the general rules of international law.

Particularly in reaching its conclusions as regards this question as well as the next, the Tribunal has given consideration to the desire of the high contracting parties "to reach a solution just to all parties concerned." As Professor Eagleton puts it (*Responsibility of States in International Law*, 1928, p. 80): "A State owes at all times a duty to protect other States against injurious acts by individuals from within its jurisdiction." A great number of such general pronouncements by leading authorities concerning the duty of a State to respect other States and their territory have been presented to the Tribunal. These and many others have been carefully examined. International decisions, in various matters, from the Alabama case[6] onward, and also earlier ones, are based on the same general principal, and, indeed, this principle, as such, has not been questioned by Canada. But the real difficulty often arises rather when it comes to determine what, *pro subjecta materie*, is deemed to constitute an injurious act.

[The tribunal considered an inter-Cantonal case from Switzerland involving target practice in which the Federal Court found that the demand of one of the Cantons "that all endangerment be absolutely abolished apparently goes too far."]

No case of air pollution dealt with by an international tribunal has been brought to the attention of the Tribunal nor does the Tribunal know of any such case. The nearest analogy is that of water pollution. But, here also, no decision of an international tribunal has been cited or has been found.

There are, however, as regards both air pollution and water pollution, certain decisions of the Supreme Court of the United States which may legitimately be taken as a guide in this field of international law, for it is reasonable to follow by analogy, in international cases, precedents established by that court in dealing with controversies between States of the Union or with other controversies concerning the

---

[6] The tribunal is here referring to the 1872 *Alabama Claims* arbitration between Britain and the United States, 1 MOORE, ARBITRATIONS 653. Editors' footnote.

quasi-sovereign rights of such States, where no contrary rule prevails in international law and no reason for rejecting such precedents can be adduced from the limitations of sovereignty inherent in the Constitution of the United States. [The tribunal proceeded to consider three U.S. Supreme Court cases concerning inter-state water pollution and two concerning inter-state air pollution. It then concluded:]

The Tribunal, therefore, finds that the above decisions, taken as a whole, constitute an adequate basis for its conclusions, namely, that, under the principles of international law, as well as of the law of the United States, no State has the right to use or permit the use of its territory in such a manner as to cause injury by fumes in or to the territory of another or the properties or persons therein, when the case is of serious consequence and the injury is established by clear and convincing evidence.

The decisions of the Supreme Court of the United States which are the basis of these conclusions are decisions in equity and a solution inspired by them, together with the regime hereinafter prescribed, will, in the opinion of the Tribunal, be "just to all parties concerned," as long, at least, as the present conditions in the Columbia River Valley continue to prevail.

Considering the circumstances of the case, the Tribunal holds that the Dominion of Canada is responsible in international law for the conduct of the Trail Smelter. Apart from the undertakings in the Convention, it is, therefore, the duty of the Government of the Dominion of Canada to see to it that this conduct should be in conformity with the obligation of the Dominion under international law as herein determined.

The Tribunal, therefore, answers Question No. 2 as follows: (2) So long as the present conditions in the Columbia River Valley prevail, the Trail Smelter shall be required to refrain from causing any damage through fumes in the State of Washington; the damage herein referred to and its extent being such as would be recoverable under the decisions of the courts of the United States in suits between private individuals. The indemnity for such damage should be fixed in such manner as the Governments, acting under Article XI of the Convention, should agree upon.

PART FOUR

The third question under Article III of the Convention is as follows: "In the light of the answer to the preceding question, what measures or regime, if any, should be adopted and maintained by the Trail Smelter?" [T]he Tribunal now decides that a regime or measure of control shall be applied to the operations of the Smelter and shall remain in full force unless and until modified in accordance with the provisions hereinafter set forth in Section 3, Paragraph VI of the present part of this decision. . . .

SECTION 3

In order to prevent the occurrence of sulphur dioxide in the atmosphere in amounts, both as to concentration, duration and frequency, capable of causing damage in the State of Washington, the operation of the Smelter and the maximum emission of sulphur dioxide from its stacks shall be regulated as provided in the following regime. [The Tribunal set forth a detailed set of requirements under the following headings: I. Instruments; II. Documents; III. Stacks; IV. Maximum Permissible Sulphur Emission (containing two tables, concerning the growing season and the non-growing season, and setting forth maximum hourly permissible emissions at various times and under various weather conditions); V. Definition of Terms and Conditions; and VI. Amendment or Suspension of Regime (providing for the establishment of a scientific commission to deal with requests for amendment or suspension of the regime).]

PART FIVE

The fourth question under Article III of the Convention is as follows:

What indemnity or compensation, if any, should be paid on account of any decision or decisions rendered by the Tribunal pursuant to the next two preceding Questions?

The Tribunal is of opinion that the prescribed regime will probably remove the causes of the present controversy and, as said before, will probably result in preventing any damage of a material nature occurring in the State of Washington in the future.

But since the desirable and expected result of the regime or measure of control hereby required to be adopted and maintained by the Smelter may not occur, and since in its answer to Question No. 2, the Tribunal has required the Smelter to refrain from causing damage in the State of Washington in the future, as set forth therein, the Tribunal answers Question No. 4 and decides that on account of decisions rendered by the Tribunal in its answers to Question No. 2 and Question No. 3 there shall be paid as follows: (a) if any damage as defined under Question No. 2 shall have occurred since October 1, 1940, or shall occur in the future, whether through failure on the part of the Smelter to comply with the regulations herein prescribed or notwithstanding the maintenance of the regime, an indemnity shall be paid for such damage but only when and if the two Governments shall make arrangements for the disposition of claims for indemnity under the provisions of Article XI of the Convention; (b) if as a consequence of the decision of the Tribunal in its answers to Question No. 2 and Question No. 3, the United States shall find it necessary to maintain in the future an agent or agents in the area in order to ascertain whether damage shall have occurred in spite of the regime prescribed herein, the reasonable cost of such investigations not in excess of $7,500 in any one year shall be paid to the United States as a compensation, but only if and when the two Governments determine under Article XI of the Convention that damage has occurred in the year in question, due to the operation of the Smelter, and "disposition of claims for indemnity for damage" has been made by the two Governments; but in no case shall the aforesaid compensation be payable in excess of the indemnity for damage; and further it is understood that such payment is hereby directed by the Tribunal only as a compensation to be paid on account of the answers of the Tribunal to Question No. 2 and Question No. 3 (as provided for in Question No. 4) and not as any part of indemnity for the damage to be ascertained and to be determined upon by the two Governments under Article XI of the Convention.

PART SIX

[The tribunal decided that investigators appointed by either government and members of the Commission provided for in Part Four, Section 3, "shall be permitted at all reasonable times to inspect the operations of the Smelter and to enter upon and inspect any of the properties in the State of Washington which may be claimed to be affected by fumes."]

The Tribunal expresses the strong hope that any investigations which the Governments may undertake in the future, in connection with the matters dealt with in this decision, shall be conducted jointly.

CORFU CHANNEL CASE (MERITS)[7]

(United Kingdom v. Albania)
International Court of Justice, 1949 I.C.J. Rep. 4

[On October 22, 1946, two British warships were seriously damaged when they struck mines while passing through the Corfu Strait in Albanian territorial waters. The explosions also resulted in the deaths of 44 British seamen and personal injuries to many more. The two governments submitted the case to the International Court of Justice by a Special Agreement they had concluded in response to a resolution of the UN Security Council. In the agreement the parties asked the court to decide upon two questions, the first of which was the following: "Is Albania responsible under international law for the explosions which occurred on the 22nd October 1946 in Albanian waters and for the damage and loss of human life which resulted from them and is there any duty to pay compensation?" In the second question the court was asked

---

[7] The Court's prior decision on the question of jurisdiction is reported in 1947–1948 I.C.J. Rep. 15. The Court's decision on the question of damages may be found in 1949 I.C.J. Rep. 244.

whether the UK had violated the sovereignty of Albania. As to the latter question, the court found that the British vessels were exercising their right of innocent passage in transiting the Straits of Corfu and thus had not violated Albanian sovereignty. As to the former, the court was confronted with a problem of proof as to which State had laid the mines and whether Albania had knowledge of their presence in its waters. The UK made a pro forma contention, unsupported by evidence, that Albania had laid the mines, but Albania had no navy and the court dispensed with this claim. In the alternative, the UK alleged that the mines had been laid by Yugoslavia with the "connivance" of Albania. The court also found insufficient evidence to support this contention. Thus, "the authors of the minelaying remain[ed] unknown." 1949 I.C.J. Rep. 4 at 17. The court's findings continue, below.]

Finally, the United Kingdom Government put forward the argument that, whoever the authors of the minelaying were, it could not have been done without the Albanian Government's knowledge.

It is clear that knowledge of the minelaying cannot be imputed to the Albanian Government by reason merely of the fact that a minefield discovered in Albanian territorial waters caused the explosions of which the British warships were the victims. It is true, as international practice shows, that a State on whose territory or in whose waters an act contrary to international law has occurred, may be called upon to give an explanation. It is also true that that State cannot evade such a request by limiting itself to a reply that it is ignorant of the circumstances of the act and of its authors. The State may, up to a certain point, be bound to supply particulars of the use made by it of the means of information and inquiry at its disposal. But it cannot be concluded from the mere fact of the control exercised by a State over its territory and waters that that State necessarily knew, or ought to have known, of any unlawful act perpetrated therein, nor yet that it necessarily knew, or should have known, the authors. This fact, by itself and apart from other circumstances, neither involves prima facie responsibility nor shifts the burden of proof.

On the other hand, the fact of this exclusive territorial control exercised by a State within its frontiers has a bearing upon the methods of proof available to establish the knowledge of that State as to such events. By reason of this exclusive control, the other State, the victim of a breach of international law, is often unable to furnish direct proof of facts giving rise to responsibility. Such a State should be allowed a more liberal recourse to inferences of fact and circumstantial evidence. This indirect evidence is admitted in all systems of law, and its use is recognized by international decisions. It must be regarded as of special weight when it is based on a series of facts linked-together and leading logically to a single conclusion.

The Court must examine therefore whether it has been established by means of indirect evidence that Albania has knowledge of minelaying in her territorial waters independently of any connivance on her part in this operation. The proof may be drawn from inferences of fact, provided that they leave no room for reasonable doubt. The elements of fact on which these inferences can be based may differ from those which are relevant to the question of connivance.

In the present case, two series of facts, which corroborate one another, have to be considered: the first relates to Albania's attitude before and after the disaster of October 22nd, 1946; the other concerns the feasibility of observing minelaying from the Albanian coast.

1.   It is clearly established that the Albanian Government constantly kept a close watch over the waters of the North Corfu Channel, at any rate after May 1946. . . .

As the Parties agree that the minefield had been recently laid, it must be concluded that the operation was carried out during the period of close watch by the Albanian authorities in this sector. This conclusion renders the Albanian Government's assertion of ignorance a priori somewhat improbable. . . .

Another indication of the Albanian Government's knowledge consists in the fact that that Government did not notify the presence of mines in its waters, at the moment when it must have known this, at the latest after the sweep on November 13th, and further, whereas the Greek Government immediately appointed a Commission to inquire into the events of October 22nd, the Albanian Government took no decision of such a nature, nor did it proceed to the judicial investigation incumbent, in such a case, on the territorial sovereign.

This attitude does not seem reconcilable with the alleged ignorance of the Albanian authorities that the minefield had been laid in Albanian territorial waters. It could be explained if the Albanian Government, while knowing of the minelaying, desired the circumstances of the operation to remain secret.

2.   As regards the possibility of observing minelaying from the Albanian coast, the Court regards the following facts, relating to the technical conditions of a secret minelaying and to the Albanian surveillance, as particularly important.

The Bay of Saranda and the channel used by shipping through the Strait are, from their geographical configuration, easily watched; the entrance of the bay is dominated by heights offering excellent observation points, both over the bay and over the Strait; whilst the channel throughout is close to the Albanian coast. The laying of a minefield in these waters could hardly fail to have been observed by the Albanian coastal defences.

On this subject, it must first be said that the minelaying operation itself must have required a certain time.... The report of the [court-appointed] Experts reckons the time that the minelayers would have been in the waters, between Cape Kiephali and St. George's Monastery, at between two and two and a half hours. This is sufficient time to attract the attention of the observation posts....

The Court cannot fail to give great weight to the opinion of the Experts who examined the locality in a manner giving every guarantee of correct and impartial information. Apart from the existence of a look-out post at Cape Denta, which has not been proved, the Court, basing itself on the declarations of the Albanian Government that look-out posts were stationed at Cape Kiephali and St. George's Monastery, refers to the following conclusions in the Experts' Report: (1) that in the case of minelaying from the North towards the South, the minelayers would have been seen from Cape Kiephali; (2) in the case of minelaying from the South, the minelayers would have been seen from Cape Kiephali and St. George's Monastery.

From all the facts and observations mentioned above, the Court draws the conclusion that the laying of the minefield which caused the explosions on October 22nd, 1946, could not have been accomplished without the knowledge of the Albanian Government.

The obligations resulting for Albania from this knowledge are not disputed between the Parties. Counsel for the Albanian Government expressly recognized that [translation] 'if Albania had been informed of the operation before the incidents of October 22nd, and in time to warn the British vessels and shipping in general of the existence of mines in the Corfu Channel, her responsibility would be involved. . . .' The obligations incumbent upon the Albanian authorities consisted in notifying, for the benefit of shipping in general, the existence of a minefield in Albanian territorial waters and in warning the approaching British warships of the imminent danger to which the minefield exposed them. Such obligations are based, not on the Hague Convention of 1907, No. VIII, which is applicable in time of war, but on certain general and well-recognized principles, namely: elementary considerations of humanity, even more exacting in peace than in war; the principle of the freedom of maritime communication; and every State's obligation not to allow knowingly its territory to be used for acts contrary to the rights of other States.

In fact, Albania neither notified the existence of the minefield, nor warned the British warships of the danger they were approaching. [The court found that even if the mines had been laid at the last possible moment Albania would have had time to warn the British vessels.] In fact, nothing was attempted by the Albanian authorities to prevent the disaster. These grave omissions involve the international responsibility of Albania.

The Court therefore reaches the conclusion that Albania is responsible under international law for the explosions which occurred on October 22nd, 1946, in Albanian waters, and for the damage and loss of human life which resulted from them, and that there is a duty upon Albania to pay compensation to the United Kingdom. . . .

NOTES AND QUESTIONS

1.   *What good are international decisions?* Despite variations in their authoritative value, cases are an important source of law in most legal systems. The international legal system is no exception. There are several major cases that most commentators regard as the principal sources of the "common law" of international environmental problems. Perhaps because of their comparative rarity, these cases seem to invite attempts to inflate their authoritative value and to apply them to problems far removed from their fact situations. One of our tasks will therefore be to examine these cases carefully with a view to determining their proper use as sources of authority and policy. *Trail Smelter* is a classic in the field, the first case decided by an international tribunal—and still one of the very few—in which a final decision was rendered in a dispute concerning transboundary pollution.

2.   *Who, me? Attribution of private conduct to the State.* The *Trail Smelter* arbitration involved a private activity in Canada that caused harm to private property in the United States, yet the arbitration was between the two States and Canada was held responsible. This is not surprising since Canada voluntarily agreed, through the convention, to pay for damage caused prior to January 1932, and to accept the tribunal's findings concerning subsequent damage, compensation therefor, and the regime to be imposed on the smelter. But what would the situation have been if Canada had not voluntarily accepted responsibility for the smelter's actions? Would Canada be responsible under international law for transboundary injury caused by a purely private activity within its borders? To put the question another way, would the smelter's conduct be "attributable" to Canada? The tribunal did say that "the Dominion of Canada is responsible in international law for the conduct of the Trail Smelter."

In his analysis of the *Trail Smelter* decision, Bleicher has written that the award goes "well beyond . . . the general principles of the law of state responsibility to aliens, which would reach only to state-controlled activities . . ." Samuel Bleicher, An Overview of International Environmental Regulation, 2 Ecology L.Q. 1, at 28–29 (1972). Indeed, the Articles on State Responsibility adopted by the United Nations International Law Commission indicate (with exceptions not pertinent here) that a state is responsible only for the acts of its organs, entities exercising government authority, or those acting on its behalf. 2001 Y.B. I.L.C. p. 30, para. 77, Chapter II, Attribution of conduct to a State, articles 4–11, pp. 40–54. The smelter would not qualify under any of these categories.

But does this principle apply in the case of transboundary pollution? Or do States have an affirmative duty to prevent activities under their jurisdiction, be they public or private, from causing transboundary pollution damage? Consider the following authorities:

- The tribunal cited Professor Eagleton, writing in 1928, for the proposition that "[a] State owes . . . a duty to protect other States against injurious acts by individuals from within its jurisdiction."

  The tribunal might also have cited Max Huber's 1928 Award in the *Island of Palmas* case, in which the arbitrator said that territorial sovereignty:

  > "has a corollary duty: the obligation to protect within the territory the rights of other States, in particular their right to integrity and inviolability in peace and in war, together with the rights which each State may claim for its nationals in foreign territory."[8]

- More recently, the same principle was applied in another inter-state arbitration in the *Indus Waters Kishenganga Arbitration*. There the Court of Arbitration declared:

  > "There is no doubt that States are required under contemporary customary international law to take environmental protection into consideration when planning and developing projects that may cause injury to a bordering State."[9]

- The *Corfu Channel* case, just considered, was decided in the same decade as *Trail Smelter*. (In fact, both *Trail Smelter* and *Corfu Channel* will resurface throughout the book in various contexts.) As we saw, in that case the International Court referred to "every State's obligation not to allow knowingly its territory to be used for acts contrary to the rights of other States." 1929 I.C.J. Rep. at 22.

- In its Advisory Opinion on the *Legality of the Threat or Use of Nuclear Weapons*, I.C.J. Reports 1996, considered briefly below, the Court stated at pp. 241–242, para. 29:

  > "The existence of the general obligation of States to ensure that activities within their jurisdiction and control respect

---

[8] Arbitral Award, 4 April 1928, *Island of Palmas (Netherlands v. United States of America), UNRIAA*, vol. II, P. 839.

[9] Partial Award, 18 February 2013, *Indus Waters Kishenganga Arbitration (Pakistan v. India)*, available at http://www.pca-cpa.org/showpageb106.html?pag_id=1392.

the environment of other States or of areas beyond national control is now part of the corpus of international law relating to the environment."

This passage was quoted approvingly in the *Gabčíkovo-Nagymaros Project* case, 1997 I.C.J. Rep. 7, at 41.

- In the *Pulp Mills* case, the International Court, after quoting the passage from *Corfu Channel* set out above, stated:

  "A State is thus obliged to use all the means at its disposal in order to avoid activities which take place in its territory, or in any area under its jurisdiction, causing significant damage to the environment of another State. This Court has established that this obligation 'is now part of the corpus of international law relating to the environment' (*Legality of the Threat or Use of Nuclear Weapons, Advisory Opinion, I.C.J. Reports 1996 (I)*, p. 242, para. 29)."

  Pulp Mills on the River Uruguay (Argentina v. *Uruguay), 2010 I.C.J. Rep.* 14, at 56, para. 101. Do you see a difference in the formulations of this obligation in the *Threat or Use of Nuclear Weapons* Advisory Opinion and in the *Pulp Mills* judgment? If so, is the difference significant? Why?

- In an analogous case, *United States Diplomatic and Consular Staff in Iran (United States* v. *Iran), 1979 I.C.J.* 7, the International Court held Iran responsible for not "taking appropriate steps to ensure the protection" of the United States embassy and staff against attacks by private persons even though the actions of these persons were not, at the time they occurred, attributable to Iran. The obligations in question were those owed by Iran to the United States under the 1961 Vienna Convention on Diplomatic Relations and other treaties. Therefore, the fact that it had not been established that the militants were in fact acting on Iran's behalf, and thus their conduct was not attributable to Iran, was not fatal to the case of the United States.

- And in its famous conclusion, the *Trail Smelter* tribunal found that "no State has the right to use *or permit the use* of its territory in such a manner as to cause injury" in or to another State (emphasis added).

- Most contemporary writers agree that the obligation in the case of transboundary pollution is in effect one of prevention. Thus it is the content of the obligation itself, rather than the strict rules of attribution in the field of State responsibility, that is determinative. See, e.g., P.-M. Dupuy, Overview of the Existing Customary Legal Regime Regarding International Pollution, in

International Law and Pollution 61, 63 (D. Magraw, ed., 1991). Cf. G. Handl, *Balancing of Interests and International Liability for the Pollution of International Watercourses: Customary Principles of Law Revisited*, 1975 Can. Y.B. Int'l L. 156, 164 (1976).

What is your assessment, based on the materials considered thus far? Should a State be responsible (liable) for the transboundary consequences of purely private conduct?

3. *From exploding mines to transboundary pollution.* Do you have any difficulty with the application to environmental cases of what the Court characterized as a "general and well-recognized principle[ ]" that "every State[ ] [has an] obligation not to allow knowingly its territory to be used for acts contrary to the rights of other States?" The U.K. was not, after all, suing to recover for environmental damage. The late Ian Brownlie, Q.C. (former holder of the Chair in International Law at Oxford), has written that "it would not occur to anyone to say that the *Corfu Channel* case was irrelevant to a pollution problem because it did not concern pollution as such." Ian Brownlie, State Responsibility and International Pollution: A Practical Perspective, in International Law and Pollution 122 (D Magraw, ed., 1991). Do you agree?

4. *I've got that right!* Does the application of the obligation just mentioned depend on the affected State's having a *right* to be from harm of the kind involved? If so, what is the scope of such a right in transboundary pollution cases?

5. *Burden, burden, who's got the burden?* Suppose toxic chemicals from a mine in developing country *A* leaked into a river that flowed from *A* into State *B,* causing harm there. In order to recover against State *A*, what would State *B* have to show according to *Corfu Channel*? That *A* had actual knowledge of the leak into the river? That *A* should have known about the leak? Does it change your answer if we assume that the mine was operated by a multinational corporation, not by State *A* itself?

6. *The proof is in the . . . inference?* In the hypothetical in the previous note, how can State *B* establish *A*'s breach unless *A* grants *B* access to *A*'s territory? It is probably not going to be enough for *B* to shout "*res ipsa loquitur*," explaining that according to its theory, the toxic chemicals came from *A*'s territory, therefore *A* is liable. Recall what the Court said about this in *Corfu Channel* and the nature of the Court's analysis in that case. Since *A* may well not grant *B* access to *A*'s territory, could *B* avail itself of circumstantial evidence?

7. *Look out!* The duty to notify and to warn identified by the Court in *Corfu Channel* will be considered in the section on Procedural Norms, below.

NOTE: LEGALITY OF THE THREAT OR USE OF NUCLEAR WEAPONS, ADVISORY OPINION, 1996 ICJ REP. 226, 35 I.L.M. 809 (1996)

On 15 December 1994 the United Nations General Assembly adopted Resolution 49/75 K, requesting an advisory opinion from the International Court of Justice on the following question: "Is the threat or use of nuclear weapons in any circumstance permitted under international law?" In its opinion, the Court observed that "some States . . . argued that any use of nuclear weapons would be unlawful by reference to existing norms relating to the safeguarding and protection of the environment, in view of their essential importance." The Court noted that States had referred in this connection to various treaties, including Additional Protocol I of 1977 to the Geneva Conventions of 1949, Article 35, paragraph 3, which prohibits the employment of "methods or means of warfare which are intended, or may be expected, to cause widespread, long-term and severe damage to the natural environment"; and the Convention of 18 May 1977 on the Prohibition of Military or Any Other Hostile Use of Environmental Modification Techniques, which prohibits the use of weapons that have "widespread, long-lasting or severe effects" on the environment (Art. 1). The Court further noted that States also cited Principle 21 of the Stockholm Declaration and Principle 2 of the Rio Declaration. It then stated:

> "29. The Court recognizes that the environment is under daily threat and that the use of nuclear weapons could constitute a catastrophe for the environment. The Court also recognizes that the environment is not an abstraction but represents the living space, the quality of life and the very health of human beings, including generations unborn. The existence of the general obligation of States to ensure that activities within their jurisdiction and control respect the environment of other States or of areas beyond national control is now part of the corpus of international law relating to the environment.

> . . .

> 33. The Court thus finds that while the existing international law relating to the protection and safeguarding of the environment does not specifically prohibit the use of nuclear weapons, it indicates important environmental factors that are properly to be taken into account in the context of the implementation of the principles and rules of the law applicable in armed conflict."

NOTES AND QUESTIONS

1. *Even advisory opinions can be tough.* The issue of the legality of the threat or use of nuclear weapons proved so controversial, even within the Court, that it had to be decided by the president's "casting vote"—i.e., a second vote the president of the Court may cast to break a tie. (There are

normally 15 members of the Court; the tie was made possible by the death of one of the judges.) The Court found that "the threat or use of nuclear weapons would generally be contrary to the rules of international law applicable in armed conflict, and in particular the principles and rules of humanitarian law." It went on to state: "However, in view of the current state of international law, and of the elements of fact at its disposal, the Court cannot conclude definitively whether the threat or use of nuclear weapons would be lawful or unlawful in an extreme circumstance of self-defence, in which the very survival of a State would be at stake; . . ." Dissenting were Vice-President Schwebel and Judges Oda, Shahabuddeen, Weeramantry, Koroma, and Higgins—albeit for different reasons. Judge Weeramantry, in dissent, found that the threat or use of nuclear weapons would be illegal in any circumstances whatsoever. (Judge Koroma agreed with this conclusion.) He noted that nuclear weapons endanger the human environment in a manner that threatens the entirety of life on the planet. 35 I.L.M. at 888. In this connection, he referred to the prohibition under international humanitarian law of causing serious damage to the environment. 35 I.L.M. at 905.

2. *Biocentricity in international humanitarian law?* The Court refers to Articles 35, paragraph 3, and 55 of Additional Protocol I of 1977 to the Geneva Conventions of 1949. Protocol Additional to the Geneva Conventions of Aug. 12, 1949, and relating to the Protection of Victims of International Armed Conflicts (Protocol I), 8 June 1977, UN Doc. A/32/144, Annex I, 1125 UNTS 3, *reprinted in* 16 I.L.M. 1391. There were 174 Parties to Additional Protocol I as of July, 2014. These instruments form part of international humanitarian law, the branch of international law that protects combatants, prisoners of war and civilians in times of armed conflict (collectively referred to as "war victims" in Article 2(a) of Additional Protocol I). The United States has signed but not ratified Additional Protocol I and is therefore not a Party to that agreement.

3. *Environments are people, too?* Article 35(3) of Additional Protocol I provides: "It is prohibited to employ methods or means of warfare which are intended, or may be expected, to cause widespread, long-term and severe damage to the natural environment." Article 55 provides in its entirety as follows:

Article 55
Protection of the Natural Environment

1. Care shall be taken in warfare to protect the natural environment against widespread, long-term and severe damage. This protection includes a prohibition of the use of methods or means of warfare which are intended or may be expected to cause such damage to the natural environment and thereby to prejudice the health or survival of the population.

2. Attacks against the natural environment by way of reprisals are prohibited.

Note that there is no requirement that humans be harmed or even threatened directly for these obligations to apply. Both provisions impose significant restrictions on State Parties during armed conflict but the Court did not say that they reflect customary international law. Thus States that are not Parties to Protocol I are not bound by the specific requirements of Articles 35(3) and 55 through custom. However, it may be that over the nearly two decades since the Court issued its Advisory Opinion the thrust, at least, of the two articles has ripened into custom.

On the other hand, the Court did state that "States must take environmental considerations into account when assessing what is necessary and proportionate in the pursuit of legitimate military objectives." It continued: "Respect for the environment is one of the elements that go to assessing whether an action is in conformity with the principles of necessity and proportionality," principles that restrict the use of force. These obligations are applicable to all states, not only those that are parties to Additional Protocol I.

PULP MILLS ON THE RIVER URUGUAY
(Argentina v. Uruguay)
2010 ICJ Rep. 14

[On 4 May 2006, Argentina brought suit against Uruguay before the International Court of Justice alleging that Uruguay had breached of the 1975 Statute of the River Uruguay (1295 UNTS 340) through "the authorization, construction and future commissioning of two pulp mills on the River Uruguay", due in particular to "the effects of such activities on the quality of the waters of the River Uruguay and on the areas affected by the river". For the "General Geographical context" see the Court's sketch-map No. 1, reproduced below. In the end only one of the mills (the Orion, or Botnia, mill, located just upstream of Fray Bentos) was constructed but by the time the Court rendered its judgment the mill had been operating for some two years. Both parties sought provisional measures, but the Court declined their requests. The following excerpt focuses on the obligation not to cause transboundary environmental harm. We will consider other aspects of the case later in this chapter, and in Chapter 12.]

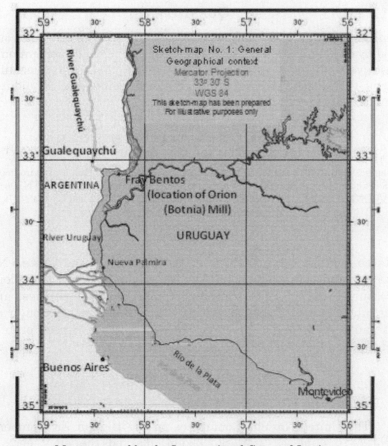

Map prepared by the International Court of Justice.

101.   The Court points out that the principle of prevention, as a customary rule, has its origins in the due diligence that is required of a State in its territory. It is "every State's obligation not to allow knowingly its territory to be used for acts contrary to the rights of other States" (*Corfu Channel (United Kingdom v. Albania), Merits, Judgment, I.C.J. Reports 1949,* p. 22). A State is thus obliged to use all the means at its disposal in order to avoid activities which take place in its territory, or in any area under its jurisdiction, causing significant damage to the environment of another State. This Court has established that this obligation "is now part of the corpus of international law relating to the environment" (*Legality of the Threat or Use of Nuclear Weapons, Advisory Opinion, I.C.J. Reports 1996 (I)*, p. 242, para. 29).

QUESTION

Pulp mills, mines, and nuclear weapons: one size fits all? Are you at all troubled by the application of this same basic "principle of prevention" to all of these very different problems? The Court mentions due diligence, suggesting that the obligation is not a strict, or absolute one. Should it be, for some kinds of activities?

STOCKHOLM DECLARATION ON THE HUMAN ENVIRONMENT, PRINCIPLE 21

Adopted 16 June 1972 at the United Nations Conference on the Human Environment,
Stockholm. Report of the U.N. Conference on the Human Environment, U.N. Doc.
A/CONF.48/14/Rev.1 at 3 (1973), U.N. Doc. A/CONF.48/14 at 2 and Corr. 1 (1972),
reprinted in 11 I.L.M. 1416 (1972)

Principle 21

States have, in accordance with the Charter of the United Nations and the principles of international law, the sovereign right to exploit their own resources pursuant to their own environmental policies, and the responsibility to ensure that activities within their jurisdiction or control do not cause damage to the environment of other States or of areas beyond the limits of national jurisdiction.

NOTES AND QUESTIONS

1.   *A Big Deal: The Stockholm Conference and Declaration:*

The United Nations Conference on the Human Environment, held 5–16 June 1972 in Stockholm, marked the emergence of international environmental law as a separate branch of international law. Much preparatory work preceded the Stockholm Conference, in which 113 States participated (the Soviet Union and other Eastern European States [except Romania] boycotted the Conference because of the exclusion of the German Democratic Republic), together with 13 specialized agencies, several intergovernmental organizations, and numerous non-governmental organizations. . . .

The Declaration on the Human Environment, which was adopted by acclamation, contains a preamble . . . and 26 principles covering many international environmental issues, including human rights, natural resource management, pollution prevention, the relation between environment and development, institutional arrangements, education, the obligation to prevent pollution (the famous principle 21), whether standards should be the same for developed and developing countries, and nuclear weapons. The Declaration does not cover some important topics, however. For example, a draft principle requiring notification of the risk of adverse transboundary effects was deleted from the Declaration.

The Stockholm Declaration was subsequently endorsed by the General Assembly on 15 December 1972 (UNGA Res. 2994), by 112 to none, with ten abstentions. Although the language of the Declaration often is normative ("shall") rather than precatory ("should"), the Declaration was intended not to be legally binding. However, at least one portion of the Declaration—Principle 21—is now generally viewed as customary international law (though there is disagreement about its precise meaning). More generally, the Stockholm Declaration has had great and widespread influence.

E. Brown Weiss, D. Magraw & P. Szasz, International Environmental Law: Basic Instruments and References 171–172 (1992).

2. *From Stockholm to Rio in 20 years.* Twenty years after the Stockholm Conference, the United Nations held a second meeting on the environment. The United Nations Conference on Environment and Development, or UNCED (popularly known as the Earth Summit), met in Rio de Janeiro from June 3–14, 1992. The 178 States participating in UNCED adopted a statement of principles, as had been done at the Stockholm Conference. The UNCED principles are entitled the Rio Declaration on Environment and Development. U.N. Doc. A/CONF.151/5/ Rev.1, 14 June 1992, adopted 14 June 1992, *reprinted in* 31 I.L.M. 874 (1992). The counterpart of Principle 21 in the Rio Declaration is Principle 2, which provides as follows:

The United Nations Conference on Environment and Development, proclaims that:

Principle 2

States have, in accordance with the Charter of the United Nations and the principles of international law, the sovereign right to exploit their own resources pursuant to their own environmental and developmental policies, and the responsibility to ensure that activities within their jurisdiction or control do not cause damage to the environment of other States or of areas beyond the limits of national jurisdiction.

Is there any difference in the wording of this principle and Principle 21 of Stockholm? If so, what is it, and is it significant? Is this principle so timeless that it does not need updating after two decades of experience?

3. *The progeny of Principle 21.* Principle 21 is incorporated verbatim in Article 3 of the Convention on Biological Diversity of June 5, 1992, 31 I.L.M. 818 (1992); and in Principle 1(a) of the Statement of Principles for a Global Consensus on the Management, Conservation and Sustainable Development of All Types of Forests (the "Forest Principles"), 31 I.L.M. 881 (1992). Either Principle 21 (Stockholm) or Principle 2 (Rio) is recited verbatim in the preambles of the Desertification Convention (Convention to Combat Desertification in Those Countries Experiencing Serious Drought and/or Desertification, Particularly in Africa, Paris, June 17, 1994, Principle 2,

fifteenth preambular paragraph, U.N. Doc. A/AC.241/15/Rev.3, 33 I.L.M. 1332 (1994)), the U.N. Framework Convention on Climate Change (New York, May 9, 1992, Principle 2, eighth preambular paragraph, 31 I.L.M. 849 (1992)) and the ECE Convention on Long-Range Transboundary Air Pollution (LRTAP) (Geneva, 13 Nov. 1979, Principle 21, fifth preambular paragraph, TIAS 10541, 18 I.L.M. 1442 (1979)).

What is the legal significance of the repetition of Principles 21 and 2? Does it indicate that they are accepted as norms of customary international law? Or does it mean that States believe these principles are not binding unless they are incorporated into an agreement?

4.   *The difficult birth of Principle 21.* The luster Principle 21 has taken on over the years tends to obscure the controversy that attended its birth. The late Professor Louis Sohn, in his commentary on the principle, describes its drafting history and discusses a number of versions proposed by different delegations, including the following:

> Each State has a sovereign right to its environment and to dispose of its natural resources and a right to take all necessary and appropriate measures to protect its environmental integrity. In support of this proposal, it was argued that as a first step in the development of international environmental law it is necessary to make clear the principle that "sovereignty includes the right to environmental integrity and the right to maintain that integrity in a wholesome and unimpaired condition." Another delegation supported this proposal, subject to the condition that any such right can be exercised only in accordance with the Charter of the United Nations and the general principles of international law. Several other delegations opposed these proposals, however. They observed that, unlike the concept of sovereignty, the concept of the human environment did not have any clearly established limits; consequently, the proposed new principle could be interpreted as "implying that each State was left free to define the extent of its environment" to the prejudice of the established principles of international law.

Louis Sohn, The Stockholm Declaration on the Human Environment, 14 Harv. Intl. L.J. 423, 488–489 (1973) (footnotes omitted).

At the Stockholm Conference, the United States made the following statement concerning its interpretation of Principle 21:

> [N]othing contained in this principle, or elsewhere in the Declaration, diminishes in any way the obligation of States to prevent environmental damage or gives rise to any right on the part of States to take actions in derogation of the rights of other States or of the community of nations. The statement on the responsibility of States for damage caused to the environment of other States or of areas beyond the limits of national jurisdiction is not in any way a

limitation on the above obligation, but an affirmation of existing rules concerning liability in the event of default on the obligation.

U.N. Doc. A/CONF.48/14, at 118 (1972). Professor Sohn describes the reaction to this and other proposals as follows:

> The consensus reached in the Working Group of the Preparatory Committee on this principle was so fragile that the Working Group of the Conference not only refused to clarify the text, as suggested by the United States, but also rejected a number of amendments of the kind that it had no trouble in accepting in connection with other principles. Thus it rejected a Brazilian proposal to delete the restrictive reference to the Charter of the United Nations and the principles of international law, as well as another Brazilian proposal to restore an earlier text allowing each state to follow, without any restriction, not only its environmental policies but also its "standards and criteria." The Working Group also refused to make a concession to the group of nine African countries, which wanted to make clear that the sovereign right to exploit resources was accompanied by the right to control them.

Louis Sohn, above, at 491 (footnotes omitted). Is this tantamount to saying, "we don't really know what it means, but if everyone else can accept it, we will"?

INTERNATIONAL LAW COMMISSION, DRAFT ARTICLES ON PREVENTION OF TRANSBOUNDARY HARM FROM HAZARDOUS ACTIVITIES

Adopted on second reading in 2001, 2001 ILC Rep. 371–374

Article 1
Scope

The present articles apply to activities not prohibited by international law which involve a risk of causing significant transboundary harm through their physical consequences.

Article 2
Use of Terms

For the purposes of the present articles:

(a) Risk of causing significant transboundary harm includes risks taking the form of a high probability of causing significant transboundary harm and a low probability of causing disastrous transboundary harm;

(b) Harm means harm caused to persons, property or the environment;

(c) Transboundary harm means harm caused in the territory of or in other places under the jurisdiction or control of a State other than the State of origin, whether or not the States concerned share a common border;

(d) State of origin means the State in the territory or otherwise under the jurisdiction or control of which the activities referred to in article 1 are planned or are carried out;

(e) State likely to be affected means the State or States in the territory of which there is the risk of significant transboundary harm or which have jurisdiction or control over any other place where there is such a risk;

(f) States concerned means the State of origin and the State likely to be affected.

Article 3
Prevention

The State of origin shall take all appropriate measures to prevent significant transboundary harm or at any event to minimize the risk thereof.

Article 4
Cooperation

States concerned shall cooperate in good faith and, as necessary, seek the assistance of one or more competent international organizations in preventing significant transboundary harm or at any event in minimizing the risk thereof.

Article 5
Implementation

States concerned shall take the necessary legislative, administrative or other action including the establishment of suitable monitoring mechanisms to implement the provisions of the present articles.

Article 6
Authorization

1. The State of origin shall require its prior authorization for:

(a) Any activity within the scope of the present articles carried out in its territory or otherwise under its jurisdiction or control;

(b) Any major change in an activity referred to in subparagraph (a);

(c) Any plan to change an activity which may transform it into one falling within the scope of the present articles.

2.   The requirement of authorization established by a State shall be made applicable in respect of all pre-existing activities within the scope of the present articles. Authorizations already issued by the State for pre-existing activities shall be reviewed in order to comply with the present articles.

3.   In case of a failure to conform to the terms of the authorization, the State of origin shall take such actions as appropriate, including where necessary terminating the authorization.

Article 7
Assessment of Risk

Any decision in respect of the authorization of an activity within the scope of the present articles shall, in particular, be based on an assessment of the possible transboundary harm caused by that activity, including any environmental impact assessment.

Article 8
Notification and Information

1.   If the assessment referred to in article 7 indicates a risk of causing significant transboundary harm, the State of origin shall provide the State likely to be affected with timely notification of the risk and the assessment and shall transmit to it the available technical and all other relevant information on which the assessment is based.

2.   The State of origin shall not take any decision on authorization of the activity pending the receipt, within a period not exceeding six months, of the response from the State likely to be affected.

Article 9
Consultations on Preventive Measures

1.   The States concerned shall enter into consultations, at the request of any of them, with a view to achieving acceptable solutions regarding measures to be adopted in order to prevent significant transboundary harm or at any event to minimize the risk thereof. The States concerned shall agree, at the commencement of such consultations, on a reasonable time-frame for the consultations.

2.   The States concerned shall seek solutions based on an equitable balance of interests in the light of article 10.

3.   If the consultations referred to in paragraph 1 fail to produce an agreed solution, the State of origin shall nevertheless take into account the interests of the State likely to be affected in case it decides to authorize the activity to be pursued, without prejudice to the rights of any State likely to be affected.

Article 10
Factors Involved in an Equitable Balance of Interests

In order to achieve an equitable balance of interests as referred to in paragraph 2 of article 9, the States concerned shall take into account all relevant factors and circumstances, including:

(a) The degree of risk of significant transboundary harm and of the availability of means of preventing such harm, or minimizing the risk thereof or repairing the harm;

(b) The importance of the activity, taking into account its overall advantages of a social, economic and technical character for the State of origin in relation to the potential harm for the State likely to be affected;

(c) The risk of significant harm to the environment and the availability of means of preventing such harm, or minimizing the risk thereof or restoring the environment;

(d) The degree to which the State of origin and, as appropriate, the State likely to be affected are prepared to contribute to the costs of prevention;

(e) The economic viability of the activity in relation to the costs of prevention and to the possibility of carrying out the activity elsewhere or by other means or replacing it with an alternative activity;

(f) The standards of prevention which the State likely to be affected applies to the same or comparable activities and the standards applied in comparable regional or international practice.

. . .

NOTES AND QUESTIONS

1.   *Prevention of harm from non-prohibited activities?* Re-read the title of this draft and Article 1. On the one hand we have "prevention of transboundary harm from hazardous activities." So far, so good: we would want to prevent transboundary harm from hazardous activities. On the other hand we have "activities not prohibited by international law." Wouldn't, or shouldn't, such activities be illegal? Can you explain this apparent contradiction?

2.   *Activities with an inherent risk of causing transboundary harm are not prohibited?* Can you give concrete examples of the kinds of activities the draft would cover?

3.   *Dueling articles?* Article 3 lays down an obligation of prevention. But Articles 9 and 10 say the States concerned are to "seek solutions based on an equitable balance of interests," rather than requiring the situs state to

prevent transboundary harm altogether. Is this satisfying? Does it apply to activities entailing a risk of causing "disastrous transboundary harm" referred to in Article 2(a)? Do States have a right to cause "disastrous transboundary harm" if the activity causing the harm is not itself prohibited?

RESTATEMENT (THIRD) OF THE FOREIGN RELATIONS LAW OF THE UNITED STATES

American Law Institute (1987)

§ 601. State Obligations with Respect to Environment of Other States and the Common Environment

(1) A state is obligated to take such measures as may be necessary, to the extent practicable under the circumstances, to ensure that activities within its jurisdiction or control

(a) conform to generally accepted international rules and standards for the prevention, reduction, and control of injury to the environment of another state or of areas beyond the limits of national jurisdiction; and

(b) are conducted so as not to cause significant injury to the environment of another state or of areas beyond the limits of national jurisdiction.

. . .

NOTES AND QUESTIONS

Muddied water? The Restatement of Foreign Relations Law is effectively the Restatement of International Law—largely as viewed by the United States. It devotes an entire chapter (Part VI) to "The Law of the Environment," a subject that is dealt with in two reporters' notes in the previous Restatement of Foreign Relations Law.[10] However, the chapter consists of only four sections: one deals with "Remedies for Violations of Environmental Obligations" and two with marine pollution, leaving only § 601 to deal with the obligations of States with regard to the environment. Commendable as it is that the ALI expanded its treatment of the subject, it is perhaps not surprising that its effort to condense the entire field of international environmental law into four sections has drawn criticism. David Caron has commented that

the resulting product constitutes only a modest step toward presenting the foreign relations law of the United States pertaining to the environment. Part VI takes a narrow view of the law of the environment, limiting itself to transfrontier pollution and, even then, relegates most of the discussion of conventional law to

---

[10] American Law Institute, Restatement (Second) of the Foreign Relations Law of the United States §§ 18, Reporters' Note 3, and 23, Reporters' Note 3 (1965).

reporters' notes. . . . As a symbolic step, Part VI is to be applauded. As a restatement of the foreign relations law of the United States pertaining to the environment, it oversimplifies and sometimes muddies the waterways of the law.

David Caron, The Law of the Environment: A Symbolic Step of Modest Value, 14 Yale J. Intl. L. 528 (1989).

Further reading: Pierre-Marie Dupuy, Overview of the Existing Customary Legal Regime Regarding International Pollution, in International Law and Pollution 61 (D. Magraw, ed., 1991).

b.   The Precautionary Principle

The precautionary "principle" or "approach" is a method of dealing with threatened environmental harm in the face of scientific uncertainty. Here we focus upon its normative status in international relations. Consider the question whether international law requires States to adopt a precautionary approach and, if so, under what circumstances and what adoption of such an approach would entail.

RIO DECLARATION ON ENVIRONMENT AND DEVELOPMENT, PRINCIPLE 15

Adopted by the United Nations Conference on Environment and Development, June 14, 1992 U.N. Doc. A/CONF.151/5/Rev.1, June 13, 1992, reprinted in 31 I.L.M. 874 (1992)

Principle 15

In order to protect the environment, the precautionary approach shall be widely applied by States according to their capabilities. Where there are threats of serious or irreversible damage, lack of full scientific certainty shall not be used as a reason for postponing cost-effective measures to prevent environmental degradation.

NOTES AND QUESTIONS

1.   *What's in a name? A "principle" or an "approach"?* Although entitled a "principle," the text of Principle 15 refers only to a precautionary "approach." Is there a normative difference in your view? Some countries, notably the United States, insisted on the use of the term "approach" rather than "principle" at Rio. Does this suggest they thought there was a distinction that would have normative consequences? Why did the United States make an issue of this given that the Rio Declaration is, in any event, non-binding? Why did it allow the term of obligation "shall" to be used?

2.   *Cost-effective measures.* Principle 15 requires only that "cost-effective" measures be taken. What does this mean in the field of environmental protection? Must the threatened harm to the environment be monetized in order to make the calculation as to whether the preventive measures are "cost-effective"? If so, does cost effectiveness depend on whether

we are risk-neutral or risk-averse? How is cost effectiveness measured in cases where the threatened damage is "serious or irreversible?" For that matter, how would you determine whether threatened damage is "serious?" "Serious" according to whose peferences and in relation to what? The effect on humans? The degree of harm to the environment? If the latter, again, in relation to what?

3. *An international obligation to look before you leap?* What do you think: Is it an international legal obligation to exercise precaution under the circumstances described in Principle 15? Or is the principle ("approach") merely advisory, or even simply descriptive of an approach?

4. *Precaution and the Climate Change Convention.* Article 3, paragraph 3 of the United Nations Framework Convention on Climate Change provides in part as follows:

> 3. The Parties should take precautionary measures to anticipate, prevent or minimise the causes of climate change and mitigate its adverse effects. Where there are threats of serious or irreversible damage, lack of full scientific certainty should not be used as a reason for postponing such measures, taking into account that policies and measures to deal with climate change should be cost-effective so as to ensure global benefits at the lowest possible cost. . . .

United Nations Framework Convention on Climate Change (UNFCCC), New York, May 9, 1992, *reprinted in* 31 I.L.M. 849 (1992). Is the use of "should" throughout this provision legally significant? Why did the drafters not use "shall"? Do you find it ironic that the Rio Declaration—a nonbinding instrument—uses "shall" in its formulation of the precautionary principle (which is, in pertinent part, nearly identical to that of the UNFCCC) while the Convention—a binding instrument—uses "should"? Is the reference to "full scientific certainty" in the UNFCCC appropriate?

5. *Precaution and the Biodiversity Convention.* The Biodiversity Convention, considered in Chapter 13, includes the precautionary principle not in one of its substantive provisions but in its preamble: *"Noting also* that where there is a threat of significant reduction or loss of biological diversity, lack of full scientific certainty should not be used as a reason for postponing measures to avoid or minimize such a threat." Do you believe this point should have been dealt with in one of the articles of the Convention rather than its preamble? What is the significance of its treatment in the preamble? How could or should such a preambular provision be used? What are the similarities and differences between this formulation and those of the Rio Declaration and UNFCCC?

6. *Precaution in other instruments.* The precautionary principle, in one form or another, has been included or reflected in a number of other instruments. For a full catalogue of treaties and other instruments, *see* Arie Trouwborst, Evolution and Status of the Precautionary Principle in

International Law, 63–133, and Annexes A (binding instruments) and B (non-binding instruments) (2002).

7. *Precaution in the World Court.*

- The precautionary principle was invoked by New Zealand in its appeal to the International Court of Justice to halt French underground nuclear testing in the South Pacific. *Nuclear Tests Case* (New Zealand v. France), request by New Zealand for an Examination of the Situation, August 21, 1995, at paragraphs 105–108. France responded that the legal status of the principle was "uncertain." ICJ, Verbatim Record, CR 95/20, September 12, 1995, at 71. In his opinion dissenting from the Court's order of September 22, 1995 (declining to reopen the case and thus to consider halting the tests), Judge Weeramantry concluded that the precautionary principle is "gaining increasing support as part of the international law of the environment."

- The precautionary principle was also relied upon by Hungary in the *Gabčíkovo-Nagymaros Project* case, 1997 ICJ Rep. 7, para. 97 ("The previously existing obligation not to cause substantive damage to the territory of another State had, Hungary claimed, evolved into an erga omnes obligation of prevention of damage pursuant to the 'precautionary principle.'") but the Court noted only that the "Parties agree on the need to take environmental concerns seriously and to take the required precautionary measures" *(id.,* para. 113) without making a finding as to whether the principle was part of international law, let alone applying it.

- In the *Pulp Mills* case, 2010 ICJ Rep. 14, Argentina referred to the precautionary principle, *id.* at 42, para. 55, using it in part in the context of the burden of proof, *id.,* at 70, para. 160, though Uruguay contested this, *id.* at 71, para. 161. "[T]he Court consider[ed] that while a precautionary approach may be relevant in the interpretation and application of the provisions of the Statute, it does not follow that it operates as a reversal of the burden of proof." *Id.* at 71, para. 164.

8. *Where's the beef? Caution and the WTO: the* Beef Hormones *Case.* In *EC Measures Concerning Meat and Meat Products (Beef Hormones),* Canada and United States v. European Community, 16 Jan. 1998, AB-1997-4, WTO Doc. WT/DS26/AB/R and WT/DS48/AB/R, the European Communities argued that "the precautionary principle is already . . . a general customary rule of international law or at least a general principle of law . . ." *Id.* The United States, on the other hand, stated that it did "not consider that the 'precautionary principle' represents a principle of customary international law; rather, it may be characterized as an 'approach'—the content of which may vary from context to context." *Id.* The Appellate Body declined to take a

position on the status of the precautionary principle in international law but indicated that it "finds reflection in" and "has been incorporated into" Article 5.7 of the 1994 WTO Agreement on the Application of Sanitary and Phytosanitary Measures (SPS Agreement), Article 5(7), 1867 UNTS 493, under which members have the right to take provisional measures where scientific evidence is insufficient. As of early 2015, the WTO has not taken a position on the status of the precautionary principle.

Further reading: *Southern Bluefin Tuna Cases (New Zealand v. Japan; Australia v. Japan),* Request for provisional measures, International Tribunal for the Law of the Sea, 1999, Cases Nos. 3 and 4, including separate opinion of Judge Treves.

c.   Sustainable Development

RIO DECLARATION ON ENVIRONMENT AND DEVELOPMENT, PRINCIPLE 1

Adopted by the United Nations Conference on Environment and Development, June 14, 1992 U.N. Doc. A/CONF.151/5/Rev.1, June 13, 1992, reprinted in 31 I.L.M. 874 (1992)

Principle 1

Human beings are at the centre of concerns for sustainable development. They are entitled to a healthy and productive life in harmony with nature.

CASE CONCERNING THE GABČÍKOVO-NAGYMAROS PROJECT
(Hungary/Slovakia)
International Court of Justice
1997 ICJ Rep. 7, 78, Judgment of September 25, 1997

[In this case, which is excerpted at length in Chapter 12 on Fresh Water, Hungary and Slovakia asked the Court to decide, inter alia, whether Hungary was entitled to suspend and subsequently abandon works being constructed on the Danube under a 1977 treaty between Hungary and Czechoslovakia. Among Hungary's arguments were that it was entitled unilaterally to terminate the treaty and that environmental considerations compelled it to stop work on the project. The Court held that Hungary had not effectively terminated the treaty and that the parties had an obligation to negotiate in good faith to implement the judgment, taking all necessary measures to ensure the achievement of the objectives of the 1977 Treaty. In the course of discussing the consequences of its holding that the treaty was still in force, the Court said the following:]

Throughout the ages, mankind has, for economic and other reasons, constantly interfered with nature. In the past, this was often done without consideration of the effects upon the environment. Owing to new scientific insights and to a growing awareness of the risks for mankind—for present and future generations—of pursuit of such interventions at an unconsidered and unabated pace, new norms and standards have been developed, set forth in a great number of instruments during the last two decades. Such new norms have to be taken into consideration, and such new standards given proper weight, not only when States contemplate new activities but also when continuing with activities begun in the past. This need to reconcile economic development with protection of the environment is aptly expressed in the concept of sustainable development.

WORLD COMMISSION ON ENVIRONMENT AND DEVELOPMENT, OUR COMMON FUTURE
43–46 (1987)

Sustainable development is development that meets the needs of the present without compromising the ability of future generations to meet their own needs. It contains within it two key concepts:

- the concept of "needs," in particular the essential needs of the world's poor, to which overriding priority should be given; and

- the idea of limitations imposed by the state of technology and social organization on the environment's ability to meet present and future needs.

NOTES AND QUESTIONS

1. *Sustainable anthropocentrism?* Look again at Principle 1 of the Rio Declaration. What is it saying ("Human beings are at the centre. . . .")? Does this formulation put the emphasis in the right place? Is the concept of sustainable development more biocentric or anthropocentric? Or is equal weight placed on human needs and environmental protection? Are human needs ultimately served by failing to protect the environment?

2. *Development assistance with strings attached?* Should environmental strings be attached to development assistance flowing from the developed world—including from bilateral donor countries and through international financial institutions such as the World Bank and regional development banks—to the developing world? They usually are. Is this ethical? Should it be left up to the recipient of development assistance how it wishes to implement sustainable development?

3. *It's a bird! It's a plane! It's the law! No, it's a . . . concept! No, it's a principle!* Much ink has been spilt over the question whether sustainable development is obligatory, whether it has some other normative value or

legal, non-legal, or quasi-legal character. Professor Vaughn Lowe has had the following to say about the character of sustainable development:

> "It lacks . . . a fundamentally norm-creating character. The argument that sustainable development is a norm of customary international law, binding on and directing the conduct of states, and which can be applied by tribunals, is not sustainable. . . . [Further,] sustainable development cannot properly be regarded as a soft law norm addressed to and purporting to constrain the conduct of states.
>
> "What, then, is left of sustainable development? Certainly, it is a convenient, if imprecise, label for a general policy goal which may be adopted by states unilaterally, bilaterally, or multilaterally. It is clearly entitled to a place in the Pantheon of concepts that are not to be questioned in polite company, along with democracy, human rights, and the sovereign equality of states. And, like those revered concepts, it is rooted in theoretical obscurity and confusion. . . . It does not follow, however, that it has no normative status whatever.
>
> ". . . Sustainable development can properly claim a normative status as an element of the process of judicial reasoning. It is a metaprinciple, acting upon other legal rules and principles—a legal concept exercising a kind of interstitial normativity, pushing and pulling the boundaries of true primary norms when they threaten to overlap or conflict with each other."[11]

Do you agree? Does calling sustainable development a "metaprinciple" give it too much status? Too little?

Further reading: International Law and Sustainable Development (Alan Boyle & David Freestone, eds., 1999); Sustainable Development and International Law (W. Lang, ed., 1995); EC Commission, The Law of Sustainable Development: General Principles (2000); Caring for the Earth: A Strategy for Sustainable Development (R.D. Munro & M. Holdgate, eds., 1991); Sustainable Development of the Biosphere (W. Clark & R. Munn, eds., 1986); Philippe Sands, *International Law in the Field of Sustainable Development*, 65 BYIL 303 (1994); Daniel Barstow Magraw, Sustainable Development, in Oxford Handbook of International Environmental Law (D. Bodansky, J. Brunnee & Ellen Hey, eds., 2008).

---

[11] Vaughn Lowe, Sustainable Development and Unsustainable Arguments, in International Law and Sustainable Development: Past Achievements and Future Challenges 19, at 30–31 (A. Boyle & D. Freestone, eds., 1999).

2. PROCEDURAL NORMS

a. Prior Notification and Consultation

PULP MILLS ON THE RIVER URUGUAY
(Argentina v. Uruguay)
2010 ICJ Rep. 14

[As we saw in the previous section, this case concerned a dispute between Argentina and Uruguay over two pulp mills that were planned to be constructed in Uruguay on the Uruguay River that forms the border between the two countries. Eventually only one of these plants, the Orion (Botnia) mill, was constructed, plans to build the other having been abandoned by the company that had proposed it. By the time the Court rendered its judgment the Botnia plant had been operating for some two years.

The parties' relations with regard to the Uruguay River are governed by the 1975 Statute of the Uruguay River, 1295 UNTS 340, an advanced agreement for its time that contains substantive and procedural obligations concerning the navigational and non-navigational uses of the watercourse. The Statute establishes the Comisión Administradora del Río Uruguay (Administrative Commission of the River Uruguay, or CARU, its Spanish acronym), a joint mechanism for the management of the River Uruguay. The Statute contains the following procedural rules:

Article 7. If one Party plans to construct new channels, substantially modify or alter existing ones or carry out any other works which are liable to affect navigation, the régime of the river or the quality of its waters, it shall notify the Commission, which shall determine on a preliminary basis and within a maximum period of 30 days whether the plan might cause significant damage to the other Party.

If the Commission finds this to be the case or if a decision cannot be reached in that regard, the Party concerned shall notify the other Party of the plan through the said Commission.

Such notification shall describe the main aspects of the work and, where appropriate, how it is to be carried out and shall include any other technical date that will enable the notified Party to assess the probable impact of such works on navigation, the régime of the river or the quality of its waters.

Article 8. The notified Party shall have a period of 180 days in which to respond in connection with the plan, starting from the date on which its delegation to the Commission receives the notification.

Should the documentation referred to in article 7 be incomplete, the notified Party shall have 30 days in which to so inform, through the Commission, the Party which plans to carry out the work.

The period of 180 days mentioned above shall begin on the date on which the delegation of the notified Party receives the full documentation.

This period may be extended at the discretion of the Commission if the complexity of the plan so requires.

Article 9. If the notified Party raises no objections or does not respond within the period established in article 8, the other Party may carry out or authorize the work planned.

Article 10. The notified Party shall have the right to inspect the works being carried out in order to determine whether they conform to the plan submitted.

Article 11. Should the notified Party come to the conclusion that the execution of the work or the programme of operations might significantly impair navigation, the régime of the river or the quality of its waters, it shall so notify the other Party, through the Commission, within the period of 180 days established in article 8.

Such notification shall specify which aspects of the work or the programme of operations might significantly impair navigation, the régime of the river or the quality of its waters, the technical reasons on which this conclusion is based and the changes suggested to the plan or programme of operations.

Article 12. Should the Parties fail to reach agreement within 180 days following the notification referred to in article 11, the procedure indicated in chapter XV shall be followed.[12]

Article 13. The rules laid down in articles 7 to 12 shall apply to all works referred to in article 7, whether national or binational, which either Party plans to carry out within its jurisdiction in the River Uruguay outside the section defined as a river and in the areas affected by the two sections.

In its suit filed in the ICJ in 2006, Argentina alleged that Uruguay had breached both substantive and procedural obligations under the treaty in relation to its approval of the Botnia mill and the effects of the

---

[12] Chapter XV, "Judicial Settlement of Disputes," consists of Article 60, which provides in part: "Any dispute concerning the interpretation or application of the Treaty and the Statute which cannot be settled by direct negotiations may be submitted by either Party to the International Court of Justice."—Eds.

mill's operation. In this section we focus on Uruguay's alleged procedural breaches.]

2.   Uruguay's obligation to inform CARU

94.   The Court notes that the obligation of the State initiating the planned activity to inform CARU constitutes the first stage in the procedural mechanism as a whole which allows the two parties to achieve the object of the 1975 Statute, namely, "the optimum and rational utilization of the River Uruguay". This stage, provided for in Article 7, first paragraph, involves the State which is initiating the planned activity informing CARU thereof, so that the latter can determine "on a preliminary basis" and within a maximum period of 30 days whether the plan might cause significant damage to the other party.

95.   To enable the remainder of the procedure to take its course, the parties have included alternative conditions in the 1975 Statute: either that the activity planned by one party should be liable, in CARU's opinion, to cause significant damage to the other, creating an obligation of prevention for the first party to eliminate or minimize the risk, in consultation with the other party; or that CARU, having been duly informed, should not have reached a decision in that regard within the prescribed period.

96.   The Court notes that the Parties are agreed in considering that the two planned mills were works of sufficient importance to fall within the scope of Article 7 of the 1975 Statute, and thus for CARU to have been informed of them. The same applies to the plan to construct a port terminal at Fray Bentos for the exclusive use of the Orion (Botnia) mill, which included dredging work and use of the river bed.

97.   However, the Court observes that the Parties disagree on whether there is an obligation to inform CARU in respect of the extraction and use of water from the river for industrial purposes by the Orion (Botnia) mill. Argentina takes the view that the authorization granted by the Uruguayan Ministry of Transport and Public Works on 12 September 2006 concerns an activity of sufficient importance ("entidad suficiente") to affect the régime of the river or the quality of its waters and that, in this matter, Uruguay should have followed the procedure laid down in Articles 7 to 12 of the 1975 Statute. For its part, Uruguay maintains that this activity forms an integral part of the Orion (Botnia) mill project as a whole, and that the 1975 Statute does not require CARU to be informed of each step in furtherance of the planned works.

98.   The Court points out that while the Parties are agreed in recognizing that CARU should have been informed of the two planned mills and the plan to construct the port terminal at Fray Bentos, they nonetheless differ as regards the content of the information which should be provided to CARU and as to when this should take place.

99.   Argentina has argued that the content of the obligation to inform must be determined in the light of its objective, which is to prevent threats to navigation, the régime of the river or the quality of the waters. According to Argentina, the plan which CARU must be informed of may be at a very early stage, since it is simply a matter of allowing the Commission to "determine on a preliminary basis", within a very short period of 30 days, whether the plan "might cause significant damage to the other party". It is only in the following phase of the procedure that the substance of the obligation to inform is said to become more extensive. In Argentina's view, however, CARU must be informed prior to the authorization or implementation of a project on the River Uruguay.

100.   Citing the terms of Article 7, first paragraph, of the 1975 Statute, Uruguay gives a different interpretation of it, taking the view that the requirement to inform CARU specified by this provision cannot occur in the very early stages of planning, because there could not be sufficient information available to the Commission for it to determine whether or not the plan might cause significant damage to the other State. For that, according to Uruguay, the project would have to have reached a stage where all the technical data on it are available. As the Court will consider further below, Uruguay seeks to link the content of the information to the time when it should be provided, which may even be after the State concerned has granted an initial environmental authorization.

101.   [This paragraph, concerning the obligation not to cause transboundary harm, is set forth in subsection 1.a, above.]

102.   In the view of the Court, the obligation to inform CARU allows for the initiation of co-operation between the Parties which is necessary in order to fulfil the obligation of prevention. This first procedural stage results in the 1975 Statute not being applied to activities which would appear to cause damage only to the State in whose territory they are carried out.

103.   The Court observes that with regard to the River Uruguay, which constitutes a shared resource, "significant damage to the other party" (Article 7, first paragraph, of the 1975 Statute) may result from impairment of navigation, the régime of the river or the quality of its waters. Moreover, Article 27 of the 1975 Statute stipulates that: "[t]he right of each party to use the waters of the river, within its jurisdiction, for domestic, sanitary, industrial and agricultural purposes shall be exercised without prejudice to the application of the procedure laid down in Articles 7 to 12 when the use is liable to affect the régime of the river or the quality of its waters".

104.   The Court notes that, in accordance with the terms of Article 7, first paragraph, the information which must be provided to CARU, at this initial stage of the procedure, has to enable it to determine swiftly and on

a preliminary basis whether the plan might cause significant damage to the other party. For CARU, at this stage, it is a question of deciding whether or not the plan falls under the co-operation procedure laid down by the 1975 Statute, and not of pronouncing on its actual impact on the river and the quality of its waters. This explains, in the opinion of the Court, the difference between the terminology of the first paragraph of Article 7, concerning the requirement to inform CARU, and that of the third paragraph, concerning the content of the notification to be addressed to the other party at a later stage, enabling it "to assess the probable impact of such works on navigation, the régime of the river or the quality of its waters".

105. The Court considers that the State planning activities referred to in Article 7 of the Statute is required to inform CARU as soon as it is in possession of a plan which is sufficiently developed to enable CARU to make the preliminary assessment (required by paragraph 1 of that provision) of whether the proposed works might cause significant damage to the other party. At that stage, the information provided will not necessarily consist of a full assessment of the environmental impact of the project, which will often require further time and resources, although, where more complete information is available, this should, of course, be transmitted to CARU to give it the best possible basis on which to make its preliminary assessment. In any event, the duty to inform CARU will become applicable at the stage when the relevant authority has had the project referred to it with the aim of obtaining initial environmental authorization and before the granting of that authorization.

106. The Court observes that, in the present case, Uruguay did not transmit to CARU the information required by Article 7, first paragraph, in respect of the CMB (ENCE) and Orion (Botnia) mills, despite the requests made to it by the Commission to that effect on several occasions, in particular on 17 October 2002 and 21 April 2003 with regard to the CMB (ENCE) mill, and on 16 November 2004 with regard to the Orion (Botnia) mill. Uruguay merely sent CARU, on 14 May 2003, a summary for public release of the environmental impact assessment for the CMB (ENCE) mill. CARU considered this document to be inadequate and again requested further information from Uruguay on 15 August 2003 and 12 September 2003. Moreover, Uruguay did not transmit any document to CARU regarding the Orion (Botnia) mill. Consequently, Uruguay issued the initial environmental authorizations to CMB on 9 October 2003 and to Botnia on 14 February 2005 without complying with the procedure laid down in Article 7, first paragraph. Uruguay therefore came to a decision on the environmental impact of the projects without involving CARU, thereby simply giving effect to Article 17, third paragraph, of Uruguayan Decree No. 435/994 of 21 September 1994, Environmental Impact Assessment Regulation, according to which the Ministry of Housing, Land

Use Planning and Environmental Affairs may grant the initial environmental authorization provided that the adverse environmental impacts of the project remain within acceptable limits.

107.   The Court further notes that on 12 April 2005 Uruguay granted an authorization to Botnia for the first phase of the construction of the Orion (Botnia) mill and, on 5 July 2005, an authorization to construct a port terminal for its exclusive use and to utilize the river bed for industrial purposes, without informing CARU of these projects in advance.

108.   With regard to the extraction and use of water from the river, of which CARU should have first been informed, according to Argentina, the Court takes the view that this is an activity which forms an integral part of the commissioning of the Orion (Botnia) mill and therefore did not require a separate referral to CARU.

109.   However, Uruguay maintains that CARU was made aware of the plans for the mills by representatives of ENCE on 8 July 2002, and no later than 29 April 2004 by representatives of Botnia, before the initial environmental authorizations were issued. Argentina, for its part, considers that these so-called private dealings, whatever form they may have taken, do not constitute performance of the obligation imposed on the Parties by Article 7, first paragraph.

110.   The Court considers that the information on the plans for the mills which reached CARU via the companies concerned or from other non-governmental sources cannot substitute for the obligation to inform laid down in Article 7, first paragraph, of the 1975 Statute, which is borne by the party planning to construct the works referred to in that provision. Similarly, in the case concerning *Certain Questions of Mutual Assistance in Criminal Matters (Djibouti* v. *France)*, the Court observed that "[i]f the information eventually came to Djibouti through the press, the information disseminated in this way could not be taken into account for the purposes of the application of Article 17 [of the Convention on Mutual Assistance in Criminal Matters between the two countries, providing that '[r]easons shall be given for any refusal of mutual assistance']" (*Judgment, I.C.J. Reports 2008*, p. 231, para. 150).

111.   Consequently, the Court concludes from the above that Uruguay, by not informing CARU of the planned works before the issuing of the initial environmental authorizations for each of the mills and for the port terminal adjacent to the Orion (Botnia) mill, has failed to comply with the obligation imposed on it by Article 7, first paragraph, of the 1975 Statute.

3.   Uruguay's obligation to notify the plans to the other party

112.   The Court notes that, under the terms of Article 7, second paragraph, of the 1975 Statute, if CARU decides that the plan might cause significant damage to the other party or if a decision cannot be

reached in that regard, "the party concerned shall notify the other party of this plan through the said Commission". Article 7, third paragraph, of the 1975 Statute sets out in detail the content of this notification, which "shall describe the main aspects of the work and . . . any other technical data that will enable the notified party to assess the probable impact of such works on navigation, the régime of the river or the quality of its waters".

113.   In the opinion of the Court, the obligation to notify is intended to create the conditions for successful co-operation between the parties, enabling them to assess the plan's impact on the river on the basis of the fullest possible information and, if necessary, to negotiate the adjustments needed to avoid the potential damage that it might cause.

114.   Article 8 stipulates a period of 180 days, which may be extended by the Commission, for the notified party to respond in connection with the plan, subject to it requesting the other party, through the Commission, to supplement as necessary the documentation it has provided. If the notified party raises no objections, the other party may carry out or authorize the work (Article 9). Otherwise, the former must notify the latter of those aspects of the work which may cause it damage and of the suggested changes (Article 11), thereby opening a further 180-day period of negotiation in which to reach an agreement (Article 12).

115.   The obligation to notify is therefore an essential part of the process leading the parties to consult in order to assess the risks of the plan and to negotiate possible changes which may eliminate those risks or minimize their effects.

116.   The Parties agree on the need for a full environmental impact assessment in order to assess any significant damage which might be caused by a plan.

117.   Uruguay takes the view that such assessments were carried out in accordance with its legislation (Decree No. 435/994 of 21 September 1994, Environmental Impact Assessment Regulation), submitted to DINAMA for consideration and transmitted to Argentina on 7 November 2003 in the case of the CMB (ENCE) project and on 19 August 2005 for the Orion (Botnia) project. According to Uruguay, DINAMA asked the companies concerned for all the additional information that was required to supplement the original environmental impact assessments submitted to it, and only when it was satisfied did it propose to the Ministry of the Environment that the initial environmental authorizations requested should be issued, which they were to CMB on 9 October 2003 and to Botnia on 14 February 2005. Uruguay maintains that it was not required to transmit the environmental impact assessments to Argentina before issuing the initial environmental authorizations to the companies, these

authorizations having been adopted on the basis of its legislation on the subject.

118.   Argentina, for its part, first points out that the environmental impact assessments transmitted to it by Uruguay were incomplete, particularly in that they made no provision for alternative sites for the mills and failed to include any consultation of the affected populations. The Court will return later in the Judgment to the substantive conditions which must be met by environmental impact assessments (see paragraphs 203 to 219). Furthermore, in procedural terms, Argentina considers that the initial environmental authorizations should not have been granted to the companies before it had received the complete environmental impact assessments, and that it was unable to exercise its rights in this context under Articles 7 to 11 of the 1975 Statute.

119.   The Court notes that the environmental impact assessments which are necessary to reach a decision on any plan that is liable to cause significant transboundary harm to another State must be notified by the party concerned to the other party, through CARU, pursuant to Article 7, second and third paragraphs, of the 1975 Statute. This notification is intended to enable the notified party to participate in the process of ensuring that the assessment is complete, so that it can then consider the plan and its effects with a full knowledge of the facts (Article 8 of the 1975 Statute).

120.   The Court observes that this notification must take place before the State concerned decides on the environmental viability of the plan, taking due account of the environmental impact assessment submitted to it.

121.   In the present case, the Court observes that the notification to Argentina of the environmental impact assessments for the CMB (ENCE) and Orion (Botnia) mills did not take place through CARU, and that Uruguay only transmitted those assessments to Argentina after having issued the initial environmental authorizations for the two mills in question. Thus in the case of CMB (ENCE), the matter was notified to Argentina on 27 October and 7 November 2003, whereas the initial environmental authorization had already been issued on 9 October 2003. In the case of Orion (Botnia), the file was transmitted to Argentina between August 2005 and January 2006, whereas the initial environmental authorization had been granted on 14 February 2005. Uruguay ought not, prior to notification, to have issued the initial environmental authorizations and the authorizations for construction on the basis of the environmental impact assessments submitted to DINAMA. Indeed by doing so, Uruguay gave priority to its own legislation over its procedural obligations under the 1975 Statute and disregarded the well-established customary rule reflected in Article 27 of the Vienna

Convention on the Law of Treaties, according to which "[a] party may not invoke the provisions of its internal law as justification for its failure to perform a treaty".

122. The Court concludes from the above that Uruguay failed to comply with its obligation to notify the plans to Argentina through CARU under Article 7, second and third paragraphs, of the 1975 Statute.

NOTES AND QUESTIONS

1. *CARU, shmaru.* Why should Uruguay be required to notify Argentina through CARU? Why shouldn't it be enough to notify the potentially affected party, Argentina, directly? What if the Commission, which consists of an equal number of members from both parties, is deadlocked?

2. *Notify as soon as the light bulb goes off in your head.* Where are the terms "environmental impact assessment," "environmental authorization," or even "environment" in the provisions of the treaty quoted above? How can the Court require a party to provide notification before issuing an environmental authorization if the treaty does not require this? What if the environmental authorization is merely an initial step in the overall approval process, which requires substantial further information for its completion? Do you think the Court went too far back in time in setting the appropriate moment for notification?

LAKE LANOUX ARBITRATION
(France v. Spain)
Ad Hoc International Arbitral Tribunal, 1957, 12 U.N. Rep. Int'l Arb. Awards 281

[This case involved a French plan to divert water which in its natural course flowed from Lake Lanoux, which is situated in France, into Spain. The Spanish government contended that the plan violated an 1866 Treaty and Additional Act between the two States and that the French project could not be executed without the prior agreement of the Parties. The following paragraphs describe the background of the dispute in some detail because the discussions between France and Spain leading to the arbitration are believed to hold important lessons concerning State practice in the field of shared natural resources.

"Lake Lanoux is situated on the south slope of the Pyrenees and on the territory of the French Republic. . . . It is fed by streams all of which rise on French territory and traverse only that territory. Its waters flow out through a single stream, the Font-Vive, which is one of the sources of the Carol River. [The latter] river, after having flowed about twenty-five kilometres measured from Lake Lanoux on French territory, crosses the Spanish boundary at Puigcerda. . . ." In 1950, Electricité de France applied to the French government for a concession to construct and operate a hydroelectric facility using water diverted from Lake Lanoux. The plan called for the construction of a dam that would increase the capacity of Lake Lanoux from 17 to 70 million cubic meters and the diversion of the lake's waters through a tunnel down a steep incline to a power station, from which it would flow toward the Ariège River. Thus, under normal conditions, no water would flow out of the lake through the Font-Vive to the Carol. The Carol and the Ariège are in different drainage basins. Waters of the former empty into the Mediterranean while those of the latter ultimately drain into the Atlantic. According to the French Memorial (brief) in the case, the project would produce sufficient electricity to meet the needs of a city of 326,000 throughout the year. The French Memorial also stated that approximately 18,000 farmers in Spain depend upon the waters of the Carol; a quarter of those waters came from Lake Lanoux.

The proposal of Electricité de France called for restoring all of the diverted waters to the Carol River in France by means of a tunnel from the Ariège to the Carol. However, the French government initially took the position that it was required to return only as much water as was necessary to satisfy the actual needs of the Spanish users. France notified Spain in 1953 that it would proceed to develop Lake Lanoux on this basis. In response, Spain requested that no work be undertaken on the project until after a meeting of the Mixed Commission of Engineers the two countries had established in 1949 to study the question of the utilization of the waters of Lake Lanoux. France agreed to a meeting of the Mixed Commission and offered assurances that no construction was planned or imminent, but noted that the relevant treaty did not require suspension of works likely to affect the system of waters at the request of the other party.

Before any meeting was held, however, France changed its position. It decided to accept the original proposal of Electricité de France to fully restore to the Carol the waters diverted from Lake Lanoux. It accordingly provided the Spanish authorities with the technical information concerning that proposal. Spain objected on the ground that the project would cause serious prejudice to Spanish interests and again requested a meeting of the Mixed Commission. France replied that since the plan in its current form would not result in any change as far as Spanish users were concerned the relevant agreement was not applicable. This meant that the agreement's requirement of prior notification did not apply. France also denied that it was under any obligation to postpone commencement of work on the project pending a meeting of the Mixed Commission. It did not object to such a meeting being held, however.

The Mixed Commission of Engineers met in August 1955, but the meeting was without result. A subsequent exchange of views between the two governments led to the formation of a Special Mixed Commission charged with preparing a proposal for the utilization of the water of Lake Lanoux for submission to the two governments. France stressed, however, that it would consider itself free to proceed, within the bounds of its rights, if the Special Commission had not concluded its work within three months. The Special Commission met in December 1955. At that meeting France offered a series of guarantees that would ensure the delivery to Spain of a quantity of water equivalent to the amount that would have flowed from Lake Lanoux but for the project. These guarantees included a double set of valves that would allow water to be released from Lake Lanoux itself in the event of technical difficulties with the restoration tunnel; a proposal to establish a mixed Franco-Spanish Commission to oversee the works and the restoration of water; the granting of access to the proposed works by a member of a Spanish Consulate who would enjoy appropriate privileges and immunities; and an assurance that irrespective of the amount of water flowing into Lake Lanoux, at least 20 million cubic meters of water per year would be restored to the Carol River, such restoration to be regulated so as to correspond to Spanish needs regardless of the quantities flowing into Lake Lanoux. Spain remained fundamentally opposed to the French plan, however, and the meeting came to naught.

A second meeting of the Special Commission was held in March 1956. France indicated at the meeting that it could offer additional guarantees to protect Spanish interests. Spain, for its part, submitted a counterproposal that involved no diversion of the waters of Lake Lanoux but would have produced 10 percent less electricity than the French plan. This initiative proved unacceptable to France. Once again, the meeting ended without result, whereupon the Special Commission terminated its work. Later in March 1956, France informed Spain that in accordance with its earlier statement it would now consider itself free to proceed with its plans, within the limits of its rights. Work on the project, which up to that point had consisted only of the construction of a road and a *telephirique,* was accordingly resumed in April. By the time the arbitral tribunal (described below) rendered its award the project had been largely completed, although no water had yet been diverted.

France and Spain referred the matter to arbitration pursuant to a 1929 Arbitration Treaty between the two countries. By a *compromis* signed in November 1956, the parties established an arbitral tribunal to which they submitted the following question:

Is the French Government justified in its contention that, in carrying out, without a prior agreement between the two Governments, works for the use of the waters of Lake Lanoux on the terms laid down in the plan and in the French proposals mentioned in the preamble to this *compromis,* it would not commit a violation of the provisions of the Treaty of Bayonne of 26 May 1866 and of the Additional Act of the same date?

The tribunal rendered its award on November 16, 1957. Excerpts from the award follow.]

1.   The public works contemplated in the French plan are situated entirely in France; the greater part, if not all, of their effects will be felt on French territory; they relate to water which is subject to French territorial sovereignty according to article 8 of the Additional Act. . . .

2.   . . . The Spanish Government bases its arguments first on the text of the Treaty and of the Additional Act of 1866. . . . But, in addition, the Spanish Government relies both on the general and traditional features of the Pyrenees boundary system and on certain rules of customary international law to interpret the Treaty and the Additional Act of 1866.

Moreover, the French Memorial . . . examines the question submitted to the Tribunal in the light of the "law of nations." The French Counter-Memorial does the same, with the following reservation: "although the question submitted to the Tribunal is clearly confined to the interpretation, in the case under consideration, of the Treaty of Bayonne . . . and of the Additional Act. . . ." In his oral pleadings, the agent of the French Government said: "the compromis does not charge the Tribunal with determining whether there are on the subject general principles of the law of nations applicable in the present case" . . ., and: "A treaty is interpreted in the context of positive international law at such time as it may be applied." . . .

Since the question submitted by the compromis relates solely to the Treaty and the Additional Act of 1866, the Tribunal will apply, with regard to each particular point, the following rules: Clear provisions of treaty law do not call for any interpretation; . . . when there is matter for interpretation, this should be done according to international law; international law does not establish any absolute and rigid system of interpretation; it is, therefore, permissible to take into consideration the spirit which governed the Pyrenees treaties as well as the rules of customary international law. . . .

3.   This dispute may be reduced to two fundamental questions:

(a) Would the works for the use of the waters of Lake Lanoux . . . constitute in themselves a violation of the rights granted to Spain by the substantive provisions of the Treaty of Bayonne of 26 May 1866 and the Additional Act of the same date?

(b) If the answer to the preceding question is in the negative, would the execution of these works constitute a violation of the provisions of the Treaty . . . and . . . the Additional Act . . ., on the ground that these provisions made execution subject in any event to a prior agreement between the two Governments or because other rules of article 11 of the

Additional Act concerning the negotiations between the two Governments had not been observed?

I.   AS TO THE FIRST QUESTION (STATED UNDER 3, A)

[The Tribunal discussed articles 9–11 and 18 of the Additional Act. Article 9 provides as follows:

For watercourses flowing from one country to the other, or which form a boundary, each government recognizes, subject to verification when appropriate, the legality of irrigations, works and domestic uses currently existing in the other state, by virtue of concession, title or by prescription, except that only such water will be used as is necessary to satisfy actual needs, that abuses must be eliminated and that this recognition will in no way infringe the respective rights of the governments to authorize works of public utility, on condition that just compensation be paid.

Article 10 provides that any water remaining after actual needs have been satisfied is to be apportioned between the parties. Article 11 requires that when new works are proposed that might affect users of a watercourse in the other country, prior notice be given to the appropriate administrative authority in that country so that the users in question may lodge a timely claim with the competent authorities in the country in which the works have been proposed. Article 18 provides that an international commission of engineers is to determine the present use of water in each country in order to allocate the necessary quantity of water and to eliminate abuses, as required by Article 9 and other articles.]

6.   Indeed, thanks to the restitution effected by the mechanism described above, no guaranteed user will be injured in his enjoyment of the waters (this has not been the subject of any claim founded on Article 9); at the lowest water level, the volume of the surplus waters of the Carol at the boundary would at no time suffer a diminution; it may even, by virtue of the minimum guarantee by France, enjoy an increase in volume assured by the waters of the Ariège that flow naturally to the Atlantic.

This conclusion might have been attacked in several ways.

It could have been argued that the works would result in the pollution of the waters of the Carol, or that the returned waters would have a chemical composition or a temperature or some other characteristic that could injure Spanish interests. Spain could then have claimed that its rights had been impaired in violation of the Additional Act. Neither the dossier nor the arguments in this case bear any trace of such an allegation.

It could also have been claimed that, by their technical character, the works contemplated by the French plan could not in fact ensure the restitution of a volume corresponding to the natural contribution of Lake

Lanoux to the Carol, because of defectiveness either of the measuring instruments or of the restoration mechanisms. The question was touched upon in the Spanish Counter-Memorial ..., which underlined the "extraordinary complexity" of the control procedures, their "very onerous" character and the "risks of damage or of negligence in the handling of the gates and of the barrier in the tunnel." But it has never been alleged that the planned works have any other character or entail any other risks than works of the same kind that are today widespread all over the world. It has not been clearly asserted that the planned works would entail a risk that is abnormal in neighborly relations or in the utilization of waters. As we have seen above, the technical guarantees for the restitution of the waters are as satisfactory as possible. If, despite the precautions that have been taken, the restitution of the waters were to suffer from an accident, such would only be an occasional occurrence and, according to the two parties, would not constitute a violation of Article 9.

7.   But the Spanish government takes a different position. In the arbitration *compromis,* it had already claimed that the French plan "alters the natural conditions of the hydrographic basin of Lake Lanoux, by diverting its waters to the Ariège and thereby making the return of the waters to the Carol physically dependent on the will of man, which will lead to the *de facto* predominance of one Party instead of the equality of the two Parties contemplated by the Treaty of Bayonne of 26 May 1866 and by the Additional act of the same date."

. . . In the statement of its case, [the Spanish government] referred to article 12 of the Additional Act:

[The lower lands are subject to receiving from the higher lands of the neighboring country the waters that naturally flow therefrom including what they carry, without the hand of man having contributed thereto. There may be constructed neither a dam nor an obstacle of any kind capable of harming the upper riparians, who are likewise prohibited from doing anything that might increase the burden of the servitude of the lower lands.]

According to the Spanish Government, this provision confirms the notion that neither of the Parties may, without the consent of the other, alter the natural order of the water's flow. The Spanish Counter Memorial. . . . acknowledges, however, that: "From the moment that the will of man intervenes to carry out any hydraulic development whatever, an extra-physical element acts on the current and alters what Nature established." Consequently, the Spanish Government does not attribute an absolute meaning to respect for natural order; according to the Counter Memorial. . . : "A State has the right to use unilaterally the part of a river which traverses it to the extent that this use is likely to cause on the territory of another State a limited harm only, a minimal inconvenience, which comes within the bounds of what is implied by good neighbourliness." In reality, it seems that the Spanish thesis is twofold and covers, on the one hand, the prohibition, without the consent of the other Party, of compensation between two basins, in spite of the equivalence of withdrawal and return and, on the other hand, the prohibition, without the consent of the other Party, of all actions that may create along with a *de facto* inequality, the physical possibility of a violation of law.

The two points should be examined in order.

8.   The prohibition of compensation between two basins, without the consent of the other Party, despite the equivalence of withdrawal and return, would result in a general bar to the taking of water from a waterway belonging to river basin A for the benefit of river basin B, even if this withdrawal was offset by a strictly equivalent return from a waterway of river basin B for the benefit of river basin A. The Tribunal, from the viewpoint of physical geography, cannot disregard the reality of each river basin, which constitutes, as the Spanish case . . . contends, "a whole." But this fact does not justify the absolute consequences which the Spanish thesis seeks to draw from it. The unity of a basin is supported at the legal level only to the extent that it conforms to the realities of life. Water, which is by nature a fungible thing, may be restored without alteration of its qualities from the viewpoint of human needs. A withdrawal with return, as contemplated in the French plan, does not alter a state of affairs established in response to the demands of life in society.

The state of modern technology leads more and more frequently to the acknowledgement that water used in the generation of electric power need not be returned to its natural course. The water is taken from a constantly higher point and it is carried still lower, and in the course of this process it is sometimes diverted to another river basin, in the same State or in another [state] within the same federation or even in a third State. In federations, court decisions have recognized the validity of this latter practice [the tribunal cited Wyoming v. Colorado, 259 U.S 419; cases cited by the authors D.J.E. Berber & G. Sauser-Hall; and case law of the Swiss Federal Tribunal].

The Tribunal considers, therefore, that withdrawal with return, as provided in the French plan and proposals, is not in conflict with the Treaty and Additional Act of 1866.

9.   In another connexion, the Spanish Government challenged the legality of works carried out on the territory of one of the signatories of the Treaty and of the Additional Act, if they were calculated to enable it, even in violation of its international commitments, to bring pressure to bear on the other signatory. This rule was said to follow from the fact that

the treaties in question established the principle of equality among States. Specifically, Spain feels that France does not have the right to procure for itself, by public works, the physical possibility of stopping the flow of the Lanoux water or the return of an equivalent quantity of water. It is not for the Tribunal to judge the reasons or experiences which might lead the Spanish Government to give expression to a certain anxiety. But it is not alleged that the purpose of the works in questions, aside from the satisfaction of French interests, is to create a means of at least potential injury to Spanish interests; that would be all the more unlikely as France could only partially exhaust the resources represented by the discharge of the Carol, as she would also affect all the French land irrigated by the Carol, and as she would expose herself along the whole boundary to formidable reprisals.

On the other hand, the French Government's proposals, which are an integral part of its plan, include "the assurance that it will not in any case, interfere with the regime thus established." . . . The Tribunal must, therefore, answer the question submitted by the *compromis* on the basis of this assurance. It could not be alleged that despite this commitment Spain would not have a sufficient guarantee, for it is a well-established general principle of law that bad faith is not presumed. Furthermore, it has not been contended that either of the two States at any time intentionally infringed a rule relating to the regime of the waters to the detriment of the other. Moreover, although based on a just spirit of reciprocity, the Treaties of Bayonne established only equality in law and not equality in fact. If it were otherwise, they would have had to forbid on both sides of the boundary any installations and works of a military order which could give to one of the States a *de facto* predominance which it might use to violate its international commitments. But it is necessary to go farther still; man's growing mastery of the forces and secrets of nature has placed in his hands instruments which he may use to violate his obligations or for the common good; the danger of misuse has not resulted, up to the present, in making the possession of these means dependent on the authorization of the States which may be threatened. Even if viewed solely from the standpoint of the relations of neighbours, the political danger alleged by the Spanish Government would be not more exceptional than the technical risk mentioned above. In any case, there is not, in the Treaty and Additional Act of 26 May 1866 or in the generally accepted principles of international law, a rule which forbids a State, acting to protect its legitimate interests, from placing itself in a situation which enables it in fact, in violation of its international obligations, to do even serious injury to a neighbouring State. It remains still to be determined whether the French plan conflicts with the substantive rules laid down by article 11. This question will be examined further on, in connexion with the general terms of this article. . . .

Subject to this last reservation, the Tribunal replies in the negative to the first question, set forth in paragraph 3 *a.*

II. AS TO THE SECOND QUESTION (STATED UNDER 3, B)

10. In the *compromis,* the Spanish Government had already declared that in its opinion the execution of the French plan required "the prior agreement of the two Governments, and that in the absence of such agreement the country that proposed the project is not free to undertake the works." In the proceedings, both written and oral, the Government developed this approach, completing it in particular by a statement of the principles which should govern the negotiations leading to this prior agreement. Two obligations were said to rest upon the State which wished to undertake the proposed works: the most important was to reach a prior agreement with the other State concerned; the other which was only secondary, was to observe the other rules laid down by article 11 of the Additional Act.

The arguments submitted by the Spanish Government are put forth, moreover, at two levels; the Spanish Government bases its position, on the one hand, on the Treaty and Additional Act of 1866, and on the other hand on the system of joint community pasturage rights *(faceries* and *compascuitis)* which exits at the Pyrenees frontier and on the generally accepted rules of international law. The last two sources would make it possible first, to interpret the Treaty and Additional Act of 1866, and then, in a broader perspective, to demonstrate the existence of an unwritten general rule of international law. There are said to be precedents establishing that rule in the traditions of the system of joint community pasturage rights, in the provisions of the Pyrenees treaties, and in the international practice of States concerning the industrial use of international waterways.

11. Before considering the Spanish arguments, the Tribunal believes it would be useful to make some very general observations on the nature of the obligations alleged to be incumbent on the French Government. To admit that in a given matter competence may no longer be exercised except on the condition of or by means of an agreement between two States is to place an essential restriction on the sovereignty of a State, and it may be allowed only if there is conclusive proof. Undoubtedly international practice discloses some specific cases in which this assumption is proved; thus, sometimes two States exercise jurisdiction jointly over certain territories (indivisum, co-imperium or condominium); similarly, in certain international institutions, the representatives of States exercise jointly a certain competence on behalf of States or on behalf of organizations. But these cases are exceptional and international case law does not readily recognize their existence, especially when they

infringe upon the territorial sovereignty of a State, which would be true in the present case.

In fact, to evaluate in its essence the need for a prior agreement, it is necessary to adopt the hypothesis that the States concerned cannot arrive at an agreement. In that case, it would have to be admitted that a State which ordinarily is competent has lost the right to act alone as a consequence of the unconditional and discretionary opposition of another State. This is to admit a "right of consent," a "right of veto," which at the discretion of one State paralyses another State's exercise of its territorial competence.

For this reason, international practice prefers to resort to less extreme solutions, limiting itself to requiring States to seek the terms of an agreement by prior negotiations without making the exercise of their competence conditional on the conclusion of this agreement. Thus reference is made, although often incorrectly, to "an obligation to negotiate an agreement." In reality, the commitments thus assumed by States take very diverse forms, and their scope varies according to the way in which they are defined and according to the procedures for their execution; but the reality of the obligations thus assumed cannot be questioned, and they may be enforced, for example, in the case of an unjustified breaking off of conversations, unusual delays, disregard of established procedures, systematic refusal to give consideration to proposals or adverse interests, and more generally in the case of infringement of the rules of good faith. (The Tacna-Arica Case, in United Nations, *Reports of International Arbitral Awards,* Vol. II, pp. 921 *et seq.;* Case concerning Railway Traffic between Lithuania and Poland, in P.C.I.J., *Series A/B* 42, pp. 108 *et seq.)* In the light of these general observations and with reference to the present case, we shall consider successively whether a prior agreement is necessary and whether the other rules established by article 11 of the Additional Act have been observed.

A) NECESSITY OF A PRIOR AGREEMENT

12. We shall consider first, therefore, whether the proposition that the execution of the French plan is conditional on the prior consent of the Spanish Government is justified by reference to the system of joint community pasturage rights or to the generally accepted principles of international law; the data collected is supposed to help, if necessary, to interpret the Treaty and Additional Act of 1866 or, better still, according to the more general form given to the Spanish thesis, to establish the existence of a general principle of law or custom which was recognized, *inter alia,* by the Treaty and the Additional Act of 1866. . . .

[After examining the question, the Tribunal concluded that] it is impossible to extend the system of joint community pasturage rights beyond the bounds assigned to it by the Treaties, or to derive from it an idea of a generalized "community" which would have any legal content whatever. As for the appeal to the idea of a "frontier zone," an obligation cannot be added to those laid down by positive law merely by the use of the vocabulary of legal doctrine.

13. The Spanish Government also attempted to establish the existing positive international law. . . . Some of the principles for which proof is offered, assuming them to be established, are without relevance to the matter now under consideration. Thus, while admittedly there is a rule prohibiting the upper riparian State from altering the waters of a river in circumstances calculated to do serious injury to the lower riparian State, such a principle has no application to the present case, since it was agreed by the Tribunal, with respect to the first question considered above, that the French plan did not alter the waters of the Carol. In fact, States today are well aware of the importance of the conflicting interests involved in the industrial use of international rivers and of the necessity of reconciling some of these interests with others through mutual concessions. The only way to achieve these compromises of interests is the conclusion of agreements on a more and more comprehensive basis. International practice reflects the conviction that States should seek to conclude such agreements; there would thus be an obligation for States to agree in good faith to all negotiations and contacts which should, through a wide confrontation of interests and reciprocal goodwill, place them in the best circumstances to conclude agreements. This point will be considered later on in establishing the obligations of France and Spain concerning contacts and negotiations prior to the execution of a plan such as the one for Lake Lanoux.

But international practice does not permit us, so far, to go beyond this conclusion; the rule that States may use the hydraulic power of international watercourses only if a *prior* agreement between the States concerned has been concluded cannot be established as a custom or, still less, as a general principle of law. In this connexion the history of the drafting of the multilateral Geneva Convention of 9 December 1923 relating to the Development of Hydraulic Power affecting more than one State is very significant. The initial draft was based on the idea of compulsory prior agreements for developing the hydraulic power of international waterways. But this proposal was rejected, and the Convention, in its final form, provided (art. 1) that it "in no way affects the right belonging to each State, within the limits of international law, to carry out on its own territory any operations for the development of hydraulic power which it may consider desirable"; it is merely provided that the signatory States concerned have an obligation to agree to a joint investigation of a scheme of development; the carrying out of this program is not compulsory except for States which have formally undertaken to do so.

No more than the traditions of the Pyrenees does generally accepted international law provide a basis for interpreting the Treaty and Additional Act of 1866 in a sense favourable to the necessity of a prior agreement or, still less, for concluding that there is a general principle of law or custom to this effect.

14. A rule requiring an agreement prior to the hydraulic development of an international waterway can exist between Spain and France only as a result of a treaty. . . . [The Tribunal, after examining the agreements in force between the parties, held that they contained no such rule.] [With respect to the other obligations under article 11 of the Additional Act, the Tribunal said:] 21. Article 11 of the Additional Act imposes a twofold obligation on States in which works or new concessions susceptible of changing the regime or the volume of a watercourse traversing the two States are proposed. One is to give prior notice to the competent authorities of the neighbouring country; the other is to develop a system of complaints and of safeguards for all the interests involved on one side and the other.

[France claimed that since it had found that the planned works would cause no harm to Spanish interests, it had no obligation to notify the Spanish authorities.] A State that may suffer the repercussions of works undertaken by a neighboring State is the sole judge of its interests, and if the latter has not taken the initiative, the right of the other [i.e., the potentially affected State] to demand notification of planned works or concessions cannot be denied.

It has not been disputed that France has satisfied the obligation of notice as far as the development of Lake Lanoux is concerned.

22. The content of the second obligation is more difficult to determine. The "complaints" mentioned in article 11 relate to the various rights protected by the Additional Act, but the main question is to establish how "all the interests involved on one side and the other" should be safeguarded. First, it is necessary to determine which "interests" should be safeguarded. A strict interpretation of article 11 would support the conclusion that only interests corresponding to a right of the riparian population were involved. Various considerations already pointed out by the Tribunal lead however to a broader interpretation. Consideration must be given to all interests, whatever their nature, which may be affected by the works undertaken, even if they do not amount to a right. Only this solution is in accord with the terms of article 16, the spirit of the Pyrenees Treaties, and the trends apparent in current international practice as regards hydro-electric development.

BASIC PRINCIPLES OF INTERNATIONAL ENVIRONMENTAL LAW

206   **CH. 4**

The second question is to determine the procedure whereby these interests can be safeguarded. Although this procedure necessarily involves negotiations, it cannot be reduced to purely formal requirements, such as taking note of complaints, protests or expressions of displeasure submitted by the lower riparian State. The Tribunal considers that the upper riparian State, under the rules of good faith, has an obligation to take into consideration the various interests concerned, to seek to give them every satisfaction compatible with the pursuit of its own interests and to show that it has, in this matter, a real desire to reconcile the interests of the other riparian with its own.

It is difficult to determine if such an obligation has been met. Nevertheless, without substituting himself for the Parties, the judge is able to undertake this determination on the basis of the evidence furnished by the negotiations.

23. In the present case, the Spanish Government charges that the French Government did not draw up the development plan for the waters of Lake Lanoux on a basis of absolute equality. This charge is twofold: it relates to both procedure and substance. With regard to procedure, it is suggested that the French Government imposed its plan unilaterally without associating the Spanish Government in a joint search for an acceptable solution. As to substance, it is contended that the French plan does not maintain an equitable balance between French interests and Spanish interests. The French plan, it is argued, perfectly serves French interests, especially those directed toward electric power production designed to meet peak demand, but does not take sufficient account of Spanish interests in respect of irrigation. According to the Spanish Government, the French Government refused to consider plans which, in the Spanish Government's opinion, would have involved a slight sacrifice for French interests and great advantages for the Spanish agricultural economy. Spain bases its argument specifically on the following facts: during the meeting of the Special Joint Commission at Madrid (12–17 December 1955), the French delegation made a comparison of three development plans for Lake Lanoux and pointed out the considerable advantages which, in its opinion, the first plan (corresponding to the final plan) had in comparison with the other two. The Spanish delegation, having no particular objection to these latter plans, declared that it was prepared to accept either of the two. The French delegation deemed itself unable to renounce the execution of plan No. 1, which was more favourable to French interests and based, in its opinion, on a right. . . .

From the standpoint of principle, the Spanish thesis cannot be accepted by the Tribunal, for it is inclined to put rights and mere interests on the same level. Article 11 of the Additional Act makes a distinction between them, which both Parties have reproduced in the fundamental statement of their theses at the beginning of the *compromis:*

Considering that, in the opinion of the French Government, the carrying out of its plan ... would not prejudice any of the rights or interests referred to in the Treaty of Bayonne of 26 May 1866 and in the Additional Act of the same date;

Considering that, in the opinion of the Spanish Government, the carrying out of this plan would prejudice Spanish interests and rights.

France may exercise its rights; it may not disregard Spanish interests. Spain may demand respect for its rights and consideration of its interests.

As to procedure, the upper riparian State has, procedurally, a right of initiative; it is not obliged to involve the lower riparian State in the preparation of its plans. If during the negotiations the lower riparian State submits plans to it, the upper riparian State should examine them, but it has the right to prefer the solution embodied in its plan, if it takes into consideration in a reasonable manner the interests of the lower riparian State.

24. In the case of Lake Lanoux, France adhered throughout to the solution which involved a diversion of the water of the Carol to the Ariège, with complete return. In making this choice, France is merely exercising a right; the Lake Lanoux development works are being carried out on French territory, the burden and the responsibility of the undertaking rests on France, and France is the sole judge of the public works to be carried out on its territory, subject to article 9 and 10 of the Additional Act, which the French plan does not infringe.

For its part, Spain may not invoke a right to have the development of Lake Lanoux based on the needs of Spanish agriculture. In fact, if France renounced all the works planned on its territory, Spain could not require other works which conformed to its wishes to be carried out. It, therefore, may assert its interests simply to obtain terms providing reasonable safeguards for them within the limits of the plan adopted by France. It remains to be decided whether this requirement has been met. ... In determining whether France, both in its negotiations and in its proposals, took Spanish interests sufficiently into consideration, note must be taken of the intimate connection between the obligation to take adverse interests into account in the course of negotiations and the obligation to give a reasonable place to such interests in the solution adopted. A State which has conducted negotiations with understanding and good faith in accordance with article 11 of the Additional Act is not released from the obligation to give a reasonable place to adverse interests in the solution adopted because the conversations have been interrupted, even by the intransigence of its partner. Conversely, in appraising the way in which a plan takes account of the interests concerned, the manner in which the negotiations have been conducted, the interests presented and the price which each of the Parties was prepared to pay to safeguard them, are the main factors in establishing the merit of the plan in relation to the obligations of article 11 of the Additional Act.

In view of all the above-mentioned circumstances of the case, the Tribunal is of the opinion that the French plan satisfies the obligations of article 11 of the Additional Act.

FOR THESE REASONS:

The Tribunal decides to reply in the affirmative to the question set forth in article 1 of the *compromis*. In carrying out, without a prior agreement between the two Governments, works for the use of the waters of Lake Lanoux on the terms laid down in the Plan for the Utilization of the Waters of Lake Lanoux, due notice of which was given to the Governor of Gerona Province on 21 January 1954 and of which the representatives of Spain on the Pyrenees Commission were informed during the Commission's session from 3 to 14 November 1955, and in accordance with the proposals submitted by the French delegation to the Special Joint Commission on 13 December 1955, the French Government would not commit a violation of the provisions of the Treaty of Bayonne of 26 May 1866 and of the Additional Act of that date.

NOTES AND QUESTIONS

1.   *Look out, here it comes!* What safeguards did the tribunal establish to prevent France from simply informing Spain that it was going to build this project, without taking Spanish interests into account?

2.   *Isn't this a treaty case?* Both France and Spain evidently believed that general international law had an important role to play in the resolution of the case, despite the fact that the question they posed to the tribunal was confined to whether the Treaty of Bayonne and the Additional Act required the prior consent of Spain for the French project. The two countries, in their memorials, extensively analyzed customary international law as it applied to the dispute. *See* J. Laylin & R. Bianchi, *The Role of Adjudication in International River Disputes: The Lake Lanoux Case*, 53 Am J. Intl. L. 30, at 42–43 (1959). And, in its award, the tribunal had broad recourse to customary international law in interpreting and filling gaps in the relevant agreements. Note in this connection that Spain appears to have argued, inter alia, that the relevant agreements simply recognized a general principle of law or custom concerning the necessity of a prior agreement. See paragraph 12 of the award. What would be the effect of the tribunal's acceptance of this argument?

3.   *No need for prior consent? Great, then, full speed ahead!* How did the tribunal mediate between the considerations favoring a requirement of prior consent and those opposed to it? Doesn't Spain's sovereignty give it a right to prior consent? What about France's sovereignty?

4. *Go into that room and talk to each other nicely!* Perhaps the most notable area in which the tribunal elaborated on principles of general international law as they applied to the dispute was that of the obligation to negotiate. In holding that France was not required to obtain Spain's consent prior to implementing its plans, the tribunal explained that "international practice prefers to resort to less extreme solutions," namely, requiring the States concerned to attempt to reach an agreement through negotiations. But is the obligation to negotiate a meaningful one? Can States satisfy it simply by being polite and appearing reasonable? Does it encourage States to inflate their initial positions in order to be able to modify their "demands" without really conceding anything of importance to them? What functions or interests of the international community does it serve, if any? Finally, do you believe France satisfied the obligation to negotiate as that obligation was defined by the tribunal?

5. *I can't define it, but I know it when I see it.* In the *North Sea Continental Shelf* cases, the Court explained the meaning of the obligation to negotiate in the following way:

> [T]he parties are under an obligation to enter into negotiations with a view to arriving at an agreement, and not merely to go through a formal process of negotiation as a sort of prior condition for the automatic application of a certain method of delimitation in the absence of agreement; they are under an obligation so to conduct themselves that the negotiations are meaningful, which will not be the case when either of them insists upon its own position without contemplating any modification of it; . . .

> . . . Defining the content of the obligation to negotiate, the Permanent Court [of International Justice], in its Advisory Opinion in the case of *Railway Traffic between Lithuania and Poland,* said that the obligation was "not only to enter into negotiations but also to pursue them as far as possible with a view to concluding agreements," even if an obligation to negotiate did not imply an obligation to reach agreement *(P.C.I.J., Series A/B, No. 42,* 1931, at p. 116). . . .

North Sea Continental Shelf cases (Germany/Denmark; Germany/The Netherlands), 1969 I.C.J. Rep. 3, at 47–48. Is the upshot that "negotiate" means . . . "negotiate?"

6. *Take your time making up your mind.* What should be the obligation of the State whose proposed project is before a tribunal in a case like *Lake Lanoux* or *Pulp Mills*? Can the State continue work on it while the tribunal is deliberating? Is your answer affected by the fact that France resumed work on the project some seven months before the arbitration tribunal was established and had largely completed it by the time the tribunal handed down its award? And recall that the Botnia plant had been operating for some two years by the time the Court issued its judgment in *Pulp Mills*. One possible solution is for the party seeking to stop a project to request the court

or arbitral tribunal for provisional measures ordering the other State to halt work on the project until the case is decided. Pakistan did this in the *Kishenganga* case, obtaining an order preventing most construction on India's Kishenganga dam project until after rendition of the award. Order of September 23, 2011, on the Interim Measures Application of Pakistan of June 6, 2011, available at http://www.pca-cpa.org/showpageb106.html?pag_id =1392. Provisional measures were also requested by Argentina in *Pulp Mills* but the Court declined the request, largely on the strength of Uruguay's assurance that it would abide by any judgment the Court rendered in the case. *Pulp Mills on the River Uruguay* (Argentina v. Uruguay), Provisional Measures, Order of 13 July 2006, *2006 I.C.J. Rep.* 113.

RIO DECLARATION ON ENVIRONMENT AND DEVELOPMENT, PRINCIPLE 19

Adopted by the United Nations Conference on Environment and Development, June 14, 1992 U.N. Doc. A/CONF.151/5/Rev.1, June 13, 1992, reprinted in 31 ILM 874 (1992)

Principle 19

States shall provide prior and timely notification and relevant information to potentially affected States on activities that may have a significant adverse transboundary environmental effect and shall consult with those States at an early stage and in good faith.

INTERNATIONAL LAW COMMISSION, DRAFT ARTICLES ON PREVENTION OF TRANSBOUNDARY HARM FROM HAZARDOUS ACTIVITIES

Adopted on second reading in 2001, 2001 ILC Rep. 373–375

[Articles 1–10 are set forth in section A, above. Articles 8 and 9 are reproduced here as well for ease of reference.]

Article 8
Notification and Information

1. If the assessment referred to in article 7 [requiring that authorization of an activity that may cause transboundary harm be based on an assessment of the possibility of such harm] indicates a risk of causing significant transboundary harm, the State of origin shall provide the State likely to be affected with timely notification of the risk and the assessment and shall transmit to it the available technical and all other relevant information on which the assessment is based.

2. The State of origin shall not take any decision on authorization of the activity pending the receipt, within a period not exceeding six months, of the response from the State likely to be affected.

Article 9
Consultations on Preventive Measures

1.   The States concerned shall enter into consultations, at the request of any of them, with a view to achieving acceptable solutions regarding measures to be adopted in order to prevent significant transboundary harm or at any event to minimize the risk thereof. The States concerned shall agree, at the commencement of such consultations, on a reasonable time-frame for the consultations.

2.   The States concerned shall seek solutions based on an equitable balance of interests in the light of article 10.

3.   If the consultations referred to in paragraph 1 fail to produce an agreed solution, the State of origin shall nevertheless take into account the interests of the State likely to be affected in case it decides to authorize the activity to be pursued, without prejudice to the rights of any State likely to be affected. . . .

Article 11
Procedures in the Absence of Notification

1.   If a State has reasonable grounds to believe that an activity planned or carried out in the State of origin may involve a risk of causing significant transboundary harm to it, it may request the State of origin to apply the provision of article 8. The request shall be accompanied by a documented explanation setting forth its grounds.

2.   In the event that the State of origin nevertheless finds that it is not under an obligation to provide a notification under article 8, it shall so inform the requesting State within a reasonable time, providing a documented explanation setting forth the reasons for such finding. If this finding does not satisfy that State, at its request, the two States shall promptly enter into consultations in the manner indicated in article 9.

3.   During the course of the consultations, the State of origin shall, if so requested by the other State, arrange to introduce appropriate and feasible measures to minimize the risk and, where appropriate, to suspend the activity in question for a reasonable period.

Article 12
Exchange of Information

While the activity is being carried out, the States concerned shall exchange in a timely manner all available information concerning that activity relevant to preventing significant transboundary harm or at any event minimizing the risk thereof. Such an exchange of information shall continue until such time as the States concerned consider it appropriate even after the activity is terminated.

Article 13
Information to the Public

States concerned shall, by such means as are appropriate, provide the public likely to be affected by an activity within the scope of the present articles with relevant information relating to that activity, the risk involved and the harm which might result and ascertain their views.

Article 14
National Security and Industrial Secrets

Data and information vital to the national security of the State of origin or to the protection of industrial secrets or concerning intellectual property may be withheld, but the State of origin shall cooperate in good faith with the State likely to be affected in providing as much information as possible under the circumstances.

NOTES AND QUESTIONS

1.   *Does the exception swallow the rule?* Does Article 14 leave the State of origin too much leeway? The fig leaf of "national security" has been used by States in the past to cover many sins, both domestically and internationally. Is a provision like Article 14 simply inevitable in light of international realities or is it unnecessary?

2.   *Look out II!* Several of the procedural rules in the hazardous activities draft are modeled on those contained in the ILC's draft articles on international watercourses, which formed the basis for the negotiation of the 1997 UN Convention on the Law of the Non-Navigational Uses of International Watercourses, U.N. Doc. A/RES/51/869, 21 May 1997, 36 ILM 700 (1997). The procedural rules in the UN Watercourses Convention are quite extensive, constituting the largest section of the treaty (Part III, articles 11–19). Why would this be so?

CORFU CHANNEL CASE (MERITS)
(United Kingdom v. Albania)
1949 I.CJ. Rep. 4, 22

[The facts of the case are given above. The following excerpt is reproduced again here for convenience of reference.]

. . . The obligations incumbent upon the Albanian authorities consisted in notifying, for the benefit of shipping in general, the existence of a minefield in Albanian territorial waters and in warning the approaching British warships of the imminent danger to which the minefield exposed them. Such obligations are based, not on the Hague Convention of 1907, No. VIII, which is applicable in time of war, but on certain general and well-recognized principles, namely: elementary considerations of humanity, even more exacting in peace than in war; the principle of the freedom of maritime communication; and every State's obligation not to allow knowingly its territory to be used for acts contrary to the rights of other States.

NOTES AND QUESTIONS

1.   *The law of "elementary considerations of humanity?"* Where did this basis of the obligations of notification and warning of known dangers come from? Natural law? Thin air? Why do you suppose the Court felt it necessary to cite these "considerations" as a basis for the obligations?

2.   *I have no duty to warn if my nuclear reactor explodes, only if mines that somehow got into my waters do.* Are the obligations of notification and warning of known dangers applicable to environmental disasters, such as the explosions at the Chernobyl nuclear plant on April 26, 1986? This situation is discussed in Chapter 6, below.

b.   Environmental Impact Assessment

RIO DECLARATION ON ENVIRONMENT AND DEVELOPMENT, PRINCIPLE 17

Adopted by the United Nations Conference on Environment and Development,
June 14, 1992

Principle 17

Environmental impact assessment, as a national instrument, shall be undertaken for proposed activities that are likely to have a significant adverse impact on the environment and are subject to a decision of a competent national authority.

QUESTION

What is the effect of this principle? Does it mean that countries are required to undertake environmental impact assessments (EIAs) for projects that won't affect any other State? And again, what is the normative character of this principle? Is it binding law? Is it soft law? If the latter, does that mean States are free to act in ways that are inconsistent with it?

PULP MILLS ON THE RIVER URUGUAY

(Argentina v. Uruguay)
2010 ICJ Rep. 14, 82–84

[The facts of this case were summarized earlier.]

(a) *Environmental Impact Assessment*

203.   The Court will now turn to the relationship between the need for an environmental impact assessment, where the planned activity is liable to cause harm to a shared resource and transboundary harm, and the

obligations of the Parties under Article 41 *(a)* and *(b)* of the 1975 Statute. [13] The Parties agree on the necessity of conducting an environmental impact assessment. Argentina maintains that the obligations under the 1975 Statute viewed together impose an obligation to conduct an environmental impact assessment prior to authorizing Botnia to construct the plant. Uruguay also accepts that it is under such an obligation. The Parties disagree, however, with regard to the scope and content of the environmental impact assessment that Uruguay should have carried out with respect to the Orion (Botnia) mill project. Argentina maintains in the first place that Uruguay failed to ensure that "full environmental assessments [had been] produced, prior to its decision to authorize the construction . . ." ; and in the second place that "Uruguay's decisions [were] . . . based on unsatisfactory environmental assessments", in particular because Uruguay failed to take account of all potential impacts from the mill, even though international law and practice require it, and refers in this context to the 1991 Convention on Environmental Impact Assessment in a Transboundary Context of the United Nations Economic Commission for Europe (hereinafter the "Espoo Convention") (*UNTS*, Vol. 1989, p. 309), and the 1987 Goals and Principles of Environmental Impact Assessment of the United Nations Environment Programme (hereinafter the "UNEP Goals and Principles") (*UNEP/WG.152/4 Annex (1987)*, document adopted by UNEP Governing Council at its 14th Session (Dec. 14/25 (1987)). Uruguay accepts that, in accordance with international practice, an environmental impact assessment of the Orion (Botnia) mill was necessary, but argues that international law does not impose any conditions upon the content of such an assessment, the preparation of which being a national, not international, procedure, at least where the project in question is not one common to several States. According to Uruguay, the only requirements international law imposes on it are that there must be assessments of the project's potential harmful transboundary effects on people, property and the environment of other States, as required by State practice and the International Law Commission 2001 draft Articles on Prevention of

---

[13] Article 41 provides as follows:

"Without prejudice to the functions assigned to the Commission in this respect, the parties undertake:

(a) to protect and preserve the aquatic environment and, in particular, to prevent its pollution, by prescribing appropriate rules and [adopting appropriate] measures in accordance with applicable international agreements and in keeping, where relevant, with the guidelines and recommendations of international technical bodies;

(b) not to reduce in their respective legal systems:

    1. the technical requirements in force for preventing water pollution, and

    2. the severity of the penalties established for violations;

(c) to inform one another of any rules which they plan to prescribe with regard to water pollution in order to establish equivalent rules in their respective legal systems."

(Editors' footnote.)

Transboundary Harm from Hazardous Activities, without there being any need to assess remote or purely speculative risks.

204.   It is the opinion of the Court that in order for the Parties properly to comply with their obligations under Article 41 *(a)* and *(b)* of the 1975 Statute, they must, for the purposes of protecting and preserving the aquatic environment with respect to activities which may be liable to cause transboundary harm, carry out an environmental impact assessment. As the Court has observed in the case concerning the *Dispute Regarding Navigational and Related Rights*,

> "there are situations in which the parties' intent upon conclusion of the treaty was, or may be presumed to have been, to give the terms used—or some of them—a meaning or content capable of evolving, not one fixed once and for all, so as to make allowance for, among other things, developments in international law" (*Dispute Regarding Navigational and Related Rights (Costa Rica v. Nicaragua), Judgment, I.C.J. Reports 2009*, p. 242, para. 64).

In this sense, the obligation to protect and preserve, under Article 41*(a)* of the Statute, has to be interpreted in accordance with a practice, which in recent years has gained so much acceptance among States that it may now be considered a requirement under general international law to undertake an environmental impact assessment where there is a risk that the proposed industrial activity may have a significant adverse impact in a transboundary context, in particular, on a shared resource. Moreover, due diligence, and the duty of vigilance and prevention which it implies, would not be considered to have been exercised, if a party planning works liable to affect the régime of the river or the quality of its waters did not undertake an environmental impact assessment on the potential effects of such works.

205.   The Court observes that neither the 1975 Statute nor general international law specify the scope and content of an environmental impact assessment. It points out moreover that Argentina and Uruguay are not parties to the Espoo Convention. Finally, the Court notes that the other instrument to which Argentina refers in support of its arguments, namely, the UNEP Goals and Principles, is not binding on the Parties, but, as guidelines issued by an international technical body, has to be taken into account by each Party in accordance with Article 41*(a)* in adopting measures within its domestic regulatory framework. Moreover, this instrument provides only that the "environmental effects in an EIA should be assessed with a degree of detail commensurate with their likely environmental significance" (Principle 5) without giving any indication of minimum core components of the assessment. Consequently, it is the view of the Court that it is for each State to determine in its domestic legislation or in the authorization process for the project, the specific

content of the environmental impact assessment required in each case, having regard to the nature and magnitude of the proposed development and its likely adverse impact on the environment as well as to the need to exercise due diligence in conducting such an assessment. The Court also considers that an environmental impact assessment must be conducted prior to the implementation of a project. Moreover, once operations have started and, where necessary, throughout the life of the project, continuous monitoring of its effects on the environment shall be undertaken.

. . .

(ii) *Consultation of the affected populations*

215.   The Parties disagree on the extent to which the populations likely to be affected by the construction of the Orion (Botnia) mill, particularly on the Argentine side of the river, were consulted in the course of the environmental impact assessment. While both Parties agree that consultation of the affected populations should form part of an environmental impact assessment, Argentina asserts that international law imposes specific obligations on States in this regard. In support of this argument, Argentina points to Articles 2.6 and 3.8 of the Espoo Convention, Article 13 of the 2001 International Law Commission draft Articles on Prevention of Transboundary Harm from Hazardous Activities, and Principles 7 and 8 of the UNEP Goals and Principles. Uruguay considers that the provisions invoked by Argentina cannot serve as a legal basis for an obligation to consult the affected populations and adds that in any event the affected populations had indeed been consulted.

216.   The Court is of the view that no legal obligation to consult the affected populations arises for the Parties from the instruments invoked by Argentina.

217.   Regarding the facts, the Court notes that both before and after the granting of the initial environmental authorization, Uruguay did undertake activities aimed at consulting the affected populations, both on the Argentine and the Uruguayan sides of the river. These activities included meetings on 2 December 2003 in Río Negro, and on 26 May 2004 in Fray Bentos, with participation of Argentine non-governmental organizations. [The Court described further consultations involving the affected populations.]

219.   In the light of the above, the Court finds that consultation by Uruguay of the affected populations did indeed take place.

NOTES AND QUESTIONS

1. *It's customary, therefore it's the law.* What is the effect of the Court's statement that "it may now be considered a requirement under general international law to undertake an environmental impact assessment where there is a risk that the proposed industrial activity may have a significant adverse impact in a transboundary context, in particular, on a shared resource?" Can the Court just pronounce something to be custom and, presto, it is? How much State practice did the Court cite? Was this finding made easier by the fact that the parties to the dispute did not disagree about the necessity of conducting an EIA with regard to the pulp mill? In fact, the Court is probably the most authoritative source on the question whether a given norm has crystallized into an obligation under customary international law. If the Court says that something has become a customary international law requirement, States generally accept the finding.

2. *You have to do it, but how you do it is up to you.* The Court says that States must conduct transboundary EIAs, but leaves the content up to them. However, note that the Court doesn't give States an entirely free hand. First, the EIA must be done prior to the project's implementation. Second, in determining the content of a particular EIA, States must "hav[e] regard to the nature and magnitude of the proposed development and its likely adverse impact on the environment as well as to the need to exercise due diligence in conducting such an assessment." Third, and interestingly, "once operations have started and, where necessary, throughout the life of the project, continuous monitoring of its effects on the environment shall be undertaken."

3. *I interpret your obligation to do X to mean that you must also do Y.* What do you think about the Court's use of interpretation of treaty obligations to bring in other, non-treaty obligations? Do you agree with the statement quoted from the *Navigational and Related Rights* case that at least under some circumstances terms in a treaty may be given an evolving meaning? Does this destroy contractual stability?

4. *Uruguay wasn't Espooed.* The Court refers to the 1991 Espoo Convention on EIA in a transboundary context, a well-known treaty concluded within the U.N. Economic Commission for Europe, a regional organization. Despite its name, however, the 56[14] member States of the ECE go well beyond "Europe," as popularly conceived, to embrace, for example, Russia and the countries that belonged to the former Soviet Union including those in Central Asia, as well as Canada and the United States. Moreover, in 2001 an amendment to the Convention was adopted which permits states that are not members of the ECE to become Parties. As of August, 2015, however, the amendment had not yet entered into force. Do you think the Court's finding that general international law requires conducting a transboundary EIA was influenced by the existence of the Espoo Convention?

---

[14] As of August, 2014.

By the fact that conducting an EIA is part of the obligation of prevention of transboundary environmental harm?

5.   *To consult or not to consult: That is the question.* Why did the Court not find that consultation of the affected populations was required by customary international law? That is a standard part of the EIA process. And, Uruguay in fact did it. Do you think the Court believed that sufficient State practice in this regard was lacking? Note that it limited its holding to basing it on the evidence submitted by Argentina.

6.   *Aarhus is your house?* Another ECE treaty of relevance is the 1998 UNECE Convention on Access to Information, Public Participation in Decision-making and Access to Justice in Environmental Matters, known by the city where it was concluded as the Aarhus Convention. Forty-six States and the European Union are parties to the treaty,[15] all of which are located in Europe and Central Asia. As its name implies, the convention grants the public rights of access to information, participation and access to justice in governmental decision-making processes concerning the local, national and transboundary environment. Why wasn't this treaty invoked by Argentina and discussed by the Court in relation to the question whether Uruguay had an obligation to consult the populations likely to be affected by the project? Is there a human right to access to information and public participation? Or is this just another European innovation that the rest of the world isn't ready for yet?

7.   *What about human rights?* As indicated in Chapter 15, human rights bodies have consistently taken the view that international human rights law requires that environmental impact assessments be conducted if environmental harm might adversely affect human rights. Why did the ICJ not mention this?

c.   Cooperation

RIO DECLARATION ON ENVIRONMENT AND DEVELOPMENT, PRINCIPLE 7

Adopted by the United Nations Conference on Environment and Development,
June 14, 1992

Principle 7

States shall cooperate in a spirit of global partnership to conserve, protect and restore the health and integrity of the Earth's ecosystem. In view of the different contributions to global environmental degradation, States have common but differentiated responsibilities. The developed countries acknowledge the responsibility that they bear in the international pursuit of sustainable development in view of the pressure

---

[15]   As of August, 2014.

their societies place on the global environment and of the technologies and financial resources they command.[16]

NOTES AND QUESTIONS

1. *Go forth and cooperate!* It sounds good, but what is the real meaning of an obligation to cooperate? How would you know if a State breached this obligation? Does the obligation obtain regardless of the status of relations between States? Can you imagine any form of cooperation between North Korea and the United States?

2. *I need to cooperate a little, but you need to cooperate a lot.* What is the meaning of "common but differentiated responsibilities?" Does the "differentiation" apply to the obligation to cooperate, so it is somehow lessened in the case of developing countries? Or does cooperation simply take a different form for those States? The UNFCCC contains the following "principle:"

Article 3
Principles

1. The Parties should protect the climate system for the benefit of present and future generations of humankind, on the basis of equity and in accordance with their common but differentiated responsibilities and respective capabilities. Accordingly, the developed country Parties should take the lead in combating climate change and the adverse effects thereof.[17]

Can you translate this principle into a practical example of how it would operate in the context of cooperation between a developed and a developing country in the protection of the climate system?

3. *Wet cooperation?* The United Nations Watercourses Convention contains the following provision on cooperation:

Article 8
General Obligation to Cooperate

1. Watercourse states shall cooperate on the basis of sovereign equality, territorial integrity, mutual benefit and good faith in order to attain optimal utilization and adequate protection of an international watercourse.

2. In determining the manner of such cooperation, watercourse States may consider the establishment of joint mechanisms or commissions, as deemed necessary by them, to facilitate cooperation on relevant measures and procedures in the

---

[16]   31 I.L.M. 874, 877 (1992).

[17]   United Nations Framework Convention on Climate Change (UNFCCC), New York, 9 May 1992, 31 I.L.M. 849, 854 (1992).

light of experience gained through cooperation in existing joint
mechanisms and commissions in various regions.[18]

It could be considered to be tautological to say that States should cooperate
with regard to shared resources. A parent gives two children a piece of cake
on a plate and says, "share it." One can imagine the possible outcomes. Each
child takes hold of the plate and starts pulling it. Or, one simply grabs the
cake and runs off. Or, one suggests cutting it in half. And so on. As seen
earlier, the Watercourses Convention contains detailed provisions on
procedures relating to prior notification of planned projects. Is effective
cooperation a necessary predicate to the proper implementation of such
procedures?

Should cooperation be institutionalized (in our metaphor, should the
parent, or a friend, be brought in), as suggested in the second paragraph of
this article? That is what Argentina and Uruguay did in the 1975 Statute of
the Uruguay River, by creating CARU. What are the advantages and
disadvantages of forming a joint body to facilitate cooperation?

d.   Emerging Procedural Norms

As is discussed below in Chapter 15 on Human Rights and
Environmental Justice, several procedural norms exist that are directly
relevant to environmental protection. These include the rights of access to
information, participation in decision-making, assembly, expression, and
access to justice.

Several of these rights also have a basis in non-human rights law,
either international agreements or emerging customary international
law. Principle 10 of the Rio Declaration on Environment and
Development, for example, provides:

> Environmental issues are best handled with participation of all
> concerned citizens, at the relevant level. At the national level,
> each individual shall have appropriate access to information
> concerning the environment that is held by public authorities,
> including information on hazardous materials and activities in
> their communities, and the opportunity to participate in
> decision-making processes. States shall facilitate and encourage
> public awareness and participation by making information
> widely available. Effective access to judicial and administrative
> proceedings, including redress and remedy, shall be provided.

After Rio, environmentalists in both Western and Eastern Europe
pressed States to give access to environmental information and
environmental decision-making processes. Some Governments, on the
other hand, had a tradition of official secrecy that needed to be overcome

---

[18] United Nations Convention on the Law of the Non-Navigational Uses of International
Watercourses, New York, 21 May 1997, UNGA Res. A/RES/51/229, 36 I.L.M. 700 (1997).

and were concerned about the lack of rules regarding public access to information. The result was the negotiation of an international agreement on the issues: the UN Economic Commission for Europe (ECE) Convention on Access to Information, Public Participation in Decision-making and Access to Justice in Environmental Matters, commonly referred to as the Aarhus Convention (and discussed elsewhere in this chapter). Under the Aarhus Convention, States are obligated upon request to make information about the environment available to the public, to implement procedures for public participation in the authorization process for certain industrial, agricultural, and commercial activities, and to establish judicial or administrative proceedings to let the public challenge the environmental decisions by governments. The Convention has a robust compliance mechanism. While the Aarhus Convention was initially open only to members of the ECE, it is now open for universal membership, though as of August 2015 no non-ECE Member States have joined it. Instead, some Latin American States are negotiating a regional agreement dealing with similar issues. This effort arose from the 2012 UN Conference on Sustainable Development (Rio+20), and is being shepherded by the UN Economic Commission for Latin America and the Caribbean. Other international agreements contain specific requirements regarding these issues. For an example of a regional watercourse agreement containing such provisions, see the 2012 Protocol to the Great Lakes Water Quality Agreement (Canada-USA).

Another emerging norm is Prior Informed Consent (PIC), also often referred to as Free, Prior and Informed Consent (FPIC). FPIC (or PIC) requires that the advance consent of indigenous peoples or other communities dependent on natural resources such as forests, fisheries, or waterways be obtained before those resources may be affected. A version of this may be found, for example, in the operating policies of the International Finance Corporation, which requires "broad community support" for projects. There is some controversy over whether FPIC requires that such communities have a "veto" over projects or whether there are circumstances in which consent may be more broadly interpreted. Some of these issues are discussed in Chapter 15, part J.

3. APPLICATION OF ENVIRONMENTAL NORMS TO DEVELOPING COUNTRIES

Earlier in this chapter we asked you to consider preliminarily the way in which environmental norms apply or should apply to developing countries. This is an issue to which increasing attention has been given since the 1972 Stockholm Conference on the Human Environment. It is a thread that runs through the entire fabric of international environmental law. Anyone who has participated in a recent multilateral diplomatic negotiation in the field can attest that the issue will be raised in one way or another in virtually any such discussions. If the instrument finally agreed upon does not make special provision for developing countries, it is likely that its provisions will have been drafted in such a way as to take their circumstances into account. Is the same true of norms of general, or customary international law? In what ways *are* the needs, interests, and special situation of developing countries taken into account in normative prescriptions? Is it appropriate to establish or recognize such a double standard? On what grounds can special—and therefore different— treatment of developing countries be justified? Practical ones (these countries are not in a position to comply with some obligations anyway, so why not recognize that and help them so that their noncompliance does not hurt us)? Political ones (it is important for developed countries to maintain good relations with developing countries—which have around three-quarters of the world's population—for a host of reasons, many of which do not concern the environment)? Moral ones (the developed countries should help developing countries, especially the least developed ones, in any way possible, including by allowing them to devote their resources to the provision of food and water and to the alleviation of absolute poverty; this is especially the case when developed countries' activities have been the predominant cause of the environmental problem)?

In the pages that follow we present, first, the relevant principles of the Stockholm and Rio Declarations, then, as an illustration of how the issue is dealt with in treaties, a provision of the UNFCCC. Finally we reproduce an analysis of the different ways in which international law takes the special situation of developing countries into account.

DECLARATION OF THE UNITED NATIONS CONFERENCE ON THE HUMAN ENVIRONMENT ("STOCKHOLM DECLARATION"), PRINCIPLE 23

Stockholm, 16 June 1972, Report of the United Nations Conference on the Human Environment, U.N. Doc. A/CONF.48/14/Rev.1, at 3 (1973), U.N. Doc. A/CONF.48/14, at 2–65, and Corr.1 (1972), reprinted in 11 I.L.M. 1416 (1972)

Principle 23

Without prejudice to such criteria as may be agreed upon by the international community, or to such standards which will have to be determined nationally, it will be essential in all cases to consider the systems of values prevailing in each country, and the extent of the applicability of standards which are valid for the most advanced countries but which may be inappropriate and of unwarranted social cost for the developing countries.

RIO DECLARATION ON ENVIRONMENT AND DEVELOPMENT, PRINCIPLES 6 AND 7

Adopted by the United Nations Conference on Environment and Development
June 14, 1992

Principle 6

The special situation and need of developing countries, particularly the least developed and those most environmentally vulnerable, shall be given special priority. International actions in the field of environment and development should also address the interests and needs of all countries.

Principle 7

States shall cooperate in a spirit of global partnership to conserve, protect and restore the health and integrity of the Earth's ecosystem. In view of the different contributions to global environmental degradation, States have common but differentiated responsibilities. The developed countries acknowledge the responsibility that they bear in the international pursuit of sustainable development in view of the pressures their societies place on the global environment and of the technologies and financial resources they command.

NOTES AND QUESTIONS

1. *Principle 6: Give special priority to the poorest but address the interests and needs of the rich ones, too?* What are the practical implications of Principle 6? Does it mean that everyone should get something? That developed countries and international financial institutions are to give "special priority" to providing financial and technical assistance to developing countries? Does it imply that international environmental obligations should be applied less strictly or perhaps sometimes not at all to developing countries?

2. *Principle 7: The developed countries have gotten theirs, at the expense of the environment, and should now help developing countries to do the same?* Again, what are the practical implications of this principle? That developed countries have a special obligation to assist developing countries in developing economically? In meeting their environmental obligations? That developed countries can continue to pollute, for example, if they are able to induce developing countries to refrain from polluting? Or that developed countries have "used up" most of their "pollution quota" whereas developing countries have considerable leeway left to engage in such environmentally harmful—but economically productive—practices as polluting and deforestation? Do you believe your conclusions are borne out by Article 3, paragraph 1 of the UNFCCC, reproduced below? For an in-depth examination of the implications of the concept of "common but differentiated

responsibilities" see Christopher D. Stone, *Common but Differentiated Responsibilities in International Law*, 98 AJIL 276 (2004).

3. *Principles 11 and 15: Have effective environmental legislation and be careful, unless you're a developing country?* Principles 11 and 15 of the Rio Declaration are also relevant in this connection.

a. *Principle 11* deals with domestic legislation rather than international law. It provides as follows:

> States shall enact effective environmental legislation. Environmental standards, management objectives and priorities should reflect the environmental and developmental context to which they apply. Standards applied by some countries may be inappropriate and of unwarranted economic and social cost to other countries, in particular developing countries.

This principle thus calls for states to enact "effective environmental legislation" but recognizes that such laws should be tailored to the conditions of the country concerned. Would it not have been enough to say only that—for example, to stop at the end of the second sentence? Why do you think the third sentence was felt to be necessary? If all developed countries regulate air pollution from automobiles and factories strictly, does this mean that developing countries should be expected to so as well? For that matter, why did the Rio Declaration deal with domestic legislation at all? Is this not a matter within the domestic jurisdiction of States and therefore within their unfettered discretion?

b. *Principle 15,* which deals with the "precautionary approach," provides that this concept is to be "widely applied by States according to their capabilities." Does this mean that where developing countries "lack . . . full scientific certainty," they may "postpon[e] cost-effective measures to prevent environmental degradation" even "[w]here there are threats of serious or irreversible damage"?

UNITED NATIONS FRAMEWORK CONVENTION ON CLIMATE CHANGE, ARTICLE 3, PARAGRAPHS 1 AND 2

Rio de Janeiro, 9 May 1992, U.N. Doc. A/CONF.151/26, 31 I.L.M. 849 (1992)

Article 3
Principles

1. The Parties should protect the climate system for the benefit of present and future generations of humankind, on the basis of equity and in accordance with their common but differentiated responsibilities and respective capabilities. Accordingly, the developed country Parties should take the lead in combating climate change and the adverse effects thereof.

2. The specific needs and special circumstances of developing country Parties, especially those that are particularly vulnerable to the adverse effects of climate change, and of those Parties, especially developing country Parties, that would have to bear a disproportionate or abnormal burden under the Convention, should be given full consideration.

NOTES AND QUESTIONS

1. *The rationale for differential treatment.* There are various possible rationales for treating developing countries differently, and they are not necessarily mutually exclusive. As noted at the outset of this section and as explored more fully in the Magraw excerpt below, differential treatment of developing countries might be justified on practical, political, or moral grounds. Is there any counterpart to the notion of "common but differentiated responsibility" on the domestic level? That is, are some individuals treated differently than others under domestic legal systems? If so, are the justifications similar to those supporting differential treatment of developing countries under international law? On the theoretical and legal implications of differential treatment, *see generally* Christopher D. Stone, *Common but Differentiated Responsibilities in International Law*, 98 AJIL 276 (2004).

2. *Article 3 and Principle 7.* To rephrase a question asked above, what does Principle 7 of the Rio Declaration mean when it states that "developed countries acknowledge the responsibility that they bear in the international pursuit of sustainable development"? Is it saying that in view of their greater contribution to global environmental problems, developed countries "acknowledge responsibility" to remedy those problems? To what extent is this interpretation supported in the case of climate change by Article 3(1) of the UNFCCC? In accepting this formula, are developed countries agreeing to reduce "the pressures their societies place on the global environment" (e.g., by changing production and consumption patterns)? Or are they agreeing to provide financial and technological assistance to developing countries so that they might develop in a sustainable manner?

3. *The Humpty-Dumpty gambit.*[19] In its "Interpretive Statements for the Record," the United States declared that it "does not accept any interpretation of Principle 7 that would imply a recognition or acceptance by the United States of any international obligations or liabilities, or any diminution of the responsibilities of developing countries." U.N. Doc. A/CONF.151/26/Rev.1 (Vol. II), at 18 (1993). Assume you are the Legal Adviser to the Foreign Ministry of the United Kingdom and that the United Kingdom made no such interpretive statement. Would it thereby be regarded as having accepted "international obligations or liabilities" in this regard? Does the fact that the United States made this statement while the United Kingdom did not make a difference?

---

[19] Quoth Humpty Dumpty: "When *I* use a word, . . . it means just what I choose it to mean—neither more nor less." Lewis Carroll, Through the Looking Glass, ch. 7.

4. *Translating principles into provisions: strengthened or lost in translation?* The notions of "global partnership" and "common but differentiated responsibilities" contained in Principle 7 have been given concrete expression in other instruments in the form of different standards, delayed compliance timetables, and less stringent commitments. Apart from other possible justifications, use of these techniques often assists in encouraging universal participation in instruments dealing with such important problems as stratospheric ozone depletion (the Montreal Protocol) and global climate change (the UNFCCC). For example, in the view of some knowledgeable observers the Montreal Protocol's combination of inducements and trade restrictions presumably led countries such as China, India and Brazil, which alone could have undermined the protective regime, to join the agreement. Examples of these techniques may be found, inter alia, in the following instruments.

a. Article 5 of the *Montreal Protocol,* entitled Special Situation of Developing Countries, entitles a developing country party "to delay its compliance with the control measures set out in [the Protocol] by ten years after that specified in [the relevant provisions]." The article also provides that parties are to "facilitate access to environmentally safe alternative substances and technology" for developing country parties and to facilitate "the provision of subsidies, aid, credits, guarantees or insurance programmes" to assist developing country parties in acquiring alternative technology and substitute products.

b. The *UNFCCC* takes the special circumstances and needs of developing countries into account in a number of ways, including the structuring of the parties' obligations (Article 4(1)) and allowing differences in reporting requirements (Article 12). That agreement's innovative provision to establish a Clean Development Mechanism (Article 12) permits a developed country party to meet a portion of its commitment to limit greenhouse gas emissions by assisting a developing country party in protecting its tropical forests, which provide a sink for those gasses.

c. The *Biological Diversity Convention* (considered in Chapter 13), which is replete with references to the special situation of developing countries, provides in Article 20(1) that developed country parties are to "provide new and additional financial resources to enable developing country Parties to meet the agreed full incremental costs to them of implementing measures which fulfil the obligations of this Convention. . . ." Paragraph 4 of that article then provides:

> The extent to which developing country Parties will effectively implement their commitments under this Convention will depend on the effective implementation by developed country Parties of their commitments . . . related to financial resources

and transfer of technology and will take fully into account the fact that economic and social development and eradication of poverty are the first and overriding priorities of the developing country Parties.

Does this provision make the provision of financial and technological resources by developed country Parties a condition precedent to the obligations of developing countries? Or is it simply a statement of fact? Does it matter? Why or why not?

d.   After listing "General obligations" in Article 4, the 1994 *Desertification Convention*[20] provides in Article 5 for additional "Obligations of affected country Parties" and then, separately, in Article 6 for additional "Obligations of developed country Parties." Among the latter are obligations to "provide substantial financial resources and other forms of support to assist affected developing country Parties" in undertaking relevant activities (Article 6 (b)) and to "promote the mobilization of new and additional funding pursuant to Article 20 [on Financial resources]."

5.   *Special treatment of former communist States?* "Countries with economies in transition"—an expression used to refer to the former Soviet bloc countries of Central and Eastern Europe—are also given beneficial treatment in certain recent instruments, including the Convention on Biological Diversity (CBD) and the UNFCCC. The CBD allows these countries to "voluntarily assume the obligations of the developed country Parties," thereby implicitly exempting them from developed country obligations under the treaty. The UNFCCC approaches the subject of classifying countries by in effect listing all nondeveloping country parties in Annex I, and listing only developed countries—members of the OECD, excluding countries with economies in transition—in Annex II. It then differentiates between countries listed in Annexes I and II, providing more stringent obligations for the OECD countries listed in Annex II. Finally, special consideration is urged for these countries in instruments adopted at universal conferences held under United Nations auspices, such as the World Summit for Social Development, Copenhagen, 1995. Paragraph 18 of the Copenhagen Declaration adopted at that meeting states that: "Countries with economies in transition, which are also [i.e., in addition to developing countries] undergoing fundamental political, economic and social transformation, require the support of the international community as well." It should further be recalled in this connection that the Montreal Protocol, concluded during the Soviet era, also makes special allowances for communist bloc countries. Article 2(6) of the Montreal Protocol in effect "grandfathers" the relevant facilities of these countries that were under construction or contracted for prior to a specified date, taking into account that the economies of these countries operated under five-year plans. More

---

[20] Convention to Combat Desertification in Those Countries Experiencing Serious Drought and/or Desertification, Particularly in Africa, 17 June 1994, U.N. Doc. A/AC.241/15/Rev.7, 33 I.L.M. 1328 (1994).

recently, certain Central and Eastern European countries requested, and in December 1995 were granted, special treatment with respect to their obligations under the Protocol.

———————

In the following excerpt, Daniel Magraw proposes three different categories of international environmental norms that may be applied to developing countries. Consider whether you believe that a single category should be applied to all developing countries with regard to all environmental problems; whether different categories should be applied to all developing countries depending upon the problem being addressed; or whether different categories should be applied to different developing countries (developing countries that are at different levels of development).

LEGAL TREATMENT OF DEVELOPING COUNTRIES: DIFFERENTIAL, CONTEXTUAL, AND ABSOLUTE NORMS

Daniel Barstow Magraw
1 Colo. J. Intl. Envtl. L. & Poly. 69, 69–76 (1990)

I.   INTRODUCTION

The treatment of developing countries arises in virtually every discussion of international environmental protection and resource management. This serious and difficult issue must be confronted successfully in order to realize effective solutions to international environmental problems.

From a practical (nonpolitical) perspective, developing countries are the source of much of the world's pollution and contain much of the world's population and natural resources. That population demands improved standards of living, and those resources are a tempting target for uncontrolled exploitation. Moreover, most of the staggering increase in world population projected for the next thirty years—from five billion now to eight-to-nine billion by 2025—will occur in developing countries, leading to further pressures on the environment. International environmental protection measures thus must involve the continuous participation of developing countries in order to be viable.

It is beyond the scope of this article to explore fully the problems of fairness between developing and developed countries in distributing the burdens of dealing with international environmental protection and resource management. It is clear, however, that these fairness issues will have to be taken seriously. Moreover, it will not be plausible either for developed countries to insist that they should be allowed to continue contributing as much pollution as they did just because they started doing it first, or for developing countries to claim that they can determine their level of pollution without reference to the condition of the biosphere as a whole.

One hopes, of course, for a consonance between the international legal regime—as it presently exists and as it evolves in the future—and the political, practical, and moral considerations just mentioned. In the remainder of this article, I examine the existing international legal regime with respect to three types of norms—differential, contextual, and absolute—and conclude that international environmental norms should be fashioned to take into account in appropriate situations the specific capabilities and needs of developing countries.

II. Analytic Framework: Types of Norms

For purposes of this article, there are three general types of international norms. These types delimit the treatment that international law can and does provide developing countries.

A. Differential Norms

The first type of norm is what I call a "differential" norm, by which I mean a norm that on its face provides different, presumably more advantageous, standards for one set of States than for another set. In theory, the sets of States can be distinguished on any ground (other than simply that one set is composed of States that are acting and the other set consists of the States that are affected by the action). The differential norms of greatest interest here are those that distinguish between developing countries and developed countries. An example of a differential environmental norm is contained in the 1987 Montreal Protocol on Substances that Deplete the Ozone Layer, which allows developed countries five years to decrease pollution to a specified level, but developing countries—defined in terms of annual per capita consumption of ozone-depleting substances—an additional ten years to reach the same level.

The Montreal Protocol is highly unusual, perhaps unique, because it defines "developing countries." The other conventions and instruments (such as UN General Assembly declarations) that provide differential treatment to "developing countries" may be relying on a common sense definition of the term or on the treatment of countries within the UN system (the United Nations, for example, maintains a list of "least-developed" developing countries). In the absence of a specific definition, countries as different as Burundi and Brazil are presumably treated the same—i.e., as "developing countries"—and disputes may arise regarding whether or not a country qualifies as "developing." By singling out one set of countries for different treatment, differential norms effectively take into account more than one type of interest. In the case of the Montreal Protocol, for example, the interests in not unduly interfering with improving standards of living in developing countries and in preserving the ozone layer are concurrently protected. That protection can be provided more or less flexibly. The Montreal Protocol provides very specific rules. In contrast, the earliest example of a different norm distinguishing between developing and developed countries is very general: It allows each developing country to decide for itself how far it will provide economic rights to nonnationals.

B. Contextual Norms

The second type of norm is what I call a "contextual" norm, by which I mean a norm on its face provides identical treatment to all States affected by the norm but the application of which requires (or at least permits) consideration of characteristics that might vary from country to country. Applying a contextual norm thus typically involves balancing multiple interests and characteristics.

Contextual norms, e.g., "reasonable" or "equitable," thus usually are indeterminate (that is also the case with differential norms that contain contextual elements). Depending on what factors may be considered, contextual norms allow disputing States wide latitude for arguing compliance or noncompliance. They also provide little, if any, certainty in predicting the outcome of the few international disputes settled by third parties such as courts and arbitral tribunals. Moreover, they permit such third parties to manipulate results within a broad range. Obviously, these effects can interfere with public order.

On the other hand, the indeterminacy of contextual norms or, in some cases, the flexibility of contextual norms that arises from the attributes that give rise to indeterminacy, can be advantageous in four types of situations. First, it is often easier to reach agreement on a contextual norm than on a more definite and precise norm, because of indeterminacy; and the fact that a contextual norm exists indicates, at the least, a recognition that the situation in question is of legitimate concern to all or part of the international community. Thus, although the existence of a contextual norm can, in some circumstances, give a false impression of progress and serve to distract attention from achieving a fully effective solution, in other circumstances a contextual norm can focus attention on a problem and lead to the subsequent formulation and acceptance of appropriate, definite norms. Moreover, the indeterminacy of contextual norms is not infinite: A contextual norm specifies the terms for discourse about the issue to which it applies and provides some bounds of acceptable behavior—bounds which, although not exact, usually are sufficiently precise that some conduct commonly will be seen as exceeding them. Even though a contextual norm might be less desirable in a given situation than a norm with clear meaning, therefore, a contextual norm might be preferable to having no applicable standard at all, which might be the only realistic alternative.

The second type of situation in which indeterminacy of contextual norms—or, more precisely, the attributes of contextual norms that create indeterminacy—is desirable involves problems that are clouded by uncertainty, either about scientific knowledge or about the range of factual situations to be covered by the norm, with the result that the precise contours of the optimal (or even suboptimal but still desirable) solution are unknowable, even by States otherwise willing to agree to an applicable norm. In such a case, an indeterminate norm is sometimes preferable to having no norm, for the reasons described in the immediately preceding paragraph. More importantly, the attributes of a contextual norm that give rise to indeterminacy also typically lead to flexibility in interpreting and applying the norm. That flexibility allows coverage of and sensitivity to a range of factual situations and of causes and effects, and it thus is desirable in dealing with the type of problem being discussed here, i.e., those so clouded by current uncertainty that a precise optimal solution is unknowable.

A related set of issues regarding which flexibility is desirable is that in which the costs of determining all the possible factual situations to be covered by a norm (or group of norms) and of articulating and agreeing on a precise norm are so high that they outweigh the benefits that would be gained from having a precise norm. A flexible contextual norm may be the most efficient means of providing a standard to deal with these issues.

Fourth, flexibility can be advantageous even with respect to issues whose current solution is clear, if significant changes in the relevant milieu are likely to occur. Examples of such changes include advances in scientific understanding about the environmental (or other) effects of particular behavior, developments in the technology applicable to solving a given pollution problem, or changes in pressures on the ecosystem at risk. Flexibility enables a contextual norm to adapt to changed circumstances and thus eliminates the need to negotiate and agree upon a new standard—a process that can be time-consuming, expensive, or impossible.

Contextual norms are either general, in which case the terms of the norm do not place a limit on the characteristics that may be considered, or limited, in which case the norm is phrased such that the set of relevant characteristics is defined (more or less precisely). Restricting the factors that may be considered in applying a contextual norm limits the indeterminacy (and flexibility) of the norm. The 1972 Convention on International Liability for Damage Caused by Space Objects, which provides for absolute liability on the part of the State from whose territory the space object was launched, contains general contextual norms: The injured State is allowed to make a claim until one year after that State "could *reasonably* be expected to have learned the facts," and compensation to be determined according to "principles of *justice* and *equity."* In contrast, an example of a limited contextual norm in the environmental area is the 1972 World Heritage Convention's requirement that a country, in protecting natural and cultural heritage, *"do all it can* to this end, to the *utmost of its own resources."* The use of contextual norms has a long history. Consider, for example, the requirement that efforts taken in self-defense must be proportional. The limited contextual norms of greatest interest here are those that permit or require consideration of factors corresponding typically, but not necessarily unvaryingly, -to the economic developmental level of a country, such as the World Heritage Convention's reference to States' "resources."

C. Absolute Norms

The third type of norm is what I call an "absolute" norm, by which I mean a norm that provides identical treatment to all countries and does not require or permit consideration of factors that vary between countries. An example of an absolute norm is the 1987 Nuclear Accident Notification Convention's requirement of "immediate" notification of pending trans-boundary harm. Applying an absolute norm often involves inquiring into the facts of the specific case (e.g., one must determine when a nuclear accident occurred and when notification occurred in order to ascertain whether notification was "immediate"); and reasonable people differ about what facts are relevant to such inquiries. No bright line thus exists between absolute and contextual norms. It is usually clear, however, on which side of the line a rule or principle falls.

Absolute norms have the capacity for being very precise (as do differential norms that do not contain contextual elements). In the area of environmental protection, precision is frequently desirable because the behavior or effect at issue is normally described specifically. Examples include emissions of hydrocarbons and exposure to ionizing radiation; it is usual to speak of these in terms of specific numbers of parts per million and rems, respectively.

Absolute norms are not necessarily precise, however. Sometimes they are ambiguous or undefined. An example would be an agreement providing that damages must be paid for transboundary harm, without defining the terms "damages" or "harm." Such a lack of clarity can, but does not automatically, result in disadvantages and advantages of flexible contextual norms.

NOTES AND QUESTIONS

1. *Making the categories fit the facts.* In what circumstances do you believe it would be appropriate to use each of the types of norms identified by Magraw? For example, should developing country A be excused for depositing toxic waste into a river that flows into developing country B solely on the ground that A is a developing country?

2.   *Role-playing I.* If you were Legal Adviser to the United States Department of State would you prefer any of these types of norms over any other? Would you instruct your delegate to the negotiation of an international agreement to try to use one type of norm or another?

3.   *Role-playing II.* Imagine now you are a judge on the International Court of Justice. Would you have any preference?

4.   *The United States and developing countries.* Is it in the interest of the United States to give differential treatment to developing countries? Why, or why not?

CONCLUDING NOTES AND QUESTIONS

Look again at the Problem that opened this chapter. Are there reasons why Canada might prefer less stringent norms for the control of transboundary pollution? What about the United States? Should it be careful not to insist on too stringent a standard for fear that could come back to haunt it?

Concerning the treatment of developing countries, is there a point at which they should be considered to be sufficiently developed to implement and comply with environmental norms in the same way as developed countries? If so, at what point would China, for example, reach that point? To what extent should international agreements make provision for such a transition? These questions are addressed in Chapter 9, at pp. 524–525.

CHAPTER 5

ACCOUNTABILITY AND COMPLIANCE

■ ■ ■

In this chapter we will begin to think about the consequences of breaching international environmental obligations. We will also consider the issue of compliance, with both hard law and soft law, as well as compliance with voluntary commitments.

A. THE PROBLEM: THE TRAIL SMELTER AND RESPONSIBILITY FOR TRANSBOUNDARY POLLUTION

In Chapter 4, we were concerned with principles of international environmental law regulating transboundary pollution. In this chapter we return to the Trail Smelter Arbitration. Now consider what the remedies should be that are available to the United States, assuming a breach of a rule of international law concerning transboundary pollution. Should the smelter have to shut down? Is there a way international law can regulate the operations of the smelter to allow it to continue operating while avoiding, insofar as possible, damage to the United States? Should Canada be held responsible for remediating, or paying for, the damage that has occurred in the United States? In approaching these questions, assume each of the roles described in connection with the problem in Chapter 4: (1) a lawyer for Canada; (2) a lawyer for the United States; (3) a lawyer for the Trail Smelter (COMINCO); and (4) a non-governmental organization (NGO) in the US state of Washington.

B. INTRODUCTION TO THE LAW OF THE RESPONSIBILITY OF STATES FOR INTERNATIONALLY WRONGFUL ACTS

The Law of the Responsibility of States for Internationally Wrongful Acts, also referred to as the law of State Responsibility, determines the circumstances under which a State will be legally "responsible" for the breach of an international obligation, whether the source of that obligation is a treaty or customary international law. The U.N. International Law Commission (ILC) studied this area of law for many years, finally adopting a complete set of articles on it in 2001.[1] Because

---

[1] Report of the International Law Commission on the Work of its Fifty-third Session, 2001 ILC Rep. p. 59, para. 77. The articles are also contained in Materials on the Responsibility of

the ILC is charged with the progressive development of international law and its codification, [2] its work can sometimes be considered as a codification of the rules of customary international law on a given subject. This is largely the case with its articles on State Responsibility.

The law of State Responsibility may be said to reflect a Civil Law approach more than one typical of Common Law countries. When a State breaches an international obligation—whether under a treaty or customary international law—it must make "reparation." In fact, a breach gives rise to a suite of new obligations: to cease the breach, if it is an ongoing one, to provide assurances and guarantees of non-repetition in appropriate cases, and to make reparation. Reparation itself has several elements: to restore the situation created by the breach to the *status quo ante* ("*restitutio in integrum*"); to provide compensation to the extent that the situation cannot be so restored; and to provide "satisfaction" in the rather unusual cases in which there is harm, usually of a moral character, that is not covered by restitution or compensation. Thus a breaching State's first and most fundamental obligation under international law is to restore the situation to the *status quo ante*, not to provide the injured State with compensation, the remedy normally applicable in the Common Law system. Only to the extent that the situation cannot be so restored may the breaching State satisfy its obligation to make reparation by paying compensation.

NOTES AND QUESTIONS

1. *It'll be good as new.* What are the advantages and disadvantages in environmental cases of the remedial system under the law of State Responsibility?

2. *Sorry about that.* Suppose State A causes environmental harm in State B—e.g., through transboundary pollution. How would the international remedial system play out? Think of the Trail Smelter problem as you consider this.

3. *Mining heaven, living hell.* What remedy would be appropriate in the following situation: In the case concerning *Certain Phosphate Lands in Nauru* (Nauru v. Australia),[3] the Republic of Nauru claimed that Australia was responsible for the rehabilitation of Nauruan phosphate lands mined during administration of Australia prior to the island's independence in 1968. Nauru's Application instituting proceedings against Australia before the International Court of Justice states that "[a]s a result of this mining process, there remained on the mined-out lands nothing but a forest of limestone

---

States for Internationally Wrongful Acts, U.N. Doc. ST/LEG/SER.B/25 (2012), together with the ILC's commentaries and a selection of international decisions making reference to the articles.

[2] ILC STATUTE, art. 1(1), United Nations, New York, U.N. Doc. A/CN.4/4/Rev.2. The ILC was established by General Assembly resolution 174(II) of 21 November 1947.

[3] Materials on the case are available on the International Court of Justice's website, www. icj-cij.org.

pinnacles, varying between 5 and 15 metres in height. The land was thus rendered completely useless for habitation, agriculture, or any other purpose unless and until rehabilitation was carried out." Application of the Republic of Nauru, filed May 19, 1989, p. 14. Australia admitted, in a report to the United Nations Trusteeship Council filed in 1948, that once the phosphate deposits were exhausted, "all but the coastal strip of Nauru will be worthless." Application, above, at 18. Nauru claimed, inter alia, that Australia had . . . a "duty of restitution [which] . . . extends to the restoration of those parts of the island, mined [during the relevant period], to a reasonable condition for habitation by the Nauruan people as a sovereign nation." Application, above, at 30. Nauru therefore claimed that Australia was "bound to make restitution or other appropriate reparation to Nauru," and reserved the right to request "an award of aggravated or moral damages. . . ." The latter would presumably have been a form of satisfaction. The case was settled by the two states by agreement concluded August 10, 1993, before the court could rule on Nauru's claims, and was accordingly removed from the court's docket. The settlement, which included a cash payment of $A107 million, was "without prejudice to Australia's long-standing position that it bears no responsibility for the rehabilitation of the phosphate lands. . . ." Article 1(1). The settlement documents are reprinted in 32 I.L.M. 1471 (1993). If you had been counsel to Nauru, would you have settled the case? For this amount?

4. *Catch a falling star and . . . let someone else clean up the mess?* *Cosmos 954* was a Soviet nuclear-powered satellite. In 1978 it fell from orbit and crashed in northern Canada, scattering radioactive debris for some 370 miles across uninhabited areas of the Northwest Territories, what is today Nunavut, Alberta and Saskatchewan. Did Canada have to permit the Soviet Union to restore the damaged area to the status quo ante insofar as possible before it had the right to claim monetary damages?

5. *A tree, or a sea otter, is worth $ . . . ?* Article 36 of the ILC's State Responsibility articles provides that only "financially assessable damage" is compensable. Doesn't this make environmental damage a square peg in the round hole of State Responsibility rules? Is it possible to assign a dollar value to natural objects? To be sure, attempts have been made in national court cases (e.g., "contingent valuation," relying on polling as to how much members of the public would pay to see a sea otter in the case of the *Exxon Valdez* oil spill).

But perhaps the foremost example of an attempt to grapple with the problem on the international level is the jurisprudence of the U.N. Compensation Commission (UNCC) formed to assess and award compensation for damage "including environmental damage and the depletion of natural resources [resulting from] Iraq's unlawful invasion and occupation of Kuwait." UNSC Res. 687 (1991). Among other things, the Commission had to deal with the harm to the marine environment caused by Saddam Hussein's intentional release of massive quantities of oil into the Persian Gulf from the Sea Island Terminal in Kuwait. It found no basis for excluding damage of a purely environmental character[4] and allowed claims for reinstatement of the *status quo ante*. It went so far as to rule that "primary emphasis must be placed on restoring the environment to pre-invasion conditions, in terms of its overall ecological functioning, rather than on the removal of specific contaminants or restoration of the environment to a particular physical condition."[5]

6.   *The victim pays?* More generally, can you think of situations in which it might make sense for the victim of pollution to pay the polluter? It might surprise you to learn that States have actually done this, on the theory that it is cheaper to pay a polluter not to pollute than it is to clean up the mess after the fact. This was the solution arrived at after many years of controversy in the Rhine Salt Case, involving waste salts from French potash mines that were dumped into the Rhine, causing harm chiefly in the Netherlands. But all Rhine riparians paid a percentage of the costs of storing the waste salts in France (according to the "1972 formula," France and Germany paid 30 per cent each; Switzerland 6 per cent; and Netherlands, the ultimate downstream State that incurred the most damage, 34 per cent). See Carel H.V. De Villeneuve, *Western Europe's Artery: The Rhine*, 36 Nat. Res. J. 441 (1996).

C. APPLICABILITY OF GENERAL PRINCIPLES OF ACCOUNTABILITY TO DEVELOPING COUNTRIES

As we have seen, international environmental obligations often take into account the special situation of developing countries. The question we deal with here is whether similar allowances are made for developing countries in rules of accountability and compliance. To a certain extent this question is addressed by the same sources we considered in the context of norms of prevention. For example, Principle 23 of the Stockholm Declaration speaks in general terms of the need to "consider . . . the extent of the applicability of standards which are valid for the most advanced countries but which may be inappropriate and of unwarranted social cost for the developing countries." And Principle 7 of the Rio Declaration embodies the concept of "common but differentiated responsibilities." Neither of these provisions is confined, by its terms, to the primary obligations of states—obligations to reduce greenhouse gas emissions, to prevent specified levels of bycatch of sea turtles in shrimp trawling or to prevent harmful transboundary water pollution, for example. They could apply as well to the issue of whether and to what extent a developing country is legally responsible or accountable for certain conduct. It may even be the case that a question of responsibility or accountability of a developing country would not arise in respect of a given norm simply because the norm is so flexible that it could not be said to have been "breached" in the formal sense. This point may in effect be

---

[4]   UNCC F4 Claims, 5th Decision, para. 57 (2006).

[5]   *Id.*, para. 82.

raised by a country as a defense to a diplomatic claim that the country had breached a particular obligation—for example, a norm providing that states are to "exercise their best efforts," use "all appropriate means," or "the best practicable means at their disposal and in accordance with their capabilities," or "exercise due diligence" to bring about a certain state of affairs. A developing country accused of having breached such an obligation could simply respond that it had in fact exercised its best efforts, and the like, and that it had therefore not breached the obligation.

A separate but increasingly important aspect of the treatment of developing countries relates specifically to compliance. Its essence is captured in the phrase, "common but differentiated responsibilities" (e.g., Principle 7 of the Rio Declaration), a concept intended to contribute to the formation of the "new and equitable global partnership" that it is the goal of the Rio Declaration to establish. The "common but differentiated responsibilities" of developing and developed states may be implemented, for example, through delayed compliance timetables, or grace periods, such as those provided for in the Montreal Protocol. Similarly, Article 26 of the 1996 Protocol to the 1972 IMO London Dumping Convention allows states joining the agreement within certain time limits to notify the secretary-general of the IMO that they "will not be able to comply with specific provisions" of the protocol, other than those concerning incineration at sea or dumping of radioactive wastes or other radioactive matter, during a transitional period. Another example is The Convention on Biological Diversity, which makes the obligations undertaken by developing country parties dependent upon the provision by developed country parties of new and additional financial resources as well as access to and transfer of technology on fair and most favorable terms (e.g., Articles 8(m), 20(2), and especially 20(4)). Under Article 4(5) of the Framework Convention on Climate Change, developed countries are to "take all practicable steps to promote, facilitate and finance, as appropriate, the transfer of, or access to, environmentally sound technologies and know-how to other Parties, particularly developing country Parties, to enable them to implement the provisions of the Convention." These actions by developed country parties might be regarded analytically as conditions precedent to the obligations of developing countries, especially those provided for in the Biodiversity Convention. But they might also be viewed as means by which developed States may assist developing States in complying with those obligations.

NOTES AND QUESTIONS

1. *From each according to its ability . . . ?* If developing country A breaches an obligation to country B, resulting in damage to country B, should A's obligations to cease the wrongful conduct and repair the damage (i.e., restore the *status quo ante* or, to the extent that that is not possible, compensate B for its loss) be in any way lessened solely by virtue of the fact

that A is a developing country? What would the policy and legal justifications be for such a result?

2.   *Environmental assistance.* Why might developed country A consider it to be in its interest to assist developing country B to comply with B's international environmental obligations? Can you think of specific examples of situations in which A's interest might be especially acute?

3.   *The case of "economies in transition."* As we have seen above in relation to norms of prevention, the countries with economies in transition (chiefly those in Central and Eastern Europe) have made claims of entitlement to special treatment, akin to that which has been accorded developing countries. Do the same considerations that might support such treatment for these countries in relation to norms of prevention also apply to norms of accountability?

D.   STATE LIABILITY FOR ENVIRONMENTAL HARM

As we have seen, international law uses the term "responsibility" to cover the consequences for a state that has breached an international obligation. We have also seen that those consequences—restoration, compensation, satisfaction—are comprised within the concept of "reparation." One of the components of reparation is compensation, sometimes called "indemnity." How then does "liability," the subject of this subsection, fit within this structure? Is it simply a duty to pay compensation (to the extent that the situation cannot be restored to the status quo ante)?

The answer is no, it doesn't fit within the remedial structure of state responsibility, at least as far as the technical use of term "liability" in the field of international responsibility is concerned. The term "liability" was in fact chosen by the International Law Commission to refer to a situation that is not covered by the rules governing the responsibility of states for internationally wrongful acts—namely, the situation in which there is no wrongful act, per se, but where there are injurious consequences for a state arising out of an act, or activity, of another state that is not prohibited by international law. Since there is no internationally wrongful act, so the theory goes, there cannot be responsibility for the injurious consequences. Yet the injured state should not have to bear loss for which it is not to blame. Et voilá! International *Liability*. The actual name of the topic the ILC invented to deal with these situations was "International Liability for Injurious Consequences Arising Out of Acts Not Prohibited by International Law." The Commission began work on this topic in 1978.

QUESTION

Can you think of examples of the kinds of acts or activities that would be covered by the "International Liability" topic? Are these the same kinds that you identified as being covered by the ILC's Draft Articles on Prevention of Transboundary Harm from Hazardous Activities, set forth above?

In fact, over the years it became clear to the ILC that the International Liability topic was not always understood by governments, and that the ones that did seem to understand it did not particularly like it. Indeed, governments have long shown an aversion to any mention of "liability" for the consequences of their conduct. When the subject came up at the 1972 Stockholm Conference, the most that States could agree upon was the following:

Principle 22

States shall cooperate to develop further the international law regarding liability and compensation for the victims of pollution and other environmental damage caused by activities within the jurisdiction or control of such States to areas beyond their jurisdiction.

And that cooperation did not produce much of significance over the twenty years between the Stockholm and Rio Conferences. At Rio, the frustration of delegations can be seen in the language of Principle 13:

Principle 13

States shall develop national law regarding liability and compensation for the victims of pollution and other environmental damage. States shall also cooperate in an expeditious and more determined manner to develop further international law regarding liability and compensation for adverse effects of environmental damage caused by activities within their jurisdiction or control to areas beyond their jurisdiction.

Thus, we have the famous Principle 21 of the Stockholm Declaration (and its counterpart in the Rio Declaration, Principle 2), making a strong statement about the responsibility of States to "ensure" that activities within their jurisdiction or control do not cause transboundary environmental harm, but then very weak statements about liability and compensation if such harm occurs. Even the following straightforward proposal by Canada, from which the "L" word is conspicuously absent, proved unacceptable:

Each state has the responsibility to compensate for damage to the environment caused by activities carried on within its territory.[6]

But the ILC did not give up. Seeing the writing on the wall, it spun two topics out of the International Liability topic and completed a draft on each: Prevention of Transboundary Harm from Hazardous Activities, which we have considered above; and Principles on the Allocation of Loss in the Case of Transboundary Harm Arising Out of Hazardous Activities. Let us consider the latter.

DRAFT PRINCIPLES ON THE ALLOCATION OF LOSS IN THE CASE OF TRANSBOUNDARY HARM ARISING OUT OF HAZARDOUS ACTIVITIES

Text adopted by the International Law Commission in 2006, and submitted to the General Assembly as a part of the Commission's report covering the work of that session, U.N. Doc. A/61/10

Principle 1
Scope of application

The present draft principles apply to transboundary damage caused by hazardous activities not prohibited by international law.

Principle 2
Use of terms

For the purposes of the present draft principles:

(*a*) "damage" means significant damage caused to persons, property or the environment; and includes:

(i) loss of life or personal injury;

(ii) loss of, or damage to, property, including property which forms part of the cultural heritage;

(iii) loss or damage by impairment of the environment;

(iv) the costs of reasonable measures of reinstatement of the property, or environment, including natural resources;

(v) the costs of reasonable response measures;

(*b*) "environment" includes natural resources, both abiotic and biotic, such as air, water, soil, fauna and flora and the interaction between the same factors, and the characteristic aspects of the landscape;

(*c*) "hazardous activity" means an activity which involves a risk of causing significant harm;

---

[6]   U.N. Doc. A/CONF/48/PC.12, Annex I, at 3 (1971).

(*d*) "State of origin" means the State in the territory or otherwise under the jurisdiction or control of which the hazardous activity is carried out;

(*e*) "transboundary damage" means damage caused to persons, property or the environment in the territory or in other places under the jurisdiction or control of a State other than the State of origin;

(*f*) "victim" means any natural or legal person or State that suffers damage;

(*g*) "operator" means any person in command or control of the activity at the time the incident causing transboundary damage occurs.

Principle 3
Purposes

The purposes of the present draft principles are:

(*a*) to ensure prompt and adequate compensation to victims of transboundary damage; and

(*b*) to preserve and protect the environment in the event of transboundary damage, especially with respect to mitigation of damage to the environment and its restoration or reinstatement.

Principle 4
Prompt and adequate compensation

1.   Each State should take all necessary measures to ensure that prompt and adequate compensation is available for victims of transboundary damage caused by hazardous activities located within its territory or otherwise under its jurisdiction or control.

2.   These measures should include the imposition of liability on the operator or, where appropriate, other person or entity. Such liability should not require proof of fault. Any conditions, limitations or exceptions to such liability shall be consistent with draft principle 3.

3.   These measures should also include the requirement on the operator or, where appropriate, other person or entity, to establish and maintain financial security such as insurance, bonds or other financial guarantees to cover claims of compensation.

4.   In appropriate cases, these measures should include the requirement for the establishment of industry-wide funds at the national level.

5.   In the event that the measures under the preceding paragraphs are insufficient to provide adequate compensation, the State of origin should also ensure that additional financial resources are made available.

Principle 5
Response measures

Upon the occurrence of an incident involving a hazardous activity which results or is likely to result in transboundary damage:

(*a*) the State of origin shall promptly notify all States affected or likely to be affected of the incident and the possible effects of the transboundary damage;

(*b*) the State of origin, with the appropriate involvement of the operator, shall ensure that appropriate response measures are taken and should, for this purpose, rely upon the best available scientific data and technology;

(*c*) the State of origin, as appropriate, should also consult with and seek the cooperation of all States affected or likely to be affected to mitigate the effects of transboundary damage and if possible eliminate them;

(*d*) the States affected or likely to be affected by the transboundary damage shall take all feasible measures to mitigate and if possible to eliminate the effects of such damage;

(*e*) the States concerned should, where appropriate, seek the assistance of competent international organizations and other States on mutually acceptable terms and conditions.

Principle 6
International and domestic remedies

1.   States shall provide their domestic judicial and administrative bodies with the necessary jurisdiction and competence and ensure that these bodies have prompt, adequate and effective remedies available in the event of transboundary damage caused by hazardous activities located within their territory or otherwise under their jurisdiction or control.

2.   Victims of transboundary damage should have access to remedies in the State of origin that are no less prompt, adequate and effective than those available to victims that suffer damage, from the same incident, within the territory of that State.

3.   Paragraphs 1 and 2 are without prejudice to the right of the victims to seek remedies other than those available in the State of origin.

4.   States may provide for recourse to international claims settlement procedures that are expeditious and involve minimal expenses.

5.   States should guarantee appropriate access to information relevant for the pursuance of remedies, including claims for compensation.

Principle 7
Development of specific international regimes

1.   Where, in respect of particular categories of hazardous activities, specific global, regional or bilateral agreements would provide effective arrangements concerning compensation, response measures and international and domestic remedies, all efforts should be made to conclude such specific agreements.

2.   Such agreements should, as appropriate, include arrangements for industry and/or State funds to provide supplementary compensation in the event that the financial resources of the operator, including financial security measures, are insufficient to cover the damage suffered as a result of an incident. Any such funds may be designed to supplement or replace national industry-based funds.

Principle 8
Implementation

1.   Each State should adopt the necessary legislative, regulatory and administrative measures to implement the present draft principles.

2.   The present draft principles and the measures adopted to implement them shall be applied without any discrimination such as that based on nationality, domicile or residence.

3.   States should cooperate with each other to implement the present draft principles.

The United Nations General Assembly noted but did not adopt the draft principles.

NOTES AND QUESTIONS

1.   *Where, oh where, has Liability gone . . . ?* Do you find the approach of the Draft Principles satisfying? Would this approach be acceptable in a domestic legal system? Is the "prompt and adequate compensation" contemplated by the Principles the same as International Liability?

2.   *Should we say "shall" or shall we say "should?"* "Shall" is normally a term of obligation in international instruments, whereas "should" is not. Note that even with "prompt and adequate compensation," States only "should" take measures to ensure that it is available under Principle 4(1). In fact, the entirety of Principle 4 is shot through with "shoulds." You might be thinking, okay, but these are only "principles." But look at Principles 5 and 6, which are dominated by "shalls." Does that mean that response measures (Principle 5) and international and domestic remedies (Principle 6) are more important than prompt and adequate compensation (Principle 4)?

3.   *You lost me at "allocation of loss."* Why should loss be "allocated?" The term "allocation" implies some kind of sharing, or apportionment. Why should the innocent victim have to bear any share of the loss? Does it, under the Draft Principles?

4.   *Channeling liability?* Are the Draft Principles like some kind of medium, channeling the duty to compensate to the (presumably private) operator and away from the State of origin itself? (Would the definition of "operator" in Principle 2 cover the State?) This is a technique adopted in treaties providing for strict liability—i.e., liability without proof of fault, as contemplated by Principle 4(2)—for harm caused by certain "hazardous" activities, such as nuclear power plants and other nuclear activities.[7] Why should the State of origin get off so easily? Is this consistent with *Trail Smelter*? Or is the *Trail Smelter* principle not applicable to transboundary damage caused by hazardous but lawful activities?

5.   *First compensation, then restoration?* The Principles give pride of place, if not more, to "prompt and adequate compensation." "Restoration or reinstatement" is mentioned in connection with the second "purpose" listed in Principle 3 but not in the subsequent provisions that implement these purposes. Is this right? Doesn't it stand the normal remedial system under international law (first restore to the extent possible, then compensate for anything you can't restore) on its head? Why would the Principles abandon this system, especially where the environment is concerned?

6.   *The activities that shall not be named.* What kinds of activities are contemplated by the Draft Principles? We have considered this question before. Do the provisions of the Draft Principles shed any new light on it? Are we talking explosions of nuclear or chemical plants here, or chronic, *Trail Smelter*-like, transboundary pollution? The ILC's commentary states:

> "(3) Following the same approach adopted in the case of the draft articles on prevention, the Commission opted to dispense with specification of a list of activities. Such specification of a list of activities is not without problems and functionally it is not considered essential. Any such list of activities is likely to be under-inclusive and might quickly need review in the light of ever evolving technological developments."

---

[7]   See the following treaties:

- The 1960 Paris Convention on Third Party Liability in the Field of Nuclear Energy, 956 UNTS 251;

- The 1962 Convention on the Liability of Operators of Nuclear Ships (not in force; see http://diplomatie.belgium.be/fr/binaries/i13_tcm313–79772.pdf);

- The 1963 Vienna Convention on Civil Liability for Nuclear Damage, 1063 UNTS 265; and

- The 1975 Convention relating to Civil Liability in the Field of Maritime Carriage of Nuclear Materials, 974 UNTS 255.

See also the 1969 International Convention on Civil Liability for Oil Pollution Damage, 973 UNTS 3; and the one treaty that establishes what it calls "absolute" liability of the State (Article II), the 1972 Convention on International liability for Damage Caused by Space Objects, 961 UNTS 187.

7.   *The da Vinci Code it's not—but is it a codification?* We have seen that some of the products of ILC work are regarded as codifications of rules of customary international law. Do you think that is the case with the Draft Principles on Allocation of Loss?

8.   *Responsible States? Even liable ones?* We have now looked behind the curtain and have seen the rather ugly truth: the traditional mechanism of State responsibility, and even new attempts at developing the law of State liability, are inadequate means of securing compliance with international environmental norms. A leading work comments as follows:

> While potentially relevant to environmental disputes, reliance on state responsibility has serious deficiencies in this context. First, claims may be brought only by states; the provision of diplomatic protection [whereby a State espouses the claim of its national against another State] is discretionary. . . . Moreover, the jurisdiction of international tribunals is rarely compulsory; without agreement to resort to litigation or a claims settlement process, claims can only proceed by negotiation.

> Second, insofar as claims may be made only by states with standing, and the remedies available may be limited or inadequate, it is potentially more difficult to use international claims as a means of protecting the environment of common areas. . . .

> Third, although compensation for the costs of transboundary environmental damage may be recovered through international claims, making states liable is an inefficient means of allocating these costs. Uncertainty surrounding liability standards, whether states or private parties should be made liable, the type of environmental damage covered, and the role of equitable balancing, means that the outcome of any claim remains inherently unpredictable and points to the absence of a fully principled basis for determining who should bear transboundary costs.

> The most important objection to state responsibility, however, is that it is an inadequate model for the enforcement of international standards of environmental protection. Like tort law, it complements, but does not displace, the need for a system of regulatory supervision.

Patricia Birnie, Alan Boyle & Catherine Redgwell, International Law and the Environment 236–37 (3d ed., 2009) (footnotes omitted).

We will therefore explore other means of securing compliance with international environmental standards. These range from private remedies and criminal responsibility to non-compliance mechanisms developed by States to assist them in ensuring that obligations under multilateral environmental agreements are properly implemented.

E. ACCOUNTABILITY FOR HARM TO THE GLOBAL COMMONS

CASE STUDY: THE WRECK OF THE BAHIA PARAISO[8]

On January 28, 1989, an Argentine ship grounded off the Antarctic Peninsula and began to leak oil into the waters and the coastline of Antarctica, causing that continent's "first major environmental crisis." The 435-foot ship *Bahia Paraiso* was on her way to deliver supplies to the Argentine government's Esperanza research station in Antarctica when rocks in the Bismarck Strait tore a 30-foot gash in her hull. She later capsized and sank, spreading a ten-mile slick. The *Bahia Paraiso* carried 250,000 gallons of diesel oil. One week after the accident, an estimated two-thirds of the fuel had leaked into the surrounding sea.

Oil from the wreckage of the *Bahia Paraiso* soon washed ashore, affecting wildlife at the nearby United States research base Palmer Station. Scientists' initial reports were grim. Thousands of krill (small crustaceans that form an essential link in the Antarctic food chain) were found dead along the coast near Palmer Station. Half of the adult skua population had abandoned their nesting grounds, leaving chicks vulnerable to predators. Penguin rookeries near Palmer Station, home to some 24,000 birds, were surrounded by oil. An early survey of 40 penguins found 38 had been "oil dipped." The oil affects the birds' natural insulation and may be deadly if swallowed.

The United States and Argentina both assisted in the cleanup of the oil spill. Immediately following the grounding, the United States dispatched a Navy transport aircraft carrying cleanup equipment. The gear was flown to Chile, where it was rerouted to a supply ship operated by the United States National Science Foundation. The Argentine government sent navy ships to assist in the cleanup effort.

––––––––––

THIRD STATE REMEDIES FOR ENVIRONMENTAL DAMAGE TO THE WORLD'S COMMON SPACES

Jonathan I. Charney
in International Responsibility for Environmental Harm 149, 175–177 (Francesco Francioni and Tullio Scovazzi eds., 1991)

International law imposes on all States certain rights and duties with respect to the environment in the world's common spaces. General customary international law requires that all States behave in a manner

––––––––––

[8] From Jonathan I. Charney, Third State Remedies for Environmental Damage to the World's Common Spaces, in Francioni & Scovazzi eds., International Responsibility for Environmental Harm, 529–531.

so as not to cause harm to the environment of areas beyond the jurisdiction of any state including, *a fortiori,* the high seas, outer space, and the Antarctic.

. . . Under some interpretations of traditional international law when no State has suffered a particular injury, no State may seek an international remedy. In the case of the world's common spaces restrictive remedy rules may permit grave injuries to be unredressed. [Professor Charney] argues that a particular injury to a State is not always necessary before a State may pursue an international remedy. In some circumstances international law finds a constructive or theoretical injury to be sufficient for standing. These occasions arise when there is no reasonable alternative to third-State remedies and substantial interests of the international community are at stake. Because there is no particular injury, a third State cannot expect that the full panoply of rights and remedies would be available. The third-State remedy is a measure born of necessity and given no more leeway than that necessity requires.

The notion of third-State remedies is especially important for [common spaces]. Because no State may suffer a particular injury upon the violation of a norm applicable to the world's common spaces, there must exist a third-State remedy or none at all. International law appears to permit all States to remedy violations of legal duties designed to protect the environment of the world's common spaces. A violation of these norms, therefore, provides standing to assert a third-State remedy against the polluting State.

That is not to say that all States are therefore competent to mount against a State accused of harming the environment of a common space the full range of remedies and pretend, as it were, to have suffered a particular injury. Third States may take some steps to protect their interest in the environment of the world's common spaces. A [S]tate certainly may exercise its *droit de regard,* or file diplomatic protests with the responsible [S]tate. These somewhat circumspect measures would doubtless comport with the limited competence possessed by third States. Other, more formidable remedies may or may not be appropriate, depending upon the circumstances.

In the case of the *Bahia Paraiso,* . . . or for that matter in any similar circumstance involving an injury to the environment of the world's common spaces, a careful application of third-State remedies may be appropriate. Indeed, if there ever were a case to be made for third-State remedies, it is present in matters like the *Bahia Paraiso* tragedy. Here, international law has imposed certain obligations on all States with respect to the Antarctic and the marine environments. A breach of these obligations affects the interests of the entire community of States. The exercise of third-State remedies in this context is especially appropriate given their necessity. No other form of remedy is available due to the absence of a particularly injured State. Furthermore, the subject-matter is of distinctly universal concern—Antarctica has been called the common heritage of mankind. . . . In sum, the resort to limited third-State remedies in situations where the damage to the environment of the world's common spaces had taken place in violation of international law is not only appropriate under the eye of international law, but necessary for the maintenance of good order among States.

NOTES AND QUESTIONS

1. *The standing problem.* For a discussion of the idea that states' obligations in the area of climate change run *erga omnes, i.e.,* to all states, *see* Frederic L. Kirgis, Jr., *Standing to Challenge Human Endeavors That Could Change the Climate*, 84 A.J.I.L. 525 (1990).

2. *Is the international community capable of responding?* Aside from third state remedies, should the international community itself not respond in some way to grave environmental injuries in the global commons? How could such a response be organized? Presumably through the United Nations, but how could or should this be done within the existing organizational framework of the UN? Would the passage of a resolution by the General Assembly concerning each case be sufficient? Would the Security Council have a role to play in such situations? What about such organs of the UN as the International Court of Justice or even the Trusteeship Council? As to the latter, could not the international community, as represented in the United Nations, be said to hold the global commons in trust for the benefit of humankind? If so, could the organized international community, perhaps through the Trusteeship Council, respond to problems such as massive pollution of the atmosphere, the oceans, or Antarctica, or even extreme overfishing? What form should such a response take?

3. *Defining the "commons."* How should the "commons" be defined? There is probably general agreement that the concept includes the high seas, the global atmosphere, Antarctica, and outer space. But what about endangered species? Is there not an important community interest in the preservation of biological diversity in general and certain species (like the whale and the elephant, for example), in particular? What if the hypothetical State of Biodiva decides to allow the unrestricted hunting, to extinction, of the Rarabong, a species that is especially valued by the international community but which is found only in Biodiva? Who (i.e., what State or States, the international community, etc.) could respond, and how?

F. PRIVATE REMEDIES FOR TRANSBOUNDARY ENVIRONMENTAL HARM

RESTATEMENT (THIRD) OF THE FOREIGN RELATIONS LAW OF THE UNITED STATES
§ 602(2) (1987)

§ 602.   Remedies for Violation of Environmental Obligations

. . . (2) Where pollution originating in a state has caused significant injury to persons outside that state, or has created a significant risk of such injury, the state of origin is obligated to accord to the person injured or exposed to such risk access to the same judicial or administrative remedies as are available in similar circumstances to persons within the state.

Comment

b. Local Remedies. . . .

Subsection (2) applies the principle of non-discrimination against foreign nationals (§ 711, Comment *f*). This principle requires that a state in which pollution originates avoid discrimination in the enforcement of applicable international rules and standards, as well as give to foreign victims the benefit of its own rules and standards for the protection of the environment, even if they are stricter than the international rules or standards. Subsection (2) applies the principle of nondiscrimination also to remedies. A state must provide the same procedures, and apply the same substantive law and the same measures of compensation, to persons outside its territory as are available to persons injured within its territory. . . .

UNITED NATIONS CONVENTION ON THE LAW OF THE SEA, 1982
Article 235(2) and (3)

Article 235
Responsibility and Liability

2.   States shall ensure that recourse is available in accordance with their legal systems for prompt and adequate compensation or other relief in respect of damage caused by pollution of the marine environment by natural or juridical persons under their jurisdiction.

3.   With the objective of assuring prompt and adequate compensation in respect of all damage caused by pollution of the marine environment, States shall cooperate in the implementation of existing international law and the further development of international law

relating to responsibility and liability for the assessment of and compensation for damage and the settlement of related disputes, as well as, where appropriate, development of criteria and procedures for payment of adequate compensation, such as compulsory insurance or compensation funds.

NOTES AND QUESTIONS

1.   *The meaning of Article 235(2).* What does paragraph 2 of Article 235 really require states to do? Must they enact new legislation if existing provisions are inadequate? What is the significance of the phrase "in accordance with their legal systems" in this regard? Does it mean they only have to offer what is already available, but on a nondiscriminatory basis? Or does it mean that they must enact new measures if none are presently in place?

2.   *"Ensuring" recourse.* How can a state *ensure that recourse is available"*? Might there not be cases in which damage was caused, but because of proof or procedural problems courts would not grant relief?

3.   *The approach of the U.N. Watercourses Convention.* These and other problems led the International Law Commission to reject a proposal to include a provision in its draft articles on international watercourses similar to Article 235(2). Instead, the commission adopted a draft article that formed the basis for Article 32 of the UN Convention on International Watercourses:

Article 32
Non-discrimination

Unless the watercourse States concerned have agreed otherwise for the protection of the interests of persons, natural or juridical, who have suffered or are under a serious threat of suffering significant transboundary harm as a result of activities related to an international watercourse, a watercourse State shall not discriminate on the basis of nationality or residence or place where the injury occurred, in granting to such persons, in accordance with its legal system, access to judicial or other procedures, or a right to claim compensation or other relief in respect of significant harm caused by such activities carried on in its territory.

United Nations Convention on the Law of the Non-Navigational Uses of International Watercourses, U.N. Doc. A/RES/51/229, May 21, 1997. Again, does the phrase "in accordance with its legal system" offer an escape route for the state that does not wish to accord access, equal or otherwise, to individuals from other countries? If you were representing such an individual, what argument(s) would you make against using that phrase as justification for not granting equal access?

INTERNATIONAL LAW AND THE ENVIRONMENT
Patricia Birnie, Alan Boyle & Catherine Redgwell
303–304 (3d ed. 2009)

There are three good reasons for encouraging resort to private law remedies in transboundary environmental disputes. First, it de-escalates disputes "to their ordinary neighborhood level," where they can be resolved using national law, and avoids turning them into interstate controversies based on problematic concepts of state responsibility in international law. Second, by allowing direct recourse against the enterprise causing the damage it facilitates implementation of a "polluter pays" approach to the allocation of environmental costs. A policy internalizing the true economic costs of pollution is endorsed in Principle 16 of the Rio Declaration and in the policy of OECD, and the EC. Third, it empowers individuals by enabling the private plaintiff to act without the intervention of a government, and facilitates further development of a rights-based approach to environmental issues. This is consistent in general terms with the policy, considered earlier in this chapter, of promoting "effective access to judicial and administrative proceedings, including redress and remedy" in accordance with Principle 10 of the Rio Declaration. Moreover, a policy of encouraging resort to transboundary civil litigation and remedies recognises the reality that many, if not most, transboundary environmental problems are mainly caused by and affect private parties, rather than states as such. In this context transboundary litigation not only provides an effective mechanism for dealing with transboundary harm, but may also offer the possibility of securing redress from multinationals whose operations in developing countries are sometimes difficult to control through local law.

Encouraging the solution of transboundary problems through national law also has disadvantages, which must be recognized. There may be no remedy, or no effective remedy, if the applicable legal system is favourable to the activities of polluters. No common legal standards will necessarily govern the availability of remedies in different states unless there is parallel progress in harmonizing environmental standards and liability for damage. Even where adequate law exists, problems of jurisdiction, the availability of remedies and enforcement in transboundary cases may limit the usefulness of this form of litigation. Public and private international law can have a role in securing access to justice by removing some or all of these disadvantages and by ensuring that adequate national remedies are available to plaintiffs in transboundary cases. These objectives can be achieved in a variety of ways, but will usually involve addressing some or all of the following elements:

(1) non-discriminatory treatment of transboundary plaintiffs and equal access to available national procedures and remedies;

(2) resolving problems of private international law, particularly jurisdiction and choice of law in transboundary cases;

(3) harmonization of national laws dealing with liability for environmental damage.

NOTE AND QUESTION

The road to a dead end is paved with good intentions? Recall that in the *Trail Smelter* case, the injured parties in Washington had sought legal advice concerning bringing a lawsuit against the smelter. They were told there was a perfect storm of blockages: they couldn't sue in Washington because (at the time) they could not get jurisdiction over the smelter; and they couldn't sue in British Columbia because of the "local action rule," a venerable common law doctrine applicable there according to which actions for damage to land must be brought at the land's situs. Is this one of those situations in which solutions that are entirely sensible run afoul of local legal impediments?

The Uniform Transboundary Pollution Reciprocal Access Act was promulgated in 1982 in both the United States and Canada to remove procedural obstacles to gaining remedies for transboundary pollution harm. It has been enacted in Colorado, Connecticut, Montana, New Jersey, Oregon, and Wisconsin, and in Canada, by the Provinces of Manitoba, Ontario and Prince Edward Island.

G. CRIMINAL RESPONSIBILITY FOR ENVIRONMENTAL HARM

CRIMES AGAINST THE ENVIRONMENT
Stephen McCaffrey
in 1 International Criminal Law 541 (M. Cherif Bassiouni ed., 1986)[9]

... [V]arious international instruments, principles and theories ... attach penal consequences to conduct resulting in serious harm to vital or scarce natural resources; and a number of states have enacted legislation, often pursuant to international instruments, making it a crime under their municipal law to cause harm to internationally shared resources. . . .

[T]here are sound reasons for criminalizing environmentally harmful conduct. And it is submitted that these reasons apply with equal vigor to resources that are shared on the domestic and international levels. In fact, the considerations which support and explain criminalization on the domestic level may apply with even greater force to internationally shared resources. It is not necessary here to enter the debate about whether such resources are *res nullius* or *res communis* because many of

---

[9] [Portions of this excerpt have been updated by the author for the purposes of this book.— Eds.]

them are, by their very nature, simply not capable of appropriation and reduction to ownership. They may, however, be used in a manner which forecloses certain uses by others or even leads to their complete destruction: air and water may be polluted, species may be extinguished.

Because it is thus likely that internationally shared resources will often be protected even less by private vigilance than their domestic counterparts, the argument for their protection by penal sanctions would seem to be stronger than that applicable to resources shared domestically. Furthermore, some internationally shared resources—such as certain species of flora and fauna—may be entirely and forever extinguished because of the "commons" effect, which may be more pronounced when the commons in question overlaps jurisdictions or is beyond the limits of national jurisdiction: to the extent that (a) national laws do not reach the conduct in question, and (b) the conduct is not governed by a relevant international regime, it will operate free of both private, and any existing public, regulatory constraints.

These considerations have led states, both individually and collectively, to attach penal sanctions to certain kinds of conduct and activities that threaten, damage or destroy those natural resources which represent internationally shared values. . . .

II. INTERNATIONAL INSTRUMENTS THAT ENVISAGE CRIMINAL RESPONSIBILITY OF PRIVATE PERSONS

Penal Characteristics

There are a number of types of provisions found in international instruments relating to nature and the environment which might be considered to be penal in nature, or to be of such a character as to be part of the field of international criminal law. Our editor has proposed the following list of characteristics, the presence of any one of which would qualify an instrument as belonging to the field of international criminal law: (1) explicit or implicit declaration of certain conduct as a crime under international law; (2) criminalization of the conduct under national law; (3) providing for the prosecution or extradition of the alleged perpetrator; (4) providing for punishment of the person found guilty; (5) cooperation through the various modalities of judicial assistance in the enforcement of the agreement; (6) establishment of a priority in theories of jurisdiction and perhaps recognition of the applicability of universal jurisdiction; (7) reference to an international criminal jurisdiction; and (8) exclusion of the defense of superior orders. These criteria have provided guidance in the identification of instruments to be included in the present study.

Conventions

The vast majority of the instruments surveyed for this study contain a blend of items (2) through (4) on the list set out above. Most commonly, these instruments require the contracting parties to take "appropriate measures to ensure the application of the provisions of the [agreement in question] and the punishment of infractions against [those] provisions." Other approaches include requiring the parties to "enact and enforce such legislation as may be necessary to make effective the ... provisions [of the agreement] with appropriate penalties for violations thereof," providing that violations "shall be an offence punishable under the laws of the territory in which the ship is registered," and providing that the parties "shall enact and enforce such legislation and other measures as may be necessary for the purpose of giving effect to [the] Agreement," which agreement includes various prohibitions. These types of provisions are found in some fifteen multilateral agreements relating to the environment. Some agreements expressly recognize their deterrent function in provisions to the effect that "the penalties specified under the law of a party shall be adequate in severity to discourage violations of the present Convention. . . ."

A number of conventions contain what might be referred to as "policing provisions" which allow parties to take action on the spot to enforce the rules of the agreement. This is true, for example, of the 1911 Convention for the Preservation of Fur Seals in the North Pacific, which provides in article 1 that persons offending against the Convention's prohibition against pelagic sealing "may be seized" by the authorities of the territory in which the violation occurs. The same convention, in article 7, provides that each party "will maintain a guard or patrol in the waters frequented by the seal herd in the protection of which it is especially interested, so far as may be necessary for the enforcement of the [Convention]." Similarly, the 1937 International Agreement for the Regulation of Whaling provides in article 1 that the parties "will maintain at least one inspector of whaling on each factory ship under their jurisdiction." The Interim Convention on Conservation of North Pacific Fur Seals of 1957 goes further, allowing a "duly authorized official of any of the Parties" to board and search "any vessel ... subject to the jurisdiction of any of the Parties" which he "has reasonable cause to believe . . . is offending against the prohibition of pelagic sealing. . . ." The Convention goes on to provide that if after searching the vessel the official "continues to have reasonable cause to believe that the vessel or any person on board thereof is offending against the prohibition, he may seize or arrest such vessel or person." Finally, what might be referred to as a "self-policing provision" is found in the Agreement between Canada and the United States on Great Lakes Water Quality of 1978. An annex to that agreement provides as follows:

> As soon as any person in charge [of a vessel] has knowledge of any discharge of harmful quantities of oil or hazardous polluting substances, immediate notice of such discharge shall be given to the appropriate agency in the jurisdiction where the discharge

occurs; failure to give this notice shall be made subject to appropriate penalties.

Recommendations and Resolutions

Various international or intergovernmental bodies have produced instruments that call for the use of penal sanctions to safeguard nature and the environment. . . .

Values Protected

[I]nternational criminal law has as its principal *raison d'être* the protection of certain shared values the international community has come to recognize as being so important that penal sanctions must be imposed on those who threaten or impair them. A survey of international instruments relating to the global environment reveals that a wide variety of values fall into this category, ranging from natural beauty and the integrity of the environment in general to specific species of flora and fauna. The following examples of these values illustrate their wide diversity.

A number of conventions with penal features include provisions on the protection of particular species or of flora and fauna in general. For example, the preamble of CITES provides that the contracting states:

RECOGNIZ[E] that wild fauna and flora in their many beautiful and varied forms are an irreplaceable part of the natural systems of the earth which must be protected for this and the generations to come; [and are] CONSCIOUS of the ever-growing value of wild fauna and flora from aesthetic, scientific, cultural, recreational and economic points of view. . . .

Perhaps more common are instruments with penal characteristics that are directed toward the protection of a specific species.

The international community has for some time now recognized the importance of protecting the ocean from pollution and has produced a number of instruments providing for the prosecution by municipal authorities of individual polluters. Interestingly, however, the same cannot yet be said of the atmosphere.

A number of instruments having penal characteristics emphasize the importance of safeguarding the beauty of nature, and aesthetic considerations in general. This is true, for example, of CITES. . . . Another example is the 1940 Convention on Nature Protection and Wildlife Preservation in the Western Hemisphere, which declares the intent of the parties "to protect and preserve scenery of extraordinary beauty, unusual and striking geologic formations, regions and natural objects of aesthetic historic or scientific value. . . ." The importance of aesthetic considerations is also recognized by intergovernmental organizations. The Committee of Ministers of the Council of Europe has declared that "the beauty of landscapes must be protected by all possible means . . . ," and the General Conference of UNESCO in 1962 adopted a recommendation, containing penal provisions, specifically addressed to "the safeguarding of the beauty and character of landscapes and sites." . . .

Finally, some instruments expressly recognize the responsibility of present generations to protect and preserve the earth's resources for future generations. Examples of this type of provision may be found both in CITES, and in the 1946 Convention for the Regulation of Whaling. The latter agreement recognizes "the interest of the nations of the world in safeguarding for future generations the great natural resources represented by the whale stocks. . . ."

IV. GENERALLY RECOGNIZED PRINCIPLES OF LAW

Article 38 of the Statute of the International Court of Justice lists as one of the sources of international law to be applied by the Court "the general principles of law recognized by civilized nations." . . .

An increasing number of states have enacted legislation providing for punishment of environment-related offenses. This trend has been given a significant boost by CITES, to which 180[10] countries are parties. . . .

NOTES AND QUESTIONS

1.   *Why criminalize?* What are the reasons for criminalizing certain conduct? Do they apply on the international level? Do you believe the available enforcement mechanisms are adequate to deter the conduct that is criminalized?

2.   *Individual versus state crimes.* Do you see the difference between criminalizing conduct by individuals, on the one hand, and states, on the other? What are the advantages and disadvantages of each form of criminal responsibility? How do you punish a state? Does history offer any lessons on the advisability of punishing countries?

3.   *The Basel Convention.* The Basel Convention on the Control of Transboundary Movements of Hazardous Wastes and Their Disposal of March 22, 1989, requires in Article 4, paragraphs 3 and 4, that:

> 3.   The Parties consider that illegal traffic in hazardous wastes or other wastes is criminal.

> 4.   Each Party shall take appropriate legal, administrative and other measures to implement and enforce the provisions of this Convention, including measures to prevent and punish conduct in contravention of the Convention.

---

[10] As of August, 2014.—Eds.

4. *The Rome Statute.* Included in the definition of "war crimes" under Article 8 of the Rome Statute of the International Criminal Court is the following:

(iv) Intentionally launching an attack in the knowledge that such attack will cause incidental loss of live or injury to civilians or damage to civilian objects or widespread, long-term and severe damage to the natural environment which would be clearly excessive in relation to the concrete and direct overall military advantage anticipated. . . .

Rome Statute, Article 8(b)(iv), U.N. Doc. A/CONF.183/9, 17 July 1998. Note that the language refers only to damage caused from intentionally launching an attack.

5. *Universal jurisdiction.* States have universal jurisdiction to prosecute individuals for a limited class of crimes regardless of the connection of the crime or the alleged perpetrator to the prosecuting state. Piracy is the paradigmatic crime that is subject to universal jurisdiction. Should Saddam Hussein's torching of the oil wells and spilling of oil into the Gulf also qualify as such a crime?

6. *A Law Against Ecocide?* In 1973 Professor Richard Falk proposed a Convention on Ecocide. In the ensuing decade States discussed defining certain environmental damage as a crime against humanity. More recently, Polly Higgins, a lawyer in the United Kingdom, has led a nongovernmental effort to draft a Law Against Ecocide to be used at the national level and submitted to the International Law Commission a proposal to add Ecocide as a fifth crime under Article 5 of the Rome Statute of the International Criminal Court. What advantages do you see to these approaches? What problems?

H. COMPLIANCE WITH HARD AND SOFT LAW

Are there approaches other than rules of responsibility and liability for encouraging compliance with norms of international environmental law? As the international community becomes increasingly organized, both through universal institutions (of which the United Nations is the foremost example) and through sectoral treaty regimes (such as those relating to climate change, biodiversity, protection of the ozone layer, and the like), it becomes possible to ever greater degrees to monitor and foster compliance with international standards of behavior, both customary and conventional. In this section we look at new treaty-based approaches to that objective and at ways to strengthen compliance with international environmental obligations.

1. NEW TREATY APPROACHES TO THE PROBLEM OF COMPLIANCE

a. Noncompliance Procedures Under the Montreal Protocol and Amendments Thereto

(*See* material in Chapter 8 on implementation of the Montreal Protocol.)

b. North American Agreement on Environmental Cooperation

NORTH AMERICAN AGREEMENT ON ENVIRONMENTAL COOPERATION, ARTICLES 14 AND 15
14 September 1993, 32 I.L.M. 1480 (1993)

Article 14
Submissions on Enforcement Matters

1.   The Secretariat may consider a submission from any non-governmental organization or person asserting that a Party is failing to effectively enforce its environ-mental law, if the Secretariat finds that the submission:

   (a) is in writing in a language designated by that Party in a notification to the Secretariat;

   (b) clearly identifies the person or organization making the submission;

   (c) provides sufficient information to allow the Secretariat to review the submission, including any documentary evidence on which the submission may be based;

   (d) appears to be aimed at promoting enforcement rather than at harassing industry;

   (e) indicates that the matter has been communicated in writing to the relevant authorities of the Party and indicates the Party's response, if any; and

   (f) is filed by a person or organization residing or established in the territory of a Party.

2.   Where the Secretariat determines that a submission meets the criteria set out in paragraph 1, the Secretariat shall determine whether the submission merits requesting a response from the Party. In deciding whether to request a response, the Secretariat shall be guided by whether:

   (a) the submission alleges harm to the person or organization making the submission;

(b) the submission, alone or in combination with other submissions, raises matters whose further study in this process would advance the goals of this Agreement;

(c) private remedies available under the Party's law have been pursued; and,

(d) the submission is drawn exclusively from mass media reports.

3.   The Party shall advise the Secretariat within 30 days or, in exceptional circumstances and on notification to the Secretariat, within 60 days of delivery of the request:

(a) whether the matter is the subject of a pending judicial or administrative proceeding, in which case the Secretariat shall proceed no further; and

(b) of any other information that the Party wishes to submit, such as

i) whether the matter was previously the subject of a judicial or administrative proceeding, and

ii) whether private remedies in connection with the matter are available to the person or organization making the submission and whether they have been pursued.

Article 15
Factual Record

1.   If the Secretariat considers that the submission, in the light of any response provided by the Party, warrants developing a factual record, the Secretariat shall so inform the Council and provide its reasons.

2.   The Secretariat shall prepare a factual record if the Council, by a two-thirds vote, instructs it to do so.

3.   The preparation of a factual record by the Secretariat pursuant to this Article shall be without prejudice to any further steps that may be taken with respect to any submission.

4.   In preparing a factual record, the Secretariat shall consider any information furnished by a Party and may consider any relevant technical, scientific or other information:

(a) that is publicly available;

(b) submitted by interested non-governmental organizations or persons;

(c) submitted by the Joint Public Advisory Committee; or

(d) developed by the Secretariat or by independent experts.

5.   The Secretariat shall submit a draft factual record to the Council. Any Party may provide comments on the accuracy of the draft within 45 days thereafter.

6.   The Secretariat shall incorporate, as appropriate, any such comments in the final factual record and submit it to the Council.

7.   The Council may, by a two-thirds vote, make the final factual record publicly available, normally within 60 days following its submission.

NOTES

Please comply? Pretty please? The positivist paradox of international law—how can there be law without a sovereign to enforce rights and duties?—has led to efforts to find alternative ways to induce compliance with newly emerging international norms. Environmentalists have tried to adapt a strategy used with some success by human rights advocates: the disclosure of information that shames a nation into changing its behavior. The negotiation of the North American Free Trade Agreement (NAFTA) produced one of the most innovative alternative environmental enforcement experiments which depends on "spotlighting" the failure of a country to adhere to national and international environmental norms. As the price for the free trade agreement, United States environmentalists obtained a side agreement, the North American Agreement on Environmental Cooperation (NAAEC), which creates a liberal citizen submission process administered by an international body with the power to investigate allegations of the under-enforcement of existing environmental laws in Canada, Mexico, and the United States. Articles 14 and 15 are the heart of the process.

The following describes the process created by the Environmental Side Agreement.

The NAAEC Submissions Procedure

The NAAEC's aim is to enhance environmental protection in North America and increase cooperation among the NAFTA Parties. Environmental organizations, particularly in the United States, had two chief fears about NAFTA. First, they feared that the increased trade that NAFTA would produce would exacerbate environmental problems in the border regions. Second, and more important, they feared that NAFTA would induce a decline in environmental protection generally. Many environmentalists believe that trade liberalization undermines environmental protection not only in terms of a race to the bottom in regulatory standards but also in a race to the bottom in implementation and enforcement. In the NAFTA context, this concern was particularly salient because Mexican environmental law, while formally strict, was in practice poorly enforced. Due to the relatively tepid political support for NAFTA in Congress in the early 1990s, environmental groups were able to successfully demand that the Clinton administration negotiate an agreement that would address this alleged race-to-the-bottom problem. Clinton, concerned that NAFTA would not pass if environmentalists opposed it, pressed for the creation of the NAAEC. Canada and Mexico ultimately accepted this as the price of NAFTA. As a result, the NAAEC was negotiated with the core objective of the "improvement of environmental laws, regulations, procedures, policies, and practices" and the enhancement of "compliance with, and enforcement of, environmental laws and regulations."

The citizen submissions procedure of the NAAEC, which in many ways is the agreement's centerpiece, permits any individual or nongovernmental organization (NGO) residing in the territory of the three Parties to tile a submission with the Secretariat of the CEC alleging that a Party is "failing to effectively enforce its environmental laws." This provision is unique in international environmental law because it focuses not on the enforcement of international law but rather on that of domestic law. In this sense, the NAAEC creates a means for the international "enforcement of enforcement. There are minor threshold requirements submitters must meet, but, unusually, submitters need not reside in or be a citizen of the Party whose enforcement practices they challenge. Thus, the process is truly transnational: Mexican NGOs can complain about enforcement failures in Nova Scotia, and—what was critical from the political perspective of securing the overall NAFTA package—U.S. NGOs can complain about enforcement failures in Tijuana.

When a submission is made, the Secretariat determines whether to request a response from the Party that is challenged. After receiving the government's reply, the Secretariat then decides whether to recommend the creation of a "factual record." The Council—the environment ministers of the three NAFTA Parties—must approve the decision by a two-thirds vote. When the factual record is complete, the Council votes again on its public release.

Kai Rausiala, Citizen Submissions and Treaty Review in the NAAEC, in Greening NAFTA: The North American Commission for Environmental Cooperation 259–260 (David L. Markel & John H. Knox, eds., 2003).

NOTES AND QUESTIONS

1.   *The screening process.* The Agreement is administered by the North American Commission on Environmental Cooperation (CEC). The CEC is composed of (1) a Council of the environmental ministers of the three countries, (2) a permanent Secretariat located in Montreal, Canada, and (3) a Joint Public Advisory Committee (JPAC). Since 1994, the Citizens

Submission Unit of the Secretariat has received some 50 submissions.[11] The submissions have come from all three NAFTA countries, but the bulk have come from Canada and Mexico. For example, in 2005, the Unit had eleven active submission files, five each from Canada and Mexico and one from the United States. The practice of the Submissions Unit, reflected in its recommendations to the Council and in published Factual Records, has created a substantial body of "precedent and jurisprudence," although the Commission is limited to the preparation of a Factual Record and is not a judicial tribunal. The preparation and release, if authorized by the Council, the factual record is the end of the Side Agreement process. The Secretariat must make many determinations during the Article 14 screening phase as well during the preparation of a Record Under Article 15. For example, what is a failure to effective enforce? Article 45 provides that it is not "a reasonable exercise of . . . discretion in respect of investigatory, prosecutorial or compliance matters or . . . results from bone fide decisions to allocate resources in respect of other environmental matters determined to have higher priorities." Should the Submissions Unit decide whether Article 45 defenses apply during the Article 14 screening phase or during the preparation of a record? Are a party's representations that Article 45 applies conclusive?

2. *Spotlight or pencil light?* The Commission has no formal enforcement power. It lacks the power to draw any conclusions about non-enforcement or future remedial steps. Thus, the primary benefit of the process is the disclosure of information about a party's non-enforcement practices which will sufficiently embarrass the party and shame it into taking action to improve enforcement. The Citizen Submissions process has a high degree of transparency, John Knox, *A New Approach to Compliance With International Environmental Law: The Submissions Procedure of the NAFTA Environmental Commission*, 28 Ecology L.Q. 1 (2001), but even this modest, and seemingly universally accepted norm, can cause a backlash. Consider the following Submission. United States NGOs alleged that the United States was not enforcing the Migratory Bird Treaty Act, 16 U.S.C. §§ 703–711. The MBTA implemented a treaty between Canada and United States which protects a wide class of migratory birds, most of which are not listed as endangered in the two countries. The Act makes it unlawful to "hunt, take, capture, kill. . . ." any migratory bird, not just those protected under the United States Endangered Species Act or the more recently enacted Canadian counterpart. The United States Supreme Court has held that the United States Department of Interior can define "take" in the ESA to include habitat modification, Babbitt v. Sweet Home Chapter of Communities of Greater Oregon, 515 U.S. 687 (1995), and environmental NGOs would like to extend this concept of "take" to the MBTA to change the ways the timber is harvested in many forests. The United States NGOs alleged "broad, programmatic failures to effectively enforce" the law, David Markell, The

---

[11] We wish to disclose that Professors Brown Weiss, McCaffrey, and Tarlock have served or are currently serving as one of the three United States Special Legal Advisors to the Submissions Unit. However, all material presented here is a matter of public record.

CEC Citizens Submissions Process: On or Off Course?, in Greening NAFTA, *supra* at 276, and Council responded as follows:

COUNCIL RESOLUTION 01–10

Instruction to the Secretariat of the Commission for Environmental Cooperation Regarding the Assertion that the Government of the United States is Failing to Effectively Enforce the *Migratory Bird Treaty Act* (SEM-99-002). . . .

THE COUNCIL . . .

HAVING REVIEWED the notification by the Secretariat of December 15, 2000 that the development of a factual record is warranted with respect to the submission (SEM-99-002); and

MINDFUL that the United States in its reply has indicated that, as a general matter, the assertions in the submission reflect, or result from, circumstances referred to in NAAEC Article 45(1), which provides that "[a] Party has not failed to "effectively enforce its environment law" or to comply with Article 5(1) in a particular case where the action or inaction in question by agencies or officials of the named Party: (a) reflects a reasonable exercise of their discretion in respect of investigatory, prosecutorial, regulatory or compliance matters; or (b) results from *bona fide* decisions to allocate resources to enforcement in respect of other environmental matters determined to have higher priorities";

HEREBY UNANIMOUSLY DECIDES:

TO INSTRUCT the Secretariat to prepare a factual record in accordance with Article 15 of the NAAEC and the *Guidelines for Submissions on Enforcement Matters under Articles 14 and 15 of the North American Agreement on Environmental Cooperation* with respect to the two specific cases identified in SEM-99-002. The first case involves the logging of several hundred trees by a private landowner during the nesting season of Great Blue Herons allegedly resulting in hundreds of crushed eggs. The second case involves a logging company's alleged intentional burning of four trees on private land, including one allegedly nested by a pair of ospreys;

TO DIRECT the Secretariat to provide the Parties with its overall work plan for gathering the relevant facts and to provide the Parties with the opportunity to comment on that plan; and

TO DIRECT the Secretariat to consider, in developing the factual record, whether the Party concerned "is failing to effectively enforce its environmental law" since the entry into force of the NAAEC on January 1, 1994. In considering such an alleged failure to effectively enforce, relevant facts that existed prior to January 1, 1994, may he included in the factual record.

Article 10 of the Agreement sets out the Council's functions. Article 10(c) authorizes the Council to "oversee the Secretariat" Does this include the specification of the content of a Factual Record?" Is this oversight, consistent with Articles 14 and 15 or the purpose of the Agreement?

3.   *So what?* Unlike the WTO Appellate Body, the CEC has no power to recommend sanctions or to monitor the party's reaction to a Factual Record. Nonetheless, Factual Records are prepared to advance one of the general goals of the Agreement, enhanced environmental protection. Tseming Yang, *The Effectiveness of the NAFTA Environmental Side Agreement's Citizen Submission Process: A Case Study of Metales y Derivados*, 76 Colo. L. Rev. 443 (2005) studied the aftermath of a factual record, Metales y Derivados, Final Factual Record (SEM 98–007 2002). Submitters alleged that waste heaps from an abandoned battery and lead waste recycling facility in Tijuana, Mexico caused groundwater contamination and more immediate health problems in the surrounding area. The record substantiated almost all the submitters' allegations, but the only post-record action was to place new warning signs at the site. Professor Yang concludes that "[t]he *Metales* case demonstrates that the citizen submission process has managed to increase regulatory enforcement transparency without accomplishing the underlying triple goal of improved environmental quality, enhanced enforcement, and broadened environmental governance. . . . The most obvious explanation for these difficulties is the weak coercive power of transparency." *Id*. at 477 and 479. Professor Yang proposes several improvements including a requirement that the Factual Record contain legal conclusions as to whether a State has failed to enforce its environmental law and that the Secretariat should be an autonomous institution free from Council supervision.

2. GETTING STATES TO COMPLY WITH INTERNATIONAL OBLIGATIONS

STRENGTHENING NATIONAL COMPLIANCE WITH INTERNATIONAL ENVIRONMENTAL AGREEMENTS

Edith Brown Weiss
27 Envtl. Pol'y & L. 297 (1997)[12]

[The following excerpt is based on research by Harold K. Jacobson and Edith Brown Weiss with more than 30 scholars that focused on nine countries and five international agreements.[13]]

In 1972, when the United Nations Conference on the Human Environment was held in Stockholm, there were only about three dozen

---

[12] This article is adapted from that presented to the 25th Anniversary of the Elizabeth Haub Prize winners in Wiesbaden, Germany, April 1997.

[13] Harold K Jacobson & Edith Brown Weiss, Strengthening Compliance with International Environmental Accords: Preliminary Observations from a Collaborative Project, 2 Global Governance 1 (1995). The research will be published as Engaging Countries: Strengthening Compliance with International Environmental Accords (Edith Brown Weiss & Harold K Jacobson, eds., 1998).

multilateral environmental agreements. Today there are more than 900 international legal instruments (mostly binding) that are either focused on environment or contain one or more important provisions concerned with environment. These instruments are viewed as primary means for affecting the behavior of states and the many other actors today: subnational governments, industries, nongovernmental organizations and individuals. They involve substantial costs to states and to the targeted and interested actors, whether in the negotiations for the agreements or their implementation. Until recently little attention has been given to the extent to which states and other actors comply with these agreements. In this brief article, I argue that compliance is a complex process involving both the intent and the capacity of states, that the three alternative compliance strategies embodied in international agreements—sunshine, incentives, and sanctions—and the institutional design of agreements affects intent and capacity, and that the choice of strategies must be targeted to individual countries' intent and capacity. Moreover, the preferred strategy choices vary across different areas of international agreements: trade, labor, human rights, arms control, and environment.

I.   THE CONCEPTUAL FRAMEWORK

The traditional stylized model of compliance assumes that countries accept international agreements only when their governments regard them as in their interest. Because of this, countries generally comply with the obligations they have assumed. If they do [not], sanctions are used to punish offenders and deter violations.

But the reality is different. While countries join agreements that are in their self-interest, there are many reasons why countries may find them to be in their self-interest. And these reasons affect their willingness and their capacity to comply. In the best of worlds, countries may join to show leadership in addressing a problem. But they also may join because others are doing so, or because governments with leverage over them are pressing them to do so, or because of domestic interests. Countries may join because the obligations require no changes in their present behavior, or they may join with no intention of immediately complying and may even lack the capacity to comply.

The traditional framework for analyzing compliance is hierarchic, static and focused on states. Governments negotiate international agreements, which are then usually put into force through implementing legislation or regulations at the national level. States ensure that other actors comply with the domestic measures. This approach is hierarchic because it moves from the international agreement and member states downward to the subgovernmental units and to the nongovernmental organizations and individual actors. It is static because it assumes a snapshot at some point in time accurately captures compliance with the agreement.

A more realistic framework for understanding compliance is non-hierarchic, includes many actors other than states and treats compliance as a process that changes over time. The agreements themselves evolve over time, both as to the obligations they contain and the implementing measures. In this framework, states continue as central and essential actors, but others actors are also very important. These include intergovernmental organizations, secretariats servicing the agreements, nongovernmental organizations, private industrial and commercial enterprises, and individual actors. These nonstate actors interact dynamically in complex ways in patterns that vary among agreements and within countries.

The international study of national compliance found, based on empirical research, that in general national compliance increases over time, with countries frequently devoting more resources to compliance over time. But compliance also declines during certain periods for certain countries and particular agreements. Economic chaos, political instability and sudden decentralization have caused compliance to decrease, especially for agreements for which there is no strongly vested interest in securing compliance.

Two critical factors explaining national compliance are a country's intent and a country's capacity to comply. Both may change over time. In designing international agreements and implementing measures, states should consider the appropriate mix of strategies to encourage member countries to have both the intent and the capacity to comply with the agreements.

II. INTENT AND CAPACITY

The study on national compliance revealed that when countries join agreements they are in quite different positions with regard to their intent to comply and their capacity to do so, and that both factors change over time.

Intent is difficult to determine. It can be generally discerned from analyzing the behavior of countries. It is not to be confused with the formal votes or positions countries may assert in international meetings. Some countries intend to comply with the obligations they assume at the time they join the agreement. Implementing legislation that fully satisfies the treaty obligations may be already in effect; the country's past practice may already be in compliance with at least the substantive obligations of the treaty. In some cases, countries may join treaties without having carefully considered the obligations; they may even be unaware of them. Others may join with no intention to comply, as in the case of certain central and east European countries becoming parties to the Protocols on Sulphur Dioxide and Nitrogen Oxide to the UN ECE Long Range Transboundary Air Pollution Convention. They may bend to international pressure, or may respond to "bribes" by other states, or they may join to foster international cooperation in general in anticipation of other returns. There may be conflicts in intent within a country which reflect internal divisions. "[A] government may be divided, the foreign ministry may intend to comply while other branches of government may have no intention of abandoning practices that contravene the accord."[6] The national government may even intend to comply, but relevant provincial governments do not. In many cases, countries may intend to comply in the abstract, but the agreements have too low priority in the country to receive the attention and resources needed for compliance.

Countries must also have the capacity to comply. Many assets are important: an effective and honest bureaucracy, economic resources, public support, and technical expertise and know-how. These assets differ among states when they join an agreement, and the assets change over time in response to domestic and international events. International environmental agreements, in particular, have targeted financial and technical assistance to states to help them develop the capacity to comply. In many cases, the acute issue for member states is one of prioritization: how much resources to devote to compliance with particular obligations contained in the agreements. This issue is particularly difficult when it involves coordination among several ministries and with provincial and local governments, which may be recalcitrant.

While the only effective strategy to increase the political intent and the capacity to comply is to engage countries in the agreement, countries can facilitate this through the strategies they adopt in designing and implementing international agreements and the institutional structure that they create with the agreement.

III. STRATEGIES FOR COMPLIANCE

International legal strategies to encourage compliance may be grouped into three categories: negative incentives in the form of penalties, sanctions and withdrawal of privileges; sunshine methods such as monitoring, reporting, transparency and NGO participation; and positive incentives, such as special funds for financial or technical assistance, access to technology or training programs. In addition there are traditional public international law remedies for breach of an agreement, as set forth in the Vienna Convention on Treaties and customary international law. The question is which methods work best under what set of circumstances. In part, this can only be answered through empirical research. . . .

A. SANCTIONS

Under the traditional framework for compliance, parties rely on sanctions, penalties, and such measures as withdrawal of privileges

---

[6] Harold K. Jacobson & Edith Brown Weiss, Compliance with International Environmental Accords: Achievements and Strategies (1996).

under the convention to enforce treaty commitments. In trade law, sanctions have been regarded as essential to achieving compliance. In international environmental law, sanctions are rarely used. When used, individual parties ban trade in certain products with violators of the agreement or deny certain status accorded under the agreement to the violating party.

Trade sanctions have been threatened to enforce CITES. For example, the CITES Standing Committee recommended that parties ban trade in wildlife products with China [and Taiwan] for violating prohibitions on trade in rhinoceros horns and tiger parts. Not long before, the Standing Committee considered a trade ban on CITES products with Italy. Using trade sanctions to enforce multilateral environmental agreements raises problems of consistency with the General Agreement on Tariffs and Trade as incorporated in the new World Trade Organization. The World Trade Organization prohibits import quotas, requires national treatment between imported and domestic products, and requires most favored nation treatment among countries—that is, the most favorable treatment offered to one exporting country must be granted to all, but provides relevant exceptions in Article XX (b) and (g). These issues are considered in Chapter 18.

Withdrawing the privileges of membership in a convention is another traditional enforcement measure. The World Heritage Convention provides for a variation of this. While the text of the convention provides only for countries to list sites on the World Heritage List, the guidelines provide for delisting a World Heritage site if the country is in violation of its obligations to conserve the site. The language is ambiguous as to whether the host country must consent to the delisting. The sanction has not been used; no site has been removed from the World Heritage List, although the integrity of several sites is severely threatened.

There are instances in which sanctions in the form of withdrawal of some of the privileges of membership in the convention apply. In the Montreal Protocol, for example, countries qualifying as Article V developing countries qualified to receive assistance from the Montreal Protocol Fund can lose that status if they do not provide baseline data on consumption levels of controlled substances within a certain time after joining the agreement.

Public international law provides remedies for breaches of treaty obligations and of rules of customary international law. The Vienna Convention on Treaties indicates under what circumstances parties may withdraw from an agreement because of a breach of an obligation by a member party. Rules of customary international law set forth rights of retorsion and counter measures. They have not been invoked generally for international environmental problems. Nonetheless, such remedies are always available to states, providing that the legal requirements have been satisfied.

In international environmental law, sanctions are a "last resort" after other methods have failed. It is not clear the extent to which sanctions are needed as a latent threat in order to make other methods of achieving compliance effective. This issue is discussed below.

B.   THE SUNSHINE APPROACH

The key way of insuring compliance is through what I have labeled the "sunshine strategy." This approach relies on monitoring behavior of various actors through regular reports, site visits, and international review procedures, on transparency and access to information, on media access and coverage to provide public awareness, on nongovernmental organization participation in monitoring compliance, and on informal pressures by parties and by secretariats to comply. It relies on what has been termed the "reputation" factor to induce compliance.

Monitoring is essential to any effective program to increase implementation and compliance with treaty obligations. Monitoring may take many forms: off site monitoring through advanced technologies of scientific baselines or other criteria; reports by parties or nongovernmental organizations; on site monitoring by parties, secretariat officials or consultants; and international review of materials submitted by parties or gathered from other sources.

Of late, reporting has become a primary monitoring instrument. Nearly all of the most recent UNEP conventions require regular reports from parties on implementation of the agreements. Indeed there is almost a "bandwagon" effect among countries to include a provision on reporting in new agreements.

A reporting requirement is useful in that it engages countries in implementing the agreement. Some official(s) in the country must be responsible for filing the report. Moreover, reports are an important tool for educating countries about their commitments under the agreement and potentially a means to build local capacity to comply with the agreement.

But there are also problems with relying on reporting as the key monitoring tool. Officials required to file reports under the burgeoning number of international agreements may find that their time is mostly occupied by preparing reports rather than by taking the actions called for under the convention, or addressing other high priority environmental actions. Indeed, in countries with a scarcity of skilled labor, the government may need to devote much of its time to meeting reporting requirements. This is a problem of "congestion in treaty reporting." Moreover, unless the reporting requirements are standardized, the data may be difficult to compare and evaluate. Great variations in content in national reports for a given agreement may occur. In other cases, national reports may begin to look alike across different issue areas as information technology makes for easy transfer of written material.

Reports are useful monitoring tools if they convey information that others can review and verify. This requires an international process of review, and means to draw violations to the attention of parties for actions. However, both secretariats and parties can be reluctant to call particular countries to account for inaccurate reports. Some studies have found low rates of compliance by parties generally with reporting requirements. Many countries do not report or do not report on a timely basis. The reports may be incomplete or may be inaccurate, as when the same data is reported for several years. It may be difficult to determine whether the data is reliable. However, the preoccupation with the relatively low rates of compliance with reporting obligations in international environmental agreements may be slightly misplaced. It is arguably much less important that all countries comply with the obligation to file regular reports than that the countries that are major players in a particular agreement comply. Here the record of compliance with reporting obligations is much stronger.

Reporting is linked with transparency—to states, to non-state actors and to individuals. Nongovernmental organizations rely upon this transparency to monitor and encourage compliance with the convention, although admittedly the information might also be used to circumvent the obligations in some circumstances. Providing other member states and non-state actors with access to information makes it generally more likely that unreliable reports and inaccurate data will be detected.

The sunshine strategy relies on nongovernmental organizations, expert communities, and corporate actors to make possible parties' compliance with international agreements. Nongovernmental organizations bring violations to the attention of governments and of Secretariats servicing the convention. International nongovernmental organizations, such as Greenpeace International and Friends of the Earth, may work with local nongovernmental organizations to pressure countries to comply or may exert pressure directly on governments or on corporate actors. Non-state actors (and individuals) bring suspected violations to the attention of the secretariats servicing the agreements, to the parties and to the media. While these organizations have been much more active in industrialized countries than in developing countries, their numbers are growing worldwide.

Under some agreements NGOs are explicitly asked to monitor the agreement. For example, the World Conservation Monitoring Unit tracks national country reports of imports and exports of listed species for CITES. Other nongovernmental organizations systematically monitor state behavior on their own initiative, as in TRAFFIC's monitoring of trade in endangered species and tropical timber.

Sometimes the most effective monitoring of compliance takes place in the private sector. Corporations have a keen interest in maintaining a "level playing field." Under the Montreal Protocol, for example, a handful of large companies that produce CFC's and other controlled substances have an important financial stake in insuring that competitors abide by the agreement. They also have the resources to monitor compliance, albeit quietly.

Finally, the sunshine strategy relies on consultation and informal pressures such as jawboning to induce compliance. Secretariats consult with governments and with nongovernmental organizations, industry, and individuals Governments consult with secretariats, nongovernmental organizations and industry. Secretariats often play an important but quiet role in bringing informal pressure to bear upon non-complying actors. The sunshine strategy builds upon the culture which surrounds the politics of environmental issues in many, but not all, countries. Publics see environment as an issue in which they ought to have access to information and an opportunity to participate in decisions affecting them. Governments are becoming accustomed to non-state actors as influential participants in the policy process, whether formally or informally. Thus, in contrast to areas such as trade and national security, the sunshine strategy finds fertile ground.

C. INCENTIVES

International agreements increasingly rely on positive incentives to induce compliance. The incentive approach is based on the belief that many problems of compliance are problems of the lack of capacity to comply. If countries have the intent to comply but lack capacity, incentives can be an effective strategy for securing compliance. They may also be effective in shaping the interests and hence the intent of the country in complying.

Incentives may take the form of training materials and seminars, special funds for financial or technical assistance, access to technology, or bilateral assistance outside the framework of the convention.

Many international environmental agreements provide for the establishment of special funds to assist parties in complying with the convention. The 1972 World Heritage Convention established a special fund, which although small, has regularly assisted countries in conserving sites on the World Heritage List. Similarly, parties to the Montreal Protocol established in 1990 the Montreal Protocol Fund to assist Article V developing countries to comply with their Protocol obligations. The two Rio conventions, the Framework Convention on Climate Change and the Biological Diversity Convention, provide for funding to countries to meet the global incremental costs of complying with the conventions, although they do not establish separate funds to do so.

The Global Environmental Facility, created in 1990 initially as a $1.2 billion, 3-year fund, provides grants and loans to developing countries for specific environmental problems: ozone depletion, biological diversity, climate change, and marine pollution. It has been restructured and become permanent. The scope now encompasses desertification. The GEF potentially provides an additional source of financial incentives to countries to build local capacity to comply with international commitments.

Developing countries have increasingly viewed provision for financial and technical assistance as prerequisites for joining international environmental conventions. India, for example, insisted that the Montreal Protocol Fund be in place before joining the Protocol. During negotiations for the Desertification Convention, countries insisted on having access to funds as a prerequisite to concluding the convention.

Financial incentives build local capacity to comply with treaty obligations. But access to funds can also be used as a "stick" to ensure compliance with treaty obligations. For example, in 1995, the GEF linked fulfillment of obligations under the Montreal Protocol to receipt of GEF funds.

Training is an important component of the incentive strategy. Generally the funds devoted to training and the numbers of people trained annually have increased for international environmental conventions. For example, funds devoted to training under the Convention on International Trade in Endangered Species have increased sharply since 1994.

Training programs build local capacity to comply with treaty obligations and engage local actors in the agreement. However, care must be taken to ensure that the proper people are trained and at least some of those who are trained will continue working with the agreements beyond six months. Various strategies can be employed: moving training to the regions or within countries, training slightly larger numbers of people than might be needed so that some may still be on the job in a year. Other techniques include: training the "trainers" who can then conduct regular seminars, providing clear training manuals, and scrutinizing training applicants for quality.

Of the three compliance strategies, only two are in frequent use: the sunshine and the positive incentive strategies. Sanctions and other enforcement measures are rarely resorted to, and then only for items in international trade. Sanctions are a blunt instrument. By contrast the sunshine and positive incentive approaches are more flexible and rather more subtle instruments to encourage compliance.

D. INSTITUTIONAL MEASURES

The institutional structure of the regime surrounding each international agreement affects compliance. Features intended to encourage compliance include the establishment of an implementation committee and noncompliance procedures, which have been unusually effective for the Montreal Protocol, engagement of an enforcement officer (as in CITES), publication of violations (as in CITES and Basel), providing a formal role for NGOs (as in UNESCO's World Heritage Convention and in CITES), developing a formal link with industry (as in the Montreal Protocol and OzonAction) and establishing scientific and technical assessment and advice bodies to ensure that the convention keeps pace with scientific advances (as in the Montreal Protocol).

The role of the institutional features in facilitating compliance often evolves over time. The implementation committee and noncompliance procedures of the Montreal Protocol were used initially to help noncomplying Article V developing countries come into compliance with reporting obligations. However, in 1995 parties were using the procedures to exert strong pressure upon several countries, such as the Russian Federation, to come into compliance with procedural and substantive obligations. In the World Heritage Convention, the role of the IUCN and organizations concerned with cultural heritage has shifted from an almost exclusive early emphasis on evaluating sites for whether they were suitable for the World Heritage List to a substantial focus on monitoring member state conservation of the listed sites. Similar changes have taken place in the functions assumed by institutions established for other international agreements. Thus, in designing international agreements, it is important to consider whether the parties will be able to use the institutional features to respond flexibly over time to new needs and demands.

Secretariats to international agreements play important roles in securing compliance by member countries and targeted nonstate actors. They have substantial influence in part because they may be the only body with comprehensive knowledge of the extent to which parties are complying. They are uniquely situated to respond to questions and to jawbone actors into compliance. One of the most important measures for securing compliance is to ensure that secretariats for the agreements have secure funding and long-term personnel contracts. In light of the financial crisis in the United Nations system, some secretariats have moved largely to short-term contracts of one to three months, and funds provided by the parties to the agreement, even if in separate bank accounts, have become subject to general restrictions on use. Secretariats need to attract and retain high quality personnel and to be able to implement long-range planning for implementing the convention and ensuring compliance by member countries.

IV. LINKING COMPLIANCE STRATEGIES WITH INTENT AND CAPACITY

With respect to each international agreement, it is possible to create a figure of four boxes joining intent and capacity: countries with intent to comply and high capacity; countries with low intent to comply but with capacity; countries with intent to comply but lacking in capacity; and countries with no intent to comply and with no capacity. In each of these four categories, member countries will always have varying degrees of intent to comply and varying degrees of capacity to comply. Strategies for compliance must be targeted to move countries toward having both the intent and the capacity to comply. Different strategies need to be emphasized for different categories of countries, although a mix of strategies should be available.

For those countries having both the intent and the capacity, the sunshine strategy may be especially important, for it facilitates monitoring by both governments and nonstate actors. Sanctions are of secondary importance, primarily to ensure that countries are not tempted to change their intent to comply. When countries have the intent to comply, but lack the capacity, incentives are especially important, although sunshine strategies may have an important secondary role in mobilizing nonstate actor support and in monitoring progress in building capacity. This category includes many developing countries. Countries that lack intent but have the capacity may be particularly susceptible to some form of sanction, but the sunshine approach may be important in reshaping intent. Incentives may also help. For those countries lacking intent and capacity, all three strategies may be essential.

One of the complications of linking intent, capacity and compliance strategies is that both the intent and the capacity of countries to comply may change over time. National compliance changes over time in response to many factors. This suggests that the suite of measures needed to promote or to ensure compliance by member countries may also change over time.

. . .

LESSONS LEARNED IN GLOBAL
ENVIRONMENTAL GOVERNANCE

Peter Sand
31–34 (1990)

COMPLAINTS AND CUSTODIAL ACTION

As an alternative to legal action against the responsible party, recourse to a non-judicial international institution may provide a first-choice remedy when environmental agreements are infringed. [Sand discusses the noncompliance procedures then being developed for the Montreal Protocol, which are examined in Chapter 8.] A much bolder step toward collective compliance control was taken by the 1957 Rome Treaty establishing the *European Economic Community* (EEC). Article 155 made the EEC Commission the guardian of the treaty's implementation, and article 169 empowered it to initiate proceedings against any member state in case of infringements, sanctioned if necessary by formal action in the European Court of Justice at Luxembourg. Over the past ten years, this "custodial" procedure has become one of the most important means of enforcing EEC environmental standards.

The EEC infringement proceedings comprise three stages: As a first step, the Commission sends "letters of formal notice" to member states that fail to enact or apply a Community directive, or to report on its enactment or application. After giving the member state an opportunity to respond, the Commission can next render a "reasoned opinion" confirming the infringement in light of all the facts gathered. If the member state still doesn't comply, the Commission may then refer the matter to the European Court of Justice. During 1988, the Commission issued 93 letters of formal notice, 71 reasoned opinions, and 11 references to the court concerning infringements of EEC environmental directives (some 70 of which were in force at that time) . . .

What may be the most significant feature of this procedure is mentioned nowhere in the treaty and evolved only gradually during its implementation. More than half of the infringement proceedings initiated against member states were based not on the Commission's own monitoring of compliance but on citizen complaints—from private individuals, associations (such as Greenpeace and Friends of the Earth), or municipalities. As a result of public information on the complaints procedure and the establishment of a "complaints registry" within the Commission secretariat in Brussels, the number of environmental complaints rose dramatically—from 10 in 1982 to 190 in 1988 and to 460 in 1989. While complaints are usually based on local non-compliance with EEC standards, some have wider effects: a single complaint by a resident in one of the United Kingdom's two non-attainment areas with regard to the 1980 EEC *Directive on Air Quality Limit Values and Guide Values for Sulphur Dioxide and Suspended Particulates* thus triggered a

Commission investigation that led to infringement proceedings against seven member states. . . .

ENVIRONMENTAL AUDITS

Besides judicial review, international organizations have developed other forms of compliance control. Probably the body with the most such experience is the *International Labour Organization* (ILO), which has enacted and monitored a long line of multilateral conventions since the 1920s—ranging from bans on white lead paint and other occupational health hazards, to work-place protection from air pollution, radiation, and toxic chemicals. All these conventions contain provisions on dispute settlement that allow states to initiate complaints and *ad hoc* inquiries against other states for not observing the treaty. However, a detailed study of ILO's enforcement record over more than sixty years shows that this adversarial procedure was used only rarely and then mostly for political potshots. Instead, ILO member states developed an entirely different procedure that turned out to be far more effective in enforcing compliance: annual or biennial reporting by governments combined with regular auditing by an independent technical Committee of Experts to ascertain compliance in each member state, followed by public debate of these audited reports by the Conference Committee on the Application of Conventions and Recommendations.

Over the years, the ILO "auditing" system—with the active participation of both trade unions and employers' associations—has turned into a worldwide public hearing that clearly induces more compliance by governments than the threat of any intergovernmental legal action would. The *U.N. Commission on Human Rights* applies a similar procedure of country reports and public hearings, in which non-governmental organizations . . . play an active role.

In the environmental field, the biennial Conference of the Parties to the *Convention on International Trade in Endangered Species of Wild Fauna and Flora* (CITES) has become a forum for international review of compliance with the treaty, again with massive NGO support. Similarly, reviews of treaty implementation by parties to the *Convention on Long-Range Transboundary Air Pollution* and its protocols are carried out and published regularly by the Executive Body for the Convention.

In all these cases, periodic audits of compliance with agreed-upon international standards are well established. Essential to this process is publicity. It facilitates collective review and mutual accountability by all member states and, even more important, exposes governmental compliance reports to scrutiny by nongovernmental groups and, through them, by the public. . . .

One strong point of environmental audits is timing. Audits can make a difference *before* things have gone seriously wrong—unlike traditional judicial review mechanisms based on liability, which can only intervene after the fact. Considering the clear need to make environmental controls preventive rather than corrective, now may be the time to envisage a global auditing body that would periodically evaluate the performance of states and organizations in complying with their international obligations. Rather than relying on *ad hoc* review by a tribunal, where "action" would inevitably turn into confrontation, it may be preferable to assign this function to a permanent intergovernmental body—such as the *United Nations Trusteeship Council*, as recently suggested by Maurice Strong, Secretary General of the U.N. Conference on Environment and Development. As in the field of standard-setting and regulation, more imaginative approaches to compliance control are needed today than those drawn from outdated legal textbooks. An obvious and largely untapped source is the rich procedural experience of existing international institutions.

QUESTIONS

Why do you suppose these compliance mechanisms and techniques have been developed? What's wrong with traditional liability rules? Do you see analogues on the domestic level to the compliance techniques and mechanisms discussed in the foregoing excerpts?

3. COMPLIANCE WITH VOLUNTARY COMMITMENTS

What if I say, "Yes, I'll do that." Am I bound by that statement? Would I be bound if I were a State? Can private companies be bound to their commitments to address international problems? In the following excerpt, the author addresses the latter questions.

VOLUNTARY COMMITMENTS AS EMERGING INSTRUMENTS IN INTERNATIONAL ENVIRONMENTAL LAW

Edith Brown Weiss
44 Envtl. Pol'y & L 83 (2014)

Since the year 2000, the rate of negotiating new multilateral environmental agreements has slowed. While binding agreements continue to be important, in part because of their provisions for dispute resolution and for mandating compliance, other forms of international nonbinding legal instruments have become ever more important, such as declarations, codes of conduct, international standards and guidelines.

. . .

Voluntary Commitments by States

In international law, States have always possessed the authority to make voluntary commitments to address an international issue. Such commitments represent an exercise of national sovereignty. In practice,

States have been reluctant to undertake such commitments in the absence of a commitment by other States to do the same. Hence, there has been the penchant for binding agreements or more recently in the environmental area, for consensus on a nonbinding legal instrument. The effort to address climate change and to promote environmental sustainability has led States to make voluntary commitments to control greenhouse gases and to take measures to promote sustainability, even in the absence of a nonbinding legal instrument. The commitments of States after the climate meetings in Copenhagen, Denmark, in December 2009, illustrate this.

At the Conference, States negotiated but then declined to adopt the Copenhagen Accord, by which States would commit to reduce greenhouse gases. They even declined to approve it as a Conference document, so that it had no legal status. Nonetheless 141 countries have engaged with the Accord, either by being associated with it or supportive of it. These countries represent about 87% of global greenhouse gas emissions. Eighty-one States have submitted targets for reducing emissions, with 46 States committing to specific targets and timetables for reducing quantities of emissions, 7 States committing to reductions from "business as usual", two States committing to carbon intensity reduction, and 26 States submitting actions designed to reduce greenhouse gas emissions or promote efficiency but without reduction targets.[31] In a few instances, increased commitments were conditional upon other States also ma[king] specific commitments.[32] In the climate meetings since Copenhagen, States have not renounced these commitments. To the contrary, at the next climate meeting in Cancun, Mexico, they built upon the foundation laid in the Copenhagen Accord.[33]

In the case of climate, these voluntary commitments take place within a broader context of binding agreements: the United Nations Framework Convention on Climate Change and, for many, the Kyoto Protocol.[34] Indeed States have agreed to negotiate a new binding agreement on climate by 2015, to take effect in 2020 for the period beyond 2020.[35] Yet, the voluntary commitments of Copenhagen represent the

---

[31] The country submissions of actions are available at US Climate Action Network, http://www.usclimatenetwork.org/policy/copenhagen-accord-commitments.

[32] Ibid. Examples include Australia, the European Union, and Norway. European Commission, Expression of willingness to be associated with the Copenhagen Accord and submission of the quantified economy-wide emissions reduction targets for 2020, 28 January 2010, http://unfccc.int/files/meetings/cop_15/copenhagen_accord/application/pdf/europeanunion cphaccord_app1.pdf.

[33] The Cancun Agreements: Outcome of the work of the Ad Hoc Working Group on Long-term Cooperative Action under the Convention, FCCC/CP/2010/7/Add.1 http://unfccc.int/resource/docs/2010/cop16/eng/07a01.pdf.

[34] United Nations Framework Convention on Climate Change, 21 May 1992, 1771 UNTS 107 (1992); Kyoto Protocol to the United Nations Framework Convention on Climate Change, 10 December 1997, 2303 UNTS 162 (1997).

[35] Establishment of an Ad Hoc Working Group on the Durban Platform for Enhanced Action, FCCC/CP/2011/9/Add.1 http://unfccc.int/resource/docs/2011/cop17/eng/09a01.pdf.

willingness of States to commit to measures even in the absence not only of a binding agreement, but even of consensus on a nonbinding legal instrument or a formal conference document. This development may presage other voluntary commitments by States to address either other global environmental commons issues or environmental issues specific to an area, in which the dangers of inaction are too severe to wait for a formal consensus.

Voluntary commitments can be especially useful in at least the following contexts: to press ahead in addressing a problem in the context of a general binding commitment, to enable differentiated commitments by States in addressing problems, or, importantly, to take actions when the dangers from inaction are too severe to wait for a formal consensus.

Nonbinding Legal Instruments and Voluntary Commitments by Corporate and Nongovernmental Organizations.

From an environmental perspective, a potentially significant development is the increase globally of voluntary commitments by private industry. The instrument may be an international one, to which companies voluntarily agree to commit themselves. One of the most important examples is the United Nations Global Compact, which sets forth ten principles, three of which directly concern environment. As of December 2013, the Compact had over 10,000 signatories in more than 140 countries, which included the major companies. In other cases, the private sector has negotiated the instrument. . . .

The globalization of corporations and the development of international supply chains mean that national regulations are often inadequate and regulation at the international level is needed. These efforts by private industry are often linked with intergovernmental organizations, private sector networks, nongovernmental organizations or other participants in civil society. . . . They can take different forms: principles, standards and certification, self-reporting of actions, or adoption of certain processes.[37] By 2010, for example, more than 46,000 firms were certified as compliant with the International Organization for Standardization's (ISO) 14001 standard for environmental management systems.[38]

Nongovernmental organizations have also developed standards with which producers are expected to comply and supply their own system of certification. . . .

The norms encapsulated here do not constitute formal binding agreements, even by the private sector. Rather they are nonbinding

---

[37] Dirk Ulrich Gilbert, Andreas Rasche and Sandra Waddock, *Accountability in a Global Economy: The Emergence of International Accountability Standards,* 21 BUSINESS ETHICS QUARTERLY 23 (2011).

[38] David Vogel, *The Private Regulation of Global Corporate Conduct,* 49 BUSINESS & SOCIETY 68 (2010).

measures that have been formulated by a consensus of mostly nonstate actors, to which the private sector voluntarily adheres. Initiatives such as Fair Trade and those applying to fisheries and forests depend upon recognition by consumers in the marketplace. Conceptually some of the voluntary private sector initiatives share similarities with the nonbinding instruments that governments negotiate in that they are generally easier to negotiate and provide some flexibility in implementation, such as through certification arrangements. When industry self-regulates, the initiatives are often attractive because they may avoid or pre-empt actions by governments. Since the instruments apply to many actors, they may also help to ensure a level playing field in trade relations, and to provide fodder in pressuring others to join or to comply. However, those participating in them to date often represent only a small fraction of those engaged in the industry.

Voluntary Commitments for Sustainability

Voluntary commitments are distinguished from other legal forms because they are not made pursuant to a consensus instrument to which [all] have agreed. They are not negotiated. They are generally independent of the commitments of other parties, though they may be in part conditioned upon similar actions by others, as in several commitments that States filed for the Copenhagen Accord. They generally provide for specific actions to be taken within a given time frame. Ideally, they provide for measurable results.

Λ growing number of international initiatives solicit and publish voluntary commitments by States and nongovernmental entities to sustainable development. Most have their own registries. Several registries aggregate and publish commitments from multiple initiatives. . . . The sites generally do not yet gather data on compliance with the commitments made.

One of the most significant initiatives of this kind is the UN Sustainable Development Knowledge Platform. In the preparations for the Rio+20 Conference, several States and nongovernmental organizations, including the US based World Resources Institute, pushed for the creation of a compendium of commitments to promote sustainable development. As part of the conference, international organizations, nongovernmental organizations, and private corporations were invited to make voluntary commitments to take actions to achieve sustainable development. More than 700 commitments were collected during the Conference, which were listed in a new online registry, the United Nations Sustainable Development Knowledge Platform.[47]

The final Report from the Conference, *The Future We Want*, explicitly endorsed this initiative.

---

[47] http://sustainabledevelopment.un.org.

"We welcome the commitments voluntarily entered into at the United Nations Conference on Sustainable Development and throughout 2012 by all stakeholders and their networks to implement concrete policies, plans, programmes, projects and actions to promote sustainable development and poverty eradication. We invite the Secretary-General to compile these commitments and facilitate access to other registries that that have compiled commitments, in an Internet-based registry. The registry should make information about the commitments fully transparent and accessible to the public, and it should be periodically updated." (para 283).[48]

. . . . Major corporations have also made commitments under the various voluntary initiatives referenced above. These may be more significant than the commitments by States. Some of the commitments are from large multinational corporations, whose revenues eclipse the economies of some countries. They are in the form of targets and timetables. Microsoft, for example, has committed to achieve net zero carbon emissions by 2013. The Bank of America has committed $50 billion over the next 10 years to finance activities that advance a low carbon economy. Bridgestone has committed to secure 100% of its materials from sustainable sources by 2030. Dell has committed to reducing its greenhouse gas emissions by 40% by 2015. . . .

While these commitments are in themselves significant, they certainly are not enough to effect a sufficient change in behavior to meet the growing need for a globally sustainable economy. But they do have the potential to leverage consumer opinion to encourage competitors and others to make similar commitments. Of course, for this to happen, the public must know about the commitments and be willing to respond accordingly.

Voluntary Commitments in a Kaleidoscopic World

. . . . In a kaleidoscopic world, individuals, *ad hoc* coalitions, informal groups, transient networks, and other such actors become important. Their actions may often be characterized as bottom-up. They may respond to both immediate issues, which may emerge and change rapidly, and to longer-term challenges. And the foci may change in response to changing conditions.

Voluntary commitments could have an important role in bottom-up empowerment. They produce "buy in" by those who make them. If we are to address the momentous environmental issues confronting us locally and globally, we need to mobilize everyone to engage in sustainable development and living patterns. Voluntary commitments are useful because they do not depend on negotiated outcomes, can be initiated

---

[48] *The Future We Want,* Report of the United Nations Conference on Sustainable Development, Rio de Janeiro, Brazil, 20–22 June 2012, UN Doc. A/CONF.216/16, Resolution 1: Annex, para 283.

quickly (at least in theory), and can be adapted to local practices and culture. They give actors flexibility, because the party making the commitment is responsible for specifying its content. Such actions should be able to draw upon best practices and to showcase best practices to facilitate learning. Voluntary commitments can inform others and build a favorable reputation for those taking them. They can build momentum toward broader efforts to live sustainably. They can provide space for cooperative efforts. Such efforts are a complement to, but not a substitute for, commitments by States and major private sector actors.

Concerns about Voluntary Commitments

While voluntary commitments are becoming an important feature in the environmental law landscape, they also raise significant issues. Such issues will increase as more actors in the kaleidoscopic world voluntarily take initiatives and other actions relevant to environmental law. Some environmental problems, especially global ones like climate change or marine pollution, require that States work together to address them and that they agree upon what needs to be done. They also require that other actors behave in certain ways. While voluntary commitments may be an important, perhaps necessary step, in the face of inaction, they cannot be regarded as a substitute for negotiated norms and requirements. Indeed they may in the long run depend upon the latter for their effectiveness.

Voluntary commitments in the private sector rest in good part upon the premise that they enhance the reputation of those making them, although there is little evidence that such commitments have been reflected in sales or share prices.[50] Scholarly literature on corporate compliance with regulations also suggests that reputation is an important factor in motivating compliance.[51] The concern with reputation can be used to encourage commitments as well as to guard against "green wash" in the commitments.

One of the most significant problems with voluntary commitments made in the absence of a negotiated consensus on the obligation is that they may not be enunciated in formats that are compatible with each other or comparable. The qualitative data, for example, may not be standardized or sufficiently comparable for civil society, investors, and others to use in assessing the overall advancement toward sustainability.

This leads to the issue of monitoring. Since there may be hundreds or thousands of commitments in different formats and with different content, it will be challenging to monitor an actor's compliance with its

---

[50] See, e.g., David Vogel, *The Private Regulation of Global Corporate Conduct,* 49 BUSINESS & SOCIETY 68 (2010). Vogel argues that corporations agree to industry regulation to protect their reputations. For analysis of the role of reputation in corporate social responsibility, see, e.g., Lorenzo Sacconi, Margaret Blair, Edward Freeman and Alessandro Vercelli (eds.), CORPORATE SOCIAL RESPONSIBILITY AND CORPORATE GOVERNANCE (Palgrave Macmillan, 2011).

[51] See e.g. Margaret Blair, OWNERSHIP AND CONTROL: RETHINKING CORPORATE GOVERNANCE FOR THE TWENTY-FIRST CENTURY (1994), for a classic work on corporate behavior.

voluntary commitments. This will be the case, even if there is full transparency of commitments and of reporting on progress in meeting them. Developments in information technology may improve this situation in the future.

Voluminous voluntary commitments also raise difficult issues of accountability. The traditional view of accountability is that the party responsible for carrying out an obligation must be held to account if it is not carried out. But this requires tracking an actor's compliance with its commitment and being able to impose consequences for not meeting the commitment. None of the international registries track compliance with voluntary commitments. Especially in a kaleidoscopic world, where many commitments may not be centrally registered, and accountability can be difficult, and can potentially involve high transaction costs.

Perhaps most of all, the growing use of voluntary commitments points to the need for platforms that compile and aggregate individual commitments and that make the commitments readily accessible online. Such platforms can be formed at the local, regional and international levels, and by civil society organizations as well as governments. A few integrating platforms should facilitate our ability to assess the comprehensiveness of voluntary commitments, to identify significant gaps, and to encourage cooperation. They also need to provide space for those making the commitments to report regularly on their implementation of them, so that it may be possible to track compliance.

The Importance of Common Values

All of the above rests on having a set of common values, from which commitments can emerge and desirable behavior can be derived. While traditionally international environmental agreements reflected such values and articulated shared commitments, which penetrated hierarchically downward within States for implementation, in the kaleidoscopic world, the common values and shared commitments will also need to flourish from the bottom up. Since individuals, *ad hoc* coalitions, and informal or transient group actors will increasingly be able to influence the development and implementation of international environmental law, common values become essential. Otherwise, voluntary commitments can be a fig leaf for inaction, or can be drastically insufficient to achieve a sustainable world. Or they may even be few in number. . . .

QUESTIONS

Why comply? What are the incentives to comply with voluntary commitments? What steps are needed to ensure that States, international organizations, corporations, nongovernmental organizations, etc., comply with the commitments they make? To what extent does the analysis of compliance with hard law apply to compliance with voluntary commitments?

CONCLUDING NOTES AND QUESTIONS

1.   Return to the Problem that opened this chapter. You have now been exposed to a variety of possible ways of holding a party accountable for causing international environmental harm, or of promoting compliance with international undertakings. Are there mechanisms, techniques, approaches, and the like that were not used in the *Trail Smelter* case but could have been, or perhaps even should have been? What are they, if so?

2.   Are you satisfied with the current state of the international system, or systems, concerning accountability and compliance in the field of the environment? If not, what would you change? Are your suggestions practical or utopian? On the inter-governmental level, do you believe the new, non-confrontational approaches hold promise? Should they be viewed as complementary to or as a replacement for inter-governmental litigation or arbitration?

3.   On the private level, is the current state of the law adequate? That is, do you believe more should be done to ensure the availability of private recourse for transboundary pollution damage?

4.   What about criminalization of environmental insults? Does this approach hold promise?

CHAPTER 6

DISASTERS AND EMERGENCIES

▪ ▪ ▪

Environmental disasters such as oil spills, industrial accidents, and floods often cause grave human and ecological harm. Partly for this reason and partly because, by definition, they strike without warning, these situations frequently capture the attention of the public and are prominently reported in the news media. This often serves to galvanize the political will of States, resulting in legal action on the domestic or international level aimed at preventing or mitigating future incidents of the kind in question. It is thus not surprising that lawmaking in the field of the environment-especially on the international plane-has been characterized as "legislation by disaster." [37] Two well-known cases illustrate the point: The Torrey Canyon spill off the English coast of 1967, and the British response of destroying the tanker without the consent of the flag State in order to protect its coastline, was followed by the conclusion of the Convention Relating to Intervention on the High Seas in Cases of Oil Pollution Casualties of November 29, 1969, 26 U.S.T. 765, 970 U.N.T.S. 211. And the international community responded to the Chernobyl accident of April 26, 1986, by concluding two agreements the following September: the Convention on Early Notification of a Nuclear Accident of September 26, 1986, *reprinted in* 25 I.L.M. 1370, and the Convention on Assistance in the Case of a Nuclear Accident or Radiological Emergency of the same date, U.N.T.S. Reg. no. 24643, *reprinted in* 25 I.L.M. 1377.

But surely no one would seriously argue that we should wait for accidents to happen before concluding agreements or enacting legislation to prevent them or minimize their effects. Or would they? The more unlikely the accident, the more expensive the preventive measures, the more powerful the forces resisting preventive measures, the less politically important the people or environment likely to be affected, and the stronger will be the argument against measures of prevention. The debate over whether to require double hulls on oil tankers—initially sparked by the Torrey Canyon spill but only resolved in the United States

---

[37] *See, e.g.,* Tammy Alcock, *Ecology Tankers and the Oil Pollution Act of 1990: A History of Efforts to Require Double Hulls on Oil Tankers,* 19 Ecology L.Q. 97 (1992), stating with regard to the history of the controversy over requiring double hulls on oil tankers: "Ultimately, it is a story of a system which seems to require a disaster to force change." *Id.* at 100.

as a result of the Exxon Valdez disaster—is but one of the many illustrations of this point.[38]

In this chapter, we examine the international legal framework governing environmental emergencies. You should evaluate the various sources included in sections B and E of the chapter to determine, as nearly as you can, (1) their authoritative value, and (2) whether they adequately take into account the forces identified in the preceding paragraph. We have chosen the term "disasters" to describe unplanned phenomena that cause or threaten damage. These events have also been referred to as "emergencies," "incidents," "emergency situations," and "accidents." They may be of human (e.g., chemical spills and industrial plant explosions) or natural (e.g., floods and ice floes) origin. You should ask yourself whether the rules expressed in a given document are appropriate to both kinds of emergency situations (for example, would rules concerning notification and responsibility apply equally to chemical spills and floods?). We will generally concentrate upon environmental emergencies that cause or threaten transfrontier harm—for example, a chemical spill in one country carried by an international watercourse into another country. But we will also touch upon other situations whose "transfrontier" character is more subtle. For example, the plant involved in the Bhopal disaster could be said to have been "exported" to India from the United States by Union Carbide, whose subsidiary operated the plant. Are these situations covered at all by the rules governing emergencies in one State causing or threatening harmful effects in another? Another example of a domestic disaster having international though not transfrontier repercussions is one that affects a world heritage site wholly within the state. The present chapter can only touch upon the important problem of marine oil spills. Marine pollution is dealt with in Chapter 11.

EXERCISE

As you read through the rest of the chapter, consider the Fukushima Daiichi nuclear disaster of 2011. In March of 2011, the Tōhoku earthquake caused a tsunami to hit the Fukushima Daiichi nuclear power plant. This in turn led the plant to release substantial amounts of radioactive material, leading to the largest nuclear accident since Chernobyl. Since then, the plant has had continued spills of radioactive water.

However, as of February 2015, the international effects of the nuclear disaster have been regarded as minimal. But what if, instead, significant nuclear pollution from Fukushima had reached the shores of China, Korea, and Russia? Read the rest of this chapter and consider the potential legal claims that might apply, as well as the types of factual determinations that must be made in order to establish a legal claim.

---

[38] *See* Oil Pollution Act of 1990, Pub. L. No. 101–380, 104 Stat. 484, requiring that double-hulled ships be phased in over a period of 25 years.

A. CASE STUDIES

The following case studies describe major and well-known industrial accidents of a non-nuclear nature. Nuclear accidents will be covered in section E of this chapter.

1. SEVESO

NATURE AND SCOPE OF THE PROBLEM
Ved Nanda & Bruce Bailey
in Transferring Hazardous Technologies and Substances 3, 3–7
(G. Handl & R. Lutz eds., 1989)

On July 10, 1976, an explosion occurred in Meda, Italy. at the Icmesa plant owned by Givaudan, a subsidiary of the Swiss-controlled Hoffmann-LaRoche chemical combine. A thick whitish cloud of trichlorophenol gas with a pungent, medicinal odour containing approximately four and one-half pounds of the substance 2, 3, 7, 8 dibenzo-paradioxin, known as TCDD or dioxin, was released into the atmosphere surrounding the plant. A northerly wind moved the cloud to the south over an area some four and one-half miles long and one-third of a mile wide before dispersing about half an hour after the initial release. The cloud eventually dispersed as droplets over parts of seven towns, the three most affected being Meda, Seveso and Cesano Maderno.

The Icmesa plant, located about 13 miles north of Milan, produced mainly trichlorophenol gas, a chemical used primarily to make hexachlorophene, an ingredient in cleansers and germicides, and 2–4–5, a defoliant employed by the American armed forces during the Vietnam war. On July 10, 1976, for an unknown reason, temperatures within the plant's system rose, causing pressure to build up. Production at the plant usually took place at a temperature of 180 degrees centigrade, while temperatures of 230 degrees centigrade could cause the process to go out of control. On that Saturday in 1976, the temperature in the system rose to 300 degrees centigrade, even though the controls were set for cooling. As a consequence of the pressure build-up, a safety valve burst, and the cloud of trichlorophenol gas was released into the atmosphere.

The head of Givaudan at that time, Guy Waldvogel, stated that the plant had two cooling plants built into its security systems, although these may not have been put into action soon enough. As would be the case at Bhopal, the Icmesa plant had been the subject of safety complaints prior to the accident, including assertions by workers at the plant that security measures for handling toxic substances were inadequate and that the plant lacked a dump tank or vapour recovery system. This latter defect meant that once the safety valve burst, the vapours were released directly into the atmosphere. A medical survey of workers at the plant also indicated that many had in the past suffered from nausea and vomiting, burns, blisters, intoxication and vertigo.

The pattern of company management failing to inform local authorities as to the type of products being in the chemical production processes, the exact nature of the production processes and the high-risk potential involved which eight years later, would characterize the Bhopal context were present at the Icmesa plant. Initially, plant officials kept quiet about the release, hoping that rain would wash away the pollution, before finally informing local authorities twenty-seven hours after the explosion took place. It then took the plant managers seven days to inform local authorities that dioxins were present in the vapour cloud which had been released by the explosion. This delay was with regard to a substance three ounces of which could injure or kill most of New York City's population. Local authorities magnified these errors of delay by taking five days to place some of the areas contaminated by the dioxin off-limits to workers and residents. In addition, the superhighway through the area remained open, and cleanup crews wore their contaminated protective clothing into non-contaminated neighbouring areas.

Once the magnitude and nature of the accident were realized by the local authorities, three zones were established around the plant, with the most contaminated zone designated as Zone A: Inside this zone, which initially encompassed about 285 acres, the 730 inhabitants were evacuated, and the area was sealed off. The 175 children of the residents living in this zone were sent to state-subsidized summer camps. All agricultural, industrial, and commercial activity in Zone A was halted, including the sale and consumption of locally produced foodstuffs. Zone B, which included about 451 acres, was classified as slightly polluted, and the 4,280 residents were allowed to remain at home, although they were urged to send their children away and pregnant women were asked to submit to medical examinations. A larger area, Zone C, was designated as a safeguard zone where the residents were advised not to eat produce grown in the area.

The immediate human medical effects of the accident were primarily in the form of more than 500 cases of chloracne and other forms of skin disease. Some of these cases persisted for more than two years from the time of the accident. The most severe biological impact came in the form of the loss of produce and domestic animals raised in the contaminated zones, all of which either died or had to be destroyed.

The indirect and more long-term effects of the accident went beyond the physical impacts upon the inhabitants of the three zones. Immediately following the accident, orders for furniture and clothes sold by local merchants were either canceled or large discounts were demanded. The plant itself was permanently closed a little more than a month after the accident.

As a consequence of the forced evacuation and relocation of the residents of the contaminated area, many families and businesses were disrupted. Houses in the most contaminated areas were demolished, while structures left standing had to be decontaminated. Initially, the Italian government allocated $48.4 million to carry out these measures, with most of that money earmarked for decontamination and health projects for affected residents.

The magnitude of the problem can be seen by the fact that for months after the accident, officials were not sure how to clean up the affected area. Demonstrations by former residents occurred, protesting at the slow pace of the government's decontamination programme. The basic reclamation plan finally approved by the regional government provided that all vegetation and soil to a depth of one foot from the directly affected areas were to be removed and incinerated at 1,000 degrees centigrade. Once an area had been sufficiently decontaminated to allow human activity again, a research and experimental laboratory to study techniques for neutralizing or reducing the effects of dioxin was constructed. Nearly three years after the accident, data supplied by the laboratory indicated that there was no sign that the toxicity of remaining dioxin-contaminated areas was diminishing.

By the time the decontamination efforts had been largely completed, more than two tons of chemical waste containing dioxin had been removed from the total of 4,400 acres of land which had been contaminated by the Icmesa plant. Even the disposal of this waste was not without mishap, as the 41 drums containing the waste disappeared during their transport out of Italy. The drums were eventually located in a storehouse in northern France after considerable public furor. Finally, more than six years after the accident, the Italian government oversaw the dismantling of the Icmesa reactor and the burial of the remaining rubble from the reactor in lead barrels in a 160,000 cubic metre ditch situated in a corner of the once highly contaminated sector. A committee of independent scientists reported that eight years after the accident, no chemical traces of the explosion were visible, except for occasional continuing cases of chloracne. The committee reported that Hoffmann-LaRoche was planning to landscape the affected area into a 40-hectare park.

Hoffmann-LaRoche indicated fairly early on that it intended to accept responsibility for the consequences of the explosion and to compensate those damaged by the accident, perhaps partly as a result of the findings of a special parliamentary investigating commission set up by the Italian government. The commission's report, issued one year after the accident, accused the Hoffmann-LaRoche subsidiary, Givaudan, of not only failing to inform the local and regional Italian authorities about the nature of the Icmesa operations, but also of failing to install automatic control and warning devices.

The Italian government and the Lombardy region reached a settlement with Givaudan with regard to compensation for the Seveso accident. Givaudan agreed to pay the two governments a total of $80 million as payment for expenses incurred by various Italian ministries, land reclamation, health work, rebuilding in the area, lost crops and decontamination.

The commune of Seveso filed suit in Geneva, Switzerland against Givaudan in early 1979 for damages to the community and its inhabitants. The suit accused Givaudan of failing to take adequate safety precautions, failing to correct those inadequacies after becoming aware of them, and attempting to cover up after the explosion. Seveso arid Givaudan reached a settlement of the suit in late 1983 when Givaudan agreed to pay about $7.2 million to Seveso as payment for damages.

Five Icmesa executives, including the plant's managing director, technical director, plant designer, company chairman, and plant engineer, were brought to trial as a result of the Seveso explosion. The five men were charged with negligence leading to a disaster, causing contamination of a vast inhabited area that had to be evacuated, and failure to have adequate safety systems. The Italian court found the five guilty and assessed sentences ranging from two and one-half to five years in prison. Four of the convictions were overturned on appeal, while the fifth sentence was suspended. Charges against the mayor of Meda and local health officials were initially filed and then later dropped. The charges had been based upon the officials' failure to apply existing legislation which could have avoided the disaster.

Two and one-half years after the Seveso accident, Italy, which had virtually no environmental legislation in force during 1976, enacted legislation which reformed its national health-care system. Provisions within the new law which had a bearing on environmental hazards caused by harmful substances included standards for the production, registration, sale and use of chemical substances capable of upsetting the biological and ecological balance; the establishment and maintenance of a national inventory of chemical substances; and the creation of "risk maps" based on requirement that all factories provide data on the toxicological characteristics of the products they use and their possible effects on humans and the environment.

NOTES AND QUESTIONS

The Seveso Directive. In connection with your consideration of the Seveso accident, you may wish to consult the "Seveso Directive" (Council Directive on Major Accident Hazards of Certain Industrial Activities, Doc. 82/501/EEC, OJ. No. 230/1, Aug. 5, 1982) adopted by the Council of the European Communities June 24, 1982, as amended March 19, 1987, which is discussed in the Brown Weiss excerpt below. Since the initial directive, the Seveso Directive has been replaced or modified twice, once in 1996 (Directive 96/82/EC—"Seveso II"), and once in 2012 (Directive 2012/18/EU—"Seveso III"). Seveso II extended the scope of Seveso I; established requirements for safety management systems, emergency planning, and land-use planning; and reinforced earlier mandates on inspections to be carried out by Member States. Seveso III increased citizen access to information regarding the risks posed by activities of nearby companies, provided more rules for public participation, created recourse provisions for citizens who were not provided sufficient access to information or participation, as well as established stricter inspection standards.

2. BHOPAL

NATURE AND SCOPE OF THE PROBLEM
Ved Nanda & Bruce Bailey
in Transferring Hazardous Technologies and Substances 7–11
(G. Handl & R. Lutz eds., 1989)

On the night of December 2–3, 1984, toxic methyl isocyanate (MIC) gas escaped from an underground storage tank at a Union Carbide chemical manufacturing plant in Bhopal, India, and leaked into the atmosphere. The leaked gas covered an area of 25 square miles, and resulted in an unparalleled catastrophe, causing the death of over 1,600 people and injuring over 200,000 people as a direct result of the leak; several hundred more died in the next few months due to the fatal effects of the lethal gas. Livestock were killed, crops damaged, and business interrupted.

In the aftermath of the world's worst industrial accident, medical authorities were uncertain about the long-term effects of exposure to the deadly gas. Two years after the disaster, it was reported that lingering effects on many Bhopal residents included: "shortness of breath, eye irritation, and depression." The Indian government reported that the death toll has risen to 2,347 people, that 30,000 to 40,000 people had suffered serious injuries in the incident, and that it had received 500,000 leak-related claims.

The accident occurred at the Bhopal plant of Union Carbide India, Ltd. (UCIL), a subsidiary of the Union Carbide Corp., a New York Corporation with headquarters in Danbury, Connecticut, which owns

50.9% of its Indian subsidiary. The Indian government blamed Union Carbide for errors in the design, management, and oversight of the Bhopal plant, and specifically asserted that "unreasonable and highly dangerous and defective plant conditions" caused the catastrophe. It cited inadequate safety measures, faulty alarm systems, storage of huge quantities of toxic chemicals, lack of cooling facilities, and poor maintenance at the factory. The company, on the other hand, contended that the responsibility must lie with its subsidiary along with the state of Madhya Pradesh where the plant was located and the central government of India; it also alleged sabotage by a disgruntled worker at the plant.

In the Bhopal district court where the case is pending, Union Carbide contended that although it owned 50.9% of the stock in its subsidiary, the government of India has barred it from running the plant. Instead, it said that "it sold general design drawings to its Indian subsidiary, which then hired companies to do detailed design and construction. The parent trained some of the plant managers, but was unable to dictate the plant's daily operations." It added that the 1973 agreement for the sale of the design, approved by the Indian government, stipulated that the parent "shall not, in any way, be liable for any loss, damage, personal injury or death" resulting from the use of the design specifications by the UCIL. The company also contended that "the Indian government had approved and inspected the plant, knew about the dangers of MIC and refused to allow American employees from Carbide to remain in India to provide technical assistance requested by its subsidiary to the Indians running the plant. . . . [T]he state government in Bhopal had allowed people to move close to the plant, hence knowing the dangers they would face in an accident." Earlier, in a federal district court in New York, similar charges and counter charges regarding the responsibility for the design of the plant, overall control and training of the personnel were exchanged by the government of India and Union Carbide.

Questions have been raised about the safety of the plant design in Bhopal, which went into production in 1980, and the adequacy of safety equipment and operating systems. None of the safety devices worked. Because of instrumentation errors, monitoring gauges did not work and hence there was no early warning of impending disaster. The mechanical valves which were supposed to act as a backstop measure were dysfunctional. Also, the vent gas scrubber (VGS) intended to neutralize any leaking gas by automatically "washing" the toxic gas with caustic soap, thereby rendering it harmless, was shut off when the leak occurred. The flair tower designed to burn leaking gas had also been shut down. However, according to one report, "because of faulty design, both the VGS and flair tower together also could not have prevented the MIC from escaping into the atmosphere." As evidence of the faults in the plant design, it was reported that there was no backup system to prevent this kind of gas escape. Safety measures used elsewhere by Union Carbide were lacking; for example, the UCIL lacked the computerized pressure/temperature sensing system, and there were no effective alternatives. A study of the design analysis of the storage area for MIC led one reporter to two conclusions:

> First, that the short-sighted design modifications made in the pipeline connections, less than a year ago, along with the dysfunctioning of some valves, were primarily responsible for water ingress in the MIC tank. And second, the original design of the MIC storage area did not provide even a single safe route for a toxic gas at a very high temperature and pressure to be neutralized before escaping into the atmosphere. In other words, the safety features were greatly under signed.

Following the Bhopal disaster, several claims on behalf of the victims were filed in India as well as in the United States, raising questions about the possible violations of Indian Law which prohibits solicitation of clients and contingency fees. Meanwhile, on February 20, the Indian government adopted the Bhopal Gas Leak Disaster Ordinance, and on March 29, 1985, enacted the Bhopal Gas Leak Disaster (Processing of Claims) Act, under which the government of India assumed responsibility as the sole representative of all the victims of the gas leak to bring a single action against Union Carbide. Subsequently, in April 1985, the Indian government, on behalf of the victims, filed as *parens patriae* a lawsuit against Union Carbide in the federal district court for the Southern District of New York, seeking both compensatory and punitive damages in an unspecified amount. Before filing the suit, which invoked six separate theories of liability on the part of Union Carbide—absolute liability, strict liability, negligence, breach of warranty, misrepresentation and the multinational enterprise liability theory—the government of India had rejected a Union Carbide offer to settle the controversy for $200 million dollars.

Two U.S. lawyers challenged the Indian government's action of filing a lawsuit on behalf of all the victims by in turn filing a suit in India. The challenge to block the Indian suit in the United States was based on the alleged violations by the Indian government's legislation of the right of Indian citizens under the Constitution of India to choose their own counsel and, on the contention that if the Indian government also shared the responsibility for the disaster by failing to enforce safety regulations, it could not represent the victims because of a conflict of interest.

The Judicial Panel on Multidistrict Litigation consolidated all the lawsuits brought in the United States in federal district court in the Southern District of New York. A year after the suit was brought, District Judge Keenan dismissed the case on the grounds of forum non conveniens under three conditions: one, that Union Carbide consent to submit to the jurisdiction of the courts of India and continue to waive defenses based on the statute of limitations; two, that Union Carbide agree to satisfy any judgment rendered against it by an Indian court, provided that the minimal requirements of due process are met; and three, that Union Carbide comply with U.S. rules on discovery under the federal rules of civil procedure.

Earlier efforts for a negotiated settlement were unsuccessful when the Indian government rejected a Union Carbide offer of $350 million dollars, which with interest would have accrued to $500–$600 million, and which was accepted by lawyers representing private plaintiffs in litigation. Union Carbide appealed the Judge's ruling contending that the Indian government must also be bound by U.S.-style discovery rules. Attorneys for the individual plaintiffs in the Bhopal case also appealed the ruling by Judge Keenan that sent the proceedings to India. Subsequently, on September 5, 1986, the Indian government sued Union Carbide in the Bhopal district court in India for damages arising out of the gas leak. The Indian government is seeking at least $3 billion from Union Carbide Corp. in claims arising from the disaster. In January 1987, the Second Circuit Court of Appeals [affirmed the judgment of] the Federal District Court [but deleted the second and third conditions]. At the end of November 1987, all ongoing efforts to reach a negotiated settlement between the government of India and Union Carbide had stalled, and the Indian government filed criminal charges to culpable homicide in Bhopal against Union Carbide.

Subsequently, on December 17, 1987, Judge M. W. Deo of the Bhopal District court ordered Union Carbide to pay $270 million in interim relief to the victims of the accident. On review, the State high court ruled that an interim payment of $193 million be paid.

The Bhopal tragedy created a momentum to seek appropriate international, regional and national action to provide proper expert safeguards for hazardous substances and technologies, and effective international assistance in establishing standards and in providing guidance to developing countries.

NOTES AND QUESTIONS

1. *Ineffective settlement?* The Supreme Court of India approved a settlement in the Bhopal case in February, 1989, under which Union Carbide and Union Carbide of India Ltd. agreed to pay $470 million to the Indian Government for the benefit of the victims of the disaster. Amnesty International stated that the government of India had, as of November 2004, failed to distribute most of the settlement money to the victims. *See* BBC News, *World "Failed" Bhopal Gas Victims* (November 29, 2004) (stating that " 'new research' revealed that more than 7,000 people had died immediately

after the gas leak, while a further 15,000 people had died of related diseases since 1984"). The report further stated that: "The site has not been cleaned up so toxic wastes continue to pollute the water which the surrounding communities rely on." *Id.* Even now, victims are demanding additional punishment and more compensation. *See* Nita Bhalla, Reuters, *Victims Call for Justice 30 Years After Bhopal Disaster* (December 3, 2014).

2. *Who should pay?* Union Carbide was taken over by Dow Chemical Company well after the settlement described in the previous note. Some have insisted that Dow pay additional compensation. Should it be liable?

3. *The Basel Convention.* The Basel Convention on the Control of Transboundary Movements of Hazardous Wastes and Their Disposal, discussed in Chapter 10, addresses the movement of hazardous wastes between different countries. When you get to that chapter, think about how the Basel system might apply in the context of accidents such as Bhopal. Are there potential liabilities arising out of the Basel Convention?

4. *Chevron in Ecuador.* In 21st century, Chevron has been involved in a very complicated set of domestic and international court and arbitral actions involving environmental and social harm caused over many years by oil extraction in Ecuador. *See, e.g., Republic of Ecuador v. Chevron Corp.*, 638 F.3d 384, 388 (2d Cir. 2011); *Aguinda v. Chevron Corp.*, No. 002–2003 (Super. Ct. of Nueva Loja, Feb. 14, 2011) (Ecuador). Why is this an international problem? Is this the same type of "disaster" addressed in the current chapter? If not, how should the relevant international legal rules differ?

3. SANDOZ

NATURE AND SCOPE OF THE PROBLEM
Ved Nanda & Bruce Bailey
in Transferring Hazardous Technologies and Substances 16–19
(G. Handl & R. Lutz eds., 1989)

Ten years after the Seveso accident, a major toxic chemical spill occurred in Europe when efforts to put out a fire at a chemical storage warehouse of Sandoz, a major Swiss chemical multinational, in Basel, on November 1, 1986, resulted in a huge discharge of toxic chemicals into the Rhine. While Swiss authorities initially reported that 30 tons of chemicals, including herbicides, pesticides and poisonous mercury, leaked into the Rhine, some French reports put the figure of the spilled chemicals as high as 1,000 tons. Eventually, Sandoz announced that much of the 1,246 tons of material inside the warehouse, including 824 tons of insecticide, 71 tons of herbicide, 39 tons of fungicide, 4 tons of solvents, and 12 tons of organic compounds containing mercury, was washed into the river by the water used by the firemen in putting out the fire.

The worst accident of this kind since Seveso caused ecological disaster, adversely affecting France, Germany and the Netherlands, in addition to Switzerland. Subsequent reports said that Basel escaped a major environmental disaster "by a whisker," for the city could have suffered toxic fumes if the fire had burned longer. Former West German Chancellor, Willy Brandt, referred to Basel as "Bhopal on the Rhine," and some political parties started calling it "Baselpal," while the French and West German press renamed the city "Chemobasel," or "Chemobale." On the evening of November 1, 2,000 demonstrators marched through the streets of Basel carrying banners which read, "Seveso-Bhopal-Schweizerhalle." Schweizerhalle is the Basel suburb where the Sandoz plant is located. Subsequently, it was revealed that several more incidents of chemical spills in the Rhine immediately preceding and in the few weeks following the Basel spill had occurred, which also involved other Swiss chemical giants such as CIBA-Geigy, though reportedly none was as serious as the Sandoz spill.

The Sandoz spill and those other incidents of chemical spills in the Rhine caused a great deal of concern in Europe. Questions raised included those of adequate notification, safety standards, violation of pollution control laws, and liability and compensation. Calls were made for European community action and for international cooperation to prevent such pollution. The Netherlands representative told a special meeting of environment ministers from the states bordering the Rhine, convened in Zurich November 12, 1986, that, following the accident, it had already spent a quarter of a million dollars on pollution control.

On December 19, 1986, the French Environment Minister presented the Swiss government with a bill for $38 million for damages to French interests arising from the spill. The figure of $38 million was estimated by an independent commission of French experts based upon short-term damages to the fishing and boating industries; medium-term damages, including the cost to restore the ecosystem; and potential damages, including the cost of building dams and other facilities linked to the Rhine, such as a water pumping system, assuming that no significant pollution of the groundwater aquifer had occurred. The Swiss government and the Sandoz and CIBA-Geigy officials showed their willingness to settle claims for damages, although it was not clear who was to assume responsibility for how much of the claimed damages. Subsequently, Sandoz paid damages to French fishermen and to the French government. Among other developments at Sandoz, safety rules related to the storage of toxic and flammable substances in the Sandoz group of companies were strengthened; Sandoz also set up the "Sandoz Rhine Fund" to help repair ecological damage from the November 1986 disaster and announced its donation of $7.3 million to the World Wildlife Fund for a three-year project to restore the flora and fauna of the Rhine River.

Among the multilateral responses to the accident, noteworthy attempts include the establishment of a working group among French, Swiss, and German representatives to update the proper functioning of the information exchange systems and emergency contacts. Also, an agreement was reached on December 19, 1986, regarding the necessary measures to prevent industrial accidents and to limit their consequences, at a ministerial conference on Rhine Pollution, and a proposal was made by the executive director of UNEP, Mostafa K. Tolba, that for the prevention of transboundary toxic pollution, treaties similar to the ones earlier adopted on international notification and mutual assistance in the event of a nuclear accident under the auspices of IAEA, be negotiated.

Tolba said at a press conference of December 15, 1986, that UNEP's existing International Register of Potentially Toxic Chemicals (IRPTC) could act as a framework for administering the two treaties. He said that as there were no existing agreements requiring international notification in the case of an accident involving toxic chemicals, a new convention on the subject was desirable. Commenting on the Sandoz incident, Tolba said that the chemical spill at Basel "shows the ecological and economic folly of assuming that if we ignore safety standards in the chemical industry somehow the problems will go away." He added that "(t)he accident reveals the full extent of the apathy, confusion and general unpreparedness of the world's most advanced nations and the deplorable inadequacy of international legislation." The notification requirement would obligate governments to provide instant information on the chemicals involved and their predicted behaviour, the location of the plant, and the safety measures undertaken. The second convention would call for prompt assistance among state parties after an accident to minimize damage and harm.

Earlier, on November 20, 1986, Tolba had suggested that "a legal package should be drafted to prevent another Bhopal or another Basel." As part of that package, he outlined the need for "instituting a programme for governments, in cooperation with industry, to work with local leaders, identify acutely toxic chemicals, help prepare control measures to limit accidental releases and deal with such accidents."

NOTES AND QUESTIONS

1. *Lessons from the Sandoz Incident.* In *The Sandoz Spill: The Failure of International Law to Protect the Rhine from Pollution*, 16 Ecology L.Q. 443, 480 (1989), Aaron Schwabach concludes as follows: "If there is anything to be gained from the Sandoz disaster, it is a realization that the existing treaty regime is inadequate to protect the Rhine from chemical pollution, and that new measures are urgently needed if the river's ecology is to be saved from complete destruction." Recalling that the Rhine basin lies in one of the most highly integrated and developed regions in the world, what lessons would you

draw from this experience for developing countries sharing an international watercourse?

2. *The Harbin spill.* On November 13, 2005, an explosion occurred at the No. 101 Petrochemical Plant in the city of Jilin, China. The plant was a subsidiary of a state owned chemical factory. The initial blast killed 5, injured 70, and released an estimated 100 tons of benzene, nitrobenzene, and other chemicals into the Songhua River, forming a toxic slick 50 miles long.

Jilin lies some 165 miles upstream from Harbin, a city with population of nearly 4 million people that is considered one of the major cities of China. Immediately following the spill, the levels of benzene in the river water rose to 108 times the domestic safety levels set by the Chinese Environmental Protection Administration. Benzene, which can kill at high-level exposures, is also a known human carcinogen.

Within 8 hours of the accident, government officials were aware of the extent of the spill and had taken steps to mitigate its impact, including releasing water from a reservoir to dilute the spill. Nevertheless, government officials publicly denied that the explosion had given rise to any pollution and continued to issue such statements for over a week after the accident.

On November 21, 2005, officials in Harbin City shut off the city's water supply after tests of the river water revealed concentrations of benzene had risen to over 100 times the lawful level. However, the government's explanation for the shut-off was that repairs were needed. It was not until November 22, 2005, amid rumors and unofficial reports of a cover-up, that the government formally acknowledged that a major toxic spill had occurred.

The Songhua is a major tributary of the Amur River, which forms the border between China and Russia for some 1000 miles before entering Russia and ultimately emptying into the Sea of Japan. The Amur flows through the Khabarovsk region of Russia and is the main water source for the area's 1.4 million people. Though China took longer to acknowledge the accident than did Russia to acknowledge the accident at Chernobyl—China did not officially apologize to Russia until November 26, 2005, almost two weeks after the explosion—because of the rate at which the slick was moving, a mere 1–1.5 kilometers per hour, Russia had ample time to prepare for its arrival; the leading edge of the plume, which had spread out over some 150km, did not reach the Amur River and the border between China and Russia until the middle of December.

Ultimately, the slick passed through the Amur River and into the Tatar Strait in the Pacific Ocean.

Should China have notified Russia of the spill earlier? What about countries bordering or whose vessels fish in the Sea of Japan? What about the international community at large regarding risk of pollution of the high seas? If the latter was required, how might China have provided such notification?

4. THE BREAKUP OF THE PRESTIGE

The Prestige, a twenty-six year old single-hulled tanker, left St. Petersburg, Russia on October 30, 2002 bound for Singapore, loaded with 77,000 metric tons of industrial fuel oil. Formerly named the Mt. Gladys, the 243 meter long vessel was registered in the Bahamas, owned by a Liberian company, managed by Mare Shipping of Greece, and chartered by a Swiss-based Russian oil company, Crown Resources. It was captained by Apostolos Mangouras of Greece and crewed by nationals of the Philippines.

During a storm on November 13, 2002, one of the ship's tanks burst off the coast of Galicia in northwestern Spain. The captain sought refuge in a Spanish port but was refused. France and Portugal also refused to accept the ailing vessel. However, the Spanish government dispatched rescue helicopters and a veteran captain, Serafin Diaz, the stricken ship to provide assistance. The Spanish rescue operation evacuated the Filipino crew from the ship, which had drifted within 4 miles of the Galician coast, and Captain Diaz informed Captain Mangouras that the Spanish government wanted him to restart the ship's engines and sail the Prestige into deeper waters. Captain Mangouras initially refused, insisting that the ship be taken into a safe harbor where repairs could be conducted and the cargo unloaded. He ultimately relented, however, to avoid involvement of the Spanish Navy, whereupon the ship made for deeper waters with the help of a Spanish tug boat.

Meanwhile, the storm continued to batter the ship, causing a forty-foot section of the starboard hull to break off, spilling a large quantity of oil. At 8:00 a.m. on November 19, the vessel split in two. The two portions of the ship sank later the same day, some 152 miles off the Spanish coast. It is estimated that the sinking of Prestige resulted in the release of over 63,000 metric tons of oil into the Atlantic, nearly twice the amount spilled by the Exxon Valdez. An additional 13,000 metric tons remained in the tanks of the broken vessel until it was removed in 2004. The remains of the ship rest on the ocean floor at a depth of some 12,000 feet. The spill dealt a severe blow to Galicia's fishing and tourism economy and destroyed over 250,000 seabirds as well as untold numbers of fish and other marine life. The cost of cleaning up the Galician coast—an operation that took over six months—has been estimated at €2.5 billion, which easily exceeds the $2 billion cost of the Exxon Valdez clean-up.

As a result of this incident, the European Union has taken measures to limit the number and type of ships, especially tankers, that can pass through their shipping lanes, recently banning single-hulled ships from docking in their ports. Additionally, measures are being taken to enforce currently existing international ship construction standards.

NOTES AND QUESTIONS

1. *How could this happen?* How could an old, rusted, single-hulled ship carrying that much oil be allowed to sail? Although the Prestige was 26 years old at the time of the break-up, it had not been inspected since 1999 because it had deliberately refueled outside harbors. *See Policing Tankers: The Transport of Oil by Sea Requires Better Governance*, Financial Times (November 21, 2002), at 20. And who is responsible for ensuring that vessels of this sort are sound and well-maintained, and that their crews are capable of navigating them safely? The Prestige disaster is yet another example of the failure of the international community to regulate seagoing vessels adequately. Given the devastating consequences of the lack of effective regulation, what accounts for this failure, and how can it be rectified?

2. *The Prestige, flags of convenience and the law of the sea.* The Prestige was sailing under a so-called "flag of convenience," or open registry flag, under which a State grants its nationality to a vessel beneficially owned by a national of another State. *See generally* William A. Lovett, United States Shipping Policies and the World Market 107–127 (1996). All ships must sail under some State's flag to enjoy the benefits accorded by international law. The 1958 Geneva Convention on the High Seas, largely codifying customary international law, gives every State the right to sail ships under its flag and to determine the conditions for granting nationality to its ships. Convention on the High Seas, 29 April 1958, Articles 4 and 5, 450 UNTS 82, 13 UST 2312, TIAS No. 5200. However, the 1958 Convention requires that there be a "genuine link between the [flag] State and the ship; in particular, the State must effectively exercise its jurisdiction and control in administrative, technical and social matters over ships flying its flag." *Id.*, Article 5(1).

Article 91 of the 1982 United Nations Convention on the Law of the Sea (UNCLOS) also requires a "genuine link" between the flag State and the ship. U.N. Doc. A/CONF.62/122 (1982), 1933 UNTS 397. However, UNCLOS elaborates considerably on the Geneva Convention's provisions on the obligations of the flag State to exercise control over the vessel. Article 94 of UNCLOS, entitled "Duties of the Flag State," contains detailed provisions requiring every flag State to "take such measures for ships flying its flag as are necessary to ensure safety at sea" including measures regarding construction, equipment and seaworthiness of ships, their "manning," and regular surveys. *Id.*, Article 94(3) and (4). In taking such measures, the flag State "is required to conform to generally accepted international regulations, procedures and practices and to take any steps which may be necessary to secure their observance." *Id.*, Article 94(5). Specifically, UNCLOS requires flag States to "ensure compliance . . . with applicable international rules and standards . . . for the prevention, reduction and control of pollution of the marine environment from vessels. . . ." *Id.*, Article 217(1).

The international regulations, rules and standards referred to in Articles 94 and 217 are largely those developed by the International Maritime Organization (IMO). *See* IMO Charter, available at http://www.imo.org.

However, the IMO has no independent enforcement authority. Instead, as in most fields of international law, responsibility for enforcement falls upon individual States. UNCLOS provides that a State having "clear grounds to believe that proper jurisdiction and control with respect to a ship have not been exercised may report the facts to the flag State," which is then required to investigate the matter and take appropriate remedial action. UNCLOS, *supra*, Article 94(6). If the flag State fails to take measures that port States consider adequate, or if a ship otherwise fails to comply with their standards, they may refuse the ship entry. This approach is being implemented increasingly in developed port States.

3. *Is the laissez faire approach adequate?* Shipping interests, which emphasize the need to keep costs down in an increasingly competitive market, resist efforts to place further controls on flag-of-convenience States. *See* Andrew Rakestraw, Note, *Open Oceans and Marine Debris: Solutions For the Ineffective Enforcement of Marpol Annex V*, 35 Hastings Int'l & Comp. L. Rev. 383, 392–93 (2012). However, the substantial savings that can result from the use of such registries can be overwhelmed if the ship is lost or liability results from an environmental disaster. Furthermore, a number of ports are now restricting entry on construction and seaworthiness grounds, as previously indicated. Is this the best way to deal with vessels like the Prestige? Or should the regulatory system be tightened? *See* the Rakestraw Note above for some of the arguments for creating a centralized information clearinghouse for port State inspections and placing pressure on flag States to disseminate educational information to sailors.

4. *The Exxon Valdez spill.* On March 23, 1989, the oil tanker Exxon Valdez, loaded with 180,000 tons of crude oil from the North Slope of Alaska, ran aground on the Bligh Reef as it was leaving Prince William Sound, a pristine marine sanctuary, home to an abundance of species of birds and fish, including salmon, as well as marine mammals such as sea otters. The vessel released an estimated 38,800 tons of oil into the sound, taking an enormous toll on the environment. All told, the cleanup effort took over a year, costing nearly $2 billion, though the environmental effects are still being felt.

5. *Exxon's liability.* Exxon was initially found liable for $350 million in actual damages and $5 billion in punitive damages. In re Exxon Valdez, 296 F. Supp. 2d 1071 (D. Alaska 2004). That judgment, however, was vacated by the 9th Circuit. In re Exxon Valdez, 490 F.3d 1066 (9th Cir. 2007). The U.S. Supreme Court upheld compensatory damages but limited punitive damages on a 1:1 ratio. Exxon Shipping Co. v. Baker, 554 U.S. 471 (2008). Hazelwood, who was captain of the Exxon Valdez at the time of the accident, was ultimately cleared of allegations that he was inebriated when the vessel struck the reef, though he was found negligent, fined $50,000 and sentenced to 1,000 hours of community service. State v. Hazelwood, 946 P.2d 875, 883–884 (Alaska 1997).

B. GENERAL NORMS APPLICABLE TO ENVIRONMENTAL EMERGENCIES

1. OVERVIEW

ENVIRONMENTAL DISASTERS IN INTERNATIONAL LAW

Edith Brown Weiss

Anuario Juridico Interamericano 1986 141 (1988)

INTRODUCTION

With the rapid industrialization of countries there are more accidents causing environmental disasters which affect many people and often many countries. Sandoz, Chernobyl, Bhopal, Seveso and Amoco-Cadiz are only the most recent and vivid examples.[1] Some of these accidents occur in factories producing toxic chemicals, others in nuclear reactors. Some involve marine pollution, while others affect shared natural resources such as lakes and airsheds. Still other natural disasters destroy natural or cultural resources of importance to the world, such as the massive forest fire in Borneo a few years ago.[2] This article is concerned with the status of international law regarding environmental disasters. It covers man-induced environmental disasters having significant transboundary effects, natural disasters affecting shared natural resources, and disasters which affect important natural and cultural resources impressed with elements of common patrimony. The last includes world natural and cultural heritages, international gene banks, and similar resources.[3] While international law regarding environmental accidents has traditionally focused on those causing significant transboundary damage, it is now timely to extend it to those disasters which threaten natural and cultural resources regarded by the international community as having elements of common patrimony.

There are three primary aspects to the management of environmental disasters: preventing the disaster, minimizing the damage, and compensating for damage. The duty to compensate for damage represents the traditional approach. It is also the least effective

---

[1] On March 16, 1978, the oil tanker Amoco-Cadiz ran aground and broke up, spilling 220,000 tons of crude oil which reached 245 miles of coastline in Brittany, France. *See Current Reports*, 6 Int'l Env't Rep. (BNA) 471 (1983).

[2] The Borneo fire of early 1984 lasted several months and destroyed over 13,000 square miles of plant and animal life. Such destruction affects timber resources, soil quality, and; reservoir and canal siltation levels. *See Wound in the World*, Asiaweek 34 (July 13, 1984); *Devastated Forest Offers a Rare View of Rebirth*, New York Times (April 24, 1984), at 61.

[3] *See* Convention for the Protection of the World Cultural and Natural Heritage, Nov. 16, 1972, 27 6 UST 37, T.I.A.S. No 8226, 11 I.L.M. 1358 (1972), by which parties designate certain sites as World Cultural Heritages. Parties are obliged to set up services to protect natural and cultural heritages (Art. 5), to assist one another in these measures if so requested, and to avoid actions which may injure these heritages either directly or indirectly (Art. 6).

in protecting the environment against disasters. The duty to minimize damage and provide emergency assistance, which is potentially more effective, appears in an increasing number of international agreements, and has emerged as a principle of customary international law. The duty to prevent accidents has been somewhat overlooked in international law, although international agreements increasingly include it in general terms.

I.   PREVENTING ENVIRONMENTAL DISASTERS

The duty to prevent environmental disasters obligates States to enact safety measures and procedures to minimize the likelihood of major environmental accidents, such as nuclear reactor accidents, toxic chemical spills, oil spills or forest fires.

Its premise is the factual awareness that it is far more effective protection for the human environment to prevent accidents than to try to compensate for the injuries caused. This is particularly true for the protection of future generations and for protection against long-term damage to the environment, which may be irreversible or reversible only at staggering costs.

The recent accidents at Chernobyl and at Sandoz illustrate this. While the immediate effects of the accident at Chernobyl on people in the vicinity of the accident were identified, the damage to crops, vegetation, and animal life in the European countries was less clear. Several countries initiated costly measures banning the sale of domestic products, such as milk, artichokes, and other produce, and banning certain food imports in the belief that these items were contaminated by radiation. Long-term damage to people, particularly children, from exposure to radiation and long-term damage to the soils and ecological systems remains unclear and will never be fully compensated.[4] Similarly in the Sandoz chemical spill on the Rhine, it is impossible to compensate fully for the short- and long-term damage to the fish and ecosystem of the river and for the as yet unclear health effects from exposure to contaminated water supplies. Moreover, the massive forest fires in Borneo in 1984 caused large-scale destruction of tropical forests rich in biological diversity, a treasure for both present and future generations. The loss of species by the fire can never be compensated.[5] Even if it were possible to

---

[4] The long-term radioactive contamination of flora and soils comes from caesium-137 and caesium 134, with half-lives of 30 and 2 years, respectively. Mathematical models which predicted that rain would wash radioactive particles into the soil have proven inaccurate, as vegetation remains contaminated in some areas. Even after radionuclides are washed off, grasses and other vegetation can take up the radio-activity from the soil. This is especially true in areas where the soil is low in clays and micas, soil types which bind caesium effectively. Howard & Livens, *May Sheep Safely Graze?*, New Scientist 46 (April 23, 1987). For the uncertainty in health and environmental effects, *see* 43 Bull. Atomic Scientists 10 (1986).

[5] Early observations after the fire showed that small plants, vines, and soft wood trees were growing quickly, while the large hardwood trees were not regenerating. Many bird and animal species are no longer found because the fire destroyed nut and fruit bearing trees upon

compensate for all the damages caused by environmental disasters, which it is not, the costs of doing so would far outweigh the costs of prevention. Thus, imposing a duty upon States to prevent environmental accidents is far more efficient than relying on compensatory measures after the accident occurs. It ensures that those who can prevent the damage, at least cost, are required to do so. Moreover, it is equitable, because those who benefit from the activity assume the costs of it, rather than shifting them to another community, such as future generations.

The duty to prevent environmental disasters is part of the principle of State responsibility, as reflected in Principle 21 of the Stockholm Declaration of the Human Environment. It is confirmed in other texts. The U.S. Restatement of Foreign Relations Law, for example, provides in Sec. 601 that "A state is obligated to take such measures as may be necessary, to the extent practicable under the circumstances, to ensure that activities within its jurisdiction or control (a) conform to generally accepted international rules and standards for the prevention, reduction and control of injury to the environment of another state or of areas beyond the limits of national jurisdiction." (Emphasis added.) If a State breaches the obligation, it is responsible for injury to the environment of another State resulting from the violation.

The duty to prevent environmental disasters posits that there are standards and procedures which States can follow to reduce the likelihood and magnitude of accidents. The specific content of these measures must, of course, be negotiated by the States themselves. Several essential elements can be identified. These include: 1) adoption of safety standards for the location and operation of industrial and nuclear plants and vehicles; 2) maintenance of equipment and facilities to ensure ongoing compliance with safety measures; 3) monitoring of facilities, vehicles, or conditions to detect dangers; and 4) training of workers and monitoring of their performance to ensure compliance with safety standards.

These safety measures will have different specific applications depending upon whether the protection is for an industrial source, a nuclear source, an important natural resources reserve, or a cultural heritage.

To date, the duty to prevent environmental disasters is found in relatively few international documents and agreements. One of the pioneering efforts to develop this duty is a 1983 resolution of the European Council on Environmental Law, "Principles Concerning International Cooperation in Environmental Emergencies Linked to Technological Development." This resolution expressly calls for limits on siting of all hazardous installations, for the adoption of safety standards

---

which they depend. *See* Asiaweek 34 (July 13, 1984) *supra* note 2; New York Times (April 24, 1984) p. 4, *supra*, note 2.

to reduce the risk of emergencies, and for monitoring and emergency planning.

The duty has been implemented primarily in those conventions governing transport of oil and hazardous substances by sea and by rail and inland waterways, in the 1982 Directive of the European Economic Community on Major Accident Hazards of Certain Industrial Activities, and in several agreements governing shared natural resources between Canada and the United States. Increasingly, the general duty is included in agreements governing emergency assistance for other potential environmental disasters. In 1975, the IAEA adopted nuclear safety standards to minimize the differences in safety standards between countries, but these were not binding. The IAEA is now working to establish more stringent, binding safety standards. [The Convention on Nuclear Safety was adopted on June 17, 1994 by a diplomatic conference convened by the International Atomic Energy Agency. IAEA Doc. INFCIRC/449, July 5, 1994, Annex; 33 I.L.M. 1514 (1994). For the historical background of the Convention, *see* IAEA Doc. GOV/INF/723, paras. 5–21, and Paul C. Szasz, *Introductory Note*, 33 I.L.M. 1514 (1994).—Eds.]

As the World Commission on Environment and Development has asserted in its Report, it is now time to make safety measures mandatory. The Report recommends that international agreement be reached on codes of practice for nuclear reactor operations, including minimum safety standards, agreed site selection criteria, as well as "consultation and notification prior to the siting of all major civil nuclear related installations," and standards for operator training and international licensing. For industrial operations the Commission recommended countries "strengthen national capabilities and the framework for bilateral and regional cooperation" by enforcing regulations or guidelines for the safe operation of industrial plants, locating plants away from population centers, and training workers adequately in safe operational procedures and emergency preparedness. If a State has a hazardous facility located on its territory in which an accident could affect one or more neighboring States, it should provide information to the potentially affected States about the plant and establish mutually agreed criteria for the location of hazardous new plants. The recommendations are important for they recognize that certain decisions about hazardous facilities which are within the sovereign domain of States should nevertheless be subject to certain international duties, if an accident at them would have transnational effects.

Since many of the relevant hazardous industrial plants are privately operated, the question arises whether the State is or should be responsible for the actions of private actors within its jurisdiction or control. As discussed above, the duty to prevent environmental disasters is appropriately viewed as a principle of State responsibility. Sec. 207 of the Restatement of Foreign Relations Law of the United States provides that "A state is responsible for any violation of its obligations under international law resulting from action or inaction by the government of the State . . . or any organ . . . or other agent." While a State is not ordinarily responsible for acts of individuals, it is responsible for its own failure to control or regulate.

To protect against environmental disasters, it is important for States to agree to a suite of safety measures which the State has responsibility for ensuring that private parties within its jurisdiction or control implement. This is the approach adopted in the 1982 EEC Directive, on industrial accident hazards, commonly known as the Seveso Directive. Article 3 provides that States "shall adopt the provisions necessary to ensure that, in the case of industrial activities specified in Article 1, the manufacturer is obliged to take all the measures necessary to prevent major accidents and to limit their consequences for man and the environment." The Directive appropriately focuses on requiring States to enact procedures to ensure that their private operators implement the safety measures necessary to prevent environmental disasters.

II. MINIMIZING DAMAGE AND PROVIDING EMERGENCY ASSISTANCE

The duty to minimize damage and to provide emergency assistance applies both to the State in which the accident occurs and to those States that are in a position to help alleviate the damage. Many bilateral and multilateral agreements contain these obligations. Certain obligations of States in responding to major environmental disasters exist as customary international law.

A State in which a major environmental disaster occurs has the duty to minimize the damage to the human environment. At a minimum this requires that a State promptly notify countries that may be affected, provide available information about the course of the accident, and inform affected States of measures it is taking to reduce the damage. States must also take necessary and practicable steps to prevent or reduce injury to other States from the accident. They must to do so for both natural and man-induced disasters, although the State may bear no responsibility for injury caused by the natural disaster. Those States potentially affected by an environmental disaster have an obligation to cooperate in minimizing the damage. The failure to do so on their own territory may be a defense available to the State in which the accident occurred, if claims for reparation are made against it. With respect to marine pollution disasters, States are obligated to develop contingency plans for responding to such incidents in their area. States have been extending this obligation to other kinds of environmental disasters.

The duty to minimize damage from environmental disasters derives from the principle of State responsibility. Principle 21 of the Stockholm Declaration . . . reflects customary international law. Support for it is contained in the resolution of earlier disputes, such as the Trail Smelter Arbitration, and in the multitude of international agreements which implement it. The U.S. Restatement on Foreign Relations Law confirms this obligation of States to "reduce and control" injury to the environment of other States and areas beyond national jurisdiction.

There are four aspects to the duty to minimize damage: the duty to notify promptly; the duty to provide information to potentially affected States; the duty to develop contingency plans; and the duty to cooperate in minimizing damage, as by providing emergency assistance.

1. The Obligation to Notify

As early as 1949, the International Court of Justice in the Corfu Channel case affirmed the obligation of a State to warn other countries exposed to dangers in its territory which could cause serious injury or death. The Court cited a State's duty not to permit knowingly the use of its territory in such a way as to violate the rights of others and "elementary considerations of humanity" as bases for this duty. The same considerations underlie the extension of the duty to notify other States of major environmental disasters which may affect them.

The duty to notify appears in many treaties concerned with environmental disasters and in Sec. 601 of the Restatement of Foreign Relations Law on the Law of Environment, Article 9 of the Montreal Rules of the International Law Association, and Article 19 of the Legal Principles proposed in the report of the World Commissions on Environment and Development.

Treaties concerned with international waterways, marine pollution, nuclear accidents, forest fires, and other environmental catastrophes embody this duty. The provisions normally call for immediate notification when the State becomes aware that an emergency exists which could affect other countries or territories. Those regional marine pollution agreements which establish a regional organization call for giving notice to that body as well as to the potentially affected States. Several agreements for forest fires and nuclear emergencies call for parties to designate national authorities to receive the notification. The duty to notify promptly and in good faith is firmly established in international law.

2. The Obligation to Provide Information

[The obligations to notify and provide information are discussed in Chapter 4.]

3. The Obligation to Develop Contingency Plans

There is arguably a duty in customary international law to develop contingency plans for responding to marine pollution disasters in nearby areas, which may soon extend to other kinds of disasters. The multilateral agreements addressing marine pollution emergencies contain such provision. The Law of the Sea Convention in Article 199 requires States to develop such plans. The U.S. Restatement of Foreign Relations Law on the Law of the Environment in Sec. 605(2) on marine pollution sets forth a State's responsibility to develop contingency plans to the extent necessary and practicable. The comments note that "neighboring states are obligated to develop and be ready to put into operation contingency plans for responding to pollution incidents affecting the marine environment in their vicinity."

The obligation to develop contingency plans is also found in certain bilateral and multilateral agreements concerned with forest fires, nuclear accidents, and other environmental catastrophes. The 1986 Convention for the Protection of the Natural Resources and Environment of the South Pacific Region provides in Article 15 that the "Parties shall develop and promote individual contingency plans and joint contingency plans for responding to incidents. . . ." Certainly the development of contingency plans is essential for effective responses to environmental disasters and should be part of customary international law applicable to major environmental disasters, particularly those that may be ultrahazardous. It is, however, doubtful that international law as yet requires States in the absence of an international agreement to develop such national contingency plans for disasters other than marine pollution.

4. The Obligation to Cooperate in Minimizing Damage

As part of the duty to minimize damage from environmental disasters, there is an emerging duty in international law which requires States to cooperate with each other in combating environmental disasters and preventing damage. This duty is reflected in the increasingly large number of bilateral and multilateral agreements which provide for emergency assistance and for mutual cooperation in mitigating damage. The details of this obligation are, however, by no means clear. For example, do all States have a duty to provide emergency assistance if requested? Must they be potentially affected by the disaster or is it sufficient that they have the capability to render assistance? What kinds of assistance must be provided? Who is responsible for paying the cost of the emergency assistance? The existing agreements address these issues in different ways.

There are an increasing number of global, regional and bilateral agreements which set forth the duty to provide emergency assistance. . . . The earliest international agreements were negotiated to facilitate assistance in the event of oil pollution spills or nuclear accidents: the Nordic Mutual Emergency Assistance Agreement in Connection with Radiation Accidents (1963), the International Convention Relating to Intervention on the High Seas in Case of Oil Pollution Casualties (1969) and the Agreement for Cooperation in Dealing with Pollution of the North Sea by Oil (1969, revised 1983). More recently, under the auspices of the IAEA, States have concluded two international agreements governing nuclear accidents, one of which addresses emergency assistance. The Director of the United Nations Environment Programme, M. Tolba, has proposed that two similar conventions be negotiated for transboundary toxic pollution. Many regional agreements provide for emergency assistance in case of marine pollution.

There are also many bilateral agreements that provide for emergency assistance to extinguish forest fires, to combat threats to international rivers such as from pollution or floods, and to contain other environmental disasters. These include agreements between France and the Federal Republic of Germany (1977), between Germany and Luxembourg (1978), between Czechoslovakia and the German Democratic Republic (1956), between France and Spain (1959), between Chile and Argentina (1961) and between Switzerland and France (for water pollution accidents) (1977). A 1986 bilateral agreement between Argentina and Brazil provides for mutual assistance in the event of nuclear accidents. In addition, there are numerous agreements in North America between Canada and the United States, between Mexico and the United States, and between States within the United States and provinces in Canada, which provide for emergency assistance for environmental catastrophes such as forest fires and accidents contaminating waters. . . .

The actions required by these agreements vary from notification and exchange of information to the development of joint contingency plans and a regional center to coordinate mutual assistance efforts. The regional seas conventions are at the forefront of using multilateral bodies to coordinate emergency assistance for environmental disasters. Some of the bilateral agreements, particularly for fire, include provisions for monitoring that accident. Almost all of the agreements provide for easing the national barriers, such as custom controls, for parties providing assistance. Indeed the easing of these barriers is a primary rationale for the agreements. Relatively few of the agreements address the difficult issue of who must bear the costs of the emergency assistance.

One of the most difficult issues in providing emergency assistance is that of assigning responsibility for the costs of the assistance. There are three basic approaches for bearing the costs: the party receiving the assistance, the party giving the assistance, or both on the basis of some mutually agreed principles for sharing the costs of accidents. The OECD has adopted the last approach to sharing the cost of oil spills. This approach may be appropriate for large-scale operations, which could affect many countries. If the party providing the assistance were to bear the full costs of doing so, there would be little incentive to provide adequate assistance. The political gains that come from providing assistance can be satisfied by only minimal assistance. On the other hand, if the party receiving the assistance must bear the full cost of compensating those who provide it, they may be unable to pay for it. If the affected government were to be responsible for the costs of assistance, this should be coupled with an obligation on other parties to provide full-scale assistance upon request.

The most effective method of allocating the costs of assistance is likely to be agreement in advance upon procedures for sharing the costs, which should be incorporated into the arrangements for providing emergency assistance. The Nordic Convention on Nuclear Disasters requires each party to pay all expenses incurred within its territory, with the assisting State having the right to reimbursement for such expenses (salaries, equipment costs, transport, etc.) from the State assisted unless otherwise agreed. The 1986 IAEA Convention offers parties a choice: to offer assistance without payment for costs or to provide it on a wholly or partly reimbursable basis. Several of the agreements regarding forest fires and other disasters between Canada and the United States and between Mexico and the United States include provisions for allocating costs as do the European bilateral agreements concerning environmental catastrophes.

If States are to be willing to offer effective emergency assistance promptly, it will generally be important to develop in advance agreed principles for the sharing of the costs. Whether this takes the form of agreement to invoke certain model guidelines offered by the international community or of [a] mutually agreed formula must be left to the States concerned. While the issue is controversial, the failure to address it may impair effective emergency assistance.

III. COMPENSATING FOR INJURIES FROM ENVIRONMENTAL DISASTERS

When accidents occur and damage results, someone must bear the costs. International law is not entirely clear on who must bear the costs under which circumstances. There appears to be a consensus that under international law breaches of obligations of State responsibility to prevent accidents and minimize damage incur responsibility for resulting injuries and that even if no breaches occur, States may be liable for injuries resulting from ultrahazardous activities or the release of highly dangerous substances. Whether they may be liable under international law for injuries resulting from other kinds of accidents is not settled.

If the State has certain duties under the principle of State responsibility to prevent accidents and to reduce or minimize damage, violation of these obligations incurs the responsibility of the State for the resulting injuries. Sec. 602 of the U.S. Restatement on Foreign Relations Law on the Law of the Environment provides, for example, that "A State is responsible for any significant injury, resulting from a violation of obligations under subsection (1) (on preventing harm to the environment and minimizing damage), to the environment of another State or to its property, or to persons or property within that State's territory or under its jurisdiction or control." Principle 21 of the legal principles proposed by the World Commission on Environment and Development similarly provides that a State is responsible under international law for a breach of an obligation regarding the environment and must "provide compensation for the harm caused." State responsibility for harm is incurred when a State fails to comply with binding rules of international law.

Even if a State complies with its obligations under the principle of State responsibility, it may nevertheless be liable for injuries resulting from environmental disasters if the activity was ultrahazardous or involved the release of highly dangerous substances, such as radiation and toxic chemicals. In these cases, States are liable for the injury under the principle of strict liability. Some commentators have contended that strict liability should apply whenever States cause environmental harm to other States or areas outside their jurisdiction and control. States would then be liable for serious environmental injury from accidents, whether or not they had complied with their obligations under the principle of State responsibility.

The International Law Commission has created a separate body to address questions of liability for environmental injuries resulting from activities that are lawful in international law. The draft principles encourage States to establish their own liability system, and if they do not to balance a number of factors in determining liability. There is no agreement yet within the Commission on the principles.

The conceptual question of whether a State can be liable for damage if it has complied with generally accepted standards and procedures for preventing injury has been addressed in the context of domestic environmental legislation, which may offer useful insights for international law. Under the U.S. Clean Air Act and the U.S. Clean Water Act, compliance with the permits and standards set forth in the Acts and associated regulations precludes liability for damage under federal common law doctrines. It does not foreclose remedies that may be available under the common law as developed within each State. This provides an incentive to comply with federal regulations but recognizes the rights of States to maintain their own standards and remedies for environmental damage. In international law, this would mean that compliance with internationally accepted safety standards and procedures could preclude liability for damage in international law (except for abnormally dangerous activities or toxic releases), but it would not foreclose the application of a country's remedies under domestic law.

Even when there is no liability in international law for injuries caused by certain environmental disasters, parties may be liable under the domestic laws of States. Such issues have traditionally been addressed by domestic courts, as in the litigation following the Amoco Cadiz oil spill off the coast of France, where French parties sued in United States courts invoking, in part, U.S. marine tort law. States can also enact domestic legislation to compensate their own nationals for damage received from accidents elsewhere. Several countries in Europe have passed legislation compensating environmental injury caused by the Chernobyl nuclear accident. Their reticence in seeking compensation from the Soviet Union may reveal in part a reluctance to implement strict liability for injuries from environmental disasters which could be applied to them in case of accidents on their soil.

CONCLUSIONS

International law regarding environmental disasters has developed significantly in the last two decades. Today there are many agreements addressing this question, which cover not only marine pollution disasters but nuclear disasters, forest fires, international water pollution accidents, and other environmental catastrophes. The duty to minimize environmental injury by giving prompt notification, providing information, and cooperating in minimizing injury is now part of customary international law and is encompassed within the principle of State responsibility. Attention must now be given to the duty to prevent environmental disasters, which also comes within the principle of State responsibility and constitutes customary international law. However, efforts to define acceptable safety standards and practices have been lagging in many important areas. It is time for States to turn their attention to this aspect of international law relating to environmental disasters. Prevention of accidents is the most effective way to protect our natural and cultural resources for present and future generations.

NOTE

International law as related to natural disasters. International environmental law is not focused on preventing and mitigating "one-off" disasters. Rather, the focus has been on inducing States to address systematically many of the sources of planetary degradation. A few systems such as Marpol and the Basel Convention do mandate technologies intended to prevent disasters. Disaster mitigation, clean up and compensation is usually done under the source or victim State's law. However, the general duty of a State not to harm another could be the basis for post-disaster compensation by a victim State. Treaties such as the United Nations Convention on the Non-Navigational Uses of Transboundary Waters combine this duty with the duty to consult and cooperate when a State undertakes a project or activity that can adversely impact other riparian States. These duties could be the basis to improve river basin climate change-induced flood management and drought responses. One useful step would be to adopt an international agreement modeled on the Conventions on Early Notification of a Nuclear Accident and Assistance in Case of a Nuclear Accident or Radiological Emergency, which impose a duty to warn other States and the international community of disasters with likely transboundary, regional or planetary impacts and require cooperation and assistance coordination between the source and victim States.

2. ARTICLE 9, MONTREAL RULES

The Montreal Rules are presented to provide an earlier example of a notice structure created to address transfrontier emergencies.

INTERNATIONAL LAW ASSOCIATION, RULES OF INTERNATIONAL LAW APPLICABLE TO TRANSFRONTIER POLLUTION, ARTICLE 9, EMERGENCY SITUATIONS

II.A, Report of the Sixtieth Conference Held at Montreal, Aug. 29, 1982, to Sept. 4, 1982
176 (1983)

Article 9
Emergency Situations

When as a result of an emergency situation or of other circumstances activities already carried out in the territory of a State cause or might cause a sudden increase in the existing level of transfrontier pollution the State of origin is under a duty: (a) to promptly warn the affected or potentially affected States; (b) to provide them with such pertinent information as will enable them to minimize the transfrontier pollution damage; (c) to inform them of the steps taken to abate the cause of the increased transfrontier pollution level.

Comment

1. Notice to potentially affected States is to be furnished not only when the risk of transfrontier pollution results from planned activities, but also whenever as a consequence of an emergency situation, activities already carried out are likely to cause an increase in the existing level of transfrontier pollution. In this case the duty to warn the neighbouring States arises from a concrete situation, as for example from the uncontrolled emission of chlorine gases from a chemical plant. Therefore it is out of the question for the polluting State to argue that the operation of the said plant does not represent a danger of transfrontier pollution, as

it usually happens when States are requested to furnish prior information. On the other hand, it seems obvious that States will not be as reluctant to warn potentially affected neighbours of emergency situations as they are in giving them in advance notice of projects likely to cause transfrontier pollution. In fact, in this latter case they always risk to get massive opposition from the public authorities and from individuals in the potentially affected country, which often leads to a standstill of the project and to the imposition of additional and costly safety measures.

2.   A duty to warn potentially affected States in cases of emergency has been laid down in several international conventions which, however, mostly relate to the utilization of international rivers, as the Draft European Convention for the protection of international watercourses against pollution, the Agreement between the United States and Canada concerning the Great Lakes water quality of 1972 and the Agreement between the Federal Republic of Germany and the German Democratic Republic on principles concerning damage control at the border of 1973. Such a duty is also foreseen in some conventions for the protection of the marine environment, for example in the Helsinki Convention of 1974 and in the Barcelona Convention 1976.

3.   Significantly, Principle 9 of the UNEP's draft guidelines on shared natural resources also formulates the duty to warn in the mandatory language "States have a duty urgently to inform" and does not use the expression "it is necessary for States" adopted for the duty of prior information. UNEP, Draft Principles of Conduct in the Field of the Environment for the Guidance of States in the Conservation and Harmonious Utilization of Natural Resources Shared by Two or More States, 19 May 1978, Principle 9, U.N.G.A. Res. 3129 (XXVIII), 17 ILM 1097 (1978). On the other hand, the Organization for Economic Cooperation and Development (OECD), consisting of 30 mostly Western industrialized countries committed to democratic governance and the market economy, prefers only to recommend the warning of potentially affected States in Title F of its Recommendation C (74) 224.

4.   In addition to the duty to warn, the States on whose territory the emergency situation arises have the duty to provide potentially polluted States such pertinent information on the matter as will enable them to take appropriate steps in order to eliminate, reduce or combat the effects of such a situation. This implies the furnishing of details about the activity at the origin of the increased transfrontier pollution danger, the circumstances which lead to the creation of the emergency and the measures already taken by the polluting State to abate the transfrontier pollution.

3. PRINCIPLE 18, RIO DECLARATION

PRINCIPLE 18, RIO DECLARATION ON ENVIRONMENT AND DEVELOPMENT

Adopted at Rio de Janeiro by the United Nations Conference on Environment and Development, June 14, 1992, U.N. Doc. A/ CONF.151/5/Rev.1, June 13, 1992, *reprinted in* 31 I.L.M. 874 (1992)

Principle 18

States shall immediately notify other States of any natural disasters or other emergencies that are likely to produce sudden harmful effects on the environment of those States. Every effort shall be made by the international community to help States so afflicted.

NOTES AND QUESTIONS

1. *Problem.* Suppose the headwaters of the River Blue are located in a remote, mountainous region of country A. Suppose further that this region experienced unusually heavy rainfall one week and that in the past rainfall of this nature had caused flooding in downstream country B (but not in country A). Does Principle 18 indicate that country A should notify country B? Of what?

2. *Is Principle 18 binding?* What is the authoritative value of Principle 18? Is it binding on States? If not, how could it be used by a State that has been the victim of an environmental disaster?

3. *Principle 18 and the Nuclear Accident Conventions.* You should compare Principle 18 with the more specific obligations contained in the two conventions adopted under the auspices of the International Atomic Energy Agency (IAEA) following the Chernobyl accident, considered below.

4. ARTICLE 14, CONVENTION ON BIOLOGICAL DIVERSITY

Article 14(d) and (e) of the Convention on Biological Diversity require notice, efforts to minimize damage, and international cooperation to deal with a domestic emergency within a State, as well as to establish joint contingency plans. Article 14(d) states: "In the case of imminent or grave danger or damage, originating under its jurisdiction or control, to biological diversity within the area under jurisdiction of other States or in areas beyond the limits of national jurisdiction, notify immediately the potentially affected States of such danger or damage, as well as initiate action to prevent or minimize such danger or damage;" and Article 14(e) requires Parties to: "[p]romote national arrangements for emergency responses to activities or events, whether caused naturally or otherwise, which present a grave and imminent danger to biological diversity and encourage international cooperation to supplement such national efforts and, where appropriate and agreed by the States or regional economic integration organizations concerned, to establish joint contingency plans."

NOTES AND QUESTIONS

Agriculture, climate change, and the Convention on Biological Diversity. As you read Chapters 9 (climate change) and 14 (food and agriculture), think about whether the Convention on Biological Diversity creates any duties to address the impact on climate change on crop diversity that might threaten food security.

5. EMERGENCIES ON INTERNATIONAL WATERCOURSES

Compare the approach taken by the ILA to the problem of transfrontier harm caused by emergencies in general to that of the 1997 United Nations Convention on the Law of the Non-Navigational Uses of International Watercourses, U.N. Doc. A/RES/51/229:

Article 28
Emergency Situations

1. For the purposes of this article, "emergency" means a situation that causes, or poses an imminent threat of causing, serious harm to watercourse States or other States and that results suddenly from natural causes, such as floods, the breaking up of ice, landslides or earthquakes, or from human conduct, such as industrial accidents.

2. A watercourse State shall, without delay and by the most expeditious means available, notify other potentially affected States and competent international organizations of any emergency originating within its territory.

3. A watercourse State within whose territory an emergency originates shall, in cooperation with potentially affected States and, where appropriate, competent international organizations, immediately take all practicable measures necessitated by the circumstances to prevent, mitigate and eliminate harmful effects of the emergency.

4. When necessary, watercourse States shall jointly develop contingency plans for responding to emergencies, in cooperation, where appropriate, with other potentially affected States and competent international organizations.

NOTES AND QUESTIONS

1. *Other instruments.* The United Nations Convention on the Transboundary Effects of Industrial Accidents, Helsinki, March 17, 1992, *reprinted in* 31 I.L.M. 1330 (1992), entered into force on April 16, 2000. As of August 2015, it has 27 signatories and 41 Parties. This Convention works

primarily by promoting active international cooperation between Parties before, during, and after industrial accidents and encouraging parties to engage in efforts to prevent industrial accidents and develop emergency preparedness plans. It applies to "the prevention of, preparedness for and response to industrial accidents capable of causing transboundary effects, including the effects of such accidents caused by natural disasters, and to international cooperation concerning mutual assistance, research and development, exchange of information and exchange of technology in the area of prevention of, preparedness for and response to industrial accidents." It does not, however, apply to "(a) Nuclear accidents or radiological emergencies; (b) Accidents at military installations; (c) Dam failures, with the exception of the effects of industrial accidents caused by such failures; (d) Land-based transport accidents with the exception of: (i) Emergency response to such accidents; (ii) Transportation on the site of the hazardous activity; (e) Accidental release of genetically modified organisms; (f) Accidents caused by activities in the marine environment, including seabed exploration or exploitation; (g) Spills of oil or other harmful substances at sea." Art. 2.

2. *The OECD weighs in.* An international effort to assign responsibility for the costs of accident prevention and mitigation was the Recommendation of the Council of the Organization for Economic Cooperation and Development (OECD) on the Application of the Polluter-Pays Principle to Accidental Pollution, OECD Doc. C(89)88 (Final), July 25, 1989, *reprinted in* 28 I.L.M. 1320 (1989). The recommendation contains a set of "Guiding Principles Relating to Accidental Pollution." According to their terms, the principles "concern some aspects of the application of the Polluter-Pays Principle to hazardous installations." (Para. 1.) They provide, inter alia, that: "the operator of a hazardous installation should bear the cost of reasonable measures to prevent and control accidental pollution from that installation which are introduced by public authorities in Member countries . . . prior to the occurrence of an accident in order to protect human health or the environment" (Para. 4); and that "(d)omestic law which provides that the cost of reasonable measures to control accidental pollution after an accident should be collected as expeditiously as possible from the legal or natural person who is at the origin of the accident, is consistent with the Polluter-Pays Principle." (Para. 5.) The principles state that while the cost of the measures referred to "is as a general rule met by the general budget, public authorities may with a view to achieving a more economically efficient resource allocation, introduce specific fees or taxes payable by certain installations on account of their hazardous nature (e.g., licensing fees), the proceeds of which to be allocated to accidental pollution prevention and control." (Para. 9.) This would not affect the recovery by public authorities of the cost of reasonable measures to control or otherwise respond to accidental pollution. (Para. 16.)

C. CONTINGENCY PLANNING AND HAZARD MANAGEMENT

INTERNATIONALIZATION OF HAZARD MANAGEMENT IN RECIPIENT COUNTRIES: ACCIDENT PREPAREDNESS AND RESPONSE

Gunther Handl
in Transferring Hazardous Technologies and Substances: The International Legal
Challenge 106, 106–107, 111–117
(G. Handl & R. Lutx eds., 1989)

INTRODUCTION

Recent large-scale industrial accidents have sharply increased latent public unease about hazardous technology and substances and prompted concerted efforts by governments, industry, and international organizations to improve hazard management worldwide. While global industrial accident experience demonstrates that hazard management has been seriously deficient in both developed and developing countries, shortcomings appear greatly accentuated when hazardous technology and substances are non-indigenous or transferred, and particularly so when the recipient nation falls into the developing country category.

The reasons for this are well known. Transboundary transfers of hazardous technology or substances often imply inter-cultural transfers of alien values and concepts. The technological, scientific, and organizational demands of any given hazardous transfer can severely tax, if not overwhelm, local hazard management abilities. For example, a recent authoritative survey of radiation protection capabilities concludes that

> many developing countries simply lack the necessary infrastructure to implement a radiation protection policy based on international standards. . . . They lack the basic legislation and supporting regulations, as well as effective national authorities, qualified manpower, and necessary equipment.

Against the yardstick of management practices in industrialized countries, much of industrial hazard management in the Third World might have to be described in similarly negative terms. . . .

Local "Risk Communication"

For present purposes local "risk communication" might be termed the routine, i.e., non-emergency, flow of information about risks of hazardous installations or processes, either from industry to government, from government to public, or from industry to the public. As an element of public policy for both minimizing the consequences of accidents and preventing them in the first place, its importance can hardly be exaggerated.

Many of the major industrial accidents of the last few years provide dramatic illustrations of the negative consequences of risk communication failures. Apart from possibly considerable political penalties, such as loss of public trust in risk management processes and institutions, failure to communicate information about risk is likely to translate into greater environmental, public health, and thus economic costs. For example, during the Flixborough[1] and Seveso accidents, counter-measures to reduce the severity of local impacts were severely hampered by the fact that local authorities, quite apart from the public, had been kept in the dark about the nature and quantity of chemicals utilized in the struck facilities. Similarly, at Bhopal, the apparent lack of public knowledge about the general hazard characteristics of methyl isocyanate-a fact that, amongst other things, points to failure by the plant operator properly to communicate risk information-may have been a major factor in the virtual absence of off-site emergency preparations for a disaster of the kind experienced. . . .

First steps towards international regulation of local dissemination of hazard information were taken in Europe. In the aftermath of the accident in Seveso, in 1982 the EC Council adopted a directive on major-accident hazards, the so-called "Seveso-Directive." To tighten risk communication obligations and, in particular, to counter a trend in national implementing legislation that would have rendered risk communication less than effective, the Directive was substantially amended in 1988. It now calls for communication of very detailed risk information-on an "active basis"-to any person liable to be affected by a major accident. If a most recent Proposal for an EC Council Directive on the freedom of access to information on the environment should be approved, the result could be a highly effective hazard management system within the European Communities.

In the summer of 1988, the OECD Council adopted a Decision-Recommendation on the subject matter of local risk-communication. As a result, member states are now under an obligation to ensure that specific risk information relating to hazardous installations be provided to the public as well as information on appropriate behaviour to reduce risk in the event of accidents. In terms of its normative quality, the OECD measure does not, however, match the revised Seveso-Directive. While EC countries are legally obliged actively to communicate detailed hazard information, active communication of comparable information is merely recommended under the OECD document.

---

[1] In 1974, an explosion at a chemical plant in Flixborough, England, killed 29 and wounded dozens of people. *See 29 Workers Dead, More Than 40 Injured and Huge Area of Surrounding Land Devastated*, The Times (June 3, 1974), at 1, col. 1.

So far, the application of formally binding international prescriptions on local risk communication has been limited to mostly Western industrialized nations. Indeed, the 1985 World Bank Guidelines for Identifying, Analyzing, and Control ling Major Hazard Installations in Developing Countries steer clear of the issue, even though the Guidelines were directly inspired by the Seveso Directive which specifically focused on local risk communication. However, recently, risk communication has begun occupying a central place in international efforts to enhance accident preparedness and response planning worldwide, and especially in developing countries.

In 1986, the United Nations Environment Programme (UNEP) started work on practical measures to help governments, particularly in developing countries, to minimize the risk of hazardous industrial accidents, especially accident consequences. To date, the result has been a formal document detailing specific elements of a process for responding to technological accidents at local level, called "APELL" (Awareness and Preparedness for Emergencies at Local Level). A key objective of APELL is to increase local awareness of industrial hazards by encouraging communication of risk information to local community members and involving them in all aspects of emergency response planning. APELL provisions on risk communication are couched in terms of mere recommendations and do not convey any particular order of priority as to the steps to be taken. There is no mistaking, however, of the importance ascribed to the basic information process, the necessity to assure a two-way flow of communication. Since its formal introduction several developing countries with widely differing political sustains have indicated their willingness to apply APELL.

APELL in turn is closely modelled on an industry-wide campaign that was launched by the United States Chemical Manufacturers Association (CMA) after the Bhopal tragedy and a chemical leak at a similar plant at Institute, West Virginia, the Community Awareness and Emergency [Response] (CAER) Program. Indeed, CMA and its European counterpart, the Conseil Europeen des Federations de l'Industrie Chimique (CEFIC), have worked hand-in-glove with UNEP in adapting CAER for worldwide use. Clearly, the chemical industry has on its own accepted local risk communication as a globally applicable policy objective, one that industry should support in developing countries as well as in Western industrialized societies.

Against this background of international/ transnational initiatives and growing domestic pressure for better risk information for local communities, it would seem that the concept of risk communication is rapidly gaining in status as a standard against which the adequacy of local hazard management might be reviewed.

TRANSBOUNDARY "RISK COMMUNICATION"

Effects of accidents at hazardous installations may not respect international boundary lines. Hazard management in recipient countries therefore must extend to exchanges of pertinent information with neighbouring countries on any significant transboundary risks associated with the use of hazardous technology or substances. On the international level, such exchanges serve accident prevention and mitigation functions similar to those assumed by local risk communication for the benefit of local host communities.

Today there can be no doubt that states are legally required to initiate such information exchanges as soon as they have reason to believe that any proposed or ongoing activity within their territory or subject to their jurisdiction carries a risk of significant transboundary harm. This international obligation to provide prior information and engage in consultations is an essential procedural counterpart to the state's substantive customary obligation to prevent significant transboundary harm.

If internationally the basic informational entitlement must be deemed non-controversial, threshold questions regarding the activation as well as the scope of the transboundary risk communication process can pose significant problems. A recent OECD Council Decision on the Exchange of Information Concerning Accidents Capable of Causing Transfrontier Damage,[2] which is aimed at hazardous industrial installations, seeks to refine the operational parameters of the obligations concerned. The Decision's significance thus lies in specifying in compulsory fashion the contents of information to be exchanged and offering a legal definition of what constitutes a "hazardous installation." For member-states of the European Community, the Seveso Directive had already established a similarly well-defined duty to provide transboundary risk information to exposed neighbouring countries.

Although formally these international standards apply only regionally, they establish guideposts of broad international significance. In other words, they are likely to be used as general yardsticks for evaluating any recipient country's performance in the internationally mandatory process of transboundary risk communication.

As presently conceived, transboundary risk communication is an intergovernmental dialogue on transboundary risk management. Rights and obligations are those of states. However, state practice points towards the emergence of at least a regional standard pursuant to which private individuals would be owed a corresponding obligation to be included in the transboundary risk communication process. Thus the

---

[2] OECD Doc. C(88) 84 (Final) (1988), reproduced in 28 I.L.M. 249 (1989).

notion of "equal rights of access," the idea that states ought to open their administrative and judicial proceedings to potentially affected residents of risk-exposed neighbouring countries, has found particularly strong support within the OECD. Principle 14 of the 1978 UNEP Principles of Conduct in the Field of the Environment,[3] recommends "equal access and treatment" as a generally applicable concept, albeit with some qualifications. A recommendation of similar import was approved by the International Law Association. More recently, the "Expert Group on Environmental' Law" of the World Commission on Environment and Development (WCED) proposed legal principles for environmental protection and sustainable development which-much like an earlier resolution on water pollution adopted by the Institute of International Law-advocates implementation of the principle as an international legal obligation of states.

Notwithstanding these strong endorsements that come on top of some supportive state practice, presently it would be difficult to characterize "equal right of access" as embodying a universal customary international legal standard applicable to national environmental resource management. On the other hand, in Western Europe as well as North America, "equal right of access" can be said to have evolved into an internationally normative concept.

D. PROVISION OF RELIEF TO ACCIDENT VICTIMS

THE BHOPAL DISASTER: STRUCTURING A SOLUTION

Daniel Magraw
57 U. Colo. L. Rev. 835, 838, 840–847 (1986)

II. BACKGROUND LEGAL ISSUES

The Bhopal litigation has raised a myriad of significant legal issues, many of which will recur if mass injuries involving United States multinational corporations occur abroad in the future. I will briefly allude to some of those issues in order to provide a background for the discussion regarding structuring a settlement to the various litigation. . . .

A final issue relates to who should bear the responsibility for the disaster. There are four possible repositories of liability: (1) Carbide (India), the immediate owner of the facility from which the gas escaped; (2) the shareholders of Carbide (India), including Carbide (U.S.); (3) the victims; and (4) the regulatory authorities, possibly including the Government of India, the Government of the State of Madhya Pradesh, the Government of Bhopal, and the United States Government. Without

---

[3]   Draft Principles of Conduct in the Field of the Environment for the Guidance of States in the Conservation and Harmonious Utilization of Natural Resources Shared by Two or More States, text in 19 I.L.M. 1097 (1978).

endorsing any of the allegations, some of the arguments for allocating liability are as follows.

It has been alleged that Carbide (India) should be liable either on a strict-liability theory or because it was negligent in operating the plant and in failing to provide sufficient warning to the potentially affected population.

It has been alleged that Carbide (U.S.) should be liable on the theory that it was negligent with respect to training persons to operate the plant, designing the plant, or controlling its subsidiary. In addition, it has been argued that a multinational enterprise as a whole should bear financial responsibility for all of its activities, regardless of corporate form and, alternately, that traditional doctrine regarding piercing the corporate veil indicates liability on the part of Carbide (U.S.). It might also be argued that Carbide (U.S.) is directly liable by analogy to the "entrustment" doctrine, i.e., that a bailor is liable to an insured third party if the bailor knew or should have known that its bailee was likely to harm the third party and failed to take reasonable precautions to protect the third party. Finally, as an alternative to holding Carbide (U.S.) directly liable, it might be argued that Carbide (India) has a right of contribution or indemnification against Carbide (U.S.), either on the basis of the entrustment doctrine argument just described or on the basis of a contractual or common-law duty on the part of Carbide (U.S.) to supply Carbide (India) with safe and up-to-date technology and assistance.

It has been argued that some of the victims are at fault, and thus should be wholly or partly liable, because they knew or should have known that there existed danger in living close to the plant and nevertheless moved onto vacant land surrounding the plant. That argument is obviously extremely harsh; it flies in the face of economic realities in India and is contrary to the usual United States law (and presumably the Indian law) of nuisance.

With respect to the regulatory authorities, it has been argued that the Government of India and the state and local governments were negligent and thus should be liable for allowing the shantytown to develop so close to the plant (possibly in violation of an Indian ordinance mandating a vacant zone around such a plant), for regulating the safety conditions in the plant in a faulty manner, or for applying pressure with respect to hiring personnel who were more qualified by their political affiliation than by their professional competence. The Government of India, however, appears to be shielded by sovereign immunity under Indian law and probably also would have been under the United States Foreign Sovereign Immunities Act if it had not brought suit itself in United States courts, and thus opened the way to counterclaims arising out of the same occurrence.

It has been alleged that the United States should be liable for not adequately regulating Carbide (U.S.); an allegation that probably is not persuasive but which has potentially far-reaching ramifications.

III. STRUCTURING A SOLUTION

A. SALIENT CHARACTERISTICS OF TILE SOLUTION

It is appropriate to begin by identifying some of the salient characteristics of a desirable solution. First, the solution should occur relatively rapidly-a goal that may already have become unattainable due to the fact that 24 months have, as of the time this article goes to press, already passed since the disaster-because of the personal suffering of victims that will occur otherwise. Speed may also be in the interest of Carbide (India) and Carbide (U.S.) because the threat of massive liability may be more harmful than the actual liability turns out to be (e.g., in terms of lost good will, depressed stock prices, and increased credit terms). In addition, the continued existence of the litigation may strain to some degree-probably small-the relationship between the United States and India, and may be detrimental to other United States interests because, for example, perceived misbehavior abroad by United States corporations tends to discredit the foreign image of the United States and may adversely affect the availability of foreign business opportunities to other United States corporations.

Second, the solution should be reached without incurring unnecessary transaction costs. The primary issue here would appear to be the desirability of avoiding excessive legal fees, but other expenses can also soar astronomically in complex tort litigation involving complicated issues (such as forum non conveniens), disputes regarding settlement proposals, and extensive and sometimes duplicative (because of the participation of separately represented plaintiffs in different courts) discovery. For example, it has been reported that an average of 63% of the recoveries in the early asbestos litigation was consumed by expenses and legal fees; that figure has reportedly dropped to 41% on more recent claims.

Third, the solution should resolve all potential claims in India and in the United States, both because of the need for speed described above and because, if it does not, the likelihood of defendants agreeing to a settlement would be greatly decreased or the amount of such a settlement would be greatly decreased. This is typically an issue in mass torts; it is complicated here by the international aspect, i.e., that the courts of at least two countries need to recognize the settlement as final and binding.

Fourth, individual claims should be determined in an impartial and reasonable manner. That goal, which is not extraordinary in itself, is particularly difficult to achieve here because of the presence of United States and Indian claimants, the vast economic disparity between the two countries (a United States judge or jury might arguably have difficulty assessing injuries suffered by shantytown inhabitants and their families in India), and the difficulty in verifying claims brought by poor residents of a country with a relatively low documentation level.

Fifth, the total amount of the settlement should be adequate to compensate injured persons in a reasonable and fair manner. Two questions must be resolved in this regard: whether the standard should reflect the realities of life in India as opposed to the greater wealth of the United States, and whether punitive damages should be awarded. The former question should be resolved by limiting damages for residents of India to the Indian realities; any greater award would be a windfall and would distort the risks of doing business in India (thus discouraging non-Indian, and particularly United States, persons from doing business in India and, as a result, hindering India's development efforts). The latter question could be answered either way, depending on what law applies and how egregious the relevant behavior turns out to have been.

Sixth, in allocating liability through a settlement, the conduct-guidance effect of that allocation must be kept in mind: how important is it to provide incentives to the various actors to behave more carefully? In addition, it should be remembered that the allocation of liability may have significant effect in discouraging or changing the nature of foreign investment in, and technology transfer to, developing countries. For example, allocating liability to the nation in which the parent corporation is headquartered (or is incorporated or is the nation of the residence of the majority shareholders) would presumably cause that nation to regulate more strictly all foreign investment and technology export. This result could increase safety levels, but could also easily lead to decreasing those types of activities and could thus hamper developing countries' efforts to create employment opportunities, increase standards of living, and decrease dependency on imports. Alternatively, capital and technology exporting states might insist on bilateral or multilateral investment treaties to allocate liability. Although hardly objectionable in theory, such treaties might inevitably allocate liability in a manner unfavorable to developing countries, because those countries most probably would have less bargaining power. Also, there would be an undesirable disruption in international trade during those negotiations, and the transaction costs of the negotiations would be high. Finally, placing liability on the "exporting" state (here, the United States) might cause a dangerous laxity on the part of the "importing" state (here, India).

Similarly, although on a different level, holding the parent corporation liable could be expected to decrease the total amount of foreign investment by increasing the risk of such investment. Such an allocation of liability might lead to the exercise of greater care in supervising the operations of foreign branches or subsidiaries, but it might also result in either exporting only simpler or older and more thoroughly tested technology-a result that presumably would increase safety but that also could leave the developing countries' products unable to compete in export markets-or in a restructuring of foreign activities, e.g., toward licensing instead of direct investment. These and other policy considerations affect the calculus of allocating liability.

B.   A PROPOSED STRUCTURE

Taking into account the foregoing considerations, and acknowledging that the proposal outlined below raises a number of novel legal questions whose outcomes are uncertain, a solution to the Bhopal litigation might be structured as follows, to be accomplished in part via a self-executing executive agreement between the United States and India, and accompanied by any implementing legislation that may be constitutionally required by either of the two countries.

First, India and the United States should agree that India will expropriate all claims arising from the Bhopal disaster. (The March 29, 1985 Indian Act may already have accomplished such an expropriation, but that result is not obvious.) Such an agreement would remove any uncertainty with respect to India's ability to act as parens patriae in United States courts. The same result might be achieved in the absence of an executive agreement on this point if India expropriated the claims and President Reagan, in accord with the Second Hickenlooper Amendment, filed a statement in United States courts that the foreign policy interests of the United States require application of the Act of State doctrine (i.e., that the courts of one country will not challenge the acts of another country taken within that country's territory).

In either event, United States involvement in effectuating the expropriation (and the solution more broadly) would not imply any fault on the part of the United States. Rather, active United States involvement in fostering a solution is indicated by the international complexion of the problem and the fact that the Bhopal situation implicates a variety of United States interests which would be furthered by settling it fairly and expeditiously. It might be argued by United States citizens and residents that either United States action, and especially direct agreement by the United States to the Indian Government's expropriation, was a "taking" requiring just compensation under the fifth amendment and that the amount ultimately received from the claims settlement tribunal (described below) did not constitute just compensation. The United States Claims Court should have jurisdiction over such a claim, notwithstanding the so-called "treaty exception" to that court's jurisdiction, but this issue is not clear.

Second, India and the United States should agree that the amount of every claim will be determined expeditiously by a claims settlement tribunal to be established in India, by India and the United States jointly, the judges of which would be appointed by India and the United States. The cost of such tribunal would be borne equally by India and the United States. The agreement should also provide that any lump-sum amount received in settlement of the Bhopal claims shall be distributed in toto (pro rata if necessary), without deduction for any tribunal expenses, by India to the claimants whose claims had been expropriated, in accordance with the determination of the tribunal. Any amounts received, concurrently with the lump-sum payment, settling specified individual claims would be passed on by India to those claimants in full, and such claimants would be barred from bringing their claims before the claims settlement tribunal. Attorneys' fees would be limited to 10% of the amount actually received by each claimant.

The provisions just described (which are similar in some respects to those leading to the currently operating United States-Iran Claims Tribunal in the Hague), would remove cases from the court systems of both India and the United States to a specialized and presumably more expeditious forum. The likelihood of reduced delay would be furthered by having tribunal expenses paid by the two countries; they would have an incentive to facilitate the efficient operation of the tribunal. Such cost sharing would also reflect the two countries' interests in fairly resolving the disputes and the savings in costs that would otherwise be incurred by their judicial systems in processing the claims, and provide an incentive-albeit modest-to those countries to regulate more vigorously in the future.

The scheme would also enable and encourage the settlement of all claims related to the Bhopal disaster at one time. Moreover, it would permit the United States and other claimants to settle individually at that time if they so desired.

The specialized tribunal, whose decisions would be limited to determining the extent of injury and the corresponding measure of damages, would presumably apply consistent standards and operate fairly. United States participation in choosing tribunal members would presumably lead to reasonable evaluation of United States residents' claims (assuming such claims were not settled separately).

Use of a tribunal located in India would also lower transaction costs for claimants overall. (Disregarding attorneys' fees for the moment, Indian claimants' costs would presumably decrease because of the tribunal; United States claimants' costs would presumably increase.) The limitation on attorneys' fees would further reduce transaction costs (the United States successfully used such a 10% limitation with respect to United States nationals' claims against the German Democratic Republic).

Finally, Carbide (U.S.) and Carbide (India) should, simultaneously with the signing of the United States-India executive agreement described above, pay to India a lump sum in full and final settlement of all claims against the Union Carbide group of companies related to the Bhopal disaster with the exception of any specified individual claims that are settled as part of the same arrangement and for which payment is made at the same time. The amount of that settlement should reflect a reasonably informed estimate of the numbers and types of injuries suffered and should be based principally on the actual damages suffered (thus, for example, loss of livelihood of an Indian resident would be measured by his or her expected income in India). Punitive damages would not be included unless investigation revealed that particularly egregious behavior had occurred and the applicable law would allow punitive damages. Such a settlement would liquidate the Union Carbide corporate group's Bhopal-related liability and would presumably lead to a generous amount for distribution among claimants.

IV. CONCLUSION

This article proposes a structure for settling the Bhopal litigation that seeks to protect, in a balanced manner, the interests of the parties— including India—to the various litigation as well as of the United States. That structure could also serve as a starting point for resolving future occurrences similar to the Bhopal disaster. The proposal outlined herein obviously depends in large part on cooperation, statesmanship and, perhaps, leadership by the United States. Given the various considerations involved, including the fact that the Bhopal disaster is likely to recur in other forms, such involvement comports with the interests of the United States in particular and is in the interest of justice generally.

Further reading: *See* Stephen C. McCaffrey, Expediting the Provision of Compensation to Accident Victims, in Transferring Hazardous Technologies and Substances 199 (G. Handl & R. Lutz eds., 1989).

E. NORMS APPLICABLE TO NUCLEAR ACCIDENTS

1. CASE STUDY: CHERNOBYL

At approximately 1:23 A.M. on Saturday, April 26, 1986, an accident occurred in nuclear power Reactor No. 4 at Chernobyl, USSR. The processes leading to the accident commenced the day before, when operators began to prepare for a test of one of the reactor's two turbogenerators. The test was essentially intended to determine whether the generator could be used, in the event of a local electricity failure, to power the reactor's emergency cooling system until emergency electricity reserves could take over. In the many hours of preparing for the test, the operators disengaged the emergency cooling system from the reactor, disconnected both generators from external electricity, and neutralized a number of automatic safety systems from both generators. These steps violated crucial provisions of the operating regulations. As the reactor's power was decreased before the test, the reactor became unstable, which ultimately caused the operators to increase and then reduce the flow rate of cooling water through the reactor.

The reactor in which the experiment was being conducted was one of 73 nuclear power reactors in the Soviet Union. Those nuclear reactors, like all nuclear power reactors, generate electricity by using controlled nuclear reactions, caused by the inherent instability of radioactive elements in the reactor core, to heat water into steam, which then turns turbines in turbogenerators that generate electricity. In the case of Reactor No. 4, the radioactive element used was uranium enriched with uranium 235. Neutrons (which are particles within atoms) emitted by the decaying uranium atoms within the core collide with other uranium atoms within the core, in turn causing these atoms to decay. Each decay releases energy in the form of heat, and under proper circumstances, the decay of the uranium atoms within the reactor core can be induced into a chain reaction leading to the continuous supply of energy.

Perhaps counterintuitively, reactors produce more energy if the neutrons emitted by the core's uranium are slowed down, at least within certain limits. In most United States nuclear power reactors, the material—called the "moderator"—used to slow down the neutrons is water. Chernobyl, however, used graphite (1,700 tons of it) as the moderator; water was used only as a coolant. The moderation occurred by moving 1,659 fuel rods containing the uranium in or out of the massive graphite block.

The use of graphite as the moderator has a number of worrisome consequences, as contrasted with the use of water. Perhaps the most problematic consequence is that the reactor becomes more unstable. Either or both of a temperature increase or a loss of water (for example, from the cooling system) causes the nuclear reaction to increase and thus more energy and heat to be released. The opposite is true regarding water-moderated reactors. Also, graphite (which is soft luminous carbon) burns, but water does not, so if there is a problem, graphite poses more of a risk than water does.

The reason that graphite was used as the moderator at Chernobyl is that the use of graphite increases the amount of plutonium that is produced as a byproduct. Plutonium, which is another radioactive element, is used in the production of nuclear weapons. The reactors at Chernobyl were part of the Soviet Union's backup system for manufacturing plutonium for military purposes. Plutonium-producing nuclear facilities in the United States also use graphite as a moderator.

When the test at Chernobyl finally began in the early hours of April 26—to quote from an English translation of the Soviet Union's official report on the accident—a "continuing decrease in the water flow rate through the channels of the reactor under conditions of an increase in power led to intense steam formation and then to a crisis," which included overheating of the fuel and its disintegration. Ensuing chemical reactions led to a massive steam explosion, followed by a thermal explosion. Those explosions—neither of which was a nuclear explosion—blasted a hole in the roof, casting aside in that process a 1,000-ton concrete shield. The explosions started at least 30 individual fires, including in the graphite core itself, and led to the immediate release of large amounts of radioactive material from the reactor.

A column of radioactive particles rose over one-half mile into the atmosphere above the plant, thus raising the likelihood of long-distance pollution from the accident. Moreover, because much of the radioactivity was carried by smoke from the burning graphite and because graphite particles are so fine, the radioactive material was not prone to fall to the earth very quickly, thus further increasing the danger of transboundary radioactive pollution.

Altogether, it was estimated that approximately 18 million curies—which is a measure of radiation—were released into the atmosphere by the Chernobyl accident. About one-quarter of that, over 4 million curies, were released the day of the explosions. By way of comparison, the accident at Three Mile Island released a total of approximately 18 curies—that is, about one-millionth as many as were released at Chernobyl.

A top Ukrainian official reached the plant 90 minutes after the first explosion. He found injured and stunned people stumbling or lying around, flames and smoke everywhere, and invisible lethal radioactivity lurking anywhere. Soviet leaders in Moscow were alerted shortly thereafter, and crisis-management teams dispatched by Moscow arrived in Chernobyl later that day. According to a member of the first team to arrive, it was only as they approached Chernobyl and saw the glowing red from the graphite core that they really appreciated the magnitude of the disaster. By that time, many severe injuries had occurred, especially among fire fighters and medical personnel, many of whom displayed extraordinary bravery. The first physicians to arrive at the reactor tried to practice triage, but with no accurate sense of how much exposure anyone had had. One hundred and twenty-nine of the most seriously injured persons were airlifted to a Moscow hospital, which had much earlier been designated as the national medical center for nuclear injuries, for longer-term medical care.

Over the next week or so, the Soviet Union engaged in a concentrated effort to try to put out the graphite fire and reduce and eliminate the release of radioactive materials. Those efforts primarily consisted of dumping from helicopters 5,000 tons of a theretofore untested mixture onto the smoldering reactor. The mixture consisted of boron (to absorb neutrons), dolomite (to create carbon dioxide to smother the fire), clay and sand (to act as a filter to trap radioactive particles), and lead (to melt into a smooth cover to absorb radiation and transfer heat).

This blanketing technique was intended to block the release of radioactive particles into the atmosphere. But it also had the unfortunate effect of increasing the temperature inside the already red-hot graphite pile, which in turn raised the possibilities of a reactor-core meltdown or the collapse of the reactor's cement foundation. Either of those events would have allowed massive amounts of radio-active material to contaminate the water table 50 feet below. An intense debate occurred within the crisis-management team regarding whether the blanketing approach should be used at all. By Sunday, April 27, the decision was made to begin, but serious doubts remained.

For five days, the blanketing technique resulted in decreasing radiation emissions but increasing core temperatures. On May 2, however, a frightening development occurred: radiation emissions also began to rise. On May 5, they reached the highest level since the explosions. Tension and doubt were intense. The blanketing continued, but new alternative steps, involving a tunnel, were also initiated. Then, unexpectedly, the radiation emissions virtually ceased the next day. The immediate crisis was over.

As a result of the emission of radioactive materials, 31 people died in the days and months immediately following the accident, most of them from radiation burns. Approximately 30 more remained hospitalized six months after the accident. About 20 countries, including the United States, volunteered to assist, or responded quickly to requests for assistance, by sending medical supplies, equipment, and personnel. Initially, estimates varied widely regarding medical difficulties that would arise in the future as a result of radiation exposure, with some predictions of numbers of dead running in the tens of thousands.

Approximately 1,000 square kilometers in the Soviet Union, in which 135,000 people formerly resided, were evacuated as uninhabitable soon after the accident, and they remain unpopulated. That area includes the town of Pripyat, where reactor workers and their families lived. On the day of the accident, the Soviet Union ordered the 49,000 inhabitants of Pripyat to stay indoors. Only a few disobeyed to sneak a look at the burning reactor, and they were among the casualties, "victims of curiosity." On Sunday morning, 1,100 buses, in a column 12 miles long, drove from Kiev and elsewhere into the radioactive danger zone to evacuate the residents of Pripyat. The town was evacuated, reportedly with almost no panic. Persons in other nearby areas were not evacuated for several more days and thus suffered greater exposure to radiation. The damage in the Soviet Union was officially stated as about $3 billion, though Western observers put the figure much higher.

Damage also occurred outside the Soviet Union. During the first two days after the accident, radioactive clouds drifted in a northwestern direction to Sweden and Finland, turned southeast across Polish territory, Czechoslovakia, southern Germany, and north again to the Netherlands. On the following days, the pollutants went directly southeastward, thus affecting Austria and northern Italy (as well as Kiev and other portions of the Soviet Union that had theretofore been relatively untouched). After several days, the radioactive pollutants reached the western United States and Japan.

Because of the nearly incomprehensible speed at which nuclear reactions occur, once prompt criticality was reached, the operators had less than one second to rectify the situation. Obviously, no warning was possible that the accident was occurring. Even after the accident, however, neither the existence of the accident nor the drift of the clouds was communicated to potentially affected countries by the Soviet Union. The first public indication of danger came from Sweden. The Soviet Union did not even acknowledge the existence of the accident until two and one-half days after it occurred, and the information disclosed after that was scanty until August, when a comprehensive report was issued to the International Atomic Energy Agency (IAEA). Affected States were essentially left to their own devices to detect the pollutants, including both their nature and amount, during the critical period during which precautionary measures were possible.

It is likely that early notification and information would have made a difference. For example, radioactive materials can affect people via a number of routes, including direct skin contact from and inhalation of materials falling from the sky, direct skin contact from and inhalation of materials lying on the ground and kicked up as dust by activities such as walking, and by ingesting food or water that has been contaminated by radioactive materials. A State that has been warned of the imminent arrival of airborne radioactive materials can instruct its residents to stay indoors and to avoid ingesting certain types of food that are likely to be contaminated, such as milk or leafy vegetables. In addition, more aggressive steps can be taken, such as providing Iodine pills to a population to minimize the intake of radioactive Iodine 131, which has a halflife of only eight days and which, together with Cesium 137 and Strontium 90, is one of the three most common and dangerous radioactive elements emitted by Chernobyl.

Many countries took efforts to minimize the harmful effects of the radiation, once they learned of the accident. Poland, for example, prohibited children in some regions from drinking milk, prohibited the pasturing of cattle, and provided children doses of Iodine. Bavaria, in the Federal Republic of Germany, removed 3,000 tons of powdered milk from circulation and paid the dairy that produced it approximately $2,000,000 in compensation; and the sale of other foodstuffs was banned in West Germany-foodstuffs that were freely available across the border in France. The contaminated powdered milk was subsequently sold to Egypt (it was intercepted and impounded before it left Germany); similar sales occurred from European countries to other developing countries.

Non-Soviet news coverage during the period immediately following the accident was extensive and, in many cases, sensationalistic and inaccurate. In at least one instance, a newspaper disregarded an explicit denial by its Moscow correspondent and reported inaccurately that 2,000 persons had died at Chernobyl and were buried in a mass grave. Western news media, as well as some others outside the Soviet Union, seemed to derive what the Germans call Schadenfreude, or joy in the suffering of others, from the Chernobyl tragedy. In any event, the inaccurate reporting gave the Soviet Union a means by which to deflect some of the criticism and doubts directed at it. If such exaggerated accounts were to appear widely in the United States following a nuclear accident here, the results might well be panic and increased casualties.

In the aftermath of Chernobyl, the Soviet Union reaffirmed its dedication to nuclear energy. Globally, 378 nuclear power plants were operating, providing 15 percent of the world's electricity. Ninety-seven of these plants were in the United States. Another 175 were scheduled for operation worldwide.

An IAEA delegation visited the Soviet Union soon after the accident and thereafter served as a channel of communication about the accident. In addition, the IAEA formed an expert working group on nuclear safety standards and convened an international conference to review the accident and to draft conventions on two of the important issues raised by it: emergency notification and assistance. Those conventions were negotiated and finalized unusually expeditiously, being opened for signature on September 26, 1986, five months after the accident. The Convention on Early Notification of a Nuclear Accident entered into force just one month later, on October 27, 1987. The Convention on Assistance in the Case of a Nuclear Accident or Radiological Emergency entered into force on February 26, 1987. (These Conventions are reprinted in 25 I.L.M. 1391 & 1377 (1986)).

The Soviet Union denied, in the period immediately after the accident, liability for damage in other States. Among other points, Soviet diplomats reportedly objected on the ground that other States' preventive measures were extreme and unnecessary. As far as is known, no States made diplomatic claims to the Soviet Union for compensation for harm from the accident, although the United Kingdom reportedly reserved its right to make such a claim.

In 2011, the United Nations Scientific Committee issued a report on the Effects of Atomic Radiation to the UN General Assembly, with Annex D discussing the health effects due to radiation from the Chernobyl Accident. *See* http://www.unscear.org/docs/reports/2008/11–80076_ Report_2008_Annex_D.pdf. It pointed out that initial predictions overestimated dose exposure, and that no cases of Acute Radiation Syndrome (ARS) developed among the general public. The "high radiation doses proved fatal for 28 of [the 134 plant staff and emergency workers]." In addition, for the exposed workers who did develop ARS, "the major health consequences from the radiation exposure . . . remain the skin injuries and radiation-induced cataracts." However, a significant increase in thyroid cancer incidence was also observed, with around 6,000 cases developing mainly in those who were children and adolescents at the time of the accident, have resulted from the resulting contamination, with only 15 proving fatal. The report also observed a possible increase in the incidence of leukemia among the recovery operation workers, but also found the data to include a number of internal consistencies making accurate resolution difficult. Beyond these effects, however, the report concluded that "there has been no persuasive evidence of any other health effect in the general population that can be attributed to radiation exposure."

NOTES AND QUESTIONS

1. *A Soviet nuclear sub accident.*

On 4 and 6 October, [1986,] the Soviet Union notified the [International Atomic Energy Agency] of the fire on, and the subsequent sinking of, one of its nuclear-powered and nuclear-armed submarines, indicating that there was no danger of nuclear explosion or radioactive contamination of the environment. Though it was not specified that this notification was made in accordance with the Early Notification Convention, it may be noted that such notification would be consistent with the undertakings by the USSR to apply the Convention provisionally and also to apply it to all nuclear activities.

Introductory Note, 25 I.L.M. 1391–1392 (1986).

2.   *Applying the general principles.* How would the general principles in section B of this chapter apply to a Chernobyl-like situation? To what extent do they differ from the obligations laid down in the Convention on Early Notification, discussed in the excerpt in the following subsection?

3.   *Chernobyl's conventional fallout.* The two agreements adopted in the aftermath of the Chernobyl disaster are the Convention on Early Notification of a Nuclear Accident, September 26, 1986, *reprinted in* 25 I.L.M. 1391 (1986) and the Convention on Assistance in the Case of a Nuclear Accident or Radiological Emergency, September 26, 1986, *reprinted in* 25 I.L.M. 1377 (1986).

4.   *Forest fires?* The no-entrance zone around the Chernobyl plant consists mostly of forests, some of which were severely damaged by radiation and all of which contain radioactive material. If forest fires were to start in these areas, significant amounts of radiation would be released in the smoke from the fires. Depending on the wind at the time, this radiation could easily reach other countries. The no-entrance zone has many signs warning of the danger of forest fires. Is Ukraine obliged to have an early warning system for other countries in the event a forest fire occurs?

2.   THE LEGAL RESPONSE

OVERVIEW OF LEGAL AND TECHNICAL ASPECTS OF NUCLEAR ACCIDENT POLLUTION

Andronico O. Adede
in International Law and Pollution 129, 129–132, 136–138 (D. Magraw ed., 1991)

INTRODUCTION

The concern with the adequacy of international legal regimes for dealing with pollution problems arising from nuclear accidents and the need to strengthen international technical standards for enhancing nuclear safety received a notable impetus following the 1986 Chernobyl nuclear accident in the U.S.S.R. Governments seemed more ready to consider specific international measures in response to the Chernobyl nuclear accident with its transboundary effects than they were following the 1979 Three Mile Island nuclear accident (TMI) in the U.S.A.

TMI, let it be observed briefly, encouraged the preparation by the International Atomic Energy Agency (IAEA) of two sets of nonlegally binding instruments, namely, the Guidelines on Emergency Assistance Arrangements in Connection with a Nuclear Accident or Radiological Emergency, and the Guidelines on Reportable Events, Integrated Planning and Information Exchange in a Transboundary Release of Radioactive Materials. As is well known, TMI also resulted in a large number of measures and programs to improve nuclear safety through improved engineering devices and more competent operation of nuclear plants. It prompted federal supervision and redesign of nuclear plants leading to more diligent evaluation of safety aspects of nuclear installations both by the U.S. government, through the National Regulatory Commission (NRC), and by the industry itself, through the Atlanta-based Institute of Nuclear Power Operations (INPO).

The Chernobyl accident, in contrast, resulted in the immediate elaboration of two legally binding international instruments by the IAEA, namely, the Convention on Early Notification of a Nuclear Accident (IAEA Notification Convention) and the Convention on Assistance in the Case of a Nuclear Accident or Radiological Emergency (IAEA Assistance Convention). Both of these have been acknowledged as landmarks in the history of the treaty-making process. It also resulted directly in the expanded program on nuclear safety and improvements by the IAEA and additional activities for the IAEA support missions in the field of nuclear safety and radiological protection. Such support missions, which are usually undertaken only upon request by a member State of the IAEA, include the Operational Safety Review Team (OSART), the Assessment of Significant Safety Event Team (ASSET), the Operational Safety Indicator Program (OSIP), the program of Integrated Safety Assessment of Research Reactor (INSARR), and the Radiation Protection Advisory Team (RAPAR). Apart from an increased demand for these support missions, at the request of member States, there was also an increased awareness of the role played by the IAEA Incident Reporting System (IAWA-IRIS) and the International Nuclear Information System (INIS). There also emerged a concern with finding ways to make legally binding the IAEA Nuclear Safety Standards (NUSS) and the evolution of the equally important questions of nuclear waste disposal through the IAEA Waste Management Advisory Program (WAMAP).

[I]t is important to note at once that, while the efforts to find appropriate remedies for the victims of nuclear-accident pollution have resulted in international measures through the elaboration of international legal instruments, international technical standards for enhancing nuclear safety have not been amendable to formulation into internationally binding legal instruments. As will be noted further, nuclear safety remains a primary responsibility of individual States enforcing their national regulations and is still the subject of the non-legally binding guidelines such as those developed by the IAEA under its NUSS program. [See footnotes 39 and 40, below, concerning the 1994 Nuclear Safety Convention.—Eds.]

TREATY LAW ON NUCLEAR ACCIDENTS BEFORE AND AFTER TMI AND CHERNOBYL

Before TMI and Chernobyl, several multilateral treaties were concluded to deal specifically with the question of civil liability for nuclear accidents in land-based nuclear installations, thus providing remedies for victims of nuclear-accident pollution. Other treaties were aimed at ensuring physical protection of nuclear material especially from theft or acts of sabotage, which could lead to exposure of the public to ionizing radiation, and treaties establishing liability for accidents arising from transportation of nuclear material and operation of nuclear ships. A checklist of these treaties, focusing on the instruments dealing specifically with the problems of pollution damage from nuclear accidents, includes:

1. the Paris Convention on Third-Party Liability in the Field of Nuclear Energy, July 29, 1960, as amended in 1964 and 1982 (adopted within the framework of Organization for Economic Co-operation and Development [OECD] and therefore regional in character);

2. the Vienna Convention on Civil Liability for Nuclear Damage, May 21, 1963 (adopted within the framework of the IAEA and therefore global in character);

3. the Brussels Convention on the Liability of Operations of Nuclear Ships, May 25, 1962;

4. the Nordic Mutual Emergency Assistance Agreement in Connection with Radiological Accidents, 1963;

5. the Brussels Convention Relating to Civil Liability in the Field of Maritime Carriage of Nuclear Material, December 17, 1971 (adopted within the framework of the International Maritime Organization [IMO]);

6. the Vienna Convention on the Physical Protection of Nuclear Material, March 3, 1980;

7. the IAEA Convention on Early Notification of a Nuclear Accident, 1986; and

8. the IAEA Convention on Assistance in the Case of a Nuclear Accident or Radiological Emergency, 1986.

There have also been a number of bilateral agreements dealing specifically with cooperation in nuclear safety matters such as exchange of information and consultation. The usefulness of these bilateral agreements was endorsed in the IAEA Assistance Convention, which regards bilateral arrangements as additional means of giving effect to the broad framework of the multilateral convention. . . .

RECOGNIZING THE FOCUS OF THE IAEA NOTIFICATION AND ASSISTANCE CONVENTIONS

As noted briefly earlier, the IAEA already succeeded in producing two conventions in direct response to Chernobyl, focusing on the matter clearly signaled in the title of each convention: the Convention on Early Notification of a Nuclear Accident; and the Convention on Assistance in the Case of a Nuclear Accident or Radiological Emergency. These two conventions were tailored to address the specific issues among those exposed by the Chernobyl accident and with respect to which the IAEA member States believed international legal instruments were achievable as a matter of urgency. The member States singled out the need to establish a treaty obligation to notify a nuclear accident with potential transboundary effects: whom to notify, how to notify, and the information to be notified. The emphasis was on the early warning following a nuclear accident that might have transboundary consequences, alerting States likely to be affected and thus enabling them to take some precautionary measures addressing, in that connection, the special needs of the developing countries. Whether or not the notification would include nuclear accidents arising from military activities of a State became a make-or-break conference issue and was indeed settled in a subtle way, as explained in the drafting history of the relevant articles of the Convention.

The IAEA also singled out the need to establish a multilateral legal framework for providing emergency assistance promptly: how to request the assistance; how to render it, the modalities for undertaking an assistance mission itself, having regard to the applicable bilateral arrangements; the question of equipment and personnel; and also the financial aspects of assistance. The financial aspects of assistance, it may be noted, also became another make-or-break conference issue, which defied solution until the last hours of negotiations of the conventions, as indicated in the drafting history of the relevant article.

The two conventions are already in force. Through the continued collaborative efforts between the IAEA, the World Meteorological Organization (WMO), and the Global Telecommunication System (GTS), the machinery established for early warning of the nuclear accident under the Notification Convention has now been successfully tested to evaluate its efficacy. It may also be observed that assistance in an actual radiological emergency has been rendered through the IAEA to a member State (Brazil) in the framework of the Assistance Convention in connection with the radiological emergency caused by the disused cesium-137 source in that member State.

The work on these two conventions clearly demonstrated the vital role played by the IAEA as an organization respected by its member

States as a forum in which they could consult and cooperate in solving a specific international problem. It is expected that such cooperation will continue to be maintained with other relevant international organizations, such as the World Health Organization (WHO), the International Labour Organisation (ILO), and other United Nations bodies, including United Nations Environment Programme (UNEP) and the United Nations Scientific Committee on the Effects of Atomic Radiation (UNSCEAR).

The basic approach of the IAEA with respect to the Notification and Assistance Conventions was to stay close to what was evidently achievable and to avoid the temptation of trying to solve, at once, all conceivable problems which might flow from a transboundary nuclear accident and radiological emergency. Thus, certain issues were deliberately left out of consideration of the two conventions in order to focus upon the obligation to notify a transboundary nuclear accident and on the framework for providing prompt assistance in the event of a nuclear accident or radiological emergency.

Commentators unfamiliar with the drafting history of the two conventions will always wonder why (and some of those who took part in the negotiations will continue to lament the fact that) the two IAEA conventions did not:

1. define the term "radiological safety significance";

2. contain provisions on intervention level which may be a trigger factor for notification of accidents; and

3. address the question of State responsibility and compensation for nuclear damage.

Apart from the last point, on which the IAEA has commenced a study toward an appropriate solution, . . . the issues were, in fact, considered during the drafting process of the two conventions. One of them— intervention level—has been singled out for subsequent scientific study under the auspices of the IAEA. Recognizing the focus chosen for the two conventions, it was necessary to limit the scope of the two instruments, in the course of their elaboration, to the specific concern articulated by the member States while leaving open the consideration of other related questions to treatment elsewhere. The two conventions clearly achieved the purpose for which they were intended and thus should be acknowledged as such. . . .

IAEA CONVENTION ON EARLY NOTIFICATION OF A NUCLEAR ACCIDENT

1439 U.N.T.S. 275 (entered into force 27 October 1986)

[Article 2 of this Convention states:]

Notification and information

In the event of an accident specified in article 1 . . . , the State Party referred to in that article shall:

(a) forthwith notify, directly or through the International Atomic Energy Agency . . . those States which are or may be physically affected as specified in article 1 and the Agency of the nuclear accident, its nature, the time of its occurrence and its exact location where appropriate; and

(b) promptly provide the States referred to in sub-paragraph (a), directly or through the Agency, and the Agency with such available information relevant to minimizing the radiological consequences in those States, as specified in article 5.

Why does this Article create the option of notifying affected States through the International Atomic Energy Agency? What would be the effect if this were not an option? What would be the effect if this were required? What sorts of information would a State be expected to give during its notification?

IAEA CONVENTION ON ASSISTANCE IN THE CASE OF A NUCLEAR ACCIDENT OR RADIOLOGICAL EMERGENCY

1457 U.N.T.S. 133 (entered into force 26 February 1987)

[This Convention provides as follows:]

Article 2
Provision of assistance

(1) If a State Party needs assistance in the event of a nuclear accident or radiological emergency, whether or not such accident or emergency originates within its territory, jurisdiction, or control, it may call for such assistance from any other State Party, directly or through the Agency, and from the Agency, or where appropriate, from other international intergovernmental organizations . . .

(3) Each State Party to which a request for such assistance is directed shall promptly decide and notify the requesting State

Party, directly or through the Agency, whether it is in a position to render the assistance requested, and the scope and terms of the assistance that might be rendered.

Article 7
Reimbursement of costs

(1) An assisting party may offer assistance without costs to the requesting State. When considering whether to offer assistance on such a basis, the assisting party shall take into account:

a. The nature of the nuclear accident of the nuclear accident or radiological emergency;

b. The place of origin of the nuclear accident or radiological emergency;

c. The needs of the developing countries;

d. The particular needs of countries without nuclear facilities; and

e. Any other relevant factors.

Do these terms create any legal obligations for assistance? What about normative obligations?

Further reading: For a discussion of treaty measures needed to prevent nuclear accidents and their transboundary effects, *see* Gunther Handl, *Transboundary Nuclear Accidents: The Post-Chernobyl Multilateral Legislative Agenda*, 15 Ecology L.Q. 203 (1988).

NOTES AND QUESTIONS

1. *The role of the international community in regulating nuclear power.* The explosion of a nuclear power plant is everyone's worst nightmare. Yet not only are nuclear power plants perfectly legal under international law, until the conclusion of the 1994 Nuclear Safety Convention there were no internationally mandated safety standards governing their design and construction.[39] Even the Nuclear Safety Convention is based on the principle that "responsibility for nuclear safety rests with the State having jurisdiction over a nuclear installation. . . ."[40] In other words, any country that can get its hands on the technology necessary to construct a nuclear power plant may do

----

[39] *See generally* Gunther Handl, *Transboundary Nuclear Accidents: The Post-Chernobyl Multilateral Legislative Agenda*, 15 Ecology L.Q. 203 (1988), especially at p. 205.

[40] Convention on Nuclear Safety, preambular paragraph (iii). The convention relies for implementation upon the submission of reports on legislative, regulatory, and administrative measures taken by State parties to carry out their obligations under the convention. The reports are submitted to periodic review meetings of the parties to the Convention, which are to be convened at least every three years.

so.[41] The rules of international law reviewed in this chapter would certainly apply to such plants, as they would to any other activity whose operation entails a risk of harm. Yet where the harm that might be caused is so potentially catastrophic, should the international community not take a more active role in the regulation of these facilities? What form might such involvement take? Would "legislation" on the international plane be sufficient? What about liability for damage caused? If there is no international legal prohibition of such activities, and if harm results from the non-negligent operation of one of them, how could the situs State be liable?

2. *Vienna Convention on the Physical Protection of Nuclear Material.* A Diplomatic Convention was convened in 2005 to amend the 1980 convention and rename it the Convention on the Physical Protection of Nuclear Material and Nuclear Facilities. Although it has not yet entered into force as of March 2015, the amendment would "make[ ] it legally binding for States Parties to protect nuclear facilities and material in peaceful domestic use, storage as well as transport [and] provide[ ] for expanded cooperation between and among States regarding rapid measures to locate and recover stolen or smuggled nuclear material, mitigate any radiological consequences of sabotage, and prevent and combat related offences." http://www.iaea.org/publications/documents/conventions/convention-physical-protection-nuclear-material.

---

[41] *See,* in this connection, Anthony D'Amato & Kirsten Engel, *State Responsibility for the Exportation of Nuclear Power Technology*, 74 Va. L. Rev. 1011 (1988).

CHAPTER 7

REGIONAL TRANSBOUNDARY POLLUTION

■ ■ ■

Transboundary pollution might be said to have catalyzed the development of international environmental law. As we will see in section B of this chapter, pollution of international watercourses has been the subject of treaty provisions for well over a century and a half. While air pollution has been known since ancient times, it has been recognized as an international problem only relatively recently. The case that many regard as the fountainhead of international environmental law, the *Trail Smelter* arbitration discussed in Chapter 4, was decided in 1941. It took another 30 years for governments to begin to appreciate the seriousness of the problem of the long-distance transport of air pollution.

In this chapter we look at the way in which States have tackled the problem of regional transboundary pollution. We deal first with transboundary air pollution and, specifically, the phenomenon commonly known as "acid rain," both in North America and in Europe. Asia's growing acid rain problems are also covered. We then move to water pollution. After considering efforts to codify general principles in this field, we focus on the efforts of Canada and the United States to protect the Great Lakes ecosystem. You should read these materials in light of the cases—in particular *Trail Smelter*—and the fundamental norms of prevention considered in Chapter 4. To what extent have the solutions suggested by the cases and the norms of prevention influenced or been carried over into the regimes considered in this chapter?

A. REGIONAL TRANSBOUNDARY AIR POLLUTION

Air pollution does not respect national boundaries; it may easily flow from one country to another, with bilateral, regional and even global effects. Not surprisingly, therefore, air pollution forms a major issue in international environmental relations. By "air pollution" we mean, generally, the use of the air as a means of waste disposal through emissions from stationary (often power or other industrial plants) or mobile (motor vehicles) sources. "Transboundary air pollution" is defined herein as "air pollution whose physical origin is situated wholly or in part within the area under the national jurisdiction of one State and which has adverse effects in the area under the jurisdiction of another State."[1]

---

[1] Convention on Long-Range Transboundary Air Pollution, Nov. 13, 1979, T.I.A.S. No. 10541.

We have already studied an example of transboundary air pollution in the *Trail Smelter* case, which many regard as the fountainhead of international environmental law. The effects of air pollution can be local (i.e., chiefly confined to one country), bilateral (i.e., involving principally two countries), regional (i.e., involving more than two countries) or even global. The latter situation is typified by depletion of the ozone layer and climate change, which are the subjects of chapters 8 and 9, respectively.

NOTES AND QUESTIONS

1. *Basic principles.* We suggest you read the following materials in light of the cases—in particular *Trail Smelter* and *Corfu Channel*—and the fundamental norms of prevention considered in Chapter 4. To what extent are the solutions suggested by the cases and the norms of prevention reflected in the regimes considered in this chapter?

2. *What approach?* Should the issues dealt with in the following case study have been dealt with as were the issues in the *Trail Smelter* case? Would it have been better to deal with the issues in *Trail Smelter* along the lines of the Canada-United States acid rain dispute? What are the advantages and disadvantages of each type of approach?

PROBLEM

State A has relatively good domestic environmental laws and as a result generates relatively little air pollution. Its skies, however, are regularly sullied by a variety of air pollutants from its neighboring States B and C. One problem involves low-level pollutants wafting into State A from a major city in State B that is located on the border of the two States. When the wind blows into State A, ozone, particulates and volatile organic compounds from vehicular traffic and industrial facilities come across the border into a city in State A, harming the health of people living in that city. A different problem exists with respect to State C: fires set in State C as part of the forestry and farming practices in that State regularly come across the border into State A with the prevailing winds, obscuring the sun during the day and causing people to experience difficulty breathing. Assume you are the Prime Minister of State A. What avenues are open to you to alleviate these situations?

1. ACID RAIN WITHIN NORTH AMERICA

a. Canada-United States Acid Rain: Background

By the early 1970s, it was known that air pollution could damage human health, natural resources such as soils, plants, and trees, aesthetic interests such as views, and historical and cultural assets such as statues and monuments. As a result of these concerns, Canada and the United States enacted Clean Air Acts intended to improve ambient air quality through the control of sulphur dioxide, nitrogen oxides, particulates, and carbon monoxide. By 1984, Canada had reduced its sulphur dioxide emissions by approximately 41 percent and the United States had reduced its emissions by approximately 24 percent. Although these reductions improved air quality in the vicinity of the emissions, they had the opposite effect regarding long-range air pollution because the Acts effectively encouraged the construction of tall stacks that dispersed pollution over a greater geographic area.

One of the results of the long-range pollution was acid deposition, more commonly referred to as acid rain, which involves the deposition (e.g., via rain, snow, mist, and fog) of acids from the atmosphere to Earth's surface. Acid rain is mainly caused by sulfur oxides and nitrogen oxides; these gases are oxidized to form sulfuric acid and nitric acid when they come into contact with water.[2] The vast majority of sulfur dioxide emissions come from industrial facilities, with the main culprits being electric utilities in the United States and metal smelters in Canada. Nitrogen oxides are primarily caused by electric utilities, transportation, and industry.[3] In the early 1980s, the United States was emitting approximately 25.7 million tons of sulphur dioxide and 23 million tons of nitrogen dioxide annually, while Canada's annual emissions totaled 5.2 million tons and 2 million tons, respectively.

By 1977, it became evident that emissions in Canada were leading to acid deposition in northeastern United States, and that emissions in the United States were leading to acid deposition in eastern Canada, thus causing significant damage to surface waters and aquatic life. A study by the International Joint Commission (Canada-United States) showed that large amounts of pollutants in the Great Lakes resulted from atmospheric deposition.[4] Negotiations between the two countries led to the formation in 1978 of a Bilateral Research Consultation Group (BRCG) on the long-range transport of airborne pollutants. The BRCG's mandate was to facilitate information exchange, to coordinate research activities, and to develop an agreed scientific database for developing solutions to the problem. Also in 1978, the United States Congress passed a resolution calling upon the president to initiate discussions with Canada in order to negotiate a cooperative agreement to protect the air quality of North America. In July 1979, Canada and the United States jointly announced their intention to develop such an agreement. On August 5, 1980, the two countries signed the Memorandum of Intent on Transboundary Air Pollution, which stated the two countries' intention of working towards developing a bilateral agreement on air quality and established five joint work groups to investigate various aspects of acid deposition. The

---

[2]   The National Acid Precipitation Assessment Program, Interim Assessment: The Causes and Effects of Acidic Deposition 1–4 (1987). Scientists assign approximately two-thirds of the blame for causing acid rain to sulphur oxides and one-third to nitrogen oxide. Id.

[3]   Acid Rain and Friendly Neighbors: The Policy Dispute Between Canada and the United States (Jurgen Schmandt & Hillary Roderick eds., 1988).

[4]   Id. at 65.

technical and scientific work groups released their final reports in February 1983 and referred them for peer review. Later in 1983, the United States peer review panel issued its report calling for reductions in emissions and rejecting the argument that more research was needed before regulatory action could be taken. Canada's peer review panel reached the same conclusion.

On January 25, 1984, President Ronald Reagan stated that the United States would intensify research into the causes and effects of acid rain rather than taking action to reduce emissions. This position caused considerable consternation in Canada. Two months later, Prime Minister Brian Mulroney and President Reagan each appointed a Special Envoy on Acid Rain to study the issue further.

Between 1977 and 1985, Canada's claim was essentially that it was taking unilateral action to reduce sulphur dioxide emissions in eastern Canada by approximately 50 percent and to reduce the transboundary flux from Canada to the United States by at least 50 percent and that the flux of sulphur dioxide from the United States to Canada was injuring lakes and streams in eastern Canada, among other natural resources, and should be reduced by 50 percent. (Throughout the negotiations, Canada focused on sulphur dioxide because it believed that the acid deposition problem in Canada is a sulphur-driven phenomenon due to the fact that the soil in eastern Canada tends to be nitrogen deficient.) During this period, negotiations regarding acid rain occurred at non-national levels: Canada and Quebec negotiated, as did Ontario and New York.

The special envoys released their report in January 1986 and concluded that acid rain is a serious transboundary problem that creates environmental hazards in both countries. In March of that year, the two leaders endorsed the special envoys' report.

The two countries took several steps to implement the special envoys' recommendations, including the formation of a Bilateral Advisory and Consultative Group and, in the United States, the establishment of a five-year, $5 billion program to develop alternative technologies to remove sulphur from coal.

By 1988, Canada claimed that 14,000 lakes and at least nine salmon-bearing rivers were dead (i.e., they could no longer support aquatic life) due to acid rain, that 150,000 other lakes were being acidified (i.e., they had a pH level less than 6.0, the acidity level at which detrimental biological effects begin to occur), and that several hundred thousand more were vulnerable to acidification. Canada also raised fears about the large percentages of the best agricultural land (85 percent) and forests (50 percent) in eastern Canada receiving high levels of acid rain.

During acid-rain discussions with the United States, Canada expressed its view that the United States is bound by international law to reduce the transboundary flow of sulphur dioxide emissions to the point where they do not cause significant damage in Canada. Canada based its view on, inter alia, the Trail Smelter,[5] Corfu Channel,[6] and Lake Lanoux[7] cases and on Principle 21 of the Stockholm Declaration on the Human Environment[8] (these are considered in Chapter 4). The United States, relying on the same authorities, was of the view that it was doing all that is required by international law. Canada did not request that the dispute be submitted to a binding dispute-settlement mechanism (despite the fact that other environmental disputes between the two countries have been so decided), preferring instead a negotiated solution.

Litigation to prompt United States action was attempted by the state of New York and environmental groups in United States courts, pursuant to section 115 of the Clean Air Act,[9] which requires the administrator of the United States Environmental Protection Agency (EPA) to give, under specified circumstances, formal notification to a state in which emissions originate that the administrator "has reason to believe ... cause or contribute to air pollution which may reasonably be anticipated to endanger public health or welfare in a foreign country. ..." (Formal notification would require a state to revise its implementation plan to prevent or eliminate the danger.) Those cases were not successful.[10] During the last four years of President Reagan's administration (1985 to 1989), the United States position was dominated by the claim that the United States needed more information before it would commit to reduce the transboundary flux. The governors of New York and Ohio also negotiated during this period and suggested an emissions-reduction program that would be funded by the two states and by the United States federal government.

The United States' insistence on the need for more information focused on perceived uncertainties regarding acid rain's causes (e.g., the role of compounds such as nitrogen oxides and volatile organic compounds), effects (e.g., the importance of naturally occurring neutralizers), and control costs. Canada argued that enough certainty existed. The debate intensified with the release in 1987 of the Interim Report of the United States National Acid Precipitation Assessment Program (NAPAP), a ten-year program established by act of Congress in

---

[5]   Trail Smelter (U.S. v. Can.), 3 R. Intl. Arb. Awards 1905 (1938 & 1941).

[6]   Corfu Channel (U.K. v. Alb.), 1949 I.C.J. 4 (Judgment of 9 Apr.)

[7]   Lac Lanoux (Fr. v. Spain), 24 I.L.R. 101 (1957) (English), 12 R. Intl. Arb. Awards 281 (1957) (French).

[8]   Stockholm Declaration on the Human Environment, Sept. 16, 1972, U.N. Doc. A/CONF. 48/14/ Rev. 1, at 3 (1973), reprinted in 11 I.L.M. 1416 (1972).

[9]   38 U.S.C. § 7415(a) (1982).

[10]   See, e.g., Thomas v. New York, 802 F.2d 1443 (D.C. Cir. 1986), cert. denied, 482 U.S. 919 (1987); Ontario v. EPA, 912 F.2d 1525 (D.C. Cir. 1990).

1980 to study acid rain in the United States. The Interim Report was highly controversial, especially the 67-page Executive Summary. Canada objected that the Executive Summary did not consider evidence in Canada, used a threshold pH level of 5.0 (which is 10 times more acidic than the 6.0 pH level at which biological damage begins), excluded lakes smaller than ten acres and waterways, assumed a 300 percent increase in United States nuclear power generation in forecasting emissions reductions, and was not peer reviewed.

After George H.W. Bush became president in January 1989, he proposed major changes in the United States Clean Air Act, which eventually were enacted in October 1990. [11] Those changes, which required utilities to reduce emissions of sulphur by ten million tons by the year 2000, were projected to meet Canada's demands for a 50 percent decrease in the transboundary flux of sulphur dioxide.

In July 1990, Prime Minister Mulroney and President Bush announced that the two countries "have agreed to begin negotiations for a practical and effective air quality accord."[12] Negotiations on that accord resulted in the Canada-United States Agreement on Air Quality of March 13, 1991, 30 I.L.M. 676 (1991) (Air Quality Agreement).

b. The Canada-United States Air Quality Agreement

Article IV of the Air Quality Agreement between Canada and the United States is entitled "Specific Air Quality Objectives." Paragraph 2 of that article provides in part that "[e]ach Party's specific objectives for emissions limitations or reductions of sulphur dioxide and nitrogen oxides, which will reduce transboundary flows of these acidic deposition precursors, are set forth in Annex 1." The agreement also establishes a bilateral Air Quality Committee to assist the parties with its implementation and assigns specific responsibilities to the International Joint Commission established by the 1909 Boundary Waters Treaty between the two countries.[13] Selected provisions follow.

AGREEMENT BETWEEN THE GOVERNMENT OF THE UNITED STATES OF AMERICA AND THE GOVERNMENT OF CANADA ON AIR QUALITY
Mar. 13, 1991, U.S.-Can., 30 I.L.M. 676 (1991)

The Government of the United States of America and the Government of Canada, hereinafter referred to as "the Parties,"

---

[11] 1990 Clean Air Act Amendments, Pub. L. No. 101–549, 104 Stat. 2399.

[12] Joint Statement, July 8, 1990, in Public Papers of the Presidents of the United States, George Bush, 1990, bk. II, p. 977 (1991).

[13] 36 Stat. 2448 (1910).

Convinced that transboundary air pollution can cause significant harm to natural resources of vital environmental, cultural and economic importance, and to human health in both countries;

Desiring that emissions of air pollutants from sources within their countries not result in significant transboundary air pollution;

Convinced that transboundary air pollution can effectively be reduced through cooperative or coordinated action providing for controlling emissions of air pollutants in both countries;

Recalling the efforts they have made to control air pollution and the improved air quality that has resulted from such efforts in both countries;

Intending to address air-related issues of a global nature, such as climate change and stratospheric ozone depletion, in other fora;

Reaffirming Principle 21 of the Stockholm Declaration . . . ;

Noting their tradition of environmental cooperation as reflected in the Boundary Waters Treaty of 1909, the Trail Smelter Arbitration of 1941, the Great Lakes Water Quality Agreement of 1978, as amended, the Memorandum of Intent Concerning Trans-boundary Air Pollution of 1980, the 1986 Joint Report of the Special Envoys on Acid Rain, as well as the ECE Convention on Long-Range Transboundary Air Pollution of 1979;

Convinced that a healthy environment is essential to assure the well-being of present and future generations in the United States and Canada, as well as of the global community;

Have agreed as follows:

Article III
General Air Quality Objective

1.   The general objective of the Parties is to control transboundary air pollution between the two countries.

2.   To this end, the Parties shall:

(a) in accordance with Article IV, establish specific objectives for emissions limitations or reductions of air pollutants and adopt the necessary programs and other measures to implement such specific objectives; (b) in accordance with Article V, undertake environmental impact assessment, prior notification, and, as appropriate, mitigation measures; (c) carry out coordinated or cooperative scientific and technical activities, and economic research, in accordance with Article VI, and exchange information, in accordance with Article VII; (d) establish institutional arrangements, in accordance with Articles VIII and IX; and (e) review and assess progress, consult, address issues of concern, and settle disputes, in accordance with Articles X, XI, XII and XIII.

Article IV
Specific Air Quality Objectives

1.   Each Party shall establish specific objectives, which it undertakes to achieve, for emissions limitations or reductions of such air pollutants as the Parties agree to address. Such specific objectives will be set forth in annexes to this Agreement.

2.   Each Party's specific objectives for emissions limitations or reductions of sulphur dioxide and nitrogen oxides, which will reduce transboundary flows of these acidic deposition precursors, are set forth in Annex I. Specific objectives for such other air pollutants as the Parties agree to address should take into account, as appropriate, the activities undertaken pursuant to Article VI.

3.   Each Party shall adopt the programs and other measures necessary to implement its specific objectives set forth in any annexes.

4.   If either Party has concerns about the programs or other measures of the other Party referred to in paragraph 3, it may request consultations in accordance with Article XI.

Article IX
Responsibilities of the International Joint Commission

1.   The International Joint Commission is hereby given, by a Reference pursuant to Article IX of the Boundary Waters Treaty, the following responsibilities for the sole purpose of assisting the Parties in the implementation of this Agreement: (a) to invite comments, including through public hearings as appropriate, on each progress report prepared by the Air Quality Committee pursuant to Article VIII; (b) to submit to the Parties a synthesis of the views presented pursuant to sub-paragraph (a), as well as the record of such views if either Party so requests; and (c) to release the synthesis of views to the public after its submission to the Parties.

2.   In addition, the Parties shall consider such other joint references to the International Joint Commission as may be appropriate for the effective implementation of this Agreement.

Article X
Review and Assessment

1.   Following the receipt of each progress report submitted to them by the Air Quality Committee in accordance with Article VIII and the views presented to the International Joint Commission on that report in accordance with Article IX, the Parties shall consult on the contents of the progress report, including any recommendations therein.

2.   The Parties shall conduct a comprehensive review and assessment of this Agreement, and its implementation, during the fifth

year after its entry into force and every five years thereafter, unless otherwise agreed.

3.   Following the consultations referred to in paragraph 1, as well as the review and assessment referred to in paragraph 2, the Parties shall consider such action as may be appropriate, including: (a) the modification of this Agreement; (b) the modification of existing policies, programs or measures.

c.   Reviews of the 1991 Agreement

On October 25, 1996, Environment Canada and the United States Environmental Protection Agency released the third biennial progress report under the 1991 United States-Canada Air Quality Agreement.[14] This report was the first five-year review of the Air Quality Agreement. Overall, the report drew a positive conclusion to the first five years of the pact. According to the report, U.S. sulphur dioxide emissions in 1995 were 5.3 million tons at 263 targeted first-stage facilities, which is a 51 percent decline since 1980.[15] The reduction in sulphur dioxide emissions led to a decrease in water sulfates, which improved water quality in both countries. [16] As a result, "substantial progress" had been made in decreasing acid rain and the damage in forests has been slowed.[17]

The report did not give the air quality policies of Canada and the United States a completely favorable review. While sulfur dioxide emissions had decreased, other atmospheric pollutants, such as acidic aerosols, had increased in both countries. Accordingly, commentators suggested that the scope of the Air Quality Agreement should be expanded to cover regional smog, ground-level ozone, toxic air contaminants, inhalable particulate matter, and acid aerosols. [18] Moreover, nitrogen deposition may offset the benefits of acid rain reduction achieved by the agreement. Sulfate deposition have continued to decline. However, there is no one-to-one correlation between sulfate

---

[14] International Joint Commission, United States-Canada Air Quality Agreement, Progress Report (1996).

[15] Id. at 1. Sulphur dioxide emissions at these facilities (most of which are utilities) were also 3.4 million tons lower than requirements established by the Clean Air Act. Id. Including Canada, total sulphur dioxides decreased from 31.4 million tons in 1980 to 24.1 million tons in 1994, a 23 percent decrease. This decrease is expected to continue, with predicted emissions in the United States of 19.1 million tons in 2000 and 17.3 million tons in 2010. Emissions in Canada will be 3 million tons in 2000 and 3.1 million tons in 2010, for an aggregate of 22.1 million tons in 2000 and 20.4 million tons in 2010 in both countries.

[16] Id. at 3. In addition, lake nitrate levels in some regions, such as the Adirondack Mountains, have also decreased. Nitrous dioxide levels, which totaled 25.3 million tons for both countries in 1980 are expected to decline to 22.8 million tons in 2000 before increasing to 23.8 million tons in 2010. Canadian NOx levels should remain constant at two million tons per year. Id.

[17] Id. The report found "no evidence" of widespread forest decline from acid rain, but it did note that there were exceptions in "especially sensitive" regions.

[18] International Joint Commission, Media Release, The International Joint Commission Releases Report on Canada-United States Air Quality Agreement, Feb. 2, 1996.

deposition reduction and the stabilization and recovery of stressed lakes and forests. Studies continued to warn that forests and lakes are still at risk from acid deposition and that the recovery time is long. The United States Environmental Protection Agency, Responses of Surface Water Chemistry to the Clean Air Act Amendments of 1990 (2003), confirmed that the 1990 Clean Air Act Amendments and similar cap and trade programs in Canada have reduced the atmospheric deposition of sulfates and led to a decline in surface water sulfate concentrations, but concluded that "the anticipated decrease in acidity corresponding to the decline in sulfate has been modest." To further complicate matters, climate change, forest maturation and continued nitrogen deposition pull against the gains from reduced sulfate deposition.

In 2000, Canada and the United States signed an Ozone Annex to the 1991 Air Quality Agreement that commits both countries to the aggressive reduction of nitrogen oxides and volatile organic compounds (VOCs). See International Joint Commission, United States-Canada Air Quality Agreement Progress Report 2004 (2004).

In 2012, the fourth 5-year report was released, constituting a 20-year review of the Air Quality Agreement. Both countries found the Agreement a success; the report commented on the mutual trust and a supportive, cooperative and committed working relationship that had developed between the countries. As of 2011, the United States had achieved a 71% decrease in SO_2 emissions and 69% decrease of NO_x emissions from power plants. As of 2010, Canada had achieved a 57% decrease in SO_2 emissions and 18% in NO_x emissions from transportation and power plant sources. Consequently the environment has gradually been recovering. Furthermore, as noted above, the Agreement laid the groundwork for the Ozone Annex, added in 2000, which called for the reduction of NO_x and VOC emissions. Within the Pollutant Emission Management Area (PEMA), the United States reduced emissions respectively 42% and 37%; meanwhile Canada by 40% and 30%, producing significant benefits for human health and the environment.

The Agreement also calls for each country to track and report progress and activities under the Agreement. According to the report, the reporting mechanism has fostered "cooperation on transboundary air pollution control, monitoring, research, and information exchange"[19] and provided data to discern what areas require further action. The countries have harmonized protocols and methodologies for monitoring, measurement, and modeling. According to the report, a significant accomplishment of the Agreement was the commitment to scientific and technical cooperation and information exchange. Through the Agreement an institutional forum for scientific cooperation on transboundary air pollution was created, which enabled joint work and the establishment of

[19] http://www.epa.gov/airmarkets/progsregs/usca/docs/2012report.pdf at 71.

common statements of fact. The existence of these data was instrumental in enabling the governments to negotiate a particulate matter (PM) Annex to the Agreement.[20] For the future, potential changes would include streamlining reporting, finalizing discussions on how to deal with transboundary PM, addressing potential air quality issues in the western border area, and strengthening notification provisions.

NOTES AND QUESTIONS

1. *Applying the principles.* Which country was right about how the great precedents, *Trail Smelter, Corfu Channel, Lac Lanoux,* and Principle 21, apply to the United States-Canada acid rain problem?

2. *Problem.* You are the United States Legal Adviser. What is your legal argument supporting the view that the United States "was doing all that is required by international law"?

3. *Negotiation vs. binding third-party settlement.* Why would Canada prefer a negotiated solution to some form of binding third-party settlement, such as arbitration or submission of the case to the International Court of Justice?

4. *The precautionary principle.* Is this a case in which the precautionary principle should be applied? Review the manner in which the principle was stated in the Rio Declaration (see Chapter 4). Would that version require abatement of the transboundary fluxes?

5. *Acid rain and the dismal science.* Assuming that there was a greater flow of air pollution from the United States to Canada than vice versa, can you state in very general terms the economic effects of this phenomenon? Can the United States be said to be imposing an "externality" on Canada?

2. ACID RAIN WITHIN THE EUROPEAN UNION REGION

a. The 1979 Long-Range Transboundary Air Pollution Convention (LRTAP)

THE EUROPEAN APPROACH TO ACID RAIN

Johan Lammers
in International Law and Pollution 265, 267–282 (Daniel Magraw ed., 1991)

The 1979 LRTAP Convention[21] was concluded by 32 European States (including the Byelorussian SSR and the Ukrainian SSR), the European Economic Community, Canada, and the United States during a High Level Meeting concerning protection of the environment held from

---

[20] *Id.* at 73.

[21] Convention on Long-Range Transboundary Air Pollution, Nov. 13, 1979, T.I.A.S. No. 10541, reprinted in 18 I.L.M. 1442 (1979). (Editors' footnote.)

November 13–16, 1979, in Geneva within the framework of the UN ECE. It entered into force on March 16, 1983. In spite of the official title of the Convention, which refers to "transboundary" air pollution only, many of its provisions deal with "air pollution, including transboundary air pollution." While this category may not be restricted to acid rain, it can be safely said that the wish to cope with long-distance acid rain constituted the main reason for concluding the Convention. Because practically all European States—whether State of origin of acid rain or victim thereof (if not both) and whether located in East or West Europe—took part in the negotiations for the Convention and eventually ratified the Convention, the Convention gives a clear indication of what written international obligations for preventing and abating acid rain appeared to be generally acceptable for European States in 1979.

Substantive obligations—or rather obligations prescribing the development of policies and strategies—are to be found in articles 2, 3, and 6 of the 1979 LRTAP Convention. Articles 2 and 3 contain fundamental principles of the Convention. Article 2 provides:

> The Contracting Parties, taking due account of the facts and problems involved, are determined to protect man and his environment against air pollution and shall endeavour to limit, and, as far as possible, gradually reduce and prevent air pollution, including long-range transboundary air pollution.

Article 3 provides:

> The Contracting Parties, within the framework of the present convention, shall by means of exchanges of information, consultation, research and monitoring, develop without undue delay policies and strategies which shall serve as a means of combating the discharge of air pollutants taking into account efforts already made at national and international levels.

Article 6, concerning air quality management, provides:

> Taking into account Articles 2 to 5, the ongoing research, exchange of information and monitoring and the results thereof, the cost and effectiveness of local and other remedies and, in order to combat air pollution, in particular that originating from new or rebuilt installations, each Contracting Party undertakes to develop the best policies and strategies including air quality management systems and, as part of them, control measures compatible with balanced development, in particular by using the best available technology which is economically feasible and low- and non-waste technology.

An important feature of the quoted provisions is their very comprehensive scope. They do not purport to protect merely certain specific interests against air pollution, but in fact all interests which could possibly be detrimentally affected by such pollution. Moreover, the provisions apply to "air pollution, including long-range transboundary air pollution," "air pollutants," or "air pollution"; that is, they do not apply to transboundary air pollution only, so that their application is not made dependent on proof of such pollution. As far as transboundary air pollution is concerned, this may be of a short- or a long-range nature. Moreover, as has already been noted, the quoted provisions cannot be deemed to apply to acid rain only, even though acid rain has beyond any doubt been the major ratio concludendi of the Convention. It is further noteworthy that the quoted provisions apply in principle to air pollution as defined in the Convention without any qualification as to the seriousness of the harm caused, so that, strictly speaking, proof of substantial harm is not required to be able to invoke the provisions.

The scope of the quoted provisions of the 1979 LRTAP Convention is thus extremely broad, a welcome feature from an environmentalist point of view. A close reading of the quoted provisions, however, makes clear that there is in fact very little reason for satisfaction.

Because of the many qualifications to which the obligation to prevent or abate air pollution has been subjected, the quoted provisions are characterized by a considerable lack of real commitment on the part of the parties to prevent or abate air pollution. The term in article 2 "taking due account of the facts and problems involved" is singularly vague and ambiguous; depending on the circumstances, it may serve to strengthen or weaken the obligation to prevent or abate air pollution. Apart from that, the parties shall only "endeavour to limit, and, as far as possible, gradually reduce and prevent" air pollution. The verb "endeavour" implies that there is not even a firm obligation on the part of the parties to prevent an increase in the amount of air pollution originating in their territory. More stringent verbs, however, such as "make every effort" or "undertake," were not generally acceptable to the negotiating States. Also, as has been noted, there is an obligation only to "gradually reduce" the air pollution. Given the cost and the technical problems involved in such an effort, this limitation is understandable. But even that obligation is weakened because there is an obligation only to reduce air pollution gradually "as far as possible." The lack of real commitment to control air pollution is also apparent from articles 3 and 6. Those articles, in fact, only impose on the parties a duty to develop air quality management policies and strategies, not to implement such policies and strategies. As to the means to develop those policies and strategies at the international level, the parties have committed themselves in article 3 only to "exchanges of information, consultation, research and monitoring." The obligation in article 6 is further circumscribed by the general reference to article 2 with its noted weak elements and by its permitting the parties to take into account "the cost and effectiveness of local and other remedies" and speaking of "control measures compatible with balanced development, in particular by using the best available technology which is economically feasible." The restriction that the control measures must be "compatible with balanced development" was inserted to cover the situation of certain less-developed European countries—for example, Romania, Spain, and Ireland—which feared that their industrial development would be unduly hampered in the future. The insertion of the restriction was a condition for those countries in order to be able to accept article 6.

The previously mentioned restrictive elements in article 6 may be deemed, in fact, to give a more specific meaning to the verb "endeavour" in article 2. Although it is true that article 6 puts some additional emphasis on the prevention of pollution from new or rebuilt installations, one should not lose sight of the fact that the qualifications mentioned earlier apply in principle also to pollution originating from such installations. In fact, this point only confirms that the Convention does not even contain a firm commitment of the parties to prevent an increase of the existing air pollution originating in their territory.

A proposal made by the Nordic countries during the negotiations to the effect that the parties would agree in the Convention to give highest priority to the conclusion in 1981 of an annex on sulphur compounds containing strategies and policies for the prevention of an increase in, and subsequently a progressive reduction of, long-range transboundary air pollution according to a timetable to be agreed on, appeared unacceptable to the pollution-exporting countries. The non-committal provisions in articles 2, 3, and 6 as eventually adopted reflect the reluctance, at least in 1979, by the COMECON countries and such other pollution-exporting West European countries as the United Kingdom and the Federal Republic of Germany to accept legally binding obligations to make meaningful air pollution control measures.

As has already been noted, the 1979 LRTAP Convention entered into force on March 16, 1983. In a resolution adopted on the occasion of the opening of the Convention for signature, however, the signatories declared that they would initiate as soon as possible and on an interim basis the provisional implementation of the Convention and carry out the obligations arising from it to the maximum extent possible pending its entry into force. This resolution had been proposed by the Nordic countries after it had become clear that the Convention would contain obligations which were considerably less stringent than those proposed by the Nordic countries. Adoption of the resolution was, in fact, considered by the Nordic countries as a sine qua non for their signing of the Convention.

It is evident that the 1979 LRTAP Convention constitutes above all a vehicle for promoting exchange of information, consultation, research, and monitoring necessary for the development of policies and strategies.

to combat air pollution. The task of promoting and reviewing the implementation of the Convention has been entrusted to the so-called Executive Body for the Convention, which consists of representatives of the parties operating within the framework of the UN ECE and the Senior Advisers to ECE Governments on Environmental Problems. The provisional implementation of the Convention pending its entry into force was promoted and reviewed by an Interim Executive Body, which met for the first time in November 1980.

THE 1985 SULPHUR PROTOCOL

As aptly stated by Hendrick Vygen, the 1979 LRTAP Convention "can only be judged fairly if it is not seen as a static event but as a point of departure for a dynamic negotiating process in pursuit of a better air quality in the ECE region." This process was to take place through the establishment of an Executive Body for the Convention that would meet at least once a year.

During the Ministerial Conference on Acidification of the Environment, which took place from June 28–30, 1982, in Stockholm following two expert meetings on the effects of acidification and on control strategies, it was agreed that the acidification problem is serious and, even if deposition remains stable, deterioration of soil and water will continue and may increase unless additional control measures are implemented and existing control policies are strengthened.

The Conference henceforth agreed that further concrete action was needed within the framework of the 1979 LRTAP Convention. Noteworthy in 1982 was also the new strong involvement of the Federal Republic of Germany after reports had shown considerable damage to the German forests as a result of acid rain.

During the first session of the Executive Body for the LRTAP Convention in June 1983, Sweden, Norway, and Finland proposed that the parties to the Convention agree to a 30% reduction of their national sulphur emissions by 1993, using 1980 as a basis for calculation. This proposal was supported by Switzerland, Austria, the Federal Republic of Germany, Canada, Denmark, and the Netherlands. Agreement (with the exception of the United States) in the Executive Body, however, could only be reached on "the need to decrease effectively [without quantitative specification] the total annual emissions of sulphur compounds or their trans-boundary fluxes by 1993–1995, using 1980 emission levels as the basis for calculations of reductions." At the Canada-Europe Ministerial Conference on Acid Rain held in Ottawa on March 21, 1984, the 30% club was enlarged by the addition of France, A further step was taken during the Multilateral Conference on the Causes and Prevention of Damage to Forests and Waters held in Munich from June 24–27, 1984, when a total of 18 countries—now including the U.S.S.R. and a number of other East European countries—agreed to reduce their annual sulphur emissions or other transboundary fluxes by at least 30% as soon as possible and at the latest by 1993, using 1980 as the base year. It was then also recognized that the contribution to air pollution by certain countries, in particular some of the smaller South European countries and Ireland, was of little significance.

At the request of the Munich Conference, the text of a formal international agreement embodying the political agreement reached at the Ottawa and Munich Conferences was elaborated within the Executive Body for the 1979 LRTAP Convention, resulting eventually in the adoption on July 9, 1985, in Helsinki of the Protocol to the 1979 Convention on Long-Range Transboundary Air Pollution on the Reduction of Sulphur Emissions or their Transboundary Fluxes by at Least 30 Per Cent (the Sulphur Protocol).[22] Article 2 of the Protocol contains the basic substantive provision: "The parties shall reduce their national annual sulphur emissions or their transboundary fluxes by at least 30 per cent as soon as possible and at the latest by 1993, using 1980 levels as the basis for calculation of reductions." Article 10(3) contains a special arrangement for States that accede to the Protocol after its entry into force. Such a State shall nevertheless implement article 2 at the latest by 1993. If the Protocol is acceded to after 1990, however, article 2 may be implemented later than 1993, but not later than 1995. The possibility of accession enables States that were not willing to sign the Protocol—for example, the United Kingdom, the United States, Spain, and Poland—to become parties to the Protocol at some appropriate moment in the future after the closing of the very short period reserved for signing it (i.e., July 5–12, 1985).

For a number of the signatories, it was clear that the Protocol constituted only a first step toward the abatement of acidification of the environment by sulphur compounds and that a much bigger reduction in emissions would be needed in the long run if a suitable decrease in acid deposition were to be achieved. This realization was expressed as follows by the Netherlands on the occasion of the signing of the Protocol: "based on a number of assumptions . . . only a reduction of SO_2 emissions by a factor of 3.5 and a reduction of NO_x emissions by a factor of 1.5 would result in an acceptable level of deposition in Western Europe." Yet, as to further reductions, the parties were able to agree in the Protocol only on a very noncommittal text. Instead of providing that "The parties shall study at the, national level the necessity for further reductions," or even better "shall endeavour to effect further reductions," article 3 of the Protocol merely provided:

The Parties recognize the need for each of them to study at the national level the necessity for further reductions, beyond those

[22] Protocol on the Reduction of Sulphur Emissions or Their Transboundary Fluxes by at Least 30%, reprinted in [1 Ref. File] Intl. Envtl. Rep. (BNA) 21:3021 (1989). (Editors' footnote.)

referred to in Article 2, of sulphur emissions or their transboundary fluxes when environmental conditions warrant.

On the opening day for signature, the Sulphur Protocol was signed by 21 out of the then 30 parties to the 1979 LRTAP Convention. On September 2, 1987, following ratification by 16 States, the Sulphur Protocol entered into force. For Luxembourg, Switzerland, and Belgium, the Sulphur Protocol entered into force later.

Notable absentees are Greece, Iceland, Ireland, Poland, Portugal, Romania, Spain, Turkey, the United Kingdom, the United States, and Yugoslavia. Of these, Romania (as of December 31, 1987) had not yet become a party to the 1979 LRTAP Convention. Among the other countries, the absence of Poland, Spain, the United Kingdom, and the United States is to be especially deplored because of the very substantial amount of SO_2 emissions caused by those countries.

Poland refused to become a party to the Sulphur Protocol because it did not have adequate modern technology to reduce its SO_2 emissions. The United States stated that since 1970 it had already considerably reduced its SO_2 emissions, and in its view these pre-1980 reductions should have been taken into account in the Protocol. Moreover, according to the United States, further SO_2 emission reductions should only be undertaken after new scientific information had been acquired indicating the need to make such reductions and if such reductions appeared to be justified by cost-benefit analyses. Also, the United Kingdom pointed to the fact that it had already considerably reduced its SO_2 emissions since 1970. It intended to reduce its emissions further after 1980, but uncertainty in the development of its (nuclear) means of energy supply made it uncertain whether the timetable imposed by the Sulphur Protocol could be met. As stated more specifically in a major speech on U.K. environmental policy by William Waldgrave, the U.K. Minister of State at the Department of Environment:

> The decision not to join the "30% Club" was not an easy one: we realise how important the 30% protocol is as a symbol of nations' concern to act on acid rain, and we thought about the issue extremely carefully before we took the position we did at the recent Helsinki meeting. To explain that position, I must mention . . . a specific difficulty. . . .

> The specific difficulty arose from domestic circumstances in the past twelve months in the UK and our projection of energy requirements towards the end of the century. I mentioned earlier the enormous improvements in air quality that we have achieved in the United Kingdom. Our emissions of sulphur dioxide have been declining steadily since 1970: they now stand some 42% below the level in that peak year. Since 1980, they have fallen by about 25%.

This trend began before a number of our European partners began to move on the downward path, and has been caused by a combination of factors, some of which I have already mentioned. The use of lower sulphur fuels, more efficient use of energy and industrial modernization has also played a substantial part.

We expect that the further development of nuclear power; continued improvements in energy efficiency; and, in the longer term, the development of new and cleaner combustion technologies will all help to ensure that this downward trend continues. However, we currently face an unusual degree of uncertainty. Our figures for 1984, in particular, are not a reliable guide, because last year industrial action compelled us to burn an atypical mix of fuels in our power stations and elsewhere. We also await the outcome of a major public inquiry into a new nuclear power station. While the Government's long-term plans indicate an increasing proportion of nuclear as a source of electricity, this depends on decisions which may have to be the subject of further detailed public enquiries.

For all these reasons we cannot be absolutely certain about the change in our sulphur dioxide emissions over the next decade, and we decided that we should not sign the protocol unless we were sure that we would meet its conditions in all respects. However, it is my government's policy to achieve further reductions in the emission of sulphur dioxide—we are aiming to get these down to 30% of 1980 levels, by the end of the 1990s. We have little reason to doubt that we shall achieve our aim, although possibly in a slightly longer timescale than envisaged in the protocol; but we do not believe that we would be justified in taking specific and costly action to meet the timetable laid down in the protocol.

Unlike the 1979 LRTAP Convention, the Sulphur Protocol entailed for the parties a highly definitive and concrete commitment to reduce their national sulphur emissions: "shall reduce . . . 30 per cent . . . at the latest by 1993, using 1980 levels as the basis for calculation." The sources from which and the measures by which the 30% reduction was to be achieved were not specified in the Protocol, however. Apart from a very general obligation in article 6 to the effect that "the parties shall . . . develop without undue delay national programmes, policies and strategies which shall serve as a means of reducing sulphur emissions or their trans-boundary fluxes," freedom of choice of sources and measures was in fact left to the parties in achieving the required reduction of sulphur emission. Another important aspect of the Sulphur Protocol was that by accepting 1980 as the base year for calculation of the reduction of the sulphur emissions, the parties to the Protocol implicitly also accepted a ceiling for sulphur emissions. As is noted above, such a ceiling was neither explicitly nor implicitly provided for in the 1979 LRTAP Convention.

While the obligation laid down in article 2 of the Protocol is clear and straightforward and for that reason must be preferred over the vague and noncommittal obligations contained in the 1979 LRTAP Convention, a few critical observations should nevertheless be made. Why was the year 1980 and not another year chosen as the base year for calculating the 30% reduction in sulphur emissions? A quick look at the survey of national SO_2 emissions compiled by the Secretariat of the UN ECE shows that for most of the parties to the Sulphur Protocol the total national emission of sulphur dioxide in 1984 or 1985 (July 9, 1985, being the date of adoption of the Protocol) was already lower—for some countries, considerably lower—than in the agreed base year 1980. For example, for France the total SO_2 emission was 3,558,000 tons in 1980 and 1,845,000 tons in 1985; for the Federal Republic of Germany these figures were 3,200,000 tons in 1980 and 2,400,000 tons in 1985; for Italy 3,800,000 tons in 1980 and 3,150,000 tons in 1983; for the United Kingdom (not a party to the Protocol) 4,670,000 tons in 1980 and 3,540,000 tons in 1984; and for the U.S.S.R. 12,800,000 tons in 1980 and 11,100,000 tons in 1985. Thus, even before the Sulfur Protocol had become binding on the parties, a clear downward trend in the total emission of SO_2 was already taking place and was perceivable in most of the major SO_2-emission-producing countries.

To a large extent, this downward trend may probably be attributed to a shift in the use from relatively high SO_2-emission-producing fuels to lessor non-SO_2-emission-producing fuels (such as, for example, the use of hydropower, geothermal energy, and nuclear energy). . . .

While the downward trend in SO_2 emissions has greatly facilitated the conclusion of the Sulphur Protocol, this does not mean that the Protocol is only of minor relevance. The Sulphur Protocol will remain important, among other reasons, in that it constitutes a legal bar against a reversal of the SO_2-emission trend when economic conditions or energy consumption patterns tend to lead again to an increasing use of relatively high-SO_2-emission-producing fuels.

Apart from the question whether there is an upward or downward trend in the use of fossil fuels after the selected base year—and this may not be the same for all countries—there also is the fact that certain countries may have already effected considerable cuts in SO_2 emissions before the base year, while others have not.

Accordingly, a 30% cut as provided for in the Sulphur Protocol will have the result that country A that already undertook considerable cuts in SO_2 emissions before the base year will in the end be obliged to reduce its sulphur emissions to a considerably larger extent than country B that only started to take control measures after the base year. This finding follows clearly from the following example in which it is assumed that countries A and B emitted the same amount of sulphur dioxide in 1970 (100 units), but country A reduced its emissions by 30% before 1980, whereas country B did not.

	1970	1980	1993
Country A:	100	70	49
Country B:	100	100	70

Another aspect of the 30% cut in the Sulphur Protocol is that it applies to all parties regardless of the size of the population and the level of industrial development. Consider the following hypothetical situation: a less developed country L having a population of, for instance, 1,000,000 inhabitants will have to reduce its SO_2 emissions, for example, from 20 to 14 units, while a more developed country M having the same population but a much higher level of economic development will have to reduce its SO_2 emissions, for example, from 100 to 70 units. Although the reduction for country M is considerably greater than for country L, it is also true that country M may still continue to emit considerably more sulphur dioxide than country L should no further control measures be taken in the future.

Given the need for drastic SO_2 emission reductions from an environmental point of view, equity would seem to require that country M be obliged to achieve a considerably higher percentage of SO_2 emission reductions than country L. It is further clear that if country M had already achieved considerable SO_2 emission reductions before the base year it would not be entitled, or in any event would be entitled much less, to invoke that fact vis-a-vis country L. As the Sulphur Protocol did not take account of considerable differences in industrial development and the resulting considerable differences in amounts of SO_2 emissions caused, this aspect could in fact be dealt with only by not putting pressure on less developed countries to become a party to the Sulphur Protocol. This solution is not an ideal one, of course, because at present no SO_2-emission limits are imposed on less developed countries that are not parties to the Sulphur Protocol. In light of this situation, the following statement by the U.K. Minister for Environment in his speech to the German Foreign Policy Society is critical:

> This brings me to the more fundamental difficulty which my government also faced—the arbitrary nature of the protocol itself. If the proposition had been a 40% reduction from the year of peak emissions, the UK would have already met that condition. If the protocol had been based on a figure for emissions per head of population, its impact on the countries concerned would also have been quite different. And if the

protocol had been designed as a first step toward reducing deposition to a level tolerable by the environment in the most vulnerable areas, it would have gained in logic and, again, been different in format.

In short, my government sees the protocol as arbitrary in its approach, and only one of several ways in which a common will to reduce emissions can be demonstrated. But I stress here that, even though we were not able to sign the protocol, we believe that our actual performance will be equal to—or better than—that of a number of countries who did. The Swedish Government, amongst others, recognizes this; in a recent assessment of the efforts being made in a number of European countries to reduce sulphur emissions, they estimated that the UK would achieve a cut of 50% between 1970 and 1995; a figure which is not dissimilar from the 55% they recorded for the Federal Republic.

A major factor to be kept in mind, of course, is the fact that in spite of the considerable reduction in SO_2 emissions already achieved before 1980, the United Kingdom was in 1980—as it was in 1985—still the greatest SO_2 emitter in Western Europe. In that year it emitted 4,670,000 tons per year compared with 3,558,000 tons for France; 3,200,000 tons for the Federal Republic of Germany; 3,800,000 tons for Italy; and 3,200,000 for Spain (not a party to the Protocol).

What has been said above amply illustrates that the 30% reduction clause in article 2 of the Sulphur Protocol was a substantive provision of a very general, simple, and straightforward nature that did not take account of any special conditions possibly existing in the member States of the UN ECE. Among the other special conditions that were not taken into account are the nature and the extent of the harm caused by sulphur compounds in each State.

As has already been noted, the Sulphur Protocol formed in the eyes of a number of its signatories only a first step toward the abatement of the acidification of the environment by sulphur compounds. Nevertheless, pleas made by the Nordic countries, Austria, Switzerland, the Federal Republic of Germany, and the Netherlands to develop a second stage to the Sulphur Protocol that would lead to a further tightening of the sulphur emission abatement goals remain so far without success.

THE NOx PROTOCOL

At its fourth session in November 1986, the Executive Body for the LRTAP Convention expanded the mandate of its Working Group on Nitrogen Oxides, allowing it to elaborate a draft protocol to the LRTAP Convention concerning control of emissions of nitrogen oxides or their transboundary fluxes. The resistance on the part of the East European countries to elaborating such a protocol—which still existed during the third session of the Executive Body in July 1985—had ceased. The East European countries, however, made their cooperation dependent on the willingness of the Western countries to agree on provisions in the future NO$_x$ Protocol obliging the parties to facilitate the transfer of technology to reduce emissions of nitrogen oxides.

The NO$_x$ Protocol eventually concluded on November 1, 1988, at Sofia, envisages a two-stage approach with regard to the substantive or basic obligations of the parties "to control and/or reduce national annual emissions of nitrogen oxides or their transboundary fluxes." As a first step, the parties shall arrive at a stabilization of the levels of NO$_x$ emissions or the transboundary fluxes thereof. In particular, they shall as soon as possible take effective measures to control and/or reduce their NO$_x$ emissions or transboundary fluxes so that these—at the latest by December 31, 1994—do not exceed the level of emissions or transboundary fluxes in the year 1987 or in any previous year to be specified by a State upon signature of, or accession to, the Protocol, provided that in addition with respect to any Party specifying such a previous year, its national average transboundary fluxes or national annual average emissions of nitrogen oxides for the period from January 1, 1987, to January 1, 1996, do not exceed its transboundary fluxes or national emissions for the year 1987.

Contrary to the 1985 Sulphur Protocol, the NO$_x$ Protocol thus does not oblige the parties to achieve certain quantified reductions of the NO$_x$ emissions or trans-boundary fluxes from the 1987 level or level of a previous year of such emissions or transboundary fluxes. Reductions or NO$_x$ emissions or transboundary fluxes are only required to the extent that such emissions or transboundary fluxes have increased after 1987 or after a selected previous base year. It follows that the stabilization provision envisaged in the Protocol does not preclude increases in NO$_x$ emissions or transboundary fluxes over present levels, provided that at the target date the level of emissions or transboundary fluxes does not exceed the level in 1987 or in a selected previous base year.

The fact that the NO$_x$ Protocol entitles the parties to select the year 1987 or any previous year as the year of reference for their duty to stabilize their NO$_x$ emissions or transboundary fluxes thereof, allows a party to select a year in which the level of its national annual NO$_x$ emissions or transboundary fluxes thereof was higher than in the year 1987. The possibility for each party to the Protocol to select the base year most suitable to it introduces in the basic obligations of the parties a flexible element that is not to be found in the 1985 Sulphur Protocol. Moreover, this possibility permits taking into account NO$_x$ emission reductions resulting from antipollution measures taken by a State before 1987 or to ignore possible reductions resulting from decreasing economic activities. However, as has been indicated above, the right to select a previous year is not unqualified. A State selecting such a previous year will be obliged to make sure that its national average annual transboundary fluxes or national average annual emissions for a period from January 1, 1987, to January 1, 1996, do not exceed its transboundary fluxes or national emissions for the year 1987. It was hoped that by means of this flexible element certain States, such as the United States, which were not able to adhere to the 1985 Sulphur Protocol, would be able to sign and ratify the NO_x Protocol.

The NO_x Protocol envisages the stabilization of NO_x emissions or transboundary fluxes only as one, albeit very important, part of the measures to be taken in the short term. The parties shall furthermore (i.e., not merely with a view to achieve the stabilization of NO_x emissions or transboundary fluxes at the agreed target date and thus involving in certain countries the possibility of NO_x emission reductions), at the latest two years after the date of entry into force of the protocol, apply national emission standards to major new or substantially modified stationary sources and new mobile sources based on the best available technologies which are economically feasible, taking into account the Technical Annex and, in respect of mobile sources, also the relevant decisions taken within the framework of the Inland Transport Committee of the UN ECE. With regard to major existing stationary sources, the parties are obliged to introduce gradually and without a final deadline control measures, taking into consideration the Technical Annex mentioned earlier, the characteristics of the plant, its age, its rate of utilization, and the need to avoid operational disruption. The Technical Annex is of recommendatory nature only; its purpose is to provide guidance for the parties in identifying economically feasible technologies they can use to effect the obligations of the Protocol.

While the measures discussed above are all short-term and first-stage, the NO_x Protocol also contains provisions on measures to be taken in its second stage. Those provisions, however, are only programmatic and cooperative. No later than six months after the date of entry into force of the Protocol, the parties shall commence negotiations on further steps to reduce NO_x emissions taking into account, among other factors, the best available scientific and technical developments and internationally accepted critical loads. To that end the parties shall cooperate to establish (1) critical loads, (2) NO_x emission reductions required to achieve agreed objectives based on critical loads, and (3) measures and a timetable commencing no later than January 1, 1996, for achieving such reductions.

The critical loads approach plays an important role in the second stage of the NO_x Protocol. By a "critical load" is meant a quantitative estimate of an exposure to one or more pollutants (i.e., nitrogen oxides in the case of the NO_x Protocol) below which significant harmful long-term effects on specified sensitive elements of the environment do not occur according to present knowledge. The development and application of the critical loads approach is hence an effect-related approach designed to determine on a scientific basis necessary reductions of NO_x emissions taking account of the sensitivity of the receptor and the impact of the pollutant on the receptor.

It follows from the foregoing that, according to the present Protocol, major reductions of NO_x emissions or transboundary fluxes from the level in 1987 or a selected previous year will in all probability be realized only in the second half of the 1990s. In this connection, it is important that the NO_x Protocol explicitly leaves open the possibility for parties to take more stringent measures than provided for in the Protocol. Indeed, a number of European States—in particular Austria, Belgium, Denmark, the Federal Republic of Germany, Finland, France, Italy, Liechtenstein, the Netherlands, Norway, Sweden, and Switzerland—consider the obligations envisaged in the Protocol as too weak and declared themselves prepared to accept an obligation to reduce NO_x emissions by at least 30% by the year 1998 at the latest, using the levels of any year between 1980 and 1986 as the basis for calculating the reduction. The refusal of other States to commit themselves already in the first stage of the Protocol to substantial NO_x emission reductions is mainly based on the grounds that, in their view, the necessary scientific, ecological, geophysical, and economic substantiation for such reductions is still lacking as the critical load approach referred to above has not yet been sufficiently developed and that, in their view, the causal relationship between NO_x emissions and damage has not yet sufficiently been demonstrated. According to those States, the first stage of the Protocol should be used not only to stabilize NO_x emissions but also to develop scientifically substantiated targets for NO_x emission reductions.

In addition to the substantive or basic obligations to control NO_x emissions, the Protocol also includes a provision specifically dealing with unleaded fuel. The parties shall as soon as possible, and no later than two years after the date of entry into force of the Protocol, make unleaded fuel sufficiently available, in particular cases as a minimum along main international transit routes, to facilitate the circulation of vehicles equipped with catalytic converters. The attenuating qualification, "in particular cases as a minimum along main international transit routes," was inserted to meet the concern of the Soviet Union, where unleaded fuel is expected not to be generally available for a long time. . . .

---

b.   The VOC Protocol

A Protocol to the LRTAP Convention on Volatile Organic Compounds (VOCs) was adopted on November 18, 1991. Protocol on the Control of

Emissions of Volatile Organic Compounds or Their Transboundary Fluxes, 31 I.L.M. 568 (1992). A member of the United States negotiating team describes VOCs as follows:

> VOCs are emitted by a wide variety of stationary sources of air pollution, as well as by motor vehicles and many commercial and consumer products. In the presence of sunlight, they react with by-products of combustion known as oxides of nitrogen (NO_x) to form tropospheric (ground-level) ozone, an important component of "smog." This tropospheric ozone is often formed far downwind from the precursor VOC and NO_x emissions. Thus, VOC emissions may lead to ozone formation in a neighboring country. Once formed, ozone also drifts across international borders.

David P. Novello, *Introductory Note*, 31 I.L.M. 568 (1992). Novello offers the following brief description of the Protocol:

> The VOC Protocol aims to limit emissions of VOCs and the formation of ozone and other "photo-chemical oxidants" through two principal mechanisms. . . . The first . . . provides several options from which countries may choose in order to freeze or reduce their VOC emissions. The second . . . requires the adoption of technology-based controls for stationary sources, motor vehicles, and products that emit VOCs. . . . This represents a compromise between the position advocated by Nordic and other European countries, which favored a fixed percentage reduction in emissions, and the position advanced by the U.S., which favored a "best available technology" approach.

Id. at 569. The VOC protocol provides for three different options for meeting emission reduction requirements: a 30 percent reduction between 1988 (or other base year between 1984 and 1990 selected by a party); reduction of emissions by 30 percent only within areas within which trans-boundary pollution actually occurs (tropospheric ozone management areas, or TOMAs); and, for countries with economies in transition (those of the former Eastern European bloc), freezing emissions by 1999, provided they emitted less than specified amounts in 1988. The TOMA option had been proposed by Canada on the ground that emissions from only a small part of its territory cross the border into the United States. TOMAs must be agreed to by all Parties to the protocol and, in any event, by 1999 total nationwide VOC emissions from a Party adopting this approach must not exceed 1988 levels.

c.   **The 1994 Sulphur Protocol**

On June 14, 1994, a new Sulphur Protocol to the LRTAP Convention was adopted at Oslo. Protocol on Further Reduction of Sulphur Emissions, reprinted in 33 I.L.M. 1540 (1994). This agreement concerns the further reduction of sulphur emissions and, for the parties, replaces the original 1985 agreement. The parties to 1994 protocol agree to reduce sulphur emissions to the lesser of their 1990 emissions or their obligation under the 1985 protocol. Article 2(5) contains specific obligations to limit emissions from new and existing sources. "Parties subject to the United States/Canada Air Quality Agreement of 1991" are exempted from the requirements of that paragraph. Annex I consists of a map setting forth critical loads ("critical sulphur depositions"). Annex II establishes a detailed list of the sulphur dioxide emission ceilings. Annex IV lists a variety of methods by which parties may control sulphur dioxide emissions. Annex V contains emission and sulphur content limit values for major stationary combustion sources and for motor vehicle fuel ("gas oil").

d.   The 1998–1999 Protocols

On March 31, 1998, members of the United Nations Economic Commission for Europe (ECE) concluded two new protocols, which were opened for signature on June 24, in Aarhus, Denmark: the Protocol on Persistent Organic Pollutants (LRTAP POPs) and the Protocol on Heavy Metals. These are addressed in Chapter 10 on Hazardous Substances. LRTAP POPs entered into force in 2003. In 1999, the Protocol to Abate Acidification, Eutrophication and Ground Level Ozone was opened for signature in Gottenberg, Sweden; it entered into force in 2005. By 2010, Europe's sulfur emissions were to be reduced by 63%, NO_x emissions by 41%, VOC emissions by 40%, and ammonia emissions by 17% percent below 1990 levels.

e.   Review of Country Performance Regarding LRTAP Protocols

Twice a year the LRTAP secretariat, in cooperation with the Centre on Emission Inventories and Projections (CEIP), compiles overview tables of the emission data by pollutant in relation to the respective emission reduction obligations set for each Party under the different protocols. These are available online.

NOTES AND QUESTIONS

1.   *Comparing the approaches.* How do the approaches to the acid rain problem taken by the United States and Canada, on the one hand, and the ECE countries, on the other, differ? Which one is preferable?

2.   *LRTAP and North America.* Why did the LRTAP Convention not solve the problem between the United States and Canada, both of which are Parties to it?

3.   *The LRTAP Convention as a model.* Do you believe the LRTAP Convention could serve as a model for a general, framework agreement on transboundary air pollution that would include both developed and

developing countries? What specific provisions mentioned by Lammers would or would not be suitable for such an agreement?

4.   *A substantial harm requirement.* Lammers notes that "proof of substantial harm is not required to be able to invoke the provisions" of the convention. What are the advantages and disadvantages of this approach? How does this feature of the convention bear, if at all, upon your answer to Note 3, above?

5.   *A license to pollute?* Does the LRTAP Convention require parties to prevent increases in existing air pollution? If not, was the conclusion of the convention just a waste of time and effort?

6.   *Inequitable reductions?* Why did the ECE countries agree in the 1985 Sulphur Dioxide Protocol to an approach that would allow a more developed country to emit considerably more SO_2 than a less developed country? Should less developed countries have been given more incentive to join the protocol, (e.g., by requiring a lower percentage of reductions or by granting them a grace period)?

7.   *Comparing the protocols.* Which approach is preferable, the stricter one of the Sulphur Protocol or the more flexible one of the Nitrogen Protocol? (The United States is a Party to the Nitrogen Protocol.)

8.   *Critical loads.* What are the advantages and disadvantages of the "critical loads" approach, as compared with the other approaches taken in the protocols?

9.   *Circumventing the Senate?* The LRTAP Convention and all of its protocols are executive agreements of the United States, rather than "treaties," and therefore do not require the advice and consent of the Senate. Do you believe the Executive Branch should have involved the Senate in the approval process of these instruments? Is their subject matter appropriate for executive agreements?

Further Reading: *See generally* Peter H. Sand, *Regional Approaches to Transboundary Air Pollution*, in Energy: Production, Consumption, and Consequences 246 (1990).

3.   TRANSBOUNDARY POLLUTION IN ASIA: COOPERATIVE APPROACHES

Several areas in Asia are subject to transboundary air pollution. One is in Northeast Asia, involving China and Korea. Another is a regional haze problem emanating from burning forests in Indonesia and involving several other Member States of the Association of Southeast Asian Nations (ASEAN). The haze problem is discussed immediately below, followed by the situation in Northeast Asia.

a. **Haze in Southeast Asia**

HAZE IN SOUTHEAST ASIA: THE ASEAN
COOPERATION PLAN

Simon SC Tay
National University of Singapore (1997)

The ASEAN Cooperation Plan on Transboundary Pollution ("ASEAN Plan") was adopted at the ASEAN Environment Ministers Meeting held in Kuala Lumpur, Malaysia on 21 October 1994. It covers three "programme areas" of transboundary pollution: atmospheric pollution, the transboundary movement of hazardous wastes, and transboundary ship-borne pollution.

The immediate catalyst for the ASEAN Plan may be traced to the problem of transboundary haze which, between August and October 1994, covered Malaysia, Singapore and parts of Indonesia. Caused by land clearing activities in the Indonesian islands of Kalimantan and Sumatra, the haze caused unhealthy atmospheric pollution levels in the three countries, resulting in a number of asthma-related hospitalizations and delayed air flights.

Despite the identification of the cause of the haze and evidence of transboundary harm, there are no express references in the ASEAN Plan to Principle 21 of the Stockholm Declaration and issues of state responsibility. Instead, it emphasizes the need for inter-state cooperation and lays out a framework for shared strategies, coordinated activities and the adoption of common standards and training.

In this, different roles are envisaged for laws and institutions at the national level and at the regional level. Differences can also be discerned in the roles of the state from which the haze originates, and those states affected, although no states are named and obligations of the different state parties are not clearly defined.

Details in respect of atmospheric pollution exemplify the approach taken. The ASEAN Plan sets objectives of cooperation to assess the origins and causes, nature and extent of local and regional haze incidents; to prevent and control the sources of haze by applying sound technologies and strengthening both national and regional capabilities; and to develop national and regional emergency response plans. To meet those objectives, short and longer term strategies are identified, as are more specific activities.

Short-term strategies emphasize the need to prevent the forest fires by timely detection, the deployment of ground forces and the involvement of local communities. It is also agreed that the burning of biomass during dry weather periods should be prohibited. Longer term strategies aim for "zero-burning" practices and technologies, with efforts to create awareness to eliminate the use of fire in clearing land. Economically sound and environmentally friendly methods in agriculture are instead to be introduced.

The ASEAN Plan sets a long list of agreed activities. Some of these are to be undertaken by each country, at the national level. These include establishing "National Focal Points" to inventorize existing resources, establish mechanisms to provide and disseminate information; and establishing procedures for reporting by Forestry and other relevant agencies. Others require inter-state cooperation, like developing a common air quality index; sharing knowledge and technology in the prevention of forest fires; and establishing a mechanism for forest fire-fighting.

Consistent with the framework of the ASEAN Plan, some cooperative efforts have been noticeable, including the supply of satellite imaging from Singapore to the Indonesian authorities, to better detect the location of fires.

Existing ASEAN institutions are also incorporated. The ASEAN Specialized Meteorological Centre, for example, is to develop a model to predict the spread of haze. The ASEAN Institute of Forest Management is asked to expand its role in strengthening national capacity in forest fire management.

The ASEAN Plan takes a similar, but less detailed, approach to the other sectors concerning the transboundary movement of hazardous waste and ship-borne pollution.

In contrast to treaties in other regions that deal with transboundary pollution, the ASEAN Plan is notable for the absence of concrete standards and binding obligations. It instead emphasizes more general cooperative efforts. This may be interpreted as being in line with the general ASEAN preference for avoiding legalistic approaches. The approach in the ASEAN Plan might also be lauded for recognizing the region as one eco-system and, therefore, that each state owes a duty to assist the other in dealing with common problems. The ASEAN Plan may also be interpreted as a pragmatic approach that recognizes the different interests and strengths of the states involved and, as such, applies the principle of a common but differentiated responsibility.

The ASEAN Plan, however, may also be criticized as a departure from the norm of state responsibility, enshrined in Principle 21. While the ASEAN Plan creates a commendable framework, it is weak in terms of establishing thresholds for action, identifying the specific obligation of each member state and allowing for monitoring and compliance of cooperative and coordinated actions that are needed to fill in that framework.

An early comment on the ASEAN Plan suggested that it "symbolizes ASEAN's promise to the people in South East Asia that their governments will strive to protect the environment from pollution." (Tookey, The ASEAN Cooperation Plan, [1996] Env. Liability, p. 36.) In the light of subsequent events that promise has yet to be fulfilled. August 1997 witnessed a return of the haze problem in the region. The causes were again fires in Indonesia used for land-clearing. Pollution levels in 1997 were higher than those in 1994, with the Pollution Standards Index reaching dangerous levels above 500 and 600 in East Malaysia, and above 200 in Singapore.

The ASEAN Environment Ministers' Meeting in September 1997, held in Indonesia, witnessed three notable events. The first was the acknowledgment of "moral responsibility" by Indonesia and a rare public apology from its head of government, President Suharto, to ASEAN countries affected by the haze. The second was the action taken at the national level, with new Indonesian laws threatening heavier fines and the cancellation of licenses for those companies which carried on clearing land by fire. The third was a continuation of ASEAN efforts towards cooperation, with Malaysia initiating discussions of a regional firefighting force.

Despite these developments, the emphasis of the ASEAN Plan on modes of cooperation over the attribution of State responsibility remains to be vindicated by effective implementation and an abatement of the haze.

Later in 1999, ASEAN adopted a "Zero Burning Policy" in order to eliminate burning as a method for land-clearance in agriculture. This policy encourages ASEAN member countries to implement it in their respective national legal systems. However, this policy could not be fully implemented due to challenges within ASEAN countries.

Eventually, 10 ASEAN governments, including Indonesia, signed the ASEAN Agreement on Transboundary Haze Pollution on June 10, 2002 in Kuala Lumpur. The agreement came into force on Nov. 25, 2003. . . . [Indonesia ratified the Agreement in 2014, the tenth ASEAN Member State to do so.—Eds.]

The agreement emphasizes the prevention and monitoring of transboundary haze pollution as a result of forest fires through national efforts and international cooperation. The agreement also led to the formation of an ASEAN Coordinating Center for Transboundary Haze Pollution that will facilitate regional anti-haze efforts and resource distribution and serve as a central focal point for emergency response efforts. In addition, the ASEAN Transboundary Haze Pollution Control Fund was also created to provide funding for the implementation of the agreement although the contribution is made on a voluntary basis.

Other principles of the agreement highlight preventive mechanisms and the precautionary approach.

NOTES AND COMMENTS

The ASEAN Haze Agreement is unusual in that ASEAN typically has avoided legally binding instruments. The haze returned as a significant problem from 2004–2010 and then again in 2013, which led ASEAN members to adopt a joint haze monitoring system that same year. In addition, Singapore offered to work directly with Indonesian farmers to encourage sustainable forestry practices and reduce the burning and subsequent haze, a project that could also assist in mitigating climate change. Indonesia is one of the world's leading greenhouse gas emitters, with about 75% of its greenhouse gas emissions coming from deforestation. How does the ASEAN approach compare with those in North America and Europe?

b.   China and Northeast Asia

China is the third largest acid rain region in the world as of 2015; and SO_2 emissions are rapidly increasing as the Chinese economy grows. China has devoted considerable resources, with international aid, to developing an environmental protection regime, with limited success. For example, in 2006, The China Daily reported that the 2000–2005 Five-Year Plan called for a 10% reduction in SO_2 emissions but in fact there had been a 27% increase. The head of the China State Environmental Protection Bureau explained that the plan was based on 1988–1999 economic levels, which assumed that in 2005 coal use would not exceed 1.5 billion tons. Instead, rapid economic growth pushed the consumption level to 2.1 billion tons. Sun Xiaohua & Yin Ping, *China's Environmental Protection Goals Not Met, China Daily,* April 13, 2006. Other Asian countries (and even the United States[23]) are suffering damage as well from China's emissions; and China in turn is affected by emissions in other Northeast Asian countries.

Unlike Southeast Asia, Europe and North America, Northeast Asia has not created a legally binding regional regime. The Northeast Asian region includes China, the Democratic People's Republic of Korea, Japan, Mongolia, the Republic of Korea, and the eastern portion of the Russian Federation—countries with significantly different political systems, economic development levels, and cultures. There also appears to be an absence of a common understanding of the problem and solutions.

Perhaps in part because of the absence of a binding regional regime, Northeast Asian countries have been developing transboundary air pollution cooperation mechanisms since the early 1990s. Cooperation is

---

[23] See, e.g., National Research Council, Global Air Quality: An Imperative for Long-Term Observational Strategies (2001); Keith Bradsher & David Barboza, *Clouds from Chinese Coal Cast A Long Shadow,* The New York Times, Sunday, June 11, 2006, p.1, col. 2.

taking place regionally, trilaterally and bilaterally. At the regional level are the North-East Asia Sub-regional Program for Environmental Cooperation (NEASPEC) and the East Asia Acid Deposition Monitoring Network (EANET). At the trilateral level is a Tri-partite Environment Ministers Meeting among the Republic of Korea, China, and Japan (TEMM). At least three bilateral cooperation mechanisms exist: the1993 Republic of Korea-Japan Agreement on Cooperation in the Field of Environmental Protection; the1993 China-Republic of Korea Agreement on Environmental Cooperation; and the 1994 Japan-China Agreement on Environmental Cooperation. In addition, international financial institutions such as the World Bank and the Asian Development Bank are involved in regional environmental cooperation.

CONCLUDING NOTES AND COMMENTS

1.   What are the advantages and disadvantages of the approaches described above?

2.   *Additional references.* Regarding Asia, see: Inkyoung Kim, Environmental cooperation of Northeast Asia: transboundary air pollution vol.7.3, Oxford Publishing Limited (2007); Inkyoung Kim, *Messages from a Middle Power: Participation by the Republic of Korea in Regional Environmental Cooperation on Transboundary Air Pollution Issues,* 14.2, Springer Science & Business Media (2014); Wakana Takahashi, *Formation of an East Asian Regime for Acid Rain Control: The Perspective of Comparative Regionalism,* 1 International Review for Environmental Strategies 97–117 (2000). Regarding Europe, see: *European Union, Europe Fights Particle Pollution—Insight into Implementation of EU Law*, 24 Natural Resources & Environment (2010).

B.   REGIONAL TRANSBOUNDARY WATER POLLUTION

The following materials address one of the major issues regarding international freshwater: pollution. The other principal issue regarding international rivers and lakes—allocation and apportionment—is dealt with in Chapter 12. Pollution of watercourses occurs primarily in a regional or bilateral context. The following excerpt provides background for the material that follows.

FRESHWATER LAW AND GOVERNANCE: GLOBAL AND REGIONAL PERSPECTIVES IN SUSTAINABILITY

UNEP, Technical background document for theme 3: "Environmental Laws and
Regulations" and theme 4: "Institutional Challenge", First International Environment
Forum for Basin Organizations—Towards Sustainable Freshwater Governance
(26–28 November 2014, Nairobi, Kenya) (Footnotes omitted)

A . . . large number of international rivers, lakes and aquifers . . . cross or extend along the border between two or more States. For example, there are roughly 276 international river basins that involve 148 States in total and as many as 19 States in one basin (the Danube River basin). These basins include nearly half of the world's land area and 40% of the world's population. Moreover, there are myriad transboundary aquifers, some of which underlie more than one international water basin (e.g. the Guarani aquifer underlies parts of the Plata and Amazon basins). Governance of such waters thus inevitably involves more than one State and raises international issues (e.g. the amount and timing of flows, water quality, access and peace and security). Water governance also has an international aspect . . . if it significantly affects some other interest of the international community, such as the survival of a species, integrity of transboundary migrations or protection of human rights, even when the activity in question occurs solely within the territory of one State.

On the legal front, watercourse treaties have existed for at least 5000 years. Indeed, the first recorded treaty of any type is a water treaty in approximately 3100 BCE between the two Mesopotamian city-states of Umma and Lagash regarding waters of the Euphrates River. At present, there are approximately 400 international water agreements at global, regional and bilateral levels. Most of these agreements establish an institution to govern the respective agreement. Unfortunately, these agreements have not been harmonised in terms of either their normative content or their organisational institutions, and there is no institutional home for watercourse agreements within the United Nations system.

The sheer number of agreements and institutions inevitably leads to complexity. In addition, many agreements and their institutions are "nested" [i.e., an agreement exists regarding part of a basin even though a separate agreement exists for the entire basin] or "parallel" [i.e., a State is Party to agreements about more than one basin] . . . , giving rise to practical and normative challenges [because the agreements to which the State is a Party contain different institutional or normative elements]. A further complication in terms of international agreements arises from the fact that many non-watercourse-specific global, multilateral and bilateral agreements [e.g., Ramsar Convention on Wetlands] and their respective institutions and activities directly involve freshwater or have important implications for freshwater, including freshwater in international watercourses and aquifers. Experience indicates that the multiplicity of norms can create duplicate reporting requirements, inconsistent norms, and confusion about what is actually required. Similarly, the multiplicity of governing bodies complicates efforts to standardize rules and coordinate enforcement and implementation efforts. On the operational level, the multiplicity of administering bodies can cause inefficiencies in coordinating, overlap in staffing, redundancy in projects and other activities, conflicting meeting schedules, and impossibility of comparing and aggregating data because of incompatible knowledge management systems and the use of inconsistent definitions of basic terms.[24] The complexity and lack of harmonisation have created a "fragmented legal architecture" for international watercourse management and resulted in a multitude of legal and operational challenges to governance.

1. INTRODUCTION TO THE PROBLEM

FOURTH REPORT ON THE LAW OF THE NON-NAVIGATIONAL USES OF INTERNATIONAL WATERCOURSES
Stephen McCaffrey
1988 Y.B. ILC, vol. 2, pt. 1, 205, 218–219 (1992)

. . . [T]he pollution of fresh water has been a concomitant of human civilization since the dawn of history.

> The sewage of human societies, all the waste and refuse of agrarian communities, have been discharged throughout the years into the waters of rivers, since there were no other means of disposal. . . . Since the earliest civilizations flourishing along the Nile, the Tigris, the Euphrates, the Indus, the Ganges, the Yangtze, etc., one of the oldest uses of river waters was the irrigation of arid lands. . . . It is well known that irrigation is one of the most common sources of pollution through the process of increase in the salinity of the waters which percolate through the soil before the water is returned to the mainstream.[76]

Of course, the concentration of people in cities meant increased potential for pollution of the rivers on which urban areas often developed. "In the days of ancient Rome the water of the Tiber river was already seriously polluted by the filth of the city."

Even by the Middle Ages, the capacity of humans to pollute fresh water had reached such proportions that water pollution has been linked to the "frequent outbreaks of terrible epidemics, such as the black plague of the 14th century which killed one-third of mankind. . . ." Cholera epidemics, as recently as the 19th century, have also been laid to water pollution.

---

[24] For discussion of this and other governance issues, see Chapter 18.

[76] J. Sette-Camara, *Pollution of International Rivers*, 186 Recueil des Cours 1983-III p. 139 (The Hague 1985).

The advent of industrialization, along with increased urbanization and the accompanying development of sewage disposal systems (originally, simply means of conveying untreated sewage to a river) exacerbated the problem tremendously. "In light of these developments it is not surprising that this pollution, which had originally often only a local or regional character, increasingly came to transcend interstate frontiers and even began to affect adversely the quality of marine waters." Unfortunately, despite the development over the years of sophisticated technology for the monitoring and control of fresh water pollution, recent studies have confirmed that the outlook for the future is not encouraging. . . .

The "Global 2000 Report" prepared by the United States Council on Environmental Quality, presented the following scenario concerning [human] use of water . . . :

> By the year 2000, worldwide urban and industrial water withdrawals are projected to increase by a factor of about 5, reaching 1.8–2.3 trillion cubic meters. . . .

> Urban and industrial effluent will be concentrated in the rivers, bays, and coastal zones near the world's largest urban-industrial agglomerations. In the developing world—where 2 billion additional persons are projected to be living by the year 2000 and where rapid rates of urbanization continue—urban and industrial water pollution will become ever more serious because many developing economies will be unable or unwilling to afford the additional cost of water treatment.

This sobering forecast is reinforced by the ["Environmental Perspective to the Year 2000 and Beyond" prepared by the United Nations Environment Programme (UNEP)][85], which adds important information concerning the use and pollution of fresh water:

> 16. There have been significant changes in weather patterns partly as a result of loss of forests and vegetation cover. This has reduced river flows and lake levels and also lowered agricultural productivity. Irrigation has greatly improved arability . . . [and] has also been playing a vital role in the Green Revolution. Inappropriate irrigation, however, has wasted water, washed out nutrients and, through salinization and alkalinization, damaged the productivity of millions of hectares. Globally, salinization

---

[85] . . . [S]tudy adopted by the UNEP Governing [Council] at its fourteenth session (decision 14/ 13 of 19 June 1987); see Official Records of the General Assembly, Forty-second Session, Supplement No. 25 (A/42/25), annex II. The study was adopted by the [United Nations] General Assembly [in 1987] "as a broad framework to guide national action and international co-operation on policies and programmes aimed at achieving environmentally sound development," and annexed to its resolution 42/186 of 11 December 1987.

alone may be removing as much land from production as the land being irrigated. . . .

20. Overuse of pesticides has polluted water and soil, damaging the ecology of agriculture and has created hazards for human health and animals. . . .

21. Use of chemical fertilizers *per capita* has increased five-fold between 1950 and 1983. In some countries excessive use of fertilizers, along with household and industrial effluents, has caused eutrophication of lakes, canals and irrigation reservoirs, and even coastal seas through run-offs of nitrogen compounds and phosphates. Ground water has also been polluted by nitrates in many places, and nitrate levels in rivers have risen steadily over the last two decades. Degradation of the quality of surface and ground water, caused by chemicals including nitrates, has been a significant problem in developed and developing countries alike.

22. . . . [S]tudy adopted by the UNEP Governing [Council] at its fourteenth session (decision 14/ 13 of 19 June 1987); *see* Official Records of the General Assembly, Fortysecond Session, Supplement No. 25 (A/42/25), annex II. The study was adopted by the [United Nations] General Assembly [in 1987] "as a broad framework to guide national action and international co-operation on policies and programmes aimed at achieving environmentally sound development," and annexed to its resolution 42/186 of 11 December 1987.

Of course, increased use and pollution of fresh water brings with it increased possibilities of disputes between watercourse States, not to mention spiraling environmental harm. Of specific relevance to the present inquiry in this connection is the following "shared perception of Governments" identified in the UNEP ["Environmental Perspective"]:

Environmental degradation can be controlled and reversed only by ensuring that the parties causing the damage will be accountable for their action, and that they will participate, on the basis of full access to available knowledge, in improving environmental conditions. . . .

i.   INTERNATIONAL AGREEMENTS

International agreements are a particularly rich source of evidence of State practice in relation to the pollution of international watercourses. In 1984, [Professor Johan] Lammers listed eighty-eight international agreements "containing substantive provisions concerning pollution of international watercourses."[25] Provisions relating to pollution have been

---

[25]   [Johan Lammers, Pollution of International Watercourses 124, et seq. (1984).—Eds.]

discovered in international agreements concluded as early as the 1860s. The approach States have taken to the pollution of international watercourses, as reflected in their agreements, has evolved considerably. The early agreements often ban such pollution outright. An example is the 1868 Final Act of the delimitation of the international frontier of the Pyrenees between France and Spain, which provides:

> . . . The discharge of foul or harmful water into the bed of the said river by riparian or other proprietors shall also be prohibited.

The object of many of the early provisions was to protect fisheries. Again, they were usually quite strict. For example, [Article 17 of] the 1904 Convention between France and Switzerland for the regulation of fishing in their frontier waters provides:

> Factories, plants or establishments of any kind situated near the Doubs shall be prohibited from discharging into the water any waste or substances that may be harmful to fish.

A characteristic of these early fishery agreements, which is quite common in modern pollution-control instruments, is that they set what amounts to a water quality standard. In the case of the 1904 Convention just referred to, the standard is very general (as is typical of these agreements)— avoidance of harm to fish. Similarly, the 1909 Boundary Waters Treaty between Canada and the United States, rather than prohibiting all pollution of boundary waters, proscribes only that which causes certain transfrontier damage:

Article IV

> It is further agreed that the waters herein defined as boundary waters and waters flowing across the boundary shall not be polluted on either side to the injury of health or property on the other. . . .

A different approach, but one that still provides a standard for determining the degree of permissible pollution, is that of the 1960 Indus Waters Treaty between India and Pakistan. Article 4, paragraph 10 of that agreement provides:

> Each Party declares its intention to prevent, as far as practicable, undue pollution of the waters of the Rivers which might affect adversely uses similar in nature to those to which the waters were put on the Effective Date, and agrees to take all reasonable measures to ensure that, before any sewage or industrial waste is allowed to flow into the Rivers, it will be treated, where necessary, in such manner as not materially to affect those uses: Provided that the criterion of reasonableness

shall be the customary practice, in similar situations on the Rivers.

Thus, rather than focusing on harm to, e.g. fish, health or property, this provision employs the standard of adverse effects upon certain uses of the waters in question. . . .

The more recent agreements concerning the pollution of international watercourses are typically more precise in defining water quality standards to be met or maintained, in setting water quality objectives, or in regulating the discharge into watercourses of different kinds of pollutants. The 1978 Agreement between Canada and the United States on Great Lakes Water Quality exemplifies this approach. . . .

Another example of a recent agreement, which classifies pollutants with regard to their character and regulates their discharge accordingly is the 1976 Convention on the protection of the Rhine against chemical pollution. Annex I of this agreement contains a so-called "black list" of dangerous substances, whose discharge into the Rhine the parties are to take appropriate steps to eliminate. Under article 3 of the Convention, "any discharge . . . that may contain one of the Annex I substances" is to be "subject to prior authorization from the competent authority of the government concerned." Annex II contains a "grey list" of less dangerous substances, whose discharge is to be reduced. The Convention also provides for national inventories of pollution discharges, which are to be reported to the International Commission for the Protection of the Rhine against Pollution. If a party to the agreement notes a "sudden and sizeable increase" in any of the substances listed in the annexes, or becomes aware of an accident that may seriously endanger the quality of the waters, Article 11 of the agreement requires that party to inform the Commission and the parties likely to be affected "without delay". . . .

Other agreements require consultation with or approval of the parties, or a joint commission, before action is taken which would alter water quality. For example, Article 4 of the 1972 Convention on the status of the River Senegal provides that no plan that may appreciably modify, inter alia, the sanitary condition of the waters, may be executed without prior approval of the contracting parties. . . . An analogous approach, reflected in a number of agreements, is to lay down only a general principle on pollution, leaving its elaboration and implementation to a joint commission. This approach, is, for example, envisaged in the 1974 Draft European Convention [for the Protection of International Watercourses Against Pollution] elaborated under the auspices of the Council of Europe, as well as in other European agreements. It is also adopted in the 1964 Convention and Statutes relating to the development of the Chad Basin.

2. GENERAL PRINCIPLES

RESOLUTION ON THE POLLUTION OF RIVERS AND LAKES AND INTERNATIONAL LAW ("ATHENS RESOLUTION")

Institute of International Law, Athens, September 12, 1979, Annuaire de l'Institut de droit international, vol. 58-I, Athens Session, Sept. 1979, at 197 (1980)[26]

THE INSTITUTE OF INTERNATIONAL LAW

Recalling its Resolutions of Madrid in 1911 and of Salzburg in 1961; Conscious of the multiple potential uses of international rivers and lakes and of the common interest in a rational and equitable utilization of such resources through the achievement of a reasonable balance between the various interests; Considering that pollution spread by rivers and lakes to the territories of more than one State is assuming increasingly alarming and diversified proportions whilst protection and improvement of the environment are duties incumbent upon States; Recalling the obligation to respect the sovereignty of every State over its territory, as a result of which each State has the obligation to avoid any use of its own territory that causes injury in the territory of another State, Hereby adopts the following articles:

Article I

1. For the purpose of this Resolution, "pollution" means any physical, chemical or biological alteration in the composition or quality of waters which results directly or indirectly from human action and affects the legitimate uses of such waters, thereby causing injury.

2. In specific cases, the existence of pollution and the characteristics thereof shall, to the extent possible, be determined by referring to environmental norms established through agreements or by the competent international organizations and commissions.

3. This Resolution shall apply to international rivers and lakes and to their basins.

Article II

In the exercise of their sovereign right to exploit their own resources pursuant to their own environmental policies, and without prejudice to their contractual obligations, States shall be under a duty to ensure that their activities or those conducted within their jurisdiction or under their control cause no pollution in the waters of international rivers and lakes beyond their boundaries.

Article III

1. For the purpose of fulfilling their obligation under Article II, States shall take, and adapt to the circumstances, all measures required

---

[26] Translation of authentic French text.

to: (a) prevent any new form of pollution or any increase in the existing degree of pollution; and (b) abate existing pollution within the best possible time limits.

2.   Such measures shall be particularly strict in the case of ultra-hazardous activities or activities which pose a danger to highly exposed areas or environments.

Article IV

In order to comply with the obligations set forth in Articles II and III, States shall in particular use the following means: (a) at national level, enactment of all necessary laws and regulations and adoption of efficient and adequate administrative measures and judicial procedures for the enforcement of such laws and regulations; (b) at international level, cooperation in good faith with the other States concerned.

Article V

States shall insure international liability under international law for any breach of their international obligations with respect to pollution of rivers and lakes.

Article VI

With a view to ensuring an effective system of prevention and of compensation for victims of transboundary pollution, States should conclude international conventions concerning in particular: (a) the jurisdiction of courts, the applicable law and the enforcement of judgements; (b) the procedure for special arrangements providing in particular for objective liability systems and compensation funds with regard to pollution brought about by ultra-hazardous activities.

Article VII

1.   In carrying out their duty to cooperate, States bordering the same hydrographic basin shall, as far as practicable, especially through agreements, resort to the following ways of cooperation:

(a) inform co-riparian States regularly of all appropriate data on the pollution of the basin, its causes, its nature, the damage resulting from it and the preventive procedures;

(b) notify the States concerned in due time of any activities envisaged in their own territories which may involve the basin in a significant threat of transboundary pollution;

(c) promptly inform States that might be affected by a sudden increase in the level of transboundary pollution in the basin and take all appropriate steps to reduce the effects of any such increase;

(d) consult with each other on actual or potential problems of trans-boundary pollution of the basin so as to reach, by methods of their own choice, a solution consistent with the interests of the States concerned and with the protection of the environment;

(e) coordinate or pool their scientific and technical research programs to combat pollution of the basin;

(f) establish by common agreement environmental norms, in particular quality norms for the whole or part of the basin;

(g) set up international commissions with the largest terms of reference for the entire basin, providing for the participation of local authorities if this proves useful, or strengthen the powers or coordination of existing institutions;

(h) establish harmonized, coordinated or unified networks for permanent observation and pollution control;

(i) develop safeguards for individuals who may be affected by polluting activities, both at the stages of prevention and compensation, by granting on a non-discriminatory basis the greatest access to judicial and administrative procedures in States in which such activities originate and by setting up compensation funds for ecological damage the origin of which cannot be clearly determined or which is of exceptional magnitude.

Article VIII

In order to assist developing States in the fulfillment of the obligations and in the implementation of the recommendation referred to in this Resolution, it is desirable that developed State and competent international organizations provide such States with technical assistance or any other assistance as may be appropriate in this field.

Article IX

This Resolution is without prejudice to the obligations which fundamental human rights impose upon State with regard to pollution occurring in their own territories.

BERLIN RULES ON THE USES OF WATERS OF INTERNATIONAL RIVERS

Presented to the 71st International Law Association (ILA) Meeting, Berlin, 2004

Article 27
Pollution

1. **States shall prevent, eliminate, reduce**, or control pollution in order to minimize environmental harm.

2.   When there is a relevant water quality standard established pursuant to Article 28, States shall take all appropriate measures to assure compliance with that standard.

3.   States shall ensure that wastes, pollutants, and hazardous substances are handled, treated, and disposed of using the best available techniques or the best environmental practices, as appropriate to protect the aquatic environment.

Commentary

The original Helsinki Rules addressed three articles to pollution, arts. IX–XI, focusing only on the risk that activities in one basin State would cause injury in other basin States. With the growing interest in protecting the environment, the International Law Association subsequently approved the Marine Pollution Rules (1972), the Belgrade Rules on the Relationship of International Water Resources with Other Natural Resources and Environmental Elements (1980), the Montreal Rules on Pollution (1982), and the Supplemental Rules on Pollution (1996). These several rules began as recommendations that States strengthen their steps to prevent or correct the pollution of internationally shared waters, and gradually strengthened the strictures into obligations. This progression matched the evolving practice of States, including multilateral and bilateral agreements, which was also moving in the direction of definite obligations regarding pollution. A similar rule was included in the UN Convention, art. 21. Today, the obligation to control pollution in order to produce the least net environmental harm is part of the customary international law of the environment. As the Rio Declaration and other instruments make clear, this obligation applies to the management of the waters within a State's jurisdiction and control as much as it applies to any other resource.

The UN Convention, art. 21, is limited to cross-border situations, but spells out in more detail the obligation of States to act against pollution. This Article sets forth the obligation in more general terms as an expression of the general obligation to minimize environmental harm as provided in Article 8. The obligation draws upon international environmental law to go beyond the earlier efforts of the Helsinki Rules and its supplements and the UN Convention. This Article not only dispenses with the limited view of preventing injury only to other basin States, but also transcends concerns limited solely to the pollution of water. It commands basin States to handle, treat, and dispose of wastes, pollutants, and hazardous materials with the best environmental practices or best available techniques as appropriate in order to minimize environmental harm.

"Best environmental practices" refers practices or prevent or reduce the effects of non-point sources of pollution, while "best available techniques" refers to techniques applied to prevent or reduce the effects of point sources of pollution. These are evolving concepts that cannot be precisely codified without preventing their further evolution. As indicated in Article 1(2), nothing in these Rules or in customary international law generally displaces the specific obligations spelled out in various treaties, including the growing body of treaties that define more precisely how wastes, pollutants, and hazardous materials are to be treated. These treaties define current standards of best environmental practices and best available techniques.

The goal of minimizing environmental harm recognizes that occasionally some degree of environmental harm must be accepted, but that overall environmental harm must be minimized if resource use is to be sustainable. The principle of integrated management further requires that the determination of how to proceed regarding wastes, pollutants, and hazardous materials should not be limited to consideration of only one medium or resource. These obligations apply to the transportation of wastes, pollutants, and hazardous materials as well as to their use or disposal.

This and other Articles do not mention the "polluter pays" principle, summarized in the Rio Declaration, pr. 16. This principle is built upon in Agenda 21, ch. 20, and has been widely embraced in European environmental law. The International Convention on Oil Pollution Preparedness, Response, and Cooperation, in its preamble, even describes "polluter pays" as a "general principle of international law." Despite such assertions, however, the polluter pays principle has not been widely adopted in international agreements outside of Europe. Most of the instruments referred to in this commentary describe the polluter pays principle as a goal ("insofar as possible") rather than as a binding norm. One cannot conclude that the polluter pays principle is in fact part of customary international law. The increasingly frequent recourse by States to economic incentives to prevent, eliminate, reduce, or control pollution is neither required nor precluded by this Article, but it serves to introduce at least some aspects of the polluter pays principle into water management.

UNITED NATIONS CONVENTION ON THE LAW OF THE NON-NAVIGATIONAL USES OF INTERNATIONAL WATERCOURSES
21 May 1997, U.N. Doc. A/RES/51/229, July 8, 1997, reprinted in 36 I.L.M. 700 (1997)

PART IV.   PROTECTION,   PRESERVATION   AND MANAGEMENT....

Article 21
Prevention, Reduction and Control of Pollution

1.   For the purpose of this article, "pollution of an international watercourse" means any detrimental alteration in the composition or

quality of the waters of an international watercourse which results directly or indirectly from human conduct.

2.   Watercourse States shall, individually and, where appropriate, jointly, prevent, reduce and control the pollution of an international watercourse that may cause significant harm to other watercourse States or to their environment, including harm to human health or safety, to the use of the waters for any beneficial purpose or to the living resources of the watercourse. Watercourse States shall take steps to harmonize their policies in this connection.

3.   Watercourse States shall, at the request of any of them, consult with a view to arriving at mutually agreeable measures and methods to prevent, reduce and control pollution of an international watercourse, such as: (a) Setting joint water quality objectives and criteria; (b) Establishing techniques and practices to address pollution from point and non-point sources; (c) Establishing lists of substances the introduction of which into the waters of an international watercourse is to be prohibited, limited, investigated or monitored.

Article 22
Introduction of Alien or New Species

Watercourse States shall take all measures necessary to prevent the introduction of species, alien or new, into an international watercourse which may have effects detrimental to the ecosystem of the watercourse resulting in significant harm to other watercourse States.

Article 23
Protection and Preservation of the Marine Environment

Watercourse States shall, individually and, where appropriate, in cooperation with other States, take all measures with respect to an international watercourse that are necessary to protect and preserve the marine environment, including estuaries, taking into account generally accepted international rules and standards.

UNITED NATIONS ECONOMIC COMMISSION FOR EUROPE (ECE) CONVENTION ON THE PROTECTION AND USE OF TRANSBOUNDARY WATERCOURSES AND INTERNATIONAL LAKES

March 17, 1992 (Helsinki Convention), reprinted in 31 LL.M. 1312 (1992)

Article 1
Definitions

For the purposes of this Convention, . . .

2.   "Transboundary impact" means any significant adverse effect on the environment resulting from a change in the conditions of transboundary waters caused by a human activity, the physical origin of

which is situated wholly or in part within an area under the jurisdiction of a Party, within an area under the jurisdiction of another Party. Such effects on the environment include effects on human health and safety, flora, fauna, soil, air, water, climate, landscape and historical monuments or other physical structures or the interaction among these factors; they also include effects on the cultural heritage or socio-economic conditions resulting from alterations to those factors; . . .

Article 2
General Provisions

. . .

2.   The Parties shall, in particular, take all appropriate measures:

(a) To prevent, control and reduce pollution of waters causing or likely to cause transboundary impact;

(b) To ensure that transboundary waters are used with the aim of ecologically sound and rational water management, conservation of water resources and environmental protection;

(c) To ensure that transboundary waters are used in a reasonable and equitable way, taking into particular account their transboundary character, in the case of activities which cause or are likely to cause transboundary impact;

(d) To ensure conservation and, where necessary, restoration of ecosystems.

3.   Measures for the prevention, control and reduction of water pollution shall be taken, where possible, at source.

4.   These measures shall not directly or indirectly result in a transfer of pollution to other parts of the environment.

5.   In taking the measures referred to in paragraphs 1 and 2 of this article, the Parties shall be guided by the following principles:

(a) The precautionary principle, by virtue of which action to avoid the potential transboundary impact of the release of hazardous substances shall not be postponed on the ground that scientific research has not fully proved a causal link between those substances, on the one hand, and the potential transboundary impact, on the other hand;

(b) The polluter-pays principle, by virtue of which costs of pollution prevention, control and reduction measures shall be borne by the polluter;

(c) Water resources shall be managed so that the needs of the present generation are met without compromising the ability of future generations to meet their own needs.

6.   The Riparian Parties shall cooperate on the basis of equality and reciprocity, in particular through bilateral and multilateral agreements, in order to develop harmonized policies, programmes and strategies covering the relevant catchment areas, or parts thereof, aimed at the prevention, control and reduction of transboundary impact and aimed at the protection of the environment of transboundary waters or the environment influenced by such waters, including the marine environment.

7.   The application of this Convention shall not lead to the deterioration of environmental conditions nor lead to increased transboundary impact.

8.   The provisions of this Convention shall not affect the right of Parties individually or jointly to adopt and implement more stringent measures than those set down in this Convention.

Article 3
Prevention, Control and Reduction

1.   To prevent, control and reduce transboundary impact, the Parties shall develop, adopt, implement and, as far as possible, render compatible relevant legal, administrative, economic, financial and technical measures, in order to ensure, inter alia, that:

(a) The emission of pollutants is prevented, controlled and reduced at source through the application of, inter alia, low- and non-waste technology;

(b) Transboundary waters are protected against pollution from point sources through the prior licensing of waste-water discharges by the competent national authorities, and that the authorized discharges are monitored and controlled;

(c) Limits for waste-water discharges stated in permits are based on the best available technology for discharges of hazardous substances;

(d) Stricter requirements, even leading to prohibition in individual cases, are imposed when the quality of the receiving water or the ecosystem so requires;

(e) At least biological treatment or equivalent processes are applied to municipal waste water, where necessary in a step-by-step approach;

(f) Appropriate measures are taken, such as the application of the best available technology, in order to reduce nutrient inputs from industrial and municipal sources;

(g) Appropriate measures and best environmental practices are developed and implemented for the reduction of inputs of nutrients and hazardous substances from diffuse sources, especially where the main sources are from agriculture (guidelines for developing best environmental practices are given in annex II to this Convention);

(h) Environmental impact assessment and other means of assessment are applied;

(i) Sustainable water-resources management, including the application of the ecosystems approach, is promoted;

(j) Contingency planning is developed;

(k) Additional specific measures are taken to prevent the pollution of groundwaters; (1) The risk of accidental pollution is minimized.

2.   To this end, each Party shall set emission limits for discharges from point sources into surface waters based on the best available technology, which are specifically applicable to individual industrial sectors or industries from which hazardous substances derive. The appropriate measures mentioned in paragraph 1 of this article to prevent, control and reduce the input of hazardous substances from point and diffuse sources into waters, may, inter alia, include total or partial prohibition of the production or use of such substances. Existing lists of such industrial sectors or industries and of such hazardous substances in international conventions or regulations, which are applicable in the area covered by this Convention, shall be taken into account.

3.   In addition, each Party shall define, where appropriate, water-quality objectives and adopt water-quality criteria for the purpose of preventing, controlling and reducing transboundary impact. General guidance for developing such objectives and criteria is given in annex III to this Convention. When necessary, the Parties shall endeavour to update this annex.

NOTES AND QUESTIONS

1.   *The approach of the 1997 UN Watercourses Convention.* The UN Watercourses Convention contains only one article on pollution, and of the three paragraphs in that article, one is devoted to defining that term. It is true that these articles should be read together with Articles 20 (Protection and preservation of ecosystems) and 22. But do they reflect a current and sophisticated approach to the control of pollution? How do they compare with the provisions of the 1992 ECE Water Convention? Can you see any reason or reasons for the differences in approach?

2.   *The UN Watercourses Convention's rules on pollution, harm, and equitable utilization.* The provisions of the United Nations Convention requiring equitable utilization (Article 5) and prohibiting harm to other states (Article 7) are set forth in Chapter 12. As is described there, the

equitable utilization and "no-harm" rules may come into conflict and if they do, the conflict would be resolved in accordance with Article 7(2). How do the convention's provisions on pollution fit in with those on equitable utilization and "no harm"? Does Article 21(2) take a "no-harm" approach? If so, why does it not flatly prohibit harmful transboundary pollution? If you believe it takes an equitable utilization approach, is this sound as a matter of policy? That is, can we speak of an "equitable right" to pollute?

3.   *The opening of the ECE Water Convention to universal participation.* The ECE is a regional organization including Europe (Western and Eastern), Russia, Central Asia, Canada and the United States. Until recently, the ECE Water Convention was, per Articles 23 and 25, for practical purposes open only to States in the ECE region and "regional economic integration organisations constituted by . . . States members of the [ECE]." (Principally the European Union.) It entered into force on October 6, 1996. Amendments to articles 25 and 26 of the convention opening it up to global participation were adopted in 2003 and entered into force on 6 February 2013. However, the amendments do not become operational until all Parties that were Parties in 2003, when the amendments were adopted, ratify them. As of this writing, Belgium, Kazakhstan and Ukraine have yet to ratify the amendments.

4.   *The ECE Water Convention and norms of allocation and use.* Is the ECE Water Convention concerned more with prevention of harm or allocation of water? If prevention of harm, why is it more concerned with this?

5.   *Mini-case study*: The Rhine Chlorides Case. Mines de Potasse d'Alsace (MDPA), a French state-owned potash mine near Mulhouse, has for many years been disposing of its waste salts by dumping them into the Rhine River. It alone was responsible for 54 percent of the total chloride content of the Rhine. The resulting salinity of Rhine water has caused various problems for downstream users. Horticulturists in the Netherlands, the lowest riparian on the Rhine, have found it necessary to treat the river's water before using it for their plants.

Three Dutch horticulturists and the Reinwater (literally, "clean water") Foundation brought suit against the MDPA in Rotterdam, seeking compensation for the damage they had suffered. After the jurisdiction of the Dutch court was confirmed by the European Court of Justice,[27] and long delays, the suit ultimately resulted in a judgment of the Netherlands Supreme Court in 1988 holding MDPA liable to compensate the plaintiffs for a share of the damage they had suffered, proportionate to MDPA's contribution to the Rhine's total chloride pollution load.[28]

In 1976 the Rhine Basin countries concluded the Rhine Chlorides Convention to address this problem. Bonn Convention on the Protection of the Rhine River Against Pollution by Chlorides, Dec. 3, 1976, *reprinted in* 16

---

[27] Handelskwekerij G.J. Bier B.V. v. Mines de Potasse d'Alsace S.A., Judgment of Nov. 30, 1976, Case 21/76.

[28] Judgment of Sept. 23, 1988, HR, 13,303 Rechtspraak van de Week 1988, at 150.

I.L.M. 265 (1977) (France, Germany, Luxembourg, the Netherlands, and Switzerland). Under the convention, the cost of reducing the discharge of salts is shared among France (30 percent), Germany (30 percent), the Netherlands (34 percent) and Switzerland (6 percent). The convention was not an immediate success, principally due to public protests in France against the alternative means of disposal it envisioned, namely, injection of the wastes underground. Protesters feared the injection could pollute groundwater used locally as a source of drinking water. Members of the French Parliament accordingly refused to ratify the Bonn Convention. The Netherlands was so angered by this refusal that it took the extraordinary step—especially for one EU Member State vis-á-vis another—of recalling its ambassador to France. The agreement eventually entered into force in July 1985, after it had been modified on the basis of new scientific studies. In September 1991 the Parties signed an additional protocol that eliminated injection as an alternative means of disposal, providing instead for discharge reductions when certain chloride levels are reached in the Rhine and for temporary storage on land. The protocol allows France to dispose of the stored chlorides by dumping them into the Rhine when the river reaches high flow levels. The costs of storage are shared by the Parties on the basis of the formula indicated above. On this case, see generally Carel H.V. De Villeneuve, *Western Europe's Artery: The Rhine*, 36 Nat. Res. J. 441, 445–448 (1996).

How does this attempted resolution of the Rhine salt problem square with the general principles contained in the above excerpts? Can you explain, in economic terms, why the Netherlands would have agreed to the arrangement contained in the Rhine Chlorides Convention? Will this arrangement result in market distortions? Do you believe private lawsuits such as the one described above can play a positive role in overall efforts to reduce Rhine pollution?

6.   *Unwanted Biodiversity.* The introduction of non-native species and organisms into watersheds can put many aquatic ecosystems around the world at risk. See Daniel Simberloff, *Non-Native Species Do Threaten the Natural Environment*, 18 J. Agri. and Envtl. Ethics 595 (2005). Mark Sagoff, *Do Non-Native Species Threaten the Natural Environment?* 18 J. Agri. and Envtl. Ethics 215 (2005), however, argues that this fear is overblown. Consider how Article 22 might have influenced the decisions that led to *Government of Manitoba v. Norton*, 338 F. Supp. 2d 41 (2005).

For years, the Bureau of Reclamation has been trying to build a large trans-basin irrigation and municipal water supply project in North Dakota. After years of opposition, the original Garrison Diversion project was drastically scaled back. The two countries sought an advisory opinion from the International Joint Commission (IJC) and in 1977 the IJC recommended that the Garrison Diversion not be constructed unless both Canada and the United States agreed that the risk to Canada was either eliminated or of no concern to her. In 1986, the United States Congress authorized a new, "lite" project, the North West Area Water Supply Project (NAWS), which is a joint

Bureau of Reclamation-North Dakota project. NAWS will transfer water from the Missouri to the Hudson Bay drainage basin. The project is driven in part by the desire to off-set downstream Canadian diversions on the Souris River which is in the Hudson Bay Basin. NAWS will divert water from a Missouri River storage reservoir, pre-treat it (chloramination), pipe it to Minot, North Dakota, which lies in the Hudson Bay Basin, where it will be again treated prior to final distribution. Manitoba has long objected to the project because of the risks to native species in Hudson Bay Basin. In 2001, the Bureau of Reclamation decided not to treat the water fully either at the point of diversion or at the Minot treatment plant. Full treatment was rejected because it would require a new $28 million plant. This contrasts to partial treatment which would require only a $16 million plant upgrade. The Bureau issued a Finding of No Significant Impact (FONSI) under the United States National Environmental Policy Act (NEPA). The FONSI concluded that the risk of the introduction of harmful biota into Canada was very low, especially compared to biota transfers from fishermen and birds.

Manitoba sued in the United States to set aside the FONSI. The federal district court held that despite years of study of the risks, the Bureau of Reclamation had not taken the "hard look" required by NEPA jurisprudence and remanded for "a more searching EA (Environmental Assessment) that considers an integrated analysis of the possibility of leakage and the potential consequences of the failure to fully treat the Missouri River water at its source given the agency's awareness of treatment-resistant biota." The court found that the Bureau's "studies are fatally flawed because they rely in large part upon water treatment standards that are too narrow to satisfy the agency's NEPA obligation to examine the potential for significant effect [sic] on the quality of the human environment." The court acknowledged that the risks of leakage were low, but found that "even a low risk of leakage may be offset by the possibility of catastrophic consequences should any leakage occur." *Government of Manitoba v. Norton*, 338 F. Supp. 2d 41 (2005). In March, 2006, the United States agreed to prepare a full EIS. 71 Fed. Reg. 11226, March 6, 2006. As of 2013, the Department of Interior had not prepared the EIS, but Minot, which is located in North Dakota's oil country, was allowed to finish upgrading its sewage plant but prohibited from constructing a new pipeline. *Manitoba v. Salazar*, Civil Action No. 02–2057 (RMC D.D.C. 2013).

7.   *Trail Smelter Redux.* Government of Manitoba v. Norton does not raise the problem that United States' statutes are presumed not to apply extraterritorially. E.g., Arc Ecology v. U.S. Dept. of Air Force, 411 F.3d 1092 (9th Cir. 2005) (U.S. Toxic waste site cleanup statute does not apply to former United States military bases in the Philippines); *F. Hoffman-La Roche Ltd. v. Empargran S.A.*, 542 U.S. 155 (2004). *Government of Manitoba* falls within the exception that the presumption does not apply when the regulated conduct occurs within the United States or outside a nation's territory. *Environmental Defense Fund, Inc. v. Massey*, 986 F.2d 528 (D.C. Cir. 1993) (U.S. NEPA applies to National Science Foundation facility in the Antarctic). See Lois J. Schiffer (Counsel for Manitoba), *The National Environmental*

Policy Act Today, with an Emphasis on its Application Across U.S. Borders, 14 Duke Envtl. L. & Policy F. 325 (2004).

United States action against the owner of the Trail Smelter, Teck Cominco, raises a harder issue. For many decades the smelter discharged heavy metals and mercury into the Columbia River. In 2003, the U.S. Environmental Protection Agency listed Lake Roosevelt, the 130-mile-long reservoir behind the Grand Coulee Dam on the Columbia and wholly within the United States, as eligible for listing on the CERCLA (Super-fund) National Priorities List. Teck Comico was ordered to investigate the extent of contamination at the site and to develop a remediation plan. *Pakootas v. Teck Comico Metals, Ltd*, 452 F.3d 1066 (9th Cir. 2006) affirmed a district court decision that the presumption against extraterritorial application did not apply when foreign-originated contamination comes to rest and causes harm in the United States. The Ninth Circuit held that the Canadian company was an arranger, that the location of the party who arranged for disposal was not controlling under CERCLA, and that the defendant was liable: "because the actual or threatened release of hazardous substances triggers CERCLA liability, and because the actual or threatened release here, the leaching of hazardous substances from slag that settled at the Site, took place in the United States, this case involves a domestic application of CERCLA." See Michael J. Robinson Dorn, *The Trail Smelter: Is What's Past Prologue? EPA Blazes a New Trail for CERCLA*, 14 N.Y. Envtl. L. J. 233 (2006); and Austen L. Parrish, *Trail Smelter Déjà Vu: Extraterritoriality, International Environmental Law, and the Search for Solutions to Canadian-U.S. Transboundary Water Pollution Disputes,* 85 B.U. L. Rev. 363 (2005).

8.   *Additional readings.* For further reading, see: Laurence Boisson de Chazournes, *International Institutions, Fresh Water and the Environment: Mutual Incentives*, 44 Envtl. Pol'y & L. 172 (2014); Edith Brown Weiss, International Law for a Water-Scarce World 7 (2013); Stephen C. McCaffrey, The Law of International Watercourses 59-60 (2nd ed. 2007); The UN Watercourse Convention in Force 6 (Flavia R. Loures & Alistair Rieu-Clarke 2013); World Wildlife Fund, International Architecture for Transboundary Water Resources Management: Policy Analysis and Recommendations (2010). For a description of good practices relating to integrating environmental protection into international and domestic water law, see UNEP, The Greening of Water Law: Managing Freshwater Resources for People and the Environment (2010), http://www.unep.org/delc/Portals/119/UNEP_Greening_water_law.pdf.

3.   CASE STUDY: PROTECTION OF THE GREAT LAKES ECOSYSTEM

CONTROLLING GREAT LAKES POLLUTION: A STUDY IN UNITED STATES-CANADIAN ENVIRONMENTAL COOPERATION

Richard Bilder
70 Mich. L. Rev. 469, 473–475, 480484 (1972)

I.   BACKGROUND

United States-Canadian cooperation regarding Great Lakes pollution problems has developed within a special geographical, economic, legal, and political context. A brief description of this setting may suggest the significance of these pollution problems and some of the reasons for the particular form this cooperation has taken.

The United States-Canadian boundary is one of the longest in the world, extending for about 3,500 miles from Passamaquoddy Bay on the Atlantic to the Fuca Straits of Vancouver on the Pacific, and along the Alaskan-Canadian boundary, for another 1,500 miles from the Pacific to the Arctic Ocean. About 2,000 miles of this boundary is water; it passes along rivers such as the St. Croix, St. John, and the St. Lawrence, through Lake Ontario, the Niagara River, Lake Erie, the Detroit River, Lake St. Clair, the St. Clair River, Lake Huron, the St. Mary's River, and Lake Superior, and on to Rainy Lake and Lake of the Woods. In addition, a number of rivers, such as the Red, the Columbia, and the Yukon, flow across the boundary.

The Great Lakes constitute the largest fresh-water system in the world, representing about a quarter of the world's total fresh-water supply. Of the total Great Lakes' water area of 95,000 square miles, about two-thirds is within United States jurisdiction and one-third in Canadian jurisdiction. Of the total Great Lakes drainage basin area of some 300,000 square miles, about 59 percent is in the United States and 41 percent in Canada. Eight states, Illinois, Indiana, Michigan, Minnesota, New York, Ohio, Pennsylvania, and Wisconsin, border on the Great Lakes, and a number of others have close economic links with the region. In Canada, only the Province of Ontario borders on the Lakes, although the Province of Quebec also has considerable concern with Great Lakes problems.

In 1966 some 30 million people lived on or near the Great Lakes, comprising about one out of every three Canadians and one out of every eight Americans. All indications are that the Great Lakes' population is rapidly expanding; projections for the year 2000 suggest the emergence of a Great Lakes megalopolis with a population approaching 60 million people.

In view of the length of this common boundary and the substantial clustering of people and industry along certain portions of it, it is not surprising that problems of boundary waters and transboundary pollution have assumed a growing importance in United States-Canadian relations. While the concern of the two governments with boundary pollution problems dates back at least to the early years of the twentieth century, these problems have assumed a new dimension and importance as a result of rapid industrial and population development during and after the Second World War. . . .

II.   THE DEVELOPMENT OF GREAT LAKES ENVIRONMENTAL COOPERATION: FRAMEWORK,   INSTITUTIONS,   AND HISTORY

A.   THE 1909 TREATY

The basic framework for American-Canadian cooperation respecting boundary waters problems is the [Boundary Waters Treaty of 1909 (1909 Treaty)],[29] which establishes the International Joint Commission between the United and Canada. The Treaty, which developed out of earlier ad hoc efforts to deal with boundary waters questions, was designed primarily to protect the levels and navigability of the Great Lakes and other boundary waters against unilateral diversion or obstruction, but it has provided the basis for an increasing involvement by the Commission in pollution and other problems as well. . . .

The Treaty distinguishes (1) "boundary waters," which are defined as those waters along which the international boundary runs; (2) "tributary waters," which are defined as the waters flowing into boundary waters; (3) waters flowing from boundary waters; and (4) the waters of rivers flowing across the boundary. For example, since the International Boundary does not run through Lake Michigan, that Lake is considered a tributary water rather than a boundary water.

The rights and obligations of the countries under the Treaty differ among these various categories of waters. Thus, the Treaty provides that navigation of all boundary waters shall be free and open to the inhabitants and vessels of each country without discrimination; this same right shall apply to the waters of Lake Michigan and to canals connecting boundary waters. On the other hand, the Treaty provides that each country retains exclusive jurisdiction and control over the use and diversion of all waters on its own side of the boundary that in their natural channels would flow across the boundary or into boundary waters. However, if through interference with or diversion of such waters

---

[29] [Treaty with Great Britain Relating to Boundary Waters and Question Arising Between the United States and Canada, Jan. 11, 1909, 36 Stat. 2448 (1910), T.S. No. 548, 12 Bevans 319, entered into force May 5, 1910. Professor Bilder explains in footnote 34: "The 1909 Treaty was signed by Great Britain on behalf of Canada, which did not acquire full powers in treaty-making until 1923. However, the Treaty has been implemented completely by Canada."—Eds.]

injury is caused on the other side of the boundary, any injured party is entitled to the same legal remedies as if that injury had taken place in the country where the diversion or interference occurred. Moreover, neither party surrenders rights it may have to object to interference with or diversion of waters on the other side of the boundary that would have the effect of materially injuring navigation on its own side of the boundary.

A principal purpose of the 1909 Treaty is the regulation of uses, obstructions, or diversions of the boundary waters, and the Commission is given broad powers in this respect, which again are stated with reference to particular categories of waters. Unless otherwise provided by special agreement, the Commission's approval is required for any uses, obstructions, or diversions of boundary waters on either side of the boundary that affect the natural level or flow of boundary waters on the other side of the boundary. Moreover, the Commission's approval is required for the construction or maintenance "of any remedial or protective works or any dams or other obstructions in waters flowing from boundary waters or in waters at a lower level than the boundary in rivers flowing across the boundary, the effect of which is to raise the natural level of waters on the other side of the boundary." In passing upon such cases, the Commission is to be guided by certain rules and principles. One of these is that each party shall have, on its own side of the boundary, equal and similar rights in the use of the boundary waters. Another is that an order of precedence is established among various uses of the waters, namely: (1) uses for domestic and sanitary purposes; (2) uses for navigation; and (3) uses for power and irrigation purposes. No use shall be permitted by the Commission that tends materially to conflict with or restrain a preferred use.

Article IV of the Treaty includes a provision that "boundary waters and water flowing across the boundary shall not be polluted on either side to the injury of health or property on the other." Neither the term "pollution" nor the term "injury" is defined, and the Treaty is silent with respect to any procedures for enforcement of this obligation.

Finally, the Treaty establishes broad and flexible provisions concerning the handling of disputes and other questions between the governments. Article IX authorizes the Commission to render advisory reports to the governments at their request. It provides that "any other questions or matters of difference arising between (the two countries) involving the rights, obligations, or interests of either in relation to the other or to the inhabitants of the other, along the common frontier . . . shall be referred from time to time to the . . . Commission for examination and report" whenever either government requests such reference. The Commission is authorized in each case so referred to examine and report upon the facts and circumstances of the particular questions, together with such conclusions and recommendations as may be appropriate, subject, however, to any restrictions that may be imposed by the terms of the reference. "Such reports of the Commission shall not be regarded as decisions of the questions or matters so submitted either on the facts or the law, and shall in no way have the character of an arbitral award." Procedures are set forth governing such advisory references. In addition, Article X provides detailed procedures under which questions or matters of difference may be referred to the Commission, by the consent of the two governments, for a binding arbitral decision or finding. To date, however, the provisions of Article X have never been utilized.

THE GREAT LAKES WATER QUALITY AGREEMENT

National Research Council of the United States and Royal Society of Canada, The Great Lakes Water Quality Agreement: An Evolving Instrument for Ecosystem Management 2, 4, 7–9, 77–78, 80, 83–84, 85–86,91–92, 93 (1985)

[The following is excerpted from a report of a group of experts appointed by the United States National Research Council and the Royal Society of Canada to review the Great Lakes Water Quality Agreement. A protocol subsequently added to the agreement reflected certain findings of the report.—Eds.]

THE GREAT LAKES BASIN AND THE 1978 AGREEMENT

The Great Lakes basin's waters include the five Great Lakes (Figure 7–1 below) and four major connecting channels, with most of the outflow eventually entering the Gulf of St. Lawrence. The relatively small land area of the basin has many urban areas and centers of industrial activity, most of which are expanding. Significant areas of the basin are devoted to agriculture and forestry in which industrialized practices predominate. There is also a hinterland that is sparsely settled but used for recreational purposes. The industrial, commercial, and residential life of some 37 million humans in the basin, and many more millions living outside of it, have the potential to produce intense impacts on the basin ecosystem.

Figure 7–1
The Great Lakes

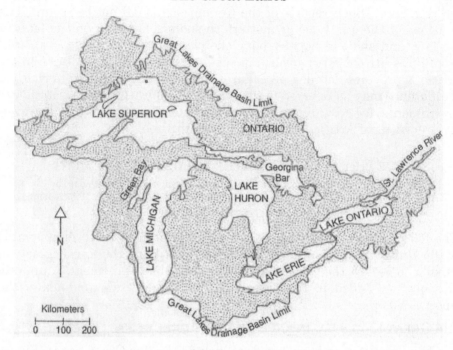

Source: National Research Council of the United States and Royal Society of Canada,
The Great Lakes Water Quality Agreement: An Evolving Instrument for Ecosystem
Management 3 (1985).

One unique characteristic of the basin . . . is the fact that two of the lakes, Michigan and Superior, have a water renewal time of 100 years or more (water renewal time is a relative indication of the time required to flush out contaminants). The two lower lakes, Erie and Ontario, can be flushed more quickly, but their inflowing water comes predominantly from the upper lakes, which, if contaminated, exert a profound influence on the lower lakes.

Both the 1972 and 1978 Great Lakes Water Quality Agreements (GLWQA) are widely recognized as among the world's pioneering international instruments designed to foster intergovernmental cooperation to correct pollution in a large river basin. As such, the committee believes that the two governments should continue and strengthen the 1978 GLWQA. These Agreements were undertaken in the context of the 1909 Boundary Waters Treaty between the United States and Canada, also a pioneering initiative for the time. That Treaty is concerned largely with water levels and flows but also with transboundary pollution. Several bi-national assessments of transboundary pollution problems were undertaken by the IJC within the framework of the Treaty between 1916 and 1968. The 1972 and 1978

Agreements are a continuing (albeit atypical) reference under the Treaty, recognizing that periodic attempts to correct damages from pollution had been unsuccessful. By 1972, management capabilities had been developed with respect to water levels and flows, but water-quality actions were mostly reactive to events after they had reached crises. Over the past century, several different types of action by human activities within the basin have led to deleterious effects on the water and aquatic biota. The problems have gradually expanded from local, to lake-wide, to a basin-wide scale. Some of these actions have caused relatively benign influences and some have been quite harmful; some have had relatively short-term consequences and others have affected the ecosystem for long periods of time. Some problems are readily apparent to laymen and some can be documented only by using advanced scientific methods. . . .

TOXIC CONTAMINANTS[30]

The parties made numerous commitments in the 1978 Agreement . . . concerning objectives and programs to control the amounts of "persistent toxic substances" and "hazardous polluting substances" entering the Great Lakes basin ecosystem. In retrospect, these goals were ambitious but probably appropriate for the time especially with respect to zero discharge. The "zero discharge" of persistent toxic substances for which no lower threshold of safety is apparent is consistent with Article IV in the 1909 Boundary Waters Treaty stating that the two countries should not pollute the boundary waters to the injury of the other.

Some progress has been made toward reduction of industrial discharges of toxic substances, although some problems remain. At the same time, toxics originating from contaminated groundwater or from atmospheric deposition are more important sources to the Great Lakes than originally thought. Although tightly regulated, certain persistent compounds such as DDT, PCBs, and dioxins apparently continue to enter Great Lakes waters. Toxic substances in sediments continue to be a source for bioaccumulation through food chains into harvestable fish, especially in areas of concern in all the state and provincial jurisdictions. Leakage of contaminants from landfill sites into the Niagara River and into the St. Clair River are of great concern. Therefore, the committee strongly endorses the 1985 Great Lakes Science Advisory Board recommendation for mapping of groundwater conditions around and under the Great Lakes basin for the necessity of data on geology and hydrology, soils, and depth to water tables. Toxic substances are carried into Great Lakes waters by vaporization from treatment plants, combustion of fossil fuels, and incineration of waste products from all

---

[30] [The U.S.-Canada Strategy for Virtual Elimination of Toxics in Great Lakes, known as the Great Lakes Binational Toxics Strategy, was signed April 7, 1997. It is available at http://www.epa.gov/greatlakes/p2/bnsintro.html.—Eds.]

parts of the basin and beyond it. Toxic substances are also transported to the lakes through the atmosphere from far outside the basin.

In this regard, the committee finds that the toxic substances control programs that were relatively easy for governments to act on have progressed furthest (e.g., controls on use of pesticides and on emissions from certain industrial point sources). However, most of the progress on these sources had been made before the 1978 Agreement without reference to the Great Lakes. The more difficult programs, such as controls on diffuse sources, remediation of contamination from landfill sites, development and implementation of measures to control in-place pollutants, and a more general comprehensive strategy to control atmospheric deposition of toxic substances, have been slow in advancing. For these difficult issues, researchers are still seeking to define and quantify the magnitude of the risks, and program managers and engineers are still considering various corrective measures. Funding for such research, which would result in the needed technological innovation, has been both limited and uncertain.

The committee concludes that the current programs for controlling persistent toxic substances in the Great Lakes Ecosystem are inadequate. Of concern are the lipophilic character of many of the chemicals (such as PCBs and dioxins), the hydrologic residence times of some of the contaminants in the lakes, the ability of the chemicals to biomagnify in the food chains, the evidence of effects on the ecosystem, and possible subtle effects on humans exposed to the chemicals. The lack of effective control measures seems likely to affect many generations to come. Thus, there is an urgency to achieve a reduction of toxic pollutants in the Great Lakes and thereby to reduce the risks to the human population using the resources of the basin.

The committee therefore recommends that measures be taken to increase the awareness of the public (including industry and politicians) as to the extent and implications of the toxic chemical problems in the Great Lakes basin.

Despite the general goal of zero discharge from known point sources, the jurisdictions on both sides of the border seem not consider the goal practicable and are accepting moderate levels of contaminant releases from industrial and other sources. The committee finds that significant sources of contamination have remained relatively uncontrolled in the Great Lakes for many years. While the Water Quality Board in 1984 began to develop plans for remedial action in the areas of concern, significant revisions of the relevant sections of the Agreement are still essential. *The committee recommends that the Agreement encourage action on the major sources of contamination at the areas of concern, that effective solutions be implemented, and that rigorous valuative case studies be undertaken and published.* Overall, the committee finds that the sources of toxic substances in the Great Lakes basin are larger and more diverse than was anticipated in 1978, and that control programs need to be much more comprehensive than anticipated.

In view of the above, the committee strongly recommends that, as part of a comprehensive toxic substances management strategy, there should be components that deal fully with the diverse sources of contamination. This will require:

- An inventory of all sources of toxic chemicals found at potentially significant levels in the Great Lakes ecosystem and, within the limits of data availability, those that are not responding to present control actions. This inventory would include extra-basin and intra-basin gaseous and particulate emissions, land-based inputs, resuspension from sediments, and inputs from contaminated groundwater.

- Actions toward an effective long-term solution to leaking toxic waste dumps recognizing that although expensive in the short run, the result can be expected to be of benefit to the health of the Great Lakes ecosystem and human population.

- Control actions against all identifiable sources of toxic chemicals to the Great. Lakes basin. Studies on the cost-effectiveness of action programs should include the long-term benefits of such programs.

- Siting and operation of modern toxic-waste treatment centers in all regions of the basin. An annex should be added to the Agreement to provide for strict management of toxic wastes, both those disposed of carelessly in the past and those in prospect for the future.

Existing toxic-waste dumps as sources of contaminants to Great Lakes water are an especially difficult problem. Removal and treatment of these toxic wastes are difficult because they are mixed with earth, debris, and other solid wastes. The nature of the chemicals in these sites is often unknown, and the groundwater may be contaminated. Although action plans are being developed for the most serious sites, the committee recommends that the Agreement recognize this issue as an area of priority action. . . .

NEW RESPONSIBILITY—DISPUTE RESOLUTION

One important issue in implementing any Agreement is the resolution of disputes concerning alleged violations of the Agreement. To date, disputes over the implementation of the 1978 Agreement have been few. Indeed, there has been only one important dispute over an alleged violation of the Agreement, the Niagara River controversy. At issue was whether the United States was in violation of the 1978 Agreement because of seepage of pollutants from landfills into the Niagara River and, hence, into Lake Ontario. This dispute was addressed outside the framework of the Agreement and the IJC in the ad hoc intergovernmental Niagara River Toxics Committee.

The committee is concerned that these disputes will increase. [T]he 1978 Agreement sets forth highly detailed obligations of the parties relating to the control of water pollution in the Great Lakes. Moreover, as scientific knowledge advances, there may be more specific standards incorporated into the Agreement. Also, the inclusion into the Agreement of implementation deadlines may become more necessary and frequent.

1978 GREAT LAKES WATER QUALITY AGREEMENT BETWEEN THE UNITED STATES AND CANADA AS AMENDED BY THE 1983 AND 1987 PROTOCOLS

Done at Ottawa Nov. 22, 1978, 30 U.S.T. 1383, T.I.A.S. 9257, as amended Oct. 16, 1983, T.I.A.S. 10798 and Nov. 18, 1987, T.I.A.S. 11551, consolidated in International Joint Commission, Revised Great Lakes Water Quality Agreement of 1978 (1988) *available at* http://www.ijc.org/files/tinymce/uploaded/GLWQA_e.pdf

Article I
Definitions

As used in this Agreement:

. . .

(g) "Great Lakes Basin Ecosystem" means the interacting components of air, land, water and living organisms, including humans, within the drainage basin of the St. Lawrence River at, or upstream from, the point at which this river becomes the international boundary between Canada and the United States. . . .

Article II
Purpose

The purpose of the Parties is to restore and maintain the chemical, physical, and biological integrity of the waters of the Great Lakes Basin Ecosystem. In order to achieve this purpose, the Parties agree to make a maximum effort to develop programs, practices and technology necessary for a better understanding of the Great Lakes Basin Ecosystem and to eliminate or reduce to the maximum extent practicable the discharge of pollutants into the Great Lakes System.

Consistent with the provisions of this Agreement, it is the policy of the Parties that:

(a) The discharge of toxic substances in toxic amounts be prohibited and the discharge of any or all persistent toxic substances be virtually eliminated;

(b) Financial assistance to construct publicly owned waste treatment works be provided by a combination of local, state, provincial, and federal participation; and

(c) Coordinated planning processes and best management practices be developed and implemented by the respective jurisdictions to ensure adequate control of all sources of pollutants.

Article III
General Objectives

The Parties adopt the following General Objectives for the Great Lakes System. These waters should be:

(a) Free from substances that directly or indirectly enter the waters as a result of human activity and that will settle to form putrescent or otherwise objectionable sludge deposits or that will adversely affect aquatic life or waterfowl;

(b) Free from floating materials such as debris, oil, scum, and other immiscible substances resulting from human activities in amounts that are unsightly or deleterious;

(c) Free from materials and heat directly or indirectly entering the water as a result of human activity that alone, or in combination with other materials, will produce color, odor, taste, or other conditions in such a degree as to interfere with beneficial uses;

(d) Free from materials and heat directly or indirectly entering the water as a result of human activity that alone, or in combination with other materials, will produce conditions that are toxic or harmful to human, animal, or aquatic life; and

(e) Free from nutrients directly or indirectly entering the waters as a result of human activity in amounts that create growths of aquatic life that interfere with beneficial uses.

Article IV
Specific Objectives

1. The Parties adopt the Specific Objectives for the boundary waters of the Great Lakes System as set forth in Annex 1, subject to the following:

(a) The Specific Objectives adopted pursuant to this Article represent the minimum levels of water quality desired in the boundary waters of the Great Lakes System and are not intended to preclude the establishment of more stringent requirements.

(b) The determination of the achievement of Specific Objectives shall be based on statistically valid sampling data.

(c) Notwithstanding the adoption of Specific Objectives, all reasonable and practicable measures shall be taken to maintain or improve the existing water quality in those areas of the boundary waters of the Great Lakes System where such water quality is better than that prescribed by the Specific Objectives, and in those areas having outstanding natural resource value.

(d) The responsible regulatory agencies shall not consider flow augmentation as a substitute for adequate treatment to meet the Specific Objectives.

(e) The Parties recognize that, in certain areas of inshore waters, natural phenomena exist which, despite the best efforts of the Parties, will prevent the achievement of some of the Specific Objectives. As early as possible, these areas should be identified explicitly by the appropriate jurisdictions and reported to the International Joint Commission.

(f) The Parties recognize that there are areas in the boundary waters of the Great Lakes System where, due to human activity, one or more of the General or Specific Objectives of that Agreement are not being met. Pending virtual elimination of persistent toxic substances in the Great Lakes System, the Parties, in cooperation with State and Provincial Governments and the Commission, shall identify and work toward the elimination of: (i) Areas of Concern pursuant to Annex 2; (ii) Critical Pollutants pursuant to Annex 2; and (iii) Point Source Impact Zones pursuant to Annex 2.

2.   The Specific Objectives for the boundary waters of the Great Lakes System or for particular portions thereof shall be kept under review by the Parties and the International Joint Commission, which shall make appropriate recommendations.

3.   The Parties shall consult on:

(a) The establishment of Specific Objectives to protect beneficial uses from the combined effects of pollutants; and

(b) The control of pollutant loading rates for each lake basin to protect the integrity of the ecosystem over the long term. . . .

NOTES AND QUESTIONS

1.   *The legal implications of the ecosystem approach.* The 1978 Protocol differs from the 1972 Agreement in that it incorporates the concept of basin

ecosystem management to indicate that the Parties are not concerned solely with contamination of the lakes themselves or direct discharges into them. What difference does this concept make in the parties' legal obligations? In implementation of the agreement?

2. *Legal obligations under the 1987 Protocol.* We have seen that as a result of the 1985 report Canada and the United States adopted the 1987 Protocol to the 1978 Agreement, which addressed groundwater contamination and atmospheric transport of toxic chemicals. Does the protocol obligate the Parties to undertake any specific activities? What problems do you foresee for the Parties in implementing obligations to control groundwater contamination? See generally George Francis, *Binational Cooperation for Great Lakes Water Quality: A Framework for the Groundwater Connection*, 65 CHI.-KENT L. REV. 359 (1989).

3. *The role of the IJC.* The 1978 Great Lakes Water Quality Agreement and its predecessor in 1972 were negotiated as a result of a Reference to the International Joint Commission (IJC) under Article IX of the 1909 Boundary Waters Treaty. Given this, could Canada or the United States use the reference procedures of Article IX for issues that arise under the Great Lakes Agreement? At various times, both Canada and the United States have advanced the argument that the Treaty preempts domestic litigation, although Article IX provides that IJC reports do not have the character of an arbitral award. It seems clear that under United States law the Treaty is not a bar to domestic legal proceedings. Ohio v. Wyandotte Chems. Corp., 401 U.S. 493, 500–501 (1971), rev'd by implication on other grounds, International Paper Co. v. Ouellette, 479 U.S. 481, 488 n.8 (1987). Nonetheless, a 2006 citizen submission to the North American Commission for Environmental Cooperation (NAAEC), SEM-06-002, alleged that Canada and the United States have failed to enforce the Boundary Waters Treaty by not referring a dispute to the IJC. The submission alleged that the construction of a drain in Devils Lake, North Dakota, will discharge toxic pollutants and alien species into the Hudson Bay drainage basin. The submission was dismissed because of the considerable uncertainty whether the Treaty was a law or regulation under either Canadian or United States law within the meaning of NAAEC Section 14 of the NAAEC limits the Commission's power concerning citizen submissions on enforcement matters to cases in which a Party is alleged to have failed to effectively enforce "environmental law." Determination in Accordance with Article 14(1) of the North American Agreement for Environmental Cooperation, SEM 06–002/04/14(1), August 21, 2006. CEC determination available at http://www.cec.org/Page.asp?PageID=2001&ContentID=2397&SiteNodeID=560&BL_ExpandID=.

4. *2012 Protocol Amending the Great Lakes Water Quality Agreement.* The 2012 Protocol emphasizes science-based management and monitoring, strengthens the process of public input and participation, and refers to the goal of "coordinating efforts to identify, quantify, understand and predict the climate change impacts on the quality of the Waters of the Great Lakes, and

sharing information that Great Lakes resource managers need to proactively address these impacts."[31]

5.   *The Virtual Elimination Strategy.* In 1997, Canada and the United States signed the Binational Strategy for the Virtual Elimination of Persistent Toxic Substances from the Great Lakes Basin. Among other things, the strategy identifies quantitative targets for reduction of anthropogenic use, discharge, and release of certain compounds of serious concern, including, PCBs (polychlorinated biphenyls), mercury, dioxin, and furans. Canada and the United States continue to implement the strategy. Lakewide Management Plans (LaMPS) have been prepared by the United States Environmental Protection Agency for four of the lakes, and these plans set out Remedial Action Plans (RAPS) for specific areas. Considerable progress has been made in reducing dioxins and furons and HCP releases, but old problems such as contaminated sediments remain. New problems such as mercury deposition have emerged. See Coal-Fired Power Plants, Submission to Commission on Environmental Cooperation SEM-04055, *available   at*   www.cec.org/Page.asp?PageID=2001&ContentID=2390& SiteNodeID=545&BL_ExpandID. International Joint Commission, 16th Biennial Report on Great Lakes Water Quality (2013) summarizes the progress and remaining problems:

> Since 1987, all seven indicators of chemical integrity have shown mostly favorable or stable results. The levels of many persistent toxic chemicals entering the Great Lakes from atmospheric deposition are lower than they were in 1987. Concentrations of most measured persistent toxic chemicals decreased in herring gulls, fish, sediments and mussels. Most reductions occurred from 1987 to 2000, but since 2000 trends vary by chemical, location, and species. However, concentrations of some chemicals of emerging concern have increased since 1987. For instance, concentrations of polybrominated diphenyl ethers (PBDEs, harmful chemicals used as flame retardants) in fish doubled every few years from 1980 to 2000 and then started to decline slightly following voluntary phase-outs of two PBDE formulations by industry. The five biological indicators show mixed results. From 1987 to 2006, 34 nonnative species became established in the Great Lakes mostly from ballast water discharges. However, no species have been introduced from ballast water since 2006. Populations of the burrowing mayfly and lake sturgeon have started to recover. The number of lake trout in four of the five Great Lakes has been stable overall with year-to-year fluctuations, largely due to stocking, but are still below targets. Diporeia, a small shrimplike invertebrate, a key part of the aquatic food web and a food source for many fish, has almost disappeared. The two physical indicators, surface water temperature and ice

---

[31] [Protocol Amending the Agreement Between Canada and the United States of America on Great Lakes Water Quality, 1978, as Amended on October 16, 1983 and on November 18, 1987, at annex 9, pt. A (Sept. 7, 2012), http://www.epa.gov/glnpo/glwqa/20120907-Canada-USA_GLWQA_FINAL.pdf.—Eds.]

cover, both indicate a warming trend, suggesting that global climate change is affecting the Great Lakes. This could lead to shifts in species composition, including increased frequency of harmful algal blooms. One of the two performance indicators evaluated progress in restoring areas that were previously identified as degraded and officially designated as areas of concern (AOCs). Of the original 43 AOCs, four have been restored to the point that they are no longer considered AOCs and they have been delisted. Approximately 25 percent of the beneficial use impairments in the remaining AOCs have been removed because of the environmental improvements. The other performance indicator evaluated progress in keeping beaches safe and open. Beach closings based on bacteria levels have remained fairly stable over the reporting period of about ten years, but are still common.

IJC, 16th Biennial Report, *available at* http://www.ijc.org.

6.   *The Great Lakes regime as a model.* On the basis of your reading of the materials in this Chapter, to what extent do you believe the treaty regime for the control of Great Lakes pollution can serve as a model for other international watercourses? Is it *sui generis*? Why or why not? In determining whether a particular water pollution control regime is applicable to other watercourses, what is most important: the characteristics (i.e., levels of development, etc.) of the countries involved and the relations between them, or the nature of the watercourses governed by the regime?

CHAPTER 8

CONTROLLING OZONE DEPLETION

■ ■ ■

In the stratosphere, high above Earth, a layer of ozone (O_3) filters ultraviolet radiation from sunlight, protecting Earth and its inhabitants. In recent years, the ozone layer has been threatened by human-made chemicals, such as chlorofluorocarbons (CFCs), which are used in air conditioners and refrigerators. As described in detail below, these chemicals can migrate into the stratosphere and destroy the ozone layer. In the Antarctic, a large hole has developed in the ozone layer, and most recently, significant thinning of the ozone layer over the Arctic has developed. Holes in the ozone layer or even depletion of the density of the ozone layer mean more ultraviolet radiation reaches Earth. This can cause skin cancer and cataracts in humans and damage flora and fauna, including phyto-plankton, which are the basis of the food chain in the ocean.

The depletion of the stratospheric ozone layer must be distinguished from the problem of ozone pollution in the lower atmosphere (the troposphere). In the air we breathe, large quantities of ozone—emitted by cars, for example—damage human health. Thus, ozone is an air pollutant that the United States and other States regulate.

Depletion of the ozone layer is an inherently long-term, intergenerational issue. Chlorine chemicals we produce today drift up to the stratosphere over time and remain there to deplete the ozone layer. They dissipate only over time. Chlorine chemical emissions today cause damage decades in the future.

Concern about the health of the ozone layer led to a historic agreement in 1985, the Vienna Convention for the Protection of the Ozone Layer, negotiated under the auspices of the United Nations Environment Programme. The agreement provided a framework for monitoring and learning about the ozone layer but did not provide specific controls on substances believed to deplete the ozone layer. In 1987, States adopted a protocol to the agreement that does provide such controls: the Montreal Protocol on Substances That Deplete the Ozone Layer. Because it is a protocol, States wishing to join the agreement must become parties to the Vienna Convention for the Protection of the Ozone Layer as well as to the Protocol.

Since the adoption of the Protocol in 1987, scientific evidence suggested that the problem of ozone depletion was more serious than originally believed and that additional chemicals were reducing the ozone layer. This has led to four amendments to the Protocol and to six "adjustments" to the target and timetable for phasing out chemicals listed under the Protocol. The Montreal Protocol includes a unique provision that enables States Parties to the Protocol to respond quickly to new scientific data by agreeing to accelerate the reductions required on chemicals already covered by the Protocol; these are referred to as "adjustments". The adjustments then apply automatically to all States Parties to the Protocol, without the need for States to ratify the provisions.

The Montreal Protocol has had four amendments, as mentioned above. Under the first amendment, the London Amendment (1990), Parties agreed to add additional chemicals to the controlled list (other fully halogenated CFCs, carbon tetrachloride, and 1,1,1-trichloroethane) and to establish a multilateral fund (the Montreal Protocol Fund). The Copenhagen Amendment (1992) added other chemicals (hydrochlorofluorocarbons, hydrobromofluorocarbons, and methyl bromide) to the list of controlled substances. States Parties also agreed to establish an annex listing products containing certain controlled substances and for each State to ban the import and export of the listed products containing controlled substances within three years, unless it objected to the annex. Within five years, States Parties were to explore the feasibility of banning the import and export of products produced with certain controlled substances.

Under the Montreal Amendment (1997), States Parties set forth a timeline by which Parties would "establish and implement a system for licensing the import and export of new, used, recycled and reclaimed of controlled substances." Under the Beijing Amendment (1999), Parties agreed to place controls on bromochloromethane.

As you read these materials, consider what general norms of international environmental law might apply in the absence of an agreement. Why could the Protocol be negotiated successfully? Why was it amended so quickly in 1990? Are the provisions in the Protocol adequate to cope with rapidly changing scientific knowledge about the ozone layer? Why do States Parties have relatively good records in implementing and complying with the agreement?

Furthermore, consider that substitutes for ozone depleting substances may be powerful greenhouse gasses. Thus, while CFCs are phased out, CFC substitutes—hydrochlorofluorocarbons (HCFCs) and hydrofluorocarbons (HFCs)—have unintended and opposing side effects.

A. THE SCIENTIFIC BACKGROUND

1.   THE OZONE LAYER

The following excerpt by Richard Benedick, the chief United States negotiator for the Montreal Protocol, discusses the historical evolution of scientific understanding of the problem of ozone depletion and the role that science played in reaching an agreement.

OZONE DIPLOMACY
Richard E. Benedick
Ch. 2, excerpt (Harvard University Press, 1991)

The Montreal Protocol was the result of research at the frontiers of science combined with a unique collaboration between scientists and policy makers. Unlike any previous diplomatic endeavor, it is based on continually evolving theories, on state-of-the-art computer models simulating the results of intricate chemical and physical reactions for decades into the future, and on satellite-, land-, and rocket-based monitoring of remote gases measured in parts per trillion. An international agreement of this nature could not, in fact, have occurred at any earlier point in history. . . .

The existence of ozone was unknown before 1839. An unstable form of oxygen composed of three, rather than the customary two, atoms of oxygen, ozone has been characterized as "the single most important chemically active trace gas in the earth's atmosphere." This significance derives from two singular properties. First, certain wavelengths of ultraviolet radiation are absorbed by the very thin "layer" of ozone molecules surrounding Earth, particularly in the upper part of the atmosphere known as the stratosphere, approximately 6 to 30 miles above the surface. If these biologically active ultraviolet (UV-B) light waves were to reach the planet's surface in excessive quantities, they could damage and cause mutations in human, animal, and plant cells. Second, the distribution of ozone throughout different altitudes could influence the temperature structure and circulation patterns of the stratosphere and thus have major implications for climate around the world. It is no exaggeration to conclude that the ozone layer, as currently constituted, is essential to life as it has evolved on Earth.

In 1973 two University of Michigan scientists, Richard Stolarski and Ralph Cicerone, were exploring the effects of possible chemical emissions from National Aeronautics and Space Administration rockets. Their research, published in 1974, indicated that chlorine released in the stratosphere could unleash a complicated chemical process that would continually destroy ozone for several decades. A single chlorine atom, through a catalytic chain reaction, could eliminate tens of thousands of the ozone molecules. This theory, though interesting, did not at first seem alarming, because the potential release of chlorine from space rocketry would be inconsequential.

In 1974 Mario Molina and Sherwood Rowland at the University of California, Irvine, became intrigued with some peculiar properties of a family of widely used anthropogenic chemicals, the chlorofluorocarbons [CFCs]. Molina and Rowland discovered that, unlike most other gases, CFCs are not chemically broken down or rained out quickly in the lower atmosphere but rather, because of their exceptionally stable chemical structure, persist and migrate slowly up to the stratosphere. Depending on their individual structure, different CFCs can remain intact from many decades to several centuries. The two researchers concluded that CFCs are eventually broken down by solar radiation and in the process release large quantities of chlorine into the stratosphere. The combined implications of these two independently-arrived-at hypotheses were deeply disturbing. The researchers had not anticipated any link between CFCs and ozone depletion. There had been no prior suspicion that CFCs were harmful to the environment. Indeed, following their invention in the 1930s, CFCs had seemed an ideal chemical. They had been thoroughly tested by customary standards and found to be safe. The possibility that dangers could originate many miles above Earth's surface was never considered.

CFCs are unusually stable, nonflammable, nontoxic, and noncorrosive—qualities that make them extremely useful in many industries, where they often replaced other chemicals, such as ammonia in refrigerators and air conditioners, as well as effective propellants in spray containers for cosmetics, household products, pharmaceuticals, and cleaners. They are also excellent insulators and are standard ingredients in the manufacture of a wide range of rigid and flexible plastic-foam materials. Their nonreactive properties make them seemingly perfect solvents for cleaning microchips and telecommunications equipment and for use in a myriad of their industrial applications. And, as an added bonus, CFCs are inexpensive to produce.

The 1974 theories came, therefore, as an economic as well as environmental bombshell.

2. THE ANTARCTIC OZONE HOLE

OZONE DIPLOMACY
Richard E. Benedick
Ch. 2, excerpt (Harvard University Press, 1991)

British scientists in 1985 published astonishing findings based on a review of land-based measurements of stratospheric ozone made at their Halley Bay station in the Antarctic. So unbelievable at first were these measurements that the scientists had delayed publication for nearly three years while they painstakingly rechecked and reviewed their data and the accuracy of their instruments. They finally concluded that ozone levels recorded during the Antarctic springtime (September November) had fallen to about 50 percent lower than they had been in the 1960s. Although concentrations recovered by mid-November, the amount of the seasonal ozone loss had apparently accelerated sharply beginning in 1979. The "ozone hole" (that is, a portion of the stratosphere in which greatly diminished ozone levels were measured) had also expanded by 1985 to cover an area greater in size than the United States.

This unexpected revelation was quickly confirmed by Japanese and U.S. scientists rechecking their own data sets. . . .

The ozone hole did not, however, provide any clear signal for policy-makers at that time. Scientists in 1986 and 1987 were far from certain that CFCs were involved in Antarctica. Nor could they confirm whether the hole was a localized phenomenon peculiar to unusual polar conditions or an ominous precursor of future ozone losses elsewhere over the planet. Since ozone concentrations over Antarctica did recover after each springtime collapse, the phenomenon was contrary to known theory and not conform to the global model predictions of gradual and pervasive long-term depletion. To add to the confusion, the downward trend was broken in late 1986—just before the start of the diplomatic negotiations—when Antarctic ozone concentrations actually improved over the previous year.

The hole over Antarctica did attract additional public attention to the ozone issue (though more in the United States than in Europe and Japan, where greater public pressure on governments was most needed). It may also have influenced some participants in the negotiations as evidence of the fragility of Earth's atmosphere. Significantly, however, Antarctica was never discussed at the negotiations, which were based solely on the global models. Even two months after Montreal, the U.S. Environmental Protection Agency had to conclude that "the Antarctic ozone hole cannot yet serve as a guide for policy decisions."

3. DEPLETION OF THE OZONE LAYER OVER THE NORTHERN HEMISPHERE

UNPRECEDENTED ARCTIC OZONE LOSS IN 2011

Gloria L. Manney et al., excerpt
Nature, Vol. 78, n.7370 (2011)

Chemical ozone destruction occurs over both polar regions in local winter-spring. In the Antarctic, essentially complete removal of lower-stratospheric ozone currently results in an ozone hole every year, whereas in the Arctic, ozone loss is highly variable and has until now been much more limited. . . . [The] chemical ozone destruction over the Arctic in early 2011 was—for the first time in the observational record—comparable to that in the Antarctic ozone hole. Unusually long-lasting cold conditions in the Arctic lower stratosphere led to persistent enhancement in ozone-destroying forms of chlorine and to unprecedented ozone loss, which exceeded 80 percent over 18–20 kilometres altitude. . . . Arctic ozone holes are possible even with temperatures much milder than those in the Antarctic."

4. THE CHEMICALS THAT CAUSE OZONE DEPLETION

The chemicals that deplete the ozone layer are found in many household products, such as refrigerators and aerosol spray cans, and in auto air conditioners. They also have a variety of other uses, such as cleaning solvents for superconductors and, in the case of halons, as fire suppressants. As of August 2015, the controlled chemicals also include carbon tetrachloride, methyl chloroform, HCFCs, HBCBs, and methyl bromide, and bromochloromethane.

There is a long lead time between the time the chemical is used and the time offending molecules reach the ozone layer. For example, when a CFC- or halon-containing product is produced and used, the chemicals escape and move up through the lower layer of the atmosphere and into the stratosphere. The release itself takes up to 30 years, depending on the product, and the traveling time usually lasts between seven and ten years. Once in the stratosphere, the stable chemical structure of the molecules allows them to remain there for long periods of time. These so-called residency times, combined with the release and travel times, result in a delay in both the depletion of ozone after the use of the CFC and in the "fixing" of the ozone after the use is stopped.

Consumption of the controlled chemicals has been widely dispersed. But, the group of producers has been highly concentrated. When the Montreal Protocol was negotiated, DuPont was the largest of only five producers in the United States and supplied a large share of the market for the chemicals. In Europe, Imperial Chemical Industries was the leader of the nine producers. Including Japan, there were only 19 companies producing almost 80 percent of the world's CFCs.

This small number of producers played a key role in making the limiting of CFC releases possible. Not only were the corporations active in negotiating the protocol, but they continue to be active in working to develop recovery methods and substitutes that are affordable alternatives to CFCs.

So far, HCFCs and HFCs are the most widely used substitutes worldwide. However, they are now known to contribute to the greenhouse effect and so are targets of international efforts to prevent harm to the global climate. The 1992 amendment to the Montreal Protocol set a phase-out schedule for HCFCs starting in 1996, to reach zero by 2030.

5.   GREENHOUSE GASES AND DEPLETION OF THE OZONE LAYER

CO_2 and other greenhouse gas emissions may accelerate the thinning of the stratospheric ozone layer. The Union of Concerned Scientists explains:

[T]emperatures in the lower stratosphere are decreasing as a result of increased carbon and other heat-trapping emissions. The reason for this apparent paradox—increasing temperatures at the Earth's surface and decreasing temperatures in higher parts of the atmosphere—can be explained using the blanket analogy. Carbon dioxide and other heat-trapping gases rise into the atmosphere, spread around the globe, and act like a blanket holding in heat around Earth. This blanket also protects the warm surface of the Earth from the cold air above it. As heat-trapping gas concentrations increase, the blanket thickness also increases. This further warms the Earth's surface; heats the blanket itself; and traps more heat in the lower atmosphere. Heat that normally (i.e. before blanket thickening) would escape the lower atmosphere and enter the stratosphere no longer does so, leaving the stratosphere cooler. Cooling of the lower polar stratosphere enhances PSC [polar stratospheric cloud] formation, and thus contributes to ozone loss. It appears unlikely that the decrease in ozone-depleting substances will lead to restabilization of the pre-1980 stratospheric ozone layer because of the competing and uncertain effects of further climate change. Union of Concerned Scientists, *Is There a Connection between the Ozone Hole and Global Warming* (last accessed Apr. 7, 2015),

B. THE MONTREAL PROTOCOL

In March 1985, the Vienna Convention for the Protection of the Ozone Layer established a framework system for addressing the multilateral environmental problems of ozone depletion. The Convention obligates States to undertake, initiate or co-operate in the conduct of research and scientific assessments and to co-operate in the exchange of scientific, technical, socio-economic, commercial and legal information relevant to the Convention. It also provides for dispute settlement and for the adoption of amendments to the Convention or to any Protocol to it. The division between representatives wanting a phase-out of CFCs and those wanting production caps prevented the adoption of any formal commitments to limit the substances, but the groundwork was laid for further work.

By 1987, the two groups were able to reach a compromise, and the Montreal Protocol was concluded. States have to first become party to the Vienna Convention and then can join the Montreal Protocol. As of August 2015, the Vienna Convention on the Ozone Layer had 197 parties. The

Montreal Protocol had 197 parties. These agreements have universal membership and are the first multilateral agreements in the United Nations history to achieve this status. By January 2015, all of the four amendments had universal membership by the States Parties to the Protocol.

The Montreal Protocol placed quantitative limits on both the production and the consumption of CFCs and halons. The Protocol adopted a system of targets and timetables. Article 2, Control Measures, provided for a baseline of 1986 for the calculated level of production and consumption, followed by progressive reductions in consumption of the controlled chemicals, down to 50% of the 1986 baseline by June 30, 1999. The Montreal Protocol is based on consumption levels of States. Consumption is determined by calculating production of the chemicals minus exports plus imports. Exports to nonmember States may not be included in the calculation. Thus, there is an incentive not only to limit production but also to trade only with States Parties to the agreement.

The Protocol makes special provision in Article V for developing States: a ten-year delay in required compliance with targets and timetables, a separate consumption limit of 0.3 kilograms per capita, access to a Multilateral Fund (1990 Amendment) to assist with the costs of compliance, and the promotion of bilateral technical assistance programs. The classification of a country as qualifying under Article V(1) to deserve special treatment is not permanent but is subject to the recommendations of an Open-Ended Working Group of the Parties.

The Protocol gives certain States flexibility in meeting their obligations. To attract the former Soviet Union, the Protocol provided in Article 2(6) that any State that already has facilities under construction or contracted for prior to September 1987 to produce the controlled chemicals may add this production to its 1986 base year level in determining its compliance with base year production. The Protocol also includes "industrial rationalization" among States. Under this policy, a State can transfer part of its calculated level of production of controlled chemicals to another State. While industrial rationalization can take place between developed member States, or between developing member States, it is not intended for transfer between developed and developing States.

The Protocol prohibits exports and imports of controlled substances with States that are not party to the treaty (although an exception exists for nonparties that are determined to be in full compliance with the control measures in Article 2 of the Protocol). In a second phase, the trade ban with nonparties would extend to products containing the controlled substances and, upon agreement of the Parties in five years, to products produced with the controlled chemicals. However, in 1992 Parties accepted the recommendation of the Technology and Economic

Assessment Panels and decided not to implement the ban based on process.

Since the 1980s, the producers and users of CFCs have been seeking means to recover, reuse, and substitute for CFCs. The recycling of CFCs is an important issue. Unless managed appropriately, it could lead to stockpiling of CFCs and undermine the effectiveness of the regime.

There are a number of factors that provide incentives for smuggling. The first and most important factor is economic. ODS [ozone depleting substances] substitutes generally remain more expensive than ODS. For example, information from the Philippines National Ozone Unit shows that in the Philippines, the market price for a kg of CFC-12 was around US$6 in 2006; but hydrofluorocarbon-134a (HFC-134a), an alternative for CFC-12, cost around US$9 per kg. This price difference alone acts as the main catalyst behind many smuggling operations. In the Asia and Pacific region, demand for CFCs in the servicing sector remains very high. For CFCs to be replaced by alternative chemicals, the equipment will often require retrofitting or will need to be completely replaced. For example, based on the UNEP [United Nations Environment Programme] surveys in Asia, retrofitting a mobile air-conditioning system to enable it to use HFC-134a in developing Asian countries could cost between US$100 and US$200. However, the cost of acquiring a 13.6 kg cylinder of CFCs, which contains enough refrigerant to service many such systems, is only about US$50. The financial incentives for continued use of CFCs will persist until all ODS-based equipment reaches its life's end or is finally replaced with newer technology that can function on ODS alternatives. However, the availability of illegal ODS holds back the replacement process by effectively extending the operating life of the equipment being used. The lifetime of ODS-containing equipment, such as refrigerators and air-conditioners, is often long. The longer these products remain on the market, the longer the demand for illegal ODS will remain.

Source: United Nations Environment Programme, Illegal Trade in Ozone Depleting Substances 4 (2007), *available at* http://www.unep.fr/ozonaction/information/mmcfiles/6075–e-illegal-trade-asia.pdf.

Besides the targets and timetables for limiting chemicals that deplete the ozone layer, the Protocol provides financial assistance to Article V States (developing States) to help them develop the capacity to comply with the Protocol. As noted previously, the Montreal Protocol Fund was part of the London Amendment of 1990. The most notable characteristic of this fund is that it is specifically not for economic development. Instead, States contribute to help offset the costs of Article V States complying with the Protocol. The Fund "shall meet all agreed incremental costs of Parties in order to enable their compliance with the control measures of the Protocol." As of May 2015, 45 countries, including countries in transition, had contributed over $3.34 billion since the Fund's inception.

The Fund secretariat has worked with OZONAction, a UNEP-industry group in Paris, France, to help develop and review State programs and proposed projects under the Fund. By 1996, most but not all Article V States had developed State programs or were in the process of doing so. As part of the State program, each State must designate an ozone action officer. These officers meet regularly on a regional basis to discuss implementation problems and to exchange views.

As of August 2015, the Executive Committee of the Montreal Protocol Fund had approved 144 country or State programs in Article V countries and 140 management plans for phasing out HCFCs. It had funded ozone offices in 145 Article V States. For a very useful historical compilation of official documents and decisions relating to the international regime protecting the ozone layer, correlated to specific articles of the Protocol, as well as other information, see UNEP Ozone Secretariat, Handbook for the International Treaties for the Protection of Ozone Layer (4th ed. 1996).

1. NEGOTIATION OF THE PROTOCOL

As discussed above, the first international agreement concerned with the high level ozone layer was the Vienna Convention on the Protection of the Ozone Layer, concluded in March 1985. At the time, States discussed including measures to control emissions of chemicals that deplete the ozone layer, but were unable to reach agreement to do so. For the next 21 months, some States discussed the issue informally. Several influential international workshops addressing the scientific and regulatory aspects were held. Finally, negotiations for a protocol opened in December 1986. What follows is a chronology of major events in the international legislative process through 1992. Many additional important events have occurred since then, as indicated elsewhere in the text.

CHRONOLOGY: INTERNATIONAL REGIME ON THE OZONE LAYER

Paul C. Szasz
International Norm-making, in Environmental Change and International Law 76–78
(Edith Brown Weiss ed., 1992) (Table adapted from original)

Protection of the ozone layer

1973–1974	Richard Stolarski and Ralph Cicerone, studies of release of chlorine in the atmosphere

1974	Mario Molina and Sherwood Rowland, studies of CFCs in the atmosphere and stratosphere
March 1977	UNEP's World Plan of Action on the Ozone Layer, Washington
April 1980	UNEP Governing Council resolution on restriction of CFC usage
May 1981	UNEP Governing Council resolution initiating negotiations towards an ozone agreement
1981	Meeting of legal experts convened by UNEP, Montevideo
January 1982	First session of Ad Hoc Working Group of Legal and Technical Experts for the Preparation of a Global Framework Convention for the Protection of the Ozone Layer, convened by UNEP, Stockholm (NB: there were seven sessions, until 1985)
1983	Establishment of the "Toronto Group"
March 1985	**Vienna Convention On The Protection of the Ozone Layer**
1986	WMO/UNEP Report on Atmospheric Ozone
May 1986	Workshop on CFC production and consumption trends, convened by EEC and UNEP, Rome
September 1986	Workshop on alternative regulatory strategies on protection of ozone, convened by USA and UNEP, Leesburg (USA)
December 1986	First negotiating session on a protocol to the Vienna Convention, convened by UNEP, Geneva
February 1987	Second negotiating session on a protocol to the Vienna Convention, convened by UNEP, Vienna
April 1987	Third negotiating session on a protocol to the Vienna Convention, convened by UNEP, Geneva
June 1987	Meeting of heads of key delegations, convened by UNEP, Brussels
September 1987	Preliminary meetings preceding the Montreal Conference, convened by UNEP, Montreal
September 1987	**Montreal Protocol On Substances That Deplete the Ozone Layer**
April–May 1989	First Meeting, of the Parties to the Vienna Convention and the Montreal Protocol, Helsinki

June 1990	Second Meeting of the Parties to the Vienna Convention and the Montreal Protocol, London (adoption of **Adjustments and Amendments to Montreal Protocol**)
June 1991	Third Meeting of the Parties to the Vienna Convention and the Montreal Protocol, Nairobi (also Executive Committee of Interim Multi-lateral Fund)
October 1992	Fourth Meeting of the Parties to the Vienna Convention and the Montreal Protocol, Copenhagen

---

As you read the following materials, consider the different interests involved in the negotiations for the Protocol. Also consider the importance of the structure of the private industries affected. Note that the CFC industry was highly concentrated, with five producers each in the United States and Japan and nine producers in the European Community (EC). DuPont was the largest American producer, estimated to account for 25 percent of world production, and Imperial Chemical Industries (ICI) was the largest European producer. The CFC-consuming industry, by contrast, was much less concentrated because of the multiple uses of CFCs. What effects did the structure of the CFC industry have on the negotiations?

WHY AN INTERNATIONAL AGREEMENT ON THE OZONE LAYER WAS POSSIBLE

Alice Enders & Amelia Porges
in The Greening of World Trade Issues 135–136
(K Anderson and R Blachhurst eds., Harvester Wheatsheaf, 1991)

The "tragedy of the commons," as popularized by Hardin (1968), is a classic problem. Individuals using a scarce common property resource engage in behavior that is individually incentive-compatible, but this leads to over-exploitation of the resource. The problem has been identified as a form of Prisoner's Dilemma. The Nash equilibrium of this non-cooperative, static, non-zero sum game leads to excessive pollution. Olson's (1965) description of free-riding in the production of a public good has also been used to describe the problem of solving global commons issues—an individual who cannot be excluded from the benefits of a collective good once it is produced has little incentive to voluntarily contribute to providing it. In Olson's problem, free-riding is inherent when the production of the collective good does not require the participation of all players.

The Prisoner's Dilemma in international pollution problems has been given a generic functional form by Barrett (1990) and by Low and Safadi (1991). Barrett's model is a symmetric Prisoner's Dilemma game where a sub-group of players have solved the cooperation problem between themselves (leaders), and they seek the cooperation of the remaining potential players (followers). Leaders may offer compensation to free riders to induce them to join but, for certain parameter values, compensation exceeds the collective benefits and an equilibrium to the leader-follower game does not exist. Note that in a symmetric Prisoner's Dilemma game where leadership is not exogenous, this division between leaders and followers is never a Nash or best-reply equilibrium.

The two leading world consumers of CFCs, the United States and the EC, each accounted for about 30 per cent of world consumption in 1986, and their shares of world production of CFCs were 30 and 45 per cent, respectively. For each entity, the impact on the ozone layer of reducing its own CFC consumption and production depends on the CFC consumption and production decisions of the other. The cost of abatement will increase as production of CFCs is reduced and their prices rise. Thus, on either the production or consumption side, the Prisoner's Dilemma can be reduced to a game played between the EC and the United States.

The United States and the European Community are the principal players in the Prisoner's Dilemma game—they constitute both the major part of the problem and its solution. Low-consuming countries are a very minor element in the game but, as discussed below, they may become more important players in the future. This is why, in our view, the leader-follower model with symmetric costs and benefits is not appropriate to the ozone layer problem.

The model we prefer to describe agreement on ozone layer depletion is the repeated Prisoner's Dilemma, where many cooperative solutions are possible provided that commitments are enforced. Two problems must be solved: (i) the problem of making credible commitments; and (ii) the problem of mutual monitoring and enforcement without an external authority.

Viewed from this perspective, the outcome of this non-cooperative game is unrelated to "the polluter pays principle." With a non-binding agreement, cooperation evolves from incentives for present and future actions. A notion of entitlement based on harm wrought by past actions is not relevant. Thus, the dominant role of high-income countries in emissions of ozone-depleting substances and the pollution of the ozone layer, compared to the insignificant contribution of low-income countries, will not shape an agreement. This does not mean that compensation will be absent from all multilateral nonbinding agreements, but simply that its basis comes from incentives of potential signatories to an agreement.

The scope for an international agreement on ozone layer depletion in a repeated game also depends on the future potential for action. Currently, there are no low-income countries that are significant consumers of CFCs. Even China, the leading low-income consumer, accounts for only 1.5 per cent of the world total. According to UNEP (1989), the U.S. Environmental Protection Agency projects annual demand growth for China, India and other developing regions in the range of 5 to 15 per cent for the period 1992–2000. Applying these growth rates to low per capita consumption figures ensures that the overall level of CFC consumption in low-income countries will still be very low by the turn of the century, but rising incomes and populations will cause demand for CFCs in low-income non-Parties to rise over time.

In the Prisoner's Dilemma described above for global CFC production and consumption, the game between the EC and the United States has two levels—the national level and the industry level. Their CFC industries are highly concentrated, and may be described by the familiar quantity-setting Cournot duopoly with restricted entry, which also has the structure of a Prisoner's Dilemma. For many years, the industry resisted any form of regulation of CFCs. Unilateral government regulation of CFCs in one entity led to the capture of market share by producers of the other entity—as the domestic industry argued after the United States' aerosol ban in 1978. Once regulation was inevitable by the mid-1980s, only coordinated regulatory actions taken simultaneously by the governments where major consuming markets are located was acceptable to producers. While ex post profits might be reduced, there are clear advantages to the industry as a whole to collusion with respect to restricting the entry of new producers in target markets. As (higher-price) substitutes looked like they were becoming available, existing producers sought an agreement that regulated CFC production in a closed "competition area."

Quantitative limits on CFC production are a form of regulation preferred by the industry. Regulation through a limit on consumption would have led to competition between producers with excess capacity, reducing profits of all. And regulation by imposing taxes would have reduced profits. According to Benedick (1991), the "adjusted production" approach of the Montreal Protocol was chosen purely for commercial reasons. (A consumption limit was included as a result of pressure from net importing countries (such as the Nordic) who were concerned that as production limits came into effect, CFC producers in the United States and the EC would favor domestic consuming industries.)

NOTES AND COMMENTS

1. *A pathbreaking agreement.* The Montreal Protocol is a pathbreaking example of States' willingness to address a problem in which the harmful

consequences of our activities today will be felt primarily by our children and their descendants. Why were States able to reach an agreement?

2. *Ozone protection and international trade.* The Montreal Protocol prohibits trade in controlled substances (and eventually in products produced with controlled substances) with non-parties. Is this consistent with the General Agreement on Tariffs and Trade? The GATT forbids import and export restrictions except for duties, taxes or other charges, and the most favored nation clause stipulates that tariffs must apply to all GATT member products. How would you go about analyzing this question? Does it matter that there is an exception for nonparties that are determined by the Conference of the Parties to be in compliance with Article 2 (Control Measures) of the Protocol? These issues are considered in detail in the chapter on environment and trade.

3. *Dispute resolution.* Note that the Montreal Protocol does not contain formal dispute resolution procedures in the text. However, the formal dispute resolution provisions in the Vienna Convention on the Protection of the Ozone Layer do apply. To date they have never been used. Why do you think that may be? (When responding, consider the material on the noncompliance procedures that have been developed under the Protocol, as outlined below.) If the dispute resolution procedures are never used, do they nonetheless serve a useful function for the parties? How?

4. *Principles of International Law.* To what extent and how does the Montreal Protocol implement various principles of international law, such as State responsibility, abuse of rights and good neighborliness, common but differentiated responsibilities (as articulated in the Rio Declaration and discussed in the next section), and intergenerational equity?

5. *Liability and compensation for injuries resulting from ozone damage.* The Montreal Protocol does not address liability. Apart from the Protocol, how would liability apply? If an abnormal number of skin cancers appeared in people living in areas of countries near Antarctica, would a principle of liability apply? Who would be liable? How would you determine liability? What would be the measure of compensation? Could you apportion liability for damage among countries on the basis of a country's percentage of global production or consumption of ozone-depleting chemicals? Is the analogy apt to the "market-share" approach of United States tort law in apportioning liability?

2. COMMON BUT DIFFERENTIATED RESPONSIBILITIES

The Rio Declaration on Environment and Development provides in Principle 7 that "States shall cooperate in a spirit of global partnership to conserve, protect and restore the health and integrity of the Earth's ecosystem. In view of the different contributions to global environmental degradation, States have common but differentiated responsibilities. The developed countries acknowledge the responsibility that they bear in the international pursuit of sustainable development in view of the pressures their societies place on the global environment and of the technologies and financial resources they command."

NOTES AND COMMENTS

1.   *The Protocol provisions*: Does the Protocol reflect this principle?

2.   *Developing States and the Montreal Protocol.* Why were developing States reluctant to join the Montreal Protocol? What incentives does the Protocol provide to attract them?

One of the major achievements of the Meeting of the Parties in London was to agree to establish a Multilateral Fund (the Montreal Protocol Fund) to help offset the costs of Article V States in complying with the Protocol. This was essential for States such as Brazil, China, and India to agree to the join the Protocol. The Indian government was not satisfied with the mere promise to establish the Fund. India indicated that it would not join the Protocol until the Fund was established.

By 2000, all the major industrialized and industrializing States had joined the Montreal Protocol. Since these are the ones with large internal and, potentially, external markets, the potential for restricting widespread usage of ozone-depleting chemicals was significantly increased. As of 2015, all 197 States were party to the Protocol and to the four amendments to it.

3.   *Delayed Implementation,* Article V. Certain States have a 10-year delay in coming into compliance with the Protocol. Is this an effective example of the principle of common but differentiated responsibilities? Can a State graduate from being an Article V State? Should it be able to?

4.   *Equity and the structure of the protocol.* Are there other equity issues embedded in the structure of the protocol?

3.   SCIENTIFIC UNCERTAINTY AND THE PRECAUTIONARY APPROACH

As you remember from the chapter addressing scientific uncertainty, new scientific information changes the way States approach their environmental problems. The more certain and serious the harm, the more willing a State is to act and spend money to prevent that harm.

The negotiators of the Montreal Protocol provided three mechanisms for adapting the substantive requirements to new scientific findings. First, the Protocol calls in Article XI(1) for a regular meeting of the Parties to monitor progress and consult on necessary modifications. Second, the Protocol provides for technical assessments prior to the meetings. Article VI of the Protocol requires that the Parties set up expert Technical and Economic Assessment Panels to report progress and help in the assessment of progress, which are to report at least once every four years. These Panels have been critical in enabling the Parties to move more quickly to phase out ozone-depleting chemicals and to add new chemicals to the list.

Third, unlike most international agreements, the Protocol does not require formal amendments to change the phase-out dates for the listed chemicals. Instead, it allows for "adjustments." *See* Article II(9) (". . . the Parties may decide whether: (i) adjustments to the one depleting potentials . . . should be made and, if so, what the adjustments should be; and (ii) further adjustments and reductions of production or consumption of the controlled substances from the 1986 levels should be undertaken and, if so, what the scope, amount and timing of any such adjustments and reductions should be"). To add new chemicals to the list, however, requires an amendment. *See* Article 11(10).

The major benefit of an adjustment rather than an amendment process is that it lets States Parties make a change without requiring national parliaments or legislatures to ratify for it to become effective. Instead, the expert committee proposes the changes, the Parties vote, and if passed, the adjustment becomes a binding modification of the Protocol. The London Meeting of the Parties in June 1990 resulted in both adjustments to the Protocol and an amendment to the Protocol. The adjustments became effective in March 1991; the amendment not until August 1992. Amendments are binding only upon those States that have ratified them. Thus, Parties may be subject to different sets of obligations, depending upon when they joined the Protocol and whether they have accepted a given amendment adopted after they became Parties. When a State becomes a Party to the Protocol, it automatically accepts those amendments that have been adopted prior to its joining the Protocol.

4. ACCELERATING CFC PHASE OUT

On April 15, 1992, 56 States agreed to speed up the phase-out of CFCs. The timetable adopted by the working group of Parties to the Protocol required a complete phase-out by January 1, 1996, four years earlier than provided for in the 1990 London Amendments. The Protocol originally only called for 50 percent reduction of 1986 consumption levels by the year 2000. A ministerial Meeting of the Parties in Copenhagen in November 1992 approved the new timetable (*see* Fourth Agreement, Annex I). Note how States agreed to phase out CFCs much more quickly than anticipated when the Protocol was negotiated, by using the Adjustment process.

The adjustment process has been used six times: 1990, 1992, 1995, 1997, 1999, and 2007. The Protocol has been amended in 1990, 1992, 1997, and 1999.

NOTES AND COMMENTS

1.   Consider the devices that were included in the Montreal Protocol to adjust to changes in scientific understanding of the problem. How would these work if States want to agree at the next Meeting of the Parties to (1) speed up the rate of phasing out methyl bromide and (2) add new chemicals to the list of controlled substances? Are these provisions adequate to respond to changes in scientific knowledge about the ozone layer and chemicals that deplete it?

2.   Consider membership of the Technical and Economic Assessment Panels. Would you expect to find the same experts as members for a significant number of years? What difference could that make?

5.   THE SPECIAL CASE OF METHYL BROMIDE

The precautionary principle or approach, discussed in Chapters 3 and 4, is raised by problems between the United States and the European Community in negotiating the phase-out of methyl bromide.

Methyl bromide is a chemical used widely in both agricultural and urban areas as a pesticide. Although good practice requires that once the chemical is sprayed on fields the dusted crops should be covered to prevent release of the bromide into the air, there have been occasions when the pesticide leaked or was incorrectly applied and escaped.

Once in the air, methyl bromide destroys ozone very efficiently. The scientific panel for the Montreal Protocol that reviewed bromide's effects in 1992 estimated that methyl bromide has an ozone depleting potential 40 times greater than that of CFCs. However, the destructive potential lasts for only two years. Unlike a ban on CFCs, which will continue destroying ozone for up to 30 years after production ends, a ban on methyl bromide could have very quick benefits for the ozone layer.

As a result, at the November 1992 Meeting of the Parties to the Montreal Protocol, the United States wanted a ban on the production of methyl bromide. However, the European Community argued that the phase-out date be held off until more findings verified the degenerative impacts of human-made methyl bromide upon ozone.

While the National Oceanic and Atmospheric Administration estimates that 25 per cent of the methyl bromide in the stratosphere comes from industrially produced bromide, not everyone agrees. Further, there is a huge demand for the chemical as a pesticide and, at the time, there was reportedly no substitute. A USDA official set the potential losses from crops at $500 million per year if a ban on its use went into effect immediately. In the end, the 1992 proposal for a ban failed. At the Ninth Meeting of the Parties in 1997, member States agreed to phase out consumption of methyl bromide by the year 2005, except that to meet basic needs, States may consume up to 15 per cent of their calculated levels in 1991. Article V developing States must reach zero consumption by the year 2015, except for uses agreed to be "critical."

At the Fifteenth Meeting of the Parties, there was disagreement over critical use exemptions for methyl bromide after 2004 where no economical or technical alternatives exist. This disagreement led to the First Extraordinary Meeting of the Parties in March 2004. Parties agreed to 13,256 tons of critical use exemptions for 2005 and set a cap for new production at 30% of 1991 baseline levels. The Second Extraordinary Meeting of the Parties in 2005 approved critical use nominations from Australia, Japan, Canada, and the United States. Parties also decided that critical use exemptions that exceed permissible levels must be drawn from existing stockpiles.

6.   THE SPECIAL CASE OF HFCS

While CFCs are phased out, CFC substitutes—HCFCs and HFCs—have unintended and opposing side effects. Consider the following:

HFCs are the third-generation chemical designed to replace HCFCs, themselves a replacement for the original ozone-eater, CFCs. HFCs do not deplete the ozone layer. However, they are very important greenhouse gases. Their global warming potential (GWP) is in the range of 1,000 to 3,000 times that of carbon dioxide.

HFCs are rapidly increasing in the atmosphere as a result of their use as ODS replacements. For example, HFC-134a, the most abundant HFC, has increased by about 10% per year from 2006 to 2010.

In the future, HFC emissions have the potential to become very large. Under current practices, the consumption of HFCs is projected to exceed the peak consumption level of CFCs in the 1980s by 2050. This would offset the benefits against climate change achieved by the reductions in ODS under the Montreal Protocol.

To appreciate the significance of projected HFC emissions, they would be equivalent to 7 to 19 per cent of the CO_2 emissions in 2050 based on the Intergovernmental Panel on Climate Change (IPCC) Special Report on Emissions Scenarios (SRES), and equivalent to 18 to 45 per cent of CO_2 emissions based on the IPCC's 450 ppm CO_2 emissions pathway scenario. There is, of course, inherent uncertainty in such projections.

If HFC emissions continue to increase, they are likely to have a noticeable influence on the climate system. *See generally* UNEP Synthesis Report, HFCs: A Critical Link in Protecting Climate and the Ozone Layer (2011), *available at* http://www.unep.org/dewa/Portals/67/pdf/HFC_report.pdf

At present, HFCs are covered under the UN Framework Convention on Climate Change and the Kyoto Protocol. However, the Kyoto Protocol limits apply only to those countries party to it. China, the United States, and other major emitters are not party to the Kyoto Protocol. Certain States would like to bring HFCs within the regulatory structure of the Montreal Protocol, since the chemicals are substitutes for those already listed. However, efforts to amend the Montreal Protocol to add HFCs have not succeeded. Canada, Mexico, and the United States reintroduced a resolution at the 2014 meeting of the Parties, which would have added 19 kinds of HFCs to the control list.

Some important bilateral progress has been made between two of the largest consumers of HFCs. In June 2013, China and the United States agreed bilaterally to reduce HFCs.

NOTES AND QUESTIONS

What legal issues do you see in adding HFCs to the Montreal Protocol list of controlled substances? Why would a country resist doing so?

C.   COMPLIANCE WITH THE MONTREAL PROTOCOL

At the 1992 Rio Conference on Environment and Development, States agreed that compliance with international agreements was one of the most important legal issues on the agenda for the next few decades. Consider how the Montreal Protocol handles the problem of compliance. What problems do you foresee with monitoring compliance and with obtaining compliance with the Protocol?

1.   CHALLENGES IN THE CONTEXT OF COMPLIANCE

THE FIVE INTERNATIONAL TREATIES: A LIVING HISTORY
Edith Brown Weiss
Chapter 2 in Engaging Countries: Strengthening Compliance with International
Environmental Accords (Edith Brown Weiss & Harold K. Jacobson eds., MIT Press,
1998)

One of the most significant innovations under the Protocol is the regime established to address issues of noncompliance, which includes the Implementation Committee of ten States and specific noncompliance procedures. The Committee meets biannually. It was established in 1990 (with only five members) and finalized in 1992. The Committee has become increasingly important to securing parties' compliance, as detailed in the discussion of monitoring and compliance.

Noncompliance procedures can be activated by one party against another, by the Secretariat, or by a party in respect of itself. Proposals to let NGOs activate the Non-Compliance Procedure were greeted warily by developing countries. In the first most significant cases of substantive violations, the parties themselves initiated the procedures because other parties and the Secretariat were reluctant to take responsibility for doing so, and preferred to exert pressure on the countries potentially in violation to do so.

The Implementation Committee reviews reports submitted by parties and addresses possible violations of targets and timetable obligations. It can make on-site visits to countries believed to be in noncompliance. In response to noncompliance, the Committee can turn either to incentives (assistance to enable countries to comply) or sticks (warnings or suspension of rights and privileges under the Protocol).

As with other environmental treaties, there have been efforts to disseminate information about the treaty and to engage industry and interested publics. In 1992, UNEP, in collaboration with industry, launched a quarterly newsletter, *OzonAction*, which provides information on relevant developments in the public and the private sectors, especially on new technology advances and technology cooperation with developing countries. It is available in six languages. The UNEP Industry Environment (IE) OzonAction Programme, based in Paris, also holds symposia that bring together government officials, industry officials, nongovernmental experts, and scholars who are directly concerned with controlling ozone-depleting substances.

. . . Monitoring of compliance is done by governments, the major industries in the private sector, and, to a much lesser extent, NGOs. The handful of large companies that produce ozone-depleting substances have an important financial stake in ensuring that competitors abide by the treaty, as well as the resources to monitor compliance, albeit quietly.

Since the Protocol has come into effect, there have been four important noncompliance issues: failure to report fully on a timely basis; failure to meet targets and timetables for controlled chemicals (in Russia and several central and east European countries); smuggling of CFCs into Western countries; and anticipated compliance problems by several article V developing countries in meeting targets and timetables when the ten-year delay period expires.

The primary tool that parties have under the Protocol to monitor compliance with the obligations to limit or phase out consumption of controlled chemicals by given dates is annual country reports. These are sent to the Secretariat for compilation and review by parties. The Implementation Committee reviews cases of noncompliance with the reporting procedures and with substantive obligations. . . .

. . . The Implementation Committee took as its first compliance issue the failure of countries to report completely and on time. The Committee chose to view such cases of noncompliance by article V countries as ones in which the countries lacked the capacity to comply. The resolution was to provide "incentives" to countries to report by helping them to develop the capacity to report and to ask the Fund Secretariat and implementing bodies to indicate how their assistance was helping to develop this capacity.

However, the Implementation Committee also initially expressed concern at the failure of some of the members of the European Community (Belgium, Greece, Italy, and Portugal) to report production data, and of the Commission of the European Communities to report consumption data. The Committee invited a European Commission representative to its next meeting "for an exchange of views on this issue." The Committee also expressed concern regarding the nonreporting of central and east European members and "the unreliability of data" reported by some countries.

NOTES AND QUESTIONS

1. *Establishing a procedure for noncompliance.* At the 1992 Copenhagen Meeting of the Parties, the member States agreed to adopt a procedure for noncompliance with the provisions of the Protocol and to set out possible measures to be taken.

Procedurally, the amendment in Annex IV provides for the creation of an Implementation Committee whose task is to take and evaluate complaints against members who are accused of not fulfilling their treaty obligations. The Committee is to report to the Meeting of the Parties, which will then decide whether action should be taken or whether there is a valid excuse.

Annex V, which sets out possible measures to be taken in the case of unexcused noncompliance, contains three compliance strategies. The first is provision of "appropriate assistance." The second and third are sanctions: "issuing cautions" (Annex V(B)) and suspending rights and privileges, "including those concerned with industrial rationalization, production, consumption, trade, transfer of technology, financial mechanism, and institutional arrangements" (Annex V(C)).

2. *The requirement to submit national reports.* Soon after the Protocol came into effect, many countries either did not provide the annual reports or failed to provide complete reports on time. In 1991, of the 48 countries required to report 1989 data, only 20 had fully complied as of March 1991. But by November 1996, 104 of the then 141 parties that should have reported data for 1994 had done so. This was a substantial improvement over 1990.

Some have questioned the value of reporting in international environmental agreements. What problems do you foresee with reporting? If a country did not file a report, what options would be open to the Implementation Committee? What factors would influence their decision on the appropriate action? How could countries make reporting an effective tool for monitoring compliance? Some have suggested that, for some agreements, on-site monitoring is preferable to reporting. Would this be feasible for the Montreal Protocol?

3. *Smuggling of controlled chemicals.* One of the most serious problems in enforcing the Protocol is that newly produced CFCs are being smuggled into certain States as recycled CFCs. Smuggling of CFCs from Mexico into the United States was perceived as a serious problem and arrests were made under United States law. In response to concerns about smuggling, the States Parties adopted an amendment in 1997 that required States to establish a licensing system by the year 2000 for the export and import of controlled chemicals listed in annexes A, B, C, and E. What problems do you foresee for States in implementing a national licensing system?

4. *Coordinating the treaties controlling trade in banned or controlled substances.* The Montreal Protocol, Basel Convention on Hazardous Wastes, Stockholm Convention on Persistent Organic Pollutants, the Rotterdam Convention for Prior and Informed Consent for Certain Hazardous Chemicals and Pesticides, and the Cartagena Protocol on Biosafety to the Convention on Biological are all multilateral environmental agreements that control trade. They have separate permitting and licensing requirements and systems. Some argue that the systems need to be integrated in order to curb illegal chemical trade efficiently and effectively. At the Sixteenth Meeting of the Parties in 2004, the Parties attempted to resolve this problem by setting forth the Prague Declaration on Enhancing Cooperation among Chemicals Related Multilateral Environmental Agreements. Among other objectives, the Prague Declaration aims to:

2. *Stress* the need in particular, to implement the relevant elements of the WSSD Plan of Implementation concerning the sound management of chemicals, including the prevention of international illegal trade in ozone-depleting substances, hazardous chemicals and hazardous wastes; . . .

6. *Seek alliance* with other multilateral instruments like the Basel, Rotterdam and Stockholm conventions to contribute to an effective strategic approach to international chemicals management; and

7. *Declare* the willingness of the Parties assembled in this City of Bridges to contribute to building bridges between the relevant multilateral environmental agreements and to help them draw inspiration from the success of the Montreal Protocol while, in turn, drawing inspiration from them in meeting future challenges.

5. *Question.* What might be done to address these issues?

2. NATIONAL IMPLEMENTATION OF THE MONTREAL PROTOCOL

Different States use different approaches in implementing international commitments within their States. For the United States, the Montreal Protocol is not a self-executing treaty. Thus, it and many other countries need national legislation or regulations to make the Protocol enforceable domestically.

a. The United States

The United States Clean Air Act was already in place when the United States signed the Montreal Protocol in September 1987. Because the Clean Air Act already required limited uses of CFCs nationally, the substantive requirements of the Montreal Protocol could be implemented under the authority granted under the act in section 602(c) (which allows the administrator to add chemicals to the lists of controlled substances to the extent consistent with the Montreal Protocol).

The original United States regulations implementing the Montreal Protocol, contained in Title VI of the Clean Air Act, were published in 1988, with minor revisions thereafter. The regulations restrict the production and consumption of controlled substances. Allowances are apportioned among companies based on their market share of national production and import levels during the baseline year. For chemicals listed before the London Amendments, the baseline year is 1986. For chemicals listed later, the baseline varies. Section 606 of the Act allows for accelerated phase-outs of chemicals consistent with the Montreal Protocol, as long as the change is announced to the public and subject to debate. Accordingly, the Copenhagen Adjustments and Amendments, which set out baselines of 1989 levels for HCFCs, 1991 levels for methyl bromide, and for the elimination of hydrobromofluorocarbons by 1996, became part of the national law. Trading of production rights is allowed. However, the timetable for phasing out methyl bromide in the Clean Air Act is shorter than that allowed by the 1997 adjustment. Should the Clean Air Act be "adjusted" to fit the longer timetable?

On January 1, 1990, taxes on ozone-depleting substances went into effect, as called for in the Omnibus Reconciliation Act of 1989. On January 1, 2013, the excise tax was raised. This increase is consistent with the plan to annually raise the tax as an additional disincentive to produce or consume the chemicals. *See* 58 Fed. Reg. 4768.

> Whether CFC taxes resulted in compliance cost savings is unclear. While taxes themselves may be costs to the taxpayer, CFC producers in this case, they are simply transfers not costs within the economy. The relevant costs are those associated with manufacturing CFCs and CFC substitutes. These costs likely

rose as a result of the program, since higher-cost substitutes were introduced more rapidly than they otherwise would have been. Presumed benefits also rose, as environmentally-damaging CFCs were phased out. Thus CFC production taxes result in market equilibrium with more costs as well as more benefits. While the CFC tax approach is likely to be more cost-effective than a command and control alternative that would yield the same environmental benefit, there appears to be no basis for estimating the magnitude of reduced compliance costs since the command and control alternative does not exist and would at best be difficult to characterize. Hence, cost savings from this program, while quite possibly substantial, cannot be determined.[1]

The excerpt below was written soon after the United States became a Party to the Protocol. It details the issues and choices facing the United States in implementing the Protocol.

IN STRATOSPHERIC OZONE: UNITED STATES REGULATION OF CHLOROFLUOROCARBONS

Orval E. Nangle

16 B.C. Envtl. Affairs L. Rev. 531 (1989)

The Montreal Protocol does not specify how its production and consumption limitations are to be met. Each party to the Protocol has discretion to choose its own method. EPA has published two rules in order to implement the Protocol in the United States: one rule for collection of the United States 1986 production and consumption data and a second rule that would implement the Protocol's substantive requirements.

Congress did not enact any special enabling legislation for these regulations. Both rules are issued under statutory authority granted in the Clean Air Act. EPA's authority to require information on 1986 production, consumption, imports, and exports of CFCs and halons is contained in section 114 of the Clean Air Act. The Act empowers the Administrator to "require any person who owns or operates an emission source or is subject to any requirement of this chapter . . . to . . . provide such other information as he may reasonably require." Likewise, authority to regulate CFCs and halons is contained in section 157(b) of the Clean Air Act. . . .

The regulations replicate the requirements of the Montreal Protocol. They regulate the same controlled substances over specified control periods, specify the same staged freezes and reductions, and restrict trade

---

[1] U.S. Environmental Protection Agency Report, National Center for Environmental Economics, Savings from Using Economic Incentives, 3.2.2. Chlorofluorocarbon Taxes and Allowance Trading (last accessed Apr. 7, 2015), *available at* http://yosemite1.epa.gov/EE/epa/eed.nsf/dcee735e22c76aef85257662005f4116/86a2750ed83fe1d88525774200597f3a!OpenDocument.

to comply with the Protocol. Moreover, the regulations become effective only after the Protocol enters into force.

A.   1986 CALCULATED LEVELS

EPA has required producers, importers, and exporters of the controlled substances listed in Annex A of the Protocol to report the amount (in kilograms) of each controlled substance: (1) produced in the United States or in its territories in 1986, (2) used and entirely consumed as a chemical intermediary in the production of other chemicals in 1986, (3) imported into the United States or its territories in 1986 (including the date, port of entry, and country of origin), and (4) exported from the United States or its territories (including the date, port of exit, country of destination, and date of arrival at destination). This information was required by January 13, 1988. The information obtained provided the basis for determining the calculated levels of production and consumption in the United States for 1986, an essential part of the regulatory scheme.

B.   REGULATORY APPROACH

Before settling on a regulatory approach, EPA considered three economic incentive approaches as well as several engineering controls and product bans. The economic incentive approaches use higher CFC and halon prices to provide incentive for firms to reduce their use of those chemicals. Higher prices should cause firms that can make relatively low-cost reductions to do so.

One of these economic incentive approaches provided for the auction of CFC permits to any interested party. The permit would allow a firm to produce a specified amount of CFCs during a specified control period, the number of permits auctioned determined by the permissible calculated levels for each group of controlled substances. Revenues from the auctions would go to the United States Treasury. It would not be permissible to hold permits for use in a later control period because such use could result in a violation of the Protocol in a future year. The trading of permits, however, would be permissible.

Another economic incentive approach involved setting production quotas based on regulatory goals. The quotas would be allocated to the five domestic CFC producers and the approximately ten United States importers based on their share of the market in 1986. Quotas could not be saved for use in a future year but could be traded among producers and importers for use in the same control year.

The third economic incentives approach considered by EPA involved the use of regulatory fees. EPA would assess fees against the regulated chemicals to encourage reduced usage, basing the amount of those fees on the chemical's ozone depletion potential and the permitted calculated levels of CFCs. A margin for error would be included to assure the target goal is met. Revenues would go to the United States Treasury.

EPA also considered developing specific engineering control measures requiring targeted CFC-user industries to reduce their consumption. EPA could, for example, ban the use of CFC-blown packaging, require additional recovery and recycling from solvent users of CFCs, and require recycling of CFCs used in sterilization. EPA could select control options based on pertinent societal considerations such as available technologies, cost of reductions, and quantity of reductions. A hybrid of these engineering controls/bans and of allocated quotas made up a fifth approach that EPA considered.

Because concerns over environmental protection and legality could undermine the program and administrative costs of controls and bans could be high, EPA chose the allocated quota approach. The sole identified drawback to the allocated quota approach was that CFC and halon producers and importers might realize substantial profits as a result of the scarcity created by regulation. Moreover, the allocated quota approach provides economically efficient reductions, involves minimal administrative costs, does not raise potential legal issues, and is the most easily enforced option . . .

F. USERS

It is important to note that no consumption allowances are required to use CFC's or halons. In fact, users of controlled substances are not involved with production allowances, consumption allowances, record keeping, or reporting. . . .

G. ENFORCEMENT

EPA will monitor compliance by reviewing the submitted reports and by inspecting sites. The Clean Air Act authorizes EPA to pursue injunctive relief, criminal prosecutions, or civil penalties of up to $25,000 per day for each violation. The regulations provide added bite to civil penalties by narrowly defining what constitutes a violation. Each kilogram of a controlled substance produced in excess of production allowances or in excess of consumption allowances constitutes a separate violation. Likewise, each kilogram imported from a non-party also constitutes a separate violation. Furthermore, the regulations provide that any producer who fails to maintain the required records and reports may be assumed to have been producing at full capacity during the period for which records or reports were not kept. The result of this approach is to allow EPA to impose substantially greater civil penalties, thus discouraging violations.

NOTES AND QUESTIONS

1. *58 Federal Register.* On January 15, 1993, the EPA issued a final ruling under section 610 of the Clean Air Act prohibiting the sale or distribution of "Non-Essential Products" that release CFCs.

The ban took effect on February 16, 1993, and resulted in the prohibition of CFC-propelled party streamers and noise horns, cleaning fluids for noncommercial photographic equipment, and flexible foams, among other things.

In determining "nonessentiality," the EPA is to take into account the availability and cost of substitutes, "health and safety" of both the product and the available substitutes, and "other relevant factors," which include the economic impact of a ban. *See* Clean Air Act, § 602 and 58 Fed. Reg. 4768.

2.   What difficulties do you foresee in implementing measures to control the ozone depleting chemicals?

b. The European Union

The European Union has implemented the Montreal Protocol through a regulation, which means it is immediately binding upon States. Generally the European Union uses the form of a directive in adopting environmental legislation, in order to give member States flexibility in bringing their legislation into conformity with that of the European Union. By contrast, a regulation is directly applicable to States and comes into effect immediately. The EU allegedly chose to use a regulation to avoid trade distortions from nonsimultaneous application of the legislation and to stress that the issue was urgent.

c. Other Countries

i. China

DuPont Corporation, one of the most active members in achieving the mandatory reductions in the Montreal Protocol, was also one of the most vigorous developers of substitutes for the banned CFCs. DuPont agreed to assist China with complying with the limits by supplying the chemical industry ministry with CFC substitutes, new technology, and expert advice. World Environment Report, July 2, 1993, at 19.

China's position as the world's most populous country and its complex administrative network make implementation of environmental regulations especially challenging. Although China was the global leader in production and consumption of CFCs, it was one of four countries to win the UNEP 2003 Outstanding National Units Ozone Award for excellence in early implementation of the Montreal Protocol in a developing country and worked to curb CFCs by embarking on dismantling its 37 CFC industrial plants. While China's environmental officials supported the objectives of the Protocol, implementation was slow. In efforts to promote a decrease in CFC production and consumption, the Multilateral Fund had already contributed about $700 million in grants to China in 2003. For a summary of China's approach to implementing the Montreal Protocol, see Daniel Magraw, International

Environmental Legal Issues, in International Occupational and Environmental Medicine 130, 134–35 (Box 13–1, by Zhao Ying) (Jessica A. Herzstein et al. eds., 1998). "In a landmark decision the Multilateral Fund's Executive Committee has agreed to provide China, the largest producer and consumer of HCFCs, an amount up to US $385 million for the entire elimination of its industrial production of ozone depleting substances (ODS) by the year 2030. China has agreed to retire current HCFC production capacity and to retire surplus production capacity that is currently not utilized." Multilateral Fund for the Implementation of the Montreal Protocol, *Multilateral Fund Approves Landmark Project for China with Ozone and Climate Benefits—Up to US $385 Million of Funding over the Next 17 Years*, Apr. 22, 2013, *available at* http://www.multilateralfund.org/InformationandMedia/default.aspx.

ii. Singapore

In Singapore, Exxon Chemical Asia became the second producer of a CFC substitute used by electronics producers for cleaning circuit boards. *See Ozone-friendly cleaner is first to be developed here*, The Straits Times, October 7, 1992. In October 1992, Actrel ED, an ozone-safe product, posed a challenge to DuPont's Axarel in Southeast Asia's computer and electronics industry. The computer and electronics industry was the largest user of CFCs in Singapore in 1991, accounting for 65 percent of the total CFCs used. The development of substitutes for ozone-depleting chemicals lowered the annual CFC consumption, which went from 4,000 tons in 1986 to 1,600 tons in 1991. As an Article V party to the Protocol, Singapore was required to freeze consumption of HCFCs on January 1, 2013 and to phase out consumption completely by January 1, 2030.

iii. Article V States

At least one large Article V State, India, produced ODSs for the export market as well as for internal consumption during the ten-year period after joining the Montreal Protocol. Is this consistent with the obligations of the protocol? What legal arguments would you make on behalf of an Article V State? On behalf of a non-Article V industrialized State?

d. CFC and HCFC Smuggling

There were increasing reports of CFCs being smuggled into the United States. The chemicals were coming in as recycled CFCs when in fact they were original production. Why do you think that this was occurring? Did the tax Congress levied on CFC producers in the United States affect the smuggling problem? How would you recommend that the United States address this problem in its regulations? What could other parties do under the Protocol? Recall that the 1997 Amendment to the Montreal Protocol called upon parties to put in place a licensing system for imports and exports of new, used, recycled, and reclaimed controlled substances listed in annexes A, B, C, and E to the Protocol by the year 2000. Moreover, "Recent HCFC seizures in the US suggest an already large black market with the potential to rival that seen with CFCs. In 2008, US customs seized 11 container loads amounting to 12,000 cylinders in Charleston, South Carolina with a market value of USD $1 million. An even bigger case came to light in 2009. The Kroy Corporation imported 29,107 cylinders containing 418 MT of HCFC-22 in 11 separate shipments with a market value of almost USD $4 million. U.S. courts prosecuted two individuals, sentencing one to 30 months imprisonment and another faces a maximum imprisonment of two years. The Kroy Corporation was fined USD $40,000 and ordered to forfeit USD $1.3 million." United Nations Environmental Programme, Risk Assessment of Illegal Trade in HCFCs 12 (2011), *available at* http://www.unep.fr/ozonaction/information/mmcfiles/7507–e-risk_assessment.pdf)

D. THE MONTREAL PROTOCOL'S EFFECTIVENESS

Many governments, international institutions, scholars, and others in the private sector hail the Montreal Protocol as a success. The U.S. Council on Environmental Quality on the occasion of the 25th anniversary of the Protocol noted the following:

> The Montreal Protocol has been and continues to be a clear and resounding success. The United Nations estimates that global production of ozone-depleting substances has fallen 98% since ratification. As a result, the ozone layer is recovering, and experts project that it will return to its pre-1960 levels as early as 2060.

> When the world first grappled with the challenge of a diminishing ozone layer, few substitutes existed for ozone-depleting chemicals and many observers warned that tackling the problem would impose tremendous economic burdens. But global innovation, led by a number of American companies, proved them wrong. An unprecedented research and development effort has led to the rapid widespread adoption of low-cost alternatives to harmful CFCs. Today, everyday products that once contained CFCs from spray cans and computers to furniture and packing peanuts, are produced with ozone-friendly materials.

> These accomplishments have produced real benefits for Americans, preventing sicknesses and deaths, and saving us money on health care costs. In fact, the U.S. Environmental Protection Agency estimates that every dollar invested in ozone protection provides $20 in health benefits here at home.

The Montreal Protocol has also played a significant role in helping to address climate change. Many ozone-depleting substances are potent greenhouse gases. By dramatically reducing the production of these substances, the Montreal Protocol has so far averted the equivalent of 135 billion metric tons of carbon dioxide worldwide, according to United Nations estimates.

NOTES AND QUESTIONS

1.   What accounts for the Protocol's success? Which of the following factors were important and how?

- Only a handful of States had companies producing most of the world's CFCs;

- The Protocol removed incentives to become a "pollution haven" or a "free rider" to receive the benefits from the Protocol;

- The Protocol provided for flexible arrangements to respond to changes in scientific understanding of the problem;

- Substitutes for the controlled substances were available;

- Obligations were perceived as equitable;

- Funds were available to assist poorer countries in complying with the Protocol;

- Companies producing the controlled chemicals wanted to ensure a level playing field among themselves

2.   The Montreal Protocol has been touted as a model for a global climate change agreement. Are its provisions and institutional arrangements useful for designing agreements related to climate change? What can we learn from our experience with the Montreal Protocol? For example, does the Montreal model depend on the ready availability of product substitutes or a similar technological solution? These questions are relevant to Chapter 9 on Climate Change.

CHAPTER 9

GLOBAL CLIMATE CHANGE

■ ■ ■

PROBLEM

A European heavy industry (Industry), which emits greenhouse gases, has decided to open a plant in a country subject to the Kyoto protocol obligations. In addition to labor cost savings, the Industry's home country is putting increasingly stringent limitations on greenhouse gas emissions. In the projected host country, the Industry's location team selected a site one-half mile inland from the ocean, although the country's climate change adaptation plan has identified the area as a high flood risk zone due to projected sea level rise. The area was selected in part because the necessary water supply was available from the nearby Clear River. However, the team has learned that Clear River's average annual flows are expected to decline in the coming three decades again due to climate change. The country's adaptation plan recommends that no new high intensity land uses that are vulnerable to flooding or water stress be located in the Clear River Basin. In addition, the host country is bumping up against its Kyoto obligations and has adopted a policy of carbon neutrality. To comply, the Industry has decided to retire a failing plant in Europe and to establish a new 2,000 acre rain forest in a tropical country 2,000 miles from the planned facility.

As part of its public relations campaign to win host country regulatory approval, the Industry's Chief Executive Officer (CEO) wants to stress its commitment to carbon neutrality. However, the public relations department is unsure of the terms to use. Initially, it touted the Industry's commitment to fight global warming, but it discovered that the term "global warming" comes with some baggage and was vetoed by the CEO as too inflammatory and inconsistent with the usage required by his industry group. The term can simply refer to the observed long-term trend of a rising average global temperature, but his industry group prefers the less frightening term "climate change". As a neutral term, "climate change" refers to the changes caused by temperature rise, which can be increased warming or cooling, and both terms have been used in the scientific literature for over forty years. The department is aware that President Obama's first science advisor, John Holdren, sought to substitute the term "climate disruption" to better describe the range of increasing non-uniform and harmful events, but the term is contested and has not been widely adopted.

A. CLIMATE CHANGE: A WICKEDLY TOUGH GLOBAL COMMONS TRAGEDY

Global climate change is perhaps the mother of all global environmental problems because it raises almost all of the economic, ethical, instrument choice, legal and scientific issues presented in this book. Climate change is a problem because long held assumptions about the planet's climate cycles no longer hold. Energy from the sun drives the earth's weather and climate and heats the earth's surface; in turn, the earth radiates energy back into space at a different wave length than it entered at, thus making our planet the only habitable one in our solar system. Greenhouse gases (GHGs), such as carbon dioxide (CO_2), methane, nitrous oxide, water vapor, ozone and chorofluorocarbons, absorb heat as it is radiated from the earth and thus retain heat in the atmosphere much as the transparent covering of a greenhouse does. For about a thousand years before the Industrial Revolution (1760–1850), the amount of greenhouse gases in the atmosphere remained relatively constant. Since then, the concentration of greenhouse gases has substantially increased due to agricultural, industrial, transportation and other activities. In addition, the concentration of nitrous oxides (NO and NO_2) and carbon monoxide (CO), is also increasing. These gases are not greenhouse gases, but they play a role in the atmospheric chemistry and have led to an increase in tropospheric ozone, a greenhouse gas, by 40% since pre-industrial times. Moreover, NO_2 is an important absorber of visible solar radiation. Chlorofluorocarbons and some other halogen compounds do not occur naturally in the atmosphere but have been introduced by human activities. Beside their depleting effect on the stratospheric ozone layer, they are strong greenhouse gases. Their greenhouse effect is only partly compensated for by the depletion of the ozone layer, which causes a negative forcing of the surface-troposphere system. See Chapter 8, page 417. The planetary greenhouse is getting warmer as concentrations of GHGs increase. Thus, the warming, which is actually a noncooling, accelerates. Climate change has been on the international environmental protection agenda since the 1980s, and many countries have taken steps to reduce greenhouse gas emissions. But, emissions continue to increase and more adverse impacts, such as species displacement, are being identified.

The focus of the international community has logically been on State actors. But, the focus is shifting to include industries and private consumers. Many national and private interests, especially in the hydrocarbon energy sector, favor the status quo. However, one industry that takes climate change is seriously is the insurance industry. Starting in the 1980s, European and Japanese insurers took the lead in pushing for early and significant reductions in GHG to head off possible increased claims resulting from property damage. Insurance industry representatives are particularly worried about the increased frequency of damaging weather events. See Stephen Schmidheiny & Frederico J.L. Zorraquin, Financing Change: The Financial Community, Eco-Efficiency, and Sustainable Development (1996) (arguing that the insurance industry should push for increased environmental protection); Charles Weiss, *Can Market Mechanisms Ameliorate the Effects of Long-Term Climate Change?,* 15 Climate Change 299 (1989); Warming of the Oceans and Implications for the (re) Insurance Industry (A Geneva Association Report 2013). The American insurance industry also takes the risks of climate change seriously. American Academy of Actuaries/Casualty Extreme Events Committee et al., Determining the Impact of Climate Change on Insurance Risk and the Global Community (2012). In general, the industry has concentrated on developing climate risk indices to use in setting rates, but the R Street Institute, a conservative organization financed largely with insurance industry money, is a strong supporter of a carbon tax to reduce greenhouse gas emissions. Industries that are heavily dependent on water, such as soft drink companies and the wine industry, are also becoming concerned about water shortages and landscape shifts. E.g., Lee Hannah et al., Climate Change, Wine, and Conservation, Proceedings of the National Academy of Sciences of the United States (2012) (predicting a possible 25% to 75% loss of land suitable for viniculture in major wine regions unless land and water use adaptation steps are taken).

There are two measures of greenhouse gases. The first is the amount of gases in the atmosphere. According to the World Meteorological Organization's annual Greenhouse Gas Bulletin, the amount of greenhouse gases in the atmosphere reached a new record high in 2013, especially from CO_2 emissions. The 2013 concentration of CO_2 was 142% of the pre-industrial era (1750), and methane and nitrous oxide concentrations were 253% and 121% over 1750 levels. The second measure is emission levels. The 2013 Global Carbon Project reported that "[g]lobal emissions due to fossil fuel alone are set to grow in 2013 at a slightly lower pace of 2.1% than the average 3.1% since 2000, reaching a level that is 61% above emissions in 1990." In fact, in 2015, the International Energy Agency reported that "global emissions of carbon dioxide from the energy sector stalled in 2014, marking the first time in 40 years in which there was a halt or reduction in emissions of the greenhouse gas that was not tied to an economic downturn." http://www. iea.org/newsroomandevents/news/2015/march/global-energy-related-emissions-of-carbon-dioxide-stalled-in-2014.html.[1] The continued increase

---

[1]   Growth rates for major emitter countries in 2012 were 5.9% (China), –3.7% (USA), –1.3% (EU28), and 7.7% (India). The 2012 carbon dioxide emissions breakdown is coal (43%), oil (33%), gas (18%), cement (5.3%) and gas flaring (0.6%). Atmospheric carbon dioxide levels increased in 2012 at a faster rate than the average over the past 10 years because of a combination of continuing growth in emissions and a decrease in land carbon sinks from very high levels in the

in emissions, despite many on-going mitigation efforts, was confirmed by the Intergovernmental Panel on Climate Change (IPCC) 2014 report. IPCC, Climate Change 2014 Synthesis Report (Approved Summary for Policymakers, 1 November 2014). Greenhouse gas budgets are used to bolster the case for a global reduction regime, but David G. Victor and Charles E. Kemmel, *Ditch the 2° C Warming Goal*, 514 Science 30 (Oct. 10, 2014), argue that the international community should abandon the goal of preventing a 2° temperature rise as unobtainable. Instead, we need scaled-down risk indexes, such as GHG concentrations, emissions such as methane that are short-lived, regional climate perturbations, ocean heat content and high altitude temperatures.

For several decades, it has been assumed that a basic reason that climate change presents such a difficult challenge is that greenhouse gas emission reduction is not amenable to uncoordinated local solutions. The level of worldwide emissions determines the concentration of greenhouse gases (GHGs) in the atmosphere and there are currently no available, effective technological fixes. *See* pages 539 to 544, *infra*. Therefore, even the largest emitting country, when acting alone, cannot meaningfully affect global concentrations of GHGs. Thus, the reduction of GHG emissions requires a globally coordinated effort. And, all States must, to some degree, participate in the project. However, in the face of the inability of the international community to agree on an effective mitigation regime, *see* Part B, page 477, *infra*, scholars have raised the question of whether the myriad national, sub-national, and private efforts now underway in developed and developing countries might be sufficient. E.g., Daniel C. Esty, Bottom-Up Climate Fix, The New York Times, September 21, 2014; see also Kirsten H. Engel and Scott R. Saleska, *Subglobal Regulation of the Global Commons: the Case of Climate Change*, 32 Ecology L. Q. 183 (2005).

As you read this chapter, ask yourself how countries should respond to what are surely the most comprehensive changes humans have wrought to our planetary systems. In particular, consider what role the level of uncertainty plays, or should play, in the development of policies, legal instruments and regimes designed to minimize the harmful impacts of global warming. Will the instruments adopted to date be as effective in countering the phenomenon and effects of climate change as the Montreal Protocol (addressed in Chapter 8) was for ozone? What kinds of policies and actions would the precautionary principle counsel or require? What are the implications of the principle of intergenerational equity, discussed in Chapter 2, for how we address climate change?

---

previous two years." CDIAC 2013 Global Carbon Budget, available at http://www.GlobalCarbon Project.org.

1. THE BASIC SCIENCE

CLIMATE CHANGE SCIENCE: AN ANALYSIS OF SOME KEY QUESTIONS

Committee on the Science of Climate Change Division on Earth and Life Sciences,
National Research Council (2001)

While all of the major greenhouse gases have both natural and anthropogenic atmospheric sources, the nature of these processes varies widely among them. Carbon dioxide is naturally absorbed and released by the terrestrial biosphere as well as by the oceans. Carbon dioxide is also formed by the burning of wood, coal, oil, and natural gas, and these activities have increased steadily during the last two centuries since the Industrial Revolution. That the burning of fossil fuels is a major cause of the CO_2 increase is evidenced by the concomitant decreases in the relative abundance of both the stable and radioactive carbon isotopes and the decrease in atmospheric oxygen. Continuous high-precision measurements have been made of its atmospheric concentrations only since 1958, and by the year 2000 the concentrations had increased 17% from 315 parts per million by volume (ppmv) to 370 ppmv. While the year-to-year increase varies, the average annual increase of 1.5 ppmv/year over the past two decades is slightly greater than during the 1960s and 1970s. A marked seasonal oscillation of carbon dioxide concentration exists, especially in the northern hemisphere because of the extensive draw down of carbon dioxide every spring and summer as the green plants convert carbon dioxide into plant material, and the return in the rest of the year as decomposition exceeds photosynthesis. The seasonal effects are quite different north and south of the equator, with the variation much greater in the northern hemisphere where most of Earth's land surface and its vegetation and soils are found.

Methane is the major component of natural gas and it is also formed and released to the atmosphere by many biologic processes in low oxygen environments, such as those occurring in swamps, near the roots of rice plants, and the stomachs of cows. Such human activities as rice growing, the raising of cattle, coal mining, use of land-fills, and natural gas handling have increased over the last 50 years, and direct and inadvertent emissions from these activities have been partially responsible for the increase in atmospheric methane. Its atmospheric concentration has been measured globally and continuously for only two decades, and the majority of the methane molecules are of recent biologic origin. The concentrations of methane increased rather smoothly from 1.52 ppmv in 1978 by about 1% per year until about 1990. The rate of increase slowed down to less than that rate during the 1990s, and also became more erratic; current values are around 1.77 ppmv. About two-thirds of the current emissions of methane are released by human activities.

. . . Nitrous oxide is formed by many microbial reactions in soils and waters, including those processes acting on the increasing amounts of nitrogen-containing fertilizers. Some synthetic chemical processes that release nitrous oxide have also been identified. Its concentration remained about 0.27 ppmv for at least 1,000 years until two centuries ago, when the rise to the current 0.31 ppmv began.

Ozone is created mainly by the action of solar ultraviolet radiation on molecular oxygen in the upper atmosphere, and most of it remains in the stratosphere. However, a fraction of such ozone descends naturally into the lower atmosphere where additional chemical processes can both form and destroy it. This "tropo-spheric ozone" has been supplemented during the 20th century by additional ozone—an important component of photochemical smog—created by the action of sunlight upon pollutant molecules containing carbon and nitrogen. The most important of the latter include compounds such as ethylene (C_2H_4), carbon monoxide (CO), and nitric oxide released in the exhaust of fossil-fuel-powered motor vehicles and power plants and during combustion of biomass.

. . . The chlorofluorocarbons (CFCs) are different from the gases considered above in that they have no significant natural source but were synthesized for their technological utility. Essentially all of the major uses of the CFCs—as refrigerants, aerosol propellants, plastic foaming agents, cleaning solvents, and so on—result in their release, chemically unaltered, into the atmosphere. The atmospheric concentrations of the CFCs rose, slowly at first, from zero before first synthesis in 1928, and then more rapidly in the 1960s and 1970s with the development of a widening range of technological applications. The concentrations were rising in the 1980s at a rate of about 18 parts per trillion by volume (pptv) per year for CFG12, 9 pptv/year for CFG11, and 6 pptv/year for CFG113 (CC12FCC1F2). Because these molecules were identified as agents causing the destruction of stratospheric ozone, their production was banned in the industrial countries as of January 1996 under the terms of the 1992 revision of the Montreal Protocol, and further emissions have almost stopped.

INTERGOVERNMENTAL PANEL ON CLIMATE CHANGE, 2014 SYNTHESIS REPORT, SUMMARY FOR POLICYMAKERS

4–6 (2014) (Figures and References Omitted)

1.2 Causes of climate change

Anthropogenic greenhouse gas emissions have increased since the pre-industrial era, driven largely by economic and population growth, and are now higher than ever. This has led to atmospheric concentrations of carbon dioxide, methane and nitrous oxide that are unprecedented in at least the last 800,000 years. Their effects, together with those of other anthropogenic drivers, have been detected throughout the climate system and are extremely likely to have been the dominant cause of the observed warming since the mid-20th century.

Anthropogenic greenhouse gas (GHG) emissions since the pre-industrial era have driven large increases in the atmospheric concentrations of CO_2, CH_4 and N_2O. Between 1750 and 2011, cumulative anthropogenic CO_2 emissions to the atmosphere were 2040 +/- 310 $GtCO_2$. About 40% of these emissions have remained in the atmosphere (880 +/- 35 $GtCO_2$); the rest was removed from the atmosphere and stored on land (in plants and soils) and in the ocean. The ocean has absorbed about 30% of the emitted anthropogenic CO_2, causing ocean acidification. About half of the anthropogenic CO_2 emissions between 1750 and 2011 have occurred in the last 40 years (high confidence).

Total anthropogenic greenhouse gas emissions have continued to increase over 1970 to 2010 with larger absolute increases between 2000 and 2010, despite a growing number of climate change mitigation policies. Anthropogenic greenhouse gas emissions in 2010 have reached 49 +/- 4.5 $GtCO_2$ eq/yr. Emissions of CO_2 from fossil fuel combustion and industrial processes contributed about 78% of the total greenhouse gas emissions increase from 1970 to 2010, with a similar percentage contribution for the increase during the period 2000 to 2010 (high confidence) (Figure SPM.2). Globally, economic and population growth continued to be the most important drivers of increases in CO_2 emissions from fossil fuel combustion. The contribution of population growth between 2000 and 2010 remained roughly identical to the previous three decades, while the contribution of economic growth has risen sharply. Increased use of coal has reversed the long-standing trend of gradual decarbonization (i.e., reducing the carbon intensity of energy) of the world's energy supply (high confidence).

The evidence for human influence on the climate system has grown since the Fourth Assessment Report. It is extremely likely that more than half of the observed increase in global average surface temperature from 1951 to 2010 was caused by the anthropogenic increase in greenhouse gas concentrations and other anthropogenic forcings together. The best estimate of the human-induced contribution to warming is similar to the observed warming over this period. Anthropogenic forcings have likely made a substantial contribution to surface temperature increases since the mid-20th century over every continental region except Antarctica. Anthropogenic influences have likely affected the global water cycle since 1960 and contributed to the retreat of glaciers since the 1960s and to the increased surface melting of the Greenland ice sheet since 1993. Anthropogenic influences have very likely contributed to Arctic sea-ice loss since 1979 and have very likely made a substantial contribution to increases in global upper ocean heat content (0–700 m) and to global mean sea-level rise observed since the 1970s.

NOTES: SCIENTIFIC CONSENSUS, LAY DOUBTS AND THE GAP BETWEEN WARNINGS AND ACTION

1.   *We Humans Are the Problem: Science or Theology?* As the 2014 IPCC Synthesis Report indicates, the widespread scientific consensus that human activities are disrupting the earth's climate remains firm. *See also* National Academy of Sciences, Climate Change Evidence & Causes: An Overview (2014). The Synthesis Report, at page 8, projects:

> Future climate will depend on committed warming caused by past anthropogenic emissions, as well as future anthropogenic emissions and natural climate variability. The global mean surface temperature change for the period 2016–2035 relative to 1986–2005 is similar for the four RCPs [Representative Concentration Pathways] and will likely be in the range 0.3°C–0.7°C (medium confidence). This assumes that there will be no major volcanic eruptions or changes in some natural sources (e.g., CH_4 and N_2O), or unexpected changes in total solar irradiance. By mid-21st century, the magnitude of the projected climate change is substantially affected by the choice of emissions scenario.

> Relative to 1850–1900, global surface temperature change for the end of the 21st century (2081–2100) is projected to likely exceed 1.5°C for RCP4.5, RCP6.0 and RCP8.5 (high confidence). Warming is likely to exceed 2°C for RCP6.0 and RCP8.5 (high confidence), more likely than not to exceed 2°C for RCP4.5 (medium confidence), but unlikely to exceed 2°C for RCP2.6 (medium confidence). The increase of global mean surface temperature by the end of the 21st century (2081–2100) relative to 1986–2005 is likely to be 0.3°C–1.7°C under RCP2.6, 1.1°C–2.6°C under RCP4.5, 1.4°C–3.1°C under RCP6.0, and 2.6°C–4.8°C under RCP8.59. The Arctic region will continue to warm more rapidly than the global mean . . . .

2.   *Not.* Despite the firm and increasing scientific consensus, there is a substantial group of climate skeptics, especially in the United States. *See e.g.*, Jim Steele, Landscapes and Cycles: An Environmentalist's Journey to Climate Skepticism (2013); Garth W. Paltridge, The Climate Caper: Facts and Fallacies of Global Warming (2010); and The Shattered Consensus: The True State of Global Warming (Patrick J. Michaels eds. 2005). The disbelief is partly due to the historical fluctuations and regional variations in temperature. *See e.g.*, Climatic Change and the Mediterranean 17 (L. Jeftic, J.D. Milliman & G. Sestini eds., 1992). Other claims include the fact that the warming trend has flattened since 2000, that temperature increases are less than the models predicted, that CO_2 emissions should not be viewed as pollution, that consensus climate scientists are chasing money at the expense

of truth and, as discussed at pages 457 to 460, *infra*, action is not justified by benefit-cost analysis. These contentions are considered and rejected by a leading student of climate change. Richard Nordhaus, *Why the Global Warming Skeptics Are Wrong*, The New York Review of Books, March 22, 2012. *See also* James Laurence Powell, The Inquisition of Climate Science (2011). Climate skepticism is especially strong in the United States. In 2013, the Pew Research Center found that 69% percent of Americans agree that there was solid evidence that earth is warming, but only 28% agreed that it was a top political priority and ranked it last on the list of choices. A separate survey found that only 40% of Americans thought that climate change was a major threat compared with a global median of 54%, the lowest of any region in the world. See also Joshua Howe, Behind the Curve: Science & the Politics of Global Warming (2014).

3.   *It's Just Weather, Not to Worry.* It is important to distinguish among weather, climate and climate change. The Intergovernmental Panel on Climate Change defines climate change as the "statistically significant variation in either the mean state of the climate or in its variability, persisting for an extended period (typically decades or longer)." In contrast, the United Nations Framework Convention on Climate Change, pages 479 to 484, *infra,* defines climate change as "a change of climate which is attributed directly or indirectly to human activity that alters the composition of the global atmosphere and which is in addition to natural climate variability observed over comparable time periods. Accordingly, climate change may result from natural internal processes, external forcings, or persistent anthropogenic changes in the composition of the atmosphere or land use." In short, the IPCC's definition of climate change encompasses variability resulting from both natural and anthropogenic causes, but it distinguishes between weather and climate. Weather describes the conditions of the atmosphere at a certain place and time with reference to temperature, pressure, humidity, wind, and other key parameters; the presence of clouds, precipitation; and the occurrence of special phenomena, such as thunderstorms, dust storms, and tornadoes. The IPCC Second Assessment Report noted that GHGs not only increase global temperatures but also disrupt weather patterns, resulting in more widely varying hydrological phenomena. When added to other meteorological occurrences such as El Niño, the results can be devastating. The El Niño phenomenon reverses the direction of winds and ocean currents and alters ocean temperature between Indonesia and the Pacific coast of the Americas, resulting, for example, in torrential rain and floods in South America. Reversal of ocean currents also alters fish migratory patterns, devastating local fishing communities. Globally, El Niño may lead to famine in Africa, floods in North America, and widespread forest fires in Indonesia. Current understanding suggests El Niño is caused by a weakening of the trade winds near Indonesia; once the trade winds weaken, warm water surges eastward across the Pacific and El Niño begins. Global warming caused by greenhouse gases may either alter trade winds off Indonesia, leading to increased occurrences of El Niño in the future, or when combined with El Niño, may create even more devastating floods and

torrential rainfall in some regions and famines in others. *See* United Nations Environmental Programme, The El Niño Phenomenon (UNEP/GEMS Environment Library No. 8, 1992); Summary for Policymakers: The Science of Climate Change, in IPCC Second Assessment. Climate Change 1995 (1995); and Summary for Policymakers, IPCC Third Assessment Report—Climate Change 2001.

4.   *Bring On Global Warming and Pass that Excellent, Inexpensive Montana Sauvignon Blanc.* Could climate change be good for humanity? Climate skeptics and others assert that there will be potential benefits from global warming, especially in the interior United States. Though there is a virtual unanimity of opinion that depletion of ozone will harm all life on Earth, this agreement does not exist for climate change. If the effects of increased temperatures are as predicted, coastal cities will be flooded, tropical forests will dry out, and temperate zones will become deserts. On the other hand, the northern countries will become warmer, with a corresponding lengthening of growing seasons and the emergence of new tourism destinations. Other likely benefits include greener rainforests, enhanced plant growth in the Amazon, increased vegetation in northern latitudes and possible increases in plankton biomass in some parts of the ocean. Lee Hannah et al., *Climate Change, Wine, and Conservation*, page 445, *supra*, predicts an expansion of viniculture acreage in the Western United States, Northern Europe, and New Zealand. Perhaps one of the most dramatic results will be in the Arctic Circle, where polar thaw has started to unlock treasures, including hints of oil and gas resources, lucrative shipping routes and important commercial fisheries. If the melting continues, as many experts expect, the mass of floating ice may largely disappear for entire summers this century; instead, the world would have a seasonally open sea nearly five times the size of the Mediterranean. Richard S.J. Tol, Climate Change: The Economic Impact of Climate Change in the Twentieth and Twenty-First Centuries, in How Much Have Global Problems Cost the World?: A Scorecard from 1900 to 2050 (Bjorn Lomborg, ed, 2013), concludes that climate change did indeed raise human and planetary welfare during the 20th century, but the adverse impacts will not kick in until 2080. However, for every benefit, there are negative impacts. For example, warmer winters would mean fewer deaths, particularly among vulnerable groups like the aged. However, the same groups are also vulnerable to additional heat, and deaths attributable to heat waves are expected to be approximately five times as great as winter deaths prevented. It is widely believed that warmer climes will encourage migration of disease-bearing insects like mosquitoes, and malaria is already appearing in places it hasn't been seen before. In Polar regions, melting can mean the loss of polar bear habitat and increased mobile ice hazards to shipping. The projected adverse impacts of climate change have been well described. The problem is that projections are based both on models and observed impacts. In Climate Change Evidence & Causes: An Overview from the Royal Society and the US National Academy of Sciences 19 (2014), the National Academy of Sciences concluded that while

some regions may benefit from climate change, "the long-term consequences overall will be disruptive."

2. PROJECTED ADVERSE IMPACTS

IPCC, CLIMATE CHANGE 2013
1139–1140 (2013)

Proxy and instrumental sea level data indicate a transition in the late 19th century to the early 20th century from relative low mean rates of rise over the previous two millennia to higher rates of rise (*high confidence*). It is likely that the rate of global mean sea level rise has continued to increase since the early 20th century, with estimates that range from 0.000 [-0.002 to 0.002] mm yr- to 0.013 [0.007 to 0.019] mm yr. It is *very likely* that the mean global rate was 1.7 [1.5 to 1.9] mm yr- between 1901 and 2010 for a total sea level rise of 0.19 [0.17 to 0.21] m. Between 1993 and 2010, the rate was *very likely* higher at 3.2 [2.8 to 3.6] mm yr[-1]; similarly high rates *likely* occurred between 1920 and 1950 . . . It is *very likely* that the rate of global mean sea level rise during the 21st century will exceed the rate observed during 1970–2010 . . . due to increases in ocean warming and the loss of mass from glaciers and ice sheets . . . For the period 2081–2100 . . . global mean sea rise is *likely* (*medium confidence*) to be in the 5 to 95% range of projections from process-based models, which give 0.26 to 0.55 m . . . .

Vulnerability to Sea Level Rise

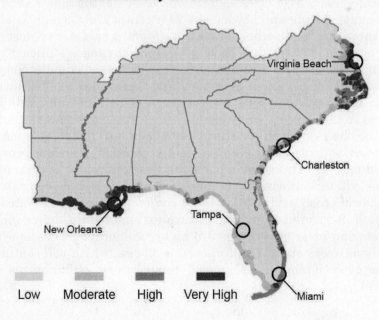

[Source: NCA, Southeast: National Climate Assessment Figure 17.6 (2014)]

INTERGOVERNMENTAL PANEL ON CLIMATE CHANGE, 2014
SYNTHESIS REPORT, SUMMARY FOR POLICYMAKERS

13–11 (2014) (Figures and References Omitted)

2.3 Future risks and impacts caused by a changing climate

Climate change will amplify existing risks and create new risks for natural and human systems. Risks are unevenly distributed and are generally greater for disadvantaged people and communities in countries at all levels of development.

Risk of climate-related impacts results from the interaction of climate-related hazards (including hazardous events and trends) with the vulnerability and exposure of human and natural systems, including their ability to adapt. Rising rates and magnitudes of warming and other changes in the climate system, accompanied by ocean acidification, increase the risk of severe, pervasive, and in some cases irreversible detrimental impacts. Some risks are particularly relevant for individual regions, while others are global. The overall risks of future climate change impacts can be reduced by limiting the rate and magnitude of climate change, including ocean acidification. The precise levels of climate change sufficient to trigger abrupt and irreversible change remain uncertain, but the risk associated with crossing such thresholds increases with rising temperature (*medium confidence*). For risk assessment, it is important to evaluate the widest possible range of impacts, including low-probability outcomes with large consequences.

A large fraction of species face increased extinction risk due to climate change during and beyond the 21st century, especially as climate change interacts with other stressors (*high confidence*). Most plant species cannot naturally shift their geographical ranges sufficiently fast to keep up with current and high projected rates of climate change in most landscapes; most small mammals and freshwater molluscs will not be able to keep up at the rates projected under RCP4.5 and above in flat landscapes in this century (*high confidence*). Future risk is indicated to be high by the observation that natural global climate change at rates lower than current anthropogenic climate change caused significant ecosystem shifts and species extinctions during the past millions of years. Marine organisms will face progressively lower oxygen levels and high rates and magnitudes of ocean acidification (*high confidence*), with associated risks exacerbated by rising ocean temperature extremes (*medium confidence*). Coral reefs and polar ecosystems are highly vulnerable. Coastal systems and low-lying areas are at risk from sea-level rise, which will continue for centuries even if the global mean temperature is stabilized (*high confidence*).

Climate change is projected to undermine food security[2]. Due to projected climate change by the mid-21st century and beyond, global marine species redistribution and marine biodiversity reduction in sensitive regions will challenge the sustained provision of fisheries productivity and other ecosystem services (*high confidence*). For wheat, rice, and maize in tropical and temperate regions, climate change without adaptation is projected to negatively impact production for local temperature increases of 2°C or more above late-20th century levels, although individual locations may benefit (*medium confidence*). Global temperature increases of ~4°C or more above late-20th century levels, combined with increasing food demand, would pose large risks to food security globally (*high confidence*). Climate change is projected to reduce renewable surface water and groundwater resources in most dry subtropical regions (*robust evidence, high agreement*), intensifying competition for water among sectors (*limited evidence, medium agreement*).

Until mid-century, projected climate change will impact human health mainly by exacerbating health problems that already exist (*very high confidence*). Throughout the 21st century, climate change is expected to lead to increases in ill-health in many regions and especially in developing countries with low income, as compared to a baseline without climate change (*high confidence*). By 2100 for RCP8.5, the combination of high temperature and humidity in some areas for parts of the year is expected to compromise common human activities, including growing food and working outdoors (*high confidence*).

In urban areas, climate change is projected to increase risks for people, assets, economies and ecosystems, including risks from heat stress, storms and extreme precipitation, inland and coastal flooding, landslides, air pollution, drought, water scarcity, sea-level rise, and storm surges (*very high confidence*). These risks are amplified for those lacking essential infrastructure and services or living in exposed areas.

Rural areas are expected to experience major impacts on water availability and supply, food security, infrastructure, and agricultural incomes, including shifts in the production areas of food and non-food crops around the world (*high confidence*).

Aggregate economic losses accelerate with increasing temperature (*limited evidence, high agreement*) but global economic impacts from

_____

[2]   Climate change is expected to have a significant impact on the ability of current food systems, not only in terms of agricultural yields, but also food prices, reliability of transport, food quality, and food safety. See Sonja J. Vermeulen, Bruce M. Campbell, and John S.I. Ingram, Climate Change and Food Systems, 37 Annual Review of Environment and Resources 195–222 (November 2012). Food systems (including agriculture as well as transport and processing) contribute have been estimated to contribute between 19%–29% of global anthropogenic greenhouse gas (GHG) emissions. The environmental issues relating to food production are covered in Chapter 14.

climate change are currently difficult to estimate. From a poverty perspective, climate change impacts are projected to slow down economic growth, make poverty reduction more difficult, further erode food security, and prolong existing and create new poverty traps, the latter particularly in urban areas and emerging hotspots of hunger (*medium confidence*). International dimensions such as trade and relations among states are also important for understanding the risks of climate change at regional scales.

Climate change is projected to increase displacement of people (*medium evidence, high agreement*). Populations that lack the resources for planned migration experience higher exposure to extreme weather events, particularly in developing countries with low income. Climate change can indirectly increase risks of violent conflicts by amplifying well-documented drivers of these conflicts such as poverty and economic shocks (*medium confidence*).

3. HAMLET'S 21ST CENTURY DILEMMA: TO MITIGATE OR TO ADAPT?

There are two basic climate change risk reduction strategies. The first is mitigation, the roll back of greenhouse gas emissions. Mitigation has been the focus of the international community since Rio 1992. The International Panel on Climate Change (IPCC) defines mitigation as "[a]n anthropogenic intervention to reduce the sources or enhance the sinks of greenhouse gases." The second strategy is adaptation. Adaptation accepts adverse impacts such as sea level rise or more frequent droughts as inevitable and seeks to minimize the damage. The IPCC defines adaptation as the "adjustment in natural or human systems to a new or changing environment exploits beneficial opportunities. Adaptation can take many forms including anticipatory and reactive adaptation, private and public adaptation, and autonomous and planned adaptation." The IPCC's 2014 Synthesis Report synthesizes the two strategies but continues to press for mitigation:

> Mitigation and adaptation are complementary approaches for reducing risks of climate change impacts over different time scales (*high confidence*). Mitigation, in the near-term and through the century, can substantially reduce climate change impacts in the latter decades of the 21st century and beyond. Benefits from adaptation can already be realized in addressing current risks, and can be realized in the future for addressing emerging risks.

> Five "Reasons For Concern" (RFCs) aggregate climate change risks and illustrate the implications of warming and of adaptation limits for people, economies, and ecosystems across sectors and regions. The Five RFCs are associated with:

(1) Unique and threatened systems, (2) Extreme weather events, (3) Distribution of impacts, (4) Global aggregate impacts, and (5) Large-scale singular events. In this report, the RFCs provide information relevant to Article 2 of UNFCCC. Without additional mitigation efforts beyond those in place today, and even with adaptation, warming by the end of the 21st century will lead to high to very high risk of severe, widespread, and irreversible impacts globally (high confidence) (Figure SPM.10). In most scenarios without additional mitigation efforts (those with 2100 atmospheric concentrations >1000ppm CO_2eq), warming is more likely than not to exceed 4°C above pre-industrial levels by 2100. The risks associated with temperatures at or above 4°C include substantial species extinction, global and regional food insecurity, consequential constraints on common human activities, and limited potential for adaptation in some cases (*high confidence*). Some risks of climate change, such as risks to unique and threatened systems and risks associated with extreme weather events, are moderate to high at temperatures 1°C to 2°C above pre-industrial levels. [p.13]

NOTE: MITIGATION AND ITS DISCONTENTS

Mitigation raises four difficult, perhaps intractable problems. The first is that the game may not be worth the candle. Mitigation requires drastic rollbacks in greenhouse emissions. The rub is that the benefits will not manifest themselves for centuries. "If emissions of CO_2 stopped altogether, it would take many thousands of years for atmospheric CO_2 to return to 'pre-industrial' levels due to its very slow transfer to the deep ocean and ultimate burial in ocean sediments. Surface temperatures would stay elevated for at least a thousand years, implying extremely long-term commitment to a warmer planet due to past and current emissions, and sea level would likely continue to rise for many centuries even after temperature stopped increasing. Significant cooling would be required to reverse melting of glaciers and the Greenland ice sheet, which formed during past cold climates. The current CO_2-induced warming of Earth is therefore essentially irreversible on human timescales. The amount and rate of further warming will depend almost entirely on how much more CO_2 humankind emits." Id. at 22 See also Meehl, G.A., et al., *2007: Global Climate Projections,* in Climate Change 2007: The Physical Science Basis. Contribution of Working Group I to the Fourth Assessment Report of the Intergovernmental Panel on Climate Change [Solomon, S., D. Qin, M. Manning, Z. Chen, M. Marquis, K.B. Averyt, M. Tignor and H.L. Miller (eds.).

The second problem is that mitigation requires a shift from carbon to non-carbon sources of energy. *See* International Energy Agency, Redrawing the Energy-Climate Map (2013). The International Energy Outlook 2013 (IEO 2013) projects that world energy consumption will grow by 56 percent between 2010 and 2040. "Total world energy use rises from 524 quadrillion British thermal units (Btu) in 2010 to 630 quadrillion Btu in 2020 and to 820 quadrillion Btu in 2040 . . . Much of the growth in energy consumption occurs in countries outside the Organization for Economic Cooperation and Development (OECD), known as non-OECD countries, where demand is driven by policies that promote strong, long-term economic growth. Energy use in non-OECD countries increases by 90 percent; in OECD countries, the increase is 17 percent. The IEO 2013 reference case does not incorporate prospective legislation or policies that might affect energy markets. Renewable energy and nuclear power are the world's fastest-growing energy sources, each increasing by 2.5 percent per year. However, fossil fuels continue to supply almost 80 percent of world energy use through 2040." Important efforts are underway in many countries to increase the use of renewable energy, but in 2012 87% of the world's energy came from coal, natural gas and oil, www.worldwatch.org/fossil-fuels-dominate-primary-energy-consumption-1.

The third problem is the assignment of responsibility to take the necessary mitigation actions. This remains largely a developed-developing world problem. As you will learn in Part B, the initial assumption in designing a global climate change regime was that the developed world would be primarily responsible for mitigation. North America and Europe were the largest historic greenhouse emitters. However, nations such as the United States balked at this idea, and as the map below indicates, the developed world is decreasing emissions while the developing world, most of Asia, including the Middle East, and northern Africa the Middle East, are increasing them.

An atlas of pollution: the world in carbon dioxide emissions

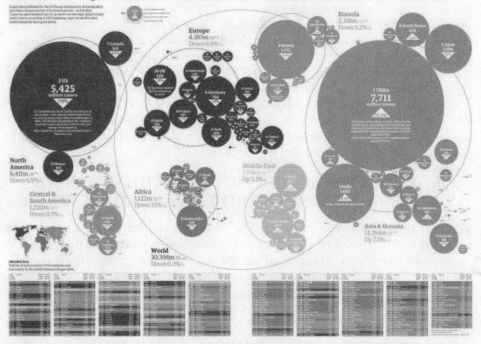

Source: The Guardian
http://co2now.org/Know-GHGs/Emissions/co2–emissions-by-country.html
http://www.theguardian.com/news/datablog/2011/jan/31/world-carbon-dioxide-
emissions-country-data-co2#data

Finally, any strategy to roll back emissions must not increase the already existing inequality within and among States. This problem has prevented the development of a comprehensive global mitigation regime. The issues are how to assign responsibility for causing and then mitigating climate change. Should responsibility be based on historic or current emission levels? The developing world advocates the former measure and the developed world, the latter. The developed world also argues that fairness requires that the countries that have benefitted most from hydrocarbon use should bear the major share of costs of rolling back greenhouse emissions. But, the problem is even more complicated because greenhouse gas emissions are the result of individual consumption choices about energy, transportation and product selection. Thus, is China responsible for the emissions caused by the manufacture of the products produced there or should or is a consumer of those products in a developed country responsible from the emissions? In Climate Change Justice (2010), Eric Posner and David Weisbach make the case against using historic emission levels. They start from the assumption that any international climate regime should not involve the redistribution of wealth from rich to poor countries. They also argue that there should be no national collective responsibility because many current residents of wealthy countries are not actually the ones responsible for climate change and the damages from climate change may be greater in richer countries. Thus, money is more efficiently allocated to address these damages. In another article, Eric Posner and Cass R. Sunstein, *Climate Justice*, 96 Geo. L. J. 1565 (2008), the authors argue that any legal responsibility for climate change damage dates only from 1990 when a sufficient causal link to anthropogenic activities was established. Professor Daniel Farber addressed and criticized these arguments in *The Case for Climate Compensation: Justice for Climate Change Victims in a Complex World*, 2008 Utah L. Rev.377 and Book Review: Climate Justice, 110 Mich. L. Rev. 985 (2012). The separate question of intergenerational equity was introduced in Chapter 2. The final problem is the challenge of adaptation. See pages 464 to 467, *infra*.

4. CLIMATE CHANGE MODELS: WHEN WILL WE KNOW WHAT WE NEED TO KNOW TO ACT?

Our ability to predict accurately the future impacts of climate change is based on the use of computer models and observed data. Thus, the use of models creates a great deal of uncertainty for policy makers. For example, expected greenhouse gas accumulations require projections about the rate of transition to a non-carbon based economy, as well as the level of the economy. The basic model is a general circulation model, but there are many such models, and they produce different outcomes. The various models must be synthesized and weighted by the IPCC. For policy makers, the important questions are what do they tell my country or region and can they predict tipping points? However, it is still more difficult to apply the models to smaller scales and to get accurate, useful impact projections. Models give ranges of impacts and confidence levels rather firm figures. For example, a well-respected model for the Mekong Basin "projects changes in annual river discharge that range from a decrease of 5.4% to an increase of 4.5%." Mark Maslin & Patrick Austin, Uncertainty: Climate Models and Their Limit?, 486 Nature 183 (2012). Thus, '[a]dvising policy makers becomes extremely difficult when models cannot predict even whether a river in a catchment system will have more or less water." The Science of Modeling is constantly being improved, Climate Change 2103: The Physical Science Basis, Working Group I Contribution to the Fifth Assessment Report of the Intergovernmental Panel on Climate Change, Chapter 9 (Thomas F. Stocker et al. eds. 2013), but the excerpt below remains an accurate summary of the problems of using the precautionary principle to move from model to policy.

CLIMATE MODELS
Charles Weiss, (2015)

The problems with scientific models are especially acute in the case of climate change. Scientists must rely on models to quantify the effect of human activities on the climate to date, and to predict their effects in the future. But to what are they to compare the results of their calculations?

Ideally, they would compare the climate on two versions of the Earth: one with human activities and one without, and ascribe the difference between the two observed climates to human activity.

Since they have no duplicate Earth on which to experiment, scientists are left with the need to compare mathematical models of the Earth's climate with and without human activity. They then test the validity of the models by "back-casting" or "post-diction"—starting the model well in the past and testing whether it reproduces the observed variations in the Earth's climate as they have happened since. They can do this with a variety of phenomena, starting with global average temperature but extending their calculations to the climate of specific regions, or the temperature of the oceans or of the atmosphere at different altitudes.

What is more, the Earth's climate is too complicated to be modeled exactly by even the most powerful computers. The physical laws that govern the climate are well known, but the range of sizes of the phenomena (from clouds of about one kilometer to El Nino of 10,000 kilometers in extent) and the climate's many feedback loops and "non-linearities" (for example, ice reflects the sun's heat while sea water absorbs it, so that melting Arctic ice sets off a feedback loop that speeds global warming) exceed the capacity of even the most powerful computers.

Fortunately, the great majority of calculations of the impact on the Earth's climate agree with each other, despite these complications. What is more, improved models have succeeded in providing reasonably accurate representations of a variety of climatic phenomena above and beyond the simple average of global temperatures—most importantly, improved representations of the responses of regional climates to human activity.

The result of this research is that the Inter-Governmental Panel on Climate Change (IPCC), the independent, authoritative committee of thousands of volunteer scientists, has declared that there is a 95% subjective probability that human activity is indeed affecting the world's climate. This subjective probability is different from the objective margin of error in the usual scientific experiments or (more familiarly) in the statistical analysis of polling data. It means that these scientists would accept odds of 19:1 that their models are leading to the correct conclusion.

MODERN GLOBAL CLIMATE CHANGE

Thomas R. Karl and Kevin E. Trenberg
302 Science, 1719, 1721–1722 (2003)

Our understanding of the climate system is complicated by feedbacks that either amplify or damp perturbations, the most important of which involve water in various phases. As temperatures increase, the water-holding capacity of the atmosphere increases along with water vapor amounts, producing water vapor feedback. As water vapor is a strong greenhouse gas, this diminishes the loss of energy through infrared radiation to space. Currently, water vapor feedback is estimated to contribute a radiative effect from one to two times the size of the direct effect of increases in anthropogenic greenhouse gases . . . Precipitation-runoff feedbacks occur because more intense rains run off at the expense of soil moisture, and warming promotes rain rather than snow. These changes in turn alter the partitioning of solar radiation into sensible versus latent heating . . . Heat storage feedbacks include the rate at which the oceans take up heat and the currents redistribute and release it back into the atmosphere at variable later times and different locations.

Cloud feedback occurs because clouds both reflect solar radiation, causing cooling, and trap outgoing long-wave radiation, causing warming. Depending on the height, location, and the type of clouds with their related optical properties, changes in cloud amount can cause either warming or cooling. Future changes in clouds are the single biggest source of uncertainty in climate predictions. They contribute to an uncertainty in the sensitivity of models to changes in greenhouse gases, ranging from a small negative feedback, thereby slightly reducing the direct radiative effects of increases in greenhouse gases, to a doubling of the direct radiative effect of increases in greenhouse gases . . . Clouds and precipitation processes cannot be resolved in climate models and have to be parametrically represented (parameterized) in terms of variables that are resolved. This will continue for some time into the future, even with projected increases in computational capability . . .

Ice-albedo feedback occurs as increased warming diminishes snow and ice cover, making the planet darker and more receptive to absorbing incoming solar radiation, causing warming, which further melts snow and ice. This effect is greatest at high latitudes. Decreased snow cover extent has significantly contributed to the earlier onset of spring in the past few decades over northern-hemisphere high latitudes . . . Ice-albedo feedback is affected by changes in clouds, thus complicating the net feedback effect.

The primary tools for predicting future climate are global climate models, which are fully coupled, mathematical, computer-based models of the physics, chemistry, and biology of the atmosphere, land surface, oceans, and cryosphere and their interactions with each other and with the sun and other influences (such as volcanic eruptions). Outstanding issues in modeling include specifying forcings of the climate system; properly dealing with complex feedback processes . . . that affect carbon, energy, and water sources, sinks and transports; and improving simulations of regional weather, especially extreme events. Today's inadequate or incomplete measurements of various forcings, with the exception of well-mixed greenhouse gases, add uncertainty when trying to simulate past and present climate. Confidence in our ability to predict future climate is dependent on our ability to use climate models to attribute past and present climate change to specific forcings. Through clever use of paleoclimate data, our ability to reconstruct past forcings should improve, but it is unlikely to provide the regional detail necessary that comes from long-term direct measurements. An example of forcing uncertainty comes from recent satellite observations and data analyses of 20th-century surface, upper air, and ocean temperatures, which indicate that estimates of the indirect effects of sulfate aerosols on clouds may be high, perhaps by as much as a factor of two. Human behavior, technological change, and the rate of population growth also affect future emissions and our ability to predict these must be factored into any long-term climate projection.

Regional predictions are needed for improving assessments of vulnerability to and impacts of change. The coupled atmosphere-ocean system has a preferred mode of behavior known as El Niño, and similarly the atmosphere is known to have preferred patterns of behavior, such as the North Atlantic Oscillation (NAO). So how will El Niño and the NAO change as the climate changes? There is evidence that the NAO, which affects the severity of winter temperatures and precipitation in Europe and eastern North America, and El Niño, which has large regional effects around the world, are behaving in unusual ways that appear to be linked to global heating (2, 31–33). Hence, it is necessary to be able to predict the statistics of the NAO and El Niño to make reliable regional climate projections.

Ensembles of model predictions have to be run to generate probabilities and address the chaotic aspects of weather and climate. This can be addressed in principle with adequate computing power, a challenge in itself. However, improving models to a point where they are more reliable and have sufficient resolution to be properly able to represent known important processes also requires the right observations, understanding, and insights (brain power). Global climate models will need to better integrate the biological, chemical, and physical components of the Earth system ... Even more challenging is the seamless flow of data and information among observing systems, Earth system models, socioeconomic models, and models that address managed and unmanaged ecosystems. Progress here is dependent on overcoming not only scientific and technical issues but also major institutional and international obstacles related to the free flow of climate-related data and information.

In large part, reduction in uncertainty about future climate change will be driven by studies of climate change assessment and attribution. Along with climate model simulations of past climates, this requires comprehensive and long-term climate-related data sets and observing systems that deliver data free of time-dependent biases. These observations would ensure that model simulations are evaluated on the basis of actual changes in the climate system and not on artifacts of changes in observing system technology or analysis methods (34). The recent controversy regarding the effects that changes in observing systems have had on the rate of surface versus tropospheric warming (35, 36) highlights this issue. Global monitoring through space-based and surface-based systems is an international matter, much like global climate change. There are encouraging signs, such as the adoption in 1999 of a set of climate monitoring principles, but these principles are impotent without implementation. International implementation of these principles is spotty at best.

We are entering the unknown with our climate. We need a global climate observing system, but only parts of it exist. We must not only take the vital signs of the planet but also assess why they are fluctuating and changing. Consequently, the system must embrace comprehensive analysis and assessment as integral components on an ongoing basis, as well as innovative research to better interpret results and improve our diagnostic capabilities. Projections into the future are part of such activity, and all aspects of an Earth information system feed into planning for the future, whether by planned adaptation or mitigation. Climate change is truly a global issue, one that may prove to be humanity's greatest challenge. It is very unlikely to be adequately addressed without greatly improved international cooperation and action.

QUESTION

Persistent uncertainty and the need to address risks are leitmotivs that run through domestic and international environmental law. The precautionary principle provides a legal foundation for regulatory and other action in the face of risks with high uncertainty levels. Opponents of addressing climate change have evoked uncertainty levels, and benefit-cost analysis as a reasoning for rejecting or not applying any version of the precautionary principle. These arguments collapsed in the case of ozone as a high level of scientific certainty about the causes of the thinning of ozone layer emerged. *See* Chapter 8, *supra*. Does the succession of IPCC reports and other analyses of the current state of climate change science provide a firm legal basis to apply a precautionary approach to both mitigation and adaptation?

5. ADAPTATION

The earth's climate has always presented challenges to civilization. E.g., Hubert H. Lamb, *Climate, History and the Modern World* (2nd ed. 1995). See Encyclopedia of Climate and Weather (Stephen H. Schneider, Terry L. Root and Michael D. Mastranada 2nd ed. 2011). Accordingly societies have always had to adapt to the constraints placed on survival based on a region's climate. E.g., Avie S. Issar & Mattanyah Zohar, Climate Change: Environment and History of the Near East (2nd ed. 2007); and Ben Orlove, *Human Adaptation to Climate Change: A Review of Three Historical Cases and Some General Perspectives*, 8 Envtl. Science & Policy 589 (2005). The collapse of some ancient civilizations is thought to be linked to extreme climate change events such as drought. E.g., Michael W. Binford et al., *Climate Variation and the Rise and Fall of An Andean Civilization*, 47 Quaternary Research 235 (1997). In the late 19th and early 20th century, the theory of geographical determinism, which paid particular attention to the role of climate on culture and society, appeared to explain the distinctive cultural and economic patterns that developed in particular regions. However, this simplistic cause and effect relationship was rejected in the United States in the 1920s, and it died after World War II. Nazi Germany had used earlier geographical determinism work to support racial explanations for the alleged superiority of northern European culture. As a result of this misuse of science, the emphasis on human adaptation to climate and the landscape gradually receded from the story of "civilization." I.G. Simmons, *Environmental History: A Concise Introduction* 179 (1993). The major reason for the rejection of the argument, which is central to modern environmental thinking, that humans should adapt to the limits on growth and settlement posed by climate, is that engineers and other applied scientists convinced governments that any constraints posed by climate could be overcome by technology such as large dams and irrigation projects, new drought resistant crops, public health systems, flood control dams, levees and sea walls, and air conditioning.

Climate change adaptation requires that countries rethink all past climate adaptation strategies.

> "At the national level, transformation is considered most effective when it reflects a country's own visions and approaches to achieving sustainable development in accordance with its national circumstances and priorities. Restricting adaptation responses to incremental changes to existing systems and structures, without considering transformational change, may increase costs and losses, and miss opportunities. Planning and implementation of transformational adaptation could reflect strengthened, altered or aligned paradigms and may place new and increased demands on governance structures to reconcile different goals and visions for the future and to address possible equity and ethical implications: adaptation pathways are enhanced by iterative learning, deliberative processes, and innovation."

2014 Synthesis Report at 13; *see also* Ian Burton, Elliot Diringer, et al., Adaptation to Climate Change: International Policy Options (Pew Center on Global Climate Change 2006); Susanne C. Moser & Julia A. Ekstrom, *A Framework to Diagnose Barriers to Climate Change Adaptation* PNAS Early Edition 1 (2010).

IPCC, FOURTH ASSESSMENT REPORT: CLIMATE CHANGE 2007, CHAPTER 4

Sector	Adaptation option/strategy	Underlying policy framework	Key constraints and opportunities to implementation (Normal font = constraints; *italics = opportunities*)
Water	Expanded rainwater harvesting; water storage and conservation techniques; water re-use; desalination; water-use and irrigation efficiency	National water policies and integrated water resources management; water-related hazards management	Financial, human resources and physical barriers; *integrated water resources management; synergies with other sectors*
Agriculture	Adjustment of planting dates and crop variety; crop relocation; improved land management, e.g. erosion control and soil protection through tree planting	R&D policies; institutional reform; land tenure and land reform; training; capacity building; crop insurance; financial incentives, e.g. subsidies and tax credits	Technological and financial constraints; access to new varieties; markets; *longer growing season in higher latitudes; revenues from 'new' products*
Infrastructure/settlement (including coastal zones)	Relocation; seawalls and storm surge barriers; dune reinforcement; land acquisition and creation of marshlands/wetlands as buffer against sea level rise and flooding; protection of existing natural barriers	Standards and regulations that integrate climate change considerations into design; land-use policies; building codes; insurance	Financial and technological barriers; availability of relocation space; *integrated policies and management; synergies with sustainable development goals*
Human health	Heat-health action plans; emergency medical services; improved climate-sensitive disease surveillance and control; safe water and improved sanitation	Public health policies that recognise climate risk; strengthened health services; regional and international cooperation	Limits to human tolerance (vulnerable groups); knowledge limitations; financial capacity; *upgraded health services; improved quality of life*
Tourism	Diversification of tourism attractions and revenues; shifting ski slopes to higher altitudes and glaciers; artificial snow-making	Integrated planning (e.g. carrying capacity; linkages with other sectors); financial incentives, e.g. subsidies and tax credits	Appeal/marketing of new attractions; financial and logistical challenges; potential adverse impact on other sectors (e.g. artificial snow-making may increase energy use); *revenues from 'new' attractions; involvement of wider group of stakeholders*
Transport	Realignment/relocation; design standards and planning for roads, rail and other infrastructure to cope with warming and drainage	Integrating climate change considerations into national transport policy; investment in R&D for special situations, e.g. permafrost areas	Financial and technological barriers; availability of less vulnerable routes; *improved technologies and integration with key sectors (e.g. energy)*
Energy	Strengthening of overhead transmission and distribution infrastructure; underground cabling for utilities; energy efficiency; use of renewable sources; reduced dependence on single sources of energy	National energy policies, regulations, and fiscal and financial incentives to encourage use of alternative sources; incorporating climate change in design standards	Access to viable alternatives; financial and technological barriers; acceptance of new technologies; *stimulation of new technologies; use of local resources*

The Report observes that "[a]daptive capacity is intimately connected to social and economic development but is unevenly distributed across and within societies." Thus, "[a] range of barriers limits both the implementation and effectiveness of adaptation measures. The capacity to adapt is dynamic and is influenced by a society's productive base, including natural and man-made capital assets, social networks and entitlements, human capital and institutions, governance, national income, health and technology. Even societies with high adaptive capacity remain vulnerable to climate change, variability and extremes."

NOTES AND QUESTIONS

Throughout history, communities have adapted to modest changes in climate. Sometimes this has been accomplished through governmental interventions, but most often it has been the result of gradual changes in patterns of behavior. Some have argued that there is no reason to adopt measures to prevent or mitigate climate change, because communities will be able to adapt readily to the changes. But poor communities are often the ones least able to adapt to change. In adapting to changes, the efforts must again be diverse, targeting the multiple areas of life that climate affects. This includes development of food crop strains that can withstand new temperatures and moisture levels, as well as changes in engineering designs to handle emergencies of floods and storms.

1. *Adaptability of developing countries.* The IPCC also explicitly recognized that developing countries would have more difficulty adapting to changes in climate than developed countries. This is due in large part to developing countries' limited research funds. However, the geographic considerations of large coastal populations and possible negative agriculture effects worsen the potential problems considerably. For additional reading, see IPCC, Coastal Zone Management, Climate Change 133, 144–146 (1991) (reporting that high population densities combined with the productivity of the coastal areas make the socio-economic effects of sea level rise associated with global warming particularly harmful).

2. *Adaptability of ecosystems.* Adaptability of natural ecosystems is expected to vary, according to the IPCC. Forested areas are expected to shift, as are growth rates and species composition found in any given area. Rangelands will generally remain the same. Perhaps the greatest effects will be found in coastal areas, where climate change and resulting rising sea levels may lead to erosion of shores, increased salinity of estuaries and freshwater aquifers, changed sediment and nutrient transport, altered chemical and microbiological contamination, and increased flooding. IPCC Second Assessment Report: Climate Change 1995, Summary for Policymakers: Scientific-Technical Analyses of Impacts, Adaptions and Mitigation of Climate Change, at 29–32 (1995).

3. *Sea level rise and depleted rivers.* One of the most talked-about impacts of global warming is the rise in sea level that would occur due to melting of the polar ice caps. Less discussed, but still important, is the role of rivers in the climate change scenario. How will the international law of rivers and waterways adapt to the differences global warming would impose? Does the Climate Convention adequately address this problem? For reading on this topic, see Ludwik A. Teclaff, *The River Basin Concept and Global Climate Change*, 8 Pace Envtl. L. Rev. 355 (1991); Gretta Goldenman, *Adapting to Climate Change: A Study of International Rivers and Their Legal Arrangements*, 17 Ecol. L.Q. 741 (1990); and A. Dan Tarlock, *How Well Can International Water Regimes Adapt to Global Climate Change*, 15 J. Land Use and Envtl. Law & Policy 423 (2000).

6. THE DEEPER POLICY IMPLICATIONS OF GREENHOUSE WARMING

The international law of climate change naturally focuses on the duties of States to limit GHG emissions. This poses difficult policy choices for States. Much of the policy and instrument choice discourse has been shaped by macro-economics. However, the issues run deeper than instrument choice debates. A deeper approach may be called for, encompassing a range of activities such as a radical reduction of fossil fuel consumption, substitution of cleaner sources of energy, and increased efficiency, the reduction of deforestation, better management of resource consumption, improved methods of agricultural production, and increased efforts to control population growth. *See* Edith Brown Weiss, *A Resource Management Approach to Carbon Dioxide During the Century of Transition*, 10 Denver J. Intl. L. & Pol'y. 487 (1981). Climate policy links economic growth and population growth with climate change mitigation and adaptation. E.g. Committee on Science, Engineering and Public Policy. The Effects of World Population and Economic Growth (National Academy of Sciences, National Academy of Engineering, Institute of Medicine (1991)); and David P. Knight, *Economic Growth, Population Growth, and Climate Change*, 26–28, *available at* http://www.feasta.org/ wp-content/uploads/2013/02/Economic_growth_Population_growth_and_ Climate_Change-23–07–2013_rbw.pdf, summarizes recent research on the issue:

Summary and policy implications

1.

The increase in global fossil fuel related greenhouse gas emissions since 1971 has not been solely or even primarily caused by population growth, least of all by rapid population growth in the countries with low incomes and high birth rates. We argue that the main driver of increasing fossil fuel related greenhouse gas emissions has been economic growth per capita. The latter has been driven by low fuel prices, cheap credit, consumerist policies, sophisticated advertising, and the pursuit of extrinsic goals including financial success, status, image and conformity. Population growth does however have a large effect by increasing both global consumption and emissions from land use change, and contributing to many other resource and environmental problems. It is extremely difficult to predict, even for the next 10 year, whether the rate of global economic growth per capita will be higher than that of global population growth and therefore whether its future contribution to fossil fuel related emissions will continue to be smaller than that of per capita economic growth.

2.

In general, population policies in the least developed countries with high birth rates are unlikely to have a large impact on global emissions within the time scale required to avoid dangerous global warming as indicated by the latest climate science.

3.

Reduction in consumption by wealthier individuals could have a quicker and larger impact than population policy in the short term. There is a strong argument that fiscal policies should be used to achieve the former. In the longer term it will probably be necessary to limit births to two per woman or less if all societies are to live within the limits imposed by the earth's life support system and their fair share of the planet's sustainable resources.

4.

Far-reaching changes in economic, technological, social and political systems are needed to reduce the risk of highly dangerous climate change and irreversible damage to biodiversity and the planetary life support systems. A combination of a radical increase in energy efficiency and carbon intensity, together with a drastic reduction in consumption is urgently needed. However, a concerted focus on a rapid adjustment of the components of the Kaya identity [3] is a necessary but in itself insufficient condition for the effective tackling of climate change. A top down, progressively constricting, upstream cap on fossil fuel introduction into the global economy seems the only practical means of guaranteeing reduction in the unabated burning of fossil fuels at a rate dictated by the latest climate science. The enormous size of the remaining fossil fuel resources and reserves particularly of coal and of planned projects to extract them make such a cap absolutely necessary. In addition to these measures, the active withdrawal of large quantities of carbon dioxide from the atmosphere probably required by 2050 to give a reasonable chance of avoiding disastrous warming and it is arguable that it would be safest to achieve this by afforestation on a gargantuan scale.

---

[3] A Japanese energy economist, Yoichi Kaya, describes total fossil fuel use carbon emissions as a product of the global population, GDP per capita, the energy intensity of GDP generation, and the carbon intensity of energy generation. P. 15

5.

A strong case can be made that the above changes require the establishment of an independent global climate commons trust to regulate the use of the finite resource of atmosphere along with that of land and water.

6.

Evidence reviewed here does not support the Environmental Kuznets theory, which justifies economic growth on the grounds that it would eventually lead to emissions reduction. It does suggest that a more equitable redistribution of income from the richer and richest individuals and countries to the poorest might on its own have a small advantageous effect on both total global energy use and fossil fuel related emissions. Such redistribution is also likely to be necessary if the developing countries are to agree to effective collective international action to prevent catastrophic climate change. A more equitable distribution of wealth and resources is arguably necessary to improve cohesion within and between countries.

NOTE: INDIVIDUAL RESPONSIBILITY, THE PROBLEM OF COLLECTIVE ACTION, AND RISK PERCEPTION

Because our present way of life and economic system revolve around activities that emit greenhouse gases, solving the climate change problem will not be possible by applying the traditional solutions adopted by the international community, such as prohibiting consumption of selected products or requiring special devices on production facilities. Limitations on large emitters are an important strategy, but the daily choices by individuals from using an automobile versus walking or using public transportation, not turning down a thermostat, not installing a low flush toilet, not installing small-scale renewable energy, flying 5,000 miles to visit a protected ecosystem or eating meat several times a week all contribute to GHG emissions. Then comes the question, why should I eat less meat if other people keep eating it? In his classic book, The Logic of Collective Action (1971), political scientist Mancur Olson, Jr. explained why individuals do not take actions to benefit the larger community. In addition, there is a large body of risk perception literature, which suggests that the lay public underappreciates risks, especially long-term risk. *See* IPCC (2014), Mitigation of Climate Change, Chapter 2, Integrated Risk and Uncertainty Assessment of Climate Change Response Policies (2014). Nonetheless, individuals do modify their behavior in response to new information. *See* Hope Babcock, *Global Climate Change: A Civic Republican Moment for Achieving Broader Changes in Environmental Behavior*, 26 Pace Envtl. L. Rev.1 (2009); Michael Vandenbergh, *The Carbon Neutral Individual*, 82 N.Y.U.L. Rev. 1673 (2007).

7. HUMAN RIGHTS AND CLIMATE CHANGE

The following petition was filed on behalf of the Inuit with the Inter-American Commission on Human Rights (IACHR), a body established by the Organization of American States in 1959. The United States is subject to the jurisdiction of the IACHR but not to the jurisdiction of the Inter-American Court of Human Rights because it is not a Party to the American Convention on Human Rights, November 22, 1969, OAS Treaty Ser. No. 36, 1144 UNTS 123, 9 I.L.M. 673 (1970).

INUIT PETITION TO THE INTER-AMERICAN COMMISSION ON HUMAN RIGHTS
(2005)

Global warming refers to an average increase in the Earth's temperature, causing changes in climate that lead to a wide range of adverse impacts on plants, wildlife, and humans. There is broad scientific consensus that global warming is caused by the increase in concentrations of greenhouse gases in the atmosphere as a result of human activity. The United States is, by any measure, the world's largest emitter of greenhouse gases, and thus bears the greatest responsibility among countries for causing global warming.

The Inuit, meaning "the people" in their native Inuktitut, are a linguistic and cultural group descended from the Thule people whose traditional range spans four countries—Chukotka in the Federation of Russia, northern and western Alaska in the United States, northern Canada, and Greenland. While there are local characteristics and differences within the broad ethnic category of "Inuit," all Inuit share a common culture characterized by dependence on subsistence harvesting in both the terrestrial and marine environments, sharing of food, travel on snow and ice, a common base of traditional knowledge, and adaptation to similar Arctic conditions. Particularly since the Second World War, the Inuit have adapted their culture to include many western innovations, and have adopted a mixed subsistence- and cash-based economy. Although many Inuit are engaged in wage employment, the Inuit continue to depend heavily on the subsistence harvest for food. Traditional "country food" is far more nutritious than imported "store-bought" food. Subsistence harvesting also provides spiritual and cultural affirmation, and is crucial for passing skills, knowledge and values from one generation to the next, thus ensuring cultural continuity and vibrancy.

. . . Nowhere on Earth has global warming had a more severe impact than the Arctic. Building on the 2001 findings of the Intergovernmental Panel on Climate Change, the 2004 Arctic Climate Impact Assessment [(ACIA)]—a comprehensive international evaluation of arctic climate change and its impacts undertaken by hundreds of scientists over four years—concluded that:

> The Arctic is extremely vulnerable to observed and projected climate change and its impacts. The Arctic is now experiencing some of the most rapid and severe climate change on Earth. Over the next 100 years, climate change is expected to accelerate, contributing to major physical, ecological, social, and economic changes, many of which have already begun. . . .

Permafrost, which holds together unstable underground gravel and inhibits water drainage, is melting at an alarming rate, causing slumping, landslides, severe erosion and loss of ground moisture, wetlands and lakes. The loss of sea ice, which dampens the impact of storms on coastal areas, has resulted in increasingly violent storms hitting the coastline, exacerbating erosion and flooding. Erosion in turn exposes coastal permafrost to warmer air and water, resulting in faster permafrost melts. These transformations have had a devastating impact on some coastal communities, particularly in Alaska and the Canadian Beaufort Sea region. Erosion, storms, flooding and slumping harm homes, infrastructure, and communities, and have damaged Inuit property, forcing relocation in some cases and requiring many communities to develop relocation contingency plans. In addition, these impacts have contributed to decreased water levels in rivers and lakes, affecting natural sources of drinking water, and habitat for fish, plants, and game on which Inuit depend. . . .

Observers have also noted changes in the location, characteristics, number, and health of plant and animal species caused by changes in climate conditions. Some species are less healthy. In the words of the Arctic Climate Impact Assessment, "[m]arine species dependent on sea ice, including polar bears, ice-living seals, walrus, and some marine birds, are very likely to decline, with some facing extinction."

Other species are becoming less accessible to the Inuit because the animals are moving to new locations, exacerbating the travel problems resulting from climate change. Still others cannot complete their annual migrations because the ice they travel on no longer exists, or because they cannot cross rivers swollen by sudden floods. More frequent autumn freeze-thaw cycles have created layers of solid ice under the snow that makes winter foraging more difficult for some game animals, including caribou, decreasing their numbers and health. These impacts on animals have impaired the Inuit's ability to subsist.

Increased temperatures and sun intensity have heightened the risk of previously rare health problems such as sunburn, skin cancer, cataracts, immune system disorders and heat related health problems. Warmer weather has increased the mortality and decreased the health of some harvested species, impacting important sources of protein for the

Inuit. Traditional methods of food and hide storage and preservation are less safe because of increased daytime temperatures and melting permafrost.

. . . Noting the particular impact these changes will have on the Inuit, the ACIA states: "For Inuit, warming is likely to disrupt or even destroy their hunting and food sharing culture as reduced sea ice causes the animals on which they depend on to decline become less accessible, and possibly become extinct."

Several principles of international law guide the application of the human rights issues in this case. Most directly, the United States is obligated by its membership in the Organization of American States and its acceptance of the American Declaration of the Rights and Duties of Man to protect the rights of the Inuit described above. Other international human rights instruments give meaning to the United States' obligations under the Declaration. For example, as a party to the International [Covenant] on Civil and Political Rights ("ICCPR"), the. United States is bound by the principles therein. As a signatory to the International [Covenant] on Economic, Social, and Cultural Rights ("ICESCR"), the United States must act consistently with the principles of that agreement.

The United States also has international environmental law obligations that are relevant to this petition. For instance, the United States also has an obligation to ensure that activities within its territory do not cause transboundary harm or violate other treaties to which it is a party. As a party to the UN Framework Convention on Climate Change, the United States has committed to developing and implementing policies aimed at returning its greenhouse gas emissions to 1990 levels. All of these international obligations are relevant to the application of the rights in the American Declaration because, in the words of the Inter-American Commission, the Declaration "should be interpreted and applied in context of developments in the field of international human rights law . . . and with due regard to other relevant rules of international law applicable to [OAS] member states."

The impacts of climate change, caused by acts and omissions by the United States, violate the Inuit's fundamental human rights protected by the American Declaration of the Rights and Duties of Man and other international instruments. These include their rights to the benefits of culture, to property, to the preservation of health, life, physical integrity, security, and a means of subsistence, and to residence, movement, and inviolability of the home. Because Inuit culture is inseparable from the condition of their physical surroundings, the widespread environmental upheaval resulting from climate change violates the Inuit's right to practice and enjoy the benefits of their culture. The subsistence culture central to Inuit cultural identity has been damaged by climate change, and may cease to exist if action is not taken by the United States in concert with the community of nations.

The Inuit's fundamental right to use and enjoy their traditional lands is violated as a result of the impacts of climate change because large tracks of Inuit traditional lands are fundamentally changing, and still other areas are becoming inaccessible. Summer sea ice, a critical extension of traditional Inuit land, is literally ceasing to exist. Winter sea ice is thinner and unsafe in some areas. Slumping, erosion, land slides, drainage, and more violent sea storms have destroyed coastal land, wetlands, and lakes, and have detrimentally changed the characteristics of the landscape upon which the Inuit depend. The inability to travel to lands traditionally used for subsistence and the reduced harvest have diminished the value of the Inuit's right of access to these lands.

The Inuit's fundamental right to enjoy their personal property is violated because climate change has reduced the value of the Inuit's personal effects, decreasing the quality of food and hides, and damaging snowmobiles, dog sleds and other tools. Their right to cultural intellectual property is also violated, because much of the Inuit's traditional knowledge, a formerly priceless asset, has become frequently unreliable or inaccurate as a result of climate change. The Inuit's fundamental rights to health and life are violated as climate change exacerbates pressure on the Inuit to change their diet, which for millennia has consisted of wild meat and a few wild plants. Climate change is accelerating a transition by Inuit to a more western store-bought diet with all of its inherent health problems. Life-threatening accidents are increasing because of rapid changes to ice, snow, and land. Traditional food preservation methods are becoming difficult to practice safely. Natural sources of drinking water are disappearing and diminishing in quality. Increased risks of previously rare heat and sun related illnesses also implicate the right to health and life.

The Inuit's fundamental rights to residence and movement, and inviolability of the home are likewise violated as a result of the impacts of climate change because the physical integrity of Inuit homes is threatened. Most Inuit settlements are located in coastal areas, where storm surges, permafrost melt, and erosion are destroying certain coastal Inuit homes and communities. In inland areas, slumping and landslides threaten Inuit homes and infrastructure.

The Inuit's fundamental right to their own means of subsistence has also been violated as a result of the impacts of climate change. The travel problems, lack of wildlife, and diminished quality of harvested game resulting from climate change have deprived the Inuit of the ability to rely on the harvest for year-round sustenance. Traditional Inuit knowledge, passed from Inuit elders in their role as keepers of the Inuit culture, is also becoming outdated because of the rapidly changing environment.

The United States of America, currently the largest contributor to greenhouse emissions in the world, has nevertheless repeatedly declined to take steps to regulate and reduce its emissions of the gases responsible for climate change. As a result of well-documented increases in atmospheric concentrations of greenhouse gases, it is beyond dispute that most of the observed change in global temperatures over the last 50 years is attributable to human actions. This conclusion is supported by a remarkable consensus in the scientific community; including every major US scientific body with expertise on the subject. Even the Government of the United States has accepted this conclusion.

However, and notwithstanding its ratification of the UN Framework Convention on Climate Change, United States has explicitly rejected international overtures and compromises, including the Kyoto Protocol to the U.N. Framework Convention on Climate Change, aimed at securing agreement to curtail destructive greenhouse gas emissions. With full knowledge that this course of action is radically transforming the arctic environment upon which the Inuit depend for their cultural survival, the United States has persisted in permitting the unregulated emission of greenhouse gases from within its jurisdiction into the atmosphere.

Protecting human rights is the most fundamental responsibility of civilized nations. Because climate change is threatening the lives, health, culture and livelihoods of the Inuit, it is the responsibility of the United States, as the largest source of greenhouse gases, to take immediate and effective action to protect the rights of the Inuit.

[The IACHR decided not to consider the petition in 2006, but the Commission did hold a hearing on the relationship between global warming and human rights. *See* Jessica Gordon, *Inter-American Commission on Human Rights to Hold Hearing After Rejecting Inuit Climate Change Petition*, 7 Sustainable Dev. L. & Pol'y 55 (2007); Donald K. Anton & Dinah Shelton, *Case Study III: Climate Change and Human Rights* in Environmental Protection and Human Rights (2011) The relationship between environmental protection and human rights is the subject of Chapter 15.]

NOTES AND QUESTIONS

1. *Arctic melting.* There is no dispute about the facts catalogued in the petition relating to the melting of Arctic ice and permafrost (which no longer seems to be permanent), and the increase of annual average arctic temperatures at a rate more than twice that of the rest of the world. New studies of Greenland's glaciers, the biggest component of Greenland's contribution to global sea level rise (0.5 millimeters out of 3 millimeters per year), show that glaciers on Greenland are slipping into the ocean twice as

fast as they were just five years ago. Rising surface air temperatures (Greenland has seen a 3 degree Celsius rise over the last 20 years) appear to be triggering the increases in glacier speed. The warmer temperatures increase the amount of melt water reaching the glacier-rock interface where it serves as a lubricant that eases glaciers' march to the ocean. Due to the recent speed-up, more ice is being dumped into the sea. The component of ice loss due to glacier flow has increased from 50 cubic kilometers of ice loss per year in 1996 to 150 cubic kilometers of ice loss per year in 2005. If the Greenland ice sheet melted completely it would raise global sea level by about 7 meters. *See* Eric Rignot & Pannir Kanagaratnam, *Changes in the Velocity Structure of the Greenland Ice Sheet*, 311 Science 986 (2006).

2.   *Would the petition survive a demurrer?* Do you think a good case has been made by the Inuit petition? What if this case were before the Inter-American Court of Human Rights? If you were a judge on the Court and the United States in effect demurred, how would you rule? What should the petitioner's burden of proof be in such a case? What would it take to shift the burden to the United States? Should the petitioners advance some variant of the market-share approach to liability, in view of the likelihood that at most, the United States only bears responsibility for a portion—even if a large portion—of their problems?

3.   *The applicability of traditional principles.* Do the fundamental principles of international environmental law examined in Chapter 4 apply to a case such as this? What about the United States' "responsibility" as that doctrine is explored in Chapter 5? What kind of remedy would be appropriate? *Restitutio in integrum*? How? Compensation? How would this be measured? Satisfaction? What form(s) would this take?

4.   *Try and Try Again.* Review the Materials on the NAFTA Side Agreement. In 2012, the Submissions Unit of the Commission for Environmental Cooperation accepted a submission which alleged that Canada did not enforce its own laws when it refused to change the status polar bears under its Species at Risk Act from "special concern" to "threatened." Commission for Environmental Cooperation, SEM-11003, Protection of Polar Bears (2011). A 2014 joint Canada-United States study found that the shrinking Artic Sea has shrunk the polar bear population from 1600 in 2004 to 900 in 2010. The Associated Press, *Study Shows Polar Bears Disappearing in Region*, N.Y. Times, Nov.18, 2014, at A13. However, in 2014, the Council, consisting of representatives from Canada, Mexico and the United States, voted 2 to 1 to reject the Submission Unit's recommendation that a factual record be prepared. Council Resolution 14–04, 5 June 2014

B. RESPONDING TO THE THREAT: THE FRAMEWORK CONVENTION ON CLIMATE CHANGE

1. THE RUN UP TO RIO 1992

The realization of the potential destructiveness of our accustomed means of achieving our standard of living resulted in states moving toward a multilateral Climate Change Convention. In June 1992, less than 18 months after the initiation of negotiations, the Framework Convention on Climate Change opened for signature. But while the formal negotiations were speedy despite the complexity of climate change, the period building up to the opening of the negotiations was longer. In 1979, a cooperative effort by UNEP, WMO, and the ICSU brought together the First World Climate Conference. This was followed by several further meetings on the carbon dioxide problem, culminating in the global warming meeting of 1985 in Villach, Austria, where international consensus on the importance of the problem was achieved.

In Geneva, in November 1988, 35 States founded the Intergovernmental Panel on Climate Change (IPCC) to assess the effects of human activities on climate change and to analyze science, policy implications, and response strategies to the greenhouse effect in three working groups. This body met periodically over the next 20 months and produced a consensus document indicating that the global temperature could be expected to rise significantly in response to human activities. This was technically a scientific panel, but governments sent other officials as well as scientists. Many have called the result "negotiated science"; in the end the process was essential for providing the international consensus necessary to open negotiations on a convention on climate change.

The call for a framework convention on the global climate started in March 1989, with the Declaration of the Hague. It continued in the same year at international meetings in Helsinki, Nairobi, and Noordwijk, the Netherlands. The Second World Climate Conference in 1990 created task groups to conduct more research and to prepare a draft convention for the Rio de Janeiro Conference.

The convention was negotiated under the umbrella of the Intergovernmental Negotiating Committee (INC), a free-standing body established by the United Nations General Assembly. The INC continued to meet until the convention went into effect and was replaced by a meeting of the parties (referred to as Conference of the Parties, or COP). The IPCC also continued to meet, even though there is no explicit mention of it in the text of the Climate Convention.

In 1992, the Framework Convention on Climate Change was opened for signature in Rio at the UN Conference on Environment and Development. It entered into force on March 21, 1993.

NOTES AND QUESTIONS

1.   *Precaution.* Did the precautionary principle or approach require countries to try to draft a formal convention to limit the emission of greenhouse gases? Whether or not it did, when you read the excerpts from the Convention below, consider whether it adequately reflects the precautionary principle or approach.

2.   *Focused or comprehensive?* Before the climate change negotiations began there was considerable scholarly debate as to whether the negotiations ought to include only those countries that were major emitters of greenhouse gases or whether they should include all countries. What arguments do you see for either position?

2.   THE CLIMATE CHANGE CONVENTION AND ITS IMPLEMENTATION

The 1992 United Nations Framework Convention on Climate Change (UNFCCC or FCCC), to which there are 198 Parties as of August 2015 (for purposes of comparison, there are 193 member States of the United Nations as of the same date), covers all greenhouse gases. Under the Convention, Parties are to provide national inventories of sources and sinks of greenhouse gases, and regular national reports on policies and measures that limit emissions of these gases and enhance the sinks for them. These inventories and reports are subject to international review by the parties. While the Convention sets up a very important process by which parties can monitor and control greenhouse gas emissions, it does not contain explicit targets and timetables for stabilizing atmospheric concentrations of the gases. For a comprehensive analysis of the negotiations of the FCCC and its provisions, see Daniel Bodansky, *The United Nations Framework Convention on Climate Change: A Commentary*, 18 Yale J. Intl. L. 451 (1993); and Negotiating Climate Change: The Inside Story of the Rio Convention (Irving M. Mintzer & J. Amber Leonard eds., 1994).

Until recently, the primary focus of the climate change policy debate was on how to deal with significant climate change induced by human activities ("anthropogenic change"). The FCCC incorporates in Article 3 (Principles) a number of legal principles that we have discussed; other legal principles are omitted. The following material highlights some of these principles and omissions. As you consider these materials, ask yourself whether you understand what they mean? If you were a government official or a lawyer advising a business entity or a nongovernmental organization, how would you describe what is required by the principles? In Article 4, the Convention sets forth the commitments of the Parties, including the commitments of developed country Parties (so-called Annex I countries) regarding limiting GHG emissions. Note that the commitments do not cover GHGs controlled by the Montreal Protocol, covered in Chapter 8. Why is that? Note also that the Parties who will actually be subject to the latter obligations are developed countries and other countries that are listed in Annex I. In particular, pay close attention to the content and structure of Article 4(2), which sets forth a timetable for developed countries to reduce greenhouse gases in section (a), but the goal of returning emissions to 1990 levels is in section (b). Why might a lay reader conclude that the Convention sets forth targets and timetables? What should a lawyer conclude?

EXCERPTS FROM THE UNITED NATIONS FRAMEWORK CONVENTION ON CLIMATE CHANGE MAY 9, 1992, U.N. DOC. A/CONF.151/26

reprinted in 31 I.L.M. 49 (1992)

Acknowledging that change in the Earth's climate and its adverse effects are a common concern of humankind.

Concerned that human activities have been substantially increasing the atmospheric concentrations of greenhouse gases, that these increases enhance the natural greenhouse effect, and that this will result on average in additional warming of the Earth's surface and atmosphere and may adversely affect natural ecosystems and humankind, . . .

Acknowledging that the global nature of climate change calls for the widest possible cooperation by all countries and their participation in an effective and appropriate international response, in accordance with their common but differentiated responsibilities and respective capabilities and their social and economic conditions, . . .

Recalling also that States have, in accordance with the Charter of the United Nations and the principles of international law, the sovereign right to exploit their own resources pursuant to their own environmental and developmental policies, and the responsibility to ensure that activities within their jurisdiction or control do not cause damage to the environment of other States or of areas beyond the limits of national jurisdiction, . . .

Article 1
Definitions

For the purposes of this Convention:

. . .

2.   "Climate change" means a change of climate which is attributed directly or indirectly to human activity that alters the composition of the

global atmosphere and which is in addition to natural climate variability observed over comparable time periods . . .

Article 2
Objective

The ultimate objective of this Convention and any related legal instruments that the Conference of the Parties may adopt is to achieve, in accordance with the relevant provisions of the Convention, stabilization of greenhouse gas concentrations in the atmosphere at a level that would prevent dangerous anthropogenic interference with the climate system. Such a level should be achieved within a time-frame sufficient to allow ecosystems to adopt naturally to climate change, to ensure that food production is not threatened and to enable economic development to proceed in a sustainable manner.

Article 3
Principles

In their actions to achieve the objective of the Convention and to implement its provisions, the Parties shall be guided, inter alia, by the following:

1.   The Parties should protect the climate system for the benefit of present and future generations of humankind, on the basis of equity and in accordance with their common but differentiated responsibilities and respective capabilities. Accordingly, the developed country Parties should take the lead in combatting climate change and the adverse effects thereof.

2.   The specific needs and special circumstances of developing country Parties, especially those that are particularly vulnerable to the adverse effects of climate change, and of those Parties, especially developing country Parties, that would have to bear a disproportionate or abnormal burden under the Convention, should be given full consideration.

3.   The Parties should take precautionary measures to anticipate, prevent or minimize the causes of climate change and mitigate its adverse effects. Where there are threats of serious or irreversible damage, lack of full scientific certainty should not be used as a reason for postponing such measures, taking into account that policies and measures to deal with climate change should be cost-effective so as to ensure global benefits at the lowest possible cost. To achieve this, such policies and measures should take into account different socio-economic contexts, be comprehensive, cover all relevant sources, sinks and reservoirs of greenhouse gases and adaption, and comprise all economic sectors. Efforts to address climate change may be carried out cooperatively by interested Parties . . .

Article 4
Commitments

1.   All Parties, taking into account their common but differentiated responsibilities and their specific national and regional development priorities, objectives and circumstances; shall:

(a) Develop, periodically update, publish and make available to the Conference of the Parties ... national inventories of anthropogenic emissions by sources and removals by sinks of all greenhouse gases not controlled by the Montreal Protocol, using comparable methodologies to be agreed upon ...

(b) Formulate, implement, publish and regularly update national, and where appropriate, regional programmes containing measures to mitigate climate change ... and measures to facilitate adequate adaption to climate change;

(c) Promote and cooperate in the development, application and diffusion, including transfer, of technologies, practices and processes that control, reduce or prevent anthropogenic emissions of greenhouse gases ... including the energy, transport, industry, agriculture, forestry and waste management sectors;

2.   The developed country Parties and other Parties included in annex I commit themselves specifically as provided for in the following:

(a) Each of these Parties shall adopt national policies and take corresponding measures on the mitigation of climate change, by limiting its anthropogenic emissions of greenhouse gases and protecting and enhancing its greenhouse gas sinks and reservoirs. These policies and measures will demonstrate that developed countries are taking the lead in modifying longer-term trends in anthropogenic emissions consistent with the objective of the Convention, recognizing that the return by the end of the present decade to earlier levels of anthropogenic emissions of carbon dioxide and other, greenhouse gases not controlled by the Montreal Protocol would contribute to such modification, and taking into account the differences in these Parties' starting points and approaches, economic structures and resources bases, the need to maintain strong and sustainable economic growth, available technologies and other individual circumstances, as well as the need for equitable and appropriate contributions by each of these Parties to the global effort regarding that objective. These Parties may implement such policies and measures jointly with other Parties and may assist other Parties in contributing to the achievement of the objective of the Convention and, in particular, that of this subparagraph;

(b) In order to promote progress to this end, each of these Parties shall communicate, within six months of the entry into force of the Convention for it and periodically thereafter . . . detailed information on its policies and measures referred to in subparagraph (a) above, as well as on its resulting projected anthropogenic emissions by sources and removals of greenhouse gases not controlled by the Montreal Protocol . . . with the aim of returning individually, or jointly to their 1990 levels these anthropogenic emissions of carbon dioxide and other greenhouse gases not controlled by the Montreal Protocol . . .

3.   The developed country Parties and other developed Parties included in annex II shall provide new and additional financial resources to meet the agreed full costs incurred by developing country Parties in Complying with their obligations under Article 12, paragraph 1. They shall also provide such financial resources, including for the transfer of technology, needed by the developing country Parties to meet the agreed full incremental costs of implementing measures that are covered by paragraph 1 of this Article and that are agreed between a developing country Party and the international entity or entities referred to in Article 11, in accordance with that Article. The implementation of these commitments shall take into account the need for adequacy and predictability in the flow of funds and the importance of appropriate burden sharing among the developed country Parties. . . .

5.   The developed country Parties and other developed Parties included in annex II shall take all practicable steps to promote, facilitate and finance, as appropriate, the transfer of, or access to, environmentally sound technologies and know-how to other Parties, in particular developing country Parties, to enable them to implement the provisions of the Convention . . .

7.   The extent to which developing country Parties will effectively implement their commitments under the Convention will depend upon the effective implementation by developed country Parties of their commitments under the Convention related to financial resources and transfer of technology and will take into account that economic and social development and poverty eradication are the first and overriding priorities of the developing country Parties. . . .

Article 7
Conference of the Parties

1.   A Conference of the Parties is hereby established.

2.   The Conference of the Parties, as the supreme body of this Convention, shall keep under regular review the implementation of the Convention and any related legal instruments that the Conference of the Parties may adopt, and shall make, within its mandate, the decisions

necessary to promote the effective implementation of the Convention. To this end, it shall:

    (a) Periodically examine the obligations of the Parties and the institutional arrangements under the Convention, in light of the objective of the Convention, the experience gained in its implementation and the evolution of scientific and technological knowledge; . . .

6.   The United Nations, its specialized agencies and . . . any State member thereof or observers thereto not Party to the Convention, may be represented at sessions of the Conference of the Parties as observers. Any body or agency, whether national or international, governmental or non-governmental, which is qualified in matters covered by the Convention, and which has informed the secretariat of its wish to be represented at a session of the Conference of the Parties as an observer, may be so admitted unless at least one-third of the Parties present object. . . .

Article 9
Subsidiary Body for Scientific and Technological Advice

1.   A subsidiary body for scientific and technological advice is hereby established to provide the Conference of the Parties and, as appropriate, its other subsidiary bodies with timely information and advice on scientific and technological matters relating to the Convention. This body shall be open to participation by all Parties and shall be multidisciplinary. It shall comprise government representatives competent in the relevant field of expertise. It shall report regularly to the Conference of the Parties on all aspects of its work. . . .

Article 10
Subsidiary Body for Implementation

1.   A subsidiary body for implementation is hereby established to assist the Conference of the Parties in the assessment and review of the effective implementation of the Convention. . . .

Article 11
Financial Mechanism

1.   A mechanism for the provision of financial resources on a grant or concessional basis, including for the transfer of technology, is hereby defined. It shall function under the guidance of and be accountable to the Conference of the Parties, which shall decide on its policies, programme priorities and eligibility criteria related to this Convention. . . .

Article 12
Communication of Information Related
to Implementation

1.   In accordance with Article 4, paragraph 1, each Party shall communicate to the Conference of the Parties, through the secretariat, the following elements of information:

(a) A national inventory of anthropogenic emissions by sources and removals by sinks of all greenhouse gases not controlled by the Montreal Protocol, to the extent its capacities permit, using comparable methodologies to be promoted and agreed upon by the Conference of the Parties;

(b) A general description of steps taken or envisaged by the Party to implement the Convention; and

(c) Any other information that the Party considers relevant

Article 14
Settlement of Disputes

1.   In the event of a dispute between any two or more Parties concerning the interpretation or application of the Convention, the Parties concerned shall seek a settlement of the dispute through negotiation or any other peaceful means of their own choice. . . .

NOTES AND QUESTIONS

1.   *Does the Convention Adopt the Precautionary Principle?* The Climate Convention provides in Article 3 that the parties "should" take precautionary measures rather than that they "shall" take such measures. Does this indicate that they are not under an obligation to do so? Isn't the whole approach of the FCCC precautionary? If so, why not say "shall?" Note also that Article 3 refers to "precautionary measures" and not to the precautionary principle. What legal difference does this make? Do you see any significant differences in the definition of "precautionary measures" from those discussed in Chapter 4? Could a country use this language to justify a carbon tax? Could an environmentally conscious non-governmental organization use this language effectively to argue that a carbon tax is required? See pages 488 to 490, *infra*.

2.   *Protection of Future Generations.* Article 3(1) provides that the parties are to protect the climate system "for the benefit of present and future generations of humankind, on the basis of equity and in accordance with their common but differentiated responsibilities and respective capabilities. Accordingly, the developed country Parties should take the lead in combating climate change and the adverse effects thereof." How would you define "equity" here? What does "intergenerational equity" mean in the context of climate change? See Edith Brown Weiss, In Fairness to Future Generations: International Law, Common Patrimony, and Intergenerational Equity 345

(1989). See also James C. Wood, *Intergenerational Equity and Climate Change*, 8 Geo. Intl. Envt'l. L. Rev. 293 (1996).

3.   *Accommodation for Developing Countries.* The reference to "common but differentiated responsibilities" may be a newly emerging principle. See Principle 7 of the Rio Declaration on Environment and Development. Is it clear to you what it means? See Christopher D. Stone, *Common but Differentiated Responsibilities in International Law*, 98 AJIL 276 (2004) (arguing that the FCCC regime has reached a stalemate, disputes over the scope of common but differentiated responsibilities being a primary cause). See also Daniel Magraw, *Legal Treatment of Developing Countries: Differential, Contextual, and Absolute Norms*, 1 Colo. J. Intl. Envtl. L. & Poly. 69 (1990) (arguing there is a customary international law requirement to take developing countries' interests into account; excerpted in Chapter 4). As you study of the implementation, especially the problems of imposing emission limitations of countries such as China and India, ask yourself is the principle "common but differentiated responsibilities" still relevant? Shoibal Chakrvarty et al., Sharing Global CO_2 Emission Reductions Among One Billion High Emitters, 106 Proceedings National Academies of Sciences 11884 (2009), answers the question, yes. The article proposes that mitigation be assigned based on summing the excess, high emitters over a treaty-established universal individual cap, regardless of their location. These emitters are identified by national income distribution and carbon intensity levels. Thus, the burden is shifted to countries with a higher percentage of high emitters. Under this scheme, the United States has the biggest abatement burden; India gets a free pass, but Africa, Russia and the Middle East do not due to high carbon intensity and inequality in nations with substantial energy industries. India has the fifth largest coal reserves behind the United States, China, Russia and Australia, and it is the third largest producer and generates 68% percent of its energy from coal. In 2014, the Supreme Court of India cancelled 214 coal leases issues from 1992 to 2009, constituting 7% of production areas, held by private companies because of the failure of authorities to follow Coal Ministry guidelines. Sharma v. Principal Secretary & Others, (2014), available at http://supremecourtofindia.nic.in/ outtoday/wr120.pdf. Nonetheless, India is expanding coal production and use. Gardiner H. Harris, Coal Rush in India Could Tip the Balance on Climate Change, The New York Times, p.A4, November 18 2014.

4.   *Stockholm Principle 21 and National Responsibility Outside the Convention.* The Convention neither explicitly obligates countries to respect Principle 21 of the Stockholm Declaration on the Human Environment nor includes the language of the principle in the obligations of the Convention. Why would countries be reluctant to include it? What would be the legal implications of doing so? When the principle was drafted in 1972, countries were concerned largely with transfrontier pollution. Do you see any problems with applying the principle to problems such as climate change or ozone depletion? Principle 21 is stated verbatim in the Convention's preamble.

5.   *Liability.* The convention also does not mention liability. Are countries liable for damage from climate change? Consider the following hypothetical case. Suppose that one of the island countries, such as the Maldives, is substantially inundated or even disappears as a result of rising sea levels from climate change. Is there any legal redress for the Maldives? Against whom could the country bring a claim? In what forum? On the basis of what theory of liability? Are your answers applicable to the Inuit case outlined in the Petition excerpted at page 471, *supra*. The considerable literature on liability includes Climate Change Liability: Transnational Law and Practice (Richard Lord et al. eds 2012) and Jennifer Klinski, *International Climate Change Liability: A Myth or Reality?* 18 J. Transnational Law & Policy 378 (2009).

Some have argued that traditional notions of liability in international law are not applicable to climate change. Rather there can only be a general notion of accountability between States. During the Climate Change Convention negotiations, the small island States were sufficiently concerned about this issue that they pressed for countries to establish a special trust fund for them to compensate for measures to adjust to future climate change. They were unsuccessful in this effort, but the issue remained before the international community and arose again during negotiations of the Kyoto Protocol (described below), as did the claim by oil-producing countries that they should be compensated because some efforts to decrease GHG emissions could hurt their economies. Are there any principles in international law that may be useful to the island countries in pressing their concerns?

6.   *The Relevance of Trail Smelter for Transfrontier Pollution Liability.* Many of the principles you have read about earlier relate directly to transfrontier pollution. Can they be applied to problems of climate change? You may wish to return to this question after reading Urgenda v. Netherlands, page 547, *infra*.

7.   *"Common Concern of Humankind."* The Framework Convention on Climate Change acknowledges in its preamble that "Earth's climate and its adverse effects are a common concern of humankind." How would you define a "common concern of humankind"? What legal obligations may flow from this? UNEP sponsored two meetings of legal experts in an effort to define this proposed principle more fully, but no formal definition has yet been adopted by the international community. Note also that this is the first time that the term "humankind" has been used rather than "mankind" in such multilateral environmental agreements. The term is also used in the Convention on Biological Diversity, which was negotiated at the same time.

8.   *"New and Additional Resources."* As mentioned above, many believe that the participation of developing countries is central to a regime for controlling climate change because of their large and growing populations and increasing greenhouse gas emission levels. What obligation do the developed States have under the Convention to help finance the developing States' efforts at reducing and controlling greenhouse gas emissions? There was considerable debate over whether the developed countries would provide

new and additional funding to developing countries under the Climate Convention. Note the formula that was agreed upon. If you were advising a government in implementing the Convention, how would you calculate the amount of financial assistance? Review Article 4, Article 4.4 (not excerpted) obligates the developed countries "to assist developing countries that are particularly vulnerable to the adverse effects of climate change in the meeting the costs of adaptation. . . ." No metric has yet developed for this mixed technical-political standard. See Richard J.T. Klein, Identifying Countries that are Particularly Vulnerable to the Adverse Effects of Climate Change: An Academic or Political Challenge?, 3CCLR 284 (2009).

There was also considerable debate as to whether the fund for the Convention would come under the umbrella of the Global Environmental Facility of the World Bank, UNDP, and UNEP or whether it would be a separate fund to be executed by State Parties to the Convention. Note the agreed formulation. Partly because the Biological Diversity Convention does not incorporate this formulation, the United States initially withheld its signature.

9.   *Planting a Tree in Indonesia to Mitigate Emissions in Europe.* One of the innovations under the FCCC is the legitimation of "joint implementation" by the Parties to the convention. Article 2 of the Convention provides that the "ultimate objective" of the convention is to achieve "stabilization of greenhouse gas concentrations in the atmosphere at a level that would prevent dangerous anthropogenic interference with the climate system." Joint implementation is a proposed strategy for achieving this; as its name suggests, it permits Parties to implement policies and measures for reducing greenhouse gas emissions jointly with other Parties. Norway introduced the concept in the negotiations in 1991; and efforts were undertaken to develop criteria for joint implementation. In theory, it could permit developed countries to focus on reducing emissions of greenhouse gases in developing countries by financing new control technologies there, rather than taking more costly measures at home to control greenhouse gases. The intent is that joint implementation will lead to measures that will provide the global benefit of stabilizing atmospheric concentrations of greenhouse gases at the lowest cost. In the negotiations of the Kyoto Protocol to the Framework Convention (discussed below), Parties took a range of positions on joint implementation, from prohibiting it to encouraging it. See Report of the Ad Hoc Group on the Berlin Mandate on the Work of its Sixth Session, Bonn, Mar. 3–7, 1997, FCCC/AGBM/1997/3/Add.1 (1997). Note, however, that the term "joint implementation" is used differently in the Kyoto Protocol (see Article 4) and that cooperation between developed country Parties to that protocol and developing countries primarily occurs through the Clean Development Mechanism provided for in Article 12 of the Protocol. For analysis of the many legal and policy issues associated with joint implementation, see Criteria for Joint Implementation under the Framework Convention on Climate Change (1994); Onno Kuik, Paul Peters & Nico Schrijiver, Joint Implementation to Curb Climate Change: Legal and Economic Aspects (1994). Glenn Wiser, *Joint Implementation: Incentives for*

Private Sector Mitigation of Global Climate Change, 9 Geo. Intl. Envtl.L. Rev.747 (1997) (exploring incentives for private sector participation in a joint implementation system and the adoption of instruments for a joint implementation market).

3. THE UNITED STATES FORCES MARKET ENVIRONMENTALISM ON THE INTERNATIONAL COMMUNITY

Climate change is an example of a tragedy of the commons. The difference between the examples of pollution previously studied and GCC is that while limitations on the amount of GHGs emitted can be adopted, it is be impossible to set a complete ban on greenhouse gas emissions. Thus, the United States and other countries have argued that the problem of controlling GHG emissions can be best handled through a market mechanisms rather than through a command and control regime.

a. Tax or Trade

Economists have been influential in the design of policy instruments. Orthodox welfare economics teaches that the way to internalize externalities is to tax them. Analytically, emissions trading has similarities to a carbon tax. A major difference is who receives the benefits. The government receives revenues generated by a carbon tax, which it may use to reduce other taxes, such as the income tax, that have distortionary effects on the economy. To date very few jurisdictions have followed the economists' advice to use a Pigovian tax to internalize externalities. For example, President Clinton proposed an energy tax in 1993, only to see the proposal soundly defeated. The Obama Administration made a push for a carbon tax in 2012 but it met with no success. The last Labor government in Australia instituted a carbon tax, but it was repealed in 2014 when the Liberal Party won the 2013 election and formed a government with the Australian National Party.

British Columbia (BC) is the major North American jurisdiction to have a carbon tax. "BC's levy started at C\$10 (\$9) a tonne in 2008 and rose by C\$5 each year until it reached C\$30 per tonne in 2012. That works out to 7 cents of the C\$1.35 per litre Vancouver residents pay at the pump to fill up their vehicles. Because the tax must, by law in BC, be revenue-neutral, the province has cut income and corporate taxes to offset the revenue it gets from taxing carbon. BC now has the lowest personal income tax rate in Canada and one of the lowest corporate rates in North America, too. BC's fuel consumption is also down. Over the past six years, the per-person consumption of fuels has dropped by 16% (although declines levelled off after the last tax increase in 2012). During that same period, per-person consumption in the rest of Canada rose by 3%." http://

www.economist.com/blogs/americasview/2014/07/british-columbias-carbon-tax.

Mexico adopted a carbon tax in 2014. Fossil fuel emitters can either pay a tax of $3.50 per metric ton of CO_2 emitted or acquire a Certified Emissions Reduction Credit from an approved UN Clean Development Mechanism project. Crude oil and natural gas producers are exempt. Thus, the projected impact on CO_2 emissions is minimal. See http://www.worldbank.org/content/dam/Worldbank/document/SDN/background-note_carbon-tax.pdf, for a summary of national carbon taxes. Chile enacted South America's first climate pollution tax in South America; the tax is $5.00 per metric ton of CO_2 (the original proposed Mexican rate) and applies to 55% of the low emitting country's emissions.

A carbon tax raises a host of technical-policy questions. What is the price that produces the desired behavioral changes from more efficient home energy use to less discretionary automobile use? The elasticity of demand for goods must be known. This may lead to high carbon tax which might spur the exit of firms from developed countries. How should the revenue be used? Should it be used to fund non-carbon-based alternatives or to fund adaptation? Is it possible that a tax would increase greenhouse gas emissions by setting a race to exploit coal, oil and gas before they decline in value? For a yes answer see Climate Policy and Nonrenewable Resources: The Green Paradox and Beyond (Karen Pittel, Rick van der Poog and Cees Witgaen eds. (2014). The carbon tax literature is enormous. E.g., Robert Kaineg, Carbon Taxes: Key Considerations for Policymakers and Stakeholders (2013); Shi-Ling Hsu, The Case for the Carbon Tax: Getting Past Our Hang-Ups on Effective Climate Policy (2nd ed. 2011).

Under an emissions trading regime, by contrast, entities that possess emissions rights can sell or trade those rights they do not need. The entities that possess those rights will thus enjoy windfall profits (unless the rights are allocated by auction) while other entities that must acquire rights to emit will have additional costs, which may be passed on to consumers. Thus, under emissions trading, consumers may face additional costs without the benefit of having other taxes reduced by the government. See Stephen Smith, Who Pays for Climate Change Policies? Distributional Side-Effects and Policy Responses, in The Economics of Climate Change 277 (1994). In addition, what about countries that do not become Parties to such an agreement—would Parties have to impose a border tax adjustment to avoid inequity and competitive disadvantage with such non-Parties? Keep this in mind when covering the materials on international trade in Chapter 16 below: Would the WTO agreements impose any restraints on the ability to utilize border tax adjustments? Instrument choice is inextricably linked the calculation of the costs and benefits of taking action. See Global Economic Commission, The Better

Growth, Better Climate (2014); Richard S.J. Tol, *The Economic Effects of Climate Change, 23 J. of Economic Perspectives* 29 (2009); Nicholas Stern, The Economics of Climate Change: The Stern Review (2007); William D. Nordhaus, Managing the Global Commons: The Economics of Climate Change (1994); and William D. Nordhaus, Climate Casino: Risk, Uncertainty, and Economics for a Warming World (2013).]

b.   Global Emissions Trading

The international community has embraced emissions trading rather than carbon taxes. It is more politically palatable than a carbon tax. Economists have enthusiastically endorsed emissions trading. In early 1997, a group of 2,000 economists, including six Nobel laureates, announced its support for either reducing carbon emissions by tradable emissions or through a carbon tax. *Action to Curb Greenhouse Emissions Wins Endorsement from 2,000 Economists*, 20 Intl. Envtl. Rep. 152 (Feb. 19, 1997). The original idea was to combine trading with a global cap and to form an international administrative agency to issue pollution permits that could be traded on private exchange markets. UNCTAD, Trading Entitlements to Control Carbon Emissions: A Practical Way to Combat Global Warming (1992). Permits would be allocated to participating countries, which would decide for themselves how to regulate the sale to companies. Each permit would allow a producer to emit one ton of CO_2 per year, so that a company producing more than this amount would have to buy extra allowances from another, less emitting source. The model was the United States Clean Air Act system of tradable SO_2 permits. CO_2 allowances could thus be traded in lots of 100 on stock exchanges. The global agency would reduce the total number of permits issued over time, spurring incentives to develop cleaner technologies and lessen the threat of global warming. That is, allocate the right to emit GHGs to specific entities within an economy and allow potential emitters to use or sell their right to emit or to buy rights to emit from others. In theory, this would keep the total emissions at the desired level, while taking advantage of the creativity spurred by profit-making. What are the advantages and disadvantages of letting the market implement environmental policy? How would the initial allocation (s) of emissions rights be accomplished? What should be the extent of the government's supervisory role? In thinking about this, it may be helpful to bear in mind that at least two different levels of trading are possible in a climate change emission trading system—within a country and between countries. With respect to the latter, should only countries be able to trade, or should private entities also be able to?

EMISSIONS TRADING AND CLIMATE CHANGE

Edith Brown Weiss & M.P.A. Kindall
(unpublished, 1992)

In the past the United States has actively promoted the use of emissions trading if any system for limiting greenhouse gas emissions were to be agreed upon at the global level.

An emissions trading program is a system that allocates—on some basis—rights to emit a given substance or substances—among various sources or potential sources. Any entity that is allocated such a right can either use it or transfer it to another entity. The entity that is able to reduce emissions below the level of its allocation thus has a valuable commodity which can be sold to someone else—presumably another entity that cannot reduce emissions to the level of its allocation without incurring a very high cost. Society achieves the same level of emissions reductions that it would have achieved if each entity had emitted no less, and no more, than its allocated amount, but the overall cost is reduced: the company that can achieve reduced emissions at the least cost will have an incentive to do so.

Promising as emissions trading is, it does not solve every problem, nor does it eliminate all administrative tasks. Emissions trading is a mechanism for accomplishing environmental goals efficiently; it cannot determine what those environmental goals should be or how much society should be willing to pay collectively to achieve those goals. Nor does emissions trading necessarily produce an equitable distribution of the burden of meeting society's environmental goals. That issue can only be addressed through the way in which emissions rights are allocated at the outset.

The U.S. experience with emissions trading indicates that an effective emissions trading program requires certain important elements: market participants with easy access to good information about the emissions credit market; a regulatory system that creates emissions rights that are relatively easy to calculate and are dependable; and regulatory agencies that are capable of approving applications quickly and monitoring compliance effectively. Thus, an emissions trading system has certain infrastructure requirements.

An emissions trading system would only be necessary if a protocol to the Climate Convention required State parties to reduce net emissions of greenhouse gases by a given amount.

The climate change issue is complicated by the fact that many gases contribute to the enhanced greenhouse effect.... Reductions in anthropogenic emissions for any one greenhouse gas might not produce sufficient reductions in overall GHG emissions to mitigate potential effects of the enhanced greenhouse effect. This is particularly true where reductions in emissions of one gas could lead to increases in emissions of other gases. Shifting from oil and coal consumption to natural gas, for example, would result in reduced CO_2 emissions, but the positive effects of this reduction could be completely offset by increases in methane emissions that occur from leaks in natural gas transmission pipelines.

The U.S. advocated a comprehensive approach that would permit countries to control net greenhouse emissions as they saw fit, rather than mandating a specific set of reductions for each greenhouse gas. Thus, one country could reduce its net emissions by concentrating on reduced net CO_2 emissions—it could encourage greater energy efficiency in the transportation and energy sectors and conduct vigorous afforestation and reforestation efforts, thus increasing its carbon dioxide "sinks." Or, if it preferred, it could concentrate on reducing methane emissions from natural gas transmissions, coal beds, and rice paddies.

This, in effect, is emissions trading between gases. It can be accomplished only if there is a scientifically sound basis for comparing the effect of one greenhouse gas to another in terms of its global warming potential. The Intergovernmental Panel on Climate Change produced such a "global warming potential" index, and it is undergoing revision as our knowledge of the science improves. The use of such an index would permit countries to allocate their global warming potential "budgets" among those activities that they determined to be most important.

The possibilities for emissions trading in a climate regime do not end there, however. The system could also be designed to allow international trading of emissions allowances. Thus, a country that did not use all of its allocated GHG emissions allowances could sell them to another country, thereby giving countries an incentive to go beyond their reduction targets. Additionally, countries could receive emissions credits for actions that they took to reduce emissions in other countries as well as in their own. This would provide added incentives for the transfer of environmentally sound technology, which all recognize to be a key component in the control of greenhouse gas emissions worldwide.

The details for designing such a system would not be trivial. Allocation of greenhouse gas emissions rights likely would be an extremely contentious issue; one could present equity arguments for allocations based on per capita emissions, historical emissions, or capacity for emitting greenhouse gases. Equally difficult would be designing an effective system for monitoring emissions and ensuring compliance. . . . The potential problems are enormous.

EMISSIONS BUDGETS: BUILDING AN EFFECTIVE INTERNATIONAL GREENHOUSE GAS CONTROL SYSTEM

Daniel J. Dudek
Environmental Defense Fund (February 1997)

This report . . . proposes an emissions budget and trading system for greenhouse gases that includes the following: national budgets; covering all sources and sinks; expressed as total GHG [greenhouse gas] emissions over a decade-long period; and in terms of carbon equivalent units (CEUs).

Nations could meet their decadal budget obligations by trading CEUs with each other and by "saving" CEUs whenever their decadal GHG emissions total was less than their total budget. Such CEUs could be used to offset GHG emissions in subsequent decadal periods and even earn "premiums" in the form of increases in their emissions value.

To ensure compliance, countries would be obligated to furnish detailed annual reports of their current and cumulative emissions and of the acquisition and/or sale of their CEUs. Countries exceeding their budgets would be subject to a two-pronged automatic sanction. The emissions value of any CEUs such countries had exported would be discounted upon their use by those holding such CEUs. In addition, cumulative GHG emissions in excess of a country's decadal budget—adjusted to reflect CEUs acquired or exported by the country—would be deducted—again automatically—from the country's budget for the decadal period immediately following.

Finally, each decade's emissions budget for affected nations would be established during the course of an ongoing review process undertaken by the Secretariat. Emissions budgets for upcoming decades would be announced at the 5-year point of the current decadal period after assessments of the atmospheric and climate science and of technology developments as well as of the performance to date of the overall regime. . . .

MECHANICS OF REPORTING, ACCOUNTING AND TRADING

One of the innovations introduced by the SO_2 emissions trading program under the U.S. Clean Air Act was that the SO_2 emissions "allowance" served—all at the same time—as i) the currency of trading, ii) the instrument of compliance for affected sources and iii) the regulatory mechanism applied by the U.S. EPA for ensuring sources' accountability and for "tracking" emissions trades. Similarly, the protocol can establish a single, simple sovereign accounting system that performs the same multiplicity of functions for an international GHG emissions budget and trading regime. At the same time, this system would be able to succeed without relying on the allocation of emissions "allowances" or marketable permits. . . .

TRADING

Through this approach, which is, in effect, one of double-entry record-keeping, the international emission trading system can accommodate GHG emissions trading between and among private firms in different nations while ensuring both the integration of private and sovereign trading and the full GHG emissions budget accountability of all nations. In addition, it does not presuppose any particular set of policy approaches that participating nations may use on a domestic level, nor does it rely on developing extensive new institutional authorities internationally.

In fact, under this system, virtually any firm operating under virtually any domestic policy regime can transact the international sale of purportedly surplus GHG emissions reductions. Meanwhile, the integrity of the system of accountability remains assured. This approach achieves this by requiring nations to report annually all emissions exports, whether initiated by the sovereign itself or any private firms operating within sovereign borders. Even private firm sales transactions, therefore, of necessity will have to be effectuated through both their being reported to the government of the selling firm and a corresponding deduction being taken from the sovereign's budget. . . .

JOINT IMPLEMENTATION AND PARTICIPATION

. . . GHG emissions from the developing world are rapidly reaching or exceeding par with those generated by the industrialized and Eastern bloc nations. Their emissions trajectory corresponds to their economies increasing importance and activity in the global marketplace. . . .

. . . Ostensibly, the most effective way of using the emissions trading market to create incentives for developing countries to participate in an international GHG regime is to condition their ability to engage in transactions in the emissions trading market on their agreement to subject themselves to a GHG emissions budget. . . . Erecting such a barrier to developing nations' participation in trading may prove to be too crude and risky a strategy, however, while also denying opportunities for achieving environmental and economic gains. In contrast, permitting international GHG emissions trading for and with nations prior to their accepting GHG emissions budget—that is, joint implementation—may offer a smoother path by which developing countries can "graduate" to full participation in the emissions budget regime. . . .

Typically, the kinds of international transaction that would result in the transfer of GHG emissions reduction credits would have the mutual economic benefits to buyer and seller characteristic of trading: sellers would gain a new, additional sources of revenue and buyers would be able to achieve compliance at lower cost. Moreover, these transactions would bring a host of benefits crucial to the credibility, durability and environmental performance of a GHG protocol. First, the very opportunity afforded firms and sovereigns in the industrialized world to meet their GHG emissions budgets at reduced cost and with greater flexibility would enhance the acceptance and credibility of an international GHG regime.

At the same time, those developing economies experiencing the greatest growth in the current economic time horizon are making substantial infrastructure investments whose environmental consequences, including GHG emissions, could have long-lasting effects for good or ill. Investments of the sort that yielded transactable GHG reductions for the host economy or the foreign investor simultaneously would help direct the host countries' economic growth along paths that were less, rather than more, GHG emissions-intensive. In addition to the environmental benefits that would result directly from this outcome, achieving growth in this way would make it that much easier for these countries to accept, eventually, a GHG emissions budget. As a result, the implicit gradualism in this strategy could speed and facilitate these countries' graduation to more rigorous international GHG obligations. . . .

————————

For a review of lessons from the use of tradeable permit schemes in other areas for climate change, see OECD, Climate Change: Designing a Tradeable Permit System (1992). For the implementation of the sulphur dioxide emissions trading system under United States law and a comparison of United States law with the global trading plan, see Acid Rain Allowance Allocation and Reserves, 40 C.F.R. 72, 73, 75 (1993); see also Edith Brown Weiss, *Environmentally Sustainable Competitiveness: A Comment*, 102 Yale L.J. 2123, 2139–2141 (1993); National Academy of Public Administration, The Environment Goes to Market (1994) (discussing experience with tradeable emission permits in California); Bernard S. Black & Richard J. Pierce, Jr., *The Choice Between Markets and Central Planning in Regulating the U.S. Electricity Industry*, 93 Colum. L. Rev. 1339 (1993) (describing United States experience with emissions trading under the Clean Air Act); and Tom H. Tietenberg, Economic Instruments for Environmental Regulation, in Economic Policy Toward the Environment 86 (Dieter Helm ed., 1991).

NOTE: THE DEVIL IS IN THE DETAILS

Emissions trading schemes raise a number of technical-policy problems. One of the major issues under an emission trading regime is allocation of the emissions rights. Allocation—which involves distributing trillions of dollars of assets (in the form of emissions rights), perhaps for eternity—offers many opportunities for corruption and political influence (both domestically and internationally) as some entities might be willing to pay political actors for scarce emission rights that they could then resell to other entities at a higher price. Concerns over potential corruption or undue political influence might thus lead one to favor a carbon tax. On the other hand, under a carbon tax, one of the major issues would be determining the proper level of the tax, with it being very likely that some entities would claim that the price was too high. With emissions trading, the market clearing price of emission rights would determine the amount of the charge, so there would probably be less criticism that the cost was too high. Instead, criticism would be focused over the amount of emissions permitted, as higher levels of permitted emissions would increase the supply of emissions available for trading and thus reduce the price of emissions in the event entities needed to purchase additional rights to emit. See OECD, Global Warming: Economic Dimensions and Policy Responses 49–51 (1995). Criticism might also be expected with respect to who is allocated the emission rights, including questions about distributive equity, political influence, and concentration of economic power. See OCED Policy Roundtable: Emission Permits and Competition (2011), www.oecd.org/competition/sectors/48204882.pdf.

The European Union embraced emissions trading three years before the global downturn of 2008. However, by 2007 the price of carbon emissions collapsed to essentially zero for three basic reasons. First, the goals for emission reduction in the pilot program were constructed under time pressure with a shortage of reliable data and were supposed to be relatively modest. Second, aggregate emission data was unavailable until almost halfway through the pilot program, and when the first tranche of actual emissions data was released in 2006 by the EU Commission, market participants realized aggregate emission levels were low vis-à-vis allowance supply. Third, emissions allowances in this pilot first phase of the program could only be used between 2005 and 2007 and could not be further banked. The too-late realization of oversupply coupled with an inability to use excess allowances sparked a dramatic fall in prices. The rationale for not allowing banking was the desire to separate Phase II (which coincided with the first Kyoto compliance period starting in 2008) from the pilot program period—but the consequences of this decision were clear: by the final quarter of 2007, spot prices were essentially zero, at €0.06/ton, even while contract futures prices for Phase II allowances hovered above €20/ton (Point Carbon 2012). Banking is now allowed in all current and future phases

Since 2008, carbon prices have fallen not risen as was expected. The combination of generous initial credits coupled with the downturn resulted in excess credits and the price of credits from 30€ per ton in 2008 to 8€ in 2012.[4]

---

[4] The European Emissions Trading System has faced three high-profile market controversies, two of which were not specific to emissions trading markets. One of these two cases involved traders manipulating value-added tax laws in different countries to defraud governments of over €1 billion from 2008–2009, while the second involved cyber-attacks which likely stole over €50 million worth of allowances on spot exchanges in 2011. The one major controversy unique to emission markets occurred when Clean Development Mechanism credits previously collected by the Hungarian government for compliance re-entered the market. It appears that the Hungarian government simply swapped the CDM credits for another type of carbon asset under the Kyoto Protocol that it needed to sell. While the swap was legal under the Kyoto Protocol, it was surprising to many participants in the European Emissions Trading System and created the appearance of possible credit "recycling" that would have negated

Thus, banked carbon credits may increase emissions in 2020 and cancel out most of the gains from renewable energy, primarily wind. Tim Liang et al, Assessing the Effectiveness of the EU Emissions Trading System (Centre for Climate Change Economics, Working Paper 126 (January 2013), available at http://www.cccep.ac.uk/Publications/Working-papers/Papers/120–129/ WP126–effectiveness-eu-emissions-trading-system.pdf. To try and stem this gap, the Commission is going back to the drawing board. It has released a number of options for structural reform, to try and lower the surplus and address the imbalance between demand and supply of carbon credits. Whilst corruption cannot necessarily be blamed as a cause of the current surplus, better governance and increased transparency over how the ETS is structured should at least be central to any reform, the EU ETS is now in its third phase, running from 2013 to 2020. A major revision approved in 2009 in order to strengthen the system means the third phase is significantly different from phases one and two and is based on rules which are far more harmonised than before. The main changes are:

- A single, EU-wide cap on emissions applies in place of the previous system of national caps;

- Auctioning, not free allocation, is now the default method for allocating allowances. In 2013 more than 40% of allowances will be auctioned, and this share will rise progressively each year;

- For those allowances still given away for free, harmonized allocation rules apply which are based on ambitious EU-wide benchmarks of emissions performance;

QUESTION

Can you have emissions trading without a cap? The efforts to trade in anticipation of a cap are instructive. In 2003, commodity traders in Chicago banked on a global trading regime or at least to be able to allow European emitters to count United States reductions and formed the Chicago Climate Exchange (CCX). CXX was a greenhouse gas (GHG) emission reduction and trading pilot program for emission sources and offset projects in the United States, Canada, and Mexico. Projects also included Brazil. CCX was self-regulatory; members made a voluntary, legally binding commitment to reduce their emissions of greenhouse gases by four percent below the average of their 1998–2001 baseline by 2006, the last year of the pilot program. See http://www.chicagoclimatex.com. The CXX closed in 2010 when carbon credits fell to 10 cents per metric ton compared to $7.50 in 2006.

---

relevant carbon reductions and diminished the integrity of the trading system. The European Commission has since revised its rules to address each of these concerns.

4. THE DEVELOPED WORLD GETS SERIOUS: KYOTO PROTOCOL

The Kyoto Protocol is the closest that the international community has come to a global greenhouse reduction regime. The Protocol's first commitment period expired in 2012; in 2012, UNFCCC Parties adopted the Doha Amendment to the Kyoto Protocol which added a second commitment period ending in 2020. Decision 1/CMP.8 in accordance with Articles 20 and 21 of the Kyoto Protocol. The amendment includes:

> "New commitments for Annex I Parties to the Kyoto Protocol who agreed to take on commitments in a second commitment period from 1 January 2013 to 31 December 2020;

> A revised list of greenhouse gases (GHG) to be reported on by Parties in the second commitment period; and Amendments to several articles of the Kyoto Protocol which specifically referenced issues pertaining to the first commitment period and which needed to be updated for the second commitment period."

a. Developments Leading to the 1997 Kyoto Protocol to the UNFCCC

At the first meeting of the UNFCCC Conference of the Parties (COP) in Berlin, Germany, in March 1995, countries agreed to a mandate to negotiate a new, legally binding international instrument to apply to the period beyond the year 2000. That instrument was to consider quantified targets and timetables for controlling greenhouse gas emissions by Annex I (developed) countries. The parties established an Ad Hoc Group on the Berlin Mandate for considering a future protocol. The target date for the instrument was 1997. See also B. Arts & Wolfgang Rudig, *Negotiating the "Berlin Mandate": Reflections on the First "COP" to the UN Framework Convention on Climate Change*, 4 Envtl. Polit. 481 (1995).

The second meeting of the Conference of the Parties, in Geneva in 1996, endorsed the conclusions of the 1995 Second Assessment Report of the Inter-governmental Panel on Climate Change (IPCC). That report stated that the increase in global mean surface temperature since the late 19th century "is unlikely to be entirely natural in origin," and that the "balance of evidence . . . suggests a discernible human influence on global climate." Perhaps the most significant event at the conference was the shift in position by the United States to support for a protocol or other instrument that would include a binding target for reducing GHG emissions, if such an instrument used an emissions trading scheme (as described below). However, the conference also saw increased conflict emerge over climate change, with OPEC countries fearful that adaptation measures would involve reducing the use of petroleum products. The meeting also reached agreement on contents of the "national communications" that developing countries were scheduled to begin submitting in April 1997, specifying what steps they are taking to reduce GHG emissions. (Annex I countries were already required to submit "national communications.")

The third meeting of the Conference of the Parties, in Kyoto, Japan, in December 1997, was projected to adopt a legal instrument that would include binding targets and timetables for reductions in GHG emissions. Various proposals were floated on how these reductions should be accomplished. The United States proposed to establish a "budget" for GHG emissions that would last up to ten years and cap each country's total emissions of all GHGs not covered by the Montreal Protocol—i.e., carbon dioxide (CO_2), methane (CH_4), nitrous oxide (NO_2), hydrogen-fluorochride (HFC), perfluorochloride (PFC), and sulfur hexafluoride (SF_6)—during this period at 1990 levels. A country could exceed this cap by "borrowing" emissions from the next budget period but would have to repay the "borrowings" with additional reductions. Developed countries could "jointly implement" GHG reduction projects with developing countries and split the emissions credits equally. The United States also proposed an international system of GHG emissions trading between industrialized nations. Finally, developing countries would be required to take "no regrets" measures—measures that make sense for other reasons, such as saving money. By contrast to the United States plan, the European Community (EC) proposed that industrialized nations reduce emissions of only three GHGs (carbon dioxide, methane, and nitrous oxide), but by a larger percentage: 15 percent from 1990 levels. Japan proposed that emissions of the same three GHGs be reduced by 5 percent. Japan also proposed an afforestation project of 5 million hectares by 2020. See Government Reportedly Set to Launch Global Afforestation Scheme, Yomiuri Shinbum, Apr. 20, 1997, at 25. A list of some proposals is available in Report of the Ad Hoc Group on the Berlin Mandate on the Work of Its Sixth Session, Bonn, Mar. 3–7, 1997, at 49–55, FCCC/AGBM/1997/3/ Add.1 (1997). None of these proposals contained a legally binding limit on the ultimately important issue of the actual concentration of GHGs in the atmosphere, though some of them had specific goals in mind in this respect.

b. Introduction to the Kyoto Protocol: Basic Characteristics

The Kyoto Protocol to the UNFCCC was adopted in 1997 after intense negotiations spanning two years and culminating in a high-level negotiation in Kyoto, Japan, at the Third Conference of the parties to the UNFCCC. The Protocol is an unusually complicated instrument, perhaps unavoidably so given the unusual degree of scientific uncertainty and importance of its subject matter. Not only must the Protocol be read with a close eye on the UNFCCC, but the Protocol's wording is occasionally unusually obtuse, and substantively related provisions are often found in different parts of the Protocol. Moreover, because details of some contentious issues were left to be decided in the future by the Conference of the Parties of the UNFCCC or by the Meeting of the Parties of the Protocol, it will be necessary to track future developments in those fora in order to understand the implications of certain provisions.

Generally speaking, some of the defining features of the Kyoto Protocol are as follows. The Protocol takes a comprehensive approach by covering both actual emissions of GHGs and sinks that sequester carbon and by covering all six GHGs not covered by the Montreal Protocol. It provides legally binding, individualized emissions targets for countries listed in Annex I of the UNFCCC (so-called Annex I countries, which are primarily OECD members, some Eastern European countries, and some former republics of the Soviet Union). These targets—which are specified in Annex B to the Protocol—are to be met over a five-year budget period, running from 2008 to 2012. The Protocol allows countries flexibility in meeting their targets, domestically, as well as internationally via a set of innovative mechanisms. These mechanisms include not only emissions trading but also joint implementation between industrialized countries— note the change in the use of the term "joint implementation" from the UNFCCC context—and cooperation among industrialized and developing countries via a Clean Development Mechanism. Article 12 permits emission-reduction projects in developing countries to earn certified emission reduction (CER) credits, each equivalent to one ton of CO_2 which can be traded and sold, and used by industrialized countries to meet a part of their Protocol emission reduction targets. Details regarding some of these aspects of the Protocol are provided below. For a more thorough discussion, see Clare Breidenich, Daniel Magraw, Anne Rowley & James Rubin, *Current Development: The Kyoto Protocol to the Framework Convention on Climate Change*, 92 Am. J. Intl. L. 322 (1998).

Critical Provisions from the Kyoto Protocol are reproduced below.

KYOTO PROTOCOL TO THE UNITED NATIONS FRAMEWORK CONVENTION ON CLIMATE CHANGE, ARTICLES 3–8, 11–12, 17–19 & ANNEX B

Kyoto Protocol to the FCCC, FCCC Conference of the Parties, 3d Sess. UN Doc.
FCCC/CP/1997/L7/Add.1 (Dec. 10, 1997)

Article 3

1.   The Parties included in Annex I shall, individually or jointly, ensure that their aggregate anthropogenic carbon dioxide equivalent emissions of the greenhouse gases listed in Annex A do not exceed their assigned amounts, calculated pursuant to their quantified emission limitation and reduction commitments inscribed in Annex B and in accordance with the provisions of this Article, with view to reducing their

overall emissions of such gases by at least 5 per cent below 1990 levels in the commitment period 2008 to 2012.

2.   Each Party included in Annex I shall, by 2005, have made demonstrable progress in achieving its commitments under this Protocol.

3.   The net changes in greenhouse gas emissions from sources and removals by sinks resulting from direct human-induced land-use change and forestry activities, limited to afforestation, reforestation and deforestation since 1990, measured as verifiable changes in carbon stocks in each commitment period, shall be used to meet the commitments under this Article of each Party included in Annex I. The greenhouse gas emissions by sources and removals by sinks associated with those activities shall be reported in a transparent and verifiable manner and reviewed in accordance with Articles 7 and 8.

4.   Prior to the first session of the Conference of the Parties serving as the meeting of the Parties to this Protocol, each Party included in Annex I shall provide, for consideration by the Subsidiary Body of Scientific and Technological Advice, data to establish its level of carbon stocks in 1990 and to enable an estimate to be made of its changes in carbon stocks in subsequent years. The Conference of the Parties serving as the meeting of the Parties to this Protocol shall, at its first session or as soon as practicable thereafter, decide upon modalities, rules and guidelines as to how, and which, additional human-induced activities related to changes in greenhouse gas emissions by sources and removals by sinks in the agricultural soils and the land use change and forestry categories shall be added to, or subtracted from, the assigned amounts for Parties included in Annex I, taking into account uncertainties, transparency in reporting, verifiability, the methodological work of the Intergovernmental Panel on Climate Change, the advice provided by the Subsidiary Body for Scientific and Technological Advice in accordance with Article 5 and the decisions of the Conference of the Parties. Such a decision shall apply in the second and subsequent commitment periods. A Party may choose to apply such a decision on these additional human-induced activities for its first commitment period, provided that these activities have taken place since 1990.

5.   The Parties included in Annex I undergoing the process of transition to a market whose base year or period was established pursuant to decision 9/CP.2 of the Conference of the Parties at its second session shall use that base year or period for the implementation of their commitments under this Article. Any other Party included in Annex I undergoing the process of transition to a market economy which has not yet submitted its first national communication under Article 12 of the Convention may also notify the Conference of the Parties serving as the meeting of the Parties to this Protocol that it intends to use an historical base year or period other than 1990 for the implementation of its

commitments under this Article. The Conference of the Parties serving as the meeting of the Parties to this Protocol shall decide on the acceptance of such notification.

6.   Taking into account Article 4, paragraph 6, of the Convention, in the implementation of their commitments under this Protocol other than those under this Article, a certain degree of flexibility shall be allowed by the Conference of the Parties serving as the meeting of the Parties to this Protocol to the Parties included in Annex I undergoing the process of transition to a market economy.

7.   In the first quantified emission limitation and reduction commitment period, from 2008 to 2012, the assigned amount for each Party included in Annex I shall be equal to the percentage inscribed for it in Annex B of its aggregate anthropogenic carbon dioxide equivalent emissions of the greenhouse gases listed in Annex A in 1990, or the base year or period determined in accordance with paragraph 5 above, multiplied by 5. Those parties included in Annex I for whom land-use change and forestry constituted a net source of greenhouse gas emissions in 1990 shall include in their 1990 emissions base year or period the aggregate anthropogenic carbon dioxide equivalent emissions by sources minus removals by sinks in 1990 from land-use change for purposes of calculating their assigned amount.

8.   Any Party included in Annex I may use 1995 as its base year for hydro-fluorocarbons, perfluorocarbons and sulphur hexafluoride, for the purposes of the calculation referred to in paragraph 7 above.

9.   Commitments for subsequent periods for Parties included in Annex I shall be established in amendments to Annex B to this Protocol, which shall be adopted in accordance with the provisions of Article 21, paragraph 7. The Conference of the Parties serving as the meeting of the Parties to this Protocol shall initiate the consideration of such commitments at least seven years before the end of the first commitment period referred to in paragraph 1 above.

10. Any emission reduction units, or any part of an assigned amount, which a Party acquires from another Party in accordance with the provisions of Article 6 or of Article 17 shall be added to the assigned amount for the acquiring Party.

11. Any emission reduction units, or any part of an assigned amount, which a Party acquires from another Party in accordance with the provisions of Article 6 or of Article 17 shall be subtracted from the assigned amount for the transferring Party.

12. Any certified emission reductions which a Party acquired from another Party in accordance with the provisions in Article 12 shall be added to the assigned amount for the acquiring Party.

13. If the emissions of a Party included in Annex I in a commitment period are less than its assigned amount under this Article, this difference shall, on request of that Party, be added to the assigned amount for that Party for subsequent commitment periods.

14. Each Party included in Annex I shall strive to implement the commitments mentioned in paragraph 1 above in such a way as to minimize adverse social, environmental and economic impacts on developing country Parties, particularly those identified in Article 4, paragraphs 8 and 9, of the Convention. In line with relevant decisions of the Conference of the Parties on the implementation of those paragraphs, the Conference of the Parties serving as the meeting of the Parties to this Protocol shall, at its first session, consider what actions are necessary to minimize the adverse effects of climate change and/or the impacts of response measures on Parties referred to in those paragraphs. Among the issues to be considered shall be the establishment of funding, insurance and transfer of technology.

Article 4

1.   Any Parties included in Annex I that have reached an agreement to fulfill their commitments under Article 3 jointly, shall be deemed to have met those commitments provided that their total combined aggregate anthropogenic carbon dioxide equivalent emissions of the greenhouse gases listed in Annex A do not exceed their assigned amounts calculated pursuant to their quantified emission limitation and reduction commitments inscribed in Annex B and in accordance with the provisions of Article 3. The respective emission level allocated to each of the Parties to the agreement shall be set out in that agreement.

2.   The Parties to any such agreement shall notify the secretariat of the teams of the agreement on the date of deposit of their instruments of ratification, acceptance or approval of this Protocol, or accession thereto. The secretariat shall in turn inform the Parties and signatories to the Convention of the terms of the agreement.

3.   Any such agreement shall remain in operation for the duration of the commitment period specified in Article 3, paragraph 7.

4.   If Parties acting jointly do so in the framework of, and together with, a regional economic integration organization, any alteration in the composition of the organization after adoption of this Protocol shall not affect existing commitments under this Protocol. Any alteration in the composition of the organization shall only apply for the purposes of those commitments under Article 3 that are adopted subsequent to that alteration.

5.   In the event of failure by the Parties to such an agreement to achieve their total combined level of emission reductions, each Party to

that agreement shall be responsible for its own level of emissions set out in the agreement.

6.   If Parties acting jointly do so in the framework of, and together with, a regional economic integration organization which is itself a Party to this Protocol, each member State of that regional economic integration organization individually, and together with the regional economic integration organization acting in accordance with Article 24, shall, in the event of failure to achieve the total combined level of emission reductions, be responsible for its level of emissions as notified in accordance with this Article.

Article 5

1.   Each Party included in Annex I shall have in place, no later than one year prior to the start of the first commitment period, a national system for the estimation of anthropogenic emissions by sources and removals by sinks of all greenhouse gases not controlled by the Montreal Protocol. Guidelines for such national systems, which shall incorporate the methodologies specified in paragraph 2 below, shall be decided upon by the Conference of the Parties serving as the meeting of the Parties to this Protocol at its first session.

2.   Methodologies for estimating anthropogenic emissions by sources and removals by sinks of all greenhouse gases not controlled by the Montreal Protocol shall be those accepted by the Intergovernmental Panel on Climate Change and agreed upon by the Conference of the Parties at its third session. Where such methodologies are not used, appropriate adjustments shall be applied according to methodologies agreed upon by the Conference of the Parties serving as the meeting of the Parties to this Protocol at its first session. Based on the work of, inter alia, the Intergovernmental Panel on Climate Change and advice provided by the Subsidiary Body for Scientific and Technological Advice, the Conference of the Parties serving as the meeting of the Parties to this Protocol shall regularly review and, as appropriate, revise such methodologies and adjustments, taking fully into account any relevant decisions by the Conference of the Parties. Any revision to methodologies or adjustments shall be used only for the purposes of ascertaining compliance with commitments under Article 3 in respect of any commitment period adopted subsequent to that revision.

3.   The global warming potentials used to calculate the carbon dioxide equivalence of anthropogenic emissions by sources and removals by sinks of greenhouse gases listed in Annex A shall be those accepted by the Intergovernmental Panel on Climate Change and agreed upon by the Conference of the Parties at its third session. Based on the work of, inter alia, the Intergovernmental Panel on Climate Change and advice provided by the Subsidiary Body for Scientific and Technological Advice, the Conference of the Parties serving as the meeting of the Parties to this

Protocol shall regularly review and, as appropriate, revise the global warming potential of each greenhouse gas, taking fully into account any relevant decisions by the Conference of the Parties. Any revision to a global warming potential shall apply only to commitments under Article 3 in respect of any commitment period adopted subsequent to that revision.

Article 6

1.   For the purpose of meeting its commitments under Article 3, any Party included in Annex I may transfer to, or acquire from, any other such Party emission reduction units resulting from projects aimed at reducing anthropogenic emissions by sources or enhancing anthropogenic removals by sinks of greenhouse gases in any sector of the economy, provided that:

(a) Any such project has the approval of the Parties involved;

(b) Any such project provides a reduction in emissions by sources, or an enhancement of removals by sinks, that is additional to any that would otherwise occur;

(c) It does not acquire any emission reduction units if it is not in compliance with its obligations under Article 5 and 7; and

(d) The acquisition of emission reduction units shall be supplemental to domestic actions for the purposes of meeting commitments under Article 3.

2.   The Conference of the Parties serving as the meeting of the Parties to this Protocol may, at its first session or as soon as practicable thereafter, further elaborate guidelines for the implementation of this Article, including for verification and reporting.

3.   A Party included in Annex I may authorize legal entities to participate, under its responsibility, in actions leading to the generation, transfer or acquisition under this Article of emission reduction units.

4.   If a question of implementation by a Party included in Annex I of the requirements referred to in this Article is identified in accordance with the relevant provisions of Article 8, transfers and acquisitions of emission reduction units may continue to be made after the question has been identified, provided that any such units may not be used by a Party to meet its commitments under Article 3 until any issue of compliance is resolved.

Article 7

1.   Each Party included in Annex I shall incorporate in its annual inventory of anthropogenic emissions by sources and removals by sinks of greenhouse gases not controlled by the Montreal Protocol, submitted in accordance with the relevant decisions of the Conference of the Parties,

the necessary supplementary information for the purposes of ensuring compliance with Article 3, to be determined in accordance with paragraph 4 below.

2.	Each Party included in Annex I shall incorporate in its national communication, submitted under Article 12 of the Convention, the supplementary information necessary to demonstrate compliance with its commitments under this Protocol, to be determined in accordance with paragraph 4 below.

3.	Each Party included in Annex I shall submit the information required under paragraph 1 above annually, beginning with the first inventory due under the Convention for the first year of the commitment period after this Protocol has entered into force for that Party. Each such Party shall submit the information required under paragraph 2 above as part of the first national communication due under the Convention after this Protocol has entered into force for it and after the adoption of guidelines as provided for in paragraph 4 below. The frequency of subsequent submission of information required under this Article shall be determined by the Conference of the Parties serving as the meeting of the Parties to this Protocol, taking into account any timetable for the submission of national communications decided upon by the Conference of the Parties.

4.	The Conference of the Parties serving as the meeting of the Parties to this Protocol shall adopt at its first session, and review periodically thereafter, guidelines for the preparation of the information required under this Article, taking into account guidelines for the preparation of national communications by Parties included in Annex I adopted by the Conference of the Parties. The Conference of the Parties serving as the meeting of the Parties to this Protocol shall also, prior to the first commitment period, decide upon modalities for the accounting of assigned amounts.

Article 8

1.	The information submitted under Article 7 by each Party included in Annex I shall be reviewed by expert review teams pursuant to the relevant decisions of the Conference of the Parties and in accordance with guidelines adopted for this purpose by the Conference of the Parties serving as the meeting of the Parties to this Protocol under paragraph 4 below. The information submitted under Article 7, paragraph 1, by each Party included in Annex I shall be reviewed as part of the annual compilation and accounting of emissions inventories and assigned amounts. Additionally, the information submitted under Article 7, paragraph 2, by each Party included in Annex I shall be reviewed as part of the review of communications.

2.   Expert review teams shall be coordinated by the secretariat and shall be composed of experts selected from those nominated by Parties to the Convention and, as appropriate, by intergovernmental organizations, in accordance with guidance provided for this purpose by the Conference of the Parties.

3.   The review process shall provide a thorough and comprehensive technical assessment of all aspects of the implementation by a Party of this Protocol. The expert review teams shall prepare a report to the Conference of the Parties serving as the meeting of the Parties to this Protocol, assessing the implementation of the commitments of the Party and identifying any potential problems in, and factors influencing, the fulfillment of commitments. Such reports shall be circulated by the secretariat to all Parties to the Convention. The secretariat shall list those questions of implementation indicated in such reports for further consideration by the Conference of the Parties serving as the meeting of the Parties to this Protocol.

4.   The Conference of the Parties serving as the meeting of the Parties to this Protocol shall at its first session, and review periodically thereafter, guidelines for the review of implementation of this Protocol by expert review teams taking into account the relevant decisions of the Conference of the Parties.

5.   The Conference of the Parties serving as the meeting of the Parties to this Protocol shall, with the assistance of the Subsidiary Body for Implementation and, as appropriate, the Subsidiary Body for Scientific and Technological Advice, consider: (a) The information submitted by Parties under Article 7 and the reports of the expert reviews thereon conducted under this Article; and (b) Those questions of implementation listed by the secretariat under paragraph 3 above, as well as any questions raised by Parties.

6.   Pursuant to its consideration of the information referred to in paragraph 5 above, the Conference of the Parties serving as the meeting of the Parties to this Protocol shall take decisions on any matter required for the implementation of this Protocol.

Article 11

1.   In the implementation of Article 10, Parties shall take into account the provisions of Article 4, paragraphs 4, 5, 7, 8 and 9, of the Convention.

2.   In the context of the implementation of Article 4, paragraph 1, of the Convention, in accordance with the provisions of Article 4, paragraph 3, and Article 11 of the Convention, and through the entity or entities entrusted with the operation of the financial mechanism of the Convention, the developed country Parties and other developed Parties included in Annex II to the Convention shall: (a) Provide new and

additional financial resources to meet the agreed full costs incurred by developing country Parties in advancing the implementation of existing commitments under Article 4, paragraph 1(a), of the Convention that are covered in Article 10, subparagraph (a); and (b) Also provide such financial resources, including for the transfer of technology, needed by the developing country Parties to meet the agreed full incremental costs of advancing the implementation of existing commitments under Article 4, paragraph 1, of the Convention that are covered by Article 10 and that are agreed between a developing country Party and the international entity or entities referred to in Article 11 of the Convention, in accordance with that Article.

The implementation of these existing commitments shall take into account the need for adequacy and predictability in the flow of funds and the importance of appropriate burden sharing among developed country Parties. The guidance to the entity or entities entrusted with the operation of the financial mechanism of the Convention in relevant decisions of the Conference of the Parties, including those agreed before the adoption of this Protocol, shall apply mutatis mutandis to the provisions of this paragraph.

3.   The developed country Parties and other developed Parties in Annex II to the Convention may also provide, and developing country Parties avail themselves of, financial resources for the implementation of Article 10, through bilateral, regional and other multilateral channels.

Article 12

1.   A clean development mechanism is hereby defined.

2.   The purpose of the clean development mechanism shall be to assist Parties not included in Annex I in achieving sustainable development and in contributing to the ultimate objective of the Convention, and to assist Parties included in Annex I in achieving compliance with their quantified emission limitation and reduction commitments under Article 3.

3.   Under the clean development mechanism:

(a) Parties not included in Annex I will benefit from project activities resulting in certified emission reductions; and

(b) Parties included in Annex I may use the certified emission reductions accruing from such project activities to contribute to compliance with part of their quantified emission limitation and reduction commitments under Article 3, as determined by the Conference of the Parties serving as the meeting of the Parties to this Protocol.

4.   The clean development mechanism shall be subject to the authority and guidance of the Conference of the Parties serving as the

meeting of the Parties to this Protocol and be supervised by an executive board of the clean development mechanism.

5. Emission reductions resulting from each project activity shall be certified by operational entities to be designated by the Conference of the Parties serving as the meeting of the Parties to this Protocol, on the basis of: (a) Voluntary participation approved by each Party involved; (b) Real, measurable, and long-term benefits related to the mitigation of climate change; and (c) Reductions in emissions that are additional to any that would occur in the absence of the certified project activity.

6. The clean development mechanism shall assist in arranging funding of certified project activities as necessary.

7. The Conference of the Parties serving as the meeting of the Parties to this Protocol shall, at its first session, elaborate modalities and procedures with the objective of ensuring transparency, efficiency and accountability through independent auditing and verification of project activities.

8. The Conference of the Parties serving as the meeting of the Parties to this Protocol shall ensure that a share of the proceeds from certified project activities is used to cover administrative expenses as well as to assist developing country Parties that are particularly vulnerable to the adverse effects of climate change to meet the costs of adaptation.

9. Participation under the clean development mechanism, including in activities mentioned in paragraph 3(a) above and in the acquisition of certified emission reductions, may involve private and/or public entities, and is to be subject to whatever guidance may be provided by the executive board of the clean development mechanism.

10. Certified emission reductions obtained during the period from the year 2000 up to the beginning of the first commitment period can be used to assist in achieving compliance in the first commitment period.

Article 17

The Conference of the Parties shall define the relevant principles, modalities, rules and guideline, in particular for verification, reporting and accountability for emissions trading. The Parties included in Annex B may participate in emissions trading for the purposes of fulfilling their commitments under Article 3. Any such trading shall be supplemental to domestic actions for the purpose of meeting quantified emission limitation and reduction commitments under that Article.

Article 18

The Conference of the Parties serving as the meeting of the Parties to this Protocol shall, at its first session, approve appropriate and effective procedures and mechanisms to determine and to address cases of non-compliance with the provisions of this Protocol, including through the development of an indicative list of consequences, taking into account the cause, type, degree and frequency of non-compliance. Any procedures and mechanisms under this Article entailing binding consequences shall be adopted by means of an amendment to this Protocol.

Article 19

The provisions of Article 14 of the Convention on settlement of disputes shall apply *mutatis mutandis* to this Protocol.

Annex B

[Annex B to the Kyoto Protocol contains the commitment of each Annex I State in the UNFCC to a quantified emission limitation or reduction, expressed as a percentage of the base year or period.]

Australia	108
Austria	92
Belgium	92
Bulgaria*	92
Canada	94
Croatia*	95
Czech Republic*	92
Denmark	92
Estonia*	92
European Community	92
Finland	92
France	92
Germany	92
Greece	92
Hungary*	94
Iceland	110
Ireland	92
Italy	92
Japan	94
Latvia*	92
Liechtenstein	92
Lithuania*	92
Luxembourg	92
Monaco	92
Netherlands	92

New Zealand	100
Norway	101
Poland*	94
Portugal	92
Romania*	92
Russian Federation*	100
Slovakia*	92
Slovenia*	92
Spain	92
Sweden	92
Switzerland	92
Ukraine*	100
United Kingdom of Great Britain and Northern Ireland	92
United States of America	93

*Countries that are undergoing the process of transition to a market economy.

DECISION 1/CP.3 OF THE UNFCCC THIRD CONFERENCE OF THE PARTIES, ADOPTION OF THE KYOTO PROTOCOL TO THE FCCC

UNFCCC Conference of the Parties, 3d Sess., UN Doc. FCCC/CP/1997/L.7/Add.1
(Dec. 10, 1997), art. 5

THE CONFERENCE OF THE PARTIES, . . .

5. Requests the Chairman of the [FCCC] Subsidiary Body for Scientific and Technological Advice and the Chairman of the [FCCC] Subsidiary Body for Implementation, taking into account the approved programme budget for the biennium 1998–1999 and the related programme of work of the secretariat (FCCC/CP/1997/ INF.1), to give guidance to the secretariat on preparatory work needed for the consideration by fourth session of the Conference of the Parties of the following matters, and to allocate work on these matters to the respective subsidiary bodies as appropriate:

(a) Determination of modalities, rules and guidelines as to how and which additional human induced activities related to changes in greenhouse gas emissions and removals in the agricultural soil and land-use change and forestry categories shall be added to, or subtracted from, the assigned amount for

Parties included in Annex I, as provided for under Article 3, paragraph 4, of the Protocol;

(b) Definition of relevant principles, modalities, rules and guidelines, in particular for verification, reporting and accountability of emissions trading, pursuant to Article 17 of the Protocol;

(c) Elaboration of guidelines for any Party included in Annex I to transfer to, or acquire from, any other such Party any emission reduction units resulting from projects aimed at reducing anthropogenic emissions by sources or enhancing anthropogenic removals by sinks of greenhouse gases in any sector of the economy, as provided for under Article 6 of the Protocol; and

(d) Consideration of and, as appropriate, action on suitable methodologies to address the situation of Parties listed in Annex B of the Protocol for whom single projects would have a significant proportional impact on emissions in the commitment period;

c. The Drama of the Protocol's Entry into Force

The Kyoto Protocol was concluded on December 11, 1997, but did not enter into force until February 16, 2005. (As of February, 2015 there were 193 Parties.) Why did it take so long for an agreement that many States believe to be critically important to become effective? The story of the Protocol's entry into force is rather dramatic.

Article 25 of the Kyoto Protocol provides that it would enter into force after it has been ratified by 55 developed States that accounted for 55% of global carbon dioxide emissions in 1990. The combination of the two factors was designed to ensure that the Protocol would not enter into force but be ineffective for want of participation by the major GHG emitters. The number of ratifications was not the problem. It was attained with Iceland's ratification on May 23, 2002. The 55% figure was what caused the difficulty. Many believed that without participation by the United States it would be all but impossible to bring the Protocol into force. According to government estimates, the U.S. was responsible for about 25% of global carbon dioxide emissions. (See http://www.eia.gov/oiaf/1605/ggccebro/chapter1.html.) The tension heightened when some countries—including even Japan, the place of the Protocol's birth—vacillated on joining the Protocol. But ultimately, with the United States effectively out of the picture, Russia was the key.

Russia had long been undecided as to whether it would be in its interest to join the Protocol and the government itself was divided on the issue. Opposition to the Protocol was led by President Vladimir Putin's economic policy advisor, Andrei Illarionov, whose strident attacks included arguments that Russia's participation in the agreement would seriously impede its economic growth. On the other hand, the European Union (EU) brought its considerable influence to bear on Russia in favor of ratification. Following talks with the EU in May 2004 on Russian accession to the World Trade Organization (WTO), President Putin announced that Russia would ratify the Protocol. However, no action was taken at the time, presumably because of internal disagreements within the government (both the Foreign Ministry and the Ministry of Natural Resources had spoken against ratification). But in September 2004 President Putin decided that Russia should join the Protocol. Russian ratification followed shortly thereafter, on November 18, 2004.

What factors were decisive for Russia? While the full picture is not entirely clear, it appears that an important consideration was that because of its economic difficulties in the wake of the collapse of the Soviet Union, Russia's emission levels were already substantially lower than its Kyoto targets. In addition, it is possible that because of the gap between its current emissions and its Kyoto targets, Russia could profit from selling emissions credits to other Parties to the Protocol, although this has been debated. Finally, it does not seem improbable that political trade-offs, such as support from the EU on Russian WTO accession, may have played a role.

Thus the Kyoto Protocol entered into in force and more than 55% (specifically, over 61.6%) of 1990 global carbon dioxide emissions are represented among the Parties. But is the entire Kyoto system flawed? Will the efforts of the EU countries and others in Annex I be straws in the wind as long as the United States, China and India remain outside the Kyoto club? The Kyoto Protocol has now entered its second commitment period (post-2012), as noted elsewhere in this chapter. What needs to be done to ensure that continued progress is made toward reducing emissions of greenhouse gases?

d. Unpacking the Protocol's Obligations

Determining the legally binding targets for industrialized countries established by the Kyoto Protocol can be somewhat complex. Essentially, these limitations are based on individualized percentage changes— usually reductions, but sometimes increases—in emissions from a base year (often referred to as 1990, but which can in fact be other years depending on the country and the particular GHG), augmented or decreased by voluntary participation in emissions trading, joint implementation, or the Clean Development Fund. Both actual emissions of GHGs and the effect of sequestering carbon in "sinks" such as forests are taken into account, although the exact procedure for doing that for sinks is not clear on the face of the Protocol and may give rise to substantial and significant debate in future years. The following excerpt describes the process of determining emissions reduction targets and of taking sinks into account

e. The Kyoto Protocol in Action

CURRENT DEVELOPMENT: THE KYOTO PROTOCOL TO THE UNITED NATIONS FRAMEWORK CONVENTION ON CLIMATE CHANGE

Clare Breidenich, Daniel Magraw, Anny Rowley & James Rubin
Reproduced with permission from 92 Am. J. Intl. 315 (1998), © The American Society of International Law (footnotes omitted)

EMISSION REDUCTION TARGETS

[A]rticle 3 of the Protocol establishes QELROs [quantified emissions limitation and reduction objectives] or emission targets for FCCC Annex I countries, with the exception of Turkey. The Protocol sets targets against base year emission levels. For most parties, 1990 is the official base year. However, certain countries with economies in transition are authorized by a decision of the Conference of the Parties to use a different base year, and other countries with economies in transition may apply to use a different base year. Also, as described in greater detail below, any Annex I country may select 1995 as the base year for the three synthetic GHGs (HFCs, PFCs and SF6). The negotiated emission targets for each Annex I country are contained in Annex B to the Protocol, and are listed as percentages of base year emission levels. For example, the target for the United States, which is listed as 93, corresponds to a 7 percent reduction from 1990 levels (or from 1995 levels for the three synthetic GHGs, as explained below). The targets range from an 8 percent reduction (i.e., 92) in the base year emissions level for the European Community (Community or EC) to a 10 percent increase (i.e., 110) in the base year emissions level for Iceland. Overall, the emission reduction among countries listed in Annex B is equivalent to about 5.2 percent of their emissions, if one does not take into account the possible use of 1995 as a base year for synthetic GHGs and the possible use of the Clean Development Mechanism by industrialized countries, both of which are discussed in more detail below.

The difference in parties' individual targets is the outcome of contentious negotiations. Several parties, notably EC member states and the United States (until the last stages of the negotiations), called for a uniform target for all industrialized-country parties (although the Community envisioned differentiation among its own member states). Other parties, led strongly by Australia, and including Japan, Norway and Iceland, argued that differentiated targets, rather than a uniform target, were appropriate, owing to the vast differences in countries' national circumstances, particularly natural resources and energy production and consumption profiles. In the final negotiations, parties were not able to reach agreement on a uniform target and opted for individual, differentiated targets.

The uniform 8 percent reduction target for the EC member states is also noteworthy. With respect to the FCCC's aim of returning emissions of Annex I countries to 1990 levels by the year 2000, parties are allowed to achieve that aim individually or jointly. Consequently, the Community developed an arrangement, often referred to as the "EC bubble," to share emission reductions among its member states. This arrangement was fundamental to the Community's ability to gain member state support for a reduction target in the Protocol. Under the EC internal burden-sharing agreement, certain member states such as Portugal and Ireland will be allowed to increase their emissions from 1990 levels. Thus, for the Community as a whole to reach the 8 percent reduction target, other member states will be required to reduce emissions by more than 8 percent. Originally, the Community based its burden-sharing arrangement on an overall 10 percent reduction. Although the FCCC allows for internal burden sharing among Annex I countries with respect to its aim of reducing GHG emissions from those countries to 1990 levels, such burden sharing was not automatically a part of the Kyoto Protocol and had to be negotiated. Under Article 4 of the Protocol, Annex B countries may jointly fulfill their commitments under its Article 3. It is possible that the internal EC arrangement may be renegotiated in light of the Kyoto Protocol's requirements. At least until the internal EC arrangement is renegotiated and the FCCC Secretariat is notified of it under Article 4, the individual targets for the member states set forth in Annex B reflect a common EC target, not in the internal burden-sharing arrangements.

Rather than a single-year, fixed-target, the Protocol establishes a cumulative target that applies to a multiyear "commitment period." Each Annex I country must ensure that its aggregate emissions during the commitment period do not exceed its "assigned amount." The first commitment period is established by the Protocol as 2008–2012. This multiyear formulation was devised to give parties greater flexibility in meeting their emission reduction commitments and to take into account annual fluctuations, for example, from business cycles. Article 3 implies that there will be subsequent commitment periods of unspecified duration Each party's initial "assigned amount" is calculated by multiplying its base year emissions by its individual target in Annex B and then multiplying the result by five—the number of years in the first commitment period. However, the assigned amount may increase or decrease, depending on the party's participation in market-based mechanisms authorized by the Protocol. . . .

SINKS

. . . The Protocol also takes emissions and sequestration from the land use change and forestry (LUCF) sector into account. The FCCC broadly directs countries to mitigate climate change by addressing "anthropogenic emissions by sources and removals by sinks" but does not specify how parties are to take account of carbon sequestration (and corresponding emissions) in the forestry sector. This vagueness led to inconsistencies in how parties account for and credit emissions from LUCF. Some parties have failed to provide any data on this sector, while those which have done so differ, some reporting the information separately and others combining it with other categories of emissions to generate a net total.

Perhaps more problematic, most countries calculate emissions from LUCF as an annual flow rate of carbon sequestered or emitted. Since the ability of trees to sequester carbon declines over time, a country with a large proportion of forested area, hence a high rate of carbon sequestration in the base year, will not be able to maintain the same rate of carbon sequestration in later years as its forestry resources age. The declining rate of carbon sequestration in these countries makes an emission target more difficult to attain. Conversely, countries that had net emissions from LUCF in their base year, due to deforestation, can ease the difficulty in attaining their target simply by decreasing the rate of deforestation. Thus, the system under the FCCC rewarded countries that historically had been deforesters and penalized countries that historically had been afforesters.

Because of these factors and the complexity of measuring emissions from LUCF, the negotiations on the sinks language in the Kyoto Protocol were some of the most difficult of the negotiations. The parties finally agreed to a compromise solution. As a general matter, sinks are not included in calculating base year emissions; however, they do play a role during the commitment period. Under the Protocol, Annex I countries must give an accounting of the net changes in LUCF emissions and removals by sinks during the commitment period that are due to human-induced activities and that began after 1990. This new accounting system will reward countries that are increasing their forestry sinks, and penalize those whose sinks are decreasing. Recognizing the difficulty that this new accounting system will create for a few parties, the Protocol requires Annex I countries with net emissions from LUCF in 1990 (i.e., those Annex I countries which were deforesting in 1990) to include those emissions in their base year which has the effect of correspondingly raising their assigned amount and allowed emissions. The meeting of the parties to the Protocol (MOP) is to provide further guidance on LUCF activities that may be counted toward emission targets. . . .

f.   Market-Based Mechanisms Redux: Efficiency Implementation or Inequitable Burden Shifting?

Article 4(2) of the FCCC states that parties may "individually or jointly" implement policies and measures aimed at reducing GHG emissions to 1990 levels by 2000. The convention does not provide any further guidance as to how such cooperation might occur, in particular as to whether the FCCC allows emissions reduction credit for joint implementation (JI) between industrialized and developing countries. Some countries argued that such JI would be efficient for Annex I countries and encourage the transfer of climate-friendly technology. Other countries countered that JI and other such mechanisms would allow rich countries to buy their way into compliance without taking any domestic corrective measures of their own and that these countries would buy up relatively cheap emissions credits, leaving developing countries to bear heavier costs later.

This debate ultimately led to the establishment at the first Conference of the Parties (COP-1) of a pilot program, referred to as "Activities Implemented Jointly" (AU), to gain experience in cooperative activities to reduce emissions. The Parties agreed to decide by 2000 whether to continue the pilot phase or to allow countries to get emissions reduction credit for such projects. The debate continued into the negotiations leading up to the meeting in Kyoto, encompassing not only JI and emissions trading but also the question of whether the European Community could share its emissions reduction among community members in an arrangement that came to be known as the "EU bubble." The following excerpt describes the outcome at Kyoto.

CURRENT DEVELOPMENT: THE KYOTO PROTOCOL TO THE UNITED NATIONS FRAMEWORK CONVENTION ON CLIMATE CHANGE

Clare Breidenich, Daniel Magraw, Anne Rowley & James Rubin
92 Am. J. Intl. L. 317, 326–327 (1998) (footnotes omitted)

[U]ltimately, four distinct mechanisms reflecting the competing proposals on transboundary emission reduction cooperation were incorporated in the Protocol. Project-based transfer credits, or JI among Annex I countries, is authorized by Article 6 and accounted for in Article 3(10) and 3(11). Through these provisions the Annex I countries and private-sector participants will be able to invest in emission reduction projects in the territory of any other Annex I country and to apply emission reduction credits for those projects toward their national emission targets. As a precondition for acquiring credit for an emission reduction through such project-based JI, parties must be in compliance with the measurement and reporting requirements of the Protocol. Article 6 does not contain rules or guidelines for the certification and tracking of projects or for attaining credit for emission reductions generated by any such projects, but these may be further developed by the MOP [the Conference of the Parties of the FCCC serving as the Meeting of the Parties of the Protocol].

In comparison to project-based trading under Article 6, a target-based emissions tradition system is authorized by Article 17 and accounted for in Article 3(10) and 3(11). Despite difficult, lengthy debate, the parties were not able to agree in Kyoto on the specific mechanism or rules for target-based emissions tradition; therefore, these articles do not provide much detail on the type of system contemplated by the parties. Instead, the Protocol simply authorizes Annex B countries to participate in emissions trading with each other and to use such trading to meet emission target commitments under Article 3. It also directs the COP (under the FCCC) to develop the rules and modalities for emissions trading (e.g., concerning accounting, verification and reporting of trades). If the COP does not agree on modalities and guidelines for emissions tradition, Annex I countries may be able to do that on a bilateral or multilateral basis with respect to emissions trading inter se. Finally, the Protocol specifies that such trading shall be "supplemental to domestic actions" to meet emission target commitments. The COP, rather than the MOP, was tasked with the duty of defining the rules and modalities of trading prior to entry into force of the Protocol.18 Authorization of the EC burden-sharing arrangement is contained in Article 4. Early in the negotiations, as a concession to other Annex I countries that viewed this arrangement as conferring a special advantage on EC member states, the Community proposed language that would allow other Annex I parties the option of "bubbling" (i.e., meeting their commitments individually or jointly). Article 4 allows Annex I parties, including those acting within the framework of regional economic integration organizations, to agree to fulfill their Article 3 commitments jointly.

A fourth mechanism for international cooperation on emission reductions is authorized by Article 12 and accounted for in Article 3(12). This mechanism reflects the evolution of a concept first proposed by Brazil to deal with noncompliance—the "Clean Development Mechanism" (CDM). Under the CDM, Annex I parties may invest in emission reduction projects in developing countries and may apply some portion of the reductions generated by these projects toward meeting their emission target under Article 3. In return, a share of the proceeds of these projects will be used to finance adaptation to climate change in particularly vulnerable developing countries, as well as to cover the administrative expenses of the mechanism. The CDM will be supervised by an executive board and subject to the guidance of the MOP, which will develop rules and guidelines for operating the mechanism, and will designate operational entities to certify and track projects. Certified emissions reductions obtained as early as the year 2000 may be used to assist in achieving compliance in the first commitment period. Hence, under the CDM, Annex I countries may be able to generate emission reduction credits applicable to their QELROs by investing in projects in developing countries that meet certain requirements.

---

g.   Implementation and Compliance

Implementation of and compliance with the Kyoto Protocol are obviously of great importance. Consider the following excerpts.

ELEMENTS OF A SUPERVISORY PROCEDURE FOR THE CLIMATE REGIME

Hermann E. Ott
39 Heidelberg J. Intl. L. 732, 744 (1997)

[T]here is still a broad consensus that the [non-compliance] procedure should be non-confrontational, non-punitive and rather facilitative in nature. These characteristics are reasonable in light of the experiences with the non-compliance procedure of the Montreal Protocol (1987) and they are also in line with academic thinking on this subject. A punitive approach does not offer much success in bringing about compliance if the reasons for non-compliance are, in general, not a willful disregard for legal obligations, but rather the incapacity of Governments, the ambiguity of norms or changing circumstances between the adoption of a treaty and its entry into force.

NOTES AND QUESTIONS

1.   *The "assigned amount."* In order to better understand how emissions targets actually work under the Kyoto Protocol, it might be useful to diagram the steps in determining what exactly a country's assigned amount is. At what point will a country know whether it is in compliance with its target? Will it matter if many emission trades have occurred in the private sector? When an emission trade occurs, on whom should the risk of nonperformance of Kyoto Protocol obligations fall—the buyer or the seller?

2.   *Measuring.* What measurement problems are likely to be encountered in implementing the Kyoto Protocol? How should sinks be calculated? Does it make sense to ignore carbon stored in soil or sinks operating in marine areas?

3.   *Noncompliance mechanisms.* Are Hermann Ott's ideas at odds with implementation and compliance provisions in the Kyoto Protocol? What additional implementation/compliance mechanisms or binding consequences for noncompliance should be adopted to strengthen the Protocol?

CURRENT DEVELOPMENT: THE KYOTO PROTOCOL TO THE
UNITED NATIONS FRAMEWORK CONVENTION ON
CLIMATE CHANGE

Clare Breidenich, Daniel Magraw, Anne Rowley & James Rubin

92 Am. J. Intl. L. 317, 329–332 (1998)

[C]ritics of the Protocol have argued that it has no effective compliance regime. Actually, the Protocol contains several elements designed to promote compliance by the parties. Most of these elements build on the existing structural and institutional components of the FCCC. The Protocol, however, expands on and improves the Convention's mechanisms in several ways. These improvements take the form of (1) strengthening the nature of the commitments to be legally binding, (2) requiring more rigorous reporting, (3) establishing a more critical review process, and (4) mandating the development of procedures and mechanisms to address cases of noncompliance. In addition, the Protocol elaborates the FCCC's approach in allowing each party flexibility with respect to how it implements its obligations and in encouraging cooperation among parties. Overall, the compliance provisions are designed to work together to form a logical progression of steps, beginning with reporting and review requirements and potentially culminating in consequences for noncompliance. Various compliance components of the Protocol and their relationship to provisions of the FCCC are described in more detail below.

LEGALLY BINDING TARGETS

A fundamental difference between the Convention and the Protocol is the nature of emissions reduction commitments. The FCCC established an aspirational commitment: each Annex I party does not actually commit itself to return to 1990 emissions levels, but rather to undertake policies and measures to mitigate climate change, and to "communicate . . . detailed information on its policies and measures . . . as well as on its resulting projected anthropogenic emissions by sources and removals by sinks of greenhouse gases not controlled by the Montreal Protocol . . . , with the aim of returning" its anthropogenic emissions of those GHGs to their 1990 levels. Verification and assessment of compliance with this obligation thus necessarily involves a subjective assessment of whether the party communicated detailed information with the aim of returning its GHG emissions to their 1990 levels, and there are no binding consequences for failure to comply with this aim. Indeed, parties do not violate the FCCC by exceeding their 1990 emissions. In contrast, the Kyoto Protocol establishes a clear, mandatory set of targets. The operative language of Article 3(1) commits parties to ensure that their emissions do not exceed their assigned amounts. Because the obligation is clear and precise, objective assessment of compliance with targets is greatly facilitated and there is a legal consequence for exceeding the targets—noncompliance with the Protocol.

FLEXIBILITY IN IMPLEMENTING

The Protocol allows flexibility at both the national and international levels with respect to how parties may implement their obligations. At the national level, each party may select its own policies and measures. At the international level, the market-based mechanisms described above provide parties with several possible choices. For example, the ability of a party to increase its assigned amount by acquiring tons through the international flexibility mechanisms provides an opportunity for parties, which might otherwise be in noncompliance at the end of a compliance period, to come into compliance. This flexibility will enhance implementation and compliance because it allows each party to design its own approach in light of its unique environmental, economic, social and political situation.

MEASUREMENT OF EMISSIONS

Under the FCCC, parties are directed to use the standard methodologies recommended by the IPCC to measure and estimate their national GHG emissions. The Protocol further defines this directive and mandates that parties have a national system for the estimation of GHG emissions from sources and the removal of such emissions by sinks in place at least one year prior to the beginning of the first commitment period (i.e., by 2007). The Protocol also requires that parties use the standardized IPCC methodologies for the preparation of national GHG inventories. While this requirement was already applicable under the FCCC, it was set forth in a Decision by the Parties, and not in the text of the Convention itself. The Kyoto Protocol goes a step further by requiring that the inventories of parties that fail to use these methods must be adjusted to account for uncertainty, which encourages parties to adopt the most current methodologies—those used by the IPCC. These new provisions on measurement will greatly enhance the accuracy, transparency and comparability of parties' national emissions inventories—features that are essential to verifying attainment of emission targets.

REPORTING

The FCCC established two basic reporting requirements: (1) annual inventories and accounts of GHG emission budgets, and (2) periodic national communications that provide detailed information on all aspects of parties' implementation of the Protocol. Under the Protocol, reporting requirements are expanded to incorporate additional information to enable the annual accounting of cumulative emission targets and international GHG trading. Article 7 of the Protocol contains the expanded reporting requirements. Article 7(1) requires each party, as part of its annual inventory, to provide the information necessary to ensure that it is in compliance with the budgetary and other commitments of Article 3. Article 7(2) requires each party to provide, in this periodic national communication, information necessary to ensure its compliance with all of its obligations under the Protocol. Guidelines to specify the additional information required and the reporting format must be adopted by the MOP at its first session. Furthermore, the parties must determine modalities for centralized accounting of emission, targets and trades. The FCCC Secretariat, which also serves as the Protocol Secretariat, is responsible for collecting, compiling and publishing national GHG inventory data. Accounting for emission targets and transactions could be a natural extension of this function.

REVIEW OF IMPLEMENTATION

The FCCC established a process for the review of information submitted by Annex I parties in national communications. Decision 3/CP.1 calls for secretariat-led expert teams to conduct in-country technical reviews of individual party communications. Although acceptance of the country visits is voluntary on the part of each party, to date all Annex I parties have undergone in-depth review of their first national communication. Reviews of the second national communications are scheduled for 1998 and 1999.

The Protocol builds upon and strengthens the in-depth review process established by the FCCC in two ways. First, under the FCCC, inventory information is collected annually, but has been published and reviewed only in conjunction with periodic national communications. Article 8(1) of the Protocol requires an annual review of national inventory and emissions target information as part of the centralized accounting of assigned amounts. Second, the review of parties' implementation under the Protocol will be conducted more thoroughly and critically than under the FCCC. Under the Protocol, teams of experts, coordinated by the secretariat and nominated by the parties to the Protocol with assistance as appropriate from intergovernmental organizations, are directed to conduct a comprehensive technical assessment of the full range of a party's implementation of the Protocol, and to identify any potential problems that a party might have in fulfilling its commitments. The secretariat will forward any problems identified in the expert teams' reports for consideration by the MOP. The MOP is authorized to take decisions on any matter required for implementation of the Protocol. In addressing potential compliance problems, the MOP is required to consider: information provided by the party in question in its relevant inventories and national communications; the reports of, and compliance issues raised by, the expert review teams; and questions raised by parties to the Protocol.

Guidelines governing review of implementation by the expert review teams are to be adopted by the MOP at its first session.

CONSEQUENCES OF NONCOMPLIANCE

Whereas the Convention called for consideration of the establishment of a multilateral consultative process to deal with implementation issues, the Protocol established two automatic consequences for compliance and, more generally, in Article 18, requires the parties to establish appropriate and effective procedures and mechanisms to determine and address cases of noncompliance, including development of an indicative list of consequences for noncompliance [The parties in fact adopted such a regime in December, 2005, as discussed below.] The parties, in developing the indicative list of consequences must take into consideration the cause, type, degree and frequency of noncompliance, as those factors relate to individual cases of potential noncompliance. The Protocol also requires that any procedures or mechanisms that involve binding consequences for noncompliance may be adopted by parties only by amending the Protocol. This language in Article 18 was adopted as a compromise between those parties that wanted binding, but unspecified consequences, on the one hand, and those that were not willing to commit themselves to binding but unspecified consequences, on the other hand. Essentially, the parties agreed to defer consideration of specific, binding consequences to a later date, but also agreed that they would adopt a list of indicative measures that could be implemented sooner, although they would not be legally binding.

NOTE: A TALE OF TWO REACTIONS TO KYOTO

The European Union more or less successfully embraced Kyoto. Corina Haita, The State of Compliance in the Kyoto Protocol 3 (International Center for Climate Governance 2012), reports that the largest 15 EU countries were 2% below the target for 2008–2012 despite the fact that Luxembourg, Austria, Spain, Denmark, Italy, the Netherlands and Ireland were above target. Other non-complying countries were Luxembourg and Canada which were the farthest from agreed emissions reductions. New Zealand, Australia, the United States, Lichtenstein, Switzerland, Slovenia, Norway, and Japan. Finland, Belgium, Croatia, the EU-15, Portugal, Germany, France, Greece, the UK, Sweden, Belarus and the Russian Federation were close to meeting their targets. The Ukraine was largest over-supplier of Kyoto credits.

On July 21, 1997, the United States Senate passed a non-binding resolution sponsored by Senator Richard Byrd[5] (the Byrd Resolution) stating:

> . . . Whereas the exemption for Developing Countries is inconsistent with the need for global action on climate change and is environmentally flawed;

---

[5] Richard Byrd was a powerful Democratic United States senator (1959–2010), from West Virginia, the second largest United States coal producing state.

Resolved, That it is the sense of the Senate that—

(1) the United States should not be a signatory to any protocol to, or other agreement regarding, the United Nations Framework Convention on Climate Change . . .—which would—

(A) mandate new commitments to limit or reduce greenhouse gas emissions for the Annex I Parties, unless the protocol or other agreement also mandates new specific scheduled commitments to limit or reduce greenhouse gas emissions for Developing Country Parties within the same compliance period, or

(B) would result in serious harm to the economy of the United States; . . .

The Kyoto Protocol was finalized later in 1997 and has not been submitted to the Senate for approval as of August 2015, nor is it expected ever to be. Ironically, the United States did reduce greenhouse gas emissions during the 2008–2012 commitment period, though it did not reduce them below the 1990 level. http://www.eia.gov/todayinenergy/detail.cfm?id=10691.

h.   Developing Countries Again

By its terms, the Berlin Mandate precluded the introduction of new commitments for developing countries in the Protocol at Kyoto. The Berlin Mandate, however, did call for parties to "advance the implementation" of existing commitments under UNFCCC Article 4.1; those commitments apply to all parties. The Protocol does allow developing countries to voluntarily assume binding emissions reductions obligations through amending Annex B, in order to be able to engage in emissions reduction trading. Either through this or some other means, it is essential over the long term to include developing countries in emissions reduction efforts. From a scientific perspective, GHG emissions from developing countries are expected to surpass those of industrialized countries sometime early in the 21st century, so the cooperation of developing countries is necessary in order to control anthropogenic climate change. From a political perspective, some countries—notably the United States—do not want to risk putting their industries at a competitive disadvantage by incurring Kyoto Protocol-related costs that facilities in other (developing) countries are not required to incur. These countries are unlikely to become parties to the protocol unless there is some sort of "meaningful participation"—a term used by President Clinton—by developing countries (although it is not obvious how much and what type of participation is needed to be "meaningful"). Developing countries, on the other hand, tend to view the climate change problem as having been caused by the economic development activities of the industrialized countries and thus believe those countries should take the first steps to alleviate it, before developing countries are asked to take steps that might slow their economic development. See, e.g., Cheng Zheng

Kang, *Equity, Special Considerations, and the Third World*, 1 Colo. J. Intl. Envtl. L. & Poly. 57, 61–63 (1990). How would you go about trying to convince developing countries voluntarily to undertake binding emission reduction commitments? Does the fact that they generally stand to suffer most from the adverse effects of climate change help you? How does your approach square with the polluter pays principle and other principles you have studied in this course? Early analyses of developing country concerns include Joyeeta Gupta, The Climate Change Convention and Developing Countries: From Conflict to Consensus? (1997); Jyoti K. Parikh, *Joint Implementation and North-South Cooperation for Climate Change*, 7 Intl. Envtl. Aff. 22 (1995) (addressing North-South equity concerns with joint implementation between developed and developing countries under the FCCC). Michael W. Wara, Building an Effective Climate Regime While Avoiding Carbon and Energy Stalemate (January 10, 2014). Available at SSRN: http://ssrn.com/abstract=2377447 or http://dx.doi.org/10.2139/ssrn.2377447.

i. Can We Plant Our Way to a Stable Climate Through Carbon Sequestration?: Reducing Emissions from Deforestation and Forest Degradation (REDD)

REDD (now REDD+) is designed to address two linked problems: (1) the biodiversity loss from deforestation, especially in temperate and tropical regions and (2) the mitigation of the rise in greenhouse gas emissions. For several decades, scientists have identified the adverse climate change impacts of deforestation. E.g. Norman Myers, *Tropical Deforestation and Climate Change*, 15 Environmental Conservation 293 (1998). Trees absorb CO_2, thus helping mitigate the greenhouse effect. In 2014, United States National Space Agency put the rate at 1.4 billion metric tons out of a total rate of 2.5 billion metric tons. http://www.jpl.nasa.gov/news/news.php?feature=4424. However, as with all climate change issues, uncertainty abounds. For example, scientists are concerned that tree growth rates are not sufficient to demonstrate that forests can absorb the necessary carbon levels. Peter van der Sleen et al., No growth stimulation of tropical trees by 150 years of CO_2 fertilization but water-use efficiency increased, Nature Geoscience, available at http://www.nature.com/ngeo/journal/v8/n1/abs/ngeo2313.html.

REDD was launched in 2008. The UN Food and Agriculture Organization of the United Nations (FAO), the United Nations Development Programme (UNDP) and the United Nations Environment Programme (UNEP) contributed to its formation. The Kyoto Protocol does not include the retention of carbon through the conservation of existing forests. Thus, negotiations for REDD have taken place under the auspices of the UNFCC, which established a separate Working Group for this purpose. The Copenhagen Accord, page 531 *infra*, expressly recognized "the crucial role of reducing emissions from deforestation and forest degradation." Under REDD, countries with tropical forests, primarily in tropical Asia, Central Africa, and South America, are incentivized to conserve forests and to prevent deforestation or degradation that would otherwise have taken place. The payments for conserving the forests come from carbon offsets paid for by actors in developed countries or direct funding that does not require an off-set, such as the funding that Norway has provided to Brazil for conserving areas in the Amazon. See William Boyd, *Ways of Seeing in Environmental Law: How Deforestation Became an Object of Climate Governance*, 37 Ecology L. Q. 843 (2011), for the ideological and political origins of the program. Anja Rosenberg and Jane Wilkinson, Demonstrating Approaches to REDD+ Lessons from the Kalimantan Forests and Climate Partnership (2013), available at http://climatepolicyinitiative.org/wp-content/uploads/2013/11/SGG-Case-Study-Lessons-from-the-Kalimantan-Forests-and-Climate-Partnership.pdf, provides an example of a forest presentation and rehabilitation project in Indonesia. See also Naomi Johnstone, *Indonesia in the REDD: Climate Change, Indigenous Peoples and Global Legal Pluralism*, 12 APLPJ 93 (2010–2011).

While States have tried to negotiate formal rules for calculating emission credits and for implementing REDD, a formal Protocol has yet to be concluded. REDD has not been integrated into international human rights law or the Convention on Biological Divdiversity. See Annalisa Savaresi, *The Role of REDD in the Harmonization of Overlapping International Obligations*, in Climate Change and the Law 427 (2013). As do all carbon-set programs, REDD raises a host of fundamental and technical issues:

- How do you ensure that REDD leads to emissions reductions that are "real and additional," meaning they would not have happened without a REDD program?

- How do you know that reducing deforestation in one place will not cause increased deforestation in another? This is what is called "leakage."

- How do you know that REDD will not just be a temporary fix, but rather will protect forests permanently?

- How do you ensure that REDD will not adversely impact the rights and livelihoods of the millions of people who live in or around forests, especially in poorly governed states?

- How do you address the complex issues of land tenure and of timber tenure, which may be separate from land tenure?

- What are the baseline scenarios against which the enhanced storage of carbon can be measured, designing credible and efficient monitoring, reporting and verification (MRV) procedures, and developing local benefit sharing and forest management strategies?

- How do you design, measure, monitor report and verify emission reductions from forests? See Conferences of the Parties to United Nations Framework Convention on Climate Change, Nineteenth Meeting, Decision 13/CP.19, Guidelines and Procedures for the Technical Assessment of Submissions from Parties on Proposed Forest Reference Emission Levels and/or Forest Reference Levels (2013).

Examples of these problems abound. Bolivia doubled the size of a national park and expelled loggers from the area, but leakage occurred when the loggers began to cut down trees in an adjacent non-protected forest. In other areas such as Indonesia, large corporations are preserving forests to earn off-sets but indigenous forest dwellers risk expulsion. See Daniel C. Nepstad et al., Systematic Conservation, REDD, and the Future of the Amazon Basin, 25 Conservation Biology 1113 (2011); Michael L. Brown, Limiting Corrupt Incentives in a Global REDD Regime, Ecology L.Q. 237 (2010); and Elizabeth Baldwin and Kenneth R. Richards, *REDD, PINC, and Other Shades of Green: Institutional Requirements for an International Forest Carbon Sequestration Treaty in a Post-Kyoto World*, 52 Nat. Res. J. 1 (2012). The initial assessments are not positive on the fundamental question: does REDD work? "As currently designed, the likelihood of broader development impact (i.e., emission reductions) largely lies beyond the Programme's reach. To achieve emission reductions and implement solutions that will address the underlying drivers of deforestation and forest degradation, the Programme posits that partner countries that graduate from the readiness phase will be able to secure long term financial support from either market or non-market sources. The future of such financing is unclear, and the road to REDD+ readiness and implementation faces important challenges." External Evaluation of the United Nations Collaborative Programme on Reducing emissions from Deforestation in developing Countries (the UN-REDD Programme), Final Report v (2014), available at http://www.un-redd.org/Portals/15/documents/UN-REDD Ëvaluation%20Final%20Report%20Volume1%20June2014ËN.pdf.

NOTES AND QUESTIONS

1. During the negotiations for the UNFCC, there was considerable debate as to whether the Convention should include a Protocol on Forests or whether forests were more appropriately addressed in the context of biodiversity. In the end, there was no protocol to the UNFCC. States negotiated a set of explicitly nonbinding principles on forests, which were adopted in 1992 in Rio, at the same time the UNFCC was opened for signature. Current international forest management strategies are discussed in Chapter 13, pages 880 to 894.

2.   Would it be better to characterize REDD+ and similar programs as forest biological diversity conservation strategies with important but limited climate change mitigation benefits?

3.   On the other hand, why should developed States receive emission credits for planting forests in other countries, but the countries themselves cannot receive credits for maintaining the forests that they do have rather than harvesting the timber in them?

5.   POST-KYOTO: THE PARTIES MEET AGAIN AND AGAIN: A SELECTIVE TRAVEL AND LESIURE GUIDE TO THE TRAVELS OF THE PARTIES

In Luigi Pirandello's famous play, Six Characters in Search of an Author, a group of actors crash a theater and put on an improvised play, but in end, the effort is unsatisfactory. The actors know neither how to create a play nor how to interpret their roles. Since the adoption of the Kyoto Protocol, the Parties sought to create a global climate regime that bridges the North-South divide (or the divide between States with emission-reduction obligations under the Kyoto Protocol and those that do not). E.g. Richard Cooper, *Toward a Real Global Warming Treaty*, 77 For. Aff. 66 (1998). This section is divided into three parts: part (a) summarizes the major meetings and the important policy decisions reached; part (b) outlines some of the unresolved technical and equity issues; and part (c) examines the arguments that there are global solutions beyond a treaty with caps on every country's emissions. The next section, 6, is a brief examination to the on-going efforts to come up with a new global regime.

The Parties to the Convention met frequently and achieved considerable progress in developing new greenhouse reduction strategies, even if a global accord has eluded them.

a.   The Major Meetings

At the Eleventh Meeting of the Conference of the Parties to the Kyoto Protocol in Montreal, Montreal, 2005, the Parties agreed to set binding targets for greenhouse-gas emission reduction in the second commitment period, post-2012, when the Protocol's then-current emission-reduction requirements would expire. Parties also adopted the so-called "Marrakesh Accords," a rulebook for the Kyoto Protocol. The Accords formally launched the emissions trading system and the clean development mechanism and established the Joint Implementation Supervisory Board to oversee investment by developed countries in other developed countries, particularly in those in central and Eastern Europe. See table, Decisions adopted by COP 11 and COP/MOP 1, available at http://unfccc.int/meetings/cop_11/items/3394.php.

The Marrakesh Accords also established the compliance regime for the Protocol to hold Parties accountable for meeting their emission reduction targets which could be amended to transform the compliance regime into a binding treaty commitment, as envisaged in Article 18 of the Protocol. The decision and annexed Procedures and Mechanisms are available at http://unfccc.int/cop7/documents/accords_draft.pdf. The compliance system is implemented by a twenty-member Compliance Committee (Section II), composed of a "facilitative branch" (Section IV) and an "enforcement branch" (Section V), each consisting of ten members. The enforcement branch is "responsible for determining whether a Party included in Annex I [developed country Parties to the FCCC] is not in compliance with [QELROs under Article 3(1) of the Protocol, the methodological and reporting requirements under Articles 5 and 7 of the Protocol and the eligibility requirements under Articles 6, 12 and 17 of the Protocol]." (Section V, para. 4.) It is also responsible "for applying the consequences set out in section XV for the cases of non-compliance mentioned [above]." (Section V, para. 6.) Section V of the Procedures and Mechanisms strongly suggests that the purpose of imposing "consequences" is not punishment: "The consequences of non-compliance with Article 3, paragraph 1, of the Protocol to be applied by the enforcement branch shall be aimed at the restoration of compliance to ensure environmental integrity, and shall provide for an incentive to comply." (Section V, para. 6.) Section XV, "Consequences applied by the Enforcement Branch," confers authority on that branch to take certain measures with respect to a non-complying state party, ranging from a declaration of non-compliance to the imposition of what amount to sanctions for violations of emission reduction commitments. The latter may include "deduction from the Party's assigned amount for the second commitment period of a number of tonnes equal to 1.3 times the amount in tonnes of excess emissions; . . ." (Section XV, para. 5(a).) Thus, it would appear that providing an incentive to comply under section V may take the form of impending punishment, in the form of a 30 percent penalty, if the Protocol's requirements are not met. The enforcement branch may also suspend the non-complying party's eligibility to make transfers (sell credits) under the emissions trading system of Article 17 of the Protocol. (Section XV, para. 5(c).)

The endorsement of joint implementation was one of the most important decisions adopted at COP/MOP 1. Article 6 of the Kyoto Protocol allows Annex I parties to invest in projects in other Annex I parties that reduce emissions or increase GHG removals by means of sinks. The investing country then receives emission reduction units (ERUs) that may be used to help meet its Kyoto target. The COP/MOP adopted a decision on "Implementation of Article 6 of the Kyoto Protocol" which established a Joint Implementation Supervisory Committee, requested it to establish and carry out a work program and made other decisions regarding implementation of the JI mechanism. The meeting also adopted a decision entitled "Guidelines for the implementation of Article 6 of the Kyoto Protocol." An annex to that decision contains detailed provisions—many of which are couched in mandatory language and thus appear to be more than "guidelines"—concerning the implementation of JI under the Protocol. These include provisions on the functions of the Article 6 Supervisory Committee, the structure of the Committee, the nomination and election of its members, and the like, requirements for participation in JI projects, and the verification procedure under the Article 6 Supervisory Committee.

QUESTION

Since JI investments are most likely to be made in countries with economies in transition (EIT countries, including the Russian Federation), and since a number of these countries are now members of the European Union, how much scope is there, in fact, for an Annex I country like the United States to earn ERUs through joint implementation (if it were a party to the Protocol)? Is there an issue of plucking the low-hanging fruit in a country under joint implementation and leaving the more expensive projects? Could joint implementation simply give emission credits for taking emissions out of service that were already not being used, which is sometimes referred to as the "hot air" problem?

Two Conferences of the Parties (COPs), one in Bali in 2007 and the other in Copenhagen in 2009, were set in order to negotiate a post-Kyoto Protocol treaty or, alternatively, to extend the period of the Kyoto Protocol. The COP in Bali resulted in the "Bali Action Plan." The Bali Action Plan is considered "[t]he primary framework for negotiating the post-Kyoto climate regime." Furthermore, "[t]he Action Plan put the world on a schedule to agree to a post-Kyoto regime by the end of 2009. The most tangible aspect of the Bali Action Plan is the establishment of the Ad-hoc Working Group on Long-term Cooperative Action. The Working Group Action Plan also reflected important concessions by many of the Parties in framing the negotiations. However, according to Chris Wold et al., Climate Change and the Law 335–336 (2209), the Bali Action Plan left unresolved three of the most important issues threatening success of future negotiations, specifically:

> "First, although the Action Plan calls for developed countries to make measurable reductions in greenhouse gasses, the countries must still reach agreement on what specifically those new commitments will be.

> Second although the Bali Action Plan commits developing countries to adopt 'nationally appropriate mitigation actions,' it

does not clarify what the nature of those mitigation actions might be. . . .

A third issue also lingers: what will be necessary for the United States to join a post-Kyoto regime? . . ."

In 2009, Parties to the UNFCCC met in Copenhagen and there were high hopes, especially after the election of United States President Barack Obama in 2008, that the Parties would negotiate a treaty to replace, or at least specify a second commitment period for, the Kyoto Protocol. A draft treaty was circulated before the meeting. However, the outcome was the Copenhagen Accord, a document negotiated very late in the process by a group of about twenty-five heads of State, heads of government, ministers, and other heads of delegations. Unexpectedly, the Conference of the Parties (COP) did not adopt the document, because several countries opposed it, and decisions to adopt the document were to be made by consensus. Instead, the COP "took note of" the Accord and the Copenhagen Accord had an uncertain legal status. The Accord is especially interesting because it invites both developed and developing countries to list in Annex 1 and Annex 2 commitments to reduce greenhouse gas emissions. More than 100 countries submitted such commitments in the few months following the Conference. These varied significantly. While developed States often expressed commitments in terms of the targets and timetables in Annex 1, some of the commitments by countries in Annex 2 were expressed in terms of limitations or reductions in the intensity of carbon used in production. China, Brazil, and India, for example, made commitments in terms of intensity. Several States, such as Brazil, included forests in determining their commitments.

b. The Copenhagen Accord

Key provisions of the Accord include:

1. We underline that climate change is one of the greatest challenges of our time. We emphasize our strong political will to urgently combat climate change in accordance with the principle of common but differentiated responsibilities and respective capabilities. To achieve the ultimate objective of the Convention to stabilize greenhouse gas concentration in the atmosphere at a level that would prevent dangerous anthropogenic interference with the climate system, we shall, recognizing the scientific view that the increase in global temperature should be below 2 degrees Celsius, on the basis of equity and in the context of sustainable development, enhance our long-term cooperative action to combat climate change. We recognize the critical impacts of climate change and the potential impacts of response measures on countries particularly vulnerable to its adverse effects and stress the need to

establish a comprehensive adaptation programme including international support.

5.   Non-Annex I Parties to the Convention will implement mitigation actions, including those to be submitted to the secretariat by non-Annex I Parties in the format given in Appendix II by 31 January 2010, for compilation in an INF document, consistent with Article 4.1 and Article 4.7 and in the context of sustainable development. Least developed countries and small island developing States may undertake actions voluntarily and on the basis of support. Mitigation actions subsequently taken and envisaged by Non-Annex I Parties, including national inventory reports, shall be communicated through national communications consistent with Article 12.1(b) every two years on the basis of guidelines to be adopted by the Conference of the Parties. Those mitigation actions in national communications or otherwise communicated to the Secretariat will be added to the list in appendix II. Mitigation actions taken by Non-Annex I Parties will be subject to their domestic measurement, reporting and verification the result of which will be reported through their national communications every two years. Non-Annex I Parties will communicate information on the implementation of their actions through National Communications, with provisions for international consultations and analysis under clearly defined guidelines that will ensure that national sovereignty is respected. Nationally appropriate mitigation actions seeking international support will be recorded in a registry along with relevant technology, finance and capacity building support. Those actions supported will be added to the list in appendix II. These supported nationally appropriate mitigation actions will be subject to international measurement, reporting and verification in accordance with guidelines adopted by the Conference of the Parties.

8.   Scaled up, new and additional, predictable and adequate funding as well as improved access shall be provided to developing countries, in accordance with the relevant provisions of the Convention, to enable and support enhanced action on mitigation, including substantial finance to reduce emissions from deforestation and forest degradation (REDD-plus), adaptation, technology development and transfer and capacity-building, for enhanced implementation of the Convention. The collective commitment by developed countries is to provide new and additional resources, including forestry and investments through international institutions, approaching USD 30 billion for the period 2010–2012 with balanced allocation between adaptation and mitigation. Funding for adaptation will be prioritized for the most vulnerable developing countries, such as the least developed countries, small island developing States and Africa. In the context of meaningful mitigation actions and transparency on implementation, developed countries commit to a goal of mobilizing jointly USD 100 billion dollars a year by 2020 to address the

needs of developing countries. This funding will come from a wide variety of sources, public and private, bilateral and multilateral, including alternative sources of finance. New multilateral funding for adaptation will be delivered through effective and efficient fund arrangements, with a governance structure providing for equal representation of developed and developing countries.

9.   To this end, a High Level Panel will be established under the guidance of and accountable to the Conference of the Parties to study the contribution of the potential sources of revenue, including alternative sources of finance, towards meeting this goal.

10. We decide that the Copenhagen Green Climate Fund shall be established as an operating entity of the financial mechanism of the Convention to support projects, programme, policies and other activities in developing countries related to mitigation including REDD-plus, adaptation, capacity-building, technology development and transfer."

11. In order to enhance action on development and transfer of technology we decide to establish a Technology Mechanism to accelerate technology development and transfer in support of action on adaptation and mitigation that will be guided by a country-driven approach and be based on national circumstances and priorities.

12. We call for an assessment of the implementation of this Accord to be completed by 2015, including in light of the Convention's ultimate objective. This would include consideration of strengthening the long-term goal referencing various matters presented by the science, including in relation to temperature rises of 1.5 degrees Celsius. [Report of the Conference of the Parties on the Fifteenth Session, held in Copenhagen from 7–19 December, 2009, available at http://unfcce.int/resource/docs/2009/cop15/eng/11.pdf.

NOTE AND QUESTIONS: WHAT HATH COPENHAGEN WROUGHT?

Does the agreement contain a long term objective on the upper bound of the concentration of greenhouse gases? Without one, is the bottom line that Copenhagen yielded few results and did not close the developed-developing country divide? Or did the submission of voluntary commitments in Annex 1 and Annex 2 suggest a way forward? China and India rejected the United States' demand that developing countries accept binding emission reduction obligations if the United States is to do so. In addition, Australia supported the George W. Bush administration's approach of promoting the development of cleaner technologies and rejecting what it views as the economically harmful measures represented by the Kyoto Protocol's binding targets and timetables. It appears that the traditional division between developed and developing countries is giving way to one between developed countries that support binding reduction obligations and those that favor voluntary reductions. Fearing that such a stalemate could prevent effective action, former President Bill Clinton suggested in an address to the Conference that countries undertake smaller initiatives to create emission reduction technologies that could be utilized by both developed and developing nations. This echoes the calls of many critics who argue that a combination of binding targets and technological advances is necessary to adequately address the problem of climate change. In addition, Daniel Bodansky, The Copenhagen Climate Change Accord 14 ASIL Insights (2010), observes that the Copenhagen Accord "establishes a bottom-up process that allows each Annex I party to define its own target level, base year and accounting rules, and to submit its target in a defined format, for compilation by the UNFCCC Secretariat." The merits of this strategy are discussed in *infra* Section 6. The bottom-up strategy has arguably proved at least partially successful if measured by voluntary GHG reeduction commitments: the developed and developing States which have formally announced targets represent over 50% of global CO_2 emissions. On the other hand, those commitments fall far short of limiting projected temperature increase to less than the 2 degrees Celsius mentioned in the Accord.

Is it inevitable that the United States will eventually accept binding GHG reduction obligations? If yes, why? The demands of U.S. multinational and other businesses for a level playing field? The economic need to take advantage of U.S. technological innovation? The increasing relative cost of fossil fuels? Moral grounds? If the answer is no, what will the environmental, political and economic consequences be? What is required for voluntary commitments to be effective?

c. Developing Country Mitigation

As with developed country emissions targets, the Copenhagen Accord establishes a bottom-up process by which developing countries will submit their mitigation actions in a defined format, for compilation by the UNFCCC Secretariat. It provides that developing countries will submit greenhouse gas inventories every two years, that developing country mitigation actions will be subject to domestic MRV, and that the results of this domestic MRV will be reported in biennial national communications, which will be subject to 'international consultations and analysis under clearly defined guidelines.' The Copenhagen Accord also establishes a registry for listing nationally appropriate mitigation actions (NAMAs) for which international support is sought, and provides that supported NAMAs will be subject to international MRV (monitoring, reporting and verification) in accordance with COP guidelines. Subsequent meetings have taken more concrete mitigation assistance actions.

The parties met in Durban in 2011 and Doha in 2012 prior to COP 16 in Cancun. In Cancun, the Parties agreed to the Cancun Agreements. One of the most important achievements was the establishment of the Green Climate Fund, which is based in South Korea and provides both mitigation and adaptation assistance. The Cancun Agreements include the following:

Green Climate Fund

In order to scale up the provision of long-term financing for developing countries, Governments at COP 16 in Cancun decided to establish a Green Climate Fund. The fund will support projects, programmes, policies and other activities in developing country Parties using thematic funding windows. A Transitional Committee selected by Parties to the UNFCCC will design the details of the new fund, which will be designated as an operating entity of the financial mechanism of the Convention and will be accountable to the COP.

Technology Mechanism

The new Technology Mechanism is expected to facilitate enhanced action on technology development and transfer to support action on mitigation and adaptation. The Mechanism consists of two key components: a Technology Executive Committee and a Climate Technology Centre and Network.

Cancun Adaptation Framework

The objective of the Cancun Adaptation Framework is to enhance action on adaptation, including through international cooperation and coherent consideration of matters relating to adaptation under the Convention. Ultimately enhanced action on adaptation seeks to reduce vulnerability and build resilience in developing country Parties, taking into account the urgent and immediate needs of those developing countries that are particularly vulnerable.

Fast-start finance

Fast-start finance refers to new and additional resources that developed country Parties pledged to mobilize through international institutions, approaching USD 30 billion for the period 2010—2012. Mitigation and adaptation should receive a balanced allocation of fast start finance, and funding for adaptation is expected to be prioritized for the most vulnerable developing countries, such as the least developed countries, small island developing States and Africa. The COP invited developed country Parties to provide information on their efforts to achieve this goal and on how developing country Parties can access these resources.

Forest Management Reference Levels

In the run-up to Copenhagen, the potential to reduce emissions from deforestation and forest degradation (known as

'REDD-plus') received considerable attention. [See *supra* p. 525.] The principal question has been whether to finance REDD-plus from public funds or by providing carbon credits. The Copenhagen Accord calls for the "immediate establishment" of a mechanism to help mobilize resources for REDD-plus from developed countries and acknowledges the "need to provide positive incentives," without resolving the issue of public vs. private support. The Conference of the Parties serving as the meeting of the Parties to the Kyoto Protocol (CMP) at its sixth session requested each Annex I Party to submit to the secretariat information on the forest management reference level (FMRL). The CMP also decided that each submission shall be subject to a technical assessment, the outcomes of which are to be considered by the CMP at its seventh session.

The Durban outcomes addressed the challenge of reducing greenhouse gas emissions "by creating a roadmap with four primary areas of coordinated and complementary action and implementation." These areas were designed to build as well as preserve trust amongst countries In November 2013, in Warsaw, Poland, States agreed to establish yet another Fund, the Warsaw Mechanism, to compensate for damage caused by climate change.

6. THE NEXT STAGE?

a. Vers Paris et Après

The United Nations Framework Convention on Climate Change identified 450 ppm as the level necessary for a 50 percent chance of holding temperatures to a 2-degree-Celsius increase above pre-industrial levels. Nonetheless, the parties are pushing ahead to fulfill Decision 1/CP.17, adopted in Durban, to develop a protocol, another legal instrument or an agreed outcome with legal force under the Convention applicable to all Parties, which is to be completed no later than 2015. The 21st meeting will take place in Paris in late 2015. The idea of aggregating individual country commitments without a legally binding agreement setting emissions caps and allocating the burden of mitigation among all emitting countries became the basis for a post-Kyoto approach to mitigation.

In 2014, the Obama Administration assumed a major leadership role on climate change by seeking to engage the developing world in taking more aggressive action at the same time the developed countries increase their emission reduction efforts. For example, in November 2014, China and the United States jointly announced that "t]he United States intends to achieve an economy-wide target of reducing its emissions by 26%–28%

below its 2005 level in 2025 and to make best efforts to reduce its emissions by 28%. China intends to achieve the peaking of CO_2 emissions around 2030 and to make best efforts to peak early and intends to increase the share of non-fossil fuels in primary energy consumption to around 20% by 2030. Both sides intend to continue to work to increase ambition over time." http://www.whitehouse.gov/the-press-office/2014/11/11/us-china-joint-announcement-climate-change. India, on the other hand, may be going in the opposite direction under the government elected in 2014. However, India's National Action Plan for Climate Change (NAPCC) sets a target for the share of renewables-based power generation from the current 4 percent to 15 percent by 2020.

In preparation for the Paris, 2015 meeting, the Parties met in Lima, Peru in December 2014. A wide range of topics were discussed, including a draft agreement, but in the end the Parties agreed to focus on six topics -- mitigation, adaptation, finance, technology transfer, capacity building and transparency of action and support—and pushed all major decisions forward. The result was the Report of the Working Group on the Durban Platform for Enhanced Action, Draft Decision CP.XX (2014), which *inter alia,* states:

2.   *Decides* that the protocol, another legal instrument, or agreed outcome with legal force under the Convention applicable to the parties shall address in a balanced manner, inter alia, mitigation, adaptation, finance, technology, develop and transfer, and capacity-building, and transparency of action and support.

9.   *Reiterates* its invitation to each Party to communicate its intended nationally determined contribution to achieving the objective of the Convention as set out in Article 2.

10. *Agrees* that each Party's intended nationally determined contribution toward achieving of the objective of the Convention as set out in Article 2 will represent a progression beyond the current undertaking of that Party.

11. *Also agrees* that the least developed countries and small island states developing States may communicate on strategies, plans and actions for low greenhouse gas emission development reflecting their special circumstances in the context of intended nationally determined contributions.

16(b).   *Requests* the secretariat to:

Prepare by 1 November 2015 a synthesis report on the on the aggregate effect of intended nationally determined contributions. . . .

QUESTIONS

What is missing from the Lima Report? The hoped for Lima result was a draft text for Paris, but a 100-plus-page draft was abandoned because the Parties could not agree on any text. In its place, at the last minute the Parties agreed to a four-page draft of elements. Section 4 "*acknowledges* the progress made in Lima in elaborating the elements for a draft text as contained in the annex." The Decision makes no direct mention of the Global Environment Facility and the funds that it administers. See Chapter 17, pages 1197 to 1202, *infra*. Section 4 exhorts developed countries to "mobilize enhanced financial support to developing country Parties for ambitious mitigation and adaptation actions, especially to the Parties that are particularly vulnerable to the adverse effects of climate change. . . ." Section 4 reflects the objection of smaller developing countries that the GDM benefits flow mainly to four countries, China, India, Brazil and Mexico. Does this represent an efficient allocation of resources given the emission levels of these countries?

What new concepts emerged in Lima? To move beyond the simple developed-developing divide, Brazil proposed to put the non-Kyoto countries into three or four concentric circles around the core industrialized countries. It was not formally adopted, but does its influence appear in the Draft Decision sections reproduced above?

If the major developing emitting countries are unwilling to commit to a new treaty, what are the alternative binding mechanisms? One option is that a Paris agreement could be styled not as a new treaty but as a protocol negotiated through the Durban Platform for Enhanced Action. The 1992 FCCC is only a framework convention, and subsequent protocols to the UNFCC itself could specify the Parties' substantive obligations that implement the general objectives of the Convention. They could bind those States accepting them. Would a Protocol or other document by which States offer specific individual voluntary commitments on what they will do to limit/reduce greenhouse gas emission be in effect a new agreement or treaty? The issue is significant for the United States. Article II, Section 2 of the United States Constitution requires the consent of two thirds of the Senate present before the President can ratify a treaty. And, the Senate can condition ratification of the treaty. See Michael J. Glennon, *The Constitutional Power of the United States Senate to Condition its Consent to Treaties*, 67 Chicago Kent L. Rev. 533 (1991). Would the President have to submit any Paris agreement to the Senate? The conventional definition of a treaty is any international agreement between States in writing and governed by international law. The Vienna Convention on the Law Treaties, art. 2(1)(a). However, the United States has entered into binding international legal instruments that are extensions of existing agreements to which it is a Party or based either on the President's express or implied constitutional authority, without seeking Senate approval for ratification. David A. Wirth, *The International and Domestic Law of Climate Change: A Binding International Areement Without the Senate or Congress?*, 39 Harv.

Envtl. L. Rev/ 515 (2015), parses the unresolved issues of shared Executive-Congressional power and concludes that the President can agree to a new climate change agreement without Senate consent or additional statutory authority.

Precedents exist for a provisional application of an amendment to the Kyoto Protocol or a new free-standing agreement. Article 25 of the Vienna Convention on the Law of Treaties provides for provisional application of a treaty. Provisional application has been used, inter alia, to prevent legal gaps between successive treaty regimes. e.g., the 1994 United Nations International Tropical Timber Agreement, 1955 U.N.T.S. 81; 33 I.L.M. 1014. international agreements that have been applied on a provisional basis include the Agreement Relating to the Implementation of Part XI of the United Nations Convention on the Law of the Sea, of Part XI of the United Nations Convention on the Law of the Sea of 10 December 1982, 28 July 1994, 1836 U.N.T.S. 3; 33 ILM 1309 (a treaty with a fixed date for provisional application to enter into effect) and The International Coffee Agreement 2001, 28 September 2000, 2161 U.N.T.S. 308; 33 I.L.M. 1309, which provides for provisional entry into force if the formal criteria for entry into force have not been met within a given period. The International Law Commission concluded that "there can be no doubt that such clauses have legal effect and bring the treaty into force on a provisional basis". Report of the International Law Commission on the Work of its Eighteenth Session, 2 YILC 210 (1966).

To mitigate greenhouse gas emissions, it seems clear that industrialized countries must move toward non-carbon or less intense carbon sources energy sources such as natural gas, nuclear power, renewable heat and power which includes hydropower, solar, wind, geothermal and bioenergy, as well as engaging in carbon dioxide capture and storage (a form of the so-called geoengineering, discussed below) and more fuel-efficient vehicles and possibly modal shifts from road transport to rail and public transport systems. Does this suggest that States should focus negotiations on emission reductions by each sector? Or perhaps a combination of binding sector reduction targets and more general voluntary pledges?

b. Geoengineering

PROBLEM

The leaders of East Raj are deeply concerned that sea level rise will inundate large areas of the coastal country and inland areas will experience, massive flooding, disrupted rainfall, and internal and external migration. Over the objections of many parties to the UNFCCC, East Raj's leaders decided to cool the country by releasing large amounts of sulphuric acid into the stratosphere by multiple flights by their military jets. The cost of doing this was far less than East Raj's leaders estimated that unremitted climate change would cost. As the East Raj Academy of Science researchers had predicted, average global temperatures decreased by about .5 degree C during the year after the SAG occurred. In neighboring countries, average temperatures also decreased, rainfall patterns were irregular, tornadoes increased, and agricultural harvests were significantly less than normal. As these conditions became evident, several neighboring States protested to East Raj. Despite stern diplomatic protests, East Raj continued "acid spreading" and as a result, a more-or-less permanent haze spread over the planet; and average global temperature decreased by 1.5 degrees C, which was more than the researchers had predicted. This time agricultural harvests in Europe were less than normal and unusually cold weather resulted in the deaths of the homeless and the elderly. Assume you represent a neighboring State. What international and domestic legal strategies would you recommend to address the exeternalities, including increased, unanticipated risks, of geoengineering experiments?

Many climate change analysts initially assumed that both mitigation and adaptation were necessary because no technological fix existed. In recent years a number of technological solutions have been proposed stemming from the widespread concern that reduction of GHG emissions and the use of "natural" sinks through, for example, afforestation, would be a prohibitively expensive and protracted endeavor. Such proposals are often described as involving "geoengineering" or "climate intervention". The Intergovernmental Panel on Climate Change (IPCC) defines "geoengineering" as "a broad set of methods and technologies that aim to deliberately alter the climate system in order to alleviate the impacts of climate change." IPCC Expert Meeting on Geoengineering Meeting Report 2 (Ottmar Edenhofer et al. eds. 2011), *available at* https://www.ipcc-wg2.gov/meetings/EMs/EM_GeoE_Meeting_Report_final.pdf.

The two primary geoengineering strategies that have been proposed as of August 2015 are carbon dioxide removal (CDR) and solar radiation management (SRM). CDR methods refer to those techniques that aim to remove CO_2 (or other GHGs) directly from the atmosphere by either (1) increasing natural sinks for carbon or (2) using chemical or biological engineering to remove CO_2 (or other GHGs) from the atmosphere or oceans with the intent of reducing atmospheric CO_2.

SRM technologies, on the other hand, are intended to alleviate climate change by increasing the reflectivity of the Earth's atmosphere or surface. The technique, also referred to as Strategic Aerosol Geoengineering (SAG), mimics volcanic eruptions that spew sulphate particles into the atmosphere, resulting in cooling.

Although the Royal Society considers CDR to have less immediate impacts than SRM, it believes there are fewer risks associated with CDR deployment. IPCC Expert Meeting on Geoengineering, *supra* at 28. The IPPC cautions that "[l]imited evidence precludes a comprehensive qualitative assessment of both Solar Radiation Management (SRM) and Carbon Dioxide Removal (CDR) and their impact on the climate system."

The United States National Academy of Sciences has evaluated CDR and SRM and concluded that more research is needed on these technologies, although they are not a substitute for greenhouse gas reductions. National Academy of Sciences, Climate Intervention: Carbon Dioxide Removal and Reliable Sequestration (2015), and National Academy of Sciences, Climate Intervention: Reflecting Sunlight to Cool Earth (2015). *Available at* http://www.nap.edu/collection/34/climate-change.

i.   *Carbon Capture and Sequestration (CCS)*

Carbon Capture and Sequestrations are used for both carbon and biomass sources of energy. The need for these technologies is driven by the increasing use of large amounts of coal to generate electricity in many areas of the world. A report issued at the United Nations Warsaw Climate Change Conference concluded that new coal plants cannot be built while simultaneously keeping global warming below the 2° Celsius threshold, unless the coal industry can deploy CCS.

After capture, CO_2 is compressed and then transported by pipeline or other means, to a site where it is injected underground for permanent storage sequestration). Geologic formations suitable for sequestration include depleted oil and gas fields, deep coal seams, and saline formations. The process of capturing CO_2 is better understood than the process of sequestration. It may be many years until CCS for fossil fuels is ready for commercial development.

Financial considerations present an initial obstacle for CCS deployment. While the price of renewables continues to decrease, the costs of using coal may increase to cover the costs of CCS. Moroeover, there are logistical and safety problems involved in carbon sequestration. For example, although the Gulf of Mexico presents one of the most viable storage sites in the United States, CO_2 is generated in significant quantities elsewhere and would require safe transportation to the Gulf. In addition, the absence of a regulatory framework to permit geological sequestration of CO_2 also presents a fundamental challenge to CCS deployment. Peter Folger, Coordinator, Carbon Capture: A Technology Assessment 12 (Congressional Research Service 2011), suggests that "[a]n integrated structure would be necessary to deploy CCS at a large scale, whether for fossil fuels or bioenergy." Such an integrated structure would involve identifying the owner of the sequestered CO_2, where to sequester the CO_2, defining what constitutes leakage, identifying where liability rests for sequestered CO_2 leaks, developing a monitoring and maintenance plan, and developing a pipeline infrastructure specifically for CO_2 that will be sequestered. Carbon leakage is also a problem because even a small earthquake has the potential to release stored carbon back into the atmosphere. *See* Mark D. Zoback and Stephen M. Gorelick, Earthquake Triggering and Large-Scale-Geologic Storage of

Carbon, 109 Proceedings of the National Academy of Sciences 10164 (2012).

ii.   Ocean-Based Storage

The basic approach to CO_2 storage in the ocean is to take captured and compressed CO_2 and transport it to the deep ocean for release at or above the sea-floor where it will dissolve and become part of the ocean carbon cycle. IPCC Expert Meeting on Geoengineering, *supra* at 282. Ocean-based methods to remove CO_2 from the atmosphere fall within three categories: "(1) physically-based methods: primarily direct injection of liquid CO_2 into the ocean; (2) chemically-based methods: primarily based on the addition of alkalinity to the ocean; and (3) biologically-based methods: primarily based on the enhancement of the ocean's biological pump." To this date, no large-scale experiments have been carried out. The risks of storage of CO_2 in the ocean are largely unknown, for example because of limited knowledge of the deep seas and deep sea-beds. As of August 2015, gaps in knowledge exist concerning biological systems in the deep sea, testing procedures, cost-effective and reliable engineering technology for pipes, diffusers, nozzles, etc., and techniques for monitoring biological and geochemical sequences. Most of the risks associated with ocean-storage appear to pertain to transporting liquid CO_2 to the deep sea, but it might be possible to recover liquid CO_2 from the ocean floor thereby diminishing some reluctance to deployment.

Another ocean-based approach is iron fertilization, i.e., the anthropogenic introduction of iron into the upper ocean in order to stimulate the growth of phytoplankton, an important marine organism. The theory is that the additional iron would lead to increased growth of phytoplankton, which would absorb carbon and sink to the bottom when they die, thus sequestering it on the ocean floor. As of August 2015, several experiemts along this line have been conducted.

iii.   Land-Based Storage Methods

Geological storage is widely considered a potentially important mitigation option. Possible storage basins include oil fields, depleted gas fields, deep coal seams, and saline formations. To determine the suitability of a particular site it is necessary to assess how much CO_2 can be stored there and for how long. However, there is no standard methodology, and site-specific data collection can be expensive. There are two basic methods: bioenergy generation coupled with CO_2 capture and storage and direct air capture.

(a) Bioenergy Generation Coupled with CO_2 Capture and Storage (BECSS)

BECS consists of three phases: (1) planting a growing a biomass crop, (2) harvesting the crop for biofuel production, and (3) capturing and storing the carbon released during this process. When biomass is used to generate electricity, the CO_2 released in the process may be captured and sequestered in geological formations or the deep sea in the same manner as a fossil-fueled generation CCS operation. However, no commercial-scale CCS facility exists and proponents of BECS expect to learn from future deployment of CCS in the context of fossil fuels. Consequently, some contend that BECS could not be administered soon enough to have significant impact on climate change. Christian Azar, Kristian Lindgren, & Eric Larson, Carbon Capture and Storage from Fossil Fuels and Biomass—Costs and Potential Role, in Stabilizing the Atmosphere, 74 Climate Change 1 (2006).

(b) Direct Air Capture (DAC)

DAC systems use a chemical solvent to selectively remove carbon dioxide from the ambient air, that solvent is then regenerated releasing a concentrated stream of CO_2, which then is compressed (most likely to a supercritical fluid) and injected into the deep subsurface and monitored for long-term permanence. Estimated deployment costs range from $50–130t CO_2 to $600–$1200/t CO_2.

(c) Capture by Genetically Engineered Micro-Organisms

Research is occurring to use genetic engineering or synthetic biology to produce algae, bacteria or other micro-organsms that are highly efficient at consuming atmostpheric carbon, in order to later sequester those organisms or otherwise use them in a climate-friendly manner. In order to counter the risk that such organisms would escape their confinement and create uncontrolled consumption of carbon, the idea is to make them dependent on a nutrient that does not occur in nature.

iv. Solar Radiation Management (SRM)

SRM seeks to cool the plant by blocking or reflecting heat and light from the sun back into space. The IPCC defines SRM as "the intentional modification of the Earth's shortwave radiative budget with the aim to reduce climate change according to a give metric (e.g., surface temperature, precipitation, regional impacts, etc.)." Capture: A Technology Assessment, *supra* at 15. SRM encompasses those engineering solutions that seek to change climate by increasing the reflectivity of the Earth or reducing the amount of incoming solar radiation that reaches the Earth without altering the atmospheric concentrations of greenhouse gasses. Although several modes of SRM have been proposed, marine cloud brightening and stratospheric aerosols are generally considered to present the most feasible options.

SRM's primary advantage over CDR is its speed. Kelsi Bracmort and Richard L. Lattanzio, Goeengineering Goverance and Technology Policy (Congressional Research Service 2013). Scientists predict that within a couple decades, SRM can restore the Earth to its pre-industrial temperature. This optimism is predicated on the cooling effects of Mt. Pinatubo's volcanic eruption in 1991. Despite the promise of rapidly cooling the earth, SRM would likely require a multiple centuries-long commitment because of the protracted lifetime of atmospheric CO_2. Implementation of large-scale SRM could also subject the earth to rapid warming if the technique employed suddenly failed; the Earth would experience more rapid warming than it would absent SRM as a result of the release of carbon stored in land and ocean reservoirs. Moreover, moderating the global-mean climate will not necessarily lead to a moderation of climate in all regions. Simulations indicate that cooling and drying in the tropics and warming in high latitudes.

Opponents of SRM most consistently argue that SRM disincentivizes countries to reduce GHG emissions today. Proponents respond that in the face of effective SRM technology it would be inefficient for States to focus on reducing GHG emissions and that the lack of effort to reduce g emissions is the is a classic free-rider problem which can be solved by government-sponsored technology research to encourage use However, at this time, SRM techniques would not mitigate CO_2 fertilization effects, ocean acidification effects, CO_2 physiological effects. In addition, modeling suggests that most SRM techniques will fail to mitigate CO_2-induced stratospheric cooling. Finally, excessive SRM could plunge the Earth into a damaging or even disastrous coolig period – a condition that could not be easily reversed.

NOTES AND QUESTIONS

1.   Note the change in language that may be occurring as this book goes to press in 2015. Until recently, scientists, politicians and others referred to "geoengineering." The latest IPCC report refers to "geoengineering", and contains a very brief discussion of it. The Report from the US National Academy of Science/National Research Council refers instead to "Climate Intervention." The political discourse at a number conferences now uses "Climate Intervention." Why do you think this has happened?

2.   Note the difference between the CCS techniques and the SRM technologies. The first take much more time to be effective, are probably more costly, but the risks in many cases are likely much less than in SRM. SRM would take less time to produce effects, may cost less, but the risks are enormous.

3.   One of the concerns motivating attention to geoengineering is that we may be reaching or will reach in the not too distant future a "tipping point," which if crossed can set in motion catastrophic changes in the climate. SRM techniques in particular could potentially offer a way to act quickly to try to prevent such tipping points from being crossed. However, note that the SRM technologies do not in any way reduce the buildup of carbon dioxide in the atmosphere. Thus, they would need to be continued to be effective. The risks from this are enormous and not at all identified or understood.

4.   Scientists and others point to the "moral hazard" problem, namely that focusing on technology "to save us", we will divert efforts from what is needed most: the reduction in emissions of greenhouse gases.

5.   As a lawyer, what do you advise? Should we draft a moratorium on all experimentation? On research? Should we develop a code of conduct, or principles, to govern scientific research and experimentation? Or should we avoid addressing the issues so that we do not encourage these developments, and focus on reducing greenhouse gas emissions?

6.   What international legal principles are relevant to geoengineering? How would you apply a principle of intergenerational equity?

c.   National and Sub-National Initiatives

i.   The United States and the EU

The numerous national greenhouse gas reduction initiatives have both international legal and national importance. For the remaining Parties to the Kyoto Protocol that have emission-reduction obligations, these initiatives are the implementation mechanism. For both non-Party developed and developed countries, national and sub-national programs can be used to resist pressure for further action or to put pressure on other nations for further action. For example, a major national initiative and a sub-national one have been used to pressure other nations to take action. In 2015, the Obama Administration issued its final regulations regulations under § 11(d) of the Clean Air Act. 42 U.S.C. § 74119d), to reduce CO_2 emissions by 32% by 2030. Carbon Pollution Emission Guidelines for Existing Stationary Sources: Electric Utility Generating Units, 40 CFR Part 60, August 3, 2015. They are based in part on California's trading scheme. In 2006, the California State Legislature passed the Global Warming Solutions Act (AB 32), which requires the California Air Resources Board to adopt a statewide GHG emissions limit equivalent to California's GHG level in 1990. AB 32 creates a cap-and-trade program. The program allows external trading. In April 2013, the Board announced a plan to link California's cap-and-trade program with the cap-and-trade program of the province of Quebec, one of Canada's largest provinces. The first action of 33.8 million carbon allowance sold out in November, 2014 and raised about $407 million. http://www.environmentalleader.com/tag/carbon-auction/#ixzz3LRBF7Vla.

Greenhouse reduction plans face a variety of legal challenges that they are inconsistent with international and domestic free trade law. California's program survived a Dormant Commerce Clause challenge, Rocky Mountain Farmers Union v. Goldstene, 730 F.3d 1070 (9th Cir. 2013), rehearing *en banc* denied sub. Nom., Rocky Mountain Farmers Union v. Corey, 740 F.3d 507, 512 (9th Cir. 2014), cert. denied, ___ U.S. ___ (2014), but other challenges have been successful and many state renewable energy programs are being challenged on this ground.

Japan and the EU, *inter alia*, challenged Ontario, Canada's feed in tariff (i.e., a payment to an ordinary energy consumer for the renewable energy he or she produces) because the domestic content requirements of wind energy facilities violated the national treatment rule of Article III:4 of the General Agreement on Tariffs and Trade (GATT). The Appellate Body upheld the Panel's conclusion that that Ontario program violated GATT 111:4, and Canada changed the content requirements to comply the WTO decision. WT/DS412/AB/R; WT/DS426/AB/R (2013). The European Court of Justice (ECJ) ruled that France's feed in tariffs were illegal State aid. "Article 107(1) TFEU must be interpreted as meaning that a mechanism for offsetting in full the additional costs imposed on undertakings because of an obligation to purchase wind-generated electricity at a price higher than the market price that is financed by all final consumers of electricity in the national territory, such as that resulting from Law No 2000–108, constitutes an intervention through State resources." Association Vent de Colere Federation, Case C-262/12 ¶ 37(2013), available at http://eur-lex.europa.eu/LexUriServ/LexUriServ.do?uri=CELEX:62012CJ0262:EN:HTML. The ECJ distinguished a 2001 case upholding Germany's feed in tariffs:

> All those factors taken together serve to distinguish the present case from that which gave rise to the judgment in PreussenElektra [2001 ECR 1–2099], in which the Court held that an obligation imposed on private electricity supply undertakings to purchase electricity produced from renewable sources at fixed minimum prices could not be regarded as an intervention through State resources where it does not lead to any direct or indirect transfer of State resources to the undertakings producing that type of electricity. [Id at ¶ 34.]

See Lincoln L. Davies and Kirstin Allen, *Feed in Tariffs in Turmoil*, 116 West Va. L. Rev. 937 (2014). The relationship between environmental regulation and international trade law is coveredin Chapter 16.

ii. The Kingdom of the Netherlands Creates Hard Law from the Work of the IPCC

URGENDA [URGENT AGENDA] FOUNDATION V. THE STATE OF THE NETHERLANDS (MINISTRY OF INFRASTRUCTURE AND THE ENVIRONMENT)

Den Haag District Court
Case No. C/09/456689/HA ZA 13–1396, June 24, 2015

[A foundation devoted to the Netherland's transition to a sustainable society, as defined by the Brundtland Commission, sued to require the reduction greenhouse gas emissions above the targets set by the state. The government challenged Urgenda's standing only in so far as it claimed to represent current and future generations in other countries. The court held that the plaintiff had met the two conditions of the Dutch Civil code: (1) the Foundation was organized to represent the interests of other persons and (2) it had made sufficient efforts to enter into dialogue with the defendant. However, the court found that the government had not violated Urgenda's personal rights. The core of the opinion follows.]

4.52. The foregoing leads the court to conclude that a legal obligation of the State towards Urgenda cannot be derived from Article 21 of the Dutch Constitution, the "no harm" principle, the UN Climate Change Convention, with associated protocols, and Article 191 TFEU with the ETS Directive and Effort Sharing Decision based on TFEU. Although Urgenda cannot directly derive rights from these rules and Articles 2 and 8 ECHR [European Charter of Human Rights], these regulations still hold meaning, namely in the question discussed below whether the State has failed to meet its duty of care towards Urgenda. First of all, it can be derived from these rules what degree of discretionary power the State is entitled to in how it exercises the tasks and authorities given to it. Secondly, the objectives laid down in these regulations are relevant in determing the minimum degree of care the State is expected to observe. In order to determine the scope of the State's duty of care and the discretionary power it is entitled to, the court will therefore also consider the objectives of international and European climate policy as well as the principles on which the policies are based.

[The court accepted the IPPC's conclusions about the causes and dire consequences of global warming, noting that the IPCC favored mitigation over adaption. It extensively reviewed the Framework Convention on Climate Change, the Kyoto Protocol, and EU climate change law. The court stressed, inter alia, that "[s]trong scientific evidence shows that urgent action to tackle climate change is imperative, Para. 2.80, and "the 2°C target has globally been taken as the starting point for the development of climate policies." Para. 4.14]

4 THE ASSESSMENT

A. Introduction

4.1. This case is essentially about the question whether the State has a legal obligation towards Urgenda to place further limits on greenhouse gas emissions—particularly CO_2 emissions—in addition to those arising from the plans of the Dutch government, acting on behalf of the State. Urgenda argues that the State does not pursue an adequate climate policy and therefore acts contrary to its duty of care towards Urgenda and the parties it represents as well as, more generally speaking, Dutch society. Urgenda also argues that because of the Dutch contribution to the climate policy, the State wrongly exposes the international community to the risk of dangerous climate change, resulting in serious and irreversible damage to human health and the environment. Based on these grounds, which are briefly summarised here, Urgenda claims, except for several declaratory decisions, that the State should be ordered to limit, or have limited, the joint volume of the annual greenhouse gas emissions of the Netherlands so that these emissions will have been reduced by 40% and at least by 25% in 2020, compared to 1990. In case this claim is denied, Urgenda argues for an order to have this volume limited by 40% in 2030, also compared to 1990.

4.2. For its part, the State argues that the Netherlands—also based on European agreements—pursues an adequate climate policy. Therefore, and for many other reasons, the State believes Urgenda's claims cannot succeed. The key motivation is that the State cannot be forced at law to pursue another climate policy. The terms "the State" and "the Netherlands" will be used interchangeably below, depending on the context. The term "the State" refers to the legal person that is party to these proceedings, while the term "the Netherlands" refers to the same entity in an international context. The government is the State's executive body.

4.3. The court faces a dispute with complicated and "climate-related" issues. The court does not have independent expertise in this area and will base its assessment on that which the Parties have submitted and the facts admitted between them. This concerns both current scientific knowledge and (other) data the State acknowledges or deems to be correct. Many of these data are available under section 2 of this judgment ("The facts"). An analysis of these data, which are sometimes repeated, will enable the court to determine the severity of the climate change problem. Based on this information, the court will assess the claim and the defence put up against it. Prior to this, the court will assess Urgenda's standing. If Urgenda is not in a position to confront the State about the issues that are the subject of these proceedings, the court is unable to proceed to assess the merits of the claim. This more in-depth assessment (if applicable) will contain all further questions, including those pertaining to the absence, or not, of the State's legal obligation towards Urgenda, and the question whether the court's options also include imposing the order claimed by Urgenda.

. . .

4.18. The aforementioned considerations lead to the following intermediate conclusion. Anthropogenic greenhouse gas emissions are causing climate change. A highly hazardous situation for man and the environment will occur with a temperature rise of over 2°C compared to the pre-industrial level. It is therefore necessary to stabilise the concentration of greenhouse gases in the atmosphere, which requires a reduction of the current anthropogenic greenhouse gas emissions.

. . .

4.37. The realisation that climate change is an extra-territorial, global problem and fighting it requires a worldwide approach has prompted heads of state and government leaders to contribute to the development of legal instruments for combating climate change by means of mitigating greenhouse gas emissions as well as by making their countries "climate-proof" by means of taking mitigating measures. These instruments have been developed in an international context (in the UN), European context (in the EU) and in a national context. The Dutch climate policy is based on these instruments to a great extent.

4.38. The Netherlands has committed itself to UN Climate Change Convention, a framework convention which contains general principles and starting points, which form the basis for the development of further, more specific, rules, for instance in the form of a protocol. The Kyoto Protocol is an example of this. The COP with a number of subsidiary organs was set up for the further development and implementation of a climate regime. Almost all COP's decisions are not legally binding, but can directly affect obligations of the signatories to the convention or the protocol. This applies, for instance, to several decisions taken pursuant to the Kyoto Protocol. These involve mechanisms which enable the trade in emission (reduction) allowances and which allow collaboration between the parties so that greenhouse gas emissions can be reduced where it is cheapest.

4.39. In this context, Urgenda also brought up the international-law "no harm" principle, which means that no state has the right to use its territory, or have it used, to cause significant damage to other states. The State has not contested the applicability of this principle.

4.40. The care and protection of the living environment is also increasingly determined by the EU. The basis for the European environmental policy is enclosed in Article 19 TFEU [Treaty on the Functioning of the European Union]. For the development and implementation of the Community's environmental policy use has mostly been made of directives. These often concern minimum harmonisation, so that on the one hand the entire Union will have a basic protection level while on the other hand the Member States still have the power to establish stricter standards for their own territories.

4.41. In view of the obligation of Member States to take reduction measures, the implementation of the ETS Directive in Chapter 16 of the Environmental Management Act (see 2.70) is relevant to these proceedings. The Directive has introduced an emission allowance trading system, with the European Commission determining the CO_2 emission ceiling for five year periods. The allowed emission level is allocated to the Member State concerned in the form of emission allowances. In the context of the EU, the Effort Sharing Decision (see 2.62) is also relevant. Based on these schemes, the Netherlands has committed itself to a 21% reduction of emissions that fall under the ETS in 2020, compared to 2005 and to a 16% reduction for non-ETS sectors in 2020, compared to 2005 (see 2.74).

4.42. From an international-law perspective, the State is bound to UN Climate Change Convention, the Kyoto Protocol (with the associated Doha Amendment as soon as it enters into force) and the "no harm" principle. However, this international-law binding force only involves obligations towards other states. When the State fails one of its obligations towards one or more other states, it does not imply that the State is acting unlawfully towards Urgenda. It is different when the written or unwritten rule of international law concerns a decree that "connects one and all". After all, Article 93 of the Dutch Constitution determines that citizens can derive a right from it if its contents can connect one and all. The court—and the Parties—states first and foremost that the stipulations included in the convention, the protocol and the "no harm" principle do not have a binding force towards citizens (private individuals and legal persons). Urgenda therefore cannot directly rely on this principle, the convention and the protocol (see, among other things, HR 6 February 2004, ECLI:NL: HR:2004:AN8071, NJ 2004, 329, Vrede et al./State).

4.43. This does not affect the the fact that a state can be supposed to want to meet its international-law obligations. From this it follows that an international-law standard—a statutory provision or an unwritten legal standard—may not be explained or applied in a manner which would mean that the state in question has violated an international-law obligation, unless no other interpretation or application is possible. This is a generally acknowledged rule in the legal system. This means that when applying and interpreting national-law open standards and concepts, including social proprietary, reasonableness and propriety, the general interest or certain legal principles, the court takes account of such international-law obligations. This way, these obligations have a "reflex effect" in national law.

4.44. The comments above regarding international-law obligations also apply, in broad outlines, to European law, including the TFEU stipulations, on which citizens cannot directly rely. The Netherlands is obliged to adjust its national legislation to the objectives stipulated in the directives, while it is also bound to decrees (in part) directed at the country. Urgenda may not derive a legal obligation of the State towards it from these legal rules. However, this fact also does not stand in the way of the fact that stipulations in an EU treaty or directive can have an impact through the open standards of national law described above.

. . .

Breach of standard of due care observed in society, discretionary power

4.53. The question whether the State is in breach of its duty of care for taking insufficient measures to prevent dangerous climate change, is a legal issue which has never before been answered in Dutch proceedings and for which jurisprudence does not provide a ready-made framework. The answer to the question whether or not the State is taking sufficient mitigation measures depends on many factors, with two aspects having particular relevance. In the first place, it has to be assessed whether there is a unlawful hazardous negligence on the part of the State. Secondly, the State's discretionary power is relevant in assessing the government's actions. From case law about government liability it follows that the court has to assess fully whether or not the State has exercised or exercises sufficient care, but that this does not alter the fact that the State has the discretion to determine how it fulfils its duty of care. However, this discretionary power vested in the State is not unlimited: the State's care may not be below standard. However, the test of due care required here and the discretionary power of the State are not wholly distinguishable. After all, the detailing of the duty of care of the person called to account will also have been included in his specific position in view of the special nature of his duty or authority. The standard of care has been attuned to this accordingly.

Factors to determine duty of care

4.54. Urgenda has relied on the "Kelderluik" ruling of the Supreme Court (HR 5 November 1965, ECLI:NL:HR:1965:AB7079, NJ 1966, 136) and on jurisprudence on the doctrine of hazardous negligence developed later to detail the requirement of acting with due care towards society. Understandably, the State has pointed out the relevant differences between this juridprudence and this case. This case is different in that the central focus is on dealing with a hazardous global development, of which it is uncertain when, where and to what extent exactly this hazard will materialise. Nevertheless, the doctrine of hazardous negligence, as explained in the literature, bears a resemblance to the theme of hazardous climate change, so that several criteria stated below can be derived from hazardous negligence jurisprudence in order to detail the concept of acting negligently towards society.

4.55. In principle, the extent to which the State is entitled to a scope for policymaking is determined by the statutory duties and powers vested in the State. As has been stated above, under Article 21 of the Constitution, the State has a wide discretion of power to organise the national climate policy in the manner it deems fit. However, the court is of the opinion that due to the nature of the hazard (a global cause) and the task to be realised accordingly (shared risk management of a global hazard that could result in an impaired living climate in the Netherlands), the objectives and principles, such as those laid down in the UN Climate Change Convention and the TFEU, should also be considered in determining the scope for policymaking and duty of care.

4.56. The objectives and principles of the international climate policy have been formulated in Articles 2 and 3 of the UN Climate Change Convention (see 2.37 and 2.38). The court finds the principles under (i), (ii), (iii) and (iv) particularly relevant for establishing the scope for policymaking and the duty of care. These read as follows, in brief:

(i) protection of the climate system, for the benefit of current and future generations, based on fairness;

(iii) the precautionary principle;

(iv) the sustainability principle.

4.57. The principle of fairness (i) means that the policy should not only start from what is most beneficial to the current generation at this moment, but also what this means for future generations, so that future generations are not exclusively and disproportionately burdened with the consequences of climate change. The principle of fairness also expresses that industrialised countries have to take the lead in combating climate change and its negative impact. The justification for this, and this is also noted in literature, lies first and foremost in the fact that from a historical perspective the current industrialised countries are the main causers of the current high greenhouse gas concentration in the atmosphere and that these countries also benefited from the use of fossil fuels, in the form of economic growth and prosperity. Their prosperity also means that these countries have the most means available to take measures to combat climate change.

4.58. With the precautionary principle (ii)[6] the UN Climate Change Convention expresses that taking measures cannot be delayed to await full scientific certainty. The signatories should anticipate the prevention or limitation of the causes of climate change or the prevention or limitation of the negative consequences of climate change, regardless of a certain level of scientific uncertainty. In making the consideration that is needed for taking precautionary measures, without having absolute certainty whether or not the actions will have sufficient effects, the Convention states that account can be taken of a cost-benefit ratio: precautionary measures which yield positive results worldwide at as low as possible costs will be taken sooner.

[The court's discussion of EU climate change policy is omitted]

4.74. In answering the question whether the State is exercising enough care with its current climate policy, the State's discretionary power should also be considered, as stated above. Based on its statutory duty—Article 21 of the Constitution—the State has an extensive discretionary power to flesh out the climate policy. However, this discretionary power is not unlimited. If, and this is the case here, there is a high risk of dangerous climate change with severe and life-threatening consequences for man and the environment, the State has the obligation to protect its citizens from it by taking appropriate and effective measures. For this approach, it can also rely on the aforementioned jurisprudence of the ECtHR. Naturally, the question remains what is fitting and effective in the given circumstances. The starting point must be that in its decision-making process the State carefully considers the various interests. Urgenda has stated that the State meets its duty of care if it applies a reduction target of 40%, 30% or at least 25% for the year 2020. The State has contested this with reference to the intended adaptation measures.

4.75. The court emphasises that this first and foremost should concern mitigation measures, as adaptation measures will only allow the State to protect its citizens from the consequences of climate change

---

[6]   The court meant iii. Eds.

to a limited level. If the current greenhouse gas emissions continue in the same manner, global warming will take such a form that the costs of adaptation will become disproportionately high. Adaptation measures will therefore not be sufficient to protect citizens against the aforementioned consequences in the long term. The only effective remedy against hazardous climate change is to reduce the emission of greenhouse gases. Therefore, the court arrives at the opinion that from the viewpoint of efficient measures available the State has limited options: mitigation is vital for preventing dangerous climate change.

4.76. The State's options are limited further by the private-law principles applicable to the State and mentioned above. After all, these principles were developed in response to the special risk of climate change and therefore limit the State's options. This also applies, for instance, to the circumstance that Annex I countries, including the Netherlands, have taken the lead in taking mitigation measures and have therefore committed to a more than proportional contribution to reduction, in view of a fair distribution between industrialised and developing countries. Due to this principle of fairness, the State, in choosing measures, will also have to take account of the fact that the costs are to be distributed reasonably between the current and future generations. If according to the current insights it turns out to be cheaper on balance to act now, the State has a serious obligation, arising from due care, towards future generations to act accordingly. Moreover, the State cannot postpone taking precautionary measures based on the sole reason that there is no scientific certainty yet about the precise effect of the measures. However, a cost-benefit ratio is allowed here. Finally, the State will have to base its actions on the principle of "prevention is better than cure".

4.77. To all these principles it applies that if the State wants to deviate from them, it will have to argue and prove sufficient justification for the deviation. A justification could be the costs. The State should not be expected to do the impossible nor may a disproportionately high burden be placed on it. However, as has been considered above, it has neither been argued, nor has it become evident that the State has insufficient financial means to realise higher reduction measures. It can also not be concluded that from a macro economic point of view there are obstructions to choosing a higher emission reduction level for 2020.

4.78. The State has argued that allowing Urgenda's claim, which is aimed at a higher reduction of greenhouse gas emission in the Netherlands, would not be effective on a global scale, as such a target would result in a very minor, if not negligible, reduction of global greenhouse gas emissions. After all, whether or not the 2°C target is achieved will mainly depend on the reduction targets of other countries with high emissions. More specifically, the States relies on the fact that the Dutch contribution to worldwide emissions is currently only 0.5%. If the reduction target of 25–40% from Urgenda's claim were met the State argues that this would result in an additional reduction of 23.75 to 49.32 Mt CO_2-eq (up to 2020), representing only 0.04–0.09% of global emissions. Starting from the idea that this additional reduction would hardly affect global emissions, the State argues that Urgenda has no interest in an allowance of its claim for additional reduction.

4.79. This argument does not succeed. It is an established fact that climate change is a global problem and therefore requires global accountability. It follows from the UNEP report that based on the reduction commitments made in Cancun, a gap between the desired CO_2 emissions (in order to reach the climate objective) and the actual emissions (14–17 Gt CO_2) will have arisen by 2030. This means that more reduction measures have to be taken on an international level. It compels all countries, including the Netherlands, to implement the reduction measures to the fullest extent as possible. The fact that the amount of the Dutch emissions is small compared to other countries does not affect the obligation to take precautionary measures in view of the State's obligation to exercise care. After all, it has been established that any anthropogenic greenhouse gas emission, no matter how minor, contributes to an increase of CO_2 levels in the atmosphere and therefore to hazardous climate change. Emission reduction therefore concerns both a joint and individual responsibility of the signatories to the UN Climate Change Convention. In view of the fact that the Dutch emission reduction is determined by the State, it may not reject possible liability by stating that its contribution is minor, as also adjudicated mutatis mutandis in the Potash mines ruling of the Dutch Supreme Court (HR 23 September 1988, NJ 1989, 743). The rules given in that ruling also apply, by analogy, to the obligation to take precautionary measures in order to avert a danger which is also the subject of this case. Therefore, the court arrives at the opinion that the single circumstance that the Dutch emissions only constitute a minor contribution to global emissions does not alter the State's obligation to exercise care towards third parties. Here too, the court takes into account that in view of a fair distribution the Netherlands, like the other Annex I countries, has taken the lead in taking mitigation measures and has therefore committed to a more than proportionte contribution to reduction. Moreover, it is beyond dispute that the Dutch per capita emissions are one of the highest in the world.

. . .

4.83. Due to the severity of the consequences of climate change and the great risk of hazardous climate change occurring—without mitigating measures—the court concludes that the State has a duty of care to take mitigation measures. The circumstance that the Dutch contribution to the present global greenhouse gas emissions is currently small does not affect this. Now that at least the 450 scenario is required to prevent hazardous climate change, the Netherlands must take reduction measures in support of this scenario.

. . .

Causal link

4.90. From the above considerations, particularly in 4.79, it follows that a sufficient causal link can be assumed to exist between the Dutch greenhouse gas emissions, global climate change and the effects (now and in the future) on the Dutch living climate. The fact that the current Dutch greenhouse gas emissions are limited on a global scale does not alter the fact that these emission contribute to climate change. The court has taken into consideration in this respect as well that the Dutch greenhouse emissions have contributed to climate change and by their nature will also continue to contribute to climate change.

Relativity

4.91. The government's care for a safe living climate at least extends across Dutch territory. In view of the fact that Urgenda also promotes the interests of persons living on this territory now and in the future, the court has arrived at the opinion that the breached security standard—exercising due care in combating climate change—also extends to combating possible damages incurred by Urgenda as a result of this, thereby meeting the so-called relativity requirement.

4.92. No decision needs to be made on whether Urgenda's reduction claim can als be successful in so far as it also promotes the rights and interests of current and future generations from other countries. After all, Urgenda is not required to actually serve that wide "support base" to be successful in that claim, as the State's unlawful acts towards the current or future population of the Netherlands is sufficient.

Conclusion regarding the State's legal obligation

4.93. Based on the foregoing, the court concludes that the State—apart from the defence to be discussed below—has acted negligently and therefore unlawfully towards Urgenda by starting from a reduction target for 2020 of less than 25% compared to the year 1990.

E.   The system of separation of powers

4.94. The main point of this dispute concerns if allowing Urgenda's main claim—an order for the State to limit greenhouse gas emissions further than it has currently planned—would constitute an interference with the distribution of powers in our democratic system. Urgenda has answered this question in the negative and the State, relying on the trias politica, has arrived at an opposing viewpoint.

4.95. The court states first and foremost that Dutch law does not have a full separation of state powers, in this case, between the executive and judiciary. The distribution of powers between these powers (and the legislature) is rather intended to establish a balance between these state powers. This does not mean that the one power in a general sense has primacy over the other power. It does mean that each state power has its own task and responsibilities. The court provides legal protection and settles legal disputes, which it must to do this if requested to do so. It is an essential feature of the rule of law that the actions of (independent, democratic, legitimised and controlled) political bodies, such as the government and parliament can—and sometimes must—be assessed by an independent court. This constitutes a review of lawfulness. The court does not enter the political domain with the associated considerations and choices. Separate from any political agenda, the court has to limit itself to its own domain, which is the application of law. Depending on the issues and claims submitted to it, the court will review them with more or less caution. Great restraint or even abstinence is required when it concerns policy-related considerations of ranging interests which impact the structure or organisation of society. The court has to be aware that it only plays one of the roles in a legal dispute between two or more parties. Government authorities, such as the State (with bodies such as the government and the States-General), have to make a general consideration, with due regard for possibly many more positions and interests.

4.96. This distinctive difference between these state powers does not automatically provide an answer to the question how the court should decide if it finds that allowing a claim in a dispute between two parties has substantial consequences for third parties which are not part of the proceedings. A decision between two private parties in itself does not have consequences for the position of third parties, so that the position of these third parties does not need to be considered in principle. However, a claim seeking an order such as is the case here, in a case against central government, could have direct or indirect consequences for third parties. This prompts the court to exercise restraint in allowing such claims, all the more if the court does not have a clear picture of the magnitude and meaning of these consequences. . . .

[The court refused to order a 40% reduction in part because Urganda had admitted that that claim concerning the proposed target was "a tall order." Para. 4.103]

5   THE RULING

The court:

5.1. orders the State to limit the joint volume of Dutch annual greenhouse gas emissions, or have them limited, so that this volume will have reduced by at least 25% at the end of 2020 compared to the level of the year 1990, as claimed by Urgenda, in so far as acting on its own behalf;

. . .

CHAPTER 10

HAZARDOUS SUBSTANCES: WASTES, TOXIC CHEMICALS, HEAVY METALS

■ ■ ■

Over the past several decades, there has been growing international concern about substances that can harm the environment or human health when manufactured, stored, transported, used or disposed of. These include industrial and agricultural wastes, nuclear wastes, toxic chemicals used in manufacturing or agriculture, dangerous substances contained in consumer goods, heavy metals, and pesticides. These materials are of international environmental concern, for example, because they move in trade across domestic borders and because they may have harmful transboundary consequences. The issues are of special concern to developing countries, many of which see themselves as the dumping ground for hazardous wastes and toxic chemicals and which typically have weaker regulatory systems for managing chemicals. In addition, some hazardous substances are of particular concern to indigenous peoples because, for example, they bioaccumulate in foods that comprise important part of those peoples' diets.

The harms caused by hazardous materials vary widely and can be extremely serious. Harmful effects include cancers (from, e.g., asbestos, benzene, diethylstilbestrol (DES) and plutonium), birth defects (from, e.g., thalidomide), heart disease (from, e.g., tobacco), organ failure (from, e.g., cadmium), respiratory illness (from, e.g., smoke from cooking fires), blindness (from, e.g., mercury), mental retardation (from, e.g., lead), harm to endocrine, immune and reproductive systems (from, e.g., persistent organic pollutants such as DDT and polychlorinated biphenyls (PCBs)), and other harms to humans, as well as harm to other forms of life and entire ecosystems. Exposure can occur in homes, in work places, in schools, out of doors—virtually anywhere depending on the circumstances.

International regulation of chemicals is complicated in several important ways. Determining whether a particular chemical is harmful encounters several uncertainties. For example, humans are exposed to possibly harmful substances in many ways, often in tandem, and testing chemicals on humans raises serious ethical issues. Thus often risk has to be determined based on epidemiological studies with many uncertainties or on animal tests, which raise their own set of ethical issues and in any event are only approximations of effects on humans. Similarly, although some chemicals can cause almost immediate harm (e.g., mercury), others cause harm only after a considerable time lag (e.g., DDT), requiring testing and observation over long periods during which exposure is or can be occurring. Further, the harm caused by some chemicals seems to increase with the amount of exposure (e.g., mercury), but some chemicals seem to be more harmful at low doses (e.g., endocrine disrupters); and it is often not clear that harm increases linearly with exposure even for the former group. These and other factors make determining the risk associated with a particular substance difficult.

An additional complication arises from the fact that activities relating to hazardous substances, such as chemical research, testing, manufacture and use vary greatly among countries, providing different countries with significantly different incentives and priorities with respect to negotiating international control measures. The uneven distribution of hazardous substances (e.g., heavy metals) among countries has a similar effect (e.g., large deposits of commercially exploitable lead occur in only a few countries). The fact that business enterprises involved with hazardous substances sometimes wield substantial economic and political power can further affect international discussions.

Complicating all of this is the fact that most chemicals in use have not been tested for harm. For example, it is generally believed that there are approximately 100,000 chemicals used internationally, the vast majority of which have never been subjected to rigorous testing for possible harm to humans and the environment. Furthermore, chemicals are ubiquitous in human society. All humans and the environment generally are exposed to chemicals, and removing chemicals from use and the stream of commerce could have substantial economic effects and social effects.

Finally, although most hazardous chemicals are human-made (anthropogenic), some dangerous substances occur in nature, such as cadmium, lead, and mercury. Trying to eliminate or control exposure to non-anthropogenic substances raises particular problems.

In spite of these and other complicating factors, the international legal system regulates hazardous substances in many respects. Instruments exist at the global, regional and bilateral levels, and both hazardous wastes and chemicals are subject to treaties and other international instruments. For example, a taxonomy of international law relating to hazardous substances includes broad multilateral agreements governing the movement of transboundary wastes; regional agreements governing the movement of transboundary wastes; and specific initiatives governing particular hazardous chemicals. This chapter focuses on two aspects of that larger set of topics: the international legal system for hazardous wastes and the emerging systems for toxic chemicals, particularly persistent organic chemicals, and for sound chemicals management more broadly.

A. HAZARDOUS WASTES

SMUGGLING EUROPE'S WASTE TO POORER COUNTRIES
Elisabeth Rosenthal
New York Times A1 (Sept. 27, 2009)

When two inspectors swung open the doors of a battered red shipping container here, they confronted a graveyard of Europe's electronic waste—old wires, electricity meters, circuit boards—mixed with remnants of cardboard and plastic.

"This is supposed to be going to China, but it isn't going anywhere," said Arno Vink, an inspector from the Dutch environment ministry who impounded the container because of Europe's strict new laws that place restrictions on all types of waste exports, from dirty pipes to broken computers to household trash.

Exporting waste illegally to poor countries has become a vast and growing international business, as companies try to minimize the costs of new environmental laws, like those here, that tax waste or require that it be recycled or otherwise disposed of in an environmentally responsible way.

Rotterdam, the busiest port in Europe, has unwittingly become Europe's main external garbage chute, a gateway for trash bound for places like China, Indonesia, India and Africa. There, electronic waste and construction debris containing toxic chemicals are often dismantled by children at great cost to their health. Other garbage that is supposed to be recycled according to European law may be simply burned or left to rot, polluting air and water and releasing the heat-trapping gases linked to global warming.

While much of the international waste trade is legal, sent to qualified overseas recyclers, a big chunk is not. For a price, underground traders make Europe's waste disappear overseas.

After Europe first mandated recycling electronics like televisions and computers, two to three tons of electronic waste was turned in last year, far less than the seven tons anticipated. Much of the rest was probably exported illegally, according to the European Environment Agency.

Paper, plastic and metal trash exported from Europe rose tenfold from 1995 to 2007, the agency says, with 20 million containers of waste now shipped each year either legally or illegally. Half of that passes through this huge port, where trucks and ships exchange goods around the clock.

In the United States, more states are passing laws that require the recycling of goods, especially electronics. But because the United States places fewer restrictions on trash exports and monitors them far less than Europe, that increasing volume is flowing relatively freely overseas, mostly legally, experts say. Up to 100 containers of waste from the United States and Canada arrive each day, according to environmental groups and local authorities in Hong Kong.

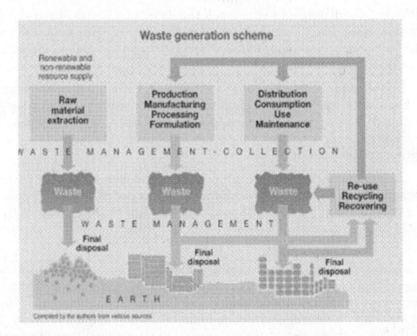

Figure 1: From United Nations Environment Programme, *A Waste at Every Stage* (2002), available at http://www.grid.unep.ch/waste/html_file/10–11_waste_cycle.html

Pollution from hazardous chemicals can occur, and waste containing hazardous chemicals can be generated, at every stage of economic activity. Figure 1 shows waste streams from raw material extraction, industrial production and processing, and consumption. The same situation exists with respect to marine and land-based agriculture. Exposure rates are discussed further in the excerpt from Peter Lallas and Steve Wolfson, below.

The rationale behind transboundary movements of hazardous waste is economic. The costs of disposing of wastes in compliance with domestic regulations in industrialized countries may be significantly higher than the costs of disposal outside the country. Developing countries may find the payments enormously attractive, especially when they rival a country's gross national product, as occurred in the case of a contract signed in 1988 by officials in Guinea-Bissau to bury 15 million tons of toxic wastes from European tanneries and pharmaceutical companies. In return, Guinea-Bissau would receive a yearly payment of $120 million (at the time, the GNP of Guinea-Bissau was $150 million). In other cases, countries simply need the hard currency that disposal of hazardous wastes provide. In yet others, the incentive to import emanates from bribes of government officials.

There are three basic approaches to addressing the growing international trade in wastes: prohibit export and import of wastes; regulate the trade in wastes, as by requiring prior informed consent; and facilitate the trade in waste by eschewing international regulation. Countries have moved from the third approach, essentially a laissez-faire approach, to relying on the second one, consisting of multilateral and bilateral regulatory agreements, and some have been flirting with the first by agreeing to ban shipments of hazardous wastes from OECD (Organisation for Economic Co-operation and Development) countries to non-OECD countries. As you read the materials below, consider the legal implications of each approach from the perspective of industrialized and developing States, and countries with economies in transition.

1. THE PREVAILING LEGAL SYSTEM

The 1989 Basel Convention in the Transboundary Movement of Hazardous Wastes, http://www.basel.int/Portals/4/Basel%20Convention/ docs/text/BaselConventionText-e.pdf, *reprinted in* 28 ILM 657 (1989), is the central multilateral agreement. We advise that you read the text of this treaty. The agreement provides that hazardous wastes may only be exported to a country with its prior informed written consent. Prior informed written consent is also needed from each transit country. Importing States have the right to prohibit the import of such wastes without providing proof of potential harm. In addition, each State must take "appropriate measures" to "[p]revent the import of hazardous wastes and other wastes if it has reason to believe that the wastes in question will not be managed in an environmentally sound manner" (Article 4(2)(g)). If an importing State has given its consent, but disposal cannot be done in an environmentally sound manner, the exporting State has the duty to make alternative arrangements, including, if necessary, to reimport the waste (Article 9).

Trade in hazardous wastes is prohibited between Parties and non-Parties unless there is an agreement or arrangement in place between the two countries that is consistent with the Convention (Article 11). The latter possibility is particularly important for the United States, which as of February 2015 is not a Party to the Convention and whose business enterprises regularly trade in hazardous wastes.

One amendment to the Basel Convention was adopted in 1995 (the so-called OECD-non-OECD Ban Amendment, or Ban Amendment). "The

'Ban Amendment' provides for the prohibition by each Party included in the proposed new Annex VII (Parties and other States which are members of the OECD, EC, Liechtenstein) of all transboundary movements to States not included in Annex VII of hazardous wastes covered by the Convention that are intended for final disposal, and of all transboundary movements to States not included in Annex VII of hazardous wastes covered by paragraph 1(a) of Article 1 of the Convention that are destined for reuse, recycling or recovery operations." *See* The Basel Convention Ban Amendment, *available at* http://www. basel.int/implementation/legalmatters/banamendment/tabid/1484/default. aspx.

One Protocol was finalized in 1999 (the Liability Protocol). "The objective of the Protocol is to provide for a comprehensive system for liability as well as adequate and prompt compensation for damage resulting from the transboundary movement of hazardous wastes and other wastes, including incidents occurring because of illegal traffic in those wastes." http://www.basel.int/TheConvention/Overview/Liability Protocol/tabid/2399/Default.aspx. As of February 2015, neither the Ban Amendment nor the Liability Protocol was in force. However, a number of policy instruments have been elaborated that are legally non-binding but nevertheless important in terms of providing technical guidelines for specific waste streams. *See, e.g.,* Development of Technical Guidelines on E-Waste, http://www.basel.int/Implementation/TechnicalMatters/Development ofTechnicalGuidelines/Ewaste/tabid/2377/Default.aspx. These guidelines, in turn, have served as good practice guidances for governments and private actors to use.

Both the Ban Amendment and the Liability protocol are described below. This section first addresses the overall international management system, and then discusses particular aspects of this system, such as prior informed consent and disposal of the waste in an environmentally sound manner.

INTERNATIONAL MANAGEMENT OF HAZARDOUS WASTES

Katharina Kummer
47–48 (1995)

Taking into account Decision II/12 of the Conference of the Parties, the fundamental principles of the Basel Convention, as it stands, can be summarized as follows:

(1) The generation of hazardous wastes should be reduced to a minimum (principle of waste minimization).

(2) Where it is unavoidable, the wastes should be disposed of as close as possible to the source of generation (principle of proximity of disposal).

(3) In a number of instances, the export of hazardous wastes is prohibited absolutely; hazardous wastes may not be exported from OECD to non-OECD countries, or from any party state to Antarctica . . .

(4) In all other cases, transboundary hazardous waste movements must conform to the provisions of the Convention or a treaty establishing equivalent standards, or to parties which have banned the import of hazardous wastes.

(5) The cornerstone of this regulatory system is the prior informed consent (PIC) of the prospective states of import and transit.

(6) Hazardous wastes that have been exported illegally, as well as legally exported hazardous wastes that cannot be safely disposed of in the state of destination, must be re-imported into the state of origin.

NOTES AND QUESTIONS

1. *Fundamental Principles.* Does Kummer include all of the principles? What about the principle that waste should be disposed of safely, in an environmentally sound manner? *See, e.g.,* Basel Convention, article 4(8); paragraphs 2(b), (e), (g) & (h) of article 4, and the penultimate paragraph of the Preamble.

2. Because of disagreements during the negotiations, the principles outlined above have not been consistently followed throughout the Convention. Sometimes they have been weakened or modified. *See* Katharina Kummer, International Management of Hazardous Wastes, 47–48 (1995); *see also* Elli Louka, Overcoming National Barriers to International Waste Trade (1994). After the Convention went into effect, parties have further refined aspects of the system.

3. *The OECD/non-OECD ban.* The second meeting of the Conference of the Parties to the Basel Convention in March 1994 adopted a decision "to prohibit immediately all transboundary movements of hazardous wastes which are destined for final disposal from OECD to non-OECD countries" and "to phase out by 31 December 1997, and prohibit as of that date, all transboundary movements of hazardous wastes which are destined for recycling or recovering operations from OECD to non-OECD states." The decision permits a non-OECD member that does not have a domestic ban on importing hazardous wastes to inform the Basel Convention Secretariat that it would allow the import of specific categories of hazardous wastes from OECD members, but only until December 31, 1997. Second Meeting of the Conference of the Parties to Basel Treaty on Control of Transboundary Movements of Hazardous Wastes, adopted March 25, 1994. The United States strongly opposed the decision, and the process of adopting it was

unusually bitter and divisive. What prompted this decision? Does it promote efficient waste management? Equitable waste management? In November 1995 at the Third Conference of the Parties, Parties decided to amend the Basel Convention to prohibit all transboundary movements of hazardous wastes from States who are members of the OECD and the European Community (EC) and from Liechtenstein to all other States. The United States opposed this amendment, as it had the earlier decision. Decision III, 1, Nov. 28, 1995, UNEP/CHW.3/35. As of February 2015, only 80 countries had ratified the ban, and the ban was thus not in effect. Can you argue that the ban is an environmentally unsound decision? In thinking about that question, consider the excerpt from Theo Colborn, Dianne Dumanoski & John Peterson Myers, in section B.1, below. Note that the U.S. Supreme Court has forbidden U.S. states to prohibit the import of wastes from other states as a burden on interstate commerce. City of Philadelphia v. New Jersey, 437 U.S. 617 (1977).

The problem of recycling, and making appropriate distinctions between recyclables and nonrecyclables in the context of the OECD/non-OECD ban is discussed further in Note 3 in the following section regarding Definition of Hazardous Wastes.

4. *The United States and Basel.* While the Basel Convention has been in effect since 1995, the United States is not yet a Party as of 2014. The Senate has given its advice and consent to ratification, but the President has not deposited its instrument of ratification on the grounds that the necessary implementing legislation to bring the United States into compliance with the agreement has not yet been enacted. The purported legal impediments are that the Resource Conservation and Recovery Act (RCRA) needs to be amended to give the United States the authority to prohibit export of hazardous wastes if they will not be disposed of in an environmentally sound manner abroad and to reimport the wastes that have been sent abroad for disposal in violation of the Convention. The Toxic Substances Control Act (TSCA), which regulations PCBs (polychlorinated biphenyls), is also implicated. The United States regularly enters into arrangements with Basel Parties to allow trade in hazardous wastes between those countries and the United States.

5. *The* Amlon Metals *case.* The case of Amlon Metals, Inc. v. FMC Corp., 775 F. Supp. 668 (S.D.N.Y. 1991), illustrates the difference that implementing legislation could make. The United States corporation FMC contracted with the United Kingdom corporation Amlon to recycle nonhazardous wastes, but the wastes that arrived in the U.K. contained xylene and other hazardous chemicals. British authorities ordered that the wastes be stored at Amlon's facilities, and Amlon sued unsuccessfully in both British and U.S. courts, with the latter finding no basis for jurisdiction under existing statutes. Amlon was stuck with the waste. If U.S. implementing legislation for the Basel Convention had been in effect then, the results might have been different because the U.S. district court would have been able to exercise jurisdiction over the contractual claims. *See* Sean D. Murphy,

Prospective Liability Regimes for the Transboundary Movement of Hazardous Wastes, 88 Am. J. Intl. L. 24 (1994).

6. *1999 Basel Convention Protocol on Liability and Compensation for Damage Resulting from Transboundary Movements of Hazardous Wastes and Their Disposal.* In December 1999, the Parties to the Basel Convention finalized the Protocol on Liability and Compensation for Damage Resulting from Transboundary Movements of Hazardous Wastes and Their Disposal ("Protocol") at the Fifth Conference of the Parties, after years of contentious negotiations. The Protocol functions as a supplement to the Basel Convention and must be ratified separately before it enters into force. As of February 2015, there are a total of 13 signatories and 11 Parties to the Protocol, and it has not yet entered into force, which requires ratification or accession by 20 Parties.

The objective of the Protocol is to provide for a comprehensive system for liability as well as adequate and prompt compensation for damage resulting from the transboundary movement of hazardous wastes and other wastes, including incidents occurring due to illegal traffic in those wastes (Article 1). The Protocol addresses who is financially responsible in the event of an incident. Each phase of a transboundary movement, from the point at which the wastes are loaded on the means of transport to their export, international transit, import, and final disposal, is considered.

There are several criticisms regarding the efficacy of the Protocol, especially in connection with the financial mechanism described in Article 15. Article 15 states, "[w]here compensation under the Protocol does not cover the costs of damage, additional and supplementary measures aimed at ensuring adequate and prompt consideration may be taken using existing mechanisms." Critics argue that developed States succeeded in creating a weak financial provision, and that the concern of developing States over the lack of funds to properly dispose of hazardous waste was not adequately addressed. Other criticism arises from Article 3, Paragraph 7, which contains exceptions. *See* http://archive.basel.int/meetings/cop/cop5/docs/prot-e.pdf; *see also* Jerrold A. Long, *Protocol on Liability and Compensation for Damage Resulting from the Transboundary Movements of Hazardous Wastes and Their Disposal*, 1999 Colo. J. Int'l Envtl. L. & Pol'y (2000).

2. DEFINITION OF HAZARDOUS WASTES

The question of which wastes should be included in the scope of the Basel Convention generated considerable debate during the negotiations and is subject to ongoing controversy. In 1988, OECD Council Decision C(88)90(Final) addressed the reporting needs of member countries and the development of an international waste identification code. The Decision identified the core list of wastes to be controlled, which was later adopted with minor variances by the Parties to the Basel Convention. The relevant annexes to the Basel Convention are closely modeled on the corresponding annexes to the relevant legislation of the European Union and the OECD.

OECD DECISION OF THE COUNCIL CONCERNING THE CONTROL OF TRANSFRONTIER MOVEMENTS OF WASTES DESTINED FOR RECOVERY OPERATIONS OECD COUNCIL DECISION

(incorporating amendments to C(92) 39, adopted on 25 February 2002—
C(2001)107/ADD1, 9 March 2004—C(2004)20, 25 November 2005—C(2005)141
18 November 2008—C(2008)156)

THE COUNCIL,

. . .

Having regard to the Basel Convention on the Control of Transboundary Movements of Hazardous Wastes and their Disposal, which entered into force on 5 May 1992, as amended on 6 November 1998 with Annexes VIII and IX listing respectively wastes characterised as hazardous pursuant to Article 1(1)(a) of the Convention and wastes not covered by Article 1(1)(a) of the Convention; and Noting that most OECD Member countries (hereafter Member countries) and the European Community have become Parties to the Basel Convention; Noting that Member countries agreed at the Working Group on Waste Management Policy (WGWMP) meeting in Vienna in October 1998 to further harmonisation of procedures and requirements of OECD Decision C(92)39/FINAL with those of the Basel Convention; Noting that recovery of valuable materials and energy from wastes is an integral part of the international economic system and that well established international markets exist for the collection and processing of such materials within Member countries; Noting further that many industrial sectors in Member countries have already implemented waste recovery techniques in an environmentally sound and economically efficient manner, thus increasing resource efficiency and contributing to sustainable development, and convinced that further efforts to promote and facilitate waste recovery are necessary and should be encouraged; Recognizing that the environmentally sound and economically efficient recovery of wastes may justify transboundary movements of wastes between Member countries; Recognizing that the operational Control System established by Decision C(92)39/FINAL has provided a valuable framework for Member countries to control transboundary movements of wastes destined for recovery operations in an environmentally sound and economically efficient manner; Desiring, therefore, to continue this agreement or arrangement under Article 11.2 of the Basel Convention; Recognizing that Member countries may, within their jurisdiction, impose requirements consistent with this Decision and in accordance with the rules of international law, in order to better protect human health and the environment; and Recognizing the need to revise Decision C(92)39/FINAL in order to improve certain elements of the Control System and to enhance harmonisation with the Basel Convention,

On the proposal of the Environment Committee:

Decides that the text of Decision C(92)39/FINAL is revised as follows:

Chapter I

I.   DECIDES that Member countries shall control transboundary movements of wastes destined for recovery operations within the OECD area in accordance with the provisions set out in Chapter II of this Decision and in the appendices to it.

II.   INSTRUCTS the Environment Policy Committee in co-operation with other relevant OECD bodies, in particular the Trade Committee, to ensure that the provisions of this Control System remain compatible with the needs of Member countries to recover wastes in an environmentally sound and economically efficient manner.

III.   RECOMMENDS Member countries to use for the Notification Document and Movement Document the forms contained in Appendix 8 to this Decision.

IV.   INSTRUCTS the Environment Policy Committee to amend the forms for the Notification Document and Movement Document as necessary.

V.   INSTRUCTS the Environment Policy Committee to review the procedure for amending the waste lists under Chapter II. B, (3) at the latest seven (7) years after the adoption of the present Decision.

VI.   REQUESTS Member countries to provide the information that is necessary for the implementation of this Decision and is listed in Appendix 7 to this Decision.

VII.   REQUESTS the Secretary General to transmit this Decision to the United Nations Environment Programme and the Secretariat of the Basel Convention.

Chapter II

A. DEFINITIONS

For the purposes of this Decision:

1.   WASTES are substances or objects, other than radioactive materials covered by other international agreements, which:

i) are disposed of or are being recovered; or

ii) are intended to be disposed of or recovered; or

iii) are required, by the provisions of national law, to be disposed of or recovered.

2.   HAZARDOUS WASTES are:

i) Wastes that belong to any category contained in Appendix 1 to this Decision unless they do not possess any of the characteristics contained in Appendix 2 to this Decision; and

ii) Wastes that are not covered under sub-paragraph 2.(i) but are defined as, or are considered to be, hazardous wastes by the domestic legislation of the Member country of export, import or transit. Member countries shall not be required to enforce laws other than their own.

3.   DISPOSAL means any of the operations specified in Appendix 5.A to this Decision.

4.   RECOVERY means any of the operations specified in Appendix 5.B to this Decision.

5.   TRANSBOUNDARY MOVEMENT means any movement of wastes from an area under the national jurisdiction of a Member country to an area under the national jurisdiction of another Member country.

6.   RECOVERY FACILITY means a facility which, under applicable domestic law, is operating or is authorised or permitted to operate in the country of import to receive wastes and to perform recovery operations on them.

7.   COUNTRY OF EXPORT means a Member country from which a transboundary movement of wastes is planned to be initiated or is initiated.

8.   COUNTRY OF IMPORT means a Member country to which a transboundary movement of wastes is planned or takes place.

9.   COUNTRY OF TRANSIT means a Member country other than the country of export or import through which a transboundary movement of wastes is planned or takes place.

10. COUNTRIES CONCERNED means the countries of export and import and any country of transit, as defined above.

11. OECD AREA means all land and marine areas, under the national jurisdiction of any Member country.

12. COMPETENT AUTHORITIES means the regulatory authorities of countries concerned having jurisdiction over transboundary movements of wastes covered by this Decision.

13. PERSON means any natural or legal person.

14. EXPORTER means any person under the jurisdiction of the country of export who initiates the transboundary movement of wastes or

who has, at the time the planned transboundary movement commences, possession or other forms of legal control of the wastes.

15. IMPORTER means any person under the jurisdiction of the country of import to whom possession or other form of legal control of the waste is assigned at the time the waste is received in the country of import.

16. RECOGNISED TRADER means any person under the jurisdiction of a Member country who, with appropriate authorisation of countries concerned, acts in the role of principal to purchase and subsequently sell wastes; such a person may act to arrange and facilitate transboundary movements of wastes destined for recovery operations.

17. GENERATOR means any person whose activities create wastes.

18. A MIXTURE OF WASTES means a waste that results from an intentional or unintentional mixing of two or more different wastes. A single shipment of wastes, consisting of two or more wastes, where each waste is separated, is not a mixture of wastes.

NOTES AND QUESTIONS

1. *Problems in defining hazardous wastes.* What problems do you foresee in defining hazardous wastes? How should a country treat wastes that are regarded domestically as nonhazardous but contain material that is covered by the Basel Convention? Suppose the exporting country considers a material as a hazardous waste, but the importing country does not, or vice versa? Do Articles 1, 2.1 and 3 of the Basel Convention mean that each Party gets to define what "hazardous waste" means?

2. *Basel Article 11.* OECD Council Decision C(2008)156 also modified the initial OECD Council Decision C(92)39 to update the OECD waste lists, require certain control procedures for the return of hazardous wastes, and add new required tracking and documentation procedures for accumulation and transfer facilities. As a legally binding, Basel-consistent agreement under Article 11 of the Convention, the Decision allows trade in hazardous wastes between a Party and a non-Party (such as the United States), if both are OECD members.

3. *Distinction between recyclables and nonrecyclables?* One controversial issue has been the absence of a distinction between "recyclable" and "nonrecyclable" wastes in the text of the Convention. The Basel Convention defines "wastes" as substances subject to disposal. It applies to both wastes subject to final disposal as well as wastes exported for recycling. It does not distinguish between wastes based on the purpose of the export. This issue is particularly controversial for the recycling of scrap metal and other recoverable materials, much of which is shipped to other countries such as China, India, and Pakistan for recycling and recovery. A technical working group was established under the Convention to consider the extent to which scrap metal and other materials destined for recovery are covered by the

Basel Convention and the ban on shipments from OECD countries to non-OECD countries at the third Conference of the Parties (COP 3) (18–22 September 1995). At the fourth conference of the parties (COP 4) in Malaysia in February 1998, the working group presented two lists of wastes: those that are hazardous and those that are nonhazardous, with the first list defining those wastes that may not be shipped from an OECD country to a non-OECD country under the amendment to the convention. COP 4 decided to incorporate List A, identifying wastes characterized as hazardous, and List B, identifying nonhazardous wastes, as Annex VII and Annex IX to the Basel Convention, respectively. The lists, however, did not define all scrap metals, most plastics, or paper as hazardous. The lists would thus allow most shipments of wastes for recycling in developing countries to continue. See also OECD Council Decision C(2008)156 (amending earlier Council Decision to address more the issue of waste recycling); EU Council Regulation 333/2011 (31 March 2011) (creating criteria for when scrap iron, steel, and aluminum cease to be waste and can instead be classified as products).

The question becomes even more complicated when contemplating the developing dynamics for electronic waste shipment. For further thoughts on this, read the subsection on electronic waste and its associated Exercise.

4.   *Question.* Why should scrap metal from OECD countries destined for recovery in developing countries be exempt from the Basel Convention and thus from the OECD-non-OECD ban (if it goes into effect)?

3.   PRIOR INFORMED CONSENT

INTERNATIONAL MANAGEMENT OF HAZARDOUS WASTES
Katharina Kummer
65–66 (1995)

[A]ny transboundary movement of hazardous wastes which is not, in principle, prohibited, and which is in conformity with the general obligations, must be carried out in accordance with the Convention's regulatory system (Article 4(1.c) and (2.f). This system, generally referred to as the PIC procedure, is regulated in Articles 5 and 7 and in Annex VI of the Convention. Party states must designate at least one competent authority responsible for administering the PIC procedure (see para. 18 below). The duties of the states involved, as outlined below, are to be carried out by their competent authorities. . . .

THE POSITION OF THE STATES OF EXPORT AND IMPORT

The state of export has the duty to notify the prospective states of import and transit of any intended transboundary movement of hazardous wastes. The state of export can either provide this information itself or require the generator or exporter to do so, through the channel of its competent authority. The information to be provided must be sufficiently detailed to enable the authorities of the states of import and transit to assess the nature and the risks of the intended movement; the content of the information is specified in Annex VA. Among other things, the reason for the export; the exporter and the generator; the site and process of generation; the nature of the wastes and their packaging; the intended itinerary; the site of disposal; the disposer; and the method of disposal as per Annex IV must be specified (Article 6(1)). In accordance with Article 6(6)–(8), the reporting state may, with the prior approval of the states of import and transit, allow the use of a general notification for shipments of wastes having the same characteristics and the same transport route, for a maximum period of 12 months.

In order to promote uniformity in this regard, the (then) Interim Secretariat of the Basel Convention prepared a form to be used for the notification of transboundary movements of hazardous wastes, which is based on the above requirements. Following a consideration of this form by the open-ended Ad Hoc Committee on Implementation, the Conference of the Parties provisionally adopted it, and recommended that states use it and provide comments to the Secretariat.

The state of import must respond to the notifier in writing, consenting to the movement with or without conditions, denying permission for the movement, or requesting further information. In its reply, the state of import must also confirm the existence of a contract between the exporter and the disposer, which specifies the environmentally sound disposal of the wastes. Copies of the importing state's final response must be sent to the competent authorities of all states involved in the transaction (Article 6(2) and (3.b)). The state of export may not allow the movement to commence until the notifier has received the importing state's written consent, along with the confirmation of the existence of the contract (Article 4(1.c), Article 6(2) and (3)). The Convention gives no time limit for the response by the importing state. Since the consent of the importing state has to be explicit and unconditional, a movement may not be permitted to commence if *no* response is given by that state. After the completion of the disposal operation, the exporter and the exporting state must be informed accordingly (Article 6(9)).

This regulation is very detailed; however, some points are again left open. For example, there is no requirement for the state of export to verify the contents of the contract concluded between the exporter and the disposer; the transaction may commence on the basis of mere confirmation of its existence.

NOTES AND QUESTIONS

1. *Foreseeable problems with the informed consent system.* What problems do you foresee in implementing the prior informed consent system for transboundary movements of hazardous wastes? Would it make a

difference whether the shipments were between industrialized countries, such as Canada and the United States, or between an industrialized country, such as Italy, and a developing one?

2. *References.* For a more detailed discussion of prior informed consent, see David Langlet, Prior Informed Consent and Hazardous Trade (2009).

4. DISPOSAL IN AN ENVIRONMENTALLY SOUND MANNER

INTERNATIONAL MANAGEMENT OF HAZARDOUS WASTES
Katharina Kummer
65–66 (1995)

Parties must require that hazardous wastes subject to transboundary movement are managed in an environmentally sound manner, whatever their place of their disposal (Article 4(8)). Thus, in accordance with the principle of nondiscrimination, the same rules and standards must be applied to hazardous wastes moved out of the state of generation as to those disposed of domestically. Article 4(10) prohibits the transfer, "under any circumstances," of the generating state's obligation to ensure the environmentally sound management of hazardous wastes to the states of import or transit. By implication, the duty to ensure environmentally sound management is thus allocated to the generating state. That state may not allow the export of hazardous wastes if it has "reason to believe" that their environmentally sound management and disposal would not be guaranteed in the prospective state of import (Article 4(2.e)). The Basel Convention does not specify the manner or the extent to which the state of export must verify this. It does not give the exporting state the right of active verification, e.g., by the means of prior EIA [environmental impact assessment—Eds.] of a disposal facility, nor is this right recognized by customary law. . . . Any such initiative might thus come up against claims to sovereignty by the importing state. Therefore, except where the lack of proper facilities is notorious, the term "reason to believe" must be interpreted to refer to the exporting state's conclusion based on relevant information received from the importing state. The prospective state of import has the parallel obligation to believe that they would not be managed in an environmentally sound manner (Article 4(2.g)).

The Basel Convention itself defines the crucial notion of "environmentally sound management" only in very general terms (Article 2(2) and (8)), a fact that has been criticized extensively. For purposes of the Convention, this term means "taking all practicable steps to ensure that hazardous wastes or other wastes are managed in a manner which will protect human health and the environment against the adverse effects which may result from such wastes." After the adoption of the

Convention, additional efforts were made to give more concrete content to the notion of environmentally sound management of hazardous wastes.

NOTES AND QUESTIONS

1. *Technical guidelines.* Many sets of Technical Guidelines have been prepared under the auspices of the Convention. The Guidelines cover topics such as POPs (persistent organic pollutants); PCBs, PCT (polychlorinated terphenyls), and PBB (polybrominated biphenyls); hazardous characteristics; DDT (dichloro-diphenyl-trichloroethane); HCB (hexachlorobenzene); dioxins and furans; pesticide wastes; surface treatment of metals and plastics; and recycling/reclamation of metals and metal compounds. The latest versions of these Guidelines may be viewed at http://www.basel.int/TheConvention/ Publications/TechnicalGuidelines/tabid/2362/Default.aspx.

2. *Environmentally sound disposal standards.* What standards should apply to determine whether the disposal might be in an environmentally unsound manner? Should U.S. standards for disposal of hazardous wastes in the United States be applied in this context to disposal abroad by U.S. waste generators?

5. REIMPORTATION OF WASTES

Under the Basel Convention, it is important to distinguish between wastes that have been legally exported and those that have been illegally exported. In the case of the illegal export of wastes, the State of export shall ensure that the wastes are "(a) taken back by the exporter or the generator or, if necessary, by itself into the State of export, or, if impracticable, (b) are otherwise disposed of in accordance with the provisions of this Convention." (Article 9.) In the case of legally exported wastes of which disposal cannot be completed in accordance with the terms of the contract, "the State of export shall ensure that the wastes in question are taken back into the State of export, by the exporter, if alternative arrangements cannot be made for their disposal in an environmentally sound manner, within 90 days from the time that the importing State informed the State of export and the Secretariat. . . . To this end, the State of export and any Party of transit shall not oppose, hinder or prevent the return of those wastes to the State of export." (Article 8.) Who has the primary responsibility for reimporting the wastes? If the wastes were legally exported, does the exporting State have the affirmative obligation to take back the wastes? Kummer, above, comments that "Article 8 . . . constitutes an innovative approach which does not as yet seem to be supported by customary law, or have precedents in treaty provisions." Suppose the wastes were illegally exported, would the exporting State have a duty to take them back? If the exporting country has such a duty, at what point in the country of disposal does the obligation begin—from the waste disposal site or only from the point of entry? Why does the answer to this question matter?

The United States and Mexico reached an understanding on the return of hazardous wastes under the bilateral Agreement of Cooperation Between the United States of America and the United Mexican States Regarding the Transboundary Shipments of Hazardous Waste and Hazardous Substances, which is memorialized in a letter of November 12, 1986, from the Deputy Legal Advisor to the United States Department of State to the Legal Advisor to the Secretariat of Foreign Relations of Mexico. The relevant portion provides:

> In accordance with Articles 4 and 9 of the Annex, the United States will allow reentry of shipments of hazardous waste and hazardous substances in compliance with domestic law where the exporter is responsible for the shipment. Further, under Article 9, the United States will readmit any shipment of hazardous substances that was not lawfully imported into Mexico when appropriate arrangements have been made with the U.S. exporter for return of the shipment and for its proper use or disposal in the United States or reexport to another country.

Does this language fully answer the legal issues raised above?

6. AGREEMENTS AND ARRANGEMENTS

There are regional and bilateral agreements that also address the transboundary movements of hazardous wastes, such as the Bamako Convention governing movements in Africa, OECD Council Decision C(2008)156 amending OECD Decision C(92)(30) (*see* above), and the bilateral agreements between the United States and Canada and between the United States and Mexico (discussed above). Some of the provisions in these agreements differ from those of the Basel Convention, and an important legal issue is the extent to which they are consistent with the provisions of the convention. Article 11 provides that

> Parties may enter into bilateral, multilateral, or regional agreements or arrangements regarding transboundary movement of hazardous wastes or other wastes with Parties or non-Parties provided that such agreements or arrangements do not derogate from the environmentally sound management of hazardous wastes and other wastes as required by this Convention. These agreements or arrangements shall stipulate provisions which are not less environmentally sound than those provided for by this Convention in particular taking into account the interests of developing countries.

Article 4 of the Bamako Convention, in contrast, states that "Hazardous Waste Import Ban. All Parties shall take appropriate legal, administrative and other measures within the area under their jurisdiction to prohibit the import of all hazardous wastes, for any reason, into Africa from non-Contracting Parties. Such import shall be deemed illegal and a criminal act."

NOTES AND QUESTIONS

1. *Arrangements*. What form and content must an agreement have to satisfy Article 11 and thus allow trade between a party and nonparty? What will be the relationship between Article 11 and the OECD-non-OECD ban if the latter becomes effective?

2. For reference materials, *see generally* OECD, Transfrontier Movements of Hazardous Wastes (1985); Katharina Kummer, International Management of Hazardous Wastes (1995); Eli Louka, Overcoming National Barriers to International Waste Trade (1995) (covering hazardous and radioactive wastes); Transferring Hazardous Technologies and Substances: The International Legal Challenge (Gunther Handl & Robert Lutz eds., 1989).

3. For an analysis of the interface between U.S. domestic law and the various international legal instruments applicable to trade in hazardous wastes, *see* L. Belenky, *Cradle to Border: U.S. Hazardous Waste Export Regulations and International Law*, 17 Berkeley J. Int'l L. 95 (1999).

4. The Bamako Convention was motivated by a number of concerns, including concerns from African States that they lacked environmentally sound disposal sites and concerns that the Basel Convention failed to adequately issues specific to underdeveloped States, such as control of general waste mixed with hazardous materials and prevention of forged or bribe-induced signatures on import documents. *See* John Ovink, *Transboundary Shipments of Toxic Waste: The Basel and Bamako Conventions: Do Third World Countries Have a Choice?*, 13 Dick. J. Int'l L. 281, 287–88 (1995). Do regional conventions such as the Bamako Convention, which contains a prohibition on trade from non-Party States with no exceptions, adequately address such concerns?

7. E-WASTE

IN DEVELOPING WORLD, A PUSH TO BRING E-WASTE OUT OF SHADOWS

Mike Ives
Yale Environment 360 (2014), *available at* http://e360.yale.edu/feature/in_developing_world_a_push_to_bring_e-waste_out_of_shadows/2736/

For two decades the global narrative around electronic waste has typically been that rich, industrialized countries were dumping used devices onto impoverished ones, where the desperately poor often recycled printed circuit boards under unsafe conditions. But experts say nascent e-waste trends are beginning to challenge that paradigm. Developing countries are now shipping more e-waste by weight to developed countries than vice versa, according to a recent analysis of United Nations trade data by Josh Lepawsky, a geographer at Canada's Memorial University of Newfoundland and an expert on the electronic waste trade. "Between 1996 and 2012 the dominant inter-regional trade pattern has been turned on its head," he says.

Meanwhile, a small but growing number of businesses . . . , often backed by international donors and lenders, are exploring ways to create incentives for informal collectors to sell e-waste to formal recycling operations. For example, the German government's development aid agency, the German Society for International Cooperation, has supported an Indian company named e-WaRDD that has piloted a project to incentivize circuit-board collection in Bangalore, India. And a Belgium-based non-profit, WorldLoop, receives corporate funding to support a range of electronics recycling programs in Africa that link informal recyclers with state-of-the-art facilities overseas that recycle printed circuit boards, transformers, and leaded glass.

Researchers say printed circuit boards, which often contain gold and other valuable metals, are a good first step for such projects because they typically represent the most valuable—as well as the most environmentally hazardous—aspect of the e-waste recycling process. The goal is to allow collectors to continue their practice of re-using or manually dismantling electronic equipment, but then sell those parts to professional facilities instead of melting them or using cyanide to extract valuable metals in backyard workshops. Advanced recycling facilities employ commodity separation, shredding, resource recovery, and pollution-control technologies that greatly reduce the health and environmental hazards associated with backyard recycling operations.

Fledgling e-waste programs and businesses offer early lessons about what may help move the informal recycling sector toward more sustainable practices, according to researchers. But they also highlight the complexities of the global e-waste market, where it can often be more profitable for backyard recyclers to continue their ad-hoc operations than sell to large-scale e-waste processors or middlemen, sometimes called "interface" outfits.

"As far as I know, there has been plenty of legislative action to ban trade and informal recycling," but insufficient action to develop alternate approaches, says Eric Williams, a professor at the Rochester Institute of Technology who led a recent study that examined how to more effectively link informal and formal e-waste recyclers.

As e-waste flows shift, manufacturers in China, India, and many other low- and middle-income countries increasingly view e-scrap as a valuable commodity—both for extracting metals or for manufacturing new devices from a product's component parts. That is partly because the value of e-waste has broadly increased in recent years in tandem with rising demand for the so-called "rare earth" elements used in laptops, cellular phones, and other electronic devices.

Policies that encourage sustainable "harvesting" of e-waste resources already exist in Singapore, Taiwan, and South Korea, says Michael Biddle, president of the California-based plastics recycler MBA Polymers, which has a facility in China. "They're doing it not just to protect their environment," he adds. "They also recognize, 'Hey, these are resources we need to remain viable as a manufacturing base.' "

E-waste experts say, however, that any effort to connect the formal and informal sectors faces major challenges. One is finding incentives to ensure safe treatment not only of lucrative components like circuit boards, but also of less valuable and potentially hazardous materials. Ramzy Kahhat, a professor of engineering at the Pontifical Catholic University of Peru, says the question for any scrap middleman becomes: "Do you want to cherry pick and take only the good stuff and leave the bad things? Or are you willing to handle the whole product?"

. . .

Over the years, numerous initiatives have attempted, with mixed results, to create laws and international agreements to help mitigate the e-waste trade's negative environmental and health effects. The best known is the 1992 Basel Convention, which imposed a patchwork of restrictions on which electronic products some rich countries could ship to poorer ones.

Since then, the amount of e-waste generated globally has only increased: A 2013 study by the group Solving the E-Waste Problem (StEP) Initiative forecasted that the amount of e-waste produced globally may rise by a third in the next five years, from nearly 49 million metric tons to 64.5 million tons. However, a few e-waste experts say the Basel Convention and related debates no longer reflect the shifting geographies of the global e-waste market. And in a forthcoming study, the geographer Josh Lepawsky notes that while Indonesia was a net importer of e-waste in 1996, it is now a net exporter whose top three export destinations are China, South Korea, and Hong Kong.

Electronics are still sent abroad by the United States and other developed countries. But researchers say the material is often critical for technology infrastructure in developing countries, and that much of the e-waste crossing the globe is actually destined for repair and reuse rather than immediate recycling.

. . .

Fledgling recycling companies in the developing world often purchase printed circuit boards from informal scrap collectors and either reprocess them in a nearby modern facility or ship them to one in a more developed country like Germany. . . . E-waste experts say that attempts at reform should begin with the recognition that informal e-scrap collectors are good at what they do—finding value in waste—and should be an integral part of any environmental solution. "Even though there is evidence of environmental problems related to recycling of e-waste, I think there are some activities in this system that are positive," says Kahhat. "Instead of saying, 'Okay, I'll put a stop on everything,' try to understand what activities are positive and do not harm the environment, and give creative solutions for those activities that are harming the environment."

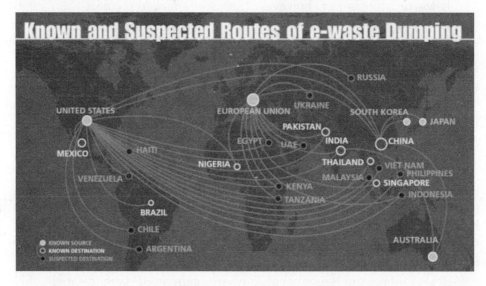

Figure 2: from Karin Lundgren, International Labour Office, *The Global Impact of E-waste: Addressing the Challenge*, at 15 (2012).

EXERCISE

Recent studies have shown that direction of electronic waste shipment is changing from the original developed country to developing country direction contemplated in the Basel Convention; developing countries are shipping more e-waste by weight to developed countries than vice versa. This phenomenon is driven by increases in value of e-waste in rare earth elements used in laptops. Fledgling recycling companies in the developing world purchase printed circuit boards from informal scrap collectors and ship them for reprocessing in more developed countries, for a fee. Regardless of the direction of e-waste shipment, Singapore, Taiwan, and South Korea (the latter of which is a Basel Party) are adopting policies to encourage the sustainable "harvesting" of e-resources.

Suppose Finland, a Basel Party, is thinking about adopting domestic policies to encourage this sort of recycling. But it doesn't want to run afoul of the Basel Convention. Discuss what it should do (and whether it should suggest modifications to the Basel Convention). In doing so, consider the exercise from the following perspectives:

- A Finnish Ministry of Foreign Affairs attorney

- A regional trade representative from a developing country that is a Party to the Basel Convention and which has adopted sustainable e-waste recycling policies

- A sustainable recycling advocate from who wants to encourage all developing countries to adopt such policies, even non Basel parties

- Nokia Corporation, who wants to use the materials

- Greenpeace Nordic, which is concerned with illegal trafficking, as well as the possibility that pro-recycling policies will "water down" Basel Convention protections

8. SHIPBREAKING

"Shipbreaking," in which obsolete merchant or military vessels are broken down for the scrap metal they contain, raises important environmental and worker safety issues. The most serious problems are raised by shipbreaking that occurs in countries such as India, Pakistan, and Turkey. For discussions of the worker safety issues, *see* the International Labour Organization's (ILO) website, www.ilo.org. In 2004, the ILO issued "Safety and Health in Shipbreaking: Guidelines for Asian Countries and Turkey."

International environmental issues are raised under the Basel Convention when vessels are transported from one country to another for dismantling if either country is Party to the Convention. These vessels frequently contain asbestos, polychlorinated biphenyls (PCBs), mercury, lead and other hazardous chemicals; and their dismantling and the subsequent processing of the scrap metal raise the risk of toxic releases, affecting both the shipbreaking workers and the broader environment, both locally and globally (discussed in section B, below). The Basel Convention Secretariat issued Technical Guidelines for Environmentally Sound Management of the Full and Partial Dismantling of Ships in 2004. The International Maritime Organization (IMO) also discussed voluntary guidelines. A Joint ILO/IMO/Basel Convention Working Group was also formed in 2004 at the fifty-first session of the IMO Marine Environment Protection Committee, and the 291st session of the ILO Governing Body. The Joint Working Group's aim was to coordinate their responsibilities and competencies of the three organizations on the issue of ship scrapping, to consider mechanisms to promote jointly their respective programs, and to consider further needs.

The United States stopped the transport of its ships for this purpose in the 1990s. Before that, the United States sought the written prior informed consent of the Government of India before allowing the transport, via an exchange of diplomatic cables. Was it required to do so? Are PCBs "hazardous"? Whose law determines that in this instance, the United States' or India's or Egypt's if the ship is to transit through the Suez Canal? What role does the Basel Convention play in that determination?

Negotiations commenced to create a convention specifically to address shipbreaking. In 2009, in Hong Kong, the International Convention for the Safe and Environmentally Sound Recycling of Ships, 2009 (the Hong Kong Convention), was adopted. The Convention aims to ensure that ships, when being recycled, do not pose any unnecessary risks to human health or safety or the environment. The Convention addresses issues involved in ship recycling, including the fact that ships sold for scrapping may contain environmentally hazardous substances such as asbestos, heavy metals, hydrocarbons, ozone-depleting substances and others. It also addresses concerns raised about the working and environmental conditions at many of the world's ship recycling locations.

The new Convention covers: the design, construction, operation and preparation of ships; the operation of ship recycling facilities, including training of workers; and the establishment of an enforcement mechanism for ship recycling, incorporating certification and reporting requirements. Ships sent for recycling will be required to have an inventory of hazardous materials, which will be specific to each ship. An annex to the convention specifies regulations for safe environmentally sound recycling of ships. Appendix 1 to the Convention provides a list of hazardous materials the installation or use of which is prohibited or restricted in shipyards, ship repair yards, and ships of Parties. Ships will be required to undergo an initial survey to verify the inventory of hazardous materials, additional surveys during the life of the ship, and a final survey prior to recycling. Ship recycling yards will be required to provide a ship-specific "Ship Recycling Plan", specifying the manner in which each ship will be recycled.

The precise relationship between the Hong Kong Convention (which is not in force as of February 2015) and the Basel Convention has yet to be determined.

B. HAZARDOUS CHEMICALS

1. THE PROBLEM

Increasing attention has been paid in recent years to the threats to human, animal, and plant health posed by hazardous chemicals, including industrial chemicals, pesticides, and heavy metals. These chemicals include heavy metals such as lead and mercury; industrial chemicals such as PCBs (polychlorinated biphenyls, a family of chemicals used to insulate electrical equipment) and methyl isocyanate (which resulted in thousands of deaths in Bhopal, India); pesticides such as DDT and chlordane; and herbicides such as paraquat. There is a thriving international market in many hazardous chemicals, involving both developed and developing countries.

The sound management of hazardous and other chemicals must consider many factors. Hazardous and other chemicals play major roles in industry, agriculture and disease prevention, and often have important beneficial effects. As pointed out above, some hazardous chemicals, such as heavy metals, occur naturally, so exposure to them could not be eliminated completely even if countries decided to do that. The risks that chemical use creates vary widely, depending not only on the attributes of the chemicals themselves but also on how they are used, the pathways through which people, animals, or plants are exposed to them, the characteristics of the exposed population, the behavior patterns of members of those populations, and the environment in which they are released.

Concerns about hazardous chemicals have increased for several reasons. The Bhopal disaster in 1984, referred to above and described in detail in Chapter 6, focused concern on single-event tragedies. Increased experience with chemicals such as leaded gasoline and some carcinogens focused attention on risks from longer-term exposure. Better understanding of bioaccumulation (the accumulation of a substance in the tissue of an organism over time), bioconcentration (the increased concentration of a substance in organisms as one progresses up the food chain, such as the concentration of DDT in bald eagles and peregrine falcons), the persistence over time of some chemicals (e.g., DDT and PCBs), and the wide geographic dispersion of chemicals (e.g., polar bears and humans in the Arctic have unusually high levels of PCBs in their bodies) raised the level of concern about the potentially widespread effect of chemicals, even those used in low amounts. Improved research allowed moving beyond risk assessments based primarily on cancer risks to include other risks, such as interference with the endocrine system and developmental and reproductive damage.[1] Examining risks to different segments of society revealed differential risks that depend on inherent susceptibility or different behavior patterns. For example, children may have increased susceptibility because they are still developing, they have relatively low body weight, and their immune systems are immature; women and men may have different susceptibilities; and people who subsist primarily on locally caught fish or eat a greater amount of fish organs may have higher than normal exposure rates to certain chemicals that bioaccumulate in those fish. Although our understanding of these

---

[1]   Theo Colborn, Dianne Dumanoski & John Peterson Myers, Our Stolen Future (1996).

and other aspects of chemical use has improved, much remains to be learned about these questions.

A final question concerns the characteristics of the chemicals themselves. It is estimated that more than 100,000 chemicals have been introduced into commerce since World War II, some in massive quantities. For the vast majority of these chemicals, no risk assessment with respect to their impact on human health and the environment has ever been conducted. That fact provided the impetus for the European Union's REACH, described below.

The following excerpt addresses many of the effects identified above.

OUR STOLEN FUTURE

Theo Colborn, Dianne Dumanoski & John Peterson Myers
91–102 (1996)

But research over the past two decades has given scientists a good understanding of how PCBs travel through ecosystems and migrate over long distances. Based on this knowledge, it is possible to imagine the journey of an individual PCB molecule. Though the specific route and events in the journey we are about to describe are hypothetical, the plot is a plausible scenario built from historical accounts and a myriad of scientific studies.

Our imaginary PCB molecule—a chemical known among scientists as PCB-153 because of the arrangement of its chlorine atoms—had already been around for some time before it set off on its global wanderings just after World War II ended. As the market for PCBs began to grow in the 1930s, the Monsanto Chemical Works expanded production at its plant in Anniston, Alabama, where it heated a mixture of the chemical biphenyl, a particular form of chlorine, and iron filings to create PCBs. During the spring of 1947, the workers at the Anniston factory made up a batch of PCBs containing fifty-four percent chlorine. As the chlorine gas bubbled through the heated biphenyl, six atoms of chlorine bonded to one of the biphenyls in the tank, and PCB-153 came into being. After an alkali wash and some distillation to purify the newly formed PCBs, Monsanto often sold the compound—which contained not only PCB-153 but dozens of other members of the large PCB family—under its brand name Aroclor-1254.

Almost half a century later, the PCBs made on that spring day might be found virtually anywhere imaginable: in the sperm of a man tested at a fertility clinic in upstate New York, in the finest caviar, in the fat of a newborn baby in Michigan, in penguins in Antarctica, in the bluefin tuna served at a sushi bar in Tokyo, in the monsoon rains falling on Calcutta, in the milk of a nursing mother in France, in the blubber of a sperm whale cruising the South Pacific, in a wheel of ripe brie cheese, in a handsome striped bass landed off Martha's Vineyard on a summer weekend. Like most persistent synthetic chemicals, PCBs are world travelers.

Our imaginary molecule of PCB-153 that would end up in a polar bear in the high Arctic might have made its first trip by train. A few weeks after the manufacture of this molecule, the freight train carrying a shipment of Aroclor-1254 rumbled over the rails in New York State headed for a plant in western Massachusetts where General Electric manufactured electrical transformers.

These ubiquitous metal cans attached to electrical poles were an essential component in the growing grid that sent electricity from generating systems over high voltage power lines and into homes to power lights, radios, vacuum cleaners, and refrigerators—the wonderful new twentieth-century electric conveniences. The transformers made at GE's Pittsfield, Massachusetts, plant reduced the high-voltage current from the transmission lines into the lower voltage required by lights and appliances.

From General Electric's perspective, the PCBs were an ideal insulating coolant for their capacitors and for transformers used in situations where flammability was a concern. Because PCBs did not catch fire and burn, they offered a safer alternative to the flammable oil used in transformers before this new synthetic product was developed. The company had developed its own custom formula for transformers called Pyranol, containing Aroclor and oils which it blended at the Pittsfield plant.

With the postwar economic boom, the demand for transformers and other electrical equipment seemed insatiable. America, was building new houses for returning GIs as fast as it could—houses that needed new appliances and increased electrical service. While it would be very difficult to retrace the precise sequence of events that led to the escape of our PCB molecule into the environment, we can imagine that the next step in its journey took place at Pittsfield, and from interviews with a former plant employee and public records, we can reconstruct what might have taken place on a typical summer day. That summer the production line in Pittsfield was working at full tilt, and the Pyranol in the factory storage tanks did not sit around for long. On a steamy day in June, a worker reached for a hose at his workstation that was connected through underground pipes to storage tanks. After making a final check on the transformer he had been finishing, he opened the valve and filled it to the top with Pyranol. In a few days, our molecule of PCB-153, sealed tightly inside that new transformer, was heading back south by train.

The oil refineries in the west Texas city of Big Spring were also scrambling that summer to keep up with the postwar economic boom, for the explosive growth of suburbs was creating a new class of commuters who needed new cars and gasoline to power them. One of the city's smaller oil and chemical companies, now no longer in business, was moving as quickly as possible to build a new refinery complex, but the project had stalled for several months while the contractors awaited the arrival of back-ordered electrical equipment. The shipment of transformers from GE to the refinery finally arrived in July. Within a week, the distribution transformer containing the molecule of PCB-153 was installed and in service in a building that housed the control room for the new installation.

Not even a month had passed before a fierce August thunderstorm tore through Big Spring, filling the air with exploding thunder and leaping lightning that struck at several places during the short, violent storm, including the power lines supplying the refinery. As the power surge hit the transformer near the control room, it responded with a metallic thump and the building went dark.

The following morning, the refinery's maintenance supervisor lifted the cover of the transformer to inspect the damage. Seeing twisted, crumbled coils, he decided that the unit was beyond repair, so he asked one of his men to empty the unit and send it off to the dump. The maintenance worker complied, hauling the transformer to the parking lot. As he tilted the transformer, its oily contents oozed out onto the red dirt of the parking lot, and PCB-153 slipped into the greasy puddle. The worker reckoned the oil might help keep down the insufferable dust. Since PCBs have an affinity for organic matter, the molecule quickly attached itself to a dust particle.

But with the roaring winds of west Texas, dust never stays put long. Four months later, a winter storm roared through and swept the molecule aloft. Stampeding curtains of dust drove toward the town of Tarzan, where they beat against barns and houses as the winds howled. The dust particle with PCB-153 rode the whirlwind, bouncing with the turbulence like a cowboy on a bronco. The wild ride ended when the dust particle sifted through the fine cracks around a doorsill and settled in a drift on the kitchen floor.

When the windstorm passed, the woman of the house surveyed her kitchen with a sigh. The fine red dust coated the windowsills and lay two inches deep before the door. With a weary efficiency, she took up her corn-straw broom and whisked the dust particle with our itinerant molecule into a dustpan. As it fell into the wastebasket, the dust particle sifted down into a crumpled, grease-stained newspaper page that the housewife had used to drain her bacon that morning. By the end of the week, PCB-153 was buried under trash in a local dump, an informal affair in a ravine with a parched creek bed. Despite the rivulets that flowed down through the growing mountain of trash during summer thunderstorms, the molecule stayed put for more than two years, for unlike many chemicals, PCBs don't dissolve readily in water.

The late winter of 1948 brought a spell of heavy rains to west Texas. After intermittent downpours, the creek surged to life in the beginning of March and roared toward the trash that tumbled down the side of the ravine. The roiling waters took a bite out of one edge of the trash mound, exposing a cross section of the town's recent history and sweeping the greasy newspaper and the molecule from the transformer spill downstream. The floodwaters subsided the following morning, leaving the soggy newspaper sheet stranded on a sandbar. Five miles away. PCB-153 was clinging to a greasy blotch on the page, shielded from the light but exposed to warm spring air.

As the sun climbed higher and winter turned to spring, the lump of paper dried and slowly warmed. With the sun beating down on the paper in early April, PCBs suddenly began disengaging from the dust particle moving upward, floating into the air as a vapor. The PCB-153 was suddenly free. The journey that would end in the rump fat of a Norwegian polar bear had begun.

The molecule caught a warm gentle breeze from the southwest, wafting north and east over the shrub-covered expanse of east Texas toward the fragrant pine forests of Arkansas. As the breeze stiffened, it sailed on unimpeded into Missouri. A rising current of spring air pushed it higher into the atmosphere, and the molecule soared upward, higher and higher on the thermal. When the air mass collided with a cold front moving down from the north, the journey ended abruptly. The clouds released their moisture in a hard, cold rain, and PCB-153 washed back to earth and landed on a bluff overlooking the Mississippi River north of St. Louis.

During three weeks of unusually cool and cloudy weather, the molecule clung to a rotting leaf in a hollow on a rocky outcropping, but as soon as the sun reemerged and the temperature climbed, the molecule floated off again. It lingered over St. Louis for several days and sloshed about in a stagnant air mass. Then, as a Bermuda high developed off the southern Atlantic coast, a torrent of air rushed through from the south and swept the PCB molecule northward over the radiant green cornfields of southern Illinois toward the Great Lakes.

The air flow generated by the Bermuda high pushed north with the speed of a freight train. The molecule tumbled onward in a great white bank of cumulus clouds. But as the warm winds rushed through Chicago and out over Lake Michigan, they met a wall of cooler air because the Great Lakes, like any large body of water, warmed more slowly in spring than the surrounding land. In the night chill, the PCB-153 suddenly condensed back into a liquid state for the first time since it had left Missouri.

The breeze died just before midnight and the molecule settled on the dark water near the lakeshore city of Racine, Wisconsin. Like all PCBs, the molecule had a predilection for surfaces, so it lingered about on the boundary between the air and water, bumping now and again into other wandering members of its extended family. The molecule found it hard, however, to remain unattached for very long. Its strong attraction to organic matter drew it to a patch of algae, rootless plants that floated like a gauzy green veil near the water's surface. When the opportunity presented itself, the molecule grabbed on to one of the tiny plants and, clinging to its waxy surface, washed back and forth along the shoreline near the mouth of the Root River, moving with the vagaries of the wind and waves.

Plant-eaters, such as the water flea, nibbled around the edges of the green veil, and some of the plants ended up as their salad course, but the tiny plant PCB-153 was riding managed to escape and live its full life span—which lasted three weeks. The alga began to yellow and grow tattered around the edges. The dead plant grew waterlogged and sank, carrying PCB-153 with it. The dead alga settled on the bottom and was quickly covered by soil washing into the lake from a city dump at the water's edge. Accumulating sediment buried the molecule ever deeper in the lake muds, and with each passing year, its chances of getting back into circulation seemed to grow slimmer. PCB-153 might be impervious to the attack of the bacteria that broke down most chemicals, but it could be entombed.

Persistence is viewed as a virtue in people. In chemicals, it is the mark of a troublemaker. The synthetic chemical industry helped bring convenience and comfort to American homes, but at the same time, it unleashed dozens of chemicals, including PCBs, that became notorious for combining the devilish properties of extreme stability, volatility, and a particular affinity for fat. Besides PCBs, this lot includes the pesticides DDT, chlordane, lindane, aldrin, dieldrin, endrin, toxaphene, heptachlor, and the ubiquitous contaminant dioxin, which is produced in many chemical processes and during the burning of fossil fuels and trash. They ride through the food web on particles of fat or vanish into vapors that gallop on the winds to distant lands. In *Silent Spring*, Rachel Carson put the persistent pesticides at the top of her most-wanted list. It didn't occur to her to include compounds such as PCBs that may not be particularly poisonous (in the usual sense of causing immediate death or cancer) but are persistent—a fact scientists did not recognize until 1966, four years after *Silent Spring* was published.

The members of the PCB family that contain fewer chlorine atoms do have a few enemies, including two bacteria from the Achromobacter genus. But chlorine heavies like PCB-153 are impervious to almost everything save ultraviolet B radiation from the sun. Because of the way

PCBs move through the environment, hidden in soil, sediments, animal tissue, and other places, these deadly rays only rarely encounter them. With the prosperity that followed the end of World War II, the lakefront in Racine began to change. For half a century, the gas plant with its huge black storage cylinders and mountains of coal had loomed over central Racine and the lakefront. With the arrival in Wisconsin of a long-planned natural gas pipeline from the southwest in 1949, the old facility that made cooking and heating gas from coal became history.

A few years later, Racine took its first step toward reclaiming its lakefront for pleasure-a vision that it would not fully realize until the 1980s. Nevertheless, the city's first waterfront park was, indeed, a significant beginning, since the plans called for converting the now-abandoned city dump into a twenty-seven-acre recreation area with trees, grassy playing fields, a boat ramp, and a scenic shore drive. . . .

During the construction of [the park], which commenced in 1954, the work crews began to fashion the new shore where the scenic drive would run. Dump trucks laden with huge chunks of rock moved back and forth in a grumbling caravan to the water's edge. Load after load of stones tumbled into water. On a spring day in 1956, a monstrous rock came hurtling down into the stretch of sediment where the PCB-153 lay buried. As the shock rippled through the buried mud, the molecule sprang free in a burst of hydrogen sulfide gas that filled the water with bubbles. The molecule rode one of the tiny glistening spheres upward toward the light and air.

Within hours, the PCB-153 was lodged in the fat of a water flea that had gobbled it up while grazing along the surface. This was a fat-loving molecule's dream, a ticket to ride, and it would take PCB-153 to the top of the food chain.

The water flea acted like a filter, sifting tiny plants and the PCBs clinging to them out of the water while it fed, so as the days passed more and more PCBs accumulated in the body fat of the tiny animal. Less persistent contaminants do not build up in this way because animals can break them down into water-soluble substances and excrete them. Many PCBs, on the other hand, resist breakdown, and once ingested, they are drawn by their chemical structure to the animal's fat, where they remain indefinitely. Over its short ten-day life, the flea's PCB concentrations grew to four hundred times the levels in the water. When it was finally eaten by a small shrimp called a mysid, the water flea passed on this legacy of fat-loving persistent chemicals to its predator, and the PCB-153 moved a rung higher on the Lake Michigan food web.

In its life, the mysid would eat hundreds of water fleas and inherit a bundle of persistent chemicals with each bite. The PCBs riding in its fat, like PCB-153, found themselves in growing company that included not only their own chemical family but other persistent compounds as well, such as DDT and toxaphene, a pesticide used heavily then in cotton fields in the South. For a time, agricultural specialists thought toxaphene was an improvement over DDT because it disappeared quickly from the fields where it was sprayed. It was some time before anybody realized that it did not disappear at all; it vaporized and moved on. Much of it came sailing on the winds to the Great Lakes.

The mysid eventually became a meal for a smelt—a small, tasty fish that darts about in offshore waters in flashing silver schools. As the smelt gorged on mysids and other smaller critters, the persistent chemical concentrations multiplied seventeen more times. Smelt were a particular favorite with the families that crowded into local eateries in Racine for the Friday-night fish fry, and over time, their body fat would also bear witness to the nights when they had popped down dozens of the succulent little fish with a side order of potato pancakes or dined grandly on lake trout or coho salmon.

The smelt containing our PCB-153 molecule cruised Lake Michigan for two years before it was ambushed by a lake trout. Now the molecule moved to the trout and rested in its fat for another five years until an angler hooked the trophy-size fish on the last day of vacation at a family cottage in Door County, Wisconsin.

The following morning, the trout, packed on ice in a cooler in the back of a station wagon, was heading eastward on the interstate toward upstate New York. The molecule was moving into new territory on this imaginary journey. The fisherman could hardly wait to get home and show off the catch of a lifetime to fishing buddies. His mouth watered at the thought of a truly memorable fish dinner with his family.

Three days later, however, the fish ended up in the family's trash barrel rather than on a platter at the dinner table. At the height of an August heat wave, the station wagon had broken down, leaving the family stranded at a gas station in rural Michigan without transportation and without ice for the cooler. When the family reached home and opened the cooler, the fish smelled like old cat food.

A blizzard of gulls swirled around the trash collection truck when it arrived at a landfill outside Rochester. As the rank fish carrying the molecule tumbled onto the growing trash mountain, the gulls dove at it like shoppers at a half-price sale, squawking and jostling each other to grab a bite. In a matter of minutes, they had picked the carcass clean.

PCB-153 wound up in the fat of a female gull, which had spent more than a dozen years feeding on the fish in Lake Ontario, so the molecule simply added to her already substantial store of contaminants. In the Great Lakes food chain, the herring gulls occupy a spot just below the bald eagles, which sometimes nab a herring gull or two. By the time PCBs have moved this high on the food chain, the concentrations have multiplied to 25 million times the levels found in the water.

The following spring, the female herring gull headed for Scotch Bonnet Island, roughly one hundred miles east of Toronto on the Canadian shore of Lake Ontario. The gull and her mate quickly set their stake on a good patch of sand in the middle of the gull colony, a location considered preferable to the edges, where the chicks might be more vulnerable to predators. The pair courted and mated. Afterward, the female scraped a hollow in the sand and laid two large lightly speckled eggs that she dutifully set about incubating.

A tiny beak broke through one shell six weeks later, but the chick could only muster feeble peeks and it died, seemingly from exhaustion. The other egg showed no signs of life at all, but the pair stayed on the nest for another week. The mother finally abandoned the nest without fledging a single offspring.

PCB-153 and its relatives had passed from the mother gull into the yolk of the lifeless egg and had contributed to its death, along with DDT, dioxin, and other contaminants. A skunk carted off the rotting egg five days later but then thought better of eating it and dropped it on a rock near the shore, where it smashed. Some of the yolk spattered into the water, and PCB-153 was off on another trip up the food chain, this time via a crayfish—a small bottom-feeding scavenger that vacuumed up the bits of fatty yolk sloshing in the shallows near shore.

Before long, the crayfish that had dined on the egg yolk became dinner for one of the American eels that hunted at night in the weedy shallows. The eel is something of a contrarian when it comes to spawning. Many species, such as salmon and herring, spend their maturity at sea and then return upriver to their birthplace to spawn. American eels, on the other hand, frequent freshwater rivers and lakes most of their lives before finally making a long pilgrimage out to the Sargasso Sea—an area in the Atlantic Ocean between the West Indies and the Azores—to spawn before dying. Curiously, the eels migrating from the Great Lakes and other northern waters are all female, while those migrating from southern rivers tend to be males.

With the approach of summer, the oldest eels in Lake Ontario, including the sixteen-year-old animal carrying the PCB-153 molecule, began to undergo changes that signal sexual maturity and preparation for the three-thousand-mile journey to the spawning ground. Their gray green backs began to darken toward silvery black, their yellow bellies whitened, and their eyes enlarged and changed to allow better vision in deeper ocean waters. Restless with the migratory urge, groups of silver eels moved toward the entrance to the St. Lawrence River waiting apparently for some sign that the time was right. Then on a stormy night when rain poured in dense silver sheets out of a black sky, a slithering multitude suddenly departed down the great river toward the North Atlantic. The eel carrying PCB-153 swam onward for more than six months with a mystifying urgency before finally reaching the floating rafts of Sargasso seaweed that give this region of warm, salty waters its name. There beneath the clear tropical waters east of the Bahamas and south of Bermuda, a roiling congregation of eels, gathered from the Gulf Coast to Newfoundland, spawned and then expired from exhaustion— their long journey ended, their compelling mission accomplished.

The eel's flesh disintegrated quickly in the warm tropical waters, and PCB-153 sloughed off in a shred of fat that floated up to the surface of the Sargasso Sea under the intense tropical sun. In the heat, the molecule suddenly vaporized once more and, carried on prevailing winds, began hopscotching north. At any cold spot it encountered, the molecule condensed and settled on any available surface, only to be off again as soon as the summer sun warmed the surface. Alternating between liquid and gas, it rode the winds farther and farther north. The waters grew colder, making it increasingly difficult for the molecule to become airborne. Instead it hitchhiked on one of the small floating plants at the bottom of the North Atlantic food web, sweeping into the Gulf Stream and from then on north and east toward Iceland.

Two hundred miles east of Iceland, a small shrimplike creature called a copepod finally nabbed the plant and PCB-153 as it filtered a meal out of the rich waters of the North Atlantic. Five days later, a cloud of copepods was swept into a swift current that carried it quickly north and east like a giant conveyer belt toward the edge of the solid pack ice in the Greenland Sea, where a large school of Arctic cod had gathered to feast on the incoming bounty.

The gray green water boiled with the feeding cod, one of the most abundant species in high Arctic waters. As one of the small fish digested its stomachful of copepods, PCB-153 migrated to the fatty tissue near its tail, which already had a considerable store of persistent chemicals. The Arctic food web, which includes the cod, is quite simple, but it includes many long-lived animals that accumulate significant amounts of contamination over a lifetime. For this reason, the Arctic food web concentrates and magnifies persistent chemicals to an even greater degree than that of the Great Lakes. Though far from a top predator, this cod carried PCBs at 48 million times the concentration found in the surrounding waters. Even so, the cod are still less contaminated than Great Lakes salmon because the ocean waters they inhabit are far cleaner.

Arctic cod spend the greater part of their lives feeding beneath the solid vault of ice that closes over high Arctic waters for most of the year. That season, the cod carrying PCB-153 followed the shifting food supply, and on the trail of a particularly abundant crop of copepods, it gradually swam toward the eastern part of the Greenland Sea. During the icebound period, ringed seals depend exclusively upon the schools of cod that wander beneath the ice.

It was only a matter of time before the cod carrying PCB-153 became a meal for a hungry adolescent seal that shot through the water, propelled by its powerful hind flippers. Like many seals searching for food, the youngster had wandered along a fracture in the sea ice west of the Svalbard Islands. The hunting had been good that winter, and the seal had added significantly to its ample blubber, which, despite its short life, contained not only PCB-153 but a high concentration of chlordane, DDT, toxaphene, and other persistent chemicals that were wending their way to the Arctic from all over the world. A seal eats hundreds of fish, ingesting and storing all the PCBs that had accumulated in them. For this reason, the PCB levels in the seals are eight times greater than in the cod, or 384 million times the concentrations in the ocean water. [A while later, the seal was caught and eaten by a polar bear, whose PCB levels are even higher, on the order of one billion times the concentration in the ocean water.]

NOTES AND QUESTIONS

Local or global threat. On the basis of the preceding except, does it matter where a persistent organic pollutant is emitted in terms of its effect on health and the environment in a particular place? POPs have been associated with significant environmental impact in a wide range of species and at virtually all trophic levels. Locally, short-term exposure to high concentrations of certain POPs has been shown to result in illness and death. As described in the excerpt from *Our Stolen Future*, POPs can also travel great distances around the globe and through the atmosphere due to their ability to volatize and evaporate, until they ultimately gather in colder climates. This cycle of long-range air transport and deposition is known as the "grasshopper effect." *See* World Bank, Persistent Organic Pollutants—Backyards to Borders (2009).

The following excerpt discusses some of the pathways by which exposure to hazardous chemicals occurs.

INTERNATIONAL COOPERATION TO ADDRESS RISKS FROM PESTICIDES AND HAZARDOUS CHEMICALS

Peter Lallas & Steve Wolfson
unpublished (1997)

B. SOURCES AND ROUTES OF EXPOSURE

. . . The probability of exposure to harmful levels of pesticides and dangerous chemicals varies with each chemical and with each stage of the life-cycle of the product or substance. The discussion below reviews several different sources and routes of exposure, and some of the consequences of these exposures, in both developed and developing countries.

Transport of these substances can occur through air or by water, and often is helped along by human action such as transport, trade in dangerous or contaminated products (e.g., foods with pesticide residues), dredging of contaminated areas, and disposal activities. This long-range transport can occur as a result of a release in any of the life-cycle stages described below.

1.   ACCIDENTS AND UNINTENDED RELEASES (ALL STAGES OF LIFE-CYCLE)

The adage "accidents will happen" certainly is true in the case of pesticides and dangerous chemicals. Some of the most serious incidents associated with these products result from accidents—whether in manufacture, handling/transport, use, or disposal.

The Bhopal disaster [in 1984], involving a U.S.-controlled pesticide formulation facility in India, illustrates the extreme consequences of accidents involving dangerous pesticides. A number of other well-known incidents have captures headlines in recent years. These include:

- the 1986 fire at a chemical warehouse in Basel, Switzerland that sent toxic fumes into France and Germany and released toxic chemicals into the Rhine river, damaging riverine ecosystems and polluting water supplies downstream;

- the 1990 pesticide spill from a train into the Sacramento River in California, illustrating the potential risks during transport; and

- the poisoning of 20,000 Swainson's Hawks, about five percent of the world's population, in the Argentine pampas in 1995, linked to the application of the pesticide monocrotophos.

Concerns over the possibility of accidental releases are magnified by data indicating that production, transport and use of many pesticides and dangerous chemicals continue to rise. In the case of pesticides, EPA estimates that about 4 billion pounds of pesticide (by volume of active ingredient) are produced annually worldwide. The U.S. produces about 1 billion pounds, while other countries produce 3 billion pounds. More than 1400 active ingredients in over 60,000 formulations are in use around the world.

The production figures are even higher with respect to chemicals more broadly. As of 1990, there were more than eight million known chemicals. Approximately 70,000 of these are in common use, and as many as 1,000 new chemicals may come onto the market each year.

The data show a large increase in recent years in the volume of manufacturing of pesticides, for example, in developing countries such as India and China and certain countries in South America. Some of these new production facilities are owned by multinational companies. . . . At the same time, locally-owned production of pesticides in developing countries has grown in response to lively and profitable markets, including export markets.

Absent improved safety practices, increases in production, transport, storage, and use may translate into more accidental releases and more adverse impacts, both to humans and the environment.

2.   EXTRACTION OF MINERALS: MINING

In some cases, dangerous substances are released at the first stage in the life-cycle of many products or substances: i.e., the extraction of raw materials. Most notable in this regard, perhaps, is mining for heavy metals, such as lead, silver, cadmium, zinc and others. Many countries throughout the world have active mine operations. In the case of many developing countries, these mines often are operated by large foreign companies (e.g., U.S., Canadian, Australian).

The mining process is a potential source of release of heavy metals or pollutants into the environment. Rain or floodwaters can quickly carry contaminant-laden tailings from mining operations into lakes or other waterways. Because these contaminants tend to be heavy and persistent, they often collect in sediments at the bottom of waterways. They can pose a risk to fish and birds that feed in contaminated areas, as well as to drinking water supplies. For many developing countries, mining can be a greater source of pollution than manufacturing or processing.

3.   PRODUCTION AND PROCESSING ACTIVITIES

[Another] potential source of release of pesticides or hazardous substances comes during the production or formulation process.

A recent study of hazards in the workplace in Canada, for example, identifies a number of serious workplace health concerns posed by chemicals. . . . As with accidents, these occupational risks seem likely only to rise as rates of manufacture and use rise also.

Other data documents the serious occupational hazards posed by the use of lead in production activities. . . .

Manufacturing operations also release a wide range of chemicals directly into the environment outside the workplace. A particularly important concern in this regard is the release of dioxins and furans as unintended by-products of certain industrial operations. Operations which release these two substances as by-products include hazardous, industrial, medical and sewage sludge incineration, municipal waste combustion, combustion of fossil fuels and organic materials containing chlorine, certain metals recovery processes, pulp and paper production, and others.

More generally, according to data gathered by the U.S. Environmental Protection Agency as part of its Toxic Release Inventory, there were more than 3000 toxic materials totaling approximately 2.2 million metric tons released by industrial activity in the U.S. in 1990. . . . While data for other countries is not readily available, recent figures indicate that Japan has larger emissions of heavy-metals than the U.S., and that China and India have larger estimated emissions than several countries of the OECD.

4.   HANDLING AND USE (INCLUDING SPECIAL RISKS FOR FARMERS)

Pesticides, in particular, are released into contact with people and the environment at the stage of handling and use. Farmers who handle and use pesticides face particularly high risks of harmful exposures. Recent data cited by the World Resources Institute, in collaboration with the United Nations Development Programme (UNDP), indicates that pesticide poisoning "is disconcertingly common in developing nations, representing a major occupational hazard for farmers and their families." Harmful exposures also occur in developed countries; however, the extent of harm appears to be much higher in developing countries. A 1990 study of the World Health Organization estimated that as many as 25 million workers in developing countries, or three percent of the entire agricultural workforce, suffer occupational pesticide poisoning each year. . . .

Pesticides extend their sphere of influence well beyond farmworkers to a much larger population. Studies in developing countries, in particular, indicate dangerously high levels of contamination in fish and on locally grown vegetables. Pesticide run-off from farming operations can pollute waterways, affecting aquatic life, birds and drinking water supplies.

The use or handling of certain other products or substances, besides pesticides, also can create serious risks of exposure and harm. Thus is true, for example, of products containing lead, asbestos, phosphates and other harmful substances.

5.   RISKS FROM UNSAFE STORAGE AND DISPOSAL

Releases also occur at the stage of storage and disposal of products or substances. An important example of this is the case of obsolete pesticides stocks. In Kenya, for example obsolete pesticide stocks total approximately 100 million tons and are left over from previous locust control campaigns. More generally, the [Food and Agriculture Organization] recently identified more than 7 million kilograms of unusable and outdated pesticides in thirty-five countries in need of safe disposal. In many cases, the containers are corroded, leaking or unlabelled.

The problem also applies to developed countries. In the U.S., for example, dangerous discarded chemicals and pesticides are found in a number of hazardous waste sites around the country.

C. THE CIRCLE OF POISON

In recent years, special attention has been given to one particular pathway for risks from pesticides; the so-called "circle of poison." This refers to the phenomenon where domestically prohibited pesticides which are exported can return in the form of dangerous residues on food items grown in other countries and imported for domestic consumption. Some have suggested this concern as a rationale for banning the export of domestically prohibited pesticides.

The extent to which such a risk exists is subject to debate. Under the Federal Food, Drug and Cosmetic Act (FFDCA), [the Environmental Protection Agency] sets, and the Food and Drug Administration (FDA) enforces, tolerance levels for the amount of residues of specific pesticides permitted on various food items imported for domestic consumption. If a pesticide is prohibited domestically on the basis of health risks to those who consumer treated food items, the tolerance for that pesticide can be revoked. Thus imports of food items with residues of such domestically prohibited pesticides would be subject to enforcement action by FDA, which monitors pesticide residues on food imports.

To the extent that exported pesticides do end up as residues on products that then move into international markets, approaches other than export controls could be employed. For example, . . . improved monitoring might be a more effective means of addressing any such problem than bans by individual countries on export of domestically prohibited pesticides. One reason for this is that even where unilateral export bans exist, food producers in other countries could obtain many domestically banned pesticides from producers in countries other than the U.S. This latter concern could be addressed at least in part, however, by "internationalizing" the bans so that other sources of supply would be similarly closed off.

. . . Perhaps a stronger basis for concern about exports is the evidence concerning the potential for exported pesticides to adversely affect health or the environment in other countries where they are used. . . .

Other types of transboundary impacts and concerns also can result from the production, transport, trade, use and disposal of pesticides or chemicals. Indeed, the discharge of chemicals used in production activities into international waterways or airsheds, whether by accident or not, has created a large number of bilateral or regional environmental issues and problems.

D.   REGULATORY SAFEGUARDS IN DEVELOPING COUNTRIES

Third World importers have no way to effectively control trade in chemicals that have been banned or severely restricted in exporting countries.

The effects of pesticides and hazardous chemicals are felt in all countries where they are available (and beyond). The degree of impact, however, varies significantly according to a variety of factors. One major factor is the level of law, regulation and implementation capacity within an individual country where these products are available and used.

The nature and degree of regulatory control over pesticides and hazardous chemicals in developing countries varies significantly, as does the level of resources available for implementation and enforcement. In many cases developing countries have not yet developed rigorous controls and procedures to guard against the risks of these products, and/or do not have the resources to implement such controls. In some cases, regulatory systems are virtually non-existent. . . .

Many developing countries have not implemented systems to generate and analyze the information needed to assess the relative dangers of a particular pesticide or chemical. As noted by UNEP:

> It is not just a question of numbers. In most cases the problem is of information: how to get it, how to spread it, and how to make sure it is used properly. The greatest obstacle to our safe use and disposal of chemicals is ignorance.

. . . The lack of regulatory infrastructure is accompanied by poor handling and storage practices, and high-risk use techniques. Risks during transport, for example, are heightened in many developing countries by improper or merely careless storage and handling and improper labeling and packaging.

For example, labels that should contain warnings and directions for safe use may not contain complete information, or may not be read or understood by the workers who handle the pesticides. Workers often fail to wear protective clothing to minimize exposure in the handling and application of pesticides, even though many pesticides readily are absorbed through the skin or the lungs, particularly in the humid and hot conditions of the tropics. Extremely dangerous situations arise due to handling by careless, illiterate workers, distribution of pesticides in inadequately protective containers, such as empty beverage bottles where they might be mistaken for a soft-drink, application by users unfamiliar with the necessary protective procedures in the mixing and application process, and inadequate warnings to people who live in areas here pesticides are applied.

Many pesticide operators do not have access to running water and are unable to clean up after application, resulting in pesticide-contaminated clothing entering the home. Households often store drinking water and food in "recycled" pesticide containers. Many developing countries also lack the infrastructure (medical and otherwise) to respond to pesticide poisonings.

Accordingly, while health and environmental problems from pesticides and dangerous chemicals also arise in developed countries, they often pale in comparison to problems facing those developing countries that have not yet developed rigorous controls and procedures to guard against the risks of these products.

NOTES AND QUESTIONS

Agriculture, food, and the environment. The regulation of pesticides, fungicide, and herbicide exposure through agricultural methods and food consumption is explored in more detail in Chapter 14. Does the context of toxics exposure through food raise unique considerations beyond traditional environmental considerations?

2. INTERNATIONAL INITIATIVES

For some harmful chemicals or harmful uses of chemicals, less harmful alternatives exist. The international community, societies and individuals have already taken some steps to control the use of harmful chemicals. For example, leaded gasoline is banned in most countries because of the developmental and other health risks, especially to children, of lead; and there is a movement towards integrated pest management (IPM) to reduce the use of pesticides, herbicides, and fungicides in agriculture. (More about the international framework addressing pesticides, herbicides, and fungicides is presented in Chapter 14.) In addition, international efforts are underway at the global, regional and bilateral levels to confront risks from hazardous chemicals cooperatively and to increase our understanding of them. Much remains to be accomplished.

The following materials address international activities with respect to some important hazardous chemicals risks.

a. UNEP's Montevideo Programme

Beginning in the 1980s, the United Nations Environment Programme (UNEP) has conducted an ambitious priority-setting exercise with respect to needed developments in environmental law for the next decade. These are referred to collectively as the Montevideo Programme, because the first blueprint was finalized in Montevideo, Uruguay. The Montevideo Programme for each decade is approved by the UNEP governing body, with input from governments, international legal experts, and other stakeholders; and it holds a mid-term review to evaluate progress and identify gaps. The Programme is widely acclaimed and has done much to galvanize action with respect to environmental law.

Protection from trade in hazardous wastes and chemicals has been emphasized in each of the four Montevideo Programmes. Montevideo Programme I (for the 1980s) identified the transport, handling and disposal of toxic and dangerous wastes as one of three major focus areas, and also called for action with respect to international trade in potentially harmful chemicals (parts I.2(a) and (b); part II.A.1.(c) and II.(e)). Montevideo Programme II (for the 1990s) included focusing on risks from hazardous wastes (part L) and international trade in potentially harmful chemicals (part M). Montevideo Programme III (for the first decade of the 21st century) included "Pollution prevention and control; waste management" in part 15; and it emphasized effective implementation of multilateral environmental agreements in the field of chemicals, including the Rotterdam Convention for the Application of Prior Informed Consent Procedure for Certain Hazardous Chemicals and Pesticides in International Trade (discussed below) and completion of negotiations on persistent organic pollutants (also discussed below) (paragraph 15(f)). Montevideo Programme IV (for the second decade of the 21st century) included supporting the development of sustainable production and consumption patterns, including those that minimize waste (Part II.F), analyzing linkages between climate change and areas of law relating to, among other areas, waste (Part III.A(c)), and "Support[ing] the effective development of national laws and policies that encourage integrated pollution prevention and control, waste minimization, the 3Rs (reduce, reuse, recycle) and the environmentally sound and safe management of chemicals and wastes, and assist developing countries, in particular the least developed among them, and countries with economies in transition, to achieve this objective"(Part III.F(j)).

b.   Agenda 21

Agenda 21 is one of the five instruments adopted at the 1992 U.N. Conference on Environment and Development (UNCED, or the Earth Summit) in Rio de Janeiro, Brazil. It is a comprehensive global plan of action for the implementation of sustainable development, and identifies the environmentally sound management of hazardous chemicals as a prominent issue. Chapter 19 of Agenda 21, "Environmentally sound management of toxic chemicals, including prevention of illegal international traffic in toxic and dangerous products," identifies six program areas to strengthen both domestic and international efforts needed to achieve an environmentally sound management of chemicals.

These program areas are: (a) expanding and accelerating international assessment of chemical risks; (b) harmonization of classification and labeling of chemicals; (c) information exchange on toxic chemicals and chemical risks; (d) establishment of risk reduction programs; (e) strengthening of domestic capabilities and capacities for management of chemicals; and (f) prevention of illegal international traffic in toxic and dangerous products. Agenda 21 calls for improved coordination and enhanced cooperation among international chemical safety activities and for the establishment of an international mechanism for chemical risk assessment and management.

c. Intergovernmental Forum on Chemical Safety (IFCS)

The Intergovernmental Forum on Chemical Safety (IFCS) was established in response to Agenda 21's call for an intergovernmental mechanism regarding chemicals. At its first meeting in 1994, at the International Conference on Chemical Safety, the Conference adopted the Terms of Reference for the IFCS, establishing the IFCS as a mechanism for cooperation among governments, intergovernmental organizations and nongovernmental organizations for the promotion of chemical risk assessment and the environmentally sound management of chemicals. The Conference also recommended priorities for action, and took steps to provide for necessary administrative and financial arrangements. The IFCS's scope included all questions related to chemical risks, and it addressed linkages not only with Chapter 19 of Agenda 21, but also other areas such as hazardous waste and human health. The IFCS met at intervals of approximately three years.

According to its website (http://www.who.int/ifcs/page2/en/index. html), "IFCS is a flexible, open and transparent brainstorming and bridge-building forum. It is a broad consensus-building mechanism that serves as a facilitator and advocate aiming to bring order to global actions taken in the interest of global chemical safety. It functions as an accountability mechanism for its participants. The IFCS provides countries the opportunity to place issues on the international agenda and emphasize special needs and concerns with respect to improving chemicals management. All participants, including developing countries and NGOs, find it a useful mechanism to bring emerging and contentious issues to the international agenda."

The 2002 World Summit on Sustainable Development (WSSD) Plan of Implementation cited the Bahia Declaration on Chemical Safety (http://www.who.int/ifcs/documents/forums/forum3/en/Bahia.pdf) and IFCS Priorities for Action as the basis for development of a strategic approach to international chemicals management (SAICM). This was later endorsed by UNEP's Governing Council/Global Environmental Ministerial Forum. At its fourth session (2003), the IFCS reviewed its progress and discussed further development of the SAICM. The outcome of these deliberations was presented to the first meeting of the Preparatory Committee for the development of a SAICM, which took place immediately after (in Bangkok). For further discussion, see the discussion on SAICM/ICCM below. The IFCS has been phased out.

d. Prior Informed Consent (PIC) and the Rotterdam Convention

Prior informed consent (PIC) is playing an increasingly important role in dealing with international environmental and social issues. We encountered PIC in the context of controlling international trade in hazardous wastes (the Basel Convention) earlier in this chapter. The materials immediately following this paragraph discuss PIC in the context of controlling trade in hazardous chemicals (the PIC Convention). A variant of PIC, referred to as Advanced Informed Agreement, is used in the Cartagena Protocol on Biosafety (a protocol to the Convention on Biological Diversity) to control trade in living modified organisms (which are genetically engineered organisms). On 29 October 2010, the Nagoya Protocol on Access to Genetic Resources and the Fair and Equitable Sharing of Benefits Arising from their Utilization (ABS) to the Convention on Biological Diversity was adopted (http://www.cbd.int/abs/text/default.shtml). Article 6 of the Protocol states that "In accordance with domestic law, each Party shall take measures, as appropriate, with the aim of ensuring that the prior informed consent or approval and involvement of indigenous and local communities is obtained for access to genetic resources where they have the established right to grant access to such resources." As of February 2015, the Nagoya Protocol has not yet entered into force. In 2009, a committee of the World Intellectual Property Organization—the Intergovernmental Committee on Intellectual Property and Genetic Resources, Traditional Knowledge and Folklore—agreed to develop an international legal instrument (or instruments) that would give traditional knowledge, genetic resources and traditional cultural expressions effective protection, with mechanisms of compliance with the Cartagena Protocol provisions of prior informed consent under discussion. The World Bank policies currently include a variant of PIC, referred to as Broad Community Support, in connection with approval of projects that affect indigenous and other local communities. Finally, in the field of human rights, the implementation of community-based property rights (i.e., the idea that indigenous or other local communities dependent on a natural resource have a right to participate in decisions about those resources and also a substantive right in those resources), involves PIC. In the context of indigenous peoples, PIC is referred to as Free, Prior and Informed Consent, or FPIC.)

The Rotterdam Convention for the Application of the Prior Informed Consent Procedure for Certain Hazardous Chemicals and Pesticides in International Trade (referred to as the Rotterdam Convention or the PIC

Convention), finalized in 1998, builds upon UNEP's nonbinding Amendment London Guidelines for the Exchange of Information and Chemicals in International Trade of UNEP and the FAO's International Code of Conduct on the Distribution and the Use of Pesticides, which is also nonbinding.

Article 1 of the PIC Convention provides that the objective of the agreement is "to promote shared responsibility and cooperative efforts among Parties in the international trade of certain hazardous chemicals . . . by facilitating information exchange about their characteristics, by providing for a national decision-making process on their import and export and by disseminating these decisions to Parties." The Convention also applies to banned or severely restricted chemicals and to hazardous pesticide formulations.

The Convention covers those chemicals that were already listed as part of the voluntary procedures preceding the treaty. As of February 2015, the Prior Informed Consent (PIC) list under the Convention included 14 industrial chemicals and 29 pesticides that are banned or severely restricted. It also included four pesticides categorized as "severely hazardous pesticides formulations." Under the Convention, States are to notify the Convention's secretariat of final regulatory actions regarding those chemicals that are banned or severely restricted for use in its territory, and the secretariat in turn notifies the parties. The Parties decide whether to list the chemical in Annex III. All Parties have to consent to the import of Annex III chemicals. Countries wishing to export chemicals banned or severely restricted by the territory of the exporting country, but not yet listed on Annex III, must notify the country of import and provide specific information, including safety data, with the export. No reservations to the agreement are permitted. On 4 July 2012, the European Union adopted Regulation (EU) 649/2012, which implements, within the European Union, the PIC Convention on prior informed consent procedure for certain hazardous chemicals and pesticides in international trade.

NOTES AND QUESTIONS

1. *Silence as acceptance?* In a prior informed consent system, should consent have to be express, or should silence on the part of the importing State be deemed to be consent? Should the answer depend on whether the importing State is a developing country or not? In the Basel Convention, does consent have to be express? Compare the bilateral agreement on hazardous waste between the United States and Canada (silence is acceptance) with that between the United States and Mexico (silence is not acceptance). Why might these agreements differ?

2. *Domestically prohibited goods*. Why is prior informed consent not required for the export of all chemicals that have been banned or severely restricted for use within the territory of the exporting country?

3. *Effectiveness*. What problems do you foresee in making the PIC Convention effective? Suppose you are exporting a banned chemical or pesticide to another country and want to be sure that the farmer who applies the pesticide knows of the dangers in its use. Would a legal obligation of the exporting country to notify the importing country be sufficient? What additional measures might be taken?

e.   Persistent Organic Pollutants (POPs)

Persistent organic pollutants (POPs) are organic chemicals that remain intact in the environment for long periods of time, become widely distributed geographically, accumulate in the tissue of living organisms, and are toxic to humans and wildlife. Some POPs are intentionally produced (e.g., DDT); others are unintended byproducts (e.g., dioxin). As illustrated by the excerpt from *Our Stolen Future*, above, POPs circulate globally and can cause damage wherever they travel.

i.   Stockholm Convention

The Stockholm Convention on Persistent Organic Pollutants is a global treaty to protect human health and the environment from POPs (adopted May 2001 at Stockholm). As of February 2015, there are 152 signatories (including the United States) and 179 Parties (not including the United States). The Convention entered into force on 17 May 2004, after the 50th ratification. In implementing the Convention, governments are to take measures to eliminate or reduce the release of POPs into the environment. *See* http://www.pops.int/.

The Stockholm Convention seeks the elimination or restriction of production and use of all intentionally produced POPs (e.g., industrial chemicals and pesticides). It also seeks the continuing minimization and, where feasible, ultimate elimination of releases of unintentionally produced POPs such as dioxins and furans. Stockpiles must be managed and disposed of in a safe, efficient, and environmentally sound manner. The Convention also imposes certain trade restrictions.

The 12 chemicals covered by the Stockholm Convention (the so-called Dirty Dozen) are the pesticides aldrin, chlordane, DDT, dieldrin, endrin, heptachlor, hexachlorobenzene (HCB), mires and toxaphene, as well as the industrial chemical polychlorinated biphenyls (PCBs), and the unintentionally produced dioxin and furan. The Convention provides a mechanism for adding POPs to its coverage, and under this mechanism, 12 POPs have been added as of February 2015.

The Convention takes a chemical-specific approach. For example, continued use of the pesticide DDT is allowed for disease vector control until safe, affordable and effective alternatives are in place. Similarly, countries must make determined efforts to identify, label and remove PCB-containing equipment from use by 2025. The Convention also seeks the continuing minimization and, where feasible, elimination of the releases of unintentionally produced POPs such as the industrial by-products dioxins and furans.

ii. Requirements of the Stockholm Convention

1. *Existing chemicals.* Article 4.4 requires Parties with regulatory and assessment schemes to take into consideration the POPs screening criteria set out in Annex D of the Convention when assessing pesticides or industrial chemicals currently in use. Article 3 states that Parties must eliminate from production and use certain of the chemicals listed in the convention.

2. *New chemicals.* Article 4.2 requires Parties with regulatory and assessment schemes to regulate with the aim of preventing the production and use of new pesticides or new industrial chemicals which exhibit the characteristics of POPs.

3. *Import/export controls.* Article 3.2 restricts the import and export of POPs to cases where, for example, the purpose is environmentally sound disposal. It also requires that POPs not be transported across international boundaries without taking into account relevant international rules, standards, and guidelines (Article 6.1).

4. *Waste management.* Article 6 obliges Parties to develop strategies for identifying POPs wastes, and to manage these in an environmentally sound manner. The POPs content of wastes is generally to be destroyed or irreversibly transformed. The Basel Convention Technical Working Group has developed technical guidelines on POPs wastes as part of its work program and at the request of the Conference that adopted the Stockholm Convention. *See* http://www.basel.int/Portals/4/Basel%20Convention/docs/pub/techguid/tg-POPs.pdf.

5. *Environmental releases.* The Convention requires Parties to take measures to reduce or eliminate releases of POPs from intentional production and use (Article 3), unintentional production (Article 5) and stockpiles and wastes (Article 6). A Conference of the Parties (COP) (SC-3/5) adopted draft guidelines on Best Available Techniques (BAT) and Best Environmental Practices (BEP).

6. *Hazard communication.* Provision is made for the obligatory communication of hazard information under Article 10.

7. *Replacement.* The Convention requires information exchange and research on POPs alternatives (Articles 9 and 11). It obliges each Party using DDT to develop an Action plan, including for implementation of alternative products (Annex B). *See* http://www.pops.int/documents/background/ hcwc.pdf.

The Stockholm Convention also provided for the establishment, by the Conference of the Parties, of a subsidiary body called the Persistent Organic Pollutants Review Committee (POPRC—pronounced "poprock"). This committee assesses chemicals that have been proposed for addition to the Convention and makes recommendations to the COP. The first meeting of the POPRC took place in Geneva on 7–11 November 2005. The Committee decided that all five chemicals it was considering for inclusion in the Convention fulfilled the screening criteria in Annex D of the Convention. Subsequently, the Committee has determined that a number of other chemicals fulfill the screening criteria as well. As of February 2015, the Committee has developed risk profiles for nine chemicals. *See* http://www.pops.int/documents/meetings/poprc/chem_review.htm.

The Convention also addresses the need for technical assistance regarding developing countries. In Article 12, the Convention provides for regional centers for training and technology transfer. Article 13 and 14 envisage a "financial mechanism" to be operated by the Global Environment Facility (GEF) on an interim basis. "Enabling activities" such as the development of National Implementation Plans are a key initial GEF focus. *See* http://www.pops.int/documents/background/hcwc. pdf.

iii. Regional and Bilateral Approaches

Several regional and bilateral approaches to managing POPs exist. Some examples follow. The North American Agreement on Environmental Cooperation (NAAEC), signed in January 1994, provided the overall framework for Canada, Mexico, and the United States to cooperate on a wide range of environmental issues in the North American Regions. The Agreement was negotiated as a parallel side agreement to the North American Agreement on Free Trade (NAFTA). The NAAEC established the North American Commission for Environmental Cooperation (CEC). The CEC provided the mechanism for these countries to cooperate with respect to the Sound Management of Chemicals (SMOC), which was agreed to on October 13, 1995, in Oaxaca, Mexico. *See* The SMOC Initiative of the CEC of North America, Overview and Update, 2003.

The SMOC is an ongoing initiative to reduce the risks of toxic substances to human health and the environment in North America. The project provides a forum for: (a) identifying priority chemical pollution issues of regional concern; (b) developing North American Regional Action Plans (NARAPs) to address these priority issues; (c) overseeing the implementation of approved NARAPs; and (d) facilitating and encouraging capacity building in support of the overall goals of SMOC, with emphasis on the implementation of NARAPs.

To date, six NARAPs (DDT, chlordane, PCBs, mercury, lindane and other isomers, and environmental monitoring and assessment) have been developed and are at various stages of implementation. Other action plans are now under development, one for dioxins, furans and hexachlorobenzene (HCB), and the other for poly brominated diphenyl ethers (PBDE). These action plans should identify regulatory and non-regulatory measures to minimize exposure to these substances, and ultimately phase out those that pose unreasonable and otherwise unmanageable risks. *See* The SMOC Initiative of the CEC of North America, Overview and Update, 2003.

The Canada-United States Strategy for the Virtual Elimination of Persistent Toxic Substances in the Great Lakes Basin, known as the Great Lakes Binational Toxics Strategy, provides a framework for actions to reduce or eliminate persistent toxic substances, especially those which bioaccumulate. The Strategy was developed jointly by Canada and the United States in 1996 and 1997, and was signed on April 7, 1997. It established reduction challenges for an initial list of persistent toxic substances targeted for virtual elimination: aldrin/dieldrin, benzo(a)pyrene, chlordane, DDT, HCB, alkyl-lead, mercury and compounds, mirex, octachlorostyrene, PCBs, dioxins and furans, and toxaphene. Recognizing the long-term nature of virtual elimination, the Strategy provided the framework for actions to achieve quantifiable reduction "challenges" in the timeframe from 1997–2006 for specific toxic substances. A November 2011 Integration Workshop Meeting between Environment Canada and U.S. EPA, reduction goals for mercury and dioxins/furans had been met by the United States and Canada; and goals for PCB reduction had been met by Canada and goals for benzo(a)pyrene/hexachlorobenzene reduction had been met by the United States, with the other country making significant progress towards those goals. *See* http://www.epa.gov/greatlakes/bns/integration/201111/index .html.

The development of baseline measurements for tracking and measuring progress toward reductions is also a key element of the Strategy. A "Technical Support Document" appended to the Strategy provides action items that will be undertaken to pursue reductions. *See* http://www.epa.gov/greatlakes/p2/bns.html#Technical Support Document Attachment 1.

In 1998, States who were members of the United Nations Economic Commission for Europe concluded two new protocols to the Convention on Long-Range Transboundary Air Pollution (LRTAP, discussed in Chapter 9 above): the Protocol on Persistent Organic Pollutants (POPs) and the Protocol on Heavy Metals (discussed in the next section).

The first protocol (POPs Protocol) addresses the problem of persistent organic pollutants that resist natural degradation and cause serious harm to human health and the environment. As the excerpt from *Our Stolen Future* indicated, the Arctic ecosystem and indigenous people who live on fish and mammals are particularly vulnerable to harm from persistent organic chemicals. Under the POPs Protocol parties agree to take effective measures "to eliminate the production and use of these substances and the transboundary movement of the substances are done in an "environmentally sound manner," (Article 3(1)(b)), to reduce the total annual emissions of each substance listed in Annex III from a baseline year to be determined individually, and to use best available techniques to reduce emissions for new stationary sources or alternative strategies that achieve comparable reductions. There are exceptions to the controls, including for laboratory-scale research.

Notably the POPs Protocol looks to public awareness and participation as a means to implement the agreement and encourage compliance. Article 6, Public Awareness, provides that the parties must "promote the provision of information to the general public, including individuals who are direct users of persistent organic pollutants" and notes that the information may cover risk assessment, ways to eliminate the use of POPs (as through integrated pest management), alternatives to POPs, and the economic and social impacts of the alternatives.

f. Heavy Metals

The term "heavy metal" refers to any metallic chemical element that has a relatively high density and is toxic or poisonous at low concentrations. Examples of heavy metals include mercury (Hg), cadmium (Cd), arsenic (As), chromium (Cr), thallium (Tl), and lead (Pb). Heavy metals are natural components of the Earth's crust. As a general matter, they cannot be degraded or destroyed. To a small extent they enter our bodies via food, drinking water and air. As trace elements, some heavy metals (e.g., copper, selenium, and zinc) are essential to maintain the metabolism of the human body. However, at higher concentrations they can lead to poisoning and death. Heavy metal poisoning could result, for instance, from drinking-water contamination (e.g., lead pipes), high ambient air concentrations near emission sources, or intake via the food chain. Heavy metals are particularly dangerous because they tend to bioaccumulate, i.e., to increase in concentration in a biological organism over time, compared to the chemical's concentration in the environment. Compounds accumulate in living things any time they are taken up and stored faster than they are broken down (metabolized) or excreted.

i.   General: LRTAP Protocol on Heavy Metals

The 1998 Protocol on Heavy Metals to the UNECE Convention on Long-Range Transboundary Air Pollution (LRTAP) obligates countries to reduce their total annual emissions into the atmosphere of the heavy metals listed in Annex I with reference to a base year of 1990 or an alternative base year from 1985 to 1995 as set by the country when it joins the agreement. The three heavy metals listed in Annex I are cadmium, lead, and mercury. Other heavy metals may be added by amendment. In addition, the protocol obligates parties to adopt the best available techniques for reducing emissions of the heavy metals for new and existing stationary sources or, in some cases, to adopt strategies to reduce emissions that achieve equivalent overall emission reductions. Annex III provides detailed guidance on determining the best available techniques for 11 categories of stationary sources of heavy metals.

NOTES AND QUESTIONS

1.   *Implementation.* What problems do you foresee in implementing technology-based obligations to control POPs and heavy metals?

2.   *The VOC Protocol.* Compare these protocols with the VOC [Volatile Organic Compounds] Protocol discussed in Chapter 9. As of February 2015, the VOC Protocol has 23 signatories and 24 Parties, and it entered into force on September 29, 2007. Why might States hesitate to join these protocols?

3.   *Compliance review.* Both protocols contain a separate identical article (Article 11—POPs, Article 9—Heavy Metals) addressed issues of compliance. The articles provide that "[c]ompliance by each Party with its obligations under the present Protocol shall be reviewed regularly. The Implementation Committee . . . shall carry out such reviews and report to the Parties." What specific measures might be suggested to increase compliance with these protocols? (Review the materials in Chapter 5 on accountability and compliance.)

ii. Lead

Several NGOs, for example, the National Resources Defense Council and the Alliance to End Childhood Lead Poisoning, as well as governments and other organizations had been taking or pressing for action to minimize exposure to lead in the early 1990s. In May 1994, the United Nations Commission on Sustainable Development (CS) recognized the severe health impacts of human exposure to lead and encouraged further efforts to reduce human exposure to lead. In November 1994, the seven Central American countries and the United States reached agreement on working to eliminate the use of lead in gasoline, an agreement that was based on a joint statement to the same effect a month earlier by the heads of State of the Central American countries. Later that month, language was agreed to among all the countries in the Western Hemisphere (except Cuba) to do the same thing. These non-legally binding agreements—the CONCAUSA and the Summit of the Americas Plan of Action, respectively—were formally adopted by heads of state at the Summit of the Americas in Miami in December 1994. Dangers from lead exposure were considered by the Organisation for Economic Co-operation and Development in 1995 and led to a declaration to phase out the use of lead in gasoline except for narrow and specialized uses (e.g., race car fuel). The CSD further discussed lead issues in 1995.

In 1996, at the Second United Nations Conference on Human Settlements (Habitat II), [2] the entire world community agreed to "eliminate as soon as possible the use of lead in gasoline." Article 42(bb) of the Habitat Agenda. The World Bank had become active in lead abatement and elimination efforts; and its statement that lead is the single most dangerous pollutant for developing countries was influential in getting the international community to commit at Habitat II to eliminate the use of lead in gasoline. The 1997 Special Session of the United Nations General Assembly also adopted non-legally binding language regarding lead in its five-year review of Agenda 21 and UNCED. As with the Summit of the Americas, the United States took the lead in these negotiations, as it did in subsequent efforts in the UN Commission on Human Settlements and UNEP to adopt action plans in this regard. As a result of these efforts, most countries now ban the use of lead in gasoline (except for narrow uses). By 2005, for example, gasoline in virtually all countries in Africa was lead-free.

iii. Mercury

Mercury, whether from natural or anthropogenic sources, is a well-known toxin. The infamous tragedy in Minamata, Japan, helped publicize this fact. According to a 2005 EPA report, 44 states, 2 tribes, and 1 territory issued advisories regarding consumption of fish because of mercury contamination. The EPA specifically advised against the consumption of shark, swordfish, king mackerel, and tilefish by women who might become pregnant, women who are pregnant, nursing mothers, and young children. This is based partly on mercury contamination and partly on contamination by POPs.

In February 2003, the UNEP Governing Council determined that there was sufficient evidence of significant global adverse impacts from mercury to warrant further international actions to reduce the risks to

---

[2] Article 42(bb) of the Habitat Agenda.

humans and wildlife from the release of mercury to the environment. It initially established a mercury programme within UNEP Chemicals, which was strengthened by the Governing Council at its 23rd session (Decision 23/9 of 25 February 2005). Initially, the priority activities of the UNEP mercury programme in 2005/2006 included raising awareness of the nature of mercury pollution problems, including through regional awareness-raising workshops and assisting countries to identify and understand any mercury problems in their countries and implement action to mitigate them and developing materials to support the reduction of risks to human health and the environment from the release of mercury to the environment.

In 2013, the Minamata Convention on Mercury was adopted. The Minamata Convention (named after the mercury disaster in Minamata, Japan, rather than after the city—Geneva—in which the convention was finalized) is a global treaty aimed at protecting human health and the environment from the adverse effects of mercury. The Convention on Mercury includes a ban on new mercury mines, the phase-out of existing mercury mines, control measures on air emissions, and the international regulation of the informal sector for artisanal and small-scale gold mining. It regulates mercury supply sources and trade (Art. 3), mercury-added products (Art. 4), and manufacturing processes in which mercury or mercury compounds are used (Art. 5). It charges States with taking measures to control mercury emissions and releases through the creation of domestic plans (Arts. 8 & 9), as well as taking measures "to ensure that the interim storage of such mercury and mercury compounds intended for a use allowed to a Party under this Convention is undertaken in an environmentally sound manner" (Art. 10).

The Minamata Convention also contains provisions for the management of mercury wastes (Art. 11) and identification of strategies for managing contaminated sites (Art. 12). It also addresses financial sources and mechanisms for all of these activities (Art. 13).

For the text of the Convention and related materials, *see* http://mercuryconvention.org/Convention/tabid/3426/Default.aspx. As of March 2015, there are 128 signatories to the Minamata Convention, and 10 parties. It will enter into force after ratification by 50 Parties.

Consider the following:

THE MINAMATA CONVENTION ON MERCURY: A FIRST STEP TOWARD PROTECTING FUTURE GENERATIONS

Rebecca Kessler

121 Environmental Health Perspectives A306–08 (Oct. 2013), *available at* http://ehp. niehs.nih.gov/wp-content/uploads/121/10/ehp.121–a304.pdf

Some developing nations initially balked at the cost of technology that removes mercury from smokestack emissions. The United States worked hard to convince China and India, in particular, that mandatory controls in this sector could be affordably achieved through the application of so-called best available techniques. . . . In the end, the United States succeeded, although a detailed description of acceptable techniques remains to be worked out, and they are required only for new sources of mercury air emissions. . . .

However, critics like IPEN's [the International POPs Elimination Network] DiGangi say that although the measure should reduce the mercury emissions per unit of energy produced, countries are free to keep building capacity, so total emissions will probably rise. "The treaty will address some mercury sources—it just will not be able to keep up with the increased mercury emissions," DiGangi says. "In other words, it will change the slope, but the amount of mercury pollution will still increase."

Critics also say the time frame for implementation is too long. Countries have 5 years before they must build new sources that comply and 10 years before they must at least establish a goal to reduce emissions from existing sources. But the clock doesn't start ticking until the convention is ratified, which is unlikely for another few years, says Susan Egan Keane, a senior environmental analyst with the Natural Resources Defense Council. "You're basically grandfathering in . . . thousands of tons of mercury emitted during that time that you're sitting around not doing anything," Keane says. "That's a lot of mercury that you're just letting go!"

Another key issue was the biggest source of mercury pollution, artisanal and small-scale gold mining, which accounts for more than a third of global emissions. Small, often temporary mining operations have boomed worldwide as the price of gold skyrocketed. Some 10–15 million people, including possibly as many as 3 million women and children, many of them extremely poor, are estimated to work in the industry.

To separate tiny particles of gold from ore, workers commonly use large quantities of mercury with no protection whatsoever for themselves, their homes, or the environment. According to Keane, mercury is cheap and readily available to miners. She recalls visiting a mine in Borneo where she watched a worker casually amalgamate gold with mercury he poured from a soda bottle. She later calculated the bottle held roughly as much mercury as 60,000 compact fluorescent light bulbs; she says the miner may well have used a bottle each day.

Various countries have tried outlawing mercury in artisanal and small-scale gold mining, but without help for miners to transition away from the practice, it has simply gone covert, Keane says. She says the convention took the right approach by directing countries to come up with their own plans to reduce or eliminate mercury in mining. Guidelines for the plans mandate strategies to formalize the industry and eliminate its most polluting practices, and to protect children and pregnant women from mercury exposure. However, the convention allows continued mercury trade for artisanal and small-scale gold mining, and there is no phase-out date for the practice.

The convention does phase out mercury in most products by 2020, including pesticides and certain batteries, bulbs, switches, cosmetics, and measuring devices. One product that sparked extensive debate was dental amalgam. The Zero Mercury Working Group, a coalition of environmental and health organizations, led the charge to include amalgam in the convention by pointing out that it is a significant source of mercury emissions from cremated human remains and amalgam waste washed down the drain. The convention "phases down"—gradually reduces but doesn't eliminate—the use of mercury-containing dental amalgam by directing countries to adopt at least two control measures from a list of nine options.

Another hotly debated product was the mercury-based vaccine preservative thimerosal. Although thimerosal has been eliminated from most children's vaccines in developed nations, it is still widely used throughout the developing world because it enables vaccines to be packaged in multidose bottles, significantly lowering costs and making it easier to transport and distribute vaccines in remote areas.

Two U.S. organizations, SafeMinds and the Coalition for Mercury-Free Drugs, pushed for the convention to phase out or phase down thimerosal, contending that it poses a risk to children's health. Numerous global health agencies led by the World Health Organization rallied to protect it, however, arguing that the preservative is safe and essential to vaccination programs that protect the world's poorest children from life-threatening diseases. A number of developing nations expressed concern about thimerosal during the negotiations, but in the end they supported its continued use, and the convention specifically exempts it.

The convention also addressed specific manufacturing processes, notably phasing out mercury in the production of acetaldehyde, the source of the contamination at Minamata. By 2020 countries must halve the use of mercury in the production of vinyl chloride monomer, the main component of PVC plastic. China is all but alone in manufacturing vinyl chloride monomer in a way that uses mercury as a catalyst, but IPEN describes the Chinese industry as an unquantified and "potentially enormous" emissions source.

Developing nations drove the negotiations on two other points of contention. One was the inclusion of an article devoted to health issues. Developed nations opposed including one, largely out of concern that it would open the door for costly public health programs to be included in the convention, according to Keane. The final convention does include a health article, albeit a brief one simply encouraging nations to implement general measures to protect their populations from mercury exposure.

Developing nations were also concerned about securing enough international funding to implement the convention effectively. After much discussion, the final convention designates the Global Environment Facility Trust Fund as the funding mechanism, but it remains to be determined how much donor countries will give to the fund or, therefore, how much recipient countries will receive. "The treaty is one thing, but now implementing it is also another process, which will bring on board a lot of other issues—capacity, capability, resources, and understanding," says Richard Mwendandu, a delegate from Kenya.

Yet the convention has drawn praise, even from some critics, as an important first step and the first unified global action to curb mercury emissions. "The treaty involved compromises, but it reflects a global consensus that mercury emissions and releases represent a serious health and environmental concern," says Evers, of the Biodiversity Research Institute.

NOTES AND QUESTIONS

What's next? What do you expect are the next steps in the implementation of the Minamata Convention? What potential tensions might arise?

g.   Endocrine Disruptors

In 1997, the International Forum on Chemical Safety (IFCS) undertook a major study of chemicals that disrupt the endocrine (hormone) system—so called endocrine disruptors—which, among other things, may cause developmental and reproductive damage. Early scientific knowledge indicates that these synthetic chemicals pose unusual challenges to policymakers and regulators, not only because the chemicals (which include PCBs, dioxin, and furans) are so widespread but also for several other reasons: effects are often noncarcinogenic; effects may not be felt directly by the person exposed but rather by that person's offspring, sometimes several decades later; effects may be caused by a single hit at a particular time in development; effects may occur at extremely low concentrations (e.g., parts per trillion); and some of the chemicals may be more dangerous at low concentrations than at high ones. *See generally* Theo Colborn, Dianne Dumanoski & John Peterson Myers, Our Stolen Future (1996).

Other initiatives include an international workshop on endocrine disrupting chemicals held at the Smithsonian Institution in January 1997, which aimed to review the status of domestic and regional assessments on the state of the science of endocrine disruptors; explore the perspective of developing countries and countries with economies in transition on the issue of endocrine disruptors; discuss the need for an international science assessment of endocrine disruptors; and identify opportunities and open a dialogue for international cooperation that could advance our understanding of the endocrine disruptor issue. *See* http://www.epa.gov/edrlupvx/Pubs/smithrep.pdf.

Also in 1997, the OECD initiated the Special Activity on Endocrine Disruptors Testing and Assessment with objectives to provide a set of internationally recognized and harmonized testing guidelines and testing and assessment strategies for regulatory use that would avoid duplication of testing and thus save resources, including animals. It has since issued a number of guidance documents in this area. *See* http://www.oecd.org/chemicalsafety/testing/seriesontestingandassessmenttestingforendocrinedisrupters.htm.

International organizations have also been performing periodic assessments of the state of the science on endocrine disruptors. The most recent assessment is State of the Science of Endocrine Disrupting Chemicals 2012: Summary for Decision-Makers, published by the World Health Organization. *See* http://apps.who.int/iris/bitstream/10665/78102/1/WHO_HSE_PHE_IHE_2013.1_eng.pdf. It provides a comprehensive review of the global peer-reviewed scientific literature where the associations between environmental exposures and adverse outcomes have been demonstrated or hypothesized to occur via mechanisms of endocrine disruption.

h. SAICM/ICCM

The United Nations Environment Programme (UNEP) Governing Council, at its seventh Special Session in February 2002, adopted Decision SS.VII/3 on a "Strategic Approach to International Chemicals Management" (SAICM). Some countries had advocated a binding framework convention on chemicals; others had opposed any new initiatives. The Governing Council decided that there was a need to further develop a strategic approach and endorsed as a foundation the Bahia Declaration and the Priorities for Action Beyond 2000 adopted by the Intergovernmental Forum on Chemical Safety (IFCS) in 2000. The initiative was subsequently endorsed by the World Summit on Sustainable Development in Johannesburg in September 2002. In February 2003, a progress report was considered by the UNEP Governing Council. The Council adopted decision 22/4 IV endorsing the concept of an international conference.

The SAICM was ultimately adopted by the International Conference on Chemicals Management (ICCM) on 6 February 2006 in Dubai, United Arab Emirates. *See* http://www.saicm.org/images/saicm_documents/saicm%20texts/SAICM_publication_ENG.pdf. It provides recommendations for measures to support the reduction of risks; improvement of knowledge and information; governance; capacity-building; reduction of illegal international traffic; and improvement of general practices. The SAICM has been formally endorsed by a number of international bodies, including the Governing Council of the United Nations Environment Programme (Decision SS.IX/1), the Council of the United Nations Food and Agriculture Organisation (FAO), and the World Health Assembly (for the World Health Organisation).

The most recent ICCM, ICCM 3, was held in Nairobi from 17 to 21 September 2012. Among other things, the ICCM "reviewed progress in the implementation of the Strategic Approach with tangible data on the 20 indicators of progress adopted at the second session. . . . evaluated implementation, addressed emerging policy issues, considered new activities for addition to the Global Plan of Action, evaluated the financing of the Strategic Approach and took strategic decisions for the future including the consideration of recommendations from the Executive Board of the Quick Start Programme regarding the future of the Programme and its trust fund. . . ." *See* http://www.saicm.org/index. php?option=com_content&view=article&id=96&Itemid=485.

i. REACH

Over 100,000 synthetic chemicals are believed to be in use worldwide, but the vast majority of these have never been tested for their effects on the environment and human health. The European Commission proposed a new European Union (EU) regulatory framework for the Registration, Evaluation and Authorisation of Chemicals (REACH) in 2003. The law entered into force on 1 June 2007 ((EC 1907/2006)). *See* http://eur-lex.europa.eu/LexUriServ/LexUriServ.do?uri=OJ:L:2006:396: 0001:0849:EN:PDF. The aim is to improve the protection of human health and the environment through the better and earlier identification of the properties of chemical substances. At the same time, innovative capability and competitiveness of the EU chemicals industry should be enhanced. The benefits of the REACH system will come gradually, as more and more substances are phased into REACH.

REACH places greater responsibility on industry to manage the risks from chemicals and to provide safety information on the substances. Manufacturers and importers are required to gather information on the properties of their substances (Annex VI) and update that information (Article 22) which will help them manage the substances more safely, and to register the information (Articles 6–7) in a central database run by the European Chemicals Agency (ECHA) in Helsinki (Article 75). In turn, EU Member States' public authorities will examine registration dossiers and substances of concern (Article 45). The minimization of animal testing is listed as a priority (Preamble 40 and 47). Use-specific authorizations are required for chemicals that cause cancer, mutations or reproduction problems, or that accumulate in our bodies and in the environment (Annex XVII). Authorization will be granted only to companies that can show that the risks are adequately controlled or if social and economic benefits outweigh the risks and suitable alternative substances do not exist. (Preamble 69). This is intended to encourage substitution of unsafe substances by safer ones.

Under REACH, the ECHA will act as a central point of the system, running the databases necessary to operate the system, co-ordinate the in-depth evaluation of suspicious chemicals and run a public database in which consumers and professionals can find hazard information (Article 77). *See* http://echa.europa.eu/. As explained on the REACH website:

Unambiguous substance identification is a pre-requisite to most of the REACH processes. Actors in the supply chain must have sufficient information on the identity of their substance.

The correct identification of a substance will enable, for example:

- The sharing of information by potential registrants and data holders to prevent the duplication of testing on animals and unnecessary costs;

- The assessment of the applicability of test data across companies who registered the same substance, the assessment of read-across proposals (categorisation approach) or the use of non test information; and

- The assessment if a substance is included in the Authorisation List, the list of restrictions or if its classification and labelling has been harmonized.

The following information on the manufactured or imported substance shall be included in the dossier in order to unambiguously identify the substance:

- Substance name and related identifiers, molecular and structural formulae, if applicable;

- Information on the composition and purity of the substance;

- Spectral data and analytical information to verify the identity and composition of the substance; and

- Clear and concise description of the analytical methods.

See http://echa.europa.eu/web/guest/regulations/reach/substance-identity.

j.   Framework Convention on Tobacco Control

There are approximately 4.9 million tobacco-related deaths per year. Many people do not consider tobacco use to be an *environmental* problem; in fact, some people claim that the Convention is the world's first *public health* treaty. It is now relatively widely known that smoking or chewing tobacco creates health risks; but it is also the case that tobacco smoke is a form of indoor air pollution. In fact, half of the world's children are exposed to smoke at home, with serious health effects.

Work on the convention began in 1999, under the auspices of the World Health Organization (WHO), based on the recognition in 1995 at the World Health Assembly that a global convention was needed. The WHO Framework Convention on Tobacco Control (FCTC) was adopted in 2003. It entered into force in 2005 and has 177 Parties as of February 2014.

The FCTC requires, inter alia, that countries impose restrictions on tobacco advertising, sponsorship and promotion; establish new packaging and labeling requirements for tobacco products; establish clean indoor air controls; and strengthen legislation to control tobacco smuggling. The following excerpt is from the WHO website (http://www.who.int/features/2003/08/en/):

Advertising, sponsorship and promotion

Tobacco products are advertised through sports events, music events, films, fashion—in fact, any place where the tobacco industry can target potential new smokers. The treaty obliges Party States to undertake a comprehensive ban on tobacco advertising, promotion and sponsorship, as far as their constitutions permit. Parties whose constitution or constitutional principles do not allow them to undertake a comprehensive ban must apply a series of restrictions on all advertising, promotion and sponsorship.

Packaging and labelling of tobacco products

As advertising restrictions are implemented, tobacco packaging plays an increasingly important role in encouraging tobacco consumption. The treaty obliges Party States to adopt and implement large, clear, visible, legible, and rotating health warnings and messages on tobacco products and its outside packaging, occupying at least 30% of the principal display areas. This is required within three years of entry into force of the Convention.

Protection from exposure to tobacco smoke

Second-hand smoke is a real and significant threat to public health. Children are at particular risk—exposure to tobacco smoke in children can cause respiratory disease, middle ear disease, asthma attacks, and sudden infant death syndrome (SIDS). The treaty obliges Party States to adopt and implement (in areas of existing national jurisdiction as determined by national law), or promote (at other jurisdictional levels), effective measures providing for protection from exposure to tobacco smoke in indoor workplaces, public transport, indoor public places and, as appropriate, other public places.

Illicit trade in tobacco products

Cigarettes are smuggled widely throughout the world. In addition to making international brands more affordable and accessible, illegal cigarettes evade restrictions and health regulations. The treaty obliges State Parties to adopt and implement effective measures to eliminate illicit trade, illicit manufacturing, and counterfeiting of tobacco products.

The Protocol to Eliminate Illicit Trade in Tobacco Products, the first Protocol to the Convention, was adopted on 12 November 2012 at the fifth session of the Conference of the Parties; as of February 2015, it has 54 signatories and 6 Parties.

THE WHO PROTOCOL TO ELIMINATE ILLICIT TRADE IN TOBACCO PRODUCTS: A NEXT STEP IN INTERNATIONAL CONTROL OF TOBACCO PRODUCTS

Lukasz Gruszczynski
4 Eur. J. Risk Reg. 91 (2013)

The Protocol repeats the very broad definition of "illicit trade" included in the Convention, understood as "any practice or conduct prohibited by law and which relates to production, shipment, receipt, possession, distribution, sale or purchase, including any practice or conduct intended to facilitate such activity." Consequently, it goes beyond the common meaning of the term and covers such acts as manufacturing or complicity in various illicit activities. Note also that this definition— and as a consequence the Protocol itself—is not limited to international illicit trade only, but also encompasses purely domestic acts. In practice, when one speaks about illicit trade, the following activities are the most common: large scale smuggling of tobacco products between different jurisdictions (with respect to either genuine or counterfeit products); bootlegging (illegal reselling in high-tax jurisdictions of tobacco products legally purchased in low-tax jurisdictions), which is one of the recent forms of smuggling; manufacturing of counterfeit tobacco products; simulated export with subsequent reintroduction of products to the original market.

Probably the most important reason that led to the adoption of the Protocol is the fact that illicit trade in tobacco products undermines a number of the FCTC provisions. In particular, it compromises price and tax measures adopted by the countries with the aim of suppressing the demand for tobacco products. It may lead to avoidance of packaging and labelling requirements enforceable in a particular jurisdiction, or facilitate sales to minors (since illicit products are frequently traded on the black market). It makes tobacco products more accessible to users and undermines applicable rules relating to the technical qualities of products (e.g., permissible ingredients, emission standards). Illicit trade therefore clearly contributes to an increase in the health problems posed by tobacco use. In addition, it also results in significant losses in state revenues and diverts portion of those funds to black market operators and organized crime.

The Protocol consists of three broad categories of provisions. The first category includes detailed rules on preventive measures to be taken by the Parties to control illegal trade in tobacco, tobacco products, and manufacturing equipment. The second category is concerned with the improvement of law enforcement, while the third deals with international cooperation. These are supplemented by a set of provisions relating to reporting obligations and dispute settlement mechanism. The section below summarizes the most important obligations in each of the categories.

1. Preventive measures: Supply chain controls

The Protocol requires the adoption of specific control measures over the supply chain. Firstly, the Protocol establishes a mandatory licensing requirement for key participants in the supply chain (manufacturers, importers and exporters of tobacco products or manufacturing equipment), and allows for a possible extension of the licensing obligations to other actors, such as wholesalers or retailers of tobacco products (Art. 6.1–2). In this context, the Protocol provides detailed instructions on information that needs to be included in a licensing application, operation of the licensing system, and its supervision. Second, it requires certain operators engaged in the supply chain to perform customer identification and verification procedures (together with a due diligence), and to monitor subsequent sales (Art. 7). The provision does not set any de minimis threshold. Third, the Protocol requires the establishment of a tracking and tracing system for all tobacco products and establishes its parameters (e.g., scope of relevant information and rules on access to this information). In this context, the Protocol distinguishes between national and global tracking and tracing systems. The former covers tobacco products that are manufactured in or imported onto the territory of an individual Party. The latter is supposed to connect national systems into one network, and its implementation is to be phased-in over for a period of five years from the Protocol's entry into force. As a part of a tracking and tracing system, each Party is expected to introduce unique, secure and non-removable identification markings on all unit packets and packaging, as well as on the individual packaging of cigarettes and other tobacco products. These can take the form of codes or stamps (Art. 8). Fourth, the Parties need to guarantee that all entities in the supply chain of tobacco, tobacco products, and manufacturing equipment comply with certain record-keeping obligations. The extent of required information depends on the type of an actor (e.g., a licensed or non-licensed entity), and covers such information as quantities of tobacco products and equipment in their possession; shipment data, including identification of contractors, transaction details, and the intended market for retail sales (Art. 9). Fifth, the Parties are expected to require all entities that are subject to licensing obligations to introduce measures preventing the diversion of legal tobacco products into illicit trade channels. This task is to be accomplished through various reporting obligations (e.g., with respect to "suspicious" transactions), restrictions on acceptable methods of payment, and requirements to supply tobacco products only in in amount necessary to satisfy the demand in the intended market of retail sale (Art. 10). Sixth, each Party has to implement control measures on the manufacturing of tobacco and tobacco products (and related transactions) in free zones (Art. 12.1), as well as control and verification measures with respect to international transit and any transfer of tobacco products and manufacturing equipment that takes place on its territory (Art. 12.3).

2. Penalization, investigation and prosecution

The Protocol requires Parties to make certain activities connected with the illicit trade of tobacco, tobacco products and manufacturing equipment unlawful. The catalogue is broad and includes, among the other things, acts such as manufacturing or selling tobacco products without the payment of applicable duties or taxes; failure to comply with applicable marking and labelling requirements; producing tobacco products with false markings or fiscal stamps; and mis-declaring on official forms the description, quantity or value of tobacco or tobacco products in order to evade payments of duties or taxes. At the same time, the Protocol leaves the Parties with the discretion as to which of these activities are to be considered as criminal offences under domestic law (Art. 14). Besides penalization, each Party needs to provide in its legal system for possibility of making legal entities liable for such acts (either in the form of criminal, administrative, or civil liability) (Art. 15).

The above acts, as well as other acts connected with the illicit trade of tobacco products as identified by the Parties, must be subject to effective, proportionate, and discouraging sanctions of either a criminal or non-criminal character (including monetary sanctions). Illegal products (e.g., tobacco products or manufacturing equipment) which are confiscated are subject to destruction (Art. 18). The Protocol also encourages the use of special investigative techniques, such as controlled deliveries or undercover operations, leaving however final decisions in this respect to each individual Party (Art. 19).

3. International cooperation

The provisions on international cooperation constitute an important part of the Protocol. The aim of these obligations is to improve enforcement capabilities with respect to transnational acts of illicit trade by establishing communication channels among the Parties, facilitating information exchange, simplifying or creating necessary procedures, and providing necessary technical assistance. The relevant rules provide for:

- general information sharing (reporting in aggregated form on seizures of tobacco, tobacco products, and manufacturing equipment, and their import, export or transit) (Art. 20);

- information sharing on enforcement if necessary for the detection or investigation of illicit trade in tobacco (e.g., records of investigations and prosecutions, payments for import, export, or duty-free sales of tobacco) (Art. 21);

- assistance and cooperation with respect to training, provision of technical assistance, and cooperation in scientific, technical and technological matters (transfer of relevant expertise or technology in areas such as protection of personal data, electronic surveillance, forensic analysis) (Art. 23);

- assistance and cooperation with respect to the investigation and prosecution of offences (Art. 24);

- law enforcement cooperation (enhancing cooperation among the competent national authorities responsible for enforcement activities) (Art. 27);

- mutual administrative assistance with respect to information required for proper enforcement of customs and other laws relevant to the prevention, detection, investigation, or prosecution of acts of illicit trade (Art. 28);

- mutual legal assistance in investigations, prosecutions and judicial proceedings in relation to acts penalized by the Protocol (e.g., executing searches and seizures, identifying or tracing the proceeds of crime) (Art. 29);

- extradition rules applicable to persons charged with the criminal offences envisaged by the protocol (subject to strict conditions) (Art. 30).

4. Other provisions

The Protocol imposes on the Parties certain reporting obligations with respect to implementation of its provisions (Art. 32). It also contains a dispute settlement clause, which refers back to the relevant rules provided in the FCTC. As a consequence, any dispute between the Parties concerning the interpretation or application of the Protocol is to be resolved through diplomatic means, and if such means fail, through compulsory ad hoc arbitration (subject to the consent of each Party upon ratification, acceptance, and approval).

NOTES AND QUESTIONS

1.   *Parallels?* In what ways do the problems encountered with hazardous chemicals parallel those of hazardous wastes?

2.   *Developing countries and domestically prohibited goods.* What attributes of developing countries might make them more (or less) vulnerable than developed countries to risks associated with hazardous chemicals? Should countries ban the export of goods whose use is banned or severely restricted domestically?

3.   *Pulling together.* International activities at different levels can reinforce each other. The issue of eliminating lead from gasoline is one example. What guidance does this provide regarding how to approach dealing with hazardous chemicals at the international level?

4.   *MDGs.* For a discussion of how sound chemical management relates to the eight Millennium Development Goals, *see* Kelly Rain, *Establishing Sound Chemicals Management Is a Prerequisite for Achieving the Millennium Development Goals*, Sustainable Development Law & Policy (Fall 2005), at 27.

5.   *SDGs.* The Sustainable Development Goals being negotiated in 2015 also relate to sound chemical management. *See, e.g.*, draft Goal 3, target 9—"by 2030 substantially reduce the number of deaths and illnesses from hazardous chemicals and air, water, and soil pollution and contamination"; draft Goal 6, target 3—"by 2030, improve water quality by reducing pollution, eliminating dumping and minimizing release of hazardous chemicals and materials . . ."; and Goal 12, target 4—"by 2020 achieve environmentally sound management of chemicals and all wastes throughout their life cycle in accordance with agreed international frameworks and significantly reduce their release to air, water and soil to minimize their adverse impacts on human health and the environment".

6.   *Body Burdens.* The term "body burden" refers to the amount of a chemical stored in the body at a given time, especially a potential toxin in the body as the result of exposure. Both governmental bodies and non-governmental organizations have conducted body burden analyses. In 2005 the U.S. Centers for Disease Control and Prevention (CDC) released an assessment of the exposure of the U.S. population to chemicals in the environment. "The National Report on Human Exposure to Environmental Chemicals provides an ongoing assessment of the U.S. population's exposure to environmental chemicals using biomonitoring. Biomonitoring is the assessment of human exposure to chemicals by measuring the chemicals or their metabolites in human specimens such as blood or urine.

This Third Report presents first-time exposure information for the U.S. population for 38 of the 148 chemicals included in the Report. The Report also includes the data from the Second Report; that is, data for 1999–2000." *See* http://www.cdc.gov/exposurereport/. A Fourth Report, updating the earlier findings and presenting data for 212 chemicals, was released in 2009.

Nongovernmental organizations such as Commonweal and the Environmental Working Group have been active with respect to body burdens. For example, in a 2005 study, researchers at two major laboratories found an average of 200 industrial chemicals and pollutants in umbilical cord blood from 10 babies born in August and September of 2004 in U.S. hospitals. Tests revealed a total of 287 chemicals in the group. The umbilical cord blood of these 10 children, collected by the American Red Cross, harbored pesticides, consumer product ingredients, and wastes from burning coal, gasoline, and garbage.

"This study represents the first reported cord blood tests for 261 of the targeted chemicals and the first reported detections in cord blood for 209 compounds. Among them are eight perfluorochemicals used as stain and oil repellants in fast food packaging, clothes and textiles—including the Teflon chemical PFOA, recently characterized as a likely human carcinogen by the EPA's Science Advisory Board—dozens of widely used brominated flame retardants and their toxic by-products; and numerous pesticides. Of the 287 chemicals we detected in umbilical cord blood, we know that 180 cause cancer in humans or animals, 217 are toxic to the brain and nervous system, and 208 cause birth defects or abnormal development in animal tests. The dangers of pre- or post-natal exposure to this complex mixture of carcinogens, developmental toxins and neurotoxins have never been studied." *See* http://www.ewg.org/research/body-burden-pollution-newborns.

7. *The precautionary approach.* Is the precautionary principle (or precautionary approach) given adequate weight in the approaches described in this chapter?

8. *What to do?* Part B of Chapter 18 analyzes environmental governance, including with respect to the so-called chemicals cluster of global multilateral environmental agreements that includes the Basel, Rotterdam, Stockholm and Minamata Conventions. The secretariats of the first three of these have been combined into a joint BRS secretariat, to which the Minamata secretariat might be added once that convention enters into force. Would a framework convention for sound chemicals management be more advisable than the joint secretariat approach, or should some other form of consolidation of chemicals management be considered? Why or why not? The Experts Group involved in the mid-term review of UNEP's Montevideo Programme IV recommended in 2015: "Conduct feasibility study on chemicals framework convention."

CHAPTER 11

MARINE AND POLAR REGIONS

• • •

A. INTRODUCTION

And yet I wish but for the thing I have.
My bounty is as boundless as the sea,
My love as deep. The more I give to thee,
The more I have, for both are infinite.

Juliet, in Romeo & Juliet, Act 2, Scene 2

Up to and well beyond Shakespeare's time the sea was conceived of as being "boundless," "infinite." But while it covers over two-thirds of Earth's surface, we know today that humans now have the capacity to reach the ocean's most abyssal depths and to cause entire species of marine life to collapse. This chapter will explore the international community's efforts to protect the marine environment from the serious threats that human activities pose to its health. We begin with a Problem designed to bring some of the challenges of regulating these activities into focus.

PROBLEM

The coastal State of Playa del Oro obtains 60% of its revenues from taxes related to its tourism industries. Many eco-resorts are situated around the State's Bay of Pirates and the estuary of the Deep River. In February, the height of the winter tourism season, an oil tanker registered in a country that provides no oversight of its registered vessels breaks apart just beyond Playa del Oro's territorial sea. Oil enters the Bay of Pirates and does substantial damage to the Deep River estuary. In a separate incident, beach patrons at the ultra chic Verde Health Spa and Eco-Resort were greeted with vast piles of plastic soft drink webbing and tarps, dead dolphins who had ingested over 50 pounds of plastic. An investigation by the national environmental protection agency revealed that the garbage came from a cluster of coastal developments, illegal under local law, in the neighboring State of Corrupt. The garbage, including the plastic, was placed in a land fill next to the Ocean; it drifted out to sea and became entangled in the nets of Corruptian fishing boats in Corrupt's Exclusive Economic Zone where crews dumped all the garbage overboard. The prevailing current took it to Playa del Oro's beaches.

As a member of the legal department of Playa del Oro's Foreign Ministry, you have been asked to prepare a memorandum setting forth the rights of the country with respect to the harm caused by these two incidents and the remedies that might be available to it.

B. THE SEA AND ITS USE BY HUMANS

The world's ocean are under stress from over-fishing, predator loss, the effects of climate change, invasive species and marine pollution from both vessels and land-based sources of marine pollution. See United Nations Environmental Programme, Ocean Atlas available at www. oceansatlas.org. Pew Oceans Commission, America's Living Oceans: Charting a Course for Sea Change (2003), described the pollution coming into the oceans from all sources as leading to a state of "silent collapse." Oceans cover approximately 71 percent of Earth's surface and comprise the great preponderance of its hydrosphere. The average depth of the sea is estimated to be 3,790 meters (12,430 feet). For purposes of comparison, the average elevation of land above sea level is only 840 meters (2,760 feet). While all the seas of the world share certain obvious characteristics, many have unique attributes. For example, shipping lanes and straits are used more intensively than other parts of the ocean for navigation, making accidents and spills there more likely; some areas of the sea are more ecologically fragile than others; seas, such as the Mediterranean and the Baltic, are semi-enclosed, inhibiting the exchange of their waters with those of the rest of the ocean and thus slowing the process of self-purification; and some parts of the ocean are utilized more intensively by humans than others, resulting in more pollution, both chronic and accidental.

For centuries humans have engaged both in fishing and hunting of marine mammals (including, e.g., whales, fur seals, and sea otters), with results that have sometime been disastrous for the specie in question, and these uses of the seas have changed and intensified over time. Originally a convenient highway for exploration, travel, trade, and food, today the sea is also used for the extraction of oil and other minerals (from the subsoil and the seabed, respectively), the laying of cables and pipelines, the placement (on the seabed) of antisubmarine warfare devices, tourism, and waste disposal. Global climate change has serious adverse impacts on ocean. Oceans are warming at the rate of about 0.2 degrees F per decade. Oceans function as carbon sinks, but greenhouse gas emissions are causing ocean acidification, coral bleaching, sea level rise, coastal inundation, coastal erosion, dead zones, new diseases, loss of marine mammals, changes in levels of precipitation, and fishery declines. Warm oceans mean more extreme weather events from droughts to hurricanes, floods and storm surges. Coastal settlement and farming also contribute substantial stresses on the oceans to absorb pollution. According to the United Nations Ocean Atlas, 44 percent of the world's population lives within 150 kilometers (93 miles) of an ocean or sea.[1] Thus, many coastal cities are vulnerable to sea level rise and could face 1 trillion dollars in annual damages. The world's most at-risk cities include Miami (No. 1), New York (No, 2), Guangzhou, China (No. 6), and Mumbai, India (No. 7).[2] The concentration of human settlements and activities near coastal areas and in river basins also results in massive pollution of the marine environment from land-based sources. Over 70 percent of marine pollution comes from these sources, while maritime transport and dumping at sea contribute only 10 percent each. In addition to ocean dumping and spills, intensive shore development funnels oil and toxic pollutants into coastal waters. Nutrient run-off from farm and yard fertilizers cause algae blooms which threaten coral reefs and seagrass beds. Subsequent studies and reports only confirm that the problem is getting worse.

Fishing is an example of the potential effects of human exploitation of marine living resources. Technological advances have enabled humans to catch fish in vast quantities to feed the growing human population, as well as animals and even plants (as fertilizer), and to reach areas of the ocean that were until recently too remote or inhospitable for significant fishing activities. What was once done with rod and small net is now accomplished with sonar, satellites, spotter planes, factory processing ships, and enormous nets. The latter include driftnets, which may be 30 miles long and may, as "ghost nets," go on catching fish, marine mammals, and birds for months or even years after they have been lost or abandoned. [3] The result of this greatly enhanced capacity has been overfishing and the collapse of a number of fish stocks. Marine fish harvests reached a high of 84.4 million tons in 1996 and has since declined to between 77 and 80 million tons per year. Several countries such as Iceland and New Zealand have taken effective conservation steps, but the Food and Agricultural Organization paints a gloomy picture of the current state of the world's fisheries:

> The proportion of non-fully exploited stocks has decreased gradually since 1974 when the first FAO assessment was completed. In contrast, the percentage of overexploited stocks has increased, especially in the late 1970s and 1980s, from 10 percent in 1974 to 26 percent in 1989. After 1990, the number of overexploited stocks continued to increase, albeit at a slower rate. Increases in production from these overexploited stocks may be possible if effective rebuilding plans are put in place. The

---

[1]   http://www.oceansatlas.org/servlet/CDSServlet?status=ND0xODc3JjY9ZW4mMz M9KiYzNz1rb3M~).

[2]   http://ens-newswire.com/2013/09/03/10–coastal-cities-at-greatest-flood-risk-as-sea-levels-rise/.

[3]   See Tegan Churcher Hoffman, identifying Opportunities to Address Issues of Marine Fisheries and Biodiversity Conservation (Macarthur Foundation Conservation White Paper Series 2010).

fraction of fully exploited stocks, which produce catches that are very close to their maximum sustainable production and have no room for further expansion and require effective management to avoid decline, has shown the smallest change over time, with its percentage stable at about 50 percent from 1974 to 1985, then falling to 43 percent in 1989 before gradually increasing to 57 percent in 2009. About 29.9 percent of stocks are overexploited, producing lower yields than their biological and ecological potential and in need of strict management plans to restore their full and sustainable productivity in accordance with the Johannesburg Plan of Implementation that resulted from the World Summit on Sustainable Development (Johannesburg, 2002), which demands that all overexploited stocks be restored to the level that can produce maximum sustainable yield by 2015, a target that seems unlikely to be met. The remaining 12.7 percent of stocks were non-fully exploited in 2009, and these are under relatively low fishing pressure and have some potential to increase their production, although they often do not have a high production potential and require proper management plans to ensure that any increase in the exploitation rate does not result in further overfishing. [Food and Agricultural Organization, World Review of Fisheries and Aquaculture 11–12 (2012)]

Curbing stresses such as over-fishing present enormous challenges. See United Nations Environmental Programme, Overfishing and Other threats to Aquatic Living Resources (2012). For starters, many countries subsidize fishing, and fish are an important source of protein for developing countries. Is the existing legal framework equipped to deal with them? Has it kept pace with the capacity of humans to develop new technologies that hold the potential for both great good and great harm? Consider these overarching questions as you read through the following materials.

This chapter is devoted to these matters. Protection of the marine environment is regulated generally by Part XII of the 1982 United Nations Convention on the Law of the Sea (UNCLOS). But, a number of separate agreements deal with the protection of regional seas, and other instruments address specific problem, such as vessel-source pollution and land-based source pollution. Land-based sources have thus far eluded global legal regulation beyond the general provisions of UNCLOS, despite regional seas agreements which address land-based sources global guidelines and a global action program negotiated under UNEP auspices. This chapter will provide a brief overview of this regulatory system. Efforts to protect marine mammals are discussed in Chapter 13, Biodiversity. It is important to view the problem of protection of the marine environment from a holistic perspective, one that is not limited to any one problem or class of problems, such a marine pollution. Article 192 of UCLOS, the first provision in Part XII, captures the essence of this approach. The article in its entirety states:

Article 192
General Obligation

States have the obligation to protect and preserve the marine environment.

This provision is striking in both its generality and lack of qualification. But what does it mean as a practical matter? What do States actually have to do, or refrain from doing, to comply with this obligation? What precisely is meant by the expression "marine environment" (the term is not defined in the convention)? Some light is shed on these questions by the historical development of the law concerning the protection of the marine environment, the more specific provisions of UNCLOS bearing on this problem, and other related instruments.

1. THE LAW OF THE MARINE ENVIRONMENT

a. Historical Development

It was not until the latter half of the present century that humans began to inflict wide-ranging harm on the marine environment. It was therefore not until well after World War II that humans, and thus States, began to recognize the need to protect the marine environment. Thus the law of the marine environment is relatively new. The law of the sea itself, however, is quite venerable. See generally R.P. Anand, Origin and Development of the Law of the Sea (1983); and W.E. Butler, Grotius and the Law of the Sea, in Grotius and International Relations 209 (H. Bull, B. Kingsbury & A. Robers eds., 1990). Two ideas have dominated the evolution of the law of the sea: freedom of the seas versis State authority over large portions of the seas. This tension is captured eloquently in the so-called battle of the books of the seventeenth century, between Hugo Grotius' Mare *Liberum* (1609) and John Selden's Mare *Clausum* (1635). As their titles indicate, these works argued, respectively, that "State may not individually or collectively acquire the high seas areas by occupation since they are res *communis omnium* or *res extra commercium*"; and that the sea "is as capable of private dominion as land, and the king of Great Britain is lord of all the sea inseparably and perpetually appendant to the British Empire." W.E. Butler, Grotious and the Law of the Sea, *supra* at 211. Ironically, Selden was a staunch opponent of the Stuart King's assertion of the Royal Prerogative. Today, his name lives on in the Selden Society, the major publisher of English legal history monographs and other materials.

By the end of the eighteenth century most claims to large areas of the sea had effectively been abandoned, and in the twentieth century, "the freedom of the seas has come to be accepted as a 'general', 'basic', or 'fundamental' principle of international law: some are even prepared to treat it as *jus cogens*." *Id.* at 212. But even this principle has been effectively eroded in the latter decade of this century as the "high seas," to which the concept of the freedom of the seas applies, have been steadily shrinking with the expansion of coastal State jurisdiction, in particular the recognition in the 1982 Convention of the 200-mile exclusive economic zone. Is this a positive or a negative development with regard to the marine environment? You should consider this question in relation to such specific problem as the control of vessel-source pollution, the protection of marine mammals, and the protection and management of fish stocks.

Is the following Canadian unilateral action an example of needed environmental stewardship or a violation of UNCLOS? Concerned about the dumping of nuclear waste from the then USSR submarines, in 1970 Canada adopted the Arctic Pollution Prevention Control Act, R.S.C., 1985, c. A-12, which now extends Canadian regulatory jurisdiction to waters 200 nautical miles from the nearest Canadian land and asserts the right to license all waste disposal from ships or mineral activities passing through this area or areas designated as safety control zones. The Act remains an integral part of Canada's evolving Arctic policy. Speaking in 2008, Canadian Prime Minister Stephen Harper said, "Canada takes responsibility for environmental protection and enforcement in our Arctic waters. This magnificent and unspoiled region is one for which we will demonstrate stewardship on behalf of our country, and indeed, all of humanity." See Burt K. Carnahan, The Canadian Arctic Waters Pollution Prevention Act: An Analysis, 31 La. L. Rev. (1971), for a discussion of the legal basis of the Act.

Reflecting the relative intensity of different use of the seas during the first half of the twentieth century, early efforts to protect the marine environment for the most part addressed living resources rather than pollution. Among the agreements concluded during this period were treaties for the protection of fur seals (1911),[4] fisheries (1923, 1930),[5] and whales (1931).[6] See Chapter 13. The pace picked up considerably after World War II, with the conclusion of additional agreements on marine living resources[7] and, in 1954, the Convention for the Prevention of

---

[4] Convention for the Preservation and Protection of Fur Seals, July 7, 1911, 37 Stat. 1542, T.S. 564, 104 B.S.F.P. 175.

[5] Convention between Canada and the United States for the Preservation of the Halibut Fishery of the Northern Pacific Ocean, Mar. 2, 1923, 32 L.N.T.S. 93; Convention Establishing an International Pacific Salmon Fisheries Commission, 1930, 184 L.N.T.S. 306.

[6] Convention for the Regulation of Whaling, Sept. 24, 1931, 155 L.N.T.S. 349, 49 Stat. 3079, T.S. 880.

[7] Among the agreements concluded shortly after World War II were the London Convention for the Regulation of the Meshes of Fishing Nets and the Size Limits of Fish, Apr. 5, 1946, 231 U.N.T.S. 199; the Washington International Convention for the Regulation of Whaling, Dec. 2, 1946, 161 U.N.T.S. 72, 62 Stat. 1716, TIAS 1849, U.K.T.S. No. 5 (1949); and the FAO

Pollution of the Sea by Oil.[8] This treaty, which addressed discharge of oil from ships, was followed four years later by the Geneva Convention on the High Seas—one of four agreements on the law of the sea adopted under United Nations auspices in 1958.[9] Article 24 of the High Seas Convention required parties to adopt rules for the prevention of marine pollution from "the discharge of oil from ships or pipeline or resulting from the exploitation and exploration of the seabed and its subsoil. . . ." The widely publicized *Torrey Canyon* disaster of March 1967—together with the United Kingdom's response[10]—highlighted the threat to the marine environment from accidental oil spills by tankers, as well as the legal issues raised by such incidents. [11] Agreements were concluded shortly thereafter to confirm the right of the coastal State to respond to threats posed by such incidents[12] and to provide for civil liability for marine oil pollution damage.[13] The 1970s saw the conclusion of several regional treaties[14] and two global agreements for the protection of the marine environment. The latter—the 1972 London Dumping Convention[15] and the 1973/1978 MARPOL Convention[16]—continue to be

---

Agreement for the Establishment of the Indo-Pacific Fisheries Commission, Feb. 26, 1948, 120 U.N.T.S. 59, 62 Stat. 3711, T.I.A.S. 1895.

[8]   May 12, 1954, 327 U.N.T.S. 3, 12 U.S.T. 2989, T.I.A.S. 4900.

[9]   Convention on the Territorial Sea and the Contiguous Zone, Apr. 29, 1958, 516 U.N.T.S. 205, 15 U.S.T. 1606; Convention on the Continental Shelf, Apr. 29, 1958, 499 U.N.T.S. 311, 15 U.S.T. 471; Convention on the High Seas, Apr. 29, 1958, 450 U.N.T.S. 82, 13 U.S.T. 2312, TIAS 5200; and Convention on Fishing and Conservation of the Living Resources of the High Seas, Apr. 29, 1958, 559 U.N.T. 25, 17 U.S.T. 138, T.I.A.S. 5969. All four agreements, done at Geneva, are known as the 1958 "Geneva Conventions" on the law of the sea.

[10]   The UK responded to the threat to its coastline posed by the breakup of the Torrey Canyon by destroying the tanker without the consent of the flag State. This incident was followed by the conclusion of the Convention Relating to Intervention on the High Seas in Cases of Oil Pollution Casualties of Nov. 29, 1969, 26 U.S.T. 765. 970 U.N.T.S. 211.

[11]   See generally R. Michael M'Gonigle & Mark W. Zacher, Pollution, Politics, and International Law: Tankers at Sea (1979).

[12]   *See* Convention, 1969 Oil Pollution Casualties, *supra* footnote 10.

[13]   Brussels International Convention on Civil Liability for Oil Pollution Damage. Nov. 29, 1973, 973 N.T.S. 3, K.T.S. No. 106 (1975), 9 I.L.M. 45 (1970), establishing strict liability of the shipowner, which may be limited under specified conditions; Brussels International Convention on the Establishment of an International Fund for Compensation for Oil Pollution Damage. Dec. 18, 1971, 1110 U.N.T.S. 57, U.K.T.S. No. 95 (1978), 11 I.L.M. 284 (1972), supplementing the compensation available under the Civil Liability Convention.

[14]   Oslo Convention for the Prevention of Marine Pollution by Dumping from Ships and Aircraft, Feb. 15, 1972, 932 U.N.T.S. 3, U.K.T. No. 119 (1975), 9 I.L.M. 359 (1970); Copenhagen (Nordic) Agreement on Cooperation in Oil Pollution, Sept. 16, 1971, 2 International Protection of the Environment: Treaties and Related Documents 502 (B. Rüster, B. Simma & M. Bock eds.); and Barcelona Convention for the Protection of the Mediterranean Sea against Pollution, Feb. 16. 1976, U.N.T.S. Reg. o. 1690, 15 1.L.M. 290 (1976); see also the Bonn Agreement for Cooperation in Dealing with Pollution of the North Sea by Oil, June 9, 1969, 704 U.N.T.S. 3, 9 I.L.M. 359 (1970).

[15]   IMO Convention on the Prevention of Marine Pollution by Dumping of Wastes and Other Matter, Dec. 29, 1972 (as amended Oct. 12, 1978), 1046 U.N.T.S. 120, 26 U.S.T. 2403, T.I.A.S. 8165, 11 I.L.M. 1294 (1972).

[16]   London International Convention for the Prevention of Pollution from Ships (MARPOL), Nov. 2, 1973, 121.L.M. 1319 (1973), as amended by the London Protocol of 17 Feb. 1978, T.I.A.S., 17 I.L.M. 546 (1978).

among the most important global instruments in force concerning the prevention of marine pollution. During this same decade, however, a major international effort was underway to negotiate an agreement covering all aspects of the law of the sea: The Third United Nations Conference on the Law of the Sea (1973–1982).

b. The Approach of the United Nations Convention on the Law of the Sea (UNCLOS)

The Law of the Sea Conference, "the largest and most complex international negotiation ever held,"[17] produced the 1982 United Nations Convention on the Law of the Sea (UNCLOS).[18] This agreement has been said to be, "after the United Nations charter itself, . . . the most far-reaching and potentially influential agreement on the peacetime conduct of nations ever attempted."[19] It is also the only global treaty dealing, albeit in a general way, with all aspects of the protection of the marine environment. Furthermore, UNCLOS "clarifies the extent of coastal States' authority in the various maritime areas [e.g., the territorial sea and the exclusive economic zone], thus contributing also to the clarification of the scope of the other existing Conventions."[20] Recent treatments include Alexander Prölss, The United Nations Convention on the Law of the Sea (2014) and Donald R. Rothwell, The International Law of the Sea (2010).

The convention devotes one entire chapter, Part XII, to the "[p]rotection and[p]reservation of the [m]arine [e]nvironment." However, other provisions on the subject are scattered throughout the treaty. This is true not only of the definition of "pollution of the marine environment," to which we will return, but also of environmental provisions in sections of the convention dealing with, inter alia, the territorial sea (Part II), straits (Part III), archipelagic waters (Part N), the exclusive economic zone (Part V), the high seas (Part VII), enclosed or semienclosed seas (Part IX), the exploration and exploitation of the seabed (Part XI), and marine scientific research (Part XIII). Part XII itself consists of 11

---

[17] William Wertenbaker, The Law of the Sea—I & II, The New Yorker, Aug. 1 and Aug. 8, 1983. This article contains an excellent description of the negotiations and their dynamic, as well as of the personalities involved.

[18] UNCLOS, supra footnote I. The convention entered into force on Nov. 16, 1994, in accordance with its Article 308. The United States has not become a party as of this writing, even though the principal objections of the United States to the treaty had been eliminated through the adoption by the UN General Assembly, on June 28, 1994, of the Agreement relating to the Implementation of Part XI of the United Nations Convention on the Law of the Sea of Dec. 10, 1982, 33 I.L.M. 1309 (1994). The vote was 121 in favor, none against, and 7 abstentions. GA Res. 48/263 (July 28, 1994). The agreement in effect amends Part XI, which contains the proposed regime for mining in the deep seabed. See Law of the Sea Forum: The 1994 Agreement on Implementation of the Seabed Provisions of the Convention on the Law of the Sea, 88 Arn.J. Intl. L. 687 (1994).

[19] Wertenbaker, *supra* footnote 17.

[20] Tullio Treves, Oceans, in World Treaties for the Protection of the Environment 149, 150 (1992).

sections,[21] which contain Articles 192–237 of the convention. These provisions "serve as a framework for existing and future conventions of a specialized kind as well as for state cooperation within International Organizations and through their lawmaking and enforcement activity."[22]

Birnie and Boyle observe that UNCLOS reflects a number of fundamental changes in the law concerning the protection of the marine environment. "Of these perhaps the most important is that pollution can no longer be regarded as an implicit freedom of the Seas; rather, its diligent control from all sources is now a matter of comprehensive legal obligation affecting the marine environment as a whole, and not simply the interests of other States."[23] What are the implications of this change? If interests of other States are not affected, are these true "obligations"? Why or why not?

Part XII begins by laying down the all-important "general obligation" to protect and preserve the marine environment in Article 192, set forth above. It then recognizes, in Article 193, the "sovereign right of States to exploit their natural resources," but provides that States must exercise this right "in accordance with their duty to protect and preserve the marine environment." Compare this formulation with that of Principle 21 of the Stockholm Declaration/Principle 2 of the Rio Declaration: Which do you consider preferable from an environmental protection point of view? Article 194 is entitled "Measures to prevent, reduce and control pollution of the marine environment." "Pollution of the marine environment" is broadly defined in Article 1(1)(4) as

> the introduction by man, directly or indirectly, of substances or energy into the marine environment, including estuaries, which results or is likely to result in such deleterious effects as harm to living resources and marine life, hazards to human health, hindrance to marine activities, including fishing and other legitimate uses of the sea, impairment of quality for use of sea water and reduction of amenities.[24]

Article 194 lays down general obligations concerning marine pollution and sets forth a nonexhaustive catalogue of sources of pollution that States are required to address. As the article encapsulates well the

---

[21] Those are: Section 1, General Provisions; Section 2, Global and Regional Cooperation; Section 3, Technical Assistance; Section 4, Monitoring and Environmental Assessment; Section 5, International Rules and National Legislation to Prevent, Reduce and Control Pollution of the Marine Environment; Section 6, Enforcement; Section 7, Safeguards; Section 8, Ice-Covered Areas; Section 9, Responsibility and Liability; Section 10, Sovereign Immunity; and Section 11, Obligation under Other Conventions on the Protection and Preservation of the Marine Environment.

[22] Treves, above footnote 20, at 150.

[23] Patricia W. Birnie & Alan E. Boyle, International Law and the Environment at 253 (1992).

[24] UNCLOS, Article 1(1)(4).

approach of the convention to the control of marine pollution, we set it forth here in full:

Article 194
Measures to Prevent, Reduce and Control Pollution of the Marine Environment

1.   States shall take, individually or jointly as appropriate, all measures consistent with this Convention that are necessary to prevent, reduce and control pollution of the marine environment from any source, using for this purpose the best practicable means at their disposal and in accordance with their capabilities, and they shall endeavor to harmonize their policies in this connection.

2.   States shall take all measures necessary to ensure that activities under their jurisdiction and control are so conducted as not to cause damage by pollution to other States and their environment, and that pollution arising from incidents or activities under their jurisdiction or control does not spread beyond the areas where they exercise sovereign rights in accordance with this Convention.

3.   The measures taken pursuant to this Part shall deal with all sources of pollution of the marine environment. These measures shall include, inter alia, those designed to minimize to the fullest possible extent:

(a) the release of toxic, harmful or noxious substances, especially those which are persistent, from land-based sources, from or through the atmosphere or by dumping;

(b) pollution from vessels, in particular measures for preventing accidents and dealing with emergencies, ensuring the Safety of operations at sea, preventing intentional and unintentional discharges, and regulating the design, construction, equipment, operation and manning of vessels;

(c) pollution from installations and devices used in exploration or exploitation of the natural resources of the sea-bed and subsoil, in particular measures for preventing accidents and dealing with emergencies, ensuring the safety of operations at sea, and regulating the design, construction, equipment, operation and manning of such installations or devices;

(d) pollution from other installations and devices operating in the marine environment, in particular measures for preventing accidents and dealing with emergencies, ensuring the safety of operations at sea, and regulating the design, construction, equipment, operation and manning of such installations or devices.

4.   In taking measures to prevent, reduce or control pollution of the marine environment, States shall refrain from unjustifiable interference with activities carried out by other States in the exercise of their rights and in pursuance of their duties in conformity with this Convention.

5.   The measures taken in accordance with this Part shall include those necessary to protect and preserve rare or fragile ecosystems as well as the habitat of depleted, threatened or endangered species and other forms of marine life.

Subsequent provisions of Part XII elaborate on the measures to be taken with regard to each of the sources enumerated in paragraph 3 of Article 194. They also specify in detail the authority of States to enforce obligations concerning marine pollution in the different maritime zones. The convention strikes a delicate balance between the traditional authority of flag States over pollution from ships and the authority of coastal and port States, which has developed more recently in response to threats to their marine environment. The subject of jurisdiction to enforce these obligations is a complex one, since more than one State may have jurisdiction over a vessel under international law at the same time. The convention also permits especially stringent measures to be applied with regard to areas as to which there is a particular risk due to oceanographic, ecological, or traffic conditions.[25]

NOTES AND QUESTIONS

1.   *The status of UNCLOS.* The Convention on the Law of the Sea entered into force on November 16, 1994. As of 2013, 165 States and the European Union are parties. The United States is not, however, a party. But in March 1983, President Reagan issued a Statement on United States Oceans Policy in which he noted the United States decision not to sign the Convention because of its deep seabed mining provisions, but went on to state that the convention "contains provisions with respect to traditional uses of the oceans [i.e., uses other than deep seabed mining] which generally confirm existing maritime law and practice and fairly balance the interests of all States" and that "the United States is prepared to accept and act in accordance with the balance of interests relating to traditional uses of the ocean. . . ."[26] He also proclaimed a 200-nautical-mile exclusive economic zone for the United States—a jurisdictional zone that did not exist prior to the convention. As you might expect, this infuriated some States because of the

---

[25]   UNCLOS , Article 211(6)(a).
[26]   19 Weekly Comp. Pres. Docs. 383 (1983), 83 Dept. State Bull., No. 2075, at 70–71 (1983), 22 I.L.M. 464 (1983).

understanding during the negotiation of the convention that the text as finally adopted was a "package deal"—a State had to accept all of it or could take advantage of none of it (other than provisions reflecting existing customary international law, of course). Does the position of the United States vis-a-vis the convention affect its right to assert violations of provisions of Part XII? Ratification has considerable bi-partisan support, including all Presidents since Ronald Reagan as well the consistent support of the Department of Defense, but the last push for ratification failed in December, 2012. Only eight Republicans supported ratification. The DOD and other proponents of ratification argue that it will give the United States more political influence and certainty for naval operations in the South China Sea as well as to assert claims in the Arctic. See Ernest Z. Bower and Gregory B. Poling, Advancing National Interests of the United States: Ratification of Law of the Sea, available at http://csis.org/publication/advancing-national-interests-united-states-ratification-law-sea.

2.   *Examining Article 194.* Article 194 is commendable in its coverage of sources of marine pollution. But is it sufficiently strict with regard to the "measures" to be taken as to those sources? What is the meaning of the phrases "the best practicable means at their disposal" and "in accordance with their capabilities"? Are these loopholes that may undermine the convention's entire regime concerning marine pollution? Why do you suppose they were included in the article? Do these phrases make Article 194 consistent or inconsistent with the norms of prevention we examined in Chapter 6?

3.   *Vessel-source pollution.* Article 211, "Pollution from vessels," provides for the "prevention, reduction and control" of marine pollution from vessels by the flag State (para. 2), the port State (para. 3) and the coastal State (paras. 4–6). Not surprisingly, a coastal State's authority over foreign vessels increases as they near its shore. In the 200-mile exclusive economic zone the laws and regulations it adopts must conform to "generally accepted international rules and standards established through the competent international organization or general diplomatic conference." This formula is used frequently in the convention, referring to widely accepted obligations adopted under the auspices of the International Maritime Organization (IMO-formerly the International Maritime Consultative Organization, IMCO) or by a diplomatic conference that prepared an international agreement. In a coastal State's 12-mile territorial sea, on the other hand, its right to adopt such laws and regulations is unrestricted, except that these measures may not hamper the innocent passage of foreign vessels through those waters. (Innocent passage is regulated by Part II Section 3 of UNCLOS, Articles 17–32.) Finally, the convention permits a State to "establish particular requirements . . . as a condition for the entry of foreign vessels into their ports or internal waters or for a call at their offshore terminals," requiring such a State to "give due publicity to such requirements" and to "communicate them to the competent international organization"—generally the IMO. This gives States importing large quantities of oil, such as the United States and Japan, considerable authority over the standards

governing foreign oil tankers. However, the fact that many tankers are also registered in such States or owned by their nationals acts as a practical check on the stringency of the regulations they are prepared to adopt. Enforcement of laws and regulations concerning marine pollution is governed by Section 6 of Part XII. Broad authority is given to port States to enforce "applicable international rule and standards" concerning a discharge occurring on the high seas or to investigate a discharge violation at the request of another State within whose jurisdiction the discharge occurred or where it caused or threatened damage (Article 218). Coastal States are also granted significant enforcement powers (Article 220).

4.   *Problem.* The good ship *MV Leaky*, a large oil tanker registered in State A, strikes a reef in the exclusive economic zone (EEZ) of State B, causing it to spill a large quantity of oil. The oil slick spread both into the territorial sea of State C and into the high seas. Which States have authority with regard to this incident? Which States' laws apply? Which States have enforcement authority? How should action on the public (State-to-state) and private (e.g., lawsuits against the ship owner seeking redress for damage) levels be coordinated in such cases, if at all?

2.   OCEAN DUMPING

Marine pollution emerged as a serious global problem in the period between 1950 and 1970. Just as there were more oil spills, discharges from ships, and dumping of waste into the ocean, so also there was a growing awareness that the oceans did not have an unlimited capacity to absorb wastes without harming the marine environment. States negotiated agreements to control the dumping and discharge of wastes into oceans long before they negotiated agreements governing air pollution or, with the notable exception of the United States-Canada Boundary Waters Agreement, fresh water.

The 1972 Convention on the Prevention of Marine Pollution by Dumping of Wastes and Other Matter (informally known as the London Dumping Convention) was a product of the 1972 Stockholm Conference preparations. The London Convention was concluded in December 1972, six months after Stockholm, and became effective in August 1975. As of February 2015, 87 States were party to the agreement. In 1996 States negotiated a Protocol to the Convention, which replaces the 1972 agreement for those countries that ratify the Protocol. As of February 2015, 48 States have ratified the 1996 Protocol, at least 5 of which are not parties to the earlier 1972 Convention. The Protocol has gone into effect. The International Maritime Organization (IMO) in London hosts the agreement. The following reading provides a concise overview of the 1972 Convention.

a.   The London Convention of 1972

SEA CHANGES? OCEAN DUMPING AND
INTERNATIONAL REGULATION
Alan B. Sielen
1 Geo. Intl. Envtl. L. Rev. 2 (1988)

Many governments today face substantial pressure to open up the oceans to greater use as a waste disposal medium. This pressure stems primarily from a growing inventory of wastes and the difficulty of finding technically suitable and politically acceptable waste-disposal sites on land. The wastes involved range from the very toxic, such as high-level radioactive wastes, to the relatively benign, such as garbage. Some parts of the scientific community have also taken greater interest lately in the oceans' potential for receiving wastes. This scientific debate results from the large strides made in recent years in understanding the scientific aspects of marine pollution, as well as the development of new analytic tools for assessing risks to humans and the environment and for monitoring the effects of pollution over time.

An important manifestation of this growing interest in the oceans as a place for waste disposal is the emergence of major global and regional marine protection treaties. To date one of the most significant agreements has been the London Dumping Convention. . . .

The Convention has provided the basic global framework for the control of the deliberate disposal (ocean dumping) of all wastes at sea since its entry into force in 1975. Ocean dumping operations usually consist of collecting wastes generated on land, loading them on a ship or barge, and then taking them out to sea for the express purpose of disposal. Although most wastes are dumped from vessels, the London Convention's definition of dumping also includes deliberate disposal from "aircraft, platforms or other manmade structures. . . ." The incineration of hazardous chemicals at sea is also regulated as a form of ocean dumping under the United States Marine Protection, Research, and Sanctuaries Act (MPRSA) and the London Convention.

Dumping does not include discharges from what are usually referred to as "land-based sources" of marine pollution: rivers, pipelines, outfalls, and runoff. Nor does it include operational discharges from vessels, offshore drilling operations, or disposal arising from or related to the exploration, exploitation, and associated offshore processing of seabed mineral resources. In the United States, these activities are regulated under separate laws and, in the case of vessel pollution, are also subject to a broad array of international conventions on vessel design, construction, operation, manning, and liability for damage from tanker spills.

Ocean dumping accounts for only about ten percent of all pollution of the seas; its impact, however, if left uncontrolled, can result in significant damage to the marine environment. For example, most dumping, for reasons of economy, takes place relatively close to shore. Thus, the waste may be deposited in or near biologically productive continental shelf areas. Moreover, the cumulative impacts of ocean dumping may significantly increase as more countries begin to look towards the oceans as a repository for industrial, chemical, agricultural, and radioactive wastes, as well as contaminated dredged material and sewage sludge.

a.   Application

Under the London Convention, national authorities in contracting States must control dumping consistently with the provisions of the Convention. Accordingly, regardless of whether the waste is actually to be dumped in the Contracting Party's territorial waters, a Contracting Party will require that all vessels loading in its ports or territorial seas for the purpose of dumping must first obtain a permit from the Contracting Party's designated agency. Any of the Contracting Party's own vessels planning to dump anywhere in the world must also obtain a permit. In addition, a Contracting Party will require foreign vessels to obtain permits before dumping in offshore areas subject to the Party's jurisdiction—usually 200-mile exclusive economic zones (EEZs). Enforcement is left for the most part to the flag States, although coastal States may apply the Convention to foreign vessels dumping in their EEZ. As in most international environmental agreements, individual countries are free to apply standards stricter than the London Convention's to their own activities. . . .

The International Maritime Organization (IMO) in London, a specialized agency of the United Nations, serves as Secretariat for the Convention. In this capacity, the IMO receives notifications from governments of dumping permits issued, distributes documents, holds regular consultative and scientific group meetings, and carries out all other administrative tasks necessary to the Convention's operation. The Contracting Parties have been rather fortunate in this respect as the IMO continues to be one of the most efficient bureaucracies on the international scene.

b.   Regulatory Structure: Blacklist/Graylist

The London Convention's basic approach to regulation is embodied in its three technical Annexes, and is relatively simple. Annex I lists those substances that may not be dumped because of their potential to harm the marine environment. These "blacklisted" substances include such highly toxic or persistent substances as high-level radioactive wastes, organohalogens, mercury, cadmium, oil, and persistent plastics. Certain of these Annex I substances, however, may be incinerated at sea in accordance with regulations set by the London Convention.

Exceptions to the Annex I prohibitions are made in cases of "emergencies, posing unacceptable risks relating to human health and admitting no other feasible solution." In addition, and most significantly, the Annex I prohibitions do not include substances that are "rapidly rendered harmless by physical, chemical, or biological processes in the seas," or apply to cases where blacklisted substances are found only as "trace contaminants" in other wastes such as sewage sludge or dredged spoils.

Annex II identifies wastes containing significant amounts of substances posing less danger to the environment. These "graylist" substances may be dumped so long as special care is taken with regard to factors such as site selection, monitoring, packaging of the wastes, and disposal methods intended to mitigate environmental contamination.

Materials not found in either Annex I or II may be clumped under a general permit issued in compliance with the requirements of Annex III. Annex III contains environmental protection criteria which national authorities must carefully consider before issuing any dumping permit. These criteria include consideration of possible effects on marine life, amenities, and other uses of the sea along with factors pertaining to the suitability of any particular disposal operation such as the characteristics and composition of the waste, description of the disposal site, method of disposal, and the practical availability of land-based alternatives.

Over the years, Contracting Parties have supplemented the Convention with additional guidance relating to the implementation of the Convention. These additions have ranged from amendments to the Convention and its Annexes to guidelines that define and interpret key technical terms used in the Annexes including "rapidly rendered harmless," "trace contaminants," and "significant amounts."

In this way, member countries have been able to both apply their practical experience gained in the disposal of common wastes, such as contaminated dredged material, and establish new controls for emerging technologies, such as ocean incineration. Some of the more significant initiatives undertaken pursuant to the Convention include regulations and technical guidelines for ocean incineration, arbitration procedures for the peaceful settlement of disputes arising under the Convention, criteria for allocating substances to the Convention's Annexes, and guidance on the application of the Annexes to dredged material.

b.   The 1996 Protocol to the London Convention

In the fall of 1996, parties to the London Convention adopted the 1996 Protocol, which supersedes the 1972 Convention for all member States that join the protocol. However, the 1972 Protocol remains in effect until a country ratifies the 1996 Protocol. The new agreement essentially updates the 1972 treaty to keep pace with changes in our understanding of marine pollution and with measures needed to protect the oceans. It adopts the "precautionary approach" and permits dumping of wastes in the ocean only if the wastes fall into those categories listed in an annex and a permit has been obtained. It prohibits the incineration of wastes at sea, bans the export of wastes to other countries for dumping or incineration at sea, provides for setting up procedures to handle complaints, obligates countries to promote technical cooperation and assistance (although it does not establish a fund for such assistance), establishes formal dispute resolution procedures, and provides in an annex for waste audits, which include alternative forms of waste disposal.

1996 PROTOCOL TO THE CONVENTION ON THE PREVENTION OF MARINE POLLUTION BY DUMPING OF WASTES AND OTHER MATTER, 1972 AND RESOLUTIONS ADOPTED BY THE SPECIAL MEETING

As adopted by the Special Meeting of Contracting Parties to the London Convention 1972 on Nov. 7, 1996

Article 2
Objectives

Contracting Parties shall individually and collectively protect and preserve the marine environment from all sources of pollution and take effective measures, according to their scientific, technical and economic capabilities, to prevent, reduce and where practicable eliminate pollution caused by dumping or incineration at sea of wastes or other matter. Where appropriate, they shall harmonize their policies in this regard.

Article 3
General Obligations

1.   In implementing this Protocol, Contracting Parties shall apply a precautionary approach to environmental protection from dumping of wastes or other matter whereby appropriate preventative measures are taken when there is reason to believe that wastes or other matter introduced into the marine environment are likely to cause harm even when there is no conclusive evidence to prove a causal relation between inputs and their effects.

2.   Taking into account the approach that the polluter should, in principle, bear the cost of pollution, each Contracting Party shall endeavor to promote practices whereby those it has authorized to engage in dumping or incineration at sea bear the cost of meeting the pollution prevention and control requirements for the authorized activities, having due regard to the public interest.

3.   In implementing the provisions of this Protocol, Contracting Parties shall act so as not to transfer, directly or indirectly, damage or

likelihood of damage from one part of the environment to another or transform one type of pollution into another.

4.   No provision of this Protocol shall be interpreted as preventing Contracting Parties from taking, individually or jointly, more stringent measures in accordance with international law with respect to the prevention, reduction and where practicable elimination of pollution.

Article 4
Dumping of Wastes or Other Matter

1.1. Contracting Parties shall prohibit the dumping of any wastes or other matter with the exception of those listed in Annex 1.

1.2. The dumping of wastes of other matter listed in Annex I shall require a permit. Contracting Parties shall adopt administrative or legislative measures to ensure that issuance of permits and permit conditions comply with provisions of Annex 2. Particular attention shall be paid to opportunities to avoid dumping in favour of environmentally preferable alternatives.

2.   No provision of this Protocol shall be interpreted as preventing a Contracting Party from prohibiting, insofar as that Contracting Party is concerned, the dumping of wastes or other matter mentioned in Annex I. That Contracting Party shall notify the Organization of such measures

Article 5
Incineration at Sea

Contracting Parties shall prohibit incineration at sea of wastes or other matter.

Article 6
Export of Wastes or Other Matter

Contracting Parties shall not allow the export of wastes or other matter to other countries for dumping or incineration at sea. . . .

Article 9
Issuance of Permits and Reporting

1.   Each Contracting Party shall designate an appropriate authority or authorities to:

  .1   issue permits in accordance with this Protocol;

  .2   keep records of the nature and quantities of all wastes or other matter for which dumping permits have been issued and where practicable the quantities actually dumped and the location, time and method of dumping; and

  .3   monitor individually, or in collaboration with other Contracting Parties and competent international organizations, the condition of the sea for the purposes of this Protocol.

2.   The appropriate authority or authorities of a Contracting Party shall issue permits in accordance with this Protocol in respect of wastes or other matter intended for dumping or, as provided for in article 8.2, incineration at sea:

.1   loaded in its territory; and

.2   loaded onto a vessel or aircraft registered in its territory or flying its flag, when the loading occurs in the territory of a State not a Contracting Party to this Protocol . . .

Article 10
Application and Enforcement

1.   Each Contracting Party shall apply the measures required to implement this Protocol to all:

.1   vessels and aircraft registered in its territory or flying its flag;

.2   vessels and aircraft loading in its territory the wastes or other matter which are to be dumped or incinerated at sea; and

.3   vessels, aircraft and platforms or other man-made structures believed to be engaged in dumping or incineration at sea in areas within which it is entitled to exercise jurisdiction in accordance with international law.

2.   Each Contracting Party shall take appropriate measures in accordance with international law to prevent and if necessary punish acts contrary to the provisions of this Protocol.

3.   Contracting Parties agree to co-operate in the development of procedures for the effective application of this Protocol in areas beyond the jurisdiction of any State, including procedures for the reporting of vessels and aircraft observed dumping or incinerating at sea in contravention of this Protocol.

4.   This Protocol shall not apply to those vessels and aircraft entitled to sovereign immunity under international law. However, each Contracting Party shall ensure by the adoption of appropriate measures that such vessel and aircraft owned or operated by it act in a manner consistent with the object and purpose of this Protocol and shall inform the Organization accordingly.

5.   A State may, at the time it expresses its consent to be bound by this Protocol, or at any time thereafter, declare that it shall apply the provisions of this Protocol to its vessel and aircraft referred to in paragraph 4, recognizing that only that State may enforce those provisions against such vessels and aircraft.

Article 11
Compliance Procedures

1.   No later than two years after the entry into force of this Protocol, the Meeting of Contracting Parties shall establish those procedures and mechanisms necessary to assess and promote compliance with this Protocol. Such procedures and mechanisms shall be developed with a view to allowing for the full and open exchange of information, in a constructive manner.

2.   After full consideration of any information submitted pursuant to this Protocol and any recommendations made through procedures or mechanisms established under paragraph 1, the Meeting of Contracting Parties may offer advice, assistance or co-operation to Contracting Parties and non-Contracting Parties. . . .

Article 16
Settlement of Disputes

1.   Any disputes regarding the interpretation or application of this Protocol shall be resolved in the first instance through negotiation, mediation or conciliation, or other peaceful means chosen by parties to the dispute.

2.   If no resolution is possible within twelve months after one Contracting Party has notified another that a dispute exists between them the dispute shall be settled at the request of a party to the dispute, by means of the Arbitral Procedure set forth in Annex 3 unless the parties to the dispute agree to use one of the procedures listed in paragraph I of Article 287 of the 1982 United Nations Convention on the Law of the Sea. The parties to the dispute may so agree, whether or not they are also States Parties to the 1982 United Nations Convention on the Law of the Sea.

3.   In the event an agreement to use one of the procedures listed in paragraph I of Article 287 of the 1982 United Nations Convention on the Law of the Sea is reached, the provisions set forth in Part XV of that Convention that are related to the chosen procedure would also apply, *mutatis mutandis.*

4.   The twelve month period referred to in paragraph 2 may be extended for another twelve months by mutual consent of the parties concerned.

5.   Notwithstanding paragraph 2, any State may, at the time it expresses its consent to be bound by this Protocol, notify the Secretary-General that, when it is a party to a dispute about the interpretation or application of article 3.1 or 3.2, its consent will be required before the dispute may be settled by means of the Arbitral Procedure set forth in Annex 3. . . .

Annex 1
Wastes or Other Matter That May Be Considered for Dumping

1.   The following wastes or oilier matter are those that may be considered for dumping being mindful, of the Objectives and General Obligation of this Protocol set out in articles 2 and 3:

.1   dredged material;

.2   sewage sludge;

.3   fish waste, or material resulting from industrial fish processing operations;

.4   vessels and platforms or other man-made structures at sea;

.5   inert, inorganic geological material;

.6   organic material of natural origin; and

.7   bulky items primarily comprising iron, steel, concrete and similarly unharmful materials for which the concern is physical impact, and limited to those circumstances where such wastes are generated at locations, such as small islands with isolated communities, having no practicable access to disposal options other than dumping . . .

3.   Notwithstanding the above, materials listed in paragraphs 1.1 to 1.7 containing levels of radioactivity greater than de minimis (exempt) concentrations as defined by the IAEA and adopted by Contracting Parties, shall not be considered eligible for dumping; provided further that within 25 years of 20 February 1994, and at each 25 year interval thereafter, Contracting Parties shall complete a scientific study relating to all radioactive wastes and other radioactive matter other than high level wastes or matter, taking into account such other factors as Contracting Parties consider appropriate and shall review the prohibition on dumping of such substances in accordance with the procedures set forth in article 22.

Annex 2
Assessment of Wastes or Other Matter That May Be Considered for Dumping

1.   The acceptance of dumping under certain circumstances shall not remove the obligations under this Annex to make further attempts to reduce the necessity for dumping. . . .

5.   Applications to dump wastes or other matter shall demonstrate that appropriate consideration has been given to the following hierarchy of waste management options, which implies an order of increasing environmental impact: .1 reuse; .2 off-site recycling; .3 destruction of

hazardous constituents; .4 treatment to reduce or remove the hazardous constituents; and .5 disposal on land, into air and in water.

6.   A permit to dump wastes or other matter shall be refused if the permitting authority determines that appropriate opportunities exist to re-use, recycle or treat the waste without undue risks to human health or the environment or disproportionate costs. The practical availability of other means of disposal should be considered in the light of a comparative risk assessment involving both dumping and the alternatives.

NOTES AND QUESTIONS

1.   *Slow Ratification.* The protocol opened for signature on April1, 1997 and entered into force in 2004. By February 2015, 48 countries had ratified the Protocol. The United States, which signed the Protocol, has not ratified it.

2.   *Disposal of Nuclear Waste.* During the 1980s the former Soviet Union's Navy disposed of high-level radioactive materials in the northern seas, which led to an international furor in 1991. The Soviet foreign ministry argued that the dumping did not violate the 1972 Convention because Article VII exempted vessels and aircraft entitled to sovereign immunity under international law. Do you agree that there is no violation of the Convention? Resolution I.C. 51(16), which entered into force in 1994, banned all dumping of nuclear waste. See Malgiosia Fitzmaurice, Contemporary Issues in International Environmental Law 52–54 (2009). What does the 1996 Protocol provide? For excellent coverage of the Soviet dumping, see William Zimmerman, Elena Nikitina, and James Clem, The Soviet Union and the Russian Federation: A Natural Experiment in Environmental Compliance in Engaging Countries: Strengthening Compliance with International Accords, Edith Brown Weiss & Harold K. Jacobson eds., 1998. What does sovereign immunity in the context of the Convention and Protocol? Does it apply only to vessels and aircrafts that are owned by the government? Suppose that a country wishes to dump low-level nuclear wastes in the oceans. May it do so under the London Convention of 1972 or the 1996 Protocol?

3.   *Bonfire at Sea.* Suppose that a country wishes to incinerate its wastes at sea. May it do so under the 1996 Protocol? Note that in 1993, parties to the London Convention decided to prohibit incineration at sea; the modification entered into force 100 days after it was adopted by the parties except for countries that filed a declaration indicating they did not accept the change. If a country ratified the 1996 Protocol and had filed a declaration under the 1972 Convention refusing to accept the ban on incineration, is it obligated to abide by the provision in the 1996 Protocol? Supposing the country had not yet ratified the Protocol?

4.   *Why Treat Sewage When the Waste Assimilative Capacity of the Ocean is Near?* Suppose that country wishes to dispose of sewage sludge at sea. What would be required for a country to do so under the 1972 Convention? Under the 1996 Protocol?

5. CO_2 *Disposal: A New Use of the Ocean Sub-seabed as Waste Sink.* Does the Protocol allow the disposal of CO_2 in the deep seabed of the ocean? In 2006, Parties agreed by Resolution LP.1(1) to amend Annex 1 to the Protocol to regulate the sequestration of carbon dioxide streams from carbon dioxide capture processes by adding such streams to Annex 1, thereby allowing the possibility of such disposal by sequestration in the sub-seabed geological formations. The Amendment further provides that the streams must consist "overwhelmingly of carbon dioxide" and that "no wastes or other matter" can be added for purposes of disposing of them. In accordance with Article 22 of the Protocol, the Amendment enters into force for each Party accepting it immediately upon notification to the IMO and 100 days after the Amendment was adopted (i.e. on February 10, 2007), for all other Parties, unless the Party declares that it does not accept the Amendment.

At the fourth meeting of the contracting parties to the London Protocol in October 2009 Parties adopted Resolution LP.3(4) on the Amendment to Article 6 of the London Protocol adds a new paragraph to Article 6:

2   Notwithstanding paragraph 1, the export of carbon dioxide streams for disposal in accordance with Annex 1 may occur, provided that an agreement or arrangement has been entered into by the countries concerned. Such an agreement or arrangement shall include:

2.1 confirmation and allocation of permitting responsibilities between the exporting and receiving countries, consistent with the provisions of this Protocol and other applicable international law; and

2.2 in the case of export to non contracting parties, provisions at a minimum equivalent to those contained in this Protocol, including those relating to the issuance of permits and permit conditions for complying with the provisions of Annex 2, to ensure that the agreement or arrangement does not derogate from the obligations of contracting parties under this Protocol to protect and preserve the marine environment.

The Amendment was adopted under Article 21 of the Protocol. As of May 2015, only 2 of the 30 necessary countries to bring it into force countries had ratified the Amendment, but several other countries arein the process of ratifying it. For a discussion of the technical issues of seabed carbon sequestration see International Energy Agency, Carbon Capture and Storage and the London Protocol (2011).

6.   *Can We Just Settle This?* Note the provision in the 1996 Protocol relating to dispute settlement. The 1972 Convention does not provide for dispute settlement, but an amendment was proposed that dealt with it. The amendment was never ratified by the requisite number of countries. Note how the 1996 Protocol provision addresses the dispute settlement mechanisms available under the Law of the Sea Treaty. Does the provision

solve the hypothetical problem of "forum shopping" to settle international disputes?

7. Other parts of this book have discussed the use of incentives as a means to induce compliance with an international agreement. Compare the 1972 and 1996 agreements in this regard. Are countries required to provide assistance under the 1996 Protocol?

8. The secretariat for the London Convention is housed in the International Maritime Organization in London, England. What branch of government in the member State do you think normally represents the countries at the IMO?

9. *Is Taking a Cruise a Good Thing to Do?* Taking a cruise might seem like a good example of eco-tourism. There is comparatively little use of terrestrial areas, other than ports of call, although some shore visits or visits to coral reefs can pose serious problems. Laurette Burke & Jon Maidens, Reefs at Risk in the Caribbean (2004). However, cruise ships can be a major source of ocean pollution. Cruise ships and ferries constitute only 13 percent of the world's shipping fleet, but these large floating cities generate a disproportionate amount of marine pollution such as sewage, graywater, hazardous waste, ballast water, and solid waste. For example, 24 percent of vessel solid waste comes from cruise ships. See Claudia Copeland, Cruise Ship Pollution: Background, Laws and Regulations, and Key Issues (Congressional Research Service, The Library of Congress, 2005). Reefs at Risk in the Caribbean, *supra*, estimates that 15 percent of the region's reefs are threatened by marine discharges. Most cruise ships are registered in Liberia or Panama. Foreign registered cruise ships are subject to the MARPOL 73/ 78, supra, pp. 7 to 8. However, the flag country is responsible for enacting the necessary domestic laws to enforce the Convention and for certifying compliance with the standards. Two MARPOL Annexes, IV and VI, regulate sewage and air pollution. Annex IV entered the force in 2003, and the Revisited Annex will enter into force in 2007. Annex V1 entered into force in 2005. Annex IV prohibits the discharge of sewage into the sea except when the ship (1) has an approved sewage treatment plant, (2) is discharging comminuted and disinfected sewage more than three nautical miles from land, or (3) is discharging uncomminuted and non-disinfected sewage more than 12 nautical miles from land. A MARPOL signatory State has the right to inspect ships within her territorial waters to verify compliance. E.g., The Act to Prevent Pollution from Ships, 33 U.S.C. §§ 1905–1915. See U.S. General Accounting Office, Marine Pollution: Progress Made to Reduce Marine Pollution by Cruise Ships, But Important Issues Remain (GAO.RCED-00-48 (2000)). A host country can enforce violations of its domestic law or of MARPOL within its territorial waters. Sections 311 and 312 of the United States Clean Water Act, 33 U.S.C. §§ 1321–1322 proscribe marine sanitation standards. The following United States Supreme Court precedent supports the increasingly large number of prosecutions under United States pollution laws against foreign flag cruise ships who discharge into United States territorial waters. Spector v. Norwegian Cruise Lines Ltd.

545 U.S. 119 (2005) holds that the Americans with Disabilities Act applies to foreign flag ships operating in United States waters. The Court found that the Act does not require structural modifications that would interfere with the internal affairs of flag States but suggested that the Act would not apply if it interfered with the ability of the ships to comply with international standards. MARPOL violations in international waters are harder to enforce. MARPOL requires that alleged violations in international waters be referred to the flag State for enforcement. Not surprisingly, the GAO report found that the flag State response rate was poor. Id. at 19–21. For a thorough analysis of the lack of compliance and enforcement incentives in many of the world's flagging countries and ports, see Alan Khee and Jin Tan, Vessel-Source Marine Pollution (2005). See also United Nations, General Assembly, Report on the Work of the United Nations Ad Hoc Open-ended Informal Working Group to study issues relating to conservation and sustainable use of marine biological diversity beyond areas of national jurisdiction, March 9, 2006.

10. *When and Where Does a Violation of National Law Occur?* United States v. Pena, 654 F.3d 1137 (11th Cir. 2012), expanded the reach of the Act to Prevent Pollution from Ships (APPS). Pena was the surveyor, the MARPOL enforcer, on a Panama flagged ship docked in a harbor south of Fort Lauderdale, Florida. He issued an International Oil Pollution Prevention certificate "under the provisions of MARPOL" which falsely stated, inter alia, that the ship had the required bilge holding tank. Pena argued that only Panama could prosecute him, but the court held that the United States prosecution of a MARPOL regulation was permissible under MARPOL Art. 4. Flag and port States have concurrent jurisdiction because the APPS surrendered the United States' exclusive but not concurrent jurisdiction over foreign commercial vessels in United States ports or navigable waters. See also United States v. Sanford Ltd, 880 F.Supp.2d 9 (D.D.C. 2012), which upheld the prosecution against the owners of a New Zealand flag commercial fishing vessel. The chief engineer recorded numerous false entries in the MARPOL required Oil Record Book (ORB) while on the high seas. The violations were discovered while the vessel was docked in a port in the United States Territory of American Samoa. The vessel's owners argued that (1) that the entries complied with New Zealand law and (2) any MARPOL violations on the high seas, such as the discharge of bilge water, could only be prosecuted by New Zealand. Citing Pena, the court held that the MARPOL and APPS violation occurred in United States territorial waters. "This result stems from the fact that the term 'maintain' contemplates more than a mere duty to record a discharge of oily waste on the high seas, divorced from commercial purposes and future plans of the vessel. . . . thus a vessel on the high seas has a duty to 'keep up' its ORB and insure that '[continues]' to be accurate in relation to the ports that it wishes to call on and with which it desires to engage in commerce." 880 F.Supp.2d at 18.

3. LAND-BASED SOURCES OF MARINE POLLUTION

a. The United Nations Convention on the Law of the Sea

The major threats to the health and productivity and biodiversity of the marine environment result from human activities on land—in coastal areas and further inland. Most of the pollution load of the oceans, including municipal, industrial and agricultural wastes and run-off, as well as atmospheric deposition, emanates from such land-based activities and affects the most productive areas of the marine environment, including estuaries and near-shore waters. These areas are likewise threatened by physical alteration of the coastal environment, including destruction of habitats of vital importance for ecosystem health.[27]

As indicated earlier, land-based sources contribute over 70 percent of marine pollution.[28] These substances are carried into the sea by rivers but can also be discharged directly into it from coastal facilities and sewage pipes. [29] According to Agenda 21: "Many of the polluting substances originating from land-based sources are of particular concern to the marine environment since they exhibit at the same time toxicity, persistence and bioaccumulation in the food chain."[30] In fact, most of the contaminants Agenda 21 identifies as posing "the greatest threat to the marine environment" derive from land-based sources. These include sewage, nutrients (largely from agricultural runoff), sediments, litter and plastics, and metals.[31] But since much of this pollution originates from so-called nonpoint sources (e.g., agricultural runoff, oil washed off of roadways and parking lots by precipitation) it is difficult to regulate on the national level and hence on the international plane. The result is that to date, there is no global agreement devoted exclusively to marine pollution from land-based sources. It is, however, the subject of regional treaties and nonbinding instruments. In addition, as we have seen, land-based marine pollution is addressed in the United Nations Convention on the Law of the Sea. Building on the requirements of Article 194(3)(a), set forth above, Article 207 of UNCLOS provides in part as follows:

---

[27] Global Programme of Action for the Protection of the Marine Environment from Land-Based Activities, Nov. 3, 1995, at 7, U.N. Doc. UNEP (OCA)/LBA/IG.2/7, Dec. 5, 1995.

[28] Agenda 21, para. 17.18, Report of the United Nations Conference on Environment and Development, vol. 1, at 243, U.N. Doc. A/ CONF.151/26/Rev.1 (Vol. I) (1993).

[29] Many of these pipes extend considerable distances out to sea. Examples may be found in southern California and in Vancouver, British Columbia. The latter has given rise to concern in Washington State, across the Strait of Juan de Fuca.

[30] Agenda 21, supra footnote 28.

[31] *Id.*

Article 207
Pollution from Land-Based Sources

1. States shall adopt laws and regulations to prevent, reduce and control pollution of the marine environment from land-based sources, including rivers, estuaries, pipelines and outfall structures, taking into account internationally agreed rules, standards and recommended practices and procedures.

Article 207 goes on to provide for action by States on the regional and global levels with regard to land-based sources. In fact, a number of protocols have already been concluded under the Regional Seas Programmes of UEP. These include the 1980 Protocol for the Protection of the Mediterranean Sea Against Pollution from Land-based Sources, the 1990 Protocol to the Kuwait Regional Convention for the Protection of the Marine Environment Against Pollution from Land-based Sources, the 1983 Protocol for the Protection of the South-East Pacific Against Pollution from Land-based Sources, and the 1992 Protocol on Protection of the Black Sea Marine Environment Against Pollution from Land-based Sources. A draft protocol on the protection of the marine environment from land-based activities is being developed under the Wider Caribbean Action Plan. See United Nations Environment Programme (UNEP), Second Meeting of the Experts on Land-based Sources of Pollution in the Wider Caribbean Region, Sanjuan (March 1994). Article 213 of UNCLOS provides for enforcement on the national level of the Convention's rules on land-based marine pollution:

Article 213
Enforcement with Respect to Pollution from
Land-Based Sources

States shall enforce their laws and regulations adopted in accordance with article 207 and shall adopt law and regulations and take other measures necessary to implement applicable international rules and standards established through competent international organizations or diplomatic conference[s] to prevent, reduce and control pollution of the marine environment from land-based sources.

The following is one of the first, important steps to define the nature of a State's obligations under Articles 207 and 213.

PROTECTION OF THE MARINE ENVIRONMENT AGAINST POLLUTION FROM LAND-BASED SOURCES: MONTREAL GUIDELINES

Reprinted in 14 Environmental Policy and the Law No. 2/3, at 77 (1985)

1.   Definitions

For the purposes of these guidelines:

(b) "Land-based sources" means:

(I) Municipal, industrial or agricultural sources, both fixed and mobile, on land, discharges from which reach the marine environment, in particular: From the coast, including from outfalls discharging directly into the marine environment and through run-off; Through rivers, canals or other watercourses, including underground watercourses; and Via the atmosphere.

. . .

2.   Basic Obligation

States have the obligation to protect and preserve the marine environment. In exercising their sovereign right to exploit their natural resources, all States have the duty to prevent, reduce and control pollution of the marine environment.

3.   Discharges Affecting Other States or Areas Beyond the Limits of National Jurisdiction

States have the duty to ensure that discharges from land-based sources within their territories do not cause pollution to the marine environment of other States or of areas beyond the limit of national jurisdiction.

4.   Adoption of Measures Against Pollution from Land-Based Sources

1.   States should adopt, individually or jointly, and in accordance with their capabilities, all measures necessary to prevent, reduce and control pollution from land-based sources, including those designed to minimize to the fullest possible extent the release of toxic, harmful or noxious substances, especially those which are persistent, into the marine environment. States should ensure that such measures take into account internationally agreed rules, criteria, standards and recommended practices and procedures.

2.   In taking measures to prevent, reduce and control pollution from land-based sources, States should refrain, in accordance with international law, from unjustifiable interference with activities carried out by other States in the

exercise of their sovereign rights and in pursuance of their duties in conformity with internationally agreed rules, criteria, standards and recommended practices and procedures.

5.   Co-operation on a Global, Regional or Bilateral Basis

1.   States should undertake, as appropriate, to establish internationally agreed rules, criteria, standards and recommended practices and procedures to prevent, reduce and control pollution from land-based sources, with a view to co-ordinating their policies in this connection, particularly at the local and regional level. Such rules, criteria, standard and recommended practices and procedures should take into account local ecological, geographical and physical characteristics, the economic capacity of States and their need for sustainable development and environmental protection, and the assimilative capacity of the marine environment, and should be reviewed from time to time as necessary. . . .

6.   Duty Not to Transfer or Transform Pollution from Land-Based Sources

In taking measures to prevent, reduce and control pollution from land-based sources, States have the duty to act so as not to transfer directly or indirectly, damage or hazards from one area to another or transform such pollution into another type of pollution. Guideline 6 does not prevent the transfer or transformation of pollution in order to prevent, reduce and control pollution of the environment as a whole.

Chapter 17 of Agenda 21 recommends that States "[c]onsider updating, strengthening and extending the Montreal Guidelines [for the Protection of the Marine Environment from Land-Based Sources[32]], as appropriate," and that they "[i]nitiate and promote the development of new regional agreements, where appropriate."[33] On November 3, 1995, the Global Programme of Action for the Protection of the Marine Environment from Land-based Activities was adopted by the High-level Segment of the Intergovernmental Conference to Adopt a Global Programme of Action for the Protection of the Marine Environment from Land-based Activities. [34] Also adopted at that meeting was the Washington Declaration on Protection of the Marine Environment from Land-Based Activities. [35] The Global Programme of Action contains detailed recommendations for action at the national, regional and

---

[32] [UNEP Governing Council Decision, May 24, 1985, U.N. Doc. UNEP/GC.13/9/Add.3, UNEP/GC/DEC/13/1811, UNEP Environmental Law Guidelines and Principles No. 7.—Eds.]

[33] Agenda 21, at 245.

[34] Document UNEP (OCA)/LBA/IG.2/6, Dec. 5, 1995, Annex II, at 16.

[35] Document UNEP (OCA)/LBA/IG.2/ 7, Dec. 5, 1995.

international levels. In addition, it recommends specific actions for different categories of pollution sources and other threats, including sewage, persistent organic pollutants (POPs),[36] radioactive substances, heavy metals, oils (hydrocarbons), nutrients, sediments, litter, and physical alteration and destruction of habitats.

NOTES AND QUESTIONS

1. *A customary norm?* Birnie and Boyle are of the view that relevant treaty provisions "support the conclusion that the diligent control of land-based sources of marine pollution required by Articles 194, 207, and 213 of the 1982 UNCLOS constitutes a rule of customary international law." Patricia W. Birnie & Alan E. Boyle, International Law and the Environment at 305 (1992). In light of the requirements for the formation of a rule of customary international law we studied in Chapter 4, do you agree? The issue came to United States courts in the Rio Tinto litigation stemming from massive land and ocean pollution from a mine in Papua New Guinea. The plaintiffs relied on the Alien Tort Claims Act and the LOS claim barely survived a motion to dismiss:

> We agree with the district court that PNG's actions taken pursuant to the Copper Act to exploit its own natural resources are "public acts of the sovereign." See Marcos I, 978 F.2d at 498 n. 10. Further, assuming that UNCLOS reflects customary international law norms actionable under the ATCA, it is not yet clear whether "the international community recognizes the norm[s] as one[s] from which no derogation is permitted." Siderman de Blake, 965 F.2d at 715 (internal quotations omitted). Without more, we cannot conclude that the UNCLOS norms are also jus cogens norms. Therefore, the UNCLOS provisions at issue do not yet have a status that would prevent PNG's acts from simultaneously constituting official sovereign acts. We further agree with the district court that to adjudicate the UNCLOS claim would require a court to judge the validity of these official acts.

> Having found that the alleged UNCLOS violations constituted official sovereign acts, the district court turned to Sabbatino to determine whether the act of state doctrine barred any further consideration. See Sabbatino, 376 U.S. at 428, 84 S.Ct. 923. The district court's application of the Sabbatino factors relied in part on the SOI's assertion regarding the potential impact of this case on United States foreign relations. See Sabbatino, 376 U.S. at 428, 84 S.Ct. 923 (identifying "implications . . . for our foreign relations" as one factor to consider in act of state analysis).

---

[36] "Persistent organic pollutants (POPs) are a set of organic compounds that: (i) possess toxic characteristics; (ii) are persistent; (iii) are liable to bioaccumulate; (iv) are prone to long-range transport and deposition; and (v) can result in adverse environmental and human health effects at locations near and far from their source." Global Programme of Action, footnote 27, above, at 37.

Because we have rejected the district court's reliance on the SOI in the context of the political question doctrine, we consider it prudent to allow the district court to revisit its reliance on the SOI in the act of state context. We have concluded that the SOI, even when given "serious weight," does not establish—on its own—the presence of any of the Baker factors. However, the act of state analysis, while related, is not identical to the political question analysis. A consideration of foreign policy concerns is one of several Sabbatino factors, and the SOI's foreign policy concerns are entitled to consideration, but only as one part of that analysis. Moreover, further factual development may be necessary to determine whether "the government which perpetrated the challenged act of state is [still] in existence." Sabbatino, 376 U.S. at 428, 84 S.Ct. 923. We therefore vacate the district court's UNCLOS act of state dismissal for reconsideration in light of our analysis of the SOI [Sarei v. Rio Tinto PLC, 487 F.3d 1192 (9th Cir en banc. 2008).

[The litigation was eventually dismissed in 2013 after the United States Supreme Court strengthened the presumption against the extraterritorial application of United States law and made it extremely difficult, if not impossible, to bring an ATC case. Kiobel v. Royal Dutch Petroleum Co., 133 S. Ct. 1659 (2013).]

2. *Enforcement by other States*? Could another State assert a violation of the obligation referred to in note 1? If so, would that other State have to have suffered a direct injury as a result of the violation? If not, how can the obligation be enforced? Is it an obligation *erga omnes*? If so, how could it be enforced? In 2001, the LOS Tribunal decided Dispute Concerning MOX Plant, International Movements of Radioactive Materials and Protection of the Marine Environment of Irish Sea (Ireland v. United Kingdom), 2001 ITLOS Case No. 10. Ireland alleged that the United Kingdom's failure to prohibit the construction of a nuclear reprocessing plant on the Irish Sea violated LOS Article 207 and 213. The Tribunal found that there was insufficient urgency to suspend construction of the plant, but held that the UK had duty to cooperate with Ireland to exchange information, monitor the effects of the operation of the plant on the Irish Sea and to "devise, as appropriate, measures to prevent pollution of the marine environment, which might result from the operation of the plant." See Daud Hassan, International Conventions Relating to Land Based Pollution Sources of Marine Pollution Control: Applications and Shortcomings, 16 Geo. Int. Envtl. L. Rev. 657 (2004) and Regional Frameworks for Land Based Sources of Marine Pollution Control: A Legal Analysis of North East Atlantic and the Baltic Sea Regions, 2004 QUT Law and Justice J.

b. The Mediterranean: A Case Study in the Disconnect Between Law and Coastal Pollution

There are many multilateral efforts to improve the condition of various regional seas and many declarations that urge States to do so.

The following is a brief discussion of the legal framework for the conservation of the Mediterranean Sea, taken from an EU funded study, which can serve as a model for other regional seas programs.

MARE NOSTRUM PROJECT: BRIDGING THE LEGAL-INSTITUTIONAL GAP IN MEDITERRANEAN COASTLINE MANAGEMENT

First Interim Report: Existing Knowledge on Legal-Institutional Frameworks for Coastline Management, The International, EU and National Levels
[Rachelle Alterman, Rachel Adam, Jesee Fox and Cygal Pellach, Editorial Team 2013]

Mediterranean countries share common environmental challenges. The coastal environments of the project's partners are marked by rising pollution levels, overexploitation of natural resources, and loss of biodiversity—all direct results of intensive urbanization and escalating tourism. Meanwhile, the loss of agricultural land has led to degradation of ecosystems, soil erosion and the loss of fertile soils and a mounting demand for water. . . .

The main factors impeding implementation of ICZM are complex institutional structures and fragmentation of authorities. Current governance structures lack mechanisms for coordination and cooperation among the multiple institutions that deal with coastal issues. While all the partner countries (except Malta) have "coastal laws" that specifically address their coastal areas, these laws are generally not comprehensive coastal-management frameworks.

Despite repeated attempts to rein in the phenomenon, illegal building continues to be the overwhelming obstacle to effective coastal management in Spain, Greece, Turkey, Malta and Sicily, comprising the key threat to these countries' coastal areas. In these countries, attempting to solve this problem through retroactive legalization has emerged as another shared baseline practice. While the terminology used often varies (in Greece the term is "regularization;" in Sicily, these laws have become known as "condoni"), the methods, as well as the unintended consequences, bear many similarities. Key threats for Israel comprise coastal construction plans approved prior to the country's 1983 national outline plan for the coastline, along with infrastructure plans that require a coastal location.

This review comprises an inventory of the key international and regional instruments and initiatives concerning ICZM in the Mediterranean. It traces the path of the ICZM concept throughout the last four decades, to its current lead role on the international agenda and recent incorporation in binding international and regional legal instruments (the Barcelona Convention's ICZM Protocol and the EU Directive for spatial planning and integrated coastal management).

Seeking the origins of the ICZM concept it is appropriate to start with the 1972 UN Conference on the Human Environment (the UNCHE or, the Stockholm Conference), the first environmental mega-conference which launched the modern international environmental movement. Principle 7 to the Stockholm Conference's Declaration proclaims that:

> States shall take all possible steps to prevent pollution of the seas by substances that are liable to create hazards to human health, to harm living resources and marine life, to damage amenities or to interfere with other legitimate uses of the sea.

Whereas Principle 13 declares that:

> In order to achieve a more rational management of resources and thus to improve the environment, States should adopt an integrated and coordinated approach to their development planning . . . to protect and improve environment for the benefit of their population.

Beyond these principles of the UNCHE Declaration, its Action Plan (Recommendation 86, paras (c) and (e)) recommended that "Governments . . . work towards the completion of . . . an over-all instrument for the control of ocean dumping" and:

> participate . . . in the 1973. . . . Conference on Marine Pollution and the Conference on the Law of the Sea scheduled to begin in 1973. . . . with a view to bringing all significant sources of pollution within the marine environment . . . under appropriate controls. . . .

[S]everal months following the Stockholm Conference the United States undertook a pioneering role in the development of coastal law by enacting the 1972 US Coastal Zone Management Act. This precedential law which established the Coastal Management Programs, called on States together with the federal government to adopt an integrative approach in managing the country's coastal areas, balancing demands and resolving conflicts over use of the coastal areas.

Escalating concern over the destructive impact of population growth and intensive development on coastal areas, that had spurred the US into enacting the Coastal Zone Management Act, soon reached Europe as well. The Council of Europe Resolution of 26 October 1973 on the protection of coastal areas defined the principles of coastal management and in particular beach setbacks and open public access to and along the beach. Addressing the critical conditions of Europe's coasts, the Resolution explained that:

> protection of the coast can only be effective if multiple interests and problems are taken simultaneously into account

... the present dispersal of responsibilities in regard to coastal belts among numerous public authorities without any co-ordination between them ... is ... an obstacle to ... action to protect the coasts; . . . .

In response to the "dispersal of responsibilities" the resolution recommended that governments adopt policies for coastal projection which should include development bans ... along the seafront;— subjecting the granting of development permits to particularly stringent conditions; proclaim[ing] the principle of free public access to the coast and give effect to this principle ... by establishing the necessary rights-of-way through private property situated on the seafront;-by purchasing, if need be, the land required to give free access to the beach. . . .

A further milestone in the evolution of ICZM policy was the 1976 Recommendation of the Organization for Economic Co-operation and Development (OECD) on Principles concerning Coastal Management. The principles that the recommendation promoted included public access to the coasts and prevention of development likely to adversely impact the environment. The Recommendation further proposed that Coastal development projects should not jeopardise coastal ecosystems. . . ." and "[e]fforts should be made to manage industrial and urban wastes by requiring pre-treatment and/or prohibiting and/or restricting discharges into the sea. Sewage treatment and disposal policies should be strengthened by various means such as recycling and making beneficial uses of effluent and sewage sludge." [F]ollowing these two decisions the European Commission undertook to conduct an in-depth analysis of coastal management, resulting in the 1978 publication Integrated Littoral Development in the European Community which called for an integrated coastal zone plan. In 1982 the European Parliament approved the European Coastal Charter that incorporated principles of integrated coastal zone planning policy. But only in the 1990s did the European Union actually decide to implement these principles, publishing in 2000 a European ICZM Strategy. . . . The Mediterranean Action Plan and the Barcelona Convention for the Protection of the Mediterranean Sea against Pollution, 1975, 1976. . . .

The fledgling United Nations Environmental Programme (UNEP), established in 1973 by a decision of the 1972 UNCHE, launched as its first project the Regional Seas Programme. The Mediterranean Sea was targeted for the first regional seas organization and in 1975 the Mediterranean Action Plan (MAP) was launched.

To create an operative tool for implementing MAP, in 1976 the Mediterranean countries adopted the Barcelona Convention for the Protection of the Mediterranean Sea Against Pollution (the 1976 Barcelona Convention). The convention committed its contracting parties to protecting the Mediterranean from a range of threats including pollution caused by dumping from ships and aircrafts (Art.5), oil spills and pollution from other harmful substances discharged from ships (art. 6), exploration and exploitation of the continental shelf and the seabed and its subsoil (Art. 7), and "pollution from land-based sources" referring to "discharges from rivers, coastal establishments or outfalls, or emanating from other land-based sources within their territories." (Art.8). The Barcelona Convention was adopted together with the dumping protocol (from ships and aircraft) and the Prevention and Emergency Protocol (oil pollution from ships and emergency situations). The Protocol for the Protection of the Mediterranean Sea against Pollution from Land-Based Sources, adopted in 1980, was an early step in interfacing between the coasts and the sea by means of a binding international instrument. . . .

The event that directly launched ICZM onto the international agenda was the 1992 Rio Earth Summit. Its outstanding output was Agenda 21, a global action plan for implementing sustainable development. Chapter 17 of Agenda 21 entitled "Protection of the Oceans, All kinds of Seas, Including Enclosed and Semi-enclosed Seas and Coastal Areas and the Protection, Rational Use and Development of their Living Resources," introduced what it heralded as "new approaches to marine and coastal area management and development. . . . that are integrated in content and are precautionary and anticipatory in ambit. . . ." Countries were called upon to "commit themselves to integrated management and sustainable development of coastal areas and the marine environment under their national jurisdiction." Chapter 17 sets out in detail a global vision of integrated coastal management, articulating the objectives to be achieved, activities to undertake, the data and information required, and the need for international and regional cooperation.

3.5. UN Framework Convention on Climate Change, 1992

Adopted at the UNCED and displaying the critical role of ICZM as a tool for confronting the impact of climate change on coastal areas, the UN Framework Convention on Climate Change commits its parties to "cooperate in preparing for adaptation to the impacts of climate change" and "develop and elaborate appropriate and integrated plans for coastal zone management." . . . .

Concerning the Mediterranean region, as of May 2013 only nine countries have ratified the Mediterranean ICZM Protocol, questioning their commitment to effective coastal management and casting doubts on the power of the Protocol to change the behavior of states. . . .

[I]n 1995 the Mediterranean States replaced the 1975 Mediterranean Action Plan with the "Action Plan for the Protection of the Marine Environment and the Sustainable Development of the Coastal Areas of the Mediterranean (MAP Phase II)." (Decision IG 20/2, Adoption of the Action Plan for the implementation of the ICZM Protocol for the

Mediterranean (2012–2019), at 11). Together with the updated Action Plan the contracting parties amended the Barcelona Convention and its protocols so as to incorporate principles of sustainable development. . . . Although the initial focus of the MAP was on marine pollution control, experience soon confirmed that socio-economic trends . . . are the root of most environmental problems, and that meaningful and lasting environmental protection is inseparably linked to social and economic development. Therefore the focus of MAP gradually shifted from a sectoral approach to pollution control to integrated coastal zone planning and management as the key tool. . . ."

The 2008 ICZM Protocol is a result of this evolution of the MAP institutional structures, from a sectoral approach to an approach embracing the cross-cutting principles of sustainable development and integrated coastal management (Rochette, Bille, 2012, 978).

This broad and diverse range of international and regional plans, programs, strategies and conventions discussed above constitute 'soft law' (Prem, 2009, 258), non-binding instruments that serve as policy papers and guidelines for best practice, rather than binding legal documents. Yet with the growing awareness of the obstacles to effective implementation, stakeholders were beginning to recognize the need for a binding instrument specifically for integrated coastal management (Prem, 2010, 257–258). The Mediterranean countries within the framework of MAP were the first to take up the challenge.

---

i. *Convention for the Protection of the Marine Environment and the Coastal Region of the Mediterranean, 1995*

To create an operating system for MAP II, the Contracting Parties adopted an amended version of the 1976 Barcelona Convention which they appropriately renamed the Convention for the Protection of the Marine Environment and the Coastal Region of the Mediterranean. The updated convention that entered into force in 2004, determined that its geographical coverage "may be extended to coastal areas as defined by each Contracting Party within its own territory." (Art.1). Under "General Obligations" in Art.3 (e), Contracting Parties are required "to promote the integrated management of the coastal zones. . . ." With the emphasis on sustainable development, in 1996 the Contracting Parties to the Barcelona Convention established the Mediterranean Commission on Sustainable Development (MCSD). By 1999 the MCSD had adopted a "Recommendation for ICZM in the Mediterranean." The Barcelona Convention already had six sectoral protocols that by imposing detailed legal obligations on countries, operate to implement the convention's objectives and principles: the Dumping Protocol (from ships and aircraft), the Prevention and Emergency Protocol (pollution from ships and emergency situations), Land-based Sources and Activities Protocol, Specially Protected Areas and Biological Diversity Protocol, Offshore Protocol (pollution from exploration and exploitation), and the Hazardous Wastes Protocol. The convention's seventh protocol would be the Protocol on Integrated Coastal Zone Management (ICZM).

ii. The ICZM Protocol, 2008

Since the amended 1995 Barcelona Convention specifically required countries to promote integrated coastal management, the next step was to draft a protocol to implement this general obligation by detailed provisions. The 12th Meeting of the Parties (MOP) held in Monaco in 2001 recommended "a feasibility study of a regional legal instrument on sustainable coastal area management," the conclusions of which demonstrated a need for a binding legal instrument (Prem, 2010, 258). On the basis of this study the 2003 MOP in Catania called for the preparation of a draft protocol and charged PAP/RAC with the task. The first draft of the protocol was presented to the 14th MOP in 2005 in Portoroz, Slovenia, which decided to establish a working group of experts to further develop a draft text, launching a series of consultations and meetings. Five rounds of negotiations were held during 2006 and 2007 and the final text of the protocol was adopted in Madrid in 2008 (Prem, 2010, 258), (Rochette, Bille, 2012, 979).

Expanding the traditional focus of coastal management beyond environmental concerns, the 2008 ICZM Protocol integrates socioeconomic considerations with environmental and ecological ones. Part I of the ICZM Protocol entitled "General Provisions," declares that the parties to the Barcelona Convention shall establish "a common framework for the integrated management of the Mediterranean coastal zone" (Art. 1). "Integrated coastal zone management" is defined as "a dynamic process for the sustainable management and use of coastal zones, taking into account at the same time the fragility of coastal ecosystems and landscapes, the diversity of activities and uses, their interactions, the maritime orientation of certain activities and uses and their impact on both the marine and land parts." (Art.2)

Art. 5 to the Protocol lists six objectives of ICZM, both procedural and substantive: facilitate the sustainable development of coastal zones; preserve coastal zones; ensure the sustainable use of natural resources; ensure preservation of the integrity of coastal ecosystems; prevent or reduce the effects of natural hazards and climate change in particular; and, "achieve coherence between public and private initiatives and between all decisions by the public authorities. . . ."

Art. 6 elaborates on a list of ten principles of ICZM to guide countries in implementing the Protocol: the marine and coastal environments as one unit the biodiversity and natural wealth of the intertidal area, the interdependency of the marine part and the land part, for a "single entity;"—"; the concept of 'carrying capacity'—". . . not to exceed the carrying capacity of the coastal zone so as to prevent the negative effects of natural disasters and development; use of the ecosystems approach to coastal planning and management; "appropriate governance allowing . . . a transparent decision-making process by local populations and stakeholders in civil society concerned with coastal zones . . ."; "Cross-sectorally organized institutional coordination . . . competent in coastal zones . . ."; "formulation of land use strategies, plans and programmes covering urban development and socio-economic activities" and "other relevant sectoral policies"; consideration of all activities taking place in coastal zones, prioritizing "public services and activities requiring. . . . the immediate proximity of the sea."; balanced allocation of uses throughout the coastal zone, avoiding urban sprawl; risk assessments of activities and infrastructures to avoid their negative impact on coastal zones; preventing damage to the coastal environment, and where required, restoration of the damaged environment.

Art. 7 addresses "Coordination." Parties are required to "ensure institutional coordination . . . to avoid sectoral approaches and facilitate comprehensive approaches"; coordinate between authorities responsible for both marine and coastal environments, as well as vertical coordination regarding "coastal strategies, plans and programmes" and regulation of activities "through joint consultative bodies or joint decision-making procedures."

iii. Status of Ratification of the ICZM Protocol

The ICZM protocol came into force in 2012 but as of May 2013 only nine out of the 21 member States of the Barcelona Convention have ratified it. The fact that less than half has ratified signals gaps in implementation of integrated coastal management at all scales, pointing to the lack of political will required to commit internationally to implement the Protocol and to balance between demands for coastal land use. Ratification can also be constrained by heavy government bureaucracy and procedures required for joining international conventions. A major obstacle is the obligation of each country to adapt their national legislation to the Protocol's provisions, to ensure its implementation and the cross-sectoral integration and coordination required for ICZM. Moreover, as pointed out by Prem, achieving Parliamentary approval for legislation incorporating the protocol's provisions could be problematic.

Within these parameters, the Land-Based Sources Protocol was completed by political compromise. The LDC were assured that atmospheric transport and river transport of pollution, radioactive wastes and technology transfer would be covered by the protocol, and that some ambient standards would be included. The DCs were satisfied by a full list of substances in the annexes that were largely consistent with EEC obligations, even though France had to accept some ambient standards and some controls exceeding those laid out in the EEC directive.

C. THE SPECIAL PROBLEMS OF ICE-COVERED LAND MASSES OR SEAS

The earth's two polar regions are governed by separate legal regimes. The Antarctic is an uninhabited ice-covered continent with multiple State claims. Its current value is for research and tourism, and it has a mature treaty regime. The Arctic is a melting ice-covered sea with multiple unresolved LOS issues which may contain substantial oil and gas reserves and become a new transportation route. There is no Arctic treaty, but there is an evolving regime to promote the sustainable development and use of the region.

1. THE ANTARCTIC: AN ICE-COVERED CONTINENT

a. Territorial Claims

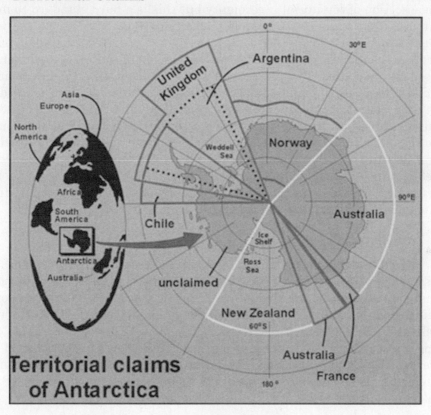

Antarctica is very fragile ice-covered continent. The Montreal Protocol on Substances that Deplete the Ozone Layer, see Chapter 8, was enacted after scientists confirmed the thinning of the ozone layer in the Antarctic. Antarctica was formed by "avulsion" as the super-continent of Gondwanaland split into Africa, Australia, the Indian sub-continent, New Zealand and South America. Under classic international law, the Antarctic is an unallocated *terra nullis* subject to a special treaty regime. See Sudhir Chopra, Antarctica as a Commons Regime: A Conceptual Framework for Cooperation and Coexistence in The Antarctic Legal Regime in The Antarctic Legal Regime (Christopher Clayton Joyner and Sudhir K. Chopra eds. 1989).

States can establish claims of territorial sovereignty over unclaimed areas by five methods: (1) subjugation, (2) accretion (this is a natural process of boundary change), cession, (4) prescription and (5) occupation of heretofore unoccupied lands. The international community initially treated Antarctica as *res nullius* and thus equally open to territorial claims by all States of the world. Seven countries, France, Australia, New Zealand, Norway, the United Kingdom, the United States and Russia, have discovery claims. Effective occupation is now the basic standard for the assertion of territorial sovereignty but this is a hard standard to meet in harsh, cold areas not amenable to permanent settlement. As the map illustrates the "Gondwanaland" countries have asserted somewhat novel sectorial claims by propinquity, an extension of national boundaries, based on the claims of the Arctic countries. See Donat Pharand, Canada's Arctic Waters in International Law (1988). Technically, the theory does not apply because the sea intervenes, and the claim has been rejected by some countries in the Arctic because it is inconsistent with the freedom of the seas. See David W.H. Walton, Discovering the Unknown Continent 1, in Antarctica: Global Science from a Frozen Continent (2013). Other theories include *uti possidetis*, inheritance from Spain, and effective occupation. David Braun, Antarctic Treaty at 50, a Beacon for Joint Management of the Earth, National Geographic 2009).

b. Antarctic Treaty

Territorial claims are now "frozen" by treaty. In the 1950s, the possibility of using Antarctica for nuclear tests and waste disposal emerged. Ultimately, the most effected nations agreed to freeze territorial claims possibility by treaty. The Antarctic Treaty entered into force in 1961 and now has fifty member States. Article 12 now allows that "any consultative Party may call for a conference to review the operation of the Treaty." See Donald Rothwell, The Polar Regions and the Development of International Law (1996) A majority decision is required for modification. Relevant portions of the Treaty are set out below:

Preamble

The Governments of Argentina, Australia, Belgium, Chile, the French Republic, Japan, New Zealand, Norway, the Union of South Africa, the Union of Soviet Socialist Republics, the United Kingdom of Great Britain and Northern Ireland, and the United States of America,

Recognizing that it is in the interest of all mankind that Antarctica shall continue forever to be used exclusively for peaceful purposes and shall not become the scene or object of international discord;

Acknowledging the substantial contributions to scientific knowledge resulting from international cooperation in scientific investigation in Antarctica;

Convinced that the establishment of a firm foundation for the continuation and development of such cooperation on the basis of freedom of scientific investigation in Antarctica as applied during the International Geophysical Year accords with the interests of science and the progress of all mankind;

Convinced also that a treaty ensuring the use of Antarctica for peaceful purposes only and the continuance of international harmony in Antarctica will further the purposes and principles embodied in the Charter of the United Nations;

Have agreed as follows:

Article I—Peaceful purposes

Antarctica shall be used for peaceful purposes only. There shall be prohibited, inter alia, any measure of a military nature, such as the establishment of military bases and fortifications, the carrying out of military maneuvers, as well as the testing of any type of weapon.

The present Treaty shall not prevent the use of military personnel or equipment for scientific research or for any other peaceful purpose.

Article II—Freedom of scientific investigation

Freedom of scientific investigation in Antarctica and cooperation toward that end, as applied during the International Geophysical Year, shall continue, subject to the provisions of the present Treaty.

Article IV—Territorial sovereignty

Nothing contained in the present Treaty shall be interpreted as:

a renunciation by any Contracting Party of previously asserted rights of or claims to territorial sovereignty in Antarctica;

a renunciation or diminution by any Contracting Party of any basis of claim to territorial sovereignty in Antarctica which it may have whether as a result of its activities or those of its nationals in Antarctica, or otherwise;

prejudicing the position of any Contracting Party as regards its recognition or non-recognition of any other State's rights of or claim or basis of claim to territorial sovereignty in Antarctica.

No acts or activities taking place while the present Treaty is in force shall constitute a basis for asserting, supporting or denying a claim to territorial sovereignty in Antarctica or create any rights of sovereignty in Antarctica. No new claim, or enlargement of an existing claim, to territorial sovereignty in Antarctica shall be asserted while the present Treaty is in force.

i.   Post Treaty Threats to the Environment: Mining and Tourism

Two major issues have arisen since the treaty: the possibility that the continent has valuable minerals and the impact of tourism. In anticipation of mining, the parties, which had operated by consensus on all major issues, created the Antarctic Minerals Resources Commission. The Commission proposed a treaty, The Convention on the Regulation of Antarctic Mineral Activities (CRAMA). CRAMA created a prospecting and exploitation regime based on the law of the sponsoring State plus international law. The proposed regime keeps party control over the decision to open an area to exploration but substituted 2/3 and 51% approval schemes for the consensus practice of the Treaty regime for the approval of plans in open areas. Christopher Joyner, The Evolving Minerals Regime for Antarctica in The Antarctic Legal Regime, *supra*, at 142–43. CARMA did not come into force, but the environmental protection mandate became the guiding principle for the regime.

In 1991, the parties adopted The Protocol on Environmental Protection, 30 I.L.M. 1461 (1991), (Madrid Protocol), which entered into force in 1998. Article 2 designates Antarctica as a "natural reserve, devoted to peace and science" and Article 3 declares that the "protection of the Antarctic environment and dependent and associated ecosystems and the intrinsic value of Antarctica, including its wilderness and aesthetic values and its value as an area for the conduct of scientific research, in particular research essential to understanding the global environment, shall be fundamental considerations in the planning and conduct of all activities in the Antarctic Treaty area.

Article 7 prohibits "any activity relating to mineral resources, other than scientific research."

Article 3 sets out the primary environmental protection duties.

3.2. To this end:

(a) activities in the Antarctic Treaty area shall be planned and conducted so as to limit adverse impacts on the Antarctic environment and dependent and associated ecosystems;

(b) activities in the Antarctic Treaty area shall be planned and conducted so as to avoid:

(i) adverse effects on climate or weather patterns;

(ii) significant adverse effects on air or water quality;

(iii) significant changes in the atmospheric, terrestrial (including aquatic), glacial or marine environments;

(iv) detrimental changes in the distribution, abundance or productivity of species or populations of species of fauna and flora;

(v) further jeopardy to endangered or threatened species or populations of such species; or

(vi) degradation of, or substantial risk to, areas of biological, scientific, historic, aesthetic or wilderness significance;

(c) activities in the Antarctic Treaty area shall be planned and conducted on the basis of information sufficient to allow prior assessments of, and informed judgments about, their possible impacts on the Antarctic environment and dependent and associated ecosystems and on the value of Antarctica for the conduct of scientific research; such judgments shall take account of:

(i) the scope of the activity, including its area, duration and intensity;

(ii) the cumulative impacts of the activity, both by itself and in combination with other activities in the Antarctic Treaty area;

(iii) whether the activity will detrimentally affect any other activity in the Antarctic Treaty area;

(iv) whether technology and procedures are available to provide for environmentally safe operations;

(v) whether there exists the capacity to monitor key environmental parameters and ecosystem components so as to identify and provide early warning of any adverse effects of the activity and to provide for such modification of operating procedures as may be necessary in the light of the results of monitoring or increased knowledge of the Antarctic environment and dependent and associated ecosystems; and

(vi) whether there exists the capacity to respond promptly and effectively to accidents, particularly those with potential environmental effects;

(d) regular and effective monitoring shall take place to allow assessment of the impacts of ongoing activities, including the verification of predicted impacts;

(e) regular and effective monitoring shall take place to facilitate early detection of the possible unforeseen effects of activities carried on both within and outside the Antarctic Treaty area on the Antarctic environment and dependent and associated ecosystems.

3.3. Activities shall be planned and conducted in the Antarctic Treaty area so as to accord priority to scientific research and to preserve the value of Antarctica as an area for the conduct of such research, including research essential to understanding the global environment.

Article 3.4 includes tourism in the activity to which the Protocol applies, but Article 8 exempts activities with "a minor or transitory impact" from prior impact assessment. 37,405 persons visited the Antarctic in 2013–2014. Do these visits require an environmental impact assessment? See Implementing the Environmental Protection Regime for the Antarctic (Davor Vidas ed (2000) and thee International Association of Antarctic Tour Operators Guidelines are available at http://iaato.org/home. At the 2013 meeting of the Environmental Protection Committee, a number of guidelines for visits to protected areas were adopted. See Cornelis Bastmeyer and Ricardo Routa, Regulating Antarctic Tourism and the Precautionary Principle, 98 American J, Int, L. 763 (2004) and Alan D. Hemings & Richrdo Roura, A Square Peg in the Round Hole: Fitting Impact Assessment Under the Antarctic Environmental protocol to Antarctic Tourism, 21 Impact Appraisal and Project Appraisal 13 (2003). Antarctica in International Law (Ben Saul and Tim Stephens eds. 2015), examines the potential impacts of global climate change, recent activity by China and other countries, and the strains on the consensus that the treaty regime has nurtured.

ii. The Antarctic Precedent in the World

The Antarctic treaty regime has been cited for the proposition that some areas are the common heritage of humankind and thus States have an *erga omnes* duty to protect these areas. Needless to say most States view the argument an unjustified intrusion in their internal affairs, e.g., Russia rejected a proposal for a world park in the Lake Baikal region. See Lake Baikal, Woods, International Environmental Aid to the States of the Former Soviet Union: A Case Study Focusing on Siberia's Lake Baikal, 5 Colo. J. Int. Envir. Law and Policy 459 (1994). The Madrid Protocol rejected it for Antarctica. See Jeffrey D. Myhre, The Antarctic Treaty System: Politics, Law and Diplomacy (1987). Brazil has long been deeply concerned about the "internationalization" of the Amazon rain forests and a possible foreign invasion to protect them. See J.R.M. Filho and Daniel Zirker, Nationalism, National Security, and Amazonia: Military Perceptions and Attitudes in Contemporary Brazil, 27 Armed Forces & Society 105 (2000).

2. THE ARCTIC: AN ICE-COVERED SEA

a. LOS and the Arctic

The Arctic, in contrast to the Antarctic, is not a continent but a semi-enclosed ice covered sea surrounded by Canada, Greenland (Denmark), Norway, Russia and the United States. Finland, Iceland and Sweden also have Arctic interests, and along with the five littoral States make up the eight Arctic States. Since Roald Amundsen's 1906 successful navigation of the Northwest Passage, nations have dreamed of the possibility of a route from Europe to Asia and the West Coast of America which would save 2,400 miles compared to the Panama canal. See United States Department of Defense, Arctic Strategy (2013). Global climate change has reduced the Sea's summer ice cover by 40% since 1979, and in 2013 the Arctic Orion shipped coal from Vancouver, British Columbia to Finland, saving $200.000.00 and four days over the Panama canal route. But the bigger prize is oil and gas. The United States Energy Information Administration estimates that the Sea could contain 22% of the world's undiscovered oil and gas reserves. http://geology.com/articles/arctic-oil-and-gas/.

Review the materials on the LOS, pages 632 to 635, *supra*. For a thorough analysis of how the Antarctic treaty regime might apply to the Arctic, see

Christopher C. Joyner, The Legal Regime for the Arctic Ocean, 18 J. Transnational L. & Policy 195 (2009).

As the map indicates the claims of coastal States are extensive and potentially overlapping. Given the nature of the Arctic, the resolution of these claims and the management of any exploitation of mineral or fishery resources are crucial problems. The Arctic legal regime is a combination of hard and soft law. The hard law is the Law of the Sea, discussed earlier in this chapter; the soft law regime is discussed below. Christopher C. Joyner, The Legal Regime for the Arctic Ocean, *supra* at 202–204, sets out the LOS regime for these claims (selected footnotes omitted and shortened):

> The 1982 LOS Convention codifies offshore jurisdiction for coastal States through various zone delimitations with important implications for Arctic states. All eight arctic States have coastlines bordering the Arctic, and thus they are all affected by these zone delimitations The Convention provides that a coastal State in the Arctic may claim a territorial sea out to twelve miles from the coastal baseline.[37] In the territorial sea, the sovereignty of the coastal State extends to the water column, the seabed, and all living and nonliving resources.[38] Foreign vessels may pass through this zone if the passage is deemed to be "innocent," i.e., "not prejudicial to the peace, good order or the security of the coastal State." [39] Fishing, polluting, testing weapons, and covert intelligence operations by foreign vessels are not considered "innocent" activities.

> The Convention creates a second offshore area, the contiguous zone. A coastal State may claim beyond the twelve nautical mile limit an additional twelve nautical mile area of ocean space—which translates into twenty-four nautical miles from the coastal baseline of the territorial sea. [40] In this contiguous zone, Arctic littoral States can continue to enforce laws in the four specified areas of pollution, taxation, customs, and immigration.

> The 1982 LOS Convention also created for coastal States a special new offshore region, the exclusive economic zone (EEZ). The EEZ extends 200 nautical miles offshore from a State's coastal baseline, or 188 miles seaward beyond a State's twelve-mile territorial sea. Within this area, the eight Arctic coastal States retain sole exploitation rights over all living and nonliving natural resources. Although this zone was introduced primarily to give coastal States greater control over fishing rights, the

---

[37] Art. 3.

[38] Art. 2.

[39] Art. 19.

[40] Art. 33.

prospect of exploring and exploiting offshore hydrocarbons within the littoral States' EEZs seems likely to become increasingly salient. Beyond the territorial seas, in the EEZ, foreign States have the freedoms of navigation and overflight, subject to regulation of the coastal States. Foreign States may also lay submarine pipes and cables in the EEZ, as well as in ocean space beyond the limits of national jurisdiction.

The final special area of ocean space created by the 1982 LOS Convention is the continental shelf. This submarine area on the ocean floor is defined as the natural prolongation of the land territory to the continental margin's outer edge, or 200 nautical miles from the coastal State's baseline, whichever is greater. Coastal States enjoy no unilateral right to assert claims to the outer continental shelf beyond 200 nautical miles. Even so, the Convention permits a State to extend its continental shelf beyond 200 nautical miles, out to 350 nautical miles, so long as that shelf formation is a natural prolongation of the State's continental shelf. However, the continental shelf may not exceed 350 nautical miles from the baseline. Similarly, it may never exceed 100 nautical miles beyond the 2,500 meter isobath (i.e., the line connecting the depth of 2,500 meters).[41] Under Article

---

[41] In full, Article 76 provides the following:

1. The continental shelf of a coastal State comprises the seabed and subsoil of the submarine areas that extend beyond its territorial sea throughout the natural prolongation of its land territory to the outer edge of the continental margin, or to a distance of 200 nautical miles from the baselines from which the breadth of the territorial sea is measured where the outer edge of the continental margin does not extend up to that distance.

2. The continental shelf of a coastal State shall not extend beyond the limits provided for in paragraphs 4 to 6.

3. The continental margin comprises the submerged prolongation of the land mass of the coastal State, and consists of the seabed and subsoil of the shelf, the slope and the rise. It does not include the deep ocean floor with its oceanic ridges or the subsoil thereof.

4. (a) For the purposes of this Convention, the coastal State shall establish the outer edge of the continental margin wherever the margin extends beyond 200 nautical miles from the baselines from which the breadth of the territorial sea is measured, by either:

(i) a line delineated in accordance with paragraph 7 by reference to the outermost fixed points at each of which the thickness of sedimentary rocks is at least 1 per cent of the shortest distance from such point to the foot of the continental slope; or

(ii) a line delineated in accordance with paragraph 7 by reference to fixed points not more than 60 nautical miles from the foot of the continental slope.

(b) In the absence of evidence to the contrary, the foot of the continental slope shall be determined as the point of maximum change in the 204 J. OF TRANSNATIONAL LAW & POLICY [Vol. 18.2] data substantiating that extended claim must be submitted by each government to a special Convention-created mechanism called the Commission on the Limits of the Continental Shelf, which will then make a determination regarding the validity of the claim asserted by each state. Critically important for the Arctic littoral states is that the 1982 LOS Convention gives coastal states the right to harvest mineral and non-living material in the subsoil of its continental shelf, to the exclusion of others. Furthermore, Arctic coastal states are permitted to assert exclusive control over living resources "attached" to the continental shelf, but not to creatures living in the water column beyond the exclusive economic zone. It is gradient at its base

76 of the 1982 LOS Convention, scientific data substantiating that extended claim must be submitted by each government to a special Convention-created mechanism called the Commission on the Limits of the Continental Shelf, which will then make a determination regarding the validity of the claim asserted by each State.

Critically important for the Arctic littoral States is that the 1982 LOS Convention gives coastal States the right to harvest mineral and non-living material in the subsoil of its continental shelf, to the exclusion of others.[42] Furthermore, Arctic coastal States are permitted to assert exclusive control over living resources "attached" to the continental shelf, but not to creatures living in the water column beyond the exclusive economic zone.[43]

b. The Arctic Council: A Soft but Hardening Regime

The international environmental regime is a soft but important evolving one. The regime originated in a 1987 suggestion by Mikhail Gorbachev, the former Soviet-Secretary General, that the Arctic States cooperate to protect the environment. The result was the 1991 Arctic Environmental Protection Strategy. Arctic Environmental Protection Strategy, 2 Yb. Int'l Env. L. 585 (1991). See Franklyn Griffiths, Artic Council Origins: A Memoir, available at http://gordonfoundation.ca/sites/default/files/images/Jan18%20-%20Griffiths_ArcticCouncilOrigins.pdf. In 1996, the eight Arctic States created the Arctic Council to further implement the Strategy. Declaration on the Establishment of the Arctic Council, para. 1(a), 35 ILM 1387 (1996) The Council has no binding

5. The fixed points comprising the line of the outer limits of the continental shelf on the seabed, drawn in accordance with paragraph 4 (a)(i) and (ii), either shall not exceed 350 nautical miles from the baselines from which the breadth of the territorial sea is measured or shall not exceed 100 nautical miles from the 2,500 metre isobath, which is a line connecting the depth of 2,500 metres.

6. Notwithstanding the provisions of paragraph 5, on submarine ridges, the outer limit of the continental shelf shall not exceed 350 nautical miles from the baselines from which the breadth of the territorial sea is measured. This paragraph does not apply to submarine elevations that are natural components of the continental margin, such as its plateaux, sea is measured shall be submitted by the coastal State to the Commission on the Limits of the Continental Shelf set up under Annex II on the basis of equitable geographical representation. The Commission shall make recommendations to coastal States on matters related to the establishment of the outer limits of their continental shelf. The limits of the shelf established by a coastal State on the basis of these recommendations shall be final and binding. 9. The coastal State shall deposit with the Secretary-General of the United Nations charts and relevant information, including geodetic data, permanently describing the outer limits of its continental shelf. The Secretary-General shall give due publicity thereto. 10. The provisions of this article are without prejudice to the question of delimitation of the continental shelf between States with opposite or adjacent coasts.

For an insightful analysis, see Alex G. Oude Elferink, The Outer Continental Shelf in the Arctic: The Application of Arctic 76 of the LOS Convention in a Regional Context, in THE LAW OF THE SEA THE SEA AND POLAR MARITIME DELIMITATION AND JURISDICTION 139–56 (Alex G. Oude Elferink & Donald R. Rothwell, eds., 2001).

[42] Art. 77.

[43] Art. 77(4).

authority, but it has six active working groups which have developed environmental protection programs for high biodiversity areas and environmental assessment guidelines. See Erika Lennon, A Tale of Two Poles: A Comparative Look At the Legal Regimes in the Arctic and the Antarctic, 8 Change in Polar Regions 32 (2008). Paula Kankaanpöäaä and Oren Young, The Effectiveness of the Arctic Council, 2012 Polar Research 31, argue that the Council has become an influential policy shaper through the production of influential scientific assessments, the participation by Arctic's indigenous people, and international initiatives such as the 2013 agreement on Cooperation on Marine Pollution Preparedness and Response in the Arctic, available at http://www.state.gov/r/pa/prs/ps/2013/05/209406.htm. Art. 77(4).

After a year delay due tensions between the Russian Federatuion and the United States over the Ukraine, in July, 2015, Canada, the Kingdom of Denmark, the Kingdom of Norway, the Russian Federation, and the United States agreed to a moririorium on a 1.1 million square mile area of the ice-covered Central Arctic high seas near the North Pole. Declaration Concerning The Prevention of Unregulated High Seas Fishing in the Central Arctic Ocean. http://um.dk/da/~/media/UM/Danish-site/Documents/Nyheder/Draft%20Declaration%20on%20Arctic%20Fisheries%2016%20July%202015.pdf. The area's commercial fishing stocks, if any, are unknown, but species currently harvested in southern Arctic waters may migrate north due to the rapid melting of the polar ice cover. However, the Agreement does not apply to States which also fish the Arctic such as China, Spain, Japan, the United Kingdom, and South Korea. The key portions of the Agreement provide:

> We therefore intend to implement, in the single high seas portion of the central Arctic Ocean that is entirely surrounded by waters under the fisheries jurisdiction of Canada, the Kingdom of Denmark in respect of Greenland, the Kingdom of Norway, the Russian Federation and the United States of America, the following interim measures:
>
> • We will authorize our vessels to conduct commercial fishing in this high seas area only pursuant to one or more regional or subregional fisheries management organizations or arrangements that are or may be established to manage such fishing in accordance with recognized international standards.
>
> • We will establish a joint program of scientific research with the aim of improving understanding of the ecosystems of this area and promote cooperation with relevant scientific bodies, including but not limited to the International Council for the Exploration of the Sea (ICES) and the North Pacific Marine Science Organization (PICES).

- We will promote compliance with these interim measures and with relevant international law, including by coordinating our monitoring, control and surveillance activities in this area.

- We will ensure that any non-commercial fishing in this area does not undermine the purpose of the interim measures, is based on scientific advice and is monitored, and that data obtained through any such fishing is shared.

We recall that an extensive international legal framework applies to the Arctic Ocean. These interim measures will neither undermine nor conflict with the role and mandate of any existing international mechanism relating to fisheries, including the North East Atlantic Fisheries Commission. Nor will these interim measures prejudice the rights, jurisdiction and duties of States under relevant provisions of international law as reflected in the 1982 United Nations Convention on the Law of the Sea, or the 1995 United Nations Agreement for the Implementation of the Provisions of the United Nations Convention on the Law of the Sea of 10 December 1982 relating to the Conservation and Management of Straddling Fish Stocks and Highly Migratory Fish Stocks, or alter the rights and obligations of States that arise from relevant international agreements.

NOTES AND QUESTIONS

In contrast to Antarctica, there is no binding agreement on the Arctic. The Arctic Council was established by a legally nonbinding instrument. Under its auspices, however, States have negotiated two binding international agreements. At the time the Arctic Council was established, there was considerable debate about whether to negotiate a binding international agreement for the Arctic or a nonbinding instrument. Why do you think the States in the Arctic region opted for a nonbinding instrument?

CHAPTER 12

FRESH WATER

• • •

A. INTRODUCTION

Water, water, everywhere,
Nor any drop to drink.

Samuel Taylor Coleridge, The Rime of the Ancient Mariner

Coleridge's Ancient Mariner was referring to salt water, of course. But in some areas of the world his second line, "Nor any drop to drink," is becoming increasingly descriptive of prevailing conditions with respect to fresh water. This is due in part to the fact that while Earth's human population continues to grow, the amount of fresh water on the planet has been the same for billions of years. But climate change is also contributing to the problem, especially in already arid countries. "Climate change is projected to reduce renewable surface water and groundwater resources in most dry subtropical regions (*robust evidence*, *high agreement* [1]). . . ." IPCC, AR5, Synthesis Report, Summary for Policymakers, p. 14 (2014).

Much of the world's fresh water is shared by two or more countries. For example, every country on the continent of Africa shares either surface water or groundwater with another country. The following map shows transboundary river basins in Africa, which cover much of the continent.

---

[1] "The degree of certainty in key findings in this assessment is based on the author teams' evaluations of underlying scientific understanding and is expressed as a qualitative level of confidence (from very low to very high) and, when possible, probabilistically with a quantified likelihood (from exceptionally unlikely to virtually certain). Confidence in the validity of a finding is based on the type, amount, quality, and consistency of evidence (e.g., data, mechanistic understanding, theory, models, expert judgment) and the degree of agreement." IPCC, Fifth Assessment Report, WG I, SPM, p. 3, available at http://www.ipcc.ch/pdf/assessment-report/ar5/wg1/WG1AR5_SPM_FINAL.pdf. (Editors' footnote.)

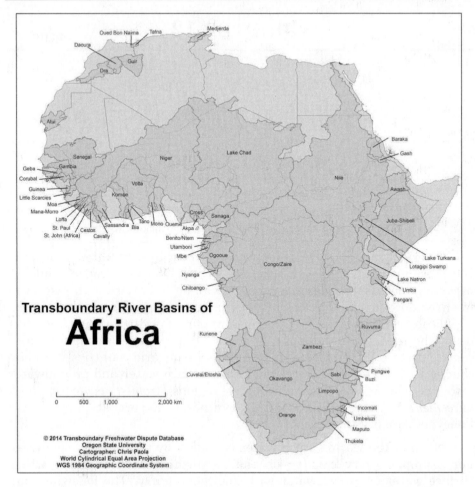

Source: http://www.transboundarywaters.orst.edu/database/register/maps/
Africa%20Basins.jpg.

It should be borne in mind that this map does not take into account some African transboundary aquifers that are not recharged significantly, which are found especially in North Africa.

There are over 260 international drainage basins in the world. They cover nearly half of Earth's land surface and account for some 60% of global freshwater flows. One hundred forty-five countries have some or all of their territories in international basins. UNEP, Atlas of International Freshwater Agreements 2 (2002).

The growing scarcity of the world's fresh water supplies on a per capita basis coupled with the proportion of these resources that is shared portends increasing competition and possibly conflict between countries over international rivers, lakes, and aquifers. Global climate change threatens to exacerbate these conflicts by altering historic flow patterns, melting glaciers and giving rise to the risk that less water will be

...se and in situ needs; but even ...lire. This chapter explores the ...tection, use and management ...defined broadly by the 1997 ...stem of surface waters and ...physical relationship a ...n different States." UN ...This chapter will also ...undary aquifers that ...receive significant

..., FIRST SERVED?

...ping country, most of whose territory is ...because of plentiful rainfall Mountainia is the ...vers that flow down to lower elevations and cross ...ring States. One of those States is Desertia, the home of ...zation that has relied on the waters of the Azure, a river ...in Mountainia, for thousands of years to support flood-recession ...rigated agriculture. In fact, the Azure River is virtually the only source ..fresh water available to Desertia. Mountainia is also home to an ancient civilization that has long grown various crops, taking advantage of the abundant precipitation to practice rainfed agriculture, there being no need to irrigate.

Until the late nineteenth and early twentieth centuries, the technology had not developed sufficiently to construct large dams that would produce hydroelectric power. By the second half of the twentieth century, Mountainia had been approached by various multilateral and bilateral development agencies offering financial and technical assistance for the construction of dams on some of Mountainia's rivers, including the Azure. Unrest in Mountainia put those plans on hold until the early twenty-first century. But then, with a stable government and other preconditions in place, Mountainia decided to proceed with several large dams, including one on the Azure that would be one of the largest on the continent in which Desertia and Mountainia are located. In announcing these plans, Mountainia's president proudly declared that the Azure Dam would produce enough electricity not only for Mountainia's needs, but for those of Desertia and other countries in the region, as well. She said that this would help to alleviate poverty in Mountainia and would provide much-needed foreign exchange. Desertia's president responded that Desertia considered the planned Azure Dam to constitute a threat to the security and very life of his country, and that Desertia would take "any necessary measures" to ensure that it did not become a reality. He stated that the dam would affect not only Desertia's water supply but also the flora and fauna downstream of the dam, and that

---

² Convention on the Law of the Non-Navigational Uses of International Watercourses, 21 May 1997, entered into force 17 August 2014, U.N. Doc. A/RES/51/869, 36 ILM 700 (1997).

Desertia could not tolerate a situation in which Mount[...]
hand on the tap" of the water on which Desertia had bee[...]
"for millennia." He also contended that Mountainia had [...]
transboundary environmental impact assessment and to [...]
with the "prior notice of its plans, together with all the re[...]
information, both of which are required by international law."[...]

1. Assume you are a lawyer working for a new i[...]
infrastructure bank, which would provide most of the funding for [...]
Dam. You have been tasked with preparing a memorandum setting [...]
rights and obligations under international law of Desertia and Mou[...]
with respect to the Azure Dam project.

2. Now assume that you have been appointed sole arbitrator[...]
Desertia and Mountainia in their dispute over the Azure Dam. How wou[...]
you rule?

3. Finally, assume you are a lawyer with a non-governmental
organization (NGO) focused on protecting the environment and ecosystems of
international watercourses. Would you recommend to your superiors that the
NGO oppose the Azure Dam? Even if so, if it became evident that the dam
would go forward, do you see any way, procedurally or substantively, in
which the NGO could press for Mountainia to manage the dam so as to
minimize its environmental consequences?

B. THE DEVELOPMENT OF INTERNATIONAL WATER LAW

1. THE "HARMON DOCTRINE"

WATER, POLITICS, AND INTERNATIONAL LAW
Stephen C. McCaffrey
in Water in Crisis 92, 96 (Peter Gleick ed., 1993)

[A] dispute [between Mexico and the United States] gave rise to what
is perhaps the most infamous legal view yet espoused publicly by a state
concerning international riparian rights. The controversy stemmed from
diversions of water from the Rio Grande in the late 19th century by
farmers and ranchers in the U.S. states of Colorado and New Mexico.
According to Mexico, these diversions reduced the supply of water to
Mexican communities in the vicinity of Ciudad Juarez. The Rio Grande
rises in Colorado, flows through New Mexico, then forms the border
between the United States state of Texas and Mexico before emptying
into the Gulf of Mexico. Mexico protested the diversions in October, 1895,
declaring that the legal claim of those living on its side of the Rio Grande
"to the use of the water of that river is incontestable, being prior to that of

the inhabitants of Colorado by hundreds of years." The U.S. Secretary of State responded that the United States was not obligated to halt the diversions. He relied on a legal opinion prepared by Attorney General Judson Harmon, which has since become known as the "Harmon Doctrine." According to the opinion:

> The fundamental principle of international law is the absolute sovereignty of every nation, as against all others, within its own territory. . . .
>
>> All exceptions . . . to the full and complete power of a nation within its own territories must be traced up to the consent of the nation itself. They can flow from no other legitimate source.[3]

While nothing in the opinion denied a duty to avoid causing harm to other countries, it has been taken as standing for the proposition that international law allows a state complete freedom of action with regard to international watercourses within its territory, irrespective of any consequence that might ensue in other countries. In fact, the response of the State Department to Mexico on the basis of Harmon's opinion took precisely this position. It declared that

> the rules of international law imposed upon the United States no duty to deny to its inhabitants the use of the water of that part of the Rio Grande lying wholly within the United States, although such use resulted in reducing the volume of water in the river below the point where it ceased to be entirely within the United States, the supposition of the existence of such a duty being inconsistent with the sovereign jurisdiction of the United States over the national domain.

The United States nonetheless joined Mexico in instructing the International Boundary Commission, which the two countries had established in 1889, to investigate and report on the Rio Grande question.

> The Commissioners' report stated that Mexico had been wrongfully deprived for many years of its equitable rights and they recommended that the matter be settled by a treaty dividing the use of the waters equally, Mexico to waive all claims for indemnity for the past unlawful use of water.[4]

---

[3] [This quotation is from The Schooner Exchange v. McFadden, 11 U.S. (7 Cranch) 116, 3 L. Ed. 287 (1812), a sovereign immunity case involving the question of whether a foreign vessel was immune from suit in United States courts, decided by the United States Supreme Court in an opinion by Chief Justice Marshall.—Eds.]

[4] United States of America, Memorandum of the State Department of Apr. 21, 1958, Legal Aspects of the Use of Systems of International Waters with reference to Columbia-Kootenay River System under Customary International Law and the Treaty of 1909, 85th Cong., 2d Sess., Senate doc. No. 118 (Washington, D.C., 1958), p. 64.

The United States and Mexico substantially followed the recommendations of the report in their agreed resolution of the dispute, which was embodied in the 1906 Convention concerning the Equitable Distribution of the Waters of the Rio Grande for Irrigation Purposes.

NOTES AND QUESTIONS

1. *Harmon's folly.* The doctrine of "absolute territorial sovereignty" epitomized by the Harmon Doctrine enjoyed a certain amount of popularity, principally among upstream States, during the nineteenth century. Its downstream-country counterpart was the idea of "absolute territorial integrity," according to which a downstream state had the right to receive the same quantity (and presumably quality) of water it had always received. The general opinion today is that both doctrines have given way to the more flexible principle of equitable utilization, which would accommodate inevitable changes in the use made of an international watercourse by the riparian states. This principle is explored below.

You should ask yourself as you read through the materials in this chapter whether you believe that the Harmon Doctrine is still "alive" and reflects "real" international practice. For a study of the practice of the United States and other countries concluding that it is not, *see* Stephen McCaffrey, The Harmon Doctrine One Hundred Years Later: Buried, Not Praised, 36 Nat. Res. J. 549 (1996). As a matter of legal analysis, are there any problems with basing an opinion concerning international water rights on a decision in a sovereign immunity case involving a foreign vessel?

Because it did not serve United States interests in cases in which it would be on the receiving end of pollution or other actions in upstream states, U. S. government lawyers have been bending over backwards to repudiate the Harmon Doctrine almost from the time it was articulated. See the State Department memorandum cited in footnote 4, above.

2. *Harmon by another name?* The view that a country can use the waters of a river that rises in its territory or flows through it regardless of the impact on existing and future uses of other states has been rejected by all bodies charged with formulating principles of international water law. However, the idea that states may act unilaterally, subject to the obligations of prior notification, equitable utilization and prevention of harm, persists in all post-Harmon formulations of the law. The Lake Lanoux Arbitration (France-Spain), Award of November 16, 1957, 53 Am. J. Int. L. 156 (1959) (discussed in Chapter 4), rejected the argument that a riparian nation cannot use an international river unless there is prior agreement with the other riparian states. Thus, states, especially upstream states, generally take the position that they may act unilaterally as long as there is no injury to other states. The result can be the construction of dams upstream on the main stem and tributaries of a river with insufficient consideration of the impact of the project on downstream interests. In recent years, we are discovering that these downstream impacts include stresses on deltas and other aquatic ecosystems.

Canada and China provide examples of Harmon "lite" at work. When the United States proposed to develop the Columbia River in a way that would preclude some upstream hydro development in Canada, Canada considered its options. Article II of the 1909 of the Boundary Waters Treaty, 36 Stat. 2448 (1909), provides in part that each State: "reserves to itself . . . the exclusive jurisdiction and control over the use and diversion, whether temporary or permanent, of all waters on its own side of the line which in their natural channels would flow across the boundary or into boundary waters; but it is agreed that any interference with or diversion from their natural channel of such waters on either side of the boundary, resulting in any injury on the other side of the boundary, shall give rise to the same rights and entitle the injured parties to the same legal remedies as if such injury took place in the country where such diversion or interference occurs; . . . ." Article II has been interpreted as a codification of the Harmon doctrine. A leading Canadian international water lawyer has written, "In the case of the Columbia River, Canada did study the feasibility of diverting waters from it for exclusive use in Canada, but, though holding to the opinion that Article II of the 1909 Treaty would justify any diversion, she did not rely on the [Harmon] doctrine, for the diversions under study were deemed to be well within Canada's right under the doctrine of equitable apportionment. . . ." Charles B. Bourne, The Right to Utilize Waters of International Rivers, 3 Can. Y.B. Int'l L. 187, 205 (1965).

China has completed three large dams on the upper Mekong River (called the Lancang Jiang in China); five more are planned or under construction in what is referred to as the Mekong Cascade. In 1995, the four lower riparian states (Cambodia, the Lao PDR, Thailand and Vietnam) entered into an agreement to share and manage the river, but China is only an observer not a party to this agreement. In response to complaints about the dams by the four lower basin states, China has concluded that its models show that either under a limited sovereignty (equitable use) or ecological benefits approach its use is consistent with international water law. Patricia K. Wouters. Sergei Vinogradov, Andrew Allan, Patricia Jones and Alistair Rieu-Clark, Sharing Transboundary Waters: An Integrated Assessment of Equitable Entitlement: The Legal Assessment Model 121 (UNESCO International Hydrological Programme Technical Document 74 2005). *See also* Fred Pearce, Chinese Dams Blamed for Mekong River's Bizarre Flow, New Scientist, 25 (March 2004).

Other current examples of strong assertions by upstream States of a right to proceed with dams in the face of objections by downstream States are the Lao PDR's Xayaburi Dam, under construction on the main stem of the Mekong at this writing, and Ethiopia's Grand Ethiopian Renaissance Dam on the Blue Nile, also under construction at this writing.

3.   *Harmon redivivus?* During the negotiation of the recently adopted UN Convention on the Law of the Non-Navigational Uses of International Watercourses, discussed below, and in their explanations of vote on the Convention, several countries lamented what in their view was the failure of

the Convention to take due account of "sovereignty." Most, if not all of these countries were upstream states. But does this necessarily mean they were embracing the Harmon Doctrine?

2. THE EVOLUTION OF THE LAW: SUBSTANTIVE RULES

INSTITUTE OF INTERNATIONAL LAW, INTERNATIONAL REGULATION REGARDING THE USE OF INTERNATIONAL WATERCOURSES FOR PURPOSES OTHER THAN NAVIGATION—DECLARATION OF MADRID, 20 APRIL 1911

Annuaire de l'Institut de Droit International, Madrid Session 1911
vol. 24, p. 365 (Paris 1911)

Statement of Reasons

Riparian States with a common stream are in a position of permanent physical dependence on each other which precludes the idea of the complete autonomy of each State in the section of the natural watercourse under its sovereignty.

International law has dealt with the right of navigation with respect to international rivers but the use of water for the purposes of industry, agriculture, etc. was not foreseen by international law.

It therefore seems expedient to remedy this lack by noting the rules of law resulting from the interdependence which undoubtedly exists between riparian States with a common stream and between States whose territories are crossed by a common stream.

With the exception of the right of navigation, as already established or to be established by international law:

The Institute of International Law is of the opinion that the following regulations should be observed from the point of view of (any) use of international streams.

I.   When a stream forms the frontier of two States, neither of these States may, without the consent of the other, and without special and valid legal title, make or allow individuals, corporations, etc. to make alterations therein detrimental to the bank of the other State. On the other hand, neither State may, on its own territory, utilize or allow the utilization of the water in such a way as to seriously interfere with its utilization by the other State or by individuals, corporations, etc. thereof.

The foregoing provisions are likewise applicable to a lake lying between the territories of more than two States.

II.   When a stream traverses successively the territories of two or more States:

1.   The point where this stream crosses the frontiers of two States, whether naturally, or since time immemorial, may not be changed by establishments of one of the States without the consent of the other;

2.   All alterations injurious to the water, the emptying therein of injurious matter (from factories, etc.) is forbidden;

3.   No establishment (especially factories utilizing hydraulic power) may take so much water that the constitution, otherwise called the utilizable or essential character of the stream shall, when it reaches the territory downstream, be seriously modified;

4.   The right of navigation by virtue of a title recognized in international law may not be violated in any way whatsoever;

5.   A State situated downstream may not erect or allow to be erected within its territory constructions or establishments which would subject the other State to the danger of inundation;

6.   The foregoing rules are applicable likewise to cases where streams flow from a lake situated in one State, through the territory of another State, or the territories of other States;

7.   It is recommended that the interested States appoint permanent joint commissions, which shall render decisions, or at least shall give their opinion, when, from the building of new establishments or the making of alterations in existing establishments, serious consequences might result in that part of the street situated in the territory of the other States.

NOTES AND QUESTIONS

1.   *Take that, Harmon!* In this early set of principles, the Institute of International Law directly contradicts Attorney-General Harmon's absolute-territorial-sovereignty based view: the "permanent physical dependence" between states sharing an international watercourse "precludes the idea of the complete autonomy of each State in the section of the natural watercourse under its sovereignty." The Institute is a prestigious body of experts in international law. It has adopted two other resolutions on international watercourses, the 1961 Salzburg Resolution on Utilization of Non-Maritime International Waters (Except for Navigation), Annuaire de l'Institut de droit international, vol. 49, II, Salzburg Session, September 1961, (Basle 1961), p. 381, and the 1979 Athens Resolution on the Pollution of Rivers and Lakes and International Law, Annuaire de l'Institut de droit international, vol. 58, II, Athens Session, September 1979, Basel München, 1980, p. 197.

2.   *From a pipe to a watershed?* In its 1961 Salzburg Resolution, the Institute opened the way to a more expansive—and realistic—view of the subject matter of legal regulation. Article I, establishing the scope of the Resolution, provides that it applies "to the use of waters which are part of a

river or of a watershed extending upon the territory of two or more States."
This idea was given more prominence in the International Law Association's
1966 Helsinki Rules, considered below.

3. *Enter the Chancellor's foot?*[5] Article III of the 1961 Resolution
provides as follows:

> If the various States disagree upon the extent of their rights of
> use, the disagreement shall be settled on the basis of equity, taking
> into consideration the respective needs of the States, as well as any
> other circumstances relevant to any particular case.

The idea that the respective rights and obligations of States sharing an
international watercourse should be governed by equitable principles has
been adopted by the U.S. Supreme Court in a series of interstate allocation
cases beginning in 1907[6] and has become the controlling legal principle of
international watercourse law. Like the IIL's 1961 Salzburg Resolution, all
formulations of the equitable utilization principle call for all relevant factors
to be taken into account in arriving at an equitable allocation.

HELSINKI RULES ON THE USES OF THE WATERS OF INTERNATIONAL RIVERS, 1966

International Law Association, Report of the Fifty-Second Conference
Helsinki, 1966, p. 484 (1966)

CHAPTER 1.   GENERAL

Article I

The general rules of international law as set forth in these chapters
are applicable to the use of the waters of an international drainage basin
except as may be provided otherwise by convention, agreement or binding
custom among the basin States.

Article II

An international drainage basin is a geographical area extending
over two or more States determined by the watershed limits of the system
of waters, including surface and underground waters, flowing into a
common terminus.

. . .

---

[5]   With apologies to John Selden, who complained in the 17th century that equity was too
vague and subjective a standard: "[It is] as if they should make the standard for the measure the
Chancellor's foot. What an uncertain measure would this be? One Chancellor has a long foot;
another a short foot; a third an indifferent foot. It is the same thing with the Chancellor's
conscience." As quoted in Joseph Story, 1 Commentaries on Equity Jurisprudence § 19, at 21.

[6]   Kansas v. Colorado, 206 U.S. 46 (1907).

CHAPTER 2.   EQUITABLE UTILIZATION OF THE WATERS OF AN INTERNATIONAL DRAINAGE BASIN

Article IV

Each basin State is entitled, within its territory, to a reasonable and equitable share in the beneficial uses of the waters of an international drainage basin.

Article V

(1) What is a reasonable and equitable share within the meaning of Article IV is to be determined in the light of all the relevant factors in each particular case.

(2) Relevant factors which are to be considered include, but are not limited to:

(a) the geography of the basin, including in particular the extent of the drainage area in the territory of each basin State;

(b) the hydrology of the basin, including in particular the contribution of water by each basin State;

(c) the climate affecting the basin;

(d) the past utilization of the waters of the basin, including in particular existing utilization;

(e) the economic and social needs of each basin State;

(f) the population dependent on the waters of the basin in each basin State;

(g) the comparative costs of alternative means of satisfying the economic and social needs of each basin State;

(h) the availability of other resources;

(i) the avoidance of unnecessary waste in the utilization of waters of the basin;

(j) the practicability of compensation to one or more of the co-basin States as a means of adjusting conflicts among uses; and,

(k) the degree to which the needs of a basin State may be satisfied, without causing substantial injury to a co-basin State.

(3) The weight to be given to each factor is to be determined by its importance in comparison with that of other relevant factors. In determining what is a reasonable and equitable share, all relevant factors are to be considered together and a conclusion reached on the basis of the whole.

UNITED NATIONS CONVENTION ON THE LAW OF THE NON-NAVIGATIONAL USES OF INTERNATIONAL WATERCOURSES

U.N. Doc. A/RES/51/869, 21 May 1997, 36 ILM 700 (1997)

PART I.   INTRODUCTION

. . .

Article 2
Use of Terms

For the purposes of the present Convention:

(a) "Watercourse" means a system of surface waters and groundwaters constituting by virtue of their physical relationship a unitary whole and normally flowing into a common terminus;

(b) "International watercourse" means a watercourse, parts of which are situated in different States;

. . .

PART II.   GENERAL PRINCIPLES

Article 5
Equitable and Reasonable Utilization and Participation

1.   Watercourse States shall in their respective territories utilize an international watercourse in an equitable and reasonable manner. In particular, an international watercourse shall be used and developed by watercourse States with a view to attaining optimal and sustainable utilization thereof and benefits therefrom, taking into account the interests of the watercourse States concerned, consistent with adequate protection of the watercourse.

2.   Watercourse States shall participate in the use, development and protection of an international watercourse in an equitable and reasonable manner. Such participation includes both the right to utilize the watercourse and the duty to cooperate in the protection and development thereof, as provided in the present Convention.

Article 6
Factors Relevant to Equitable and Reasonable Utilization

1.   Utilization of an international watercourse in an equitable and reasonable manner within the meaning of article 5 requires taking into account all relevant factors and circumstances, including:

(a) Geographic, hydrographic, hydrological, climatic, ecological and other factors of a natural character;

(b) The social and economic needs of the watercourse States concerned;

(c) The population dependent on the watercourse in each watercourse State;

(d) The effects of the use or uses of the watercourses in one watercourse State on other watercourse States;

(e) Existing and potential uses of the watercourse;

(f) Conservation, protection, development and economy of use of the water resources of the watercourse and the costs of measures taken to that effect;

(g) The availability of alternatives, of comparable value, to a particular planned or existing use.

2.   In the application of article 5 or paragraph 1 of this article, watercourse States concerned shall, when the need arises, enter into consultations in a spirit of cooperation.

3.   The weight to be given to each factor is to be determined by its importance in comparison with that of other relevant factors. In determining what is a reasonable and equitable use, all relevant factors are to be considered together and a conclusion reached on the basis of the whole.

Article 7
Obligation Not to Cause Significant Harm

1.   Watercourse States shall, in utilizing an international watercourse in their territories, take all appropriate measures to prevent the causing of significant harm to other watercourse States.

2.   Where significant harm nevertheless is caused to another watercourse State, the States whose use causes such harm shall, in the absence of agreement to such use, take all appropriate measures, having due regard for the provisions of articles 5 and 6, in consultation with the affected State, to eliminate or mitigate such harm and, where appropriate, to discuss the question of compensation.

Article 8
General Obligation to Cooperate

1.   Watercourse States shall cooperate on the basis of sovereign equality, territorial integrity, mutual benefit and good faith in order to attain optimal utilization and adequate protection of an international watercourse.

2.   In determining the manner of such cooperation, watercourse States may consider the establishment of joint mechanisms or commissions, as deemed necessary by them, to facilitate cooperation on relevant measures and procedures in the light of experience gained through cooperation in existing joint mechanisms and commissions in various regions.

Article 10
Relationship Between Different Kinds of Uses

1.   In the absence of agreement or custom to the contrary, no use of an international watercourse enjoys inherent priority over other uses.

2.   In the event of a conflict between uses of an international watercourse, it shall be resolved with reference to articles 5 to 7, with special regard being given to the requirements of vital human needs.

NOTES AND QUESTIONS

1.   *Déjà vu all over again?* Do the words of that well-known sage, Yogi Berra, describe developments in the concept of the subject-matter to be regulated by international water law, as indicated in the more recent instruments (the 1961 IIL Salzburg Resolution, the 1966 Helsinki Rules and the 1997 UN Convention)? Are "watershed," "drainage basin," and "system of surface waters and groundwaters" equivalent expressions? If not, how are they different, and does this have any practical implications?

2.   *I can harm you equitably!* Note that both the Helsinki Rules and the UN Convention contain provisions on equitable utilization. The UN Convention also contains a separate article on the prevention of significant harm. Where is the counterpart in the Helsinki Rules (hint: it's not in one of the articles not reproduced above). Is it possible that obligations of equitable utilization and prevention of harm could clash? If so, how? Can you give examples of how they could/could not come into conflict?

3.   *No, thanks, I'd rather not participate. Even equitably.* What is meant by "equitable and reasonable participation" within the meaning of Article 5(2) of the UN Convention? Can a state be obligated to participate in cooperation in the protection and development of an international watercourse—i.e., to engage in affirmative conduct of the kinds contemplated?

In the *Gabčíkovo-Nagymaros Project* case, considered below, the International Court found that the parties were under an obligation to re-establish the joint management regime provided for under the 1977 treaty between them involved in the case. The Court referred to Article 5(2) in the following way:

> 147. Re-establishment of the joint régime will . . . reflect in an optimal way the concept of common utilization of shared water resources for the achievement of the several objectives mentioned in the [1977] Treaty, in concordance with Article 5, paragraph 2, of the Convention on the Law of the Non-Navigational Uses of International Watercourses, according to which:
>
> > Watercourse States shall participate in the use, development and protection of an international watercourse in an equitable and reasonable manner. Such participation includes both the right to utilize the watercourse and the duty to cooperate in the

protection and development thereof, as provided in the present
Convention."

1997 ICJ Rep. 7, 80. Does this help you to understand Article 5(2)? Does it
surprise you that the Court quoted from the Convention a mere four months
after it was concluded, and years before it entered into force?

4. *From Helsinki to Berlin in 40 years.* In 2006 the International Law
Association (ILA) adopted The Berlin Rules on Water Resources at its
conference in Berlin. Revision of the Helsinki Rules on the Use of the Waters
of International Rivers, Report of the Seventy-First Conference, Berlin
(1966). Like the IIL, the ILA is a non-governmental organization that adopts
resolutions on subjects of international law. The purpose of what became the
Berlin Rules was to update the Helsinki Rules in light of developments since
their adoption in 1966. As indicated by their title, the Berlin Rules actually
go far beyond the Helsinki Rules in that they apply to wholly domestic water
resources as well as those that are internationally shared.

5. *The law of supply and . . . supply.* International water law has been
focused largely on problems of supply. It generally doesn't deal with demand.
Should it? E.g., should Ethiopia be required to use more efficient irrigation
techniques so more water would flow down the Blue Nile to Egypt, as Egypt
contends? Since some 85% of the water reaching Egypt comes from Ethiopia,
largely via the Blue Nile, Egypt has historically been wary of any Ethiopian
projects that would interfere with this flow. Ethiopia is currently
constructing the enormous Grand Ethiopian Renaissance Dam (GERD) on
the Blue Nile just upstream of the Ethiopia-Sudan border. On March 23,
2015, the three countries signed a Declaration of Principles (DOP) concerning
the GERD at Khartoum after four years of controversy about the dam. An
unofficial English translation of the DOP is available at http://english.ahram.
org.eg/News/125941.aspx. The DOP distills key principles from the 1997 UN
Watercourses Convention and the Nile River Basin Cooperative Framework
Agreement (CFA), which is not yet in force.

6. *Please pass the salt—the other way.* To what extent should the
possibility of desalination of sea water figure into the picture? Specifically, if
country A has the possibility of desalinating, should that be taken into
account in arriving at an equitable apportionment of a river or aquifer shared
with country B? Consider the factors set forth Article V of the Helsinki Rules
and Article 6 of the UN Convention. Israel has recently increased its
desalination capacity significantly. Should this mean it should take less
water from aquifers and the Jordan River, shared with Palestine and, in the
case of the river, Jordan? *See* A. Dan Tarlock, *International Water Law and
Adaptation,* in THE LAW OF ADAPTATION TO CLIMATE CHANGE 771, 779-780
(Michael B. Gerrard & Katrina Fischer Kuh eds., 2012).

7. *No harm to the environment?* Note that article 5 of the UN
Watercourses Convention ends with the proviso that an otherwise equitable
use nevertheless must be consistent with protecting the watercourse. Is that
the same as protecting the environment of the watercourse? If not, what does

it mean? See in this connection Article 20 of the Watercourses Convention, set forth below in connection with the discussion of protection of aquatic ecosystems.

8.   *My polluting use is as important as your drinking water use.* What? How can it be that "no use of an international watercourse enjoys inherent priority over other uses" as Article 10(1) says? Part of the explanation lies in the historical priority given to navigation over all other uses. (Where do you think this inherent priority developed? In the arid countries of North Africa?) One of the chief purposes of Article 10(1) was to lay that idea to rest. As far as drinking water is concerned, are you satisfied with the phrase at the end of Article 10(2), referring to the need to give "special regard" to "the requirements of vital human needs?" Is this enough? You will have an opportunity to think further about these issues in the section on the human right to water, below.

3.   THE EVOLUTION OF THE LAW: PROCEDURAL RULES

Thus far, we have been focusing chiefly on what may be characterized as "substantive" norms of international water law: the role of sovereignty in defining a state's obligations; equitable utilization; and the prevention of significant harm. But procedural rules are at least as important. They serve to allow States to keep their utilization within equitable bounds; to keep States informed of any development by other States that may affect an international watercourse; and thus possibly to nip in the bud proposed projects that may have harmful or inequitable consequences by encouraging dialogue between the States concerned. Set forth below are procedural rules contained in the 1997 UN Watercourses Convention as an illustration of how such rules operate.

UNITED NATIONS CONVENTION ON THE LAW OF THE NON-NAVIGATIONAL USES OF INTERNATIONAL WATERCOURSES
U.N. Doc. A/RES/51/869, 21 May 1997, 36 ILM 700 (1997)

Article 9
Regular Exchange of Data and Information

1.   Pursuant to article 8, watercourse States shall on a regular basis exchange readily available data and information on the condition of the watercourse, in particular that of a hydrological, meteorological, hydrogeological and ecological nature and related to the water quality as well as related forecasts.

2.   If a watercourse State is requested by another watercourse State to provide data or information that is not readily available, it shall employ its best efforts to comply with the request but may condition its compliance upon payment by the requesting State of the reasonable costs of collecting and, where appropriate, processing such data or information.

3.   Watercourse States shall employ their best efforts to collect and, where appropriate, to process data and information in a manner which facilitates its utilization by the other watercourse States to which it is communicated.

. . .

PART III.   PLANNED MEASURES

Article 11
Information Concerning Planned Measures

Watercourse States shall exchange information and consult each other and, if necessary, negotiate on the possible effects of planned measures on the condition of an international watercourse.

Article 12
Notification Concerning Planned Measures with Possible Adverse Effects

Before a watercourse State implements or permits the implementation of planned measures which may have a significant adverse effect upon other watercourse States, it shall provide those States with timely notification thereof. Such notification shall be accompanied by available technical data and information, including the results of any environmental impact assessment, in order to enable the notified States to evaluate the possible effects of the planned measures.

Article 13
Period for Reply to Notification

Unless otherwise agreed:

(a) A watercourse State providing a notification under article 12 shall allow the notified States a period of six months within which to study and evaluate the possible effects of the planned measures and to communicate the findings to it;

(b) This period shall, at the request of a notified State for which the evaluation of the planned measures poses special difficulty, be extended for a period of six months.

Article 14
Obligations of the Notifying State During the Period for Reply

During the period referred to in article 13, the notifying State:

(a) Shall cooperate with the notified States by providing them, on request, with any additional data and information that is available and necessary for an accurate evaluation; and

(b) Shall not implement or permit the implementation of the planned measures without the consent of the notified States.

Article 15
Reply to Notification

The notified States shall communicate their findings to the notifying State as early as possible within the period applicable pursuant to article 13. If a notified State finds that implementation of the planned measures would be inconsistent with the provisions of articles 5 or 7, it shall attach to its finding a documented explanation setting forth the reasons for the finding.

Article 16
Absence of Reply to Notification

1.   If, within the period applicable pursuant to article 13, the notifying State receives no communication under article 15, it may, subject to its obligations under articles 5 and 7, proceed with the implementation of the planned measures, in accordance with the notification and any other data and information provided to the notified States.

2.   Any claim to compensation by a notified State which has failed to reply within the period applicable pursuant to article 13 may be offset by the costs incurred by the notifying State for action undertaken after the expiration of the time for a reply which would not have been undertaken if the notified State had objected within that period.

Article 17
Consultations and Negotiations Concerning Planned Measures

1.   If a communication is made under article 15 that implementation of the planned measures would be inconsistent with the provisions of articles 5 or 7, the notifying State and the State making the communication shall enter into consultations and, if necessary, negotiations with a view to arriving at an equitable resolution of the situation.

2.   The consultations and negotiations shall be conducted on the basis that each State must in good faith pay reasonable regard to the rights and legitimate interests of the other State.

3.   During the course of the consultations and negotiations, the notifying State shall, if so requested by the notified State at the time it makes the communication, refrain from implementing or permitting the implementation of the planned measures for a period of six months unless otherwise agreed.

Article 18
Procedures in the Absence of Notification

1.   If a watercourse State has reasonable grounds to believe that another watercourse State is planning measures that may have a significant adverse effect upon it, the former State may request the latter

to apply the provisions of article 12. The request shall be accompanied by a documented explanation setting forth its grounds.

2.   In the event that the State planning the measures nevertheless finds that it is not under an obligation to provide a notification under article 12, it shall so inform the other State, providing a documented explanation setting forth the reasons for such finding. If this finding does not satisfy the other State, the two States shall, at the request of that other State, promptly enter into consultations and negotiations in the manner indicated in paragraphs 1 and 2 of article 17.

3.   During the course of the consultations and negotiations, the State planning the measures shall, if so requested by the other State at the time it requests the initiation of consultations and negotiations, refrain from implementing or permitting the implementation of those measures for a period of six months unless otherwise agreed.

Article 19
Urgent Implementation of Planned Measures

1.   In the event that the implementation of planned measures is of the utmost urgency in order to protect public health, public safety or other equally important interests, the State planning the measures may, subject to articles 5 and 7, immediately proceed to implementation, notwithstanding the provisions of article 14 and paragraph 3 of article 17.

2.   In such case, a formal declaration of the urgency of the measures shall be communicated without delay to the other watercourse States referred to in article 12 together with the relevant data and information.

3.   The State planning the measures shall, at the request of any of the States referred to in paragraph 2, promptly enter into consultations and negotiations with it in the manner indicated in paragraphs 1 and 2 of article 17.

NOTES AND QUESTIONS

1.   *The Rolling Stones gambit.* Can the notifying state simply go through the motions of complying with Part III's procedures, singing "Time Is On My Side," and go ahead with its project after all applicable time periods have expired? If not, what would prevent the notifying state from doing that? If so, how would you draft a provision or set of provisions that would check such a temptation?

2.   *Pulp fiction?* Recall the coverage of the procedural norms of prior notification and consultation in Chapter 2, above. In particular, consider the excerpts from the *Pulp Mills* judgment of the International Court of Justice reprinted there, including the following:

113.   In the opinion of the Court, the obligation to notify is intended to create the conditions for successful co-operation between the

parties, enabling them to assess the plan's impact on the river on the basis of the fullest possible information and, if necessary, to negotiate the adjustments needed to avoid the potential damage that it might cause.

Sounds reasonable enough. So why was Uruguay reluctant to follow the notification procedures of the treaty involved there? Would the same concern apply to the procedures under the Watercourses Convention set forth above?

C. APPLYING THE LAW TO THE FACTS: CASE LAW AND A CASE STUDY

1. CASE STUDY: THE TIGRIS-EUPHRATES BASIN

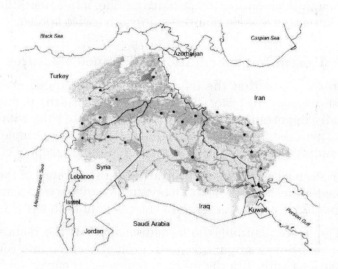

Tigris and Euphrates Watershed

Revenga, C., S. Murray, J. Abramovitz, and A. Hammond, 1998. Watersheds of the World: Ecological Value and Vulnerability. Washington, DC: World Resources Institute.

http://earthtrends.wri.org/text/water-resources/map-336.html

WATER, POLITICS, AND INTERNATIONAL LAW

Stephen C. McCaffrey
in Water in Crisis 92, 93 (Peter Gleick ed., 1993)[7]

The Tigris and Euphrates River systems are often treated as one basin because they unite in the Shatt-al-Arab waterway shortly before emptying into the Persian Gulf. Both rivers rise in Turkey and flow through or along Syrian territory before entering Iraq. While the Euphrates flows through Syria for a considerable distance, the Tigris never enters Syria entirely but only forms the border of that country with Turkey briefly before flowing into Iraq. Tributaries flowing from the Zagros Mountains in Iran also contribute importantly to the Tigris. The Euphrates is currently the subject of the greatest development efforts, especially in Turkey, but the flow of the Tigris system is approximately 65 percent greater than that of the Euphrates. Iraq is more heavily dependent upon water from the Tigris and Euphrates than Syria or Turkey, with a majority of the Iraqi population relying upon those rivers for all of their water needs.

Since the 1980s Turkey has been constructing an immense, multifaceted water project on the Euphrates and Tigris called the Southeastern Anatolia Project (GAP by its name in Turkish), which has given rise to considerable concern on the part of Syria and Iraq. The GAP project will ultimately consist of 22 dams which will be used for the production of hydroelectric power and for the irrigation of up to 1,500,000 hectares. It has been estimated that when completed, the project could cause Syria to lose up to 40 percent of its water from the Euphrates and Iraq as much as 90 percent. The largest dam in the project, the Ataturk dam, was completed in 1990. In order to begin filling the reservoir behind the dam, Turkey stopped the flow of the Euphrates entirely for one month, from mid-January to mid-February of 1990.

Needless to say, this action disturbed the two lower riparians greatly. Turkey has stated that it will guarantee a flow of 500 cubic meters per second (CMS) below the project and maintains that increased releases before the January, 1990 stoppage of the Euphrates kept the average flow at that level. Iraq, however, was not satisfied with that amount. At a ministerial level meeting of the three states in June of 1990, Iraq requested 700 CMS, basing its claim on what it termed its "acquired rights" to the use of Euphrates waters for irrigation. According to Iraq, these rights derived from use of the waters for that purpose for thousands of years. Indeed, the waters of the Tigris and Euphrates have been used for irrigation in what is now Iraq since the time of ancient Mesopotamia, some 6,000 years ago.

---

[7]   Certain updates have been made to this excerpt by the Editors.

Unlike the situation in the Jordan basin, the relations between the countries in the Tigris-Euphrates basin have not been marked by military conflict over water. There are, in fact, bilateral agreements between Turkey and Iraq and between Syria and Iraq concerning certain aspects of their water relations. Furthermore, beginning in 1983 Syria participated in the work of a Joint Technical Regional Rivers Committee that had been established by Iraq and Turkey in 1980, at the invitation of those two countries. Subsequent political developments in Syria and Iraq have left this situation uncertain. Yet water is undeniably a source of tension in the region and a crucial element in the overall political relations between the three countries.

Turkey has accused both Syria and Iraq of providing sanctuary to the Marxist Kurdish Workers' Party (PKK), which waged a violent and bloody independence campaign against the Turkish government. In October, 1989, then prime minister Turgut Ozal, who later became Turkey's president, declared that Euphrates water would be cut off unless activities of the PKK were curtailed. But after assuming the presidency, Ozal . . . stated that Turkey "will never use the control of water to coerce or threaten [our neighbors]." While this should be of some comfort to Turkey's neighbors, Turkish officials have denied any obligation to provide water to downstream countries. For example, Turkey's Minister of State, Kamran Inan, has been reported to have stated that "We have no international obligations" concerning the Tigris and Euphrates. [Turkey has taken the position that international watercourses are only those that run along a boundary, not across it.[8]]

Even if coercion or pressure is not an objective, however, the GAP project poses a significant threat to downstream water users. Syria, for example, depends heavily upon the Euphrates for drinking water, irrigation and industrial uses, and to a lesser extent for electricity. According to one account, "With its population growing at 3.7% per year, Syria would be running short of water by the end of the [20th] century even without the GAP. With it, Syria faces a water catastrophe." While Iraq may look to the Tigris as an alternative source of supply, it is sufficiently concerned with the flow of the Euphrates that in 1974 it threatened to bomb the al-Thawra dam in Syria and massed troops along the border, alleging that the dam reduced the river's flow. It is not only water quantity, but also water quality that is at stake. Return flows from the massive irrigation projects that are part of GAP will carry salts as well as fertilizer and pesticide residues back into the Euphrates. This may render the water unfit for drinking, unless treated, and reduce its suitability for irrigation and some industrial uses.

---

[8] *See* A. Kibarorglu et al., *Cooperation on Turkey's Transboundary Waters*, Status Report Commissioned by the German Federal Ministry for Environment, Nature Conservation and Nuclear Safety 20 (2005). This position is a significant issue regarding Turkey's efforts to join the EU because of the EU Water Framework Directive.

Subsequent Developments: From Bad to Worse. More recent developments must be divided into two phases: prior to the 2003 United States-British led coalition invasion of Iraq; and post-invasion events. Prior to the invasion, Syria and Iraq agreed in 1990 that Syria would release 58 percent of the flow of the Euphrates to Iraq. Turkey then tried to shift the debate from a rights-based to a needs-based plan. It proposed that the three riparian states perform a basin wide inventory of water and land followed by an evaluation of land and water resources which would provide the basis for an equitable apportionment. Iraq and Syria did not accept this process; Iraq's historic entitlement (if any) thus remains unquantified. The Iraq War begun with the United States 2003 invasion brought basin cooperation to a virtual standstill, to the benefit of Turkey. The portions of the Tigris and Euphrates in Iraq's territory were polluted by everything from agricultural run-off to dead bodies and hazardous leaks from abandoned weapons facilities. Since that conflict, the civil war in Syria and general destabilization of the region have prevented progress on cooperation concerning the Tigris-Euphrates Basin.

2. THE GABČÍKOVO-NAGYMAROS PROJECT CASE

CASE CONCERNING THE
GABČÍKOVO-NAGYMAROS PROJECT
(Hungary/Slovakia)
International Court of Justice
Judgment of Sept. 25, 1997, 1997 I.C.J. Rep. 7

[Hungary and Slovakia brought this case to the Court on July 2, 1993, by Special Agreement signed on April 7, 1993. The case concerned a project on the Danube River, provided for by a 1977 treaty between Hungary and Czechoslovakia, consisting of a series of dams and barrages on a stretch of approximately 200 kilometers of the Danube between Bratislava, the capital of Slovakia, and Budapest, the capital of Hungary. For most of the length of this stretch the Danube forms the border between the two countries. Upstream of the point at which it begins to form the border it is for a short distance wholly within what is now Slovak territory; downstream of the border sector it passes into Hungary. According to the treaty, its purposes were chiefly to improve navigation, provide flood protection, and produce electricity. The treaty provided for the construction of two series of locks, one at the Czechoslovak town of Gabčíkovo, on a 31-kilometer bypass canal in Czechoslovak (now Slovak) territory, and the other at the town of Nagymaros, in Hungarian territory. In order to fill the bypass canal and thus operate the hydroelectric power plant and ship locks at Gabčíkovo, the treaty called for the Danube to be dammed at the Hungarian town of Dunakiliti. This diversion dam was Hungary's responsibility under the agreement. The Court's sketch map no. 2 depicts the design of the "original project."

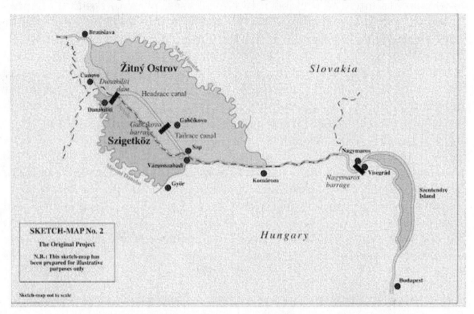

Sketch-Map prepared by the International Court of Justice

[Citing environmental concerns, and in response to a growing protest movement organized by a group called the Danube Circle,[9] Hungary stopped work on both the Nagymaros and the Dunakiliti portions of the project in 1989 and purported to terminate the treaty unilaterally in May, 1992. Czechoslovakia decided to put the upper part of the project into operation by damming the Danube, beginning on October 24, 1994, at Čunovo, a point at which the river is solely in Czechoslovak (now Slovak) territory. This diversion dam, which substituted for the non-operational Dunakiliti Dam, created a reservoir (although a smaller one than foreseen under the treaty) and, as envisioned in the treaty, diverted most of the flow of the Danube (80 to 90 percent) into the bypass canal until the point at which the canal rejoins the bed of the Danube. The Čunovo Dam and related structures are known as "Variant C"—the title given to one of the possible "provisional solutions" considered by Czechoslovakia after Hungary's abandonment of the project. (See the Court's sketch map no. 3, depicting Variant C. Although indicated on the sketch map, the Dunakiliti dam was not put into operation by Hungary.) On January 1, 1993, Slovakia became an independent state.

---

[9] Protests against the Hungarian Government coalesced around this movement and contributed to the downfall of the communist government in 1989.

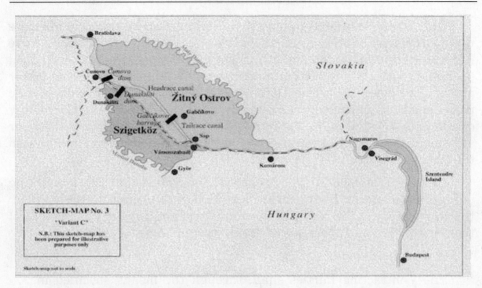

Sketch-Map prepared by the International Court of Justice

[As will appear below, the court essentially held that both parties had breached their international obligations, Hungary by stopping work on the project and Slovakia, as successor to Czechoslovakia, by putting into operation Variant C. It also held that Hungary's purported termination of the 1977 treaty was ineffective, that the project—including the Čunovo dam—would have to be placed under a joint operational regime, and that—unless the parties agree otherwise—they must compensate each other for the injurious consequences of their respective breaches.

[The court's opinion and some of the separate and dissenting opinions contain a wealth of material pertaining to the field of international environmental law. The following passages of the court's opinion are relevant to the field in general and to the subject of allocation and use of shared natural resources.]

17. The Danube has always played a vital part in the commercial and economic development of its riparian States, and has underlined and reinforced their inter-dependence, making international co-operation essential. Improvements to the navigation channel have enabled the Danube, now linked by canal to the Main and thence to the Rhine, to become an important navigational artery connecting the North Sea to the Black Sea. In the stretch of river to which the case relates, flood protection measures have been constructed over the centuries, farming and forestry practised, and, more recently, there has been an increase in population and industrial activity in the area. The cumulative effects on the river and on the environment of various human activities over the years have not all been favourable, particularly for the water regime.

Only by international co-operation could action be taken to alleviate these problems. Water management projects along the Danube have frequently sought to combine navigational improvements and flood protection with the production of electricity through hydroelectric power plants. The potential of the Danube for the production of hydroelectric power has been extensively exploited by some riparian States. The history of attempts to harness the potential of the particular stretch of the river at issue in these proceedings extends over a 25-year period culminating in the signature of the 1977 Treaty.

18. ... Article 15 [of the 1977 treaty] specified that the contracting parties "shall ensure, by the means specified in the joint contractual plan, that the quality of the water in the Danube is not impaired as a result of the construction and operation of the System of Locks." . . .

It was stipulated in Article 19 that:

The Contracting Parties shall, through the means specified in the joint contractual plan, ensure compliance with the obligations for the protection of nature arising in connection with the construction and operation of the System of Locks.

Article 20 provided for the contracting parties to take appropriate measures, within the framework of their national investments, for the protection of fishing interests in conformity with the Convention concerning Fishing in the Waters of the Danube, signed at Bucharest on 29 January 1958. . . .

[Hungary had contended that even though its stoppage of work was in breach of the 1977 treaty, it was justified by a "state of ecological necessity" to which the implementation of the project might have given rise.]

49. The Court will now consider the question of whether there was, in 1989, a state of necessity which would have permitted Hungary, without incurring international responsibility, to suspend and abandon works that it was committed to perform in accordance with the 1977 Treaty and related instruments.

50. In the present case, the Parties are in agreement in considering that the existence of a state of necessity must be evaluated in the light of the criteria laid down by the International Law Commission in Article 33 of the Draft Articles on the International Responsibility of States ["State Responsibility"] that it adopted on first reading. That provision is worded as follows:

ARTICLE 33

STATE OF NECESSITY[10]

1.   A state of necessity may not be invoked by a State as a ground for precluding the wrongfulness of an act of that State not in conformity with an international obligation of the State unless:

> (a) the act was the only means of safeguarding an essential interest of the State against a grave and imminent peril; and

> (b) the act did not seriously impair an essential interest of the State towards which the obligation existed.

2.   In any case, a state of necessity may not be invoked by a State as a ground for precluding wrongfulness: . . .

> (c) if the State in question has contributed to the occurrence of the state of necessity.

(Yearbook of the International Law Commission, 1980, Vol. II, Part 2, p. 34.) In its Commentary, the Commission defined the "state of necessity" as being

> the situation of a State whose sole means of safeguarding an essential interest threatened by a grave and imminent peril is to adopt conduct not in conformity with what is required of it by an international obligation to another State" (ibid., para. 1). . . .

51. The Court . . . observes . . . that [the state of necessity] can only be accepted on an exceptional basis. . . .

[A]ccording to the Commission, the state of necessity can only be invoked under certain strictly defined conditions which must be cumulatively satisfied; and the State concerned is not the sole judge of whether those conditions have been met.

52. In the present case, the following basic conditions set forth in Draft Article 33 are relevant: it must have been occasioned by an "essential interest" of the State which is the author of the act conflicting with one of its international obligations; that interest must have been threatened by a "grave and imminent peril"; the act being challenged must have been the "only means" of safeguarding that interest; that act must not have "seriously impair[ed] an essential interest" of the State towards which the obligation existed; and the State which is the author of

---

[10]   The final articles on Responsibility of States for Internationally Wrongful Acts adopted in 2001 are annexed to General Assembly resolution 56/83 of 12 December 2001. The final version of the Article 33, Article 25, Necessity, largely corresponds with Article 33 of the draft articles.— Eds.

that act must not have "contributed to the occurrence of the state of necessity." Those conditions reflect customary international law.

The Court will now endeavour to ascertain whether those conditions had been met at the time of the suspension and abandonment, by Hungary, of the works that it was to carry out in accordance with the 1977 Treaty.

53. The Court has no difficulty in acknowledging that the concerns expressed by Hungary for its natural environment in the region affected by the Gabčíkovo-Nagymaros Project related to an "essential interest" of that State, within the meaning given to that expression in Article 33 of the Draft of the International Law Commission.

The Commission, in its Commentary, indicated that one should not, in that context, reduce an "essential interest" to a matter only of the "existence" of the State, and that the whole question was, ultimately, to be judged in the light of the particular case (see Yearbook of the International Law Commission, 1980, Vol. II, Part 2, p. 49, para. 32); at the same time, it included among the situations that could occasion a state of necessity, "a grave danger to . . . the ecological preservation of all or some of [the] territory [of a State]" (ibid., p. 35, para. 3); and specified, with reference to State practice, that "It is primarily in the last two decades that safe-guarding the ecological balance has come to be considered an 'essential interest' of all States." (Ibid., p. 39, para. 14.) The Court recalls that it has recently had occasion to stress, in the following terms, the great significance that it attaches to respect for the environment, not only for States but also for the whole of mankind:

> the environment is not an abstraction but represents the living space, the quality of life and the very health of human beings, including generations unborn. The existence of the general obligation of States to ensure that activities within their jurisdiction and control respect the environment of other States or of areas beyond national control is now part of the corpus of international law relating to the environment.

Legality of the Threat or Use of Nuclear Weapons, Advisory Opinion, I.C.J. Reports 1996, pp. 241–242, para. 29.

54. The verification of the existence, in 1989, of the "peril" invoked by Hungary, of its "grave and imminent" nature, as well as of the absence of any "means" to respond to it, other than the measures taken by Hungary to suspend and abandon the works, are all complex processes.

As the Court has already indicated . . . , Hungary on several occasions expressed, in 1989, its "uncertainties" as to the ecological impact of putting in place the Gabčíkovo-Nagymaros barrage system, which is why it asked insistently for new scientific studies to be carried out.

The Court considers, however, that, serious though these uncertainties might have been they could not, alone, establish the objective existence of a "peril" in the sense of a component element of a state of necessity. The word "peril" certainly evokes the idea of "risk"; that is precisely what distinguishes "peril" from material damage. But a state of necessity could not exist without a "peril" duly established at the relevant point in time; the mere apprehension of a possible "peril" could not suffice in that respect. It could moreover hardly be otherwise, when the "peril" constituting the state of necessity has at the same time to be "grave" and "imminent." "Imminence" is synonymous with "immediacy" or "proximity" and goes far beyond the concept of "possibility." As the International Law Commission emphasized in its commentary, the "extremely grave and imminent" peril must "have been a threat to the interest at the actual time" (Yearbook of the International Law Commission, 1980, Vol. II, Part 2, p. 49, para. 33). That does not exclude, in the view of the Court, that a "peril" appearing in the long term might be held to be "imminent" as soon as it is established, at the relevant point in time, that the realization of that peril, however far off it might be, is not thereby any less certain and inevitable.

The Hungarian argument on the state of necessity could not convince the Court unless it was at least proven that a real, "grave" and "imminent" "peril" existed in 1989 and that the measures taken by Hungary were the only possible response to it. . . .

57. The Court concludes . . . that, with respect to both Nagymaros and Gabčíkovo, the perils invoked by Hungary, without prejudging their possible gravity, were not sufficiently established in 1989, nor were they "imminent"; and that Hungary had available to it at that time means of responding to these perceived perils other than the suspension and abandonment of works with which it had been entrusted. What is more, negotiations were under way which might have led to a review of the Project and the extension of some of its time-limits, without there being need to abandon it. The Court infers from this that the respect by Hungary, in 1989, of its obligations under the terms of the 1977 Treaty would not have resulted in a situation "characterized so aptly by the maxim *summum jus summa injuria*". . . .

. . . [A]lthough the principal object of the 1977 Treaty was the construction of a System of Locks for the production of electricity, improvement of navigation on the Danube and protection against flooding, the need to ensure the protection of the environment had not escaped the parties, as can be seen from Articles 15, 19 and 20 of the Treaty. . . .

The Court infers from all these elements that, in the present case, even if it had been established that there was, in 1989, a state of necessity linked to the performance of the 1977 Treaty, Hungary would not have been permitted to rely upon that state of necessity in order to justify its failure to comply with its treaty obligations, as it had helped, by act or omission to bring it about. . . .

[The Court then turned to the legality of "Variant C."]

78. [I]n practice, the operation of Variant C led Czechoslovakia to appropriate, essentially for its use and benefit, between 80 and 90 per cent of the waters of the Danube before returning them to the main bed of the river, despite the fact that the Danube is not only a shared international watercourse but also an international boundary river.

Czechoslovakia submitted that Variant C was essentially no more than what Hungary had already agreed to and that the only modifications made were those which had become necessary by virtue of Hungary's decision not to implement its treaty obligations. It is true that Hungary, in concluding the 1977 Treaty, had agreed to the damming of the Danube and the diversion of its waters into the bypass canal. But it was only in the context of a joint operation and a sharing of its benefits that Hungary had given its consent. The suspension and withdrawal of that consent constituted a violation of Hungary's legal obligations, demonstrating, as it did, the refusal by Hungary of joint operation; but that cannot mean that Hungary forfeited its basic right to an equitable and reasonable sharing of the resources of an international watercourse. . . .

[In discussing whether Czechoslovakia's putting into operation of Variant C could be justified as a countermeasure,[11] 14 the Court stated, *inter alia*, as follows:]

85. In the view of the Court, an important consideration is that the effects of a countermeasure must be commensurate with the injury suffered, taking account of the rights in question.

In 1929, the Permanent Court of International Justice, with regard to navigation on the River Oder, stated as follows:

> [the] community of interest in a navigable river becomes the basis of a common legal right, the essential features of which are the perfect equality of all riparian States in the user of the whole course of the river and the exclusion of any preferential privilege of any one riparian State in relation to the others. *Territorial Jurisdiction of the International Commission of the River Oder, Judgment No. 16, 1929, P.C.I.J., Series A, No. 23,* p. 27.

Modern development of international law has strengthened this principle for non-navigational uses of international watercourses as well, as evidenced by the adoption of the Convention of 21 May 1997 on the

---

[11] That is, a measure that would be unlawful but for the fact that it was a legitimate response to the prior wrongful act of another state.—Eds.

Law of the Non-Navigational Uses of International Watercourses by the United Nations General Assembly.

The Court considers that Czechoslovakia, by unilaterally assuming control of a shared resource, and thereby depriving Hungary of its right to an equitable and reasonable share of the natural resources of the Danube—with the continuing effects of the diversion of these waters on the ecology of the riparian area of the Szigetköz—failed to respect the proportionality which is required by international law.

86. Moreover, . . . the fact that Hungary had agreed in the context of the original Project to the diversion of the Danube (and, in the Joint Contractual Plan, to a provisional measure of withdrawal of water from the Danube) cannot be understood as having authorized Czechoslovakia to proceed with a unilateral diversion of this magnitude without Hungary's consent. . . .

97. Finally, Hungary argued that subsequently imposed requirements of international law in relation to the protection of the environment precluded performance of the Treaty. The previously existing obligation not to cause substantive damage to the territory of another State had, Hungary claimed, evolved into an erga omnes obligation of prevention of damage pursuant to the "precautionary principle." On this basis, Hungary argued, its termination was "forced by the other party's refusal to suspend work on Variant C." . . .

112. Neither of the Parties contended that new peremptory norms of environmental law had emerged since the conclusion of the 1977 Treaty, and the Court will consequently not be required to examine the scope of Article 64 of the Vienna Convention on the Law of Treaties [providing for termination of a treaty through the emergence of a peremptory norm of international law (jus cogens) with which the treaty is in conflict]. On the other hand, the Court wishes to point out that newly developed norms of environmental law are relevant for of the Treaty and that the parties could, by agreement, incorporate them through the application of Articles 15, 19 and 20 of the Treaty. These articles do not contain specific obligations of performance but require the parties, in carrying out their obligations to ensure that the quality of water in the Danube is not impaired and that nature is protected, to take new environmental norms into consideration when agreeing upon the means to be specified in the Joint Contractual Plan.

By inserting these evolving provisions in the Treaty, the parties recognized the potential necessity to adapt the Project. Consequently, the Treaty is not static, and is open to adapt to emerging norms of international law. By means of Articles 15 and 19, new environmental norms can be incorporated in the Joint Contractual Plan.

The responsibility to do this was a joint responsibility. The obligations contained in Articles 15, 19 and 20 are, by definition, general and have to be transformed into specific obligations of performance through a process of consultation and negotiation. Their implementation thus requires a mutual willingness to discuss in good faith actual and potential environmental risks.

It is all the more important to do this because as the Court recalled in its Advisory Opinion on the *Legality of the Threat or Use of Nuclear Weapons*, "the environment is not an abstraction but represents the living space, the quality of life and the very health of human beings, including generations unborn" (I.C.J. Reports 1996, para. 29; see also paragraph 53 above).

The awareness of the vulnerability of the environment and the recognition that environmental risks have to be assessed on a continuous basis have become much stronger in the years since the Treaty's conclusion. These new concerns have enhanced the relevance of Articles 15, 19 and 20.

113. The Court recognizes that both Parties agree on the need to take environmental concerns seriously and to take the required precautionary measures, but they fundamentally disagree on the consequences this has for the joint Project. In such a case, third-party involvement may be helpful and instrumental in finding a solution, provided each of the Parties is flexible in its position. . . .

[In discussing the legal consequences of its judgment, the court stated in part as follows:]

140. It is clear that the Project's impact upon, and its implications for, the environment are of necessity a key issue. The numerous scientific reports which have been presented to the Court by the Parties—even if their conclusions are often contradictory—provide abundant evidence that this impact and these implications are considerable.

In order to evaluate the environmental risks, current standards must be taken into consideration. This is not only allowed by the wording of Articles 15 and 19, but even prescribed, to the extent that these articles impose a continuing—and thus necessarily evolving—obligation on the parties to maintain the quality of the water of the Danube and to protect nature.

The Court is mindful that, in the field of environmental protection, vigilance and prevention are required on account of the often irreversible character of damage to the environment and of the limitations inherent in the very mechanism of reparation of this type of damage.

Throughout the ages, mankind has, for economic and other reasons, constantly interfered with nature. In the past, this was often done without consideration of the effects upon the environment. Owing to new scientific insights and to a growing awareness of the risks for mankind—for present and future generations—of pursuit of such interventions at an unconsidered and unabated pace, new norms and standards have been developed, set forth in a great number of instruments during the last two decades. Such new norms have to be taken into consideration, and such new standards given proper weight, not only when States contemplate new activities but also when continuing with activities begun in the past. This need to reconcile economic development with protection of the environment is aptly expressed in the concept of sustainable development. For the purposes of the present case, this means that the Parties together should look afresh at the effects on the environment of the operation of the Gabčíkovo power plant. In particular they must find a satisfactory solution for the volume of water to be released into the old bed of the Danube and into the side-arms on both sides of the river.

141. It is not for the Court to determine what shall be the final result of these negotiations to be conducted by the Parties. It is for the Parties themselves to find an agreed solution that takes account of the objectives of the Treaty, which must be pursued in a joint and integrated way, as well as the norms of international environmental law and the principles of the law of international watercourses. The Court will recall in this context that, as it said in the *North Sea Continental Shelf* cases:

> [the Parties] are under an obligation so to conduct themselves that the negotiations are meaningful, which will not be the case when either of them insists upon its own position without contemplating any modification of it (*I.C.J. Reports 1969,* p. 47, para. 85). . . .

147. Re-establishment of the joint régime will . . . reflect in an optimal way the concept of common utilization of shared water resources for the achievement of the several objectives mentioned in the Treaty, in concordance with Article 5, paragraph 2, of the Convention on the Law of the Non-Navigational Uses of International Watercourses, according to which:

> "Watercourse States shall participate in the use, development and protection of an international watercourse in an equitable and reasonable manner. Such participation includes both the right to utilize the watercourse and the duty to cooperate in the protection and development thereof, as provided in the present Convention." . . .

148. . . . Now the Court will turn to the legal consequences of the internationally wrongful acts committed by the Parties.

149. The Permanent Court of International Justice stated in its Judgment . . . in the case concerning the *Factory at Chorzów*:

reparation must, as far as possible, wipe out all the consequences of the illegal act and reestablish the situation which would, in all probability, have existed if that act had not been committed.

P.C.I.J., Series A, No. 17, p. 47.

150. Reparation must, "as far as possible," wipe out all the consequences of the illegal act. In this case, the consequences of the wrongful acts of both Parties will be wiped out "as far as possible" if they resume their co-operation in the utilization of the shared water resources of the Danube, and if the multi-purpose programme, in the form of a coordinated single unit, for the use, development and protection of the watercourse is implemented in an equitable and reasonable manner. . . .

155. For these reasons, THE COURT,

(1) . . .

A. Finds, by fourteen votes to one, that Hungary was not entitled to suspend and subsequently abandon, in 1989, the works on the Nagymaros Project and on the part of the Gabčíkovo Project for which the Treaty of 16 September 1977 and related instruments attributed responsibility to it;

. . .

B. Finds, by nine votes to six, that Czechoslovakia was entitled to proceed, in November 1991, to the "provisional solution" as described in the terms of the Special Agreement;

. . .

C. Finds, by ten votes to five, that Czechoslovakia was not entitled to put into operation, from October 1992, this "provisional solution";

. . .

D. Finds, by eleven votes to four, that the notification, on 19 May 1992, of the termination of the Treaty of 16 September 1977 and related instruments by Hungary did not have the legal effect of terminating them;

. . .

(2) . . .

B. Finds, by thirteen votes to two, that Hungary and Slovakia must negotiate in good faith in the light of the prevailing situation, and must take all necessary measures to ensure the achievement of the objectives of the Treaty of 16 September 1977, in accordance with such modalities as they may agree upon; . . .

C. Finds, by thirteen votes to two, that, unless the Parties otherwise agree, a joint operational régime must be established in accordance with the Treaty of 16 September 1977;

. . .

D. Finds, by twelve votes to three, that, unless the Parties otherwise agree, Hungary shall compensate Slovakia for the damage sustained by Czechoslovakia and by Slovakia on account of the suspension and abandonment by Hungary of works for which it was responsible; and Slovakia shall compensate Hungary for the damage it has sustained on account of the putting into operation of the "provisional solution" by Czechoslovakia and its maintenance in service by Slovakia; . . .

[Declarations, separate opinions and dissenting opinions by various judges are omitted.]

NOTES AND QUESTIONS

1.   *Uncertain about uncertainty?* Do you believe the court handled correctly the question of "scientific uncertainty" as to the possible effects of the project? What about its treatment of the "precautionary principle"? If you believe these were dealt with correctly, see if you can restate what in the court's view a State in the position of Hungary in 1989 should do. If not, how would you strike the balance between the values of the stability of treaty regimes, on the one hand, and environmental protection, on the other?

2.   *Sustainable dams?* Did the outcome of the case give effect to the "concept" of sustainable development, as the court called it? (Judge Weeramantry, in his separate opinion, maintains it is a "principle.") If you do not believe so, how would you strike *that* balance? If sustainable development is the standard, shouldn't tribunals also consider social impacts, not just economic and environmental ones?

Large dams have been criticized for destroying aquatic ecosystems, displacing populations, often poor and indigenous, and for failing to deliver the promised benefits. There have been several efforts to develop a more inclusive and comprehensive dam planning strategy to make them more sustainable. See World Commission on Dams, Dams and Development: A New Framework for Decisionmaking (2000); Thayer Scudder, The Future of Large Dams: Dealing with Social, Environmental, Institutional and Political Costs 61 (2005); Int'l Inst. For Envt. & Dev., Sharing the Benefits of Large Dams In West Africa (Jamie Skinner, Madiodio Niasse & Lawrence Haas eds., 2009).

3.   *Why do you need a treaty when you've got custom?* This case provides a rather dramatic illustration of the interplay between treaties and customary international law. There was a treaty, but the parties had an obligation to negotiate to implement its general terms (in particular, those of Articles 15, 19, and 20); and a party that breached the treaty had to conform

its conduct to the requirements of the customary international law of international watercourses.

4. *Darwinian treaties?* Let's say there is a treaty concluded in 1858 between States A and B, and that the countries become involved in a dispute in the 21st century about the treaty's interpretation. Do you interpret the treaty in light of its meaning in 1858, when it was concluded, or, say, in 2005, when the dispute was submitted to the Court? In the *Navigational and Related Rights* case, the ICJ found that "generic" terms in a treaty must have been intended by the parties to be interpreted in an evolutionary way: "[W]here the parties have used generic terms in a treaty, the parties necessarily having been aware that the meaning of the terms was likely to evolve over time, and where the treaty has been entered into for a very long period or is 'of continuing duration', the parties must be presumed, as a general rule, to have intended those terms to have an evolving meaning." *Dispute Regarding Navigational and Related Rights (Costa Rica v. Nicaragua)*, 2009 ICJ Rep. p. 213, p. 243, para. 66.) This idea, which is supported by Article 31(3)(c) of the Vienna Convention on the Law of Treaties and a growing body of case law, is reflected in the *Gabčíkovo-Nagymaros Project* judgment. See in particular paragraphs 112 and 140.

3.   THE PULP MILLS CASE

PULP MILLS ON THE RIVER URUGUAY

(Argentina v. Uruguay)
2010 ICJ Rep. p. 14

[We have already had occasion to consider the substantive and procedural principles discussed by the Court in this case in Chapter 4. We revisit it here because of its importance in the field of international watercourses.]

[Please see the summary of the facts of this case and the accompanying map in Chapter 4. Briefly, the case involved a suit by Argentina against Uruguay concerning two planned pulp mills on Uruguay's side of the Uruguay River, only one of which was ultimately built. Argentina alleged that Uruguay had breached the 1975 Statute of the River Uruguay (1295 UNTS 340), a treaty between the two countries that is quite advanced for its time. Argentina contended that the mills would adversely affect the quality of the waters of the River Uruguay.]

55. Argentina asserts that the 1975 Statute constitutes the law applicable to the dispute before the Court, as supplemented so far as its application and interpretation are concerned, by various customary principles and treaties in force between the Parties and referred to in the Statute. Relying on the rule of treaty interpretation set out in Article 31, paragraph 3(c) of the Vienna Convention on the Law of Treaties, Argentina contends notably that the 1975 Statute must be interpreted in the light of principles governing the law of international watercourses

and principles of international law ensuring protection of the environment. It asserts that the 1975 Statute must be interpreted so as to take account of all "relevant rules" of international law applicable in the relations between the Parties, so that the Statute's interpretation remains current and evolves in accordance with changes in environmental standards. In this connection Argentina refers to the principles of equitable, reasonable and noninjurious use of international watercourses, the principles of sustainable development, prevention, precaution and the need to carry out an environmental impact assessment. It contends that these rules and principles are applicable in giving the 1975 Statute a dynamic interpretation, although they neither replace it nor restrict its scope. . . .

57. Uruguay likewise considers that the 1975 Statute must be interpreted in the light of general international law and it observes that the Parties concur on this point. It maintains however that its interpretation of the 1975 Statute accords with the various general principles of the law of international watercourses and of international environmental law, even if its understanding of these principles does not entirely correspond to that of Argentina. . . .

64. The Court next briefly turns to the issue of how the 1975 Statute is to be interpreted. . . . The Parties . . . are in agreement that the 1975 Statute is to be interpreted in accordance with rules of customary international law on treaty interpretation, as codified in Article 31 of the Vienna Convention on the Law of Treaties.

65. . . . The 1975 Statute is . . . a treaty which predates the entry into force of the Vienna Convention on the Law of Treaties. In interpreting the terms of the 1975 Statute, the Court will have recourse to the customary rules on treaty interpretation as reflected in Article 31 of the Vienna Convention. Accordingly the 1975 Statute is to be "interpreted in good faith in accordance with the ordinary meaning to be given to the terms of the [Statute] in their context and in light of its object and purpose". That interpretation will also take into account, together with the context, "any relevant rules of international law applicable in the relations between the parties". . . .

III. THE ALLEGED BREACH OF PROCEDURAL OBLIGATIONS

. . .

93. [T]he Court considers that, because of the scale and diversity of the functions they have assigned to CARU [from the Spanish acronym for "Comisión Administradora del Río Uruguay," the Administrative Commission of the River Uruguay], the Parties intended to make that international organization a central component in the fulfilment of their obligations to co-operate as laid down by the 1975 Statute.

. . .

101. The Court points out that the principle of prevention, as a customary rule, has its origins in the due diligence that is required of a State in its territory. It is "every State's obligation not to allow knowingly its territory to be used for acts contrary to the rights of other States" (*Corfu Channel (United Kingdom v. Albania), Merits, Judgment, I.C.J. Reports 1949,* p. 22)). A State is thus obliged to use all the means at its disposal in order to avoid activities which take place in its territory, or in any area under its jurisdiction, causing significant damage to the environment of another State. This Court has established that this obligation "is now part of the corpus of international law relating to the environment" (*Legality of the Threat or Use of Nuclear Weapons, Advisory Opinion, I.C.J. Reports 1996 (I),* p. 242, para. 29). . . .

149. The Court concludes . . . that by authorizing the construction of the mills and the port terminal at Fray Bentos before the expiration of the [180-day] period of negotiation [provided for in Article 12 of the Statute], Uruguay failed to comply with the obligation to negotiate laid down by Article 12 of the Statute. . . .

[The Court then addressed the question whether Uruguay was required to suspend work on the projects after Argentina had referred the dispute to the Court after the parties failed to reach an agreement during the 180-day negotiation period.]

152. According to Uruguay, the 1975 Statute does not give one party a "right of veto" over the projects initiated by the other. It does not consider there to be a "no construction obligation" borne by the State initiating the projects until such time as the Court has ruled on the dispute. Uruguay points out that the existence of such an obligation would enable one party to block a project that was essential for the sustainable development of the other. . . .

154. . . . The Court points out that, while the 1975 Statute gives it jurisdiction to settle any dispute concerning its interpretation or application, it does not however confer on it the role of deciding in the last resort whether or not to authorize the planned activities. Consequently, the State initiating the plan may, at the end of the negotiation period, proceed with construction at its own risk. . . .

IV. SUBSTANTIVE OBLIGATIONS

. . .

B. *Alleged Violations of Substantive Obligations*

. . .

1. The obligation to contribute to the optimum and rational utilization of the river (Article 1)

170. . . . Argentina . . . maintains that, in interpreting the 1975 Statute . . . according to the principle of equitable and reasonable use, account must be taken of all pre-existing legitimate uses of the river, including in particular its use for recreational and tourist purposes.

171. For Uruguay, the object and purpose of the 1975 Statute is to establish a structure for co-operation between the Parties through CARU in pursuit of the shared goal of equitable and sustainable use of the water and biological resources of the river. Uruguay contends that it has in no way breached the principle of equitable and reasonable use of the river and that this principle provides no basis for favouring pre-existing uses of the river, such as tourism or fishing, over other, new uses. . . .

177. Regarding Article 27,[12] it is the view of the Court that its formulation reflects not only the need to reconcile the varied interests of riparian States in a transboundary context and in particular in the use of a shared natural resource, but also the need to strike a balance between the use of the waters and the protection of the river consistent with the objective of sustainable development. The Court has already dealt with the [procedural] obligations arising from Articles 7 to 12 of the 1975 Statute. . . . The Court wishes to add that such utilization could not be considered to be equitable and reasonable if the interests of the other riparian State in the shared resource and the environmental protection of the latter were not taken into account. Consequently, it is the opinion of the Court that Article 27 embodies this interconnectedness between equitable and reasonable utilization of a shared resource and the balance between economic development and environmental protection that is the essence of sustainable development. . . .

3. The obligation to co-ordinate measures to avoid changes in the ecological balance (Article 36)

. . .

183. It is recalled that Article 36 provides that "[t]he parties shall coordinate, through the Commission, the necessary measures to avoid any

---

[12] Article 27 provides: "The right of each Party to use the waters of the river, within its jurisdiction, for domestic, sanitary, industrial and agricultural purposes shall be exercised without prejudice to the application of the procedure laid down in articles 7 to 12 when the use is liable to affect the retime of the river or the quality of its waters."—Eds

change in the ecological balance and to control pests and other harmful factors in the river and the areas affected by it". . . .

185. In the view of the Court, the purpose of Article 36 of the 1975 Statute is to prevent any transboundary pollution liable to change the ecological balance of the river by co-ordinating, through CARU, the adoption of the necessary measures. . . . As the Court emphasized in the *Gabčíkovo-Nagymaros* case:

"in the field of environmental protection, vigilance and prevention are required on account of the often irreversible character of damage to the environment and of the limitations inherent in the very mechanism of reparation of this type of damage" (*Gabčíkovo-Nagymaros Project (Hungary/Slovakia), Judgment, I.C.J. Reports 1997*, p. 78, para. 140).

. . .

188. This vigilance and prevention is all the more important in the preservation of the ecological balance, since the negative impact of human activities on the waters of the river may affect other components of the ecosystem of the watercourse such as its flora, fauna, and soil. The obligation to co-ordinate, through the Commission, the adoption of the necessary measures, as well as their enforcement and observance, assumes, in this context, a central role in the overall system of protection of the River Uruguay established by the 1975 Statute. It is therefore of crucial importance that the Parties respect this obligation.

189. In light of the above, the Court is of the view that Argentina has not convincingly demonstrated that Uruguay has refused to engage in such co-ordination as envisaged by Article 36, in breach of that provision.

4. The obligation to prevent pollution and preserve the aquatic environment (Article 41)

190. Article 41 provides that:

"Without prejudice to the functions assigned to the Commission in this respect, the parties undertake:

(a) to protect and preserve the aquatic environment and, in particular, to prevent its pollution, by prescribing appropriate rules and [adopting appropriate] measures in accordance with applicable international agreements and in keeping, where relevant, with the guidelines and recommendations of international technical bodies;

(b) not to reduce in their respective legal systems:

    1. the technical requirements in force for preventing water pollution, and

    2. the severity of the penalties established for violations;

(c) to inform one another of any rules which they plan to prescribe with regard to water pollution in order to establish equivalent rules in their respective legal systems."

191. Argentina claims that by allowing the discharge of additional nutrients into a river that is eutrophic and suffers from reverse flow and stagnation, Uruguay violated the obligation to prevent pollution, as it failed to prescribe appropriate measures in relation to the Orion (Botnia) mill, and failed to meet applicable international environmental agreements, including the Biodiversity Convention and the Ramsar Convention. It maintains that the 1975 Statute prohibits any pollution which is prejudicial to the protection and preservation of the aquatic environment or which alters the ecological balance of the river. Argentina further argues that the obligation to prevent pollution of the river is an obligation of result and extends not only to protecting the aquatic environment proper, but also to any reasonable and legitimate use of the river, including tourism and other recreational uses.

192. Uruguay contends that the obligation laid down in Article 41*(a)* of the 1975 Statute to "prevent . . . pollution" does not involve a prohibition on all discharges into the river. It is only those that exceed the standards jointly agreed by the Parties within CARU in accordance with their international obligations, and that therefore have harmful effects, which can be characterized as "pollution" under Article 40 of the 1975 Statute. Uruguay also maintains that Article 41 creates an obligation of conduct, and not of result, but that it actually matters little since Uruguay has complied with its duty to prevent pollution by requiring the plant to meet best available technology ("BAT") standards.

193. Before turning to the analysis of Article 41, the Court recalls that:

"The existence of the general obligation of States to ensure that activities within their jurisdiction and control respect the environment of other States or of areas beyond national control is now part of the corpus of international law relating to the environment." (*Legality of the Threat or Use of Nuclear Weapons, Advisory Opinion, I.C.J. Reports 1996 (I)*, pp. 241–242, para. 29.)

194. The Court moreover had occasion to stress, in the *Gabčíkovo-Nagymaros Project* case, that "the Parties together should look afresh at the effects on the environment of the operation of the Gabčíkovo power plant". . . . The Court is mindful of these statements in taking up now the examination of Article 41 of the 1975 Statute.

195. In view of the central role of this provision in the dispute between the Parties in the present case and their profound differences as to its interpretation and application, the Court will make a few remarks

of a general character on the normative content of Article 41 before addressing the specific arguments of the Parties. . . .

197. Thirdly, the obligation to "preserve the aquatic environment, and in particular to prevent pollution by prescribing appropriate rules and measures" is an obligation to act with due diligence in respect of all activities which take place under the jurisdiction and control of each party. It is an obligation which entails not only the adoption of appropriate rules and measures, but also a certain level of vigilance in their enforcement and the exercise of administrative control applicable to public and private operators, such as the monitoring of activities undertaken by such operators, to safeguard the rights of the other party. The responsibility of a party to the 1975 Statute would therefore be engaged if it was shown that it had failed to act diligently and thus take all appropriate measures to enforce its relevant regulations on a public or private operator under its jurisdiction. . . .

(a) *Environmental Impact Assessment*

[Relevant portions of this section are reprinted in Chapter 4. In it, the Court found that "it may now be considered a requirement under general international law to undertake an environmental impact assessment where there is a risk that the proposed industrial activity may have a significant adverse impact in a transboundary context, in particular, on a shared resource," and that this was a due diligence obligation. (Para. 204.)] . . .

(c) *Impact of the discharges on the quality of the waters of the river*

229. [T]he Parties have over the last three years presented to the Court a vast amount of factual and scientific material containing data and analysis of the baseline levels of contaminants already present in the river prior to the commissioning of the plant and the results of measurements of its water and air emissions after the plant started its production activities and, in some cases, until mid-2009. . . .

237. The particular parameters and substances that are subject to controversy between the Parties in terms of the impact of the discharges of effluent from the Orion (Botnia) mill on the quality of the waters of the river are: dissolved oxygen; total phosphorus (and the related matter of eutrophication due to phosphate); phenolic substances; nonylphenols and nonylphenolethoxylates; and dioxins and furans. The Court now turns to the assessment of the evidence presented to it by the Parties with respect to these parameters and substances.

[After evaluating each parameter and substance individually the Court found in essence that there was insufficient evidence to support Argentina's contention that discharges of effluent from the Botnia mill were adversely impacting the river. The Court also evaluated Argentina's contentions regarding effects on biodiversity (paras. 260–262) and air pollution (paras. 263–264).] . . .

(f) *Conclusions on Article 41*

265. It follows from the above that there is no conclusive evidence in the record to show that Uruguay has not acted with the requisite degree of due diligence or that the discharges of effluent from the Orion (Botnia) mill have had deleterious effects or caused harm to living resources or to the quality of the water or the ecological balance of the river since it started its operations in November 2007. Consequently, on the basis of the evidence submitted to it, the Court concludes that Uruguay has not breached its obligations under Article 41.

(g) *Continuing obligations: monitoring*

266. The Court is of the opinion that both Parties have the obligation to enable CARU, as the joint machinery created by the 1975 Statute, to exercise on a continuous basis the powers conferred on it by the 1975 Statute, including its function of monitoring the quality of the waters of the river and of assessing the impact of the operation of the Orion (Botnia) mill on the aquatic environment. Uruguay, for its part, has the obligation to continue monitoring the operation of the plant in accordance with Article 41 of the Statute and to ensure compliance by Botnia with Uruguayan domestic regulations as well as the standards set by CARU. The Parties have a legal obligation under the 1975 Statute to continue their co-operation through CARU and to enable it to devise the necessary means to promote the equitable utilization of the river, while protecting its environment. . . .

281. Lastly, the Court points out that the 1975 Statute places the Parties under a duty to co-operate with each other, on the terms therein set out, to ensure the achievement of its object and purpose. This obligation to co-operate encompasses ongoing monitoring of an industrial facility, such as the Orion (Botnia) mill. In that regard the Court notes that the Parties have a long-standing and effective tradition of co-operation and co-ordination through CARU. By acting jointly through CARU, the Parties have established a real community of interests and rights in the management of the River Uruguay and in the protection of its environment. They have also co-ordinated their actions through the joint mechanism of CARU, in conformity with the provisions of the 1975 Statute, and found appropriate solutions to their differences within its framework without feeling the need to resort to the judicial settlement of disputes provided for in Article 60 of the Statute until the present case was brought before the Court.

282. For these reasons,

THE COURT,

(1) By thirteen votes to one,

Finds that the Eastern Republic of Uruguay has breached its procedural obligations under Articles 7 to 12 of the 1975 Statute of the River Uruguay and that the declaration by the Court of this breach constitutes appropriate satisfaction; . . .

(2) By eleven votes to three,

Finds that the Eastern Republic of Uruguay has not breached its substantive obligations under Articles 35, 36 and 41 of the 1975 Statute of the River Uruguay; . . .

(3) Unanimously,

Rejects all other submissions by the Parties.

NOTES AND QUESTIONS

1.   *Pulp fiction?* Historically, pulp mills were often the worst polluters of rivers. Are you surprised, in light of this, at the outcome of the case? While the case was *sub judice*, an observer without detailed knowledge of the proof offered by the two sides might have been forgiven for taking something resembling a *res ipsa loquitur* approach: it's a pulp mill, therefore it's going to pollute the river horribly. But this particular plant was of Finnish design and was built and operated according to the exacting standards of the European Union. It even had its own wastewater treatment plant; the adjacent town of Fray Bentos did not, discharging fluid waste, including untreated sewage, directly into the river. The Botnia plant arranged to pass that waste through its plant, resulting in a reduction of the pollution entering the river.

2.   *Tommy, that was bad, but it's enough punishment that I've said that.* What? "[T]he declaration of this breach [of procedural obligations] constitutes appropriate satisfaction?" This form of remedy is actually not all that unusual in international law. As we have seen in Chapter 5, Accountability and Compliance, the obligation of a breaching State is known broadly as "reparation." The breaching state must repair the injury caused by its breach. The Court found the first two forms of reparation—restitution and, to the extent that is not possible, compensation—inapplicable in this case. That leaves the third form, "satisfaction," which is intended to provide a remedy when an injury cannot be made good by restitution or compensation. The ILC's commentary explains that satisfaction "is the remedy for those injuries, not financially assessable, which amount to an affront to the State. These injuries are frequently of a symbolic character, arising from the very fact of the breach of the obligation, irrespective of its material consequences for the State concerned."[13] Satisfaction can itself take various forms, from an

---

[13] UNITED NATIONS, MATERIALS ON THE RESPONSIBILITY OF STATES FOR INTERNATIONALLY WRONGFUL ACTS, p. 249 (2012).

acknowledgement of the breach and apologies to declarations by international tribunals, to the payment of exemplary damages. The Court found a declaration to be the most appropriate form in this case.

3. *The Chickenman*[14] *of international water law?* Did you notice how many times the Court and the parties referred to equitable and reasonable utilization? Are you surprised at this, given that the expression does not figure in the 1975 Statute? Can you articulate why both the parties and the Court seem to use it as a standard?

4. THE KISHENGANGA ARBITRATION

INDUS WATERS KISHENGANGA ARBITRATION
(Pakistan v. India)
Partial Award of 18 February 2013, Final Award of 20 December 2013, *available at the website of the Permanent Court of Arbitration,* http://www.pca-cpa.org/showpageb106. html?pag_id=1392; the awards and other decisions are reprinted in THE INDUS WATERS KISHENGANGA ARBITRATION (PAKISTAN V INDIA), RECORD OF PROCEEDINGS (2010–2013), Permanent Court of Arbitration Award Series, Award No. 2011–01 (2014)

[The following excerpts are from the Partial Award of February 18, 2013.]

. . .

4.   Through a Request for Arbitration dated 17 May 2010, Pakistan initiated proceedings against India pursuant to Article IX and Annexure G of the [1960 Indus Waters] Treaty.[15]

5.   In its Request for Arbitration, Pakistan stated that the Parties had failed to resolve the "Dispute" concerning the Kishenganga Hydro-Electric Project (the "KHEP") by agreement pursuant to Article IX(4) of the Treaty. Pakistan identified "two questions that are at the centre" of the dispute in the following manner:

a.   Whether India's proposed diversion of the river Kishenganga (Neelum) into another Tributary, i.e. the Bonar-Madmati Nallah, being one central element of the Kishenganga Project, breaches India's legal obligations owed to Pakistan under the Treaty, as interpreted and applied in accordance with international law, including India's obligations under Article III(2) (let flow all the waters of the Western rivers and not permit any interference with those waters) and Article IV(6) (maintenance of natural channels)?

b.   Whether under the Treaty, India may deplete or bring the reservoir level of a run-of-river Plant below Dead Storage Level

---

[14] Of whom it was said, "He's everywhere, he's everywhere!"—Eds.

[15] Indus Waters Treaty 1960 between the Government of India, the Government of Pakistan and the International Bank for Reconstruction and Development, 19 September 1960, 419 U.N.T.S. 126.

(DSL) in any circumstances except in the case of an unforeseen emergency? [We will focus here on the first question.]

. . .

II. BACKGROUND

126. This arbitration marks the first instance that a court of arbitration has been constituted since the Indus Waters Treaty was concluded over half a century ago. The proceedings have arisen out of a dispute between Pakistan and India concerning the interpretation and implementation of the Treaty in relation to the construction and operation of the Kishenganga Hydro-Electric Project. The Treaty sets forth the rights and obligations of the Parties on the use of the waters of the Indus system of rivers. The KHEP is an Indian hydro-electric project located on one such river—known as the "Kishenganga" in India-administered Jammu and Kashmir and as the "Neelum" in Pakistan-administered Jammu and Kashmir (the "Kishenganga/Neelum River," "Kishenganga/Neelum," or "River").

127. The KHEP is designed to generate power by diverting water from a dam site on the Kishenganga/Neelum River (within the Gurez valley, an area of higher elevation) to another river of the Indus system (lower in elevation and located near Wular Lake) through a system of tunnels, with the water powering turbines having a capacity of up to 330 megawatts. In essence, the Parties disagree as to whether the planned diversion of water and other technical design features of the KHEP are in conformity with the provisions of the Treaty. The Parties also disagree over the permissibility under the Treaty of the use of the technique of drawdown flushing for sediment control in Run-of-River Plants.

A. THE GEOGRAPHY

128. The Indus system of rivers is composed of six main rivers: the Indus, the Jhelum and the Chenab (together with their tributaries, the "Western Rivers"), and the Sutlej, the Beas and the Ravi (together with their tributaries, the "Eastern Rivers"). These rivers and their tributaries rise primarily in the Himalayas and course through Afghanistan, China, India and Pakistan before merging into the Indus river and draining into the Arabian Sea south-east of the port of Karachi in Pakistan. The Indus system of rivers and its catchment are depicted on the following map provided by Pakistan:

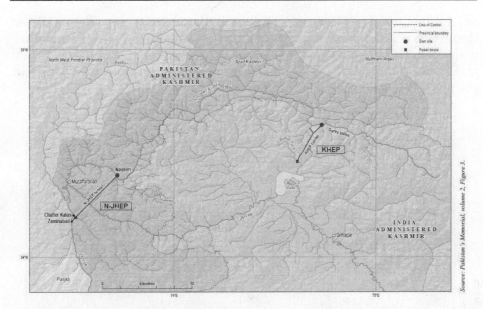

Source: Pakistan's Memorial, volume 2, Figure 3.

129. The Kishenganga/Neelum River, on which the KHEP is located, is a tributary of the Jhelum. The River originates in India-administered Jammu and Kashmir . . . at an elevation of 4400 metres. It flows through India-administered Jammu and Kashmir, crosses the Line of Control separating India-administered Jammu and Kashmir from Pakistan-administered Jammu and Kashmir, and joins the Jhelum River at Muzaffarabad in Pakistan-administered Jammu and Kashmir. The flow in the Kishenganga/Neelum River is strongly seasonal. The highest flows occur from May to August, associated with seasonal snowmelt in the upper catchment, and monsoon rain in the lower reaches. In contrast, there is a long low flow season from early October to the middle of March. . . .

D. THE KHEP AND THE NJHEP—TECHNICAL CHARACTERISTICS

. . .

155. The KHEP was re-designed in 2006. . . . The new design comprises: (1) a 35.48 metre high dam over the Kishenganga/Neelum River located in the Gurez valley in India-administered Jammu and Kashmir, . . . approximately 12.07 kilometres upstream of the Line of Control; (2) a reservoir with a gross storage capacity of 18.35 MCM [million cubic metres], located behind the dam; (3) a 23.5 kilometre head-race tunnel through which up to 58.4 m^3/s of water can be diverted from the Kishenganga/Neelum River at the dam site to the powerhouse; (4) a powerhouse at the downstream end of the tunnel . . . ; and (5) a tail-race channel which, after power generation, will deliver water diverted from the Kishenganga/Neelum River into the Bonar Nallah, another tributary

of the Jhelum. The diverted water will then rejoin the Jhelum River through Wular Lake, at a point upstream of the Jhelum River's juncture with the Kishenganga/Neelum River. The design of the KHEP thus makes use of the natural 666-metre denivelation between the dam and the powerhouse for the generation of power.

156. Pakistan renders the KHEP schematically as follows:

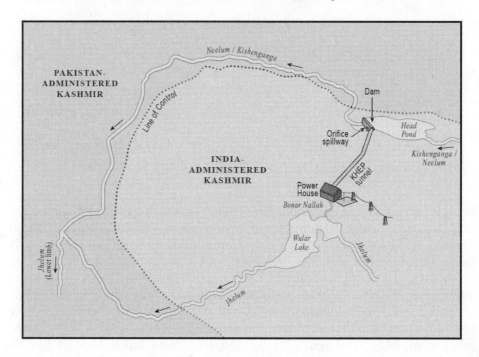

. . .

158. As described in Pakistan's Memorial, the NJHEP's [Pakistan's Neelum-Jhelum Hydro-Electric Project's] design includes: (1) a 41.5-metre dam to be constructed on the Kishenganga/Neelum River at Nauseri, in Pakistan-administered Jammu and Kashmir, 158 kilometres downstream of the KHEP and a short distance upstream of Muzaffarabad; and (2) a tunnel of approximately 30 kilometres through which water will be diverted from the Kishenganga/Neelum River to an underground powerhouse at Chatter Kalas. After power generation, the water will be returned to the Jhelum River near Zaminabad. The NJHEP has a design capacity of 969 megawatts. . . .

E.   THE IMPACT OF THE KHEP ON THE NJHEP

160. It is undisputed between the Parties that the operation of the KHEP would to some extent affect the power-generating capacity of the NJHEP, although the precise numbers cited by the Parties differ somewhat. The Parties' contentions as to the potential effect of the KHEP on the volume of water in the Kishenganga/Neelum River available for

power generation at Nauseri (from where water is diverted to the NJHEP's power station) and on potential energy production by the NJHEP may be summarized as follows:

	Average Flow Reduction at Nauseri (in percent)		Average Energy Production Reduction at NJHEP (in percent)	
	In Pakistan's submission	In India's submission	In Pakistan's submission	In India's submission
October to March	33	29.88	35	29.9
April to September	11	4.59	6	4.6
Annually	14	11.2	13	11.2

. . .

IV. ANALYSIS OF THE COURT

358. At the outset of its analysis, the Court considers it appropriate to note the extraordinary contribution of the World Bank to the conception, mediation, negotiation, drafting and financing of the Indus Waters Treaty, an instrument critical to the life and well-being of hundreds of millions of people of India and Pakistan. The conclusion of the Indus Waters Treaty in 1960, in which the leaders and staff of the World Bank lent vital support to the Parties, was and remains a great achievement of international cooperation.

. . .

(a) The permissibility of inter-tributary transfers in general

378. Whether Annexure D permits inter-tributary transfers is answered by the plain text of Paragraph 15(iii). This Paragraph provides that "where a Plant is located on a Tributary of The Jhelum . . ., the water released below the Plant may be delivered . . . into another Tributary . . . ," thus allowing the diversion of water from one tributary to another, provided that the works in question fall within the terms of that Paragraph.

379. With respect to the scope of permissible diversion, the Court is not convinced that Paragraph 15(iii) was intended only to permit the occasional diversion of water in the course of Operation [as Pakistan had argued], rather than diversion as an integral part of the design and operation of a Plant on the Kishenganga/Neelum River similar to the KHEP as now presented. No such distinction is evident from the text itself. Moreover, whether effected by tunnel or canal, any release of water

from one tributary into another will be a major undertaking, involving substantial engineering works constructed at great expense. The Court can see no purpose that would be served by investing in the extensive infrastructure required for transfer, only to carry out such transfers on an occasional basis and in a manner ancillary to the *raison d'être* of a Plant—power generation.

. . .

(b) The KHEP as a Run-of-River Plant located on a tributary to the Jhelum

381. Paragraph 15(iii) of Annexure D provides:

. . .

(iii) where a Plant is located on a Tributary of The Jhelum on which Pakistan has any Agricultural use or hydro-electric use, the water released below the Plant may be delivered, if necessary, into another Tributary but only to the extent that the then existing Agricultural Use or hydro-electric use by Pakistan on the former Tributary would not be adversely affected.

382. For India to take advantage of the possibility of inter-tributary transfer provided for in Paragraph 15(iii), the KHEP must meet the following three conditions: (1) it must be a Run-of-River Plant; (2) it must be located on a tributary of the Jhelum; and (3) the inter-tributary transfer must be within the terms laid down in Paragraph 15(iii). The Court will consider these three requirements in turn. [The Court's discussion of the first two requirements and part of the third are omitted.]

3.   The interpretation of the "then existing Agricultural Use or hydro-electric use by Pakistan" in Paragraph 15(iii) . . .

401. In seeking the proper meaning of Paragraph 15, the Court is guided by the fundamental rules of treaty interpretation as set out in Article 31(1) of the [Vienna Convention on the Law of Treaties]: "[a] treaty shall be interpreted in good faith and in accordance with the ordinary meaning to be given to the terms of the treaty in their context and in the light of its object and purpose." . . .

403. Read on its own, Paragraph 15 seems to be operational in character. . . .

404. In the same vein, sub-paragraph (iii) is phrased as an operational provision: its function is to qualify the general operational constraints found in the chapeau of Paragraph 15 where a Plant "is located on a Tributary of The Jhelum on which Pakistan has any Agricultural Use or hydroelectric use." The present tense structure ("*is* located"; "*has*" any agricultural or hydro-electric use) suggests that the

determination whether Pakistan has any agricultural or hydro-electric uses should take place throughout the operational life of a Run-of-River Plant, whenever India diverts water through an inter-tributary transfer.

405. Sub-paragraph (iii) then continues with the words "the water released below the Plant may be delivered, if necessary, into another Tributary but only to the extent that the then existing Agricultural Use or hydro-electric use by Pakistan on the former Tributary would not be adversely affected." Here again, the choice of the words *"then existing* Agricultural Use or hydro-electric use" suggests that the sub-paragraph is to be given an operational meaning, as any delivery of water by the KHEP for purposes of power generation can occur "only to the extent" that Pakistan's "then existing" agricultural or hydro-electric uses "would not be adversely affected." The formulation of Paragraph 15(iii) thus lends credence to what has been termed in these proceedings an "ambulatory" interpretation of Paragraph 15. [This interpretation was urged by Pakistan.] . . .

409. In the Court's view, the various paragraphs contained in Part 3 of Annexure D must be interpreted in a mutually reinforcing manner to avoid forbidding with one provision what is permitted by others. It would make little sense, and cannot have been the Parties' intention, to read the Treaty as permitting new Run-of-River Plants to be designed and built in a certain manner, but then prohibiting the operation of such a Plant in the very manner for which it was designed. Such an interpretation of the various paragraphs of Part 3 in isolation from one another would render ineffective those provisions that specifically permit the development of hydro-electric power in accordance with the design constraints of Annexure D. . . .

4. Challenges of the application of Paragraph 15(iii) to the KHEP . . .

(d) The Treaty's balance between the rights of both Parties

433. The Court considers that neither of the two approaches to interpretation discussed above—the ambulatory and critical period approaches—is fully satisfactory. Rather, the proper interpretation of Paragraph 15(iii) of Annexure D combines certain elements of both approaches. The Court is guided by the need to reflect the equipoise which the Treaty sets out between Pakistan's right to the use of the waters of the Western Rivers (including the Jhelum and its tributary, the Kishenganga/Neelum) and India's right to use the waters of those rivers for hydro-electric generation once a Plant complies with the provisions of Annexure D.

434. Pakistan's relevant uses in this context are, in the Court's view, essentially its hydro-electric uses. As for agricultural uses, the Court notes the observation of India—not contradicted by Pakistan—that there

are no significant existing agricultural uses of the Kishenganga/Neelum's main river. It appears to the Court that agricultural uses in the Neelum Valley are largely met by the tributary streams that feed the river.

435. Accordingly, the Court considers that its interpretative task consists of two principal elements. The Court must first establish the critical period at which the KHEP crystallized. Consistent with Part 3 of Annexure D (particularly the notice provisions of Paragraph 9), and using the same critical period criteria, the Court must then determine whether the NJHEP was an "existing use" that India needed to take into account at the time the KHEP crystallized. As shown below, the Court's determination of the critical period leads to the conclusion that the KHEP preceded the NJHEP, such that India's right to divert the waters of the Kishenganga/Neelum for power generation by the KHEP is protected under the Treaty.

436. Second, India's right to divert the waters of the Kishenganga/Neelum cannot be absolute. The premise underlying Paragraph 15(iii)—that Pakistan's existing uses are to be taken into account in the operation of India's Plants—remains a guiding principle (albeit not to the preclusive extent of the ambulatory approach). Paragraph 15(iii) protects Pakistan's right to a portion of the waters of the Kishenganga/Neelum throughout the year for its existing agricultural and hydro-electric uses.

5. The import of the Court's interpretation for the construction and operation of the KHEP

(a) India's vested right to build and operate the KHEP

437. The Court faces a difficult task: it must determine which Party has demonstrated not only that it planned its respective hydro-electric project "first," but also that it was the first to take concrete steps toward the realization of those plans. The Court has meticulously reviewed the evidence submitted by both Parties, including internal correspondence, letters between the Parties, the records of the meetings of the Commission and environmental impact assessments. What emerges for both projects is a succession of stops and starts, of plans communicated and plans revised, of permits given but not implemented, of financing purportedly obtained and withheld, of tenders on particular project plans that are not consistent with the final design, and other vagaries. Nonetheless, a decision must be made, and having weighed the totality of the record, the Court concludes that India has a stronger claim to having coupled intent with action at the KHEP earlier than Pakistan achieved the same at the NJHEP, resulting in the former's priority in right over the latter with respect to the use of the waters of the Kishenganga/Neelum for hydro-electric power generation. . . .

442. Thus, within the critical period of 2004–2006, India demonstrated a serious intent to move ahead with the project and took steps to make the KHEP a reality (through a combination of design, tender, financing, public consultations, environmental assessments and, crucially, national and local government approvals) of which Pakistan was aware. . . . This suffices to convince the Court that the KHEP had progressed to a stage of firm intention to proceed before that same point was reached with respect to the NJHEP. While it is clear that there were many "bumps in the road" in the progression of the KHEP—the ineffectiveness of the Commission process in arriving at an orderly resolution of questions in this case being particularly striking to this Court—it is clear that, by 2004–2006, the plans for the KHEP were being finalized. The same cannot be said for the NJHEP. . . .

(b) The preservation of downstream flows

445. India's right under the Treaty to divert the waters of the Kishenganga/Neelum to operate the KHEP is subject to the constraints specified by the Treaty, including Paragraph 15(iii) of Annexure D as discussed above and, in addition, by the relevant principles of customary international law to be applied by the Court pursuant to Paragraph 29 of Annexure G when interpreting the Treaty. As discussed in the following paragraphs, both of these limitations require India to operate the KHEP in a manner that ensures a minimum flow of water in the riverbed of the Kishenganga/Neelum downstream of the Plant.

446. Accepting that the KHEP crystallized prior to the NJHEP under the critical period analysis set out above, Pakistan nonetheless retains the right to receive a minimum flow of water from India in the Kishenganga/Neelum riverbed. That right stems in part from Paragraph 15(iii) of Annexure D, which gives rise to India's right to construct and operate hydro-electric projects involving inter-tributary transfers but obliges India to operate those projects in such a way as to avoid adversely affecting Pakistan's "then existing" agricultural and hydro-electric uses. The requirement to avoid adverse effects on Pakistan's agricultural and hydro-electric uses of the waters of the Kishenganga/Neelum cannot, however, deprive India of its right to operate the KHEP—a right that vested during the critical period of 2004–2006. Both Parties' entitlements under the Treaty must be made effective so far as possible: India's right to divert water for the operation of the KHEP is tempered by Pakistan's right to hydro-electric and agricultural uses of the waters of the Western Rivers, just as Pakistan's right to these uses is tempered by India's right to divert the waters for the KHEP's operation. Any interpretation that disregards either of these rights would read the principles of Paragraph 15(iii) out of the Treaty, to one or the other Party's injury.

447. India's duty to ensure that a minimum flow reaches Pakistan also stems from the Treaty's interpretation in light of customary international law. . . .

448. Well before the Treaty was negotiated, a foundational principle of customary international environmental law had already been enunciated in the *Trail Smelter* arbitration. There, the Tribunal held that

> no State has the right to use or permit the use of its territory in such a manner as to cause injury by fumes in or to the territory of another or the properties or persons therein, when the case is of serious consequence and the injury is established by clear and convincing evidence.

A broader restatement of the duty to avoid transboundary harm is embodied in Principle 21 of the 1972 Stockholm Declaration, pursuant to which States, when exploiting natural resources, must "ensure that activities within their jurisdiction or control do not cause damage to the environment of other States or of areas beyond the limits of national jurisdiction."

449. There is no doubt that States are required under contemporary customary international law to take environmental protection into consideration when planning and developing projects that may cause injury to a bordering State. Since the time of *Trail Smelter*, a series of international conventions, declarations and judicial and arbitral decisions have addressed the need to manage natural resources in a sustainable manner. In particular, the International Court of Justice expounded upon the principle of "sustainable development" in *Gabčíkovo-Nagymaros*, referring to the "need to reconcile economic development with protection of the environment."

450. Applied to large-scale construction projects, the principle of sustainable development translates, as the International Court of Justice recently put it in *Pulp Mills*, into "a requirement under general international law to undertake an environmental impact assessment where there is a risk that the proposed industrial activity may have a significant adverse impact in a transboundary context, in particular, on a shared resource." The International Court of Justice affirmed that "due diligence, and the duty of vigilance and prevention which it implies, would not be considered to have been exercised, if a party planning works liable to affect the regime of the river or the quality of its waters did not undertake an environmental impact assessment on the potential effects of such works." Finally, the International Court of Justice emphasized that such duties of due diligence, vigilance and prevention continue "once operations have started and, where necessary, throughout the life of the project."

451. Similarly, this Court recalls the acknowledgement by the Tribunal in the *Iron Rhine* arbitration of the "principle of general international law" that States have "a duty to prevent, or at least mitigate" significant harm to the environment when pursuing large-scale construction activities.[16] As the *Iron Rhine* Tribunal determined, this principle "applies not only in autonomous activities but also in activities undertaken in implementation of specific treaties," such as, it may be said, the present Treaty.

452. It is established that principles of international environmental law must be taken into account even when (unlike the present case) interpreting treaties concluded before the development of that body of law. The *Iron Rhine* Tribunal applied concepts of customary international environmental law to treaties dating back to the mid-nineteenth century, when principles of environmental protection were rarely if ever considered in international agreements and did not form any part of customary international law. Similarly, the International Court of Justice in *Gabčíkovo-Nagymaros* ruled that, whenever necessary for the application of a treaty, "new norms have to be taken into consideration, and . . . new standards given proper weight." It is therefore incumbent upon this Court to interpret and apply this 1960 Treaty in light of the customary international principles for the protection of the environment in force today.

453. In this context, the Court takes note of India's commitment to ensure a minimum environmental flow downstream of the KHEP at all times. . . .

(c) The insufficiency of the data on record to determine a precise minimum downstream flow; the Court's request for further data

455. There is . . . no disagreement between the Parties that the maintenance of a minimum flow downstream of the KHEP is required in response to considerations of environmental protection. The Parties differ, however, as to the quantity of water that would constitute an appropriate minimum; thus, the precise amount of flow to be preserved remains to be determined by the Court. The evidence presented by the Parties does not provide an adequate basis for such a determination, lacking sufficient data with respect to the relationship between flows and (1) power generation, (2) agricultural uses, and (3) environmental factors downstream of the KHEP below the Line of Control. Accordingly, the Court finds itself unable . . . to make an informed judgment as to whether a minimum flow of 3.94 m3/s (said to correspond to the lowest recorded flow over a 30-year period), which India committed to maintain in its operation of the KHEP, is sufficient to accommodate Pakistan's right

---

[16] *Arbitration Regarding the Iron Rhine* ("Ijzeren Rijn") *Railway between the Kingdom of Belgium and the Kingdom of the Netherlands*, Award, 24 May 2005, *PCA Award Series* (2007), para. 59. [Renumbered footnote.]

under the Treaty and customary international law to the avoidance or mitigation of environmental harm.

456. The Court therefore defers its determination of the appropriate minimum flow downstream of the KHEP to a further, Final Award, to be issued after it has had the benefit of considering further written submissions on the matter from the Parties.

[In its Final Award, the Court of Arbitration determined that India is required to release a minimum flow of 9 cumecs into the Kishenganga/Neelum River below the Kishenganga dam. The Court explained in paragraph 109 of the Final Award:

> In balancing India's right to operate the KHEP effectively with the needs of the downstream environment, the Court has decided that, on the basis of the evidence currently available, India should have access to at least half of the average flow at the KHEP site during the driest months. In the Court's view, it would not be in conformity with the Treaty to fix a minimum release above half the minimum monthly average flow for the purpose of avoiding adverse effects on the NJHEP.

If the daily average flow of the river upstream of the dam is less than 9 cumecs, India is to release 100 percent of the flow. The Court also included the innovative possibility for either party to seek reconsideration of the minimum flow requirement beginning seven years after the initial diversion of water from the Kishenganga River. Final Award, part V, paragraphs A and B, p. 43.]

NOTES AND QUESTIONS

1. *Abracadabra!* Did the Court of Arbitration conjure something from nothing when it required protection of the environment downstream of the Kishenganga dam? Did it impermissibly shoehorn environmental principles into the 1960 Treaty, using customary international law as the shoehorn? The Court stated in paragraph 110 of its Final Award:

> As India has recalled to the Court, recourse to customary international law is conditioned by Paragraph 29 of Annexure G to the Indus Waters Treaty, which provides as follows:

> > Except as the Parties may otherwise agree, the law to be applied by the Court shall be this Treaty and, whenever necessary for its interpretation or application, but only to the extent necessary for that purpose, the following in the order in which they are listed:

> > (a) International conventions establishing rules which are expressly recognized by the Parties.

> > (b) Customary international law.

The Court recalled that it had relied in part on the finding of the *Iron Rhine* tribunal that "principles of international environmental law must be taken into account even when interpreting treaties concluded before the development of that body of law" (Final Award, para. 111), but then observed: "Unlike the treaty at issue in *Iron Rhine*, this Treaty expressly limits the extent to which the Court may have recourse to, and apply, sources of law beyond the Treaty itself." Did the Court respect that limit? Did it go far enough in giving effect to the evolving customary international law of the environment? Why did the Court not take into account the effect of increased flow on Wular Lake, which is on the Ramsar Convention's List of Wetlands of International Importance, particularly since both India and Pakistan are Parties to the Ramsar Convention? Compare Certain Activities Carried Out by Nicaragua in the Border Area (Costa Rica v. Nicar.), Provisional Measures, 2011 I.C.J. 6, para. 79 (Mar. 8), where the ICJ expressly took into account the convention in both its reasoning and its order (*id.* at paras. 79, 80, 86).

2. *You don't like the final judgment? Come back in 7 years.* What do you think of the Court's allowing either party to seek reconsideration of the minimum flow requirement after seven years of operation of the KHEP? Does this do violence to the principle of the finality of judgments and awards? The Court said that it "considers it important not to permit the doctrine of *res judicata* to extend the life of this Award into circumstances in which its reasoning no longer accords with reality along the Kishenganga/Neelum." Final Award, para. 118. Could this not be said about virtually any judgment or award concerning shared natural resources? If so, which way does that cut? Open all of them to reconsideration; or open none of them? In this case, which State do you think is most likely to take advantage of this possibility, if either?

Further reading: For general sources on the law of international watercourses, see Edith Brown Weiss, International Law for a Water-Scarce World (2013); and Stephen C. McCaffrey, The Law of International Watercourses (2nd ed., 2007).

D. TRANSBOUNDARY GROUNDWATER

Developments in the mapping of aquifers—water-bearing geologic formations—have revealed a number of important groundwater basins that straddle borders throughout the world. For example, there are significant transboundary aquifers in arid areas along the United States-Mexico border and a number in North Africa and the Middle East. It is not uncommon for withdrawals to have been made from these water sources historically without realizing that they are shared with the country across the border.

Transboundary aquifer depletion can impact food production and drinking water availability. Yoshihide Wada and Lena Heinrich, Assessment of transboundary aquifers of the world—vulnerability arising from human water use, 2013 Environ. Res. Lett. 8 024003. But depletion can also stress wetlands. In addition, aquifers are vulnerable to saline intrusion from sea level rise but may be able to be managed to offset some of the adverse consequences climate change. See Magdalena A. K. Muir, Managing Transboundary Aquifers for Climate Change: Challenges and Opportunities, UNESCO-IAH-UNEP Conference, Paris, 6–8 December 2010, *available at* http://www.eucc.net/en/climate_change/January2011-ISARM2010-MAKMuir-RevisedVersion.pdf.

The UN Watercourses Convention covers both surface water and related groundwater, by virtue of the way in which it defines the term "watercourse," as has been seen. This is the most common form of groundwater globally. But what about the more rare form, that which does not receive significant recharge from the surface and thus is not related to surface water bodies? This type of aquifer is often found thousands of feet below the Earth's surface, as is the case in North Africa and the Middle East. It is sometimes referred to as "fossil water" because of its prehistoric origins.

In adopting its draft articles on International Watercourses in 1994, the ILC also adopted a resolution on what it called "confined transboundary groundwater." 1994 ILC Report at 89. This expression was meant to refer to groundwater that is not related to surface water and would thus not be covered by the articles on International Watercourses. In the resolution the ILC recommended that in view of the importance of this form of groundwater, (a) there is a need for the elaboration of rules concerning it, and (b) in the meantime states should be guided by the principles contained in the Watercourses articles in regulating transboundary groundwater.

In 2008 the ILC adopted a set of nineteen draft articles on the Law of Transboundary Aquifers. 2008 ILC Report at 19. These articles go beyond what was originally envisioned and cover all forms of transboundary groundwater, largely tracking the Watercourses Convention with appropriate adjustments. The ILC benefitted during the draft's preparation from advice from UN specialized agencies such as UNESCO. The articles thus represent a potential contribution to the law and practice in the field of transboundary groundwater.

However, the ILC's Transboundary Aquifers articles depart from the Watercourses Convention in an important respect. The first provision in the draft's section on "General Principles," Article 3, is entitled "Sovereignty of Aquifer States." The draft article on definition of terms and four of the provisions on general principles are reproduced below.

THE LAW OF TRANSBOUNDARY AQUIFERS

UNGA Res. 63–124, 11 Dec. 2008, UN Doc. A/RES/63/124.

. . .

Part One
Introduction

. . .

Article 2
Use of terms

For the purposes of the present articles:

(*a*) "aquifer" means a permeable water bearing geological formation underlain by a less permeable layer and the water contained in the saturated zone of the formation;

(*b*) "aquifer system" means a series of two or more aquifers that are hydraulically connected;

(*c*) "transboundary aquifer" or "transboundary aquifer system" means, respectively, an aquifer or aquifer system, parts of which are situated in different States;

(*d*) "aquifer State" means a State in whose territory any part of a transboundary aquifer or aquifer system is situated;

(*e*) "utilization of transboundary aquifers or aquifer systems" includes extraction of water, heat and minerals, and storage and disposal of any substance;

(*f*) "recharging aquifer" means an aquifer that receives a non-negligible amount of contemporary water recharge;

(*g*) "recharge zone" means the zone which contributes water to an aquifer, consisting of the catchment area of rainfall water and the area where such water flows to an aquifer by run-off on the ground and infiltration through soil;

(*h*) "discharge zone" means the zone where water originating from an aquifer flows to its outlets, such as a watercourse, a lake, an oasis, a wetland or an ocean.

Part Two
General principles

Article 3
Sovereignty of aquifer States

Each aquifer State has sovereignty over the portion of a transboundary aquifer or aquifer system located within its territory. It shall exercise its sovereignty in accordance with international law and the present articles.

Article 4
Equitable and reasonable utilization

Aquifer States shall utilize transboundary aquifers or aquifer systems according to the principle of equitable and reasonable utilization, as follows:

(*a*) They shall utilize transboundary aquifers or aquifer systems in a manner that is consistent with the equitable and reasonable accrual of benefits therefrom to the aquifer States concerned;

(*b*) They shall aim at maximizing the long-term benefits derived from the use of water contained therein;

(*c*) They shall establish individually or jointly a comprehensive utilization plan, taking into account present and future needs of, and alternative water sources for, the aquifer States; and

(*d*) They shall not utilize a recharging transboundary aquifer or aquifer system at a level that would prevent continuance of its effective functioning.

Article 5
Factors relevant to equitable and reasonable utilization

1.   Utilization of a transboundary aquifer or aquifer system in an equitable and reasonable manner within the meaning of article 4 requires taking into account all relevant factors, including:

(*a*) The population dependent on the aquifer or aquifer system in each aquifer State;

(*b*) The social, economic and other needs, present and future, of the aquifer States concerned;

(*c*) The natural characteristics of the aquifer or aquifer system;

(*d*) The contribution to the formation and recharge of the aquifer or aquifer system;

(*e*) The existing and potential utilization of the aquifer or aquifer system;

(*f*) The actual and potential effects of the utilization of the aquifer or aquifer system in one aquifer State on other aquifer States concerned;

(*g*) The availability of alternatives to a particular existing and planned utilization of the aquifer or aquifer system;

(*h*) The development, protection and conservation of the aquifer or aquifer system and the costs of measures to be taken to that effect;

(*i*) The role of the aquifer or aquifer system in the related ecosystem.

2.   The weight to be given to each factor is to be determined by its importance with regard to a specific transboundary aquifer or aquifer system in comparison with that of other relevant factors. In determining what is equitable and reasonable utilization, all relevant factors are to be considered together and a conclusion reached on the basis of all the factors. However, in weighing different kinds of utilization of a transboundary aquifer or aquifer system, special regard shall be given to vital human needs.

Article 6
Obligation not to cause significant harm

1.   Aquifer States shall, in utilizing transboundary aquifers or aquifer systems in their territories, take all appropriate measures to prevent the causing of significant harm to other aquifer States or other States in whose territory a discharge zone is located.

2.   Aquifer States shall, in undertaking activities other than utilization of a transboundary aquifer or aquifer system that have, or are likely to have, an impact upon that transboundary aquifer or aquifer system, take all appropriate measures to prevent the causing of significant harm through that aquifer or aquifer system to other aquifer States or other States in whose territory a discharge zone is located.

3.   Where significant harm nevertheless is caused to another aquifer State or a State in whose territory a discharge zone is located, the aquifer State whose activities cause such harm shall take, in consultation with the affected State, all appropriate response measures to eliminate or mitigate such harm, having due regard for the provisions of articles 4 and 5.

———————

The implications of draft Article 3 are not clear. Article 4, on "Equitable and reasonable utilization" and the other principles in the Transboundary Aquifers draft largely adapt to groundwater the provisions of the UN Watercourses Convention.

NOTES AND QUESTIONS

1.   *King of the shared aquifer?* What does it mean for a State to have "sovereignty" over "its" portion of a shared aquifer? Does this refer only to the "rock," the geologic formation, or to the water it contains, as well? The ILC's draft defines "aquifer" to include both.

2. *Now you have it, now you don't?* Does the second sentence of Article 3 take away what the first sentence seems to give? If so, what's the point of saying that a State "has sovereignty" over the portion of a transboundary aquifer located in its territory? Is there any danger in saying this? With apologies to "There Will Be Blood," does it mean, in effect, that the biggest straw wins?

3. *Shared Sovereignty?* On 30 April 2015, Jordan and Saudi Arabia concluded the Agreement between the Government of the Hashemite Kingdom of Jordan and the Government of the Kingdom of Saudi Arabia for the Management and Utilization of the Ground Waters in the Al-Sag/Al-Disi Layer, available in unofficial English translation and the original Arabic on the International Water Law Project website, http://internationalwaterlaw. org/documents/regionaldocs/Disi_Aquifer_Agreement-English2015.pdf. Article 3 of the agreement provides in part as follows:

> 1. A Joint Saudi/Jordanian Technical Committee shall be established, and shall be composed of five members from each Party to the this Agreement, and headed from the Saudi side by the Undersecretary of the Ministry of Water and Electricity, and from the Jordanian a side by the Secretary-General of the Ministry of Water and Irrigation.

> . . .

> 4. The Joint Technical Committee shall be responsible for the following:

>> a. The supervision of the implementation of the terms of this Agreement.

>> b. The supervision and observation of the groundwaters, from the point of view of the quantity of water extracted, its quality and level. . . .

Does this provision reflect an attitude by the contracting parties that each has sovereignty over the portion of the Disi Aquifer—a very important water source in the region—located within its territory?

CASE STUDY: THE GUARANI AQUIFER AGREEMENT[17]

The Acuerdo sobre el Acuífero Guaraní (Guarani Aquifer Agreement) focuses on an aquifer system, rather than on a basin. . . . The agreement flowed from a World Bank-sponsored project (for which Organization of American States was the implementing agency) called the Project for Environmental Protection and Sustainable Development of the Guarani

---

[17] Guarani Aquifer Agreement, unofficial English translation available at http://www. internationalwaterlaw.org/documents/regionaldocs/Guarani_Aquifer_Agreement-English.pdf. This material is from UNEP, Freshwater law and Governance: Global and Regional Perspectives for Sustainability, Technical background document for theme 3: "Environmental Laws and Regulations" and theme 4: "Institutional Challenge" (2014).

Aquifer System (PGAS). The PGAS is referred to in the final preambular paragraph of the agreement.

The original purpose was to fully understand the Guarani hydrological system and have clarity on its location as it previously was described as different hydrological bodies. However the study evolved into a project with the main objective to "implement a shared institutional, legal, and technical framework to preserve and manage the Guarani Aquifer System (GAS) for current and future generations."[18] The purpose of the management mechanism is to prevent pollution, and provide socio-economic and environmental benefits at a local and transboundary scale.

GAS is one of the world's largest groundwater reservoirs, with storage capacity of around 37,000 cubic kilometres and a natural recharge of 166 cubic kilometres per year. It lies beneath parts of Argentina, Brazil, Paraguay, and Uruguay, covering 1,087,879 square kilometres.[19] The Guarani aquifer extends below parts of the Plata River and Amazon River basins. The aquifer primarily supplies drinking water to populations living within its area (estimated at 70 million) but is also used for industrial and agricultural irrigation purposes.[20]

Argentina, Brazil, Paraguay, and Uruguay signed the Guarani Aquifer Agreement in August 2010. However, as of 31 July 2014 the agreement has only been ratified by Argentina and Uruguay and thus is not yet in force. The agreement reflects the principles outlined in United Nations General Assembly Resolution 63/124 (on the Law of Transboundary Aquifers), [21] including sovereignty, the equitable and reasonable use of water resources, the obligation not to cause harm, cooperation, and the exchange of data and information. [22] The administrative mechanism for the Guarani Aquifer Agreement is to be the Intergovernmental Coordinating Committee of La Plata Basin Countries (CIC) established through La Plata Basin Treaty, which concerns the basin that exists over most of the Guarani aquifer.

---

[18] Global Environmental Facility, From Community to Cabinet: Two decades of GEF Action to Secure Transboundary River Basins and Aquifers 35 (2012) [hereinafter From Community to Cabinet].

[19] Organization of American States, Guarani Aquifer: Strategic Action Program 62 (2009), http://www.oas.org/en/sedi/dsd/IWRM/Past_Projects/Documents/Guarani_SAP.pdf [hereinafter Guarani SAP].

[20] Organization of American States Office for Sustainable Development & Environment, Guarani Aquifer System: Environmental Protection and Sustainable Development of the Guarani Aquifer System 1 (2005), http://www.oas.org/dsd/Events/english/Documents/OSDE_7Guarani.pdf.

[21] The Law of Transboundary Aquifers, G.A. Res. 63/124 A, U.N. Doc. A/RES/63/124 (Jan. 15, 2009), http://www.un.org/en/ga/search/view_doc.asp?symbol=A/RES/63/124&Lang=E [hereinafter Law of Transboundary Aquifers].

[22] Guarani Aquifer Agreement, *supra*, at arts. 1, 3, 4, 8, 12, 14.

NOTES AND COMMENTS

1. As noted above, the Guarani Agreement is not yet in force, and the regional follow-up steps recommended by the Strategic Action Program of the PGAS have not been carried out. At the national level, however, countries have implemented some of the recommended steps pertaining to those countries. Moreover, the agreement and the process of formulating it are interesting in several respects.

The data gathered fills 26 volumes and is available to the countries and in libraries, universities and hydrological institutions. The process of determining the aquifer's location and size not only provided the information necessary to begin to manage and protect the aquifer, but it also provided stakeholders and policy-makers a better understanding of how the aquifer countries would need to work together to protect the aquifer. In addition, water governance-related reforms identified during the process of designing the agreement, which involved substantial outreach to indigenous peoples and others and public input, have occurred in each country. Examples include: (a) the six Guarani aquifer provinces of Argentina are now represented on the Federal Water Resources Council; (b) Brazil has integrated groundwater considerations into its National Water Resources Plan and allocated $8.26 million to support the implementation of its Surface and Groundwater Integrated Management Program; (c) Paraguay's 2007 Water Resources Law includes groundwater; and (d) Uruguay has established a national Guarani Management Unit. [23]

2. The Guarani Agreement includes dispute resolution clauses that ultimately result in arbitration, the details of which are to be set forth in an additional protocol to be negotiated in the future. In the meantime, the PGAS led to the resolution of a burgeoning dispute between Argentina and Uruguay:

> One of the pilot programs conducted under PGAS concerned Salto-Concordia, a popular thermal tourist location on the border between Argentina and Uruguay and a source of income for both countries. Previous to the pilot, unregulated and wasteful extractions of water caused controversies between the two countries. As a result of the pilot, the disputes ended. Mathematical modelling allowed the countries to determine the best locations to open new wells and settled some misunderstandings about one Party's depleting aquifer water from the other Party. Also both countries approved new legislation to better manage the aquifer and signed a cooperation agreement to promote sustainable development of the thermal corridor.[24]

---

[23] Freshwater Law and Governance: Global and Regional Perspectives For Sustainability—Technical background document for theme 3: "Environmental Laws and Regulations" and theme 4: "Institutional Challenge", at the First International Environment Forum for Basin Organizations Towards Sustainable Freshwater Governance 26-28 November 2014, Nairobi, Kenya, at 94 (UNEP 2014).

[24] *Id.* at 96.

E. WATER SECURITY: THREATS AND APPLICATIONS

Water security has three dimensions: economic, social, and environmental. The first focuses on increasing water productivity; the second on assuring equitable access; and the third on the sustainable management of aquatic ecosystems and the restoration of aquatic ecosystem services. Eelco van Beck and Wouter Lincklaen Arriens, Water Security: Putting the Concept into Practice 12–13 (Global Water Partnership, Background Paper No. 20 2014). In this section we will consider two threats to water security, global climate change and the deterioration of freshwater ecosystems, and how the concept of water security applies in the case of access by individuals to clean water.

1. GLOBAL CLIMATE CHANGE

Chapter 9 discusses the nature of global climate change in detail as well as the existing regimes to mitigate the projected consequences of a changed climate. However, the possible adverse impacts on freshwater systems cannot wait for the chimera of mitigation. Existing management regimes may have to adapt, not least because the current science indicates that climate change is accelerating the hydrologic cycle at nearly twice the rate predicted by models. The following excerpt from the Fifth Assessment Report of the Intergovernmental Panel on Climate Change (IPCC),[25] released in 2014, summarizes the IPCC's conclusions about the possible impacts of a warmer climate on freshwater resources and human uses thereof.

3.5. Projected Impacts, Vulnerabilities, and Risks

In general, projections of freshwater-related impacts, vulnerabilities, and risks caused by climate change are evaluated by comparison to historical conditions. Such projections are helpful for understanding human impact on nature and for supporting adaptation to climate change. However, for supporting decisions on climate mitigation, it is more helpful to compare the different hydrological changes that are projected under different future GHG [greenhouse gas] emissions scenarios, or different amounts of global mean temperature rise. One objective of such projections is to quantify what may happen under current water resources management

[25] Jiménez Cisneros, B.E., T. Oki, N.W. Arnell, G. Benito, J.G. Cogley, P. Döll, T. Jiang, and S.S. Mwakalila, 2014: Freshwater resources. In: Climate Change 2014: Impacts, Adaptation, and Vulnerability. Part A: Global and Sectoral Aspects. Contribution of Working Group II to the Fifth Assessment Report of the Intergovernmental Panel on Climate Change, 229–269, at 248–251 (Field, C.B., V.R. Barros, D.J. Dokken, K.J. Mach, M.D. Mastrandrea, T.E. Bilir, M. Chatterjee, K.L. Ebi, Y.O. Estrada, R.C. Genova, B. Girma, E.S. Kissel, A.N. Levy, S. MacCracken, P.R. Mastrandrea, & L.L. White, eds., 2014), *available at* http://ipcc-wg2.gov/AR5/images/uploads/WGIIAR5–Chap3_FINAL.pdf.

practice, and another is to indicate what actions may be needed to avoid undesirable outcomes. . . .

The studies compiled in [a table not included here] illustrate the benefits of reducing GHG emissions for the Earth's freshwater systems. Emissions scenarios are rather similar until the 2050s. Their impacts, and thus the benefits of mitigation, tend to become more clearly marked by the end of the 21st century. For example, the fraction of the world population exposed to a 20th century 100-year flood is projected to be, at the end of the 21st century, three times higher per year for [a very high emissions scenario] than for [a low emissions scenario]. . . . Each degree of global warming (up to 2.7°C above preindustrial levels . . .) is projected to decrease renewable water resources by at least 20% for an additional 7% of the world population. The number of people with significantly decreased access to renewable groundwater resources is projected to be roughly 50% higher under [an emissions scenario for the 2080s] than for [one for the 1980s]. The percentage of global population living in river basins with new or aggravated water scarcity is projected to increase with global warming, from 8% at 2°C to 13% at 5°C. . . .

3.5.1.   Availability of Water Resources

About 80% of the world's population already suffers serious threats to water demand, and pollution. . . . Climate change can alter the availability of water and therefore threaten water security as defined by UNESCO (2011).

Global-scale analyses so far have concentrated on measures of resource availability rather than . . . multi-dimensional indices. . . . All have simulated future river flows or groundwater recharge using global-scale hydrological models. Some have assessed future availability based on runoff per capita [citing eight studies], whilst others have projected future human withdrawals and characterized availability by the ratio of withdrawals to availability from runoff or recharge [citing three studies]. A groundwater vulnerability index was constructed that combined future reductions of renewable groundwater resources with water scarcity, dependence on groundwater, and the Human Development Index. . . . There are several key conclusions from this set of studies. First, the spatial distribution of the impacts of climate change on resource availability varies considerably between climate models, and strongly with the pattern of projected rainfall change. There is strong consistency in projections of reduced availability around the Mediterranean and parts of southern Africa, but much greater variation in projections for south and East Asia. Second, some water-stressed areas see increased runoff in the future . . . , and therefore less exposure to water resources stress. Third, over the next few decades and for increases in global mean temperature of less than around 2°C above preindustrial, changes in population will generally have a greater effect on changes in resource availability than will climate change. Climate change would, however, regionally exacerbate or offset the effects of population pressures. Fourth, estimates of future water availability are sensitive not only to climate and population projections and population assumptions, but also to the choice of hydrological impact model . . . and to the adopted measure of stress or scarcity.

As an indication of the potential magnitude of the impact of climate change, Schewe et al. (2013) estimated that about 8% of the global population would see a severe reduction in water resources (a reduction in runoff either greater than 20% or more than the standard deviation of current annual runoff) with a 1°C rise in global mean temperature (compared to the 1990s), rising to 14% at 2°C and 17% at 3°C; the spread across climate and hydrological models was, however, large.

Under climate change, reliable surface water supply is expected to decrease due to increased variability of river flow that is due in turn to increased precipitation variability and decreased snow and ice storage. Under these circumstances, it might be beneficial to take advantage of the storage capacity of groundwater and to increase groundwater withdrawals. . . . However, this option is sustainable only where, over the long term, withdrawals remain well below recharge, while care must also be taken to avoid excessive reduction of groundwater outflow to rivers. Therefore, groundwater cannot be expected to ease freshwater stress where climate change is projected to decrease groundwater recharge and thus renewable groundwater resources. . . . The percentage of projected global population (SSP2 population scenario) that will suffer from a decrease of renewable groundwater resources of more than 10% between the 1980s and the 2080s was computed to range from 24% (mean based on five GCMs [general circulation models] . . .). The land area affected by decreases of groundwater resources increases linearly with global mean temperature rise between 0°C and 3°C. For each degree of global mean temperature rise, an additional 4% of the global land area is projected to suffer a groundwater resources decrease of more than 30%, and an additional 1% to suffer a decrease of more than 70% (Portmann et al., 2013).

The IPCC Working Group 2 report summarizes freshwater-related risks of climate change as follows:

> **Climate change is projected to reduce renewable surface water and groundwater resources significantly in most dry subtropical regions (*robust evidence, high agreement*). . . .** This will intensify competition for water among agriculture, ecosystems, settlements, industry, and energy production, affecting regional water, energy, and food security (*limited evidence, medium to high agreement*). . . . In contrast, water resources are projected to increase at high latitudes. Proportional changes are typically one to three times greater for runoff than for precipitation. The effects on water resources and irrigation requirements of changes in vegetation due to increasing GHG concentrations and climate change remain uncertain. . . .

> **Climate change is *likely* to increase the frequency of meteorological droughts (less rainfall) and agricultural droughts (less soil moisture) in presently dry regions by the end of the 21st century under the RCP8.5 scenario (*medium confidence*). . . .** This is *likely* to increase the frequency of short hydrological droughts (less surface water and groundwater) in these regions (*medium evidence, medium agreement*). . . . Projected changes in the frequency of droughts longer than 12 months are more uncertain, because these depend on accumulated precipitation over long periods. There is no evidence that surface water and groundwater drought frequency has changed over the last few decades, although impacts of drought have increased mostly due to increased water demand. . . .

> **Climate change negatively impacts freshwater ecosystems by changing streamflow and water quality (*medium evidence, high agreement*).** Quantitative responses are known in only a few cases. Except in areas with intensive irrigation, the streamflow-mediated ecological impacts of climate change are expected to be stronger than historical impacts owing to anthropogenic alteration of flow regimes by water withdrawals and the construction of reservoirs. . . .

> **Climate change is projected to reduce raw water quality, posing risks to drinking water quality even with conventional treatment (*medium evidence, high agreement*).** The sources of the risks are increased temperature, increases in sediment, nutrient and pollutant loadings due to heavy rainfall, reduced dilution of pollutants during droughts, and disruption of treatment facilities during floods. . . .

In regions with snowfall, climate change has altered observed streamflow seasonality, and increasing alterations due to climate change are projected (*robust evidence, high agreement*). . . . Except in very cold regions, warming in the last decades has reduced the spring maximum snow depth and brought forward the spring maximum of snowmelt discharge; smaller snowmelt floods, increased winter flows, and reduced summer low flows have all been observed. River ice in Arctic rivers has been observed to break up earlier. . . .

Because nearly all glaciers are too large for equilibrium with the present climate, there is a committed water resources change during much of the 21st century, and changes beyond the committed change are expected due to continued warming; in glacierfed rivers, total meltwater yields from stored glacier ice will increase in many regions during the next decades but decrease thereafter (*robust evidence, high agreement*). Continued loss of glacier ice implies a shift of peak discharge from summer to spring, except in monsoonal catchments, and possibly a reduction of summer flows in the downstream parts of glacierized catchments. . . .

There is little or no observational evidence yet that soil erosion and sediment loads have been altered significantly due to changing climate (*limited evidence, medium agreement*). However, increases in heavy rainfall and temperature are projected to change soil erosion and sediment yield, although the extent of these changes is highly uncertain and depends on rainfall seasonality, land cover, and soil management practices. . . .[26]

NOTES AND QUESTIONS

As one might expect, most international customary and treaty law predates the concern over global climate change. If it can be demonstrated that global climate change has reduced the previously estimated flow of an international river, how should shortages be shared? Should each country bear its pro rata share or should the doctrine of equitable apportionment be used to decide which uses should be curtailed. Does the state which is most adversely impacted by global climate change now have a stronger case to dam available supplies? Article X of the Treaty Respecting Utilization of Waters of Colorado and Tijuana Rivers and of the Rio Grande, 59 Stat. 1219 (1944), provides that the United States does not have to deliver Mexico's full Colorado River entitlement in the case of extraordinary drought. Is reduced

---

[26] *Id.*, pp. 232–233.

flow due to global warming an extraordinary drought? *See* Joseph Dellapenna, Adapting the Law of Water Management to Global Climate Change and Other Hydropolitical Stresses, 35 J. Am. Water Resources Ass'n 1301 (1999); A. Dan Tarlock, How Well Can International Water Allocation Regimes Adapt to Global Climate Change, 15 J. Land Use & Envir. L. 423 (2000); and Greta Goldenman, Adapting to Climate Change: A Study of International Rivers and Their Legal Arrangements, 17 Ecology L.Q. 741 (1990).

2. PROTECTION OF AQUATIC ECOSYSTEMS

We have already seen that specialists, policymakers and governments are increasingly recognizing the need to protect and nurture aquatic ecosystems. Article 20 of the 1997 U.N. Watercourses Convention provides simply as follows:

Article 20

Protection and Preservation of Ecosystems

Watercourse States shall, individually and, where appropriate, jointly, protect and preserve the ecosystems of international watercourses.

There is nothing in the text of the article to indicate that it only applies where failure to protect aquatic ecosystems would adversely affect another riparian State. As we have seen, protection of aquatic ecosystems has played an important part in two of the most recent cases decided by international tribunals, the *Pulp Mills* case and the *Kishenganga* arbitration. In *Kishenganga*, the Court of Arbitration noted that there was "no disagreement between the Parties that the maintenance of a minimum flow downstream of the KHEP is required in response to considerations of environmental protection." (Para. 455.) It also referred to "Pakistan's right under the Treaty and customary international law to the avoidance or mitigation of environmental harm" from the project. (*Id.*) The tribunal proceeded to order India to release a minimum flow through the dam.

The following case study concerns a new development in treaty practice, specifically, that of the United States and Mexico under their 1944 water treaty, aimed in part at restoring the delta of the Colorado River.

CASE STUDY: THE RESTORATION OF MEXICO'S COLORADO RIVER DELTA[27]

Mexico's Colorado River Delta is one of the world's many stressed deltic aquatic ecosystems. The Colorado River originates in the United States Rocky Mountains, enters Mexico at the Arizona-California border, and drains into the Gulf of California. A 1922 Interstate Compact among seven federal United States states and the 1944 Mexico-United States Water Treaty (Treaty) allow users in both nations to divert the entire average flow upstream from its mouth, thus cutting off both the necessary seasonal sediment deposits and water flows to sustain the Delta. Until 2012, the two nations had no treaty obligation to supply any flows to the Delta; remnant marshes survived precariously on wet year surplus "pulses" and upstream agricultural return flows. For years, both Mexico and the United States took the position that the degradation of the Delta was an irremediable consequence of the Treaty. This position was consistent with both the Treaty and customary international water law which does not generally recognize a nation's right to the entire pre-dam flow of a river. Lake Lanoux Arbitration (France v. Spain), Chapter 4, page 194. But, after a two decade long campaign by NGOs to protect the Delta, in 2012 the two countries adopted Minute 319, in effect amending the Treaty to provide a modest experimental Delta flow maintenance regime.

Minute 319, Interim International Cooperative Measures in the Colorado River Basin through 2017 and Extension of Minute 318 Cooperative Measures to Address the Continued Effects of the April 2010 Earthquake in the Mexicali Valley, Baja California (November 20, 2012), sets three important precedents, broadly defined. First, it is *a de facto* implementation the ecosystem conservation mandates of the U.N. Watercourses Convention and other recent drafts by expert bodies. Second, Minute 319 is equally a recognition of the duty of riparian nations to cooperate in the long term management of shared rivers. See CHRISTINA LEB, COOPERATION IN THE LAW OF TRANSBOUNDARY WATER RESOURCES (2013); and P. Wouters and A.D. Tarlock, The Third Wave of Normativity in International Water Law, 23 Journal of Water Law 51 (2013). Third, although Minute 319 de facto amended a treaty through inter-governmental negotiations, it would not have happened were it not for the efforts of non-governmental organizations (NGOs). Mexican and United States environmental NGOs both prodded the two nations to address the Delta's problems and helped to provide the financing to acquire the necessary "wet water" for the flows on an over-allocated river system.

---

[27] Adapted from A. Dan Tarlock, *Mexico and the United Assume a Legal Duty to Provide Colorado River Delta Restoration Flows: An Important International Environmental and Water Law Precedent,* 23 RECIEL 76 (2014).

MINUTE 319

A. The Legal Basis

Minute 319 is a de facto amendment to the Mexico-United States Water Treaty. See C. Cadena, *A Minute of Clarity After Decades of Confusion: "Extraordinary Drought" in the Lower Rio Grande Basin*, 24 GEORGETOWN J. INT'L ENVTL. L. 605, 622–626 (2012). The Treaty is more flexible than other treaties because the parties can de facto amend it through "interpretive" Minutes negotiated through the International Boundary and Water Commission (IBWC). The IBWC traces its roots back to the 1848 Treaty of Guadalupe de Hildago by which Mexico ceded much of the present Southwestern United States including California to the United States.[28] The Commission's current authority derives from the 1944 Treaty. Article 2 of that agreement renamed the previous boundary commission the IBWC and, along with other provisions of the Treaty, gives it broad powers. Article 25 provides that IBWC decisions are to "be recorded in the form of minutes" which become effective unless either Mexico or the United States objects to them. Thus, matters recorded in Minutes are de facto amendments.

B. Why Was Minute 319 Possible?

Water sharing agreements are hard to negotiate because entrenched entitlement holders, as is the case on the Colorado River, tend to see them as zero sum games. Thus, at least one of three conditions must be present. First, the entitlement holders must perceive that a non-agreement would make them worse off. Second, the agreement must minimize the risk that entitlement holders will be seriously injured. Third, the agreement must provide a wide spectrum of entitlement holders benefits that they could not otherwise obtain. Minute 319 did not meet the first condition because there is little political risk that either the Compact or Treaty would be renegotiated to include Delta flows. But, Minute 319 met the second two conditions.

United States water users in both the Lower and Upper Basins benefit from the Minute and face no risk of curtailment. The upstream benefits partially derive from the benefits that Mexico gained in the Minute. Mexico obtained a major benefit because Minute 319 opens Lake Mead, between Arizona and Nevada, to Mexican storage for the first time. The United States had consistently resisted the idea of any Mexico rights

---

[28] See R.J. McCarthy, *Executive Authority, Adaptive Treaty Interpretation, and the International Boundary and Water Commission*, U.S.-Mexico', 14 Den. L. Rev. 197, at 208–216 (2011). The Treaty has an adaptive mechanism to allow the parties to adjust to changed conditions. The International Boundary Commission has the power to interpret the treaty. These interpretations are recorded as Minutes. However, interpretation does not accurately describe the effect of an interpretations. Minutes such as 319 are de facto amendments because they share two essential characteristics of an amendment. First, Minutes can deal with problems that were never contemplated when the treaty was drafted. Second, Minutes agreed upon by the two parties are accorded deference by both parties. For those reasons, much of scholarship about Commission refers to Minutes as amendments

in the Colorado north of the border. During the 1944 Treaty negotiations, Mexico initially proposed that it be awarded 8% of the Lower Basin states' diversions. However, this was rejected by the United States, under pressure from Arizona and California, because "it meant that Mexico's eyes could reach north of the border when the terms of the treaty were being administered." See C.J. Meyers and R.L. Noble, *The Colorado River: The Treaty with Mexico*, 19 STAN. L. REV. 367, at 384 (1967).

Minute 319 allows the creation of an Intentionally Created Mexican Allocation (ICMA). The Minute abandons the long held United States position that Mexico is entitled to its 1,500,000 acre feet (1,850,000mcm) whether it needs it or not. Mexico can now decide to leave water in Lake Mead rather than taking delivery at the border in wet years. Minute 319 III.4. It provides for releases from 40,000 (19,000mcm) to 200,000 acre feet (247,000 mcm) in wet years. Minute 319 III.2.b. Thus, Mexico is not forced to take her yearly allocation, whether she needs it not, or see the water used by the United States. The United States first changed its position in 2010 for humanitarian reasons. In that year, Mexican canals and water storage infrastructure were damaged by a 7.2 magnitude earthquake, and Mexico was allowed to store temporarily water in Lake Mead.

United States users benefit in several ways. Both basins benefit from the prospect of high levels in Lake Mead, especially as the predictions are that climate change will reduce the flow of the Colorado. Upper Basin states benefit because they may not have to release as much water into Lake Mead as required by the 2007 reservoir balancing Agreement. Record of Decision, Colorado River Interim Guidelines for Lower Basin Shortages and the Coordinated Operations for Lake Powell and Lake Mead, found at: http://www.usbr.gov/lc/region/programs/strategies/Record ofDecision.pdf. In addition, in the Linear Basin the water-short Metropolitan Water District of Southern California (which supplies the Los Angeles area) can make a one time purchase of more than 47,500 acre-feet of water from Mexico at a cost of $5 million. The Southern Nevada Water Authority (which serves Las Vegas) and Central Arizona Water Conservation District can also make purchases. Mexico, in turn, will use part of the revenue from those water sales and funding from other sources to repair the earthquake damage. Finally, Minute 319 shifts some of the risks of curtailing uses in a drought year to Mexico.

The 1944 Treaty has a vague provision for allocating water in periods of "extraordinary drought," Section X, but it provides no guidance about when and how shortages are to be apportioned. Minute 319 takes a step in this direction by specifically reducing Mexico's right by 50,000 acre feet when Lake Mead falls below 1,075 feet and by 125,000 when it falls below 1,025 feet.

C.   Delta Flows

The environmental core of Minute 319 is the creation of a pilot program to deliver some 158,088 acre feet (195,000 mcm) base flow to the Colorado River limitrophe and Delta. The water will come from two sources, a one time pulse flow of 105,392 and a base flow of 52,696 acre feet per year. The Minute provides that the pulse flow is to take place by 2016 at the latest and will come entirely from water saved by Mexico by building more efficient water infrastructure to replace the earthquake damaged facilities. The base flow is being assembled in Mexico through NGO water trust purchases of Mexican water rights. The water trust was established in 2010 and of 2013 about 40% of the amount had been acquired. Minute 319 is only an interim measure, but it is first step toward a permanent adaptive management regime for the Delta. The expectation is that by the end of 2016, Minute 319 will be replaced by "a comprehensive Minute that extends or replaces the substantive provisions of this Minute . . ." Minute 319 III. The Minute expressly calls for an evaluation of the success of the program in contributing to the Delta's sustainability and restoration. Minute 319 III.6.c

The first of three planned pulse flows was a success:

"As provided in Minute 319 of the U.S.-Mexico Water Treaty of 1944, a pulse flow of approximately 130 million cubic meters (105,392 acre-feet) was released to the riparian corridor of the Colorado River Delta from Morelos Dam at the U.S.-Mexico border. The water was delivered over an eight-week period that began on March 23, 2014 and ended on May 18, 2014. Peak flows were released early in this period to simulate a spring flood. Some pulse flow water was released to the riparian corridor via Mexicali Valley irrigation canals.

Base flow volumes totaling 65 mcm (52,696 acre-feet) are also being delivered to new and pre-existing restoration areas during the term of Minute 319 through December 31, 2017. One hundred and twentynine hectares (320 acres) of non-native vegetation in the Laguna Grande area were cleared and graded to promote regeneration of native vegetation. Portions of the site were hydro-seeded with native vegetation and 38 hectares (94 acres) of the site were planted with native trees. In the Miguel Aleman restoration site, 35 hectares (86 acres) were cleared and graded and of these, 10 hectares (25 acres) were planted with native trees.

The monitoring program established by Minute 319 assembled baseline information on the hydrology and biology of the riparian corridor and deployed binational, multi-agency teams of scientists during and after the pulse flow. Results of these efforts through July 24, 2014 are reported in this interim report.

Ground-based and remotely-sensed data were collected to evaluate the ecosystem response to the pulse flow.

Surface water from the pulse flow rapidly infiltrated into the sandy subsurface in the first 60 km (37 miles) downstream of Morelos Dam. Scour and deposition modified the channel bed topography, but bank erosion of the existing channel was minor. Smaller volumes inundated the river channel farther downstream, including areas that had been prepared for restoration of native vegetation. Pulse flow surface water reached the Gulf of California on May 15, 2014."

International Boundary Water Commission, United States and Mexico et al., Minute 319 Colorado Delta Flows Monitoring: Initial Progress Report, December 4, 2014 pp. 4–5.

D.   The Precedential Implications of Minute 319

International water allocation treaties routinely deal with the duty of upstream states to maintain minimum flows for the benefit of downstream states, usually for power generation and consumptive uses. However, most major river treaties ignore the impact of upstream development and diversions on the river's delta. While traditional customary international law did not recognize a specific duty to protect aquatic ecosystems, modern formulations the applicable customary norms recognize such a duty. The duty can be derived from the international environmental law of state responsibility for transboundary harm [discussed in Chapter 4, *supra*]. The duty not to cause harm was developed in the context of air and water pollution but the foundational principle, that states have a duty not to allow state agencies and private parties subject to the state's regulatory jurisdiction to use the territories under their control in a manner that causes significant harm to other states and their nationals, can encompass ecosystem risk as the *Kishenganga* case illustrates.

The 1997 United Nations Convention on the Law of the Non-Navigational Uses of International Watercourses extends the duty not to cause harm from a negative to positive one. Article 20 recognizes that the shared use of international water includes ecosystem protection. The Convention does not control the Delta because its provisions make it subordinate to pre-existing treaties and other agreements and because the U.S. and Mexico are not parties to it, in any event. Nonetheless, the Convention, as a codification of basic principles of international water law, can inform the evolution of new duties by recognizing that the core right to an equitable and reasonable share of a river includes environmental uses of a river. Equitable apportionment has been characterized as a theory of limited territorial sovereignty because it imposes minimum limitations on exclusive territorial sovereignty claims. But, consistent with the principles of international environmental law and sustainable development, the emerging vision of international water law posits that international watercourses are both commodities and heritage resources which support a variety of human consumptive and non-consumptive uses and ecosystem services and that both purposes must be equally respected in decisions about the use and management of these resources. See Jonathan King, Peter W. Gulp, and Carlos de LaParra, *Getting to the Right Side of the River: Lessons for International Cooperation on the Road to Minute 319*, 18 DENVER WATER L. REV. 36, (2014).

Minute 319 also illustrates the application of the emerging construct of water security to identify and remedy water scarcity risks. Water security builds off of two primary concepts. The first is the distinction between "green" and "blue" water. "Green" water is water consumed in plants, by humans and by evaporation; "blue" water is water left in rivers, lakes and aquifers. The second concept is water stress. Water stress has two meanings. The first applies to countries with poor hydrology. Scarcity is a risk in poor countries with permeable soils and agriculture-dependent economies; land conversion can reduce evaporation rates, potentially causing droughts. "Blue" water scarcity can result when these countries, especially arid ones, compensate by increasing irrigation, thus reducing stream flows and aquifer recharge. M. Falkenmark et al., Overcoming the Land-Water Disconnect in Water-Scare Regions: Time for IWRM to Go Contemporary, 30 Int. J. Water Resources Development 381 (2014), available at http://dx.doi.org/10.1080/07900627.2014.897157. The second meaning of water stress is the lack of institutional capacity, such as storage, strong allocation systems and effective management, to manage the risks of scarcity. The American southwest is stressed by the first but not by the second.

NOTE ON THE IRAQ MARSHES IN THE TIGRIS AND EUPHRATES DELTA

One of the most publicized examples of the plight of deltas is the Tigris and Euphrates Delta and its inhabitants, the Iraqi Marsh Arabs. Upstream dams in Turkey and Iraq reduce the downstream flow, but in the 1980s the government resumed work on reclamation projects began in the 1950s. However, the Third River Canal prevented water from the two rivers from reaching two-thirds of the marsh lands, not to open land to agricultural production but to oppress the Marsh Arabs for heeding the United States call to rebel after the 1991 Gulf War. See generally The Iraqi Marshlands: A Human and Environmental Study (Emma Nicholson & Peter Clark eds., 2002).

U.N. General Assembly Resolution 688, passed April 6, 1991, requires the Iraqi government to provide free access to United Nations and nongovernmental humanitarian agencies to all parts of the marshes so that "essential humanitarian assistance can be provided." In January 1995, the European Parliament (EP) also passed a resolution "characterizing the [M]arsh Arabs as a persecuted minority 'whose very survival is threatened by the Iraqi Government.' The EP resolution described the Government's treatment of the marsh inhabitants as 'genocide.'" In March 1995, the European Parliament adopted another resolution deploring the continuing attacks on Marsh Arabs. Furthermore, the U.N. Human Rights Commission in March 1995, passed a resolution calling for an end to military operations and efforts to drain the swamplands. However, the government of Iraq never included the lands in the Ramsar wetlands convention. United States actions after the invasion of Iraq in 2003 have begun to restore the flow. *See* Curtis J. Richardson et al., The Restoration Potential of the Mesopotamian Marshes of Iraq, Science, Vol. 307, Issue 5713, at 1307–1311, 25 February 2005. But the marshes remain stressed. The International Criminal Court has jurisdiction over the crime against humanity of genocide. Article 6 of the Rome Statute, U.N.Doc.A/Conf.183/9 (1998), defines genocide to include the deliberate "physical destruction in whole or in part" of a national, ethnic, racial or religious people." Review pp. 169–170. Could any former Iraqi officials charged with the destruction of the marshes and their people defend the action as the exercise of the right to sustainable development? The United Nations Compensation Commission, established after the 1991 Gulf War, awarded damages against Iraq for lost ecosystem services in Jordan, Kuwait, and Saudi Arabia. The Panel agreed that the novel claims were appropriate when "there is sufficient evidence that primary restoration will not fully compensate for any identified loses." Panel of Commissioners Concerning Fifth Installment of "F4" Claims, U.N. Doc. S/AC.26/2005/10 (2005) Paragraphs 81–82, available at http://www.uncc.ch. The damage included degraded refuges, damaged wildlife habitats, rangelands and shore preserves. The panel based the awards on the cost of compensatory projects. *See generally* Eric T. Jensen, The International Law of Environmental Warfare: Active and Passive Damage During Armed Conflict, 38 Vand. L.J. Transnat'l L. 145 (2005); Peter Sharp, Prospects for Environmental Liability in the International Criminal Court, 18 Va. Envt'l L. J. 217 (1999); and Linda A. Malone and Scott Pasternack, Defending the Environment: Civil Society Strategies to Enforce International Environmental Law 186–193 (2004).

3.   THE HUMAN RIGHT TO WATER

In many parts of the world, millions of people lack access to safe drinking water or to sanitation systems. According to a World Health Organization (WHO) report, in 2014 748 million people lacked access to an improved drinking water source and in 2012, 2.5 billion people did not have access to an improved sanitation facility. WHO, Progress on sanitation and drinking-water—2014 update. A part of the solution to this problem may be the increasing recognition since the early 2000s of a human right to water. While there is no express recognition of a fundamental right to water in any of the documents that compromise the

International Bill of Human Rights, such a right has been derived from the International Covenant on Economic, Social and Cultural Rights by the Committee responsible for overseeing the implementation of that Covenant. General Comment No. 15 (2002) on the Right to Water.

The Committee relied on Articles 11 and 12 of the International Covenant on Economic, Social, and Cultural Rights, General Assembly Resolution 2200, 22nd Sess., Supp. 49, U.N. Doc. A/6318 (167), reprinted 6 ILM 360 (1967). Article 11 recognizes "the right of everyone to an adequate standard of living for himself and his family, including adequate food, clothing and housing, and to the continuous improvement of living conditions." As the following excerpt explains, the United Nations Committee on Economic, Social and Cultural Rights adopted a non-binding comment which for the first time in a UN document recognized a human right to water.

THE HUMAN RIGHT TO WATER

Stephen C. McCaffrey
in FRESH WATER AND INTERNATIONAL ECONOMIC LAW 93, 102–103, 104, 107
(Brown Weiss, Boisson de Chazournes & Bernasconi-Osterwalder eds., 2005)

At its twenty-ninth session in 2002, the U.N. Committee on Economic, Social, and Cultural Rights (ESC Committee) adopted General Comment No. 15 (2002) on the Right to Water (Articles 11 and 12 of the International Covenant on Economic, Social and Cultural Rights).[50] ["The human right to water entitles everyone to sufficient, safe, acceptable, physically accessible and affordable water for personal and domestic uses." General Comment 15, para. 2.] This is the first recognition by a United Nations human rights body of an independent and generally applicable human right to water.[51] As such, it is deserving of attention and examination. First, some background regarding the ESC Committee will help to place General Comment 15 in context.

3.1 Background: The ESC Committee

Unlike the Committee on Civil and Political Rights, which is established in the CP Covenant, the ESC Committee is not provided for in the ESC Covenant.[52] This may be because the rights recognized in the latter instrument are for the most part to be achieve[d] progressively,[53] to the extent permitted by a State's available resources. The Committee was established by a 1985 resolution of the Economic and Social Council

---

[50] U.N. Doc. E/C.12/2002/11, 26 November 2002, adopted at the ESC Committee's 29th session, held in Geneva from 11–29 November 2002 (hereinafter General Comment 15).

[51] An earlier general comment by the ESC Committee, General Comment No. 6 (1995) on the economic, social, and cultural rights of older persons, recognized in that context that the right to water is a human right contained in Art. 11(1) of the ESC Covenant.

[52] [*See* the Committee's website, http://www.ohchr.org/en/hrbodies/cescr/pages/cescrindex. aspx visited 3 August 2015—Editors' revised footnote.]

[53] ESC Covenant, *supra* footnote 49, Art. 2(1).

(ECOSOC)[54] and began functioning in 1987.[55] It replaced a Working Group composed of government representatives which, due to its very representative character, had not enjoyed success in monitoring government implementation. The eighteen members of the Committee are elected by the ECOSOC, on nomination of States Parties to the Covenant, for four year terms and serve in their individual, expert capacities, not as government representatives.[56] Like the Working Group, the Committee's main function is to monitor the implementation of the ESC Covenant by the States that are Parties. It performs this function chiefly through receiving reports from the Parties,[57] posing questions to them on the reports, and issuing "concluding observations," stating the Committee's opinion concerning the status of the Parties' implementation of the Covenant.

The ECOSOC authorized the ESC Committee to adopt general comments on the ESC Covenant to assist the parties in fulfilling their obligations and to indicate its interpretation of particular provisions.[58] The Committee was not authorized to adopt general comments that would be binding on the States Parties to the ESC Covenant.[59] The ESC Committee's sister body, the Human Rights Committee under the CP Covenant, generated a storm of controversy when it purported to do just that in a general comment on the permissibility of reservations.[60] This

---

[54] ECOSOC Res. 1985/17.

[55] *See generally* Philip Alston and Bruno Simma, The First Session of the UN Committee on Economic, Social and Cultural Rights, 81 AJIL 747 (1987).

[56] [See the Committee's website, http://www.ohchr.org/en/hrbodies/cescr/pages/cescrindex. aspx, visited 3 August 2015], also indicating that the Committee meets twice a year in Geneva.— Editors' revised footnote.

[57] "Under articles 16 and 17 of the Covenant, States parties undertake to submit periodic reports to the Committee—within two years of the entry into force of the Covenant for a particular State party, and thereafter once every five years—outlining the legislative, judicial, policy and other measures which they have taken to ensure the enjoyment of the rights contained in the Covenant. States parties are also requested to provide detailed data on the degree to which the rights are implemented and areas where particular difficulties have been faced in this respect." *Id.*

[58] ECOSOC Res. 1987/5; Rule 65, CESCR, Rules of Procedure of the Committee, 1 Sept. 1993, U.N. Doc. E/C.12/1990/4/Rev.1. Rule 65 reads: "The Committee may prepare general comments based on the various articles and provisions of the Covenant with a view to assisting States parties in fulfilling their reporting obligations." *Id.* According to the Committee's website, "The Committee decided in 1988 to begin preparing 'general comments' on the rights and provisions contained in the Covenant with a view to assisting States parties in fulfilling their reporting obligations and to provide greater interpretative clarity as to the intent, meaning and content of the Covenant. . . . General comments are a crucial means of generating jurisprudence, providing a method by which members of the Committee may come to an agreement by consensus regarding the interpretation of norms embodied in the Covenant." Thus the Committee does not claim the authority to adopt interpretations that are binding on the States Parties.

[59] *See* ECOSOC Res. 1987/5, containing no such authorization. This is not surprising, since the Committee's counterpart for Civil and Political Rights was also not so authorized. *See* the following notes and accompanying text.

[60] General Comment No. 24 (52) of 2 Nov. 1994, U.N. Doc. CCPR/C/Rev.1/Add.6, 34 ILM 839 (1995), stating that the consequence of an unacceptable reservation will be that the "reservation will generally be severable, in the sense that Covenant will be operative for the

experience counsels caution in attributing sweeping effect to pronouncements such as the ESC Committee's new General Comment on the human right to water. The General Comment reflects the Committee's interpretation of Articles 11 and 12 of the ESC Covenant. Eminently sensible though this interpretation may be, it must be accepted by the States parties to the Covenant in order to be binding upon them. This is also true, a fortiori, of States that are not parties to the Covenant. The fact that States have not yet accepted explicitly a general human right to water suggests that the ESC Committee's General Comment may be somewhat ahead of State practice and therefore may be more in the nature of a statement de lege ferenda rather than lex lata. Even so, the ESC Committee will expect States parties to the ESC Covenant, in reporting on their implementation of the Covenant, to indicate what progress they have made in achieving the full realization of the human right to water. At the very least, this will help to raise awareness of the urgent need to ensure availability of, and ready access to, clean drinking water in sufficient quantity to sustain health.

NOTES AND QUESTIONS

1. *Who's on and who's off the HRW bandwagon?* In 2010, the U.N. General Assembly adopted Resolution A/64/292 on "the human right to water and sanitation." While a resolution of this kind would normally be adopted by consensus, the United States called for a vote. The resolution was adopted by a vote of 122 in favor, none against, with 41 abstentions. A number of developed countries, including many major donors in the water sector including Australia, Austria, Canada, Denmark, Greece, Iceland, Ireland, Japan, the Netherlands, New Zealand, Sweden, the United Kingdom and the United States, were among those that abstained. The United States explained that "there was no 'right to water and sanitation' in an international legal sense, as described by the resolution." UN Press Release on the 108th Meeting (AM) of the 64th General Assembly (28 July 2010), found at http://www.un.org/News/Press/docs/2010/ga10967.doc.htm. The

reserving party without benefit of the reservation." *Id.*, para. 18. France, the United Kingdom, and the United States were all critical of the Committee's assumption of the power to make such a binding determination, on the ground that it was not authorized to do so in the CP Covenant. *See* Observations, [1996] Report of the Human Rights Committee, vol. 1, GAOR, 51st session, Supp. No. 40, U.N. Doc. A/51/40, 104 Annex VI (France); Observations, [1995] Report of the Human Rights Committee, vol. 1, GAOR, 50th session, Supp. No. 40, U.N. Doc. A/50/40, 130, Annex VI B (U.K.); and Observations, [1995] Report of the Human Rights Committee, vol. 1, GAOR, 50th session, Supp. No. 40, U.N. Doc. A/50/40, 126, Annex VI A (U.S.). *See* Human Rights as General Norms and a State's Right to Opt Out 185–207 (J. Gardner ed., 1997). Some commentators have defended the ESC Committee's action. *See, e.g.*, Rosalyn Higgins, Human Rights as General Norms and a State's Right to Opt Out xv, xxvi–xxviii (Christine Chinkin et al. eds., 1997); and C.J. Redgwell, *Reservations to Treaties and Human Rights Committee General Comment No. 24* (52), 46 ICLQ 390 (1997). *But see, e.g.*, the reaction of the Special Rapporteur of the International Law Commission on the topic of Reservations to Treaties: Alain Pellet, Second Report on Reservations to Treaties, U.N. Doc. A/ CN.4/447/Add.1, 13 June 1996, para. 226–230, arguing that the Human Rights Committee's General Comment No. 24 "takes no account whatsoever of the consensuality that is the very essence of any treaty commitment." *Id.*, para. 228.

United Kingdom stated that "there was no sufficient legal basis for declaring or recognizing water or sanitation as freestanding human rights, nor was there evidence that they existed in customary law." *Id.* Later in 2010 the Human Rights Council adopted a resolution by consensus on "Human Rights and Access to Safe Drinking Water and Sanitation," affirming the conclusions expressed by the ESC Committee in General Comment 15. U.N. Doc. A/HRC/15/L.14, 24 September 2010. What is the significance of the reluctance of some important developed countries to recognize a human right to water and sanitation? Can they prevent the development of a customary norm recognizing these rights? Or would they just be "persistent objectors" and not bound by such a right, assuming it crystallizes or has already emerged?

2.   *A transboundary human right to water?* If State A uses an international watercourse in a way that deprives those in downstream State B of sufficient water to meet their basic needs, do those people in State B have a claim against State A for denial of their human right to water? Or must they raise their claim with the government of State B, hoping it would then make an inter-state claim against State A? As we have seen in subsection 4, above, Article 10(2) of the UN Watercourses Convention provides: "In the event of a conflict between the uses of an international watercourse, it shall be resolved with reference to articles 5 to 7, with special regard being given to the requirements of vital human needs." Is this tantamount to saying that the human right to water enjoyed by those in State B may be asserted against State A? If not, what is the meaning of Article 10(2)? *See* Inga T. Winkler, The Human Right to Water and Implications for Allocation (2012); and Takele Soboka Bulto, The Extraterritorial Application of the Human Right to Water in Africa (2014).

3.   *A commodified human right to water?* Is the recognition of a human right to water inconsistent with treating water as a commodity or economic good? Water policy students often argue that water is a subsidized good in many parts of the world and that this leads to excessive consumption at the expense of aquatic ecosystems. If a country moves to price water at market rates, would this violate the human right to water? Conversely, since the right includes a right to safe drinking water, does this require increased pollution and water protection standards? *See* Eric E. Bluemel, *The Implications of Formulating a Right to Water*, 31 Ecology L.Q. 957 (2004) and Amy Hardberger, *Life, Liberty, and the Pursuit of Water: Evaluating Water as a Human Right and the Duties and Obligations It Creates*, 4 Northwestern J. Int'l L. 331 (2005). What are the implications for riparian states on international watercourses?

CONCLUDING NOTES AND QUESTIONS

1.   *Water, water . . . nowhere?* No. Water isn't going away. The law of the indestructability of matter/conservation of mass tells us that. But its distribution is changing, and relative to the size of the human population it is decreasing in quantity. Given the fact that more fresh water is shared

between countries than isn't, are conflicts, sometimes military ones, inevitable? What indications are there that they are, or aren't?

2.   *Is the Problem still a problem?* Do you see the Problem that opened this chapter through a different lens now? Or does it look the same to you? If you were a sole arbitrator tasked with solving the conundrum presented by the Problem, what would your solution be?

3.   *Some other issues:*

a.   Could fresh water now be considered a "common concern of humankind," like climate change and biodiversity in the UN Framework Convention on Climate Change and the Convention on Biodiversity? What would be the implications of this?

b.   International water law has focused on issues of supply, both allocation and quality. Brown Weiss argues that it is time to focus on the demand for water. What are the international legal implications of doing so?

c.   There has been much discussion about water markets. Limited water markets already exist within certain western states in the United States. To what extent does international water law accommodate water markets?

See Edith Brown Weiss, International Law for a Water-Scarce World (2013).

CHAPTER 13

BIOLOGICAL DIVERSITY

■ ■ ■

PROBLEM

The football mad country of Novo Terra has some 75 million hectares of rain forest. Novo Terra implemented the Convention on Biological Diversity by creating a Biodiversity Commission to advise the government about how to comply. The Commission recommended that 20% of the country's rain forest be placed in protected nature reserves based on an index of biodiversity richness, that Novo Terra allow bio-prospecting in all rain forest areas, and that the national legislature create a new property right in traditional, indigenous knowledge. The Novo Terra President studied the report, but she recommended that the national legislature place only 10% of the rainforest in protected areas and allow intensive ecotourism development in 75% of the area. The protected and non-protected areas are home to Leopold's Jaguar, an Appendix I CITES species. The President's recommendations, which were adopted by the legislature, excluded two areas with two species of tropical hardwood listed in Appendix 2 of CITES. In the head waters of the country's major river, the President designated two wetland areas under the Ramsar Convention. However, in 2012, the Novo Terra Ministry of Energy authorized oil exploration in one of the Ramsar wetlands.

Instead of allowing prospecting, the legislature enacted a law which declares "the genetic knowledge contained in all flora and fauna is the patrimony of Novo Terra and can only be exploited by National Scientific University which has the exclusive right to bio-prospect within Novo Terra and to license the fruits of any useful applications of the genetic structure of the nation's flora and fauna. Traditional indigenous knowledge, however, is subject to the exclusive control of native peoples who have the exclusive right to license its use." Big Pharm heard that a native tribe, the Cloud People, in Novo Terra was using a plant for a number of medical purposes, including relief from many severe forms of arthritis. Big Pharm sent one of its scientists to Novo Terra on an ecotourism trip. The trip included the primary native village of the Cloud People and the scientist was able to convince a tribal member to reveal the name of the plant. Big Pharm subsequently obtained a patent under United States law for a powerful and popular arthritis relief medicine derived from the plant.

In 2014, a group of wealthy game hunters from Europe approached the President and asked for permission to hunt Leopold's Jaguar. The President subsequently promulgated an executive order which allows Jaguar hunting licenses to be issued so long as the survival of the population in Novo Terra is not endangered, but no monitoring institution was created. In the same year, the neighboring state of Tordesillas allowed extensive land clearing by burning in its rain forest, and the resulting smoke and haze resulted in a sharp drop in Nova Terra's ecotourism and the population of the Leopold's Jaguar.

A. INTRODUCTION

The conservation of biological diversity, or biodiversity, emerged as an over-arching construct in the 1980s to justify the protection of functioning ecosystems versus individual ecosystem components, including both biotic (living) and abiotic (non-living) elements. See David Takacs, The Idea of Biodiversity: Philosophies of Paradise (1996). But, the project has a history because countries have long been concerned with protecting particular species of fauna and flora and with preserving areas of high scenic beauty or scientific interest. The United States established its first national park, Yellowstone, in 1872. Wildlife laws have existed since at least the time of the Romans. However, older laws were used mainly to define what constituted private ownership of wildlife. Early efforts did not seek to eliminate wildlife exploitation, but rather to manage populations sustainably. Nonetheless, these efforts began to change the public's perception of the value of conserving wildlife and to raise ethical questions about humanity's obligations toward it. After he left office, the great conservation president Theodore Roosevelt (1900–1908) wrote, "The game belongs to the people. So it does; and not merely to the people now alive, but to the unborn people." A Book-Lover's Holidays in the Open (1916). TR's creation of the first national wildlife refuges helped to establish the scientific connection between species protection and habitat conservation. Today, there are more than 100 international agreements protecting wildlife. For a history of these early wildlife laws, see Michael J. Bean, The Evolution of National Wildlife Law (1977) and William F. Sigler, Wildlife Law Enforcement 1–9, 29–31 (1980). While motivated largely by the wish to preserve populations for human use, the protection of fur seals and especially migratory birds in the late nineteenth and early twentieth centuries marks the beginning of international environmental law. See Alexander Gillespie, Conservation, Biodiversity and International Law (2011). While that concern continues to be an important component of international environmental law and is the subject of section A of this chapter, the primary international focus is no longer on protecting only endangered species but rather on the health and integrity of ecosystems, especially large scale ones.

The importance of ecosystem conservation can be traced to Article II of the 1940 Convention on Nature, Wildlife Preservation in the Western Hemisphere, which urged the creation of national parks, national reserves, nature monuments, and "strict wilderness areas." See Michael Bonman, Peter Davis and Catherine Redgwell, Lyster's International

Wildlife Law, Chapter 8 (2nd ed. 2010), but little was done to implement it. Other legal instruments negotiated later have given increasing attention to ecosystem protection. For example, the 1982 World Charter for Nature, A/RES/37/7, a nonbinding instrument adopted by the UN General Assembly, identified nature as the human life-support system. In 1992, countries concluded the Convention on Biological Diversity which—for the first time—obligates States to establish a monitoring network for biological diversity. However, the protection and management of forests, one of the major reservoirs of biodiversity, is only subject to an evolving but still non-binding legal regime for forests, which is implemented at the national level.

The protection of biodiversity is not easy because much of the biodiversity that needs protection is within the territory of sovereign states, except the oceans. Thus, the focus of international efforts has been to convince states to adopt effective laws to protect the biological diversity within their own territories. At the highest conceptual level, the term is not self-defining and its utility remains contested. E.g., Sahotra Sarkarm, Biodiversity and Environmental Philosophy: An Introduction (2005). The relative newness of the construct means that biodiversity protection is often incidental to legal regimes with other objectives. However, in the past twenty years, concern over global climate change has led to a sharpened focus on biodiversity conservation as we learn more about the possible impacts of climate change on vital ecosystems. See Elizabeth Kolbert, The Sixth Extinction: An Unnatural History (2014). Acknowledging these difficulties, we start with a rough definition offered by the United States Council on Environmental Quality's Eleventh Annual Report (1985). The Report defined "biological diversity" as "a broad catchall term including the inter-connected and related concepts of genetic diversity, species or ecological diversity . . . ; and habitat or natural diversity . . ." (at 273). *See also* Fred P. Bosselman, *Extinction and the Law: Protection of Religiously-Motivated Behavior*, 68 Chi.-Kent L. Rev. 15 (1992) (discussing United States laws enacted to prevent the extinction of species and cultures). The problems of transforming the broad concept of biodiversity into a set of legal standards are discussed in section C, infra.

Ecosystem protection is the core component of biodiversity conservation. But, while the ecosystem construct has emerged as a major organizing principle for public policy, it has not produced consistent, comprehensive, strong legal protection norms either within states or as a matter of international environmental law. The problem is exacerbated by the lack of a clear legal definition of an ecosystem. Scientists understand ecosystems as biological communities of interdependent plants, animals and microorganisms that occur in a specific place associated with particular soils, temperatures and disturbance patterns, and the physical and chemical factors that make up that communities' abiotic, nonliving, environment. However, in many legal instruments, the term ecosystem is also often used carelessly and interchangeably with other similar terms such as environment, nature, balance of nature, ecological balance, or ecological stability and thus has no consistent meaning. It can equally refer to the perspective of a decision process as well as to a substantive obligation to protect a defined resource or geographical area. For example, the term "environment" is often equated with "ecosystem." An illustration is provided by the 1988 Convention on the Regulation of Antarctic Mineral Resources Activities (CRAMRA), which defines as harm "any harm on the living and non-living components of that environment or those ecosystems. . . ." Minors Oposa v. Secretary of the Department of Environment and Natural Resources, 33 International Legal Materials 174 (1994), which granted standing to the children of a Philippine citizen to challenge logging permits, spoke of the "right to a healthful ecology" and to a "sound environment." Philippe Sands Jacqueline Peel and Adriana Fabria Aguillar, Principles of International Environmental Law I: Frameworks, Standards and Implementation 13 (3rd ed. 2012) distinguishes environment from ecosystem because the former "encompasses both features and products of the natural world and those of human civilization" while the latter is concerned with "plants and animals occurring together plus that part of the environment over which they have an influence." This distinction has considerable support, but others argue that the definition of environment should be confined to the natural environment. M.A. Fitzmaurice, International Protection of the Environment, 293 Recueil des Courses: Collected Courses of the Hague Academy of International Law 22–28 (2001).Thus transnational eco-systems are often studied and mapped more than they are protected because there is little formal recognition of ecosystems as distinct areas subject to international protection duties. In addition, boundaries are hard to define because there are over-arching systems such as the North American ecosystem with many sub-systems embedded within it. In international law, ecosystems are still viewed primarily as simply parts of a State's territory over which it exercises complete sovereignty. See Dan Tarlock, Ecosystems in The Oxford Handbook of International Law 574 (D. Bodansky, J. Brunnee and Ellen Hey eds. 2007).

Foundational sources include Vandana Shiva et al., Biodiversity: Social and Ecological Perspectives (1991); Office of Technology Assessment, Technologies to Maintain Biological Diversity, Summary (1987) (setting out OTA's results of a presentation to Congress on the problems and policy options for maintaining biological diversity); Jeffrey McNeely et al., Conserving the World's Biological Diversity (1990) (including a bibliography of sources); WRI/IUCN/UNEP, Global Biodiversity Strategy: Guidelines for Action to Save, Study, and Use Earth's Biotic Wealth Sustainably and Equitably (1992) (creating an

action plan for conserving biodiversity); and Bryan G. Norton, Why
Preserve Natural Variety? (1987) (discussing the economic and intrinsic
values of biodiversity). An ambitious survey of the status of the world's
ecosystems is United Nations Environmental Programme, Millennium
Ecosystem Assessment, and Living Beyond Our Means: Natural Assets
and Human Well-Being (2006).

This chapter thus covers a wide set of topics. Section B traces the
history of efforts to protect specific species and area conservation efforts.
These are still in place and in many respects remain the main
international biodiversity conservation instruments. It covers two major
kinds of specific resource protection instruments, the specific sites as in
the UNESCO World Heritage Convention and the Ramsar Wetlands
Convention, and the specific species, as in the Convention on
International Trade in Endangered Species (CITES) and the protection of
certain migratory species (e.g., whales). Section C explores the overall
problem of the loss of biological diversity, including what the term
"biodiversity" means, and examines the options for conserving biological
diversity, including the Convention on Biological Diversity. Sections C.3–
4 discuss the special significance of forests and forest preservation, and of
deserts.

QUESTION

As you read these materials, you see that the two primary means of
protecting biodiversity are to conserve individual species at risk of extinction
or to wall off large areas of nature from substantial use. You should ask
yourself whether these strategies are sufficient in the face of climate change
and efforts to convince developing countries to practice sustainable
development. What new legal strategies would you suggest?

B. THE ANTECEDENTS OF THE CONVENTION ON BIOLOGICAL DIVERSITY

1. WORLD CULTURAL AND NATURAL HERITAGE CONVENTION

a. History and Structure of the Convention

The 1972 Convention for the Protection of the World Cultural and
Natural Heritage provides that certain natural and cultural sites can be
designated as world heritages and conserved for present and future
generations. The Convention was prepared in parallel with the
preparations for the historic 1972 United Nations Conference on the
Human Environment in Stockholm, Sweden. As of July, 2015, 191
countries were party to the Convention, and 1031 sites in 163 countries
were included on the World Heritage List. This list includes 802 cultural

sites, 197 natural sites, and 32 mixed cultural and natural sites. http://whc.unesco.org/en/list/. The Convention derives from two separate initiatives. One attempts to conserve the world's built cultural heritage, and the other attempts to protect natural properties of special scientific or cultural importance. The origins of the Convention lie in World War II which saw severe damage to Europe's cultural heritage. E.g. Lynn H. Nicholas, The Rape of Europa: The Fate of Europe's Treasures in the Third Reich and the Second World War (1995). After the War, countries were determined to conserve important cultural properties for the future. The subsequent initiatives were centered in the United Nations Education, Scientific and Cultural Organization (UNESCO). In 1954, countries negotiated the Hague Convention on the Protection of Cultural Property in the Event of Armed Conflict. This was followed by campaigns under the auspices of UNESCO to save specific cultural sites and three years later by the establishment of an international nongovernmental organization dedicated to conserving cultural properties—the International Council on Monuments and Sites (ICOMOS). UNESCO adopted a series of resolutions that authorized the negotiation of a new international agreement to protect cultural properties, and by spring 1971 draft text was ready. At the same time, the International Union for the Conservation of Nature and Natural Resources (IUCN) prepared a draft convention to protect national parks, some historic structures, certain natural sites, and important wildlife areas which were to become part of a World Heritage Trust.

The United States, and especially the leadership of Russell Train, was instrumental in encouraging the creation of a trust and a new convention. But, eventually in 1972 the two drafts were combined into a single convention, which was opened for signature in November of that year and went into effect in 1977. The preamble to the Convention notes that "parts of the cultural or natural heritage . . . need to be preserved as part of the world heritage of mankind as a whole." The approach of the Convention is to conserve important national and cultural sites through the use of a World Heritage List. Individual countries nominate national and cultural sites for inclusion on the List. The Convention provides for a World Heritage Committee composed of Party member and a "representative of the International Centre for the Study of the Preservation and Restoration of Cultural Property (ICCROM), a representative of the International Council of Monuments and Sites (ICOMOS) and a representative of the International Union for Conservation of Nature and Natural Resources (IUCN), to whom may be added, at the request of States Parties to the Convention meeting in general assembly during the ordinary sessions of the General Conference of the United Nations Educational, Scientific and Cultural Organization . . . ." In addition, representatives of other intergovernmental or non-governmental organizations, with similar objectives, may attend the meetings of the Committee in an advisory capacity." Art. 8. The Committee may assist the Parties to decide whether to apply for a listing. Only a small portion of the sites nominated are approved. There is an informal understanding that every country that joins the Convention is entitled to have one site put on the World Heritage List.

Under the Convention, states that have natural and cultural properties on the list are obligated to protect them, and other states are also obligated to refrain from actions that would endanger them. If they are put on the List of World Heritage Sites in Danger, the sites will be afforded such protections. As of July, 2015, there were 48 world heritage sites on the danger list including the Rio Plátano Biosphere Reserve in Honduras, barrier reefs in Belize, the tropical rainforest heritage of Sumatra, Indonesia and several national parks and a wildlife refuge in Democratic Republic of the Congo. Despite a multi-billion dollar on-going restoration effort, the Florida Everglades were placed on the list in 2010.

The Convention provides for a World Heritage Fund to assist developing countries in maintaining world heritage sites. Countries with a site on the endangered list are eligible for special funds to protect the site. The secretariat has also tried to enlist the support of the World Bank's Global Environmental Facility to fund natural heritage conservation projects, with limited success to date. The treaty created three new institutions: the general assembly, the committee, and the bureau. The General Assembly, which meets biannually, has very limited powers. Its main task is to elect members of the World Heritage Committee, which is comprised of 21 member states serving six-year terms. The Committee, which meets annually, approves the listing of sites on the World Heritage List, changes in the Operational Guidelines, changes in listing criteria, and programmatic developments, such as monitoring and conservation of sites. It has always operated by consensus. The Bureau, composed of the chairman of the committee, five vice-chairs, and the rapporteur, is elected by members of the committee. The Bureau meets twice a year and prepares the agenda for the upcoming Committee meetings, deals with emergency assistance requests and other problems, and serves as an important forum for considering new initiatives, such as the Strategic Plan in 1992 and considering the monitoring reports of the International Council on Monuments and Sites (ICOMOS) and the International Union for the Conservation of Natural Resources (IUCN) for 60 sites. The secretariat for the Convention is located at UNESCO headquarters in Paris, France. Until May 1992, administration of the natural and the cultural sites was handled within separate divisions of UNESCO.

In 1992, a separate secretariat to unify administration of the Convention for both natural and cultural sites was created. Since the Convention came into effect, states have expanded its scope and assumed new powers in implementing it. All of this has been accomplished not through amendment, but through the development of Operational Guidelines and alterations to the Guidelines. In 1993 the parties added landscapes to the categories of properties that could be listed as world heritage sites. While countries have always had the capacity to indicate that a world heritage site within the country should be placed on the List of World Heritage Sites in Danger, it is only within the last few years that member states have taken it upon themselves to put a site on the danger list in the absence of a request from the host country. Members voted to inscribe Dubrovnik in Croatia, which was shelled by the Yugoslav People's Army in 1991–1992, and Manas National Park in India on the endangered list without the consent of the host countries. In 1993, the World Heritage Committee placed the Everglades National Park on the danger list, even though the United States had not requested this and abstained in the voting. The Committee continues to assert the power to list sites in danger without the consent of the host State, Operation Guidelines IV.B. Para. 177, but Para. 183 requires that the Committee consult with the state to develop a corrective action program.

The World Heritage Convention is an early and outstanding example of an international agreement that explicitly provides for non-governmental organizations to assist in its implementation. Articles 13 and 14 explicitly reference three intergovernmental and non-governmental organizations: the International Centre for the Study of the Preservation and Restoration of Cultural Property (the Rome Centre), ICOMOS, and IUCN. ICOMOS and IUCN, in particular, have played important roles. They evaluate requests to put cultural properties and natural sites, respectively, on the World Heritage List; review requests from countries for financial and technical assistance; and, more recently, monitor at least some of the sites. They have routinely participated in the meetings of the bureau and of all the parties. However, few non-governmental organizations, other than those specified in the Convention, have been closely involved with the Convention. For the above and further details on the World Heritage Convention, see Edith Brown Weiss, *The Five International Treaties: A Living History,* Chapter 5, in Engaging Countries: Strengthening Compliance with International Environmental Accords (1998).

As you read the following excerpts, consider whether the World Heritage Convention offers a useful legal framework for conserving unique sites located within national borders. What are the incentives to list sites on the World Heritage List or to maintain them in the face of local threats? Consider also the content of member countries' obligations under the Convention. How specific are the obligations? How does this affect countries' implementation of the convention? Can you argue that the generality or specificity of the obligations makes Countries more or less willing to join the World Heritage Convention?

INTERNATIONAL WILDLIFE LAW: AN ANALYSIS OF INTERNATIONAL TREATIES CONCERNED WITH THE CONSERVATION OF WILDLIFE

Simon Lyster
222–226 (1993)

Articles 4 and 5 of the Convention set out the obligations to conserve sites in the World Heritage List which are situated in their territories.

Article 4 states:

Each State Party to this Convention recognizes that the duty of ensuring the identification, protection, conservation, presentation and transmission to future generations of the cultural and natural heritage referred to in Articles 1 and 2 and situated on its territory belongs primarily to that State. It will do all it can to this end, to the utmost of its own resources and, where appropriate, with any international assistance and cooperation, in particular, financial, artistic, scientific and technical, which it may be able to obtain.

Article 5 states:

To ensure that effective and active measures are taken to the protection, conservation and presentation of the cultural and natural heritage situated on its territory, each State Party to this Convention shall endeavor, in so far as possible, and as appropriate for each country: a) to adopt a general policy which aims to give the cultural and natural heritage a function in the life of the community and to integrate the protection of that heritage into comprehensive planning progammes; b) to set up within its territories, where such services do not exist, one or more services to the protection, conservation and presentation of the cultural and natural heritage with an appropriate staff and possessing the means to discharge their functions; c) to develop scientific and technical studies and research and to work out such operating methods as will make the State capable of counteracting the dangers that threaten its cultural or natural heritage; d) to take the appropriate legal, scientific, technical, administrative and financial measures necessary for the identification, protection, conservation, presentation and rehabilitation of this heritage; and e) to foster the establishment or development of national or regional centres for training in the protection, conservation and presentation of the cultural and natural heritage and to encourage scientific research in this field.

The only court to have considered the nature of the obligations imposed on Parties by Articles 4 and 5 is the High Court of Australia in the . . . case of Commonwealth of Australia v. The State of Tasmania (1983), 46 A.L.R. 625. The case arose because of plans by the State of Tasmania to construct a dam on the Gordon River, downstream of its junction with the Franklin River in an area known as the Western Tasmania Wilderness National Parks which the Commonwealth of Australia (i.e. the federal Australian government) nominated for inclusion in the World Heritage List on 13 November 1981. The World Heritage Committee accepted the nomination in December 1982 although, aware of Tasmania's plans, it expressed "serious concern" at the likely effect of the proposed dam and recommended that "the Australian authorities take all possible measures to protect the integrity of the property." The Commonwealth of Australia then took two steps to protect the site. The Governor-General exercising his authority under Section 69 of National Parks and Wildlife Conservation Act of 1975 issued the World Heritage (Western Tasmania Wilderness) Regulations (S.R. Nos. 31 and 66 of 1983) and the Australian Parliament adopted the World Heritage Properties Conservation Act of 1983. Both the Regulations and the Act made construction of the dam illegal. The State of Tasmania challenged the constitutional authority of the Commonwealth of Australia to make a law or to adopt regulations prohibiting construction of the dam and the Commonwealth sought a ruling from the High Court that the measures taken to protect the Western Tasmania Wilderness National Parks were valid. A key question in the argument before the Court was whether the World Heritage Convention imposes a legal duty on each Party to protect a site in the World Heritage List which is situated on its territory. The Commonwealth of Australia contended that the Convention does impose such a duty while the State of Tasmania argued that the Convention imposed no real obligation but is merely a statement of aspiration or political accord. Since it is the only case in which this issue has been considered, the findings of the Court bear consideration in some detail. By a 4–3 majority decision the Court upheld the authority of the Commonwealth to stop the dam, and the opinions of the four Justices who formed the majority all state categorically that the Convention imposes a legal duty on Australia to protect Western Tasmania Wilderness National Parks. The Court recognized that the key sections of the Convention are Articles 4 and 5. Asking himself the question "does the Convention impose an obligation on Australia to protect the area which has been entered on the World Heritage List and, if so, what kind of obligation?", Justice Mason stated in The Commonwealth of Australia v. The State of Tasmania that Article 5

> . . . imposes obligations on each state with the object set out in the opening words of the article "[t]o ensure that effective and active measures are taken for the protection, conservation" etc. of the heritage in the discharge of the responsibility acknowledged by Article 4. Article 5 cannot be read as a mere

statement of intention. It is expressed in the form of a command
. . . Indeed, there would be little point in adding the
qualifications "in so far as possible" and "as appropriate for each
country" unless the Article imposed an obligation. The first
qualification means "in so far as is practicable" and the second
takes account of the difference in legal systems. Neither the
qualifications nor the existence of an element of discretion is
inconsistent with the existence of an obligation. There is a
distinction between discretion as to the manner of performance
and discretion as to performance or non-performance. The latter,
but not the former, is inconsistent with a binding obligation to
perform. (see Thorby v. Goldberg (1964) 112 C.L.R. 597, at pp.
604–605, 613, 614–615.)

Justice Brennan stated that the last part of Article 4 and the first
part and (d) of Article 5 are critical. In considering whether the want of
specificity in Articles 4 and 5 and the discretion they leave to each Party
as to how it will protect World Heritage sites makes them merely
hortatory, he concluded that the Articles are not merely hortatory and
that there is a clear obligation on Australia to act under Articles 4 and 5,
though the extent of that obligation may be affected by decisions taken by
Australia in good faith. Justice Brennan went on to say that

the obligation under Article 4 of the Convention leaves no
discretion in a Party as to whether it will abstain from taking
steps in discharge of the "duty" referred to in that Article. Each
Party is bound to "do all it can . . . to the utmost of its own
resources," and the question whether it is unable to take a
particular step within the limits of its resources is a justifiable
question. No doubt the allocation of resources is a matter for
each Party to decide, and the allocation of resources for the
discharge of the obligation may thus be said to be discretionary,
but the discretion is not large. It must be exercised "in good
faith," as Article 26 of the Vienna Convention requires. If a Party
sought exemption from the obligation on the ground that it had
allocated its available resources to other purposes, the question
whether it had done so in good faith would be justiciable.

In a strongly worded dissenting opinion the Chief Justice, Sir Harry
Gibbs, disagreed with the Court's decision, stating

that it is unnecessary to consider whether if the words of Arts. 4
and 5 which purport to impose an obligation had appeared in, for
example, a commercial contract, they would in an appropriate
context have imposed a duty to do what was reasonably possible
and fitting in the circumstances. It is however impossible to
conclude that Arts. 4 and 5 were intended to impose a legal duty
of that kind on the States Parties to the Convention. If the

conduct which those articles purport to prescribe was intended to be legally enforceable, the obligations thereby created would be of the most onerous and far reaching kind. The obligations would extend to any property which might reasonably be regarded as cultural or natural heritage within the meaning of Arts. 1 and 2 of the Convention, whether or not it was included on the World Heritage List, and would require a State Party to the convention to take all legal measures within its constitutional power that might reasonably be regarded as appropriate for the identification and protection of such property, and to apply all of its financial resources that it could possibly make available for the same purpose; there would of course be further obligations, but what I have said suffices to indicate the nature of the burden which the articles would impose. The very nature of these obligations is such as to indicate that the State Parties to the Convention did not intend to assume a legal obligation to perform them.

———————

Commonwealth of Australia v. The State of Tasmania is a landmark decision both because it is the first test of the scope of the Convention in a court of law and because the majority of judges stated so clearly that each Party has a legal duty to do all it can to protect sites in the World Heritage List which are situated within its own territorial boundaries. Although non-binding the case has been widely studied, but its influence is hard to discern outside of Australia. The Commonwealth's duty to protect World Heritage Convention sites was upheld in *Richardson v. Forestry Commission*, 164 CLR 261 (1988) and *Queensland v. Commonwealth*, 167 CLR 232 (1989). *See* Global Change and the Great Barrier Reef: Australia's Obligations Under the World Heritage Convention (2004), *available at* http://sydney.edu.au/law/scigl/SCIGL FinalReport21_09_04.pdf.

b. Conservation of Sites Not in the World Heritage List but Which Are Part of the Cultural and Natural Heritage Referred to in Articles 1 and 2

The conservation obligations imposed on Parties by Articles 4 and 5 are not limited to sites in the World Heritage List. Also included are sites which are part of the cultural and natural heritage as defined by Articles 1 and 2 of the Convention. Article 4 states that [e]ach State Party to this Convention recognizes that the duty of ensuring the identification, protection, conservation, presentation and transmission to future generations of the cultural and natural heritage referred to in Articles 1 and 2 and situated on its territory, belongs primarily to the State. . . . (emphasis added). Article 5 starts with the words: [t]o ensure that effective and active measures are taken for the protection, conservation and presentation of the cultural and natural heritage situated on its territory, each State Party shall endeavor . . . (emphasis added).

This is an important point since the cultural and natural heritage within the meaning of Articles 1 and 2 may include substantially more sites than those in the World Heritage List. As was pointed out earlier in this chapter, it is up to each Party to identify sites on its territory which it deems to be part of the cultural and natural heritage within the meaning of Articles 1 and 2, while the compilation of the World Heritage List is the responsibility of the World Heritage Committee. It is quite conceivable, therefore, that a Party might decide that a site in its territory is part of the cultural and natural heritage as defined by Articles 1 and 2, notwithstanding that it is not on the World Heritage List. Australia, for example, has declared a 780 hectare area and numerous cultural sites in Tasmania, which are outside the Western Tasmania Wilderness National Parks and not on the World Heritage List, to be part of the natural and cultural heritage as defined by Articles 1 and 2 of the Convention. Furthermore, Section 3(2) of Australia's World Heritage Properties Conservation Act states that the provisions of the Act apply to sites submitted to the World Heritage Committee for listing and to sites "declared by the regulations to form part of the cultural and natural heritage" as well as to sites that the World Heritage Committee has actually agreed to include on the World Heritage List.

c. Delisting and Gerrymandering

In the 1990s the issue of whether and how to delist a site already on the World Heritage List arose. No site had ever been taken off the World Heritage List, although in December 1993 Germany, Thailand, and the United States indicated that the step should be considered for Manas National Park. Mount Nimba Nature Reserve in Guinea, which was put on the danger list in 1992, poses the issue dramatically, because it had become a promising source of minerals since its inscription on the World Heritage List. The World Heritage Convention does not address the issue, but the Operational Guidelines provide detailed delisting procedures that are intended to ensure that all possible measures are taken to prevent deletion but to authorize the World Heritage Committee to delist if these fail. There was considerable controversy over whether delisting could take place over the host State's opposition and whether a site must be delisted at a host country's request. After a long period of discussion, the Committee decided that it would delist a site with the host country's consent. Operational Guidelines, IV.C. Paras. 192–198. However, there have been two unilateral delistings. In 2008, the World Heritage Committee decided to remove Germany's Elbe Valley near Dresden, listed in 2004, from UNESCO's World Heritage List after a bridge was built in the heart of the cultural landscape. The Committee decided that the property no longer had its "outstanding universal value" as an 18th and 19th century landscape. The Oman's Arabian Oryx Sanctuary was delisted in 2007.

Countries which face development pressure in World Heritage sites have sometimes complied with the Convention by redrawing the site's boundaries to allow development such as mineral exploitation. In 2012, Tanzania persuaded the World Heritage Committee to "modify" the boundaries of the Selous Game Reserve to allow uranium mining. http://www.africannaturalheritage.org/Selous-Game-Reserve-Tanzania/. A similar request was made to allow oil exploration in the Virunga National Park in the democratic Republic of Congo. Jeffrey Gettlemen, Oil Dispute Takes a Page from Congo's Bloody Past, The New York Times, p.A6, November 16, 2014. However, in 2014, the Committee panel unanimously rejected a bid by Australia's newly elected government to remove 74,039 hectares of Tasmania wilderness from a designated World Heritage Site. http://news.sciencemag.org/asiapacific/2014/06/unesco-rejects-australias-bid-shrink-tasmanian-world-heritage-site.

d. The United States and the World Heritage Convention

The United States has 21 sites on the World Heritage List. There has been only one addition since 1995. The George W. Bush administration (2001–2008) defended its no-new-nominations policy because further U.S. nominations might compete with "those of other States Parties which may have no sites yet inscribed on the list." United States Department of Interior, Application of the World Heritage Convention by the United States 8 (2004). In 2010, Papahnaumokuākea, an isolated linear cluster of small, low lying islands and atolls, with their surrounding ocean, roughly 250 km to the northwest of the main Hawaiian Archipelago was added. The area has deep cosmological and traditional significance for living Native Hawaiian culture, as an ancestral environment, as an embodiment of the Hawaiian concept of kinship between people and the natural world, and as the place where it is believed that life originates and to where the spirits return after death. The student may consult the Convention's web site, www.whc.unesco.org, for a list of World Heritage sites. The United States abstained in voting to put the Everglades on the endangered list and requested that Yellowstone National Park be put on the endangered list.

Yellowstone National Park has been the focus of considerable controversy because of private efforts to develop mineral resources just outside the park. During the George W. Bush administration, there were proposals to lease lands outside the park for geothermal drilling; no leases were issued but could be in the future. What legal effect does the listing of Yellowstone National Park on the World Heritage List have in controlling private mining activity near the site? Does it make any difference that the site has been put on the endangered list? In the past few years, the United States and the state of Florida have embarked on a multi-billion dollar experiment to restore the Everglades ecosystem. The Convention has been cited as one among many reasons for the program.

The Department of Interior has primary responsibility for implementing the convention. In practice, the Secretary of the Interior has delegated authority to the National Park Service, which is part of the Interior Department, to implement the agreement. A representative from the National Park Service usually heads the United States delegation to meetings of the parties to the convention. For additional references, see International Union for the Conservation of Nature/United Nations Education, Scientific, and Cultural Organization's World Heritage Committee, The World Heritage Twenty Years Later (1992); J.G. Nelson & E.A. Alder, Toward Greater Understanding and Use of the World Heritage Convention (1992). When the U.S. Congress passed legislation forbidding the U.S. to contribute to UNESCO, the question arose as to whether that applied to U.S. contributions to the World Heritage Convention's Fund, since the Convention's secretariat is housed in UNESCO. The State Department at least initially thought that it did. Do you agree?

e. International Law and Park Protection: A Global Responsibility

IN OUR COMMON LANDS: DEFENDING THE NATIONAL PARKS

Daniel Magraw
143, 148–50, 162–163 (David J. Simon ed., 1988)

I. INTRODUCTION

National parks and other areas administered by the National Park Service (hereinafter referred to jointly as "national parklands") currently face a variety of threats from outside their borders. Such threats are commonly referred to as "external threats." Many, probably most, external threats are domestic threats, that is threats to national parklands originating in the United States. Others, however, are international threats to national parklands that originate outside the United States. International threats can be either continuous and long-term, such as acid rain resulting from ongoing industrial activity, or instantaneous or short term, such as radioactive fallout from the accident at the Soviet Union's Chernobyl nuclear power reactor. Some national parklands adjoin a U.S. boundary with another nation and are threatened by sources in that nation. Glacier National Park, which is threatened by water pollution from the proposed Cabin Creek coal mine in British Columbia, Canada, and by logging in Canada, is one example. Approximately twenty-four national parklands immediately adjacent to

U.S. borders with Canada and Mexico may be so affected.[1] Four of those national parklands and sixty other national parklands are on U.S. seacoasts and thus face possible threats from pollution occurring in international or foreign waters. . . .

The legal effect and meaning of the World Heritage Convention is not entirely clear. The only case to analyze the Convention is an Australian case, Australia v. Tasmania. It is beyond cavil that the Convention is binding (on the United States, Canada, and the other states that are parties to it) as international law. Nevertheless, there is no international forum that automatically has jurisdiction to hear disputes arising under the Convention, and none appears likely. Thus, it might be impossible for a nation alleging that another nation is violating the Convention to be able to obtain an international adjudicatory determination of that allegation. With respect to enforceability in U.S. domestic courts, a crucial question is whether the Convention requires implementing legislation in order to be effective, that is, whether the Convention is "self-executing." The Tasmania case did not address that question because under Australian law, treaties cannot be self-executing. If it is not self-executing, it will not be effective as domestic law within the United States (although it remains in force as international law and binding on the countries that are parties to it) unless implementing legislation is passed. The Solicitor of the Department of the Interior has concluded that the World Heritage Convention is not self-executing. That result is not free from doubt, however. The Secretary of the Interior has been designated to direct and coordinate U.S. participation in the Convention, and the Secretary has issued rules setting forth policies and procedures in that regard, which may give rise to enforceable domestic legal rights.

Articles 4 and 5 of the Convention place obligations for protecting cultural and natural heritage sites on the nation in which those sites are located. In addition, Article 6.2 imposes an obligation on parties to the Convention to aid in "the identification, protection, conservation and preservation of the cultural and natural heritage" identified in the World Heritage List, if the nation in which the site is located so requests. The extent of the obligation is not clear from the face of the Convention, and research has revealed no source that analyzes that question. Nevertheless, vis-a'-vis other nations that are parties to the Convention, Article 6.2 offers protection of some sort to national parklands that are on the World Heritage List.

Article 6.3 of the Convention imposes an obligation on parties "not to take any deliberate measures which might damage directly or indirectly the cultural and natural heritage referred to in Articles 1 and 2 situated on the territory of other" parties to the Convention. The meaning of

---

[1]   See also David K. W. Wilson, Jr., Cabin Creek and International Law—An Overview, 5 Public Land and Resources L. Rev. 109 (1984).

Article 6.3 is subject to debate. For instance, the important term "damage directly or indirectly" is subject to widely differing interpretations. Further, Article 6.3 applies by its terms regardless of whether the heritage site has been placed on the World Heritage List, an interpretation that is supported by the structure of the Convention as a whole and by several opinions in the Tasmania case. If that interpretation is correct, Canada may be obligated to prevent British Columbian approval of the Cabin Creek coal mine, even though Glacier National Park, which would seem to qualify easily as a natural area of "outstanding value from the point of view of science, conservation, or natural beauty," has not yet been approved at the international level for placement on the World Heritage List. The constitutional powers of the Canadian provinces complicate the analysis, however. Article 34 of the Convention provides that if the federal government has the authority to prevent the prohibited action, it must do so; but if the federal government does not have that authority, it is obligated only to inform the competent authorities at the provincial level with its recommendations. . . .

————————

Another possible source of international obligations is the Man and the Biosphere Program, which operates under the auspices of UNESCO. Perhaps the primary component of that program is the biosphere reserve project, which began in the early 1970s and is not based on an international agreement per se. Each participating country voluntarily establishes its own national autonomous committee. The activities of those committees are coordinated to some degree by UNESCO, but UNESCO does not control their operations. As of August 2015, there were 120 participating countries and 651 biosphere reserves in 117 countries, including 12 transboundary sites. Two hundred fifty-two biosphere reserve sites now exist in 66 countries.

The need for stronger protection of areas of international environmental and cultural significance was underlined in 2001. The then Taliban-led government of Afghanistan deliberately destroyed two third and fifth century A.D. Buddha statues carved into the sandstone cliffs of the country Bamiyan Valley. Destruction was justified by a fatwa that declared the statues the "gods of infidels." See Francesco Francioni and Federico Lenzerini, *The Destruction of the Buddhas of Bamiyan and International Law*, 14 European J. Envtl. L. 619 (2003). There were several UN General Assembly resolutions condemning the Taliban's actions, but only the Ukraine characterized the act as a breach of the Convention and a flagrant violation of international law. See Rodger O'Keefe, *World Heritage Convention: Obligations to the International Community as a Whole?*, 53 Int. & Comp. L. Q. 189, 198 (2004). In 2003, after an application from the new, non-Taliban government of Afghanistan, the World Heritage Committee placed the remains and the valley on the World Heritage list, "which confirms that the Buddhas of Bamiyan represented an element of general interest to humanity in the safeguarding of cultural heritage." *Id.* at 651. However, in 2011 Afghanistan and UNESCO reached an agreement that the site is sufficiently protected to be removed from the danger list. In August 2015, the Islamic State of Iraq and the Levant destroyed the Baal Shamin temple in Palmyra, Syria, a UNESCO World Heritage Site since 1980.

The United States, which continues to participate in the Man and the Biosphere Program even though it has withdrawn from membership in UNESCO, has designated all or part of twenty-six national parklands as biosphere reserves. Preliminary research has not revealed any basis for concluding that the biosphere reserve project creates binding legal obligations for the participating nations with respect to biosphere reserves in other nations. Nevertheless, the project may give rise to expectations that warrant some legal protection and contains, at the very least, an element of moral suasion. That result might particularly follow where two adjacent parks are both biosphere reserves, as is the case with the United States' Glacier National Park and Canada's Waterton Lakes National Park. Recently proposed legislation would direct the Secretary of the Interior to give priority attention to biosphere reserves.

. . .

The World Heritage Convention obligates member Statess in which outstanding natural or cultural resources are located to engage in some activities, although the extent of that obligation is uncertain. Article 4, for example, provides that each State Party to the Convention:

> recognizes that the duty of insuring the identification, protection, conservation, presentation and transmission to future generations of the cultural and natural heritage referred to in Articles 1 and 2 and situated on its territory, belongs primarily to that State. It will do all it can to this end, to the utmost of its own resources and, where appropriate, with any international assistance and cooperation.

The inclusion of the word "duty" is reassuring; the qualification implied by the terms "do all it can," "to the utmost of its own resources," and "where appropriate," reduce the strength of that obligation considerably.

Similarly, Article 5 provides that each State Party to the Convention "shall endeavor, insofar as possible, and as appropriate for each country" to take a number of enumerated measures, including "the appropriate legal, scientific, technical, Convention . . . established a general good faith responsibility for each signatory to protect heritage properties, but left latitude for implementation to each country." (The 1981 memorandum further says that 16 U.S.C. § 470a–1 "implements these provisions . . .

and [restricts] that latitude" in such a way that "the Secretary [of the Interior] must be satisfied that each nominated site has adequate legal protection to ensure its preservation.") There does not appear to be a definitive answer at present regarding the extent of the obligations imposed by Articles 4 and 5 of the Convention, but it is clear that the obligations exist and that they at least require good faith efforts.

NOTES AND QUESTIONS

1. *A Postscript to Cabin Creek.* Canada and the United States supported a Reference to the International Joint Commission concerning this proposed project, see pages 771 to 773 *supra.* The resulting report recommended that the mine not be built. International Joint Commission, Impacts of Proposed Coal Mine in the Flathead River Basin (1988). See also Note, *Mountaintop Removal at the Crown of the Continent: International Law and Energy Development in the Transboundary Flathead River Basin*, 32 Vermont L. Rev. 547 (2008).

2. *The international community's interest.* Does the international community have an interest in natural or cultural resources that are located within the borders of one country? Are World Heritage sites part of the common heritage of humankind subject to duties beyond the Convention?

3. *Outside pressure.* Would a government resent or welcome pressure from the international community, an international organization, or another country to protect one of its natural or cultural resources? What if the pressuring party were a non-governmental organization?

4. *Compliance.* How would you measure compliance with the World Heritage Convention?

5. *A hypothetical.* Consider a hypothetical in which Queensland, Australia, permits a foreign oil company to explore for oil in an area adjacent to the Great Barrier Reef. Could the United Kingdom, for example, bring a claim against Australia to the International Court of Justice to try to stop the exploration from continuing? What procedural and substantive problems do you foresee? From what you have read about the Tasmania case, could a case be brought by the federal government against Queensland? As is increasingly the case, private entities can de facto enforce the Convention. In May 2014, Deutsche Bank and HSBC refused to finance a billion-dollar expansion of a coal terminal in Queensland, Australia. The Australian government had approved the project, but the banks wanted assurance from UNESCO that the project would not damage the Great Barrier Reef. *See* http://www.db.com/cr/en/positions/activities-in-the-close-proximity-to-world-heritage-sites.htm.

2. THE RAMSAR CONVENTION ON WETLANDS

a. Introduction

Wetlands, which include marshes, fens, peat lands, and marine waters less than six meters deep, are one of Earth's most important systems for protecting wildlife habitats and controlling floods. The health of wetlands depends on both the quantity and the quality of water available to them. In some cases, human activities that affect wetlands occur only within the borders of states. In other cases, offending activities occur beyond national borders and cause transnational air and water pollution, which jeopardize wetlands. In addition, some important wetlands straddle international boundaries. In response to concern about the alarming rate of wetlands loss throughout the world, 18 countries in 1971 concluded the Convention on Wetlands of International Importance Especially as Waterfowl Habitat, 11 I.L.M. 963 (1971), popularly known as "the Ramsar Convention" after the Iranian city in which it was adopted. The convention was amended in 1982 and 1987. As of 2015, 168 countries are parties to the convention.

The Ramsar Convention is intended to promote the conservation and wise use of wetlands, including preventing harm to them from human activities such as from pollution and water drainage. Parties are obligated to designate suitable wetlands in their territory for inclusion in the List of Wetlands of International Importance (with special attention to migratory waterfowl), to promote conservation of wetlands on the list, to promote the conservation of all wetlands (whether or not on the list), and to promote and maintain nature reserves. In contrast to the World Heritage Convention, listing under the Ramsar Convention is unilateral. Parties do not screen any wetland proposed for inclusion on the list. Each State is required to list a wetland at the time it consents to be a party. It may of its own volition substitute one wetland for another wetland if the matter raises "urgent national interest," but the overall area of protected wetlands insofar as possible must not decrease. As of 2015, 2208 wetland sites wetlands were listed covering 210,734,269 hectares. [There are 2.47 acres per hectare] The Convention's activities are funded by annual contributions from the contracting parties. There are three small assistance funds to help countries comply with the Convention. IUCN is home to the secretariat of the Convention in Gland, Switzerland. Parties to the Ramsar Convention meet every three years to review policies and activities and to set new initiatives. Each member country reports to the conference on its national protection of wetlands. The Convention has played a major role in supporting host country protection capacity, coordinating conservation efforts with local and international NGOs, spotlighting threats to wetlands and in bringing the latest science and economic analysis to bear on implementation of the Convention. For example, at the Kampala, Uganda, Conference of the Parties, a declaration was adopted stressing the continued degradation of the world's wetlands and the need to focus on the services that they provide to human well-being and disaster mitigation.

b. Conservation Duties

The Convention has been criticized because it does not impose stringent binding obligations on the parties. However, the Convention has induced widespread participation. Formally, the Convention speaks only of an obligation to "promote" the conservation of listed sites and to "promote" establishment of nature reserves. Frequently a country, particularly a developing country that has put a particular wetland on the Ramsar Wetlands List will have a plaque prominently displayed at the entrance to the wetland indicating that it is a protected site. Whether this effort to enlist effective public support for the wetland is successful, however, is doubtful, particularly in those cases in which there are no effective environmental laws in place or local officials can be easily corrupted so as to ignore threatening pollution or pillaging of migratory waterfowl. Nonetheless countries seem pleased to be able to cite to wetlands that are listed as important under the Ramsar Convention, and international monitoring of protected sites by on-site visits of secretariat officials and their consultants can be important measures to foster compliance by States with the Convention.

There is some evidence that placing a site on the Ramsar list leads to efforts by a country to address broader problems in the larger watershed. *See* Jonathan Verschuuren, *The Case of Transboundary Wetlands Under the Ramsar Convention: Keep the Lawyers Out!*, 19 Colo. J. Int. Envtl. L. & Pol'y, (2008). *See also* Pamela Griffen, The Ramsar Convention: A New Window for Environmental Diplomacy? (Institute for Environmental Diplomacy & Security, University of Vermont, 2012). The Secretariat has worked to broaden the focus to ecosystem conservation and to integrate the Convention with the Convention on Biological Diversity and the 2008 Millennium Assessment. Its "Wise Use" Handbook (3rd ed. 2007), defines the wise use of wetlands as "the maintenance of their ecological character, achieved through the implementation of ecosystem approaches, within the context of sustainable development." By advocating this approach, Ramsar therefore necessitates that all Parties use the ecosystem approach when managing wetlands to account for the linkages and interdependence between wetlands and forests. *See* David Farrier and L Tucker, *Wise Use of Wetlands under the Ramsar Convention: a Challenge for Meaningful Implementation of International Law*. 12 J. Envt'l L. 21 (2000).

In 2005, Costa Rica brought an action against Nicaragua in the International Court of Justice contesting Nicaraguan military presence in the Isla Calero which Costa Rica claims as its own. Costa Rica alleged that Nicaragua's activities had damaged two interconnected Ramsar, one listed by each country. The Court entered an Order prohibiting both countries from sending personnel to the area, except that Costa Rica was entitled to protect the wetland that it had listed in the disputed area.

Certain Activities Carried Out by Nicaragua in the Border Area (Costa Rica v. Nicaragua), Provision Measures, 2011 IJC 6, para 79. The Order was reaffirmed in 2013 after Nicaragua brought an action against Costa Rica for the construction of a road in Costa Rica adjacent to the contested area. *Construction of a Road in Costa Rica along the San Juan River (Nicaragua v. Costa Rica); Certain Activities Carried Out by Nicaragua in the Border Area (Costa Rica v. Nicaragua),* Provisional Measures, Order of 13 December 2013, I.C.J. Reports 2013, p. 398. As of July, 2015, the cases had been argued, but the IJC had not issued its opinion on the merits.

The Ramsar Convention can also reinforce national law. Recall the Australian High Court decision in *Commonwealth v. Tasmania*, page 765, *supra*. Australia has a federal-state program to create sustainable, environmental flows in its major inland river basin, The Murray-Darling. Under Australia's Constitution, the allocation of water is an exclusive state, not federal, function. However, after an early cooperative state-federal effort did not produce the desired outcome, the Commonwealth passed a federal legislative program. Both the Ramsar and Biodiversity Conventions were cited justifications for the assertion of the External Affairs power as interpreted by the High Court in *Commonwealth v. Tasmania*. Amy Sennett et al., *Changes and Responses in the Murray-Darling Basin*, 16 Water Policy 117, 140 (2014).

c. Enforcement Through Spotlighting

The Ramsar Convention provides for a spotlighting process similar to that provided by the Environmental Side Agreement of NAFTA described in Chapter 5, pages 260 to 266. Article VI has been supplemented by the Ramsar Advisory Mission, a technical assistance mechanism formally adopted by Recommendation 4.7 of the 1990 Conference of the Parties. The main objective of this mechanism is to provide assistance to both developed and developing countries alike in solving the problems or threats that make inclusion in the Montreux Record of shame unnecessary. The Record is a list of some 45 wetlands where human interference, e.g. dams, pollution, mining, is degrading the ecology of the wetland.

There have been at least 75 missions under the auspices of the Ramsar Convention to observe the condition of the wetlands. For example, a mission investigated the Ukraine's plans to construct a shipping canal, the Bystroe canal, through its portion of the Danube Delta Wetlands, a Ramsar site, and basically concluded that the Ukraine had chosen the most environmentally destructive alternative. Ramsar Advisory Mission No. 55, Ukraine, Kyliski Mouth (2003). A similar inquiry, requested by Romania, under the Convention on Environmental Impact Assessment in a Transboundary Context (ESPOO Convention), Chapter 4, page 217, documented significant transboundary environmental impacts. United Nations Economic Commission for Europe, Espoo Convention, Opinion of Inquiry Commission, Danube-Black Sea Deep Water Navigation Canal in the Ukrainian Sector of the Danube Delta (2006). http://www.unece.org/fileadmin/DAM/env/eia/ documents/inquiry/Final%20Report%2010%20July%202006.pdf. The case would have undoubtedly come before the newly-established Implementation Committee of the UNECE Water Convention if it had been in existence. Information about the committee is *available at* http:// www.unece.org/index.php?id=32997. The canal goes through the heart of the Ukrainian Danube Delta Biosphere Reserve, an area of global ecological importance, and has questionable economic benefits. Starting in 2004, The Ukraine constructed Phase I of the Canal, but it quickly silted up past its previous depth, which precluded its use by ocean going vessels. Dredging began in 2006 and was completed in April 2007. Since then, ships have been able to use the canal. Phase II of the project, which included deepening of the canal as well as construction of a dike into the Black Sea, was begun in 2007 but as of August 2015 had not yet been completed.

The broader lesson of the Bystroe Canal conflict is that being "caught up" in a spotlighting process may have long term consequences and provides victim states with some leverage to mitigate expected damages. "In February 2012 Ukrainian authorities sent a full report highlighting that the works related to the implementation of Phase II of the Bystroe Channel project have not started. Moreover, according to the report, Ukraine prepared an EIA which was handed to the Government of Romania and discussed by a panel of international experts before being amended—in 2008—according to the comments made; a separate analysis of the impacts of the full implementation of the Channel in a transboundary context was also available; public hearings on the issue were organized without the cooperation of the Romanian government. The Ukrainian government further affirmed that it had looked into all possible alternatives to the route of the waterway before deciding to consider the Bystroe one. Regarding the ecological compensation and mitigation of possible damages to the environment, the Ukrainian government indicated that it had identified specific measures to mitigate the potential negative transboundary environmental impact of the Bystroe project; furthermore, the authorities stated that appropriate measures had been taken over the past years to enhance the conservation status of the Danube Delta Biosphere Reserve and to expand its territory.' Convention on the Conservation of European Wildlife and Natural Habitats: Cases and Complaints (2012). As of July, 2015, the Convention had not made a formal recommendation on Phase II. https:// www.coe.int/t/dg4/cultureheritage/nature/Bern/Institutions/Documents/ 2014/Misc_2014_34eCP_EN_final_adopted%20(2).pdf.

NOTES AND QUESTIONS

1. What leverage does the Convention provide to national officials interested in protecting their country's wetlands? Consider the following: In 1995, the Colombia Superintendence of Notaries denied property rights over lands that serve to protect the environment or conserve natural resources. Its instructions said that wetlands are inalienable, that they serve vital regulatory functions in the environment, and that for these reasons they must be considered as goods for public use. The existence of acquired rights over wetlands was therefore not permissible and the granting of any such contract illegal. Most of the 50,000 hectares of wetlands in the savannah region around Bogota, the primary target of the ruling, have been destroyed in the last 60 years.

2. The Convention permits a country to delete one wetland that is listed and substitute wetlands elsewhere. Can one wetland really be substituted for another without thwarting the purposes of wetland protection? Many scientists are very skeptical of this approach. Why is this provision included in the Convention? Would countries simply refuse to comply with the agreement when it became seriously inconvenient for them if such a provision were not included?

3. What measures would you recommend to increase compliance with the Convention and why?

4. Consider the following problem: Brazil, Argentina, Uruguay, Bolivia, and Paraguay want to construct a controversial waterway (the Hidrovia waterway) along the borders of the countries from a Uruguayan port to the remote interior of Brazil. The last fifth of the waterway would be through the Pantanal wetlands. Environmentalists contend that as much as 40 percent of the Pantanal wetlands, which encompass 56,000–80,000 square miles, could be destroyed. They also predict alteration of the hydrological regime, water quality deterioration, increased flooding in the area, loss of biodiversity, decline in bioproductivity, and loss of landscape complexity. Read the text of the Wetlands Convention. If the four countries were parties to the Ramsar Convention, could it affect the outcome of the proposal? How? (Note that Latin American countries have been slow to join the Convention, with the exception of Chile, Uruguay, and Venezuela.)

Further reading: Simon Lyster, International Wildlife Law ch. 10 (1993); Daniel Navid, *The International Law of Migratory Species: The Ramsar Convention*, 29 Nat. Res. J. 1001 (1989); Cyril de Klemm, *La Convention de Ramsar et La Conservation des Zones Humides Cotieres*, Particulierment en Mediterranee, Revue-Juridique de L'environnement 577 (1990); and Royal C. Gardner, The Ramsar Convention, in Wetlands—Integrating Multidisciplinary Concepts (Ben A. LePage ed., 2010).

3. CONSERVATION OF ENDANGERED SPECIES

The increasingly rapid disappearance of species around the globe is cause for concern both because of the loss of individual species and the broader loss of biodiversity. Traditionally this concern has taken the form of trying to protect certain species that are endangered, primarily through limiting international trade in them. But, the basic idea remains increasingly contested.

International trade in endangered species has been very profitable. While this trade dates back centuries, the volume of trade greatly expanded after World War II. In 1963 the International Union for the Conservation of Nature, a hybrid non-governmental/governmental organization, called for a convention to control the international trade in endangered species. Such a treaty, the Convention on International Trade in Endangered Species of Wild Fauna and Flora (CITES) was concluded ten years later. As of August 2015, 185 countries and the European Union were party to the Convention, with more than 975 species and sub-species of animals and plants on the Appendix I Endangered List and more than 34,400 species and sub-species on the Appendix II List of Threatened Species.

a.   Basic Elements of the Convention

The Convention is designed to protect species, defined as a group of organisms that can breed and produce offspring, of fauna and flora from extinction by commercial trade. States are required to give varying degrees of protection depending on the status of the particular species. The Convention's protection extends to any parts derivative of endangered animals or plants. Thus, ivory is a protected part of the endangered elephant. Under the treaty, regulated species are listed on one of three appendices: those threatened with extinction (Appendix I), those that could face extinction if their trade is not controlled (Appendix II), and those facing over-exploitation in a particular country (Appendix III). Member countries decide multilaterally to list a species on the first two appendices; a country may unilaterally put one of its species on Appendix III.

The agreement operates through a permit system that requires export and import permits for species listed in Appendix I and export permits for species in the other two appendices. Every state is required to designate a Management Authority and a Scientific Authority to supervise the review of permit applications. Traders in endangered species listed on Appendix I must present an export permit to the customs agency of the exporting country and both the export and import certificates to the importing country's custom officials. In theory this provides a double check against illegal trade. The Management Authority must certify that (1) the trade will not adversely affect species survival; (2) the specimen was not obtained illegally and will be transported in a manner minimizing the risk of death, damage, or cruel treatment; and (3) an import permit has been granted.

Species listed under Appendices II and III receive less protection. No import permit is required, and the specimens may be used for commercial purposes. But the same conditions for granting an export for Appendix I species apply to Appendix II species, and importation of them requires presentation of an export permit or re-export certificate prior to import. If a country has placed a species on Appendix III, an export permit is still required, but since the listing only means that the species is endangered in the listing country, no general assessment that the species is not endangered is needed for the export permit. To implement the treaty, countries must designate ports of entry and exit, and create a detailed record of trade in specimens of listed species.

CITES provides six exceptions from the requirements of the three appendices: specimens owned as household or personal effects, bred or propagated in captivity for commercial purposes, acquired before regulation of them took effect, loaned noncommercial between registered scientific institutions, transshipped while in customs' control, or transported as part of a travelling exhibition. While these exemptions are intended to relieve the burden of CITES, the effect of the household use, captive bred, and prior acquisition exceptions have been particularly prone to abuse and have undermined the objectives of CITES.

To encourage countries to join CITES, countries can opt out of any listing of species on Appendix I or II—i.e., make a reservation to the listing—within 90 days before the listing becomes effective. In this case, the reserving country is not treated as a party to the agreement for purposes of trade in the particular species. From 1975 to 1990, countries filed 289 reservations to changes in the listing of species under CITES appendices. The most high profile reservations were those taken by five African countries (Botswana, Burundi, Malawi, Mozambique, and Zimbabwe) to the October 1989 decision of the CITES parties to move the African elephant from Appendix II to Appendix I, effectively banning trade in ivory and other elephant products. As a result these five countries were not bound by the Appendix I trade restrictions. You should consider this as you read the materials later in this chapter on the elephant controversy.

Nongovernmental organizations have been integral to the operation of CITES. NGOs participate in the meetings of the parties and lack only the right to vote. Over time the number of NGOs participating in conference meetings has increased dramatically to the point where they significantly outnumber the state parties participating. In 1994, for example, 96 percent of the parties (119 states) attended the Conference of the Parties, with 221 nongovernmental observers and several non-party governments attending as observers. The NGOs were highly influential in pushing for the listing of elephants on Appendix I. NGOs have had a pivotal role in monitoring compliance with the agreement. The World

Conservation Monitoring Unit, in Cambridge, England, has been responsible for the computerized tracking of exports and imports, and provides the data to the CITES secretariat. TRAFFIC, a division of the World Wildlife Fund, has also been very active and effective in monitoring illegal trade in wildlife. NGOs have also assisted with scientific and technical studies and have provided valuable expertise.

The IUCN publishes a "Red List" of Threatened Animals, which the organization has tracked and recorded with the help of the World Conservation Monitoring Centre and the International Council for Bird Preservation, among others. The list includes the family, genus, and species name, the common name, the area in which the species is found, and a rating indicating the severity of the threat of extinction. The analyses are sophisticated and under constant review. See generally Simon Lyster, International Wildlife Law: An Analysis of International Treaties Concerned with the Conservation of Wildlife 239–277 (1985).

The 186 members of CITES meet periodically to assess its implementation and expand the list of threatened species. For example, the 1992 Kyoto, Japan meeting parties extended protection to 45 additional species. Thirty-five that had been listed in Appendix II were switched to Appendix I, thereby prohibiting trade in these species. Approximately 17 species were dropped from either annex. Four were downgraded from Appendix I to Appendix II. Among the additions to CITES, the Brazilian rosewood and the Central American mahogany became the first tropical tree species to come under the control of the Convention. The rosewood, which is used to make musical instruments and decorations, was placed in Annex I. Mahogany was listed in Annex II. At the 2002 Santiago, Chile conference, a proposal by Australia to list the Patagonian Toothfish, better known as Chilean Sea Bass, was turned back by Chile, although the parties did agree to a voluntary program to monitor the species' harvesting and trade, and as a result many restaurants have removed the item from their menus. Thirty-two species of seahorses were also added to Appendix I. At the request of the United States, the 2010 Doha, Qatar meeting directed the Secretariat to consider adding additional coral products to Appendixes I and II. At the 2013, Bangkok, Thailand meeting, Resolution 16.9 recognized that elephant poaching had reached 'unsustainable' levels and urged that parties fund and implement the Elephant Action Plan adopted at the 2010 Doha, Qatar meeting.

Fauna generally receive more protection than flora; but a significant tropical timber protection decision was made at the 12th Conference of Parties held in Santiago, Chile in late 2002. After a ten-year campaign, the parties agreed to list the Big Leaf or American Mahogany Tree in Appendix II. The listing applies only from southern Mexico to the Amazon where the tree is native; it does not apply to countries such as Indonesia and Malaysia which grow introduced trees on plantations. However, despite the listing, unsustainable harvesting continues in Central and South America.

b. Problems of Implementation of and Compliance with CITES

The Convention on International Trade in Endangered Species has frequently been criticized on the ground that countries do not enforce it effectively. Consider the following article. Think about the issues of implementation and compliance in the framework of the tools that other international environmental conventions use and consider whether some would be more effective than the ones included in CITES.

THE CONVENTION ON INTERNATIONAL TRADE IN ENDANGERED SPECIES OF WILD FAUNA AND FLORA: IMPROVING THE PROSPECTS FOR PRESERVING OUR BIOLOGICAL HERITAGE

John B. Heppes & Eric J. McFadden
5 Boston U. Intl. L.J. 229, 232–234, 237–239, 241–242 (1987)

I. PARTY IMPLEMENTATION AND COMPLIANCE WITH CITES: PROBLEMS AND PROSPECTS

A. National Record-Keeping

Article VII of CITES outlines the record-keeping and reporting requirements of the Treaty, providing:

> 6.   Each Party shall maintain records of trade in specimens of species included in Appendices I, II and III which shall cover: a) the names and addresses of exporters and importers; and b) the number and type of permits and certificates granted; the States in which such trade occurred; the numbers or quantities and types of specimens, names of species as included in Appendices I, II and III and, where applicable, the size and sex of the specimens in question.

Accurate and detailed record-keeping and reporting of international wildlife transactions by national actors is a critical component of CITES. In the absence of such pertinent statistics, it is difficult for the Secretariat or parties to CITES to discern trends in the trade of endangered species or to become aware of suspicious transactions that may warrant further investigation. Trade statistics also are essential for updating the CITES Appendices and to gauge the effectiveness of the Treaty. Finally, records and reports provided by the parties to the Secretariat help to reveal discrepancies among the parties concerning the interpretation of treaty provisions or the regulation of trade in certain species. Despite the passage of several resolutions at the biennial conferences of the parties calling for improved record-keeping and reporting of wildlife trade statistics, national compliance has continued to be woefully inadequate.

A recent study by the World Wildlife Fund (WWF) of CITES record-keeping and of the reporting practices of the members of the European Economic Community (EEC) is emblematic of the problem. . . . In general, the WWF study found an appalling lack of compliance with CITES record-keeping and reporting requirements among EEC nations. In recent years most of the EEC's member states have failed to submit annual reports to the CITES Secretariat on time, severely hampering its effectiveness. In addition, virtually all of the EEC nations have neglected to provide any information about importation and exportation of plant species. The WWF found the quality of the data provided by most EEC nations to be poor, usually providing no indication of the contents or status of individual shipments and often based only on records or permits that have been issued, rather than actual trade data.

B. Enforcement of the Convention by Member States

The efficacy of CITES has been hampered severely in most member nations by inadequate development of an infrastructure to enforce its provisions. Under the Convention, enforcement is vested solely in national authorities. One of the most severe problems in this context is an egregious shortage of personnel to conduct inspections of wildlife and wildlife products during the importation or exportation process. This problem is prevalent even in affluent member nations, such as the United States. For example, a recent study by the World Wildlife Fund of the psittacine importation process revealed that over 60,000 of such birds, many listed on Appendix I or II of CITES, may have entered the United States illegally in one year. One of the major factors contributing to this distressing situation is staff shortages at the Fish and Wildlife Service, the agency assigned to inspect psittacine shipments as they enter the United States. Because of manpower shortages, the Fish and Wildlife Service is unable to inspect the vast majority of psittacine shipments. As a consequence, the agency is compelled to rely upon importer's paperwork which purportedly certifies that the shipments are in compliance with CITES. Parrot smugglers have capitalized on this situation by exporting large numbers of endangered birds to the United States with inaccurate or wholly spurious documents obtained in other nations. As one analyst comments, "the bird market is extremely profitable and big importers have both the financial resources and the contacts in the countries of origin to ensure that the paperwork appears in order, regardless of which species may be involved. If FWS does not physically inspect the birds, they will not pick up on the illicit importation."

Manpower shortages are even more critical in member states with more limited economic resources. For example, in Argentina, national customs inspectors lack both the time and manpower to corroborate the legitimacy of transit documents for wildlife products that have been issued by provincial officials. This is distressing because provincial officials often establish quotas on the basis of market demand rather than the mandates of CITES. Similar problems plague efforts by Central American nations to staunch the flow of illegal exportation of endangered species.

Recent studies also indicate that national inspectors in most member nations lack adequate training to discharge effectively their responsibilities under CITES. In Bolivia the Forestry Development Center, a division of the Ministry of Agriculture, is responsible for issuing CITES permits. Unfortunately, most of the members of the Center have forestry backgrounds and often are unable to identify species by anything other than their common names. It is little wonder that Bolivia has had one of the worst records of compliance with CITES over the last decade.

Other nations are also plagued by similar problems. In Paraguay several government agencies that are authorized to issue import and export permits have no staff members with the expertise to ensure CITES compliance. Such shortcomings also are pervasive in developed countries such as the United States. For example, customs officials generally assign a low priority to wildlife law enforcement and only receive perfunctory training in species identification.

TRAFFIC, a program of the World Wildlife Fund which monitors international trade in animals and plants, conducted an experiment in an effort to assess the expertise of customs officials in CITES nations. TRAFFIC officials declared or displayed a cactus to customs officials in several countries, including the United Kingdom, the Soviet Union, Switzerland, Germany, Sweden, Denmark, and the United States. Despite the fact that virtually all cacti are protected under CITES, no questions were asked by officials in any of these countries about the species of the plant or its origins. While confiscation either occurred or was threatened, in the United States and the Soviet Union the officials' rationale was not related to possible CITES violations, but rather to health regulations. Officials in the United Kingdom also asked no questions when TRAFFIC sought to bring an orchid into the country from France, despite the fact that all species of orchids are listed in the CITES Appendices.

C. Trade with Non-Parties

Under CITES, parties to the Treaty are permitted to trade listed species with non-party states. In recent years, it has been estimated that trade between CITES parties and non-parties comprises approximately thirty percent of all wildlife transactions. Article X of CITES conditions such trade merely upon the issuance of "comparable documentation" by the non-party state which "substantially conforms with the requirements of the present Convention for permits and certificates."

Unfortunately, the Convention does not define the terms "comparable documentation," or "substantially conforms." The absence of objective standards to govern trade between CITES parties and non-parties has proven to be extremely detrimental to the protection of endangered species. One of the primary reasons that many nations have refused to ratify CITES is because it enables them to maintain a virtual monopoly in trade of certain species. For example, Mexico exported more than 73,000 kilograms of turtle leather and skins over a five-year period utilizing "comparable documentation" most of which was derived from Appendix I species of sea turtles. Mexican trade currently threatens the green sea turtle (chelonia mydas) with extinction. Trade between CITES parties and non-parties has similarly pushed the saltwater crocodile perilously close to extinction in recent years.

Under CITES, wildlife or wildlife products cannot be imported or exported unless a scientific finding has been made that the transaction does not threaten the continued viability of the species in question. This crucial element of CITES is jeopardized when transactions with non-parties are contemplated. . . . Smugglers have capitalized on the vague standards of Article X to obtain "comparable documentation" from officials in nonparty states that often contains inaccurate or wholly falsified information. The decision of many CITES members to accept shipments supported by such fraudulent documents has contributed to the imperiled existence of many species.

---

c.   CITES Enforcement

Since the late 1980s there has been growing concern among countries and among secretariat staff with the enforcement of CITES, especially with respect to African animals. In September 1994 countries in southern Africa adopted the Lusaka Agreement on Cooperative Enforcement Operations Directed at Illegal Trade in Wild Fauna and Flora, which provided a forum for a pilot experiment in a regional enforcement network. African elephants have been a major focus as poaching is exterminating them. Rural Africans kill elephants or destroy their habitat in order to survive or to sell their tusks. Elephants are dangerous competitors who drink water supplies dry, tear up trees and trample crops. In countries such as Kenya and Tanzania where over 80 percent of the people live off agriculture and human populations are rising at 3 or 4 percent each year, few families are willing to endure hunger so an elephant can live to provide a job for an urban-based tourist guide or a photo opportunity for a foreign tourist. The elephant was moved to Appendix I of the Convention from Appendix II by a 1989 decision of the

CITES parties, which meant that international trade in the elephant or elephant products, namely ivory, was banned. Five African countries entered reservations to the decision and were not, therefore, bound by the ban. Three of these countries—Botswana, Namibia, and Zimbabwe— proposed transfer of elephants to Appendix II in 1997 for the purpose of limited trade in elephant ivory to one trading partner, Japan, as well as limited trade in live animals, hides, and hunting trophies to other destinations. Satisfied with the precautions planned by these countries for controlling the elephant trade and with the strength of elephant populations, either stable or growing, in each country, the CITES secretariat recommended acceptance of the transfer, and the transfer was approved at the Tenth Meeting of the CITES Conference of the Parties in June 1997, in Zimbabwe. Further changes were made at the Eleventh and Twelfth Conferences of the Parties in 2000 and 2002 (see Conf. 10.10 (Rev. CoP12)).

Significantly, the controversial ban on ivory trade was retained at the Kyoto meeting. Five South African countries—Botswana, Malawi, Namibia, South Africa, and Zimbabwe—proposed an amendment that would downgrade the African elephant. They argued that the elephant population in their countries was stabilized and hunting should be strictly regulated, but not banned. A majority of CITES members, however, opposed the amendment, arguing that allowing the elephant to be hunted would cause poaching to increase dramatically. In theory, the Bush administration supported removal of the ban, believing it to be a "means of providing African governments with an economic incentive to preserve the elephant herds." The United States, however, opposed the amendment at the conference, asserting that some countries would not be able to protect the herds sufficiently. Countries were concerned about enforcement of the Convention and unanimously adopted a resolution indicting the EU for its illicit trading in endangered animals, mostly reptiles. Council Directive 92/65/EEC is concerned primarily with the prevention of infectious diseases from trade among member and non-member States.

As noted in the introduction to this section, however, Botswana, Namibia, and Zimbabwe prevailed in the effort to downgrade protection of the elephant in 1997. The web-published text of the CITES secretariat's recommendations to the CITES parties regarding the elephant proposals stated, in part:

> If the proposals were adopted, the Secretariat believes that, as the intention is only to allow export of ivory from the registered stocks direct from the proponent States to Japan in secure containers, under strictly controlled conditions, in one supervised shipment a year, there would be no significant risk of

ivory being illegally added to the shipments and thus traded in contravention of CITES.

In this context, it is noteworthy that the Panel of Experts has concluded that the import and export controls in place in Japan are adequate, although there is a need to strengthen internal controls of the retail trade to prevent the laundering of illegally obtained ivory at this level.

The proposed trade in live animals and hunting trophies seems unobjectionable. The same applies to the proposed trade in hides and the noncommercial trade (personal effects) in leather articles from Zimbabwe.

There is speculation that renewed trade in elephant ivory may lead to an escalation of poaching and an increase in illegal trade in elephant ivory. There is no way to assess these risks but the Secretariat believes that the proposed conditions would minimize them. In this connection, the Secretariat is concerned that those who spread stories to indicate that the proposals are designed to re-open "free" trade in ivory are acting against the conservation of the African elephant. In fact they should make every endeavor to ensure that the public is well informed that this is not the case.

Namibia and Zimbabwe have proposed that, in the event that their proposals are accepted and subsequently a Party becomes aware of abuses or aware that the proponent State is not honouring its commitments, the Standing Committee should be informed. If it is satisfied that there has been an abuse, it would request the Depositary Government to propose the retransfer of the population concerned to Appendix I by the postal procedure. A similar procedure could apply if the Standing Committee was satisfied that there was a significant increase in illegal trade in African elephant ivory as a result of the transfer to Appendix II.

No trade in elephant products should be permitted from any of the proponent States until its reservation on the inclusion of the African elephant in Appendix I has been withdrawn.

The parties, by secret ballot, approved the proposals by an approximate ratio of 3:1.

NOTE AND QUESTIONS

1. *It Gets Worse.* CITES has not stemmed the slaughter of elephants. Since 1997, there have been sustained attempts by certain countries to weaken the ban. In 1999, Botswana, Namibia and Zimbabwe were allowed an 'experimental one-off sale' of over 49,000kg of ivory to Japan. Then in 2002, a

further one off-sale was approved, which finally took place in 2008—and resulted in 105,000kg of ivory being shipped to China and Japan. Today, levels of poaching and illegal trade are spiraling out of control once again. In many areas, rates of poaching are now the worst they have been since 1989. In 2009, over 20,000kg of ivory was seized by police and customs authorities worldwide and in 2011, just thirteen of the largest seizures amounted to over 23,000kg, breaking all records since the ivory ban. http://www.bloodyivory. org/stop-the-ivory-trade. In July 2012 CITES recognized that elephant poaching had reached 'unsustainable' levels, which was prompted by soaring prices for ivory products

2. *Trade Versus Host Country Conservation.* Is controlling trade in endangered species an effective approach to species conservation? Many ecologists have noted that habitat loss is the primary threat facing species today. There has been a lively debate among experts about the best way to staunch the loss of CITES protected species. Laura H. Kosloff & Mark C. Trexler, *The Convention On International Trade In Endangered Species: No Carrot, but Where's the Stick?* 17 Envtl. L. Rep. 10, 222 (1987), criticize CITES because (1) it does not address the root problem of species survival, habitat loss, (2) trade is difficult to regulate because of the sheer volume of legal and illegal trade, and (3) "[t]o effectively control this trade, one would have to change the behavior of the hundreds of thousands of individuals involved in the harvesting, trading, processing, and marketing of relevant species. For many, the change would threaten their economic livelihood and is likely to be resisted. To actually monitor the trade controls would require tracking what leaves a particular country, what intermediate steps are made for processing, what products are manufactured from raw skins and other precursors to finished products, and where all these products ultimately go. Given the hundreds of thousands of shipments involved in the trade, and the many avenues by which they can move between a particular point of origin and their final point of consumption, this tracking presents an arguably insurmountable challenge." The remedy is therefore to create incentives in host countries to be stewards of their (and the world's) wildlife heritage. See Michael Glennon, *Has International Law Failed the Elephant?*, 84 Am. J. Intl. L. 1, (1990), which argues that poaching is the number one threat to elephants and See also Timothy Swanson, *Regulating Endangered Species*, Economic Policy 16 (Apr. 1993) argues that "[b]anning trade reduces the incentive for African countries to keep poachers out of the parks or to preserve elephant-friendly habitats."

3. *The Private Sector Role.* Do controlled hunts have a role in listed species conservation? A permit to kill a black rhino in Namibia, one of about 1,800 in the country, was auctioned by the Dallas Safari Club. The price, $350,000.00, was dedicated to rhino conservation in the host country. Private big game reserves have risen rapidly in Africa, but poaching continues. In 2012, "the insatiable demand for horns has sparked the worst recorded year of rhino poaching in South Africa in decades, with at least 588 rhinos killed so far, their carcasses rotting in private farms and national parks." http://

www.independent.co.uk/environment/nature/rhino-killings-for-horns-rise-rapidly-in-south-africa-8364209.html.

4.   *Supply or Demand?* Does it make sense to try control cross border trade without addressing the demand for products derived from species? Importing countries generally have the resources to enforce CITES compared with exporting ones, especially in Africa. The slaughter of African elephants is driven by the high ivory demand, especially in China, France, Japan and the United States. The largest consumer of ivory is China, but the demand for ivory manifests itself in many cultures. For example, the Philippines is also a major consumer. "Priests, . . . are major customers, according to Manila's most prominent ivory dealer. An antique dealer from New York City makes regular buying missions, as does a dealer from Mexico City, gathering up new ivory crucifixes, Madonnas, and baby Jesuses in bulk and smuggling them home in their luggage. Wherever there is a Filipino, I was often reminded, there is an altar to God." Bryan Christy, *Ivory Worship,* The National Geographic, May, 2014.

Curbing China's ivory consumption is difficult because carved ivory is a status symbol, especially for the many wealthy Chinese who buy ivory statues and carvings as investments. In a 2007 survey, the International Fund for Animal Welfare discovered that 70% of Chinese polled did not know that ivory came from dead elephants. To make things worse, in 2008 CITES allowed China to buy ivory at auction from various African countries. 15.5 million dollars were raised for conservation, but China was able to buy at low prices. It then raised prices when it sold the legal ivory, a step that created more incentives for poaching. Should countries such as China be encouraged to remove ivory from the market and take steps to reeducate its population? China and Hong Kong have begun to seize and destroy major stocks of ivory. Supporters of eliminating domestic markets argue that behavior can be changed. A poll by National Geographic and Ifop Asia, a company which has done extensive market surveys on luxury goods, found that 1 in 5 Chinese said they would stop buying ivory if their leaders denounced it. Others argue that efforts such as large, publicized burns are only feel good gestures that do not influence demand and leads to ivory hording on the expectation that prices will continue to rise in the future.

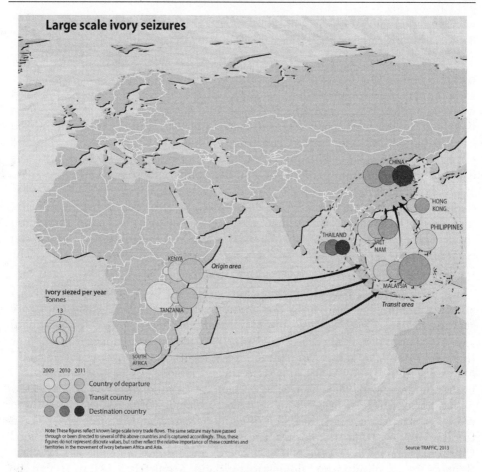

(UNEP/GRID-Arendal)

5. *Old fashioned Remedies.* The demand for tiger bones and rhino
horns in Asian traditional medicine is another problem. Tiger bone wine, for
example, is popular among China's government, military and business elite
because it is thought to impart the animal's strength to the drinker. China
has been condemned by environmental groups, such as Tiger Trust, for the
large illegal trade in tiger bones that is carried on in contravention to its
obligations under CITES. Three of the original eight sub-species of tiger are
now extinct. The number of wild tigers is estimated to be less than 7700 as of
early 2006, and tigers continue to be poached and traded from the East Asia.
China is one of the largest markets for tiger bones, a major ingredient in
traditional medicines. China is also the source of many illegal exports of tiger
products to the West. Declared by the Chinese government of the 1960s to be
pests, the number of tigers dropped to 100 in the late 1980s, as the revived
ancient medicinal values of the bones encouraged poaching. In 1986 China
set up a tiger breeding farm. The government argues that legalizing the trade
will deprive the poachers of profits, and thus help save the species. See

Richard Ellis, Tiger Bone & Rhino Horn: The Destruction of Wildlife For Traditional Medicine (2005).

d. Enforcing CITES in the United States

CITES is implemented through national legislation in the member countries. In the United States, The Endangered Species Act of 1973, 16 U.S.C. § 1538, and regulations issued pursuant thereto, 50 C.F.R. § 17.23 (1990) implement the Convention. How difficult is it to enforce the Convention in the United States? Consider Lujan v. Defenders of Wildlife, 504 U.S. 555 (1992), which made it significantly harder for environmental and other public-interest groups to gain standing to sue. The case involved the environmental group's challenge to a 1986 rule issued pursuant to the Endangered Species Act of 1973. The rule narrowed the scope of review of potentially threatening agency actions. The Defenders of Wildlife based its position on affidavits of two of its members, both of whose careers as professional naturalists who observed animals in their natural habitats were jeopardized by the rule. Writing for the Court, Justice Scalia dismissed the action for lack of standing, asserting that the plaintiffs did not exhibit the required injury in fact. In addition to narrowing the rule of standing, *Lujan* also put into doubt the constitutionality of citizen-suit provisions in many environmental laws and excluded some types of rules from judicial review. Nonetheless, the United States Fish and Wildlife Service can enforce CITES by reviewing an exporting State's decision.

CASTLEWOOD PRODUCTS, L.L.C. v. NORTON
United States Court of Appeals, District of Columbia, 2004
365 F.3d 1076

HARRY T. EDWARDS, CIRCUIT JUDGE:

This case concerns the United States' detention of several shipments of bigleaf mahogany from Brazil. The United States and Brazil are both signatories to the Convention on International Trade in Endangered Species of Wild Fauna and Flora, Mar. 3, 1973, 27 U.S.T. 1087 ("CITES" or "Convention"). The Convention governs trade in endangered species that are listed in its appendices. Article V provides that an export permit for species included in Appendix III can be granted by the exporting country only when, interalia, the designated Management Authority of the exporting country is satisfied that the specimen was not obtained in contravention of its laws. CITES, art. V(2)(a), 27 U.S.T. at1097. Brazil has included bigleaf mahogany in Appendix III. In the United States, the Endangered Species Act, 16 U.S.C. §§ 1531–44 (2000) ("ESA"), prohibits trade in violation of the Convention and authorizes the Secretary of the Interior and the Secretary of Agriculture to enforce the ESA. This case arose when the Animal and Plant Health Inspection Service ("APHIS") of the United States Department of Agriculture ("USDA") refused entry at U.S. ports to certain shipments of bigleaf mahogany after Brazil's Management Authority gave information to the United States Department of the Interior's Fish and Wildlife Service ("FWS") suggesting that the specimens in the shipments were not legally obtained. . . . The plaintiffs claimed that, because the export permits accompanying the shipments were signed and issued by Brazil's Management Authority, APHIS's detention of the shipments was arbitrary and capricious. The District Court denied the plaintiffs' motion for summary judgment and granted summary judgment to the Government, holding that the decision to detain the shipments was authorized by treaty, statute, and regulation. Castlewood Prods. v. Norton, 264 F.Supp.2d 9, 14 (D.D.C.2003). [Defendants] appealed and we now affirm the judgment of the District Court.

I.   BACKGROUND

A.   Regulatory Background

The Convention governs the import and export of certain species of endangered fauna and flora that are listed in its appendices. This case concerns bigleaf mahogany, which Brazil has included in Appendix III. Article V of CITES provides that the export of any species listed in Appendix III requires "the prior grant and presentation of an export permit." CITES, art. V(2), 27 U.S.T. at 1097. That article provides:

An export permit shall only be granted when the following conditions have been met:

(a) a Management Authority of the State of export is satisfied that the specimen was not obtained in contravention of the laws of that State for the protection of fauna and flora;

(b) a Management Authority of the State of export is satisfied that any living specimen will be so prepared and shipped as to minimize the risk of injury, damage to health or cruel treatment. Id. A Management Authority is designated by each state to "grant permits or certificates on behalf of that Party." Id., art. IX(1)(a), 27 U.S.T. at 1103. The United States has designated the Secretary of the Interior as the CITES Management Authority, and the Secretary's functions in this capacity are carried out through FWS. See 16 U.S.C. § 1537a(a). In Brazil, the Instituto Brasileiro do Meio Ambiente e dos Recursos Naturais Renovaveis or the Brazilian Institute of the Environment and Renewable Natural Resources (also known as "IBAMA") is the Management Authority under CITES.

Article VIII of the Convention provides:

(1) The Parties shall take appropriate measures to enforce the provisions of the present Convention and to prohibit trade in specimens in violation thereof. These shall include measures:

(a) to penalize trade in, or possession of, such specimens, or both; and

(b) to provide for the confiscation or return to the State of export of such specimens.

CITES, art. VIII(1)(a), 27 U.S.T. at 1101. Article XIV makes it clear that the Convention does not purport to limit the right of the Parties to adopt "stricter domestic measures regarding the conditions for trade, taking possession or transport of specimens of species included in Appendices I, II, and III, or complete prohibition thereof. . . ." Id., art. XIV(1)(a), 27 U.S.T. at 1108. Article XI provides for regular meetings of the Parties to the Convention, at which they may, inter alia, "make recommendations for improving the effectiveness of the present Convention." Id., art. XI(3)(e), 27 U.S.T. at 1105. These recommendations, adopted through resolutions, are intended to give guidance to the Parties in implementing the Convention. Since ratification, the Parties have adopted two resolutions recommending specific measures to strengthen enforcement of the Convention. One, Resolution 11.3, recommends that,

(c) if an importing country has reason to believe that an Appendix-II or -III species is traded in contravention of the laws of any country involved in the transaction, it:

(i) immediately inform the country whose laws were thought to have been violated and, to the extent possible, provide that country with copies of all documentation relating to the transaction; and

(ii) where possible, apply stricter domestic measures to that transaction as provided for in Article XIV of the Convention.

CITES, Resolution 11.3 (2000). The other, Resolution 12.3, recommends that "the Parties refuse to accept any permit or certificate that is invalid, including authentic documents that do not contain all the required information . . . or that contain information that brings into question the validity of the permit or certificate." CITES Resolution 12.3 § XIV(d) (2002) (recalling and incorporating CITES Resolution 10.2 § II(h) (1997)).

Congress implemented the Convention into U.S. law in the Endangered Species Act of 1973, Pub.L. No. 93–205, 87 Stat. 884 (codified as amended at 16 U.S.C. §§ 1531–44 (2000)).The ESA makes it unlawful to "engage in any trade in any specimens contrary to the provisions of the Convention." 16 U.S.C. § 1538(c)(1). It provides that any fish, wildlife or plants possessed or transferred in violation of the ESA or its regulations "shall be subject to forfeiture to the United States." 16 U.S.C. § 1540(e)(4)(A). The Secretary of the Interior is authorized to promulgate regulations as may be appropriate to enforce the ESA. 16 U.S.C. § 1540(f). The statute also provides for the coordination of the administration of the ESA between the Secretary of Agriculture and the Secretary of the Interior. 16 U.S.C. § 1540(h). FWS and APHIS work together to enforce the provisions of CITES.

The Department of the Interior has promulgated regulations to implement the ESA. See 50 C.F.R. pt. 23 (2003). One regulation provides: "In order to import into the United States any wildlife or plant listed in appendix III from a foreign country that has listed such animal or plant in appendix III, a valid foreign export permit or re-export certificate issued by such country must be obtained prior to such importation." 50 C.F.R. § 23.12(a)(3)(i). Another regulation states: "Only export permits, re-export certificates, certificates of origin, or other certificates issued and signed by a management authority will be accepted as a valid foreign document from a country that is a party to the Convention." 50 C.F.R. § 23.14(a).

B.   Factual Background

The facts are largely undisputed. In the fall of 2001, FWS and APHIS learned that the Brazilian government had imposed a moratorium on the logging, transport, and export of bigleaf mahogany timber. In February 2002, APHIS placed holds on shipments of bigleaf mahogany from Brazil. FWS sent a letter to IBAMA, noting that "none of the permits accompanying the shipments were endorsed . . . by the export inspection authorities in Brazil," and stating that USDA was detaining the shipments until officials in the United States could gain "verification of the validity of accompanying CITES permits." See Letter from Mark Albert, Branch of CITES Operations, FWS, to IBAMA of 2/15/02, Joint Appendix ("J.A.") 203–04. IBAMA informed FWS that recent shipments of bigleaf mahogany arriving in the United States from Brazil were accompanied by export permits hat IBAMA had issued pursuant to preliminary judicial injunctions. IBAMA stated that its issuance of these permits did not reflect its independent judgment that the mahogany had been obtained lawfully. . . . IBAMA informed FWS that it had appealed these decisions, the merits of which were pending. IBAMA pointed out that one injunction had been reversed, and that it was confident that "in the appeals, the second instance judges will probably follow the same guide, since the injunctions were being provided 'in audita altera parte' (Latin term to express 'without hearing the other part'). . . ." Id. at 2. The letter noted that bigleaf mahogany trade had ceased by law in Brazil, with an exception for certified timber. It also acknowledged that bigleaf mahogany continued to be logged illegally. FWS and IBAMA had a similar exchange about two other shipments of mahogany in March 2002. . . . In May 2, 2002, the President of IBAMA, Rômulo José Fernandes Barreto Mello, sent a letter to FWS invalidating Zachow's statements. Mello informed FWS that Zachow's letters did not express the point of view of the Brazilian government or IBAMA, and that Zachow had since been dismissed from his post. Letter from Mello to Thomas of 5/2/02, J.A. 227–29. Mello's letter also stated that IBAMA's law enforcement officials and technicians would determine the entire wood chain of custody for bigleaf mahogany from the forests and the trading companies in 2000 and 2001. The study would take into account the diminished volume of mahogany resulting from exports prior to the October 2001 ban. This was intended to determine the balance of sawn wood that could have been commercialized after the ban, and would therefore determine how much bigleaf mahogany came from a legal and known origin.

In a letter dated May 22, 2002, Mello clarified IBAMA's position regarding the permits issued pursuant to judicial command. He wrote that IBAMA "must not say that a judicial decision is not legal or not valid." Letter from Mello to Thomas of 5/22/02, J.A. 234. Mello stated further that "it has never been mentioned that CITES permits were not legal or not valid." However, Mello also noted that "the controls available nowadays at IBAMA do not allow us to state exactly the legality of each particular shipment." The letter provided survey data indicating that shipments of mahogany up to a certain volume had legal origin, but that "the legal origin of such exceeding volume is not confirmed by IBAMA, as required in Article V, paragraph 2(a) of the Convention." Subsequently, IBAMA presented tables to the CITES Secretariat showing the total volume of legally harvested timber by exporter. However, APHIS continued to detain other shipments of bigleaf mahogany. On July 23, 2002, the plaintiffs commenced this action in the United States District Court for the District of Columbia to compel the delivery of the mahogany shipments that were still being detained. They filed a complaint for injunctive and declaratory relief against APHIS, FWS, Gale A. Norton, in her official capacity as the Secretary of the Interior, Steven A. Williams, in his official capacity as the Director of FWS, Ann M. Veneman, in her official capacity as the Secretary of Agriculture, and Craig A. Reed, in his official capacity as Administrator of APHIS. The plaintiffs argued that, pursuant to the ESA and its implementing regulations, APHIS is required to validate a shipment for import upon presentment of all documentation required by the implementing regulations, and that a valid foreign export permit is the only document from the exporting country that is required under the Convention.

On January 23, 2003, APHIS entered a Memorandum for the Record "to document the decision of the U.S. Department of Agriculture (USDA) to refuse entry into the United States of certain shipments of bigleaf

mahogany lumber and veneers that the Convention on International
Trade in Endangered Species (CITES) management authority of Brazil
(known as IBAMA) has been unable to confirm originated from legal
sources." USDA, Memorandum for the Record, January 23, 2003, at 1,
J.A. 291. The memorandum stated:

> IBAMA confirmed that although it had issued the CITES export
> permits for the shipments, it had done so under court injunctions
> which it was appealing. IBAMA indicated it had not determined
> whether the mahogany had been legally acquired, which is a
> prerequisite to the issuance of a CITES export permit for this
> species. For that reason, APHIS has held those and subsequent
> mahogany shipments imported into the United States in order to
> determine from IBAMA if the mahogany was legally acquired.

The memorandum explained APHIS's position that, since it had the
express authority to seize and forfeit articles traded in violation of the
CITES treaty, it also had the discretion to choose a less drastic action,
such as to refuse entry to a commodity. It pointed out that its action
complied with CITES Resolution 10.2 § II(h), which recommended that
the signatories "not authorize the import of any specimen if they have
reason to believe that it was not legally acquired in the country of origin."
See USDA, Memorandum for the Record, January 23, 2003, at 3, J.A. 293
(quoting CITES Resolution 10.2 § II(h) (1997)) (recalled and incorporated
into CITES Resolution 12.3 (2002)).

The parties then filed cross-motions for summary judgment in the
District Court. The District Court determined that the decision to seize,
detain, and confiscate contraband specimens under the ESA was within
the agency's clear statutory and regulatory authority. Castlewood Prods.,
264 F.Supp.2d at 12–13. Based on the record before it, the District Court
found that APHIS and Brazilian officials had agreed to adopt a
"chronological approach," under which the United States would allow the
release of shipments in chronological order of shipping, until the total
amount released equaled the amount calculated by IBAMA to be of legal
origin. It noted that, "in every instance in which IBAMA has confirmed
the legality of a shipment, APHIS has released that shipment." The
District Court concluded that "the defendants' actions were in all respects
authorized by treaty, statute, and regulation, and that the government
did not act arbitrarily, capriciously, nor did it abuse its discretion in the
matter." It therefore granted the Government's motion for summary
judgment.

II. ANALYSIS

B. The Requirement of a "Valid Foreign Export Permit"

Appellants challenge the decision by FWS and APHIS to detain the
mahogany shipments as arbitrary and capricious, claiming that it rests

on impermissible interpretations of 50 C.F.R. §§ 23.12(a) and 23.14(a). We find no merit in this challenge.

Section 23.12(a)(3)(i) provides:

In order to import into the United States any wildlife or plant listed in appendix III from a foreign country that has listed such animal or plan in appendix III, a valid foreign export permit or re-export certificate issued by such country must be obtained prior to such importation.

50 C.F.R. § 23.12(a)(3)(i). APHIS detained the mahogany shipments at issue here, because, in its representations to FWS, "IBAMA indicated it had not determined whether the mahogany had been legally acquired, which is a prerequisite to the issuance of a CITES export permit for this species." USDA, Memorandum for the Record, January 23, 2003, at 1, J.A. 291. This application of the regulation reflects the Government's position that a foreign export permit cannot be "valid" under CITES absent an assurance from the exporting country "that the specimen was not obtained in contravention of the laws of that State." See CITES, art. V(2)(a), 27 U.S.T. at 1097.

Appellants argue that the Government's interpretation of § 23.12(a)(3)(i) is at odds with the plain text of § 23.14(a), which states:

Only export permits, re-export certificates, certificates of origin, or other certificates issued and signed by a management authority will be accepted as a valid foreign document from a country that is a party to the Convention.

50 C.F.R. § 23.14(a). Appellants contend that, under § 23.14(a), once the Management Authority of the exporting state has issued an export permit, the permit must be accepted as "valid" by authorities in the United States. In other words, according to appellants, the plain language of § 23.14(a) precludes United States agencies from imposing other conditions precedent to the import of Appendix III species. See Appellants' Br. at 16. This "plain language" argument is plainly wrong.

Section 23.12(a)(3)(i) merely requires a valid foreign export permit, but it does not specify the conditions that a foreign export permit must meet in order for U.S. officials to regard the permit as valid, i.e., to conclude that the exporting Management Authority was "satisfied that the specimen was not obtained in contravention of the laws of that State." CITES, art. V(2)(a), 27 U.S.T. at 1097. Section 23.14(a) requires that an export permit be issued and signed by the foreign Management Authority in order be accepted, but it does not say that these requirements are the only conditions that an agency may lawfully require before accepting a permit. Therefore, the language of the regulations is ambiguous as to whether U.S. officials may "look behind" a lawfully signed and issued export permit to determine whether the substantive requirements of

CITES (i.e., that the Management Authority was satisfied that the specimen was not obtained unlawfully) had actually been met.

The Supreme Court has held that, "[i]n situations in which 'the meaning of [regulatory] language is not free from doubt,' the reviewing court should give effect to the agency's interpretation so long as it is 'reasonable.'" Martin v. OSHRC, 499 U.S. 144, 150–51, 111 S.Ct. 1171, 1176, 113 L.Ed.2d 117 (1991) (quoting Ehlert v. United States, 402 U.S. 99, 105, 91 S.Ct. 1319, 1323, 28 L.Ed.2d 625 (1971)). Here, FWS and APHIS read § 23.12(a)(3)(i) as allowing U.S. officials to require more than facial satisfaction of § 23.14(a), at least in cases where the United States has reason to doubt whether the export permits in question were issued in compliance with CITES. The regulations were promulgated pursuant to the Secretary of the Interior's clear statutory authority under the ESA to "promulgate such regulations as may be appropriate to enforce" the ESA. See 16 U.S.C. § 1540(f). The ESA makes it "unlawful for any person subject to the jurisdiction of the United States to engage in any trade in any specimens contrary to the provisions of the Convention, or to possess any specimens traded contrary to the provisions of the Convention." 16 U.S.C. § 1538(c)(1). And, the stated purpose of the regulations at 50 C.F.R. pt. 23 is to "implement the Convention on International Trade in Endangered Species of Wild Fauna and Flora." 50 C.F.R. § 23.1(a). In light of these statutory and regulatory provisions, the Government acted reasonably in requiring more than facial satisfaction of § 23.14(a) when determining whether an export permit is "valid" (i.e., issued in compliance with CITES) under § 23.12(a)(3)(i). The regulations were promulgated to implement the ESA, which was itself passed, in part, to implement the Convention. The ESA specifically prohibits trade contrary to the provisions of the Convention, 16 U.S.C. § 1538(c), and provides that any specimens that are imported in violation of the ESA are subject to forfeiture to the United States, 16 U.S.C. § 1540(e)(4)(A). The Convention requires that an export permit for an Appendix III species shall only be granted when "a Management Authority of the State of export is satisfied that the specimen was not obtained in contravention of the laws of that State for the protection of fauna and flora." CITES, art. V(2)(a), 27 U.S.T. at 1097. Furthermore, Article XI provides for regular meetings of the Parties to the Convention, at which they may, inter alia, "make recommendations for improving the effectiveness of the present Convention." Id., art. XI(3)(e), 27 U.S.T. at 1105. These recommendations, adopted through resolutions, are intended to give guidance to the Parties in implementing the Convention. Resolution 11.3 recommends that, "if an importing country has reason to believe that an Appendix III species is traded in contravention of the laws of any country involved in the transaction, it ... immediately inform the country whose laws were thought to have been violated." CITES Resolution 11.3 (2000). And Resolution 12.3 recommends that "the Parties refuse to accept any permit or certificate that is invalid, including authentic documents that do not contain all the required information . . . or that contain information that brings into question the validity of the permit or certificate." CITES Resolution 12.3 § XIV(d) (2002) (repealing and incorporating CITES Resolution 10.2 § II(h) (1997)). These provisions, taken together, make it clear that the agencies' interpretation of the applicable regulations is perfectly reasonable. It is also clear here that, to date, there are no "valid" export permits for the disputed shipments. There is no dispute that Brazil's Management Authority questioned whether the goods in the disputed shipments were obtained legally. The United States thus had a reasonable basis for inquiring further and detaining the shipments until a finding of legal acquisition could be made. Appellants argue, and the Government does not dispute, that the CITES resolutions are merely recommendations to the Parties and, therefore, they are not binding on the United States. See Appellants' Br. at 22. This does not render the resolutions meaningless, however. There would be no point in the contracting states agreeing on resolutions only to then completely ignore them. Therefore, while not binding, it was surely reasonable for FWS and APHIS to look to the CITES resolutions for guidance in interpreting the regulations implementing CITES.

Furthermore, appellants' claim that they did not have notice of the Government's interpretation is meritless. It is clear from the text of the Convention that signatories may only issue export permits for Appendix III goods upon determining that they were legally obtained, so appellants can claim no surprise or confusion over this.

We also reject appellants' argument that the decision by a Brazilian federal court in Bianchini E Serafim LTDA v. IBAMA, Writ of Mandamus No.2002.001437–0 (10th Fed. Dist. Ct. of Curitiba, June 28, 2002), J.A. 262–65 (trans. Berlitz GlobalNet, J.A. 253–61), compels reversal in this case. See Appellants' Reply Br. at 12. The decision in Bianchini has no bearing on the shipments at issue in this case. The Government acknowledges that the United States will release detained shipments when judicial review in a foreign state concludes that the goods were legally obtained, regardless of whether the foreign Management Authority disagrees with the judicial decision. There is no serious dispute over this point. Indeed, the Government followed this precept in this case in response to the Bianchini decision.

The Brazilian federal district court's decision in Bianchini upheld a mandatory injunction directing IBAMA to issue an export permit for one exporter's shipment of bigleaf mahogany. The court explained:

> It appears that the exploitation of lumber and all of the subsequent operations were made in a proper manner and authorized by the autarchy until the issuance of the challenged [moratorium], which surprised the petitioner who already had

the merchandise in its warehouses and had signed contracts for export. Now, if from the time of the extraction, to the transport from Pará to this state, the merchandise had been handled properly and with the authorization of IBAMA, there could have been no grounds for suspicion that the lumber might have been extracted improperly . . . the fact that the extraction was done properly prior to suspension of the authorization for exploitation of the mahogany should not now complicate deals already signed. Bianchini (trans. Berlitz GlobalNet) at 5, J.A. 256. Following this decision, IBAMA informed FWS that, pursuant to that final judicial decision, "such wood was legally acquired and must be released." Although IBAMA had appealed the Bianchini decision, IBAMA declared that "such appeal must not uphold (impede) its accomplishment." Letter from Mello to Thomas of 9/26/02, J.A. 281. APHIS then authorized the release of the shipment at issue in Bianchini. See Letter from James (Bud) Petit de Mange, CITES and Plant Inspection Station Coordinator, USDA, APHIS, PPQ, to Indira Singh/Martin Feinstein, PPQ of 10/10/02, J.A. 282. However, Bianchini does not detract in any way from the reasonableness of APHIS's decision to detain other shipments for which no court or Management Authority has confirmed legal acquisition. Bianchini held that "the petitioner purchased, transported, and marketed the lumber before issuance of the restrictive regulation, in other words, with the permission previously granted by the environmental autarchy itself." Bianchini (trans. Berlitz GlobalNet) at 6, J.A. 257. That holding applied only to the wood in the specific shipment at issue in that case.

FRANKS V. SALAZAR

United States Court of Appeals, District of Columbia, 2011
816 F.Supp.2d 49

MEMORANDUM OPINION

ROYCE C. LAMBERTH, CHIEF JUDGE.

Thrill-seeking safari hunters willingly pay thousands of dollars for the privilege of shooting an African elephant. Sport hunting is legal in many African countries and can often benefit threatened elephant populations where the practice is carefully managed and revenue from hunting licenses is recycled into conservation programs. Without an effective wildlife management plan, however, the haphazard sport-killing of elephants may—intuitively enough—be detrimental to their survival as a species. For this and other reasons, the United States Fish & Wildlife Service ("the Service") determined that sport hunting in Mozambique would not "enhance" the survival of African elephants in that country—a prerequisite for allowing the import of a sporthunted trophy into the United States. See 50 C.F.R. 17.40(e)(3)(iii)(C). Accordingly, the Service denied plaintiffs' request for permission to import their elephant trophies from Mozambique into the United States. The agency's decision is rational and is supported by the administrative record, and defendants are therefore entitled to summary judgment.

I. BACKGROUND

Owing in large part to a violent civil war that plagued the country from 1977 to 1992, Mozambique has struggled to maintain a healthy population of African elephants since the mid-1970's. The number of elephants in Mozambique appears to have declined from between 50,000 and 65,000 in 1974 to an estimated 11,000 to 13,000 in 2002, though accurate population numbers during this time are somewhat elusive. Administrative Record ("AR") 13, 725. Much of the decline is directly attributable to illegal poaching for ivory, which the country has been unable to control effectively due to a lack of adequate resources. AR 942–44, 1993–95. But elephant populations have also suffered from defensive killings (to protect crops and property) and from the destruction of habitat. Id. Although Mozambique banned sport hunting in 1990, the ban was lifted in 1999 to allow a limited number of hunting licenses. AR 947, 1998.

Mozambique and the United States are both parties to the Convention on International Trade in Endangered Species of Wild Fauna and Flora ("CITES"), Mar. 3, 1973, 27 U.S.T. 1087, T.I.A.S. No. 8249, which governs the import and export of threatened species between signatories. [The discussion of the three Appendices is omitted] "Trade" in Appendix I specimens requires a permit from the designated Scientific Authority of both the importing and exporting nations. Id. art. III. Before issuing an export permit for an Appendix I specimen, the Scientific Authority of the exporting country—here, Mozambique's National Directorate of Forestry and Wildlife ("DNFFB")—must find that the export of such a trophy "will not be detrimental to the survival of that species." Id. art. III(2)(a). Similarly, before issuing an import permit, the Scientific Authority of the importing country—here, the Service—must make a separate, independent determination that the import of an African elephant trophy "will be for purposes which are not detrimental to the survival of the species involved." Id. art. III(3)(a); see 50 C.F.R. § 23.61(a).

These are commonly known as "non-detriment" findings. The United States implements CITES through the Endangered Species Act ("ESA"), 16 U.S.C. § 1531 et seq., which prohibits "trade in any specimens contrary to the provisions of the Convention." 16 U.S.C. § 1538(c)(1). Exercising its authority under § 1540(f), the Service has promulgated regulations setting out the various factors it considers in making non-detriment findings. See 50 C.F.R. § 23.61. The Service considers, for example, whether removal of an animal from the wild represents "sustainable use," id. § 23.61(c)(1), is part of a "management plan that is designed to eliminate over-utilization of the species," id. § 23.61(c)(2), or would "stimulate additional trade in the species," id. § 23.61(e)(3). These findings are based on the "best available biological information," and in cases where "insufficient information is available," the Service "take[s] precautionary measures and [is] unable to make the required finding of nondetriment." Id. § 23.61(f)(4). A special rule for African elephants— created pursuant to 16 U.S.C. §§ 1533(d) and 1539(a)(1)(A)—flatly prohibits the "[i]mport or export [of] any African elephant," with a narrow exception for sport-hunted trophies. 50 C.F.R. § 17.40(e)(3)(iii). The sport-hunted trophy exception requires the Service to determine that "the killing of the animal whose trophy is intended for import would enhance survival of the species." Id. § 17.40(e)(3)(iii)(C). This is commonly known as an "enhancement" finding. Thus, in addition to the permit requirements of 50 C.F.R. § 23.61 regarding non-detriment findings, a successful permit application must comply with the special "enhancement" rule for African elephants. See id. § 17.40(e)(3)(iii)(C).

The Service periodically receives permit applications from hunters seeking to bring home their trophies from African safaris. In November 1998, several years after the end of hostilities in Mozambique, the Service opened a line of communication with officials in the DNFFB, Mozambique's wildlife agency, requesting their help in assessing the status of the country's elephant population. Over the next several years, the Service sent Mozambique officials a series of written requests for information about the existence of an elephant management plan, domestic legislation related to elephant conservation, current population figures and sport-hunting quotas, the status of protected areas since the end of the civil war, and current estimates of illegal poaching activity. AR 84–91, 500–03, 688–89. Though Mozambique officials responded to these requests, the Service found their responses to be superficial and lacking in specific detail and scientific support. See AR 92–96, 569–72, 851–53. After several attempts to verify the requested information, the Service concluded that it did not have sufficient information to determine whether Mozambique had an elephant management plan, an accurate estimate of its elephant population, or the resources to control illegal poaching. AR 627–35, 725–27. These findings acquired significance for the plaintiffs in this case. Lawrence A. Franks, Steve Sellers and George J. Brown each shot and killed at least one elephant in Mozambique between 2000 and 2006. With the help of Conservation Force (a nonprofit organization acting as the hunters' "authorized representative"), they applied for permits to import their trophies into the United States. Am. Compl. ¶ 99 (Doc.29); see AR 318–19, 608–09, 671–72, 1047–48. Charles F. Robbins and Jesse R. Flowers, Jr., who both intended to hunt elephants in Mozambique between 2003 and 2005, filed similar permit applications prospectively. AR 490–91, 736–37. 1 The Service did not act on these requests for several years. While the administrative record reflects that the delay was caused in part by the DNFFB's failure to provide adequate responses to the agency's written questionnaires, the record also establishes that the Service did not "prioriti[ze]" these permit applications. AR 504. The Service eventually apologized for the "extreme delay in responding to [plaintiffs'] request[s]" when it ultimately denied most of these applications in July 2006. AR 1021–24. 2 The Service explained that after repeated attempts to obtain information from Mozambique on the benefits of sport hunting, it was unable to make the required enhancement and non-detriment findings. Id.

The Service gave several reasons for this conclusion. First, it had been unable to verify whether Mozambique had an effective elephant management plan. Though the plaintiffs had accompanied their permit applications with a copy of the DNFFB's National Strategy for the Management of Elephants in Mozambique, AR 97–122, the Service concluded that this was merely the "first step" in the process of implementing an effective wildlife management plan. AR 1022. Second, the Service had been unable to obtain adequate information from Mozambique regarding its elephant population. For example, the DNFFB could not provide an accurate headcount of elephants in Mozambique or quantify the extent of illegal poaching and defensive killings, and its sporthunting quotas were irrational and without scientific basis. Id. Finally, the Service expressed its view that Mozambique simply did not have the resources to enforce its existing conservation laws. Id.

After exhausting their administrative appeals, plaintiffs sued for declaratory and injunctive relief under the Administrative Procedure Act ("APA"), 5 U.S.C. § 702 et seq., seeking judicial review of the denial of their import permit applications. Shortly after the plaintiffs filed their complaint in May 2009, the Service denied Brown's remaining permit applications on September 3, 2009. AR 1974–77. Plaintiffs then filed an amended complaint raising nine claims, including additional claims related to the denial of Brown's remaining permit applications. Am Compl. ¶ 162–206. The parties then moved for judgment on the administrative record, and the case is now ripe for summary judgment.

II. STANDARD OF REVIEW

[The court's discussion of the arbitrary and capricious standard is omitted.]

III. ANALYSIS

Defendants are entitled to summary judgment because the administrative record demonstrates that the Service acted rationally in denying plaintiffs' permit applications. The Court will begin with several claims in plaintiffs' amended complaint that confront insurmountable procedural obstacles. For the remaining claims, application of the arbitrary and capricious standard leads to the conclusion that the Service acted rationally in denying plaintiffs' request to import their elephant trophies.

[In] . . . Conservation Force v. Salazar, 811 F.Supp.2d 18, 30–31, 2011 WL 3874816, at *9 (D.D.C.Sept. 1, 2011) [and] Marcum, 810 F.Supp.2d at 66–68, 2011 WL 3805666, at *8–*9. . . . plaintiffs' claims regarding the Service's alleged failure to process their permit applications were moot because, while the litigation was pending, the Service denied the outstanding permit applications. Thus, as is the case here, the requested declaratory relief would amount to an improper advisory opinion. . . .

B.   Plaintiffs' wrongful-permit-denial claims cannot be enforced via the ESA's citizen-suit provision.

. . . because they allege merely a "maladministration" of the ESA—not any violation of its substantive prohibitions. See Bennett v. Spear, 520 U.S. 154, 174, 117 S.Ct. 1154, 137 L.Ed.2d 281 (1997). . . .

In Claim V, plaintiffs argue that the ESA obligates the Service to "encourage, cooperate with and support" the conservation programs of foreign nations, see 16 U.S.C. § 1537(b)(1), and to "do all things necessary and appropriate to carry out" its designated functions under CITES, see id. § 1537a(b). Am. Compl. ¶¶ 182(b), 185. In Claim IX, plaintiffs further argue that the ESA requires the Service to "consult with" the Secretary to "insure that any action authorized, funded, or carried out by such agency . . . is not likely to jeopardize the continued existence of any endangered species." 16 U.S.C. § 1536(a)(2); see Am. Compl. ¶ 204. Plaintiffs claim that the Service's denial of their permit applications violated these affirmative duties.

These claims cannot be enforced via the ESA's citizen suit provision, 16 U.S.C. § 1540(g)(1), because they allege merely a "maladministration" of the ESA. See Bennett, 520 U.S. at 174, 117 S.Ct. 1154. Section 1540(g)(1) provides in relevant part:

> [A]ny person may commence a civil suit on his own behalf—(A) to enjoin any person, including the United States and any other governmental instrumentality . . . who is alleged to be in violation of any provision of this chapter or regulation issued under the authority thereof; or . . . (C) against the Secretary where there is alleged a failure of the Secretary to perform any act or duty under section 1533 of this title which is not discretionary. . . .

C. The Service did not engage in formal rulemaking requiring compliance with the APA's notice and comment procedures.

. . .

Plaintiffs nevertheless argue that the Service's decision to deny their permit applications in part because Mozambique did not have a national management plan or accurate population numbers violated a stipulation in Safari Club International v. Babbitt, No. 91–2523, 1994 U.S. Dist. LEXIS 18183 (D.D.C. Dec. 14, 1994), a case previously before this Court. In that case, Safari Club challenged the Service's internal guidelines for issuing elephant trophy permits on the ground that these guidelines had not undergone public notice and comment. This Court agreed, and thereafter, in exchange for the Service's withdrawal of the guidelines, the parties stipulated to dismissal of Safari Club's complaint. Plaintiffs in this case claim—with some justification—that the withdrawn guidelines overlap somewhat with the regulatory factors the Service applied in denying their permit applications. Am. Compl. § 180. However, as this Court concluded in Marcum, that by itself does not mean the Service has reinstated the withdrawn guidelines in violation of the stipulation. See Marcum, 810 F.Supp.2d at 72 n. 3, 2011 WL 3805666, at *14 n. 3. Nothing in plaintiffs' motion for summary judgment suggests the Service relied on the withdrawn guidelines as opposed to simply applying the regulatory factors under 50 C.F.R. §§ 23.61 and 17.40(e)(3)(iii)(C). For all of these reasons, defendants are entitled to summary judgment on Claim IV.

D. The Service acted rationally in denying plaintiffs' permit applications.

That leaves plaintiffs' final argument—that the Service's denial of their permit applications was arbitrary and capricious. Plaintiffs' remaining claims fail on the merits under the "highly deferential" arbitrary and capricious standard of review. See Costle, 657 F.2d at 283. The administrative record demonstrates that the Service acted rationally in denying plaintiffs' permit applications because the agency considered the relevant statutory and regulatory factors and provided a rational explanation for its decision. See id. Plaintiffs therefore cannot rebut the "strong presumption in favor of upholding decisions of the Service." American Wildlands v. Kempthorne, 478 F.Supp.2d 92, 96 (D.D.C.2007) (internal quotation marks omitted).

Recall that to grant a permit application, the Service must find that the import would be for purposes that are "not detrimental" to the survival of the species, 50 C.F.R. § 23.61(a), and indeed would serve to "enhance" the survival of the species, id. § 17.40(e)(3)(iii)(C). In making these decisions, the Service considers the various factors set out in § 23.61(c) and (e), see 16 U.S.C. § 1540(f), and makes factual findings regarding these factors based on the "best available biological information," 50 C.F.R. § 23.61(f)(4). Where "insufficient information is available," the Service "take[s] precautionary measures and [is] unable to make the required finding of non-detriment." Id. Importantly, the permit applicant bears the burden of providing sufficient information to support a non-detriment finding. Id. § 23.61(c).

The administrative record demonstrates that the Service considered the relevant statutory and regulatory factors and provided a rational explanation for its findings with respect to each factor. First, the Service considered whether the sport hunting at issue was "part of a biologically based sustainable use management plan that is designed to eliminate overutilization of the species." 50 C.F.R. § 23.61(c)(2). Based on the responses it received from Mozambique officials, the Service concluded that it lacked "sufficient information" to find that Mozambique had implemented an effective elephant management plan. AR 1022. Indeed, the record suggests that Mozambique's conservation efforts were poorly organized, underfunded, and in no position to oversee the controlled killing of elephants. AR 866–67. Plaintiffs claim that Mozambique had such a plan: the DNFFB's National Strategy for the Management of Elephants in Mozambique. AR 97–122. But the Service found that the National Strategy was just a "first step" toward a comprehensive wildlife management plan, and that it had not yet been implemented—or even ratified—by the Government of Mozambique. As the Service explained:

> No details were provide on specific research or survey projects to be conducted, how DNFFB's capacity to manage and protect elephants would be accomplished both legislatively and financially, and nothing to indicate what would be done about human elephant conflicts. We are not aware of any comprehensive plan that provided local communities with a stake in managing, protecting, and conserving elephants as both a natural and economic resource. In addition, it is not clear what level of legislative or financial commitment the Government of Mozambique would provide towards managing its elephant populations.

AR 1022. In light of this uncertainty, the Service could rationally take "precautionary measures" and find that the "best available" information did not establish the existence of an effective elephant management plan. See 50 C.F.R. § 23.61(f)(4). And contrary to plaintiffs' suggestion, the record reflects that the Service expressly considered and discussed the National Strategy in processing plaintiffs 'permit applications. AR 1022. Plaintiffs simply dislike the Service's discretionary finding that this was not a "management plan." See 50 C.F.R. § 23.61(c)(2).

Plaintiffs resist this conclusion, pointing to the existence of two community-based conservation projects in Mozambique—the Tchuma Tchato Community Project and the Niassa Game Reserve—which provide localized oversight of elephant herds through the financial support of private donors and non-government organizations like the World Wildlife Fund. Plaintiffs tout the success of these local projects and argue that because Franks, Sellers and Brown each shot their elephants in one of these community-based reserve areas, the Service should have evaluated the existence of an elephant "management plan" at the local level—rather than, as it did, at the "nationwide" level. Pls.' Mem. at 21–22.

But the Service had good reason to adhere to its "countrywide" approach. The administrative record reflects that these community-based projects were designed by professional wildlife biologists from other countries and are totally dependent on private donations and NGO funding for their survival. Although the Government of Mozambique has given its blessing to these projects, they are not government-sponsored programs and include only a fraction of the country's elephant population. And while revenue from the sale of hunting licenses in these areas was being distributed among the national and local governments and the community, AR 869, there is no evidence that this money was actually being recycled back into the maintenance of local elephant reserves.

Plaintiffs point out that in the letters informing them of the denial of their requests for reconsideration, the Service stated that it "supports the formulation of a comprehensive plan for community-based management of natural resources that could provide local communities with a stake in the management and conservation of elephants." AR 1958. But it was precisely the lack of a "comprehensive plan" for the use of these local projects that the Service found troubling. And even the existing community-based projects to which plaintiffs refer were not financially self-sustaining at the time plaintiffs submitted their requests. AR 1958 ("Although some community-based projects have been established and are currently operating in Mozambique, they were not functioning at the time you took your trophy."). Thus, the Service acted rationally in finding that the Tchuma Tchato and Niassa projects were not the equivalent of a "biologically based sustainable-use management plan." See 50 C.F.R. § 23.61(c)(2).

Second, the Service considered a number of factors generally addressing whether, despite the absence of a management plan, the sport-hunting of elephants in Mozambique was nevertheless "sustainable." 50 C.F.R. § 23.61(c)(1). These factors include, for example, whether sport hunting "would not contribute to the over-utilization of the species," id. § 23.61(c)(3), "would pose no net harm to the status of the species in the wild," id. § 23.61(c)(4), and "would not stimulate additional trade in the species," id. § 23.61(e)(3). The Service again concluded that it lacked "sufficient information" to make these findings because it had been unable to obtain adequate responses from the Mozambique government regarding its elephant population. AR 1021–24.

The Service found several deficiencies in the information supplied by Mozambique. For one thing, the DNFFB could not provide actual population numbers for elephants in Mozambique or quantify the extent of illegal poaching and defensive killings. Id. at 1022. The Service explained that:

> [M]ost of the information on elephant population size, distribution, and dynamics is based on informed guesses. As of 2005, there has been a lack of adequate research and survey work to be able to establish the actual population numbers and the extent that migration impacts population estimates.

Id. For another thing, the Service found that there was insufficient evidence that Mozambique's elephant hunting quotas were scientifically based and sustainable. Id. The Service explained that the hunting quotas were irrational and disconnected from the government's own policy on sport hunting. AR 1022–23. For example, in 1997 and 1998, Mozambique established export quotas of 50 and 20 elephants respectively, even though there was a ban on sport hunting of elephants until 1999. AR 1022. But after the ban on sport-hunting was lifted, Mozambique officials claimed that the quota was reduced to 10 elephants per year. Id. There was apparently "no scientific basis upon which these quotas have been established each year" since "the actual elephant population in Mozambique is not currently known." Id. And for a third thing, the DNFFB's vague responses regarding the extent of illegal poaching and defensive killings "raise[d] concerns about what impact any level of take involving elephant sport-hunting is having on the wild population." Id. at 1023.

Plaintiffs claim that the Service's insistence on "actual population numbers" was unlawful, arguing that the ESA was amended in 1982 to eliminate population estimates as a precondition for non-detriment findings. See 16 U.S.C. § 1537a(c)(2) ("[T]he Secretary . . . is not required to make, or require any state to make, estimates of population size in making such determinations."). Plaintiffs rely on Defenders of Wildlife v. Endangered Species Scientific Auth., 725 F.2d 726 (D.C.Cir.1984), in which the D.C. Circuit stated that population estimates are no longer a valid requirement for non-detriment findings. But the fact that the Service "is not required to make . . . estimates of population size" does not mean the Service may not consider the absence of reliable population data as a factor in making a discretionary nondetriment finding. After all, the Service must still base its determination on the "best available biological evidence." 16 U.S.C. § 1537a(c)(2). And even Defenders of Wildlife recognizes that the statutory amendment preserves "the discretion of the Secretary" to consider population estimates. 725 F.2d at 731.

Third, the Service concluded that Mozambique simply did not have the financial or human resources to manage the sport hunting of elephants. AR 1023. The Service reasoned that although domestic laws relating to elephant conservation in Mozambique had been in place for many years, it was difficult for the DNFFB to enforce these laws due to inadequate resources. Id. . . .

NOTE: THE UNITED STATES' ROLE IN IVORY TRADE

The worked ivory has been either sold domestically or shipped to consumer states such as the United States. The United States has imported about 30 percent of worked ivory that enters the international trade. About a third of Hong Kong's worked ivory exports have been sent to the United States. It has been estimated that about 80 percent of the ivory sold in the United States was obtained illegally. Ivory now sells for $1,500 per pound. Africa is losing an estimated 35,000 elephants a year to poaching, with total numbers down to less than 500,000. In 2014, the United States Fish and Wildlife Service issued a strict Enforcement Directive:

United States Fish and Wildlife Service, Director's Order 210, February 25, 2014:

a.   Service employees must strictly implement and enforce all criteria under the ESA antique exception (16 U.S.C. 1539(h)). The ESA requires that any person claiming the benefit of a statutory exemption has the burden of proving that the exemption is applicable (16 U.S.C. 1539(g)) so the burden of proof is on the importer, exporter, or seller to definitively show that an item meets all of the criteria under the exception. The burden of proof standard is high to ensure that items that people claim are antiques under the ESA exception are authentic and qualify for the exception. See Appendix 1 for additional guidance.

b.   Service employees must strictly implement and enforce the June 9, 1989, (AECA moratorium, 54 Fed. Reg. 24758) on the importation of raw and worked African elephant ivory while, as a matter of law enforcement discretion, allowing importation of certain parts and products, as follows:

(1) Raw or worked African elephant ivory imported by an employee or agent of a Federal, State, or tribal government agency for law enforcement purposes.

(2) Raw or worked African elephant ivory imported for genuine scientific purposes that will contribute to conservation of the species.

(3) Worked African elephant ivory imported for personal use as part of a household move or as part of an inheritance, provided that the worked elephant ivory:

- Was legally acquired prior to February 26, 1976;

- Has not subsequently been transferred from one person to another person for financial gain or profit since February 26, 1976; and

- The item is accompanied by a valid Convention on International Trade in Endangered Species of Wild Fauna and Flora (CITES) pre-Convention certificate.

(4) Worked African elephant ivory imported as part of a musical instrument, provided that the worked elephant ivory:

- Was legally acquired prior to February 26, 1976;

- Has not subsequently been transferred from one person to another person for financial gain or profit since February 26, 1976;

- The person or group qualifies for a CITES musical instrument certificate; and

- The musical instrument containing elephant ivory is accompanied by a valid CITES musical instrument certificate or an equivalent CITES document that meets all of the requirements of CITES Resolution Conf. 16.8.

(5) Worked African elephant ivory imported as part of a travelling exhibition, provided that the worked elephant ivory:

- Was legally acquired prior to February 26, 1976;

- Has not subsequently been transferred from one person to another person for financial gain or profit since February 26, 1976;

- The person or group qualifies for a CITES travelling exhibition certificate; and

- The item containing elephant ivory is accompanied by a valid CITES travelling exhibition certificate or an equivalent CITES document that meets the requirements of 50 CFR 23.49.

NOTES AND QUESTIONS

A rising concert pianist in California has a 100-year-old Steinway piano with ivory keys given to her by her teacher. In 2015, the pianist decided to stop playing an instrument with ivory keys and purchased a new Bösendorfer piano from Vienna. To finance the purchase, the pianist found a buyer in another state. However, the buyer has refused to complete the sale because although the piano was acquired prior to 1976, the seller cannot prove the ivory in the keys had entered the country through one of 13 American ports authorized to sanction ivory goods. In 2014, the Budapest Festival Orchestra members had their violin bows confiscated when they landed in Newark, New Jersey. A Fish and Wildlife Service agent found that the tips of seven of the bows were made from elephant ivory and the Orchestra lacked a CITES certificate proving that they were antique. Given that none of those entry points had such legal power until 1982, the regulations would make it virtually impossible to legitimize the piano's ivory, the experts said. That predicament would apply to virtually all the antique ivory in the country, barring millions of Americans from ever selling items as innocuous as teacups, dice or fountain pens. The Orchestra was, however, allowed to re-export the bows to Hungary. In 2014, New York enacted a ban of ivory sales with only four exceptions: 100-year-old antiques comprised of less than 20 percent elephant ivory with documented proof of provenance, musical instruments (string, wind and piano) manufactured prior to 1975, elephant ivory where transfer of ownership is for education and scientific purposes, including to a museum authorized by a special charter from the legislature, and elephant ivory where transfer is to a legal beneficiary of a trust or estate What do the prohibition of sales of old ivory items have to do with the slaughter of elephants? In July, 2015, the Fish and Wildlife service announced its intention to propose new ivory trade rules which allow very limited sales to address the concerns of those with "undocumented" antique ivory items.

The African Elephant Conservation Act provides that "[w]hoever knowingly violates" the prohibition against illegal ivory imports is criminally liable, including fines and imprisonment. United States v. Grigsby, 111 F.3d 806 (11th Cir. 1997), holds that government must prove specific rather than general intent:

"The initial draft provided criminal penalties for '[a]ny person who willfully commits an act which violates any provision of this Act.'" Id. at § 6(b) (emphasis added). Responding to the request for views on the proposed legislation, B. Wayne Vance, General Counsel of the United States Department of Transportation, emphasized the apparent interpretive confusion in the legislative description of the civil and criminal violative acts:

> Section 6(a)(1) (page 5, lines 23–4) creates civil penalties against a person who "knowingly violates" the bill, but section 6(b) (page 7, lines 18–9) creates criminal penalties against a person who "willfully commits an act" which violates the bill. If a distinction between "knowingly" and "willfully" is intended, it should be clarified in some way.

African Elephant Conservation: Hearing on H.R. 2999 and H.R. 4849 Before the Subcomm. on Fisheries and Wildlife Conservation and the Environment of the House Comm. on Merchant Marine and Fisheries, 100th Cong., 2d Sess. 64–65 (1988) (letter of B. Wayne Vance, General Counsel, U.S. Dept. of Transp.) (emphasis added).

In the final version of the AECA, codified at 16 U.S.C. § 4224(a), "[w]hoever knowingly violates section 4223," is subject to criminal penalties and "[w]hoever violates section 4223" is subject to civil penalties. 16 U.S.C. § 4224(a) & (b) (emphasis added). While "knowingly" is omitted from the codified civil penalties provision, it significantly is included in the criminal penalties provision. Thus, in the final version of the statute, the adverb "knowingly" modifies the verb "violates" and connotes deliberate, cognitive or specific intent as a requirement for criminal violation of section 4224(a).Thus, the government must provide both that defendant was aware that he or she was bringing ivory into the United and that the person knew that importation was illegal.

Who bears the burden of proof for proving or disproving an illegal sale under the 2014 regulations? Are they consistent with the holding in Grigsby?

NOTE: THE KILLING OF CECIL

In July, 2015, a Minneapolis dentist killed a thirteen year old lion, Cecil, in Zimbabwe. Cecil lived in a sanctuary in the Hwange National Park and was apparently lured into unprotected territory. The dentist first shot Cecil with a crossbow and then tracked him for two days before shooting the lion. Kate Rogers, American Hunter Kills Cecil, Beloved Lion Who was Lured Out of His Sanctuary, The New York Times, July 28, 2015. The dentist returned to the United States, but Zimbabwean officials announced that they planned to request his extradition under a 1997 treaty between the two countries. On July 31, 2015, the White House was presented with a 140,000 signature petition to extradite the hunter, and under United States extradition policy, any petition over 100,000 signatures mandates an administration response. See Machael John Garcia and Charles Doyle, Extradition To and From the United States: Overview of the Law and Recent Treaties (Congressional Research Service 2010), *available at* https://www.fas.org/sgp/crs/misc/98-958. pdf.

4. REGIONAL WILDLIFE PROTECTION AGREEMENTS

a. Western Hemisphere/OAS—The Convention on Nature Protection and Wildlife Preservation in the Western Hemisphere (Oct. 12, 1940, Effective Apr. 30, 1942)

One of the earliest of the multilateral agreements concerning wildlife preservation is the 1940 Organization of American States' Convention on Nature Protection and Wildlife Preservation in the Western Hemisphere.[2] This convention covers both flora and fauna and land areas of "extraordinary beauty." Under the convention states have a duty to establish wildlife parks as nature reserves and to prohibit commercial profitmaking in them. They must notify the OAS when the reserves are established.

In the second half of the 1970s, in connection with the Panama Canal Treaty, parties adopted an Agreement Pursuant to Article VI of the Convention on Nature Protection and Wildlife Preservation in the

---

[2]   T.S. 981, Bevans 630, U.N.T.S. 193.

Western Hemisphere to establish additional nature reserves, including one on Barro Colorado Island.[3] Article IX of the 1940 Convention specifies that export permits must be required for trade of endangered species. However, there are no mechanisms for resolving disputes or ensuring compliance with the treaty's provisions. Since most of the parties are also members of CITES, the lack of enforcement of the 1940 Convention is less critical than it otherwise might be.

NOTES AND QUESTIONS

CITES Implementation in the western hemisphere. For an early discussion of the implementation of CITES in the western hemisphere and the relation between national laws and CITES, *see* Kathryn S. Fuller & B. Swift, Latin American Wildlife Trade Laws (1985); Kathryn S. Fuller et al., *Wildlife Trade law Implementation in Developing Countries: The Experience in Latin America,* 5 B.U. Intl. L.J. 289 (1987).

b. Africa—African Convention on the Conservation of Nature and Natural Resources (Sept. 15, 1968, Effective June 16, 1969)

Africa is home to remarkable wildlife. To protect this resource, the members of the Organization of African Unity concluded the African Convention on the Conservation of Nature and Natural Resources. (1001 U.N.T.S. 3 (9/15/68).) Using language that sounds similar to a call for sustainable development and use, the Convention calls for members to protect natural resources by "all necessary measures" (Article VI) in order "to ensure conservation, utilization and development . . . in the best interests of the people." (Article II.) Trade in endangered species is addressed in Article IX, which calls for regulation of all trade of certain species.

NOTES AND QUESTIONS

1. *African wildlife laws.* An excellent source that lists and summarizes wildlife laws in Africa by country was produced by an IUCN project aimed at helping to implement CITES. *See* IUCN Environmental Law Centre, Cyril de Klemm, & Barbara Lausche, African Wildlife Laws (1987).

2. *Environmental conservation.* For an early work promoting environment conservation in Africa, *see generally* N.C. Pollock & B. Litt, Animals, Environment and Man in Africa (1975).

---

[3] United States International Trade Commission, International Agreements to Protect the Environment and Wildlife 5–33–5–36 (1991).

c. South East Asia—Association of South East Asian Nations (ASEAN) Agreement on the Conservation of Nature and Natural Resources, July 9, 1985 (Not Yet in Force)

ASEAN members include Brunei Darussalam, Cambodia, Indonesia, Lao PDR, Malaysia, Myanmar (Burma), Philippines, Singapore, Thailand, and Viet Nam.

The 1985 ASEAN Agreement illustrates the evolution of regional natural resources protection agreements from ones that focus on controlling trade in endangered species to ones that rely primarily on protection of ecosystems. The Agreement covers conservation of both species and ecosystems, however, including issues related to biological diversity, establishment of reserves, environmental impact assessment, scientific research, and public participation in the planning and implementation of conservation measures.

Article 5 of the Agreement regulates trade in both endangered and endemic species and obligates parties "wherever possible" to prohibit the taking of "endangered species recognized by the Contracting Parties as of prime importance to the Region and deserving special attention." However, the Agreement does not require export and import permits as does CITES.

NOTES AND QUESTIONS

1. *Asian compliance with CITES.* For compliance with CITES, see Eric McFadden, *Asian Compliance with CITES: Problems and Prospects*, 5 B.U. Intl. L.J. 311 (1987). In recent years, one of the major CITIES compliance problems has been trade in snakes, whose skins are used in luxury goods. *See* CITES Decision 15.75, http://www.cites.org/sites/default/files/eng/com/sc/61/E61–46–01.pdf. In 2013, Kering, which owns a number of the top luxury good brands, entered into the 'Python Conservation Partnership', a collaboration with the International Trade Centre and the International Union for Conservation of Nature, to help facilitate industry-wide change. *See* more at: http://www.kering.com/en/communiques-de-presse/kering_luicn_et_le_cci_forment_un_partenariat_pour_contribuer_a_un_commerce_de.

2. *Japan and CITES.* For a detailed discussion of Japanese compliance with CITES, *see* James V. Feinerman and Koichiro Fujikura, *Japan: Consensus-Based Compliance*, in Engaging Countries: Strengthening Compliance with International Environmental Accords (Edith Brown Weiss & Harold K Jacobson eds., 1998). For an overview of Japan's 1987 law regulating internal trade in endangered species and how it relates to CITES, *see* Hiroji Isozaki, *Japan's New Law on Endangered Species*, 7 B.U. Intl. L.J. 211 (1989) (examining Law for Regulation, etc., of the Transfer of Endangered Species of Wild Fauna and Flora (No. 58), June 2, 1987 (Japan)). *See also* Gray-Schofield, Trends in Wildlife Trade from India to the United States, TRAFFIC (U.S.A.) (1983).

d. Europe—Declaration on the Conservation of Flora, Fauna, and Their Habitats, 1988

In 1988, the members of the then Economic Commission for Europe (ECE) adopted a declaration to conserve endangered species and species native to Europe. (Declaration on the Conservation of Flora, Fauna and Their Habitats, ECE/ ENVWA/6 (1988).) This Declaration was intended to foster in situ conservation efforts in Europe and led to the creation of the European Red List of Globally Threatened Animals and Plants, which applies to any species put on the list, even if not threatened in that country. (ECE/ ENVWA/20 (1991).)

In 1992, the governments of the then ECE have adopted a Code of Practice for the Conservation of Threatened Animals and Plants and Other Species of International Significance. (ECE/ENVWA/24 (1992).) This Code, including a list of birds and mammals that live mainly in Europe, was intended to help member governments formulate and implement conservation policies for the protection of their biological resources.

Of particular importance are the basic principles set out in Part II of the Code, "[c]ountries should strive to maintain biological diversity within their jurisdiction and control"; "[m]easures to safeguard species should be based on the precautionary principle"; "[c]onservation of wild animals and plants should be integrated with economic activities as an integral component of sustainable development." (Code of Practice for the Conservation of Threatened Animals and Plants, ECE/ENVWA/24, 11(10), (11), (12) (1988).) Additionally, the Code includes a provision for updating the list of significant species. (Code, III (21).) While not explicit, the requirement of including the relevant data on each species' population seems to suggest that a species may be taken off, as well as put on, a list.

The Code includes separate provisions on public participation in implementing conservation measures. (Public awareness and participation. Code, IV (51)–(59).) The media, NGOs, and individual citizens are among those groups named specifically by the Code, as are formal organizations and the scientific community.

5. PROTECTING WHALES AND OTHER MARINE MAMMALS[4]

Whales are mostly found in marine areas outside a state's territorial sea, but they are often present within a country's 200 nautical mile Exclusive Economic Zone. Thus, protection of them raises intriguing legal issues regarding the conservation of marine mammals in shared areas and States' compliance with international resource regimes.

---

[4] See Lanie Kropp, Memorandum on Whales and Other Species, 1992, edited and updated by authors and on file with authors. Footnotes not included.

The following material provides a historical review of efforts to develop an effective regime to ensure the conservation of whales.

a. Introduction

When Earth's whale population sharply decreased in the early 1900s, several countries attempted to regulate whaling off their coasts in order to preserve populations for future commercial whaling. They were not successful, however, because most whaling takes place on the high seas, where the traditional doctrine of freedom of the seas governed. This doctrine was interpreted to allow harvesting without restriction. The International Council for the Exploration of the Sea, established in 1902, tried to bypass the inability of individual countries to control the high seas by calling for an international effort to regulate whaling see A. Went, 70 Years A-growing, ICES (1972). Resulting from this and other efforts, the 1931 International Convention for the Regulation of Whaling banned the harvest of two species and imposed other restrictions.[5] The absence of several major whaling states from the Convention, combined with the lack of enforcement devices, specific penalties, or basic amendment procedures to take account of new scientific data, rendered the Convention too weak to combat the severity of the whaling problem.

To remedy these defaults, in 1946, countries the International Convention for the Regulation of Whaling (ICRW). In contrast to the earlier Convention, it introduced a schedule that annually identified protected species and set catch quotas, size limits, and whaling methods for various whale species in light of new scientific evidence. Further, it established the International Whaling Commission (IWC) to implement the guidelines set out in the schedule. However, the IWC, like the 1931 Convention, is not equipped with an enforcement mechanism adequate to ensure that its recommendations are followed. In addition, a provision was added that allows countries to opt out of whaling regulations by objecting to them in a timely manner. This provision has proved troublesome to the IWC, especially in enforcing a 1982 whaling moratorium.

Contrary to popular perception today, the Convention was designed to preserve the whaling industry by initiating measures to conserve whale stocks, not to put a halt to whaling altogether. The preamble to the Convention provides that it is the parties' desire "to establish a system of international regulation for the whale fisheries to ensure proper and effective conservation and development of whale stocks . . . and thus make possible the orderly development of the whaling industry." 3 International Convention for the Regulation of Whaling, 161 U.N.T.S. 2/24, (1964). In 1982 the IWC adopted a moratorium on all commercial whaling, to which Japan, Norway, Peru, and the USSR objected. Peru

---

[5]   49 Stat. 3079, TS 880.

since withdrew its objection, as has Japan with respect to commercial pelagic whaling and coastal whaling for minke, Bryde's, and sperm whales. As long as the moratorium continues in force, the only whaling that is legal for the countries which have not objected must fall under the aboriginal whaling exception or the scientific research exception. Both exceptions have been troublesome. The first allows aborigines to take whales as long as they are used and consumed by the community alone. Because the term "aborigine" was never defined, some States, particularly Japan, argue that any community that is culturally and economically dependent on whaling should qualify under the exception. Such arguments have been continuously rejected by the IWC. States that claim to hunt under the scientific-research exception have been accused of hiding their commercial kills under the mask of "research" and thus undermining the moratorium. See the 2014 decision of the International Court of Justice in Australia v. Japan, discussed in section iv, below. Although this problem is partially alleviated by having the scientific committee review all research applications, the committee's recommendations are not binding. In addition, the inefficiency of any type of observer scheme means that "pirating," taking whales clandestinely, goes largely unchecked. Today, the consumption of whale meat is primarily limited to Canada, Greenland, Iceland, Norway, Japan and the Inuit people of Alaska in of the United States. Whale meat consumption in Norway is falling, despite government subsidies, as whale meat is expensive and considered old-fashioned. Consumption is even falling rapidly in Japan, and the operation of the fleet is dependent upon government subsidies. But, whaling still has its moral defenders. See Arne Kalland, Unveiling the Whale: Discourses on Whales and Whaling (2010).

In defiance of the IWC moratorium, Norway, which had objected to the IWC's whaling ban, announced in 1992 that it would allow commercial whaling of the minke whale beginning in 1993. Norway contended that sound scientific evidence exists that the minke whale was no longer endangered and hence should not be covered by the moratorium. The IWC questioned the reliability of this evidence. Moreover, a continuation of the moratorium would, in Norway's eyes, violate the basis of the Convention, which was intended to manage whales on a scientific basis not to prohibit their hunting indefinitely. The IWC, at its annual meetings in 1995 and 1996, urged Norway to stop whaling and to reconsider its objection to the moratorium. In 1996 this caused Norway to walk out of the IWC meeting, though the delegation maintained that they had no intention of withdrawing from the IWC permanently. Norway continued to hunt whales, with a 1996 quota almost double that of 1995, and in April 1996, Norwegian ships were caught by Japanese officials trying to smuggle whale meat from Oslo marked "mackerel" into that country. At its meeting in 1996, the IWC passed a resolution that called on the commission to play a role in the development and monitoring of whale watching, a fast growing tourist industry. The IWC feared that whale watching, a nonconsumptive and economically profitable use of whales, could pose a threat to whales if not correctly regulated. Increases in boat traffic can affect the behavior of whales and interrupt their breeding patterns. The noise and pollution, if excessive, could disturb the whales' sensitive hearing necessary for communication underwater. The World Wildlife Federation estimated that more than four million people went on whale watching trips in 1992. A 2008 study put the number at 13 million. O'Connor, S., Campbell, R., Cortez, H., & Knowles, T. Whale Watching Worldwide: tourism numbers, expenditures and expanding economic benefits, a special report from the International Fund for Animal Welfare, Yarmouth MA, USA, prepared by Economists at Large (2009).

Japan argued strongly for lifting the moratorium on whaling, and many of the countries that joined the Convention after 1998 (some of which have no sea coast or do not engage in whaling) were sympathetic. Japan used its foreign aid program to "induce" some countries to support its position on whaling.

b.   The Scientific Basis for Protecting Whales

In the 1990s and more recently, most of the debate in the IWC has centered on issues of science. Originally, whaling countries believed that scientific data would be applied so as to maximize the growth of the whaling industry while minimizing the threat to the species. What occurred, however, was not a tempered and controlled harvesting, but an unrestrained worldwide slaughter of the whale, rationalized by its alleged "scientific" basis. As the severity of this onslaught became known, antiwhaling countries pointed to the lack of accurate data and the need for a new system for measuring whale stocks, claiming that until such gaps were filled, commercial whaling would extinguish the whales. The success of their efforts culminated in 1982 with the adoption of the moratorium on commercial whaling. Purposefully kept out of the amendment was any language referring to a "permanent" ban, the mention of which would certainly have blocked its passage. Rather, the "cessation" of commercial whaling was to begin in the 1985–86 season and be kept under review based upon "the best scientific advice" until 1990. By that year, the scientific committee was to assess the status of the whale stocks as well as develop a "Revised Management Procedure" (RMP) which would set optimum population and catch sizes. Based on this information, the Convention would then determine whether to continue the moratorium, modify it, or end it altogether.

In 1991, the IWC adopted a management procedure that used computer models to set quotas. It determined that the moratorium should remain in force until the computer model was modified to incorporate more safety features. Whaling countries, particularly Iceland, Norway, and Japan, argued that this delay was simply a procrastination device, an attempt to "hide behind the science." Their argument continued in 1992 since a resolution adopting the RMP was again made dependent upon obtaining more data and creating an inspection and observation system. The IWC was criticized by pro-whaling organizations for its "non-decision making process." So angered was Iceland by the continuance of the moratorium that it withdrew from the commission. Norway, although still a member, announced that it would begin whaling by the 1993 season. Japan has also repeatedly expressed dissatisfaction. After the 1996 IWC meeting, the moratorium remained in effect, though more countries were rumored to favor weakening it. At the 1997 meeting, Ireland proposed the completion and adoption of the RMP. At the 1998 meeting the IWC adopted a resolution confirming how the RMP will take into account anthropogenic removals other than commercial catches, such as incidental catches, catches under scientific permit, and aboriginal whaling, but it decided not to fully adopt the RMP until an inspection and observer system is completed. Michael Heazle, Scientific Uncertainty and the Politics of Whaling (2012), explains how the United States and other anti-whaling countries persuaded the Commission to adopt the precautionary principle as a justification for the moratorium.

Even though the debate is usually framed in terms of science versus economics, some members of the scientific committee and analysts do not believe this to be the "true" argument. Rather, they believe that the controversy results from differences in ethics. In the viewpoint of the pro-whaling States, the anti-whaling majority does not delay the use of scientific management procedures because the data is in any way incomplete, but because their true objections are grounded in morality, and thus outside the authority of the IWC. They oppose whaling because they see whales as "special." Whether whales are in some way special cannot be scientifically shown, as theories of intelligence, compassion, and other "human" qualities are bandied about among scientists and biologists. The scientific issues are further raised in the 2014 decision of the International Court of Justice in *Australia v. Japan*, discussed in section d below.

c. Small Cetaceans

When most of us picture whales, we think of the large storybook creature or the calendar "pinup." Yet other cetaceans include the dolphin and porpoise as well as smaller whales like the orca. The IWC regulates only a small percentage of the small cetaceans. In 1971, the IWC's Scientific Committee organized a Sub-committee on Small Cetaceans to monitor the status of small cetaceans and indicate which needed protection. The subcommittee recommended that a separate international body be set up to oversee those cetaceans not covered by the IWC, but no organization was established . . . Some officials and observers doubt the IWC's legal competence on the issue of small cetaceans. The late Patricia Birnie, an expert on the IWC argued that the commission does have authority to regulate small cetaceans. She asserted that because the ICRW listed no definitions for "whale" or "whaling," the terms could cover small cetaceans, allowing the IWC to regulate them. At its 1996 meeting, the IWC passed a resolution keeping the issue of small cetaceans on the agenda of the Scientific Committee and asking governments to provide information on kills of small cetaceans worldwide.

d. The Scientific Research Exception

As discussed above, the scientific research exception to the moratorium allows States to issue special permits under Article VIII to take and process for scientific research purposes as many whales and in whatever manner as that state dictates, free from any restrictions of the Convention. The potential for abuse of this exemption prompted the commission to amend the scientific committee's procedural rules and the schedule during the late 1970s. The amended version required States to submit all proposed permits to the committee for it to review them and recommend changes. Because States could ignore the committee's comments, and sometimes did, concerns arose among the antiwhaling countries that the new provisions were not effective enough. To address these concerns, the IWC passed resolutions in 1986 and 1987 that set criteria for the scientific committee to analyze the merit of the proposed research. In addition, the Commission could examine the scientific committee's analysis and when necessary, advise States to abstain from issuing the permit. A major legal debate ensued. Iceland, joined by Norway, Japan, and the former USSR, argued that by authorizing the commission to scrutinize the permits, Article VI of the ICRW was violated and the exclusive rights of the States were not being respected.[6] The United States, supported by Australia and the United Kingdom, asserted that because no State was required to follow the commission's recommendations, the recommendations would likely activate certification under United States law. Discussing the debate over national sovereignty, At its 1995 annual meeting, the IWC passed two resolutions with the intention of making scientific research whaling more difficult. The first requested that governments refrain from authorizing research programs unless they satisfy a review by the IWC's Scientific Committee using criteria contained in the resolution. The second requested that governments use nonlethal research methods in IWC whale sanctuaries. Japan and Norway voted against both resolutions.

---

[6]   Article VI reads "[t]he Commission may from time to time make recommendations to any or all Contracting Governments on any matters which relate to whales or whaling and to the objectives and purposes of this Convention."

In practice, the IWC's ability to propose changes has had limited effect. Although proposals by Japan, Norway, and Iceland to increase their commercial quotas have continuously been rejected by the commission, catches have continued. In May, 2010, Australia decided unilaterally to prevent a tragedy of the commons and brought an action in the International Court of Justice challenging Japan's use of the scientific exemption.

WHALING IN THE ANTARCTIC

(Australia v. Japan: New Zealand Intervening)
International Court of Justice, March 31, 2014, *available at* http://www.icj-cij.org/docket/
files/148/18136.pdf

127. ... Based on the information before it, the Court thus finds that the JARPA [Japanese Whale Research Program under Special Permit in the Antarctic] II activities involving the lethal sampling of whales can broadly be characterized as "scientific research". There is no need therefore, in the context of this case, to examine generally the concept of "scientific research". Accordingly, the Court's examination of the evidence with respect to JARPA II will focus on whether the killing, taking and treating of whales in pursuance of JARPA II is for purposes of scientific research and thus may be authorized by special permits granted under Article VIII, paragraph 1, of the Convention. To this end and in light of the applicable standard of review, the Court will examine whether the design and implementation of JARPA II are reasonable in relation to achieving the programme's stated research objectives. * * *

141. [T]here is no evidence of studies of the feasibility or practicability of non-lethal methods, either in setting the JARPA II sample sizes or in later years in which the programme has maintained the same sample size targets. There is no evidence that Japan has examined whether it would be feasible to combine a smaller lethal take (in particular, of minke whales) and an increase in non-lethal sampling as a means to achieve JARPA II's research objectives. The absence of any evidence pointing to consideration of the feasibility of non-lethal methods was not explained. * * *

156. These weaknesses in Japan's explanation for the decision to proceed with the JARPA II sample sizes [i.e., the number of whales hunted every year] prior to the final review of JARPA lend support to the view that those sample sizes and the launch date for JARPA II were not driven by strictly scientific considerations. These weaknesses also give weight to the contrary theory advanced by Australia that Japan's priority was to maintain whaling operations without any pause, just as it had done previously by commencing JARPA in the first year after the commercial whaling moratorium had come into effect for it. * * *

172. In considering these contentions by the Parties, the Court reiterates that it does not seek here to pass judgment on the scientific merit of the JARPA II objectives and that the activities of JARPA II can broadly be characterized as "scientific research". With regard to the setting of sample sizes, the Court is also not in a position to conclude whether a particular value for a given variable (e.g., the research period or rate of change to detect) has scientific advantages over another. Rather, the Court seeks here only to evaluate whether the evidence supports a conclusion that the sample sizes are reasonable in relation to achieving JARPA II's stated objectives. * * *

198. Taken together, the evidence relating to the minke whale sample size, like the evidence for the fin and humpback whale sample sizes, provides scant analysis and justification for the underlying decisions that generate the overall sample size. For the Court, this raises further concerns about whether the design of JARPA II is reasonable in relation to achieving its stated objectives. * * *

219. The Court notes that the Research Plan uses a six-year period to obtain statistically useful information for minke whales and a 12-year period for the other two species, and that it can be expected that the main scientific output of JARPA II would follow these periods. It nevertheless observes that the first research phase of JARPA II (2005–2006 to 2010–2011) has already been completed, but that Japan points to only two peer-reviewed papers that have resulted from JARPA II to date. These papers do not relate to the JARPA II objectives and rely on data collected from respectively seven and two minke whales caught during the JARPA II feasibility study. . . In light of the fact that JARPA II has been going on since 2005 and has involved the killing of about 3,600 minke whales, the scientific output to date appears limited. * * *

224. The Court finds that the use of lethal sampling per se is not unreasonable in relation to the research objectives of JARPA II. However, as compared to JARPA, the scale of lethal sampling in JARPA II is far more extensive with regard to Antarctic minke whales, and the programme includes the lethal sampling of two additional whale species. Japan states that this expansion is required by the new research objectives of JARPA II, in particular, the objectives relating to ecosystem research and the construction of a model of multi-species competition. In the view of the Court, however, the target sample sizes in JARPA II are not reasonable in relation to achieving the programme's objectives.

225. First, the broad objectives of JARPA and JARPA II overlap considerably. To the extent that the objectives are different, the evidence does not reveal how those differences lead to the considerable increase in the scale of lethal sampling in the JARPA II Research Plan. Secondly, the sample sizes for fin and humpback whales are too small to provide the information that is necessary to pursue the JARPA II research objectives

based on Japan's own calculations, and the programme's design appears to prevent random sampling of fin whales. Thirdly, the process used to determine the sample size for minke whales lacks transparency, as the experts called by each of the Parties agreed. In particular, the Court notes the absence of complete explanations in the JARPA II Research Plan for the underlying decisions that led to setting the sample size at 850 minke whales (plus or minus 10 per cent) each year. Fourthly, some evidence suggests that the programme could have been adjusted to achieve a far smaller sample size, and Japan does not explain why this was not done. The evidence before the Court further suggests that little attention was given to the possibility of using non-lethal research methods more extensively to achieve the JARPA II objectives and that funding considerations, rather than strictly scientific criteria, played a role in the programme's design.

226. These problems with the design of JARPA II must also be considered in light of its implementation. First, no humpback whales have been taken, and Japan cites non-scientific reasons for this. Secondly, the take of fin whales is only a small fraction of the number that the JARPA II Research Plan prescribes. Thirdly, the actual take of minke whales has also been far lower than the annual target sample size in all but one season. Despite these gaps between the Research Plan and the programme's implementation, Japan has maintained its reliance on the JARPA II research objectives—most notably, ecosystem research and the goal of constructing a model of multi-species competition—to justify both the use and extent of lethal sampling prescribed by the JARPA II Research Plan for all three species. Neither JARPA II's objectives nor its methods have been revised or adapted to take account of the actual number of whales taken. Nor has Japan explained how those research objectives remain viable given the decision to use six-year and 12-year research periods for different species, coupled with the apparent decision to abandon the lethal sampling of humpback whales entirely and to take very few fin whales. Other aspects of JARPA II also cast doubt on its characterization as a programme for purposes of scientific research, such as its open-ended time frame, its limited scientific output to date, and the absence of significant co-operation between JARPA II and other related research projects.

227. Taken as a whole, the Court considers that JARPA II involves activities that can broadly be characterized as scientific research (*see* paragraph 127 above), but that the evidence does not establish that the programme's design and implementation are reasonable in relation to achieving its stated objectives. The Court concludes that the special permits granted by Japan for the killing, taking and treating of whales in connection with JARPA II are not "for purposes of scientific research" pursuant to Article VIII, paragraph 1, of the Convention. * * *

244. In addition to asking the Court to find that the killing, taking and treating of whales under special permits granted for JARPA II is not for purposes of scientific research within the meaning of Article VIII and that Japan thus has violated three paragraphs of the Schedule, Australia asks the Court to adjudge and declare that Japan shall:

> "(a) refrain from authorizing or implementing any special permit whaling which is not for purposes of scientific research within the meaning of Article VIII;

> (b) cease with immediate effect the implementation of JARPA II; and

> (c) revoke any authorization, permit or licence that allows the implementation of JARPA II."

245. The Court observes that JARPA II is an ongoing programme. Under these circumstances, measures that go beyond declaratory relief are warranted. The Court therefore will order that Japan shall revoke any extant authorization, permit or licence to kill, take or treat whales in relation to JARPA II, and refrain from granting any further permits under Article VIII, paragraph 1, of the Convention, in pursuance of that programme.

246. The Court sees no need to order the additional remedy requested by Australia, which would require Japan to refrain from authorizing or implementing any special permit whaling which is not for purposes of scientific research within the meaning of Article VIII. That obligation already applies to all States parties. It is to be expected that Japan will take account of the reasoning and conclusions contained in this Judgment as it evaluates the possibility of granting any future permits under Article VIII, paragraph 1, of the Convention.

[The Court found violations of Article VIII, paragraph 1 of the ICRW and paragraphs 7(b), 10(d) and 10(e) as well as paragraph 30 of the Schedule to the International Convention for the Regulation of Whaling in relation to the killing, taking and treating of fin whales in pursuance of JARPA II.]

QUESTIONS

In response to the opinion, a spokesman from the Japanese Foreign Affairs Ministry stated that, "as a state that respects the rule of law . . . and as a responsible member of the global community, Japan will abide by the ruling of the court." Does this mean that Japan will stop all harvesting for scientific research? Does the ICJ's judgment require this? Should there be an exception for historic cultural practices? *See* Gerry Nagtzaam, *Righting the Ship?: Australia, New Zealand and Japan at the ICJ and the Barbed Issue of*

"Scientific Whaling," 2014 Australian J. Int. L. 71. Japan's answer is that the decision still permits scientific harvesting. In August, 2015 Japan announced a plan to take 3,996 minke whales over the next 12 years, but The International Whaling Commission (IWC) has demanded that the country provide more information to prove that its revised Antarctic whaling programme was in fact for scientific research. http://www.theguardian.com/environment/2015/jun/19/japan-asked-to-prove-whaling-for-scientific-research.

e. Aboriginal Whaling

The legal controversy surrounding the aboriginal whaling exception centers on the definition of "aboriginal," or more precisely, the lack of one. In 1977, the United States suffered political humiliation when the aboriginal exception for the Yupik and Inuit of Alaska was hastily revoked after reports were issued of the severe depletion in the bowhead whale population, the Eskimos' primary hunt. The United States disputed the revocation on the grounds that the ban on whaling did not apply to these two peoples, as they did not engage in "commercial" whaling.[7] The outcome of this dispute was a compromise, with the Alaska Natives allowed to hunt only a limited number of the bowheads. The confusion continued, however, as other countries questioned whether the exception covers small coastal communities with a cultural history of whaling. Japan, for instance, claimed that its fishing villages were culturally and economically dependent on whaling, thus qualifying as "aboriginal."[8] The IWC rejected the argument. The reason seemed to revolve around the Japanese sale of whale products commercially. Japan requested that a group be organized to define "commercial whaling," "aboriginal subsistence whaling," and other categories. This group, the Definitions Working Group, was to work with the Aboriginal Subsistence Whaling Sub-Committee to clarify the problem. The confusion was apparent when trying to reconcile the IWC's dismissal of the United States' argument that the ban prohibits only commercial whaling with the explanation the commission gave for not recognizing an aboriginal exception for Japan's fishing villages.

Similar requests to permit aboriginal whaling were put forth by both Russia and the United States at the 1996 IWC meeting. Russia asked for a five whale quota for the Chukotka people of its polar region, who revere whales, and the United States asked for a five whale quota for the Makah tribe of its Olympic peninsula. Both requests were withdrawn after much discussion in the face of intense opposition, though the United States promised to renew its request in 1997. Despite the withdrawals, whaling

---

[7]   Patricia Birnie cites the legal opinion of D. Bowett, Q.C., who rejected the United States' argument by determining that the IWC's action was within the scope of ICRW's Art. V; Opinion of Nov. 16, 1977 (on file IWC).

[8]   *See* Hankins, 24 U.C. Davis L.Rev. 489, at n.201. Hankins explains that Japan uses a "cultural-dependence rationale" as grounds for an exception from the moratorium.

States gained a toehold for their own requests for whaling permits, and the IWC lost ground in its efforts to keep the worldwide commercial whaling moratorium strongly in place. The dispute was a major issue at the 1996 meeting.

The subsistence harvest of bowhead whales provides for important dietary needs for several Native communities in northern and western Alaska and eastern Chukotka (Russia). *See* Jeremy Firestone and Jonathan Lilley, *Aboriginal Subsistence Whaling and the Right to Practice and Revitalize Cultural Traditions and Customs*, 8 J. Int. Wildlife L. & Pol'y 177 (2005). The Alaska Eskimo Whaling Commission (AEWC) locally manages the harvest through an agreement with the National Oceanic and Atmospheric Administration (NOAA). However, the level of allowable harvest is determined under a quota system in compliance with the International Whaling Commission based on the nutritional and cultural needs of Alaskan Eskimos as well as on estimates of the size and growth of the Bering-Chukchi-Beaufort seas stock of bowhead whales. The subsistence hunt typically takes place in spring and autumn as whales migrate between the Bering and Beaufort seas. Hunters on St. Lawrence Island may take whales during the winter as well. In recent years, the quota is 67 strikes per year, and between 40 to 50 are killed. Alaska has 90% of the world's bowheads, and the Alaska Department of Fish and Game estimates that the population is about 10,000 and growing. http://www.adfg.alaska.gov/index.cfm?adfg=wildlife news.view_article & articles_id=42

http://wildlifefactsandfindings.blogspot.com/2012/11/whales-in-crosshairs-photograph-by.html.

Aboriginal whaling also faces threats from oil exploration in the Chukchi sea. 76 Fed. Reg. 69.958 (Nov. 9, 2011) (incidental harassment authorization for Shell's drilling).

f.   Unilateral Sanctions

One of the most noticeably absent features of the IWC is any mechanism for enforcing its quotas or regulations. Although all members remain bound by regulation unless they object, there are no sanctioning or enforcement powers provided by the IWC. It must rely on national laws to enforce the IWC regulations. "The only effective sanctions to implement decisions of the IWC are provided by the United States. America pulled the IWC's teeth in the first place, and America now provides the IWC's dentition"[9] (referring to the ironic fact that the enforcement provision in the original draft of the ICRW was only taken out at the insistence of the United States). In 1971, the United States enacted the Pelly amendments to the U.S. Fisherman's Protective Act and the Packwood-Magnuson amendments to the Magnuson Fishery Conservation and Management Act 1979. These laws enable the United States Secretary of Commerce to certify, or identify, any foreign state that conducts fishing operations in a way that "diminishes the effectiveness" of the Whaling Convention. If a state is certified by the secretary, the president can respond as harshly as a full trade embargo against the state. Its quotas for access to fish within the 200 mile coastal waters of the United States, or Exclusive Economic Zone (EEZ), is automatically reduced by 50 percent. Access to the EEZ is completely restricted if by the next year the State has not altered its behavior.

Beginning in 1984, the Pelly and Packwood-Magnuson amendments came under heated debate in the case of Japan Whaling Association v. American Cetacean Society.[10] In November of that year, Japan was harvesting sperm whales in direct violation of the zero quota. However, instead of certifying Japan and restricting their quota in America's EEZ under the Packwood-Magnuson amendment, the United States entered into a compromise with Japan. Under this deal, known as the Baldrige-Murazumi Agreement, the United States allowed Japan to hunt for two more seasons despite the moratorium. Japan, in turn, agreed to withdraw its objection to the moratorium at the end of this period. A group of nongovernmental organizations immediately challenged the agreement, arguing that when the Secretary of Commerce is notified by the Marine Mammal Commission of whaling violations, the Secretary has no discretion to decide whether to certify the violator, but rather must do so. Although the NGOs were victorious in the lower courts, the United States

---

[9]   Jermey Cherfas, The Hunting of the Whale: A Tragedy That Must End 113 (1988).

[10]   Japan Whaling Association v. American Cetacean Society, 78 U.S. 221 (1986).

Supreme Court held that certification was a discretionary matter. Not surprisingly there was criticism from some groups:

"The United States has provided enforcement leverage for IWC quotas through the Pelly and Packwood Magnuson Amendments. Most whaling nations, therefore, have based—or will base—their decisions on whether or not to observe an IWC quota on their assessment of the United States' intentions. They will watch to see whether the United States actually imposes the sanctions written in its laws.... Now that the United States has entered into a bilateral agreement with Japan that circumvents the IWC limits under which Japan may whale under objection without being certified, other whaling nations may demand similar concessions."[11]

International politics, coupled with discretionary enforcement by the United States, has proven to be an obstacle to uniform enforcement of IWC rules. In December 1995, then Commerce Secretary Ron Brown certified that Japan was weakening the worldwide moratorium on whaling by killing them in the Southern Ocean Sanctuary, which had been created in 1994 by the IWC to provide whales with a safe mating habitat. The President was then authorized to impose trade sanctions on Japan. However, he decided not to do so, saying that there was not enough evidence to challenge Japan's claim that its research was scientific and required killing the whales. Groups claimed that the tenuous trade relationship between the United States and Japan was more likely the reason. Since then, the United States' role in preventing whaling has come into question. Its lack of action against whaling nations and its 1996 request for an aboriginal whaling permit for a Native American culture have illustrated the unwillingness of the United States to take a strong stand on the issue of whaling and exposed the weakness of the IWC in enforcing its resolutions.[12] Internationally, unilateral sanctions such as those imposed by the United States have met with a dual response. On the one hand, they have been welcomed for their deterrent effects. "The Pelly and Packwood-Magnuson Amendments unquestionably have had a salutary effect on the ability of the IWC to achieve its conservation objectives."[13] On the opposite spectrum, "some members regard such action as an invasion of their sovereignty and contrary to UN Charter requirements on the use of force against the sovereignty of states."[14]

---

[11] Christopher Gibson, *Narrow Grounds for a Complex Decision: The Supreme Court's Review of an Agency's Statutory Construction in Japan Whaling Association v. American Cetacean Society*, 14 Ecology L.Q. 509, 510 (1987).

[12] Kate O'Connell, *The 1996 International Whaling Commission Meeting*, Cetacean Society International.

[13] Gene S. Martin, Jr. & James W. Brennan, *Enforcing the International Convention for the Regulation of Whaling: The Pelly and Packwood-Magnuson Amendments*, 17:2 Den. J. Ind. L. & Poly. 293, 315 (1989).

[14] Patricia Birnie, Natural Resources Journal 29 (1989), at 927. *Id.* at 909.

NOTES AND QUESTIONS

1.   *Are permanent bans possible*? Read the Convention carefully. Could
the parties agree to a permanent ban on whaling? Of certain species? *See*
Mike Danaher, *Why Japan Will Not Give Up Whaling*, 14 Pacific Review:
Peace, Security & Global Change 105 (2002). But *see* Andrew Hoek, Sea
Shepard Conservation Society v. Japanese Whalers, the *Showdown: Who is
the Real Villain?*, 3 Stanford J. Animal L. & Pol'y 159 (2010), which predicts
that the declining internal demand for whale meat will eventually force
Japan to stop whaling.

2.   *Defeating the Convention's purpose*? Consider Article V carefully.
Note how any State that does not wish to be bound by an amendment can file
a timely objection and be exempted from it. Does this defeat the purpose of
the Convention? Would States join the Convention without having this
option? Consider the material on the Convention on International Trade in
Endangered Species in this connection.

3.   *When is a species no longer endangered*? Changes in our scientific
understanding of problems may indicate either that the risk is greater than
we thought or that it is less. How can the international community effectively
address the situation in which scientific evidence indicates a species is no
longer endangered? Does the Whaling Convention adequately address this
situation? If a certain sub-species of whales is no longer threatened, how does
a ban on its harvest relate to sustainable development? See also the
philosophical considerations discussed in Note/Question 5 below in this
connection.

4.   *NAMMCO v. IWC*. On September 15, 1992, Norway, Iceland,
Greenland, and the Faroe Islands established the North Atlantic Marine
Mammal Commission. The Commission is in opposition to the International
Whaling Commission. NAMMCO advocates sustainable commercial whale
hunting. It will also control hunting of small cetaceans, including seals and
small whales.

5.   *Are whales special? Philosophical considerations*. Western
philosophy has posited that humans are apart from nature and that only
sentient beings, the human race, can have a legal personality.
Environmentalists such as Aldo Leopold have argued that we should reject
this hubris. What would it mean to give whales a legal personality? The
classic treatment is Anthony D'Amato & Sudhir K. Chopra, *Whales: Their
Emerging Right to Life*, 85 Am. J. Int'l L. 21 (1991). Would they be entitled to
protected ocean areas? *See generally* Elisa Morgera, *Whale Sanctuaries: An
Evolving Concept within the International Whaling Commission,* 35 Ocean
Dev. & Int'l L. 319 (2004). Are there alternative preservation options? *See*
Hope Babcock, *Putting A Price On Whales To Save Them: What Do Morals
Have To Do With It?*, 43 Envtl. L. 1 (2013).

6.   *Other Marine and Polar Animals*. Conservation regimes exist for fur
seals, polar bears, and migratory wild animals. *See* Treaty for the
Preservation and Protection of Fur Seals, 7 July 1911, 37 Stat. 1542, TS 564;

Oslo Agreement on the Conservation of Polar Bears, May 26, 1976, 27 U.S.T. 3918, T.I.A.S. 8409, *reprinted* in 13 I.L.M. 13 (1973), UNEP3 #61, at 401, IPE 2276, IELMT 973:85.

C. LOSS OF BIOLOGICAL DIVERSITY: THE PROBLEM AND IMPORTANCE OF BIOLOGICAL RESOURCES

1. TWO QUESTIONS: WHAT IS BIODIVERSITY AND HOW CAN IT BE CONSERVED?

a. What Is Biodiversity?

Biodiversity is a carefully considered word that attempts to capture both a positive and a normative idea. The positive idea is the entire process of evolution; the normative idea, of course, is that humankind should conserve this process to the maximum extent possible. Lawyers and other policymakers must understand that the term "biodiversity" is not self-defining. In fact, efforts to define the term raise difficult, complex, and unresolved scientific questions with contestable normative implications. The late Professor Fred Bosselman explored these ideas in *A Dozen Biodiversity Puzzles*, 12 N.Y.U. Envtl. L. J. 364–406 (2004). The editors remain indebted to the late Professor Fred Bosselman for the following condensed version of the longer article prepared for an earlier incarnation of this casebook.

This article provides a summary of some of the "puzzles" inherent in the concept of biodiversity; these puzzles are examples from the biological literature[15] in which the complexities of the ideas within biodiversity are discussed. The focus here will be on the scientific puzzles within the concept of biodiversity, though in some instances it is difficult to separate science from ethics, aesthetics, and religion.[16] Lawmakers may not be qualified to solve these puzzles from a scientific perspective, but they need to take them into account.

---

[15] I do not claim to have been the original discoverer of any of these biological puzzles, each of which is being written about extensively in the biological literature, but only a few have been addressed in the legal literature.

[16] A wide range of arguments for protecting biodiversity have been marshaled, including economic, religious, ethical, and aesthetic arguments. David Takacs, The Idea of Biodiversity: Philosophies of Paradise 194–287 (1996). A good summary of these arguments is found in Holly Doremus, *Patching the Ark: Improving Legal Protection of Biological Diversity*, 18 Ecology L. Q. 265, 269–81 (1991); *see also* Holly Doremus, *Listing Decisions under the Endangered Species Act: Why Better Science Isn't Always Better Policy*, 75 Wash. U. L.Q. 1029, 1134–38 (1997) (arguing that listing of endangered species should not be based solely on scientific criteria). It is not my intent to downplay the importance of these arguments, but the biological puzzles are complex enough to support my thesis.

Thirteen puzzles are identified in this article:

1. To what extent does a lack of genetic variability itself threaten a species or population's existence? How much should genetic variability be protected?

2. Should we protect phenotypic diversity, or plasticity of species, which enables species to adapt to future environmental change?

3. Can scientific criteria be developed for designating focal species to serve as proxies for biodiversity?

4. Should we treat species differently depending on the extent to which they have an evolutionary history or hidden traits that are similar to other species?

5. Should we give priority to locally endemic species and lesser protection to peripheral populations of species that interact with abundant populations of the same species living outside the United States?

6. Should we continue to utilize the traditional concept of species to determine species richness and species endangerment, or should we switch to newer systems of classifying organisms that emphasize similarity of genetic lineage?

7. Where two or more species appear to perform the same ecological function, should we focus more on ensuring that the function is performed, or on the protection of each individual species?

8. What criteria should be used to decide whether a species of plant or animal has an adverse effect on biodiversity because it arrived at its present location by the wrong method or at the wrong time? What should "wrong" mean in this context?

9. What criteria should decide whether a hybrid species has a positive or adverse effect on biodiversity? When should the potential to create new hybrid species be considered an addition or threat to biodiversity?

10. Do we need to give special priority to those species that are likely to have difficulty in dispersing to appropriate habitats in response to environmental change?

11. Should we encourage all increases in biodiversity that result from natural selection, even though this may include resistant antibiotics or pesticides, or should we only emphasize protection of the biodiversity of existing species?

12. Should we protect groups of organisms that result from captive breeding or bioengineering in the same way that we protect groups of "natural" origin?

13. Should we try to maintain existing biodiversity or to promote new mixtures of species that can better adapt to continuing environmental change?

What do we do if we are forced to make a trade-off between maintaining present biodiversity and creating conditions that we think will foster biodiversity in the future? This issue arises in a number of contexts, including the following: (1) Do we need to assist those species that have difficulty reacting to environmental change? (2) Should we foster or discourage natural speciation? (3) Should we actively create biodiversity through captive breeding and biotechnology? (4) Are there situations in which we need to concede that loss of local diversity is a necessary adaptive strategy?

i.   Anticipating Environmental Change

Over the last few decades, science has given us new tools to chart the distribution of species over space and time at far larger scales than were available earlier, and we now know that many species are reacting to a warming climate by gradually moving away from lower altitudes or toward the poles. As one researcher has noted, "[e]nvironmental change is now occurring on a global scale due to human activities, and many species will have to adapt to this change or experience an ever-increasing chance of extinction."

We now know that many species exist as metapopulations scattered about in heterogeneous landscapes—landscapes that are not only highly complex at any given point in time, but are continually changing in highly complex ways. DNA analysis, field tracking technologies, computer modeling, and other scientific and technological advances are beginning to make it possible to understand how species in metapopulations live and die. Even with these tools, though, can we devise resource management methods that are designed to protect and enhance the future biodiversity of species in metapopulations?

For a species to propagate, individual members of a species must allocate energy resources among two key functions: survival—including the need for appropriate habitat—and reproduction.[17] Species evolve strategies to adapt these functions to changing environmental conditions, and most existing species have survived ice ages, sea level changes, and tectonic plate movements, not to mention innumerable disturbances from storms, volcanoes, and other natural phenomena.[18] However, the rapid

---

[17] Robert E. Bennetts et al., *Methods for Estimating Dispersal Probabilities and Related Parameters Using Marked Animals, in* Dispersal 3 (Jean Clobert et al. eds., 2001) ("In the study of population ecology, all population change results from births, deaths, immigration, and emigration.").

[18] We have mistakenly tended to think of natural systems in the condition we first studied them as having been "natural," ignoring what may have been a long history of fluctuations that occurred before that time. Jeremy B.C. Jackson, *What Was Natural in the Coastal Oceans?*, 98

growth of human populations and technology—is leading scientists to believe that humans are now causing environmental change at a rate far faster than has occurred at any time in the past. Species' needs for new habitat—what biologists call "dispersal"—may grow at a rate that exceeds any past adaptive experience. Should humans help maintain biodiversity by reinforcing and enriching the abilities of other species to adapt to these changes?

Biologists today recognize that environmental change is a natural feature of the history of the world, and that some kinds of change are necessary in order to retain diverse environments. Humans have accelerated the rate of change—sometimes gradually through increasing greenhouse gas emissions, emitting toxic chemicals, or expanding agriculture, and sometimes rapidly by destroying wetlands or tropical forests—but change has always been inevitable even absent human intervention.[19]

Disturbances such as wildfire, flood, and epidemic often play a key role in maintaining ecological functions.[20] Given the proper perspective, many of the things that our society has called "natural disasters" are a vital part of ecological processes. [21] Viewed at the proper scale, disturbances can be seen to be a necessary part of the ecological system and a stabilizing factor. Unfortunately, as Duke University ecologist Norman Christensen has emphasized, the predictability of such disturbances is limited:

"Patterns of change are neither perfectly cyclic nor linear. Rather successional transitions are often complex and patterns of disturbance and recovery are often greatly affected by "chance" events, that is, phenomena such as variations in weather that are controlled by factors

---

Proc. Nat'l Acad. Sci. 5411 (2001). *See generally* Seth R. Reice, The Silver Lining: The Benefits of Natural Disasters (2001).

[19] Peter M. Vitousek, *Community Turnover and Ecosystem Nutrient Dynamics, in* The Ecology of Natural Disturbance and Patch Dynamics 325, 333 (S.T.A. Pickett & P.S. White eds., 1985) (describing limited conditions under which ecological processes can maintain rough constancy). In many cases, lack of a long sequence of historical records may make it difficult to determine whether dramatic change in species composition is the result of human activities or part of a natural cycle. *See* Richard B. Aronson & William F. Precht, Stasis, *Biological Disturbance, and Community Structure of a Holocene Coral Reef*, 23 Paleobiology 326 (1997) (use of core data to reconstruct history of coral composition); Robert E. Ricklefs & Eldredge Bermingham, *Nonequilibrium Diversity Dynamics of the Lesser Antillean Avifauna*, 294 Sci. 1522 (2001) (using phylogenic methods to trace history of colonization of island chain by birds).

[20] Steward Pickett and Peter White produced the pioneering synthesis of the important role of disturbance in ecology in 1985. *See generally* The Ecology of Natural Disturbance and Patch Dynamics (S.T.A. Pickett & P.S. White eds., 1985).

[21] *See*, e.g., Peter R. Grant et al., Effects of El Nino Events on Darwin's Finch Productivity, 81 Ecology 2442 (2000) (stating that finches in the Galapagos breed prolifically in el nino years, but they also take into account the length of time since the last similar event; "[t]hus perturbations of natural systems can be fully understood only in a broad temporal context."). *See also* Anthony W. King, *Hierarchy Theory: A Guide to System Structure for Wildlife Biologists, in* Wildlife and Landscape Ecology: Effects of Pattern and Scale 185, 208 (John A. Bissonette ed., 1997).

external to the system being managed."[22] Thus, in order to cope with disturbances in the past, species have had to evolve some degree of "resilience" to unpredictable environmental change.

(a) Metapopulations

Given the likelihood of environmental change, biologists have increasingly realized the need to understand how species have coped with past changes in the environment. In doing so they have discovered that many species of plants and animals have evolved a "metapopulation" strategy for coping with environmental change.[23] They aggregate in clusters that are separated from other clusters of individuals of the same species, but retain a certain amount of interaction with the other clusters.[24]

Wetland species, for example, often form metapopulations because wetlands tend to be scattered around the landscape, enlarging and contracting as environmental conditions change, silting up in one place and re-forming somewhere else.[25] For the organisms that inhabit the wetlands, it "is the fate of these local populations to wink off and on over time." Many forest species also use metapopulation strategies because storms and fires create forest gaps that disappear as trees mature, while new storms, fires, or insect infestations create new gaps elsewhere. Metapopulation ecologists study the way that metapopulations change and move over decades, centuries, and millennia. Most species that exist today have been in existence through many changes in their environmental conditions. Many species have learned to live in patches of habitat that change their locations over relatively short time spans and that interact at close range with other kinds of habitat. Research into the adaptations by species in metapopulations to the dynamic aspect of their habitat has provided new insight on the local survival or extinction of particular species.[26] We know that in order to avoid extinction each species must be prepared to adapt to change in regard to at least three

---

[22] Norman L. Christensen, Jr., *Managing for Heterogeneity and Complexity on Dynamic Landscapes*, *in* The Ecological Basis of Conservation: Heterogeneity, Ecosystems, and Biodiversity 167, 178 (Steward Pickett et al. eds., 1997).

[23] Biologists use the term "population" to mean a group of individuals of the same species living in the same habitat area. A Dictionary of Ecology, *supra* note 243, at 324. If different populations of the same species occupy separate habitat patches within the same general area, the aggregate of such clusters is called a "metapopulation." Thus metapopulation is defined as "[a] group of conspecific populations that exist at the same time, but in different places." *Id.* at 259.

[24] Robert E. Ricklefs, The Economy of Nature 362–63 (4th ed. 1996).

[25] *See* Alyson C. Flournoy, *Preserving Dynamic Systems: Wetlands, Ecology and Law*, 7 Duke Envtl. L. & Pol'y Forum 105, 114 (1996).

[26] One branch of this study is known as "metapopulation ecology," which has attracted a great deal of attention in the last two decades. Seellkka Hanski, Metapopulation Ecology 1–3 (1999). *See also* Peter H. Thrall et al., *The Metapopulation Paradigm: A Fragmented View of Conservation Biology*, *in* Genetics, Demography and Viability of Fragmented Populations 75 (Andrew G. Young & Geoffrey M. Clarke eds., 2000).

key functions: (1) staying alive (or as the biologists would say, regulating mortality); (2) reproducing; and (3) exploring new territory (dispersing). Even if we succeed with our traditional methods of reducing mortality, and if we successfully explore more ways to control threats to reproduction, it may not be sufficient to save some of the species that lack adequate dispersal mechanisms.

(b) Dispersal

Biologists know that the ability of clustered populations to exchange individuals or genes with other populations has an important effect on their potential survival when environmental conditions change. A species accomplishes this exchange through dispersal—movement of individual organisms away from their site of origination. It is dispersal that "gives populations, communities, and ecosystems their characteristic texture in space and time."[27]

Dispersal takes many forms; for example, plants often rely on the wind or birds to disperse their seeds, and many animals typically drive away their mature young to colonize new habitat areas. Much dispersal is unsuccessful, in the sense that the area at which the species arrives is unsuitable as a place in which it can reproduce and prosper—think of the millions of Cottonwood or maple seeds that are deposited on lawns each year. Such areas are known as "sinks," because the species cannot survive there without continual immigration.[28] But in some cases, the dispersing species will find a hospitable new home, which may then become a "source" for future dispersal elsewhere.[29] Ecological resilience is fostered by population levels which maintain enough surplus to allow dispersal to

---

[27] John A. Wiens, *The Landscape Context of Dispersal, in* Dispersal 96, 97 (Jean Clobert et al. eds., 2001). Peter Waser makes an amusing and useful analogy to certain human dispersal patterns:

> Because the range of ideas and systems discussed in this book is so broad, readers might well question whether dispersal is a unitary phenomenon. Academics, like other species, disperse, and the dispersal of academics seems parallel in many regards to other cases of dispersal discussed in this book. Suppose we could determine what mix of academic kin competition and inbreeding avoidance leads to the observed dispersal rates, what patterns of patch choice, interpatch movement and demographic stochasticity lead to the observed dispersal distributions, or what patterns of academic dispersal maximize population persistence. Would we expect the answers to be generalizable to other species? Each reader will have to decide whether a grand unified theory of dispersal is on the horizon. Peter Waser, Foreword to Dispersal ix, x (Jean Clobert et al. eds., 2001).

[28] Vincent A. A. Jansen & Jin Yoshimura, *Populations Can Persist in an Environment Consisting of Sink Habitats Only*, 95 Proc. Nat'l Acad. Sci. 3696, 3696 (1998). To further complicate the terminology, some areas are referred to as "pseudo-sinks" if they would not support their current population without immigration, but would appear to support a smaller but stable population. Ilkka Hanski, *Population Dynamic Consequences of Dispersal in Local Populations and in Metapopulations, in* Dispersal 283, 290 (Jean Clobert et al. eds., 2001).

[29] H. Ronald Pulliam, *Sources, Sinks, and Population Regulation*, 132 Amer. Naturalist 652 (1988). The scale of this process may vary greatly. One study suggests that speciation and dispersal of reef fish from a source area between Indonesia and the Philippines is responsible for reef fish diversity patterns throughout the Pacific and Indian Oceans. Camilo Mora et al. *Patterns and Processes in Reef Fish Diversity*, 421 Nature 933, 934 (2003).

respond to changing environmental conditions. This provides room for populations of particular species to rise and fall over time, and thus enables the ecological systems to adapt to environmental change without any drastic change in the mix of species. Niles Eldredge describes each separate population of a species as a "genetic reservoir" whose reproduction renews the supply of players in the local ecological arena and also supplies players to other arenas in need of colonization. For example, moose, which had been exterminated from the Adirondacks years ago, are becoming reestablished through migration from Canada and Vermont.[30]

The importance of dispersal has long been recognized, but research has proven to be difficult because of the problem of tracking huge numbers of organisms, and because dispersal takes place in complex, heterogeneous milieus. New technology is helping; DNA analysis makes it possible to estimate some dispersal abilities by measuring the extent to which genetic material travels among separate populations. [31] Field studies with marked animals show that the path and rate of dispersal can be highly dependent on the characteristics of the intervening landscape, and that animals select new habitat using a wide variety of cues, including presence of members of the same or compatible species, absence of predators, or habitat similar to that in which the animal originated. As metapopulation ecologists have begun building increasingly realistic models to predict the behavior of clusters of individual species in response to future environmental changes, they realized the importance of dispersal methods to the processes that allow species to survive. For metapopulations to survive, the decolonization rate must exceed local extinction rates. Conservation biologists often find that even a "trickle of dispersal" may be enough to make the difference in whether a population stays viable. And with prospects for ever more rapid environmental change, dispersal is taking on heightened importance.[32]

Those organisms that have good dispersal abilities may be at less risk from habitat destruction than other species, including even those species that are currently dominant. Metapopulation models often suggest that the species most likely to become extinct are not necessarily

---

[30]   Niles Eldredge, Reinventing Darwin 194–195 (1995).

[31]   Marie L. Hale et al., *Impact of Landscape Management on the Genetic Structure of Red Squirrel Populations*, 293 Sci. 2246, 2246–47 (2001) (DNA tests on museum specimens of various ages show how increasing forest connectivity over time improved gene flow throughout the metapopulation).

[32]   For a critique of metapopulation analysis that questions the extent to which it accurately represents the real structure of metapopulations, *see* Susan Harrison, *Do Taxa Persist as Metapopulations in Evolutionary Time?*, *in* Biodiversity Dynamics: Turnover of Populations, Taxa, and Communities 19 (Michael L. McKinney & James A. Drake eds., 1998). *See also* Daniel Simberloff, *Biogeographic Approaches and the New Conservation Biology*, *in* The Ecological Basis of Conservation: Heterogeneity, Ecosystems, and Biodiversity 274, 280 (Steward Pickett et al. eds., 1997) (discussing the ambiguity of appearance of a metapopulation, which may be a dwindling species or the result of a failure of metapopulation dynamics).

the rarest species, but those that are the poorest dispersers. In other words, those species that fail to adapt to environmental change by moving to new habitats may be at risk even though they are superior competitors and have become abundant in their current environment. This suggests that current numbers of individuals of a species may not be a key to long-term biodiversity, and that the status of local biodiversity at any given time may not be a satisfactory predictor of post-disturbance biodiversity.

(c) Habitat Heterogeneity

Many ecologists fear that the current emphasis on protecting only large reserves of homogeneous habitat[33] may be ignoring the need for organisms to be able to disperse to a variety of habitats over both space and time.[34] The preference for homogeneous reserves has relied heavily on studies of forest birds in the United States. Ironically, perhaps, the growth of forest in the Eastern states has been so significant that some of the birds living at the forest edge are now declining rather rapidly.[35] Patchy landscapes offer the possibility of regional coexistence of species in spite of local extinctions.

Today ecologists recognize that "landscape heterogeneity is an important component for the persistence and abundance of many species."[36] Historical research has shown that many areas that early European settlers called unbroken wilderness were actually quite patchy.[37] Similarly, as biologists have made more detailed analyses of current conditions in tropical forests, they also tend to find more patchiness than in the old popular image of the "jungle."[38]

---

[33] For an example of the prevailing emphasis on large reserves, see Continental Conservation: Scientific Foundations of Regional Reserve Networks (Michael E. Soule & John Terborgh eds., 1999).

[34] See James H. Brown & Mark V. Lomolino, Biogeography 565 (2nd ed. 1998) (concluding that it is not clear whether large reserves or small reserves better protect biodiversity). Vandermeer, supra note 529, at 61 ("When the history of how we saved the world's biodiversity is written, probably very little will be written about biological preserves. Almost all the story will be about how we got our act together to readjust our managed ecosystems in light of the need to preserve biodiversity."). See also Larry D. Harris et al., Landscape Processes and Their Significance to Biodiversity Conservation, in Population Dynamics in Ecological Space and Time 319, 323, 339 (Olin E. Rhodes, Jr. et al. eds., 1996).

[35] Robert A. Askins, Restoring North America's Birds: Lessons from Landscape Ecology 1–42 (2000). See also M.K. Trani et al., Patterns and Trends of Early Successional Forests in the Eastern United States, 29 Wildlife Society Bulletin 413, 414 (2001); W.C. Hunter et al., Conservation of Disturbance-Dependent Birds in Eastern North America, 29 Wildlife Society Bulletin 440, 453–54 (2001); J.A. Litvaitis, Importance of Early Successional Habitats to Mammals in Eastern Forests, 29 Wildlife Society Bulletin 466, 467 (2001); F.R. Thompson III & R.M. DeGraaf, Conservation Approaches for Woody, Early-Successional Communities in the Eastern United States, 29 Wildlife Society Bulletin 483, 483–85 (2001).

[36] Lenore Fahrig, Effect of Habitat Fragmentation on the Extinction Threshold: A Synthesis, 12 Ecological Applications 346, 352 (2002).

[37] See, e.g., Anthony Godfrey, Bureau of Indian Affairs, A Forestry History of Ten Wisconsin Indian Reservations under the Great Lakes Agency: Precontract to Present 4 (1996).

[38] S. Joseph Wright, Plant Diversity in Tropical Forests: A Review of Mechanisms of Species Coexistence, 130 Oecologia 1, 7 (2002).

A review of recent research by Carleton University ecologist Lenore Fahrig casts doubt on the idea that heterogeneity of habitat always affects biodiversity adversely; it shows that in regard to birds, at least, habitat fragmentation may have both positive and negative effects.[39] An extensive study of butterflies in Borneo also concluded that "future management to reduce impacts of logging on biodiversity should aim to preserve environmental heterogeneity as far as possible. . . ." The heterogeneous landscapes also may often serve as a barrier to the rapid spread of pathogens, fire or other disturbance.[40] The rate of change in landscape pattern, and the opportunity for organisms to find patches of habitat of various sizes, may be important factors in assuring survival of populations.

Although the growing recognition of the value of heterogeneity is an important advance in ecological science, it is important not to carry the idea to the same extremes that characterized some of the advocates of large homogeneous reserves.[41] What we now know is that the effects of disturbance on natural habitats should not be characterized in black-and-white terms because the impacts are highly dependent on both local and regional conditions. To generalize that heterogeneity enhances biodiversity is an oversimplification at least as misleading as the wholesale condemnation of fragmentation.

Puzzle #10: Do we need to give special priority to those species that are likely to have difficulty in dispersing to appropriate habitats in response to environmental change?

ii. Speciation as a Source of Biodiversity

Evolution of a new species increases species richness.[42] Evolution is naturally creating new species all the time, and at a faster pace than scientists had realized until recently. [43] Should we encourage such speciation or discourage it? What if the new species pose dangers to our health or productivity? And even more controversially, should we use genetic engineering to speed up the process of speciation?

The diversity of species that we now have is the result of speciation that took place in the past. Molecular biology and microbiology have made

---

[39] Lenore Fahrig, *Effect of Habitat Fragmentation on the Extinction Threshold: A Synthesis*, 12 Ecological Applications 346, 352 (2002).

[40] Macdonald & Johnson, Dispersal (Jean Clobert et al. eds., 2001), at 363–364.

[41] Michael A. Rosenzweig, Win-Win Ecology: How the Earth's Species Can Survive in the Midst of Human Enterprise 143–152 (2003).

[42] *See generally* Hope Hollocher, *Theories of Speciation*, 5 Encyclopedia of Biodiversity 383 (Simon A. Levin id. 2001) (explaining concepts of speciation and evolutionary forces).

[43] Nicholas H. Barton, *Speciation*, 16 Trends in Ecology and Evolution 325 (2001) ("The past few years have seen a resurgence of interest in speciation. . . ."). *See* Anurag A. Agrawal, *Community Genetics: New Insights into Community Ecology by Integrating Population Genetics*, 84 Ecology 543 (2003) (introducing a special feature with articles on the interaction between genes within a species and populations of other species in a community).

us much more aware of the continuing role of speciation in enhancing biodiversity, sometimes in ways that cause concern.[44]

Many evolutionary biologists believe that most speciation is "allopatric," which means that it begins when a population of a species is isolated from the main body of the species and develops special adaptations to the local environment. There is an increasing awareness that such speciation can take place quite rapidly in response to environmental change, and that some types of organisms are more likely to develop new species than others.

Recent research is beginning to suggest that speciation can take place without geographic separation if different populations develop specialized ecological niches. Evidence is accumulating that this kind of "sympatric" speciation may have been the origin of many species groups.[45] Much of this research has been stimulated by investigation into the wide variety of cichlid fish species found in the lakes of the African rift valley.[46] This research suggests that each species evolved by occupying a unique niche in the lake environment.[47]

Paleoecological analysis suggests that over evolutionary time scales there have been roughly equal rates of speciation and extinction, except during the few periods of mass extinction, but that increased human occupation of natural areas is likely to increase extinction rates and decrease speciation rates. However, invasions of species often encourage allopatric speciation if the invasive species becomes isolated and adapts to new environmental conditions, or if native species are unable to disperse effectively and individual populations begin to speciate allopatrically. Moreover, entire native species can sometimes evolve rapidly in response to threats posed by invasive species.

Recent research in evolutionary biology leads some scientists to believe that many organisms have the ability to increase their rate of

---

[44] Stephen R. Palumbi, The Evolution Explosion: How Humans Cause Rapid Evolutionary Change 9–10, 35–36 (2001) (development of resistance to antibiotics and pesticides through speciation).

[45] Michael Doebeli & Ulf Dieckmann, *Evolutionary Branching and Sympatric Speciation Caused In Different Types of Ecological Interactions*, 156 Am. Naturalist 577, 593 (2000); Ulf Dieckmann & Michael Doebeli, *On the Origin of Species by Sympatric Speciation*, 400 Nature 354 (1999); Kerstin Johannesson, *Parallel Speciation: A Key to Sympatric Divergence*, 16 Trends in Ecology and Evolution 148 (2001) (citing repeated and independent examples of speciation by the same mechanism and in the absence of extrinsic barriers).

[46] Herbert R. Axelrod & Warren E. Burgess. African Cichlids of Lakes Malawi and Tanganyika 250 (11th ed. 1989).

[47] *See* George W. Barlow, The Cichlid Fishes: Nature's Grand Experiment in Evolution (2000); David Quammen, The Song of the Dodo: Island Biogeography in an Age of Extinctions 232–34 (1990); Doebeli & Dieckmann, Evolutionary Branching, *supra* note 61, at 593; Erik Verheyen et al., Origin of the Superflock of Cichlid Fishes from Lake Victoria, East Africa, 300 Sci. 325, 325 (2003). *But see* Irv Korn-field & Peter F. Smith, *African Cichlid Fishes: Model Systems for Evolutionary Biology*, 31 Ann. Rev. of Ecology & Systematics 163, 184 (2000) ("We caution against premature adoption of particular divergence scenarios in the absence of sufficiently strong evidence.").

mutations when they sense rapid environmental change. In particular, insects, bacteria, and other organisms have developed resistance to antibiotics, pesticides, and herbicides with troubling rapidity. As the National Research Council has observed, "[b]ecause of their rapid growth rate and large populations, microbes can evolve very quickly, allowing them to adapt to new hosts, produce new toxins, and bypass immune responses." [48] Microbial resistance to antibiotics is a growing and understudied problem in managing disease. The processes by which resistance develops outside the laboratory are still poorly understood, but the fact that resistance is occurring nonetheless highlights the underlying question of whether speciation arising from these anthropogenic causes should be considered as contributing to biodiversity.

Puzzle #11: Should we encourage all increases in biodiversity that result from natural selection, even though this may include species that are resistant to antibiotics or pesticides, or should we only emphasize protection of the biodiversity of existing species?

iii. Can Loss of Biodiversity Be Adaptive?

Evolution "generates, sustains, shapes, and sometimes even diminishes biodiversity."[49] Is loss of local biodiversity sometimes essential to allow organisms to adapt to changing conditions? Wildlife Conservation Society marine biologist Andrew Baker has put forward a hypothesis that suggests that one of the most dreaded examples of loss of biodiversity— the bleaching of coral reefs—may be a necessary process by which coral adapts to increasing water temperature. [50] His example, which is analogous to other potential adaptations to climate change, provides a reason to list a thirteenth puzzle, thus creating a Baker's dozen.

Most coral species are naturally white. The brilliant colors that we see are provided by a remarkably complex, and poorly understood, array of algae and other microorganisms. During the late 1990s, coral reefs throughout the world experienced episodes of "bleaching" in which the microorganisms disappeared, leaving only the white coral skeletons. The bleaching has generally been attributed to increased water temperatures, and some commentators have suggested that the bleaching events could serve as an indicator of the dangerous effects of climate change.

Baker ran experiments in which he transferred corals between differing depths of water, causing them to become exposed to differing levels of sunlight. He found that corals that were raised closer to the surface (and thus closer to brighter light) tended to bleach, but that the bleached coral subsequently attracted new kinds of algae that were adapted to higher light levels. Baker argues that the fact that these corals

---

[48] Nat'l Research Council, Grand Challenges in the Environmental Sciences 39 (2001).

[49] Nat'l Research Council, Perspectives on Biodiversity 21 (1999).

[50] Andrew C. Baker, *Reef Corals Bleach to Survive Change*, 411 Nature 765 (2001).

survived well is evidence in support of a hypothesis that bleaching is the coral's way of expelling algae that are no longer adapted to the environment in order to attract new algae that are better adapted.

Today humans are causing incremental changes in the environment that are one-directional and do not replicate cyclical patterns in nature. The increasing concentrations of greenhouse gases and urbanized land use are only the most conspicuous of many examples. University of Arizona ecologist Michael Rosenzweig argues that the decline in biodiversity is inevitable in the long run because the number of species is proportional to the size of natural areas, and that size seems to be decreasing inexorably.[51] Ecologists fear that many species will have great difficulty in adapting to this rate of natural area loss, and that the resulting loss of biodiversity will make it more difficult to maintain ecological processes capable of coping with these trends of environmental change.

Is Baker's hypothesis applicable in a wide range of other contexts? With the increasing air temperatures of the past twenty-five years, similar cases have been widely noted in which both terrestrial and marine organisms are reacting to increased temperature by various mechanisms, including changes in the flowering times of plants, the egg-laying times of birds, and the altered performance of insect herbivores. Species that reproduce rapidly can often adapt to environmental change by evolving through natural selection of the traits best suited to the new environmental conditions. Other animals and some relatively mobile plant species have extended their range northward or upwards, leaving behind areas to which they are now poorly adapted. Some data suggests that birds in habitats that are experiencing warming trends may be experiencing the most rapid population declines; this might indicate that they have dispersed northward in response to the higher temperatures. Although this may reduce local biodiversity at any given time and place, such adaptations may be necessary to the long-run survival of the species.

Where local biodiversity declines as a result of climate change, should we try to restore the former diversity in the hope that the climate change can be reversed? Or should we look at the reduction of diversity as the creation of new ecological niches that may become filled by species that are more adaptable to future conditions?

b. Options for Conserving Biological Diversity

There are two basic ways to conserve biological diversity: in situ, which means conservation of habitats, and ex situ, through gene banks and zoos or botanical gardens. The latter is a stop gap measure at best,

---

[51] Michael L. Rosenzweig, *The Four Questions: What Does the Introduction of Exotic Species Do to Diversity?*, 3 Evolutionary Ecology Res. 361, 366 (2001).

although it is an attractive approach for educating people about animals and plants and enlisting their support in conservation efforts.

In situ conservation involves keeping a species in its natural environment and protecting that environment from anthropogenic damage. Consistent with the predominating preference for in situ over ex situ conservation, Walter V. Reid and Kenton R. Miller explain that "[i]n situ conservation maintains not only a variety's genetic diversity but also the evolutionary interactions that allow it to adapt continually to shifting environmental conditions, such as changes in pest populations or climate." Walter V. Reid & Kenton R. Miller, Keeping Options Alive: The Specific Basis for Conserving Biodiversity (1989). Areas such as wildlife reserves, national parks, and protected landscapes offer the opportunity to maintain not only the targeted endangered species, but also to keep the entire local ecosystem intact. For early articles on issues in the United States, *see generally* Craig A. Arnold, *Conserving Habitats and Building Habitats: The Emerging Impact of the Endangered Species Act on Land Use Development*, 10 Stan. Envtl. L.J. 1 (1991); George Cameron Coggins & Irma S. Russell, *Beyond Shooting Snail Darters in Pork Barrels: Endangered Species and Land Use in America*, 70 Geo. L.J. 1433 (1982).

Wildland management is the least costly—and in many cases the only—means available for effectively maintaining biological diversity. For certain groups of plants and animals, off-site (ex situ) preservation techniques can be useful supplements to the in situ preservation provided by wildlands. But ex situ techniques—zoos and other captive breeding facilities; botanical gardens; arboreta; cryogenic storage of embryos, eggs, and sperm; seed and pollen banks; and tissue cultures—cannot be expected to meet most biological conservation needs.

i. National Parks and Wildlife Reserves

National parks exist in most countries of the world, and are among the most prominent ways for a government to show support for the environment. Parks, wildlife reserves, and protected areas are examples of in situ conservation techniques, as the entire ecosystem (or at least a substantial part of it) is kept intact, and species coexist as in nature. In 1969, the International Union for the Conservation of Nature and Natural Resources suggested that "national park" should be a term exclusively used for areas "where (a) ecosystems are not materially altered by human exploitation, and plant and animal species, geomorphological sites, and habitats are of special interest, (b) authority has prevented exploitation or occupation in the whole area and ecological, geomorphological, or aesthetic features are respected, and (c) visitors are allowed to enter under special conditions for inspirational, educative, cultural, and recreational purposes. N.C. Pollock & B. Litt, Animals, Environment and Man in Africa 90–91 (1975) (this book also gives a brief overview of the history of national parks, starting with Yellowstone National Park's founding in 1872).

As they allow in situ conservation, national parks can maintain a fuller diversity than can ex situ methods.

Further, parks and protected areas that are open to the public can increase interest in the environment and also bring in much needed currency to fund conservation efforts. This may, however, infringe on the way of life of native populations or local people living in the area.

Because parks, other protected areas, and wildlife reserves have been treated as areas of sovereign national interest, the legal rules controlling the use of land within the boundaries of these protected areas park are overwhelmingly national or local. For a good discussion of the legal structure of the Canadian national park system, see H. Ian Rounthwaite, *The National Parks of Canada: An Endangered Species?*, 46 Saskatchewan L. Rev. 43 (1981); for an historical view of the development of some of the state parks in the western United States, see Thomas R. Cox, The Park Builders: A History of State Parks in the Pacific Northwest (1988).

In February 1992, the IUCN World Congress on National Parks, Protected Areas and the Human Future took place in Venezuela. The Congress takes place once a decade. The Congress adopted the Caracas Declaration, which stressed the importance of "well-managed national parks and protected areas." The Declaration viewed the park system as necessary for the maintenance of biological diversity, and crucial for the support of human and nonhuman life. For humankind, the protected areas have "immense scientific, educational, cultural, recreational and spiritual value," in addition to being necessary for agriculture and medicine.

The Declaration urged national and international bodies to "consolidate and enlarge national systems of well-managed protected areas with buffer zones and corridors, so that by the year 2000 they safeguard the full representative range of land, fresh water, coastal and marine ecosystems of each country." It asked governments to be sensitive to the interests of the indigenous people, women, and children of the present and future generations. *See* The Conservation Foundation, Managing National Park System Resources: A Handbook on Legal Duties, Opportunities, and Tools (Michael A. Mantell ed., 1990).

In November 2014, the IUCN World Parks Congress, which was held in Sydney, Australia, was attended by over 5,000 people and adopted the Sydney Promise, which sets forth a plan of action for the next decade. It rests on four pillars, which included the creation of a portal to collate case studies of successful solutions for conserving protected areas and the making of promises by countries, groups of countries, funders, organizatons, and other parties to take take actions and provide support for protected areas. The IUCN now maintains an online portal called Panorama, which lets practitioners share approaches to conserving protected areas, or Pas. http://www.panorama.solutions/. In addition, the IUCN environmental law centre in Bonn, Germany, has been developing modules for a course on protected areas, which will be available worldwide.

The creation of national parks and other protected areas is a major legacy of the 19th conservation movement. These areas, originally created for aesthetic and commercial reasons, can function as a major component of modern biodiversity protection. Large protected areas are also necessary component of species adaptation to global climate change, although as the following excerpt counsels, adaptation may be constrained by existing landscapes. Thomas E. Lovejoy & Lee Hannah, Global Greenhouse Gas Levels and Future of Biodiversity, in Climate Change and Biodiversity 387, 389–390 (Thomas E. Lovejoy & Lee Hannah eds., 2005):

> Rapid responses, dispersal modes, and community reorganization all carry major implications for conservation. Systems to conserve biodiversity in the face of such dynamics must engage entire landscapes. Chapters in this book have described how to design static and dynamic elements in a landscape, and suggested priorities for their management. These systems will be able to better respond to climate change than past, "parks only" strategies. However, there are clear limits to the change they can accommodate.
>
> Rapid responses provide a precedent on which to base strategies for conversation during rapid future climate change. However, the potential for rapid response is greatly constrained by habitat loss. Both rapid and genetic responses and range shifts are jeopardized by existing levels of habitat loss.
>
> Rapid genetic response is comprised where high levels of habitat fragmentation result in loss of genetic diversity. In human-dominated landscapes, natural habitat may remain as small fragments, implying small populations of resident species which lose genetic diversity. Since the recessive traits necessary for rapid response to climate change are frequently less competitive in current climates, they may be lost in small, fragmented populations. This will reduce the pool of individuals capable of rapid response to climate change or eliminate the genetic variants for rapid response altogether.
>
> Rapid range shifts, by whatever mechanism, will be limited by transformed landscapes. Long-distance dispersal is dependent on population size, destination area, and intermediate suitable

habitats, all of which are greatly reduced in human-dominated landscapes. Similarly, micropockets may be eliminated by human land uses, and where they do survive they cannot serve as centers of expansion if surrounded by transformed land.

Limitations on response are compounded when communities reorganize in distributed landscapes. As species' individualistic responses to climate change unfold, community composition will change. Constituents may leave and arrive randomly, sometimes leaving resources available for new species. Where this process unfolds surrounded by human landscapes harboring many weedy species, composition may shift toward human comensals. There will be no barrier to species leaving, since this only involves the death of individuals at a site. However, species arriving will have to traverse fragments of natural habitat, whereas weeds will be able to enter from abundant surrounding human-converted lands. The net effect may be one of simplification and dominance by weedy species.

For all these reasons, natural response to climate change will be constrained. Emerging tools in conservation can nonetheless allow this capacity to be tapped, but there are strong limitations on what can be accomplished. Range shift modeling can help identify where suitable new climate space may appear, but it is difficult to estimate species' ability to reach newly suitable sites. Reserve selection algorithms can identify efficient configurations for sites where species' present and future ranges overlap, but s species that must move substantial distances ate excluded. (Connectivity can be tailored for individual target species, but it will break down when too many species move long distances or where changes increase without limits.

Therefore, improved strategies will be meaningless unless change is kept within limits. Critical limits will be specific to each species, each site, and each region. Some species at some sites, such as the golden toad at Monteverde, may already have seen changes in excess of their critical limits. Other limits will be reached soon, affecting mounting numbers of species. The further into the future change is allowed to continue, the question then becomes, "How much climate change is too much?"

Reliance on national parks to conserve biodiversity raises the question, is this is an imperfect strategy? Consider these problems. First, experiences in the developing world have produced a paradigm shift in protected area philosophy. The original idea that these areas could be walled off from most human use has given way to the idea that parks are part of a larger landscape shared with humans. Humans, especially local indigenous communities, increasingly share protected landscapes. The

British National Park system, with 74% their lands in private ownership, is a model of a park as working landscape. *See* Frederico Cheever, British National Parks for North Americans: *What We Can Learn From a More Crowded Nation Proud of Its Countryside*, 26 Stan. Envtl. L. J.247 (2007). These landscapes are also increasingly a mix of classic reserves and settlement and sustainable exploitation areas. *See* IUCN Bulletin No. 2, Vth IUCN World Parks Congress, Benefits Beyond Boundaries (2003). Whether this conception of protection areas will promote biodiversity conservation is an open question. Second, a major objective of biodiversity is the conservation of sustainable ecosystems. *See* World Resources, People and Ecosystems: The Fraying Web of Life (2000). Protected areas, especially older ones, seldom correspond to the relevant ecosystem to be conserved and managed and are not always rich in biodiversity. Thus, parks must be linked, as in the Yukon to Yellowstone proposal, by corridors which often land in private ownership. In addition, in recent years ecosystem tourism has developed with almost no international guidance. *See* Francoise Simon, *Regulating Ecotourism: Legal Frameworks and Market Guidelines*, *in* The Ecotourism Equation: Measuring the Impacts 192 (Elizabeth Malek-Zadeh Yale School of Forestry and Environmental Studies Bulletin 99 1996); International Handbook of Ecotourism (Ray Ballantyne & Jan Packer 2013).

ii. Pricing Ecosystem Services and Other Options

Biodiversity resources have traditionally been viewed as public goods, such as national defense, which are incapable of being priced and traded in markets. However, in the past two decades, this view has changed. To counter, the persistent marginalization of non-monetizable benefits in formal and informal benefit-cost analysis, proponents of biodiversity and ecosystem conservation have adopted the utilitarian argument that ecosystems should be conserved and sustained because they provide valuable, monetizable services to society. The very idea of valuation of resources without established market prices and the methods used to do so remain extremely controversial. Review Chapter 3, pages 122 to 125. *See also* Deiter Helm, Natural Capital: Valuing the Planet (2015); Harold A. Mooney & Paul R. Ehrlich, *Ecosystem Services: A Fragmentary History*, *in* Nature's Services: Societal Dependence on Natural Ecosystems 11 (Gretchen C. Daily ed., 1997). The numbers can be staggering. In 1997, a team of researchers estimated that the global value of ecosystem services was $33 trillion per year. In 2014, the team recalculated the value in 2011 dollars and came up with the figure $125 trillion. Robert Constanza et al., *Changes in the Global Value of Ecosystem Services*, 26 Global Envtl. Change 152 (2014). The fullest effort to date to catalog the state of the world's ecosystems and the services that they provide is Millennium Ecosystem Assessment, Living Beyond Our Means: Natural Assets and Human Well-Being (2005). The loss of systems and their services contribute to the loss of biodiversity so efforts to conserve ecosystems should promote biodiversity. However, ecosystem conservation involves discrete landscapes whereas biodiversity conservation is a more abstract idea, not always anchored in a landscape. And, the emphasis on conserving high producing ecosystem services may come at the expense of identifying and conserving crucial, but not conventionally valuable, biodiversity processes.

Ecosystem services contribute to decline as the loss of biodiversity continues. Changes in the Global Value of Ecosystem Services, *supra*, estimated the yearly service losses from land conversion at between 4.3 and $20.2 trillion. The Millennium Ecosystem Assessment surveyed 24 services. Four were increasing their ability to benefit humans, but three of these were agriculture, livestock and aquaculture. Fifteen services were declined. These include ocean fisheries, wood fuel, genetic resources, fresh water, air quality, soils and wet-land buffers. Five were in a steady state. These were timber, cotton and hemp fibers, water regulation, disease regulation and recreation and ecotourism. Living Beyond Our Means, *supra*, at 13–14. World Watch Institute, Vital Signs 2005 86–87 (2005), reports that nearly one out of four mammals are in serious decline due to uncontrolled hunting, habitat fragmentation and loss and now global climate change. Butterfly and bird species are declining in Europe for similar reasons. http://www.eea.europa.eu/highlights/populations-of-grassland-butterflies-decline. The IUCN's 2006 Red List of Threatened Species reports that 16,119 out of 40,177 assessed species are threatened with extinction, http://www.iucn.org/en/news/archive/2006/o5/ 02_pr_red_Jist.htm. Subsequent reports confirm the continued rapid rate of biodiversity loss. *See, e.g.*, David U. Hooper et al, *A Global Synthesis Reveals Biodiversity Loss as a Major Driver of Ecosystem Change*, 486 Nature 105, (2012); Bradley J. Cardinal et al., *Biodiversity Loss and Its Impact on Humanity*, 486 Nature 59 (2011). The Worldwatch Institute, State of the World 2012: Moving Toward Sustainable Prosperity (2012), reports that the current rate of species extinction is up to 1,000 times above the Earth's normal extinction rate, a level of loss that has not occurred since the extinction of the dinosaurs 65 million years ago. *See also* Elizabeth Kolbert, The Sixth Extinction: An Unnatural History (2014)

2. THE BIODIVERSITY CONVENTION

a. Background

INTERNATIONAL LAW AND THE PROTECTION OF BIOLOGICAL DIVERSITY

Daniel M. Bodansky
28 Vand.J. Transnatl. L. 623, 627 (1995)

Over the last twenty to twenty-five years, international environmental law has developed a number of general principles that are relevant to biodiversity protection. . . . Regardless of whether these principles have the status of customary international law . . . they represent an orientation or framework for discussions of environmental issues.

The three principles most relevant to biological diversity are: (1) the precautionary principle, (2) the principle of intergenerational equity, and (3) the principle of differentiated responsibilities. The precautionary principle says that the international community need not await scientific certainty before taking action to protect the environment, particularly when the potential environmental harms are irreversible. This principle is clearly relevant to the biodiversity question, given the substantial uncertainties about the magnitude of the problem. . . .

The second relevant principle is intergenerational equity, which says that people have a duty to conserve resources for the benefit not only of the present generation but of future generations as well. . . .

Finally, the principle of differentiated responsibilities addresses the concerns of developing countries, where most biodiversity is found. According to this principle, countries should contribute differently to international environmental efforts, depending on their capabilities and their historical responsibility. In practice, this principle has meant preferential treatment of poor, developing countries, and a greater contribution by wealthy, developed countries.

These three principles provide the general framework for efforts to conserve biological resources. However, they are not a panacea. They do not answer the hard questions about exactly how much evidence is needed before undertaking conservation measures or how much protection is warranted, nor do they dictate any particular regulatory policies.

The more specific rules and mechanisms to conserve biological diversity are found primarily in treaties. Over the last fifty to sixty years, a whole range of treaties has been negotiated. One general category includes wildlife protection treaties addressing particular species, such as migratory birds or whales. The primary purpose of these treaties is to protect against over-exploitation of species by humans.... The bigger threat to species, however, is not over-harvesting by humans but rather habitat loss. To protect biological diversity, emphasis needs to be placed not simply on protecting particular species, but on protecting the broader ecosystems in which they live. A number of international treaties have been developed to address the need for habitat conservation.... A final category of wildlife treaties are regional treaties that address nature conservation in a comprehensive fashion through both species protection and habitat protection. The first of these was developed in Africa. Subsequently, regional treaties have been developed for the Western Hemisphere, Europe, and Southeast Asia.

When the idea of developing a global biodiversity convention first began to gather momentum in the late 1980's, some suggested that it should serve as an umbrella agreement, consolidating and subsuming the many wildlife treaties developed since the turn of the century. Ultimately, this plan did not prove practicable. Instead, the 1992 Convention on Biological Diversity has served as a framework agreement that builds upon, rather than subsumes, existing treaties. In contrast to earlier treaties, it does not include any lists or annexes of protected species or areas. The Biodiversity Convention, however, goes beyond previous treaties by dealing with the problem of biodiversity in a more comprehensive fashion, addressing all aspects of biodiversity including access to biological resources, biotechnology, and financial resources.

The Convention on Biological Diversity was negotiated under the auspices of the United Nations Environment Programme and opened for signature at the United Nations Conference on Environment and Development in Rio de Janeiro, Brazil, in June 1992. The Convention provides for national monitoring of biological diversity, the development of national strategies, plans and programs to protect biological diversity, national in situ and ex situ conservation measures, environmental impact assessments of projects for adverse effects on biological diversity, and national reports on implementing measures and the effectiveness of these measures.

The United States did not sign the Convention when it opened for signature in Rio. (Brazil was the first country to sign.) Then-President Bush indicated that the United States was concerned about constraints on technology transfer and "global pirating" of intellectual property rights under Articles 16 and 22, biotechnology and biosafety under Article 19, and the failure to designate the permanent financial mechanism under Articles 39 and 21. Subsequently, on Earth Day 1993, President Clinton announced that the United States would sign the agreement and provide an interpretive statement regarding the controversial provisions. On Earth Day 1993, President Clinton announced that the United States would sign the Biological Diversity Convention without requesting changes in Articles 16 and 19. When President Clinton submitted the convention to the Senate for ratification in November 1993, he included an interpretive statement to the convention: "with respect to technology subject to patents and other intellectual property rights," the United States understands that "the Convention requires all Parties to ensure that access or transfer of technology is consistent with the adequate and effective protection of intellectual property rights." *See* U.S. Treaty Doc. 103–20, November 16, 1993, VI–VII. The Convention remains unapproved by the Senate. As of August 2015, the United States was not among the 196 States that had ratified the Convention. *See* William J. Snape III, *Joining the Convention on Biological Diversity: A Legal and Scientific Overview of Why the United States Must Wake Up*, 3 Sustainable Development Law & Policy 6 (2010).

b. The Text

Excerpts from the Convention are reproduced below.

CONVENTION ON BIOLOGICAL DIVERSITY

UNEP/Bio. Div./CONF/L.2, reprinted in 31 I.L.M. 818 (1992), June 5, 1992

[See Document Supplement]

PREAMBLE. *Affirming* that the conservation of biological diversity is a common concern of humankind

ARTICLE 6. GENERAL MEASURES FOR CONSERVATION AND SUSTAINABLE USE.

Each Contracting Party shall, in accordance with its particular conditions and capabilities:

> (a) Develop national strategies, plans or programmes for the conservation and sustainable use of biological diversity or adapt for this purpose existing strategies, plans or programmes. . . .

ARTICLE 11.   INCENTIVE MEASURES

Each Contracting Party shall, as far as possible and as appropriate, adopt economically and socially sound measures that act as incentives for the conservation and sustainable use of components of biological diversity.

ARTICLE 15.   ACCESS TO GENETIC RESOURCES

1. Recognizing the sovereign rights of States over their natural resources, the authority to determine access to genetic resources rests with the national governments and is subject to national legislation.

2. Each Contracting Party shall endeavor to create conditions to facilitate access to genetic resources for environmentally sound uses by

other Contracting Parties and not to impose restrictions that run counter to the objectives of this Convention.

3.   For the purpose of this Convention, the genetic resources being provided by a Contracting Party, as referred to in this Article and Articles 16 and 19, are only those that are provided by Contracting Parties that are countries of origin of such resources or by the Parties that have acquired the genetic resources in accordance with this Convention.

4.   Access, where granted, shall be on mutually agreed terms and subject to the provisions of this Article.

5.   Access to genetic resources shall be subject to prior informed consent of the Contracting Party providing such resources, unless otherwise determined by that Party.

6.   Each Contracting Party shall endeavor to develop and carry out scientific research based on genetic resources provided by other Contracting Parties with the full participation of and where possible, in such Contracting Parties.

7.   Each Contracting Party shall take legislative, administrative or policy measures, as appropriate, and in accordance with Articles 16 and 19 and, where necessary, through the financial mechanism established by Articles 20 and 21 with the aim of sharing in a fair and equitable way the results of research and development and the benefits arising from the commercial and other utilization of genetic resources with the Contracting Party providing such resources. Such sharing shall be upon mutually agreed terms.

ARTICLE 16.   ACCESS TO AND TRANSFER OF TECHNOLOGY

1.   Each Contracting Party, recognizing that technology includes biotechnology, and that both access to and transfer of technology among Contracting Parties are essential elements for the attainment of the objectives of this Convention, undertakes subject to the provisions of this Article to provide and/or facilitate access for and transfer to other Contracting Parties of technologies that are relevant to the conservation and sustainable use of biological diversity or make use of genetic resources and do not cause significant damage to the environment.

2.   Access to and transfer of technology referred to in paragraph 1 above to developing countries shall be provided and/or facilitated under fair and most favorable terms, including on confessional and preferential terms where mutually agreed, and, where necessary, in accordance with the financial mechanism established by Articles 20 and 21. In the case of technology subject to patents and other intellectual property rights, such access and transfer shall be provided on terms which recognize and are consistent with the adequate and effective protection of intellectual

property rights. The application of this paragraph shall be consistent with paragraphs 3, 4 and 5 below.

3.   Each Contracting Party shall take legislative, administrative or policy measures, as appropriate, with the aim that Contracting Parties, in particular those that are developing countries, which provide genetic resources are provided access to and transfer of technology which makes use of those resources, on mutually agreed terms, including technology protected by patents and other intellectual property rights, where necessary through the provisions of Articles 20 and 21 and in accordance with international law and consistent with paragraphs 4 and 5 below.

4.   Each Contracting Party shall take legislative, administrative or policy measures, as appropriate with the aim that the private sector facilitates access to, joint development and transfer of technology referred to in paragraph 1 above for the benefit of both governmental institutions and the private sector of developing countries and in this regard shall abide by the obligations included in paragraphs 1, 2 and 3 above.

5.   The Contracting Parties, recognizing that patents and other intellectual property rights may have an influence on the implementation of this Convention, shall cooperate in this regard subject to national legislation and international law in order to ensure that such rights are supportive of and do not run counter to its objectives.

ARTICLE 17.   EXCHANGE OF INFORMATION

1.   The Contracting Parties shall facilitate the exchange of information, from all publicly available sources, relevant to the conservation and sustainable use of biological diversity, taking into account the special needs of developing countries.

2.   Such exchange of information shall include exchange of results of technical, scientific and socio-economic research, as well as information on training and surveying programmes, specialized knowledge, indigenous and traditional knowledge as such and in combination with the technologies referred to in Article 16, paragraph 1. It shall also, where feasible, include repatriation of information.

ARTICLE 18.   TECHNICAL AND SCIENTIFIC COOPERATION

1.   The Contracting Parties shall promote international technical and scientific cooperation in the field of conservation and sustenance of biological diversity, where necessary, through the appropriate international and national institutions.

2.   Each Contracting Party shall promote technical and scientific cooperation with other Contracting Parties, in particular developing countries, in implementing this Convention, inter alia, through the development and implementation of national policies. In promoting such cooperation, special attention should be given to the development and

strengthening of national capabilities, by means of human resources development and institution building.

3.   The Conference of the Parties, at its first meeting, shall determine how to establish a clearing-house mechanism to promote and facilitate technical and scientific cooperation.

4.   The Contracting Party shall, in accordance with national legislation and policies, encourage and develop methods of cooperation for the development and use of technologies, including indigenous and traditional technologies, in pursuance of the objectives of this Convention. For this purpose, the Contracting Parties shall also promote cooperation in the training of personnel and exchange of experts.

5.   The Contracting Parties shall, subject to mutual agreement, promote the establishment of joint research programmes and joint ventures for the development of technologies relevant to the objectives of this Convention.

ARTICLE 19.   HANDLING   OF   BIOTECHNOLOGY   AND DISTRIBUTION OF ITS BENEFITS

1.   Each Contracting Party shall take legislative, administrative or policy measures, as appropriate, to provide for the effective participation in biotechnological research activities by those Contracting Parties, especially developing countries, which provide the genetic resources for such research, and where feasible in such Contracting Parties.

2.   Each Contracting Party shall take all practicable measures to promote and advance priority access on a fair and equitable basis by Contracting Parties, especially developing countries, to the results and benefits arising from biotechnologies based upon genetic resources provided by those Contracting Parties. Such access shall be on mutually agreed terms.

3.   The Parties shall consider the need for and modalities of a protocol setting out appropriate procedures, including, in particular, advance informed agreement in the field of the safe transfer, handling and use of any living modified organism resulting from biotechnology that may have adverse effect on the conservation and sustainable use of biological diversity.

4.   Each Contracting party shall, directly or by requiring any natural or legal person under its jurisdiction providing the organisms referred to in paragraph 3 above, provide any available information about the use and safety regulations required by that Contracting Party in handling such organisms, as well as any avail-able information on the potential adverse impact of the specific organisms concerned to the Contracting Party into which those organisms are to be introduced.

ARTICLE 20.   FINANCIAL RESOURCES

1.   Each Contracting Party undertakes to provide, in accordance with its capabilities, financial support and incentives in respect to those national activities which are intended to achieve the objectives of this Convention, in accordance with its national plans, priorities and programmes.

2.   The developed country Parties shall provide new and additional financial resources to enable developing country Parties to meet the agreed full incremental costs to them of implementing measures which fulfil the obligations of this Convention and to benefit from its provisions and which costs are agreed between a developing country Party and the institutional structure referred to in Article 21 in accordance with policy, strategy, programme priorities and eligibility criteria and an indicative list of incremental costs established by the Conference of the Parties. Other Parties, including countries undergoing the process of transition to a market economy, may voluntarily assume the obligations of the developed country Parties. For the purpose of this Article, the Conference of the Parties, shall at its first meeting establish a list of developed country Parties and other parties which voluntarily assume the obligations of the developed country Parties. The Conference of the Parties shall periodically review and if necessary amend the list. Contributions from other countries and sources on a voluntary basis would also be encouraged. The implementation of these commitments shall take into account the need for adequacy, predictability and timely flow of funds and the importance of burden-sharing among the contributing Parties included in the list.

3.   The developed country Parties may also provide, and developing country Parties avail themselves of, financial resources related to the implementation of this Convention through bilateral, regional and other multilateral channels.

4.   The extent to which developing country Parties will effectively implement their commitments under this Convention will depend on the effective implementation by developed country Parties of their commitments under this Convention related to financial resources and transfer of technology and will take fully into account the fact that economic and social development and eradication of poverty are the first and overriding priorities of the developing country Parties.

5.   The Parties shall take full account of the specific needs and special situation of least developed countries in their actions with regard to funding and transfer of technology.

6.   The Contracting Parties shall also take into consideration the special conditions resulting from the dependence on, distribution and

location of, biological diversity within developing country Parties, in particular small island States.

7. Consideration shall also be given to the special situation of developing countries, including those that are most environmentally vulnerable, such as those with arid and semi-arid zones, coastal and mountainous areas.

ARTICLE 21.   FINANCIAL MECHANISM

1. There shall be a mechanism for the provision of financial resources to developing country Parties for purposes of this Convention on a grant or confessional basis the essential elements of which are described in this Article. The mechanism shall function under the authority and guidance of and be accountable to, the Conference of the Parties for purposes of this Convention. The operations of the mechanism shall be carried out by such institutional structure as may be decided upon by the Conference of the Parties at its first meeting. . . . The mechanism shall operate within a democratic and transparent system of governance.

2. Pursuant to the objectives of this Convention, the Conference of the Parties shall at its first meeting determine the policy, strategy and programme priorities, as well as detailed criteria and guidelines for eligibility for access to and utilization of the financial resources including monitoring and evaluation on a regular basis of such utilization. . . .

ARTICLE 22.   RELATIONSHIP   WITH   OTHER INTERNATIONAL CONVENTIONS

1. The provisions of this Convention shall not affect the rights and obligations of any Contracting Party deriving from any existing international agreement, except where the exercise of those rights and obligations would cause a serious damage or threat to biological diversity.

2. Contracting parties shall implement this Convention with respect to the marine environment consistently with the rights and obligations of States under the law of the sea.

NOTES AND QUESTIONS

1. *Assuming responsibility for damages beyond one's borders.* Article 3 of the convention provides that

Principle

States have, in accordance with the Charter of the United Nations and the principles of international law, the sovereign right to exploit their own resources pursuant to their own environmental policies, and the responsibility to ensure that activities within their jurisdiction or control do not cause damage to the environment of other States or of areas beyond the limits of national jurisdiction.

This provision restates Principle 21 of the Stockholm Declaration on the Human Environment. It has been said that this is the first time that it has ever appeared as an explicit obligation in the text of a natural resources convention. Is it an explicit obligation? Note the title of the article. What is the significance of this? The United Nations Framework Convention on Climate Change includes the principle in its preamble, not in the text of the convention. What legal differences does it make to include the provision in the text of the convention? The protection of aquatic ecosystem biodiversity often requires transnational cooperation. The UN Watercourses Convention discussed in Chapter 12 has "a complete and detailed set of rules and mechanisms for enabling cooperation to unfold. The CBD, on the other hand, has emphasized the need for States to address transboundary river basin management issues, but still lacks principles and specific provisions governing and guiding cooperation between watercourse states." Secretariat of the Convention on Biological Diversity (Sabine Brels, David Coates & Flavia Loures), Transboundary Water Resources Management: The Role of International Watercourse Agreements in Implementation of CBD 19 (CBD Technical Series No. 40 2008). How should this regulatory gap be closed?

2. *Implementing the Convention.* If you were asked to help draft implementing guidelines for the Convention, what issues would you need to address and how would you address them?

3. *Bioprospecting* If you were advising a corporate client who relies on gathering natural plants in tropical forests for medicinal products, what protection does the Biological Diversity Convention give to the client? The next section addresses these problems.

c. The Special Problem of Intellectual Property Rights in Nature

i. *Products of Nature Not Patentable*

Access to the knowledge contained in biodiversity poses two distinct intellectual property issues. One is the ownership of useful information contained in flora and fauna. The second is control of use of local knowledge possessed by indigenous peoples or other traditional communities. The assignment of the ownership of biodiversity, the flora and fauna of a nation, may be critical to its conservation. In the 1990s, there was great hope that areas such as tropical rainforests would yield major medical cures. However, the hoped-for market in biotechnological products has not substantially evolved since 1992. Merck abandoned its search for new drugs from the natural world in 2008, along with most of the other major pharmaceutical companies, and shifted their attention to synthetic compounds and vaccines. Then last year, as if to mark the anniversary of its Costa Rican folly, the company gave away its entire library of natural compounds—100,000 extracts representing 60 percent of all known plant genera, ready to be screened for the next big miracle drug. And it wasn't just Merck: Pfizer, Eli Lilly, Bristol-Myers Squibb, and most other Big Pharma companies have also abandoned the direct search for drugs from the natural world

As a matter of intellectual property law, the question of who owns biodiversity is simple: nature is incapable of ownership. One can only obtain a property right such as a patent when one uses or manipulates nature to produce a useful product. The issue arose in Association for Molecular Pathology v. Myriad Genetics, Inc., 568 U.S. 1794 (2012), 133 S.Ct. 2107 (2012). A company discovered the gene sequence for BRCA 1 and 2 genes, which allowed the company to identify women with a high risk of breast and ovarian cancer. The Court unanimously held that the naturally occurring DNA in the gene sequence alone could not be the subject of a patent:

Section 101 of the Patent Act provides:

"Whoever invents or discovers any new and useful . . . composition of matter, or any new and useful improvement thereof, may obtain a patent therefor, subject to the conditions and requirements of this title." 35 U. S. C. § 101.

We have "long held that this provision contains an important implicit exception[:] Laws of nature, natural phenomena, and abstract ideas are not patentable." Mayo, 566 U. S., at ___ (slip op., at 1) (internal quotation marks and brackets omitted). Rather, " 'they are the basic tools of scientific and technological work' " that lie beyond the domain of patent protection. Id., at ___ (slip op., at 2). As the Court has explained, without this exception, there would be considerable danger that the grant of patents would "tie up" the use of such tools and thereby "inhibit future innovation premised upon them." Id., at ___ (slip op., at 17). This would be at odds with the very point of patents, which exist to promote creation. Diamond v. Chakrabarty, 447 U. S. 303, 309 (1980) (Products of nature are not created, and " 'manifestations . . . of nature [[**134] are] free to all men and reserved exclusively to none' "). The rule against patents on naturally occurring things is not without limits, however, for "all inventions at some level embody, use, reflect, rest upon, or apply laws of nature, natural phenomena, or abstract ideas," and "too broad an interpretation of this exclusionary principle could eviscerate patent law." 566 U. S., at ___ (slip op., at 2). As we have recognized before, patent protection strikes a delicate balance between creating "incentives that lead to creation, invention, and discovery" and "impeding the flow of information that might permit, indeed spur, invention." Id., at ___ (slip op., at 23). We must apply this well-established standard to determine whether Myriad's patents claim any "new and useful

. . . composition of matter," § 101, or instead claim naturally occurring phenomena.

It is undisputed that Myriad did not create or alter any of the genetic information encoded in the BRCA1 and BRCA2 genes. The location and order of the nucleotides existed in nature before Myriad found them. Nor did Myriad create or alter the genetic structure of DNA. Instead, Myriad's principal contribution was uncovering the precise location and genetic sequence of the BRCA1 and BRCA2 genes within chromosomes 17 and 13. The question is whether this renders the genes patentable.

Myriad recognizes . . . that our decision in Chakrabarty is central to this inquiry. Brief for Respondents 14, 23–27. In Chakrabarty, scientists added four plasmids to a bacterium, which enabled it to break down various components of crude oil. 447 U. S., at 305, and n. 1. The Court held that the modified bacterium was patentable. It explained [*2117] that the patent claim was "not to a hitherto unknown natural phenomenon, but to a nonnaturally occurring manufacture or composition of matter—a product of human ingenuity 'having a distinctive name, character [and] use.'" Id, at 309–310 (quoting Hartranft v. Wiegmann, 121 U. S. 609, 615 (1887); alteration in original). The Chakrabarty bacterium was new "with markedly different characteristics from any found in nature," 447 U. S., at 310, due to the additional plasmids and resultant "capacity for degrading oil." Id, at 305, n. 1. In this case, by contrast, Myriad did not create anything. To be sure, it found an important and useful gene, but separating that gene from its surrounding genetic material is not an act of invention.

[133 S.Ct. at 2116–2117]

Intellectual property law thus creates a disincentive for countries to conserve biodiversity because they will not reap the economic benefits. Cyrille de Klemm, *Conservation of Species: The Need for a New Approach*, 9 Envtl. Pol'y & L. 122 (1982), proposed that all flora and fauna should be assigned an economic value, the benefits of species should be open to all nations, States should assume a stewardship duty to conserve species under their jurisdiction but poor but biodiversity-rich States should be compensated for the costs of assessing their biodiversity resources and conserving them. In the case of the discovery of valuable products such as drugs, royalties should be paid to the host country to finance conservation by analogy to the polluter pays principle. Others have suggested that the host country should have the choice of declaring State ownership of biodiversity or assigning it to individual land owners. Roger A. Sedjo, *Property Rights For Plants*, 97 Resource Magazine 1 (1989).

ii. TRIPS and Biodiversity

Article 15 of the Convention on Biodiversity is a departure from the structure of the major international patent protection regime, The Agreement on Trade-Related Aspects of Intellectual Property Rights (TRIPS). Nunes Pires de Carvalho, The TRIPS Regime of Patent Rights 186 (2002). There is no formal conflict between the Convention and TRIPS. TRIPS, like all conventional intellectual property law, does not apply to nature *per se*; it only applies to human modifications of natural processes that merit property protection. Thus, a country remains free to set the ground rules for access to naturally occurring resources just as they set the ground rules for access to valuable minerals. However, the objectives of the Convention and TRIPS can diverge. The basic objective of TRIPS is to promote international trade in intellectual property. It does so by reducing the distortions and impediments to international trade that result from the under-protection of patent rights and by recognizing "that intellectual property rights are private rights." Preamble, paragraph 4. These objectives basically favor the intellectual property rights protected in developed countries and assume that private individuals such as pharmaceutical complies can freely prospect in nature and does not protect traditional uses of natural products. Developing countries have long argued that intellectual property law does not permit a country to capitalize on its biodiversity heritage . . . any tensions remain largely theoretical. Suppose a country denies an otherwise qualified patent because traditional knowledge has been used to identify useful generic resources. Can a party justify the decision under Article 15(7) of the Convention? Can it also invoke the precautionary principle to protect traditional uses of biodiversity, and, if so, under what circumstances? Can a country exercise its sovereignty to declare that biodiversity is a national patrimony and is either not subject to private exploitation or subject to exploitation by licenses which do not meet the minimum standards of TRIPS? TRIPS requires national treatment and exclusive rights for a minimum of twenty years. Can a country require that the revenues from any patent obtained with traditional knowledge be shared with the State or a local community? *See* Pires de Carvalho, The Trips Regime of Patent Rights, *supra*, at 202–208, for an argument that there is no inconsistency between TRIPS and the Convention and that there are various theories available to void patents based on misappropriated knowledge.

Nonetheless, a serious gap remains between host countries' treatment of biodiversity and the use of a natural product to obtain a patent. The Himalayan Yew is a source of the cancer treatment drug, Taxol, and the Yew was listed as Appendix II CITES species in 2004. But, the chemical precursors to taxol were not. This has resulted in reduced Yew populations or even extinction in northwest Yunnan Province in China. George Friswold and Kelly Day-Rubenstein, *Bioprospecting and*

Biodiversity Conservation: What Happens When Discoveries Are Made?,
50 Ariz. L. Rev. 545, 575–576 (2008), draw broader lessons from the taxol
experience:

> "A final lesson we can draw from the experience of taxol is that
> simply creating a market demand for genetic resources with
> medical applications will not necessarily promote biodiversity
> conservation. Asian yews are being harvested rapidly in areas
> with less well-defined property-rights regimes, even where
> government policies designate them as "endangered."
> Bioprospecting can exchange one extinction threat (habitat
> conversion because a species is not valued) for another (over-
> harvesting because the resource is valued in an open-access
> setting). To date, 64 plant species have been listed under CITES
> expressly because of the threat of over-harvest for medicinal
> uses. The case of taxol illustrates that creating market demand
> for genetic resources without clearly defining property rights
> over them can lead to resource depletion rather than
> conservation. As the newest wave of bioprospecting focuses on
> the Antarctic, oceans, and other areas with more open-access
> property regimes, new questions will arise over bioprospecting's
> impact on biodiversity conservation.

Article 9 of the Nagoya Protocol, discussed, at pages 867 to 868, *infra,*
attempts to address this problem: "The Parties shall encourage users and
providers to direct benefits arising from the utilization of genetic
resources towards the conservation of biological diversity and the
sustainable use of its components."

Many countries have sought to integrate intellectual property law
and the Convention through disclosure requirements: However, the
existence of a disclosure requirement without further analysis of its
binding nature, scope and consequences for lack of fulfilment, could paint
a false picture. For instance, many countries provide only a non-binding,
voluntary disclosure requirement (such as in the EC and its member
states), provide only legal consequences for limited cases contrary to
public morality (such as in New Zealand with respect to obvious
misappropriation of Maori TK), or only require certificates of origin for
national GR [Genetic Resources] and TK [Traditional Knowledge] (such
as in Costa Rica). Furthermore, for a lot of countries, the status of
implementation of the disclosure requirement is unclear as it has been
introduced in general terms in biodiversity legislation, and the laws make
no concrete reference to patent law or IP law. Only a few countries have
introduced the disclosure of origin in patent law through clear and
detailed regulation and therefore provide instructive examples for this
study.

Disclosure can be voluntary, mandatory, and additionally require evidence of legal provenance (certificate of origin, PIC, ABS). A strong form of mandatory disclosure connects patentability, nullity or revocation of patents with disclosure of origin. An intermediate type of mandatory disclosure does not link patentability or nullity with disclosure, but sanctions the lack of fulfilment of disclosure with criminal or administrative sanctions. Independently, regulations on access to GR and TK in the country of origin provide criminal penalties and civil liability. Finally, voluntary disclosure as part of the formalities without consequences on patent application is the weakest form of disclosure.

The linking of patentability, nullity or revocation, and disclosure of origin can be found in a growing number of countries such as Switzerland, China, India, Brazil, Costa Rica, the Andean Communities, Peru and South Africa. In some countries the patentability is even subordinated to the biodiversity and TK legislation and requires a certificate of legal provenance, but as these laws are still new, one will have to wait to see how the obligation will be implemented in IP legislation on patent application or how it will be handled in administrative practice. This is the case for the constitutional provisions in Bolivia (2009) and Ecuador (2008), and the executive decrees in the Philippines (2009) and the Kyrgyz Republic (2008).

Some countries provide additional measures. Peru (on the basis of the model of the Andean Community) will even review *ex officio* foreign patents on GR and TK to work on revocations if conditions of disclosure are not respected. In India, the Biodiversity Authority is given the power to oppose the granting of patents outside of India. The model law of the African Union calls for practical cooperation of different offices to exchange information on access to GR and TK. In another group of countries, including Norway and Denmark, patentability is not linked to disclosure [Thomas Henniger, Disclosure Requirements in Patent Law and Related Measures A Comparative overview of existing national and regional legislation on IP and Biodiversity, (2009) *available at* http://ictsd. org/downloads/2009/11/henninger-biodiversity-ip-think-piece-final.pdf Footnotes Omitted.]

QUESTION

Article 29 of TRIPs provides:

Conditions on Patent Applicants

1.   Members shall require that an applicant for a patent shall disclose the invention in a manner sufficiently clear and complete for the invention to be carried out by a person skilled in the art and may require the applicant to indicate the best mode for carrying out the invention known to the inventor at the filing date or, where priority is claimed, at the priority date of the application.

2. Members may require an applicant for a patent to provide information concerning the applicant's corresponding foreign applications.

Are the disclosure laws consistent with these provisions?

iii. TRIPS and Local Knowledge

Indigenous people and other traditional communities often have invaluable information about how the environmental system functions in areas of biological diversity and about the usefulness of plant and animal life to people. However, the western system of intellectual property is intended to encourage innovation and is not designed to protect the traditional knowledge of indigenous peoples. How do we protect their intellectual property rights in the knowledge they have acquired? Alejandro Madrazo, *Biocolonialism: TRIPS and the Genetic No Man's Land,* 25 Geo. Int'l Envtl. L. Rev. 487, 516–517 (2013), argues that the net result of denying traditional communities profiting from their knowledge "keeps them from obtaining sustenance from traditional activities and pushes to seek sustenance elsewhere . . . exploiting the resources that they have in hand: sale of land or deforestation for sustenance agriculture." What measures should we adopt? *See* Andrew Jacoby & Charles Weiss, *Recognizing Property Rights in Traditional Biocultural Contribution,* 16 Stan. Envtl. L.J. 74 (1997). *See* Andrew Gray, The Impact of the Biodiversity Conservation on Indigenous Peoples, in Biodiversity: Social and Ecological Perspectives 59, 66–69 (Vandana Shiva et al. eds., 1991); Lee Breckenridge, *Rights in Ecosystems under International Environmental Law,* 59 Tenn. L. Rev. 735, 757–758 (1992). In practice, research and conservation groups have developed model guidelines and research protocols to help indigenous peoples protect their interest. To redress the balance, the Fourth Session of the WTO Ministerial Conference in Doha instructed the TRIPS Council to examine the relations between the Convention on Biological Diversity and TRIPS relating to the protection of traditional knowledge and folklore. Article 8(j) of the Convention admonishes the parties to "respect, preserve and maintain knowledge, innovations and practices of indigenous and local communities . . ." and to "encourage the equitable sharing of the benefits arising from the utilization of such knowledge, innovations and practices." Traditional knowledge is often the sum of natural ingredients and cultural practices and beliefs. As has been observed, intellectual property law "may protect the individual elements of traditional knowledge, but [it] does not attend to its holistic nature." The TRIPS Regime of Patent Rights, *supra* at 194. Portugal adopted a sui generis approach to traditional knowledge. Portuguese Decree—Law 118, April 20, 2002, defines traditional knowledge as "all the intangible elements associated to the commercial or industrial use of local varieties, and other endogenous material developed by local communities, collectively or individually, in a non-systematic manner and that are inserted in cultural or spiritual traditions of those communities . . ." It allows local communities to protect their traditional knowledge against commercial exploitation if the knowledge can be identified and has not been known beyond the community and commercially used.

NOTES AND QUESTIONS

1.   What benefit would an intergovernmental agreement provide? Are there any possible costs associated with such an agreement? Article 7 of the Nagoya Protocol, discussed, at pages 867 to 868, *infra*, provides "[i]n accordance with domestic law, each Party shall take measures, as appropriate, with the aim of ensuring that traditional knowledge associated with genetic resources that is held by indigenous and local communities is accessed with the prior and informed consent or approval and involvement of these indigenous and local communities, and that mutually agreed terms have been established." Article 12 provides in part:

> 1.   In implementing their obligations under this Protocol, Parties shall in accordance with domestic law take into consideration indigenous and local communities' customary laws, community protocols and procedures, as applicable, with respect to traditional knowledge associated with genetic resources.

> 2.   Parties, with the effective participation of the indigenous and local communities concerned, shall establish mechanisms to inform potential users of traditional knowledge associated with genetic resources about their obligations, including measures as made available through the Access and Benefit-sharing Clearing-House for access to and fair and equitable sharing of benefits arising from the utilization of such knowledge.

2.   *Biodiversity conservation in review.* For analysis of the Biodiversity Convention, see IUCN Environmental Law Centre, A Guide to the Convention on Biological Diversity (1994).

d.   Developments Since the Convention Was Opened for Signature

In May 1993, the parties met in Trondheim, Norway to begin preparations for implementing the Convention on Biodiversity. The meetings focused on drafting protocols to the Biodiversity Convention and debating questions that were not resolved in Rio de Janerio in 1992. The major issues in dispute were whether to have a biotechnology protocol, how to handle intellectual property rights in the context of conserving biological diversity, technology transfers, and how to develop a scheme to fund low-income states' efforts at protecting their biological resources.

i. The First Conference of the Parties (COP-1)

The First Conference of the Parties to the Biodiversity Convention took place in Nassau, the Bahamas, from November 28 to December 9, 1994. The UN Environment Programme (UNEP) was designated as the secretariat for the convention, the Global Environmental Facility (GEF) was designated as the interim financing arrangement, and a work program was developed for the years 1995–1997. The work plan included reports on biodiversity particularly under threat, coastal and marine biodiversity, and intellectual property; compilations of existing legislation regarding access to genetic resources and sharing of their benefits; investigation into the need for a biosafety protocol; and exploration of private funding sources to help developing countries. Agricultural biodiversity, linking decisions with the UN Commission on Sustainable Development (CSD), and promoting technology development and transfer were also key elements of the plan. Discussion of forest protection was postponed until the next Conference of the Parties.

ii. The Second Conference of the Parties (COP-2)

The parties held their Second Conference in Jakarta, Indonesia, from November 6–17, 1995. They chose Montreal, Canada, as the home to the Biodiversity Convention's permanent secretariat. Failing to reach an agreement on a permanent financing mechanism, the parties agreed that GEF would continue as an "interim" financing mechanism and endorsed guidelines for preparing national biodiversity reports.

The most controversial issue at COP-2 was the decision to draw up a biosafety protocol to cover transfer, handling, and use of genetically modified organisms. An ad hoc working group was to complete work by 1998. Observers noted that any protocol was unlikely to be successful unless the United States ratified the treaty, as the United States houses a large majority of the biotechnology firms in the world.

The COP-2 also addressed forestry. The delegates agreed to ask the secretariat to carry out studies on forest biodiversity and to submit them to the Intergovernmental Panel on Forestry (IPF) but rejected establishing a working panel on forests for budget concerns and possible overlap with the IPF.

A controversial issue that has yet to be resolved is in the area of intellectual property rights: namely, reconciling fair and equitable access to biotechnology with legal patents over products. The conference called on the secretariat to work with the World Trade Organization (WTO) on a study of the relationship between the objectives of the Biodiversity Convention and those of the Uruguay Round Agreement on Trade-Related Aspects of Intellectual Property Rights (TRIPS). Environmental groups have claimed that any conflict between the two must be resolved in favor of the Biodiversity Convention, citing the rule that the general gives way to the specific to support the primacy of the Biodiversity Convention over TRIPS.

iii. The Fifth–Eighth Conferences of Parties (COP-5-8)

The most important post-Rio achievements is the negotiation of the Cartagena Protocol on Biosafety, discussed in Chapter 14, adopted at COP-5, Subsequent meetings, especially COP-6, adopted recommendations on a wide variety topics such as agricultural biodiversity, biodiversity in dry and sub-humid climates, marine and coastal biodiversity, alien species invasions and assessment procedures. COP-8, meeting in the green city of Curitiba, Brazil in 2006, focused on the implementation of the Cartagena Protocol. The extensive reports of the meetings are important steps toward the development of coordinated biodiversity protection strategies, but the danger signs continued to mount that more urgent action was needed.

iv. The Tenth Conference of the Parties (COP-10)

The Tenth Conference held in Nagoya, Japan produced two important protocols, one on liability and the other on intellectual property rights. Articles 5 and 6 are the core of the Intellectual Rights Protocol.

Art. 5

1.   In accordance with Article 15, paragraphs 3 and 7 of the Convention, benefits arising from the utilization of genetic resources as well as subsequent applications and commercialization shall be shared in a fair and equitable way with the Party providing such resources that is the country of origin of such resources or a Party that has acquired the genetic resources in accordance with the Convention. Such sharing shall be upon mutually agreed terms.

Art. 6

1.   In the exercise of sovereign rights over natural resources, and subject to domestic access and benefit-sharing legislation or regulatory requirements, access to genetic resources for their utilization shall be subject to the prior informed consent of the Party providing such resources that is the country of origin of such resources or a Party that has acquired the genetic resources in accordance with the Convention, unless otherwise determined by that Party.

2.   In accordance with domestic law, each Party shall take measures, as appropriate, with the aim of ensuring that the prior informed consent or approval and involvement of indigenous and local communities is obtained for access to

genetic resources where they have the established right to grant access to such resources.

3.   Each Party shall take legislative, administrative or policy measures, as appropriate, with the aim of ensuring that benefits arising from the utilization of genetic resources that are held by indigenous and local communities, in accordance with domestic legislation regarding the established rights of these indigenous and local communities over these genetic resources, are shared in a fair and equitable way with the communities concerned, based on mutually agreed terms.

NOTES AND QUESTIONS

1.   Does the Protocol substantially alter the TRIPS international intellectual property regime which enshrines national laws which reward inventors who manipulate nature? Or does the Protocol institutionalize property rights for traditional holders of useful knowledge? Can developing countries effectively regulate and capitalize on bio-prospecting should major pharm decide to re-enter the field? Are shared benefits such as up-front payments, royalty or license fees or non-monetary ones such as technology transfer an adequate substitute for the host country or community's loss of a full property right in the knowledge? *See* Simon West, *Institutionalized Exclusion: The Political Economy of Benefit Sharing and Intellectual Property*, 8 J. L. Env't. & Dev. 19 (2012).

2.   The Parties also adopted A Supplementary Protocol on Liability and Dedress to the Cartagena Protocol on Biosafety, which had not yet enetered into force as of mid-2015. The Liability Protocol "applies to damage resulting from living modified organisms which find their origin in a transboundary movement." Article 3.1 Article 4 requires that a causal link between damage and the living modified organism must be established under domestic law. The primary duties are contained in Article 5 which requires that the person causing the damage" (a) Immediately inform the competent authority, (b) Evaluate the damage; and (c) Take appropriate response measures. Under Article 12, the determination of remediable damages and civil liability will be determined by existing or specially enacted domestic laws.

e.   GMOs and Biodiversity

The 1992 Biodiversity Convention also contemplated a specific agreement on biosafety. This agreement, the Cartagena Protocol, was approved by the Conference of Parties in 2000 and entered into force in 2003. The United States signed the Protocol but has not ratified it. The Protocol is covered in Chapter 14.

New biodiversity risks from GMOs, which society not yet faced, continue to emerge. For example, GMOs that have been modified to survive in drier or saltier conditions than their ancestors could have survived in may tend to push out or otherwise affect the indigenous species that formerly lived in those dry or salty conditions. Similarly, as this book goes to press, the American chestnut tree is being modified to resist the blight that killed billions of these trees in the United States. If it is introduced, it may have significant impacts on biological diversity where that occurs. In addition, the gene drive technology described in Chapter 3 may have major impacts on biological diversity. That may occur not only by changing the genome of the entire species of the organism that was genetically engineered, but also as a result of the myriad effects that such a change may have on other species in that ecosystem.

f. Implementation

i. State Judicial Legislative-Administrative Implementation

The Convention is a binding international instrument, but it has not been relied upon by domestic or international tribunals. An Indian court did cite it along with the Stockholm Conference 1972, Brundtland Commission Report, 1987, Caring of the Earth Report, 1991, Rio Conference, 1992, Convention on Climate Change, 1992, and Agenda-21 (A programme of Action for Twenty-first Century) in a case applying the principle of sustainable development, the polluter pays principle and the precautionary principles to hold a group of tanneries liable for water pollution. Vellore Citizens Welfare Forum vs. Union of India and Others [AIR 1996 SC 2715]. Australia relied on the Convention to enact a federal protection regime for its major river system. *See* page 778, *supra*. Nonetheless, many States party to the Convention are taking important legal steps to implement it. We focus on a country in South Asia as an example, for the report contains a wealth of detail of efforts underway in surrounding countries.

IMPLEMENTATION OF THE CONVENTION ON BIOLOGICAL DIVERSITY: A RETROSPECTIVE ANALYSIS IN THE HINDU KUSH-HIMALAYAN COUNTRIES

Bharat H. Desai et al.
International Centre for Mountain Development, 2010

Bangladesh

Despite its relatively small geographical area, Bangladesh harbours a great diversity of ecosystems. It is bounded to the north by the Khasi, Jaintia, and Jowai hills of North East India and to the east by the Lusai and Arakan Yoma hills of western Myanmar, which house a diversity of plants and are the site of a biodiversity hotspot. The country is a biogeographical transition area between the Indo-Gangetic plains and the eastern Himalayas and is part of the Indo-Chinese sub-region of the Oriental realm. The ecosystem types include tropical rainforests, mangrove forests, floodplains, the extensive jhum fields of the Chittagong Hill tracts, freshwater and coastal wetlands, and the littoral, sub-littoral, and benthic communities of the Bay of Bengal. Only 20 per cent of the country's land area is considered as forest, although large parts of the alluvial and coastal plains have been reclaimed for agriculture and human habitation over the years. Approximately 12 per cent of the country's land area consists of mountain ecosystems, largely confined to the north, northeast, and southeastern areas. The Chittagong Hill Tracts and Chittagong together contain a substantial part of the hill ecosystems; the mostly low elevation hill ecosystem of Sylhet represents nine percent of the hills. The vegetation of the hill forests has generally been classified as tropical evergreen and semi-evergreen.

Ecosystem conservation

Bangladesh has 18 protected areas, which together cover 2,400 sq.km or 1.6 per cent of the country's surface area and just over 9 per cent of the forested area, and are managed by the Forestry Department. The Bangladesh Wildlife Preservation (Amendment) Act 1974, recognises three categories of protected areas: national parks, wildlife sanctuaries, and game reserves. The Bangladesh Environment Conservation Act (Act I of 1995) deals exclusively with environmental issues. Bangladesh has various policies, strategies, and action plans that contain provisions for promoting the conservation of biodiversity of ecosystems, habitats, and biomes, as discussed below.

Policy instruments

The following policy instruments have some bearing on environmental conservation: Environment Policy (1992); National Agriculture Policy (1999); National Water Policy (1999); National Forest Policy (1994); National Fisheries Policy (1992); Livestock Development Policy (1992); National Seed Policy (1998); National Land Use Policy (2002); Renewable Energy Policy (Draft) (October 2002); Coastal Zone Policy (2004); Wetland Policy (Draft) (1998); and National Energy Policy (1995).

These policy instruments are supported by the following strategies and action plans: National Conservation Strategy (NCS); National Biodiversity Strategy and Action Plan (NBSAP); National Environment Management Action Plan (NEMAP); Freshwater Fisheries Strategy; Coastal Zone Development Strategy (Draft); Forestry Master Plan (1995); Barind Environmental Action Plan 2003; National Adaptation Program of Action (NAPA); National Action Plan under United Nations Convention to Combat Climate Change (UNCCD) (NAP); and the Inland Capture Fisheries Strategy (2005). Bangladesh's Third National Report to the CBD reiterates the government's commitment to restoring and conserving the country's precious biodiversity and affirms that the country has indeed taken up its international biodiversity obligations seriously. The report notes, inter alia, that the following are under development: an eco-park covering the hill ecosystem in Sitakundoo, Chittagong; a safari park in Cox's Bazar; and a National Park in the Chittagong Hill Tracts. Afforestation programmes are being implemented to restore degraded ecosystems in the hill areas of Bangladesh including Chittagong, the Chittagong Hill Tracts (Rangamati, Khagrachari, and Bandarban), Sylhet, and Mymensingh, and in the wet deciduous sal forests. Moreover, the Nishorgo Support Project is addressing co-management of five of the protected areas in the country.

Mountain biodiversity

The country has taken some measures to prevent and mitigate the negative impacts of the key threats to mountain biodiversity, including the afforestation programme in the denuded hill areas mentioned above. The Third Report refers to activities undertaken for the conservation of important biodiversity hotspots in Chittagong, the Chittagong Hill Tracts, and Rampahar and Sitapahar (in the Chittagong Region) and cites these as illustrative examples of the resolve to prevent and mitigate the threats to mountain biodiversity. The following activities are also included as examples of efforts designed to protect, recover Implementation of the Convention on Biological Diversity and restore mountain biodiversity: 1) co-management of protected areas in Chunati and Teknaf; 2) conservation of Sitakundu Hill as an eco-park; and 3) conservation activities in Lawachara and Rema-kalenga of Sylhet. The Third Report notes that Bangladesh is also considering measures to promote the sustainable use of mountain biological resources and to maintain genetic diversity in mountain ecosystems, and lists several initiatives which have been planned and executed in this regard. Bangladesh has prepared a draft law on 'Biodiversity and Community Knowledge Protection' for sharing the benefits arising from the use of biological resources and associated traditional knowledge. This is a very progressive measure that will entrust communities with rights over the use of their biological resources and ensure that they benefit from the biogenetic resources and associated traditional knowledge. This bill is still being debated. Bangladesh is currently engaged in strengthening its legal, policy, and institutional framework for the conservation and sustainable use of mountain biodiversity, as well as for implementing the CBD Programme of Work (PoWMB). As part of this, ICIMOD has identified the Chittagong Hill Tracts and Cherapunji (in India) as a potential site for conservation and management as a transboundary landscape. This work is in the initial stages, and details of how to develop transboundary cooperative agreements for managing mountain ecosystems are still being worked out. At the same time, several national measures for identifying, monitoring, and assessing mountain biodiversity are also in the pipeline.

Similarly, measures for improving research, technical and scientific cooperation, and capacity building for conservation and sustainable use of mountain biodiversity are also being evolved at the respective levels. The Third Report gauges the country's mood on environmental protection and affirms that general awareness on biodiversity conservation has increased. Capacity for plantation programmes has improved as a result of targeted training programmes. A social forestry campaign in the mountain areas is helping to rehabilitate denuded hill areas. The government is considering establishing new protected areas. Nevertheless, in spite of the good progress that has been made, the persistent problems of absence of effective community-based institutional mechanisms, lack of awareness, lack of inter-sectoral coordination, lack of human capacity, lack of financial resources, and a rapidly growing population continue to undermine the country's efforts at biodiversity conservation. In brief Bangladesh has clearly taken some measures towards promoting the sustainable use of mountain biodiversity and towards helping to preserve genetic diversity in the mountains. As yet, no concrete measures have been taken to share benefits arising out of the utilization of mountain genetic resources and associated traditional knowledge, or to protect such knowledge, although a draft law on 'Biodiversity and Community Knowledge Protection' is being discussed. The country needs to initiate a programme for developing effective institutional mechanisms at different levels to raise awareness, support inter and intra sectoral collaboration, and provide financial resources. . . .

ii. Ex Situ Conservation: Gene Banks

Ex situ conservation is the protection of genetic varieties by putting a small population of the species in a collection that people maintain. In this way, gene pools in the greatest danger of extinction can be saved in their present form, and potentially the population can be rebuilt. However, ex situ techniques, including greenhouses, botanical gardens, and zoos, stop any evolutionary development of a species that would be present in nature. See Walter V. Reid & Kenton R. Miller, Keeping the Options Alive: The Scientific Basis for Conserving Biodiversity 62 (1989) ("the evolution of the species is 'frozen' so no further adaptation to pests or environmental change can take place. For this reason, ex situ storage should be considered preservation" . . .).

Ex situ preservation is fundamental for conserving for future breeding the wild relatives of crop plants as well as traditional crop varieties that are being displaced by high-yielding varieties. But ex situ preservation has limitations. First, some crop species are difficult or costly to maintain ex situ. Second, important but rare genotypes are often absent from ex situ collections. Third, collections can be destroyed by mechanical breakdowns or accidents. Fourth, coevolution of a crop plant with other organisms, such as pollinators and potential pests and diseases, cannot continue ex situ. Fifth, the peculiar characteristics of each crop variety may be more difficult to study ex situ. Sixth, pollinators, propagule distributors (for example, birds that eat fruit and excrete the seeds), and other species-specific necessities may be difficult or impossible to include in ex situ trials. For these reasons, wildlands that contain wild relatives of crops have a high priority as areas to be preserved. It is also advisable to encourage the planting of "museum strips" of traditional crop varieties alongside new high-yielding varieties.

For most other types of biological resources, ex situ preservation is simply not practical. The costs and difficulties of storage are too great, and, as noted above, a great proportion of the world's plants and animals have yet to be inventoried and collected. Furthermore, ex situ methods cannot preserve the numerous ecological interrelations among species that are so evident in natural systems and that encourage the evolution of new varieties. Plants and animals in a natural setting continuously coevolve, but when they are removed and isolated for any length of time, they are often maladapted or completely unable to survive when reintroduced into the wild. Maintaining dead specimens in museums and herbaria provides an historical record of their existence and structure but none of the benefits of living species.

For more detailed analysis of issues related to in situ conservation, see Walter V. Reid & Kenton R. Miller, Keeping the Options Alive: The Scientific Basis for Conserving Biodiversity 61–66 (1989).

IN FAIRNESS TO FUTURE GENERATIONS: INTERNATIONAL LAW, COMMON PATRIMONY AND INTERGENERATIONAL EQUITY

Edith Brown Weiss
204–205 (1989)

Gene banks are a necessary complement to in situ conservation areas. The International Board for Plant Genetic Resources, established in 1974, has worked to develop an international network of gene banks for crop germplasm. As of 1986 about fifty such gene banks were operational. Most are field gene banks, which do not provide long-term storage of seeds. Less than 20 percent are banks that store collections for the long-term under low temperatures. The banks include both cultivated varieties and wild cultivars, although the emphasis to date has been upon the former. National centers for storing germplasm may consist of many local gene banks linked in a national network. Brazil, for example, has a national network under the Brazilian Enterprise for Agricultural Research (EMBRAPA) that includes about seventy gene banks, many of which have germplasm that is not stored at the central depository in

Brasilia. There are now also efforts to conserve animal genetic resources, as by conserving embryos and semen of important races of bovines, poultry, etc. Some microorganisms are being conserved by the Microbiological Resources Centers, an international network of research centers supported by the United Nations Environment Programme.

Gene banks provide plant breeders with the genetic resources necessary to develop crops that will resist pests more effectively and produce higher yields. . . . Most of these banks store germplasm only of the major crops, such as cereals, grain legumes, and potatoes. There is as yet little attention to conserving the germplasm of medicinal herbs, fruit and timber trees, or plantation crops.

NOTES AND QUESTIONS

1. *Storing and sharing germplasm.* Who has access to germplasm stored in gene banks? Does it make a difference whether the banks are only under national auspices or whether they are part of an international network? Consider the following:

> Issues of access also arise in connection with the exchange of germplasm. Generally, countries exchange germplasm relatively freely, except for the germplasm of certain export-oriented cash crops. . . . The policy of the United States, which reportedly stores about 1/5 of the world's germplasm, has been "for many years to freely exchange germplasm with most countries of the world." Developing countries exchange germplasm with each other, although a country may occasionally refuse to exchange germplasm of a particular commercially valuable crop, or if it exchanges germplasm, to provide that of a suboptimal strain. The cost to countries of such restrictions can be enormous.

> The experience with the international centers for storing germplasm reveals the evolution of an effective system of free gathering and exchange of germplasm, in the form of seeds. Again, the experience with the International Germplasm Center for Rice is instructive. While countries in the past expressed some reluctance to gather and send germplasm to the Center, they now do so routinely. Countries that may refuse to provide particular germplasm directly to their neighbor have been willing to provide it to an international center, even though they realize their neighbor will then have access to it. They are willing to provide the germplasm because they know that they, in turn, will have access to germplasm from other countries that they can use in improving their own crops. . . .

Edith Brown Weiss, In Fairness to Future Generations: International Law, Common Patrimony, and Intergenerational Equity 209–210 (1989).

2.   *Will germplasm be available for future generations?* Gene banks are intended to preserve germplasm for future generations as well as the present. Does this raise any legal issues? Consider the following:

> Gene banks retain information on the physical characteristics of the stored germplasm and their native locations. They do not, however, collect photographs of the plants in their native habitats or otherwise keep a visual record. Such a record might be very useful to future generations, although perhaps difficult to obtain in dense tropical vegetation. . . .

> If we fail to allocate funds for maintaining gene banks, we will spend funds to construct a facility and to gather germplasm for the benefit of only the present generation. Equity demands that we make the benefits available to future generations. Moreover, the loss . . . may cause important economic losses to members of the present generation as well.

Edith Brown Weiss, In Fairness to Future Generations: International Law, Common Patrimony, and Intergenerational Equity 205–207 (1989).

The International Treaty on Plant Genetic Resources for Food and Agriculture entered into force in 2004 and as of August 2015 has 139 Parties. The objectives of the Treaty are the conservation and sustainable use of Plant Genetic Resources for Food and Agriculture (PGRFA) and the fair and equitable sharing of the benefits arising out of their use, in harmony with the Convention on Biodiversity, for sustainable agriculture and food security. Articles 5 and 6 set down general provisions regarding conservation, exploration, collection, characterization, evaluation and documentation of PGRFA and their sustainable use. Article 5.1.(b) requires each Contracting Party, subject to national legislation, to promote the collection of PGRFA that are under threat or are of potential use, along with relevant associated information. Under paragraph 5.1.(e), Contracting Parties are required to cooperate to promote the development of an efficient and sustainable system of ex situ conservation, giving due attention to the need for adequate documentation, characterization, regeneration and evaluation, and to promote the development of appropriate technologies for this purpose. They are also to monitor the maintenance of the viability, degree of variation and genetic integrity of collections of PGRFA. Article 5.1.(f). The Treaty does specify what an "efficient and sustainable" system of ex situ conservation must include, *See* Ad Hoc Advisory Technical Committee on the Standard Material Transfer Agreement and the Multilateral System of the Treaty (hereinafter "the Ad Hoc Advisory Technical Committee") in the report on its first session in 2010, *available at* ftp://ftp.fao.org/ag/agp/planttreaty/gb4/AC_SMTA_MLS1/ac_smta_mls1_repe.pdf.

3. FORESTS

a. Introduction to the Value of Forests as a Natural Resource

Forests cover one-third of the land area of Earth. They cover 42 percent of the land in tropical countries and substantial portions in the temperate countries. About two-thirds of the forests are considered to be "closed forests," meaning that a substantially complete cover of trees exists over the whole land surface. The rest are "open forests." In the tropics and southern hemisphere, forests contain predominantly hardwoods; in the northern hemisphere, predominantly softwoods. The latter have been more readily viable commercially.

There are many different types of forests. The primary classifications are:

Tropical rainforests are characterized by year-round high temperatures and abundant rainfall makes this a dense, lush forest. Tropical rainforests are found near the equator. They are vital storehouses of biodiversity on the planet, and yet face severe threats today, with much of their original extent depleted.

Sub-tropical forests are found to the south and north of the tropical forests. The trees here are adapted to resist the summer drought.

Mediterranean forests are found to the south of the temperate regions around the coasts of the Mediterranean, California, Chile and Western Australia. The growing season is short and almost all trees are evergreen, but mixed hardwood and softwood.

Temperate forests exist in such places as eastern North America, northeastern Asia, and western and Eastern Europe. Temperate forests are a mix of deciduous and coniferous evergreen trees. Usually, the broad-leaved hardwood trees shed leaves annually. There are well-defined seasons with a distinct winter and sufficient rainfall.

Coniferous forests inhabit the cold, windy regions around the poles. There are both hardwoods and conifers found in this region. The conifers are evergreen and structurally adapted to withstand the long drought-like conditions of the long winters, whereas the hardwoods are deciduous.

Montane forests are, also known as cloud forests because they receive most of their precipitation from the mist or fog that comes up from the lowlands. Some of these montane woodlands and grasslands are found in high-elevation tropical, subtropical and temperate zones. Plants and animals in these forests are adapted to withstanding the cold, wet conditions and intense sunlight. Trees are mainly conifers.

Plantation forests or planted forests constitute around 140 million hectares, accounting for around 7% of global forest cover. The productivity of planted forests, in terms of supplying a sustainable volume of timber and fibre, is usually greater than natural forests. Plantations produce around 40% of industrial wood. Both the plantation area and contribution to world wood production are projected to continue to increase in the foreseeable future.

b.   The Role of Forests in Biodiversity Conservation

IN FAIRNESS TO FUTURE GENERATIONS: INTERNATIONAL LAW, COMMON PATRIMONY, AND INTERGENERATIONAL EQUITY

Edith Brown Weiss
219–223 (1989)

Forests have been exceedingly useful resources for people. As Spears and Ayensu note, "they protect watersheds and the natural environment as well as providing innumerable products vital to man. They provide sustenance, shelter, and employment as well as resources for the development of other sectors. They comprise the most biologically diverse, readily convertible, and potentially self-regenerating natural store of biological wealth on the planet. If all the shrubs, trees and forests in the developing countries were eliminated overnight, food production would decline by at least 20 percent in part because of the disruptive impact on irrigation water and fodder supplies." We may distinguish at least five classes of benefits that forests confer on present and future generations. First, they provide direct economic benefits through timber production and minor forest products, such as gums, resins, oils, medicines, fibers, fruits, wild nuts, etc., and through exploitation in tropical forests, in particular, for agricultural, medicinal, or industrial products. Secondly, they are important sources of fuelwood for people in rural areas of developing countries, of livestock, fodder, and even food. As population increases, the importance of tropical forests in particular will rise as people depend upon them increasingly to satisfy basic needs. Third, they provide amenity benefits, such as recreation and hunting, and have important cultural value for many societies, more or less independently of how frequently they are used. Fourth, they provide essential environmental services in conserving watersheds, as by preventing soil erosion, maintaining soil productivity, facilitating water recharge, harboring wildlife and buffering climate. They are important in the hydrological cycle and in regional, and perhaps global, climate systems. Finally, their environmental services provide direct economic benefits to areas downstream, such as increased electricity production or irrigation water due to reduced siltation of dams and streams, decreased need for dredging of navigable waterways and reduced risk of flood damage.

Today we are witnessing accelerated destruction of forests, particularly of tropical forests, at rates that will be difficult, perhaps impossible, to reverse. Forests in developing countries have declined by nearly half in this century. Over 11 million hectares of tropical forests, an area approximately the size of Austria and Switzerland combined, are being converted each year, primarily due to unplanned agricultural settlement. If this continues, the World Resources Institute estimates that at least 225 million hectares of tropical forests will be cleared by the year 2000. While the temperate climate forest area of most developed countries has stabilized in recent decades, recent studies indicate that pollution is affecting the quality of many forests in Europe and to a lesser extent in North America. Mismanagement of the forest ecosystem continues to be a problem.

Forests are threatened by several developments: population pressures, which lead to the denuding of nearby forests, destructive or unsustainable exploitation of forests for economic gain, and degradation by atmospheric pollution, which may lead to death of the forest. The first two reduce the volume of forest directly; the last indirectly.

I.   PROBLEMS OF INTERGENERATIONAL EQUITY

Forests are renewable resources that can be used by present generations and also be available to future generations if they are exploited on a sustainable basis. The problem is that they are often exploited with little attention to sustainability or to their crucial role in protecting upland watersheds, and through this, lowland watersheds. The degradation of soils, which accompanies unsustainable forestry, and pollution, which changes the chemistry of forest soils, have long-term detrimental effects on future productivity. Mismanagement of forests and their soils, together with the elimination of the diverse genetic resources in tropical forests, raises serious problems of intergenerational equity, which must be addressed.

A. DEPLETION OF RESOURCES

The most serious form of depletion is the loss of the diverse genetic resources found in tropical forests. This occurs whenever primary forests are eliminated, even though they may be reforested with plantations of selected trees. Tropical forests have enormous as yet untapped genetic reserves, which are in danger of being eliminated before they are even known. These have great potential value for food and cash crops for medicines, for industrial applications, and for developing new strains resistant to disease and pests. They will become more valuable as biotechnology advances. Destruction of forests rich in genetic diversity impoverishes future generations by reducing the resource options available to them.

Depletion of resources also occurs in yet another form: the loss of the environmental services that forests provide. These include flood control, recharge of ground water, maintenance and restoration of fertility in the soils, control of erosion, prevention of sedimentation in rivers and irrigation systems, protection of navigation, stabilization of plant and animal populations, purification of air and water, promotion of hydrological cycling, and buffering of the climate system. When forests are destroyed, these services are lost, which results in extensive costs of present and future generations as they search for technological solutions to replace these services or adapt to changed rainfall patterns, waterways filled with sedimentation, etc. In particular, the denuding of forested slopes can lead to disastrous floods for future generations, as illustrated by those that have occurred in the Po River valley. Such floods can be expected in the hilly areas of Central America and other parts of the developing world.

Depletion occurs whenever forests are not used and maintained on a sustainable basis. Sometimes this may occur intentionally through the conversion of forests to other uses, such as pasture for cattle, which may reap a higher economic return. But in tropical areas with fragile soils this use may be unsustainable, with the result that the lands become barren and unproductive. Often forest depletion occurs inadvertently through mismanagement, as by harvesting of forest products with insufficient attention to maintenance of soils and sustainable reforestation, or as a consequence of population pressures. One of the most serious causes of deforestation is excessive removal of wood for fuel and for domestic use by rural populations living in poverty. U.N. Food and Agricultural Organization studies show that three-fourths of the two billion in developing countries depend on fuelwood and other traditional fuels for all their daily energy needs. One billion rural dwellers suffer increasing shortages and can meet minimum needs only at the expense of exhausting available resources. Such depletion may raise the real price of commercial forest products for future generations and imposes hardships upon those members of both present and future generations who depend upon nearby forests for basic needs.

B. DEGRADATION IN QUALITY OF RESOURCES

Loss in the quality of forests and their genetic resources occurs primarily from mismanagement in the exploitation of forests or from pollution. Mismanagement causes soil degradation, decline in productivity, and the triumph of undesired species of fauna and flora.

These effects of pollution on the quality of forests are only beginning to become known. Atmospheric pollution of forests can result in the disfigurement of existing trees, the stunting of tree growth, the acidification of soils, and the loss of productivity in the forests. It can also reduce the variety of uses to which the forest is put. The symptoms of decline in the forests due to pollution have been so stark that people have labeled the phenomenon "Waldsterben," or death of the forests.

Large portions of the forests in western and central Europe are now suffering severe damage from air pollution. The effects first became apparent in the mid-1970s in West Germany among the silver fir and Norway spruce trees. Now the decline is apparent in the forests of the other European countries and extends to deciduous trees such as oak and beech. In 1986, the estimated forest damage in Europe was more than thirty million hectares, or 22% of the total land area.

Extensive forest damage appears in Germany, Austria, Czechoslovakia, Poland, Yugoslavia, Belgium, France, the Netherlands, Sweden, Switzerland, Hungary and Romania and is believed to exist in the [former] Soviet Union. Forests in North America, in both Canada and the United States, are also affected.

While there is still some scientific controversy about the causes of the damage to forests in Europe and in North America, very substantial evidence indicates that sulfur dioxide, ozone and ammonia are major contributors. However, the pollutants causing forest damage in different areas may not always be the same, and different trees are affected in varying degrees by the stresses of air pollution. This makes the problem of controlling air pollution damage to forests more difficult. Moreover, some scientific uncertainty about the causes of "Waldsterben" persists. For example, a West German scientist has suggested that a virus may be responsible for some European forest damage. The scientific uncertainty which still surrounds some aspects of forest damage means that we must continue to conduct research to confirm cause and effect relationships and to identify all causes of damage. In the tropics, recent scientific work indicates that pollution from burning may contribute to the acidification of soils in forest areas. The air pollutants that cause the quality of forests to decline may come from distant areas outside national borders, which makes control more difficult, as illustrated by the experiences in western and central Europe.

———————

For a recent evaluation of the state of the world's forests see Robert A. Askins, Saving the World's Deciduous Forests: Ecological Perspectives from East Asia, North America, and Europe (2014).

c. **The Incomplete but Evolving International Law of Forest Protection**

Forests present an interesting dilemma for international environmental law. Claude Martin, On the Edge: The State and Fate of the World's Tropical Rainforests (A Report to the Club of Rome 2015), surveys the recent history of concern over tropical rainforests and advances in deforestation measurement. They are not traditional global commons, but parts of the sovereign land mass of most countries in the world. However, the host countries management choices can have significant transboundary or global consequences. For example, the deforestation of tropical rainforests causes biodiversity loss and may add more carbon dioxide to the atmosphere than the sum total of cars and trucks on the world's roads. *See* L.V. Gatti et al., *Drought Sensitivity of Amazonian Carbon Balance Revealed by Atmospheric Measurements*, 506 Nature 76 (2014). The United Nations Food and Agricultural Organization (FAO), The Global Forest Resources Assessment 2005 (FRA 2005), reported that each year about 13 million hectares of the world's forests are lost due to deforestation, but the rate of net forest loss is slowing down, due to new reforestation projects and the natural expansion of existing forests. The annual net loss of forest area between 2000 and 2005 was 7.3 million hectares/year—an area about the size of Sierra Leone or Panama, but the land area lost was down from an estimated 8.9 million ha/yr between 1990 and 2000. This is equivalent to a net loss of 0.18 percent of the world's forests annually.

There are rich histories of forest management of both public and private almost every place in the world and forest management legal regimes have been in place in most countries for many decades. The history of the integration of forest management into international law is one of the transition from efforts to negotiate a comprehensive international forest management regime to the acceptance of a new governance model based on the voluntary acceptance of basic management principles, which build on the long tradition of national forest management, to guide national forest management. The over-arching goal of a global consensus on sustainable forest management has given way to more modest objectives. *See, e.g.*, Laura Horn, *RIO+20 United Nations Conference on Sustainable Development: Is This the Future We Want?*, 9 MqJICEL 1 (2013); Akiva Fishman, *From Broken Promises to Sustainable Forestry: Regulation of Private Forests in Liberia*, 21 N.Y.U. Envtl. L.J. 451 (2014). The 1992 Rio Conference promulgated a set of Forest Principles which called for international cooperation. After Rio, the United Nations Commission on Sustainable Development failed to develop a Convention, but adopted a substitute approach. United Nations Resolution 62/98 (2008) adopted a set of non-binding Forest Principles which can be adapted to individual countries. The core is the following four global objectives:

Global objective 1

Reverse the loss of forest cover worldwide through sustainable forest management, including protection, restoration, afforestation and reforestation, and increase efforts to prevent forest degradation;

Global objective 2

Enhance forest-based economic, social and environmental benefits, including by improving the livelihoods of forest-dependent people;

Global objective 3

Increase significantly the area of protected forests worldwide and other areas of sustainably managed forests, as well as the proportion of forest products from sustainably managed forests;

Global objective 4

Reverse the decline in official development assistance for sustainable forest management and mobilize significantly increased, new and additional financial resources from all sources for the implementation of sustainable forest management.

UNITED NATIONS FORUM ON FORESTS, REPORT OF THE SECRETARY GENERAL: ASSESSMENT OF PROGRESS MADE ON THE IMPLEMENTATION OF THE NON-LEGALLY BINDING INSTRUMENT ON ALL TYPES OF FORESTS AND TOWARDS THE ACHIEVEMENT OF THE FOUR GLOBAL OBJECTIVES

6–7, 9, 12, 14 (2013)

B.   Forest instrument and the global objectives on forests

Global objective 1: reverse the loss of forest cover worldwide through sustainable forest management, including protection, restoration, afforestation and reforestation, and increase efforts to prevent forest degradation.

Some progress has been made towards reversing the loss of forest cover at the global level. According to the FAO Global Forest Resources Assessment 2010, the world's total forest area is just over 4 billion hectares, which is equivalent to 31 per cent of total land area. While the rate of deforestation is slowing, it is still high, from 16 million hectares per year in the 1990s to an average of approximately 13 million hectares per year over the past decade. The highest deforestation rates and loss of forest cover remain in South America and Africa. Gains in forest cover have occurred in temperate and boreal zones, mainly thorough afforestation and the natural expansion of forests. The total forest area of the 55 States that submitted reports to the tenth session of the Forum is approximately 1.5 billion hectares, which constitutes just over 37 per cent of the global forest cover. The aggregate data for those reporting countries show a positive trend in achieving global objective 1 since there has been a 0.3 per cent increase in forest cover between 2005 and 2010, according to the Global Forest Resources Assessments prepared for those years. The progress in reversing the loss of forest cover is reflected in the numerous actions taken by the reporting countries towards the achievement of global objective 1.

Many of the actions have been prompted by international commitments agreed through the United Nations Forum on Forests. Developments and/or enhancements of national forest programmes, national forest policies and forest legislation are clear examples of that trend. Since the adoption of the forest instrument in 2007, a majority of the reporting States (46 out of 53) have undertaken concerted efforts to strengthen their forest-related legislations, including law enforcement and governance in support of sustainable forest management. Strengthening political commitment to sustainable forest management and? -Increased attention and interest in forests, at many levels, has been reflected in the various commitments of the reporting countries to sustainable forest management, in particular through the development and revisions of national forest policies, legislation and/or national forest programmes. According to the Global Forest Resources Assessment 2010, 75 per cent of the world's forests are covered by national forest programmes.

Forest law enforcement and governance

22. Three quarters of the reporting countries have amended their forest legislation since 2007. Significant efforts have been taken by countries to combat illegal trade in forest products. The most commonly reported actions, for example, by Germany, Ghana, Guyana, Italy, Jamaica and Liberia, were linked to implementation of European Union legislation, such as the European Union Forest Law Enforcement, Governance and Trade Action Plan, the new European Union timber regulation, and the voluntary partnership agreements between non-European Union countries and the European Union. Several countries provided examples of forest law enforcement and measures taken to enhance the trade of legal forest products. The United States reported on the amended Lacey Act (2008), which prohibits trade in wood and plant products taken in violation of domestic and international law. The United States also highlighted its engagement with the Experts Group on Illegal Logging and Associated Trade of the Asia-Pacific Economic Cooperation and the signing of bilateral agreements with several countries to combat illegal logging. Support for the wildlife crime working group of the International Criminal Police Organization was also mentioned. The reporting countries also highlighted bilateral cooperation on forest law enforcement. Viet Nam, for example, reported on its cooperation with the Lao People's Democratic Republic, Cambodia, China and the Republic of Korea. Nepal reported on the launch of the South Asia Wildlife Enforcement Network, opening a new chapter in regional cooperation in South Asia for strengthening wildlife law enforcement. E/CN.18/2013/2

Global objective 2: enhance forest-based economic, social and environmental benefits, including by improving the livelihoods of forest-dependent people.

Economic benefits of forests.

From a purely economic point of view, timber, in particular industrial roundwood, remains the main viable source of income from forests. According to the Global Forest Resources Assessment 2010, the total value of forest product removals in 2005 was $121.9 billion, of which 71 per cent were from industrial roundwood, 15 per cent were non-wood forest products and 14 per cent were from fuel wood. According to the Statistics Division of FAO, the global export of all wood products, including all roundwood and processed products, in 2011 was around $246 billion. Globally, however, the social and environmental benefits of forests are gaining importance, as reflected in current national and international policy dialogues and the national reports on forests.

Globally, the area of forest for roundwood production, as a primary function, has been slowly but steadily decreasing, and countries are embarking on more processed and semi-processed forest products to generate more value-added goods and services. This has generated improved conditions for forest-based employment. Moreover, according to the Global Forest Resources Assessment 2010, there has been an increase at the global level in the area of forests within protected areas, in forests managed for conservation of biological diversity (by almost 2 per cent between 2000 and 2010) and in forests managed for the provision of social services and cultural functions, which currently constitute around 3.7 per cent of the world's forests.

While timber products are easier to quantify in economic terms, putting a value on and calculating the revenue from the social and environmental benefits of forests has remained a challenge for many countries. Nevertheless, recently there have been cases that indicate progress towards natural capital accounting to measure the total value of natural assets through, for example, payments for ecosystem services. In that regard, a number of the reporting countries described the potential of payments for ecosystem services to enhance the economic, social and environmental benefits of forests. Over 30 per cent of the reporting States (16 out of 53) established some sort of mechanisms for payments for ecosystem services.

Global objective 3: increase significantly the area of protected forests worldwide and other areas of sustainably managed forests, as well as the proportion of forest products from sustainably managed forests.

According to the Global Forest Resources Assessment 2010, the area of forests in protected areas worldwide was around 460 million hectares, which equals 12.5 per cent of the global forest area. The area of forests in protected areas increased from 1990 to 2010 by 94 million hectares. The increasing trend towards protecting forest areas is reflected among the reporting countries whose protected areas constitute around 13 per cent of the total forest area. There was a 4.16 per cent increase in forests in protected areas between 2005 and 2010.

Many countries reported on the enactment of new or amendments of existing legislation related to the protection of natural resources and/or the establishment of new protection systems.

Global Objective No 4

Public domestic funding was reported as the main source of funding for forests. Over 90 per cent of the reporting countries stated that they had Government budgets specifically for forests. Half of the countries reported having funding for forests spread among other sectors. The two main sectors receiving funding for forests were nature conservation and agriculture, followed by issues related to climate change, water and energy. A couple of countries also mentioned education, research and rural development. Several countries indicated that the forest sector received separate funding from the annual budgets of their Governments.

---

d. Trade in Tropical Timber

After World War II, Europe and Japan needed cheap timber to reconstruct their economies and turned to the tropical forests in Southeast Asia, Africa, and South America. By 1978, world trade in tropical timber reached $7 billion annually causing massive rainforest losses. The best one can say about the current state of rainforest loss is that the rate has declined in recent decades but the rates are uneven. South and Central America show small declines, but deforestation is increasing in Indonesia and other parts of South Asia. Of course, continued population growth continues to stress biodiversity. Experts do not expect to see the growth rates of the past century, from 1.6 to 6.1 million in this century. Fertility rates are down, but nonetheless the developing world and the United States continue to grow rapidly. Even where population is declining, Europe, or slowing, Brazil and China, the increase in household units poses new threats to biodiversity because more resources are consumed. On the plus side, unlike biodiversity, countries have substantial financial and social incentives to manage their forests more sustainably. And, there is a long tradition of scientific sustainable forest management reaching back at least 250 years. *See, e.g.,* Sustainable Forest Management in a Changing World: a European Perspective (Peter Spathelf ed., 2009); Forests and Nature Governance (B Arts. et al eds., 2013); Rowena Maguire, Global Forest Governance— Legal Concepts and Policy Trends (2012); Collaborative Governance of Tropical Landscapes (Carol J. Pierce & Jean-Laurent Pfund eds., 2013). Is the goal of zero net deforestation possible? Martin, On the Edge, *supra* at 246–247 suggests that it is: "Between 2000 and 2012, the world has been losing about 0.43 percent of its remaining tropical rainforests per year: about 1.2 times the size of Switzerland. . . . If the decline . . . were to continue in linear fashion, it would reach the current level of reforestation . . . a few years after 2030."

In response to concerns about developing countries' abilities to process their own raw materials and about tropical deforestation, several UN bodies and NGOs began to advocate trade controls and higher timber prices. The United Nations Conference on Trade and Development (UNCTAD) requested its Secretary-General to convene preparatory meetings for international negotiations on a new tropical timber agreement. In 1983, the International Tropical Timber Agreement (ITTA) was concluded under the auspices of UNCTAD and opened to both producer and consumer countries.

The International Tropical Timber Agreement

The 1983 treaty benefited both producer and consumer countries. For producer countries, it offered opportunities to expand trade and to receive technological transfers and financial assistance from consuming countries. Consumer countries enjoyed expanded and stable supplies of tropical timber as well as increased esteem in the eyes of domestic constituents and international organizations.

The Treaty was opened for signature in November 1983 and went into effect in April 1985. As of June 1997, the Treaty had 53 member countries: 26 producer countries and 27 consumer countries (including the European Union), accounting for 90 percent of the world's tropical forests and 90 percent of the world trade in tropical timber.

On January 26, 1994, countries concluded a successor treaty to the ITTA, which entered into force on January 1, 1997. The 1994 ITTA pays more attention to sustainable forestry, particularly whether countries would be required to engage in sustainable forestry by the year 2000 and whether this would apply to all forests.

In the 1994 ITTA, those countries producing tropical timber agreed to try to export wood only from sustainably managed forests by the year 2000. In return, consumer countries agreed to establish a new fund, the "Bali Partnership Fund," to help producer countries meet the objective of sustainably managed forests. In addition, the consuming countries issued a separate formal statement (not a formal part of the treaty) pledging to respect comparable forest conservation guidelines for their own forests and committing themselves to the "national objective of achieving sustainable management of their forests by the year 2000." The 1983 ITTA was designed to facilitate trade in tropical timber, defined as nonconiferous tropical wood for industrial uses, which grows or is produced in countries situated between the Tropic of Cancer and the Tropic of Capricorn. The Treaty promoted research and development to improve forest management and wood utilization, to improve market intelligence, to encourage processing of tropical timber in producer countries, and to promote reforestation and forest policies to conserve tropical forests and their genetic resources. The Treaty's preamble and Article 1, Objects, have served as the levers to advance conservation activities. Article 1 "encourages the development of national policies aimed at sustainable utilization and conservation of tropical forests and their genetic resources, and at maintaining the ecological balance in the regions concerned." The ITTA tried to balance power between the producer and consumer countries. Almost all producers are developing countries located in the tropical belts of Latin America, Africa, and Asia. The consuming countries are for the most part developed countries from North America, Europe, and the Far East.

The ITTA obligates States to provide detailed information about their tropical timber trade to the secretariat, contribute to the administrative account (and for the developed countries, to the special projects account), and make their best efforts to promote the objectives of the Treaty and comply with decisions made under the Treaty.

To implement the Treaty, parties established an International Tropical Timber Organization (ITTO), which functions through an International Tropical Timber Council (ITTC) and three permanent committees: the Committee on Economic Information and Market Intelligence; the Committee on Reforestation and Forest Management; and the Committee on Forest Industry. The Council's voting system is designed to balance power between producer and consumer countries and among the various factions of each group. As a large consumer of tropical hardwoods, Japan has a significant share of the votes. However, matters are in fact settled by consensus. No decision has ever been put to a vote.

In 2006, the International Tropical Timber Council adopted a new Tropical Timber Agreement which entered into force in 2011. TD/TIMBER.3/L.9, *available at* http://www.iisd.ca/forestry/itto/itta4. The new agreement stresses forest restoration and the role of forests in promoting sustainable development in addition to the more traditional efforts to halt the continued loss of rainforests.

The following summarizes the final agreement and the negotiations that led to its current formulation, noting where agreement had already been achieved at previous sessions:

SUMMARY OF THE UN CONFERENCE FOR THE NEGOTIATION OF A SUCCESSOR AGREEMENT TO THE INTERNATIONAL TROPICAL TIMBER AGREEMENT, 1994, FOURTH PART: 16–27 JANUARY 2006

24 Earth Negotiations Bulletin (January 30, 2006)
available at http://www.iisd.ca/vol24/enb2475e.html

Preamble: The Preamble contains 20 clauses addressing: the importance of the multiple benefits provided by forests, NTFPs and environmental services; the role of good governance in achieving sustainable forest management; the need to improve the standard of living and working conditions within the forest sector; and the need for enhanced and predictable finance resources to achieve the objectives of the Agreement.

On "the importance of the multiple economic, environmental and social benefits provided by forests," including "timber and non-timber products and ecological services," India, opposed by Mexico, Switzerland, Togo and the US, suggested deleting "ecological services." Mexico proposed keeping "ecological services" or "environmental services." Brazil opposed using the term "ecological services" anywhere in the text, but was open to using "environmental services" in areas other than the Preamble and Objectives. Malaysia objected to both terms. The US observed that this is a hortatory statement and would not affect the scope of the agreement. Brazil, on behalf of the Producers, favored using "environmental services," as long as it was mentioned "in the context of sustainable forest management (SFM)." Delegates agreed to use the term "environmental services."

On the need to improve standards of living and working conditions within the forest sector, Norway agreed to withdraw its proposed inclusion of "peoples" after "indigenous," but wanted to retain reference to the International Labor Organization (ILO) with respect to improving working conditions. After further debate, Norway proposed, and delegates agreed to, text that takes into account relevant internationally recognized principles on these matters and relevant ILO Conventions and instruments.

After lengthy discussion on the issue of including language on certification and voluntary market-based mechanisms, delegates agreed to delete reference to this text.

Brazil, for Producers, called for preambular text "recognizing the need for higher levels of financial resources which are adequate, predictable and available from a wider ITTO consumer donor community to achieve the objectives of this agreement." Norway suggested deleting "ITTO." Switzerland, supported by Brazil and the EU, proposed discussing the issue together with articles on the Special Account and the Bali Partnership Fund. Brazil noted Producers' preference for retaining this text in both the Preamble and Objectives. The EC, supported by Switzerland, agreed to maintain this clause but only in the Preamble. The final text reads that "further recognizing the need for enhanced and predictable financial resources from a broad donor community to help achieve the objectives of this Agreement."

Final Text: The Preamble, inter alia:

Recognizes the importance of multiple economic, environmental and social benefits provided by forests, including timber and NTFPs and environmental services in the context of SFM;

Recognizes the importance of collaboration among members, international organizations, the private sector and civil society, including indigenous and local communities and other stakeholders in promoting SFM and for improving forest law enforcement and promoting trade from legally harvested timber;

Recognizes the need for increased investment in SFM, including through reinvesting revenues generated from forests including from timber-related trade; and

Recognizes the need for enhanced and predictable financial resources from a broad donor community to help achieve the objectives of this Agreement.

Chapter I. Objectives

Objectives (Article 1): This article contains a chapeau that describes two overarching objectives and lists 19 clauses in order to achieve such objectives.

In the chapeau, India requested deletion of reference to "ecological services" and "legally harvested" timber. Indonesia, supported by Switzerland, Japan, and the US, requested maintenance of language on legally harvested timber, and this was agreed. Switzerland recalled that the current reference to "ecological services" is a compromise and is necessary in order to reflect ITTO's evolution. Suriname, opposed by the US, preferred language maintaining the Organization's focus on timber trade. Brazil, for Producers, proposed deleting "taking into account the contribution of non-timber forest products and ecological services" and inserting language mentioning "environmental services in the context of SFM" in another paragraph. After informal consultation, delegates agreed to delete text on "taking into account the contribution of NTFPs and ecological services" from the chapeau.

On contributing to the process of sustainable development, the EU, supported by Norway, Indonesia and Suriname, suggested adding a reference to poverty reduction. The US suggested replacing "reduction" with "alleviation," to which delegates agreed to a paragraph saying "contributing to sustainable development and to poverty alleviation."

The US proposed new language on "encouraging information sharing on the use of voluntary market based mechanisms, such as certification, to promote trade in tropical timber from sustainably managed forests." Brazil, for Producers, proposed "encouraging information sharing for a better understanding of transparent and voluntary mechanisms such as certification to promote sustainable management of tropical forests and assisting members with their efforts in this area without prejudice to members' rights under other international agreements, in particular those related to trade." India noted that accepting reference to certification required great compromise among Producers, while Malaysia stressed that reference to certification could prejudice other trade agreements. Delegates agreed to text "encouraging information sharing for better understanding of voluntary mechanisms such as, inter alia, certification, to promote SFM of tropical forests, and assisting members with their efforts in this area."

After informal consultations, delegates agreed to a paragraph saying "strengthening the capacity of members to improve forest law enforcement and governance, and address illegal logging and related trade in tropical timber."

On the issue of strengthening capacity of members for collection, processing and dissemination of statistics on their trade in timber, delegates agreed to remove reference to improving forest law enforcement and governance.

On "encourage members to develop national policies aimed at sustainable utilization and conservation of timber-producing forests and their genetic resources," Mexico, responding to Cameroon's concerns regarding the term "genetic resources," proposed adding "as defined in the Convention on Biological Diversity." Switzerland proposed, opposed by Venezuela and Colombia, to include "genetic resources" without reference to other treaties. Delegates decided to delete reference to "genetic resources." Despite objection by the EC and Indonesia, reference to "maintaining ecological balance" was retained. The final text says that "encouraging members to develop national policies aimed at sustainable utilization and conservation of timber producing forests and their genetic resources and maintaining ecological balance, in the context of the tropical timber trade."

On "developing and contributing towards mechanisms for the provision of new and additional financial resources," Norway, supported by Switzerland, suggested deleting this phrase since it already appears in the Preamble. Malaysia, for Producers, favored keeping both references. The US suggested adding at the end of the paragraph "with a view to promoting the adequacy and predictability of funding as provided for in Article 20 (Special Account) of this Agreement." Delegates finally approved the objective of "Developing and contributing towards mechanisms for the provision of new and additional financial resources with a view to promoting the adequacy and predictability of funding and expertise needed to enhance the capacity of producer members to attain the objectives of this Agreement.

On promoting understanding of the contribution of NTFPs and environmental services, delegates discussed Switzerland's proposal to add "with the aim of enhancing the capacity of members to develop strategies for achieving increased revenues from the forests." Indonesia cautioned against broadening the scope of the agreement beyond tropical forests. Switzerland suggested limiting it to sustainable management of "tropical" forests. Brazil, for Producers, offered a compromise, adding reference to the contribution of both NTFPs and environmental services to the sustainable management of tropical forests with the aim of enhancing the capacity of Producer members to develop strategies and cooperating with relevant institutions and processes to this end. The US, supported by Egypt and the EC, noted that since the section refers to tropical forests, limiting it to Producers may unnecessarily exclude a developing Consumer country like China. After informal consultations, Brazil announced a consensus in the Producers' Group on "enhancing the capacity of Producer members to develop strategies to strengthen such contributions in the context of SFM and cooperating with relevant institutions and processes to this end." China, Egypt and Nepal, opposed by Brazil, for Producers, suggested deleting "Producer." The US highlighted the importance of enhancing the capacity of all "members," not just Producer members. After informal discussion, delegates decided to delete "Producer" before "members," and agreed to the text.

Final Text: This article states the objectives of the ITTA, 2006, are to promote the expansion and diversification of international trade in tropical timber from sustainably managed and legally harvested forests and to promote the sustainable management of tropical timber producing forests by, inter alia: Contributing to sustainable development and to poverty alleviation;

Developing and contributing towards mechanisms for the provision of new and additional financial resources with a view to promoting the adequacy and predictability of funding and expertise needed to enhance the capacity of producer members to attain the objectives of this Agreement;

Promoting market intelligence and encouraging information sharing on international timber market with a view to ensuring greater transparency and better information on markets and market trends;

Strengthening the capacity of members for the collection, processing and dissemination of statistics on their trade in timber and information on the sustainable management of their tropical forests;

Encouraging members to develop national policies aimed at sustainable utilization and conservation of timber producing forests and maintaining ecological balance, in the context of the tropical timber trade;

Strengthening the capacity of members to improve forest law enforcement and governance, and address illegal logging and related trade in tropical timber; and

Promoting better understanding of the contribution of NTFPs and environmental services to the sustainable management of tropical forests with the aim of enhancing the capacity of members to develop strategies to strengthen such contributions in the context of SFM, and cooperating with relevant institutions and processes to this end.

Chapter II. Definitions

Definitions (Article 2): This article contains 12 definitions for the purpose of the Agreement, including: Tropical timber, sustainable forest management, members, producer member, consumer member, Organization, Council and special vote.

On SFM, Switzerland and Cote d'Ivoire favored keeping the definition, while Togo preferred deleting it. The US proposed, and delegates agreed, that "SFM will be understood according to the Organization's relevant policy documents and technical guidelines."

Delegates agreed to the European Union (EU) proposal to define "member" as "a Government, the EC or any intergovernmental organization referred to in Article 5 (Membership)" bound by this Agreement.

On "Producer member," the ITTO Secretariat explained that a possible definition of "producer member" is any country situated between the Tropics of Cancer and Capricorn with tropical forest resources "and/or" a "net" exporter of tropical timber in volume terms. He said if delegates delete "net" and retain "and/or," many consumer members would become producer members. He said that if delegates kept "or" and "net," the current system would continue. The EU, Canada and Mexico supported referring to Producer "members," as opposed to "countries," and delegates agreed. Japan, opposed by the EC, favored deleting the term "net" before "exporters." Delegates agreed to this with the specification of Producer "member." On defining Producer and Consumer members, India favored language in ITTA, 1994, opposing any changes in membership categories. Delegates agreed to the definitions of Producer and Consumer.

On including "natural closed forests and forest plantations" within "tropical forest resources" used in the calculation of the distribution of votes, Egypt emphasized the importance of including plantations, and India added that, since the ITTA is a commodity agreement, its focus should remain on forest products, not forest types. On agreed text defining forest resources for the purpose of distribution of votes, WGI Chair Attah suggested inserting "tropical" natural closed forests and forest plantations. Switzerland noted that if "tropical" was inserted before "natural closed forests," it should also appear before "plantations." However, he noted that he agreed to use "between the Tropics of Cancer and Capricorn" after "plantations." The EU added "located" in front of "between," and delegates agreed to this text.

The US and Switzerland were persuaded to retain the current name of the Organization, as proposed by Togo and supported by Brazil, Japan, Panama, Malaysia and Thailand, although they noted that they preferred a name that would reflect the evolution of the ITTO.

On "Special Vote," the EU, supported by Suriname, suggested equal thresholds for both groups. The US agreed, but expressed reservations regarding the complexity of the voting system, and supported by Switzerland, suggested adding "Council may adjust the minimum percentages required for a special vote if it deems necessary," noting the possibility that otherwise the EU might have a blocking minority. The EU noted, with Switzerland, that the minimum vote requirement should apply to both Consumers and Producers, and proposed qualifying "by special vote" with the term "in accordance with Article 12." After consultation, the group agreed that a special vote would require "60%" of the votes of consumer members rather than "two-thirds." Delegates ultimately agreed that "special vote" requires at least 60% (as opposed to "two-thirds") of the votes of Producers and 60% of those of Consumers, cast by at least half of those present and voting.

Delegates agreed to refer to Food and Agriculture Organization (FAO) data on natural closed forests and forest plantations to calculate votes.

Final Text: The definitions of "Council," "Simply distributed majority vote," "Financial biennium," and "freely convertible currencies" were not discussed during ITTA-4. For the purpose of this Agreement, this article defines, inter alia:

Tropical timber as tropical wood for industrial uses, which grows or is produced in the countries situated between the Tropics of Cancer and Capricorn, and the term covers logs, sawn wood, veneers, sheets and plywood;

Producer member as any member situated between the Tropics of Cancer and Capricorn with tropical forest resources and/or net exporter of tropical timber in volume terms, which is listed in Annex A and which becomes a party to this Agreement;

Consumer member as any member that is an importer of tropical timber listed in Annex B that becomes a party to this Agreement, or any member that is an importer of tropical timber not so listed which becomes a party of this Agreement.

––––––––––

For an argument that illegal logging should be an international crime, see Rudy S. Salo, *When the Logs Roll Over: The Need for an International Convention Criminalizing Involvement in the Global Illegal Timber Trade*, 16 Geo. Int'l Envtl. L. Rev. 126 (2003).

4. CREEPING DESERTS

In the 1970s the international community began to recognize that desertification is a serious problem in arid regions. At the 1992 United Nations Conference on Environment and Development in Rio de Janeiro, African countries pressed for the conclusion of a convention on desertification. This led to the 1994 United Nations Convention to Combat Desertification. Desertification is a result of natural and human causes. The main drivers are water and wind erosion, chemical degradation and physical degradation from a range of human activities. Article 1(a) defines desertification as "land degradation in arid, semi-arid and dry sub-humid areas resulting from various factors, including climatic variations and human activities. . . ." The core article, 5, relies on "victim" States taking the following actions:

(a) give due priority to combating desertification and mitigating the effects of drought, and allocate adequate resources in accordance with their circumstances and capabilities;

(b) establish strategies and priorities, within the framework of sustainable development plans and/or policies, to combat desertification and mitigate the effects of drought;

(c) address the underlying causes of desertification and pay special attention to the socio-economic factors contributing to desertification processes;

(d) promote awareness and facilitate the participation of local populations, particularly women and youth, with the support of non-governmental organizations, in efforts to combat desertification and mitigate the effects of drought; and

(e) provide an enabling environment by strengthening, as appropriate, relevant existing legislation and, where they do not exist, enacting new laws and establishing long-term policies and action programmes.

By most measures the Convention must be judged a failure. "Global assessments indicate that the percentage of total land area that is highly degraded has increased from 15% in 1991 to 25% by 2011. While the world's drylands continue to be the most vulnerable, land degradation is a global phenomenon; some findings indicate that 78% of the total land being degraded between 1981 and 2003 is located in terrestrial ecosystems other than drylands. . . . If the current scenario of land degradation continues over the next 25 years, it may reduce global food production, from what it otherwise would be, by as much as 12% resulting in world food prices as much as 30% higher for some commodities (IFPRI 2012). This comes at a time when population growth, rising incomes and changing consumption patterns are expected to increase the demand for food, energy and water, by at least 50%, 45% and 30%, respectively by 2030. . . ." A Stronger UNCCD for a Land-Degradation Neutral World Issue Brief (UNCCD Secretariat 2013). Degraded land can function as a carbon sink compared to "greened" land. B.D. Poulter et al., *Contribution of semi-arid ecosystems to interannual variability of the global carbon cycle*, 509 Nature 600–603 (2014).

The implementation of the Convention has been hampered by many factors, including the position of the developed world that the problem is not a global but a local or regional one. Kannan Ambalan, The United Nations Convention to Combat Desertification: Issues and Challenges, International Relations, April 14, 2014, *available at* http://www.e-ir.info/2014/04/30/united-nations-convention-to-combat-desertification-issues-and-challenges/:

> The current status of the UNCCD implementation can be assessed through the Mid-term Evaluation Report on the 10-year Strategic Plan and Framework (2008–2018) to enhance the implementation of the UNCCD. The evaluation considered earlier UNCCD reports and documents. The evaluation process covered not only the status of implementation of the Convention, but also identified possible causes and potential solutions where implementation is incomplete.

> For some of the objectives related with the UNCCD implementation, there is not sufficient evidence to show the extent of progress which has been made. In some of the areas, the progress, or lack thereof, has yet to be determined. The level of implementation of most regional and subregional action programmes (RAPs and SRAPs) have been low and not aligned with the Strategy. The thematic programme networks launched to support RAP implementations are not connected with the Committee on Science and Technology, and most of them are reportedly not effective.

> The complexity of the indicators used in reporting and the limited capacity on data collection and analysis affected the reporting process. These factors are responsible for the low levels of reporting through the performance review and assessment of

implementation system (PRAIS). Many affected countries did not receive the needed technical assistance and timely financial support to undertake the reporting process.

Another difficulty in monitoring and reporting on progress towards achieving the operational objectives has been ambiguity on how to measure the indicators. It is difficult to assess whether the plan targets were reached, due to a lack of comparable data. Another challenge is establishing a connection between the indicators and the activities connected with the Convention. Nevertheless, there is evidence of progress in realizing many of the outcomes related to the operational objectives, although the progress has been uneven.

With regard to realignment, there is little evidence that they helped advance the implementation or alignment of action programmes, nationally or regionally. Only eleven countries aligned their national action programme (NAP) with the Strategy, although an additional 54 countries planned to finalise by 2015. In general, there is little evidence to conclude that the UNCCD objectives are being appropriately incorporated into relevant national policy areas and plans.

Notes and Questions

Both biodiversity and forest conservation can be said to be local problems. Is desertification any different? If not, what explains the lack of progress compared to both biodiversity and forest conservation? We have case studies, e.g., Combating Desertification and Land Degradation: Proven Practices from Asia and the Pacific (Park Chung-ho et al. eds. Korean Forest Service 2011), but no generally accepted statement of principles or best practices. Is the problem a lack of engagement, especially in Africa, by States in the north despite the existence of degraded soils in Europe and North America? "Victim" countries often lack the technical capacity to measure and monitor desertification. The Secretariat bears some blame as "in contrast with other environmental agreements, the UNCCD has not yet specified quantitative and verifiable reduction commitments and conservation goals in a time-bound manner." Ambalan, The United Nations Convention to Combat Desertification, *supra*. There are also technical-capacity problems. We have good indicators of the process but there is no general agreement on how to measure them. For analysis of the necessity of local participation and the limitations of actions plans as implementing instruments in the Desertification Convention, see Edith Brown Weiss & Tanya Katrina Lat, *Engaging the World's Poor in Sustainable Development*, 51 German Yearbook of International Law 143, 170–177 (2008).

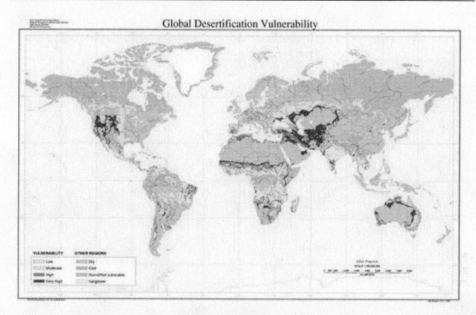

Global Desertification Vulnerability

[Soil map and soil climate map, USDA-NRCS, Soil Science Division, World Soil Resources, Washington D.C.]

A FINAL WORD

Recall the questions asked at the beginning of the chapter, page 761, *supra*. A 2014 assessment of the struggle to conserve biodiversity concluded "[c]onservation policies could slow extinctions, but current trends do not give much comfort. Although nations are expanding the number of land and ocean areas that they set aside for protection, most measures of biodiversity show pressures on species are increasing." Richard Monastersky, *Life—A Status Report*, 516 Nature 158 (December 2014). What are the next steps that the international community needs to take?

CHAPTER 14

FOOD AND AGRICULTURE

. . .

Governments, international bodies, nongovernmental organizations, and scholars have been increasingly recognizing the complex interrelationships between agriculture and the environment. The 2002 World Summit on Sustainable Development (WSSD) Plan of Action placed special emphasis on the agricultural sector, highlighting it as necessary for the protection and management of the natural resource base. Agricultural systems are especially relevant due to the many natural resource issues they implicate—from water to habitat degradation to climate change in the release of carbon to pollution in the form of pesticides, fungicides and herbicides; the relevant international law pertaining to these natural resource issues as a general matter (as opposed to the specific context of agriculture) is discussed in earlier chapters. Moreover, the relationship between agriculture and the environment is often multidirectional; environmental problems such as climate change and heavy metal contamination often feed back into agricultural production, creating negative impacts for food safety and security. *See* UNEP, The Environmental Food Crisis: The Environment's Role in Averting Future Food Crises (Christian Nellemann et al. eds., 2009). Finally, the actual agricultural products themselves may have their own associated environmental concerns. Regulation of these products, for example beef raised with growth hormones, and tobacco, is discussed in other chapters of this casebook.

This chapter discusses some of the developing international system addressing agriculture, food, and the environment. As you read this chapter, you should keep in mind that as of right now, there is no comprehensive international binding or even soft law system for agriculture. Instead, the governance of agriculture falls primarily under domestic law. To the extent that binding international agreements are implicated, it is either through WTO disputes (discussed in Chapter 16), or in particular environmental agreements that happen to touch upon agriculture or food. The latter are discussed in this chapter, as are calls for greater international agreements and norms.

A. INTRODUCTION TO AGRICULTURE, FOOD SECURITY, AND THE ENVIRONMENT

The following excerpts provide an overview of the ways in which agricultural production impacts the environment, as well as some of the tensions between issues of food security and environmental sustainability.

CAN WE FEED THE WORLD AND SUSTAIN THE PLANET?

Jonathan A. Foley
Scientific American 62–63 (November 2011)

Right about now one billion people suffer from chronic hunger. The world's farmers grow enough food to feed them, but it is not properly distributed and, even if it were, many cannot afford it, because prices are escalating.

But another challenge looms.

By 2050 the world's population will increase by two billion or three billion, which will likely double the demand for food, according to several studies. Demand will also rise because many more people will have higher incomes, which means they will eat more, especially meat. Increasing use of cropland for biofuels will make meeting the doubling goal more difficult still. So even if we solve today's problems of poverty and access—a daunting task—we will also have to produce twice as much to guarantee adequate supply worldwide.

And that's not all.

By clearing tropical forests, farming marginal lands and intensifying industrial farming in sensitive landscapes and watersheds, humankind has made agriculture the planet's dominant environmental threat. Agriculture already consumes a large percentage of the earth's land surface and is destroying habitat, using up freshwater, polluting rivers and oceans, and emitting greenhouse gases more extensively than almost any other human activity. To guarantee the globe's long-term health, we must dramatically reduce agriculture's adverse impacts.

The world's food system faces three incredible, interwoven challenges, then. It must guarantee that all seven billion people alive today are adequately fed; it must double food production in the next 40 years; and it must achieve both goals while becoming truly environmentally sustainable.

Could these simultaneous goals possibly be met? An international team of experts, which I coordinated, has settled on five steps that, if pursued together, could raise by more than 100 percent the food available for human consumption globally, while significantly lessening greenhouse gas emissions, biodiversity losses, water use and water pollution.

Tackling the triple challenge will be one of the most important tests humanity has ever faced. It is fair to say that our response will determine the fate of our civilization.

BUMPING UP AGAINST BARRIERS

At first blush, the way to feed more people would seem clear: grow more food, by expanding farmland and improving yield—the amount of edible crops harvested per hectare. Unfortunately, the world is running into significant barriers on both counts.

Society already farms roughly 38 percent of the earth's land surface, not counting Greenland or Antarctica. Agriculture is by far the biggest human use of land on the planet; nothing else comes close. And most of that 38 percent covers the best farmland. Much of the remainder is covered by deserts, mountains, tundra, ice, cities, parks and other unsuitable growing areas. The few remaining frontiers are mainly in tropical forests and savannas, which are vital to the stability of the globe, especially as stores of carbon and biodiversity. Expanding into those areas is not a good idea, yet over the past 20 years five million to 10 million hectares of cropland a year has been created, with a significant portion of that in the tropics. These additions enlarged the net area of cultivated land by only 3 percent, however, because of farmland losses caused by urban development and other forces, particularly in temperate zones.

Improving yield also sounds enticing. Yet our research team found that average global crop yield increased by about 20 percent in the past 20 years—far less than what is typically reported. That improvement is significant, but the rate is nowhere near enough to double food production by midcentury. Whereas yields of some crops improved substantially, others saw little gain and a few even declined.

Feeding more people would be easier if all the food we grew went into human hands. But only 60 percent of the world's crops are meant for people: mostly grains, followed by pulses (beans, lentils), oil plants, vegetables and fruits. Another 35 percent is used for animal feed, and the final 5 percent goes to biofuels and other industrial products. Meat is the biggest issue here. Even with the most efficient meat and dairy systems, feeding crops to animals reduces the world's potential food supply. Typically, grain-fed cattle operations use 30 kilograms of grain to make one kilogram of edible, boneless beef. Chicken and pork are more efficient, and grass-fed beef converts nonfood material into protein. No matter how you slice it, though, grain-fed meat production systems are a drain on the global food supply.

Another deterrent to growing more food is the cost in damage to the environment, which is already extensive. Only our use of energy, with its profound impacts on climate and ocean acidification, rivals the sheer magnitude of agriculture's environmental insults. Our research team estimates that agriculture has already cleared or radically transformed 70 percent of the world's prehistoric grasslands, 50 percent of the savannas, 45 percent of the temperate deciduous forests and 25 percent of the tropical forests. Since the last ice age, nothing has disrupted ecosystems more. Agriculture's physical footprint is nearly 60 times that of the world's pavements and buildings.

Freshwater is another casualty. Humans use an astounding 4,000 cubic kilometers of water per year, mostly withdrawn from rivers and aquifers. Irrigation accounts for 70 percent of the draw. If we count only consumptive water use—water that is used and not returned to the watershed—irrigation climbs to 80 or 90 percent of the total. As a result, many large rivers such as the Colorado have diminished flows, some have dried up altogether, and many places have rapidly declining water tables, including regions of the U.S. and India.

Water is not only disappearing, it is being contaminated. Fertilizers, herbicides and pesticides are being spread at incredible levels and are found in nearly every ecosystem. The flows of nitrogen and phosphorus through the environment have more than doubled since 1960, causing widespread water pollution and enormous hypoxic "dead zones" at the mouths of the world's major rivers. Ironically, fertilizer runoff from farmland—in the name of growing more food—compromises another crucial source of nutrition: coastal fishing grounds. Fertilizer certainly has been a key ingredient of the green revolution that has helped feed the world, but when nearly half the fertilizer we apply runs off rather than nourishes crops, we clearly can do better.

Agriculture is also the largest single source of greenhouse gas emissions from society, collectively accounting for about 35 percent of the carbon dioxide, methane and nitrous oxide we release. That is more than the emissions from worldwide transportation (including all cars, trucks and planes) or electricity generation. The energy used to grow, process and transport food is a concern, but the vast majority of emissions come from tropical deforestation, methane released from animals and rice paddies, and nitrous oxide from overfertilized soils.

THE GLOBAL FOOD SYSTEM, ENVIRONMENTAL PROTECTION, AND HUMAN RIGHTS

Carmen G. Gonzalez
26 Natural Resources & Environment 7–8 (Winter 2012)

The global food system is exceeding ecological limits while failing to meet the food needs of a large segment of the world's population. According to the United Nations Food and Agriculture Organization (FAO) more people are undernourished today than 40 years ago. Approximately 925 million people experience chronic food insecurity, and we are not on target toward achieving the Millennium Development Goal of cutting world hunger in half between 1990–92 and 2015. The widespread industrialization of agricultural production places enormous pressure on the world's ecosystems, causing soil degradation, deforestation, loss of agrobiodiversity, and the contamination and depletion of freshwater resources.... Agriculture is currently the principal driver of biodiversity loss, primarily through the conversion of forests, grasslands, and wetlands to large-scale agricultural production, but also through unsustainable rates of water use, pollution of lakes and rivers, and introduction of nonnative species. The United Nations Millennium Ecosystem Assessment concluded that approximately 60 percent of the ecosystem services examined have been degraded or used unsustainably to satisfy growing demands for food, water, timber, and fuel. This degradation of ecosystem services disproportionately impacts rural poor and impedes efforts to combat poverty and hunger.

The genetic diversity of the world's food supply is also threatened. Seventy-five percent of the world's food crop diversity was lost in the twentieth century as farmers abandoned traditional food crops in favor of a narrow range of domesticated plant species. Only 12 crops currently supply 80 percent of our dietary energy from plants. Genetic diversity within these crops has been declining as well because high-yielding varieties have supplanted traditional local varieties. This loss of genetic diversity increases the risk of catastrophic crop failure akin to the Irish potato famine and deprives plant breeders of germplasm essential for the development of crops capable of thriving in a changing and warming climate.

Climate change will exacerbate food insecurity and loss of biodiversity. Water scarce regions of the world are predicted to experience chronic drought as the climate becomes hotter and drier, with severe impacts in the semi-arid areas of Latin America and Sub-Saharan Africa. Coastal areas will be buffeted by hurricanes, rising sea levels, and floods. Climate change is also anticipated to have devastating impacts on biodiversity—reducing the productivity of the world's fisheries and accelerating the extinction of species and the loss of ecosystem services vital to food production. The households and countries most likely to be adversely affected are those most reliant on local agricultural production, which already face chronic food insecurity.

[. . .]

INTERRELATED PROBLEMS: INTEGRATED SOLUTIONS

When designing system-based solutions to the converging food, climate, and agrobiodiversity crises, it is useful to keep in mind three key propositions. First, poverty rather than food scarcity is generally the cause of chronic malnutrition. Global food production has outpaced population growth since 1950, and there is currently sufficient food to satisfy the nutritional needs of every human being. People go hungry, even in countries where food is abundant, because they are poor. The majority of the world's undernourished people are small farmers in developing countries who are net buyers of food. These farmers' income is often too low for them to purchase the food available on the market. Thus, combating hunger requires increasing the income of small farmers in the developing world rather than simply boosting food production.

Second, agrobiodiversity is essential to the integrity and resilience of the world's food supply. Cultivating a variety of crops provides insurance against environmental shocks, diversifies food sources, enhances soil fertility, and conserves the genetic resources necessary to breed plant varieties that can withstand the stresses associated with climate change, including salinity, heat, flood, and drought. Historically, small farmers have played an essential role in conserving and enhancing the world's agrobiodiversity. However, the rapid expansion of industrial agriculture has produced a worldwide decline in agrobiodiversity, marginalized small farmers, eroded farmers' self-sufficiency, and diminished traditional agricultural knowledge while fostering dependence on expensive seeds, pesticides, fertilizers, and machinery produced by a small number of transnational corporations. Thus, trade and production policies that enhance the livelihoods of small farmers and encourage the cultivation of diverse crops and diverse genetic varieties are essential for the health and resilience of the world's agroecosystems.

Finally, agriculture can play a significant role in climate change mitigation and adaptation. Sustainable agriculture seeks to maximize natural pest, nutrient, soil, and water management technologies while reducing agrochemical use and enhancing agrobiodiversity. By minimizing the use of fossil fuel-based agrochemicals, sustainable farming practices produce fewer greenhouse gas emissions than industrial agriculture. By utilizing animal manure, crop rotation, intercropping, and agroforestry, sustainable agriculture reduces soil erosion and enhances carbon sequestration in both soils and aboveground vegetation. By increasing the organic matter in soils and enhancing the soil's water retention capacity, sustainable farming practices boost agricultural productivity and increase resilience to floods and droughts. The cultivation of genetically diverse crop varieties improves resistance to weather-related events, pests, and diseases. Thus, agricultural trade and production policies that promote sustainable agriculture will enhance food security, conserve biological diversity, and contribute to climate change mitigation and adaptation.

Indeed, there is a growing consensus among policymakers at the international level that promoting sustainable agriculture is a vital step toward addressing the environmental and food security challenges of the twenty-first century. Sustainable agriculture has produced significant increases in agricultural yields in Asia, Africa, and Latin America while increasing the incomes of small farmers, enhancing environmental quality, reducing dependence on external inputs, and preserving the traditional agroecological knowledge of local and indigenous communities. A recent U.N. report concludes that small farmers can double food production in the next 10 years in the regions of the world plagued by food insecurity by shifting to sustainable methods.

B. LEGAL SYSTEMS FOR ENVIRONMENTAL ISSUES RAISED BY AGRICULTURAL/FOOD PRODUCTION

As described earlier, the agricultural sector implicates a wide variety of environmental issues, many of which are addressed in a more media-specific way and are described in earlier chapters of this casebook. This section describes some of the interrelationships between food systems and the international initiatives not discussed elsewhere. If you are interested in the ways in which legal systems discussed elsewhere in the casebook intersect with agriculture/food production, please also read the Notes section at this end of this part.

EXERCISE

In reading the following material, think about this hypothetical. CerealCo is considering buying land in Ethiopia and the water rights to produce a breakfast cereal grown from genetically modified seeds. The company plans to market its cereal for export to the United States, as well as to Germany, France, and Italy. The company plans to use pesticides to produce the product. Scientists at the local university lab in Addis Ababa are concerned about the effects of the pesticides on the quality of Ethiopian soil and water resources. The people living in the area of the prospective land purchase are very concerned about CerealCo's buying the land and water rights, because all the villagers depend on the area for subsistence farming. Their concerns are twofold: some villagers are concerned that after CerealCo purchases the water rights, they will no longer have enough water to raise their own crops; others believe that food prices will be driven up by the CerealCo's use of the land, and worry that they will no longer be able to purchase enough food to survive.

What legal instruments are implicated by this hypothetical? What additional research might you need to conduct to determine whether and how these instruments apply?

1. GENETICALLY MODIFIED ORGANISMS

Humans have been changing the genetic content of crops for thousands of years through conventional breeding techniques such as selection of, and cross-breeding, plants with traits that are deemed to be desirable. In the 1980s, a new technology emerged: Genetic modification (GM), also referred to as genetic engineering (GE), involves the use of recombinant deoxyribonucleic acid (DNA) technology to change the genetic structure of an organism in order to attain a desired trait not present in the original organism. Initially this involved moving genetic material from one species into another, such as moving an Arctic flounder gene into a tomato in the hopes that the resulting tomatoes would be more resistant to frost and cold storage (that product was never marketed). Some methods of introducing the new genetic material were quite imprecise, including coating small spheres with the new genetic material and bombarding the organism to be modified with them: a small percentage would hit and stick to a chromosome and cause the desired change. GE techniques have now evolved to be more precise and to no longer require material from a species other than the organism being modified. In some cases of gene editing, GE does not require material from any organism; either synthetic material is inserted or the change consists of removing genetic material. Virtually all types of living organisms—animals, plants, fungi, microbes—are being genetically engineered as of January 2015, for an extremely wide variety of purposes. GE frequently involves "stacking" genetic changes, so that the target organism will have more than one genetic modification and exhibit more than one engineered trait. Epigenetic traits (i.e., heritable traits that are not genetic) are also being engineered. GE technology undoubtedly will continue to develop.

Agricultural crops have been genetically engineered in several ways, including most notably to create their own pesticide (Bacillus thuringia, or Bt, a naturally occurring pesticide) and to be resistant to a commercially available herbicide (Round-up, or glyphosate). Other crops such as papaya have been genetically engineered to be resistant to viruses. These crops caught on relatively quickly in the United States; as of January 2015, for example, more than 90% of corn and soy bean grown in the United States is genetically engineered. Other countries have varied in their regulatory and consumer responses, with some countries welcoming them, other countries essentially banning genetically engineered crops, and still others approving the food safety of such crops but not their release into the environment (with the result that genetically engineered crops may be imported for consumption but not grown in those countries). As a general matter, GE has been criticized by some for causing risks to food safety and the environment, as well as for causing undesirable concentration in the seed industry, harming some segments of agricultural producers, and leading to resistance in weeds to relatively safe pesticides and herbicides. On the other hand, again as a general matter, GE has been praised by some as offering a safe answer to world hunger, improving farmers' income, and reducing the environmental impact of farming. A third group falls into neither of the critic or supporter camps but argues that GE requires careful regulation.

In the United States, different aspects of GE are regulated by several agencies (U.S. Department of Agriculture (USDA), Environmental Protection Agency (EPA), and Food and Drug Administration (FDA)) under what is referred to as the Coordinated Framework, which utilizes existing regulatory authority. Genetic engineering has been the subject of several research studies by the National Research Council, a part of the National Academy of Sciences. *See, e.g.*, National Research Council, Environmental Effects of Transgenic Plants: The Scope and Adequacy of Regulation (2002); National Research Council, The Impact of Genetically Engineered Crops on Farm Sustainability in the United States (2004); National Research Council & Institute of Medicine, Safety of Genetically Engineered Foods: Approaches to Assessing Unintended Health Effects (2010). As this casebook goes to press, a National Academy of Science (NAS) research committee is evaluating all aspects of GE crops; another NAS research committee is considering gene drives, discussed in Chapter 3; both reports are expected to be published in 2016.

The use of genetically engineered organisms in agriculture presents a number of potential environmental impacts, the risk assessment of which is discussed in Chapter 3, part E. The relationship between trade and genetically engineered crops is covered in Chapter 16. The United States is the leader in the development of GE. Genetically engineered crops and products are widely produced in, consumed in, and exported from the country. In contrast, Europe is much more skeptical of GE and between 1999–2003 imposed a de facto moratorium on the approval of biotech products. Argentina, Canada, and the United States successfully challenged the moratorium before the World Trade Organization. The first excerpt below describes the differences between the EU and United States approaches to regulation. The second excerpt below describes the differences between the EU and United States approaches to labeling. The final excerpt is from the Cartagena Protocol on Biosafety, which directly addresses genetically engineered organisms—referred to in that instrument as "living modified organisms," or LMOs.

THE DOOR OPENS SLIGHTLY: RECENT EUROPEAN REGULATIONS ON GENETICALLY MODIFIED PRODUCTS AND ONGOING UNITED STATES-EUROPEAN GM DISPUTES

Brian P. Rafferty
16 Georgetown Intl. L. Rev. 281, 283, 287–88, 294–96 (2004)

II. GENETICALLY MODIFIED PRODUCTS

In the United States, the definition of GM products is product centered. This product-oriented approach dictates that if a GM product is not fundamentally different from a conventional product it does not require separate regulatory treatment. . . . the U.S. position only considers products that exhibit different risk characteristics to be GM products. . . .

In the EU, the definition of GM products is process oriented. The process-oriented regulatory regime is based on the premise that different production processes require different regulatory treatment. If GM materials are used in the production process, the final product requires treatment different from that for conventional products, even if the final product is demonstrated to pose no risks different from those posed by the conventional product.

IV. THE U.S. EXPERIENCE AND REGIME

C. SYSTEMATIC DIFFERENCES AND THE MANIFESTATION OF PRECAUTION IN THE UNITED STATES

The U.S. government's stance on GM products is an expression of the relative disinterest of the U.S. public in the issue, as well as the result of the structure of the U.S. government and the manner in which it historically conducts its regulatory policy. The U.S. government's stance on GM product regulation may be attributable in a large part to public disinterest, although other factors, such as the U.S. farm and biotech lobbies, may also have significant effects. A loud public outcry against GM products, as has occurred in the EU, might shape the U.S. position differently. There has been no widespread opposition to GM products in the United States, and EU Commissioner for the Environment Margot Wallström has said that "[p]art of the explanation may be connected with the greater regulatory transparency in the United States and hence greater public trust in the process." The domination of the regulatory process by scientists and the exclusion of non-scientists in the EU create suspicion of the process and possibly apprehension as to its results. "Transparency and trust are vital." The relative openness of the U.S. regulatory system, such as the notice and comment rule-making procedure, may account for the lack of public outcry against GM products. U.S. citizens may be more inclined than EU citizens to trust that if there were a danger, their government would deal appropriately with that danger.

The United States is no less precautionary than the EU; precaution is simply expressed differently in the United States because of the manner in which the U.S. regulatory system deals with risks. The nature of the U.S. legal system, specifically its openness to citizen advocacy groups and judicial review, makes it more likely to enforce precautionary measures once adopted. The reluctance of the United States to agree to a strong version of the precautionary principle in an international treaty may be "precisely because the U.S. legal system is more likely to enforce treaty provisions on precaution through citizen suits, judicial review, and direct legislative and executive implementation." As the CAA [Clean Air

Act] and CWA [Clean Water Act] examples above demonstrate, U.S. courts are comfortable with permitting wide discretion on the part of the executive in implementing legal commitments. As the United States expects that commitments to precaution will be significantly implemented, it may be loath to make bold, sweeping commitments. Instead, the United States may be more inclined to undertake more discrete measures while avoiding bold, sweeping commitments that could have unintended results.

Other features of the U.S. legal system also make the United States appear less committed to safety than is the case. The United States has a strong tort liability system that provides for substantial recovery from at-fault parties. Ex ante precaution may be less necessary in states where ex post remedies like the U.S. tort system are strong. Accordingly, "U.S. reluctance to agree to stringent versions of precaution may reflect confidence in the U.S. legal system as a whole—not opposition to protecting health and the environment." The United States is not opposed to safety; U.S. policymakers just may not feel the need to be as precautionary as some other States because they are more confident in the ability of the U.S. tort system to address any resulting harms after they occur.

V. THE EU EXPERIENCE AND REGIME

A belief exists that the EU has acted more swiftly to regulate GM products because of its more precautionary nature. This belief is based on a misunderstanding of the EU legal and regulatory systems, on a failure to examine closely factors particular to the risk that GM products represent, and on a lack of knowledge about Europeans' previous experiences with similar risks. EU citizens approach issues involving food and food safety from a unique perspective, shaped both by the role that food plays in their lives and their view of government as a regulator. The EU regulatory apparatus is designed and operated in a manner making it prone to broad declarations of policy. In the case of the GM product debate, the particular experience of the BSE [bovine spongiform encephalopathy] outbreak casts a particularly strong shadow over the entire issue in the EU. By looking at these factors, it becomes apparent that the highly precautionary approach taken by the EU with respect to GM products is not the result of overall greater precaution by the EU, but of system-specific factors that cause precaution to manifest itself in certain ways and by factors specific to the case of GM products.

A. PRECAUTION IN THE CONTEXT OF FOOD IN THE EUROPEAN UNION

There has been widespread public outcry over GM products in the EU. This widespread concern has its roots in European views on food and the role of science, and in a general mistrust of government. In many European countries there is a strong link between culture and food, and this makes issues involving food all the more sensitive. David Byrne, the

EU Health and Consumer Safety Commissioner, has said, referring to food quality, that "[f]or some member states it's nearly synonymous with sovereignty." European objections to GM products often seem to take on a moral or pseudo-religious tone, with one British consumer saying that "[i]t's not the natural order of things." These opinions on GM products are not the result of the excessive precautionary nature of Europeans, but of the way they conceptualize food in their lives. Food represents more than just a means of survival, and the degree of risk of GM products may not be as important in shaping Europeans' opinions as the fact that this risk touches something of great symbolic importance.

The European public's reaction to GM products may also be the result of the European public's beliefs as to the governments' ability or willingness to protect them from these risks. The risks associated with GM products may produce overreactions because GM products are manufactured by large faceless transnational corporations, which people may believe the government cannot adequately control. The vigilance of the European public in reacting to the GM products issue may be largely the result of a feeling that they must intervene because the government cannot properly assesses the risk. . . .

B.   THE MANIFESTATION OF PRECAUTION IN THE EUROPEAN UNION

The design and function of the EU legal and regulatory systems makes the EU appear to be far more precautionary than it in fact is. In EU Member States, the judiciary and citizens' advocacy groups have historically done little to enforce government proclamations. EU states may thus be willing to make bold statements of policy, knowing that the chances of them being held to their specifics are slim. Ex ante regulation is a more viable option for controlling a risk in the EU than an ex post tort regime, given the relative weakness of the tort system in the EU. The legal and regulatory structure of the EU is suited to a regulation based approach, and to one involving bold encompassing statements.

The precautionary principle in the EU is understood in the wider context of EU regulatory policy . . . In the EU, "the precautionary principle is understood in tandem with the principle of proportionality." The proportionality principle allows regulators to moderate precautionary regulations if they appear unreasonable for the given situation. . . .

GENETICALLY MODIFIED FOOD AND INFORMED CONSUMER CHOICE: COMPARING U.S. AND E.U. LABELING LAWS

Valery Federici
35 Brooklyn J. Int'l L. 515, 533, 535, 537–38, 540–41, 541–46 (2010)

III. THE LABELING REGIME IN THE UNITED STATES

American laws governing the approval of new varieties of GMOs and their labeling are much laxer than E.U. laws due to social priorities and two facets of the relative regulatory approaches. Socially, American consumers have been more tolerant of GMOs and have not demanded harsher laws. In terms of regulatory approach, the U.S. is more tolerant of risk than the E.U., evaluating only the product of biotechnology rather than both the product and its method of production (or process).

American consumers have not been as troubled by GMOs as European consumers: the International Food Information Council ("IFIC") released a survey in early 2008 that deemed U.S. consumer confidence in the domestic food supply "high," at 68%. . . . Because of this tolerance, there is no current federal law requiring labeling of GMOs or GM food products. . . .

[One] regulatory difference is that regulators in the United States focus on the end product resulting from a new technology, whereas European regulators focus on the product as well as the process by which it is produced. . . . Thus, genetically modified foods and food products are evaluated pursuant to the same laws as their conventionally produced counterparts under the Coordinated Framework promulgated by the White House's Office of Science and Technology Policy. Consistent with the end-product approach, the FDA has maintained the position that:

> Labeling of GM foods should only be mandatory if they are shown to differ significantly in composition from their conventional counterparts in some way that might pose a risk to the consumer—such as through the presence of an allergen, a changed level of a major dietary nutrient, an increased level of toxins, or a change in the expected storage or preparation characteristics of the food.

While FIFRA [Federal Insecticide, Fungicide and Rodenticide Act], the TSCA [Toxic Substances Control Act, and the FPPA [Federal Plant Pest Act, *see also* Plant Protection Act of 2000] all regulate the products of biotechnology, only the FDCA [Food, Drug and Cosmetic Act, also referred to as FFDCA] sets regulations concerning food-labeling requirements . . . The FDA applied the FDCA requirements to biotech foods as follows:

- If a bioengineered food is significantly different from its traditional counterpart such that the common or usual name no longer adequately describes the new food, the name must be changed to describe the difference.

- If an issue exists for the food or a constituent of the food regarding how the food is used or consequences of its use, a statement must be made on the label to describe the issue.

- If a bioengineered food has a significantly different nutritional property, its label must reflect the difference.

- If a new food includes an allergen that consumers would not expect to be present based on the name of the food, the presence of that allergen must be disclosed on the label.

Thus, while the label need not say specifically, for example, "this tomato has been genetically engineered to contain a Brazil nut gene," it must say something to the effect of, "this tomato contains proteins that may engender allergic responses in people allergic to Brazil nuts." Further, the FDA identified examples of voluntary statements that companies could use, such as: "[t]his product contains cornmeal that was produced using biotechnology"; "[t]his product contains high oleic acid soybean oil from soybeans developed using biotechnology to decrease the amount of saturated fat"; or "[t]hese tomatoes were genetically engineered to improve texture."

The cumulative effect of these regulations is that U.S. producers are not required to label their products as genetically modified, but are free to label their products as not genetically modified—in others words, "GM-free"—to the extent that such labeling is not misleading. In addition, consumers who wish to avoid GM foods may limit their purchases to foods bearing the "USDA-Organic" label. But even with this seeming variety, U.S. consumers do not enjoy informed choice—they cannot assume that foods that do not bear labels are not GM, and they likely do not understand what labels they do encounter.

IV. THE LABELING REGIME IN THE EUROPEAN UNION

Regulations regarding approval and labeling of GMOs are much stricter in Europe than in the U.S. for two reasons. Distrust of regulators has led consumers to demand harsher regulations, and European regulators approach risk regulation conservatively—they evaluate both the product and the production process, and they use the precautionary principle. The E.U. would prefer to ban the importation and growth of GMOs altogether, as discussed in Part I. As this is not a viable option, regulators have instituted the world's broadest and harshest regulations. These regulations have led to a de facto ban on GMOs in the E.U.

The strong distrust of government and opposition to GMOs in Europe are the result of regulatory failures. . . . The strongest driver of the intensely negative consumer reaction to the BSE scare was not the fact that humans contracted the disease, or that some died, but the anger over E.U. regulators' "belated failure to recognize" the health hazards of BSE. This failure "severely undermined public trust in E.U. food safety regulations and the scientific expertise on which they were based." Both the government of Britain and the European Commission denied the validity of consumer concerns and placed no restrictions on the sale of British beef until there had been a significant number of human deaths.

As a result of these food supply scandals and regulatory failures, European consumers are distrustful of food modification in general, and they are not confident in their national and supranational regulators' abilities to ensure the safety of the food supply. This general distrust also applies to GM foods: "a majority of Europeans do not support GM foods. [They] are judged not to be useful and to be risky to society." Interestingly, the level of support differs by country: "[w]hile GM crops are supported in Spain, Portugal, Ireland, Belgium, [the United Kingdom], Finland, Germany, and the Netherlands," the public is generally opposed to GM crops in "France, Italy, Greece, Denmark, Austria, and Luxembourg."

Before the integration of the European Union, food safety was regulated at the national level in each member country by myriad individual state agencies. With the creation of the European Common Market, the free flow of goods took priority over food safety. In 1985, the European Community ("EC") moved to a labeling regime as an alternative to attempting to harmonize member countries' regulations regarding approval of individual biotech varieties. The labeling "indicate[d] the differences in composition and production methods," which aimed to allow consumers to make informed decisions.

The labeling regime was considered a success, but as the E.U. succeeded at integrating the markets and the political systems of its member countries, the regulatory focus shifted to ensuring food safety. In 2000, responding to calls from various groups for increased "excellence, transparency, and independence" of food regulation, the European Commission created the European Food Safety Authority (EFSA). While the EFSA is charged with risk assessment, risk management remains entrusted to each individual member state.

Under the old guidelines, which were part of the E.U. novel food regulation of 1997, "[g]enetically modified foods required labeling only if GM content could be detected in the final product. Proof of GM content could be obtained by testing for characteristic, genetically modified DNA fragments." In April 2004, the European Union replaced the previous product-oriented set of labeling laws covering genetically modified foods and animal feed with a more conservative, process-oriented set of regulations. The Directive on Genetically Modified (GM) Food and Feed and the Directive on the Traceability and Labelling of GMOs require producers to label more products and the food production industry to put in place a compliance system for monitoring the presence of GM material throughout the supply chain.

The stated goals of the new regulations are to protect "human life and health, animal health and welfare, [and] environment and consumer interests," to ensure "the effective functioning of the internal market," to "lay down provisions for the labeling of genetically modified food and feed," to promote "the right of consumers to information," and to "enable[ ] the consumer to make an informed choice and facilitate[ ] fairness of transactions between seller and purchaser." This is not a hierarchy of purposes, as nothing is explicitly given priority, and the various goals are distributed throughout the regulations.

The labeling requirements apply to virtually all foodstuffs, including "processed, pre-cooked or packaged food . . . bulk or unpacked goods, and catered food in restaurants and canteens." There are two important exceptions, however. Processing aids are exempt, and "[u]nintentional and technically unavoidable mixing only needs to be labeled if the GM content exceeds 0.9 percent (of the original ingredient)."

The regulations divide food into three categories: pre-cooked or packaged food with a list of ingredients, packaged food without a list of ingredients, and unpackaged food or very small package sizes. For each category, the regulations detail the exact form, location, and content of the label. For pre-cooked or packaged foods with a list of ingredients, the GM ingredient "must be labeled, in the form of an addition to the ingredient concerned, either as 'genetically modified', or as 'produced from genetically modified' material." This text may be added in a footnote to the list of ingredients. For packaged foods without a list of ingredients, the text must be clearly visible on the label. Lastly, for unpackaged foods or for very small package sizes, the text must be attached to the display, or be displayed in direct connection with the relevant product. The use of symbols or logos is not allowed for any of the three categories.

The E.U. is not alone in requiring labeling; many other countries have some form of labeling law. Canada and Argentina (the other large producers of GM crops) allow voluntary labeling, as does the United States. Australia and New Zealand require that GM content that makes up more than 1% of the total weight of a product be labeled, and provide exemptions for "vegetable oils, food additives, and food processing aids (such as enzymes used in cheese and brewing)." Japan similarly requires labeling, but with a threshold of at least 5% GM content, and provides exemptions for "feedstuffs, alcoholic beverages, and processed foods, such as soya sauce, corn flakes, and other vegetable oils." South Korea and Indonesia require labeling, with 3% thresholds.

The complexity and scope of the E.U.'s current labeling laws render them the harshest in the world. The effect of these regulations, combined with strict approval procedures for introducing GMOs to the E.U. market, has been to maintain the prior legal moratorium on the importation and growth of GMOs de facto. Producers and grocers do not want to run the risk of consumer boycotts or penalties for incorrect labeling, so GMOs are not commercially available in the E.U.

NOTES AND QUESTIONS

1. *Note on Post-2003 EU Regulation.* EU Regulation 1829/2003 of the European Parliament and of the Council on 22 September 2003, on Genetically Modified Food and Feed, covers food and feed produced from a GMO but not food and feed with a GMO, which basically is defined as processing aids with GMOs. The regulation provides a procedure to authorize the sale of foods and feeds. An applicant must submit an application to the "national competent authority" that complies, inter alia, with Annex II of the Cartagena Protocol, infra. If a domestic authority approves the food, the European Commission can review the decision and approve or reject the domestic protocol. EU Regulation 1830/2003 also sets out a framework the traceability of GMOs throughout the food chain. These rules apply not only to GMOs used in food, but GMOs used in crops (such as seeds). The objective is to enhance consumer information and to create a "safety net" based on the "traceability of GMOs at all stages of production and placing on the market."

On June 12, 2014, the Council adopted a political agreement that will allow the co-legislators to get one step closer towards the adoption of a proposal to allow Member States to restrict or ban GMO cultivation in their territory. Under the proposal, the "Member State will be able, before the authorisation of a GMO, to request the applicant company, via the Commission, to specify in the application that the GMO cannot be cultivated on all or part of its territory." No justification need be provided for the first step. "Secondly, the Member State in question will be able, by adopting an opt-out measure, to have the final say not to cultivate an EU authorised GMO on its territory." "After authorisation of the GMO, the Member States' opt out measures have to be based on a wide range of reasons such as: environmental or agricultural policy objectives, town and country planning, land use, socio-economic impacts, avoidance of GMO presence in other products, or public policy, to name a few."

2. *How different are they?* Although the EU and United States approaches to regulation genetically engineered organisms differ, the approaches they utilize to test food safety and environmental safety are essentially the same. Because of the explicit political element in decision-making, the EU approach allows greater consideration of socio-economic impacts. The food safety tests, for example, are based on guidelines established by *Codex Alimentarius,* described below.

3. *Who said this was easy?* An assessment of the proper role of GE in agriculture is complicated by the facts that GE involves agronomic, food safety, environmental and socio-economic considerations and that individuals and groups assign different values and priorities to these considerations. How would you go about making such an assessment? Is there one answer? What political process would be ideal? Should there be one international set of rules or does it suffice to leaving this to domestic and regional organizations such as the EU?

4. *Open or shut?* The GE-related reports of the National Academy of Sciences, as well as the excerpts above, emphasize the importance of both transparency and the opportunity for public participation in GE governance. *See, e.g.,* National Research Council, Biological Confinement of Genetically Engineered Organisms (2004); see also National Research Council, Understanding Risk: Informing Decisions in a Democratic Society (1996). Do you agree? What about protecting confidential business information and national security? Is international human rights law relevant here?

5. *Canada's novel approach.* Canadian law requires pre-market notification for all "novel foods", whether genetically engineered or not. "Novel foods" can be generally described as (1) products that do not have a history of safe use as food; (2) foods which have been subjected to a process that has not previously been used for that food and which causes the food to undergo a major change; and (3) foods derived from plants or animals that have been genetically modified—including changes by traditional breeding and chemical or radiation mutagenesis—to introduce or delete traits or to change the anticipated range of characteristics. B.28.001 C.R.C., c. 870 (2014). Canada does not require labeling of GE food.

Because GMOs pose potential environmental and health risks, the 1992 Biodiversity Convention contemplated a specific agreement on biosafety. The Cartagena Protocol was approved by the Conference of Parties in 2000 and entered into force in 2003. The United States signed the Protocol but has not ratified it.

CARTAGENA PROTOCOL ON BIOSAFETY TO THE CONVENTION ON BIOLOGICAL DIVERSITY
2226 U.N.T.S. 208; 39 ILM 1027 (2000)

The Parties to this Protocol,

Being Parties to the Convention on Biological Diversity, hereinafter referred to as "the Convention",

Recalling Article 19, paragraphs 3 and 4, and Articles 8 (g) and 17 of the Convention,

Recalling also decision II/5 of 17 November 1995 of the Conference of the Parties to the Convention to develop a Protocol on biosafety, specifically focusing on transboundary movement of any living modified organism resulting from modern biotechnology that may have adverse effect on the conservation and sustainable use of biological diversity, setting out for consideration, in particular, appropriate procedures for advance informed agreement,

Reaffirming the precautionary approach contained in Principle 15 of the Rio Declaration on Environment and Development,

Aware of the rapid expansion of modern biotechnology and the growing public concern over its potential adverse effects on biological diversity, taking also into account risks to human health,

Recognizing that modern biotechnology has great potential for human well-being if developed and used with adequate safety measures for the environment and human health,

Recognizing also the crucial importance to humankind of centres of origin and centres of genetic diversity,

Taking into account the limited capabilities of many countries, particularly developing countries, to cope with the nature and scale of known and potential risks associated with living modified organisms,

Recognizing that trade and environment agreements should be mutually supportive with a view to achieving sustainable development,

Emphasizing that this Protocol shall not be interpreted as implying a change in the rights and obligations of a Party under any existing international agreements,

Understanding that the above recital is not intended to subordinate this Protocol to other international agreements,

Have agreed as follows:

Article 1
Objective

In accordance with the precautionary approach contained in Principle 15 of the Rio Declaration on Environment and Development, the objective of this Protocol is to contribute to ensuring an adequate level of protection in the field of the safe transfer, handling and use of living modified organisms resulting from modern biotechnology that may have adverse effects on the conservation and sustainable use of biological diversity, taking also into account risks to human health, and specifically focusing on transboundary movements.

Article 2
General Provisions

1.   Each Party shall take necessary and appropriate legal, administrative and other measures to implement its obligations under this Protocol.

2.   The Parties shall ensure that the development, handling, transport, use, transfer and release of any living modified organisms are undertaken in a manner that prevents or reduces the risks to biological diversity, taking also into account risks to human health.

3.   Nothing in this Protocol shall affect in any way the sovereignty of States over their territorial sea established in accordance with

international law, and the sovereign rights and the jurisdiction which States have in their exclusive economic zones and their continental shelves in accordance with international law, and the exercise by ships and aircraft of all States of navigational rights and freedoms as provided for in international law and as reflected in relevant international instruments.

4. Nothing in this Protocol shall be interpreted as restricting the right of a Party to take action that is more protective of the conservation and sustainable use of biological diversity than that called for in this Protocol, provided that such action is consistent with the objective and the provisions of this Protocol and is in accordance with that Party's other obligations under international law.

5. The Parties are encouraged to take into account, as appropriate, available expertise, instruments and work undertaken in international forums with competence in the area of risks to human health.

Article 3
Use of Terms

For the purposes of this Protocol:

(a) "Conference of the Parties" means the Conference of the Parties to the Convention;

(b) "Contained use" means any operation, undertaken within a facility, installation or other physical structure, which involves living modified organisms that are controlled by specific measures that effectively limit their contact with, and their impact on, the external environment;

(c) "Export" means intentional transboundary movement from one Party to another Party;

(d) "Exporter" means any legal or natural person, under the jurisdiction of the Party of export, who arranges for a living modified organism to be exported;

(e) "Import" means intentional transboundary movement into one Party from another Party;

(f) "Importer" means any legal or natural person, under the jurisdiction of the Party of import, who arranges for a living modified organism to be imported;

(g) "Living modified organism" means any living organism that possesses a novel combination of genetic material obtained through the use of modern biotechnology;

(h) "Living organism" means any biological entity capable of transferring or replicating genetic material, including sterile organisms, viruses and viroids;

(i) "Modern biotechnology" means the application of:

a.   In vitro nucleic acid techniques, including recombinant deoxyribonucleic acid (DNA) and direct injection of nucleic acid into cells or organelles, or

b.   Fusion of cells beyond the taxonomic family,

that overcome natural physiological reproductive or recombination barriers and that are not techniques used in traditional breeding and selection;

(j) "Regional economic integration organization" means an organization constituted by sovereign States of a given region, to which its member States have transferred competence in respect of matters governed by this Protocol and which has been duly authorized, in accordance with its internal procedures, to sign, ratify, accept, approve or accede to it;

(k) "Transboundary movement" means the movement of a living modified organism from one Party to another Party, save that for the purposes of Articles 17 and 24 transboundary movement extends to movement between Parties and non-Parties.

Article 4
Scope

This Protocol shall apply to the transboundary movement, transit, handling and use of all living modified organisms that may have adverse effects on the conservation and sustainable use of biological diversity, taking also into account risks to human health.

Article 5
Pharmaceuticals

Notwithstanding Article 4 and without prejudice to any right of a Party to subject all living modified organisms to risk assessment prior to the making of decisions on import, this Protocol shall not apply to the transboundary movement of living modified organisms which are pharmaceuticals for humans that are addressed by other relevant international agreements or organisations.

Article 6
Transit and Contained Use

1.   Notwithstanding Article 4 and without prejudice to any right of a Party of transit to regulate the transport of living modified organisms through its territory and make available to the Biosafety Clearing-House, any decision of that Party, subject to Article 2, paragraph 3, regarding the transit through its territory of a specific living modified organism, the provisions of this Protocol with respect to the advance informed

agreement procedure shall not apply to living modified organisms in transit.

2.   Notwithstanding Article 4 and without prejudice to any right of a Party to subject all living modified organisms to risk assessment prior to decisions on import and to set standards for contained use within its jurisdiction, the provisions of this Protocol with respect to the advance informed agreement procedure shall not apply to the transboundary movement of living modified organisms destined for contained use undertaken in accordance with the standards of the Party of import.

Article 7
Application of the Advance Informed Agreement Procedure

1.   Subject to Articles 5 and 6, the advance informed agreement procedure in Articles 8 to 10 and 12 shall apply prior to the first intentional transboundary movement of living modified organisms for intentional introduction into the environment of the Party of import.

2.   "Intentional introduction into the environment" in paragraph 1 above, does not refer to living modified organisms intended for direct use as food or feed, or for processing.

3.   Article 11 shall apply prior to the first transboundary movement of living modified organisms intended for direct use as food or feed, or for processing.

4.   The advance informed agreement procedure shall not apply to the intentional transboundary movement of living modified organisms identified in a decision of the Conference of the Parties serving as the meeting of the Parties to this Protocol as being not likely to have adverse effects on the conservation and sustainable use of biological diversity, taking also into account risks to human health.

Article 8
Notification

1.   The Party of export shall notify, or require the exporter to ensure notification to, in writing, the competent national authority of the Party of import prior to the intentional transboundary movement of a living modified organism that falls within the scope of Article 7, paragraph 1. The notification shall contain, at a minimum, the information specified in Annex I.

2.   The Party of export shall ensure that there is a legal requirement for the accuracy of information provided by the exporter.

Article 9
Acknowledgement and Receipt of Notification

1.   The Party of import shall acknowledge receipt of the notification, in writing, to the notifier within ninety days of its receipt.

2.   The acknowledgement shall state:

(a) The date of receipt of the notification;

(b) Whether the notification, prima facie, contains the information referred to in Article 8;

(c) Whether to proceed according to the domestic regulatory framework of the Party of import or according to the procedure specified in Article 10.

3.   The domestic regulatory framework referred to in paragraph 2 (c) above, shall be consistent with this Protocol.

4.   A failure by the Party of import to acknowledge receipt of a notification shall not imply its consent to an intentional transboundary movement.

Article 10
Decision Procedure

1.   Decisions taken by the Party of import shall be in accordance with Article 15.

2.   The Party of import shall, within the period of time referred to in Article 9, inform the notifier, in writing, whether the intentional transboundary movement may proceed:

(a) Only after the Party of import has given its written consent; or

(b) After no less than ninety days without a subsequent written consent.

3.   Within two hundred and seventy days of the date of receipt of notification, the Party of import shall communicate, in writing, to the notifier and to the Biosafety Clearing-House the decision referred to in paragraph 2 (a) above:

(a) Approving the import, with or without conditions, including how the decision will apply to subsequent imports of the same living modified organism;

(b) Prohibiting the import;

(c) Requesting additional relevant information in accordance with its domestic regulatory framework or Annex I; in calculating the time within which the Party of import is to respond, the number of days it has to wait for additional relevant information shall not be taken into account; or

(d) Informing the notifier that the period specified in this paragraph is extended by a defined period of time.

4.   Except in a case in which consent is unconditional, a decision under paragraph 3 above, shall set out the reasons on which it is based.

5.   A failure by the Party of import to communicate its decision within two hundred and seventy days of the date of receipt of the notification shall not imply its consent to an intentional transboundary movement.

6.   Lack of scientific certainty due to insufficient relevant scientific information and knowledge regarding the extent of the potential adverse effects of a living modified organism on the conservation and sustainable use of biological diversity in the Party of import, taking also into account risks to human health, shall not prevent that Party from taking a decision, as appropriate, with regard to the import of the living modified organism in question as referred to in paragraph 3 above, in order to avoid or minimize such potential adverse effects.

7.   The Conference of the Parties serving as the meeting of the Parties shall, at its first meeting, decide upon appropriate procedures and mechanisms to facilitate decision-making by Parties of import.

Article 11
Procedure for Living Modified Organisms Intended for Direct Use as Food or Feed, or for Processing

1.   A Party that makes a final decision regarding domestic use, including placing on the market, of a living modified organism that may be subject to transboundary movement for direct use as food or feed, or for processing shall, within fifteen days of making that decision, inform the Parties through the Biosafety Clearing-House. This information shall contain, at a minimum, the information specified in Annex II. The Party shall provide a copy of the information, in writing, to the national focal point of each Party that informs the Secretariat in advance that it does not have access to the Biosafety Clearing-House. This provision shall not apply to decisions regarding field trials.

2.   The Party making a decision under paragraph 1 above, shall ensure that there is a legal requirement for the accuracy of information provided by the applicant.

3.   Any Party may request additional information from the authority identified in paragraph (b) of Annex II.

4.   A Party may take a decision on the import of living modified organisms intended for direct use as food or feed, or for processing, under its domestic regulatory framework that is consistent with the objective of this Protocol.

5.   Each Party shall make available to the Biosafety Clearing-House copies of any national laws, regulations and guidelines applicable to the

import of living modified organisms intended for direct use as food or feed, or for processing, if available.

6.   A developing country Party or a Party with an economy in transition may, in the absence of the domestic regulatory framework referred to in paragraph 4 above, and in exercise of its domestic jurisdiction, declare through the Biosafety Clearing-House that its decision prior to the first import of a living modified organism intended for direct use as food or feed, or for processing, on which information has been provided under paragraph 1 above, will be taken according to the following:

(a) A risk assessment undertaken in accordance with Annex III; and

(b) A decision made within a predictable timeframe, not exceeding two hundred and seventy days.

7.   Failure by a Party to communicate its decision according to paragraph 6 above, shall not imply its consent or refusal to the import of a living modified organism intended for direct use as food or feed, or for processing, unless otherwise specified by the Party.

8.   Lack of scientific certainty due to insufficient relevant scientific information and knowledge regarding the extent of the potential adverse effects of a living modified organism on the conservation and sustainable use of biological diversity in the Party of import, taking also into account risks to human health, shall not prevent that Party from taking a decision, as appropriate, with regard to the import of that living modified organism intended for direct use as food or feed, or for processing, in order to avoid or minimize such potential adverse effects.

9.   A Party may indicate its needs for financial and technical assistance and capacity-building with respect to living modified organisms intended for direct use as food or feed, or for processing. Parties shall cooperate to meet these needs in accordance with Articles 22 and 28.

Article 12
Review of Decisions

1.   A Party of import may, at any time, in light of new scientific information on potential adverse effects on the conservation and sustainable use of biological diversity, taking also into account the risks to human health, review and change a decision regarding an intentional transboundary movement. In such case, the Party shall, within thirty days, inform any notifier that has previously notified movements of the living modified organism referred to in such decision, as well as the Biosafety Clearing-House, and shall set out the reasons for its decision.

2. A Party of export or a notifier may request the Party of import to review a decision it has made in respect of it under Article 10 where the Party of export or the notifier considers that:

(a) A change in circumstances has occurred that may influence the outcome of the risk assessment upon which the decision was based; or

(b) Additional relevant scientific or technical information has become available.

3. The Party of import shall respond in writing to such a request within ninety days and set out the reasons for its decision.

4. The Party of import may, at its discretion, require a risk assessment for subsequent imports.

Article 19
Competent National Authorities and National Focal Points

1. Each Party shall designate one national focal point to be responsible on its behalf for liaison with the Secretariat. Each Party shall also designate one or more competent national authorities, which shall be responsible for performing the administrative functions required by this Protocol and which shall be authorized to act on its behalf with respect to those functions. A Party may designate a single entity to fulfil the functions of both focal point and competent national authority.

2. Each Party shall, no later than the date of entry into force of this Protocol for it, notify the Secretariat of the names and addresses of its focal point and its competent national authority or authorities. Where a Party designates more than one competent national authority, it shall convey to the Secretariat, with its notification thereof, relevant information on the respective responsibilities of those authorities. Where applicable, such information shall, at a minimum, specify which competent authority is responsible for which type of living modified organism. Each Party shall forthwith notify the Secretariat of any changes in the designation of its national focal point or in the name and address or responsibilities of its competent national authority or authorities.

3. The Secretariat shall forthwith inform the Parties of the notifications it receives under paragraph 2 above, and shall also make such information available through the Biosafety Clearing-House.

Article 20
Information Sharing and the Biosafety Clearing-House

1. A Biosafety Clearing-House is hereby established as part of the clearing-house mechanism under Article 18, paragraph 3, of the Convention, in order to:

(a) Facilitate the exchange of scientific, technical, environmental and legal information on, and experience with, living modified organisms; and

(b) Assist Parties to implement the Protocol, taking into account the special needs of developing country Parties, in particular the least developed and small island developing States among them, and countries with economies in transition as well as countries that are centres of origin and centres of genetic diversity.

2.   The Biosafety Clearing-House shall serve as a means through which information is made available for the purposes of paragraph 1 above. It shall provide access to information made available by the Parties relevant to the implementation of the Protocol. It shall also provide access, where possible, to other international biosafety information exchange mechanisms.

3.   Without prejudice to the protection of confidential information, each Party shall make available to the Biosafety Clearing-House any information required to be made available to the Biosafety Clearing-House under this Protocol, and:

(a) Any existing laws, regulations and guidelines for implementation of the Protocol, as well as information required by the Parties for the advance informed agreement procedure;

(b) Any bilateral, regional and multilateral agreements and arrangements;

(c) Summaries of its risk assessments or environmental reviews of living modified organisms generated by its regulatory process, and carried out in accordance with Article 15, including, where appropriate, relevant information regarding products thereof, namely, processed materials that are of living modified organism origin, containing detectable novel combinations of replicable genetic material obtained through the use of modern biotechnology;

(d) Its final decisions regarding the importation or release of living modified organisms; and

(e) Reports submitted by it pursuant to Article 33, including those on implementation of the advance informed agreement procedure.

4.   The modalities of the operation of the Biosafety Clearing-House, including reports on its activities, shall be considered and decided upon by the Conference of the Parties serving as the meeting of the Parties to this Protocol at its first meeting, and kept under review thereafter.

Article 21
Confidential Information

1. The Party of import shall permit the notifier to identify information submitted under the procedures of this Protocol or required by the Party of import as part of the advance informed agreement procedure of the Protocol that is to be treated as confidential. Justification shall be given in such cases upon request.

2. The Party of import shall consult the notifier if it decides that information identified by the notifier as confidential does not qualify for such treatment and shall, prior to any disclosure, inform the notifier of its decision, providing reasons on request, as well as an opportunity for consultation and for an internal review of the decision prior to disclosure.

3. Each Party shall protect confidential information received under this Protocol, including any confidential information received in the context of the advance informed agreement procedure of the Protocol. Each Party shall ensure that it has procedures to protect such information and shall protect the confidentiality of such information in a manner no less favourable than its treatment of confidential information in connection with domestically produced living modified organisms.

4. The Party of import shall not use such information for a commercial purpose, except with the written consent of the notifier.

5. If a notifier withdraws or has withdrawn a notification, the Party of import shall respect the confidentiality of commercial and industrial information, including research and development information as well as information on which the Party and the notifier disagree as to its confidentiality.

6. Without prejudice to paragraph 5 above, the following information shall not be considered confidential:

(a) The name and address of the notifier;

(b) A general description of the living modified organism or organisms;

(c) A summary of the risk assessment of the effects on the conservation and sustainable use of biological diversity, taking also into account risks to human health; and

(d) Any methods and plans for emergency response.

Article 22
Capacity-Building

1. The Parties shall cooperate in the development and/or strengthening of human resources and institutional capacities in biosafety, including biotechnology to the extent that it is required for biosafety, for the purpose of the effective implementation of this Protocol,

in developing country Parties, in particular the least developed and small island developing States among them, and in Parties with economies in transition, including through existing global, regional, subregional and national institutions and organizations and, as appropriate, through facilitating private sector involvement.

2.   For the purposes of implementing paragraph 1 above, in relation to cooperation, the needs of developing country Parties, in particular the least developed and small island developing States among them, for financial resources and access to and transfer of technology and know-how in accordance with the relevant provisions of the Convention, shall be taken fully into account for capacity-building in biosafety. Cooperation in capacity-building shall, subject to the different situation, capabilities and requirements of each Party, include scientific and technical training in the proper and safe management of biotechnology, and in the use of risk assessment and risk management for biosafety, and the enhancement of technological and institutional capacities in biosafety. The needs of Parties with economies in transition shall also be taken fully into account for such capacity-building in biosafety.

Article 22
Public Awareness and Participation

1.   The Parties shall:

(a) Promote and facilitate public awareness, education and participation concerning the safe transfer, handling and use of living modified organisms in relation to the conservation and sustainable use of biological diversity, taking also into account risks to human health. In doing so, the Parties shall cooperate, as appropriate, with other States and international bodies;

(b) Endeavour to ensure that public awareness and education encompass access to information on living modified organisms identified in accordance with this Protocol that may be imported.

2.   The Parties shall, in accordance with their respective laws and regulations, consult the public in the decision-making process regarding living modified organisms and shall make the results of such decisions available to the public, while respecting confidential information in accordance with Article 21.

3.   Each Party shall endeavour to inform its public about the means of public access to the Biosafety Clearing-House.

Article 26
Socio-Economic Considerations

1.   The Parties, in reaching a decision on import under this Protocol or under its domestic measures implementing the Protocol, may take into

account, consistent with their international obligations, socio-economic considerations arising from the impact of living modified organisms on the conservation and sustainable use of biological diversity, especially with regard to the value of biological diversity to indigenous and local communities.

2.   The Parties are encouraged to cooperate on research and information exchange on any socio-economic impacts of living modified organisms, especially on indigenous and local communities.

Article 27
Liability and Redress

The Conference of the Parties serving as the meeting of the Parties to this Protocol shall, at its first meeting, adopt a process with respect to the appropriate elaboration of international rules and procedures in the field of liability and redress for damage resulting from transboundary movements of living modified organisms, analysing and taking due account of the ongoing processes in international law on these matters, and shall endeavour to complete this process within four years.

Article 28
Financial Mechanism and Resources

1.   In considering financial resources for the implementation of this Protocol, the Parties shall take into account the provisions of Article 20 of the Convention.

2.   The financial mechanism established in Article 21 of the Convention shall, through the institutional structure entrusted with its operation, be the financial mechanism for this Protocol.

3.   Regarding the capacity-building referred to in Article 22 of this Protocol, the Conference of the Parties serving as the meeting of the Parties to this Protocol, in providing guidance with respect to the financial mechanism referred to in paragraph 2 above, for consideration by the Conference of the Parties, shall take into account the need for financial resources by developing country Parties, in particular the least developed and the small island developing States among them.

4.   In the context of paragraph 1 above, the Parties shall also take into account the needs of the developing country Parties, in particular the least developed and the small island developing States among them, and of the Parties with economies in transition, in their efforts to identify and implement their capacity-building requirements for the purposes of the implementation of this Protocol.

5.   The guidance to the financial mechanism of the Convention in relevant decisions of the Conference of the Parties, including those agreed before the adoption of this Protocol, shall apply, mutatis mutandis, to the provisions of this Article.

6. The developed country Parties may also provide, and the developing country Parties and the Parties with economies in transition avail themselves of, financial and technological resources for the implementation of the provisions of this Protocol through bilateral, regional and multilateral channels.

Article 29
Reservations

No reservations may be made to this Protocol.

Annex I
Information Required in Notifications Under Articles 8, 10 and 13

(a) Name, address and contact details of the exporter.

(b) Name, address and contact details of the importer.

(c) Name and identity of the living modified organism, as well as the domestic classification, if any, of the biosafety level of the living modified organism in the State of export.

(d) Intended date or dates of the transboundary movement, if known.

(e) Taxonomic status, common name, point of collection or acquisition, and characteristics of recipient organism or parental organisms related to biosafety.

(f) Centres of origin and centres of genetic diversity, if known, of the recipient organism and/or the parental organisms and a description of the habitats where the organisms may persist or proliferate.

(g) Taxonomic status, common name, point of collection or acquisition, and characteristics of the donor organism or organisms related to biosafety.

(h) Description of the nucleic acid or the modification introduced, the technique used, and the resulting characteristics of the living modified organism.

(i) Intended use of the living modified organism or products thereof, namely, processed materials that are of living modified organism origin, containing detectable novel combinations of replicable genetic material obtained through the use of modern biotechnology.

(j) Quantity or volume of the living modified organism to be transferred.

(k) A previous and existing risk assessment report consistent with Annex III.

(*l*) Suggested methods for the safe handling, storage, transport and use, including packaging, labelling, documentation, disposal and contingency procedures, where appropriate.

(m) Regulatory status of the living modified organism within the State of export (for example, whether it is prohibited in the State of export, whether there are other restrictions, or whether it has been approved for general release) and, if the living modified organism is banned in the State of export, the reason or reasons for the ban.

(n) Result and purpose of any notification by the exporter to other States regarding the living modified organism to be transferred.

(o) A declaration that the above-mentioned information is factually correct.

Annex II
Information Required Concerning Living Modified Organisms Intended for Direct Use as Food or Feed, or for Processing Under Article 11

(a) The name and contact details of the applicant for a decision for domestic use.

(b) The name and contact details of the authority responsible for the decision.

(c) Name and identity of the living modified organism.

(d) Description of the gene modification, the technique used, and the resulting characteristics of the living modified organism.

(e) Any unique identification of the living modified organism.

(f) Taxonomic status, common name, point of collection or acquisition, and characteristics of recipient organism or parental organisms related to biosafety.

(g) Centres of origin and centres of genetic diversity, if known, of the recipient organism and/or the parental organisms and a description of the habitats where the organisms may persist or proliferate.

(h) Taxonomic status, common name, point of collection or acquisition, and characteristics of the donor organism or organisms related to biosafety.

(i) Approved uses of the living modified organism.

(j) A risk assessment report consistent with Annex III.

(k) Suggested methods for the safe handling, storage, transport and use, including packaging, labelling, documentation, disposal and contingency procedures, where appropriate.

Annex III
Risk Assessment
Objective

1. The objective of risk assessment, under this Protocol, is to identify and evaluate the potential adverse effects of living modified organisms on the conservation and sustainable use of biological diversity in the likely potential receiving environment, taking also into account risks to human health.

Use of Risk Assessment

2. Risk assessment is, inter alia, used by competent authorities to make informed decisions regarding living modified organisms.

General Principles

3. Risk assessment should be carried out in a scientifically sound and transparent manner, and can take into account expert advice of, and guidelines developed by, relevant international organizations.

4. Lack of scientific knowledge or scientific consensus should not necessarily be interpreted as indicating a particular level of risk, an absence of risk, or an acceptable risk.

5. Risks associated with living modified organisms or products thereof, namely, processed materials that are of living modified organism origin, containing detectable novel combinations of replicable genetic material obtained through the use of modern biotechnology, should be considered in the context of the risks posed by the non-modified recipients or parental organisms in the likely potential receiving environment.

6. Risk assessment should be carried out on a case-by-case basis. The required information may vary in nature and level of detail from case to case, depending on the living modified organism concerned, its intended use and the likely potential receiving environment.

Methodology

7. The process of risk assessment may on the one hand give rise to a need for further information about specific subjects, which may be identified and requested during the assessment process, while on the other hand information on other subjects may not be relevant in some instances.

8. To fulfill its objective, risk assessment entails, as appropriate, the following steps:

(a) An identification of any novel genotypic and phenotypic characteristics associated with the living modified organism that may have adverse effects on biological diversity in the likely potential receiving environment, taking also into account risks to human health;

(b) An evaluation of the likelihood of these adverse effects being realized, taking into account the level and kind of exposure of the likely potential receiving environment to the living modified organism;

(c) An evaluation of the consequences should these adverse effects be realized;

(d) An estimation of the overall risk posed by the living modified organism based on the evaluation of the likelihood and consequences of the identified adverse effects being realized;

(e) A recommendation as to whether or not the risks are acceptable or manageable, including, where necessary, identification of strategies to manage these risks; and

(f) Where there is uncertainty regarding the level of risk, it may be addressed by requesting further information on the specific issues of concern or by implementing appropriate risk management strategies and/or monitoring the living modified organism in the receiving environment.

Points to Consider

9.   Depending on the case, risk assessment takes into account the relevant technical and scientific details regarding the characteristics of the following subjects:

(a) Recipient organism or parental organisms. The biological characteristics of the recipient organism or parental organisms, including information on taxonomic status, common name, origin, centres of origin and centres of genetic diversity, if known, and a description of the habitat where the organisms may persist or proliferate;

(b) Donor organism or organisms. Taxonomic status and common name, source, and the relevant biological characteristics of the donor organisms;

(c) Vector. Characteristics of the vector, including its identity, if any, and its source or origin, and its host range;

(d) Insert or inserts and/or characteristics of modification. Genetic characteristics of the inserted nucleic acid and the function it specifies, and/or characteristics of the modification introduced;

(e) Living modified organism. Identity of the living modified organism, and the differences between the biological characteristics of the living modified organism and those of the recipient organism or parental organisms;

(f) *Detection and identification of the living modified organism.* Suggested detection and identification methods and their specificity, sensitivity and reliability;

(g) *Information relating to the intended use.* Information relating to the intended use of the living modified organism, including new or changed use compared to the recipient organism or parental organisms; and

(h) *Receiving environment.* Information on the location, geographical, climatic and ecological characteristics, including relevant information on biological diversity and centres of origin of the likely potential receiving environment.

NOTES AND QUESTIONS

1. *How precautionary is the Protocol?* Which view of precaution does the Protocol adopt: the EU or the United States view? Is the Protocol consistent with WTO jurisprudence on the precautionary principle discussed in Chapter 16? Does the Protocol apply to issues such as the relationship between sustainable development and the use of genetically engineered organisms? The Secretariat of the Convention on Biological Diversity, the Cartagena Protocol on Biosafety: A Record of the Negotiations 18 (2003) reports that "[c]onsensus was not reached on whether the Protocol would deal with LMO-related activities other than transboundary movements, while references to animal health and sustainable development were removed." Article 4 defines the scope of the treaty. Does it apply to the products of LMOs? The parties could not reach agreement on the issue, *id.* at 24–25, but addressed it in exemptions in Articles 5 and 11. Must an importer give its expressed consent to an import under Article 10? Is the Annex III risk assessment procedure the same for LMOs and Article II products? Annex III is the primary risk assessment standard. There was considerable division among the parties over the nature of risk assessment. Many developed countries favored a science-based standard whereby many developing countries wanted to explore the impacts on sustainable use and biodiversity and to include ethical considerations such as the precautionary principle. *Id.* at 50–52. The final version of Article 15 provides that "risk assessments shall be based, at a minimum, on information provided in Article 8 and other available scientific information in Article 8 and other available scientific evidence in order to identify and evaluate possible adverse effects of living modified organisms on the conservation and sustainable use of biological diversity, taking into account risk to human health."

2. *Risk of what?* Much of the concern with genetically engineered organisms has focused on the possible health risks. The environmental risks include the promotion of monocultures which can lead to genetic erosion. Monocultures may perpetrate high pesticide use and decreased alternative,

less chemically based, pest management options. There are also benefits, although these also pose risks. Many transgenic crops such as canola, corn and soybeans are herbicide resistant, but the price may be less crop diversification and increased weed resistance on acreage treated with herbicides. Pests may also develop resistance to the toxins in transgenic crops and, especially in developing countries the result may either increase crop losses as existing biocontrol mechanisms are disrupted or increase pesticide use to offset their existence. *See* Miguel A. Altieri, Agroecology: The Science of Sustainable Agriculture (1996). The U.S. National Academy of Sciences is also expected to come out with a report on these issues in 2016. Are these risks covered by the Protocol? If not, does the Convention on Biodiversity require their assessment? The main international system for sustainable agriculture is the International Treaty on Plant Genetic Resources for Food and Agriculture, discussed in the next subsection.

3.   *Interpretational questions.* Does the Protocol apply to ketchup made with genetically engineered tomatoes? Does the advance notification procedure apply to genetically engineered fish to be released into the environment? What about genetically engineered corn intended for human or livestock consumption? Can a State prohibit the import of a LMO? What is the difference between the Protocol's risk assessment standards and the WTO Agreement on Sanitary and Phytosanitary Measures, discussed in Chapter 16?

2.   SEED PATENTS

Responding to rising concern about the equitable and fair distribution of plant genetic resources for food and agriculture, the International Treaty on Plant Genetic Resources for Food and Agriculture (PGR Treaty) entered into force in 2004. 2400 U.N.T.S. 303 (entered into force 26 June 2004), *available at* ftp://ftp.fao.org/docrep/fao/011/i0510e/i0510e.pdf.[1] The objectives of the PGR Treaty are as follows:

> [T]he conservation and sustainable use of plant genetic resources for food and agriculture and the fair and equitable sharing of the benefits arising out of their use, in harmony with the Convention on Biological Diversity, for sustainable agriculture and food security.

PGR Treaty art. 1.1. In turn, the Treaty defines the "sustainable use of plant genetic resources" as including measures such as:

> (a)   pursuing fair agricultural policies that promote, as appropriate, the development and maintenance of diverse farming systems that enhance the sustainable use of agricultural biological diversity and other natural resources;

---

[1]   Although the United States is a signatory to this treaty, as of March 2015 it has not yet ratified it.

(b) strengthening research which enhances and conserves biological diversity by maximizing intra- and inter-specific variation for the benefit of farmers, especially those who generate and use their own varieties and apply ecological principles in maintaining soil fertility and in combating diseases, weeds and pests;

(c) promoting, as appropriate, plant breeding efforts which, with the participation of farmers, particularly in developing countries, strengthen the capacity to develop varieties particularly adapted to social, economic and ecological conditions, including in marginal areas;

(d) broadening the genetic base of crops and increasing the range of genetic diversity available to farmers;

(e) promoting, as appropriate, the expanded use of local and locally adapted crops, varieties and underutilized species;

(f) supporting, as appropriate, the wider use of diversity of varieties and species in onfarm management, conservation and sustainable use of crops and creating strong links to plant breeding and agricultural development in order to reduce crop vulnerability and genetic erosion, and promote increased world food production compatible with sustainable development; and

(g) reviewing, and, as appropriate, adjusting breeding strategies and regulations concerning variety release and seed distribution.

Id. art. 6.2.

The Treaty contains several key components: the establishment of farmers' rights to plant genetic resources for food and agriculture, the creation of a multilateral system for access and benefit-sharing, and various infrastructure-related provisions. With respect to farmers' rights, the PGR Treaty requires Parties to, as appropriate and subject to domestic legislation, take measures to protect farmers' rights, including protection of traditional knowledge related to these resources, the right to equitably participate in the sharing of benefits arising from these resources, and the right to participate in making decisions at a national level regarding conservation and sustainable use of these resources. PGR Treaty art 9.

The multilateral system created by the PGR Treaty is effectively a pooling system for the conservation and sustainable use of plant genetic resources of the list of crops set forth in Annex I of the Treaty and the fair and equitable sharing of benefits arising out of those resources. The crops listed in Annex I, in turn, were "established according to criteria of food security and interdependence," PGR Treaty art. 11.1, and include crops such as breadfruit, chickpeas, apples, cassava, maize, and various legumes and grasses. Under this multilateral system, the parties share information on the conservation, characterization, and use of these listed species, as well as access to related technologies. The multilateral system also contains requirements for sharing the "monetary and other benefits of commercialization," for example, through the use of material transfer agreements such that recipients who commercialize a product that is a "plant genetic resource for food and agriculture and that incorporates material accessed from the Multilateral System, shall pay [to the financial pooling system of the Treaty] an equitable share of the benefits arising from the commercialization of that product." *Id.* art 13.2. The PGR Treaty urges that benefits arising from the use of plant genetic resources for food and agriculture "should flow primarily, directly and indirectly, to farmers in all countries, especially in developing countries, and countries with economies in transition, who conserve and sustainably utilize plant genetic resources for food and agriculture." *Id.*

Finally, the PGR Treaty contains a number of infrastructure-related provisions for implementation. For example, it urges the establishment of international networks for information exchange and research. *Id.* art. 16. It also requires the Parties to implement a funding strategy for implementing the terms of the Treaty, with some degree of equitable distribution of contributions from developed versus developing countries and countries with economies in transition. *Id.* art 18.4. The Treaty also establishes a Governing Body for further implementation of the Treaty, *id.* art. 19, and to establish compliance mechanisms, *id.* art 20.

NOTE

Weaknesses of the PGR Treaty. In an interim report submitted to the United Nations General Assembly by the Special Rapporteur on the right to food, Olivier De Schutter, pointed out that although the PGR Treaty contemplates that farmers and developing countries receive the primary benefits of the multilateral pooling system, the actual amount awarded by the PGR Treaty governing body to projects in developing countries is well below their needs. *See* Report A/64/170, Seed Policies and the Right to Food: Enhancing Agrobiodiversity and Encouraging Innovation para. 23, *available at* http://www.srfood.org/images/stories/pdf/officialreports/20091021_report-ga64_seed-policies-and-the-right-to-food_en.pdf.

3.   LAND GRABS

Another rising issue of concern with respect to agriculture is the phenomenon of "land grabs"—that is, the purchase or leasing of large swaths of land in developing countries, usually for the purposes of food or biofuel production. The following excerpt describes the phenomenon and presents two international frameworks that grapple with this problem in different ways.

THE GLOBAL LAND RUSH: MARKETS, RIGHTS, AND THE POLITICS OF FOOD

Smita Narula
49 Stanford J. Int'l L. 101, 101–16, 117–19, 120–24, 126–32 (2013)

Introduction

In 2011, Saudi Star PLC leased roughly 25,000 acres of Ethiopia's most fertile farmland from the Ethiopian government to produce rice for export to the Middle East. The investment sought to capitalize on Saudi Arabian state subsidies for the foreign production of staple crops, which is part of the country's strategy for ensuring its own food security. The Ethiopian government signed the Saudi Star contract, and others like it, seeking to revolutionize domestic agricultural production, employ local farmers, and produce more food for local consumption. Ethiopian officials claim that land earmarked for agricultural development is "unused" or "under-utilized," and that no communities have been displaced as part of the land deals. But investigations reveal that the Ethiopian government has actively worked to remove communities from land that is earmarked for commercial agricultural development. According to a report by the Oakland Institute:

> Prior to relocation, no community consultation was carried out, either by Saudi Star or the government. Villagers only knew that their land had been given to investors once the bulldozers began clearing the area. When they expressed concern to the government about the clearing of their ancestral lands, government officials reportedly replied, 'You don't have any land, only government has land.'

Since 2008, the Ethiopian government has leased out at least 8.9 million acres of land to foreign and domestic investors through arrangements like the Saudi Star contract. At this writing, another 5.2 million acres were on offer through the Ethiopian government's land bank for agricultural investment. In some regions, the government planned to relocate 1.5 million people by 2013. The relocation program, or "villagization process" in Ethiopia's Gambella region—the site of the Saudi Star investment—has been particularly devastating for indigenous communities cut off from sources of food, water, healthcare, and education. Many of these relocations have been forced and have taken place without meaningful consultation or compensation. The Ethiopian government has reportedly threatened, assaulted, or detained those resisting the relocation process. As of January 2012, government security forces enforcing the relocations were implicated in at least twenty incidents of rape.

These troubling developments threaten to destroy livelihoods and exacerbate widespread hunger and malnutrition in a country that is already well known for its cyclical famines. . . . Investors have expressed little concern for the rights of host populations and have instead praised Ethiopia for its low labor costs, tax and duty exemptions, relaxed regulations, and abundant amounts of "undeveloped" land. For its part, the Saudi Star is hoping to expand its investment to 500,000 acres within the next ten years. The going rate for this land is approximately $4 per acre per year.

The Ethiopian experience is not singular. In the past five years, interest in purchasing and leasing agricultural land in developing countries has skyrocketed. The commodification of foreign land is admittedly nothing new, but the scale and intensity with which recent investments have proceeded is startling. Reliable measurements are difficult to obtain, and even figures derived from in-country empirical research may underestimate the scale of investments because of constrained access to data or the exclusion of deals that are still under negotiation. All sources agree, however, that the amount of land being targeted for purchase or lease is dramatic. According to the World Bank Group, foreign investors targeted more than 56 million hectares (138 million acres) of agricultural land between 2008 and 2009. More than 75% of these deals took place in Sub-Saharan Africa. . . .

This trend, which was facilitated by the 2008 food and financial crises, is being led by state and private investors, both domestic and foreign. In some cases, investments are to produce food for export, while other investments are to produce biofuels or to benefit from carbon emissions credits for clean development mechanism projects. In still other cases, entities invest for purely speculative reasons. The World Bank Group has helped facilitate these deals by actively supporting the creation of investment-friendly climates and land markets in developing countries. This global drive to invest in land and boost agricultural production is justified with reference to the ongoing food crisis, which has seen basic commodity prices soar beyond the reach of vulnerable populations. Although renewed investment in agriculture presents a number of opportunities to improve food security and promote economic development, few substantive checks have been placed on these investments. As a result, in countries like Ethiopia, there are "[l]arge discrepancies between publicly stated positions, laws, policies and procedures and what is actually happening on the ground."

A wealth of evidence—largely in the form of investment case studies—reveals that many large-scale land investments are not servicing the goal of ensuring equitable development and sustainable food security in host countries and, in fact, may be further jeopardizing the rights of host populations. Land transfers are taking place in countries already suffering from acute poverty, food insecurity, and water shortages and in environments that lack oversight and regulation. Deals often lack transparency, disregard land users' rights, and are concluded without meaningful consultation with affected communities. These factors increase the risk of serious human rights violations for host populations, further marginalizing already vulnerable groups—small-scale farmers, pastoralists, indigenous peoples, and artisanal fishers who are being displaced from their land and from resources essential to their survival.

The scale, scope, and impacts of these land transfers—both potential and realized—have elevated the debate around large-scale land deals to the global level. Many agricultural investments to date have been denounced by civil society groups and farmers' organizations as "land grabs" that "depriv[e] the poorest from their access to land, and increas[e] concentration of resources in the hands of a minority." According to one editorial on the issue, rural communities throughout Latin America, Africa, and Asia "are being crushingly pushed aside in deals that are forcing large-scale migration, violent conflicts, unemployment, deepening poverty and hunger."

In response to the din of local and international protest, two dominant frameworks have emerged to assess and contest the global land rush. The first approach, led by the World Bank Group, balances the harms arising from land deals against the benefits of generating greater agricultural investment. This approach privileges market-led processes as engines for economic growth and increased agricultural productivity, but also recognizes the need for proper business, legal, and regulatory environments to help investments flourish. This approach is attuned to the rights and needs of vulnerable communities and readily acknowledges that land deals entail significant risks. A heightened focus on rights and a more frank acknowledgment of risks arguably distinguishes the current response of influential international economic actors to land investments from the purely market-based responses of past decades. For this reason . . . , I call this approach the market-plus approach. . . .

The market-plus approach argues that if carefully disciplined and appropriately regulated, large-scale land transfers can achieve win-win outcomes for both the investor and host populations. It is argued that such regulation can be achieved through continued facilitation of an appropriate investment climate and adherence to a set of good governance principles. The market-plus approach treats land as a commodity and seeks to revitalize land that is deemed idle and nonproductive to help boost global food production. The formalization of existing land rights, as a means of both clarifying use and ownership rights and facilitating land markets, is central to this approach.

The market-plus approach's insistence that host communities' rights can be protected through the creation of robust land markets, coupled with good governance measures, has been met with great skepticism from the human rights community and civil society groups. In response, human rights advocates have put forward an alternate framework. This rights-based approach—which is led by the U.N. Special Rapporteur on the Right to Food ("Special Rapporteur")—seeks to focus the analytical framework on the positive fulfillment of human rights. Under the rights-based approach, states' human rights obligations must trump other considerations.

Land is also instrumentalized under this approach; access to land is seen as a gateway to the realization of multiple human rights, including the right to food. The rights-based approach encourages legal reforms to strengthen security of tenure, and agrarian reforms that lead to more equitable distribution of land for the benefit of small-scale farmers. This approach also encourages investments that support small-scale farming, and that do not involve land transfers or evictions. To the extent that large-scale land transfers do move forward, the rights-based approach offers a set of principles for regulating these transactions—principles that are grounded in and give expression to states' obligations under international human rights law.

This Article critically assesses both approaches. It is an important time to undertake these assessments as countries and leading international bodies are currently deliberating how best to move forward with reforms to agricultural investment and land tenure policies. The Committee on World Food Security (CFS), for instance, is preparing to undertake worldwide consultations to develop a set of principles that will garner broad ownership by states and other key actors. These consultations will consider proposals put forward under both frameworks. But little effort has been made to consolidate all of the dimensions of the debate: assessing the practice of large-scale agricultural land transfers from a broader and more considered perspective; comprehensively documenting the harms to local populations; attending seriously to the arguments of proponents; and critically evaluating the recommendations of skeptics. This Article seeks to address this gap in the literature, distilling and critically assessing the underlying normative frameworks employed by the market-oriented international financial institutions that facilitate these land transfers and the human rights advocates who oppose them. The Article concludes with concrete recommendations for empowering affected communities and securing rights guarantees, a challenge in a world where such rights are so often inadequately protected.

[. . .]

I.   Large-Scale Land Transfers: Drivers, Transactions, and Impacts

In the span of just five years, the global agricultural sector has been hit by two interrelated phenomena: first, a dramatic and unprecedented rise in food prices and, second, a renewed international interest in agricultural land investments. These two trends are related in a complex and bidirectional manner. Studies have identified multiple underlying causes of the global spike in food prices, including long-term underinvestment in agriculture, higher fuel prices, climate change, the diversion of food crops to biofuels, speculative investment, and an increased demand for more resource intensive food in emerging market countries. A *110 number of these same trends, coupled with the international community's response to the food crisis, have also served as drivers for large-scale land investments. Notably, the investment that has taken place includes not only support and loans to existing agricultural producers but also the purchase or lease of large tracts of "underutilized" or "under-producing" agricultural land.

[. . .]

A.   Drivers and Actors Behind Large-Scale Land Transfers

International food prices have been highly volatile since 2006, and in 2007–08 food prices soared, with basic commodities doubling their average 2004 prices. The surge in food prices led to widespread social unrest. . . . The global food crisis generated an appropriately global response, which emphasized the need for greater investment in agriculture in developing countries. The World Bank Group has been at the forefront of this response.

To help increase foreign direct investment in agriculture the World Bank Group works through its private sector subsidiary, the International Finance Corporation (IFC), and its partner organization, the Foreign Investment Advisory Service (FIAS), to provide direct financing and advisory support to agribusiness operations. . . . These policies have made agricultural land investments even more attractive to Western investors. With the certainty of a steadily rising demand for food and emerging climate change markets, many Western investors increasingly view direct investments in land as a safe investment in an otherwise shaky financial climate.

Since the 2008 food crisis, certain states have also begun to seek opportunities to invest in foreign farmland in order to secure reliable food sources for their domestic populations. This is particularly evident in relation to investments made by many "resource-poor but cash rich" Gulf States whose scarce water and soil resources make them heavily dependent on international markets for their food supply. Countries with food security concerns and fast-growing populations, such as China,

South Korea, and India, have also begun to seek opportunities to produce food overseas.

International and domestic responses to climate change have also triggered a renewed interest in agricultural land. The surging demand for biofuels has led investors to target vast tracts of land in developing countries for biofuel production. Additionally, projects like the Kyoto Protocol's Clean Development Mechanism have incentivized some states to meet their compliance requirements by launching emission-reduction projects abroad, such as planting forests in developing countries. Implementation of the Reducing Emissions from Deforestation and Forest Degradation (REDD) Scheme, which offers financial incentives for preserving extant forests, may also prove to be a driver of large-scale land acquisitions.

B.   Land Transfers and Transactions: Documented Problems

The specific form and mechanisms of agricultural land transfers are quite diverse. Land transfers can encompass a range of land use and ownership changes, which are undertaken for a wide variety of reasons and which occur through highly diverse legal and political mechanisms. Investors are national and international, public and private, individuals, companies, and investment entities. Precise legal arrangements are to a large extent dictated by national laws and policies and can include contractual arrangements, long-term leases (some up to ninety-nine years) or outright purchase. . . . These transactions may be mediated by a central government authority, approved at a local governance level, or negotiated directly with a private title-holder. Despite this diversity, several clear and problematic patterns have emerged in relation to land-related transactions.

Dozens of case studies across a range of industries and countries reveal that large-scale land deals frequently disregard existing land users' rights, lack transparency and accountability, and move forward without meaningful participation by those most affected by these investments. . . . Many host countries do not formally recognize the land rights of populations that have customarily occupied and used the land and instead vest all untitled lands in the state, thereby obviating the need for local approval for land transfers. . . . Even where local land rights are legally recognized, they may not be honored in practice or negotiations between investors and rights-holders may be plagued with procedural flaws that taint the actual terms of the agreements. . . . The extent to which governments and investors are required to consult with local host communities also varies considerably. Few states require significant input from the communities most affected by the land deals, and the states that do require input often inadequately enforce the protective measures included for the affected communities' benefit.

When affected communities are consulted, the timetables for concluding transactions may be too short to allow for adequate input. . . . Furthermore, many contemporary land deals result in problematic contract terms that may systematically disfavor local communities. In many cases, there are no contracts. When contracts do exist, they may fail to delineate specific obligations or provide mechanisms for ensuring investor accountability. The terms of the deals are often vague or clearly favor the investor. The benefits that do fall to the host state may not reach the communities affected by the deals in the first place. . . .

C. Negative Impacts on Host Communities

The agricultural sector in the developing world has historically been under-funded, leading to a decline in agricultural production. Agricultural land investments have the potential to create much-needed infrastructure and reduce poverty in host states. They can, for example, generate employment, encourage the transfer of technology, improve local producers' access to credit and markets, and increase public revenues from taxation and export duties. They can also increase production of food crops to supply local, national, and international consumers. For countries acquiring land abroad to grow staple foods, such investments reduce reliance on international markets and increase food security for investor-country populations.

Although increased investment in land may have potentially beneficial impacts for host communities, to date this potential has not been realized. To the contrary, the results for many of these communities have been far from positive. In 2010, the Bank published the findings of an in-depth study of agricultural land investments in a controversial report entitled Rising Global Interest in Farmland: Can It Yield Sustainable and Equitable Benefits? The study finds that many investments have "failed to live up to expectations and, instead of generating sustainable benefits, contributed to asset loss and left local people worse off than they would have been without the investment." Numerous other studies echo these findings and conclude that host communities rarely benefit from these deals.

In many cases, local populations lose their most fertile and profitable land in acquisitions by foreign investors and national elites. Existing land users are often displaced from land that they have occupied for generations, resulting in diminished livelihoods and increased tenure insecurity. In fact, because the targeted land is often irrigable and close to existing infrastructure, "conflict with existing land users [is] more likely." Compensation for resource loss is "rarely adequate," because ownership rights are not recognized and the new agricultural operations' real resource requirements, especially water, are not properly taken into account. Affected communities are often not compensated for their loss of livelihood and employment opportunities generated by the investment may be limited or exaggerated, and may offer unfavorable terms, low wages, or be of a temporary nature during the "initial construction phase." Further, the number of jobs created may not compensate for the impact of displacement. Such was the case in Mali, where according to one study, the few thousand workers employed in a land deal compensated neither for the displacement of 112,537 farm families, nor for diminished access to food for well over half a million people.

Though taxation and export duties may serve as a source of revenue for the host state, tax revenues are often small because host country governments provide tax incentives in order to attract investors. Taxes are also usually not payable until the investor's operation becomes profitable, and weak enforcement mechanisms often leave due taxes uncollected. Benefits such as duty-free equipment imports and special free zones for agricultural products further decrease the government's revenue. The possible benefits of large-scale land acquisition can additionally be subverted by the unpredictability of speculative foreign investments, which may fail to materialize or perform as promised.

The transfer of land to foreign investors—many of whom export all that they reap—can also induce greater reliance on food imports, especially for the number of host countries that are already net food importers. Food security is additionally threatened by the loss of farmland-generated employment and income. In some countries, land transfers are undermining land reform gains that are seen by some as essential to addressing the global food crisis. Investment in biofuels can also have implications for food security when arable land is diverted from food to fuel production.

Large-scale land transfers can have a serious and negative impact on local water supplies—though this has been explored in less detail than the issue of food security. Abundant water supply is an important consideration for investors, especially for the production of water-intensive biofuels. Host populations may therefore face rising competition for limited water resources, which in some cases constitutes the most salient harm to a local community. The repercussions of unsustainable water use can also extend far beyond farming, reaching both rural and urban populations. In the longer term, there are also troubling signs that large-scale land transfers have the potential to generate conflict and contribute to environmental harms. The potential for conflict is especially pronounced where socio-economic and ethnic divisions are already profound and life-sustaining resources are already scarce.

II. Contesting the Global Land Rush: Market vs. Rights-Based Approaches

Two dominant frameworks have emerged that take distinct perspectives on, and propose differentiated responses to, the recent flood of land deals: a market-led approach and a rights-based approach. . . .

A.   The Market-Plus Approach

Led by the World Bank Group, the market-plus approach is essentially a market-driven approach with a special sensitivity to the need for regulation. At the most fundamental level, it privileges market-led processes as engines for economic growth and increased food production. The market-plus approach is premised on the idea that the market is the most effective mechanism for increasing global wealth and that it is the most efficient distributor of that wealth. If market processes fail, however, then government intervention may become necessary to mitigate any adverse impacts.

The market-plus approach takes existing distributions of wealth as the baseline and seeks to ensure that populations, in the aggregate, are made better off or at least not worse off than they were before. Here, progress is measured by looking at averages rather than the satisfaction of individual entitlements to resources. In seeking to promote general welfare, the market-plus approach directly prioritizes securing a larger pool of resources so that there are ultimately more resources to spread around. The market-plus approach accepts that there may be trade-offs across individuals—and across states—reasoning that net increases in welfare might offset contingent declines. It also accepts that certain risks may be necessary in order to maximize economic gains. Thus, in the context of land deals, the market-plus approach weighs the possible harms (risks) of investment to affected communities against the possibility that investment will produce economic gains (benefits) that will support the broader public interest. . . .

1.   The Market-Plus Approach to Land: Land as a Commodity

The land-as-commodity framework of the market-plus approach aims to facilitate the flow of capital into developing countries while simultaneously pushing for the increasingly efficient use of land. The logic of this approach proceeds as follows: There are a number of obstacles to meeting future food demand, including climate change and constraints on the supply of land, water, and energy. These hurdles, when combined with growing demand for food and uncertainty about the future, make food prices more vulnerable to shock-induced fluctuation. If we eliminate market shocks by increasing investment to boost agricultural productivity and build sustainable production systems, food prices should stabilize. What is needed is a productivity revolution. But greater yields can only be assured if arable land is first identified, and then transferred to the most efficient user. To achieve these ends, the World Bank Group has adopted a two-pronged strategy.

First, the World Bank seeks to identify agricultural land that can be used more productively, as well as "marginal" or "unused" land that can be converted to agricultural use, especially in Africa and Latin America. . . . Second, the World Bank promotes the formalization of land rights in order to develop robust land markets and facilitate the transfer of land to the most efficient producer. Agrarian communities in developing countries often employ communal visions of land ownership that are not easily reducible to the conventional Western property rights regime of individual land ownership. Even where property is not strictly viewed as a communal resource, title may be secured by informal mechanisms, leaving local individuals' claims to property "insecure" from a formal legal perspective. In response, the World Bank has long promoted and supported land registration and titling programs in line with the philosophy that security of tenure can help facilitate integration into the market.

In line with its land-as-commodity framework, the World Bank Group has actively facilitated large-scale agricultural land transfers in developing countries, as detailed in Part I. By 2010, however, the negative impacts of these land deals were well-documented and the accompanying public alarm was widespread. The World Bank's own studies176 bolstered these concerns to such an extent that it became widely acknowledged that safeguards had to be put in place in order to ensure that the benefits would materialize while minimizing the risks.

2. "Principles for Responsible Agricultural Investment That Respects Rights, Livelihoods and Resources"

In January 2010, the World Bank Group, together with the U.N. Food and Agriculture Organization (FAO), the International Fund for Agricultural Development (IFAD), and the U.N. Conference on Trade and Development (UNCTAD) promulgated the "Principles for Responsible Agricultural Investment that Respects Rights, Livelihoods and Resources" ("RAI Principles"). These voluntary principles, which build on similar initiatives aimed at promoting corporate social responsibility in other industries, are intended to serve as the basis for elaborating best practices, guidelines, governance frameworks, and possible codes of practice for the private sector. The seven RAI Principles are as follows:

1) "Existing rights to land and associated natural resources are recognized and respected";

2) "Investments do not jeopardize food security but rather strengthen it";

3) "Processes for accessing land and other resources and then making associated investments are transparent, monitored, and ensure accountability by all stakeholders, within a proper business, legal, and regulatory environment";

4) "All those materially affected are consulted, and agreements from consultations are recorded and enforced";

5) "Investors ensure that projects respect the rule of law, reflect industry best practice, are viable economically, and result in durable shared value";

6) "Investments generate desirable social and distributional impacts and do not increase vulnerability"; and

7) "Environmental impacts due to a project are quantified and measures taken to encourage sustainable resource use while minimizing the risk/magnitude of negative impacts and mitigating them."

B.   The Rights-Based Approach

The U.N. Special Rapporteur on the Right to Food has proposed an alternative framework for assessing large-scale land deals. Instead of disciplining and reacting to market failures, this rights-based approach prioritizes the positive fulfillment of human rights. The rights-based approach is premised on the idea that individuals are entitled to specific rights guarantees that cannot be traded away in the context of large-scale land deals. This approach begins by evaluating the claims of rights-holders and the corresponding obligations of duty-bearers. It then seeks to develop strategies that both build up the capacity of rights-holders to claim their rights and helps ensure that duty-bearers fulfill their obligations. Specifically, the rights-based approach proposes strategies to secure and strengthen the entitlement of relevant groups to land as a productive, rights-fulfilling asset.

1.   The Rights-Based Approach to Land: Land as a Gateway to Human Rights

An explicit and substantive right to land is not codified under international human rights law, but secure and stable access to land is seen as a gateway to the realization of numerous human rights, including: the right to water; the right to adequate housing; the right to health; the right to an adequate standard of living; and, most especially, the right to food. The right to food is codified under the International Covenant on Economic, Social and Cultural Rights (ICESCR), and requires states to ensure that individuals, either "alone or in community with others, have physical and economic access at all times to adequate food or means for its procurement." Under international human rights law, states must take measures to respect, protect, and fulfill this right.

According to the U.N. Committee on Economic, Social and Cultural Rights (ESCR Committee), to further their obligation to respect the right to food, states must "refrain from taking measures that may deprive individuals of access to productive resources on which they depend when they produce food for themselves." The Special Rapporteur argues that respecting the right to food, first and foremost, requires states to ensure security of tenure, and proposes the following measures in that regard:

First, states should confer legal security through formal titles to land and recognize both use and ownership rights, as well as customary and collective rights. Second, states should adopt strict anti-eviction laws and strengthen expropriation frameworks to provide clear procedural safeguards for landowners. Third, states should respect the needs of special groups by ensuring the rights of indigenous peoples under international law and by protecting access to common resources (including fishing and grazing grounds) for fisherfolk, pastoralists, and herders. Finally, respecting the right to food requires that states "prioritize development models that do not lead to eviction, disruptive shifts in land rights and increased land concentration."

In furthering their obligation to protect the right to food, the Special Rapporteur counsels that states should protect access to productive resources from encroachment by foreign and domestic private parties. This includes mapping various land users' rights and strengthening customary systems of tenure, as highlighted above. The obligation also requires states to ensure that investment agreements comply with relevant obligations under international human rights law.

Finally, under the obligation to fulfill the right to food, states must "seek to strengthen people's access to and utilization of resources and means to ensure their livelihoods, including food security." The Special Rapporteur cautions that in situations of highly unequal land distribution, efforts to secure tenure or land use rights may not be sufficient to fulfill this obligation. Instead, states should pursue "agrarian reform that leads to more equitable land distribution for the benefit of smallholders" on the reasoning that small-scale owner-operated farms are more productive and encourage more responsible uses of the soil. The Special Rapporteur encourages states to channel agricultural investment into small-scale farming, instead of transferring land rights to large-scale investors. To the extent that large-scale land transfers do move forward, the Special Rapporteur also offers a set of principles for regulating these transactions.

2. "Eleven Principles: Minimum Human Rights Principles Applicable to Large-Scale Land Acquisitions or Leases"

The Special Rapporteur's "Minimum Human Rights Principles Applicable to Large-scale Land Acquisitions or Leases" ("Eleven Principles") are based on—and give concrete expression to—minimum standards applicable to large-scale land transactions as required by international human rights law. Although the Eleven Principles are seen as essential to minimizing the negative impacts from land deals, the Special Rapporteur notes that adherence to the Principles does not necessarily justify the land investment in question. Instead, states must "balance the advantages of entering into [an investment] agreement against the opportunity costs involved, in particular when other uses" of the land might better service the needs and human rights of the local population. Where large-scale land deals do take place, the Eleven Principles call on relevant parties to meet their respective responsibilities to:

1) Conduct investment negotiations in full transparency with the participation of host communities;

2) Consult with local populations prior to any shifts in land use, with a view towards obtaining their free, prior, and informed consent for the investment project;

3) Enact and enforce legislation that safeguards the rights of host communities;

4) Ensure that investment revenues are used for the benefit of local populations;

5) Adopt labor-intensive farming systems that maximize employment creation;

6) Adopt modes of agricultural production that respect the environment;

7) Ensure that investment agreements include clear obligations and predefined sanctions, with non-compliance determined by independent and participatory ex post impact assessments;

8) Ensure that investment agreements require that a minimum percentage of food crops produced be sold locally;

9) Conduct participatory impact assessments prior to the completion of negotiations;

10) Comply with indigenous peoples' rights under international law; and

11) Provide agricultural waged workers with adequate protection of their fundamental human and labor rights.

The Eleven Principles have much in common with the RAI Principles. For example, both sets of principles call for transparency and consultation with local communities. They both call for measures to enhance food security, secure land rights, and ensure sustainable environmental practices. Both sets of principles also call for assurances that investments benefit host communities, including through investment agreements that contain clear enforceable obligations.

The fact that both sets of principles cover roughly the same terrain is not surprising. Both the RAI Principles and the Eleven Principles are, after all, meant to guide important transactional matters surrounding land deals. The Eleven Principles—which preceded the promulgation of the RAI Principles—were also intended to "inform . . . the adoption of guidelines on land policies and governance by international and regional organizations." Furthermore, the principles of transparency, accountability, and participation—which both frameworks emphasize— are key values common to both development and rights-based discourses.

The Special Rapporteur has pointed out that, despite "superficial" similarities, his "minimum" principles differ significantly from the RAI Principles. First, the Eleven Principles focus the inquiry on determining what use of land will promote human rights. Thus, in line with the land-as-gateway framework described above, the Eleven Principles call for prioritizing alternative development pathways that do not lead to significant transfers of land use and ownership rights. Second, the Eleven Principles "are not optional; they follow from existing international human rights norms" and give rise to specific obligations that attach to multiple actors, including host states, investors, investor home states, and international financial institutions. By contrast, the voluntary RAI Principles "neglect the essential dimension of accountability." Though the RAI Principles outline investors' responsibility to respect human rights, they are silent on the human rights obligations of other actors.

NOTES AND QUESTIONS

What are the differing effects of the World Bank approach versus the U.N. Rights-based approach? In contemplating this question, consider the drivers behind these different approaches. What are the pros and cons of each of these approaches? What would you do?

4. RIGHT TO FOOD

The right to adequate food as a human right also intersects with environmental considerations, especially given how the developing approach to the right to food addresses the right to the availability of food, which can include the ability to produce food on one's own, and adequate food, that is, food free from harmful substances. In reading the following excerpt, consider the ways in which the right to food can implicate environmental considerations.

FAO/UN OFFICE OF THE HIGH COMMISSIONER FOR HUMAN RIGHTS, FACT SHEET NO. 34, THE RIGHT TO ADEQUATE FOOD 2010
Pages 1–3, 7–9, 17–26

INTRODUCTION

According to the Food and Agriculture Organization of the United Nations (FAO), more than one billion people are undernourished. Over two billion suffer from a lack of essential vitamins and minerals in their food. Nearly six million children die every year from malnutrition or related diseases, that is about half of all preventable deaths. The majority of those suffering from hunger and malnutrition are smallholders or landless people, mostly women and girls living in rural areas without access to productive resources. Although many people might imagine that deaths from hunger generally occur in times of famine and conflict, the fact is that only about 10 per cent of these deaths are the result of armed conflicts, natural catastrophes or exceptional climatic conditions. The other 90 per cent are victims of long-term, chronic lack of access to adequate food. Combating hunger and malnutrition is more than a moral duty or a policy choice; in many countries, it is a legally binding human rights obligation. . . .

At the World Food Summit organized by FAO in 1996, States agreed to halve the number of undernourished people by 2015. They also called for the obligations arising from the right to food as provided for under international human rights law to be clarified. In response, the Committee on Economic, Social and Social Rights issued its general comment No. 12 (1999), which defines the right to food. In the United Nations Millennium Declaration, adopted by the General Assembly in 2000, States committed themselves to halving the proportion of people suffering from hunger by 2015. In 2004, FAO adopted the Voluntary Guidelines to Support the Progressive Realization of the Right to Adequate Food in the Context of National Food Security, providing practical guidance to States in their implementation of the right to adequate food.

I.   WHAT IS THE RIGHT TO FOOD?

A.   Key aspects of the right to food

The right to food is an inclusive right. It is not simply a right to a minimum ration of calories, proteins and other specific nutrients. It is a right to all nutritional elements that a person needs to live a healthy and active life, and to the means to access them.

The right to food can be described as follows:

> The right to adequate food is realized when every man, woman and child, alone or in community with others, has physical and economic access at all times to adequate food or means for its procurement.

Committee on Economic, Social and Cultural Rights

> The right to have regular, permanent and free access, either directly or by means of financial purchases, to quantitatively and qualitatively adequate and sufficient food corresponding to the cultural traditions of the people to which the consumer belongs, and which ensures a physical and mental, individual and collective, fulfilling and dignified life free of fear.

United Nations Special Rapporteur on the right to food

It is important to emphasize certain elements of the right to food.

Food must be *available*, *accessible* and *adequate*:

- Availability requires on the one hand that food should be available from natural resources either through the production of food . . . or through other ways of obtaining food. . . . On the other hand, it means that food should be available for sale in markets and shops.

- Accessibility requires economic and physical access to food to be guaranteed. Economic accessibility means that [i]ndividuals should be able to afford food for an adequate diet without compromising on any other basic needs, such as school fees, medicines or rent. . . . Physical accessibility means that food should be accessible to all, including to the physically vulnerable, such as children, the sick, persons with disabilities or the elderly. . . . Access to food must also be guaranteed to people in remote areas and to victims of armed conflicts or natural disasters, as well as to prisoners. . . .

- Adequacy means that the food must satisfy dietary needs, taking into account the individual's age, living conditions, health, occupation, sex, etc. For example, if children's food does not contain the nutrients necessary for their physical and mental development, it is not adequate. . . . Food should be safe for human consumption and free from adverse substances, such as contaminants from industrial or agricultural processes, including residues from pesticides, hormones or veterinary drugs. Adequate food should also be culturally acceptable. . . .

[. . .]

D.   The right to food in international law

The right to food is a human right recognized by international human rights law. The Universal Declaration of Human Rights recognizes, in the context of an adequate standard of living, that: "Everyone has the right to a standard of living adequate for the health and well-being of himself and of his family, including food, . . ." (art. 25).

The International Covenant on Economic, Social and Cultural Rights, which is part of the International Bill of Human Rights, recognizes the right to adequate food as an essential part of the right to an adequate standard of living (art. 11 (1)). It also explicitly recognizes "the fundamental right of everyone to be free from hunger" (art. 11 (2)).

The right to food is also recognized in other international conventions protecting specific groups, such as the Convention on the Elimination of All Forms of Discrimination against Women (1979), the Convention on the Rights of the Child (1989) and the Convention on the Rights of Persons with Disabilities (2006). The right to food is also recognized in some regional instruments. . . .

[. . .]

Several non-legally binding international human rights instruments, including recommendations, guidelines, resolutions or declarations, are relevant to the right to food, too. They are also called soft-law instruments. They are accepted by States and serve as guidance for the implementation of the right to food.

One such soft-law instrument, and by far the most direct and detailed, is the Voluntary Guidelines to Support the Progressive Realization of the Right to Adequate Food in the Context of National Food Security (hereinafter: Right to Food Guidelines). The Right to Food Guidelines were adopted by consensus in November 2004 by the Council of FAO. . . . While they are not legally binding as such, they seek to reflect existing human rights standards and provide useful guidance to States on how they can implement their existing obligations. . . . Considering the wide recognition in international and national laws as well as States' commitments through soft-law instruments, there is a view that at least freedom from hunger can be considered as a norm of international customary law, which is binding on all States, regardless of whether they have ratified specific treaties.

III. WHAT ARE THE OBLIGATIONS ON STATES AND THE RESPONSIBILITIES OF OTHERS?

States have the primary obligation to protect and promote human rights. Human rights obligations are defined and guaranteed by international customary and international human rights treaties, creating binding obligations on the States that have ratified them to give effect to these rights. Several national constitutions also recognize the right to food and corresponding obligations of the State.

A. Three types of obligations

The obligations of States in relation to the right to food are expressed differently from instrument to instrument. However, in general, they fall into three categories, namely the obligations to respect, protect and fulfil.

The obligation to respect the right to food

States have to respect people's existing access to food and means of obtaining food. This means that any measure which results in preventing access to food, for example denying food assistance to political opponents, is prohibited. States cannot suspend legislation or policies that give people access to food (e.g., social welfare legislation, nutrition-related programmes), unless fully justified. States should ensure public institutions, including State-run enterprises or the military, do not undermine people's access to food by, for example, contaminating or destroying farmland or through forced evictions. States should also regularly review their national policies and programmes related to food to ensure that they effectively respect the equal right of everyone to food.

The obligation to protect the right to food

States have to protect individuals' enjoyment of the right to food against violations by third parties (e.g., other individuals, groups, private enterprises and other entities). For example, States should prevent third parties from destroying sources of food by, for instance, polluting land, water and air with hazardous industrial or agricultural products or destroying the ancestral lands of indigenous peoples to clear the way for mines, dams, highways or industrial agriculture. The obligation to protect also includes ensuring that food put on the market is safe and nutritious. States must therefore establish and enforce food quality and safety standards, and ensure fair and equal market practices. Furthermore, States should take the legislative and other measures needed to protect people, especially children, from advertising and promotions of unhealthy food so as to support the efforts of parents and health professionals to encourage healthier patterns of eating and physical exercise. A State must also take into account its international legal obligations regarding the right to food when entering into agreements with other States or with international organizations.

The obligation to fulfil the right to food

The obligation to fulfil incorporates both an obligation to facilitate and an obligation to provide. The obligation to fulfil (facilitate) means the States must be proactive in strengthening people's access to and use of resources and means of ensuring their livelihoods, including food security. Typical measures include the implementation of agrarian reform programmes or minimum income regulations. When adopting food policies, Governments would also need to balance carefully investment in cash crops for export and support for domestic food crops. Other possible measures could be implementing and improving food and nutrition programmes and ensuring that development projects consider nutrition. Facilitating the full realization of the right to food also requires States to inform the population about its human rights and strengthen its ability to participate in development processes and decision-making.

Whenever individuals or groups are unable, for reasons beyond their control, to enjoy the right to food by the means at their disposal, States have the obligation to fulfil (provide) it, for example by providing food assistance or ensuring social safety nets for the most deprived and for victims of natural or other disasters.

According to the first Special Rapporteur on the right to food, to comply fully with their obligations under the right to food, States must also respect, protect and support the fulfilment of the right to food of people living in other territories. This implies that States have to ensure that their own citizens, as well as other third parties subject to their jurisdiction, such as private companies, do not violate the right to food in other countries.

B.   Progressive and immediate obligations

Progressive realization

Some treaties and national constitutions permit States to achieve the full realization of the right to food progressively. For example, article 2 (1) of the International Covenant on Economic, Social and Cultural Rights provides:

Each State Party to the present Covenant undertakes to take steps, individually and through international assistance and cooperation, especially economic and technical, to the maximum of its available resources, with a view to achieving progressively the full realization of the rights recognized in the present Covenant by all appropriate means, including particularly the adoption of legislative measures.

This is an implicit recognition that States may have resource constraints and that it may take time to fully implement the obligations towards the right to food. However, this does not mean that States do not need to do anything until they have sufficient resources. On the contrary, it means that States must lay down a roadmap towards the full realization of the right to food immediately, and demonstrate that they are making every possible effort, using all available resources, to better respect, protect and fulfil the right to food.

Obligations of immediate effect

While some aspects of the right to food are subject to progressive realization, other State obligations are of immediate effect. Below are four categories of obligations of immediate effect under the International Covenant on Economic, Social and Cultural Rights.

(a) The elimination of discrimination

States must immediately prohibit discrimination in access to food and to the related resources on the basis of race, colour, sex, language, age, religion, political or other opinion, national or social origin, property, birth, disability or other status, and adopt measures to eradicate discrimination on these grounds.

[. . .]

(b) Obligation to "take steps"

As mentioned above, under the obligation of progressive realization, States are not allowed to be inactive, but have to make constant efforts to improve the enjoyment of the right to food. This means that, while the full realization of the right to food may be achieved progressively, steps towards that goal must be taken within a reasonably short time. Such steps should be deliberate, concrete and targeted as clearly as possible, using all appropriate means and resources.

[. . .]

(c) Prohibition of retrogressive measures

States cannot allow the existing level of fulfilment of the right to food to deteriorate unless there are strong justifications for it. For example, withdrawing without justification existing services vital for smallholders, such as extension services or support to access productive resources, could constitute a retrogressive measure. To justify it, a State would have to demonstrate that it adopted the measure only after carefully considering all the options, assessing the impact and fully using its maximum available resources.

(d) Protection of minimum essential level of the right to food

Under the International Covenant on Economic, Social and Cultural Rights, there are obligations considered to be of immediate effect to meet the minimum essential levels of each of the rights, including the right to food. They are called minimum core obligations. For the right to food, States have to ensure the satisfaction of, at the very least, the minimum essential level required to be free from hunger, even in times of natural or other disasters. If a State fails to meet these obligations owing to resource restraints, it must demonstrate that it has made every effort to use all available resources to satisfy, as a matter of priority, these core obligations. Even if the resources at its disposal are clearly inadequate, the Government must still introduce low-cost and targeted programmes to assist those most in need so that its limited resources are used efficiently and effectively.

C. Obligations with international dimensions

A State is primarily responsible for respecting, protecting and fulfilling the right to food of people within its borders. However, in a globalized world, structural causes of food insecurity have international dimensions beyond the control of one State. For example, the international trade in foodstuffs is making domestic prices of food increasingly dependent on the international market, the impact of climate change is affecting people's capacity to produce food, and international development cooperation may negatively affect the right to food of marginalized groups when a human rights perspective is not integrated.

In order to address such causes, coordinated efforts among States are required.

Under the International Covenant on Economic, Social and Cultural Rights, States have obligations to take steps to realize rights recognized in it, including the right to food, individually as well as through international assistance and cooperation (art. 2). Article 11 (2) of the Covenant specifically obliges State parties to take measures, including through international cooperation, to improve methods of production, conservation and distribution of food and to ensure an equitable distribution of world food supplies. The role of international assistance and cooperation is also reflected in other legal instruments and policy documents, such as the Charter of the United Nations (Arts. 1 (3), 55 and 56), the Universal Declaration of Human Rights (arts. 22 and 28), the Convention on the Rights of the Child (arts. 4, 24 and 27), the Convention on the Rights of Persons with Disabilities (art. 32) and the Rome Declaration of the World Food Summit.

International cooperation is not a substitute for domestic obligations. However, if a State is not able to give effect to the right to food on its own, it should actively seek the necessary assistance from other States or coordinate as necessary with other States to address obstacles to realizing the right to food that have cross-border dimensions. Also, States should refrain from taking measures which undermine the enjoyment of the right to food in other countries, and take measures, through international assistance and cooperation, to enable other States to meet their obligations in relation to the right to food. In this regard, States should ensure that the protection and promotion of the right to food is given due attention when concluding international agreements or adopting domestic measures which have an extraterritorial impact.

NOTE AND QUESTIONS

The U.S. and the Right to Food. In February of 2014, the American Bar Association adopted a resolution urging "the United States government to make the realization of a human right to adequate food a principal objective of U.S. domestic policy." ABA, Resolution 107 (2014). What sorts of actions might such a principal objective entail? How might an advocate urge the U.S. government to pursue such actions? What legal opposition might this advocate encounter?

5. DEVELOPMENT AND FOOD

Agenda 21, introduced earlier in Chapter 10, is a comprehensive global plan of action for the implementation of sustainable development agreed to in 1992 at the United Nations Conference on Environment and Development. Chapter 14 of Agenda 21, "Promoting Sustainable Agriculture and Rural Development," stresses the need "to create the conditions for sustainable agriculture and rural development" through methods such as "natural resource management and environmental protection." Part 14.2. To achieve these ends, the chapter identifies eleven program areas: (a) agricultural policy review, (b) public participation and promotion of human resource development for sustainable agriculture, (c) improvement of agricultural systems through diversification of infrastructure, (d) land-resource planning and education, (e) land conservation and rehabilitation, (f) water, (g) conservation and sustainable utilization of plant genetic resources, (h) conservation and sustainable utilization of animal genetic resources, (i) integrated pest management and control, (j) sustainable plant nutrition, (k) rural energy transition, and (l) evaluation of the effects of ultraviolet radiation on agricultural systems caused by depletion of the stratospheric ozone layer.

The stated basis for focusing on agricultural policy review expressly addresses some of the difficulties involved with addressing agriculture and environmental issues, and emphasizes that these concerns are not limited to developing countries:

14.5.   There is a need to integrate sustainable development considerations with agricultural policy analysis and planning in all countries, particularly in developing countries. Recommendations should contribute directly to development of realistic and operational medium- to long-term plans and programmes, and thus to concrete actions. Support to and monitoring of implementation should follow.

14.6.   The absence of a coherent national policy framework for sustainable agriculture and rural development (SARD) is widespread and is not limited to the developing countries. In particular the economies in transition from planned to market-oriented systems need such a framework to incorporate environmental considerations into economic activities, including agriculture. All countries need to assess comprehensively the impacts of such policies on food and agriculture sector performance, food security, rural welfare and international trading relations as a means for identifying appropriate offsetting measures. The major thrust of food security in this case is to bring about a significant increase in agricultural production in a sustainable way and to achieve a substantial improvement in people's entitlement to adequate food and culturally appropriate food supplies.

14.7.   Sound policy decisions pertaining to international trade and capital flows also necessitate action to overcome: (a) a lack of awareness of the environmental costs incurred by sectoral and macroeconomic policies and hence their threat to sustainability; (b) insufficient skills and experience in incorporating issues of sustainability into policies and programmes; and (c) inadequacy of tools of analysis and monitoring.

In many of these program areas, the Chapter also calls for international and regional cooperation. For example, with respect to agricultural policy review, Agenda 21 urges "United Nations agencies, such as the FOA, the World Bank, IFAD [the International Fund for Agricultural Development], and GATT" to work with national governments to implement integrated and sustainable agricultural development and food security strategies, encourage "a more open and non-discriminatory trading system and the avoidance of unjustifiable trade barriers which together with other policies will facilitate the further integration of agricultural and environmental policies so as to make them mutually supportive," and to facilitate the exchange of information. Other roles contemplated for these international organizations include strengthening technical working groups and developing systems of data collection.

Although the outcome of Rio+20 resulted mainly in nonbinding declarations, prior to the conference, a number of proposals for goals were submitted with respect to food security and sustainable agriculture.

UNCSD SECRETARIAT, FOOD SECURITY AND SUSTAINABLE AGRICULTURE

5–6 (Dec. 2011)
available at
http://www.uncsd2012.org/index.php?page=view&type=400&nr=227&menu=45

Several submissions to the Compilation Text put food security and sustainable agriculture at the top of their priorities for Rio+20 and even at the center of the green economy. Several submissions also highlight that CSD 17 serves as a good basis for the Rio+20 outcome on the topic."

Some groups proposed even more specific goals:

The farmers' major groups has proposed the following goals:

- Increase the proportion of overseas development assistance focused on agriculture and rural development to 20%;

- countries meeting their l'Aquila and CAADP commitments;

- Increase yields on women's farms by 2.5% to 4%.

The Bonn DPI/NGO conference declaration from 1400 Civil Society Organizations has proposed:

- By 2030, global agricultural production is transformed from industrial to sustainable. Chemical inputs, herbicides, and pesticides are largely replaced with organic and biological alternatives. Interspersed natural areas are protected and restored as sources of pollination, pest control and soil fertility. Food for export is secondary to food for local consumption. Cultivated crop strains are diversified, as are production techniques and the mix of agricultural producers.

- Best management practices reduce erosion by 90% and nitrogen runoff by 50% or more.

UNSGAB proposed 70% of irrigated land using technology that increases crop per drop by 20x.

How SDGs [Sustainable Development Goals] could be structured in this area

An overarching goal in this area could be universal access to nutritious foods, produced in a sustainable and resilient way, creating decent jobs, using less water, energy, land, and pesticides while preserving biodiversity. Several specific targets have been proposed in various submissions to the compilation text. These include: (1) zero net land degradation; (2) 20% increase in total food supply-chain efficiency—reducing losses and waste from field to fork; (3) 20% increase in water efficiency in agriculture—more nutrition and crop per drop; (4) 70% of irrigated land using technology that increases crop per drop. Means of implementation targets could include: (1) increase the proportion of overseas development assistance focused on agriculture, food security and rural development to 20%; (2) target an increasing share of these funds and extension services to smallholders and women farmers to support local production; and (3) support integrated food and nutrition security and sustainable agriculture and rural development action plans and policies, including through enhanced technical cooperation among countries and regions.

NOTES AND QUESTIONS

1. *RIO+20 Review.* For the Rio+20 United Nations Conference on Sustainable Development (UNCSD), the UNCSD Secretariat produced an evaluation report on Food Security and Sustainable Agriculture. *See* UNCSD Secretariat, Food Security and Sustainable Agriculture (Dec. 2011), *available at* http://www.uncsd2012.org/index.php?page=view&type=400&nr=227&menu=45. Among other things, the Report evaluated the progress made in a number of time-bound commitments related to sustainable agriculture, including those made in Agenda 21. While the Report observed that progress was made in a few of the program areas (such as land conservation), in other areas progress was more mixed (such as the development of multisectoral plans to enhance sustainable food production and food security), had formal establishment but lacked funding (such as the conservation and sustainable utilization of plant genetic resources), or simply not achieved (such as the sustainable plant nutrition to increase food production). Overall, the Report stated, "Global delivery of the food security and sustainable agriculture-related commitments has been disappointing." Why do you think such

progress has not been made? What kinds of international mechanisms might make progress more likely?

2. *"Open and non-discriminatory trading environment"* and *"integration of agricultural and environmental policies."* Agenda 21 assumes that the former will facilitate the latter. What do you think is the basis behind this reasoning? Do you agree with this statement?

3. *Proposed goals for Rio+20.* Some of the diplomatic dynamics leading to the outcome of Rio+20 have already been discussed in earlier chapters. However, had some of these goals actually been adopted, what issues might be involved with implementation? Given the observed failures to make progress on the agricultural sustainability goals set forth in Agenda 21, can you think of concrete measures that might avoid similar outcomes?

4. *Sustainable Development Goals.* The SDGs had not been finally adopted by Heads of State as of this writing, but a draft had been adopted. The SDG most relevant to agriculture is number 2:

> Goal 2: End hunger, achieve food security and improved nutrition and promote sustainable agriculture

- End hunger and ensure access by all people to safe and nutritious food all year round

- End all forms of malnutrition and address the nutritional needs of adolescent girls, pregnant and lactating women, and older persons

- Double the agricultural productivity and the incomes of small farmers, respecting the environment and the biodiversity of each region

- Prevent problems such as drought, floods and other disasters

- Protect the variety of species of seeds, crops and farm animals and fairly distribute the benefits of these resources

- Increase investment in rural infrastructure, agricultural research, technology development, and plant and livestock gene banks to improve agricultural productive capacity in developing countries

- Correct and prevent trade restrictions and distortions in world agricultural markets

- Adopt measures to ensure the proper functioning of food commodity markets and their derivatives to help limit extreme food price volatility

6. AGRICULTURE AND SOIL PRODUCTIVITY

Many agricultural practices can negatively impact soil quality. To address these impacts, the FAO adopted a World Soil Charter. This charter provided basic principles and guidelines for the protection and sustainable management of the soil.

WORLD SOIL CHARTER
(1982)

Principles

1. Among the major resources available to man is land, comprising soil, water and associated plants and animals: the use of these resources should not cause their degradation or destruction because man's existence depends on their continued productivity.

2. Recognizing the paramount importance of land resources for the survival and welfare of people and economic independence of countries, and also the rapidly increasing need for more food production, it is imperative to give high priority to promoting optimum land use, to maintaining and improving soil productivity and to conserving soil resources.

3. Soil degradation means partial or total loss of productivity from the soil, either quantitatively, qualitatively, or both, as a result of such processes as soil erosion by water or wind, salinization, waterlogging, depletion of plant nutrients, deterioration of soil structure, desertification and pollution. In addition, significant areas of soil are lost daily to nonagricultural uses. These developments are alarming in the light of the urgent need for increasing production of food, fibres and wood.

4. Soil degradation directly affects agriculture and forestry by diminishing yields and upsetting water regimes, but other sectors of the economy and the environment as a whole, including industry and commerce, are often seriously affected as well through, for example, floods or the silting up of rivers, dams and ports.

5. It is a major responsibility of governments that land-use programmes include measures toward the best possible use of the land, ensuring long-term maintenance and improvement of its productivity, and avoiding losses of productive soil. The land users themselves should be involved, thereby ensuring that all resources available are utilized in the most rational way.

6. The provision of proper incentives at farm level and a sound technical, institutional and legal framework are basic conditions to achieve good land use.

7. Assistance given to farmers and other land users should be of a practical service-oriented nature and should encourage the adoption of measures of good land husbandry.

8. Certain land-tenure structures may constitute an obstacle to the adoption of sound soil management and conservation measures on farms. Ways and means should be pursued to overcome such obstacles with respect to the rights, duties and responsibilities of land owners, tenants and land users alike, in accordance with the recommendations of the World Conference on Agrarian Reform and Rural Development (Rome, 1979).

9. Land users and the broad public should be well informed of the need and the means of improving soil productivity and conservation. Particular emphasis should be placed on education and extension programmes and training of agricultural staff at all levels.

10. In order to ensure optimum land use, it is important that a country's land resources be assessed in terms of their suitability at different levels of inputs for different types of land use, including agriculture, grazing and forestry.

11. Land having the potential for a wide range of uses should be kept in flexible forms of use so that future options for other potential uses are not denied for a long period of time or forever. The use of land for non-agricultural purposes should be organized in such a way as to avoid, as much as possible, the occupation or permanent degradation of good-quality soils.

12. Decisions about the use and management of land and its resources should favour the long-term advantage rather than the short-term expedience that may lead to exploitation, degradation and possible destruction of soil resources.

13. Land conservation measures should be included in land development at the planning stage and the costs included in development planning budgets.

Guidelines for action

Acceptance of these Principles would require the following action:

By governments

i. Develop a policy for wise land use according to land suitability for different types of utilization and the needs of the country.

ii. Incorporate principles of rational land use and management and conservation of soil resources into appropriate resource legislation.

iii. Develop an institutional framework for monitoring and supervising soil management and soil conservation, and for coordination between organizations involved in the use of the countries' land resources in order to ensure the most rational choice among possible alternatives.

iv. Assess both new lands and the lands already being used for their suitability for different uses and the likely hazards of degradation. Provide decision makers with alternative land uses which both satisfy communities' aspirations and use the land according to its capabilities.

v. Implement education, training and extension programmes at all levels in soil management and conservation.

vi. Disseminate as widely as possible information and knowledge about soil erosion and methods of controlling it both at the farm level and at the scale of entire watersheds, stressing the importance of soil resources for the benefit of people and development.

vii. Establish links between local government administrations and land users for the implementation of the soils policy and emphasize the need to put proven soil conservation techniques into practice, and to integrate appropriate measures in forestry and agriculture for the protection of the environment.

viii. Strive to create socio-economic and institutional conditions favourable to rational land resource management and conservation. These conditions will include providing security of land tenure and adequate financial incentives (e.g., subsidies, taxation relief, credit) to the land user. Give encouragement particularly to groups willing to work in cooperation with each other and with their government to achieve appropriate land use, soil conservation and improvement.

ix.   Conduct research programmes which will provide sound
      scientific backing to practical soil improvements and soil
      conservation work in the field, and which give due
      consideration to prevailing socio-economic conditions.

By international organizations

i.   Continue and intensify efforts to create awareness and
      encourage cooperation among all sectors of the
      international community, by assisting where required to
      mount publicity campaigns, conduct seminars and
      conferences and to provide suitable technical publications.

ii.   Assist governments, especially of developing countries, on
      request, to establish appropriate legislation, institutions
      and procedures to enable them to mount, implement and
      monitor appropriate land-use and soil-conservation
      programmes.

iii. Promote cooperation between governments in adopting
      sound land-use practices, particularly in the large
      international watersheds.

iv.   Pay particular attention to the needs of agricultural
      development projects which include the conservation and
      improvement of soil resources, the provision of inputs and
      incentives at the level of the farm and of the watershed,
      and the establishment of the necessary institutional
      structures as the major components.

v.   Support research programmes relevant to soil conservation,
      not only of a technical nature hut also research into social
      and economic issues which are linked to the whole question
      of soil conservation and land resource management.

vi.   Ensure the storage, compilation and dissemination of
      experience and information related to soil conservation
      programmes and of the results obtained in different agro-
      ecological regions of the world.

———————————

In 2011, the FAO also launched a Global Soil Partnership for Food
security and Climate Change Adaptation and Mitigation. The partnership
is an "interactive, responsive and voluntary partnership, open to
governments, regional organizations, institutions and other stakeholders
at various levels." It provides expert advice on soil management and has
works with national soil entities through an interactive and consultative
approach.

The Sustainable Development Goals include attention to soil. Goal 15 reads: *Sustainably manage forests, combat desertification, halt and reverse land degradation, halt biodiversity loss.* One of the Goal 15's targets specifically deals with soils: *By 2020, combat desertification, and restore degraded land and soil, including land affected by drought and floods.*

OTHER NOTES

1. *Climate Change.* As discussed in the introduction, climate change is likely to have a significant impact on agricultural production. How might food security issues may play a role in climate change mitigation and adaptation measures? Bear in mind that agriculture provides the potential to act as carbon sinks. Consider also the role that agriculture may play in climate change mitigation through agricultural land capacity to function as carbon sinks.

2. *Freshwater.* Agricultural production often impacts the availability of freshwater for non-agricultural purposes, including fisheries and drinking water. Conversely, the lack of available freshwater (due to its other uses) may also impact the productivity of agriculture. The UN Convention to Combat Desertification art 2.2 calls upon Parties to adopt and implement long-term integrated strategies that focus simultaneously, in affected areas, on improved productivity of land, and the rehabilitation, conservation and sustainable management of land and water resources, leading to improved living conditions. Could the use of organic agriculture play a role in combating desertification?

3. *Hazardous Substances.* Consider the role of agriculture as a source of hazardous substances, as well as the relevance of the Cartagena Protocol on Biosafety with regards to agricultural inputs and products. What more should be done in this regard?

4. *Biological Diversity.* Agriculture has had—and continues to have—a huge impact on habitat (both agricultural lands as habitat, as well as the cause of habitat destruction). Between 2006 and 2010, production of corn and soybeans expanded in North and South Dakota, Nebraska and Kansas, resulting in a net loss of 1,300,000 acres of grasslands. This land included several environmentally sensitive land forms, including wetlands, highly erodible land, and land removed from the Conservation Reserve Program. *See* C.K. Wright & M.C. Wimberly, *Recent Land Use Change in the Western Corn Belt Threatens Grasslands and Wetlands*, 110 Proceedings of the National Academy of Sciences, 4134–4139 (2013). It seems certain that this resulted in significant impacts on biodiversity. Also consider the biodiversity of agricultural products, as related to the Convention on Biological Diversity.

5. *Environment and Justice.* In reading Chapter 15 consider the relevance of food security and land grabs to the issue of environment and justice.

6. *Environment and Trade.* In reading Chapter 16, consider the relationships between systems governing GMO production and labeling with the role of trade regulation.

C. RELEVANT INTERNATIONAL INSTITUTIONS

1. INTERNATIONAL FUND FOR AGRICULTURAL DEVELOPMENT

The International Fund for Agricultural Development (IFAD) was established as an international financial institution in 1977 pursuant to discussions in the 1974 World Food Conference, organized by the FAO as a response to the famines that afflicted a number of Sahelian countries of Africa. The IFAD focuses primarily on the reduction and elimination of rural poverty, hunger, and malnutrition, and improvement in the life quality, income, and productivity of poor rural populations in developing countries. Its current project areas include addressing food security impacts of climate change, desertification, and water scarcity and promoting rain-fed agriculture and sustainable livelihoods.

2. INTERNATIONAL PLANT GENETIC RESOURCES INSTITUTE

The International Plant Genetic Resources Institute (IPGRI) is a global research organization "with a mandate to advance the conservation and use of genetic diversity for the well-being of present and future generations. It is a Centre of the Consultative Group on International Agricultural Research (CGIAR)." U.N. Food and Agriculture Organization, International Plant Genetic Resources Institute (IPGRI), http://www.fao.org/forestry/4994/en/.

3. FAO COMMISSION ON GENETIC RESOURCES FOR FOOD AND AGRICULTURE

The FAO Commission on Genetic Resources for Food and Agriculture "was established in 1983 to deal with issues related to plant genetic resources. In 1995, the FAO Conference broadened the Commission's mandate to cover all components of biodiversity of relevance to food and agriculture.

The Commission provides the only permanent forum for governments to discuss and negotiate matters specifically relevant to biological diversity for food and agriculture. The Commission aims to reach international consensus on policies for the sustainable use and conservation of genetic resources for food and agriculture and the fair and equitable sharing of benefits derived from their use.

Since its establishment, the Commission has overseen global assessments of the state of the world's plant and animal genetic resources for food and agriculture and negotiated major international instruments, including the International Treaty on Plant Genetic Resources for Food and Agriculture." http://www.fao.org/nr/cgrfa/cgrfa-about/cgrfa-history/en/.

4.   INTERNATIONAL FOOD POLICY RESEARCH INSTITUTE

The International Food Policy Research Institute (IFPRI) was founded as a non-profit in 1975 as a member of the CGIAR consortium. Its mission is to "provide research-based policy solutions that sustainably reduce poverty and end hunger and malnutrition." http://www.ifpri.org/ourwork/about. Its research areas include Gender and Development, Climate Change, Malnutrition, and Transgenic Crops.

5.   CODEX ALIMENTARIUS COMMISSION

The Codex Alimentarius Commission was established in November of1961 by the FAO. Its mission is to protect consumer health and safety, and promote fair practices in the trade of food. In doing so, it promulgates the Codex Alimentarius, which provides "harmonised international food standards, guidelines and codes of practice to protect the health of the consumers and ensure fair practices in the food trade." http://www.codex alimentarius.org/.

CHAPTER 15

HUMAN RIGHTS AND ENVIRONMENT

■ ■ ■

The integration of international environmental law and human rights law is one of the success stories of the international legal system and of sustainable development over the past several decades. The environmental issues involved have included all the major aspects of international environmental law: prevention and control of pollution, preservation and allocation of natural resources, and protection of culture; and the integration has involved all levels of human rights institutions and all regional human rights systems. The path to this integration has not been smooth, however, and important challenges remain. Some of those challenges are primarily domestic, such as how to respect, protect and fulfill human rights domestically and how to achieve environmental justice within a society. Other challenges and questions are international, such as whether there is an international human right to a healthy environment and the degree to which a State is responsible for environmental harm that occurs outside its territory or control—an issue that is often described by the term "extraterritorial" but is more accurately described as "transboundary".

After providing a very brief overview of the human rights system as context in part A, this chapter examines the overall relationship between human rights and environmental protection, including, as always in this book, human health and culture (part B); and harm resulting in human rights violations and environment-related duties arising from human rights law, including the question of how human rights might apply in a transboundary context (part C). Part D discusses environmental refugees and Part E discusses environmental human rights defenders. The chapter then addresses: whether there is a right to a healthy environment (part F); environmental justice (part G) and intergenerational equity (part H); the human rights aspects of climate change (part I); and the rights of indigenous peoples (part J).

CASE STUDY/PROBLEM

Re-read the excerpts from the Inuit petition to the Inter-American Commission on Human Rights contained in Chapter 9, regarding the Inuit claim that the United States was violating the Inuit's human rights because of its behavior vis-à-vis climate change.

NOTES AND QUESTIONS

1. *An environmentalist's perspective.* Why might an environmentalist view the plight of the Inuit in the case study as a human rights issue and not one governed only by environmental law? What advantages and disadvantages might ensue from taking a human rights-based approach?

2. *A human rights advocate's perspective.* How might a human rights activist react to the proposition that climate change and other types of environmental harm can be addressed via human rights law, and why? Would they welcome novel claims of human right abuses?

3. *A climate change activist's perspective.* How might a proponent of taking measures to mitigate or adapt to climate change react to a human rights-based climate change claim, and why? Would they welcome the introduction of new and politically sensitive issues into the climate change debate and negotiations?

A. INTRODUCTION TO HUMAN RIGHTS LAW

THE NEW INTERNATIONAL LAW: PROTECTION OF THE RIGHTS OF INDIVIDUALS RATHER THAN STATES

Louis B. Sohn
32 Am. U.L. Rev. 1, 17–21 (1982)

THE DYNAMIC CHANGES IN INTERNATIONAL LAW SINCE THE SECOND WORLD WAR

The modern rules of international law concerning human rights are the result of a silent revolution of the 1940's, a revolution that was almost unnoticed at the time. Its effects have now spread around the world, destroying idols to which humanity paid obeisance for centuries. Just as the French Revolution ended the divine rights of kings, the human rights revolution that began at the 1945 San Francisco Conference of the United Nations has deprived the sovereign states of the lordly privilege of being the sole possessors of rights under international law. States have had to concede to ordinary human beings the status of subjects of international law, to concede that individuals are no longer mere objects, mere pawns in the hands of states.

Before dwelling on the various aspects of this revolution, however, it is useful to turn first to its prehistory, to the various strands of international law from which this new tapestry was woven. The human rights revolution did not appear suddenly full-grown, like Minerva springing from Jupiter's head. Its main substantive rules and its procedural safeguards can be traced back many centuries, to the origin of international law itself. . . .

THE NATURE OF "HUMAN RIGHTS"

Up to this point it has been assumed that "human rights" is a well-known concept and does not require detailed explanation. That assumption is, however, confronted by two problems. First, the theoretical nature of human rights has been debated fiercely, without resolution, since ancient time. In the play Antigone, Sophocles described Antigone's dilemma when King Creon prohibited the burial of her brother, who had been killed while rebelling against the King. When she was arrested for violating that order, she defended her action by claiming that the King could not override the "immutable, unwritten laws of heaven." The King replied that traitors must be punished; a state must have laws and they must be obeyed in all things, just and unjust alike; otherwise, there will be anarchy, and there is no evil worse than anarchy.

Similarly, when rebelling against the English King, the American revolutionaries in 1776 relied in their Declaration of Independence on the concept of "inalienable rights" endowed by their Creator. In the same spirit, the French National Assembly in 1789 set forth in the Declaration of the Rights of Man and of the Citizen "the natural and imprescriptible rights of man." More recently, Jacques Maritain pointed out:

> [The] human person possess[es] rights because of the very fact that it is a person, a whole, a master of itself and of its acts . . . by virtue of natural law, the human person has the right to be respected, is the subject of rights, possesses rights. These are things which are owed to a man because of the very fact that he is a man.

The United Nations' concept of human rights embraces this natural law concept of rights, rights to which all human beings have been entitled since time immemorial and to which they will continue to be entitled as long as humanity survives. Thus, both the Universal Declaration of Human Rights and the two Covenants assert in the first paragraphs of their preambles that "recognition of the inherent dignity and of the equal and inalienable rights of all members of the human family is the foundation of freedom, justice and peace in the world."

More recently, in specifying the guiding concepts for future human rights work within the United Nations' system, the General Assembly listed among those concepts the natural law idea that "human rights and fundamental freedoms of the human person and of peoples are inalienable."

These "inalienable" rights, both permanent and universal, differ from rights, bestowed by positive law, that a state can give and take away. . . . No state is allowed to deprive individuals of these inalienable rights; such rights are part of a higher law that no positive law can overrule.

There are two other categories of rights: first, those which a state can limit in times of emergency, such as freedom from compulsory labor, right to liberty and security of person, right to humane treatment in prison, right to certain minimum guarantees in criminal proceedings, and freedom from interference with privacy, family, home, or correspondence; and, second, those which the state can limit in order to protect national security, public order (ordre public), and public health or morals. The second category includes the following rights listed in the Covenant on Civil and Political Rights: the right to liberty of movement; the freedom to choose one's residence; the right to a public hearing; freedom to manifest one's religion or beliefs in public; freedom of expression and to seek, receive, and impart information and ideas, orally or in print; right of peaceful assembly; and freedom of association. Of the rights listed in the International Covenant on Economic, Social and Cultural Rights, only the rights relating to trade unions are subject to similar restrictions. Other rights arising under the Covenant can be limited solely "for the purpose of promoting the general welfare in a democratic society." Some scholars may find these differentiations petty. Nevertheless, they show the marriage of positivist and natural law doctrines, the positive law helping to enforce natural law distinctions.

THE INTERNATIONAL COVENANTS: OVERVIEW

When the Commission on Human Rights finished the Universal Declaration, it began preparing the other part of the International Bill of Rights, a convention containing precise obligations that would be binding on the States Parties. There were initial fears that the various rights would drown in a sea of limitations and exceptions, but this danger was avoided by careful delineation of the conditions under which rights could be limited, and identification of those rights that could not be limited under any circumstances. Another difficulty did, however, arise. It proved impossible to formulate in a parallel manner all the rights listed in the Universal Declaration; it became necessary to divide the materials into two categories: civil and political rights; and economic, social, and cultural rights. These two categories were embodied in two separate Covenants—a name that was preferred to the less solemn "convention"— each differing from the other in several respects.

The main difference was in their treatment after coming into force. States Parties were to give the Covenant on Civil and Political Rights immediate effect through appropriate legislative or other measures and by making available an effective remedy to any person whose rights have been violated. In contrast, each State Party to the Covenant on Economic, Social and Cultural Rights agreed only to take steps, to the maximum of its available resources, toward a progressive realization of the rights recognized in that Covenant. The Covenant thus contained a loophole: because a state's obligation was limited to the resources available to it, a poor state could proceed slowly, progressing only as fast as its resources permitted. If its resources should diminish, for example, during an economic crisis, its progress could wane. In contrast, the Covenant on Civil and Political Rights permits no such excuses; a state must guarantee civil and political rights fully on ratification, subject only to the limitations previously discussed.

Although doubts have been expressed about the legal force of the Declaration, the Covenants are now binding on more than [one hundred sixty—updated figure by Eds.] states, [over three-quarters—updated ratio by Eds.] of the members of the world community. Among the parties to the Covenants are states from all regions: Africa, Asia, the Americas, Western Europe, and Eastern Europe. . . .

. . .

Another general point must be made. Although the rights protected by the Covenants are stated with greater precision than those listed in the Universal Declaration, the former are broad enough in scope to surmount differences among various political, economic, and social systems, as well as among widely differing cultures and stages of development. Consequently, only the last factor—differences in stages of development, especially economic development—need be taken into account in applying the Covenant on Economic, Social and Cultural Rights. In contrast, even that factor does not excuse non-implementation of the Covenant on Civil and Political Rights.

The Covenants and national constitutions or laws are meant to coexist. The Covenants do not supersede any constitutions or laws that provide more protection to individuals. Where the Covenants go beyond a domestic law in protecting a particular right, the state concerned has the duty to adopt any additional legislative or other measures that may be necessary to give effect to the right recognized in the Covenants. . . .

WHAT ARE HUMAN RIGHTS?

United Nations Office of the High Commissioner for Human Rights
http://www.ohchr.org/EN/Issues/Pages/WhatareHumanRights.aspx

Human rights are rights inherent to all human beings, whatever our nationality, place of residence, sex, national or ethnic origin, colour, religion, language, or any other status. We are all equally entitled to our human rights without discrimination. These rights are all interrelated, interdependent and indivisible.

Universal human rights are often expressed and guaranteed by law, in the forms of treaties, customary international law, general principles and other sources of international law. International human rights law lays down obligations of Governments to act in certain ways or to refrain from certain acts, in order to promote and protect human rights and fundamental freedoms of individuals or groups.

Universal and inalienable

The principle of universality of human rights is the cornerstone of international human rights law. This principle, as first emphasized in the Universal Declaration on Human Rights in 1948, has been reiterated in numerous international human rights conventions, declarations, and resolutions. The 1993 Vienna World Conference on Human Rights, for example, noted that it is the duty of States to promote and protect all human rights and fundamental freedoms, regardless of their political, economic and cultural systems.

All States have ratified at least one, and 80% of States have ratified four or more, of the core human rights treaties, reflecting consent of States which creates legal obligations for them and giving concrete expression to universality. Some fundamental human rights norms enjoy universal protection by customary international law across all boundaries and civilizations.

Human rights are inalienable. They should not be taken away, except in specific situations and according to due process. For example, the right to liberty may be restricted if a person is found guilty of a crime by a court of law.

Interdependent and indivisible

All human rights are indivisible, whether they are civil and political rights, such as the right to life, equality before the law and freedom of expression; economic, social and cultural rights, such as the rights to work, social security and education, or collective rights, such as the rights to development and self-determination, are indivisible, interrelated and interdependent. The improvement of one right facilitates advancement of the others. Likewise, the deprivation of one right adversely affects the others.

Equal and non-discriminatory

Non-discrimination is a fundamental principle in international human rights law. The principle is present in all the major human rights treaties and provides the central theme of some of international human rights conventions such as the International Convention on the Elimination of All Forms of Racial Discrimination and the Convention on the Elimination of All Forms of Discrimination against Women.

The principle applies to everyone in relation to all human rights and freedoms and it prohibits discrimination on the basis of a list of non-exhaustive categories such as sex, race, colour and so on. The principle of non-discrimination is complemented by the principle of equality, as stated in Article 1 of the Universal Declaration of Human Rights: "All human beings are born free and equal in dignity and rights."

Both Rights and Obligations

Human rights entail both rights and obligations. States assume obligations and duties under international law to respect, to protect and to fulfil human rights. The obligation to respect means that States must refrain from interfering with or curtailing the enjoyment of human rights. The obligation to protect requires States to protect individuals and groups against human rights abuses. The obligation to fulfil means that States must take positive action to facilitate the enjoyment of basic human rights. At the individual level, while we are entitled our human rights, we should also respect the human rights of others.

THE ENVIRONMENT RIGHTS REVOLUTION: A GLOBAL STUDY OF CONSTITUTIONS, HUMAN RIGHTS, AND THE ENVIRONMENT

David R. Boyd
8–9 (2012)

Rights represent reasonable minimum demands upon society that are rooted in moral values and thus place compelling principles on the side of the person asserting a right. As Ignatieff wrote, "Rights are not just instruments of the law, they are expressions of our moral identity as a people." Because rights provide recognition for society's most cherished values, such as dignity, equality, and respect, the language of rights has considerable symbolic force and can be a source of political power. The power of rights discourse is demonstrated by the considerable progress achieved in some battles about justice, including those against racism and the oppression of women. However, one of the key messages of the modern human rights movement is that moral rights are not adequate and must be supplemented with enforceable legal rights to make them meaningful. Legal rights are said to empower rights holders to control the behavior of others, and are famously described as "trumps" by Dworkin. Shapiro argues that "rights review almost always places courts on the side of the less politically powerful," protecting minority interests against majority tyranny and fecklessness.

Not everyone has been seduced by the siren song of the rights revolution. It can be argued that rights are inherently undemocratic to the extent that they constrain governments from enforcing the preferences of the majority. . . . Human rights are criticized for being individualistic, disregarding duties to others and the interests of the broader community. Despite their purported universality, the Western conception of human rights has been criticized as a form of cultural imperialism. Rights can be divisive when there are conflicts between deeply held values (as in the ongoing abortion debate that pits the rights of women against the rights of the fetus). Glendon called for more thought to be given to "whether a particular issue is best conceptualized as a right; the relation a given right should have to other rights and interests; the responsibilities, if any that should be correlative with a given right; the social cost of rights; and what effects a given right can be expected to have on the setting of conditions for the durable protection of freedom and human dignity." Other criticisms take aim at the processes used to create rights, particularly when rights are established or enlarged through court decisions. For example, Bork argues that creating rights through judicial interpretation is "heresy" because the role of judges is to interpret law, not make law.

Critics also argue that the focus on rights obscures underlying societal problems and their root causes. Capitalism and globalization, with their emphasis on free trade and market-based solutions, are accused of contributing to the erosion of human rights. States are responsible for respecting, protecting, and fulfilling human rights, but critics argue the power of states is declining relative to international institutions (e.g., the World Trade Organization) and transnational corporations. For example, Baxi questions whether the right to food can be reconciled with a global agribusiness industry dominated by a handful of large corporations.

Perhaps the most trenchant critique is that the unprecedented global diffusion of rights on paper is not matched by global respect for rights in practice. Violations of human rights remain commonplace, even in wealthy Western nations. As Falk observes, "The achievements in human rights over the course of the last fifty years are extraordinary, but the obstacles to full realization seem as insurmountable as ever." The right to a healthy environment reflects these broader debates, as . . . the right has contributed to environmental progress, yet ecological sustainability remains a distant goal.

THE DECAMERON (SIXTH DAY—SEVENTH STORY)[1]

Giovanni Boccaccio
Start Publ'g LLC, eBook 2012, at 537–541 (1351)

There was, then, aforetime, in the city of Prato, a statute in truth no less blameworthy than cruel, which, without making any distinction, ordained that any woman found by her husband in adultery with . . . her lover should be burnt, even as she who should be discovered to have sold her favours for money. [While] this statute was in force, it befell that a noble and beautiful lady, by name Madam Filippa, who was of a

---

[1] The Decameron is a collection of 100 novelas (stories), told by seven young women and three young men who had gone to a villa near Florence, Italy, to escape the plague. Each person tells one story on each of ten days, over a period of two weeks. The novella reproduced here was the seventh story on the sixth day. It was told by Filostrato, one of the three men.—Eds.

singularly amorous complexion, was one night found by Rinaldo de'
Pugliesi her husband, in her own chamber in the arms of Lazzerino de'
Guazzagliotri, a noble and handsome youth of that city, whom she loved
even as herself.

Rinaldo, seeing this, was sore enraged and scarce contained himself
from falling upon them and slaying them; and but that he feared for
himself, . . . he had certainly done it. However, he forbore from this, but
could not refrain from seeking of the law of Prato that which it was not
permitted him to accomplish with his own hand, to wit, the death of his
wife. Having, therefore, very sufficient evidence to prove the lady's
default, no sooner was the day come than, without taking other counsel,
he lodged an accusation against her and caused . . . her [to be summoned]
before the provost.[2]

Madam Filippa, being great of heart, as women commonly are who
are verily in love, resolved, although counseled to the contrary by many of
her friends and kinsfolk, to appear, choosing rather, confessing the truth,
to die with an undaunted spirit, than, meanly fleeing, to live an outlaw in
exile and confess herself unworthy of such a lover as he in whose arms
she had been the foregoing night. Wherefore, presenting herself before
the provost, attended by a great company of men and ladies and exhorted
of all to deny the charge, she demanded, with a firm voice and an assured
air, what he would with her.

The magistrate, looking upon her and seeing her very fair and
commendable of carriage and according as her words testified, of a lofty
spirit, began to have compassion of her, fearing lest she should confess
somewhat wherefore it should behoove him, for his own honour's sake, to
condemn her to die. However, having no choice but to question her of that
which was laid to her charge, he said to her, 'Madam, as you see, here is
Rinaldo your husband, who complaineth of you, avouching himself to
have found you in adultery with another man and demanding that I
should punish you therefore by putting you to death, according to the
tenor of a statute which here obtaineth; but this I cannot do, except you
confess it; wherefore look well what you answer and tell me if that be true
whereof your husband impeacheth you.'

The lady, no wise dismayed, replied very cheerfully, 'Sir true it is
that Rinaldo is my husband and that he found me last night in the arms
of Lazzarino, wherein, for the great and perfect love I bear him, I have
many a time been; nor am I anywise minded to deny this. But, as I am
assured you know, laws should be common to all and made with the
consent of those whom they concern, and this is not the case with this
statute, which is binding only upon us unhappy women, who might far
better than men avail to satisfy many; more by token that, when it was

---

[2]   Referred to as the "Podesta" in the original, this was the Chief Magistrate of Prato.—Eds.

made, not only did no woman yield consent thereunto, but none of us was even cited to do so; wherefore it may justly be styled naught. However, if you choose, to the prejudice of my body and of your own soul, to be the executor of this unrighteous law, it resteth with you to do so; but, ere you proceed to adjudge aught, I pray you do me one slight favour, to wit, that you question my husband if at all times and as often as it pleased him, without ever saying him nay, I have or not vouchsafed him entire commodity of myself.'

Rinaldo, without waiting to be questioned [by] the provost, straightway made answer that undoubtedly the lady had, at his every request, accorded him his every pleasure of herself; whereupon, 'Then, my lord provost,' straightway rejoined she, 'if he have still taken of me that which was needful and pleasing to him, what, I ask you, was or am I to do with that which remaineth over and above his requirements? Should I cast it to the dogs? Was it not far better to gratify withal a gentleman who loveth me more than himself, than to leave it waste or spoil?'

Now well nigh all the people of Prato had flocked thither to the trial of such a matter and of so fair and famous a lady, and hearing so comical a question, they all, after much laughter, cried out as with one voice that she was in the right of it and that she said well. Moreover, ere they departed thence, at the instance of the provost, they modified the cruel statute and left it to apply to those women only who should for money make default to their husbands. Thereupon Rinaldo, having taken nought but shame by so fond an emprise, departed the court, and the lady returned in triumph to her own house, joyful and free and in a manner raised up out of the fire.

NOTES AND QUESTIONS

1. *Whence do they come?* Note the different bases for human rights asserted by Sohn and the UN Office of the High Commissioner for Human Rights (OHCHR). With which do you agree? If human rights depend on State consent, how can some be inalienable and non-derogable *jus cogens*? If they do not depend on State consent, why are they all not non-derogable?

2. *Madonna Filippa.* What three arguments did Madonna Filippa make? The first two are among the first assertions of women's equal rights in Western literature. The third can be viewed several ways, including as a claim to the right of personal autonomy. Which of Madonna Filippa's arguments obviously were persuasive to the people of Prato and the Podesta. Are they convincing to you? Would they have been convincing to you in the absence of post-World War II human rights law? If so, why? Madonna Filippa was appealing to something other than the written law. What was it?

3. *What about reality?* If evidence of State practice is necessary, does the fact that, historically, societies have often destroyed the environment and that environmental sustainability remains a distant goal pose an

insurmountable difficulty to the existence of environmental rights? Cf. Joseph L. Sax, The Search for Environmental Rights, 94 J. Land Use & Planning 6 (1990). What about Boyd's argument that violations of human rights are commonplace? Is this State practice?

4.   *Only States?* It is clear that States must observe human rights, but what about private business entities and international organizations? In the *Unocal* case, described below, a United States court held that a corporation could be held liable for human rights violations when acting under color of law. Does that make sense or should the State be the only liable party? For many years, a World Bank legal opinion drafted by the World Bank's General Counsel held that the Bank may not consider the human rights implications of its projects because the World Bank Articles of Agreement (its charter) directs it to make loans on the basis of economic considerations and forbids it from interfering in the internal affairs of borrowers. In 2006, the Bank's General Counsel drafted an opinion reversing that and stating "there are instances in which the Bank may take human rights into account, and others in which it should. Indeed, there are some activities which the Bank cannot properly undertake without considering human rights" (January 27, 2006, from a new General Counsel, Roberto Danino). However, the World Bank Board of Executive Directors, which must formally adopt the draft for it to constitute a formal legal opinion of the World Bank and binding upon the Bank, has not done so.

5.   *Is it happening again?* What do you think about the criticisms recounted by Boyd, particularly that human rights are a form of cultural imperialism?

1. REGIONAL HUMAN RIGHTS SYSTEMS

The Inter-American system of human rights includes two tribunals: the Inter-American Commission on Human Rights in Washington, DC and the Inter-American Court of Human Rights in San Jose, Costa Rica. The Court has jurisdiction to hear cases brought by a State or by the Commission. The Commission has jurisdiction to hear cases brought by individuals, and it also holds thematic hearings and issues thematic reports. The Inter-American system has three legal instruments: the American Declaration of the Rights and Duties of Man, which was adopted by the Organization of American States in 1948; the American Convention on Human Rights, which has 22 Parties as of February 2015 (not including the United States), and the Additional Protocol to the American Convention on Human Rights in the area of Economic, Social and Cultural Rights, which has 16 Parties as of February 2015 (also not including the United States). Because the United States is not a Party to the convention, it is not subject to the jurisdiction of the Inter-American Court of Human Rights.

The European human rights system has been a leader and has influenced other international and national human rights bodies. See

Thomas Buergenthal, *The Evolving International Human Rights System*, 100 Am. J. Int'l L. 783, 792–94 (2006). The basic instrument is the European Convention for the Protection of Human Rights and Fundamental Freedoms, which was adopted in 1950 and has had many protocols. The Convention has been ratified by all 47 members of the Council of Europe, from the Atlantic Ocean to the Pacific Ocean and the North Sea to the Mediterranean Sea. The institution is the European Court of Human Rights, which has been creative in deriving environmental rights from other rights such as the right to privacy and family life.

The African human rights system is governed by the African Charter on Human and Peoples' Rights, which has 53 Parties as of February 2015, and by a protocol to that charter that went into force in 2005. The system has two tribunals. The charter created the African Commission on Human and Peoples Rights in Arusha, Tanzania; and the 2005 protocol to the charter created the African Court on Human and Peoples Rights in Bajul, The Gambia.

An Asia-wide human right system does not exist. The 10 Member States of the Association of Southeast Asian Nations (ASEAN) adopted the ASEAN Human rights Declaration in 2012. It does not provide for any dispute settlement tribunals. Article 28(f) provides that every person and his or her family has the right to an adequate standard of living, including "The right to a safe, clean and sustainable environment."

The regional human rights systems have different norms, and in some instances they contain norms that may be identical though the wordings of the norms differ. With respect to the right to life, for example, the African Charter on Human and Peoples' Rights provides "Human beings are inviolable. Every human being shall be entitled to respect for his life and the integrity of his person. No one may be arbitrarily deprived of this right." (art. 4); the American Convention on Human Rights provides "Every person has the right to have his life respected. This right shall be protected by law and, in general, from the moment of conception. . . ." (art. 2); the ASEAN Human Rights Declaration provides "Every person has an inherent right to life which shall be protected by law. . . ." (art. 1); and the European Convention on Human Rights provides "Everyone's right to life shall be protected by law. . . ." (art. 4).

In practice, human rights tribunals (as well as other human rights bodies) tend to refer to and rely on each others' jurisprudence, much like common law courts apply precedents. See, e.g., *Social and Economic Rights Center v. Nigeria*, African Comm'n on Human ad Peoples' Rights, ACHPR/Comm/A044/1, Dec. re: Comm. No. 155/96 (2001), citing the European Court of Human Rights' jurisprudence. This has resulted in a high degree of coherence in the jurisprudence among the three regional systems with tribunals.

2. CONTENT OF HUMAN RIGHTS LAWS AND RELATED INSTITUTIONS

The various human rights instruments contain a wide variety of norms, which are sometimes divided into so-called substantive and procedural rights. For purposes of the relationship between human rights and environment, the most important of the global substantive human rights include: the rights to life, health, adequate standard of living, to enjoy culture, and to own and use property. The right to an adequate standard of living has been interpreted by various authorities to include the right to safe drinking water and sanitation and the right to a healthy environment. Two other rights—which sometimes are referred to as "impartiality rights"—have also been significant: equal protection and due process. Because regional human rights provisions differ from global provisions, some regional human rights that do not use the global terminology have also (and sometimes somewhat surprisingly) been central to the integration of environment and human rights. An example is the right to privacy and family life in article 8 of the European Convention on Human Rights, which is applied in the *Taskin* case, below.

Six procedural rights have been critically important to environmental protection and to the integration of human rights and environment. These are the rights to: access to information, freedom of expression, freedom of assembly, freedom of opinion, freedom to participate in decision-making, and access to justice.

Many human rights norms contained in treaties are also considered to be customary international law. Examples include the right to life and the six procedural rights mentioned above.

A wide variety of global and regional human rights institutions exist. At the global level, the most important is the United Nations Human Rights Council (HRC), which is assisted by the Office of the High Commissioner for Human Rights (OHCHR). Each of the global human rights treaties also has a committee responsible for overseeing the rights in that treaty.

In addition, the HRC appoints special rapporteurs, independent experts and other forms of what are referred to as "special procedures" with respect to the human rights aspects of various issues, typically with three-year terms and prescribed mandates. In reality, it is the mandate of a special procedure that is more important than the title, though the two are often related.

Building on several resolutions related to human rights and the environment and human rights and climate change, the Human Rights Council established the mandate for an Independent Expert on Human Rights and the Environment during its 19th session in 2012 (HRC Resolution 19/10). The official title was "Independent Expert on human rights obligations relating to the enjoyment of a safe, clean, healthy and sustainable environment". Professor John Knox of Wake Forest University in the United States began working on the mandate in August 2012. Several of his reports are excerpted below.

In 2015, the Human Rights Council decided to extend the mandate of Knox as a Special Rapporteur on the issue of human rights obligations relating to the enjoyment of a safe, clean, healthy and sustainable environment, for a period of three years (UN Human Rights Council Resolution 28/11 (2015)). The Human Rights Council requested the Special Rapporteur, among other things, to:

- Continue to study the human rights obligations relating to the enjoyment of a safe, clean, healthy and sustainable environment;

- Continue to identify, promote and exchange views on good practices relating to human rights obligations and commitments to inform, support and strengthen environmental policy making, especially in the area of environmental protection;

- Promote and report on the realization of human rights obligations relating to the enjoyment of a safe, clean, healthy and sustainable environment, and to disseminate his findings by, inter alia, continuing to give particular emphasis to practical solutions with regard to their implementation; and

- Work on identifying challenges and obstacles to the full realization of human rights obligations relating to the enjoyment of a safe, clean, healthy and sustainable environment and protection gaps thereto, including in the context of sustainable development.

On a related topic, in 2014, the HRC appointed Baskut Tuncak (of the Center for International Environmental Law) to be the third Special Rapporteur on Human Rights and Toxic Substances. Other special procedures deal with rights that are related to environmental issues, as well, such as the Special Rapporteur on the Rights of Indigenous Peoples, the Special Rapporteur on the Right to Food, Special Rapporteur on the Human Right to Water, and the Special Representative of the Secretary General on Human Rights and Transnational Corporations and Other Business Enterprises. Regional human rights institutions also appoint special procedures.

At the national level, over 100 countries have National Human Rights Institutions (NHRIs) with the general mandate to monitor and facilitate the implementation of human rights in the particular country. The specific mandate varies among countries, as does the legal source that established the NHRI, which ranges from executive orders to constitutional provisions.

3.   RECOGNITION OF ENVIRONMENTAL RIGHTS IN NATIONAL CONSTITUTIONS

The following material deals with the recognition of environmental rights of all types in national constitutions. National legal provisions regarding the right to a healthy environment are further addressed below in part F.

THE ENVIRONMENTAL RIGHTS REVOLUTION: A GLOBAL STUDY OF CONSTITUTIONS, HUMAN RIGHTS, AND THE ENVIRONMENT

David R. Boyd

47, 49–50, 52–53, 59, 66–68, 290–291 (2012)

Over the past four decades, there has been a remarkable and ongoing shift toward constitutional recognition of the importance of protecting the environment. At the time of the *Stockholm Declaration* in 1972, there were no constitutions that incorporated environmental rights and only a handful of constitutions that imposed modest environmental responsibilities. Today, three quarters of the world's constitutions (147 out of 193) include explicit references to environmental rights and/or responsibilities. . . . This majority holds for nations belonging to the Organisation for Economic Co-operation and Development, the Commonwealth, La Francophone, and even the Organization of Petroleum Exporting Countries. The majority applies in all regions, including Africa, the Americas (except North America), Asia-Pacific, Europe and the Middle East/Central Asia.

. . .

National legal systems provide another pattern that partially explains the variation in the presence of constitutional environmental provisions. The UN's 193 member states can be divided into fifteen categories according to the type of legal system. There is a striking difference between common and civil law nations in the extent to which they do or do not incorporate environmental provisions into their constitutions. Of the twenty-three nations employing exclusively common-law systems, only three have environmental provisions in their constitutions. This reflects the Anglo-American caution regarding constitutional recognition of social and economic rights. While the constitutions of most former British colonies contain bills of rights, these bills adopt the classic liberal approach to human rights—i.e., they focus on civil and political rights while economic, social, and cultural rights are not protected (except for property). In contrast, among the seventy-seven nations with exclusively civil law systems, seventy-two have environmental provisions in their constitutions. . . .

The distribution of constitutional environmental provisions across the world provides a convincing rebuttal to the charge of cultural imperialism leveled by critics who assert that environmentalism is a Western conception. The 147 nations whose constitutions contain provisions related to environmental protection include a majority of nations in Central and South America, Africa, Asia, the Middle East, and Eastern Europe. In fact, it is in the Western nations—the United States, Canada, the United Kingdom, Australia, and others—where constitutional recognition of the value of environmental protection lags.

Types of Environmental Protection Provisions in Constitutions

Constitutional provisions related to environmental protection can be grouped into five categories: government's responsibility to protect the environment; substantive rights to environmental quality; procedural environmental rights; individual responsibility to protect the environment; and a miscellaneous "catch-all" category of less common provisions. . . .

Government's Environmental Duties

The most common form of constitutional provision related to environmental protection is the imposition of a duty on the government, found in 140 constitutions. . . . In the majority of cases, the governmental duty is explicitly articulated, as in, for example, the *Instruments of Government Act*, which is part of Sweden's constitution:

> Article 2. . . .
>
> The public institution shall promote sustainable development leading to a good environment for present and future generations.
>
> . . .

Sustainable Environment Rights

Ninety-two national constitutions recognize that citizens have a substantive right to live in a healthy environment . . . , illustrated by this example in Norway's constitution (1992):

> Article 110(b).   Every person has a right to an environment that is conducive to health and to natural surroundings whose productivity and diversity are preserved. Natural resources should be made use of on the basis of comprehensive long-term considerations whereby this right will be safeguarded for future generations as well.

The environmental rights entrenched in constitutions are universal (i.e., held by all individuals in a nation), except in the case of El Salvador, where the right to a healthy environment appears to be limited to children, and the Maldives, where the right appears to be limited to Muslims. . . .

. . .

Procedural Environmental Rights

Thirty national constitutions provide procedural rights specifically related to environmental protection, including the right to information, the right to participate in decision making, and the right of access to the judicial system to challenge particular decisions, unconstitutional laws, or alleged violations of individual rights (see Table 3.2). The Czech Republic's constitution provides an example:

Article 35.   (2) Everybody is entitled to timely and complete information about the state of the environment and natural resources.

Many constitutions incorporate generic procedural rights that apply to a broad spectrum of issues including the environment. As well, in many industrialized nations these procedural rights are already available because of existing laws and policies, although constitutional affirmation will generally strengthen the individual's position. In every case except Austria, procedural environmental rights are included in constitutions that also contain a substantive right to live in a healthy environment. This suggests that procedural environmental rights are viewed as a complement to, rather than a substitute for, substantive environmental rights.

. . .

Other Environmental Protection Provisions

Not surprisingly, given the diverse legal systems of the world, there is a broad variety of constitutional environmental provisions, ranging from generic to highly detailed. Among the most common provisions in this miscellaneous category are authorization of restrictions on the use of private property in order to protect the environment; prohibitions on importing toxic, hazardous, or nuclear waste; recognition of the right to clean water; and value statements regarding the importance placed on protecting the environment. In a handful of constitutions, provisions related to environmental protection are extremely comprehensive, with a level of detail that in most nations would be found in environmental legislation.

. . .

At the end of the day, however, human rights matter only if they make a difference in people's lives. Measured by this yardstick, the constitutional right to a healthy environment is beginning to matter. There are hundreds of inspiring stories of individuals, NGOs, and communities seizing the eloquent words printed in their national constitutions and bringing them to life. The right to a healthy environment is gaining momentum, law by law, case by case, place by place, and nation by nation. As a result of the right to a healthy environment, people in many communities have gained access to safe drinking water. Millions of people are breathing cleaner air. Law-breaking polluters and despoilers have been hauled into court, fined, and forced to clean up their act. And while the right to a healthy environment is focused primarily on people, Nature too has benefited. The habitats of endangered species—sea turtles in Greece, green macaws in Costa Rica, salamanders in the Netherlands, and many others—have been protected. Damages to eco-systems from Argentina to the Philippines are being restored.

While constitutional environmental law slowly spreads its wings, the ongoing environmental challenges facing the world—climate change, toxic pollution, resource depletion, and the decline of biological diversity—indicate that we have a long way to go in achieving a sustainable future. Environmental protection remains more an aspiration than a goal that has been achieved. A parallel can be drawn with the fact that despite the long history of human rights, people throughout the world still experience inequality, poverty, oppression, and hunger. The right to a healthy environment recognizes that humanity's most common link is that we all share this small planet. We all breathe the same air. We all cherish our children's future. Constitutional protection for the environment, especially the right to healthy environment, has the legal and symbolic power to both change the rules of the game and alter our vision of the world, bringing us closer to the elusive goal of achieving sustainability.

NOTES AND QUESTIONS

1. *Sub-national constitutions.* The constitutions of sub-national units also contain provisions dealing with environmental rights and responsibilities. Article II, section 3 of the Montana State Constitution (in the United States), for example, provides: "All persons are born free and have certain inalienable rights. They include the right to a clean and healthful environment. . . ."

2. *A general principle?* Given the proliferation of national constitutional provisions regarding environmental rights and responsibilities, can it be said that there exists a "general principle of law recognized by civilized nations" (to use the language of the Statute of the International Court of Justice) to the effect that environmental rights and responsibilities exist?

B. RELATION BETWEEN HUMAN RIGHTS AND ENVIRONMENTAL PROTECTION

1. OVERVIEW

Environmentalists taking a human rights-based approach to environmental protection tended to do so for both substantive and strategic reasons. For further reading, see David K. Anton & Dinah L. Shelton, Environmental Protection and Human Rights (2011); Svitlana Krachenko & John E. Bonine, Human Rights and the Environment: Cases, Law and Policy (2008).

HUMAN RIGHTS, ENVIRONMENTAL RIGHTS, AND THE RIGHT TO THE ENVIRONMENT
Dinah Shelton
28 Stan. J. Intl. L. 103, 103–105 (1991)

There is no doubt that the global environment is deteriorating and that failure to alleviate current environmental degradation may threaten human health and human life. However, the necessary and appropriate international legal response remains unclear. These problems generate a host of questions and public policy alternatives. A fundamental question is whether human rights and environmental protection are premised upon fundamentally different social values, such that efforts to implement both simultaneously will produce more conflict than improvement, or, on the other hand, whether human rights and environmental protection are complementary, each furthering the aims of the other.

Some theorists suggest that environmental issues belong within the human rights category, because the goal of environmental protection is to enhance the quality of human life. Opponents argue, however, that human beings are merely one element of a complex, global ecosystem, which should be preserved for its own sake. Under this approach, human rights are subsumed under the primary objective of protecting nature as a whole.

A third view, which seems to best reflect current law and policy sees human rights and environmental protection as each representing different, but overlapping, societal values. The two fields share a core of common interests and objectives, although obviously not all human rights violations are necessarily linked to environmental degradation. Likewise, environmental issues cannot always be addressed effectively within the human rights framework, and any attempt to force all such issues into a human rights rubric may fundamentally distort the concept of human rights. This approach recognizes the potential conflicts between environmental protection and other human rights, but also the contribution each field can make to achieving their common objectives.

NOTES AND QUESTIONS

1.   *Tensions or synergies.* Are protecting the environment (including, as always, human health) and human rights mutually supportive? What substantive and institutional tensions, if any, exist between the two areas? Can you think of environmental issues in conflict with the right to housing, the right to food, or the right to family? What synergies exist between the two areas? Possible responses are provided under point 5, below. Are there ways of ameliorating any tensions that do exist?

2.   *Nature for humans?* The article by Professor Shelton alludes to the controversial assertion that some environmentalists fear may be the outcome of a "human-centered" (anthropocentric) view of environmental law. The problem arises from the concept of "human rights" as a species-chauvinistic approach that reduces the protection of nature to its value to humans. See Edith Brown Weiss, Our Rights and Obligations to Future Generations for the Environment, 84 Am. J. Intl. L. 198 (1990). Consider this in light of the materials in Chapter 1, e.g., Rio Declaration Principle 1.

3.   *Humans for nature?* Approaching environmental protection from a natural (biocentric) perspective poses the question of whether and to what extent humans have a moral obligation to preserve nature for its own sake and to what extent humans should sacrifice for this preservation. For example, assume the spotted owl has no direct or indirect economic value. Should it be preserved even though this would hurt the timber industry economically? From the perspective of protecting nature, what essential elements are left unprotected by traditional human rights?

4.   *Is it as bad as it seems?* Is it accurate to say that human rights only consider humans and that environmental protection efforts consider humans as just another part of nature? Will developing a rights-based approach to environmental protection necessarily diminish the emphasis on traditional human rights issues? Will it create political pressure adverse to human rights generally?

5.   *Possible responses regarding Question 1.* Regarding tensions: opposition to urban sprawl; protection of wildlife habitat; population control programs. Regarding synergies: concerns about human health, e.g., safe drinking water; concerns about worker health and safety, e.g., International Labor Organization conventions; concerns about indigenous peoples, land and culture; importance of the roles of civil society in each area; and the role of non-legally binding (soft) law in each area.

6.   *Not satisfied?* For coursebooks providing in-depth treatment to the area of human rights and environment, see Donald K. Anton & Dinah L. Shelton, Environmental Protection and Human Rights (2011); Svitlana Krachenko & John E. Bonine, Human Rights and the Environment: Cases, Law and Policy (2008).

2. JURISPRUDENTIAL APPROACH IN LIGHT OF ABSENCE OF SPECIFIC HUMAN RIGHTS STANDARDS

Analysts and tribunals in cases alleging that environmental harm violates a human right are faced with the question of how much environmental harm is required before a human rights violation occurs. Human rights norms often do not contain specific standards and in any event typically do not expressly address environmental criteria. Consider the following excerpts.

DEVELOPING SUBSTANTIVE ENVIRONMENTAL RIGHTS

Dinah Shelton
1 Journal of Human Rights and the Environment 89, 95–96 (March 2010)
(footnotes omitted)

Interpreting human rights by reference to other legal instruments and principles is increasingly common. The European Court in 2008 described its methodology in detail and provided a useful framework for future cases. *Demir and Baykara v. Turkey* [[GC] (App no 34503/97) 12 November 2008], a case concerning trade union freedoms, is the fullest exposition to date of the Court's views on the relevance of other legal instruments and general principles in instances where the European Convention is silent or lacking precision. The Turkish Government argued against reliance on international instruments other than the Convention, on the ground that such reliance would risk wrongly creating, by way of interpretation, new obligation not contained in the Convention. In particular, the Government contended that an international treaty to which the party concerned had not acceded could not be relied upon against it by reference to VCLT [Vienna Convention on the Law of Treaties] Article 31(3)(c). The court disagreed.

The Court began with a summary of the principal VCLT rules of interpretation, which it deemed mandatory to determine the meaning of the terms and phrases used in the Convention. Thus 'The Court is required to ascertain the ordinary meaning to be given to the words in their context and in the light of the object and purpose of the provisions from which they are drawn'. VCLT Article 32 allows recourse to supplementary means of interpretation, either to confirm a meaning or to establish the meaning where it would otherwise be ambiguous, obscure or manifestly absurd or unreasonable.

The Court referenced VCLT Article 31(3)(c) in particular, in adding that the Court 'has never considered the provisions of the Convention as the sole framework of reference for the interpretation of the rights and freedoms enshrined therein. On the contrary, it must also take into account any relevant rules and principles of international law applicable in relations between Contracting Parties'.

The Court also cited its earlier jurisprudence on the Convention as a 'living instrument', which 'must be interpreted in the light of present-day conditions', taking into account 'evolving norms of national and international law in its interpretation of Convention provisions'.

The remainder of the Court's analysis pointed to the variety of sources that are relevant to this general approach, first looking at other international human rights treaties that are applicable in the particular sphere, and then to 'general principles of law recognized by civilized nations' as mentioned in Article 38 sec. 1(c) of the Statute of the International Court of Justice. According to the European Court, general principles of law may be identified in texts of universal and regional scope (not only human rights treaties) and in the jurisprudence of international and domestic courts that apply these instruments. In addition, the Court may use 'intrinsically non-binding instruments of Council of Europe organs, in particular recommendation and resolutions of the Committee of Ministers and the parliamentary Assembly'. The Court may further 'support its reasoning' by reference to norms emanating from other Council of Europe organs, whether supervisory mechanisms or expert bodies.

> In sum, the European Court considers the object and purpose of the Convention provisions, but it also takes into account the international law background to the legal question before it. Being made up of a set of rules and principles that are accepted by the vast majority of States, the common international or domestic law standards of European States reflect a reality that the Court cannot disregard when it is called upon to clarify the scope of a Convention provision that more conventional means of interpretation have not enabled it to establish with a sufficient degree of certainty. [*Id.,* para. 80]

TASKIN ET AL. V. TURKEY

App. No. 46117/99 Eur. Ct. H.R.
2004-X Reports of Judgments and Decisions (Nov. 10)—ch. 6
available at
http://hudoc.echr.coe.int/eng?i=001-67401

[In holding that Turkey had violated article 8 (right to privacy and family life) of the European Convention on Human Rights with respect to allowing the operation of a gold mine, the court relied on "the danger of the use of sodium cyanide for the local ecosystem, and human health and safety" (para. 121), and identified as "relevant international texts" several instruments, as follows.]

98. In June 1992 the United Nations Conference on Environment and Development, meeting in Rio de Janeiro (Brazil), adopted a Declaration ("the Rio Declaration on Environment and Development", A/CONF.151/26

(Vol. 1)) intended to advance the concept of States' rights and responsibilities with regard to the environment. "Principle 10" of this Declaration provides:

> "Environmental issues are best handled with the participation of all concerned citizens, at the relevant level. At the national level, each individual shall have appropriate access to information concerning the environment that is held by public authorities, including information on hazardous materials and activities in their communities, and the opportunity to participate in decision-making processes. States shall facilitate and encourage public awareness and participation by making information widely available. Effective access to judicial and administrative proceedings, including redress and remedy, shall be provided."

99. The Aarhus Convention ("Convention on Access to Information, Public Participation in Decision-making and Access to Justice in Environmental Matters", ECE/CEP/43) was adopted on 25 June 1998 by the United Nations Economic Commission for Europe in application of Principle 10 of the Rio Declaration, and came into force on 30 October 2001. To date, thirty countries have ratified it. Turkey has not signed the Aarhus Convention and has not acceded to it.

The Aarhus Convention may be broken down into the following areas:

— Developing public access to information held by the public authorities, in particular by providing for transparent and accessible dissemination of basic information.

— Promoting public participation in decision-making concerning issues with an environmental impact. In particular, provision is made for encouraging public participation from the beginning of the procedure for a proposed development, "when all options are open and effective public participation can take place". Due account is to be taken of the outcome of the public participation in reaching the final decision, which must also be made public.

— Extending conditions for access to the courts in connection with environmental legislation and access to information.

100. On 27 June 2003 the Parliamentary Assembly of the Council of Europe adopted Recommendation 1614 (2003) on environment and human rights. The relevant part of this recommendation states:

> "9. The Assembly recommends that the Governments of member States:
>
> i. ensure appropriate protection of the life, health, family and private life, physical integrity and private property of persons in accordance with Articles 2, 3 and 8 of the

European Convention on Human Rights and by Article 1 of its Additional Protocol, by also taking particular account of the need for environmental protection;

ii.   recognise a human right to a healthy, viable and decent environment which includes the objective obligation for States to protect the environment, in national laws, preferably at constitutional level;

iii. safeguard the individual procedural rights to access to information, public participation in decision making and access to justice in environmental matters set out in the Aarhus Convention; . . . ."

NOTES AND QUESTIONS

1.   *Are they relevant?* Why did the Court in *Taskin* refer to the Aarhus Convention and Recommendation 1614? Why did it mention that Turkey has neither signed nor acceded to the Aarhus Convention?

2.   *But what to do?* If you were a judge hearing an environment-and-human rights claim, how would you determine whether a particular environmental harm violated a human right? How would you resolve any scientific or other factual uncertainties? What specific standard(s) would you apply to judge the behavior alleged to have resulted in a human rights violation?

ENVIRONMENTAL PROTECTION AND RULE OF LAW

Daniel Barstow Magraw
44 Envtl. Pol'y & Law 201, 205–207 (2014) (footnotes omitted).

To answer [the question of exactly how much environmental harm is allowed before a human right is violated], human rights tribunals tend to look to the domestic standards of the State accused of violating human rights: "the [European Court of Human Rights] has specifically emphasised the need for national authorities to respect national law and policy on environmental issues where domestic decisions have been taken in contempt of such laws and policies". As a practical matter, human rights tribunals are assisted greatly in that inquiry by the requirement that claimants must exhaust local remedies before resorting to an international tribunal; thus there is often a record that details the relevant domestic laws and their enforcement vi-s-vis the case at hand.

This approach contains an important and obvious rule-of-law element and maintains a focus on the standards in the respondent State (thus avoiding the prospect of an international tribunal imposing external standards on the State); but at the same time it presents an obvious difficulty. Reliance on domestic legal standards is subject to changes in those standards by the respondent State. Human rights tribunals have held that there are limits to a State's ability to change behaviour in a way that affects the State's liability or accountability for what would otherwise be a human rights violation, so some changes may not be legally permissible. . . .

If the change is made in accordance with all relevant domestic requirements (procedural and substantive), it may well be that the claimant loses in the end unless the tribunal looks to another source, *i.e.*, an international source. A case that was almost in point is *Zander v. Sweden*, in which a municipal decision increased the permitted level of cyanide in drinking water, but the claimant was unable to obtain judicial review of the change under Swedish law. The European Court of Human Rights held that the claimant's right of access to justice had been denied and thus did not reach the question of whether the new standard violated the claimant's rights.

. . .

Human rights tribunals do not limit themselves to examining domestic environmental law and policy, however, but also look to international standards binding on the respondent State if they exist and sometimes to international standards even if they are not binding on the respondent State. If the standard is legally binding on the respondent State, no problem would be raised in terms of rule of law—the State would be held to behave according to a standard that it is legally bound to observe. However, holding a State to a standard that it is not otherwise legally bound to observe raises significant issues.

An example of tribunals looking to international instruments that are not binding on the defendant State is *Oneryildiz v. Turkey*, where the European Court looked to the Convention on Civil Liability for Damage Resulting From Activities Dangerous to the Environment and the Convention on the Protection of the Environment Through Criminal Law even though the respondent State, Turkey, and most EU Member States had neither signed nor ratified either convention. Similarly, in *Taskin and Others v. Turkey*, the Court relied on its earlier environment-related jurisprudence based on the Aarhus Convention, despite the fact that Turkey was not a Party to that Convention. In *Tatar v. Romania*, in a chamber judgment delivered 27 January 2009, the European Court, in holding that Romania had violated human rights in connection with an ecological disaster at a gold mine that released high levels of sodium cyanide and heavy metals, relied on best practices of the mining industry, the Rio Declaration on Environment and Development, the Stockholm Declaration on the Human Environment, and the International Court of Justice's decision in the *Gabčíkovo-Nagymaros Project (Hungary/Slovakia)* case.

Even putting aside the fact that some of these international instruments do not contain precise standards but rather general principles or statements, the application of a "standard" to a State that is not legally bound by it raises important questions. . . . From a policy perspective, does this use of international standards broaden their use and thus make them specifically, and the international legal system generally, more effective? And does the imposition of a non-legally binding standard on a respondent State have implications for the likelihood of compliance with the tribunal's holding or for the credibility of the human rights system as a whole? From a legal perspective, how does this square with the need for consent in international law? One could argue that utilising non-binding norms is impermissible because the respondent State has not consented to be bound by them. The better argument according to this author is that the respondent State is bound by international human rights law and thus has either explicitly or implicitly consented to it, and that giving effect to human rights law requires in this case resort to non-binding standards in order to provide specific content to the human rights norm.

From a rule of law perspective, one could argue that this is not application of "law" because the standard is not legally binding on the respondent State. On the other hand, because the respondent State is bound by international human rights norms, the better argument is that this is a rule of (human rights) law and that the use of a standard not binding on the respondent State is necessary to provide specific substance to the relevant human rights norm—which is binding on the respondent State—in order to avoid that norm's become meaningless and unenforceable. According to this reasoning, human rights tribunals should look to non-binding standards only when there is nowhere else to look.

In fact, there are relatively few international environmental measurable performance standards that are legally binding and provide specific, measurable standards of behaviour. Many legally binding international environmental norms are general in nature. Others are phrased in a form that allows for considerable leeway to the States through the use of so-called "wiggle words" such as "shall, in accordance with its particular conditions and capabilities" or "shall endeavour, in so far as possible, and as appropriate for each country". Is it possible to apply such norms rigorously? Another impediment to using binding international environmental standards arises when a measurable international environmental standard is provided in a legally binding instrument, but the respondent State is not a Party to that instrument. A further impediment is that many measurable international environmental standards are intentionally non-legally binding such as those of the World Health Organization, Food and Agriculture Organization, and Codex Alimentarius. Ultimately, a human rights tribunal may have to resort to non-binding international environmental standards or the tribunal will be powerless and the claimant will lose his or her case regardless of the merits.

The resort to un-specified international standards, including non-binding ones, is not unique to human rights tribunals, however. Such resort is often seen in non-human rights fields. . . .

There is no . . . explicit agreement in any of the international human rights . . . agreements [to the approach described above], but there is consent—explicit or implicit—to international human rights law and thus it should be presumed there is consent to the effective application of human rights law. It is thus acceptable for human rights tribunals to apply non-binding international standards in order to provide substantive content to a human rights norm in deciding a claim that environmental harm violates that norm.

NOTES AND QUESTIONS

1. *Did I mean that?* Is this line of reasoning convincing? Is it appropriate to hold—on human rights grounds—a State to an international environmental standard it has agreed to in a treaty that does not specify an enforcement mechanism involving human rights (which is typically the case with environmental treaties)?

2. *Really?* Is it ever permissible to hold States to a standard they have not agreed to, other than one that has achieved the status of customary international law? Is that what is happening in these cases?

3. *But what else to do?* Are there other approaches that human rights tribunals could take to find standards? Why don't tribunals just set the standards by themselves on a case-by-case basis?

4. *Margin of Appreciation and Second-guessing?* The court in *Taskin* stated: "After weighing the competing interests in the present case against each other, the [national court] based its decision on the applicants' effective enjoyment of the right to life and the right to a healthy environment and concluded that the permit did not serve the public interest. . . . In view of that conclusion, no other examination of the material aspect of the case with regard to the margin of appreciation generally allowed to the national authorities in this area is necessary." The "margin of appreciation" is a doctrine (used, for example, in Council of Europe documents and practice) according to which international tribunals give deference to decisions by competent national authorities, which serves to preserve some authority in national authorities and to prevent some second guessing.

5. *Does it matter?* Would it matter if human rights tribunals were to declare themselves unable to proceed beyond fact finding in human rights-and-environment cases?

C. THE ENVIRONMENT AND TRADITIONAL HUMAN RIGHTS AND DUTIES

1. SUBSTANTIVE RIGHTS

Human rights are often described as being either substantive or procedural. This distinction is not entirely satisfying, at least partly because so-called procedural rights typically are based on substantive policy or legal bases. Moreover, the so-called impartiality rights—equal protection and due process—which have proven critical to environmental protection, do not fit neatly in either category. Nevertheless, we adopt that categorization because it assists in understanding the types of rights that are relevant. As John Knox wrote in his first report to the Human Rights Council regarding the effort to relate human rights and environment:

> This effort, as well as similar efforts in other forums, has identified two sets of rights closely related to the environment: (a) rights whose enjoyment is particularly vulnerable to environmental degradation; and (b) rights whose exercise supports better environmental policymaking. At the risk of oversimplification, many of the rights in the first category—that is, those at risk from environmental harm—are often characterized as *substantive* rights, while many of the rights in the second category—those whose implementation supports stronger environmental policies—are often considered *procedural* rights. Examples of the former are rights to life, health and property; examples of the latter are rights to freedom of expression and association, to information, to participation in decision-making and to effective remedies. . . .

NOTES AND QUESTIONS

In reading the following materials, consider the following questions.

1.   In what ways might human rights be related to environmental harm generally and to climate change specifically? Do efforts to combat environmental harm, including climate change, differ in human rights terms from other governmental activities? Do the impacts of climate change (or other environmental harm) interfere with individuals' ability to enjoy their human rights?

2.   What substantive human rights might be violated in the Inuit case study?

3.   Have the human rights of individuals dispossessed of their land by climate change been violated?

4.   If any rights are violated, who is responsible for that violation given that literally all States contribute to causing climate change?

5. Recalling that human rights analyses are fact-specific, what additional information would you need to determine whether human rights are being violated by environmental harm, including with respect to the Inuit case study? Who is likely to have such information? How would you obtain it?

6. How would you press such a human rights claim? Which institutions might be open to hearing such a claim? Who could bring such a claim?

7. How should a human rights tribunal deal with cases involving competing rights regarding the environment? Suppose, for example, a State argues that an increase in permissible cyanide levels was necessary in order to enable the population to have access to drinking water. Presumably a tribunal should approach this as it does other cases involving competing rights, including allowing an appropriate margin of appreciation.

REPORT OF THE INDEPENDENT EXPERT ON THE ISSUE OF HUMAN RIGHTS OBLIGATIONS RELATING TO THE ENJOYMENT OF A SAFE, CLEAN, HEALTHY AND SUSTAINABLE ENVIRONMENT

John H. Knox
Preliminary report, A/HRC/22/43 (24 December 2012) (footnotes omitted)

10. With the rise of a stronger environmental consciousness [over the past few decades] came calls for formal recognition of the importance of environmental protection to human well-being. These calls often sought expression in the language of human rights. This is unsurprising, even inevitable. Human rights are grounded in respect for fundamental human attributes such as dignity, equality and liberty. The realization of these attributes depends on an environment that allows them to flourish. At the same time, effective environmental protection often depends on the exercise of human rights that are vital to informed, transparent and responsive policymaking. Human rights and environmental protection are inherently interdependent.

11. The recognition of the close relationship between human rights and the environment has principally taken two forms: (a) adoption of an explicit new right to an environment characterized in terms such as healthy, safe, satisfactory or sustainable; and (b) heightened attention to the relationship to the environment of already recognized rights, such as rights to life and health.

. . .

16. . . . The Commission and Council, as well as other United Nations human rights bodies and mechanisms, have continued to study the interaction of human rights and the environment, but their attention has been directed primarily at the relationship of the environment with already recognized human rights. In other words, they have concentrated not on proclaiming a new right to a healthy environment, but rather on

what might be called "greening" human rights—that is, examining and highlighting the relationship of existing human rights to the environment.

. . .

18. The recognition that environmental harm can interfere with the full enjoyment of human rights is not new; it dates from the very beginning of the modern environmental movement. In the 1968 resolution deciding to convene the Stockholm Conference, the General Assembly, in the preamble of its resolution 2398 (XXIII), noted its concern about the effects of "the continuing and accelerating impairment of the quality of the human environment . . . on the condition of man, his physical, mental and social well-being, his dignity and his enjoyment of basic human rights, in developing as well as developed countries". And the first paragraph of the proclamation of the 1972 Stockholm Declaration states that "both aspects of man's environment, the natural and the man-made, are essential to his well-being and to the enjoyment of basic human rights—even the right to life itself" (para. 1).

19. In a real sense, all human rights are vulnerable to environmental degradation, in that the full enjoyment of all human rights depends on a supportive environment. However, some human rights are more susceptible than others to certain types of environmental harm. In recent years, in addition to reaffirming the general point that "environmental damage can have negative implications, both direct and indirect, for the effective enjoyment of human rights" (res. 16/11, preamble), the Human Rights Council has identified environmental threats to particular rights. To give three examples, it has: affirmed that illicit traffic in, and improper management and disposal of, hazardous substances and wastes constitute a serious threat to a range of rights, including the rights to life and health; underlined that climate change has a wide range of implications for the effective enjoyment of human rights, including the rights to life, health, food, water, housing and self-determination; and recognized that "environmental degradation, desertification and global climate change are exacerbating destitution and desperation, causing a negative impact on the realization of the right to food, in particular in developing countries".

20. . . . [A]t the request of the Council, the Office of the High Commissioner for Human Rights (OHCHR) conducted a study in 2008–2009 on the effects of climate change on the enjoyment of human rights (A/HRC/10/61). The study concluded that climate change will pose direct and indirect threats to many rights, including: the rights to life and food, as a result of malnutrition and extreme weather events; the right to water, as a result of melting glaciers and reductions in snow cover; and the right to the highest attainable standard of health, as a result of malnutrition, extreme weather, and an increasing incidence of malaria

and other diseases that thrive in warmer weather. The study noted that rising sea levels caused by global warming threaten the very existence of small island States, which has "implications for the right to self-determination, as well as for the full range of rights for which individuals depend on the State for their protection" (para. 41). In December 2009, before the Copenhagen meeting of the parties to the United Nations Framework Convention on Climate Change, the special procedure mandate holders issued a joint statement drawing attention to the dangers that climate change presents to the enjoyment of human rights.

21. Special procedures have further analysed the effects of environmental degradation on human rights. One mandate, in particular, was created to examine the human rights effects of a specific environmental problem: the illicit disposal of hazardous substances and waste in developing countries. Since 1995, the special rapporteurs appointed to carry out this mandate have identified many human rights that may be infringed by such toxic dumping, . . .

22. Other special procedures have drawn the connections between environmental harm and impairment of the rights within their mandates. The following are a few of many possible examples. The former Special Rapporteur on adequate housing as a component of the right to an adequate standard of living, and on the right to non-discrimination in this context informed the 2002 World Summit on Sustainable Development that "the realization of the right to adequate housing loses its meaning unless processes are put into place to ensure that people and communities can live in an environment that is free from pollution of air, water and the food chain" and the current Special Rapporteur has issued a detailed report on the effects of climate change on the right (A/64/255). The Special Rapporteur on the human right to safe drinking water and sanitation has carefully examined the effects of climate change on those rights. The Special Rapporteur on the right of everyone to the enjoyment of the highest attainable standard of physical and mental health has underscored that the right extends to the underlying determinants of health, such as safe water, adequate sanitation, and healthy environmental conditions generally (A/62/214, para. 104). The Special Rapporteur on the right to food has emphasized that agricultural productivity depends on the services rendered by ecosystems (A/HRC/13/33/Add.2, para. 21) and his most recent report focuses on the impact of the destruction of the world's fisheries on the right to food (A/67/268).

23. Some global human rights treaties explicitly refer to environmental threats to human rights, particularly the right to health. The Convention on the Rights of the Child states that environmental pollution poses "dangers and risks" to nutritious foods and clean drinking-water, which Parties are required to take appropriate measures

to provide in the course of pursuing full implementation of the right of the child to the highest attainable standard of health (art. 24, para. 2(c)). Similarly, article 12, paragraph 2(b) of the International Covenant on Economic, Social and Cultural Rights provides that the steps Parties must take to achieve the full realization of the right to health "shall include those necessary for . . . the improvement of all aspects of environmental and industrial hygiene". The Committee on Economic, Social and Cultural Rights has interpreted this phrase to comprise, inter alia, "the requirement to ensure an adequate supply of safe and potable water and basic sanitation; [and] the prevention and reduction of the population's exposure to harmful substances such as radiation and harmful chemicals or other detrimental environmental conditions that directly or indirectly impact upon human health".

24. Finally, the regional human rights tribunals have contributed a great deal of jurisprudence to the relationship of human rights and the environment. In a series of carefully reasoned decisions, the African Commission on Human and Peoples" Rights, the European Court of Human Rights, and the Inter-American Commission and Court of Human Rights have found that environmental harm can give rise to violations of rights to life, health, property and privacy, among others.

. . .

34. As this brief description of the evolution of environmental rights makes clear, some aspects of the relationship between human rights and the environment are now firmly established. To highlight two: first, as many human rights bodies at the global, regional and national levels have recognized, environmental degradation can and does adversely affect the enjoyment of a broad range of human rights, including rights to life, health, food and water. Second, the exercise of certain rights can and does benefit environmental policymaking, resulting in better environmental protection and, as a consequence, greater protection of the human rights that may be threatened by environmental degradation. These protective rights include rights of free expression and association, rights of information and participation, and rights to remedy. They have been affirmed in a wide range of international instruments, including environmental as well as human rights agreements.

35. The *obligations* that human rights law imposes regarding environmental protection are less clearly understood. . . .

---

a. Rights to Life and Health

As indicated in Independent Expert (now Special Rapporteur) John Knox's report, above, there are many connections between environmental risks and the human rights to life and health. Two examples of cases follow.

In E.H.P. v. Canada, residents alleged that 200,000 tons of radioactive waste remaining in Port Hope posed serious health risks in violation of Article 6(1) of the International Covenant on Civil and Political Human Rights. The International Human Rights Committee abstained from determining the merits of the case due to jurisdictional defects, but it observed that the case "raised serious issues with regard to the obligation of States parties to protect human life." E.H.P. v. Canada, No. 67/1980 at 27, 2 Selected Decisions of the Hum. Rts. Comm. Under the Optional Protocol 20 (1990).

In 1997, the Inter-American Commission on Human Rights issued a study on Ecuadorian conditions that made the link between pollution and human rights. In that study, the Commission concluded that "[c]onditions of severe environmental pollution, which may cause serious physical illness, impairment and suffering on the part of the local populace, are inconsistent with the right to be respected as a human being." Inter-American Comm'n on Human Rights, Report on the Situation of Human Rights in Ecuador, OEA/Ser.L/V/II.96, doc.10, rev.1 (1997), at 92–93. The first case to test this approach was the San Mateo case, described below.

On February 28, 2003 the Inter-American Commission on Human Rights received a petition from the community of San Mateo, Peru, claiming that the State of Peru violated the "fundamental individual and collective rights of the members of the Community of San Mateo de Huanchor, because of the effects being suffered by the members of the community from the environmental pollution caused by a field of toxic waste sludge. . . ." The State of Peru alleged that the petition was inadmissible due to petitioners' not having exhausted all remedies under domestic law. The Commission found the petition to be admissible according to articles 46 and 47 of the American Convention. An excerpt from the case follows.

COMMUNITY OF SAN MATEO DE HUANCHOR AND ITS MEMBERS V. PERU

Case 504/03, Inter-Am, Comm'n H.R., Report No. 69/04, OEA/Ser.L/V/II.122, doc. 5 rev.
¶ 66 (2004), http://cidh.org/annualrep/2004eng/Peru.504.03eng.htm

The Commission considers that the events that were denounced with regard to the effects of the environmental pollution of the Mayoc sludge, which has created a public health crisis in the population of San Mateo de Huanchor, if proven, could be characterized as a violation of the right to personal security, right to property, rights of the child, right to fair trial and judicial protection and the progressive development of economic, social, and cultural rights enshrined in Articles 4, 5, 8, 17, 19, 21, 25, and

26 of the American Convention, related to Articles 1(1) and 2 of the same instrument. (para. 66).

As a result of the Commission's admitting the petition on precautionary measures, the State of Peru was required to contain and/or remove the toxic waste sludge. In September 2005, the State of Peru initiated the removal of the toxic waste; such efforts concluded in January 2006.

Thereafter, in June 2006, the community of San Mateo submitted a brief on the merits to the Commission requesting that the State of Peru be held responsible for violating the human rights of the community. Their brief included the following arguments:

> First of all, the State did not comply with several of the precautionary measure requested by the IACHR [the Commission]—they did not fully implement a program for specialized medical care for the San Mateo residents affected by the toxic mine tailings, and they did not carry out remediation of the environment, soil, subsoil, water, or community members' homes that had been contaminated by the toxic mine tailings. These measures should be carried out, as requested by the IACHR. Also, special attention should be given to the children that were affected by the contamination since heavy metal contamination has been shown to have long and sometimes irreversible impacts on health, including to children's intellectual development. Finally, the State has not compensated the victims in San Mateo for the physical harms and material losses, which include lost crops, animals, and time at work, and this compensation should be paid to the victims.

> The Commission was also informed that the mine workers in San Mateo were threatening to harm and kill community leaders who supported the petition on precautionary measures to the Commission. A request was submitted to the Commission to require that the State of Peru adopt measures to "guarantee the life and physical integrity of Ms. Perez" (a community leader). The State of Peru thereafter has provided police protection.

A final decision in the case is pending decision as of August 2015.

b.   Right to Water

Many States and human rights bodies now recognize that there is a human right to water, though the exact parameters of that right are unsettled as of January 2015. This is discussed in Chapter 12—Fresh Water.

c. Right to Food

The right to food was also found to exist within the right to an adequate standard of living (as was the right to housing). This is discussed further in Chapter 14—Food and Agriculture.

d. Right to Home and Family Life and Privacy

Environmental threats may also violate other human rights. Indeed, Courts have been creative in interpreting rights that do not expressly refer to the environment to encompass environmental threats and harm. This is presumably due in part to the fact that the modern environmental movement and its attendant laws and regulations did not exist when the relevant instruments were drafted. Courts have not defined the scope of all of these rights including their related duties and limits. However, it is clear that some of them can be violated by environmental harm.

In one of the earliest human-rights-and-environment cases, the European Court of Human Rights held that Spain's failure to regulate a waste treatment plant resulting in the plaintiff and her family being exposed to noxious gases (e.g., hydrogen sulfide) and being forced to leave their house for health reasons violated Article 8 of the European Convention on Human Rights, López Ostra v. Spain, Eur. Ct. H.R. (9 Dec. 1994). Article 8 reads:

1. Everyone has the right to respect for his private and family life, his home and his correspondence.

2. There shall be no interference by a public authority with the exercise of this right except such as is in accordance with the law and is necessary in a democratic society in the interests of national security, public safety or the economic well-being of the country, for the prevention of disorder or crime, for the protection of health or morals, or for the protection of the rights and freedoms of others.

This case is discussed further in the mini case study, below.

In Powell and Rayner, cited by the Court in López Ostra v. Spain, the Court recognized that noise pollution can prevent the realization of this right when it affects the quality of one's family and home life. The court left open the possibility that a State may have a duty under certain circumstances to prevent harm from activities by infringing on privacy, yet it determined that these interests must be balanced against broader community interests. Powell and Rayner Case, 172 Eur. Ct. H.R. (ser. A) at 18–19 (1990).

2. PROCEDURAL RIGHTS

REPORT OF THE INDEPENDENT EXPERT ON THE ISSUE OF HUMAN RIGHTS OBLIGATIONS RELATING TO THE ENJOYMENT OF A SAFE, CLEAN, HEALTHY AND SUSTAINABLE ENVIRONMENT

John H. Knox
Preliminary report, A/HRC/22/43 (24 December 2012) (footnotes omitted)

25. The human rights whose enjoyment can be affected by environmental harm are not the only rights directly relevant to the environment. Another approach to clarifying the relationship of already recognized rights with the environment is to identify rights whose implementation is vital to environmental policymaking. In general, these are rights whose free exercise makes policies more transparent, better informed and more responsive. They include rights to freedom of expression and association, rights to receive information and participate in decision-making processes, and rights to legal remedies. When directed at environmental issues, the exercise of such rights results in policies that better reflect the concerns of those most concerned and, as a result, that better safeguard their rights to life and health, among others, from infringement through environmental harm.

26. Procedural rights are protected by many human rights instruments. For example, rights of freedom of expression, freedom of peaceful assembly and association, participation in government and effective remedies for violations of rights are recognized in the Universal Declaration (arts. 7, 8, 19, 20 and 21) and elaborated on in the International Covenant on Civil and Political Rights (arts. 2, 19, 21, 22 and 25), both of which also make clear that the rights are not subject to discrimination. Even though these instruments do not explicitly address environmental issues, they undoubtedly encompass the exercise of the rights for environmental ends.

. . .

29. The procedural rights that support environmental protection may be found in sources other than human rights instruments. One of the most often-cited sources is principle 10 of the 1992 Rio Declaration, which states:

> Environmental issues are best handled with participation of all concerned citizens, at the relevant level. At the national level, each individual shall have appropriate access to information concerning the environment that is held by public authorities, including information on hazardous materials and activities in their communities, and the opportunity to participate in decision-making processes. States shall facilitate and encourage

public awareness and participation by making information widely available. Effective access to judicial and administrative proceedings, including redress and remedy, shall be provided.

30. Principle 10 has been influential in the development of international and domestic environmental law and policy. The clearest example may be the Aarhus Convention, which sets out detailed obligations with respect to access to information, public participation and access to justice in environmental matters.

During his second year as Independent Expert on Human Rights and Environment, John Knox undertook an unprecedented survey—referred to as a "mapping"—of how human rights law applies to environmental issues. Together with other experts, including pro bono assistance, he surveyed human rights instruments, statements of human rights treaty bodies, UN General Assembly resolutions, Human Rights Council resolutions, decisions of regional human rights tribunals, national court decisions, statements by States in the context of the Human Rights Council's Universal Periodic Review, reports by Special Rapporteurs, and international environmental instruments. He also held five public consultations in different regions of the world. The results of Knox's research and consultations were included in 14 reports, each of which describes how a particular international body or process has applied human rights to environmental protection. These conclusions are summarized in his second report to the Human Rights Council. The reports can be found at: http://www.ohchr.org/EN/NewsEvents/Pages/DisplayNews.aspx?NewsID=15274 & LangID=E#sthash.gETwvCRx.dpuf. Some of the results of the survey are described below.

REPORT OF THE INDEPENDENT EXPERT ON THE ISSUE OF HUMAN RIGHTS OBLIGATIONS RELATING TO THE ENJOYMENT OF A SAFE, CLEAN, HEALTHY AND SUSTAINABLE ENVIRONMENT, MAPPING REPORT

John H. Knox
A/HRC/25/53 (30 December 2013) (footnotes omitted)

29. One of the most striking results of the mapping exercise is the agreement among the sources reviewed that human rights law imposes certain procedural obligations on States in relation to environmental protection. They include duties (a) to assess environmental impacts and make environmental information public; (b) to facilitate public participation in environmental decision-making, including by protecting the rights of expression and association; and (c) to provide access to remedies for harm. These obligations have bases in civil and political rights, but they have been clarified and extended in the environmental

context on the basis of the entire range of human rights at risk from environmental harm.

1. Duties to assess environmental impacts and make information public

30. The Universal Declaration of Human Rights (art. 19) and the International Covenant on Civil and Political Rights (art. 19) state that the right to freedom of expression includes the freedom "to seek, receive and impart information". The right to information is also critical to the exercise of other rights, including rights of participation. In the words of the then Special Rapporteur on the adverse effects of the illicit movement and dumping of toxic and dangerous products and wastes on the enjoyment of human rights, the rights to information and participation are "both rights in themselves and essential tools for the exercise of other rights, such as the right to life, the right to the highest attainable standard of health, the right to adequate housing and others" (A/HRC/7/21, p. 2).

31. Human rights bodies have repeatedly stated that in order to protect human rights from infringement through environmental harm, States should provide access to environmental information and provide for the assessment of environmental impacts that may interfere with the enjoyment of human rights.

32. For example, in its general comment No. 15 (2002) on the right to water, the Committee on Economic, Social and Cultural Rights stated that individuals should be given full and equal access to information concerning water and the environment (para. 48), and in its responses to country reports, it has urged States to assess the impacts of actions that may have adverse environmental effects on the right to health and other rights within its purview. Similarly, the Special Rapporteur on the situation of human rights defenders has stated that information relating to large-scale development projects should be publicly available and accessible (A/68/262, para. 62), and the Special Rapporteur on the human right to safe drinking water and sanitation has stated that States need to conduct impact assessments "in line with human rights standards" when they plan projects that may have an impact on water quality (A/68/264, para. 73).

33. Regional bodies have also concluded that States must provide environmental information and provide for assessments of environmental impacts on human rights. For example, on the basis of the right to respect for private and family life as set out in the European Convention on Human Rights (art. 8), the European Court has stated:

> Where a State must determine complex issues of environmental and economic policy, the decision-making process must firstly involve appropriate investigations and studies in order to allow

them to predict and evaluate in advance the effects of those activities which might damage the environment and infringe individuals' rights and to enable them to strike a fair balance between the various conflicting interests at stake. The importance of public access to the conclusions of such studies and to information which would enable members of the public to assess the danger to which they are exposed is beyond question.

34. International instruments illustrate the importance of providing environmental information to the public. Principle 10 of the Rio Declaration states: "At the national level, each individual shall have appropriate access to information concerning the environment that is held by public authorities, including information on hazardous materials and activities in their communities ... States shall facilitate and encourage public awareness and participation by making information widely available." Many environmental treaties, including the Rotterdam Convention on the Prior Informed Consent Procedure for Certain Hazardous Chemicals and Pesticides in International Trade (art. 15), the Stockholm Convention on Persistent Organic Pollutants (art. 10), and the United Nations Framework Convention on Climate Change (art. 6(a)), require environmental information to be provided to the public. The Aarhus Convention includes particularly detailed obligations. Illustrating the link between its obligations and those of human rights law, many Aarhus parties have discussed their compliance with that agreement in their reports under the universal periodic review process.

35. Most States have adopted environmental impact assessment laws, in accordance with principle 17 of the Rio Declaration, which states that "environmental impact assessment, as a national instrument, shall be undertaken for proposed activities that are likely to have a significant adverse impact on the environment and are subject to a decision of a competent national authority." The World Bank requires environmental assessment of all Bank-financed projects to "ensure that they are environmentally sound and sustainable".

2. Duties to facilitate public participation in environmental decision-making

36. The baseline rights of everyone to take part in the government of their country and in the conduct of public affairs are recognized in the Universal Declaration of Human Rights (art. 21) and the International Covenant on Civil and Political Rights (art. 25), respectively. Again, human rights bodies have built on this baseline in the environmental context, elaborating a duty to facilitate public participation in environmental decision-making in order to safeguard a wide spectrum of rights from environmental harm.

37. The Special Rapporteur on hazardous substances and wastes and the Special Rapporteur on the situation of human rights defenders

have stated that governments must facilitate the right to participation in environmental decision-making (see A/HRC/7/21 and A/68/262). The Committee on Economic, Social and Cultural Rights has encouraged States to consult with stakeholders in the course of environmental impact assessments, and has underlined that before any action is taken that interferes with the right to water, the relevant authorities must provide an opportunity for "genuine consultation with those affected" (general comment No. 15 (2002), para. 56). Regional human rights tribunals agree that individuals should have meaningful opportunities to participate in decisions concerning their environment.

38. The need for public participation is reflected in many international environmental instruments. Principle 10 of the Rio Declaration states: "Environmental issues are best handled with participation of all concerned citizens, at the relevant level . . . Each individual shall have . . . the opportunity to participate in decision-making processes." In 2012, in *The Future We Want*, the outcome document of the United Nations Conference on Sustainable Development (Rio+20 Conference), States recognized that "opportunities for people to influence their lives and future, participate in decision-making and voice their concerns are fundamental for sustainable development" (A/CONF.216/16, para. 13). Environmental treaties that provide for public participation include the Stockholm Convention on Persistent Organic Pollutants (art. 10), the Convention on Biological Diversity (art. 14(1)), the United Nations Convention to Combat Desertification (arts. 3 and 5), and the United Nations Framework Convention on Climate Change (art. 6(a)). The Aarhus Convention has particularly detailed requirements (arts. 6–8).

39. The rights of freedom of expression and association are of special importance in relation to public participation in environmental decision-making. The Special Rapporteur on the situation of human rights defenders has said that those working on land rights and natural resources are the second-largest group of defenders at risk of being killed (A/HRC/4/37), and that their situation appears to have worsened since 2007 (A/68/262, para. 18). Her last report described the extraordinary risks, including threats, harassment, and physical violence, faced by those defending the rights of local communities when they oppose projects that have a direct impact on natural resources, the land or the environment (A/68/262, para. 15).

40. States have obligations not only to refrain from violating the rights of free expression and association directly, but also to protect the life, liberty and security of individuals exercising those rights. There can be no doubt that these obligations apply to those exercising their rights in connection with environmental concerns. The Special Rapporteur on the situation of human rights defenders has underlined these obligations in

that context (A/68/262, paras. 16 and 30), as has the Special Rapporteur on the rights of indigenous peoples (A/HRC/24/41, para. 21), the Committee on Economic, Social and Cultural Rights, the Inter-American Court of Human Rights, and the Commission on Human Rights, which called upon States "to take all necessary measures to protect the legitimate exercise of everyone's human rights when promoting environmental protection and sustainable development" (resolution 2003/71).

3.   Duty to provide access to legal remedies

41. From the Universal Declaration of Human Rights onward, human rights agreements have established the principle that States should provide for an "effective remedy" for violations of their protected rights. Human rights bodies have applied that principle to human rights infringed by environmental harm. For example, the Committee on Economic, Social and Cultural Rights has urged States to provide for "adequate compensation and/or alternative accommodation and land for cultivation" to indigenous communities and local farmers whose land is flooded by large infrastructure projects, and "just compensation [to] and resettlement" of indigenous peoples displaced by forestation. The Special Rapporteur on the situation of human rights defenders has stated that States must implement mechanisms that allow defenders to communicate their grievances, claim responsibilities, and obtain effective redress for violations, without fear of intimidation (A/68/262, paras. 70–73). Other special rapporteurs, including those for housing, education, and hazardous substances and wastes, have also emphasized the importance of access to remedies within the scope of their mandates.

42. At the regional level, the European Court has stated that individuals must "be able to appeal to the courts against any decision, act or omission where they consider that their interests or their comments have not been given sufficient weight in the decision-making process." More generally, the Inter-American Commission on Human Rights and the Inter-American Court of Human Rights have stated that the American Convention on Human Rights requires States to provide access to judicial recourse for claims alleging the violation of their rights as a result of environmental harm. The Court of Justice of the Economic Community of West African States has stressed the need for the State to hold accountable actors who infringe human rights through oil pollution, and to ensure adequate reparation for victims.

43. International environmental instruments support an obligation to provide for effective remedies. Principle 10 of the Rio Declaration states: "Effective access to judicial and administrative proceedings, including redress and remedy, shall be provided." Many environmental treaties establish obligations for States to provide for remedies in specific areas. For instance, the United Nations Convention on the Law of the Sea

requires States to ensure that recourse is available within their legal systems to natural or juridical persons for prompt and adequate compensation or other relief for damage caused by pollution of the marine environment (art. 235). Some agreements establish detailed liability regimes; a leading example is the International Convention on Civil Liability for Oil Pollution Damage.

NOTES AND QUESTIONS

Environmental Impact Assessment. As indicated above in Chapter 4, the International Court of Justice held in the *Pulp Mills* case that general international law requires that an environmental impact assessment be conducted where an activity may cause transboundary harm. Why did the Court not cite to any human rights authorities for that proposition? How do the obligation in *Pulp Mills* and the human rights obligation to conduct an environmental impact assessment when environmental harm might impact human rights relate to one another?

3. A STATE'S OBLIGATION TO PROTECT HUMAN RIGHTS OUTSIDE ITS TERRITORY

It is clear that a State is obligated to respect, protect and fulfill human rights within its territory. Beyond a State's territory, it is less clear. Consider the following excerpt:

REPORT OF THE INDEPENDENT EXPERT ON THE ISSUE OF HUMAN RIGHTS OBLIGATIONS RELATING TO THE ENJOYMENT OF A SAFE, CLEAN, HEALTHY AND SUSTAINABLE ENVIRONMENT, MAPPING REPORT

John H. Knox
A/HRC/25/53 (30 December 2013) (footnotes omitted)

62. Many grave threats to the enjoyment of human rights are due to transboundary environmental harm, including problems of global scope such as ozone depletion and climate change. This raises the question of whether States have obligations to protect human rights against the extraterritorial environmental effects of actions taken within their territory.

63. There is no obvious reason why a State should not bear responsibility for actions that otherwise would violate its human rights obligations, merely because the harm was felt beyond its borders. Nevertheless, the application of human rights obligations to transboundary environmental harm is not always clear. One difficulty is that human rights instruments address jurisdiction in different ways. Some, such as the Universal Declaration of Human Rights and the African Charter, contain no explicit jurisdictional limitations, and the International Covenant on Economic, Social and Cultural Rights may

even provide an explicit basis for extraterritorial obligations (art. 2, para. 1). But other treaties, including the International Covenant on Civil and Political Rights, the Convention on the Rights of the Child, the European Convention on Human Rights and the American Convention on Human Rights, limit at least some of their protections to individuals subject to or within the jurisdiction of the State, leaving it unclear how far their protections extend beyond the State's territory. Another problem is that many human rights bodies have not addressed extraterritoriality in the context of environmental harm.

64. Nevertheless, most of the sources reviewed that have addressed the issue do indicate that States have obligations to protect human rights, particularly economic, social and cultural rights, from the extraterritorial environmental effects of actions taken within their territory. The Committee on Economic, Social and Cultural Rights has interpreted the International Covenant on Economic, Social and Cultural Rights as requiring its parties "to refrain from actions that interfere, directly or indirectly, with the enjoyment of the right to water in other countries" (general comment No. 15, para. 31), and has stated that parties should also take steps to prevent third parties within their jurisdiction, such as their own citizens and companies, from violating the rights to water and health in other countries (general comment No. 15, para. 33; and general comment No. 14, para. 39). Several special rapporteurs have adopted similar interpretations. In 2011, the Special Rapporteur on the right to food and the Special Rapporteur on extreme poverty and human rights joined with scholars and activists to adopt the Maastricht Principles on Extraterritorial Obligations of States in the area of Economic, Social and Cultural Rights. The Special Rapporteur on the human right to safe drinking water and sanitation recently cited those Principles as underscoring "the obligation of States to avoid causing harm extraterritorially" and affirming "the obligation of States to protect human rights extraterritorially, i.e., to take necessary measures to ensure that non-State actors do not nullify or impair the enjoyment of economic, social and cultural rights. This translates into an obligation to avoid contamination of watercourses in other jurisdictions and to regulate non-State actors accordingly" (A/68/264, para. 46).

65. Such interpretations are in accord with the fundamental obligation of States to carry out their treaty commitments in good faith, which requires them to avoid taking actions calculated to frustrate the object and purpose of the treaty. The International Court of Justice has read this principle of *pacta sunt servanda* as requiring the parties to a treaty to apply it "in a reasonable way and in such a manner that its purpose can be realized". This suggests that parties to a human rights treaty should not engage in conduct that makes it harder for other parties to fulfil their own obligations under the treaty.

66. Other sources, such as the Special Representative of the Secretary-General on business and human rights, have taken a more restrictive view of the scope of extraterritorial human rights obligations. The Special Representative also stated, however, that "there is increasing encouragement at the international level . . . for home States to take regulatory action to prevent abuse by their companies overseas" (A/HRC/8/5, para. 19), and urged States to do more to prevent corporations from abusing human rights abroad (A/HRC/14/27).

67. Although work remains to be done to clarify the content of extraterritorial human rights obligations pertaining to the environment, the lack of complete clarity should not obscure a basic point: States have an obligation of international cooperation with respect to human rights, which is contained not only in treaties such as the International Covenant on Economic, Social and Cultural Rights (art. 2, para. 1), but also in the Charter of the United Nations itself (arts. 55 and 56). This obligation is of particular relevance to global environmental threats to human rights, such as climate change (A/HRC/10/61, para. 99). As the Human Rights Council noted in its resolution 16/11, principle 7 of the Rio Declaration states that "States shall cooperate in a spirit of global partnership to conserve, protect and restore the health and integrity of the Earth's ecosystem."

68. Indeed, much of international environmental law reflects efforts by States to cooperate in the face of transboundary and global challenges. Further work to clarify extraterritorial obligations in respect of environmental harm to human rights can receive guidance from international environmental instruments, many of which include specific provisions designed to identify and protect the rights of those affected by such harm.

In an earlier report, the OHCHR had elaborated on the duty to cooperate in the context of climate change. Consider the following excerpt.

REPORT OF THE OFFICE OF THE UNITED NATIONS HIGH COMMISSIONER FOR HUMAN RIGHTS ON THE RELATIONSHIP BETWEEN CLIMATE CHANGE AND HUMAN RIGHTS

UN Doc. A/HRC/10/61 (15 January 2009) (footnotes omitted)

B. Obligations of international cooperation

84. Climate change can only be effectively addressed through cooperation of all members of the international community. Moreover, international cooperation is important because the effects and risk of climate change are significantly higher in low-income countries.

85. International cooperation to promote and protect human rights lies at the heart of the Charter of the United Nations. The importance of such cooperation is explicitly stated in provisions of the International Covenant on Economic, Social and Cultural Rights, the Convention on the Rights of the Child, the Convention on the Rights of People with Disabilities and in the Declaration on the Right to Development. According to CESCR and the Committee on the Rights of the Child, the obligation to take steps to the maximum of available resources to implement economic, social and cultural rights includes an obligation of States, where necessary, to seek international cooperation. States have also committed themselves not only to implement the treaties within their jurisdiction, but also to contribute, through international cooperation, to global implementation. Developed States have a particular responsibility and interest to assist the poorer developing States.

86. The Committee on Economic, Social and Cultural Rights identifies four types of extraterritorial obligations to promote and protect economic, social and cultural rights. Accordingly, States have legal obligations to:

- Refrain from interfering with the enjoyment of human rights in other countries

- Take measures to prevent third parties (e.g. private companies) over which they hold influence from interfering with the enjoyment of human rights in other countries

- Take steps through international assistance and cooperation, depending on the availability of resources, to facilitate fulfilment of human rights in other countries, including disaster relief, emergency assistance, and assistance to refugees and displaced persons

- Ensure that human rights are given due attention in international agreements and that such agreements do not adversely impact upon human rights

87. Human rights standards and principles are consistent with and further emphasize "the principle of common but differentiated responsibilities" contained in the United Nations Framework Convention on Climate Change. According to this principle, developed country Parties (annex I) commit to assisting developing country Parties (non-annex I) in meeting the costs of adaptation to the adverse effects of climate change and to take full account of the specific needs of least developed countries in funding and transfer of technology. The human rights framework complements the Convention by underlining that "the human person is the central subject of development", and that international cooperation is not merely a matter of the obligations of a State towards other States, but also of the obligations towards individuals.

88. Human rights standards and principles, underpinned by universally recognized moral values, can usefully inform debates on equity and fair distribution of mitigation and adaptation burdens. Above all, human rights principles and standards focus attention on how a given distribution of burden affects the enjoyment of human rights.

NOTES AND QUESTIONS

1.   *How can a State not be responsible?* Suppose a State takes and action or makes a decision within its own territory that results in the death of a person in another State or in territory beyond a State's jurisdiction? Why should not the acting State be responsible for its action?

2.   *"Extraterritorial" or "Transboundary"?* In international legal parlance, "extraterritoriality" means the exercise by a State of jurisdiction acting outside its territory. The competence to exercise extraterritorial jurisdiction is not normally assumed; and in fact in such a situation another recognized basis for exercising jurisdiction or taking action must be found (e.g., the effects principle or protection of nationals principle). In contrast, with respect to human rights, the action in question often occurs within the jurisdiction of the State. Thus another term, e.g., "transboundary", might be more accurate and appropriate.

3.   *The duty to cooperate.* If there is no duty to protect human rights outside a State's territory and jurisdiction, how much does the duty to cooperate replace that duty? What does the duty to cooperate mean, exactly?

4.   *Obligation to comply with treaties in good faith.* Again assuming that there is no duty to protect human rights outside a State's territory, does the obligation of States to carry out their treaty commitments in good faith, which requires them to avoid taking actions calculated to frustrate the object and purpose of the treaty (including human rights treaties) at issue, replace that duty? How could it be in good faith to make it more difficult for another State to fulfill its human rights obligations?

D. ENVIRONMENTAL REFUGEES

International law has considered the plight of international political refugees and those fleeing persecution for many decades. In contrast, the issue of migration caused by environmental causes is relatively recent. Especially because climate change is expected to lead to large migration—both internal and across borders—the question of environmental refugees is of growing concern.

THE ENVIRONMENTAL CAUSES AND CONSEQUENCES OF MIGRATION: A SEARCH FOR MEANING OF "ENVIRONMENTAL REFUGEES"

David Keane
16 Geo. Intl Envtl. L. Rev. 209, 210–19 (2004)

I. INTRODUCTION

The 1951 Convention Relating to the Status of Refugees defines a refugee as any person who, owing to a well-founded fear of being persecuted for reasons of race, religion, nationality, membership in a particular social group or political opinion, is outside the country of his nationality and is unable or, owing to such fear, unwilling to avail himself of the protection of that country; or who, not having a nationality and being outside the country of his former habitual residence as a result of such events, is unable or, owing to such fear, is unwilling to return to it. In 1985, El-Hinnawi identified a new class of persons known as "environmental refugees." He defined environmental refugees as "those people who have been forced to leave their traditional habitat, temporarily or permanently, because of a marked environmental disruption (natural and/or triggered by people) that jeopardized their existence and/or seriously affected the quality of their life." It is currently estimated that there are 10 million environmental refugees worldwide. [Estimates for 2015 are much higher.—Eds.]

El-Hinnawi focused on whether migrants were likely to return to their homes. He identified three broad categories of environmental migrants: persons who are displaced temporarily but who can return to their original home when the environmental damage has been repaired; persons who are permanently displaced and have resettled elsewhere; and persons who migrate from their original home in search of a better quality of life when their original habitat has been degraded to such an extent that it does not meet their basic needs. These categories have been confirmed by further studies as describing the principal, causes of environmental migration. The international community has been urged to officially recognize environmental refugees and to better understand the causes of environmental migration. . . .

II. THE CAUSES OF ENVIRONMENTAL MIGRATION

It is difficult to distinguish the different causes of displacement because often displacement occurs as the result of a combination of different factors. There can be political, economic, and demographic factors involved. However, there is a consensus among scholars on five broad causes of displacement—natural disasters, long-term environmental degradation, development, industrial accidents and remnants of war. . . .

III. DOES INTERNATIONAL LAW PROTECT ENVIRONMENTAL REFUGEES?

There are four principal elements to the definition of a refugee contained in the Refugee Convention. They must be outside their country of origin; they must be unwilling or unable to avail themselves of the protection of their country or return there; such inability or unwillingness must be attributable to a well-founded fear of being persecuted; and the persecution feared must be based on reasons of race, religion, nationality, membership of a particular social group, or political opinion. The definition does not include "those people who have been forced to leave their traditional habitat, temporarily or permanently, because of a marked environmental disruption (natural and/or triggered by people) that jeopardized their existence and/or seriously affected the quality of their life," as defined by El-Hinnawi. Astri Suhrke formulated a narrower definition of an environmental refugee. She distinguishes between environmental migrants and environmental refugees and states that migrants make a voluntary, rational choice to leave their country whereas refugees are compelled to flee by sudden, drastic environmental change that cannot be reversed. However, neither definition falls within the terms of the 1951 Refugee Convention. Therefore, the term "environmental refugees" is a misnomer, as environmentally displaced persons are not recognized as refugees. The Convention was not drafted with such persons in mind, nor can it be reasonably interpreted in modern times to include those persons. The United Nations High Commissioner for Refugees (UNHCR), the International Organization for Migration (IOM) and the Refugee Policy Group, have all opted not to use the term "environmental refugee" and instead to use the term "environmentally displaced persons." Environmentally displaced persons are defined as "persons who are displaced within their own country of habitual residence or who have crossed an international border and for whom environmental degradation, deterioration or destruction is a major cause of their displacement, although not necessarily the sole one."

It is possible to expand the 1951 definition along human rights lines. The five freedoms contained in the definition, i.e., freedom from persecution for reasons of race, religion, nationality, membership of a social group and political opinion, are all rights set forth in the Universal Declaration of Human Rights. The Refugee Convention clearly recognizes that refugee status results from the denial of human rights. The Refugee Convention also recognizes the right to seek safety, as contained in Article 14(1) of the Universal Declaration. Both the International Covenant for Civil and Political Rights and the International Covenant for Economic and Social Rights acknowledge the "inherent right of all peoples to enjoy and utilize fully and freely their natural wealth and resources" and "in no case may a people be deprived of its own means of subsistence." Therefore, a solution to the problem of environmentally displaced persons would be to extend the 1951 definition contained in the Refugee Convention in line with those developments in international human rights law. However, such an extension would meet severe opposition from States for a number of reasons.

First, expanding the definition would lead to a devaluation of the current protection for refugees. This is because migration due to environmental factors is rarely, if ever, a result of governmental oppression. Second, the vast majority of environmentally displaced persons are internally displaced because they are not fleeing State persecution. Internally displaced persons do not meet the definitional requirements of Article 1 of the Refugee Convention. Third, only a limited expansion of the definition would be possible given the enormous number of environmentally displaced persons. . . .

Therefore, neither of these expanded definitions recognizes the environment as a single cause of migration, and neither provides protection for environmental refugees. This is in line with academic writing on the subject that asserts that environmental change, as a cause of migration, cannot be meaningfully separated from political, economic and social changes. . . .

V. THE ENVIRONMENT OR THE DISPLACED PERSON: WHOSE PLIGHT IS BEING HIGHLIGHTED?

The term "environmental refugees" has been severely criticized for being legally meaningless and confusing. It is difficult to see the benefits of the term. It has been suggested that its popularity is due to the fact that it allows governments to deny applicants refugee status. Thus it was invented "at least in part to depoliticize the causes of displacement, so enabling States to derogate their obligation to provide asylum." However, the difficulty with this explanation is that most of the academic literature surrounding the issue is arguing for an extension of asylum law to incorporate this new category, rather than a restriction of the numbers being granted asylum. Therefore, the above explanation would constitute a manipulation of the term, rather than a deliberate invention of a category with a view towards reducing the number of persons being granted refugee status.

If we accept that the category of "environmental refugees" was not invented in order to restrict the numbers of persons receiving asylum, and we also accept that there can be no extension of existing international refugee law to cover this category, what then is the benefit in separating environmental causes of migration from other political, social or economic causes? A possible answer lies not in asylum literature, but in environmental literature. Norman Myers, who is a strong advocate of the notion of environmental refugees, is an ecologist, not an international refugee lawyer. His concern regarding the rising number of environmental refugees is related to the environmental problems of deforestation, desertification, and climate change that these migrations highlight. If the international community wishes to prevent huge numbers of "refugees" or migrants, it must prevent the environmental causes of those migrations. . . .

Similarly, if we return to one of the causes of environmentally displaced persons highlighted above, namely conflicts and wars, we see that while environmental destruction can result from conflicts, and environmental refugees can result from this destruction, the main causes of those conflicts can often be traced back again to the environment. Homer-Dixon proposed three hypotheses on the relationship between conflict and the environment. First, that environmental scarcity leads to simple scarcity conflicts between States. Second, that environmental scarcity causes large population movement, which in turn causes group-identity conflict. Third, that environmental scarcity causes economic deprivation and disrupts social institutions, leading to "deprivation conflicts." Again, by highlighting the large numbers of environmentally displaced persons resulting from a conflict, the focus is on the environment and its protection as a means of combating migrations. . . .

Regarding the likelihood of large-scale migration due to climate change, consider, the materials in Chapter 9 and the following excerpt.

TURNING THE TIDE: RECOGNIZING CLIMATE CHANGE REFUGEES IN INTERNATIONAL LAW
Angela Williams
30 Law & Policy 502 (2008)

There is no obvious provision for refugees created by environmental change within [the definition in the Refugee convention]. Some have sought to argue that environmental refugees do currently fit within the Refugee Convention definition by claiming that government-induced environmental degradation is a form of persecution and, furthermore, that such persecution is taking place "for reasons of" environmental refugees' membership in a social group. . . . Examples suggested include the desertification of the African Sahel where it is claimed the governments of the Sahel region "could have enacted policies and programs to cut population growth, to improve agricultural techniques, or to heighten food production". . . .

The United Nations Refugee Agency has recognized the concept of internally displaced persons in paragraph 2 of the Guiding Principles on Internal Displacement. This paragraph provides "persons or groups of persons who have been forced or obliged to flee or to leave their homes or places of habitual residence, in particular as a result of or in order to avoid the effects of armed conflict, situations of generalised violence, violations of human rights or natural or human-made disasters, and who have not crossed an internationally recognised State border."

Immigration and Protection Tribunal New Zealand, D. 501370–371 (2014), considered the claim of citizens of Tuvalu that deportation would subject them to "the risk of suffering the adverse impacts of climate change and socio-economic deprivation." The Tribunal granted the petitioners the requested residency visas to reunite the family with members who were either New Zealand citizens or residents. Thus, the Tribunal did not need to reach the climate change issue, but it did consider the risks to Tuvalu and added, that future claims "must establish not simply the existence of a matter of broad humanitarian concern, but that there are exceptional circumstances of a humanitarian nature such that it would be unjust or unduly harsh to deport *the particular appellant* from New Zealand." See also International Bar Association, Achieving Justice and Human Rights in an Era of Climate Disruption (2014).

The United Nations Refugee Agency has recognized the concept of internally displaced persons in paragraph 2 of the Guiding Principles on Internal Displacement. This paragraph provides "persons or groups of persons who have been forced or obliged to flee or to leave their homes or places of habitual residence, in particular as a result of or in order to avoid the effects of armed conflict, situations of generalised violence, violations of human rights or natural or human-made disasters, and who have not crossed an internationally recognised State border."

NOTES AND QUESTIONS

1. *Environmental refugees and climate change.* The plight of people forced to migrate because of deteriorating ecosystems has the potential to worsen in the coming years because of the threat of global warming. Most scientists estimate that the greenhouse effect could cause average global temperatures to rise significantly in coming decades. (See Chapter 9.) The United Nations High Commissioner for Refugees (UNHCR) says 36 million people were displaced by natural disasters in 2009. Scientists predict this number will rise to at least 50 million by 2050. Some say it could be as high as 200 million.

2. *Classifying the causes.* There are at least five circumstances that indirectly result in displacement: (1) systematic human rights violations, (2) war, armed conflict, communal violence, and aggression, (3) development-induced relocation, (4) industrial accidents, and (5) damage to the environment. Presently, displacement is not viewed as a human rights violation and does not trigger international concern in a workable manner.

Recognizing a person's right not to be displaced would shift the burden to the relocator and give primacy to the human rights aspect rather than the developmental one, or at a minimum puts the two on equal footing. Maria Stavroupoulou, *The Right Not to Be Displaced*, 9 Am. U. J. Intl. L. & Poly. 689, 701, 728–732 (1994). Envision a discourse about a proposed project that would cause dislocation if the human rights concerns received such recognition.

3.   *Do you agree with Keane's analysis?* For different views, see Dana Zartner Falstrom, *Stemming the Flow of Environmental Displacement: Creating a Convention to Protect Persons and Preserve the Environment*, 2001 Colo. J. Int'l Envtl. L. & Pol'y 1 (2001); Jessica B. Cooper, *Environmental Refugees: Meeting the Requirements of the Refugee Definition*, 6 N.Y.U. Envtl. LJ. 480 (1998).

E.   ENVIRONMENTAL HUMAN RIGHTS DEFENDERS

Persons trying to protect their own or their communities' environmental rights have been found to be in unusual danger. A study reported that globally almost three people were killed every week in 2013 as a result of their environmental protection efforts. Global Witness, Deadly Environment: The Deadly Rise in Killings of Environmental and Land Defenders (2014). This means that environmental human rights defenders are among those human rights advocates most at risk around the world. Consistent with this, Independent Expert John Knox wrote in his Preliminary Report, supra, that:

> 28. In practice, environmental human rights defenders have proved to be especially at risk when trying to exercise [procedural] rights. The Special Rapporteur on the situation of human rights defenders has reported (A/HRC/19/55) that she receives many communications concerning environmental activists, "including those working on issues related to extractive industries, and construction and development projects; those working for the rights of indigenous and minority communities; women human rights defenders; and journalists" (ibid., para. 64). Environmental rights defenders face a high risk of killings, attacks, assault, threats and intimidation from both State and non-State actors (ibid., paras. 64–92). Needless to say, the primary effect of these human rights violations is felt by the individuals and communities who suffer from them. But the violations also have secondary effects on the environment that the individuals were trying to protect and on all of those whose full enjoyment of human rights depends upon that environment.

Human rights tribunals have responded to these threats by specifying duties that States have with respect to environmental human rights defenders. For example, the Inter-American Commission on Human Rights has issued preliminary measures to protect environmental human rights defenders. See, e.g., *Mauricio Meza v. Colombia* (2009) (precautionary measures requiring Colombia to adopt measures to protect a human rights defender and environmentalist who had been harassed and subjected to an attempted kidnapping for his activities); *Marco Arana, Mirtha Vásquez* (2007) (requiring the State to provide perimeter surveillance for the headquarters of the NGO under threat).

The Inter-American Court of Human Rights, in *Kawas Fernández v. Honduras* (2009), held that Honduras' failure to adopt the measures necessary to protect an activist who led an organization that, among other things, denounced environmental contamination and illegal logging and forest degradation in a national park, violated the right of the activist (who had been killed) to freedom of association. The Court required that Honduras compensate relatives of Ms. Fernández for pecuniary and non-pecuniary damages. The Court also required Honduras to: (i) publish excerpts from its judgment in major newspapers; (ii) publicly acknowledge its international responsibility for this human rights violation; and (iii) conduct a national awareness campaign regarding the importance of the work performed by environmentalists in Honduras.

NOTES AND QUESTIONS

1. Why are environmental rights defenders at such an unusually high risk?

2. What should be done to remedy this situation?

F. RIGHT TO A HEALTHY ENVIRONMENT

Debate has existed for decades regarding the existence of a human right to a healthy environment. Other formulations of the same purported right include the right to a "clean" or "safe" environment and the "fundamental right to an environment capable of supporting human society and the full enjoyment of human rights". Consider the following materials.

HUMAN RIGHTS, ENVIRONMENTAL RIGHTS, AND THE RIGHT TO THE ENVIRONMENT

Dinah Shelton
28 Stan. J. Intl. L. 103, 103–105 (1991)

There is no doubt that the global environment is deteriorating and that failure to alleviate current environmental degradation may threaten human health and human life. However, the necessary and appropriate international legal response remains unclear. These problems generate a host of questions and public policy alternatives. A fundamental question is whether human rights and environmental protection are premised upon fundamentally different social values, such that efforts to implement both simultaneously will produce more conflict than improvement, or, on the other hand, whether human rights and environmental protection are complementary, each furthering the aims of the other.

Some theorists suggest that environmental issues belong within the human rights category, because the goal of environmental protection is to enhance the quality of human life. Opponents argue, however, that human beings are merely one element of a complex, global ecosystem, which should be preserved for its own sake. Under this approach, human rights are subsumed under the primary objective of protecting nature as a whole.

A third view, which seems to best reflect current law and policy sees human rights and environmental protection as each representing different, but overlapping, societal values. The two fields share a core of common interests and objectives, although obviously not all human rights violations are necessarily linked to environmental degradation. Likewise, environmental issues cannot always be addressed effectively within the human rights framework, and any attempt to force all such issues into a human rights rubric may fundamentally distort the concept of human rights. This approach recognizes the potential conflicts between environmental protection and other human rights, but also the contribution each field can make to achieving their common objectives.

In order to contribute to environmental protection using a human rights approach—or vice versa—this third view suggests several alternatives. First, environmental problems may be combated through the assertion of existing human rights, such as the rights to life, personal security, health, and food. In this regard, a safe and healthy environment may be viewed either as a pre-condition to the exercise of existing rights or as inextricably intertwined with the enjoyment of these rights. A second, intermediate position proposes a set of "environmental rights" (rights of the environment as well as to the environment) based upon existing rights to information about and involvement in the political design-making process. Third, and most ambitiously, a specific "right to the environment" could be formulated and added to the current catalogue of human rights. . . .

THE RIGHT TO A CLEAN ENVIRONMENT

Noralee Gibson
54 Sask. L. Rev. 5, 12, 16–17 (1990)

1. CULTURAL LEGITIMACY THEORY

The first theory asserts the right to a clean environment derives from cultural legitimacy. Cultural legitimacy is defined as "the quality or state of being in conformity with recognized principles or accepted rules and standards of a given culture." If the theoretical basis of the right to a clean environment is a value or norm accepted by a wide range of cultural traditions, it may be recognized as a human right.

2. INDISPENSABILITY THEORY

The threat to human existence and survival provides a second basis for the right to a clean environment. The right to a clean environment is indispensable to the exercise of other human rights. A clean and healthy environment is a prerequisite for the enjoyment of other human rights. Under the indispensability theory, the right to a clean environment is an essential condition for the fulfillment of all human rights.

3. SURVIVAL NEED THEORY

In conjunction with the broader international goal of saving the ecosystem, one can formulate an international right to a clean environment. This right would be extended to all members of the ecosystem including humans. It is a right based on need. This right would be viewed as the most basic need of all living organisms. It is even more fundamentally important than individual human rights; it is concerned with the collective survival of all human beings. It is this most important objective to which the right to a clean environment should be linked and not to individual human rights. Granting the rights to the environment as a whole is a recognition of its value, not to us as consumers of environmental amenities, but as an integral part of life itself. . . .

Also, if the right to a clean environment can be viewed as a survival need, it is truly a "universal" right since the cultural aspect of legitimization is not a factor. The need for survival is universal due to every organism's inherent need and desire to survive.

NOTES AND QUESTIONS

1. *What world do advocates live in; how can the environment be "healthy" or safe"?* One criticism raised against the right to a healthy environment is that the environment is inherently unsafe. Carnivores such as mountain lions kill and injure people; other fauna such as snakes kill and harm people in defense; diseases such as malaria and Ebola kill and harm people; natural disasters such as hurricanes, earthquakes, tsunamis and volcanic eruptions occur that kill or injure thousands and destroy entire population centers. Is there an answer to this?

2.   *A human right to tourism?* A wide range of special interest groups perceive the usefulness of attaching the "human rights" label to further their cause. For example, the World Tourism Organization has proclaimed "tourism has become increasingly a basic need, a social necessity, a human right." The World Tourism Organization's Global Code of Ethics (1999) states in article 7 (Right to Tourism): "The universal right to tourism must be regarded as the corollary of the right to rest and leisure, including reasonable limitation of working hours and periodic holidays with pay, guaranteed by Article 24 of the Universal Declaration of Human Rights and Article 7.d of the International Covenant on Economic, Social and Cultural Rights." The Global Code of Ethics for Tourism was officially recognized by the UN General Assembly in 2001 (A/RES/56/212 (21 Dec. 2001). Do you think there is a human right to tourism?

3.   *What level of support?* Although the right to a clean environment is certainly not a frivolous claim, does declaring it a human right without support at the highest international levels threaten the integrity of the entire process of human rights recognition? See Noralee Gibson, *The Right to a Clean Environment*, 54 Sask. L. Rev. 5, 9 (1990); Philip Alston, *Conjuring Up New Human Rights: A Proposal for Quality Control*, 78 Am. J. Intl. L. 607 (1984).

4.   *What States and others are doing.* In his third report (A/HRC/28/61), John Knox, the UN Independent Expert on human rights and the environment "describes good practices of Governments, international organisations, civil society organisations, corporations and others in the use of human rights obligations relating to the environment, including (a) procedural obligations to make environmental information public, to facilitate public participation in environmental decision-making, to protect rights of expression and association, and to provide access to legal remedies; (b) substantive obligations, including obligations relating to non-state actors; (c) obligations relating to transboundary harm; and (d) obligations relating to those in vulnerable situations."

5.   *Direct or indirect protection?* As a rule, an individual's environment is indirectly protected when the environment in general is protected. However, an individual's particular environment could also be legally protected in a direct manner through recognition of an individual's right to a clean and healthy environment.

6.   *The nature of human rights, revisited.* As noted at the beginning of this chapter, substantial disagreement exists as to the precise nature of human rights, their sources and their practical implications. International human rights law is developing in ways that attempt to balance diverse ideologies and garner allegiances of widely varying cultural traditions. See Philip Alston, *Making Space for New Human Rights: The Case for the Right to Development*, 1 Harv. Hum. Rts. J. 3, 29 (1988); Kamenka & Tay, *Philosophy and Human Rights: A Survey and Select Annotated Bibliography of Recent English Language Literature*, 70 Archiv Far Rechts-und Sozialphilosphie 291, 297 (1984). Proponents of new human rights such as

the right to a clean environment contend that these rights have already become part of customary international law. Opponents argue that these rights are not legal rights but are either political or social principles. Is the right to a clean environment a "moral" right, without any legal force? See Louis B. Sohn, *The New International Law: Protection of the Rights of Individuals Rather Than States*, 32 Am. U. L. Rev. 1, 61 (1982); Noralee Gibson, *The Right to a Clean Environment*, 54 Sask. L. Rev. 5, 15 (1990).

1. ARTICULATIONS OF A HUMAN RIGHT TO A HEALTHY ENVIRONMENT

a. Multilateral Instruments

DECLARATION OF THE UNITED NATIONS CONFERENCE ON THE HUMAN ENVIRONMENT [STOCKHOLM DECLARATION], UNITED NATIONS CONFERENCE ON THE HUMAN ENVIRONMENT, STOCKHOLM, SWED., JUNE 5–16, 1972

Stockholm Declaration on the Human Environment, U.N. Doc. A/Conf.48/14/Rev.1 (June 16, 1972), http://www.un-documents.net/aconf48–14r1.pdf

Principle 1

Man has the fundamental right to freedom, equality, and adequate conditions of life, in an environment of a quality that permits a life of dignity and well-being, and he bears a solemn responsibility to protect and improve the environment for present and future generations. . . .

RIO DECLARATION ON ENVIRONMENT AND DEVELOPMENT, UNITED NATIONS CONFERENCE ON ENVIRONMENT AND DEVELOPMENT, RIO DE JANEIRO, BRAZ., JUNE 3–14, 1992

Rio Declaration on Environment and Development, U.N. Doc. A/CONF.151/26/Rev.1 (vol. I), annex I (Aug. 12, 1992), http://www.un.org/documents/ga/conf151/aconf15126–1annex1.htm

Principle 1

Human beings are at the centre of concerns for sustainable development. They are entitled to a healthy and productive life in harmony with nature.

JOHANNESBURG PRINCIPLES ON THE ROLE OF LAW AND SUSTAINABLE DEVELOPMENT

August 20, 2002, adopted at the Global Judges Symposium

We emphasize that the fragile state of the global environment requires the Judiciary . . . to boldly and fearlessly implement and enforce applicable international and national laws, which in the field of environment and sustainable development will assist in alleviating poverty and sustaining an enduring civilization, and ensuring that the present generation will enjoy and improve the quality of life of all peoples, while also ensuring that the inherent rights and interests of succeeding generations are not compromised.

We recognize that the people most affected by environmental degradation are the poor, and that, therefore, there is an urgent need to strengthen the capacity of the poor and their representatives to defend environmental rights, so as to ensure that the weaker sections of society are not prejudiced by environmental degradation and are enabled to enjoy their right to live in a social and physical environment that respects and promotes dignity.

[T]he programme of work should include . . . (b) The improvement in the level of public participation in environmental decision-making, access to justice for the settlement of environmental disputes and the defense and enforcement of environmental rights, and public access to relevant information.

NOTES AND QUESTIONS

1. *The Stockholm Declaration, the Rio Principles, and the right to environment.* At the international level, the Stockholm Declaration in 1972 formulated the first evidence of a right to a clean environment. Although the text does not explicitly state that there is a right to a clean environment, it does express the issue in human rights terms. The General Assembly adopted the declaration but has not specifically proclaimed the existence of a right to a clean environment, despite proposals that it do so. Does Principle 1 of the Rio Declaration imply a right to a healthy environment or to an environment that allows a healthy and productive life? Why did States not use the language from Stockholm Principle 1 when drafting the Rio Declaration?

2. *The Stockholm Declaration: additional provisions.* Article 2 of the Stockholm Declaration is also read as being a source of environmental rights. It declares that protection of the human environment is a precondition for the well-being of present and future generations and "the duty of all Governments." Iveta Hodkova, *Is There a Right to a Healthy Environment in the International Legal Order?* 7 Conn. J. Intl. L. 65, 66 (1991).

3. *The General Assembly and a right to environment.* In December 1989, the UN General Assembly considered a resolution that would have recognized a "healthy environment" as a human right. The resolution was blocked by the government of Brazil under former President Jose Sarney, who was sensitive to criticism of Brazil's environmental practices.

4. *The Brundtland Commission and a right to environment.* The Legal Experts Group of the World Commission on Environment and Development (WCED or the Brundtland Commission) explicitly incorporated into its report, General Principles Concerning Natural Resources and Environmental Interferences, the provision that "[a]ll human beings have the fundamental

right to an environment adequate for their health and wellbeing." (Principle 1) Although the term "adequate" is vague and may have many different meanings according to the socio-economic situation of a country, one author argues this provision does provide the basis for "an international obligation on the part of the State vis-à-vis another State . . . to protect the environment for all individuals. . . ." Iveta Hodkova, above, at 67 (1991) (citing Experts Group on Environmental Law of the World Commission on Environment and Development, Environmental Protection and Sustainable Development: Legal Principles and Recommendations 40 (1986)).

5.   *The Small Island Developing States speak up.* The 2007 Male' Declaration on the Human Dimension of Global Climate Change expressly recognizes the "fundamental right to an environment capable of supporting human society and the full enjoyment of human rights". Excerpts follow.

> We the representatives of the Small Island Developing States having met in Male' from 13 to 14 November 2007,
>
> *Aware* that the environment provides the infrastructure for human civilization and that life depends on the uninterrupted functioning of natural systems;
>
> . . .
>
> *Persuaded* that the impacts of climate change pose the most immediate, fundamental and far-reaching threat to the environment, individuals and communities around the planet, and that these impacts have been observed to be intensifying in frequency and magnitude;
>
> *Emphasizing* that small island, low-lying coastal, and atoll states are particularly vulnerable to even small changes to the global climate and are already adversely affected by alterations in ecosystems, changes in precipitation, rising sea-levels and increased incidence of natural disasters;
>
> . . .
>
> *Noting* that the fundamental right to an environment capable of supporting human society and the full enjoyment of human rights is recognized, in varying formulations, in the constitutions of over one hundred states and directly or indirectly in several international instruments;
>
> . . .
>
> *Concerned* that climate change has clear and immediate implications for the full enjoyment of human rights including *inter alia* the right to life, the right to take part in cultural life, the right to use and enjoy property, the right to an adequate standard of living, the right to food, and the right to the highest attainable standard of physical and mental health; . . . .

6.   *The Hague Declaration.* The Conference on the Environment drafted the Hague Declaration of 1989 following WCED's efforts. This document's relevant provision states "[b]ecause of the nature of the dangers involved, remedies to be sought involve not only the fundamental duty to preserve the ecosystem, but also the right to live in dignity in a viable global environment. . . ." Hague Declaration on the Environment, March 11, 1989, 28 I.L.M. 1308, 1309 (1989). Is there a correlation between the right to live and the global environment? The declaration also ties the implementation of a human right to live (which includes environment protection obligations) to the development of a UN organization to create and enforce international agreements to control pollution. Although the document does not have the force of law, it demonstrates States' recognition that cooperation on such issues is essential. Twenty-four States have adopted the Hague Declaration.

7.   *The World Charter.* The World Charter for Nature, adopted by the UN General Assembly in 1982 by a vote of 111 to 1, with 18 abstentions, sets out General Principles that include: "Nature shall be respected . . .; the genetic viability of life forms shall be protected; all areas of the earth shall be subject to principles of conservation with special protection being given to habitats of rare or endangered species; and ecosystems, organisms and land, marine and atmospheric resources shall be managed in a way to achieve optimum sustainable productivity." 1982 U.N.Y.B. 1023; World Charter for Nature, G.A. Res. 27/7, 37 U.N. GAOR Supp. (No. 51) at 17, U.N. Doc. A/37/51 (1982), reprinted in 22 I.L.M. 455 (1983). At least one commentator has argued that while the World Charter lacks an explicit pronouncement of a human right to environment, its General Principles—along with other similarly worded international statements—can be used to infer such a right. See Melissa Thorme, *Establishing Environment as a Human Right*, 19 Denv. J. Intl. L. & Poly. 301, 317 (1991). Can you see how one might make such an argument? The United States cast the lone dissenting vote on the World Charter. Why do you suppose the United States cast that vote?

8.   *Johannesburg Principles on the Role of Law and Sustainable Development.* The United States Department of State disagreed with the Johannesburg Principles on the Role of Law and Sustainable Development, which are excerpted above; the United States judges participating in the Global Judges Symposium did not.

9.   *UNESCO's contribution.* An additional source for the right to a clean environment can be found in a 1980 UNESCO colloquium on new human rights. The colloquium discussed "the right to a healthy and ecologically balanced environment." See UNESCO, Symposium on New Human Rights: The Rights of Solidarity, Mexico City, 1980, at 1, UNESCO Doc. 55 81/CONF 806/4 (1981).

10. *Environmental rights of children.* For a discussion of this topic, see The Right of the Child to a Clean Environment (A. Fijalkowski & M. Fitzmaurice eds., 2000).

11. *An international court for the environment?* The 1989 International Congress on "A More Efficient International Law on the Environment and Establishing an International Court for the Environment within the United Nations System" stressed in its Final Statement the need for "obligatory and legal procedures for preventing and regulating any conflicts" at the international level. The Final Statement called for a body that would plan and manage the world environment, establish an international court for the environment accessible to States, United Nations organs, and private citizens. See Final Statement, International Congress on a More Efficient International Law on the Environment and Establishing an International Court for the Environment within the United Nations System (1989), reprinted in 19 Envtl. Pol'y. & L. 138 (1989). See also George & Catherine Pring, Greening Justice: Creating and Improving Environmental Courts and Tribunals, in G. Pring & V. Nanda, International Environmental Law & Policy for the 21st Century (2d ed. 2012).

b. Regional Instruments

Regional instruments are able to promote the right to a clean environment in a unique way that global treaties cannot. Regional bodies are comprised of fewer States, which have closer ties to each other geographically, culturally, historically, and politically. How can these commonalities aid in reaching regional agreements to recognize the right to a clean environment? Do they have a role in the progressive development of universal norms?

AFRICAN CHARTER OF HUMAN AND PEOPLES' RIGHTS
June 26, 1981, Article 24, 21 I.L.M. 59

All peoples shall have the right to a general satisfactory environment favorable to their development.

ADDITIONAL PROTOCOL TO THE AMERICAN CONVENTION ON HUMAN RIGHTS (THE SAN SALVADOR PROTOCOL)
Nov. 14, 1988, Article 11, 28 LL.M. 161

1. Everyone shall have the right to live in a healthy environment and to have access to basic public services.

2. The States Parties shall promote the protection, preservation and improvement of the environment.

NOTES AND QUESTIONS

1. *The African Charter.* The African Charter became effective in 1986 making it the first international document to delineate the right "to a general satisfactory environment" (African Charter on Human and Peoples' Rights, entered into force Oct. 21, 1986). The charter differs from other documents

stipulating this general right by recognizing that social and economic rights are a precondition for the recognition of civil and political rights and in that it defines the right as a collective right to "peoples" rather than individuals. The charter lacks specific legal obligations, providing only that: "State parties . . . shall allow the establishment and improvement of appropriate national institutions entrusted with the promotion and protection of the rights and freedoms guaranteed by the present Charter." (Art. 26).

2. *The OAS*. Article 11 expresses an explicit right to environmental protection, and the rights adopted in the Protocol are "promised the protection of the inter-American human rights system." See Dinah Shelton, *Improving Human Rights Protections: Recommendations for Enhancing the Effectiveness of the Inter-American Commission and Inter-American Court of Human Rights*, 3 Am. U.J. Intl. L. & Poly. 323, 323–325 (1988). One major impediment to actions by individuals may be Article 1. It requires States to cooperate on an international level and to adopt all necessary measures "to the extent allowed by their available resources, and taking into account their degree of development" to protect the guaranteed rights. The Parties must also adopt domestic legislation to realize the rights. Do these provisions swallow up the right and render the protocol's protection to individuals useless? Further, the protocol does not grant individuals the right to petition for violations of the right to the environment, but allows the Inter-American Commission on Human Rights to conduct investigations and make recommendations on the status of the rights enunciated in the protocol. (Art. 19(7)). Is this a political way to restrict by procedural requirements the individual right to a healthy environment?

The OAS has adopted several resolutions regarding human rights and the environment. See Human Rights and the Environment, AG/RES. 1926 (XXXIII-O/03), June 10, 2003; AG/RES. 1896 (XXXII-O/02); AG/RES. (XXXI-O/01).

The Inter-American human rights system contains two institutions: the Inter-American Commission of Human Rights and the Inter-American Court of Human Rights. The Commission has jurisdiction over all countries that belong to the OAS, but it can only issue studies and non-legally binding decisions. The Court can issue legally binding decisions but has jurisdiction over a more limited number of States. There have been several cases in the Commission and the Court that address environment-related rights, as discussed below.

3. *The Council of Europe*. The Council of Europe is dedicated to "the maintenance and further realization of human rights and fundamental freedoms." In light of this purpose, it adopted the European Convention on Human Rights (European Convention for the Protection of Human Rights and Fundamental Freedoms, Nov. 4, 1950, 213 U.N.T.S. 221) and the European Social Charter (opened for signature, Oct. 18, 1961, 529 U.N.T.S. 89) which together implement civil, political, economic, social, and environmental human rights. Since the 1970s the Council of Europe has

strived to create a human right to a healthy environment, but objections have prohibited its adoption.

In 1990, the Assembly of the Council of Europe adopted the Recommendation to the Parliamentary Assembly on the Formulation of a European Charter and a European Convention on Environmental Protection containing not only an individual's definitive right to a healthy environment but also a respective legal duty:

1.   Every person has the fundamental right to an environment and living conditions conducive to his good health, well-being and full development of the human personality.

2.   Every Contracting European State has a duty to preserve and protect the environment in the interests of the health and well-being of all people inside and outside of Europe, for the benefit of present and future generations.

Eur. Parl. Assem., 42d Sess., Recommendation 1130, at 2 (1990).

The draft of the ECE Charter on Environmental Rights and Obligations also espouses the right to an adequate environment and the responsibility of everyone to contribute to the environment's protection and conservation. In addition, it contains the right to information on environmental issues and access to decision making. (Draft ECE, at 2).

4.   *Mini-case study*: *The European Convention on Human Rights.* Gregoria Lopez Ostra lived with her family in the vicinity of Lorca, in the region of Murcia, Spain. In 1988 she suffered health problems from a waste treatment plant located on government property twelve meters from her home. The facility was being operated without a required permit. Despite a temporary evacuation of people in the area by the municipality, they continued to experience health problems. Doctors confirmed that living in this highly polluted area caused Lopez Ostra's daughter to suffer from nausea, vomiting, allergic reactions, bronchitis, and anorexia. Lopez Ostra sought relief in Spain without success. She therefore applied to the European Commission of Human Rights, established by Article 19 of the European Convention for the Protection of Human Rights and Fundamental Freedoms, Nov. 4, 1950, 213 U.N.T.S. 222. Lopez Ostra claimed that the problems caused by the plant violated her rights under Articles 3 and 8 of the European Convention, which provide as follows:

Article 3

No one shall be subjected to torture or to inhuman or degrading treatment or punishment.

Article 8

(1) Everyone has the right to respect for his private and family life, his home and his correspondence.

(2) There shall be no interference by a public authority with the exercise of this right except such as is in accordance with the law

and is necessary in a democratic society in the interests of national security, public safety or the economic well-being of the country, for the prevention of disorder or crime, for the protection of health or morals, or for the protection of the rights and freedoms of others.

The commission rejected the Article 3 claim but found a violation of Article 8. The European Court of Human Rights, in its decision of December 9, 1994,[3] held unanimously that Spain's failure to prevent harmful pollution from the plant violated Article 8 of the European Convention. In explaining its reasoning, the Court stated:

> 51. Naturally, severe environmental pollution may affect individuals' well-being and prevent them from enjoying their homes in such a way as to affect their private and family life adversely, without, however, seriously endangering their health.
>
> Whether the question is analysed in terms of a positive duty on the State—to take reasonable and appropriate measures to secure the applicant's rights under paragraph 1 of Article 8 . . ., as the applicant wishes in her case, or in terms of an "interference by a public authority" to be justified in accordance with paragraph 2 . . ., the applicable principles are broadly similar. In both contexts regard must be had to the fair balance that has to be struck between the competing interests of the individual and of the community as a whole, and in any case the State enjoys a certain margin of appreciation. Furthermore, even in relation to the positive obligations flowing from the first paragraph of Article 8 . . ., in striking the required balance the aims mentioned in the second paragraph . . . may be of a certain relevance (see, in particular, the Rees v. the United Kingdom judgment of 17 October 1986, Series A no. 106, p. 15, para. 37, and the Powell and Rayner v. the United Kingdom judgment of 21 February 1990, Series A no. 172, p. 18, para. 41).
>
> . . .
>
> 58. Having regard to the foregoing, and despite the margin of appreciation left to the respondent State, the Court considers that the State did not succeed in striking a fair balance between the interest of the town's economic well-being—that of having a waste-treatment plant—and the applicant's effective enjoyment of her right to respect for her home and her private and family life.

The court held Spain liable for four million pesetas in damages and more than one million pesetas for costs and expenses. The decision is significant, inter alia, because the European Convention contains no provision on "environmental rights" per se.

5.   Do you see any danger in relying on Article 8 for protection such as that sought by Lopez Ostra? Why do you suppose she did not base her case on

---

[3]   Series A: Judgments and Decisions, vol. 303, C, Case of Lopez Ostra v. Spain.

the right to life (Article 2) or the right to physical integrity and health (Article 3), neither of which is subject to broad exceptions?

c. National Laws Regarding the Right to a Healthy Environment

A diverse number of States are beginning to recognize and articulate the right to a healthy environment—expressed with a variety of qualifiers such as "healthy", "healthful", "safe" and "sustainable"—in national legislation and constitutions.

As indicated in the excerpt from David Boyd above, both developed and developing countries, in the last couple of decades, have incorporated a right to the environment into their constitutions. Over 90 countries' constitutions now include such a right, and legislation or courts in other countries have provided for such a right.

i. Constitutional Provisions of a Right to a Healthy Environment

National constitutions include various versions of the right to a healthy environment. Examples include. The Constitution of Peru (1993) authorizes the State to "determine national environmental policy" and directs it to promote "the sustainable use of its natural resources", "the preservation of biological diversity and protected natural areas" and "sustainable development of the Amazon Region through proper legislation." The Portuguese Constitution (1975) provides: "[a]ll have the right to a human, healthy and ecologically balanced human environment and the duty to protect it." The 2002 Constitution of the Kingdom of Bahrain directs the State to "take the necessary measures for the protection of the environment and the conservation of wildlife." The Democratic Republic of East Timor's 2002 Constitution recognizes the right of everyone to "a humane, healthy and ecologically balanced environment" and imposes the duty "to protect it and improve it for the benefit of future generations." The Constitution further obliges the State to "recognize the need to preserve and rationalize natural resources" and to "promote actions aimed at protecting the environment and safeguarding the sustainable development of the economy."

Article 33 of the 2005 Draft Constitution of the Republic of Iraq recognizes that "[e]very individual has the right to live in a correct environmental atmosphere." The same article obliges the State to guarantee "protection and preservation of the environment and biological diversity." Thus, in Article 112, the federal and regional authorities are tasked with "drawing up environmental policy to guarantee the protection of the environment from pollution and the preservation of its cleanliness, in cooperation with the regions." The former Yugoslavian Constitution of 1974 in Article 192 proclaimed: "[m]an shall have the right to a healthy environment. Conditions for realization of this right shall be ensured by the social community."

Generally no rules were adopted to guarantee or enforce any human rights in the former Communist countries. These rights were considered effectuated by the interests of the socialist community. See Hodkova, above, at 77. Since the collapse of the Communist regime, the Czechoslovak Federal Assembly adopted in 1991 a new constitution entitled Charter of Fundamental Rights and Freedoms. See The Charter of Fundamental Rights and Freedoms of the Czech and Slovak Federative Republic, A Constitutional Law, adopted Jan. 9, 1991, Prague. Article 35 of the Charter contains an explicit right to a healthy environment:

1.   Everyone has the right to live in a favorable environment;

2.   Everyone is entitled to timely and complete information about the state of the environment and natural resources;

3.   In exercising his or her rights nobody may endanger or cause damage to the environment, natural resources, the wealth of natural species, and cultural monuments beyond limits set by law.

The charter attests that international agreements on human rights ratified by the state are obligatory and supersede national law. (Art. 2 at 1). Still, many of the environmental rights contained in the charter may remain merely declarative for some time given the economic conditions and the outdated industrial and power facilities that produce great amounts of ground, water, and air pollution.

Due to the enormous amount of deforestation of the Amazon, the Brazilian government enacted the 1988 constitution implementing Chapter VI as a safeguard for the region. It states: "[e]veryone is entitled to an ecologically balanced environment, which is an asset of everyday use to the common man and essential to a healthy quality of life; this imposes a duty on the government and the community to protect and preserve it for the present and future generations." Albert P. Blaustein, *Federative Republic of Brazil* (1988), reprinted in 3 Constitutions of the Countries of the World (Albert P. Blaustein & Gisbert H. Flanz eds., 1990). Chapter VII imposes responsibility on the Brazilian government to preserve' and restore ecosystems and biological diversity, and protect the flora and fauna, and for practices that place them at risk of extinction. The effectiveness of this bold step remains to be seen given the country's high foreign debt and reliance on the timber and cattle ranching industries.

The 1990 Constitution of the Republic of Namibia in Article 91(c) delegates authority to an "Ombudsman" to "investigate complaints concerning the over-utilization of living natural resources, the irrational exploitation of non-renewable resources, the degradation and destruction of ecosystems and failure to protect the beauty of Namibia." This authority may be the most extensive in that it provides a specific body power with respect to certain actions.

Other constitutions tend to be more restrictive and allow only citizens to be beneficiaries of the right. The constitution of the Republic of Korea (1988) in Article 35(1) proclaims: "[a]ll citizens have the right to a healthy and pleasant environment." What restrictions does this mean for foreigners harmed by a neighboring government's actions? Does such a right have any force if an action against the polluting government is prevented by the act of State doctrine in the victim State's court and the polluter's domestic law does not recognize foreign citizen actions?

Sub-national units also have provided such rights, again using varying terminology. For example, in the United States individual state constitutions began in 1960 to recognize the right. Five states explicitly, and perhaps 11 states implicitly, recognize the right to the environment. The constitutions of Illinois and Hawaii explicitly guarantee the right to a clean environment, providing that "[e]ach person has the right to a clean and healthful environment." See Haw. Const. art. XI, § 9; and III. Const. art. IX, § 2. See also the constitutions of California, Florida, Massachusetts, Montana, Pennsylvania, Rhode Island, and Virginia.

ii. National Cases Regarding a Right to a Healthy Environment

Caselaw has played an important role in establishing the right to a healthy environment in some countries. For example, in some countries the right to the environment is inferred from other obligations imposed on individuals, governments, and states. The 1982 Netherlands Constitution, Article 21, proclaims: "It shall be the concern of the authorities to keep the country habitable and to protect and improve the environment." Furthermore, the Indian Constitution (1974), in Article 48A, declares: "The states shall endeavor to protect and improve the environment and to safeguard the forests and wildlife of the country."

In the landmark case of *Oposa v. Factoran* (G.R. No. 101083 July 30, 1993), a group of minors, represented and joined by their respective parents, instituted a taxpayers' class suit against the Secretary of the Department of Environment and Natural Resources (DENR) to compel him to cancel all timber license agreements in the country, as well as to stop issuing new ones. Claiming to represent not only their generation but also generations yet unborn, the minors asserted that continued felling of trees in Philippine rainforests would lead to deforestation and consequent irreparable damage. The lower court dismissed the complaint on the ground that the plaintiffs failed to allege a specific legal right they were seeking to enforce and protect. On certiorari, the Philippine Supreme Court recognized the locus standi of the complainants-minors and set aside the assailed judgment, as discussed in Chapter 2, above. In addition, the Court disagreed with the trial court's conclusion that the plaintiffs failed to allege with sufficient definiteness a specific legal right:

> The complaint focuses on one specific fundamental legal right—the right to a balanced and healthful ecology which, for the first time in our nation's constitutional history, is solemnly incorporated in the fundamental law. Section 16, Article II of the 1987 Constitution explicitly provides:
>
> > Sec. 16. The State shall protect and advance the right of the people to a balanced and healthful ecology in accord with the rhythm and harmony of nature.
>
> This right unites with the right to health which is provided for in the preceding section of the same article:
>
> > Sec. 15. The State shall protect and promote the right to health of the people and instill health consciousness among them.
>
> While the right to a balanced and healthful ecology is to be found under the Declaration of Principles and State Policies and not under the Bill of Rights, it does not follow that it is less important than any of the civil and political rights enumerated in the latter. Such a right belongs to a different category of rights altogether for it concerns nothing less than self-preservation and self-perpetuation—aptly and fittingly stressed by the petitioners—the advancement of which may even be said to predate all governments and constitutions. As a matter of fact, these basic rights need not even be written in the Constitution for they are assumed to exist from the inception of humankind. If they are now explicitly mentioned in the fundamental charter, it is because of the well-founded fear of its framers that unless the rights to a balanced and healthful ecology and to health are mandated as state policies by the Constitution itself, thereby highlighting their continuing importance and imposing upon the state a solemn obligation to preserve the first and protect and advance the second, the day would not be too far when all else would be lost not only for the present generation, but also for those to come—generations which stand to inherit nothing but parched earth incapable of sustaining life.
>
> The right to a balanced and healthful ecology carries with it the correlative duty to refrain from impairing the environment.

The Supreme Court granted the petition for certiorari and found a prima facie violation of the complainants-minors' rights as a result of the granting of timber licenses by the government.

In October 4, 2000, the Constitutional Court of South Africa handed down its decision in the case of *Government of the Republic of South Africa and Others v. Grootboom*, which "was acclaimed among international academics for its creative and politically astute reasoning— carving out space for itself in the policy process without usurping the space for political decision-making." At issue in this case were the applicants' right to housing and the right of children to shelter. The applicants were evicted from private land they were unlawfully occupying and camped on a nearby sports field. They subsequently applied for a court order requiring the government to provide them with basic shelter. Although the Constitutional Court "did not recognize a directly enforceable claim to housing on the part of the litigants," it issued a declaratory order requiring the government to act to meet its obligations and "implement a reasonable policy for those who are destitute." See Siri Gloppen, *Social Rights Litigation as Transformation: South African Perspectives,* in Ivar Kolstad and Hugo Stokke eds., Writing Rights: Human Rights Research at the Chr. Michelsen Institute 198402994; Bergen: Fagbokforlaget pp. 172–188.

NOTES AND QUESTIONS

1.   *Effect of State constitutions and other laws?* What is the probative value of these national constitutions and other laws that include a right to a healthy environment? Do they mean that these States automatically recognize and respect the right domestically and/or internationally and that they consider themselves legally responsible for their actions? Consider the factors identified by David Boyd above with respect to assessing the impact of constitutional provisions.

2.   *Standing.* A critical issue often is whether anyone has standing to sue to enforce an environmental provision, whether it is constitutional or statutory, in a domestic court. This can be quite complicated and is primarily a matter of the relevant domestic law, though the human right to access to justice may play a role. For an early analysis, see Robert E. Lutz, II and Stephen C. McCaffrey, *Standing on the Side of the Environment: A Statutory Prescription for Citizen Participation*, 1 Ecology L.Q. 561 (1971).

3.   *International legal norm?* What amount of State practice would be sufficient to show a firm commitment to be bound for purposes of customary international law or a general principle of law recognized by civilized nations (to use the ICJ Statute's terminology)?

4.   *So what?* What would—or does, if such a right already exists—a human right to a healthy environment (variously phrased) add, given that so many other human rights are directly relevant to protecting the environment and human health?

G. ENVIRONMENTAL JUSTICE

The concept of "environmental justice" originated in the United States, in large part as a result of studies indicating that hazardous waste facilities were being located in areas that were populated by minorities, regardless of the wealth levels of those communities. See, e.g., Robert Bullard, *Anatomy of Environmental Racism and the Environmental Justice Movement,* in Confronting Environmental Racism: Voices from the Grassroots (Robert D. Bullard ed. 1993). Subsequent research cast doubt on those studies, but the fundamental concern has not subsided. In 1994, President William Clinton issued an Executive Order (12898) regarding environmental justice, 59 Federal Register 7629, February 11, 199, as amended Exec. Order No. 12, 948, 60 Fed. Reg. 6,381 (1995).

THE NON-DISCRIMINATION PRINCIPLE IN UNITED STATES AND INTERNATIONAL ENVIRONMENTAL LAW
A. Dan Tarlock
in Annales de la Faculté de Droit, Economie et Administration de Metz No. 7637 (2007)
(France)

Executive Order 12898 . . . mandates that each federal agency "shall make achieving environmental justice part of its mission . . ." The Order legitimizes the environmental justice movement and insures that environmental justice will be a factor to be considered in the administration of existing programs and the development of new ones. [Section 6–609 of the] Order binds federal agencies and those state and local agencies that receive federal grant money, but it creates no private right against the United States.

The Executive Order does not comprehensively define the term "environmental justice" because the concept is an evolving one. The Order's lack of precision reflects the multifaceted nature of the concept. Executive Order 12898 is primarily designed to create a process to understand and to define the issues. The process, however, is informed by the belief that there are defined population groups and communities who are insufficiently protected by existing environmental programs. Thus, disproportionate impact is the only substantive standard that the Order adopts to measure existing regulatory programs. All federal agencies must now develop agency-wide justice strategies which identify and address the "disproportionately high and adverse human health or environmental effects of its programs, policies, and activities on minority populations and low-income populations.

The U.S. Environmental Protection Agency defines environmental justice as follows (http://www.epa.gov/environmentaljustice):

> Environmental Justice is the fair treatment and meaningful involvement of all people regardless of race, color, national origin, or income with respect to the development, implementation, and enforcement of environmental laws, regulations, and policies. EPA has this goal for all communities and persons across this Nation. It will be achieved when everyone enjoys the same degree of protection from environmental and health hazards and equal access to the decision-making process to have a healthy environment in which to live, learn, and work.

The EPA's definition thus appears to focus on (1) protection from disproportionate impact from environmental harm and (2) meaningful opportunity for participating in all aspects of environmental protection. Others believe it has the additional elements of ensuring equal access to environmental amenities, such as sanitation, clean drinking water and parks, as well as the achievement of an adequate level of environmental protection and the provision of access to remedies for environmental harm. E.g., Daniel Magraw & Owen Lynch, *One Species, One Planet: Environmental Justice and Sustainable Development*, in 2 World Bank Legal Review: Law, Equity and Development 441 (Ana Palacio ed., 2006).

The precise "justice" concern varies by society. For example, in India there have been concerns about unequal treatment according to caste, and in Sri Lanka according to ethnic community.

NOTES AND QUESTIONS

1. *International efforts regarding environmental justice within societies.* The United States attempted to include the concept of environmental justice in the documents at the Second United Nations Conference on Human Settlements at Istanbul in 1996. Other States objected to the inclusion of the term "environmental justice" and to the concept of "disproportionality", but did agree to include many of the individual elements of that concept in the final action plan. See Habitat Agenda, A/CONF.165/14 (1996).

2. *International efforts regarding environmental justice between societies.* The concept of environmental justice has also been used to analyze inequalities between States, including the environmental and related impacts that one State can have on other States. In this sense, it is related to the doctrine of Common But Differentiated Responsibilities as expressed in Principle 7 of the Rio Declaration on Environment and Development.

3. *Climate change.* The international discussion about climate change includes reference to "climate justice". That term, for which there is no fixed definition, refers generally to the ethical aspects of climate change and the impacts it has on environmental justice and social justice, both within and between societies.

H. INTERGENERATIONAL EQUITY

Intergenerational equity has an important rights component. For a discussion of this, see Chapter 2.

I. CLIMATE CHANGE

Human rights treaties do not mention climate change, and climate change treaties do not mention human rights. Nevertheless, although official recognition of the relationship between climate change and human rights is still developing, it is clear that climate change has critical human rights aspects. At the broadest level, these include that climate change interferes with the enjoyment of human rights and with governments' efforts to protect human rights, and that efforts to mitigate and adapt to climate change must respect, protect and fulfill human rights (just as do any other government actions).

Indeed, given the seriousness of the likely impacts of climate change and the nature and scope of efforts likely to be undertaken to mitigate and adapt to it, climate change is one of the most serious and important human rights challenges of the twenty-first century. It is already impacting the human rights of people around the world, especially those of vulnerable individuals and communities, and it will do the same for future generations.

This recognition that there is a relationship between climate change and human rights involved several steps. The first major step was the filing of the Inuit petition against the United States in the Inter-American Commission on Human Rights in 2005. See http://www.ciel.org/Publications/ICC_Petition_7Dec05.pdf. That petition is excerpted in Chapter 9 and referred to above; we suggest that you review it at this stage. The petition aroused derision in some quarters as substantively unfounded or hopeless; others welcomed it as a means for examining legal issues and putting a human face on climate change. Although the Commission chose not to proceed with the Inuit petition, it did accept a request to hold a hearing on climate change and human rights, which took place soon thereafter.

Soon after that, the Republic of the Maldives, a nation of approximately 1200 islands southwest of India with a high point of 2 meters above sea level, began an effort to develop an instrument recognizing that climate change impacts the enjoyment of human rights. Those efforts led to the Male' Declaration on the Human Dimension of Climate Change (14 November 2007), http://www.ciel.org/Publications/Male_Declaration_Nov07.pdf, which states:

> **We** the representatives of the Small Island Developing States having met in Male' from 13 to 14 November 2007,

Aware that the environment provides the infrastructure for human civilization and that life depends on the uninterrupted functioning of natural systems;

. . .

Persuaded that the impacts of climate change pose the most immediate, fundamental and far-reaching threat to the environment, individuals and communities around the planet, and that these impacts have been observed to be intensifying in frequency and magnitude;

Emphasizing that small island, low-lying coastal, and atoll states are particularly vulnerable to even small changes to the global climate and are already adversely affected by alterations in ecosystems, changes in precipitation, rising sea-levels and increased incidence of natural disasters;

. . .

Noting that the fundamental right to an environment capable of supporting human society and the full enjoyment of human rights is recognized, in varying formulations, in the constitutions of over one hundred states and directly or indirectly in several international instruments;

. . .

Concerned that climate change has clear and immediate implications for the full enjoyment of human rights including *inter alia* the right to life, the right to take part in cultural life, the right to use and enjoy property, the right to an adequate standard of living, the right to food, and the right to the highest attainable standard of physical and mental health;

Do solemnly request:

- . . .

- The Conference of the Parties of the United Nations Framework Convention on Climate Change, with the help of the Secretariat, under article 7.2(l), to seek the cooperation of the Office of the United Nations High Commissioner for Human Rights and the United Nations Human Rights Council in assessing the human rights implications of climate change.

- The Office of the United Nations High Commissioner for Human Rights to conduct a detailed study into the effects of climate change on the full enjoyment of human rights, which includes relevant conclusions and recommendations thereon, to be submitted prior to the tenth session of the Human Rights Council.

- The United Nations Human Rights Council to convene, in March 2009, a debate on human rights and climate change. . . .

In 2008, the OHCHR conducted a study of the effects of climate change on the enjoyment of human rights. The report of that study, which recognizes there is a relationship, was published in January 2009 and is excerpted above. A high-level workshop later in January of that year further publicized the relationship and led the holders of several UN Special Procedures to study the impact of climate change on the human rights that their Special Procedure focused on, and eventually to a joint statement just before the 2009 15th Conference of the Parties (COP) of the UN Framework Convention on Climate Change (UN FCCC) in Copenhagen. Moreover, the Human Rights Council did consider the relationship between climate change and human rights in March 2009. As Marc Limon describes it, by the Council discussion in 2009,

> no delegation argued with the notion that climate change has implications for a wide-range of explicitly identified, internationally-protected human rights; that already vulnerable 'climate frontline' countries are most at risk (and the least able to adapt); and that the human rights impacts do not fall evenly across a given population, but rather target marginalized or vulnerable groups, such as women and children.

Marc Limon, *Human Rights Obligations and Accountability in the Face of Climate Change*, 38 GA. J. INT'L & COMP. L. 543, 567–68 (2010).

In 2011, the Conference of the Parties of the UNFCCC also acknowledged the relationship, quoting from the 2009 Human Rights Council resolution that "the adverse effects of climate change have a range of direct and indirect implications for the effective enjoyment of human rights" (UNFCCC Conference of the Parties, 2011).

A further step in this process is that in 2014, the Human Rights Council passed a resolution in which it

> 1. *Reiterates its concern* that the adverse effects of climate change have a range of direct and indirect implications for the effective enjoyment of human rights, including the right to development, and that the effects of climate change will be felt most acutely by individuals and communities around the world that are already in vulnerable situations owing to geography, poverty, gender, age, indigenous or minority status or disability;
>
> 2. *Expresses concern* that climate change has contributed to the increase of both sudden-onset natural disasters and slow-

onset events, and that these events have adverse effects on the full enjoyment of all human rights;

3.   *Emphasizes* the urgent importance of continuing to address the adverse consequences of climate change for all, particularly in developing countries and its people whose situation is most vulnerable to climate change, especially those in a situation of extreme poverty, and deteriorating livelihood conditions, with regard to the human rights obligations of States;

In January 2015, 18 States issued the Geneva Declaration on Climate Change and Human Rights, pledging to take action in this respect. The declaration is open to accession by other States.

In sum, it is generally recognized, including by States in the contexts of both the human rights and environmental protection legal systems, that climate change affects the enjoyment of human rights and that States must observe human rights with respect to actions they take relating to climate change. As of August 2015, it is unknown how human rights will be treated in the international instrument on climate change supposed to emerge from the December 2015 UN FCCC COP in Paris.

NOTES AND COMMENTS

1.   *To everyone?* Does a State have an obligation to protect the human rights of persons outside its territory or jurisdiction from the impacts of climate change? Must a State observe human rights if it undertakes or supports climate change mitigation or adaptation activities outside its territory or jurisdiction? What does the duty to cooperate in protecting human rights mean in this context?

2.   *Who and how much?* How should responsibility for causing climate change be allocated among States, given how many sources and sinks exist? This was one of the issues that arose in the Inter-American Commission's hearing on climate change and human rights. Should States be responsible for private emissions? Should historical emissions be taken into account?

3.   *Redressability.* Suppose a State is held to be responsible for climate change damages, what remedies would be appropriate?

J. RIGHTS OF INDIGENOUS PEOPLES

1. OVERVIEW

REPORT OF THE INDEPENDENT EXPERT ON THE ISSUE OF HUMAN RIGHTS OBLIGATIONS RELATING TO THE ENJOYMENT OF A SAFE, CLEAN, HEALTHY AND SUSTAINABLE ENVIRONMENT, MAPPING REPORT

John H. Knox

A/HRC/25/53 (30 December 2013) (footnotes omitted)

76. Because of their close relationship with the environment, indigenous peoples are particularly vulnerable to impairment of their rights through environmental harm. As the Special Rapporteur on the rights of indigenous peoples has stated, "the implementation of natural resource extraction and other development projects on or near indigenous territories has become one of the foremost concerns of indigenous peoples worldwide, and possibly also the most pervasive source of the challenges to the full exercise of their rights" (A/HRC/18/35, para. 57).

77. International Labour Organization convention 169 and the United Nations Declaration on the Rights of Indigenous Peoples are designed to protect the rights of indigenous peoples, but human rights bodies have also interpreted other human rights agreements to protect those rights. The interpretations have reached generally congruent conclusions about the obligations of States to protect against environmental harm to the rights of indigenous peoples. In his reports, the Special Rapporteur on the rights of indigenous peoples has described in detail the duties of States to protect those rights. This section therefore only outlines certain main points.

78. Firstly, States have a duty to recognize the rights of indigenous peoples with respect to the territory that they have traditionally occupied, including the natural resources on which they rely. Secondly, States are obliged to facilitate the participation of indigenous peoples in decisions that concern them. The Special Rapporteur has stated that the general rule is that "extractive activities should not take place within the territories of indigenous peoples without their free, prior and informed consent," subject only to narrowly defined exceptions (A/HRC/24/41, para. 27). Thirdly, before development activities on indigenous lands are allowed to proceed, States must provide for an assessment of the activities' environmental impacts. Fourthly, States must guarantee that the indigenous community affected receives a reasonable benefit from any such development. Finally, States must provide access to remedies, including compensation, for harm caused by the activities.

2. UNITED NATIONS DECLARATION ON THE RIGHTS OF INDIGENOUS PEOPLES

The United Nations Declaration on the Rights of Indigenous Peoples (UNDRIP) was adopted by a vote of 143 in favor, 4 opposed (including Australia and the United States), and 11 abstentions. Australia and the United States later accepted UNDRIP. Excerpts follow.

UNITED NATIONS DECLARATION ON THE RIGHTS OF INDIGENOUS PEOPLES
UN Doc. A/RES/61/295 (13 Sept. 2007).

. . .

Concerned that indigenous peoples have suffered from historic injustices as a result of, inter alia, their colonization and dispossession of their lands, territories and resources, thus preventing them from exercising, in particular, their right to development in accordance with their own needs and interests,

Recognizing the urgent need to respect and promote the inherent rights of indigenous peoples which derive from their political, economic and social structures and from their cultures, spiritual traditions, histories and philosophies, especially their rights to their lands, territories and resources,

. . .

Recognizing that respect for indigenous knowledge, cultures and traditional practices contributes to sustainable and equitable development and proper management of the environment,

Solemnly proclaims the following United Nations Declaration on the Rights of Indigenous Peoples as a standard of achievement to be pursued in a spirit of partnership and mutual respect:

. . .

Article 8

1.   Indigenous peoples and individuals have the right not to be subjected to forced assimilation or destruction of their culture.

2.   States shall provide effective mechanisms for prevention of, and redress for:

(a) Any action which has the aim or effect of depriving them of their integrity as distinct peoples, or of their cultural values or ethnic identities;

(b) Any action which has the aim or effect of dispossessing them of their lands, territories or resources;

(c) Any form of forced population transfer which has the aim or effect of violating or undermining any of their rights;

(d) Any form of forced assimilation or integration;

(e) Any form of propaganda designed to promote or incite racial or ethnic discrimination directed against them.

. . .

Article 10

Indigenous peoples shall not be forcibly removed from their lands or territories. No relocation shall take place without the free, prior and informed consent of the indigenous peoples concerned and after agreement on just and fair compensation and, where possible, with the option of return.

. . .

Article 18

Indigenous peoples have the right to participate in decision-making in matters which would affect their rights, through representatives chosen by themselves in accordance with their own procedures, as well as to maintain and develop their own indigenous decision-making institutions.

Article 19

States shall consult and cooperate in good faith with the indigenous peoples concerned through their own representative institutions in order to obtain their free, prior and informed consent before adopting and implementing legislative or administrative measures that may affect them.

. . .

Article 24

1. Indigenous peoples have the right to their traditional medicines and to maintain their health practices, including the conservation of their vital medicinal plants, animals and minerals. Indigenous individuals also have the right to access, without any discrimination, to all social and health services.

2. Indigenous individuals have an equal right to the enjoyment of the highest attainable standard of physical and mental health. States shall take the necessary steps with a view to achieving progressively the full realization of this right.

Article 25

Indigenous peoples have the right to maintain and strengthen their distinctive spiritual relationship with their traditionally owned or otherwise occupied and used lands, territories, waters and coastal seas and other resources and to uphold their responsibilities to future generations in this regard.

Article 26

1.   Indigenous peoples have the right to the lands, territories and resources which they have traditionally owned, occupied or otherwise used or acquired.

2.   Indigenous peoples have the right to own, use, develop and control the lands, territories and resources that they possess by reason of traditional ownership or other traditional occupation or use, as well as those which they have otherwise acquired.

3.   States shall give legal recognition and protection to these lands, territories and resources. Such recognition shall be conducted with due respect to the customs, traditions and land tenure systems of the indigenous peoples concerned.

Article 27

States shall establish and implement, in conjunction with indigenous peoples concerned, a fair, independent, impartial, open and transparent process, giving due recognition to indigenous peoples' laws, traditions, customs and land tenure systems, to recognize and adjudicate the rights of indigenous peoples pertaining to their lands, territories and resources, including those which were traditionally owned or otherwise occupied or used. Indigenous peoples shall have the right to participate in this process.

Article 28

1.   Indigenous peoples have the right to redress, by means that can include restitution or, when this is not possible, just, fair and equitable compensation, for the lands, territories and resources which they have traditionally owned or otherwise occupied or used, and which have been confiscated, taken, occupied, used or damaged without their free, prior and informed consent.

2.   Unless otherwise freely agreed upon by the peoples concerned, compensation shall take the form of lands, territories and resources equal in quality, size and legal status or of monetary compensation or other appropriate redress.

Article 29

1.   Indigenous peoples have the right to the conservation and protection of the environment and the productive capacity of their lands

or territories and resources. States shall establish and implement assistance programmes for indigenous peoples for such conservation and protection, without discrimination.

2.   States shall take effective measures to ensure that no storage or disposal of hazardous materials shall take place in the lands or territories of indigenous peoples without their free, prior and informed consent.

3.   States shall also take effective measures to ensure, as needed, that programmes for monitoring, maintaining and restoring the health of indigenous peoples, as developed and implemented by the peoples affected by such materials, are duly implemented.

Article 30

1.   Military activities shall not take place in the lands or territories of indigenous peoples, unless justified by a relevant public interest or otherwise freely agreed with or requested by the indigenous peoples concerned.

2.   States shall undertake effective consultations with the indigenous peoples concerned, through appropriate procedures and in particular through their representative institutions, prior to using their lands or territories for military activities.

Article 31

1.   Indigenous peoples have the right to maintain, control, protect and develop their cultural heritage, traditional knowledge and traditional cultural expressions, as well as the manifestations of their sciences, technologies and cultures, including human and genetic resources, seeds, medicines, knowledge of the properties of fauna and flora, oral traditions, literatures, designs, sports and traditional games and visual and performing arts. They also have the right to maintain, control, protect and develop their intellectual property over such cultural heritage, traditional knowledge, and traditional cultural expressions.

2.   In conjunction with indigenous peoples, States shall take effective measures to recognize and protect the exercise of these rights.

Article 32

1.   Indigenous peoples have the right to determine and develop priorities and strategies for the development or use of their lands or territories and other resources.

2.   States shall consult and cooperate in good faith with the indigenous peoples concerned through their own representative institutions in order to obtain their free and informed consent prior to the approval of any project affecting their lands or territories and other resources, particularly in connection with the development, utilization or exploitation of mineral, water or other resources.

3.   States shall provide effective mechanisms for just and fair redress for any such activities, and appropriate measures shall be taken to mitigate adverse environmental, economic, social, cultural or spiritual impact.

. . .

Article 46

1.   Nothing in this Declaration may be interpreted as implying for any State, people, group or person any right to engage in any activity or to perform any act contrary to the Charter of the United Nations or construed as authorizing or encouraging any action which would dismember or impair, totally or in part, the territorial integrity or political unity of sovereign and independent States.

2.   In the exercise of the rights enunciated in the present Declaration, human rights and fundamental freedoms of all shall be respected. The exercise of the rights set forth in this Declaration shall be subject only to such limitations as are determined by law and in accordance with international human rights obligations. Any such limitations shall be non-discriminatory and strictly necessary solely for the purpose of securing due recognition and respect for the rights and freedoms of others and for meeting the just and most compelling requirements of a democratic society.

3.   The provisions set forth in this Declaration shall be interpreted in accordance with the principles of justice, democracy, respect for human rights, equality, non-discrimination, good governance and good faith.

3.   CASES

The following excerpts represent the types of analyses found in human rights cases regarding indigenous peoples in the Americas.

TIM COULTER ET AL. V. BRAZIL (YANOMAMI INDIANS)

Case 7615, Inter-Am, Comm'n H.R., Report No. 12/85, OEA/Ser.L/V/II.66, doc. 10 rev. at
Considerando ¶ 10 & Resuelve ¶ 1 (1985)
http://www.cidh.org/annualrep/84.85sp/Brasil7615.htm
(unofficial translation by Andrea Martinez)

10. After the careful examination of the facts realized by the Commission, including the answers provided by the Brazilian government, the following is concluded:

e.   With the initial motivation, in 1973, of the construction of the BR-210 highway (*Rodovia Perimetral Norte*), the territory that for immemorial times has been inhabited by the Yanomami Indians was invaded by highway construction workers, geologists, mining explorers and individuals with the desire to settle down in such territory;

f. That such invasions were carried out without any previous and appropriate protection for the security and health of the Yanomami Indians, which resulted in a considerable number of deaths due to epidemics of influenza, tuberculosis, measles, malaria, venereal diseases, etc.;

g. That indigenous communities living near the BR-210 highway (*Rodovia Perimetral Norte*) route abandoned their villages and became beggars and prostitutes without the Brazilian government adopting any necessary measures to prevent such situations;

h. After the discovery, in 1976, of tin and other metals in the region where the Yanomami Indians lived, serious conflicts began that led to violent exchanges between the explorers and exploiters and the indigenous communities. Such conflicts mainly took place in *Serra dos Surucucus, Couto de Magalhaes* and *Furo de Santa Rosa* and affected the life, security, health and cultural integrity of the Yanomami.

. . .

The Inter-American Human Rights Commission

Resolves:

1. To declare that there is sufficient record and evidence to conclude that due to the omission of the Brazilian Government to adopt opportune and effective measures in favor of the Yanomami Indians it has created a situation that has resulted in the violation, to the detriment of the Indians, of the following rights recognized in the American Declaration of the Rights and Duties of Man: the right to life, liberty and personal security (article 1); the right to residence and movement (article 8); and the right to the preservation of health and to well-being (article 9 [sic]).

THE MAYAGNA (SUMO) AWAS TINGNI COMMUNITY V. NICARAGUA

Judgment, Inter-Am. Ct. H.R. (ser. C) No. 79, ¶¶ 107, 109–112, 115–116, 121–124,127–
128, 134, 163–164 (Aug. 31, 2001), http://www1.umn.edu/humanrts/iachr/AwasTingni
case.html
(unofficial translation by the University of Minnesota)

Considerations of the Court

107. Article 1(1) of the Convention affirms that

[t]he States Parties to this Convention undertake to respect the rights and freedoms recognized herein and to ensure to all

persons subject to their jurisdiction the free and full exercise of those rights and freedoms, without any discrimination for reasons of race, color, sex, language, religion, political or other opinion, national or social origin, economic status, birth, or any other social condition.

. . .

109. The Commission argues, as a key point, lack of recognition of the rights of the Community of Awas Tingni by Nicaragua, and more specifically the ineffectiveness of the procedures set forth in legislation to make those rights of the indigenous communities effective, as well as the lack of demarcation of the lands possessed by that Community. The Commission adds that, despite multiple steps taken by the Community, official recognition of the communal property has not yet been attained, and furthermore it has been prejudiced by a logging concession granted to a company called SOLCARSA on the lands occupied by that community.

110. The State, in turn, argues basically that the Community has disproportionate claims, since its possession is not ancestral, it is requesting title to lands that have been claimed by other indigenous communities of the Atlantic Coast of Nicaragua, and it has never made a formal titling request before the competent authorities. Nicaragua also maintains that there is a legal framework which regulates the procedure of land titling for indigenous communities under the authority of the Nicaraguan Agrarian Reform Institute (INRA). As regards the logging concession granted to SOLCARSA, the State points out that the Awas Tingni Community suffered no prejudice, as that concession was not executed but rather was declared unconstitutional.

111. The Court has noted that article 25 of the Convention has established, in broad terms,

> the obligation of the States to offer, to all persons under their jurisdiction, effective legal remedy against acts that violate their fundamental rights. It also establishes that the right protected therein applies not only to rights included in the Convention, but also to those recognized by the Constitution or the law.

112. The Court has also reiterated that the right of every person to simple and rapid remedy or to any other effective remedy before the competent judges or courts, to protect them against acts which violate their fundamental rights, "is one of the basic mainstays, not only of the American Convention, but also of the Rule of Law in a democratic society, in the sense set forth in the Convention".

. . .

115. In the present case, analysis of article 25 of the Convention must be carried out from two perspectives. First, there is the need to analyze whether or not there is a land titling procedure with the characteristics mentioned above, and secondly whether the amparo remedies submitted by members of the Community were decided in accordance with article 25.

a) Existence of a procedure for indigenous land titling and demarcation:

116. Article 5 of the 1995 Constitution of Nicaragua states that:

> Freedom, justice, respect for the dignity of the human person, political, social, and ethnic pluralism, recognition of the various forms of property, free international cooperation and respect for free self-determination are principles of the Nicaraguan nation.

> . . . The State recognizes the existence of the indigenous peoples, who have the rights, duties and guarantees set forth in the Constitution, and especially those of maintaining and developing their identity and culture, having their own forms of social organization and managing their local affairs, as well as maintaining communal forms of ownership of their lands, and also the use and enjoyment of those lands, in accordance with the law. An autonomous regime is established in the [. . .] Constitution for the communities of the Atlantic Coast.

> The various forms of property: public, private, associative, cooperative, and communitarian, must be guaranteed and promoted with no discrimination, to produce wealth, and all of them while functioning freely must carry out a social function.

> . . .

121. Law No. 14, published on January 13, 1986 in La Gaceta No. 8, Official Gazette of the Republic of Nicaragua, called "Amendment to the Agrarian Reform Law", establishes in article 31 that:

> The State will provide the necessary lands for the Miskito, Sumo, Rama, and other ethnic communities of the Atlantic of Nicaragua, so as to improve their standard of living and contribute to the social and economic development of the [N]ation.

122. Based on the above, the Court believes that the existence of norms recognizing and protecting indigenous communal property in Nicaragua is evident.

123. Now then, it would seem that the procedure for titling of lands occupied by indigenous groups has not been clearly regulated in Nicaraguan legislation. According to the State, the legal framework to carry out the process of land titling for indigenous communities in the country is that set forth in Law No. 14, "Amendment to the Agrarian

Reform Law", and that process should take place through the Nicaraguan Agrarian Reform Institute (INRA). Law No. 14 establishes the procedures to guarantee property to land for all those who work productively and efficiently, in addition to determining that property may be declared "subject to" agrarian reform if it is abandoned, uncultivated, deficiently farmed, rented out or ceded under any other form, lands which are not directly farmed by their owners but rather by peasants through medieria, sharecropping, colonato, squatting, or other forms of peasant production, and lands which are being farmed by cooperatives or peasants organized under any other form of association. However, this Court considers that Law No. 14 does not establish a specific procedure for demarcation and titling of lands held by indigenous communities, taking into account their specific characteristics.

124. The rest of the body of evidence in the instant case also shows that the State does not have a specific procedure for indigenous land titling. . . .

127. In light of the above, this Court concludes that there is no effective procedure in Nicaragua for delimitation, demarcation, and titling of indigenous communal lands.

b) Administrative and judicial steps:

128. Due to the lack of specific and effective legislation for indigenous communities to exercise their rights and to the fact that the State has disposed of lands occupied by indigenous communities by granting a concession, the "General diagnostic study on land tenure in the indigenous communities of the Atlantic Coast", carried out by the Central American and Caribbean Research Council, points out that " 'amparo remedies' have been filed several times, alleging that a concession by the State (normally to a logging firm) interferes with the communal rights of a specific indigenous community".

. . .

134. In light of the criteria established on the subject by this Court, and bearing in mind the scope of reasonable terms in judicial proceedings, it can be said that the procedure followed in the various courts which heard the amparo remedies in this case did not respect the principle of a reasonable term protected by the American Convention. According to the criteria of this Court, amparo remedies will be illusory and ineffective if there is unjustified delay in reaching a decision on them.

. . .

139. From all the above, the Court concludes that the State violated article 25 of the American Convention, to the detriment of the members of the Mayagna (Sumo) Awas Tingni Community, in connection with articles 1(1) and 2 of the Convention.

. . .

163. In the instant case the Court established that Nicaragua breached articles 25 and 21 of the Convention in relation to articles 1(1) and 2 of the Convention. In this regard, the Court has reiterated in its constant jurisprudence that it is a principle of international law that any violation of an international obligation which has caused damage carries with it the obligation to provide adequate reparation for it.

164. For the aforementioned reason, pursuant to article 2 of the American Convention on Human Rights, this Court considers that the State must adopt the legislative, administrative, and any other measures required to create an effective mechanism for delimitation, demarcation, and titling of the property of indigenous communities, in accordance with their customary law, values, customs and mores. Furthermore, as a consequence of the aforementioned violations of rights protected by the Convention in the instant case, the Court rules that the State must carry out the delimitation, demarcation, and titling of the corresponding lands of the members of the Awas Tingni Community, within a maximum term of 15 months, with full participation by the Community and taking into account its customary law, values, customs and mores. Until the delimitation, demarcation, and titling of the lands of the members of the Community has been carried out, Nicaragua must abstain from acts which might lead the agents of the State itself, or third parties acting with its acquiescence or its tolerance, to affect the existence, value, use or enjoyment of the property located in the geographic area where the members of the Awas Tingni Community live and carry out their activities.

Another important case is Mercedes Julia Huenteao Beroiza et al. v. Chile (Ralco Dam), Case 4617/02, Inter-Am, Comm'n H.R., Report No. 30/04, OEA/Ser.L/V/II.122, doc. 5 rev. (2004), http://cidh.org/annualrep/2004eng/Chile.4617.02eng.htm.

On December 10, 2002 the petitioners submitted a petition to the Inter-American Commission on Human Rights alleging a violation of the American Convention on Human Rights. The petitioners also made a request for precautionary measures to prevent irreparable harm from flooding the lands of the Mapuche Pehuenche from the Upper Bio Bio. In 1993 ENDESA Chile (a company) was authorized to build a hydroelectric plant in Ralco (where the petitioners live). However, the construction was only to take place if the indigenous population living there willingly provided consent and a proper swap of land that satisfied the indigenous community with approval from the National Corporation for Indigenous Development.

Though the Mapuche community opposed the construction of the dam, ENDESA Chile began construction in 1993. The Chilean government carried out an appraisal of the relevant land, despite opposition from the Mapuche community. By the time the petition was submitted to the Commission, 70% of the dam had already been constructed.

On December 12 the State of Chile received the petition from the Commission with a notice to respond and a request to "refrain from taking any steps that might alter the *status quo* in the matter," (¶ 5) until the Commission adopts a final decision. On December 19, the State of Chile wrote to the Commission asking it to "explain precisely the content and scope of the request made to the State." (¶ 6) The Commission replied to this request in a note on December 23: "the purpose of the request made to the State of Chile is to ensure that the decisions of the organs of the inter-American system of human rights are not rendered meaningless efforts to protect the human person. Accordingly, the State should refrain from any act that might broaden or exacerbate the dispute and impair the effectiveness of any decision that the Commission might potentially adopt." (¶ 6)

Ultimately the State of Chile and the petitioners reached a "Friendly Settlement Agreement" on October 17, 2003, and on March 11, 2004 the Commission approved the Friendly Settlement Agreement and requested the parties to regularly report on compliance with the Agreement. In that agreement, the State of Chile stated:

> The State of Chile reiterates its respect for the rights of indigenous peoples and their communities, as well as its will to promote, through the mechanisms provided under the country's laws, full recognition and protection for said rights. In this context, recognizing that the indigenous question is an affair of State, and convinced that its adequate solution is essential to ensure social unity and peace, it has been agreed to implement the following measures to strengthen the legal institutions for protection of indigenous peoples, together with the activities mentioned in each case (§ III.1)

The Friendly Settlement Agreement included six requirements: (1) improve the legal institutions protecting the rights of indigenous peoples and their communities; (2) strengthen the territorial and cultural identity of the Mapuche Pehuenche people, as well as mechanisms for participation in their own development; (3) foster development and environmental conservation in the Upper Bio Bio sector; (4) agree on urgent measures with respect to the lawsuits against indigenous leaders who have been persecuted for acts connected with the construction of the Ralco Plant; (5) satisfy the private demands of the Mapuche Pehuenche families concerned; (6) the agreement is a single whole in which each item has the same value; and (7) to report to the Inter-American Commission on Human Rights. In practice, this included: the Chilean government's promise to try to reform the Chilean constitution to recognize indigenous rights; an indigenous-community municipality to secure political autonomy; provision of contiguous and high quality land (the original offer had involved non-continuous, low-quality land spread among several existing non-indigenous municipalities); and monetary compensation of US$300,000 per extended family.

NOTES AND QUESTIONS

1. *Free, prior and informed consent.* It is generally, though not universally, recognized that indigenous peoples have a right to free, prior and informed consent (FPIC) regarding decisions affecting the natural resources that they rely on. It is at least arguable that other communities that rely on natural resources, such as forests, waterways and fisheries, have a similar right to FPIC. See, e.g., D. Magraw & L. Baker, *Emerging Human Rights Norms: Community-Based Property Rights and Prior Informed Consent by Communities*, 35 U. Denver L.J. 413 (2007).

2. *A veto right?* Does FPIC give an indigenous or other community the right to veto a proposed project? Consider the effect of paragraph 2 of article 46 of the UN Declaration on the Rights of Indigenous Peoples (UNDRIP), above. Analysis concluding that article 46 allows the State to proceed with eminent domain without a veto right allowed the United States to accept UNDRIP.

CHAPTER 16

ENVIRONMENT AND TRADE

∎ ∎ ∎

Environmental protection and free trade are inherently linked. Measures to protect the environment often affect trade between countries; for example, protecting against pesticide-contaminated food may require regulating imports. Similarly, trade measures certainly affect environmental conditions; for example, trade disciplines place limits on what environmental protection measures are permissible, and trade may lead to the introduction of exotic species that alter local ecosystems, such as zebra mussels in the Great Lakes. Until recently, most discussions of trade and environmental issues have focused on facilitating freer trading relationships and on fitting environmental concerns into the framework of trade law. The traditional approach has been to identify trade issues raised by environmental measures, to assess their consistency with the General Agreement on Tariffs and Trade (GATT), and then to assess how the measures might be made consistent with GATT. Those concerned with environmental protection have criticized this approach as not giving sufficient weight to environmental concerns.

The materials that follow are intended to introduce readers to some of the major environment-and-trade issues. Note that this chapter focuses on trade in goods, and by and large does not include consideration of trade in services, intellectual property or investment. The latter three areas raise important issues, but the texts of the relevant agreements, the jurisprudence and (for investment) the dispute settlement mechanisms differ. More generally, bear in mind that trade law (including trade in goods and services, investment and intellectual property law) is an unusually complex area of international law, and that these materials only touch on some aspects of it, even with respect to trade in goods.

A. OVERVIEW: ENVIRONMENT AND TRADE IN INTERNATIONAL LAW

1. HISTORICAL INTRODUCTION

Modern international concern with trading relationships dates back to just after World War I. The first trade negotiations thereafter led to a 1927 agreement on abolishing import and export restrictions, which never came into effect. In 1929 countries faced a world depression, and in the

1930s national protectionism reigned, as exemplified by the U.S. Smoot-Hawley Tariff Act of 1930. After World War II, countries concerned with avoiding another world depression sought to create a regime that would promote free trade and squash protectionism. They tried to establish an International Trade Organization, but in the end settled in 1947 for the General Agreement on Tariffs and Trade (GATT), which eventually became the venerable framework for trading relationships. Only in 1994, after the end of the Cold War between the United States and the former Soviet Union, did countries successfully conclude a new World Trade Organization (WTO) Agreement, which includes several agreements and incorporates the GATT (now sometimes referred to as GATT 1994). Regional trade relationships had been created (e.g., the European Community in 1954 via the Treaty of Rome). Also, in the early 1990s Canada, Mexico, and the United States concluded the North American Free Trade Agreement (NAFTA), an innovative regional trade agreement facilitating open and free trade among the three countries.

In contrast, countries were not as yet concerned in the immediate post-World War II period with environmental protection because they had not recognized their capacity to degrade the environment irreversibly on a large scale, except by using nuclear weapons. Rachel Carson's famous book, *The Silent Spring*, which promoted environmental consciousness in the United States and abroad, was published only in 1962. The first major piece of United States national environmental legislation, the National Environmental Policy Act, was enacted in 1969, and the United States Environmental Protection Agency was established only in 1971. Internationally, the picture is similar. In 1972 countries held the first United Nations conference concerned with environmental issues, which led directly to the formation of the United Nations Environment Programme. At the time there were only about three dozen multilateral environmental agreements concerned with the environment, and these included agreements primarily concerned with promoting use of living natural resources.

Unlike the trade area, where GATT and the WTO have provided the basic law on tariffs and trade, there is no general international agreement on environmental and natural resource protection. Rather there are many separate legal instruments, some with overlapping provisions and each with a differing set of countries as Parties. Thus, it is perhaps not surprising that the environment/trade debate has been focused on how environmental measures can fit into the one internationally accepted global legal framework that exists—GATT, and now the WTO. (The text of the original GATT, adopted in 1947, was incorporated as one of the WTO agreements; the 1947 GATT expired on December 31, 1995, one year after the WTO agreements, including GATT 1994, went into effect).

In order to integrate environment and trade, it is helpful to identify what each community is trying to accomplish, i.e., their values and goals, and on that basis to examine why each community is concerned about the other.

The fundamental goal of trade liberalization is promoting free trade, and the subsidiary goal is to remove barriers to trade in goods and services. These goals are based on the theory of comparative advantage, i.e., that every country will be better off if it produces and exports those goods and services which it can most efficiently produce given its mix of inputs and if it imports goods and services which it has a comparative disadvantage producing, and that this will lead, in theory, to an increase in trade, economic growth and living standards. Trade barriers interfere with this outcome and thus should be eliminated. The various techniques used to do this vary according to the type of economic activity and non-trade policy involved. They include limits on tariff levels, requirements of most-favored nation treatment and national treatment, prohibitions on quotas, and requirements that least-trade-restrictive measures be used to achieve non-trade policy goals. These and other trade rules, referred to as "disciplines," are described elsewhere in this chapter.

Regarding environmental protection, the fundamental environmental goals are to protect human, animal and plant health and ecosystems and to conserve the natural and cultural environment. As developed in previous chapters, various techniques are used to protect the environment, such as emission limits (e.g., to water, air or soil), ambient environmental standards (e.g., in air, water or soil), reporting requirements (e.g., toxic release inventories), inspection requirements (e.g., of goods being imported), performance requirements (e.g., regarding waste disposal), permitting requirements (e.g., for emissions into water bodies), remediation requirements (e.g., clean-up standards), cap-and-trade systems (e.g., regarding sulphur dioxide), access and use restrictions (e.g., regarding protected areas), private remedies (e.g., nuisance cases), technology requirements (e.g., regarding process and production methods such as using turtle excluder devices while fishing for shrimp), and restrictions on imports (e.g., requirements that new chemicals must be proven to be safe before they may be imported and prohibitions on importing endangered species of plants or animals). Unlike trade liberalization (which is based on the theory of comparative advantage), there is no overarching paradigm for environmental protection. Differing threats, resources and political realities lead to different approaches. Opinions differ sharply on issues such as whether the value of nature depends only on its utility to humans. Different States and communities have different risk preferences.

Why, then, is each community concerned about the other?

Advocates of free trade are concerned about environmental protection efforts because environmental laws and regulations can act as trade barriers and interfere with free trade. Two types of trade barriers exist: tariffs and non-tariff barriers (NTBs). Tariffs are relatively unimportant in terms of integrating environment and trade. NTBs, however, include quotas and other measures that have the effect of restricting trade even if they are not phrased in trade terms and relate to other areas of human behavior. Importantly, many measures designed to protect health, safety and the environment qualify as NTBs. For example, a requirement that automobiles contain a catalytic converter of specific characteristics and a prohibition against DDT residues on food are NTBs because imported goods must comply with them. Trade advocates are concerned that sometimes environmental measures having trade effects are intentionally onerous ("disguised protectionism" or "disguised barriers to trade") in order to advantage economically the country imposing the environmental measure. Trade regimes thus include rules defining the circumstances under which such environmental measures are permissible.

In addition, developing countries often express a different concern, i.e., that attempts to protect the environment via measures that affect trade are either intended to, or have the effect of, conditioning developing countries' access to markets on adherence to prescribed environmental standards. They point to the fact that complying with even legitimate environmental standards can be financially costly, technically complex and administratively complicated.

The environmental community, in turn, is concerned about trade liberalization because international trade rules designed to eliminate NTBs can be unnecessarily strict, thus leaving too little policy space to enact and enforce necessary environmental measures or undercut or eviscerate existing ones. This process can also lead to a downward harmonization of environmental protection standards. Alternatively, the environmental community is concerned that economic integration can lead to "pollution havens", including the potential that countries might relax their health, safety and environmental standards in order to attract international investment or gain a competitive advantage (a "race to the bottom"). Further, there is a serious lack of transparency and public participation in the development and implementation of trade agreements, and in related dispute settlement. These issues are particularly significant to the environmental community because of the critical roles that transparency and public participation play in environmental protection, both domestically and internationally.

It thus is obvious that trade liberalization and environmental protection are integrally related and that the legal regime about each must appropriately consider the other. In addition to the legal complexities created by that reality, lack of a common knowledge base, terminology differences and "cultural" differences exist that complicate the relationship.

There often is no common knowledge base between trade and environmental experts, with the result that they do not understand the values and approaches important to the other area. Without such an understanding, the process of integrating the two areas is impossible. This problem arises for a variety of reasons, including that the areas are distinct, that each area is complex and multi-layered, and that officials and staff typically work only in one area and do not move between them.

Terminology can be a barrier to integrating environment and trade because the meaning of important terms differs between the two communities. Three examples will suffice: "protection", "discrimination" and "transparency". Trade experts want to prevent and eliminate protectionalism that interferes with free trade; for them protection is the devil incarnate. In contrast, for the environmental community, protection (e.g., of human health, a species or an ecosystem) is a fundamental goal. "Discrimination" raises a similar problem. Trade experts think of discrimination in terms of the Most Favored Nation and National Treatment disciplines common in the trade area, and they know that discrimination is allowed under a limited set of circumstances that include protecting human, animal and plant health (e.g., GATT Article XX(b)). Environmental experts, in contrast, tend to think of discrimination on the basis of race, religion, gender, national origin, etc.— something that is not allowed under virtually any circumstances. "Transparency" in trade parlance means that laws must be publicly available and knowable. In contrast, in environmental parlance, transparency also refers to decision-making processes being publicly knowable and open to public participation. This is particularly important because public participation, which is impossible without transparency (in the environmental sense), has played a critical role in environmental protection, both domestically and internationally. These examples illustrate how terminology can interfere with efforts to communicate and integrate.

There is also a difference in what might be called the "culture" of the two communities that can interfere with integration efforts. This difference turns on the values and interests that have traditionally been at stake in the two areas. Especially when only tariffs were involved, a trade negotiator could trade off different items as long as the overall economic package came out in a defined range. Thus, for example, just as a banker can trade off a higher interest rate for a higher initiation fee, trade negotiators might be able to trade off a given deal on wheat tariffs or controls for a better deal on soy beans. Environmentalists, in contrast, tend to be wary of trade-offs and instead to view the process like mountain climbers: everyone needs to be roped together because they don't know who might fall and they may need everyone if someone does fall. There are several reasons for this view: environmental issues are inter-connected; most environmental values are not monetizable or interchangeable on a quantitative (or often even on a qualitative) basis; many environmental problems cannot be solved by one country acting alone; and the risk of free riders exists. These cultural differences also can impede communication and cooperation between the two communities and thus integration of environment and trade.

Beginning in 1991, the OECD recognized the need for the trade and the environment communities to talk to each other, and joint meetings of the OECD's committees on trade and on environment were initiated. The GATT also held in November 1991 the first meeting of its Working Group on Trade and Environment.

On April 14, 1994, parties to the GATT signed a Final Act embodying the results of the Uruguay Round of Multilateral Trade Negotiations at Marrakesh, Morocco, thus creating the WTO. In this document, the Ministers decided "to direct the first meeting of the General Council of the WTO to establish a Committee on Trade and Environment open to all members of the WTO." The Committee was directed to address seven issues initially, as follows:

- the relationship between the provisions of the multilateral trading system and trade measures for environmental purposes, including those pursuant to multilateral environmental agreements;

- the relationship between environmental policies relevant to trade and environmental measures with significant trade effects and the provisions of the multilateral trading system;

- the relationship between the provisions of the multilateral trading system and (a) charges and taxes for environmental purposes and (b) requirements for environmental purposes relating to products, including standards and technical regulations, packaging, labeling and recycling;

- the relationship between the provisions of the multilateral trading system with respect to the transparency of trade measures used for environmental purposes and environmental measures and requirements that have significant trade effects;

- the relationship between the dispute settlement mechanisms in the multilateral trading system and those found in multilateral environmental agreements;

- the effect of environmental measures on market access, especially in relation to developing countries, in particular

to the least developed among them, and environmental
benefits of removing trade restrictions and distortions; and

- the issue of exports of domestically prohibited goods.

The Doha Agenda, adopted in 2001 at the Fourth WTO Ministerial
Conference, specified several environment-and-trade topics for specific
negotiation. Paragraph 28 deals with fishing subsidies, a problem that is
both distorting of trade and destructive of the environment and thus
considered to be a classic "win-win" situation. In December 2008, the
Chair of the Negotiating Group on Rules issued a "roadmap" on fisheries
subsidies for further discussions, but progress on the issue has stalled.

Paragraph 31(i) of the Doha Agenda identified other areas for
negotiation: the relationship between existing WTO rules and
multilateral environmental agreements (MEAs), the collaboration
between the WTO and MEA secretariats, and the elimination of tariff and
non-tariff barriers to environmental goods and services (Note: the term
"environmental services" here means something entirely different from
ecological services discussed in earlier chapters). In July 2014, 14 WTO
members (Australia, Canada, China, Costa Rica, the European Union,
Hong Kong (China), Japan, Korea, New Zealand, Norway, Singapore,
Switzerland, Chinese Taipei, and the United States), which account for
86% of the world trade in environmental goods, formally opened
negotiations in the WTO on the Environmental Goods Agreement (EGA)
to remove tariffs on environmental goods or so-called "green goods". The
negotiations are to build on the list of 54 environmental goods agreed by
the Asia-Pacific Economic Cooperation (APEC) in 2012 to reduce tariffs.

Regional, including bilateral, trade relations have received mounting
attention since roughly 2000. The European Union and the United States,
for example, have negotiated and concluded many bilateral trade
agreements, sometimes including chapters on investment. Many bilateral
investment treaties, or BITs, have been negotiated. As of August 2015,
more than 3200 existed.

ADDITIONAL READINGS

For general references on environment and trade issues, *see*, e.g.,
Daniel C. Esty, Greening the GATT (1994) Ernst-Ulrich Petersmann,
International and European Trade and Environmental Law After the
Uruguay Round (1995); Asia Dragons and Green Trade (Simon S.C. Tay
& Daniel C. Esty, eds. 1996); Thomas Schoenbaum, International Trade
and Protection of the Environment: The Continuing Search for
Reconciliation, 91 Am. J. Intl. L. 268 (1997); Nathalie Bernasconi-
Osterwalder, Daniel Magraw, Maria Julia Oliva, Marcos Orellana &
Elisabeth Tuerk, Environment and Trade: A Guide to Jurisprudence
(2006); Reconciling Environment and Trade, 2nd ed. (Edith Brown Weiss,
John H. Jackson, & Natalie Bernasconi-Osterwalder, eds. 2008); Erich

Vranes, Trade and the Environment: Fundamental Issues in International Law, WTO Law, and Legal Theory (2009); Chris Wold, Sanford Gaines & Greg Block, Trade and the Environment: Law and Policy (2011); James K.R. Watson, The WTO and the Environment: Development of Competence Beyond Trade (2013).

2. DISPUTE SETTLEMENT IN THE WORLD TRADE ORGANIZATION

The agreements establishing the World Trade Organization (WTO) brought important changes to the settlement of trade disputes. These changes are found in the Dispute Settlement Understanding (DSU), which is Annex 2 to the WTO Agreement. The DSU is administered by the Dispute Settlement Body (DSB), which is basically the WTO Council. The importance of the DSU is reflected in Article III of the WTO Agreement, which states that a principal function of the WTO is administering the DSU. As a general matter, these changes were designed to increase the likelihood that disputes would be settled within the WTO and thereby to reduce the need for countries (such as the United States) to take unilateral measures to protect their rights.

There are up to ten steps in the full WTO dispute settlement process. The process starts with consultations between the parties to attempt to resolve their differences (DSU, Article 4.7). If these consultations are unsuccessful, parties may use the GATT conciliation or mediation services. A party may also opt, however, to establish a Panel to decide the dispute. If parties opt to establish a Panel, a Panel is chosen and terms of reference are decided. The Panel hears submissions by the disputing parties and other interested parties and issues a report. Thereafter, the DSB must adopt the report unless there is a consensus against adoption. If either of the disputing parties is dissatisfied with the results of a panel decision, it may appeal the decision to the Appellate Body, which is composed of seven persons appointed for four-year terms, who serve in panels of three. Prior to the DSU, there was no Appellate Body. The Appellate Body can only consider issues of law and legal interpretations developed by the original panel and must issue a report 60 to 90 days after hearing the submissions of the parties. Like the original panel report, the report of the Appellate Body is to be adopted automatically unless there is a consensus to the contrary, and the losing party must implement the recommendations and inform the DSB. The DSB monitors implementation and, in the event the recommendations are not implemented, authorizes the withdrawal of trade concessions, unless there is a consensus to the contrary. The WTO dispute settlement process differs markedly from the GATT dispute settlement process. The GATT process offered multiple opportunities for parties to delay or prevent decisions. For example, prior to 1989, there was no right to have a panel established; the right was not completely clarified until the DSU came into effect. A party could also delay decisions by disputing composition of a panel and its terms of reference.

Most importantly, any party, even the losing party, could block adoption of a panel report. On the one hand, this led some countries, principally the United States, that were frustrated with their inability to force compliance with a report to take action unilaterally. The United States usually acted under Section 301 of the Trade Act of 1974, as amended, which was a source of intense friction with the United States' trading partners, who viewed the law as a heavy-handed means to allow the United States to enforce its will on them. On the other hand, the ability to block adoption of a panel report allowed countries to blunt the effect of panel reports they did not like, such as the tuna-dolphin reports (discussed in Section D, below). In contrast, under the DSU, panel reports will be adopted unless there is a consensus to the contrary or a party appeals. In return, WTO members are required by Article 23.1 to use the DSU process exclusively if they "seek the redress of a violation of obligations or other nullification or impairment of benefits under the covered agreements."

While the DSU dramatically strengthened the WTO dispute resolution process, it has not resolved all problems with the process. Those concerned with the environment have made three related complaints about the process. First, although the DSU gives third parties who have a "substantial interest" in a dispute the right to make a presentation to the deciding panel, this right is extended only to WTO members. As a result, environmental groups do not have the right under the DSU to present their views directly to a dispute resolution panel and can participate only by either submitting an amicus curiae brief or indirectly by lobbying trade officials of their country to present their view. In United States courts, in contrast, environmental groups may be able to submit amicus curiae briefs or intervene in a case either permissively or by right. Second, proceedings of panels are secret unless the parties to the dispute agree otherwise. Thus, the public and other WTO Members are able to learn what is happening in the panel proceedings only if informed by an official of a party to the dispute or through leaks to the media. The WTO held its first open hearing in the fall of 2005, in the *Beef Hormones* case, in which the main parties (the United States and the European Commission) agreed to open the proceedings to the public. The hearing could be viewed in another room via closed circuit television; interestingly, most of those viewing were WTO delegates from other WTO Members. Third, panels are composed of trade experts, not environmental or scientific experts, with the result that needed expertise and perspective are missing, and so, the environmentalists argue, the decisions are flawed. The WTO Agreement provides for the use of subgroups of scientific experts, but the decision-making power still lies with the members of the panels.

Environmentalists are not the only group in the United States concerned about the DSU. Many conservatives have been concerned that the DSU will transfer United States sovereignty to the WTO. As a result, in order to secure United States participation in the WTO, President William Clinton made a number of concessions to Congress, which are found in the statute implementing the WTO Agreement and the Statement of Administrative Action submitted by President Clinton to Congress. Key requirements include reporting and congressional consultation (to the House Ways and Means and Senate Finance Committees) concerning WTO decision-making and dispute settlement, five-year reviews of United States participation in the WTO, and support for consensus-based resolution of the dispute. More importantly, the implementing act establishes a three-judge panel to review all cases that the United States loses. In the event that the United States loses three or more cases, the panel is to decide whether to recommend continued United States participation in the WTO.

In 2001, at the Doha Ministerial, Trade Ministers agreed to improve and clarify the DSU, based on an earlier review of the DSU and various proposals submitted by Members. The United States and some other Members advocated increased transparency and opportunities for public participation. But considerable disagreement arose with respect to whether to open dispute settlement procedures to the public, provide timely access to submissions and Panel and Appellate Body reports, and formalize the treatment of amicus curiae briefs. Negotiators failed to meet a 2003 deadline for concluding the DSU negotiations, just as Members had failed to meet previous deadlines with respect to the DSU. In June 2003, Dr. Supachai Panitchpakdi, WTO Director-General at the time, constituted the Consultative Board, chaired by Peter D. Sutherland, to examine the functioning of the WTO as an institution and to prepare a report on the future of the WTO. The report, known as the Sutherland Report, discusses the WTO Dispute Settlement System, and calls for opening hearings and arbitrations to the public. Though these suggestions have not led to agreement, panel and Appellate Body proceedings are becoming increasingly transparent in practice. Between 2005 and 2012, 19 hearings and arbitrations were opened to the public, including both Panel and Appellate Body proceedings. In addition, parties are increasingly choosing to make their written submissions open to the public, and panels and the Appellate Body are increasingly accepting and considering amicus briefs in deciding their cases. *See* Gabrielle Marceau and Mikella Hurley, *Transparency and Public Participation in the WTO: A Report Card on WTO Transparency Mechanisms*, 4 Trade Law and Development 19 (2012). Notably, the Sutherland Report also suggests that, while the DSU has traditionally focused on the WTO texts, "the Appellate Body has, on occasion, been forced to confront strong arguments that its interpretation should not be totally confined to embellishing trade policies, but on the contrary, it must weigh, or balance, such policies in certain situations against other kinds of policies, such as environmental protection." (Sutherland Report para. 236).

In July 2008 the Chairman of the Special Session of the Dispute Settlement Body issued under his own responsibility a consolidated draft text for a proposed amendment to the DSU. Negotiations have taken place since then on the basis of this draft legal text, but as of August 2015, States had not reached agreement to reform the DSU.

3. RELEVANT GATT PROVISIONS

Two main types of environmentally related disputes have come before the GATT and now the WTO: (1) those involving domestic laws ostensibly directed to protecting the national environment; and (2) those involving unilateral measures to protect the global environment. Both types of disputes have usually involved issues of consistency with the following GATT/WTO provisions: Article I (requirement of unconditional most favored nation treatment), Article III (requirement of national treatment of so-called like products), Article XI (prohibition of import restraints), and Article XX(b) and (g) (exceptions that apply should a violation of a GATT article occur). As Frieder Roessler, former Director of Legal Affairs for both the GATT and then the WTO, has explained for Article I, "its fundamental function is to ensure that each contracting party accord access to its markets independently of any of the policies of the trading partner, including domestic policies." Frieder Roessler, *Diverging Domestic Policies and Multilateral Trade Integration*, 2 Fair Trade and Harmonization 21, 31 (J. Bhagwati & R. Hudec, eds. 1996). The relevant parts of Articles I, III, XI, and XX follow, together with Article XXI providing for "Security Exceptions."

THE GENERAL AGREEMENT ON TARIFFS AND TRADE 1994 EXCERPTS
55 UNTS 187 (1947)

ARTICLE I: GENERAL MOST-FAVOURED NATION TREATMENT

1.   With respect to customs duties and charges of any kind imposed on or in connection with importation or exportation or imposed on the international transfer of payments for imports or exports, and with respect to the method of levying such duties and charges, and with respect to all rules and formalities in connection with importation and exportation, and with respect to all matters referred to in paragraphs 2 and 4 of Article III, any advantage, favour, privilege or immunity granted by any contracting party to any product originating in or destined for any other country shall be accorded immediately and unconditionally to the like product originating in or destined for the territories of all other contracting parties. . . .

ARTICLE III: NATIONAL TREATMENT ON INTERNAL TAXATION AND REGULATION . . .

4. The products of the territory of any contracting party imported into the territory of any other contracting party shall be accorded treatment no less favourable than that accorded to like products of national origin in respect of all laws, regulations, and requirements affecting their internal sale, offering for sale, purchase, transportation, distribution or use. The provisions of this paragraph shall not prevent the application of differential internal transportation charges which are based exclusively on the economic operation of the means of transport and not on the nationality of the product.

ARTICLE XI: GENERAL ELIMINATION OF QUANTITATIVE RESTRICTIONS

1. No prohibitions or restrictions other than duties, taxes or other charges, whether made effective through quotas, import or export licenses or other measures, shall be instituted or maintained by any contracting party on the importation of any product of the territory of any other contracting party or on the exportation or sale for export of any product destined for the territory of any other contracting party. . . .

ARTICLE XX: GENERAL EXCEPTIONS

Subject to the requirement that such measures are not applied in a manner which would constitute a means of arbitrary or unjustifiable discrimination between countries where the same conditions prevail, or a disguised restriction on international trade, nothing in this Agreement shall be construed to prevent the adoption or enforcement by any contracting party of measures:

(a) necessary to protect public morals;

(b) necessary to protect human, animal or plant life or health;

(c) relating to the importations or exportations of gold or silver;

(d) necessary to secure compliance with laws or regulations which are not inconsistent with the provisions of this Agreement, ...

(e) relating to the products of prison labour;

(f) imposed for the protection of national treasures of artistic, historic or archaeological value;

(g) relating to the conservation of exhaustible natural resources if such measures are made effective in conjunction with restrictions on domestic production or consumption; . . . (h, i, j. . . .)

ARTICLE XXI: SECURITY EXCEPTIONS

Nothing in this Agreement shall be construed

(a) to require any contracting party to furnish any information the disclosure of which it considers contrary to its essential security interests; or (b) to prevent any contracting party from taking such action which it considers necessary for the protection of its essential security interests (i) relating to fissionable materials or the materials from which they are derived; (ii) relating to the traffic in arms, ammunitions and implements of war and to such traffic in other goods and materials as is carried on directly or indirectly for the purpose of supplying a military establishment; (iii) taken in time of war or other emergency in international relations; or (c) to prevent any contracting party from taking any action in pursuance of its obligations under the United Nations Charter for the maintenance of international peace and security.

The mode of analysis of the GATT provisions is as follows. First, the panel must find a violation of one or more provisions of GATT. If such a violation is found, then the panel proceeds to examine the Article XX exceptions, either XX(b) or XX(g). If the dispute comes within one of the two exceptions, then the panel will look at the chapeau language in Article XX to see whether these conditions are fully satisfied. It is important to note that the panel does not go directly to Article XX, but rather must first find a problem under the other provisions of GATT and then it must determine whether the measure satisfies Article XX. Similarly, the panel can only analyze the case in terms of the chapeau after it has determined that the dispute falls within either XX(b) or XX(g).

4. OTHER WTO AGREEMENTS

Some environmentally related disputes may involve the Technical Barriers to Trade Agreement (TBT), the Sanitary and Phytosanitary Measures Agreement (SPS), and the Trade-Related Aspects of Intellectual Property Rights Agreement (TRIPS), all of which are part of the WTO. (See Chapter 13 on biodiversity, for TRIPS related issues.)

The TBT covers technical regulations, voluntary standards and the procedures designed to ensure that these are met. The type of measure determines whether it comes within the TBT. The TBT provides for non-discrimination in the measures covered, encourages the development of international standards, and requires the establishment of a national "Enquiry Point" or information office. Relevant provisions of the TBT are contained in the material related to cigarettes and to ecolabeling later in this chapter.

The SPS Agreement, as noted by the WTO, "sets out basic rules for food safety and animal and plant health standards. It allows countries to set their own standards, but it also says regulations must be based on science. They should be applied only to the extent necessary to protect human, animal or plant life or health. And they should not arbitrarily or unjustifiably discriminate between countries where identical or similar conditions prevail." The SPS encourages countries to use international standards, but they may use measures resulting in higher standards if there is scientific justification. The SPS Agreement was relevant in the Beef Hormones dispute, discussed later in this chapter.

5. MULTILATERAL ENVIRONMENTAL AGREEMENTS

Some multilateral environmental agreements (MEAs) use trade restrictions as a primary instrument to accomplish the purposes of the agreements. With respect to conserving natural resources, these include the Convention on International Trade in Endangered Species (CITES), which restricts trade in species listed by countries in three appendices, and the International Whaling Convention. Regional agreements on conserving biological diversity also incorporate this approach. In the area of hazardous wastes, both the Basel Convention on the Transboundary Movement of Hazardous Wastes and regional/bilateral hazardous waste agreements restrict trade in covered wastes. In respect of toxic chemicals, the Rotterdam Convention on Prior Informed Consent, the Stockholm Convention on Persistent Organic Pollutants and the Minamata Convention on Mercury utilize trade measures. The Montreal Protocol on Substances that Deplete the Ozone Layer also contains important provisions restricting trade with non-Parties to the agreement, as does the Cartagena Biosafety Protocol to the Convention on Biological Diversity. The provisions differ in important details, including under what circumstances nonparties to the agreement can still trade with Parties to the agreement. The legal question is in case of an apparent conflict between the MEA and the GATT which agreement prevails.

The answer to that question is not clear. If all the parties to the dispute (or perhaps all the Parties to the WTO, see below) are Parties to all of the agreements involved in the dispute, one might argue that either the more specific (using the doctrine of *lex specialis* and the Vienna Convention on the Law of Treaties) or the later-in-time (using the doctrine of *lex posterior* and the Vienna Convention on the Law of Treaties) should control. This could result in peculiar results, however, where trade measures are concerned, because it may be purely fortuitous which agreement is later-in-time. The Montreal Protocol on Substances that Deplete the Ozone Layer (though not all of its amendments) pre-dates the WTO agreements. Should that fact mean that disputes between Parties to both agreements must disregard the Montreal Protocol (or disregard the WTO if the amendments have the effect of renewing the date of the Montreal Protocol)? That sort of either-or choice may not be the most preferable way to cast the question. Another approach would be to refer to the obligation of States under article 31.3(c) of the Vienna Convention on the Law of Treaties to take into account in interpreting international agreements "any relevant rules of international law applicable in the relations between the two parties". Another way to reconcile apparent conflicts would be to make use of what the UN International Law Commission (ILC) refers to as the "harmonization principle" of interpretation: "when several norms bear on a single issue they should, to the extent possible, be interpreted so as to give rise to a single set of compatible obligations." Rep. of the Int'l Law Comm'n, 58th sess., May 1–June 9, July 3–Aug. 11, 2006, para. 251 § 1(4), U.N. Doc. A/61/10; GAOR 61st Sess., Supp. No. 10 (2006).

The problem is probably even more complicated with respect to countries that are not party to the MEA at issue in a dispute. Several international environmental agreements contain explicit provisions prohibiting import and export of products unless the exporting and importing countries are parties to the agreement or are complying with it. Such provisions provide incentives both to join the agreement and, in certain cases, to comply with the provisions of the agreement. For example, the Montreal Protocol on Substances That Deplete the Ozone Layer contains such provisions.

A further level of complication arises when new norms of international law might appear to be in conflict with WTO law (or otherwise affect it). The International Court of Justice has held that new norms must be taken into account even with respect to continuing activities governed by existing international agreements. In discussing new norms relating to environmental protection and sustainable development, the ICJ said: "Such new norms have to be taken into consideration, and such new standards given proper weight, not only when States contemplate new activities but also when continuing with activities begun in the past *Gabčíkovo-Nagymaros Project (Hung./Slovk.)* 1997 I.C.J. Rep. 7 (Sept. 25), at 78, para. 140. The doctrine of inter-temporal law has been applied in at least two subsequent cases involving international rivers governed by basin agreements, once by the ICJ in the *Pulp Mills* case (*Pulp Mills on the River Uruguay (Arg. v. Uru.)* 2010 I.C.J. Rep. 14 at para. 177, 204–205 (Apr. 20)), and once by the Court of Arbitration established pursuant to the Indus Waters Treaty of 1960. *Indus Waters Kishenganga Arbitration (Pak. v. India)* Final Award (2013).

a. The Role of MEAs and International Environmental Law in Deciding WTO Disputes

Two WTO cases deal with MEAs. The Appellate Body in the 1998 *Shrimp-Turtle* case took the Convention on Biological Diversity (CBD) and the Convention on International Trade in Endangered Species (CITES) into account. In contrast, in the *EC—Biotech* case brought by the United States, Canada and Argentina against the European Communities (EC) with respect to its alleged moratorium on approving genetically modified organisms (GMOs), the Panel held that it was not required to take into account the CBD or the Cartagena Protocol on Biosafety (to the CBD), and that it would not do so on its own initiative.

Following is a critique by an environmental group (which had submitted an amicus curiae brief in the case) of the MEA portion of the Panel's then interim report, which was leaked and thus available for public review (interim reports normally are released only to the parties to the dispute, who then have the opportunity to comment on the interim report before the Panel finalizes it, sometimes with changes reflecting the parties' comments, and releases it to the public). The Panel's final report did not deviate from the interim report in this respect, and thus the critique is relevant.

EC—BIOTECH: OVERVIEW AND ANALYSIS OF THE PANEL'S INTERIM REPORT

Center for International Environmental Law—Nathalie Bernasconi-Osterwalder &
Maria Julia Oliva 2006 (footnotes omitted)

Interpreting WTO Law and the Relevance of Multilateral Environmental Agreements (MEAs)

In the EC—Biotech case, the EC argued that the WTO agreements had to be interpreted and applied by reference to relevant rules of international law arising outside the WTO context. It criticized the approach by the complaining parties to treat the legal issues concerning the authorization and international trade of GMOs as though they were regulated exclusively by WTO rules, making no reference whatsoever to the relevant rules of public international law which have been adopted to regulate the concerns and requirements which arise from the particular characteristics of GMOs. The EC referred to the US–Shrimp decision—in which the Appellate Body looked at several treaties, including treaties which at least one party to the dispute had not signed or had signed but not ratified. In line with the Appellate Body's approach, the EC argued that the Panel in the EC—Biotech case had to take the 1992 CBD (ratified by the EC, Argentina and Canada; and signed by the United States) and the 2000 Biosafety Protocol (ratified by the EC and signed by Argentina and Canada) into account when interpreting the relevant WTO rules. Specifically, the EC argued that the rules of international law

reflected in the Biosafety Protocol on the precautionary principle and on
risk assessment should be taken into account to inform the meaning and
effect of the relevant provisions of the WTO agreements.

[The *amicus curiae* brief of the Center for International
Environmental Law (CIEL)] also argued that customary rules of
interpretation of public international law, recognized by the WTO dispute
settlement system, require that WTO agreements be considered as a part
of the broader corpus of international law and principles. Moreover, the
Appellate Body has emphasized the importance, in certain circumstances,
of interpreting terms in the WTO Agreements in light of the
"contemporary concerns of the community of nations." CIEL's submission
also noted that international law and principles may provide particularly
significant interpretative guidance to the Panel in the present case for
two reasons. First, the concerns of the international community regarding
the transboundary movement of GMOs are reflected in the first
comprehensive international agreement on the subject at issue, the
Biosafety Protocol. Second, the precautionary principle reflected in the
SPS Agreement, and particularly in Article 5.7, provides critical
interpretative guidance for regulators and adjudicators in cases where
uncertainty renders scientific evidence insufficient to adequately
determine sanitary and phytosanitary risks.

A.   The Panel's Reasonings & Findings

The Panel confirmed, in line with previous jurisprudence, that it had
to interpret the WTO agreements "in accordance with customary rules of
interpretation of public international law" reflected, in part, in Article 31
of the Vienna Convention.

In this context, the Panel concentrated primarily on the meaning of
Article 31(3)(c), which directs the interpreter to "take into account,
together with the context" "any relevant rules of international law
applicable in the relations between the parties." It found that "rules of
international law" seemed sufficiently broad to encompass all generally
accepted sources of public international law, including treaties,
customary international law, and the recognized general principles of
law. With respect to the latter, it noted that the Appellate Body in US—
Shrimp made it clear that pursuant to Article 31(3)(c) general principles
of international law are to be taken into account in the interpretation of
WTO provisions.

The Panel also addressed the phrase "applicable in the relations
between the parties" in the same article. It found that this reference
limited the application of Article 31(3)(c) to the rules of international law
applicable in the relations between all the parties to the treaty that is
being interpreted. In the present case, this would cover those rules that
are applicable in the relations between the WTO Members. However, the
Panel did not take a position on the situation where the relevant rules of

international law are applicable between all parties to the dispute, but not between all WTO Members. As a consequence, the Panel rejected the idea that it was required to take into account either the CBD, or the Biosafety Protocol, in light of the fact that several WTO Members, including the complaining parties to this dispute, were not parties to the agreements in question.

The Panel also rejected the notion that it should consider the fact that some of the disputing parties, while not ratifying, had signed the agreement, and that pursuant to Article 18 of the Vienna Convention a State which has signed a treaty must refrain from acts which would defeat the object and purpose of that treaty. The Panel's reasoning was based on the argument that "the 'object and purpose' of a treaty cannot be reasonably considered to constitute a 'rule' of international law." [Paragraph 7.74, FN 200]

1. *The Precautionary Principle*

. . .

With respect to the precautionary principle, the Panel found that if the "precautionary principle" was a general principle of law, it should be taken into account. Noting that the EC had not explained exactly what it meant by the term "general principle of international law," the Panel found that the term could be understood as encompassing either rules of customary law or the general principles of law recognized by States or both, and that it would consider whether the precautionary principle fit within either of these categories. In doing so, the Panel relied primarily on the Appellate Body's handling of this question in its report in EC— Hormones. In that case, the Appellate Body, noting that it was unclear whether the precautionary principle has been widely accepted by Members as a principle of general or customary international law, refrained from taking position on the status. In line with that approach, the EC—Biotech Panel also refrained from expressing a view on the issue. [Paragraph 7.87]

. . .

2. *Other International Law Rules*

Finally, the Panel examined whether it could consider, in interpreting WTO agreements, rules of international law that are not applicable in the relations between the WTO Members and thus do not fall within the category of rules which is at issue in Article 31(3)(c). Referring to the EC argument that in US—Shrimp the Appellate Body interpreted WTO rules by reference to treaties that were not binding on all parties to the proceedings (including the CBD), the Panel concluded that it could consider such rules when interpreting the terms of WTO agreements if it deemed such rules to be informative. It stressed, however, that it need not necessarily rely on these. [Paragraphs 7.91–

7.93] To come to this conclusion, the Panel relied on Article 31(1) of the Vienna Convention, according to which the terms of a treaty must be interpreted in accordance with the "ordinary meaning" to be given to its terms "in their context and in the light of its object and purpose." It noted:

> The ordinary meaning of treaty terms is often determined on the basis of dictionaries. We think that, in addition to dictionaries, other relevant rules of international law may in some cases aid a treaty interpreter in establishing, or confirming, the ordinary meaning of treaty terms in the specific context in which they are used. Such rules would not be considered because they are legal rules, but rather because they may provide evidence of the ordinary meaning of terms in the same way that dictionaries do. They would be considered for their informative character. It follows that when a treaty interpreter does not consider another rule of international law to be informative, he or she need not rely on it. [Paragraph 7.92, footnotes omitted]

Applying these considerations to the EC—Biotech case, the Panel concluded without further explanation that it was not necessary or appropriate to rely on the particular provisions of the CBD and the Biosafety Protocol invoked by the EC in interpreting the WTO agreements at issue in this dispute. [Paragraph 7.95] . . .

B. Preliminary Conclusions

US—Shrimp has become the leitmotiv of those who believe that the WTO and MEA question has been cleverly resolved. Any concerns expressed that MEAs might not be adequately considered in a WTO dispute, were brushed off as irrelevant in light of the jurisprudence laid down by the Appellate Body in US—Shrimp. The EC—Biotech Panel's reasoning with respect to the MEA-WTO relationship and the relationship between the WTO and public international law more generally, serves as a wake-up call. The Panel rejected the notion that rules of interpretation might require that international conventions that were not ratified by all WTO Members be taken into account. Having to address the fact that the Appellate Body previously had taken into account treaties to which not all disputing parties were parties (and as a consequence not all WTO Members were parties), the Panel found that a treaty interpreter could rely on such a treaty only if found useful, but that under no circumstance was he or she obliged to do so.

While the Panel's interpretation of the reference in Article 31(3)(c) of the Vienna Convention to "rules applicable in the relations between the parties" may not be manifestly wrong, it does not contribute to building channels of dialogue in an increasingly fragmented international legal system. The Panel's apparent attempt to avoid conflicts between relevant rules of international law led it to conclude that the Vienna Convention did not establish a legal obligation for interpreting bodies to take into account treaties that were not ratified by all parties to the treaty being interpreted. However, this conclusion stands at odds with the responsibility of an interpreting body to take into account those treaties, especially when they address issues of global concern where the interests of the international community are involved.

While the particular wording of the Vienna Convention on the Law of Treaties may lead to differing interpretations, it should also be noted that the customary rules of treaty interpretation reflect a State-centered view of international law. Indeed, under such view, a State cannot acquire obligations that it has not consented to and the interpretation of rules applicable to it cannot take into account other rules the State has not consented to. In addition, the rules of interpretation in the Vienna Convention were developed at a time where most treaty-making activity focused on bilateral treaties, and where multilateral agreements were only beginning to appear. The limitations of this State-centered paradigm and its impact on the interpretation of the rules of treaty interpretation are particularly evident in regards to issues of common concern to humanity, such as those addressed by multilateral environmental agreements. Where the concerns of the international community are at stake, such as the preservation of biodiversity and life on planet earth, the State-centered paradigm and its rules of treaty interpretation must give way to the recognition of superior values and interests. In that regard, international environmental law must have an impact and be given proper weight in the interpretation of treaties.

. . .

Finally, countries regularly refer to the concept of mutual supportiveness between trade and environment. Taking an MEA into account for the interpretation of WTO agreements and vice versa allows different regimes to co-exist and for one regime to support the other. This approach does not result, as the Panel appears to believe, in new obligations for WTO Members that are not party to the MEA. The attitude of the Panel to ignore the importance of internationally negotiated instruments outside the WTO runs counter to the notion of mutual supportiveness.

NOTES AND QUESTIONS

1.   *Note on the EC Biotech case.* The EC did not appeal the Panel's decision, and the Panel reports were adopted in November 2006. The EU did not implement the DSB recommendations within an agreed timeframe, and the United States made a retaliation request to suspend concessions in January 2008. The EC objected and the matter was referred to arbitration under Article 22.6 of the WTO Dispute Settlement Understanding. However in February 2008, the EC and the United States agreed to a sequencing agreement and requested the Arbitrator to suspend the arbitration

proceedings. The EU had reached a settlement agreement with Argentina and Canada (two other complainants in the EC Biotech dispute) in 2010 and 2009, respectively, but had not reached an agreement with the United States as of August 2015. The European Commission announced plans in April 2015 to let EU member States opt out of an EU-wide approval program for genetically modified organisms, which did not please the United States.

2.   Do you agree with the analysis by the Center for International Environmental Law? The final term, "mutual supportiveness" is used in many international instruments to describe the proper relationship between trade rules and MEAs. What does it mean? Is it required by the concept of sustainable development, discussed in chapters 1 and 6, above? Does "mutual supportiveness" require that environmental measures purportedly taken in support of an MEA be taken in good faith, or not run afoul of the concepts in the chapeau to Article XX of the GATT, above? Who should have the burden of proof on various aspects of these arguments?

3.   What if provisions restricting trade with nonparties were incorporated in legal instruments that were not formal agreements but only guidelines or codes of conduct? What if there were a rule of customary international law that countries were using trade measures to enforce?

4.   Does it matter whether trade provisions in international agreements are directed to products that would be in themselves harmful in the importing country or rather to the processes (PPMs) by which the products are produced? If the latter is the case, does it matter whether the PPMs relate to the safety or other characteristics of the product?

5.   Does it matter whether the international agreement is directed to protecting the so-called global commons or to the environment (including species) within a country?

6.   Must the measure adopted in the agreement be the least trade restrictive measure available to meet the environmental goal? Cf. Article 5 of the SPS Agreement. Should that be required?

7.   In what forum should disputes over conflicts between provisions in environmental and in trade agreements be resolved? The Protocol on deep seabed mining to the U.N. Convention on the Law of the Sea provides that trade-related disputes shall be brought in the WTO.

8.   What means might be available to confirm that the multilateral environmental provisions limiting trade are consistent with GATT/WTO?

9.   *Inter-temporal law.* As noted above, the International Court of Justice has held that new norms of customary international law must be taken into account even with respect to continuing activities governed by existing international agreements. Should the inter-temporal doctrine apply in WTO and other trade jurisprudence, at least when environmental issues are involved?

b. The Multilateral Agreements and Their Provisions

As a case study, consider whether the provisions in three international agreements restricting trade in controlled items to nonparties are consistent with the WTO: The Montreal Protocol on Substances That Deplete the Ozone Layer, the Basel Convention on Control of Transboundary Movements of Hazardous Wastes and Their Disposal, and the Convention on International Trade in Endangered Species of Fauna and Flora. As you read the provisions, note the differences among the conventions.

THE MONTREAL PROTOCOL, ARTICLE 4: CONTROL OF TRADE WITH NON-PARTIES

1. Within one year of the entry into force of this Protocol, each Party shall ban the import of controlled substances from any State not party to this Protocol.

2. Beginning on 1 January 1993, no Party operating under paragraph 1 of Article 5 may export any controlled substance to any State not party to this Protocol.

3. Within three years ... the Parties shall ... elaborate in an annex a list of products containing controlled substances. Parties that have not objected to the annex in accordance with those procedures shall ban, within one year of the annex having become effective, the import of those products from any State not party to this Protocol.

8. Notwithstanding the provisions of this Article, imports referred to in paragraphs I, 3 and 4 may be permitted from any State not party to this Protocol if that State is determined, by a meeting of the Parties, to be in full compliance with Article 2 [control measures] and this Article, and has submitted data to that effect as specified in Article 7 [reporting of data].

CONVENTION ON INTERNATIONAL TRADE IN ENDANGERED SPECIES, ARTICLE X: TRADE WITH STATES NOT PARTY TO THE CONVENTION

Where export or re-export is to, or import is from, a State not a party to the present Convention, comparable documentation issued by the competent authorities in that State which substantially conforms with the requirements of the present Convention for permits and certificates may he accepted in lieu thereof by any Party.

BASEL CONVENTION ON THE CONTROL OF TRANSBOUNDARY MOVEMENTS OF HAZARDOUS WASTES AND THEIR DISPOSAL, ARTICLE 4(5) & ARTICLE 11

Article 4(5): A Party shall not permit hazardous wastes or other wastes to be exported to a non-Party or to be imported from a non-Party.

Article 11: . . .Notwithstanding the provisions of Article 4 paragraph 5, Parties may enter into bilateral, multilateral, or regional agreements or arrangements regarding transboundary movement of hazardous wastes or other wastes with Parties or non-Parties provided that such agreements or arrangements do not derogate from the environmentally sound management of hazardous wastes and other wastes as required by this Convention. . . . The provisions of this Convention shall not affect transboundary movements which take place pursuant to such agreements, provided that such agreements are compatible with the environmentally sound management of hazardous wastes and other wastes as required by this Convention.

Note that the Montreal Protocol bans trade in the controlled substances with nonparties and allows Parties to ban trade in products containing the substances and eventually products produced with the controlled substances (although Parties have decided not to pursue the latter). However, Article 4(8) provides an escape: imports may be permitted from a nonparty if a meeting of the Parties determines the nonparty is in full compliance with the control measures and the reporting of data.

CITES permits export, re-export, or import from nonparty States only "if comparable documentation issued by the competent authorities in that State . . . substantially conforms to the requirements of the present Convention for permits and certificates."

Article 4(5) of the Basel Convention restricts imports and exports of controlled hazardous wastes from and to nonparties, but Article 11 allows such trade if there is an agreement or arrangement in place between the countries that is consistent with the Convention.

NOTES AND QUESTIONS

1.   Do the differences in the provisions in the three agreements affect whether they are consistent with the WTO?

2.   Who determines whether documentation is comparable under CITES, or if the agreement or arrangement does not derogate from the Basel Convention's environmentally sound management?

3.   Should it make any difference to the outcome of a dispute that the Party complaining about the validity of a trade measure in an environmental agreement is or is not a Party to the relevant environmental agreement?

4.   The United States is not yet a Party to the Basel Convention. The Senate has at long last given its advice and consent, but the United States has not yet deposited its instrument of ratification. The United States has bilateral agreements with both Canada and Mexico for the shipment of hazardous wastes; both Canada and Mexico are parties to the treaty and are members of the OECD. May Canada and Mexico engage in transboundary shipments of hazardous wastes consistent with the Basel Agreement? Who decides?

5.   A 1995 Amendment to the Basel Convention bans trade between OECD and non-OECD States. Is the 1995 Amendment consistent with the GATT?

c.   The North American Free Trade Agreement and Multilateral Environmental Agreements

The North American Free Trade Agreement addressed the question of the consistency of multilateral environmental agreements with it by including a provision by which the trade obligations set out in specific international agreements "trump" the NAFTA provisions to the extent of any inconsistency:

NAFTA, ARTICLE 104: RELATIONS TO ENVIRONMENTAL AND CONSERVATION AGREEMENTS

1.   In the Event of any inconsistency between this Agreement and the specific trade obligations set out in: (a) the Convention on International Trade in Endangered Species of Wild Fauna and Flora, done at Washington, March 3, 1973, as amended June 22, 1979, (b) the Montreal Protocol on Substances that Deplete the Ozone Layer, done at Montreal, September 18, 1987, as amended June 29, 1990, (c) the Basel Convention on the Control of Transboundary Movements of Hazardous Wastes and Their Disposal, done at Basel, March 22, 1989, on its entry into force for Canada, Mexico and the United States, or (d) the agreements set out in Annex 104.1, such obligations shall prevail to the extent of the inconsistency, provided that where a Party has a choice among equally effective and reasonably available means of complying with such obligations, the Party chooses the alternative that is the least inconsistent with the other provisions of this Agreement.

2.   The Parties may agree in writing to modify Annex 104.1 to include any amendment to an agreement referred to in paragraph 1, and any other environmental or conservation agreement.

Annex 104.1

Bilateral and Other Environmental Conservation Agreements

1.   The Agreement Between the Government of Canada and the Government of the United States of America Concerning the Transboundary Movement of Hazardous Waste, signed at Ottawa, October 28, 1986.

2.   The Agreement Between the United States of America and the United Mexican States on Cooperation for the Protection and Improvement of the Environment in the Border Area, signed at La Paz, Baja California Sur, August 14, 1983.

QUESTIONS

1.   *Verbal agreements.* The United States received a verbal agreement from Canada and Mexico to add the U.S.-Mexican Convention for the Protection of Migratory Birds and Game Animals and the U.S.-Canada Convention on the Protection of Migratory Birds to Annex 104.1. What trade implications would arise if either Canada or Mexico did not agree to include their bilateral convention with the United States in Annex 104.1 while the other country did? Must all three countries agree to modify Annex 104.1?

2.   *Does Article 104 really help?* What protection does Article 104 actually provide? Suppose Mexico or Canada complained about the Sea Turtle Protection Act, and the United States responded that the Act implements the objective of CITES. Would Article 104 protect against a challenge under NAFTA?

3.   *WTO Article 104?* What problems do you foresee if the WTO were to adopt such a provision? Should only multilateral agreements be eligible? Must they be global or would regional (including bilateral) ones qualify? Should there be a requirement that a certain number of WTO Parties must also be Party to the environmental agreement to qualify for listing? Who could decide, and by what procedures, whether to list the environmental agreement? Or do we need an additional exception to Article XX for multilateral environmental agreements for those States that are Party to them? What problems would this raise?

6.   UNILATERAL ENVIRONMENTAL ACTIONS AFTER THE RIO CONFERENCE

The 1992 Rio Declaration on Environment and Development addressed the acceptability of unilateral actions relating to extraterritorial environmental problems that have effects on trade. Principle 12 provides as follows:

> States should cooperate to promote a supportive and open international economic system that would lead to economic

growth and sustainable development in all countries, to better address the problems of environmental degradation. Trade policy measures for environmental purposes should not constitute a means of arbitrary or unjustifiable discrimination or a disguised restriction on international trade. Unilateral actions to deal with environmental challenges outside the jurisdiction of the importing country should be avoided. Environmental measures addressing transboundary or global environmental problems should, as far as possible, be based on an international consensus.

Two other international legal instruments adopted at Rio also address the question of unilateral measures. The Framework Convention on Climate Change provides in Article 3(5) that "Measures to combat climate change, including unilateral ones, should not constitute a means of arbitrary or unjustifiable discrimination or a disguised restriction on international trade." Principles 13 and 14 of the Forest Principles provide as follows:

> Trade in forest products should be based on non-discriminatory and multilaterally agreed rules and procedures consistent with international law and practices. (Principle 13)

> Unilateral measures, incompatible with international obligations or agreements, to restrict and/or ban the international trade in timber or other forest products, should be removed or avoided. . . . (Principle 14)

The Forest Principles are explicitly nonbinding, but a similar provision is included in the 1994 International Tropical Timber Agreement (which replaced the earlier agreement by that name). The 2006 version of the agreement differs, stating in Article 34 (Non-Discrimination) that "Nothing in this Agreement authorizes the use of measures to restrict or ban international trade in, and in particular as they concern imports of, and utilization of, timber and timber products."

The legitimacy of unilateral measures taken for environmental purposes remains an important issue. Can you think of situations where a State might want to take unilateral measures to protect an environmental resource before an international consensus on action could be reached? Under what conditions might these be allowed? Brown Weiss has suggested the possibility of provisional unilateral measures (PUMs), which would be valid for only a few years pending an international arrangement, would be subject to scientific criteria as to the need for the measures, and would be accompanied by a dispute resolution procedure to evaluate the scientific need for the measures. What advantages would this approach have? What problems do you foresee? How would you apply PUMs if a country wanted to impose a carbon tax to protect against global warming from greenhouse gases?

For early discussions on the general issue of unilateral measures and the trade regime, *see* Office of Technology Assessment, Trade and Environment: Conflicts and Opportunities (1992); and Robert A. Reinstein, *Trade and Environment: The Case for and against Unilateral Actions*, in Sustainable Development and International Law (Winfried Lang, ed. 1995). For a particularly thorough treatment of the use of trade measures as sanctions, *see* Howard F. Chang, *An Economic Analysis of Trade Measures to Protect the Global Environment*, 83 Geo. L.J. 2121 (1995).

NOTES AND QUESTIONS

Is the term "unilateral" a helpful one in this context? Isn't all domestic legislation (including that necessary to implement an international obligation) a unilateral act by a sovereign State? Suppose a country takes an action in support of a non-legally binding United Nations General Assembly resolution such as that condemning driftnet fishing—is that "unilateral"? Suppose the action supports an international agreement but is not required by it? Suppose the action is required by, or in support of, an international agreement to which the target country is not a Party? How do these situations differ in terms of being "unilateral" or not?

B. HEALTH AND SAFETY MEASURES

Many of the environmentally related disputes before the WTO involve national measures that are arguably designed to protect the health and safety of the country's people. Some of these involve both the GATT and the SPS. The materials that follow are intended to highlight the key disputes that have arisen and to stimulate discussion as to whether the WTO has drawn the correct balance between protecting human health and safety, on the one hand, and guarding against protectionist measures and ensuring a level playing field among countries in international trade, on the other.

1. THE ASBESTOS CASE

EC—MEASURES AFFECTING ASBESTOS AND PRODUCTS CONTAINING ASBESTOS
(Canada v. European Community)
WT/DS135R (18 September 2000); WT/DS135/AB/R (12 Marcdh 2001)

[In 1998, Canada challenged a French ban on the manufacture, processing, sale and import of asbestos fibers and products containing asbestos fibers. France stated that the ban was intended to protect workers and consumers from asbestos' carcinogenic effects. Canada argued that this violated Article 2 of the Technical Barriers to Trade Agreement and Articles III.4 (national treatment), XI (quantitative restrictions) and XXIII.1(b) (non-violation nullification or impairment) of the GATT.

The panel ruled for France, and Canada appealed. The Appellate Body (AB) also ruled for France and, among other things, ruled that health effects may be taken into account in analyzing whether products are "like" for purposes of deciding whether they receive national treatment, and that asbestos products are not "like" other fibrous products used for similar purposes, because of the different effects on human health. [1] The AB also made three important observations: (1) Members have the right to determine their own appropriate levels of protection for human, animal and plant health; (2) either quantitative or qualitative evaluation of health could qualify in determining the application of Article XX(b); and (3) Members may rely in adopting health measures not only on majority scientific views, but also on respected divergent scientific opinions. (Paras. 168 & 178 of the AB Report.)]

2.   THE THAI CIGARETTE CASE

THAILAND—RESTRICTIONS ON IMPORTATION OF AND INTERNAL TAXES ON CIGARETTES
(United States v. Thailand)
GATT B.I.S.D. (37th Supp.) at 200 (1991)

[In this dispute between the United States and Thailand (which was decided in 1990 before the WTO Dispute Settlement Understanding was in place), the Royal Thai Government enacted restrictions on imports of and internal taxes on cigarettes, under which all imports required a license. No license had been granted within the last decade. Thailand justified its import restrictions on grounds of public health, noting that the restrictions were to protect the public from harmful ingredients in imported cigarettes and to reduce the consumption of cigarettes in Thailand. Domestic cigarettes continued to be for sale. The United States contended that the import ban was in fact a protectionist measure directed to promoting local tobacco companies, in violation of GATT Article XI:1.

At Thailand's request, the Panel asked the World Health Organization (WHO) to present its conclusions on technical aspects of the case, such as the health effects of cigarette use and consumption. In its submission, the WHO explained the health effects of smoking, including lung cancer, pulmonary and cardiovascular diseases, increased risk of miscarriage and stillbirths, and reduced birth weight. The WHO findings on trends in smoking showed that once a market was opened, the United States tobacco industry wielded great influence and that with limited

---

[1]   *European Communities—Measures Affecting Asbestos and Products Containing Asbestos,* *Appellate Body Report,* 12 March 2001, WTO Doc. WT/DS135/AB/R.

budgets the governments could not compete with the vast capital of the companies to carry out public health policies. While the Panel accepted the view that smoking constituted a serious harm to human health that fell within the scope of Article XX(b), it found that the measure had to be "necessary" and had to satisfy the chapeau requirements for Article XX, which the Thai regulation did not. The Panel thus agreed with the United States but noted that a nondiscriminatory regulation requiring complete disclosure of ingredients, coupled with a ban on unhealthy substances, would be an alternative that would be consistent with the GATT.

In another important aspect of the case, the Panel suggested that a ban on advertising of all cigarettes, both domestic and imported, would be consistent with the GATT. The United States tobacco companies contended that a ban on advertising would make it much more difficult for new, foreign suppliers to sell cigarettes within the country, even if imports were permitted. The Panel noted that even if this argument were accepted, "such an inconsistency would have to be regarded as unavoidable and therefore necessary within the meaning of Article XX(b), because additional advertising rights would risk stimulating demand for cigarettes." (Panel report, para. 78).]

NOTES AND QUESTIONS

1.   Suppose that it could be shown that United States cigarettes contained much higher levels of nicotine than locally produced cigarettes and that these levels were intended to induce addiction, particularly in young people. Could a Panel find the measure consistent with the GATT? Would the foreign cigarettes still be considered a "like product" for purposes of the national treatment required by Article III of the GATT? If so, would Article XX save the day? For an interesting and potentially important analysis of "like products," *see* the *Euromotors* case (also called the *CAFE Standards* case), brought under the GATT by the EC against the United States and decided in 1993.

2.   In Canada, there was a proposal more than two decades ago to require plain packaging of all cigarettes sold in Canada. The proposed package would be white with only the brand name written in black letters on the package. Would such a measure be consistent with the GATT/WTO?

3.   In 2011, Australia enacted the Tobacco Plain Packaging Act as part of regulatory measures designed to discourage tobacco use. The statute sets out guidelines for all tobacco products sold in Australia and requires that the retail packaging of tobacco products be in drab dark brown with no trademarks. Five countries brought challenges against the plain packaging regime and argued that the regulations violated Australia's obligations under the Trade Related Aspects of Intellectual Property Rights (TRIPS) Agreement to protect foreign trademarks and prevented trademark holders from exercising their intellectual property rights. Australia has released studies showing the favorable impact of plain packaging on tobacco use. The United

Kingdom and Ireland have beome the second and third countries to pass plain packaging laws similar to Australia's. The findings of the Panel will determine the extent to which States will be able to further their public health objectives through plain packaging legislation. As of August 2015, the Tobacco Plain Packaging Case was pending at the WTO.

3.   US—CLOVE CIGARETTES CASE

US—MEASURES AFFECTING THE PRODUCTION AND SALE OF CLOVE CIGARETTES

(Indonesia v. United States)
WT/DS406/R (2 September 2011); WT/DS406/AB/R (4 April 2012)

[In 2010, Indonesia initiated dispute procedures against the United States regarding US legislation banning certain flavored cigarettes. Indonesia claimed that the ban violated the national treatment obligation under the Agreement on Technical Barriers to Trade (TBT) because it prohibited clove cigarettes, the majority of which are imported from Indonesia, but not menthol cigarettes, which are produced by companies in the United States. The United States argued that the ban reflected a legislative decision to target cigarettes smoked primarily by young people, such as clove cigarettes, without incurring the level of costs that would result from banning cigarettes more widely used by smokers of all ages, such as menthol cigarettes and non-flavored cigarettes.

The Panel found that the US ban was inconsistent with article 2.1 of the TBT Agreement, which states:

> Members shall ensure that in respect of technical regulations, products imported from the territory of any Member shall be accorded treatment no less favourable than that accorded to like products of national origin and to like products originating in any other country.

The Panel analyzed whether clove cigarettes and menthol cigarettes were "like products," and whether imported clove cigarettes were accorded less favorable treatment. [2] It considered the public health objectives of the ban in both determinations, but concluded that differentiating between clove cigarettes and menthol cigarettes did not serve the stated objective of reducing youth smoking, and that the costs associated with banning menthol cigarettes was not sufficient to show that they were not like products or that treatment of clove cigarettes was no less favorable.

The Appellate Body upheld the Panel's finding that the measure violated article 2.1 of the TBT, but held that it should not have considered

---

[2]   *United States—Measures Affecting the Production and Sale of Clove Cigarettes*, Panel Report, 2 September 2011, WTO Doc. WT/DS406/R

public health objectives in its like products determination, except insofar as they provide evidence of different health risks of different products that could affect the competitive relationship. [3] In assessing whether imported clove cigarettes were afforded less favorable treatment, it analyzed whether the differential impact on imported cigarettes was the result of "a legitimate regulatory distinction." The Appellate Body stated:

> We recall that the stated objective of [the measure] is to reduce youth smoking. One of the particular characteristics of flavoured cigarettes that makes them appealing to young people is the flavouring that masks the harshness of the tobacco, thus making them more pleasant to start smoking than regular cigarettes. To the extent that this particular characteristic is present in both clove and menthol cigarettes, menthol cigarettes have the same product characteristic that, from the perspective of the stated objective of [the measure], justified the prohibition of clove cigarettes. Furthermore, the reasons presented by the United States for the exemption of menthol cigarettes from the ban on flavoured cigarettes do not, in our view, demonstrate that the detrimental impact on competitive opportunities for imported clove cigarettes does stem from a legitimate regulatory distinction. . . . [A]ccording to the United States, the exemption of menthol cigarettes from the ban on flavoured cigarettes is justified in order to avoid risks arising from withdrawal symptoms that would afflict menthol cigarette smokers in case those cigarettes were banned. We note, however, that the addictive ingredient in menthol cigarettes is nicotine, not peppermint or any other ingredient that is exclusively present in menthol cigarettes, and that this ingredient is also present in a group of products that is likewise permitted under [the measure], namely, regular cigarettes. Therefore, it is not clear that the risks that the United States claims to minimize by allowing menthol cigarettes to remain in the market would materialize if menthol cigarettes were to be banned, insofar as regular cigarettes would remain in the market.[4]

NOTES AND QUESTIONS

1.   Unlike the national treatment obligation under the GATT, the national treatment obligation under the TBT is not subject to exceptions in the TBT for measures necessary to protect human health. The Panel refrained from considering whether Article XX of the GATT can be used as a defense to justify a violation of the TBT Agreement. However, the Panel did determine that the jurisprudence developed under Article XX(b) of the GATT

---

[3]   *United States—Measures Affecting the Production and Sale of Clove Cigarettes*, Appellate Body Report, 4 April 2012, WTO Doc. WT/DS406/AB/R.

[4]   *Id.* at para. 225 (internal footnotes omitted).

is relevant in analyzing whether the ban on clove cigarettes is "more trade restrictive than necessary" under Article 2.2 of the TBT. To what extent should the absence of an exception equivalent to Article XX of the GATT affect the Panel and Appellate Body reasoning in these cases?

2.   In its analysis of the exemption of menthol cigarettes, is the Appellate Body second-guessing the US legislature's decision on how best to regulate to protect the health of its citizens? Should national health measures be subject to such international oversight? Conversely, might such questioning of the stated objectives of national legislation be necessary to prevent disguised restrictions on trade? As some would ask, why should Philip Morris, the primary producer of menthol cigarettes, be able to convince the U.S. Congress to exclude clove cigarettes, a potential competitor on the domestic market?

4.   THE BEEF HORMONES CASE

EC—MEASURES CONCERNING MEAT AND MEAT PRODUCTS

(Canada and United States v. European Community)
WT/DS406/R (2 September 2011); WT/DS406/AB/R (4 April 2012

[In the WTO Beef Hormones Case, the United States and Canada lodged complaints in 1996 against the European Community (EC) on the ground that the EC prohibition on importing meat and meat products derived from cattle to which specific natural and synthetic hormones had been administered to promote growth violated one of the WTO agreements, viz. the Agreement on the Application of Sanitary and Phytosanitary Measures (the SPS Agreement). This was the first case under that agreement. The 1997 Panel report held against the EC on the grounds that a country could adopt a higher standard than the international standard but only in an exceptional case, that there was insufficient scientific basis for an exception here, and that the application of the SPS measure constituted a disguised restriction on trade because the EC accepted certain natural hormones but prohibited synthetic ones that had the same effect. The Appellate Body reversed some of the findings of the Panel, although it ultimately found in favor of the United States.[5] Most importantly, the Appellate Body held that the burden of proof is on the country challenging the SPS measure and that the right of a Party (in this case the EC) to establish a higher standard was a basic rule, not an exception, and rejected the Panel's assessment of the scientific risk by noting that the issue was whether there was any scientific evidence to serve as a rational basis for the prohibition. This potentially provides broad latitude to states to adopt environmental

---

[5]   World Trade Organization Appellate Body, *EC Measures Concerning Meat and Meat Products (Hormones)*, WT/DS26/AB/R, WT/DS48/AB/R, 1998.

measures that may be more environmentally protective than relevant international standards.

With regard to the precautionary principle, the Appellate Body first declined to take a position on the status of the precautionary principle as to whether it has become customary international law or a general principle of law as suggested by the European Communities. The Appellate Body stated that "it is unnecessary, and probably imprudent, for the Appellate Body in this appeal to take a position on this important, but abstract, question." It noted that the precautionary principle "still awaits authoritative formulation" citing *Case Concerning the Gabčíkovo-Nagymaros Project* to the effect that the International Court of Justice did not identify the precautionary principle as a principle. The Appellate Body agreed with the Panel's finding that the precautionary principle does not "override" provisions of the SPS Agreement and stated that it cannot be invoked "as a ground for justifying SPS measures that are otherwise inconsistent with the obligations" of the SPS Agreement. However, the Appellate Body held that the precautionary principle was "reflected" in paragraph 6 of the Preamble, Article 3.3, and Article 5.7 of the SPS Agreement which all "explicitly recognize the right of Members to establish their own appropriate level of sanitary protection, which level may be higher (i.e., more cautious) than that implied in existing international standards, guidelines and recommendations." It noted that in determining whether "sufficient scientific evidence" exists, the Panels should "bear in mind that responsible, representative governments commonly act from perspectives of prudence and precaution where risks of irreversible, e.g. life-terminating, damage to human health are concerned."

The dispute continued, with the EC challenging the imposition of trade sanctions by the United States and Canada in response to the EC ban on growth hormone-treated beef. The EC claimed that neither country had removed its trade sanctions even though the EC had modified its rules to (allegedly) comply with the WTO ruling. After several additional sets of consultations, the EC and the US signed a Memorandum of Understanding in 2009 in relation to this dispute, which gave U.S. producers additional access to the EU market with no duties for beef produced without growth-promoting hormones in exchange for the United States reducing the retaliatory tariffs on EU products from 116 million to 38 million dollars. The 2009 MOU expired in 2013, but a revised MOU was agreed in 2013 for a two-year extension. For a detailed description of the legal issues involved in this case, *see* Nathalie Bernasconi-Osterwalder et al., Environment and Trade: A Guide to WTO Jurisprudence 268–70 (2005).]

5.   RETREADED TYRES CASE

Excessive import of used and recycled products can also cause problems, especially in developing countries, as such products may not last as long and therefore become waste sooner, or may dampen domestic recycling industries, resulting in domestic used products going straight to landfills. In the early 2000s, Brazil passed legislation intended to address health and environmental problems associated with the build-up of tyre waste, which included, among other measures, a ban on the import of retreaded tyres—used tyres that had been given new treads in order to make them reusable. Brazil reasoned that such tyres were replacing new tyres, which had a longer lifespan, and tyres retreaded from used tyres within the country led to more tyres in Brazilian landfills.

This ban first raised issues within the Mercado Común del Sur (MERCOSUR), a regional trade agreement among several countries of South America. Following an order from a MERCOSUR tribunal, Brazil amended the ban on retreaded tyres to exempt tyres imported from MERCOSUR member countries.

This exemption created new problems under the WTO. A WTO Panel established in 2006 at the request of the European Community found that the ban was inconsistent with article XI of the GATT, which prohibits restrictions on trade other than tariffs. The Panel went on to find that the ban was not justifiable under the article XX(b) exception for measures necessary to protect human health, because under the chapeau of Article XX, the MERCOSUR exemption resulted in "arbitrary or unjustifiable discrimination." However, in its article XX analysis, the Panel found that the import ban could be considered "necessary to protect human, animal, or plant life or health" under article XX(b), and that it constituted "arbitrary or unjustifiable discrimination" only insofar as the volume of imports from MERCOSUR countries is sufficient to undermine the objectives of the ban.

The Appellate Body upheld the Panel's finding that the import ban was inconsistent with Article XI and not justified under Article XX of the GATT, but reversed its specific finding regarding "arbitrary or unjustifiable discrimination". Excerpts from its Article XX analysis are reproduced below.

BRAZIL—MEASURES AFFECTING IMPORTS OF RETREADED TYRES

(European Community v. Brazil)
WTO Doc. WT/DS332/AB/R (3 December 2007) [internal footnotes omitted]

IV. Background and the Measure at Issue

119. At the end of their useful life, tyres become waste, the accumulation of which is associated with risks to human, animal, and plant life and health. Specific risks to human life and health include:

> (i) the transmission of dengue, yellow fever and malaria through mosquitoes which use tyres as breeding grounds; and (ii) the exposure of human beings to toxic emissions caused by tyre fires which may cause loss of short-term memory, learning disabilities, immune system suppression, cardiovascular problems, but also cancer, premature mortality, reduced lung function, suppression of the immune system, respiratory effects, heart and chest problems.

Risks to animal and plant life and health include: "(i) the exposure of animals and plants to toxic emissions caused by tyre fires; and (ii) the transmission of a mosquito-borne disease (dengue) to animals."

120. Governments take actions to minimize the adverse effects of waste tyres. Policies to address "waste" include preventive measures aiming at reducing the generation of additional waste tyres, as well as remedial measures aimed at managing and disposing of tyres that can no longer be used or retreaded, such as landfilling, stockpiling, the incineration of waste tyres, and material recycling.

121. The Panel observed that the parties to this dispute have not suggested that retreaded tyres used on vehicles pose any particular risks compared to new tyres, provided that they comply with appropriate safety standards. Various international standards exist in relation to retreaded tyres, including, for example, the norm stipulating that passenger car tyres may be retreaded only once. One important difference between new and retreaded tyres is that the latter have a shorter lifespan and therefore reach the stage of being waste earlier.

. . .

V. The Panel's Analysis of the Necessity of the Import Ban

139. We begin by recalling that the analysis of a measure under Article XX of the GATT 1994 is two-tiered. First, a panel must examine whether the measure falls under at least one of the ten exceptions listed under Article XX. Secondly, the question of whether the measure at issue satisfies the requirements of the chapeau of Article XX must be considered.

140. We note at the outset that the participants do not dispute that it is within the authority of a WTO Member to set the public health or environmental objectives it seeks to achieve, as well as the level of protection that it wants to obtain, through the measure or the policy it chooses to adopt.

144. It is against this background that we must determine whether the Panel erred in assessing the contribution of the Import Ban to the realization of the objective pursued by it, and in the manner in which it weighed this contribution in its analysis of the necessity of the Import Ban. We begin by identifying the objective pursued by the Import Ban. The Panel found that the objective of the Import Ban is the reduction of the "exposure to the risks to human, animal or plant life or health arising from the accumulation of waste tyres", and noted that "few interests are more 'vital' and 'important' than protecting human beings from health risks, and that protecting the environment is no less important." The Panel also observed that "Brazil's chosen level of protection is the reduction of the risks of waste tyre accumulation to the maximum extent possible." Regarding the trade restrictiveness of the measure, the Panel noted that it is "as trade-restrictive as can be, as far as retreaded tyres from non-MERCOSUR countries are concerned, since it aims to halt completely their entry into Brazil."

. . .

150. As the Panel recognized, an import ban is "by design as trade-restrictive as can be". We agree with the Panel that there may be circumstances where such a measure can nevertheless be necessary, within the meaning of Article XX(b)

153. . . . The Panel's conclusion with which we agree was that, "if the domestic retreading industry retreads more domestic used tyres, the overall number of waste tyres will be reduced by giving a second life to some used tyres, which otherwise would have become waste immediately after their first and only life." For these reasons, the Panel found that a reduction of waste tyres would result from the Import Ban and that, therefore, the Import Ban would contribute to reducing exposure to the risks associated with the accumulation of waste tyres.

. . .

156. In order to determine whether a measure is "necessary" within the meaning of Article XX(b) of the GATT 1994, a panel must assess all the relevant factors, particularly the extent of the contribution to the achievement of a measure's objective and its trade restrictiveness, in the light of the importance of the interests or values at stake. If this analysis yields a preliminary conclusion that the measure is necessary, this result must be confirmed by comparing the measure with its possible

alternatives, which may be less trade restrictive while providing an equivalent contribution to the achievement of the objective pursued.

. . .

174. In evaluating whether the measures or practices proposed by the European Communities were "alternatives", the Panel sought to determine whether they would achieve Brazil's policy objective and chosen level of protection, that is to say, reducing the "exposure to the risks to human, animal or plant life or health arising from the accumulation of waste tyres" to the maximum extent possible. In this respect, we believe, like the Panel, that non-generation measures are more apt to achieve this objective because they prevent the accumulation of waste tyres, while waste management measures dispose of waste tyres only once they have accumulated. Furthermore, we note that, in comparing a proposed alternative to the Import Ban, the Panel took into account specific risks attached to the proposed alternative, such as the risk of leaching of toxic substances that might be associated to landfilling, or the risk of toxic emissions that might arise from the incineration of waste tyres. In our view, the Panel did not err in so doing. Indeed, we do not see how a panel could undertake a meaningful comparison of the measure at issue with a possible alternative while disregarding the risks arising out of the implementation of the possible alternative. In this case, the Panel examined as proposed alternatives landfilling, stockpiling, and waste tyre incineration, and considered that, even if these disposal methods were performed under controlled conditions, they nevertheless pose risks to human health similar or additional to those Brazil seeks to reduce through the Import Ban. Because these practices carry their own risks, and these risks do not arise from non-generation measures such as the Import Ban, we believe, like the Panel, that these practices are not reasonably available alternatives.

175. With respect to material recycling, we share the Panel's view that this practice is not as effective as the Import Ban in reducing the exposure to the risks arising from the accumulation of waste tyres. Material recycling applications are costly, and hence capable of disposing of only a limited number of waste tyres. We also note that some of them might require advanced technologies and know-how that are not readily available on a large scale. Accordingly, we are of the view that the Panel did not err in concluding that material recycling is not a reasonably available alternative to the Import Ban.

. . .

182. In sum, the Panel's conclusion that the Import Ban is necessary was the result of a process involving, first, the examination of the contribution of the Import Ban to the achievement of its objective against its trade restrictiveness in the light of the interests at stake, and, secondly, the comparison of the possible alternatives, including associated

risks, with the Import Ban. The analytical process followed by the Panel is consistent with the approach previously defined by the Appellate Body. . . .

183. In the light of all these considerations, we are of the view that the Panel did not err in the manner it conducted its analysis under Article XX(b) of the GATT 1994 as to whether the Import Ban was "necessary to protect human, animal or plant life or health".

VI. The Panel's Interpretation and Application of the Chapeau of Article XX of the GATT 1994

213. After finding that the Import Ban was provisionally justified under Article XX(b) of the GATT 1994, the Panel examined whether the application of the Import Ban by Brazil satisfied the requirements of the chapeau of Article XX.

214. The chapeau of Article XX of the GATT 1994 reads:

> Subject to the requirement that such measures are not applied in a manner which would constitute a means of arbitrary or unjustifiable discrimination between countries where the same conditions prevail, or a disguised restriction on international trade, nothing in this Agreement shall be construed to prevent the adoption or enforcement . . . of measures [of the type specified in the subsequent paragraphs of Article XX].

. . .

226. The Appellate Body Reports in *US—Gasoline*, *US—Shrimp*, and *US—Shrimp* (*Article 21.5—Malaysia*) show that the analysis of whether the application of a measure results in arbitrary or unjustifiable discrimination should focus on the cause of the discrimination, or the rationale put forward to explain its existence. In this case, Brazil explained that it introduced the MERCOSUR exemption to comply with a ruling issued by a MERCOSUR arbitral tribunal. This ruling arose in the context of a challenge initiated by Uruguay against Brazil's import ban on remoulded tyres, on the grounds that it constituted a new restriction on trade prohibited under MERCOSUR. The MERCOSUR arbitral tribunal found Brazil's restrictions on the importation of remoulded tyres to be a violation of its obligations under MERCOSUR. These facts are undisputed.

227. We have to assess whether this explanation provided by Brazil is acceptable as a justification for discrimination between MERCOSUR countries and non-MERCOSUR countries in relation to retreaded tyres. In doing so, we are mindful of the function of the chapeau of Article XX, which is to prevent abuse of the exceptions specified in the paragraphs of that provision. In our view, there is such an abuse, and, therefore, there is arbitrary or unjustifiable discrimination when a measure provisionally

justified under a paragraph of Article XX is applied in a discriminatory manner "between countries where the same conditions prevail", and when the reasons given for this discrimination bear no rational connection to the objective falling within the purview of a paragraph of Article XX, or would go against that objective. The assessment of whether discrimination is arbitrary or unjustifiable should be made in the light of the objective of the measure ... Accordingly, we have difficulty understanding how discrimination might be viewed as complying with the chapeau of Article XX when the alleged rationale for discriminating does not relate to the pursuit of or would go against the objective that was provisionally found to justify a measure under a paragraph of Article XX.

228.   In this case, the discrimination between MERCOSUR countries and other WTO Members in the application of the Import Ban was introduced as a consequence of a ruling by a MERCOSUR tribunal. The tribunal found against Brazil because the restriction on imports of remoulded tyres was inconsistent with the prohibition of new trade restrictions under MERCOSUR law. In our view, the ruling issued by the MERCOSUR arbitral tribunal is not an acceptable rationale for the discrimination, because it bears no relationship to the legitimate objective pursued by the Import Ban that falls within the purview of Article XX(b), and even goes against this objective, to however small a degree. Accordingly, we are of the view that the MERCOSUR exemption has resulted in the Import Ban being applied in a manner that constitutes arbitrary or unjustifiable discrimination.

. . .

232.   Like the Panel, we believe that Brazil's decision to act in order to comply with the MERCOSUR ruling cannot be viewed as "capricious" or "random". Acts implementing a decision of a judicial or quasi-judicial body—such as the MERCOSUR arbitral tribunal—can hardly be characterized as a decision that is "capricious" or "random". However, discrimination can result from a rational decision or behaviour, and still be "arbitrary or unjustifiable", because it is explained by a rationale that bears no relationship to the objective of a measure provisionally justified under one of the paragraphs of Article XX, or goes against that objective.

. . .

234.   This being said, we observe, like the Panel, that, before the arbitral tribunal established under MERCOSUR, Brazil could have sought to justify the challenged Import Ban on the grounds of human, animal, and plant health under Article 50(d) of the Treaty of Montevideo. Brazil, however, decided not to do so. It is not appropriate for us to second-guess Brazil's decision not to invoke Article 50(d), which serves a function similar to that of Article XX(b) of the GATT 1994. However, Article 50(d) of the Treaty of Montevideo, as well as the fact that Brazil might have raised this defence in the MERCOSUR arbitral proceedings,

show, in our view, that the discrimination associated with the MERCOSUR exemption does not necessarily result from a conflict between provisions under MERCOSUR and the GATT 1994.

. . .

239. . . . We explained above why we believe that the Panel erred in finding that the MERCOSUR exemption would result in arbitrary or unjustifiable discrimination only if the imports of retreaded tyres from MERCOSUR countries were to take place in such amounts that the achievement of the objective of the Import Ban would be significantly undermined. As the Panel's conclusion that the MERCOSUR exemption has not resulted in a disguised restriction on international trade was based on an interpretation that we have reversed, this finding cannot stand. Therefore, we also *reverse* the Panel's findings, in paragraphs 7.354 and 7.355 of the Panel Report, that "the MERCOSUR exemption . . . has not been shown to date to result in the [Import Ban] being applied in a manner that would constitute . . . a disguised restriction on international trade."

C. ENDANGERED SPECIES AND BIOLOGICAL DIVERSITY

1. THE TUNA-DOLPHIN CONTROVERSIES

As evidenced by the preceding materials, one of the major conflicts facing the environment and trade communities is the consistency with the WTO Agreement (including GATT) of unilateral national measures to protect the environment. These measures may have several characteristics, each of which raises different consistency issues: measures directed to products; measures targeting the process by which products are produced (so-called process and production methods or PPMs); and national measures targeting natural resources and environmental conditions located outside national boundaries. PPMs further fall into two types: PPMs that affect the safety or other characteristics of the product (referred to as product-related PPMs) and PPMs that do not affect the product (non-product related PPMs, or NPR PPMs). The following case study on the tuna-dolphin dispute raises these issues in the context of protecting resources outside national borders. As you read the material, consider what arguments you would marshal in support of the United States' measures to protect dolphins.

a. United States Actions and Court Decisions

EARTH ISLAND INSTITUTE V. MOSBACHER
929 F.2d 1449 (9th Cir. 1991)

[In 1972, the United States Congress enacted the Marine Mammal Protection Act ("MMPA") to address the problem of dolphins being killed as a byproduct of fishing for yellowfin tuna in the eastern tropical Pacific Ocean by using the purse seine method of fishing. Because yellowfin tuna swim below schools of dolphins in the region, fishing vessels often set the purse seine nets on dolphins to catch the tuna below the dolphins. The dolphins were often killed or injured in the process. Although the MMPA successfully reduced the number of dolphins being killed by U.S. fishing vessels, it could not reduce the dolphin slaughter by foreign fishing vessels. To ensure that foreign fishing fleets would also reduce the number of dolphins being killed, Congress amended the MMPA in 1984 and 1988 to mandate an embargo on the importation of yellowfin tuna or its products from foreign countries unless the Secretary of Commerce certified that the foreign country's incidental kill rate of dolphins was comparable to that of the United States ("comparability finding"). The relevant provision of the MMPA provided that an embargo was required unless "the total number of eastern spinner dolphins (Stenella longirostria) incidentally taken by vessels of the harvesting nation during the 1989 and subsequent fishing seasons does not exceed 15 percent of the total number of all marine mammals incidentally taken by such vessels *in such year*." The National Marine Fisheries Service ("NMFS"), a federal agency, promulgated a regulation to implement the MMPA, which required that foreign countries had to supply data to the NMFS by July 31 of each year regarding the number of dolphins killed during the previous calendar year. The regulation further stated that if a foreign country exceeded the limitations for the previous year, the Secretary could nonetheless "reconsider" the embargo and certify compliance with the MMPA if the number of dolphins killed during the six month following the year that exceeded the limits "improved to the acceptable level."

In September 1990, the Earth Island Institute along with other environmental groups sought for a temporary restraining order ("TRO") banning the import of yellowfin tuna from Mexico, after the NMFS lifted the embargo based on the reconsideration regulation that Mexico was within the limits of numbers of dolphins killed for the first six months of 1990, even though Mexico had exceeded the limits for 1989. The district court granted the TRO in October 1990 finding that the regulation allowing "reconsideration" of the embargo based on the six months of 1990 data was beyond the agency's authority, because the language of the MMPA was clear that the comparability finding of the numbers of dolphins killed must be based on an entire year of data. The government filed an appeal arguing that the six-month "reconsideration" provision was within the discretion delegated by Congress to the agency for regulation implementation of the MMPA. The Ninth Circuit affirmed the district court's order and held that the clear language of the MMPA required an embargo unless the number of dolphins killed in the previous year was within the limits, and the regulation's reconsideration provision was at odds with the purpose of the amendments to the MMPA, which was to hold foreign fishing vessels to U.S. dolphin protection standards.]

b. The GATT Tuna/Dolphin Panel Report (Tuna-Dolphin I)

US—RESTRICTIONS ON IMPORTS OF TUNA

(Mexico v. United States)
General Agreement on Tariffs and Trade
Report of the Panel
Sept. 3, 1991

[Dolphins swimming in eastern tropical areas of the Pacific Ocean were often killed when they were trapped in the purse seine nets harvesting yellowfin tuna. As noted in the Earth Island case, summarized above, the United States enacted the Marine Mammal Protection Act (MMPA) to address this issue and banned the importation of yellowfin tuna and yellowfin tuna products from countries unless the countries proved to U.S. authorities that they met the dolphin protection standards established in the MMPA. Specifically, the MMPA required a ban on importation of tuna products from countries unless the average incidental taking rate (dolphins killed each time in the purse-seine nets) by vessels of those countries was no more than 1.25 times that of U.S. vessels for the same period. In 1990, the United States imposed an embargo against Mexico on imports of yellowfin tuna and yellowfin tuna products harvested with purse seine nets because Mexico had exceeded the incidental taking rate. In 1991, Mexico complained under the GATT dispute settlement procedure (which was pre-WTO), that the embargo violated GATT Article XI (prohibition of quantitative restrictions). The United States argued that the embargo was consistent with Article III:4 (enforcement of an internal regulation), and even if the measures were found not consistent with Article III, they were justified by exceptions in Article XX(b) (necessary to protect animal life) and Article XX(g) (relating to the conservation of exhaustible natural resources).

Two key questions in *Tuna/Dolphin I* were 1) whether member States may restrict trade based on the process used to produce goods (as opposed to the products themselves); and 2) whether Article XX would justify trade restrictions in order to protect the life or the environment outside its jurisdiction.

1. **Categorization of restrictions on importation as internal regulations (Article III) or quantitative restrictions (Article XI)**

Mexico argued that the measures prohibiting importation of yellowfin tuna and yellowfin tuna products were quantitative restrictions on importation prohibited by Article XI. The United States argued that the disputed measures were not covered by Article XI but were "internal regulations" under Article III:4 and the Note Ad Article III, and the United Sates were merely enforcing the import prohibition consistent with Article III:4 on a non-discriminatory basis. The Note Ad Article III provided that "[a]ny internal ... regulation ... referred to in [Article III:1] which applies to an imported product and the like domestic product ... is accordingly subject to the provisions of Article III."

The Panel concluded that the MMPA import prohibition of yellowfin tuna for the purpose of reducing the incidental killing of dolphins did not constitute "internal regulations" covered by Article III, and therefore Article III was not applicable. In reaching this conclusion, the Panel stated that only those measures that were applied to *products* would be covered by Article III, and measures regulating *process* (the method in which tuna was caught) did not fall under the scope of Article III. Because the MMPA import prohibition did not "directly regulate the sale of tuna" or "possibly affect tuna as a product," the MMPA was not regarded as being applied to tuna products and did not constitute internal regulations covered by Article III. The Panel further concluded that even if the MMPA import prohibition were regarded as regulating the sale of tuna products, it did not meet the requirements of Article III as Article III required a "comparison of the treatment of imported tuna as a *product* with that of domestic tuna as a *product*," and the MMPA provisions regulating the incidental taking of dolphins "could not possibly affect tuna as a product." The Panel then found that the ban on Mexican tuna was a quantitative restriction violating Article XI.

2. **Article XX: General Exceptions**

Parties may argue that Article XX would justify measures that would otherwise be inconsistent with the GATT. Article XX provides that:

> Subject to the requirement that such measures are not applied in a manner which would constitute a means of arbitrary or unjustifiable discrimination between countries where the same conditions prevail, or a disguised restriction on international trade, nothing in this Agreement shall be construed to prevent the adoption or enforcement by any contracting party of measures ...

> (b) necessary to protect human, animal or plant life or health; ...

(g) relating to the conservation of exhaustible natural resources if such measures are made effective in conjunction with restrictions on domestic production or consumption; . . .

Article XX(b)

The United States argued that the import prohibition of yellowfin tuna and its products from Mexico was justified under Article XX(b) because it was "necessary" to protect the life and health of dolphins. Mexico argued that Article XX(b) could not justify a measure intended to protect human, animal or plant life or health outside the jurisdiction of the party, and the import prohibition was not "necessary" because other alternative means such as international co-operation were available to protect dolphin lives while being consistent with the GATT obligations.

The Panel first acknowledged that each party was free to set its own environmental standards to protect human, animal or plant life or health, and Article XX may allow parties to impose trade restrictive measures inconsistent with the GATT obligations in order to "pursue overriding public policy goals to the extent that such inconsistencies were unavoidable." However, the Panel concluded that parties could not impose trade restrictions for the purpose of protecting human, animal or plant life or health outside its jurisdiction, because otherwise it would be subject to abuse as any parties could unilaterally impose trade restrictions against other countries for merely having different environmental protection policies.

The Panel further concluded that the MMPA import prohibition was not "necessary" under Article XX(b) because the United States failed to demonstrate that it had "exhausted all options reasonably available to it to pursue its dolphin protection objectives through measures consistent with" the GATT, particularly "through the negotiation of international cooperative arrangements."

Article XX(g)

The United States argued that Article XX(g) would justify the import prohibition because it was "relating to" the conservation of dolphins as exhaustible natural resources. Mexico argued that like Article XX(b), Article XX (g) was unavailable for the conservation of exhaustible natural resources outside its jurisdiction, and the disputed import prohibition was not "relating to" the conservation of dolphins.

Acknowledging that parties were free to adopt its own conservation policies under Article XX(g), the Panel concluded that like Article XX(b), Article XX(g) did not allow parties to impose trade restrictions in order to conserve exhaustible natural resources outside its jurisdiction because of the same concern expressed in Article XX(b) analysis (unilateral trade restrictions based on different conservation policies in other countries). The Panel further concluded that even if Article XX(g) could be applied extraterritorially, the import prohibition was not "relating to" the conservation of dolphins because it was found not primarily aimed at the conservation of dolphins. The Panel recalled that the United States linked the maximum incidental dolphin-taking rate, which Mexico had to meet during a particular period in order to be able to export tuna to the United States, to the taking rate actually recorded for United States fishermen during the same period. Consequently, the Mexican authorities could not know whether, at a given point of time, their conservation policies conformed to the United States conservation standards. The Panel considered that a limitation on trade based on such unpredictable conditions could not be regarded as being primarily aimed at the conservation of dolphins.

Note that the Panel focused on the fact that the United States was not regulating a product but the process by which the product was obtained, (i.e., a PPM), namely by the use of purse seine nets which captured dolphins in the process, and that the process did not affect the product in any way (e.g., it did not improve its safety). Note also that the Panel first determined whether Article III applied (no) and whether the import ban violated Article XI (yes) before considering whether Article XX exceptions applied. The Reformulated Gasoline case, decided under the WTO agreements and described later in this chapter, followed precisely the same analytic structure. It is important to remember that Article XX becomes relevant only if there is a violation of some other provision of GATT/WTO.]

---

c. The Secondary Boycott of Yellowfin Tuna (Tuna-Dolphin II)

In addition to the primary embargo on tuna imported from countries that failed to meet standards discussed above, the US Congress also provided for a secondary embargo against countries that import tuna from countries that do not satisfy the statutory requirements of the Marine Mammal Protection Act and then export the tuna to the United States. Congress wanted to protect against "tuna laundering." The relevant section of the MMPA (§ 1371(a)(2)(C)) provided that the Secretary of the Treasury "shall require the government of any intermediary nation from which yellowfin tuna or tuna products will be exported to the United States to certify and provide reasonable proof that it has acted to prohibit the importation of such tuna and tuna products from any nation from which direct export to the United States of such tuna and tuna products is banned under this section within sixty days following the effective date of such ban on importation to the United States."

Earth Island Institute brought suit to enforce the secondary embargo. The plaintiff argued, among other things, that the scope of the secondary embargo applies not only to yellowfin tuna and tuna products harvested with purse seine nets in the eastern tropical Pacific from countries not meeting MMPA comparability standards but applies to the import of all yellowfin tuna and tuna products containing yellowfin from intermediary countries, unless the Secretary of the Treasury obtains proof that the intermediary country has prohibited imports of tuna and tuna products from the embargoed country.

The court agreed with plaintiff's argument and ordered a preliminary injunction. *Earth Island Institute v. Robert Mosbacher et al.,* January 31, 1992, 1992 U.S. Dis. LEXIS 1866.

The EC and the Netherlands, on behalf of the Netherlands Antilles, complained to the GATT that the embargoes were inconsistent with Article XI of the GATT, did not qualify as a border adjustment under Article III, and were not covered by Article XX exceptions. In July 1992 the GATT established a Panel to hear the claims. The Panel, which operated under the pre-WTO procedures, concluded that both the primary and the intermediary country embargoes against States that export yellowfin tuna or tuna products to the United States and import these items were inconsistent with Article XI, since they banned imports from countries not adopting certain policies, and that Article III could not apply to restrictions based on practices and not the product. It rejected the Article XX exceptions but on the basis of reasoning that differed somewhat from that in the Tuna Dolphin I Panel report.

Most notably, the Panel concluded that Article XX(g) on conserving exhaustible natural resources does not limit the location of the resources that must be conserved, thus allowing for the possibility of extraterritorial jurisdiction under these exceptions. This differs from the reasoning of the Panel in the Tuna Dolphin I dispute. However, the Panel rejected the argument that the measures were within Article XX. The Panel concluded that, because the embargo went beyond prohibiting the import of tuna caught in a dolphin-unsafe manner, to prohibiting the import of all tuna from countries that allowed any tuna to be caught in a manner endangering dolphins (or in this case, from countries that imported any tuna from such a country), the embargo was an impermissible attempt to force other countries to change their policy. This reasoning left open the possibility that a more narrowly drawn measure— (e.g., one aimed more precisely at preventing the United States' purchasing power from being an incentive to kill dolphins)—might be GATT/WTO-consistent. GATT, *United States—Restrictions on Imports of Tuna* (June 16, 1994), 33 I.L.M. 839 (1994). Like the Panel report in Tuna-Dolphin I, this Panel report was never adopted.

In May 1992, the United States and nine other countries (Costa Rica, France, Japan, Mexico, Nicaragua, Panama, Spain, Venezuela, and Vanuatu) concluded a new Inter-American Tropical Tuna Commission Agreement. The agreement, which went into effect in January 1993, extended through 1999. Under the agreement, parties aimed to reduce dolphin mortality rates to near zero by the end of the century. Countries were to reduce the dolphin mortality rate by 30 percent in 1993, 24 percent in 1994, 19 percent in 1995, 14 percent in 1996, 11 percent in 1997, 10 percent in 1998, and 8 percent in 1999.

This was followed in 1999 by the Agreement on the International Dolphin Conservation Program (AIDCP). The AIDCP is a legally binding instrument for dolphin conservation and ecosystem management in the eastern tropical Pacific Ocean. It is intended to reduce incidental dolphin mortality in the tuna purse-seine fishery through the setting of annual limits, to seek alternative means (i.e., non-dolphin-related means) of capturing large yellowfin tunas, and to ensure the long-term sustainability of tuna stocks and marine resources in the ETP. As of August 2015, Belize, Colombia, Costa Rica, Ecuador, El Salvador, the European Union, Guatemala, Honduras, Mexico, Nicaragua, Panama, Peru, the United States, and Venezuela were Parties to the AIDCP. Bolivia and Vanuatu were applying the AIDCP provisionally.

NOTES AND QUESTIONS

1. *Terminology: Extraterritoriality.* Is the term "extraterritorial" helpful in this context? Would it be more useful analytically to distinguish among efforts by one country: to protect its territory against a threat arising outside its territory; to protect the environment of another country; and to protect the global commons? Also, can (should) countries condition their acceptance of a multilateral environmental agreement on a change in other countries' domestic law?

2. *Environmental or ethical?* Some sub-species of dolphin protected by the United States law were (and are) not endangered or threatened. Should this affect the characterization of the dispute as environmental? Was the United States legislation primarily ethically motivated?

3. *Protecting the commons.* Suppose a resource is found in the high seas, or suppose it is endangered: should this affect the WTO analysis? Does a country have no right to protect the global commons? Did countries give up any such right in joining the GATT in 1948 or the WTO in 1994?

2. THE SHRIMP-TURTLE DISPUTE

There are seven species of sea turtles in the world, which are found in subtropical or tropical areas. All the species are included in Appendix I of the Convention on International Trade in Endangered Species (CITES, examined in Chapter 13, above) as endangered, and all except one species are listed in Appendices I and II of the 1979 Convention on Migratory Species of Wild Animals (CMS) and appear in the IUCN (International Union for the Protection of Nature and natural Resources) Red List as endangered or vulnerable.

In the United States, the Endangered Species Act lists all sea turtles as endangered or threatened and prohibits the taking of all endangered sea turtles within the United States, its territorial sea, or the high seas without authorization by the Secretary of Commerce. One human activity that has proven highly dangerous to sea turtles is catching shrimp using mechanical shrimp trawlers.

In 1987, the United States issued regulations requiring all shrimp trawlers to use turtle excluder devices (TEDs), which are highly effective in preventing turtles from being killed in the nets shrimp trawlers use; and in 1989 United States legislation (the Sea Turtle Protection Act) called upon the United States government to negotiate bilateral or multilateral agreements to protect sea turtles. The legislation banned imports of shrimp unless the President certified to Congress that the harvesting country had a regulatory program and incidental take rate for sea turtles comparable to that of the United States or that the fishing environment of the harvesting country did not pose a threat to sea turtles. The subsequent 1991 United States guidelines required countries to use TEDs or a program with comparable results but limited the application to the Caribbean/western Atlantic region. The 1993 Guidelines eliminated the alternative program option to TEDs.

The United States government conducted workshops in various countries around the world demonstrating the TEDs and how they could be made cheaply from local materials.

In 1995, the United States Court of International Trade (CIT) found that the 1991 and 1993 Guidelines were contrary to law in limiting the geographical coverage and directed the Department of State to prohibit by May 1, 1996, the importation of shrimp or shrimp products harvested in the wild with commercial fishing technology that could affect sea turtles adversely. The subsequent regulations required all imports of shrimp to be accompanied by a declaration indicating that they were fished under conditions not adversely affecting sea turtles or in waters from a country that had been certified as sea turtle safe. The 1996 Guidelines required that certifications to other countries could be done only if they used TEDs at all times. The CIT ruled that the embargo applied to all shrimp and shrimp products from countries that had not been certified and nullified the alternative declaration method from noncertified countries. The United States government appealed that ruling to the U.S. Court of Appeals for the Federal Circuit.

India, Malaysia, Pakistan, and Thailand, which are large exporters of shrimp and shrimp products, brought a claim against the United States to the WTO in 1997. The dispute Panel issued its final report to the parties in 1998.

The Panel held that the United States law restricting imports violates Article XI:1 of the GATT and did not rule on the claims that the law also violates Articles I:1 and XIII:1. Rather it proceeded directly to examine whether the measures could come within the Article XX exceptions and found they did not.

Contrary to previous panels, which had first determined whether the measures came within any of the explicit exceptions (b) and (g) of Article XX, the Shrimp-Turtle Panel first determined whether the measures satisfied the chapeau (opening paragraph) of Article XX. This provides that:

> Subject to the requirement that such measures are not applied in a manner that would constitute a means of arbitrary or unjustifiable discrimination between countries where the same conditions prevail, or a disguised restriction on international trade, nothing in this Agreement shall be construed to prevent the adoption or enforcement by any contracting party of measures: . . .

Noting that the Sea Turtle Protection Act (as interpreted by the CIT) bans the import of all shrimp from a country that does not require that all its mechanized shrimp trawlers use TEDs—rather than banning the import only of shrimp caught by mechanized trawlers not using TEDs—the Panel invoked reasoning somewhat similar to that used by the Panel in Tuna-Dolphin II: the United States is impermissibly pressuring another country to change its policy. The Panel's analysis was radically different in one sense, however, because it created a new test for applying the Article XX chapeau, viz. whether a challenged action would threaten the multilateral trading system. The Panel stated:

> 7.43. Therefore, we are of the opinion that the chapeau Article XX, interpreted within its context and in the light of the object and purpose of GATT and of the WTO Agreement, only allows Members to derogate from GATT provisions so long as, in doing so, they do not undermine the WTO multilateral trading system, thus also abusing the exceptions contained in Article XX. [We] find that when considering a measure under Article XX, we must determine not only whether the measure on its own undermines the WTO multilateral trading system, but also whether such type of measure, if it were to be adopted by other Members, would threaten the security and predictability of the multilateral trading system.

After the Panel issued its report, the CIT decision was reversed by the United States Court of Appeals, on the ground that the plaintiff in the

CIT case had withdrawn before the CIT issued its ruling. The Court of Appeals did not reach the question of how the Act should be interpreted.

The United States appealed the WTO Panel's Article XX finding. The Appellate Body (AB) also found that the United States' approach did not satisfy Article XX, but its ruling differed from the Panel's in several important respects.

- The AB found that the Panel had erred in its Article XX analysis by reversing the required sequence of the two-tiered analysis set out in the Reformulated Gasoline case, above. The proper sequence is first to examine whether any of the specific exceptions in Article XX applies, and only then to analyze whether the conditions in the chapeau (headnote) are satisfied.

- In analyzing paragraph (g) of Article XX, the AB found that the term "exhaustible natural resources" includes not only minerals and other non-living natural resources, but also living natural resources. The AB concluded that sea turtles are both "exhaustible" and "natural resources" (and also that the "related to" and "made effective in conjunction with" requirements were also met, applying the Reformulated Gasoline case's criteria of "even-handedness").

With respect to Article XX's chapeau, the AB held that "discrimination results not only when countries in which the same conditions apply are treated differently, but also when the application of the measure at issue does not allow for any inquiry into the appropriateness of the regulatory program for the conditions prevailing in those existing countries" (paragraph 165). The AB found that the United States measure, as implemented, had an "intended and actual coercive effect on . . . foreign governments [to adopt] essentially the same policies and enforcement practices as the United States." (Paragraph 161.)

The AB focused on the importance of trying to resolve this type of issue through international agreements. The AB found an additional incident of unjustifiable discrimination because the United States' had failed to pursue sufficiently the conservation of sea turtles through bilateral or multilateral agreements with the target countries before resorting to its unilateral measure. (Paragraph 166–172.)

The AB based another part of its reasoning on what it referred to as "basic fairness and due process". (*See* paragraphs 177–181.) It found that the United States measure constituted arbitrary discrimination because of how it was applied.

a. Excerpts from the Appellate Body Report

US—IMPORT PROHIBITION OF CERTAIN SHRIMP AND SHRIMP PRODUCTS ("SHRIMP/TURTLE I")

(India, Malaysia, Pakistan, and Thailand v. United States)
Report of the Appellate Body
WT/DS58/AB/R, adopted on 6 November 1998 (most footnotes deleted)

VI. Appraising Section 609 Under Article XX of the GATT 1994

111. We turn to the second issue raised by the appellant, the United States, which is whether the Panel erred in finding that the measure at issue constitutes unjustifiable discrimination between countries where the same conditions prevail and, thus, is not within the scope of measures permitted under Article XX of the GATT 1994.

A. The Panel's Findings and Interpretative Analysis

115. In the present case, the Panel did not expressly examine the ordinary meaning of the words of Article XX. The Panel disregarded the fact that the introductory clauses of Article XX speak of the "manner" in which measures sought to be justified are "applied". In United States—Gasoline, we pointed out that the chapeau of Article XX "by its express terms addresses, not so much the questioned measure or its specific contents as such, but rather the manner in which that measure is applied." (emphasis added) The Panel did not inquire specifically into how the application of Section 609 constitutes "a means of arbitrary or unjustifiable discrimination between countries where the same conditions prevail, or a disguised restriction on international trade." What the Panel did, in purporting to examine the consistency of the measure with the chapeau of Article XX, was to focus repeatedly on the design of the measure itself. For instance, the Panel stressed that it was addressing "a particular situation where a Member has taken unilateral measures which, by their nature, could put the multilateral trading system at risk." (emphasis added)

116. The general design of a measure, as distinguished from its application, is, however, to be examined in the course of determining whether that measure falls within one or another of the paragraphs of Article XX following the chapeau. The Panel failed to scrutinize the immediate context of the chapeau: i.e., paragraphs (a) to (j) of Article XX. Moreover, the Panel did not look into the object and purpose of the chapeau of Article XX. Rather, the Panel looked into the object and purpose of the whole of the GATT 1994 and the WTO Agreement, which object and purpose it described in an overly broad manner. Thus, the Panel arrived at the very broad formulation that measures which "undermine the WTO multilateral trading system" must be regarded as "not within the scope of measures permitted under the chapeau of Article

XX." Maintaining, rather than undermining, the multilateral trading system is necessarily a fundamental and pervasive premise underlying the WTO Agreement; but it is not a right or an obligation, nor is it an interpretative rule which can be employed in the appraisal of a given measure under the chapeau of Article XX. In United States—Gasoline, we stated that it is "important to underscore that the purpose and object of the introductory clauses of Article XX is generally the prevention of 'abuse of the exceptions of [Article XX]'." The Panel did not attempt to inquire into how the measure at stake was being applied in such a manner as to constitute abuse or misuse of a given kind of exception.

117. The above flaws in the Panel's analysis and findings flow almost naturally from the fact that the Panel disregarded the sequence of steps essential for carrying out such an analysis. The Panel defined its approach as first "determin[ing] whether the measure at issue satisfies the conditions contained in the chapeau." If the Panel found that to be the case, it said that it "shall then examine whether the US measure is covered by the terms of Article XX(b) or (g)." . . .

. . .

118. In United States—Gasoline, we enunciated the appropriate method for applying Article XX of the GATT 1994:

In order that the justifying protection of Article XX may be extended to it, the measure at issue must not only come under one or another of the particular exceptions—paragraphs (a) to (j)—listed under Article XX; it must also satisfy the requirements imposed by the opening clauses of Article XX. *The analysis is,* in other words, *two-tiered: first, provisional justification by reason of characterization of the measure under XX(g); second, further appraisal of the same measure under the introductory clauses of Article XX.* (emphasis added)

. . .

120. The task of interpreting the chapeau so as to prevent the abuse or misuse of the specific exemptions provided for in Article XX is rendered very difficult, if indeed it remains possible at all, where the interpreter (like the Panel in this case) has not first identified and examined the specific exception threatened with abuse. The standards established in the chapeau are, moreover, necessarily broad in scope and reach: the prohibition of the application of a measure "in a manner which would constitute a means of arbitrary or unjustifiable discrimination between countries where the same conditions prevail" or "a disguised restriction on international trade." When applied in a particular case, the actual contours and contents of these standards will vary as the kind of measure under examination varies. What is appropriately characterizable as "arbitrary discrimination" or "unjustifiable discrimination", or as a

"disguised restriction on international trade" in respect of one category of measures, need not be so with respect to another group or type of measures. The standard of "arbitrary discrimination", for example, under the chapeau may be different for a measure that purports to be necessary to protect public morals than for one relating to the products of prison labour.

122. We hold that the findings of the Panel quoted in paragraph 112 above, and the interpretative analysis embodied therein, constitute error in legal interpretation and accordingly reverse them.

123. Having reversed the Panel's legal conclusion that the United States measure at issue "is not within the scope of measures permitted under the chapeau of Article XX", we believe that it is our duty and our responsibility to complete the legal analysis in this case in order to determine whether Section 609 qualifies for justification under Article XX.

. . .

B. Article XX(g): Provisional Justification of Section 609

125. In claiming justification for its measure, the United States primarily invokes Article XX(g). Justification under Article XX(b) is claimed only in the alternative; that is, the United States suggests that we should look at Article XX(b) only if we find that Section 609 does not fall within the ambit of Article XX(g). We proceed, therefore, to the first tier of the analysis of Section 609 and to our consideration of whether it may be characterized as provisionally justified under the terms of Article XX(g).

126. Paragraph (g) of Article XX covers measures:

> relating to the conservation of exhaustible natural resources if such measures are made effective in conjunction with restrictions on domestic production or consumption;

1. "Exhaustible Natural Resources"

127. We begin with the threshold question of whether Section 609 is a measure concerned with the conservation of "exhaustible natural resources" within the meaning of Article XX(g). The Panel, of course, with its "chapeau-down" approach, did not make a finding on whether the sea turtles that Section 609 is designed to conserve constitute "exhaustible natural resources" for purposes of Article XX(g). In the proceedings before the Panel, however, the parties to the dispute argued this issue vigorously and extensively. India, Pakistan and Thailand contended that a "reasonable interpretation" of the term "exhaustible" is that the term refers to "finite resources such as minerals, rather than biological or renewable resources." In their view, such finite resources were exhaustible "because there was a limited supply which could and would

be depleted unit for unit as the resources were consumed." Moreover, they argued, if "all" natural resources were considered to be exhaustible, the term "exhaustible" would become superfluous. They also referred to the drafting history of Article XX(g), and, in particular, to the mention of minerals, such as manganese, in the context of arguments made by some delegations that "export restrictions" should be permitted for the preservation of scarce natural resources. For its part, Malaysia added that sea turtles, being living creatures, could only be considered under Article XX(b), since Article XX(g) was meant for "nonliving exhaustible natural resources". It followed, according to Malaysia, that the United States cannot invoke both the Article XX(b) and the Article XX(g) exceptions simultaneously.

128. We are not convinced by these arguments. Textually, Article XX(g) is not limited to the conservation of "mineral" or "non-living" natural resources. The complainants' principal argument is rooted in the notion that "living" natural resources are "renewable" and therefore cannot be "exhaustible" natural resources. We do not believe that "exhaustible" natural resources and "renewable" natural resources are mutually exclusive. One lesson that modern biological sciences teach us is that living species, though in principle, capable of reproduction and, in that sense, "renewable", are in certain circumstances indeed susceptible of depletion, exhaustion and extinction, frequently because of human activities. Living resources are just as "finite" as petroleum, iron ore and other non-living resources.[106]

. . .

132. We turn next to the issue of whether the living natural resources sought to be conserved by the measure are "exhaustible" under Article XX(g). That this element is present in respect of the five species of sea turtles here involved appears to be conceded by all the participants and third participants in this case. The exhaustibility of sea turtles would in fact have been very difficult to controvert since all of the seven recognized species of sea turtles are today listed in Appendix 1 of the Convention on International Trade in Endangered Species of Wild Fauna and Flora ("CITES"). The list in Appendix 1 includes "all species threatened with extinction which are or may be affected by trade." (CITES, Article II.1.)

133. Finally, we observe that sea turtles are highly migratory animals, passing in and out of waters subject to the rights of jurisdiction of various coastal states and the high seas. . . . The sea turtle species here at stake, i.e., covered by Section 609, are all known to occur in waters

---

[106] We note, for example, that the World Commission on Environment and Development stated: "The planet's species are under stress. There is growing scientific consensus that species are disappearing at rates never before witnessed on the planet. . . ." World Commission on Environment and Development, Our Common Future (Oxford University Press, 1987), p. 13.

over which the United States exercises jurisdiction.[119] Of course, it is not claimed that all populations of these species migrate to, or traverse, at one time or another, waters subject to United States jurisdiction. Neither the appellant nor any of the appellees claims any rights of exclusive ownership over the sea turtles, at least not while they are swimming freely in their natural habitat—the oceans. We do not pass upon the question of whether there is an implied jurisdictional limitation in Article XX(g), and if so, the nature or extent of that limitation. We note only that in the specific circumstances of the case before us, there is a sufficient nexus between the migratory and endangered marine populations involved and the United States for purposes of Article XX(g).

134. For all the foregoing reasons, we find that the sea turtles here involved constitute "exhaustible natural resources" for purposes of Article XX(g) of the GATT 1994.

2.   *"Relating to the Conservation of [Exhaustible Natural Resources]"*

137. In the present case, we must examine the relationship between the general structure and design of the measure here at stake, Section 609, and the policy goal it purports to serve, that is, the conservation of sea turtles.

138. Section 609(b)(1) imposes an import ban on shrimp that have been harvested with commercial fishing technology which may adversely affect sea turtles. This provision is designed to influence countries to adopt national regulatory programs requiring the use of TEDs by their shrimp fishermen. In this connection, it is important to note that the general structure and design of Section 609 cum implementing guidelines is fairly narrowly focused. There are two basic exemptions from the import ban, both of which relate clearly and directly to the policy goal of conserving sea turtles. First, Section 609, as elaborated in the 1996 Guidelines, excludes from the import ban shrimp harvested "under conditions that do not adversely affect sea turtles". Thus, the measure, by its terms, excludes from the import ban: aquaculture shrimp; shrimp species (such as pandalid shrimp) harvested in water areas where sea turtles do not normally occur; and shrimp harvested exclusively by artisanal methods, even from non-certified countries. The harvesting of such shrimp clearly does not affect sea turtles. Second, under Section 609(b)(2), the measure exempts from the import ban shrimp caught in waters subject to the jurisdiction of certified countries.

---

[119] *See* Panel Report, para. 2.6. The 1987 Regulations, 52 Fed. Reg. 24244, 29 June 1987, identified five species of sea turtles as occurring within the areas concerned and thus falling under the regulations: loggerhead (Caretta caretta), Kemp's ridley (Lepidochelys kempi), green (Chelonia mydas), leatherback (Dermochelys coriacea) and hawksbill (Eretmochelys imbricata). Section 609 refers to "those species of sea turtles the conservation of which is the subject of regulations promulgated by the Secretary of Commerce on 29 June, 1987."

139. There are two types of certification for countries under Section 609(b)(2). First, under Section 609(b)(2)(C), a country may be certified as having a fishing environment that does not pose a threat of incidental taking of sea turtles in the course of commercial shrimp trawl harvesting. There is no risk, or only a negligible risk, that sea turtles will be harmed by shrimp trawling in such an environment.

140. The second type of certification is provided by Section 609(b)(2)(A) and (B). Under these provisions, as further elaborated in the 1996 Guidelines, a country wishing to export shrimp to the United States is required to adopt a regulatory program that is comparable to that of the United States program and to have a rate of incidental take of sea turtles that is comparable to the average rate of United States' vessels. This is, essentially, a requirement that a country adopt a regulatory program requiring the use of TEDs by commercial shrimp trawling vessels in areas where there is a likelihood of intercepting sea turtles. This requirement is, in our view, directly connected with the policy of conservation of sea turtles. It is undisputed among the participants, and recognized by the experts consulted by the Panel, that the harvesting of shrimp by commercial shrimp trawling vessels with mechanical retrieval devices in waters where shrimp and sea turtles coincide is a significant cause of sea turtle mortality. Moreover, the Panel did "not question . . . the fact generally acknowledged by the experts that TEDs, when properly installed and adapted to the local area, would be an effective tool for the preservation of sea turtles."

141. In its general design and structure, therefore, Section 609 is not a simple, blanket prohibition of the importation of shrimp imposed without regard to the consequences (or lack thereof) of the mode of harvesting employed upon the incidental capture and mortality of sea turtles. Focusing on the design of the measure here at stake, it appears to us that Section 609, cum implementing guidelines, is not disproportionately wide in its scope and reach in relation to the policy objective of protection and conservation of sea turtle species. The means are, in principle, reasonably related to the ends. The means and ends relationship between Section 609 and the legitimate policy of conserving an exhaustible, and, in fact, endangered species, is observably a close and real one, a relationship that is every bit as substantial as that which we found in United States—Gasoline between the EPA baseline establishment rules and the conservation of clean air in the United States.

142. In our view, therefore, Section 609 is a measure "relating to" the conservation of an exhaustible natural resource within the meaning of Article XX(g) of the GATT 1994.

3. *"If Such Measures are Made Effective in conjunction with Restrictions on Domestic Production or Consumption"*

143. In United States—Gasoline, we held that the above-captioned clause of Article XX(g),

> ... is appropriately read as a requirement that the measures concerned impose restrictions, not just in respect of imported gasoline but also with respect to domestic gasoline. The clause is a requirement of even-handedness in the imposition of restrictions, in the name of conservation, upon the production or consumption of exhaustible natural resources.

In this case, we need to examine whether the restrictions imposed by Section 609 with respect to imported shrimp are also imposed in respect of shrimp caught by United States shrimp trawl vessels.

144. We earlier noted that Section 609, enacted in 1989, addresses the mode of harvesting of imported shrimp only. However, two years earlier, in 1987, the United States issued regulations pursuant to the Endangered Species Act requiring all United States shrimp trawl vessels to use approved TEDs, or to restrict the duration of tow-times, in specified areas where there was significant incidental mortality of sea turtles in shrimp trawls. These regulations became fully effective in 1990 and were later modified. They now require United States shrimp trawlers to use approved TEDs "in areas and at times when there is a likelihood of intercepting sea turtles", with certain limited exceptions. Penalties for violation of the Endangered Species Act, or the regulations issued thereunder, include civil and criminal sanctions. The United States government currently relies on monetary sanctions and civil penalties for enforcement. The government has the ability to seize shrimp catch from trawl vessels fishing in United States waters and has done so in cases of egregious violations. We believe that, in principle, Section 609 is an even-handed measure.

145. Accordingly, we hold that Section 609 is a measure made effective in conjunction with the restrictions on domestic harvesting of shrimp, as required by Article XX(g).

C. The Introductory Clauses of Article XX: Characterizing Section 609 under the Chapeau's Standards

146. As noted earlier, the United States invokes Article XX(b) only if and to the extent that we hold that Section 609 falls outside the scope of Article XX(g). Having found that Section 609 does come within the terms of Article XX(g), it is not, therefore, necessary to analyze the measure in terms of Article XX(b).

147. Although provisionally justified under Article XX(g), Section 609, if it is ultimately to be justified as an exception under Article XX,

must also satisfy the requirements of the introductory clauses—the "chapeau"—of Article XX, that is,

Article XX

General Exceptions

Subject to the requirement that such measures are *not applied* in a manner which would constitute a means of arbitrary or unjustifiable discrimination between countries where the same conditions prevail, or a disguised restriction on international trade, nothing in this Agreement shall be construed to prevent the adoption or enforcement by any Member of measures: (emphasis added)

We turn, hence, to the task of appraising Section 609, and specifically the manner in which it is applied under the chapeau of Article XX; that is, to the second part of the two-tier analysis required under Article XX.

1. *General Considerations*

. . .

150. We commence the second tier of our analysis with an examination of the ordinary meaning of the words of the chapeau. The precise language of the chapeau requires that a measure not be applied in a manner which would constitute a means of "arbitrary or unjustifiable discrimination between countries where the same conditions prevail" or a "disguised restriction on international trade." There are three standards contained in the chapeau: first, arbitrary discrimination between countries where the same conditions prevail; second, unjustifiable discrimination between countries where the same conditions prevail; and third, a disguised restriction on international trade. In order for a measure to be applied in a manner which would constitute "arbitrary or unjustifiable discrimination between countries where the same conditions prevail", three elements must exist. First, the application of the measure must result in discrimination. As we stated in United States—Gasoline, the nature and quality of this discrimination is different from the discrimination in the treatment of products which was already found to be inconsistent with one of the substantive obligations of the GATT 1994, such as Articles I, III or XI.[138] Second, the discrimination must be arbitrary or unjustifiable in character. We will examine this element of arbitrariness or unjustifiability in detail below. Third, this discrimination must occur between countries where the same conditions prevail. In United States—Gasoline, we accepted the assumption of the participants in that appeal that such discrimination could occur not only between different exporting Members, but also between exporting Members and

---

[138] In United States—Gasoline, adopted 20 May 1996, WT/DS2/AB/R, p. 23, we stated: "The provisions of the chapeau cannot logically refer to the same standard(s) by which a violation of a substantive rule has been determined to have occurred."

the importing Member concerned. Thus, the standards embodied in the language of the chapeau are not only different from the requirements of Article XX(g); they are also different from the standard used in determining that Section 609 is violative of the substantive rules of Article XI:1 of the GATT 1994.

. . .

159. The task of interpreting and applying the chapeau is, hence, essentially the delicate one of locating and marking out a line of equilibrium between the right of a Member to invoke an exception under Article XX and the rights of the other Members under varying substantive provisions (e.g., Article XI) of the GATT 1994, so that neither of the competing rights will cancel out the other and thereby distort and nullify or impair the balance of rights and obligations constructed by the Members themselves in that Agreement. The location of the line of equilibrium, as expressed in the chapeau, is not fixed and unchanging; the line moves as the kind and the shape of the measures at stake vary and as the facts making up specific cases differ.

160. With these general considerations in mind, we address now the issue of whether the application of the United States measure, although the measure itself falls within the terms of Article XX(g), nevertheless constitutes "a means of arbitrary or unjustifiable discrimination between countries where the same conditions prevail" or "a disguised restriction on international trade". We address, in other words, whether the application of this measure constitutes an abuse or misuse of the provisional justification made available by Article XX(g). We note, preliminarily, that the application of a measure may be characterized as amounting to an abuse or misuse of an exception of Article XX not only when the detailed operating provisions of the measure prescribe the arbitrary or unjustifiable activity, but also where a measure, otherwise fair and just on its face, is actually applied in an arbitrary or unjustifiable manner. The standards of the chapeau, in our view, project both substantive and procedural requirements.

2. "Unjustifiable Discrimination"

161. We scrutinize first whether Section 609 has been applied in a manner constituting "unjustifiable discrimination between countries where the same conditions prevail". Perhaps the most conspicuous flaw in this measure's application relates to its intended and actual coercive effect on the specific policy decisions made by foreign governments, Members of the WTO. Section 609, in its application, is, in effect, an economic embargo which requires all other exporting Members, if they wish to exercise their GATT rights, to adopt essentially the same policy (together with an approved enforcement program) as that applied to, and enforced on, United States domestic shrimp trawlers. As enacted by the Congress of the United States, the statutory provisions of Section

609(b)(2)(A) and (B) do not, in themselves, require that other WTO Members adopt essentially the same policies and enforcement practices as the United States. Viewed alone, the statute appears to permit a degree of discretion or flexibility in how the standards for determining comparability might be applied, in practice, to other countries.[158] However, any flexibility that may have been intended by Congress when it enacted the statutory provision has been effectively eliminated in the implementation of that policy through the 1996 Guidelines promulgated by the Department of State and through the practice of the administrators in making certification determinations.

162. According to the 1996 Guidelines, certification "shall be made" under Section 609(b)(2)(A) and (B) if an exporting country's program includes a requirement that all commercial shrimp trawl vessels operating in waters in which there is a likelihood of intercepting sea turtles use, at all times, TEDs comparable in effectiveness to those used in the United States. Under these Guidelines, any exceptions to the requirement of the use of TEDs must be comparable to those of the United States program. Furthermore, the harvesting country must have in place a "credible enforcement effort". The language in the 1996 Guidelines is mandatory: certification "shall be made" if these conditions are fulfilled. However, we understand that these rules are also applied in an exclusive manner. That is, the 1996 Guidelines specify the only way that a harvesting country's regulatory program can be deemed "comparable" to the United States' program, and, therefore, they define the only way that a harvesting nation can be certified under Section 609(b)(2)(A) and (B). Although the 1996 Guidelines state that, in making a comparability determination, the Department of State "shall also take into account other measures the harvesting nation undertakes to protect sea turtles", in practice, the competent government officials only look to see whether there is a regulatory program requiring the use of TEDs or one that comes within one of the extremely limited exceptions available to United States shrimp trawl vessels.[163]

163. The actual application of the measure, through the implementation of the 1996 Guidelines and the regulatory practice of administrators, requires other WTO Members to adopt a regulatory program that is not merely comparable, but rather essentially the same, as that applied to the United States shrimp trawl vessels. Thus, the effect

---

[158] Pursuant to Section 609(b)(2), a harvesting nation may be certified, and thus exempted from the import ban, if:

    (A) the government of the harvesting nation has provided documentary evidence of the adoption of a program governing the incidental taking of such sea turtles in the course of such harvesting that is comparable to that of the United States; and

    (B) the average rate of that incidental taking by vessels of the harvesting nation is comparable to the average rate of incidental taking of sea turtles by United States vessels in the course of such harvesting. . .

[163] Statements by the United States at the oral hearing.

of the application of Section 609 is to establish a rigid and unbending standard by which United States officials determine whether or not countries will be certified, thus granting or refusing other countries the right to export shrimp to the United States. Other specific policies and measures that an exporting country may have adopted for the protection and conservation of sea turtles are not taken into account, in practice, by the administrators making the comparability determination.[164]

165. Furthermore, when this dispute was before the Panel and before us, the United States did not permit imports of shrimp harvested by commercial shrimp trawl vessels using TEDs comparable in effectiveness to those required in the United States if those shrimp originated in waters of countries not certified under Section 609. In other words, shrimp caught using methods identical to those employed in the United States have been excluded from the United States market solely because they have been caught in waters of countries that have not been certified by the United States. The resulting situation is difficult to reconcile with the declared policy objective of protecting and conserving sea turtles. This suggests to us that this measure, in its application, is more concerned with effectively influencing WTO Members to adopt essentially the same comprehensive regulatory regime as that applied by the United States to its domestic shrimp trawlers, even though many of those Members may be differently situated. We believe that discrimination results not only when countries in which the same conditions prevail are differently treated, but also when the application of the measure at issue does not allow for any inquiry into the appropriateness of the regulatory program for the conditions prevailing in those exporting countries.

166. Another aspect of the application of Section 609 that bears heavily in any appraisal of justifiable or unjustifiable discrimination is the failure of the United States to engage the appellees, as well as other Members exporting shrimp to the United States, in serious, across-the-board negotiations with the objective of concluding bilateral or multilateral agreements for the protection and conservation of sea turtles, before enforcing the import prohibition against the shrimp exports of those other Members.

. . .

167. A propos this failure to have prior consistent recourse to diplomacy as an instrument of environmental protection policy, which produces discriminatory impacts on countries exporting shrimp to the United States with which no international agreements are reached or even seriously attempted, a number of points must be made. First, the Congress of the United States expressly recognized the importance of

---

[164] Statement by the United States at the oral hearing.

securing international agreements for the protection and conservation of the sea turtle species in enacting this law. . . . Apart from the negotiation of the Inter-American Convention for the Protection and Conservation of Sea Turtles (the "Inter-American Convention") which concluded in 1996, the record before the Panel does not indicate any serious, substantial efforts to carry out these express directions of Congress.

168. Second, the protection and conservation of highly migratory species of sea turtles, that is, the very policy objective of the measure, demands concerted and cooperative efforts on the part of the many countries whose waters are traversed in the course of recurrent sea turtle migrations. The need for, and the appropriateness of, such efforts have been recognized in the WTO itself as well as in a significant number of other international instruments and declarations.

. . .

169. Third, the United States did negotiate and conclude one regional international agreement for the protection and conservation of sea turtles: The Inter-American Convention.

. . .

170. The juxtaposition of (a) the consensual undertakings to put in place regulations providing for, inter alia, use of TEDs jointly determined to be suitable for a particular party's maritime areas, with (b) the reaffirmation of the parties' obligations under the WTO Agreement, including the Agreement on Technical Barriers to Trade and Article XI of the GATT 1994, suggests that the parties to the Inter-American Convention together marked out the equilibrium line to which we referred earlier. The Inter-American Convention demonstrates the conviction of its signatories, including the United States, that consensual and multilateral procedures are available and feasible for the establishment of programs for the conservation of sea turtles. Moreover, the Inter-American Convention emphasizes the continuing validity and significance of Article XI of the GATT 1994, and of the obligations of the WTO Agreement generally, in maintaining the balance of rights and obligations under the WTO Agreement among the signatories of that Convention.

171. The Inter-American Convention thus provides convincing demonstration that an alternative course of action was reasonably open to the United States for securing the legitimate policy goal of its measure, a course of action other than the unilateral and non-consensual procedures of the import prohibition under Section 609. It is relevant to observe that an import prohibition is, ordinarily, the heaviest "weapon" in a Member's armoury of trade measures. The record does not, however, show that serious efforts were made by the United States to negotiate similar agreements with any other country or group of countries before (and, as

far as the record shows, after) Section 609 was enforced on a world-wide basis on 1 May 1996. Finally, the record also does not show that the appellant, the United States, attempted to have recourse to such international mechanisms as exist to achieve cooperative efforts to protect and conserve sea turtles[174] before imposing the import ban.

172. Clearly, the United States negotiated seriously with some, but not with other Members (including the appellees), that export shrimp to the United States. The effect is plainly discriminatory and, in our view, unjustifiable. . . . The principal consequence of this failure may be seen in the resulting unilateralism evident in the application of Section 609. As we have emphasized earlier, the policies relating to the necessity for use of particular kinds of TEDs in various maritime areas, and the operating details of these policies, are all shaped by the Department of State, without the participation of the exporting Members. The system and processes of certification are established and administered by the United States agencies alone. The decision-making involved in the grant, denial or withdrawal of certification to the exporting Members, is, accordingly, also unilateral. The unilateral character of the application of Section 609 heightens the disruptive and discriminatory influence of the import prohibition and underscores its unjustifiability.

173. The application of Section 609, through the implementing guidelines together with administrative practice, also resulted in other differential treatment among various countries desiring certification. Under the 1991 and 1993 Guidelines, to be certifiable, fourteen countries in the wider Caribbean/western Atlantic region had to commit themselves to require the use of TEDs on all commercial shrimp trawling vessels by 1 May 1994. These fourteen countries had a "phase-in" period of three years during which their respective shrimp trawling sectors could adjust to the requirement of the use of TEDs. With respect to all other countries exporting shrimp to the United States (including the appellees, India, Malaysia, Pakistan and Thailand), on 29 December 1995, the United States Court of International Trade directed the Department of State to apply the import ban on a world-wide basis not later than 1 May 1996. On 19 April 1996, the 1996 Guidelines were issued by the Department of State bringing shrimp harvested in all foreign countries within the scope of Section 609, effective 1 May 1996. Thus, all countries that were not among the fourteen in the wider Caribbean/western Atlantic region had only four months to implement the requirement of compulsory use of TEDs. We acknowledge that the greatly differing periods for putting into operation the requirement for use of TEDs resulted from decisions of the

---

[174] While the United States is a party to CITES, it did not make any attempt to raise the issue of sea turtle mortality due to shrimp trawling in the CITES Standing Committee as a subject requiring concerted action by states. In this context, we note that the United States, for example, has not signed the Convention on the Conservation of Migratory Species of Wild Animals or UNCLOS, and has not ratified the Convention on Biological Diversity.

Court of International Trade. Even so, this does not relieve the United States of the legal consequences of the discriminatory impact of the decisions of that Court. The United States, like all other Members of the WTO and of the general community of states, bears responsibility for acts of all its departments of government, including its judiciary.

    . . .

177. Differing treatment of different countries desiring certification is also observable in the differences in the levels of effort made by the United States in transferring the required TED technology to specific countries. Far greater efforts to transfer that technology successfully were made to certain exporting countries—basically the fourteen wider Caribbean/western Atlantic countries cited earlier—than to other exporting countries, including the appellees;.

176. When the foregoing differences in the means of application of Section 609 to various shrimp exporting countries are considered in their cumulative effect, we find, and so hold, that those differences in treatment constitute "unjustifiable discrimination" between exporting countries desiring certification in order to gain access to the United States shrimp market within the meaning of the chapeau of Article XX.

3. "Arbitrary Discrimination"

177. We next consider whether Section 609 has been applied in a manner constituting "arbitrary discrimination between countries where the same conditions prevail". We have already observed that Section 609, in its application, imposes a single, rigid and unbending requirement that countries applying for certification under Section 609(b)(2)(A) and (B) adopt a comprehensive regulatory program that is essentially the same as the United States' program, without inquiring into the appropriateness of that program for the conditions prevailing in the exporting countries. Furthermore, there is little or no flexibility in how officials make the determination for certification pursuant to these provisions. In our view, this rigidity and inflexibility also constitute "arbitrary discrimination" within the meaning of the chapeau.

    . . .

181. The certification processes followed by the United States thus appear to be singularly informal and casual, and to be conducted in a manner such that these processes could result in the negation of rights of Members. There appears to be no way that exporting Members can be certain whether the terms of Section 609, in particular, the 1996 Guidelines, are being applied in a fair and just manner by the appropriate governmental agencies of the United States. It appears to us that, effectively, exporting Members applying for certification whose applications are rejected are denied basic fairness and due process, and

are discriminated against, vis-à-vis those Members which are granted certification.

. . .

184. We find, accordingly, that the United States measure is applied in a manner which amounts to a means not just of "unjustifiable discrimination", but also of "arbitrary discrimination" between countries where the same conditions prevail, contrary to the requirements of the chapeau of Article XX. The measure, therefore, is not entitled to the justifying protection of Article XX of the GATT 1994. Having made this finding, it is not necessary for us to examine also whether the United States measure is applied in a manner that constitutes a "disguised restriction on international trade" under the chapeau of Article XX.

185. In reaching these conclusions, we wish to underscore what we have not decided in this appeal. We have not decided that the protection and preservation of the environment is of no significance to the Members of the WTO. Clearly, it is. We have not decided that the sovereign nations that are Members of the WTO cannot adopt effective measures to protect endangered species, such as sea turtles. Clearly, they can and should. And we have not decided that sovereign states should not act together bilaterally, plurilaterally or multilaterally, either within the WTO or in other international fora, to protect endangered species or to otherwise protect the environment. Clearly, they should and do.

186. What we have decided in this appeal is simply this: although the measure of the United States in dispute in this appeal serves an environmental objective that is recognized as legitimate under paragraph (g) of Article XX of the GATT 1994, this measure has been applied by the United States in a manner which constitutes arbitrary and unjustifiable discrimination between Members of the WTO, contrary to the requirements of the chapeau of Article XX. For all of the specific reasons outlined in this Report, this measure does not qualify for the exemption that Article XX of the GATT 1994 affords to measures which serve certain recognized, legitimate environmental purposes but which, at the same time, are not applied in a manner that constitutes a means of arbitrary or unjustifiable discrimination between countries where the same conditions prevail or a disguised restriction on international trade. As we emphasized in United States—Gasoline, WTO Members are free to adopt their own policies aimed at protecting the environment as long as, in so doing, they fulfill their obligations and respect the rights of other Members under the WTO Agreement.

VII. Findings and Conclusions

187. For the reasons set out in this Report, the Appellate Body:

. . .

(b) reverses the Panel's finding that the United States measure at issue is not within the scope of measures permitted under the chapeau of Article XX of the GATT 1994, and

(c) concludes that the United States measure, while qualifying for provisional justification under Article XX(g), fails to meet the requirements of the chapeau of Article XX, and, therefore, is not justified under Article XX of the GATT 1994.

NOTES AND QUESTIONS

1.   What factors contributed to the Appellate Body's finding that the United States' measure was unjustifiable discrimination?

2.   What factors contributed to the Appellate Body's finding that the United States' measure was arbitrary discrimination?

b. The Appellate Body Report Regarding US Conformity with the Appellate Body Shrimp-Turtle Report

The WTO Dispute Settlement Body (DSB) requested in 1998 that the United States conform its import prohibition, as requested by the AB. The United States undertook to remedy the application of its measures by taking several steps: it unsuccessfully engaged with Pacific Island and Asian countries regarding an international agreement regarding sea turtles; it issued Revised Guidelines that provided more flexibility to countries desiring to import shrimp; and it provided greater transparency and notification regarding certification decisions.

Malaysia objected to the WTO regarding these measures under DSU Article 21.5, arguing that the United States' remedial actions did not comply with the AB's and DSB's recommendations and rulings. The DSB referred the dispute to the original Panel, which ruled in the United States' favor. *Inter alia*, the Panel found that the AB's recommendations had been followed as long as the United States demonstrates "ongoing serious good faith efforts to reach multilateral agreement." Malaysia appealed to the AB.

The AB found in favor of the United States. Excerpts from the AB's Article 21.5 decision follow.

US—IMPORT PROHIBITION OF CERTAIN SHRIMP AND SHRIMP PRODUCTS ("SHRIMP/TURTLE 21.5")

(India, Malaysia, Pakistan, and Thailand v. United States)
Report of the Appellate Body
WT/DS58/AB/RW, adopted on 21 November 2001 (most footnotes omitted)

VI. The Chapeau of Article XX of the GATT 1994

111. The second issue raised in this appeal is whether the Panel erred in finding that the new measure at issue is applied in a manner that no longer constitutes a means of "arbitrary or unjustifiable discrimination between countries where the same conditions prevail" and is, therefore, within the scope of measures permitted under Article XX of the GATT 1994.

. . .

The Nature and the Extent of the Duty of the United States to Pursue International Cooperation in the Protection and Conservation of Sea Turtles

115. Before the Panel, Malaysia asserted that the United States should have negotiated and concluded an international agreement on the protection and conservation of sea turtles before imposing an import prohibition. Malaysia argued that "by continuing to apply a unilateral measure after the end of the reasonable period of time pending the conclusion of an international agreement, the United States failed to comply with its obligations under the GATT 1994". The United States replied that it had in fact made serious, good faith efforts to negotiate and conclude a multilateral sea turtle conservation agreement that would include both Malaysia and the United States, and that these efforts, as detailed and documented before the Panel, should, in view of our previous ruling, be seen as sufficient to meet the requirements of the chapeau of Article XX. The Panel found as follows:

> . . . The Panel first recalls that the Appellate Body considered "the failure of the United States to engage the appellees, as well as other Members exporting shrimp to the United States, in serious across-the-board negotiations with the objective of concluding bilateral or multilateral agreements for the protection and conservation of sea turtles, before enforcing the import prohibition against the shrimp exports of those other Members" bears heavily in any appraisal of justifiable or unjustifiable discrimination within the meaning of the chapeau of Article XX. From the terms used, it appears to us that the Appellate Body had in mind a negotiation, not the conclusion of an agreement. If the Appellate Body had considered that an agreement had to be concluded before any measure can be taken by the United States, it would not have used the terms "with the

objective"; it would have simply stated that an agreement had to be concluded.

. . .

We are consequently of the view that the Appellate Body could not have meant in its findings that the United States had the obligation to conclude an agreement on the protection and conservation of sea turtles in order to comply with Article XX. However, we reach the conclusion that the United States has an obligation to make serious good faith efforts to reach an agreement before resorting to the type of unilateral measure currently in place. We also consider that those efforts cannot be a "one-off" exercise. There must be a continuous process, including once a unilateral measure has been adopted pending the conclusion of an agreement. Indeed, we consider the reference of the Appellate Body to a number of international agreements promoting a multilateral solution to the conservation concerns subject to Section 609 to be evidence that a multilateral, ideally non-trade restrictive, solution is generally to be preferred when dealing with those concerns, in particular if it is established that it constitutes "an alternative course of action reasonably open".

. . .

We understand the Appellate Body findings as meaning that the United States has an obligation to make serious good faith efforts to address the question of the protection and conservation of sea turtles at the international level. We are mindful of the potentially subjective nature of the notion of serious good faith efforts and of how difficult such a test may be to apply in reality.

116. Malaysia appeals these findings of the Panel. According to Malaysia, demonstrating serious, good faith efforts to negotiate an international agreement for the protection and conservation of sea turtles is not sufficient to meet the requirements of the chapeau of Article XX. Malaysia maintains that the chapeau requires instead the conclusion of such an international agreement. . . .

118. The chapeau of Article XX establishes three standards regarding the application of measures for which justification under Article XX may be sought: first, there must be no "arbitrary" discrimination between countries where the same conditions prevail; second, there must be no "unjustifiable" discrimination between countries where the same conditions prevail; and, third, there must be no "disguised restriction on international trade". The Panel's findings appealed by Malaysia concern the first and second of these three standards.

129. With this in mind, we examine what the Panel did here. In its analysis of the Inter-American Convention in the context of Malaysia's

argument on "unjustifiable discrimination", the Panel relied on our original Report to state that "the Inter-American Convention is evidence that the efforts made by the United States to negotiate with the complainants before imposing the original measure were largely insufficient". The Panel went on to say that "the Inter-American Convention can reasonably be considered as a benchmark of what can be achieved through multilateral negotiations in the field of protection and conservation."

130. At no time in United States—Shrimp did we refer to the Inter-American Convention as a "benchmark". The Panel might have chosen another and better word perhaps, as suggested by Malaysia, "example". Yet it seems to us that the Panel did all that it should have done with respect to the Inter-American Convention, and did so consistently with our approach in United States—Shrimp. The Panel compared the efforts of the United States to negotiate the Inter-American Convention with one group of exporting WTO Members with the efforts made by the United States to negotiate a similar agreement with another group of exporting WTO Members. The Panel rightly used the Inter-American Convention as a factual reference in this exercise of comparison. It was all the more relevant to do so given that the Inter-American Convention was the only international agreement that the Panel could have used in such a comparison. As we read the Panel Report, it is clear to us that the Panel attached a relative value to the Inter-American Convention in making this comparison, but did not view the Inter-American Convention in any way as an absolute standard. Thus, we disagree with Malaysia's submission that the Panel raised the Inter-American Convention to the rank of a "legal standard". The mere use by the Panel of the Inter-American Convention as a basis for a comparison did not transform the Inter-American Convention into a "legal standard". Furthermore, although the Panel could have chosen a more appropriate word than "benchmark" to express its views, Malaysia is mistaken in equating the mere use of the word "benchmark", as it was used by the Panel, with the establishment of a legal standard.

131. The Panel noted that while "factual circumstances may influence the duration of the process or the end result, . . . any effort alleged to be a 'serious good faith effort' must be assessed against the efforts made in relation to the conclusion of the Inter-American Convention." Such a comparison is a central element of the exercise to determine whether there is "unjustifiable discrimination". The Panel then analyzed the negotiation process in the Indian Ocean and South-East Asia region to determine whether the efforts made by the United States in those negotiations were serious, good faith efforts comparable to those made in relation with the Inter-American Convention.

. . .

132. On this basis and, in particular, on the basis of the "contribution of the United States to the steps that led to the Kuantan meeting and its contribution to the Kuantan meeting itself", the Panel concluded that the United States had made serious, good faith efforts that met the "standard set by the Inter-American Convention." In the view of the Panel, whether or not the South-East Asian MOU is a legally binding document does not affect this comparative assessment because differences in "factual circumstances have to be kept in mind".[93] Furthermore, the Panel did not consider as decisive the fact that the final agreement in the Indian Ocean and South-East Asia region, unlike the Inter-American Convention, had not been concluded at the time of the Panel proceedings. According to the Panel, "at least until the Conservation and Management Plan to be attached to the MOU is completed, the United States efforts should be judged on the basis of its active participation and its financial support to the negotiations, as well as on the basis of its previous efforts since 1998, having regard to the likelihood of a conclusion of the negotiations in the course of 2001."

133. We note that the Panel stated that "any effort alleged to be a 'serious good faith effort' must be assessed against the efforts made in relation to the conclusion of the Inter-American Convention." In our view, in assessing the serious, good faith efforts made by the United States, the Panel did not err in using the Inter-American Convention as an example. In our view, also, the Panel was correct in proceeding then to an analysis broadly in line with this principle and, ultimately, was correct as well in concluding that the efforts made by the United States in the Indian Ocean and South-East Asia region constitute serious, good faith efforts comparable to those that led to the conclusion of the Inter-American Convention. We find no fault with this analysis.

134. In sum, Malaysia is incorrect in its contention that avoiding "arbitrary and unjustifiable discrimination" under the chapeau of Article XX requires the conclusion of an international agreement on the protection and conservation of sea turtles. Therefore, we uphold the Panel's finding that, in view of the serious, good faith efforts made by the United States to negotiate an international agreement, "Section 609 is now applied in a manner that no longer constitutes a means of unjustifiable or arbitrary discrimination, as identified by the Appellate Body in its Report".[97]

---

[93] Panel Report. It appears that the United States was in favour of a legally binding agreement for the Indian Ocean and South-East Asia region, but a number of other parties were not, and the latter view prevailed. *See,* Panel Report, para. 5.83.

[97] Panel Report, para. 5.137. We do wish to note, though, that there is one observation by the Panel with which we do not agree. In assessing the good faith efforts made by the United States, the Panel stated that:

> The United States is a demandeur in this field and given its scientific, diplomatic and financial means, it is reasonable to expect rather more than less from that Member

NOTES AND QUESTIONS

1. *A global standard?* The United States argued that the use of TEDs has become "a recognized multilateral environmental standard." Nineteen countries require TEDS on shrimp trawl vessels subject to their jurisdiction (either as a result of the Inter-American Convention on the Protection and Conservation of Sea Turtles or of countries' own initiatives). Why shouldn't this be sufficient to serve as the basis of legislation to ban shrimp imports caught by methods that desecrate the endangered sea turtles? What more could be required?

2. *Hypothetical.* Suppose a global agreement banning shrimp unless caught by TEDs or harvested through aquaculture were negotiated and the four claimant States did not join the agreement. Would a ban on their imports be consistent with the GATT, according to the Shrimp-Turtle Panel? Should it be?

3. *Relationship to CITES.* In a situation in which species are already listed as endangered under Appendix I of CITES, why shouldn't countries be able to adopt legislation that discourages fishing methods that contribute to the extinction of the species? Or to put it another way, why should countries be forced to keep their markets open to fish that have been caught by methods that lead to the extinction of species that the international community has designated as endangered? Should the parties to the CITES take any action? Could they do so consistent with GATT 1994?

4. *"Same conditions."* Notes and Questions 1 and 3 immediately above consider aspects of whether discrimination is "arbitrary or unjustifiable" (in the language of the Article XX chapeau). The chapeau also is limited by its terms to discrimination "between countries where the same conditions apply." Why isn't the use or non-use of TEDs a valid basis for determining whether the "same conditions prevail"? Hasn't the United States decided, in effect, that it is?

5. *The shoe on the other foot.* Suppose Canada or Brazil bans the import of forest products from the United States (or from the Pacific Northwest region) on the ground that U.S. forestry practices endanger the spotted owl and the marbled murelet (both endangered species). Would this be consistent with GATT 1994 and the WTO Agreement?

6. *The role of exceptions.* The *Beef Hormones* Appellate Body decision, *see* above, referred to "abuses" of Article XX. The *Shrimp/Turtle* Panel was concerned that recognizing exceptions within the plain meaning of Article XX would threaten the multilateral trading system as established by GATT 1994

---

in terms of serious good faith efforts. Indeed, the capacity of persuasion of the United States is illustrated by the successful negotiation of the Inter-American Convention.

(Panel Report, para. 5.76)

We are not persuaded by this line of reasoning. As we stated in our previous Report, the chapeau of Article XX is "but one expression of the principle of good faith". (Appellate Body Report, United States—Shrimp, *supra*, footnote 24, para. 158) This good faith notion applies to all WTO Members equally.

and the WTO Agreement. How could that be? Isn't Article XX an essential component of that system? If so, would it be more accurate to say that failing to apply Article XX would threaten the multilateral trading system? The preamble to the WTO Agreement places trade liberalization in the context of sustainable development and also mentions the need to protect the environment. Does this affect your analysis?

7. *Unsustainable production and consumption patterns.* The Rio Declaration, Agenda 21, and various other international instruments call for countries, especially industrialized countries, to adopt production and consumption patterns that are sustainable. Is the Sea Turtle Protection Act an example of this? If so, how should that affect the legal analysis in the *Shrimp/Turtle* case?

3. EC—SEAL PRODUCTS CASE

EC—MEASURES PROHIBITING THE IMPORTATION AND MARKETING OF SEAL PRODUCTS

(Canada and Norway v. European Community)
WT/DS400R, WT/DS401/R (25 November 2013);
WT/DS400/AB/R, WT/DS401/AB/R(22 May 2014)

[In 2011, Canada and Norway filed complaints against the European Community's regulations prohibiting the importation and the marketing of seal products ("EU Seal Regime"). The regulations included exceptions for seal products (1) obtained from seals hunted by Inuit or other indigenous communities (IC exception), (2) obtained from seals hunted for purposes of marine resource management (MRM exception), and (3) brought by travelers into the European Union in limited circumstances (Travelers exception). The European Community stated that the regulations were aimed at addressing public moral concerns regarding the welfare of seals. Canada and Norway argued that the IC and MRM exceptions violated the European Union's obligations under the Agreement on Technical Barrier to Trade.

While the Panel found that the EU Seal regime was a technical regulation within the TBT, the Appellate Body reversed the finding. The Panel also found that the EU Seal Regime was inconsistent with both GATT Article 1.1 and GATT Article III.4, which the Appellate Body upheld. The Panel further found that the policy objective of the EU in addressing public moral concerns regarding seal welfare fell within the scope of protecting public morals in the GATT 1994, Article XX(a). But the Panel also found that the IC and MRM exceptions were not justified under XX(a) because they did not meet the chapeau requirements.[6] Canada and Norway appealed. The Appellate Body upheld the Panel's finding that the EU Seal Regime is "necessary to protect public morals"

---

[6] *European Communities—Measures Prohibiting the Importation and Marketing of Seal Products*, Panel Report, 25 November 2013, WTO Doc. WT/DS400/R and WT/DS401/R.

within the meaning of Article XX(a) of the GATT, but disagreed with the Panel's analysis of the chapeau and undertook its own analysis. The Appellate Body also concluded, though, that the European Union had not shown that the EU Seal Regime met the requirements of the chapeau of Article XX. [7] The European Union agreed to implement the DSB recommendations and bring the Seal Regime into compliance with its WTO obligations by 18 October 2015. This dispute is especially noteworthy, because it is the first time that the Article XX(a) exception has been recognized in a case.]

NOTES AND QUESTIONS

Environmental protection and public morals. How might Article XX(a) apply in the context of other environmental cases, such as the *Shrimp/Turtle* case or the *Tuna/Dolphin* case? Should it matter that sea turtles are endangered, whereas dolphin are not?

D. POLLUTION CONTROL

Many environmental measures are aimed at controlling air, water or land pollution, and may raise concerns about consistency with GATT obligations. Measures that restrict trade in natural resources may arguably be justified on grounds of protecting against pollution or may be intended to protect the resources domestically for a competitive edge. The two disputes below raise and address these issues.

1. THE REFORMULATED GASOLINE CASE

US—STANDARDS FOR REFORMULATED AND CONVENTIONAL GASOLINE

(Venezuela and Brazil v. United States)
WT/DS2/R (29 January 1996); WT/DS2/AB/R (29 April 1996)

[On January 17, 1996, the first WTO Panel decision was handed down in a dispute between the United States and Venezuela/Brazil, which involved implementation of the U.S. Clean Air Act. The Panel continued a trend of previous GATT panels in rejecting environmental justifications for laws that expressly discriminate between foreign and domestic producers to the disadvantage of the former, a position the Appellate Body upheld. However, in one sense the report of the Appellate Body was more sensitive to environmental concerns in that it strengthened the hand of environmentalists against the protectionist interests of domestic producers who pressured Congress to require the discriminatory measures.

---

[7] *European Communities—Measures Prohibiting the Importation and Marketing of Seal Products*, Appellate Body Report, 22 May 2014, WTO Doc. WT/DS400/AB/R and WT/DS401/AB/R.

The dispute began in 1990 when Congress amended the Clean Air Act to instruct the United States Environmental Protection Agency (EPA) to issue regulations reducing vehicle emissions caused by gasoline.[8] The EPA subsequently promulgated regulations in December 1993 that tied gasoline emissions to the emission levels in effect in 1990. Conventional gasoline could have emission levels no higher than those in 1990. Reformulated gasoline had to reduce toxic air pollutants and volatile organic compounds by 15 percent compared with 1990 levels and have corresponding NO_x emission levels no higher than those of 1990.

The problem in this case arose over how to determine the baselines for the reduction in air pollutants for reformulated gas. Domestic refineries that were in existence prior to 1990 could use one of several methods to determine their baseline, including an "individual baseline" derived from refinery specific data. In contrast, United States refineries built after 1990 and all foreign refineries whenever built were required to use a statutory baseline. This statutory baseline in some circumstances was more disadvantageous than the baselines used by domestic refineries. The EPA justified this discriminatory treatment of foreign refineries by arguing that there might be insufficient reliable information to determine the baseline for individual foreign refineries.

After the regulation was implemented in December 1993, Venezuela strongly protested the disparate treatment of domestic and foreign refineries and threatened to bring a complaint under the GATT (which was still in effect at that time). Instigation of a GATT action was avoided when the United States and Venezuela concluded an agreement in 1994 under which Venezuela dropped the action in return for the EPA's altering its regulations. The EPA then issued proposed regulations that would have permitted foreign refineries to use individual baselines. However, domestic oil producers joined with some United States environmental groups and successfully persuaded Congress to prevent the EPA from implementing the proposed regulations. [9] Following continued United States inaction, Venezuela (later joined by Brazil) brought an action in the WTO (which had by then gone into effect) in January 1995.

Venezuela's main allegation was that the EPA regulation violated Article III:4 of the GATT,[10] which states that imported products "shall be accorded treatment no less favorable than that accorded to like products of national origin in respect of all laws, regulations, and requirements affecting their internal sale." There are two key elements to finding a violation of Article III:4. The products in question must be "like" products

---

[8]   Pub. L. No. 101–549 (1990).

[9]   108 Stat. 2322 (1994).

[10]   Although the WTO has replaced the GATT, the GATT rules have been absorbed into the WTO structure, and the GATT is referred to as GATT 1994.

and the imported product must be treated less favorably than the domestic product. The Panel found that imported gas and domestic gas were "like" products and that by not giving foreign refineries the chance to use an individual baseline, the EPA regulation treated importers less favorably than domestic producers, and hence violated Article III:4.

The United States had argued that importers were not in fact treated less favorably because while some refineries were disadvantaged by use of the statutory baseline, other refineries were helped. However, the Panel rejected this argument, stating that favorable treatment of some importers could not be used to counterbalance unfavorable treatment of other importers. Further, the United States contended that the EPA regulation only applied to annual shipments by refineries, so any particular shipment did not have to meet the baseline. However, the Panel concluded that the EPA regulation nevertheless created a more favorable sales condition for domestic gasoline than for imported gasoline.

In addition to rejecting United States defenses to Venezuela's charges under Article III, the Panel also rejected United States defenses based on Article XX(b) and (g) exceptions. Article XX(b) provides an exception for measures "necessary to protect human, animal or plant life or health." The Panel agreed that the Clean Air Act fit within the general scope of Article XX(b) but said that the United States had not established that there was no "reasonably available" alternative measure that was consistent with GATT rules or less inconsistent with GATT rules. In particular, although the EPA claimed that it would be feasible neither to determine the refinery of origin for imported gasoline nor to compile enough information to create an individual baseline, the Panel disagreed with these arguments. Instead, the Panel suggested that the EPA could have given foreign refineries the chance to compile enough information to establish an individual baseline and apply the statutory baseline only in the event the refinery was unable to establish enough information.

The Panel also rejected the United States' defense based on Article XX(g) and appeared to incorporate a "necessity" test into the article. Article XX(g) provides an exception for measures "relating to conservation of exhaustible natural resources if such measures are made effective in conjunction with restrictions on domestic production or consumption." According to previous GATT jurisprudence, for a measure to be "related" to the conservation of an exhaustible natural resource, it must be "primarily aimed" at such conservation. The Panel recognized that clean air is an exhaustible natural resource. However, in determining whether the EPA regulation was "primarily aimed" at conservation, the Panel did not examine the intent behind the whole statute but seemed to ask whether the "precise aspects" of the parts of the Act that violated Article III were necessary to achieve conservation. The Panel determined that since the EPA could have implemented equivalent measures in a form that would have been consistent with Article III, the Article XX(g) exception did not apply.

On appeal to the Appellate Body, the Appellate Body upheld the Panel concerning Article XX(g) but rejected the implication that Article XX(g) contains a necessity test.

Note that the logical sequence of the legal argument is that first a violation of a provision of the WTO must be found and only then are the Article XX exceptions relevant, and further that in applying Article XX, the first step is to determine whether any of the specific exceptions apply, followed by an analysis of whether the chapeau (headnote) conditions are met.

The Reformulated Gasoline Case is noteworthy, *inter alia*, because the WTO dispute settlement bodies based their reports not on the characteristics of the product but on the treatment accorded to the producers of the product, namely the methods by which they were permitted to calculate their baselines for the reduction in air pollutants for reformulated gasoline.]

NOTES AND QUESTIONS

1.   *Does process matter?* Can you argue that this case begins to lay a basis (if inadvertently) for finding that regulations based on the process by which products are produced could be consistent with the GATT/WTO? Why or why not? Is it relevant that paragraph (e) of Article XX (products of prison labor) relates to a process?

2.   *Domestic politics.* This dispute illustrates the importance of domestic politics in the development of a regulation, which could violate the GATT. Do you think the U.S. Environmental Protection Agency was pleased or displeased with this decision?

2.   THE RARE EARTH MINERALS CASE

CHINA—MEASURES RELATED TO THE EXPORTATION OF RARE EARTHS, TUNGSTEN AND MOLYBDENUM
(United States v. China)
WT/DS/421/R,WT/DS/422R, WT/DS/423/R (26 March 2014);
WT/DS/421/AB/R, WT/DS/422/AB/R, WT/DS/423/AB/R (7 August 2014)

[In 2012, the European Union, Japan and the United States brought a complaint against China for imposing export restrictions (export duties and export quotas) on rare earths, tungsten and molybdenum. China produces more than 90% of the world's rare earths, which are crucial elements in manufacturing high-technology products such as hybrid car batteries and wind turbines. The States argued that the export restrictions gave an unfair advantage to Chinese manufacturers because it increased the price of rare earths for foreign manufacturers while Chinese domestic manufacturers could obtain the same rare earths at a lower price and produce lower-priced products.

The complaining States first argued that China was in violation of paragraph 11.3 of China's Accession Protocol for not eliminating export duties. China argued that Article XX(b) of the GATT 1994 "necessary to protect human, animal or plant life or health" was applicable because mining rare earth minerals would cause pollution and processing of rare earths would cause harm to human health. The majority of the Panel first concluded that China could not invoke Article XX to justify a breach of obligation under paragraph 11.3 of the Accession Protocol.[11] The Panel nonetheless examined the merits of Article XX(b) and concluded that even if paragraph 11.3 of the Accession Protocol were subject to Article XX, export duties were not "necessary" to protect human health because China had failed to demonstrate how export duties would decrease the overall production of rare earths. A price increase in foreign markets would be likely to be counterbalanced by increased consumption in the domestic market because of a lower price.

The complaining States also argued that export quotas were in violation of Article XI:1 of the GATT 1994. China argued that it was permitted under Article XX(g) "relating to the conservation of exhaustible natural resources if such measures are made effective in conjunction with restrictions on domestic production or consumption." The Panel first agreed with China that the term "conservation" was not limited to a preservation of exhaustible natural resources but also encompassed policy considerations of using natural resources to promote a Member State's sustainable economic development.[12] In reaching this definition of "conservation," the Panel recognized two general international law principles of 1) sovereignty over natural resources; and 2) sustainable development, citing Rio Declaration Principle 2 (States' sovereignty over natural resources), Principle 4 (sustainable development) and the WTO preamble (resources are to be used "in accordance with the objective of sustainable development"). However, the Panel disagreed with China's argument that its sovereign right over its natural resources allowed China to control distribution of rare earths in the domestic and international market, and concluded that China's export quotas were not "relating to" the conservation of rare earths but were designed for China's industrial policy to "reserve amounts of rare earths products for domestic consumption" so that domestic downstream industries can use them and export their final products.

---

[11] One panelist disagreed and wrote a separate opinion that GATT Article XX was available to all WTO obligations unless such obligation explicitly provided otherwise.

[12] Panel Report, *China—Measures Related to the Exportation of Rare Earths, Tungsten, and Molybdenum*, 26 March 2014, WT/DS431/R, WT/DS432/R, and WT/DS433/R.

The Panel also found that a requirement of "made effective in conjunction with restrictions on domestic production or consumption" in Article XX(g) was not met because there were no restrictions on domestic consumption or production. The Panel further suggested that member States must satisfy an "even-handedness" requirement, a showing that the burden of conservation-related measures are distributed between foreign and domestic consumers in a balanced way, in addition to the express conditions set out in Article XX(g).

In April 2014, China appealed on certain issues of law and legal interpretations developed by the Panel. The Appellate Body first clarified the Panel's finding that obligations under the Accession Protocol were not subject to Article XX of the GATT 1994 unless "a thorough analysis of the relevant provisions on the basis of the customary rules of treaty interpretation and the circumstances of the dispute" finds that exception provisions may apply. Second, the Appellate Body affirmed the Panel's finding that China's export quotas were not "relating to" conservation, agreeing with the Panel's reasoning that any "conservation signals" sent to foreign users were undermined by the "perverse signals" stimulating domestic demands. However, the Appellate Body rejected the Panel's suggestion that "even-handedness" was an additional requirement in Article XX(g).[13]

E. ENVIRONMENTAL LABELING

1. INTRODUCTION TO ENVIRONMENTAL LABELING

CRITERIA IN ENVIRONMENTAL LABELING: A COMPARATIVE ANALYSIS OF ENVIRONMENTAL CRITERIA IN SELECTED ECO-LABELING SCHEMES

United Nations Environmental Programme 2–6 (excerpts) (Feb. 1996)
(reporting results of a study)

1. INTRODUCTION

Environmental labelling is defined as "the use of labels in order to inform consumers that a labelled product is environmentally more friendly relative to other products in the same category."[18] Labels may be granted by a government or privately sponsored agency to applicants from enterprises.

Environmental labelling represents a voluntary, market-based instrument of environment policy. Its major aims are to raise consumer

---

[13] Appellate Report, *China—Measures Related to the Exportation of Rare Earths, Tungsten, and Molybdenum*, 7 August 2014, WT/DS431/AB/R, WT/DS432/AB/R, WT/DS433/AB/R.

[18] International Cooperation on Eco-Labeling and Eco-Certification Programmes and Opportunities for Environmentally Friendly Products. 1994. UNCTAD Ad hoc Working Group on Trade, Environment and Development TD/B/WG.6/2.

awareness about environmental effects of products so as to inform consumers about the environmental characteristics of a product and to promote the adoption of more environmentally sound production methods and technologies. Environmental labelling is only one among a whole range of domestic environment policy tools. It is an example of informational tools, which have recently gained importance alongside with the more traditional legislative, administrative, and economic policy instruments.

In principle, eco-labels are awarded on the basis of an overall assessment of the environmental impact of a good during its entire life cycle, including the procurement of raw materials, production, distribution, consumption and disposal. Therefore, eco-labels differ from single-criteria labels, which address only one environmental quality of a product, or from "negative labels" containing warnings about the possible dangers of the product.

In recent years, the number of environmental labelling schemes in developed countries has multiplied rapidly, and several developing countries are in the process of establishing programmes. The majority of schemes are operated by the national authorities or bodies closely linked to them. . . . The criteria used for awarding eco-labels primarily reflect domestic environmental priorities. An issue of some concern is the extent to which environmental criteria of the importing country may and should be extended to imported products. Labelling might fail to have the desired effects of alleviating the environmental problems if the criteria address non-relevant environmental considerations (i.e., issues that are not of overriding concern to the producing/exporting country). Moreover, there is concern—which is now under study in the WTO Committee on Trade and Environment—that different eco-labelling schemes may constitute a technical barrier of trade, because domestic producers are better positioned to influence the choice of the product groups and the criteria used for awarding the labels, than exporters.

Thus, concerns have been raised that environmental criteria may discriminate against imports of like products. Finally labelling schemes are sometimes seen [as] problematic from the point of view of international trade agreements, because the criteria often include the process and production methods (PPMs) and not to the qualities of the product itself.

Developing countries may be particularly vulnerable to possible discriminatory trade impacts of labelling: on one hand, products earmarked for eco-labelling are often among the most important export items of developing countries (e.g., textiles); on the other, the developing country exporters frequently lack resources to undergo costly testing, verification, plant inspection, and certification procedures required.

1.1 TYPES OF ENVIRONMENTAL LABELLING

Three types of environmental labeling can be identified: Type I, based on criteria set by a third party; Type II, based on self-declaration by manufacturers; and Type III, based on product information covering several environmental aspects, but without comparing or weighing such aspects.

Type I eco-labels are "third-party," typically voluntary schemes, which identify products that are relatively less harmful to the environment than similar products in the same category. The selection of product categories and determination of criteria for awarding the label are, in the case of official national schemes, generally undertaken by a national environmental authority. . . .

Type II labelling schemes are based on self-declaration by companies, claiming their products to have specific "environment-friendly" properties. For the moment there are no pre-established definitions or criteria with which products must comply to bear the label.

Type III labels do not establish pass/fail criteria on a product by product basis, but report the findings of a life-cycle assessment on a group of preset indices. It is suggested that the indices should include, at a minimum, information pertaining to extraction of natural resources, energy consumption, air and water pollution emissions, and generation of solid waste . . . A parallel can be drawn between the nutritional labels that provide information about the nutritional constituents of foods, and Type III labels containing information about the relative environmental burdens associated with products.

2. ENVIRONMENTAL LABELING AND TRADE REGULATION

ENVIRONMENT AND TRADE: A GUIDE TO WTO JURISPRUDENCE
Nathalie Bernasconi-Osterwalder, Daniel Magraw, Maria Julia Oliva,
Marcos Orellana & Elisabeth Tuerk
206–207 (2006)

Eco-labels provide consumers, retailers, government officials and other interested parties with information about the environmental characteristics and impacts of labelled products and services. (The term eco-label has not been officially defined; here, the term is used broadly to include mandatory and voluntary labeling schemes that relate directly to the product or are 'non-product-related'.) Eco-labels allow purchases to make more informed choices about the goods and services they buy and signal their preferences to manufacturers and service providers. Often eco-labels provide information on how products were produced; thus, they are closely linked to the debate on PPM-based measures, and non-product-related PPM-based measures in particular. Some perceive eco-labelling schemes as trade restrictions, reducing access to the markets of countries applying the schemes and increasing costs for producers and exporters.

With respect to eco-labelling, a host of legal questions arise in the context of WTO rules: (i) which WTO rules and agreements apply to labelling schemes, (ii) do these rules also apply to voluntary labelling schemes; (iii) do these rules apply to labelling schemes that are based on the production method, including those schemes that apply criteria that are not directly related to the end-product; and (iv) if so, do those rules allow the use of non-product-related PPMs?

The WTO Agreements that potentially apply to eco-labelling schemes include the GATT, the Agreement on Technical Barriers to Trade (TBT), and the Agreement on Sanitary and Phytosanitary Measures (SPS). Each agreement contains its own set of rules, some of which overlap with the scope and rules contained in other agreements. The GATT contains several obligations that could apply to mandatory labels, notably its prohibitions of discrimination and quantitative restrictions, and its exceptions for environmental measures (Articles III, XI and XX). However, although the question has not been fully tested, labelling schemes for products are most likely to fall under the TBT Agreement rather than the GATT. According to the TBT Agreement both technical regulations (mandatory measures) and standards (voluntary measures) are documents that may 'include or deal exclusively with ... labelling requirements as they apply to a product, process or production method' (Annex 1, paragraphs 1 and 2 of the TBT Agreement). At the same time, the SPS Agreement is also relevant for labels. The SPS Agreement applies to all sanitary and phytosanitary measures taken by Members, including packaging and labelling requirements, as long as they are aimed at protecting humans, animals and plants within the territory of the Member applying the measure from risks arising from the spread of pests, diseases and disease-causing organisms, as well as from additives, contaminants and toxins or disease-causing organisms in food, beverages and feedstuffs. For example, concerns have been raised in the SPS Committee rather than the TBT Committee with respect to the EU's regulation on the labelling and traceability of genetically modified organisms (Note of the Secretariat to the SPS Committee, Specific Trade Concerns, items 54 and 55, G/SPS/GEN/204/Rev. 4, 2 March 2004). To date, however, only one WTO dispute, EC—Sardines, has specifically addressed a labelling scheme. In that case, the mandatory labelling scheme at issue was examined under the TBT Agreement. No case has yet addressed an eco-labelling scheme.

The only agreement that would appear to apply to voluntary labelling schemes is the TBT Agreement. It is the only agreement to explicitly cover documents 'with which compliance is not mandatory', also referred to as 'standards' (TBT Agreement, Annex 1, paragraph. 2). Provisions for voluntary labels, including privately administered labels, are contained in the TBT Agreement's Code of Good Practice for the Preparation, Adoption and Application of Standards in Annex 3 of the TBT Agreement. The Code of Good Practice incorporates many of the same elements that are applicable to mandatory labels, but in a form that can be characterized as guidance. Standardization bodies may, on their own initiative, notify the WTO that they have chosen to accept and comply with the Code of Good Practice. While WTO Members are called to ensure that their central government's standardizing bodies accept and comply with the Code of Good Practice, they are only called to 'take such reasonable measures as may be available to them' to ensure that local governmental bodies and non-governmental organizations within their territories comply with the relevant provisions for standards (TBT Agreement, Article 4). It is currently unclear what types of actions Members must take to satisfy the 'reasonable measures' requirement. No jurisprudence has addressed issues relating to voluntary standards.

3. THE WTO TUNA-DOLPHIN LABELING DISPUTE

Almost two decades after the original dispute, tensions flared up again between Mexico and the United States over unilateral measures to protect dolphins from tuna fishing operations. This time, the dispute centered on "dolphin-safe" labeling standards under the US Dolphin Protection Consumer Information Act and its implementing regulations, as well as a United States Circuit Court of Appeals (for the 9th Circuit) ruling in a case brought by Earth Island Institute, decided in 2007.

The WTO Panel found that the labeling provisions were technical regulations within the scope of the Agreement on Technical Barriers to Trade (TBT). The Panel found that though the provisions did not constitute less favorable treatment under Article 2.1 of the TBT, they were "more trade-restrictive than necessary", and therefore inconsistent with Article 2.2 of the TBT. The Panel also discussed Mexico's claims that the United States should allow use of the alternative labeling standards promulgated under the International Dolphin Conservation Program (AIDCP), according to Article 2.4 of the TBT which requires Members to use relevant international standards as a basis for their technical regulations. It found that although the AIDCP standards do constitute relevant international standards, they would not be effective in achieving the United States' objectives in these circumstances.

The Appellate Body reversed several parts of the Panel's decision, finding that the dolphin-safe labeling provisions do afford imported Mexican tuna less favorable treatment than domestic tuna and tuna imported from other origins, but that they are not "more trade-restrictive than necessary" to achieve legitimate objectives. The Appellate Body also found that the AIDCP was not an international standardizing organization within the meaning of TBT Article 2.4. The Appellate Body report was adopted in June, 2012, and the United States agreed to implement the report's recommendations by July, 2013. Excerpts from the Appellate Body report follow.

US—MEASURES CONCERNING THE IMPORTATION, MARKETING AND SALE OF TUNA AND TUNA PRODUCTS

(Mexico v. United States)
Appellate Body Report, 16 May 2012, WTO Doc WT/DS381/AB/R
[internal footnotes omitted]

IV. Background and Overview of the Measure at Issue

172. This dispute arises out of a challenge brought by Mexico against certain legal instruments of the United States establishing the conditions for the use of a "dolphin-safe" label on tuna products. In particular, Mexico identified the following legal instruments as the object of its challenge: the *United States Code*, Title 16, Section 1385 (the "Dolphin Protection Consumer Information Act" or "DPCIA"); the *United States Code of Federal Regulations*, Title 50, Section 216.91 and Section 216.92 (the "implementing regulations"); and a ruling by a US federal appeals court in *Earth Island Institute v. Hogarth* (the "Hogarth ruling"). Taken together, the DPCIA, the implementing regulations, and the Hogarth ruling set out the requirements for when tuna products sold in the United States may be labelled as "dolphin-safe". More specifically, they condition eligibility for a "dolphin-safe" label upon certain documentary evidence that varies depending on the area where the tuna contained in the tuna product is harvested and the type of vessel and fishing method by which it is harvested. In particular, tuna caught by "setting on" dolphins is currently not eligible for a "dolphin-safe" label in the United States, regardless of whether this fishing method is used inside or outside the Eastern Tropical Pacific Ocean (the "ETP"). The DPCIA and the implementing regulations also prohibit any reference to dolphins, porpoises, or marine mammals on the label of a tuna product if the tuna contained in the product does not comply with the labelling conditions spelled out in the DPCIA. However, they do not make the use of a "dolphin-safe" label obligatory for the importation or sale of tuna products in the United States. We refer to the legal instruments challenged by Mexico collectively as the "measure at issue", the "US measure", or "the US 'dolphin-safe' labelling provisions" for ease of reference and uniformity with the Panel.

. . .

V. Legal Characterization of the Measure at Issue

199. As noted, a determination of whether a particular measure constitutes a technical regulation must be made in the light of the characteristics of the measure at issue and the circumstances of the case. In this case, we note that the US measure is composed of legislative and regulatory acts of the US federal authorities and includes administrative provisions. In addition, the measure at issue sets out a single and legally mandated definition of a "dolphin-safe" tuna product and disallows the use of other labels on tuna products that do not satisfy this definition. In doing so, the US measure prescribes in a broad and exhaustive manner the conditions that apply for making any assertion on a tuna product as to its "dolphin-safety", regardless of the manner in which that statement is made. As a consequence, the US measure covers the entire field of what "dolphin-safe" means in relation to tuna products. For these reasons, we *find* that the Panel did not err in characterizing the measure at issue as a "technical regulation" within the meaning of Annex 1.1 to the *TBT Agreement*.

VI. Article 2.1 of the *TBT Agreement*

201. Article 2.1 of the *TBT Agreement* provides that, with respect to their central government bodies:

> Members shall ensure that in respect of technical regulations, products imported from the territory of any Member shall be accorded treatment no less favourable than that accorded to like products of national origin and to like products originating in any other country.

202. Article 2.1 of the *TBT Agreement* consists of three elements that must be demonstrated in order to establish an inconsistency with this provision, namely: (i) that the measure at issue constitutes a "technical regulation" within the meaning of Annex 1.1; (ii) that the imported products must be like the domestic product and the products of other origins; and (iii) that the treatment accorded to imported products must be less favourable than that accorded to like domestic products and like products from other countries. Mexico's appeal concerns only the Panel's finding in respect of the third element, namely, the "treatment no less favourable" standard in Article 2.1. We further note that the United States has not appealed the Panel's finding that Mexican tuna products are "like" tuna products of United States' origin and tuna products originating in any other country within the meaning of Article 2.1 of the *TBT Agreement*.

. . .

213. The sixth recital of the preamble [of the TBT] recognizes that a WTO Member may take measures necessary for, *inter alia*, the protection of animal or plant life or health, or for the prevention of deceptive

practices, at the levels it considers appropriate, subject to the requirement that such measures "are not applied in a manner which would constitute a means of arbitrary or unjustifiable discrimination" or a "disguised restriction on international trade" and are "otherwise in accordance with the provisions of this Agreement". Although the sixth recital does not explicitly set out a substantive obligation, we consider it nonetheless sheds light on the meaning and ambit of the "treatment no less favourable" requirement in Article 2.1, by making clear, in particular, that technical regulations may pursue legitimate objectives but must not be applied in a manner that would constitute a means of arbitrary or unjustifiable discrimination.

214. Regarding the context provided by other covered agreements, we further note that the expression "treatment no less favourable" can be found in Article III:4 of the GATT 1994. In the context of that provision, the Appellate Body has indicated that whether or not imported products are treated "less favourably" than like domestic products should be assessed "by examining whether a measure modifies the *conditions of competition* in the relevant market to the detriment of imported products. . . .

215. As the Appellate Body has previously explained, when assessing claims brought under Article 2.1 of the *TBT Agreement*, a panel should therefore seek to ascertain whether the technical regulation at issue modifies the conditions of competition in the relevant market to the detriment of the group of imported products *vis-à-vis* the group of like domestic products or like products originating in any other country. The existence of such a detrimental effect is not sufficient to demonstrate less favourable treatment under Article 2.1. Instead, in *US—Clove Cigarettes*, the Appellate Body held that a "panel must further analyze whether the detrimental impact on imports stems exclusively from a legitimate regulatory distinction rather than reflecting discrimination against the group of imported products."

. . .

233. The Panel found that the "dolphin-safe" label has "significant commercial value on the US market for tuna products". The Panel further found that Mexico had presented evidence concerning retailers' and final consumers' preferences regarding tuna products, which, in the Panel's view, confirmed the value of the "dolphin-safe" label on the US market. On this basis, the Panel agreed with Mexico that access to the "dolphin-safe" label constitutes an "advantage" on the US market. These findings have not been appealed.

235. In our view, the factual findings by the Panel clearly establish that the lack of access to the "dolphin-safe" label of tuna products containing tuna caught by setting on dolphins has a detrimental impact

on the competitive opportunities of Mexican tuna products in the US market.

236. Mexico and the United States disagree as to whether any detrimental impact on Mexican tuna products results from the measure itself rather than from the actions of private parties. In assessing whether there is a genuine relationship between the measure at issue and an adverse impact on competitive opportunities for imported products, the relevant question is whether governmental action "affects the conditions under which like goods, domestic and imported, compete in the market within a Member's territory".

239. These findings by the Panel suggest that it is the governmental action in the form of adoption and application of the US "dolphin-safe" labelling provisions that has modified the conditions of competition in the market to the detriment of Mexican tuna products, and that the detrimental impact in this case hence flows from the measure at issue. Moreover, it is well established that WTO rules protect competitive opportunities, not trade flows. It follows that, even if Mexican tuna products might not achieve a wide penetration of the US market in the absence of the measure at issue due to consumer objections to the method of setting on dolphins, this does not change the fact that it is the measure at issue, rather than private actors, that denies most Mexican tuna products access to a "dolphin-safe" label in the US market. The fact that the detrimental impact on Mexican tuna products may involve some element of private choice does not, in our view, relieve the United States of responsibility under the *TBT Agreement*, where the measure it adopts modifies the conditions of competition to the detriment of Mexican tuna products.

240. In the light of the above, we consider that it is the measure at issue that modifies the competitive conditions in the US market to the detriment of Mexican tuna products. We turn next to the issue of whether this detrimental impact reflects discrimination.

. . .

282. The United States argued before the Panel that to the extent that there are any differences in criteria that must be satisfied in order to substantiate "dolphin-safe" claims, they are "calibrated" to the risk that dolphins may be killed or seriously injured when tuna is caught. In this regard, the United States emphasized the uniqueness of the ETP in terms of the phenomenon of tuna-dolphin association, which is used widely and on a commercial basis to catch tuna, and causes observed and unobserved mortalities that, in the United States' view, are not comparable to dolphin mortalities outside the ETP. The United States further alleged that there is a clear relationship between the objectives of the measure and the conditions under which tuna products may be labelled "dolphin-safe". This clear relationship, the United States argued, does not support the

conclusion that the "dolphin-safe" labelling provisions are inconsistent with Article 2.1 of the *TBT Agreement*.

284. In the light of the findings of fact made by the Panel, we concluded earlier that the detrimental impact of the measure on Mexican tuna products is caused by the fact that most Mexican tuna products contain tuna caught by setting on dolphins in the ETP and are therefore not eligible for a "dolphin-safe" label, whereas most tuna products from the United States and other countries that are sold in the US market contain tuna caught by other fishing methods outside the ETP and are therefore eligible for a "dolphin-safe" label. The aspect of the measure that causes the detrimental impact on Mexican tuna products is thus the difference in labelling conditions for tuna products containing tuna caught by setting on dolphins in the ETP, on the one hand, and for tuna products containing tuna caught by other fishing methods outside the ETP, on the other hand. The question before us is thus whether the United States has demonstrated that *this* difference in labelling conditions is a legitimate regulatory distinction, and hence whether the detrimental impact of the measure stems exclusively from such a distinction rather than reflecting discrimination.

. . .

297. In the light of the above, we conclude that the United States has not demonstrated that the difference in labelling conditions for tuna products containing tuna caught by setting on dolphins in the ETP, on the one hand, and for tuna products containing tuna caught by other fishing methods outside the ETP, on the other hand, is "calibrated" to the risks to dolphins arising from different fishing methods in different areas of the ocean. It follows from this that the United States has not demonstrated that the detrimental impact of the US measure on Mexican tuna products stems exclusively from a legitimate regulatory distinction. We note, in particular, that the US measure *fully* addresses the adverse effects on dolphins resulting from setting on dolphins in the ETP, whereas it does "not address mortality (observed or unobserved) arising from fishing methods other than setting on dolphins outside the ETP". In these circumstances, we are not persuaded that the United States has demonstrated that the measure is even-handed in the relevant respects, even accepting that the fishing technique of setting on dolphins is particularly harmful to dolphins.

298. In the light of uncontested facts and factual findings made by the Panel, we consider that Mexico has established a *prima facie* case that the US "dolphin-safe" labelling provisions modify the conditions of competition in the US market to the detriment of Mexican tuna products and are not even-handed in the way in which they address the risks to dolphins arising from different fishing techniques in different areas of the ocean. We consider further that the United States has not met its burden

of rebutting this *prima facie* case. . . . Thus, in our view, the United States has not justified as non-discriminatory under Article 2.1 the different requirements that it applies to tuna caught by setting on dolphins inside the ETP and tuna caught by other fishing methods outside the ETP for access to the US "dolphin-safe" label. The United States has thus not demonstrated that the detrimental impact of the US measure on Mexican tuna products stems exclusively from a legitimate regulatory distinction.

299. For these reasons, we *reverse* the Panel's finding, in paragraphs 7.374 and 8.1(a) of the Panel Report, that the US "dolphin-safe" labelling provisions are not inconsistent with Article 2.1 of the *TBT Agreement*. We *find*, instead, that the US "dolphin-safe" labelling provisions provide "less favourable treatment" to Mexican tuna products than that accorded to tuna products of the United States and tuna products originating in other countries and are therefore inconsistent with Article 2.1 of the *TBT Agreement*.

. . .

VII. Article 2.2 of the *TBT Agreement*

311. We begin by considering the text of Article 2.2 of the *TBT Agreement*, which provides:

> Members shall ensure that technical regulations are not prepared, adopted or applied with a view to or with the effect of creating unnecessary obstacles to international trade. For this purpose, technical regulations shall not be more trade-restrictive than necessary to fulfil a legitimate objective, taking account of the risks non-fulfilment would create. Such legitimate objectives are, *inter alia:* national security requirements; the prevention of deceptive practices; protection of human health or safety, animal or plant life or health, or the environment. In assessing such risks, relevant elements of consideration are, *inter alia:* available scientific and technical information, related processing technology or intended end-uses of products.

. . .

322. In sum, we consider that an assessment of whether a technical regulation is "more trade-restrictive than necessary" within the meaning of Article 2.2 of the *TBT Agreement* involves an evaluation of a number of factors. A panel should begin by considering factors that include: (i) the degree of contribution made by the measure to the legitimate objective at issue; (ii) the trade-restrictiveness of the measure; and (iii) the nature of the risks at issue and the gravity of consequences that would arise from non-fulfilment of the objective(s) pursued by the Member through the measure. In most cases, a comparison of the challenged measure and possible alternative measures should be undertaken. In particular, it may

be relevant for the purpose of this comparison to consider whether the proposed alternative is less trade restrictive, whether it would make an equivalent contribution to the relevant legitimate objective, taking account of the risks non-fulfilment would create, and whether it is reasonably available.

. . .

326. Before the Panel, Mexico argued that "a 'reasonably available alternative measure' for the United States would be to permit the use in the US market of the AIDCP 'dolphin safe' label." It was for the Panel, therefore, in assessing Mexico's claim that the US "dolphin-safe" labelling provisions "are more trade-restrictive than necessary" within the meaning of Article 2.2, to examine, *inter alia*, the contribution that the US measure makes to the achievement of its objectives; the trade-restrictiveness of the US "dolphin-safe" labelling provisions; whether Mexico had identified a "reasonably available" and less trade-restrictive alternative measure, and to compare the degree of the US measure's contribution with that of the alternative measure, which is reasonably available and less trade restrictive, taking account of the risks non-fulfilment would create.

329. . . . [I]t would appear that, in respect of the conditions for labelling as "dolphin-safe" tuna products containing tuna harvested *outside* the ETP, there is no difference between the measure at issue and the alternative measure identified by Mexico, namely, the coexistence of the US "dolphin-safe" labelling provisions with the AIDCP rules. We recall that the geographic scope of application of the AIDCP rules is limited to the ETP. Thus, the conditions for fishing outside the ETP would be identical under the alternative measure proposed by Mexico, since only those set out in the US measure would apply. Therefore, for fishing activities *outside* the ETP, the degree to which the United States' objectives are achieved under the alternative measure would not be higher or lower than that achieved by the US measure, it would be the same. *Inside* the ETP, however, the measure at issue and the alternative measure set out different requirements. Under the alternative measure identified by Mexico, tuna that is caught by setting on dolphins would be eligible for a "dolphin-safe" label if the prerequisites of the AIDCP label have been complied with. By contrast, the measure at issue prohibits setting on dolphins, and thus tuna harvested in the ETP would only be eligible for a "dolphin-safe" label if it was caught by methods other than setting on dolphins.

330. . . . Since under the proposed alternative measure tuna caught in the ETP by setting on dolphins would be eligible for the "dolphin-safe" label, it would appear, therefore, that the alternative measure proposed by Mexico would contribute to both the consumer information objective and the dolphin protection objective to a lesser degree than the measure

at issue, because, overall, it would allow more tuna harvested in conditions that adversely affect dolphins to be labelled "dolphin-safe". We disagree therefore with the Panel's findings that the proposed alternative measure would achieve the United States' objectives "to the same extent" as the existing US "dolphin-safe" labelling provisions, and that the extent to which consumers would be misled as to the implications of the manner in which tuna was caught "would not be greater" under the alternative measure proposed by Mexico.

331. For these reasons, we find that the Panel's comparison and analysis is flawed and cannot stand. Therefore, the Panel erred in concluding, in paragraphs 7.620 and 8.1(b) of the Panel Report, that it has been demonstrated that the measure at issue is more trade restrictive than necessary to fulfil the United States' legitimate objectives, taking account of the risks non-fulfilment would create. Accordingly, we *reverse* the Panel's findings that the measure at issue is inconsistent with Article 2.2 of the *TBT Agreement*.

VIII.   Article 2.4 of the *TBT Agreement*

. . .

349. The text of Article 2.4 of the *TBT Agreement* reads as follows:

Where technical regulations are required and relevant international standards exist or their completion is imminent, Members shall use them, or the relevant parts of them, as a basis for their technical regulations except when such international standards or relevant parts would be an ineffective or inappropriate means for the fulfilment of the legitimate objectives pursued, for instance because of fundamental climatic or geographical factors or fundamental technological problems

. . .

396. We now proceed to evaluate whether the Panel erred in finding that the AIDCP standard is a "relevant international standard" within the meaning of Article 2.4 of the *TBT Agreement*. As noted, the Panel's finding is based on its intermediate conclusions that the AIDCP "dolphin-safe" definition and certification constitute a standard, that the AIDCP is an "international standardizing organization", and that the AIDCP standard was made available to the public.

397. We begin by considering whether the Panel erred in concluding that the AIDCP is "international", that is, that membership in the AIDCP is open to the relevant bodies of at least all Members.

398. Mexico suggests that being invited to accede to the AIDCP is a "formality". Mexico also states that "[n]o additional countries or regional economic integration organizations have expressed interest in joining the AIDCP" and that "it is common that during the AIDCP meetings, Parties

to the Agreement invite observer countries that regularly attend such meetings with the intention in the future to become Parties." We have stated above that, in order to show that an invitation to accede to the AIDCP is a "formality", Mexico would have to prove that the issuance of an invitation occurs automatically once a WTO Member has expressed interest in joining. This Mexico has not shown. It is uncontested that the parties to the AIDCP have to take the decision to issue an invitation by consensus. Overall, we are not persuaded that being invited to join the AIDCP is a mere "formality". In the light of the provisions for accession to the AIDCP, it therefore appears that the AIDCP is not an "international" body for the purposes of the *TBT Agreement*.

It follows that the Panel also erred in finding, in paragraph 7.707 of the Panel Report, that the "AIDCP dolphin-safe definition and certification" constitute a "relevant international standard" within the meaning of the *TBT Agreement*.

NOTES AND QUESTIONS

1. *The aftermath.* After the DSB adopted the Appellate Body report in 2012, the United States amended the disputed regulation in July 2013 to require that in order to use the label, captains of vessels or other approved observers must certify that "no dolphins were killed or seriously injured in the sets or other gear deployments in which the tuna were caught" occurring outside the eastern tropical Pacific Ocean (ETP). Previously, the certification requirement existed for fishing operations inside the ETP but not for tuna caught outside the ETP. The United States claimed that because this new condition made the labeling program "even-handed" in the treatment of tuna harvested in different oceans, it had fully complied with the WTO findings. However, Mexico disagreed and in November 2013 requested a Compliance Panel to review the changes. The Compliance Panel was formed in January 2014 and in April 2015 findings were circulated to the Parties reportedly indicating the amended measures were still inconsistent.

2. *When are environmental labels consistent with trade law?* The use of environmental labels on goods and products is becoming increasingly common. Under what conditions are such government labels consistent with the GATT and the TBT provisions? In the 1991 GATT Panel Report on US Restrictions on Imports of Tuna, the Panel found that the optional use of a "Dolphin Safe" label was consistent with the GATT because it did not restrict the sale of tuna products whether or not they carried a dolphin safe label nor did it grant any other governmental trade benefit. But as we have seen, in the *2012 Tuna-Dolphin* report, the WTO Appellate Body found that the US Dolphin Safe label requirement did not satisfy the Technical Barriers to Trade Agreement.

3. *Private labels.* Labels set by private groups would not be subject to the TBT or GATT unless a national government adopts them. However, under Article 4.1 of the TBT, States are to take reasonable measurs to ensure

that non-gernmental standardizing bodies in their country comply with the Code of Good Practice included as Annex 3 of the TBT Agreement.

4. *Labels for forest products.* One well known labeling group is the Forest Stewardship Council (FSC), an international network which promotes "environmentally appropriate, socially beneficial, and economically viable management of the world's forests." The FSC had its beginnings in California in 1990 when a group of timber users, traders and representatives of environmental and human-rights organizations recognized the need for "an honest and credible system for identifying well-managed forests as acceptable sources of forest products." The FSC's international center is located in Bonn, Germany and links with four regional centers in Africa, Asia, Europe and Latin America. The FSC has embarked on several programs including the setting up of international standards for responsible forest management through consultative processes, the establishment of an accreditation/certification system that monitors adherence to its standards and the institution of a product labeling system to reward responsible forest managers. The FSC trademark and product label are intended to allow worldwide consumers to recognize organizations that support the growth of responsible forest management, as well as their products.

5. *Labels for fisheries.* The Marine Stewardship Council (MSC) is an independent, London-based organization that "works to enhance responsible management of seafood resources, to ensure the sustainability of global fish stocks and the health of the marine ecosystem." It seeks to utilize the consumer purchasing power to promote environmentally responsible management of the world's fisheries. The MSC was originally established in 1997 by Unilever and the World Wildlife Fund (WWF) and has been operating independently since 1999. It has brought together people from over 100 organizations in more than 20 countries. The MSC has developed an environmental standard for sustainable fisheries and uses a product label to allow recognition of environmentally responsible fishery management and practices. This is intended to permit consumers to choose seafood products that have not contributed to overfishing, a serious environmental problem. The MSC has also established an independent certification of fisheries that comply with the MSC Standard.

6. *A carbon footprint label?* There have been proposals to establish a carbon footprint label for certain products to increase awareness about the extent to which they are contributing to climate change. Similar proposals have been advanced for a label on goods or products that would disclose the amount of water used to produce them. What issues would arise? How might you address them consistently with the TBT? For an analysis of water labeling and trade issues, *see* Edith Brown Weiss & Lydia Slobodian, *Virtual Water, Water Scarcity, and International Trade Law*, 17 Journal International Economic Law 717, 730–737 (2014).

7. As noted above, there has been a very significant growth in the use of environmental labels, also referred to as ecolabels. For an index for ecolabels, *see* http://www.ecolabelindex.com. Do you regard this as a good

development? What problems do you foresee? Are you confident that consumers will be able to know what a particular ecolabel means, who awarded it, and how it was awarded? Might it be useful to have a central international repository for ecolabels? Might the TBT serve as a forum for the registration of ecolabels, which could provide information on the entity awarding the label and the criteria for qualifying for the label?

F. REGIONAL TRADE AGREEMENTS

1. THE NORTH AMERICAN FREE TRADE AGREEMENT

The United States, Mexico, and Canada began negotiating the North American Free Trade Agreement (NAFTA) in 1991, with the goal of a free trade area. Free trade areas involve common internal tariffs but, unlike a customs union such as the European Union, no common external tariffs. Both free trade areas and customs unions are allowed by the WTO.

NAFTA was intended to lower tariffs (hopefully to zero) and to create more open markets for trade and investment among the three countries. It was designed to cover a wide variety of economic activity, including trade in goods, investment, agriculture (including sanitary and phytosanitary measures), standards-related measures, energy, and services. From the beginning of the negotiations, there was a debate about the environmental implications of NAFTA.

NAFTA AND THE ENVIRONMENT: SUBSTANCE AND PROCESS

Daniel Magraw
3–6 (1995) [footnotes omitted]

C. ENVIRONMENTAL CONCERNS ABOUT A NORTH AMERICAN FREE TRADE AREA

Threat to domestic environmental laws and to international environmental agreements. Perhaps the most significant environmental concern raised by the prospect of negotiating and implementing the NAFTA was the potential threat to U.S. domestic environmental laws and regulations posed by the "trade disciplines" contained in trade agreements. Trade disciplines are intended to prevent countries from unduly interfering with international trade by restricting imports or exports. These disciplines potentially affect environmental protection efforts because such efforts often require prohibiting trade in banned products. For example, to protect the U.S. health and environment from DDT (a toxic pesticide), it is necessary not only to prohibit DDT's use in the U.S., but also to prohibit the import of foodstuffs containing DDT residues.

Pollution havens. The possibility that industry would be attracted to locales with low environmental protection standards or enforcement was another concern, especially given the risk that a government might lower its standards or reduce its enforcement in order to attract or retain investment. The antipathy towards pollution havens had both environmental and competitiveness underpinnings.

Environmentally damaging growth. The fact that liberalized trade would create economic growth and increased investment gave rise to other concerns. This was particularly the case along the U.S.-Mexican border. The growth of the maquiladora program—under which components may be imported duty-free into Mexico from the United States for processing or further manufacturing by factories (which are concentrated along the border) and then exported duty-free to the United States—had already caused serious health problems and environmental degradation. Some commentators were not convinced that the international trade paradigm of comparative advantage—the theory that free trade is good for all countries because it allows each country to exploit its particular advantage in inputs—makes environmental sense; some distrusted growth as a general matter; and others feared that the rapid pace of growth would outpace the creation of environmental infrastructure, some of which requires large capital outlays.

Other indirect effects. There were also other expected effects of increased trade and investment that have environmental implications, though several of these are positive. For example, increased trade in environment-friendly services and technologies will make pollution prevention and clean-up more efficient. Increased contact and information flow between companies will result in better environmental-management techniques. Perhaps most important, increased trade and investment was expected by some to result in increased resources being devoted to environmental protection, particularly in Mexico. This belief is based on historical evidence that the ratio of Gross National Product spent on environmental protection increased markedly once a country's per capita income exceeded $5000. Others are less optimistic, based on an assumption that the increased wealth from trade liberalization would not be spread equitably among the Mexican population.

INTERNATIONAL ECONOMICS, TRADE, AND THE ENVIRONMENT

Adapted from Peter Lallas and Andreas Ziegler
International Occupational and Environmental Medicine
(Jessica Herzstein et al., eds., Mosby 1998)

The U.S. Administrations, for their part, became very engaged in these debates [about NAFTA and the environment]. Both the Bush and the Clinton Administrations prepared an environmental review of the NAFTA, and carried out extensive public consultations on these issues.

In the end, a number of actions were taken. First, a political decision was made during the negotiation of NAFTA to diverge from the Uruguay Round "model" in order to address specific environmental concerns. This included, in particular, a new approach to provisions in the NAFTA Chapters on Standards, Sanitary and Phytosanitary measures, and Investment, as well as the introduction of a provision intended to safeguard the use of trade measures specified in MEAs from challenge under NAFTA, subject to a specified proviso.

Beyond this, the three countries transformed the NAFTA from a single trade agreement (the NAFTA) into a "package" of agreements focused more broadly on trade, environment and labor, with the broad objective of sustainable development. The core of this approach was the development of parallel environmental and labor-related agreements and initiatives. On the environmental side, these included:

- the North American Agreement for Environmental Cooperation (NACEC), designed *inter alia* to promote cooperation on environmental issues and maintain and enhance enforcement against violation of environmental laws;

- the Border Environmental Cooperation Commission and related NADBank, designed *inter alia* to identify and fund environmental infrastructure needs in the U.S.-Mexico Border Area.

In addition, the U.S. and Mexico reinforced existing efforts to address environmental problems in the U.S.-Mexico border area, including through the adoption of an integrated border environmental plan.

NAFTA AND THE ENVIRONMENT: SUBSTANCE AND PROCESS

Daniel Magraw
12–19 (1995) [footnotes omitted]

E. PROVISIONS IN THE NAFTA TEXT

The NAFTA text contains several provisions intended to make it more environmentally sensitive. In almost every instance, these provisions . . . are more protective of the environment than the equivalent provisions in the so-called Dunkel text, the then-operative text of the Uruguay Round of the GATT negotiations, which were occurring simultaneously with the NAFTA negotiations.

Although the Objectives article of the NAFTA does not refer to implementing the agreement in an environmentally protective manner, the NAFTA Preamble commits the countries to undertake the increased trade and investment envisioned by the NAFTA in "a manner consistent with environmental protection and conservation." It further commits the countries to "promote sustainable development" and "strengthen the development and enforcement of environmental laws and regulations." Domestic environmental laws are protected in several ways. Provisions on Sanitary and Phytosanitary measures (SPS) (Chapter 7B) and on Standards Related measures (Chapter 9) ensure that the United States has the right to choose its own level of protection in those areas, and they establish committees to strive to enhance levels of protection. Domestic laws may exceed international standards and may exist in the absence of scientific certainty. The problem of downward harmonization is thus dealt with. The potential problem of "dueling science" in disciplines upon SPS measures is avoided by requiring that an SPS measure be supported simply by a scientific basis, rather than a standard that would allow a dispute over whose science is "better." The United States may determine whether another country's testing is equivalent to its own. States and localities retain their right to adopt standards that are stricter than federal and international standards.

Environmentalists expressed concern about several provisions in chapters 7B and 9, especially the use of the word "necessary" in article 712(5) as a trade discipline. The term "necessary" is problematic for many in the environmental community, because it has been interpreted narrowly by GATT dispute settlement panels when applying GATT article XX(b), which is the exception for trade measures taken to protect human, animal or plant life or health. In a letter dated September 13, 1993 to the Natural Resources Defense Council (reprinted in Part III), U.S. Trade Representative Michael Kantor explained this and several other points about the NAFTA text to the satisfaction of at least some in the environmental community.

Article XX of the GATT—which contains exceptions that permit otherwise-prohibited trade measures, inter alia, if they are necessary to protect human, animal, or plant life or health or if they relate to conserving exhaustible natural resources—formed the basis for the tuna/dolphin cases referred to above and is incorporated into NAFTA with respect to environment-based trade measures not already covered by chapters 7B and 9. Although new language clarifies that article somewhat in an environmentally sensitive manner, the outcome of the tuna/dolphin case, referred to above, most probably would remain unchanged. The inability to resolve this problem troubled many environmentalists deeply.

The trade-related obligations in specified international environmental agreements are protected by article 104, which gives them precedence over the NAFTA in certain circumstances. The list of such agreements can be added to by a relatively simple procedure. Some environmentalists believed, however, that the list in NAFTA was inadequate. During the political process leading to congressional approval of NAFTA, it was agreed to add the U.S.-Canada and U.S.-Mexico migratory birds treaties to the list and to consider adding other agreements.

Moreover, unlike those in the GATT, the dispute settlement provisions of NAFTA place the burden of proof in some circumstances on the country challenging an environmental regulation. In addition, a country defending an environmental standard under chapters 7B or 9 or article 104 may choose to have the case decided by a NAFTA dispute settlement panel, even if the challenging country desires to have the case decided by a GATT panel. This provision ensures the applicability of more environmentally sensitive rules and procedures. Finally, the provisions allow panels to obtain advice from scientific experts if such issues are present in a case. On the other hand, they embody the principle that panel hearings, deliberations, and written submissions shall be confidential. Environmentalists continue to be troubled by some aspects of dispute settlement. In particular, they argue for more environmental expertise on the panels and increased opportunities for public involvement in the process.

NAFTA also includes a provision regarding pollution havens, which states that countries should not encourage investment by relaxing or derogating from domestic health, safety or environmental measures. The article uses the hortatory word "should," rather than the normative "shall." Article 1114 further provides that if a country believes another country is engaging in this type of behavior, there shall be consultations if the first country requests them; but formal NAFTA dispute settlement is not provided.

NOTES AND QUESTIONS

1.   *Balance?* Does the NAFTA package provide proper balance to environmental and trade concerns? For literature assessing NAFTA and the environment, *see* Shawkat Alam, Sustainable Development and Free Trade (2008) (Chapter 6 discusses the NAFTA and the Environment); Gary Clyde Hufbauer and Jeffrey J. Schott, NAFTA Revisited: Achievements and Challenges (2005) (Chapter 3 discusses the environment); Gary Clyde Hufbauer et al, NAFTA and the Environment: Seven Years Later (2000)

2.   *The FTAA.* In 1994, the 34 countries in the Western Hemisphere (all countries except Cuba) agreed to create a Free Trade Area of the Americas (FTAA). Would the NAFTA model fit the FTAA? Brazil, Argentina, and Uruguay had formed their own regional trade area, MERCOSUR. These three countries, as well as others, were not enthusiastic about adopting the NAFTA model. Chile, however, was; and negotiations commenced to

accomplish that. Political disagreements in the United States interrupted these negotiations, however. Why would MERCOSUR countries be opposed to the NAFTA model?

2. THE DOMINICAN REPUBLIC-CENTRAL AMERICA-UNITED STATES FREE TRADE AGREEMENT (CAFTA-DR)

The CAFTA-DR was signed in 2004 by five Central American countries (Costa Rica, El Salvador, Guatemala, Honduras and Nicaragua), Dominican Republic and the United States. Like the NAFTA, the CAFTA-DR was intended to eliminate tariffs and other trade barriers between the Central American countries and the United States and to facilitate trade and investment. The CAFTA-DR contains an Environmental Chapter in which countries agree to ensure that their domestic laws provide for high levels of environmental protection and to enforce effectively their domestic environmental laws. Unlike the NAFTA where the citizen submissions procedure was established in a separate North American Agreement on Environmental Cooperation (NAAEC), the submissions mechanism is contained in the CAFTA-DR Environmental Chapter itself. Under the CAFTA-DR citizen submissions procedure, any national or an enterprise of a Party can file a submission with the Secretariat for Environmental Matters (SEM) asserting that a Party is failing to effectively enforce its environmental laws. However, the CAFTA-DR citizen submissions procedure is not available to U.S. persons claiming that the United States is not enforcing its environmental laws; such U.S. persons must use the NAAEC submissions procedure. After receiving a submission which must meet certain requirements, the SEM prepares and publishes a Factual Record if approved by one vote of any Party. From 2007 to 2013, the SEM received twenty-nine submissions and published three Factual Records.

The CAFTA-DR Environmental Cooperation Agreement (ECA) was signed among parties in February 2005 as a supplemental agreement to implement the CAFTA-DR Environmental Chapter. The ECA sets out a framework for an environmental cooperation program between parties. The CAFTA-DR Environmental Cooperation Program focuses on four themes: institutional strengthening for the enforcement of environmental laws; protecting biodiversity and conservation by implementing obligations under multilateral environmental agreements such as the Convention on Trade in Endangered Species of Flora and Fauna (CITES); promoting market-based conservation through environmentally sustainable income generating activities; and encouraging private sector environmental performance.

3. OTHER REGIONAL FREE TRADE AGREEMENTS

The proposed Trans-Pacific Partnership (TPP) is a comprehensive free trade agreement in the Asia-Pacific region that as of August 2015 was still being negotiated. The 12 negotiating States are Australia, Brunei, Canada, Chile, Japan, Malaysia, Mexico, New Zealand, Peru, Singapore, the United States and Vietnam, which together represent nearly 40% of global GDP and one third of world trade. The proposed TPP has an Environmental Chapter, which is controversial. One of the issues relates to the inclusion of an enforcement mechanism for domestic environmental laws.

The United States and the European Union have initiated negotiations for a Transatlantic Trade and Investment Partnership (TTIP), which would provide another important free trade agreement.

NOTES AND QUESTIONS

1.   Just as the WTO brought together the various separate codes that had existed into one comprehensive international agreement, the growth of regional trade agreements now raises the question of consistency between the various provisions of the regional trade agreements and the WTO agreements. What issues might you foresee and how do you think they could be resolved?

2.   The NAFTA is complemented by a separate agreement, the North American Agreement on Environmental Cooperation. The CAFTA has a separate environmental chapter within the agreement to addresses the issue of enforcement of national environmental laws. Which approach do you prefer and why? Would such an agreement be viable in other regions?

3.   Would it be timely and appropriate to consider a regional or international agreement that articulates best practices for national environmental laws and regulations? Should it be linked to a trade agreement?

CHAPTER 17

FINANCING SUSTAINABILITY

■ ■ ■

A major concern facing the international community is how to finance effective environmental protection and natural resources conservation. Many countries are still economically poor, with people living on less than $1.25 per day. Some are politically fragile, or the governance structure is in disarray. Many lack the resources and capacity to undertake effective environmental protection, especially for issues of global environmental concern. As explored previously, the benefits and costs of environmental protection and natural resource conservation are short-term and long-term, sometimes far into the future. Financing the measures needed to mitigate climate change and assisting countries to adapt to it will be especially challenging, as noted in Chapter 9 on climate change.

One of the themes in this book has been equity or fairness. This issue is prominent in the problems of financing sustainable development. Why should developing countries sacrifice opportunities to industrialize to "save" the environment, when developed countries had no such concern during their industrial development years ago, and even had the largest role in causing global environmental damage (such as depletion of the ozone layer)? Why should developing countries limit their development options when developed countries, which on a per capita basis pollute far more, will not proportionately curb their polluting activities? The Rio Declaration Principle of "common but differentiated responsibilities," described in Chapter 4, reflects many of these concerns, and has been at the heart of the debates about agreement on actions to address climate change.

On the other hand, sustainable development is arguably most important to poor communities around the world. Otherwise, poor communities may shoulder a disproportionate share of the costs, but not receive a proportionate share of the benefits. To the extent that new practices and technologies enable communities to leapfrog the environmental harms associated with earlier ones, they may save costs, even in the short term.

From the perspective of the industrialized world, the issue may be put differently: Why should developed countries pay the costs of measures undertaken by developing countries, especially when developing countries argue that such aid should be in addition to assistance already given by the developed countries? There are also important issues of equity within countries, as to who bears the burden of environmental protection.

In recent years, there has been a significant shift in the distribution of wealth, economic activity, and political engagement among countries. Many formerly "developing countries" have experienced rapid economic growth and development in the past decade, and previous distinctions between "industrialized/developed" and "developing" countries have become less clear. The changing international landscape may not alter the importance of basic principles of sustainability highlighted in this chapter (and elsewhere in the text), but it does provide a new set of conditions and dynamics going forward.

While States have been the traditional source of assistance to countries for sustainable development, other financing avenues have become increasingly important. These include public-private partnerships, private sector investment, foundations and individuals, nongovernmental organizations, and bottom-up initiatives, such as crowd sourcing.

This chapter begins by addressing the role of States and of multilateral development banks in financing sustainable development. The chapter then turns to the role of the private sector, debt relief including debt-for-nature swaps, microfinance, bottom-up initiatives, such as Kiva, and more recently, crowd-sourcing.

TWO PROBLEMS

In this hypothetical, Lesotho, an independent State entirely surrounded by South Africa, is considering building a dam on the upper reaches of a river that flows into South Africa. One of the world's largest dams already exists on the upper reaches of a river in Lesotho. South Africa is eager for the dam because it needs the hydroelectric power, especially at a time when its construction of new coal fired plants has come under attack. Lesotho is attracted to the revenue that the plant could generate from power sales to South Africa. A French company has made a proposal to build the dam. Lesotho will need to arrange financing, either from a multilateral development bank, a foreign government, or private sources in order to afford the dam. Meanwhile, the people living in the area of the proposed dam are very concerned. Most are traditional farmers, who eke out their living on the land, or fishermen. According to the plans, many will need to be resettled. None of the communities have electricity or running water. They are aware that as a result of the other dam, the communities in the area of the reservoir still do not have electricity or running water, and that some people have been cut off from ready access to roads or other means of transport.

Consider what sources of financing you would prefer and why. You should try to answer this question from the perspective of the government of Lesotho, the French company, the local community, and an international nongovernmental organization such as International Rivers. What legal issues arise in relation to different funding sources? You may want to revisit your responses to these questions after finishing the entire chapter.

In the second hypothetical problem, you are to assume that a logging company from North America is proposing to log a large tropical forest in Guyana, a country located on the northeast corner of Latin America, which borders Brazil. A native Indian tribe inhabits part of the tropical forest being considered for cutting. A road system (an infrastructure project) will then be constructed across the deforested land, which may be financed by a regional or multilateral development bank. Countrybank, a hypothetical North American Bank, owns a very substantial amount of debt from Guyana, which was incurred from earlier projects in the country. You are to assume that your interest is to ensure sustainable development in the country. What are the options, and what do you recommend and why? What are the important legal issues raised by each source of financing? You are to consider this problem as you read the chapter, and you may want to revisit your answers after you have finished the entire chapter.

A. STATES AS SOURCES OF FINANCING

1.   POST 2015 AND MILLENNIUM DEVELOPMENT GOALS

Governments are a primary source of financing for sustainable development. In 2000, the United Nations adopted the Millennium Development Goals (MDGs). *See supra* Chapter 1. The eight goals establish different priorities for meeting the needs of the world's poorest people by 2015. Most are concerned with issues other than financing of development. The UN Millennium Declaration, Article 13 states: "Success in meeting these objectives depends, *inter alia*, on good governance within each country. It also depends on good governance at the international level and on transparency in the financial, monetary and trading systems. We are committed to an open, equitable, rule-based, predictable and nondiscriminatory multilateral trading and financial system."

The eighth goal, a Global Partnership for Development, is concerned with financing the MDGs through partnerships between developed and developing countries. Developed countries pledged to increase aid from $80 billion in 2004 to $130 billion in 2010. However, in 2013, only six donor countries had achieved the longstanding United Nations aid target of 0.7 percent of their gross national income (Denmark, Luxembourg, Norway, Sweden, the Netherlands, and the United Kingdom). Five more indicated they intended to do so soon.

In addition to money for official development assistance, debt relief is seen as a significant step toward enabling developing countries to meet the MDGs. By April 2005, twenty-seven countries were receiving debt relief under the Heavily Indebted Poor Countries (HIPC) Initiative. Eighteen of these countries had reached "completion point" and were receiving irrevocable debt relief. These 18 countries benefited from an agreement reached by the major developed countries in June 2005 to provide for the full cancellation of the $40 billion they owe to the World Bank, the International Monetary Fund and the African Development Bank.

According to the Millennium Development Goals Report 2014, several MDG targets have been met, such as increased access to an improved drinking water by 89% of world's population in 2012 compared to 76% in 1990. More than 2.3 billion people gained access to improved drinking water between 1990 and 2012. Countries have nearly eliminated ozone-depleting substances as a result of the Montreal Protocol. Other MDGs require more efforts to reach the targets. Global emissions of carbon dioxide have increased by more than 50% since 1990, and the loss of forests continues even though net forest loss decreased from 8.3 million hectares in the 1990s to 5.2 million hectares between 2000 and 2010.

The United Nations has developed a new set of Sustainable Development Goals for the period post-2015. In July 2012, the UN Secretary-General established the High-Level Panel of Eminent Persons on the Post-2015 Development Agenda to provide recommendations. In May 2013, the Panel issued a report titled *A New Global Partnership: Eradicate Poverty and Transform Economies through Sustainable Development* with a central message to eradicate extreme poverty by 2030. The Panel proposed five transformative shifts for the post-2015 agenda, which are: (1) leave no one behind; (2) put sustainable development at the core; (3) transform economies for jobs and inclusive growth; (4) build peace and effective, open and accountable institutions for all; and (5) forge a new global partnership. The report can be accessed at http://www.post2015hlp.org/. The Heads of State and Government Summit at the United Nations in September 2015 adopted the Sustainable Development Goals, which form the 2030 Development Agenda.

2.   THE 1992 RIO SUMMIT AND AGENDA 21

The Rio Conference on Environment and Development in 1992, was held on the twentieth anniversary of the 1972 Stockholm Conference on the Human Environment, the initial international conference on environmental issues. At the Rio Conference, countries adopted the concept of sustainable development and drafted an Agenda 21 to detail their commitments for implementing sustainable development.

The text of Agenda 21 specifically addressed the need to provide substantial new and additional financial resources to developing countries, targets for national levels of Overseas Development Assistance

(ODA) in terms of percent of GNP, and the need to make use of various types of funding sources and mechanisms. It provided as follows:

> 33.10. The implementation of the huge sustainable development programmes of Agenda 21 will require the provision to developing countries of substantial new and additional financial resources. Grant or concessional financing should be provided according to sound and equitable criteria and indicators. . . .

> 33.13   . . . Developed countries reaffirm their commitments to reach the accepted United Nations target of 0.7 per cent of GNP for ODA and, to the extent that they have no target, agree to augment their aid programmes in order to reach that target as soon as possible and to ensure prompt and effective implementation of Agenda 21.

3.   WORLD SUMMIT ON SUSTAINABLE DEVELOPMENT (WSSD), JOHANNESBURG 2002

On the 10th anniversary of the 1992 Rio Conference on Environment and Development, countries met in Johannesburg, South Africa, and developed the Johannesburg Plan of Implementation (JPOI). This Plan called for significant increases in the flow of financial resources to developing countries, including through debt relief.

As compared to the 1992 Rio Summit, however, the WSSD put a higher emphasis on the importance of foreign direct investment flows in support of sustainable development. The JPOI called for fully implementing agreements from the World Trade Organization's Doha Declaration, including accession of developing countries to the WTO; improved developing countries' market access to developed countries; fuller integration of small, vulnerable economies into the multilateral trading system; and greater capacity of commodity-dependent countries to diversify exports. It also addressed environment and trade issues.

The WSSD process led to a stronger emphasis than before on the use of voluntary partnerships to tackle major global health and environmental problems. Partnerships are voluntary, multi-stakeholder initiatives to implement the commitments in the JPOI and Agenda 21. They are generally collaborative, limited in size and scope, and focused on finding innovative solutions to specific sustainable development challenges. They are seen as having many of the benefits of business enterprises. Many partnerships use pilot projects to test their strategies, before replicating their models at higher levels. The bulk of funding has come from governments and intergovernmental organizations, with limited funding from grants from nongovernmental organizations and private sector donors. The success of these partnerships is varied as of July 2015.

4.   RIO+20, JUNE 2012, AND THE GREEN ECONOMY

In June 2012, States met in Rio de Janeiro to consider once again the problem of sustainable development, to reaffirm the principles in the Rio Declaration on Environment and Development and Agenda 21, and to put forward a plan for the future, titled *The Future We Want*. The Conference included a new focus on a green economy. Although there is no internationally agreed definition of "green economy", UNEP defines green economy as an economy that "results in improved human well-being and social equity, while significantly reducing environmental risks and ecological scarcities." In another words, green economy aims to transform the current economy to an "inclusive, resource-efficient, low-carbon" economy. Relevant portions of the final report, *The Future We Want,* follow:

> 59. We view the implementation of green economy policies by countries that seek to apply them for the transition towards sustainable development as a common undertaking, and we recognize that each country can choose an appropriate approach in accordance with national sustainable development plans, strategies and priorities.
>
> . . .
>
> 66. Recognizing the importance of linking financing, technology, capacity building and national needs for sustainable development policies, including green economy in the context of sustainable development and poverty eradication, we invite the United Nations system, in cooperation with relevant donors and international organizations, to coordinate and provide information upon request on:
>
>> (a) Matching interested countries with the partners that are best suited to provide requested support;
>>
>> (b) Toolboxes and/or best practices in applying policies on green economy in the context of sustainable development and poverty eradication at all levels;
>>
>> (c) Models or good examples of policies on green economy in the context of sustainable development and poverty eradication;
>>
>> (d) Methodologies for evaluation of policies on green economy in the context of sustainable development and poverty eradication;
>>
>> (e) Existing and emerging platforms that contribute in this regard.

The Conference pointed to the need to engage all sources of financing for achieving a green economy and equitable sustainable development. In response to *The Future We Want*, four UN agencies—the United Nations Environment Programme (UNEP), the International Labour Organization (ILO), the United Nations Industrial Development Organization (UNIDO) and the United Nations Institute for Training and Research (UNITAR)—launched the Partnership for Action on Green Economy (PAGE) in February 2013 to "provide a comprehensive suite of green economy services that will enable countries to transform their national economic structures." PAGE is to assist 30 countries over the next seven years to build national green economy strategies and to shift their investments and policies toward creating clean technologies, resource efficient infrastructure, well-functioning ecosystems, green skilled labor and good governance. The first PAGE conference in March 2014 attracted 450 participants from 66 countries. In January 2012 the Global Green Growth Institute, the Organisation for Economic Co-operation and Development (OECD), UNEP and the World Bank established the Green Growth Knowledge Platform (GGKP), a global network of international organizations and experts to assist policymakers to make a transition to a green economy,

NOTES AND QUESTIONS

1.   *The 0.7 percent commitment. How much is enough?* Is the 1992 commitment by developed States of 0.7 percent of GNP (usually referred to in the United States as Gross Domestic Product, or GDP) too little or too much? How do you suppose such a figure was calculated? In 2013, only five countries met 0.7 percent of their GNP for official development assistance. These were Denmark, Luxembourg, Norway, Sweden and the United Kingdom. Of the industrialized countries, only the United States expressly stated that it refused to commit to the 0.7 percent level.

2.   *Conditionalities. Should we attach conditions?* Many bilateral aid agreements attach conditions. One common condition requires that the donor country's technology must be used. The price of such technology may be inflated above market price. Developing countries frequently demand the removal of conditions on aid from developed countries (referred to as "conditionalities"). Do conditionalities raise legal issues? Are there equity issues?

3.   *Additionality. New funds or reprogram the old?* The notion that the aid for global environmental protection be in addition to existing forms and amounts of assistance provided by developed countries is referred to as "additionality." This concept is not new. At the 1972 U.N. Conference on the Human Environment in Stockholm, developing countries made this demand. *See* Peter Thatcher, *The Role of the UN*, in The International Politics of the Environment 194, 201 (A. Horrel & B. Kingsbury eds., 1992). The concern was that funds for other aspects of development would be "shifted" to

environmental protection, with the result that no "additional funding" is provided.

4. *IFC and MIGA. What role for the private sector?* In addition to multilateral development banks (MDBs), discussed below, private sector sources may be facilitated through international organizations such as the International Finance Corporation (IFC) and the Multilateral Investment Guarantee Agency (MIGA), both of which are part of the World Bank Group. The IFC was established to promote private sector development through financing of private enterprise in developing countries. IFC can make equity investments or loans within the private sector, whether or not there is governmental participation, and puts deals together that involve private banks and other lending institutions to leverage its capital. The World Bank established MIGA in 1988 to promote and protect private foreign aid direct investment for economic and social development in the World Bank member countries. MIGA provides investment guarantees against the risks of expropriation, war, civil disturbance, and breach of contract by the host government, thereby helping countries create an attractive investment climate for private foreign direct investment.

5. *Role of partnerships. Do they work?* Reliance on public-private partnerships has been criticized because they are voluntary and lack accountability. There is no mechanism in place for ensuring that these programs follow their stated objectives and promote sustainable development. Some countries may be wary of relying too heavily on voluntary partnerships to implement international commitments. Why might this be so? What legal provisions might be appropriate in partnerships to further accountability?

6. *Role of Foreign Direct Investment. Can it support sustainable development?* Do you agree with the increased emphasis at the WSSD on the role and importance of foreign direct investment in support of sustainable development? Much information suggests that while such investment may bring significant benefit, it also can result in significant negative environmental and social effects. *See, e.g.,* Inspection Panel Investigation Report, Cambodia: Forest Concession Management and Control Pilot Project, April 11, 2006, Chapter 2 (noting the activities of an "all too vigorous" timber industry in the Philippines, Malaysia, Indonesia and now Cambodia, operations of which are "not even close to sustainable"); Doe v. Unocal Corp., 395 F.3d 932 (9th Cir. 2002) (addressing human rights violations in connection with construction by Unocal, a company from the United States, of gas pipeline in Burma). Did the governments get it right in Johannesburg? Does something seem to be missing in placing such high hopes on foreign investment flows, from a normative perspective or otherwise? What would you recommend?

B. MULTILATERAL AND DEVELOPMENT BANKS

1. THE WORLD BANK

Multilateral Development Banks (MDBs) play a significant role in financing economic development in the Global South, and such development in turn can have significant environmental and social impacts.

After the end of World War II, countries negotiated to establish three international organizations to address economic and financial issues: The International Bank for Reconstruction and Development (the World Bank), the International Monetary Fund, and the International Trade Organization. Only the first two institutions came into being.

In 1946 when the World Bank began operations, its primary mission was the reconstruction of countries destroyed or heavily damaged during World War II. In the decades since, the World Bank has moved from financing post-war reconstruction to financing economic development in developing countries, with a primary mission to reduce/eliminate poverty. The institutional structure of the World Bank has expanded, with the establishment of the International Finance Corporation (IFC)—the private sector arm—in 1956; the International Development Association (IDA)—which provides grants and very low interest loans—in 1959; the International Centre for Settlement of Investment Disputes (ICSID) in 1966; the Multilateral Investment Guarantee Agency (MIGA) in 1988; and the Global Environment Facility (GEF) in 1991. All of these institutions are included within the "World Bank Group."

From 2010 to 2014, the World Bank Group's total lending reached more than $209 billion. The World Bank's total lending in 2014 was $40.8 billion. Of the $40.8 billion, the World Bank provided $22.2 billion in IDA credit and grants. In 2014, the IFC committed $17 billion compared to $18.3 billion in 2013, and MIGA provided $3.2 billion in guarantees compared to $2.8 billion in 2013.

The World Bank borrows money from world private capital markets and relends to more advanced developing countries (called "Bank borrowers") at a small profit. Because the Bank's borrowing is guaranteed by its member governments, it can borrow at a rate normally afforded only to the best private borrowers, and relend at a rate advantageous to its developing country borrowers. Part of the loans are for projects involving well-defined components and procurement of goods and services for specific purposes. Part of the loans are program or sector loans providing general budgetary support for broad changes in economic policy. According to the World Bank, its development policy lending, previously referred to as adjustment lending, has on average accounted for 20 to 25 % of Bank lending. However, from 2009-2011 during the financial crisis, it accounted for 40% of Bank lending.

The IDA is of special interest for the poorest countries with little or no access to market-based financing, because it provides interest-free loans and grants for programs in these countries. IDA lends to 82 countries to help 2.5 billion people, most of whom live on less than $2 a day. Forty of these countries are in Africa. IDA shares the same staff and headquarters with the World Bank.

Since IDA loans are highly concessional, IDA's resources must be periodically replenished, through contributions from richer member countries. The sixteenth replenishment of the IDA (IDA16) occurred in 2011 covering fiscal years 2012 to 2014, with approximately U.S. $49.3 billion made available for the three-year period ending June 30, 2014, the largest expansion of IDA resources in two decades. The largest pledges were made by the United Kingdom, the United States, Japan, Germany, France, Canada and Spain; less wealthy countries eligible to borrow from IBRD (but not IDA) also contributed. The IDA 17 Replenishment covering fiscal years 2015 to 2017 was agreed to in December 2013, where countries committed to provide $52 billion for IDA.

Consider the following excerpts to get an idea of the controversy that has surrounded these institutions and of the links to debates over globalization.

TROPICAL GANGSTERS

Robert Klitgard
8–12, 207 (1991)

Faced with these grave and worsening problems, most African countries are experimenting with radical economic reforms that can be compared to Eastern Europe's. (Few, however, are emulating Eastern Europe's move toward democracy.) Why the sudden upheaval in economic strategy? Bluntly put, most African countries have gone broke. Private banks will no longer lend to them, so they need financing of the International Monetary Fund and the World Bank. The IMF and the Bank are the preachers of free-market economic reforms. To get their blessing, the Africans are converting.

The influence of the Fund and the Bank has grown tremendously over the past decade. The two institutions work closely together—their headquarters are on adjacent streets in Washington. Both are multilateral organizations set up near the end of the Second World War to help the shattered global economy. Today both concentrate on the developing countries, to which they offer low-interest loans with strings attached. But the two institutions tend to differ in their economic concerns. Although the lines have been blurring, the IMF tends to worry about economic stability in the short run—say, over a year or two—while the World Bank struggles with economic growth in the medium run—say, three to five years. The IMF tends to focus on money supplies and budget balances, whereas the Bank homes in on public investment and pricing policies. Both the Fund and the Bank emphasize exports as the key to growth, as opposed to the old strategy of import substitution, which promoted industries producing goods for domestic consumption. And both institutions stress the move toward free markets.

For a developing country, an agreement with the IMF has become something like a Good Housekeeping Seal of Approval. Unless the IMF says your economic strategy is sound, many aid donors and commercial lenders will not ante up. The World Bank's role is less dramatic, but having a structural adjustment program with the Bank is frequently a facilitator if not a prerequisite for aid from other sources. An agreement with the IMF and a structural adjustment program with the Bank typically contain common elements. The country devalues its currency, cuts government spending, frees up domestic and international trade and turns public enterprises over to private management or joint ventures. In the parlance of the World Bank,

> The objective of structural adjustment programs is to restore rapid economic growth while simultaneously supporting internal and external financial stability. As such, these programs have macroeconomic and microeconomic aspects. The major macro objectives are to improve the external balance and domestic fiscal balance. An adjustment program thus commonly includes a combination of (1) fiscal and monetary policies to bring about overall demand reduction and (2) trade policies (mainly the exchange rate and import/export taxes and subsidies) to alter the relative incentives between tradable and non-tradable goods. On the micro side, the major objective is to improve efficiency in the use of resources by removing price distortions, opening up more competition, and dismantling administrative controls (deregulation). Such programs include those for government expenditures and the management of public enterprises, including reduction in the government's presence in areas where private enterprise can operate more efficiently.

Structural adjustment means less government, freer trade, and more private enterprise. But the change can be painful. It is often accompanied by a recession. Public spending on schooling and health collapses, while prices rise for food and housing and transport.

Since so many poor countries are bankrupt and up to their eyes in debt, they virtually have to do what the IMF and the Bank say. Consequently, the Fund and the Bank often play the role of outside heavies. They insist on reform, design it, and monitor its implementation.

No wonder such foreign aid is controversial: to many, it smacks of neo-imperialism. And there is controversy over the adequacy of the IMF-World Bank recipe. Not only politicians but also academicians and even Bank staff have qualms.

. . .

[But] First of all, the IMF and the World Bank do not exactly dictate. A country has to ask for loans from the Fund or the Bank. Some countries have not—Cuba, for example. It is in a strict sense voluntary that a nation submit to some impingements on its autonomy—as private companies sometimes do when they are in financial trouble and allow bankers to sit on their boards or venture capitalists to help manage the company. Or, as patients sometimes do with their physicians.

On the other hand, do bankrupt countries have a real choice? Leverage can restrict sovereignty. Benevolence can undermine autonomy. Fundamental dilemmas like these often drive people to extremes. We seem to need to find bad guys, someone to blame, and to put ourselves on the other side. We seem to seek simple truths.

"Look," says one extreme position, "these countries want to borrow money and the only way they will be creditworthy is if they follow this advice. We've seen our recipes work elsewhere. And by imposing these conditions, by using our leverage, we are doing good. Not least, we are saving the people of these countries a little bit from their corrupt and inefficient governments." "The governments of places like Equatorial Guinea are composed of predatory figures who cloak themselves in concepts of 'African socialism' and 'poorest of the poor' but spend their time with their hands in the till. Those beating the drum of sovereignty loudest are often, in the words of Kid Creole and the Coconuts, the truest tropical gangsters." In these difficult circumstances, how can the outside world help without hurting, apply leverage without trampling sovereignty? . . . How can we work for change while respecting what exists? How can we exercise analytical skills and make critical judgments while still affirming the imperfect people and situations we encounter? And how can we extend our limits in order to receive from the people to whom we are trying to give? . . .

GLOBALIZATION AND ITS DISCONTENTS
Joseph E. Stiglitz
3–20, 241 (2002)

International bureaucrats—the faceless symbols of the world economic order—are under attack everywhere. Formerly uneventful meetings of obscure technocrats discussing mundane subjects such as concessional loans and trade quotas have now become the scene of raging street battles and huge demonstrations. . . . Virtually every major meeting of the International Monetary Fund, the World Bank, and the World Trade Organization is now the scene of conflict and turmoil. . . .

Why has globalization—a force that has brought so much good—become so controversial? Opening up to international trade has helped many countries grow far more quickly than they would otherwise have done. . . . Globalization has reduced the sense of isolation felt in much of the developing world and has given many people in the developing countries access to knowledge well beyond the reach of even the wealthiest in any country a century ago. . . . Foreign aid, another aspect of the globalized world, for all its faults still has brought benefits to millions. . . . But to many in the developing world, globalization has not brought the promised economic benefits.

A growing divide between the haves and have-nots has left increasing numbers in the Third World in dire poverty, living on less than a dollar a day. . . . In Africa, the high aspirations following colonial independence have been largely unfulfilled. Instead, the continent plunges deeper into misery, as incomes fall and standards of living decline. . . .

What is this phenomenon of globalization that has been subject, at the same time, to such vilification and such praise. Fundamentally, it is the closer integration of the countries and peoples of the world which has been brought about by the enormous reduction of costs of transportation and communication, and the breaking down of artificial barriers to the flows of goods, services, capital, knowledge, and (to a lesser extent) people across borders. Globalization has been accompanied by the creation of new institutions that have joined existing ones to work across borders. . . .

To understand what went wrong, it's important to look at the three main institutions that govern globalization: the IMF, the World Bank, and the WTO. There are, in addition, a host of other institutions that play a role in the international economic system—a number of regional banks, smaller and younger sisters to the World Bank, and a large number of UN organizations. . . . These organizations often have views that are markedly different from the IMF and the World Bank. . . .

Underlying the problems of the IMF and the other international economic institutions is the problem of governance: Who decides what they do. The institutions are dominated not just by the wealthiest industrial countries but by commercial and financial interests in those countries, and the policies of the institutions naturally reflect this. The choice of heads for these institutions symbolizes the institutions' problem, and too often has contributed to their dysfunction. While almost all of the activities of the IMF and the World Bank today are in the developing world (certainly, all of their lending), they are led by representatives from the industrialized nations. (By custom or tacit agreement the head of the IMF is always a European; that of the World Bank an American.) . . .

Part of the reason that I remain hopeful about the possibility of reforming the international economic institutions is that I have seen change occur at the World Bank. It has not been easy, nor has it gone as far as I would have liked. But the changes have been significant . . . Reforms involved changes in philosophy in three areas: development; aid in general and the Bank's aid in particular; and relationships between the Bank and the developing countries.

NOTES AND QUESTIONS

1. *A response to the critiques.* How would you respond to these critiques?

2. *Giving member countries a voice.* The Board of Directors of the World Bank (and IDA) consists of 25 Executive Directors representing the member countries. As part of the 2010 reforms, an additional Executive Director was added to the long-existing limit of 24, to represent countries in Sub-Saharan Africa. China, France, Germany, Japan, the United Kingdom, the Russian Federation, Saudi Arabia, and the United States have their own Executive Director representing them on the Board. Other countries share an Executive Director, with one Executive Director sometimes representing over a dozen countries. Some countries have complained that the Board needs to give more representation to borrowing countries. What factors should affect representation? The Group of 20 States have in practice become more influential at the World Bank. What are the implications of this development?

3. *New issues for the World Bank?* As suggested, the World Bank has evolved as an institution, in good part in response to changes in the international system. What role do you foresee in the future for the Bank in financing sustainable development? How could the MDBs address the issues related to globalization? To climate change? Or to violations of human rights? The institution does evolve. In the early days, health and environment were not included in the Bank's portfolio, but they have been now for several decades. The World Bank has also announced a number of measures to address climate change.

2. REGIONAL MULTILATERAL DEVELOPMENT BANKS

Typically grouped with the World Bank are the four main regional development banks, covering Africa, Asia, Europe, and the Americas. Modeled on the World Bank, they provide long-term loans at market interest financed from borrowing in the international capital markets, and longer-term loans with below-market interest funded from contributions by donor countries. Some also provide grant financing. Their members include both borrowing developing countries and developed donor countries, and membership is not limited to countries from the region of the regional development bank. The majority of capital is held by regional member States and borrower States generally enjoy greater influence than they do at the World Bank.

Regional banks only finance projects in member States in their region. Their general purpose is to promote sustainable economic and social development in member countries. To this end, they provide loans for investments in the public sector and for private-sector promotion. They also provide technical assistance to help borrower countries implement their programs.

a.   African Development Bank

The African Development Bank (AfDB) was founded in 1964 at the impetus of politicians from several newly independent African States; all Bank presidents have been African. It is based in Tunis, Tunisia, and has 77 member countries, which are represented on the Board of Governors. Non-regional members were not admitted until 1982. The 53 regional countries retain 60 percent of voting power. Nigeria has the single largest voting power, followed by the United States and Japan. The Bank supports regional member States primarily by providing loans to promote the economic and social sectors, technical assistance with development projects, and consultancy and advisory services. The AfDB gauges borrowing countries' adherence to sound economic policies through the Country Performance Assessment, modeled after assessment policies at the World Bank. The Bank also provides no-interest loans with 50-year repayment periods to its most impoverished members.

b.   Asian Development Bank

Located in Manila, the Asian Development Bank (AsDB) was founded in 1966. Of the 67 members, 48 are from the Asia and Pacific region. Japan and the United States are coequally the largest shareholders, each with 15.8 percent of total subscribed capital. Japan was the driving force behind the AsDB's creation and by tradition, its president is Japanese. 60 percent of voting power belongs to regional countries, including developed country members Japan, Australia and New Zealand.

The Bank created an Environment Policy in 2002 in order to ensure environmental protection in AsDB-funded projects. The AsDB estimates that the annual economic costs of environmental degradation range from 4 to 8 percent of GDP in various developing member countries, and public expenditures on the environment are less than 1 percent of many of those countries' GDP. In many ways, the Environment Policy is modeled after the World Bank's environmental policy, such as the use of environmental and social safeguards, and individual environmental assessment of most AsDB programs.

c. Inter-American Development Bank Group

The Inter-American Development Bank (IDB) was founded in 1959 and is headquartered in Washington, D.C. It has provided the largest souce of development financing for Latin American and Caribbean countries. The IDB has 48 member States, 26 of which are regional borrowing countries. The IDB's charter provides that borrower country members as a group have at least 50 percent of total voting power. (They have 50.02% of voting power.) The United States is the largest voting power, at 30 percent. Argentina and Brazil have the next largest voting power at 11.03%.

The IDB has an Ordinary Capital of $105 billion. Of this amount, 4% has been paid in by member States and the rest remains as callable capital. The IDB's other major source of funding is the Fund for Special Operations (FSO). Its loans are more concessional and are limited to the region's weakest economies. At the end of 2014, the total subscription for the FSO was $10.2 billion. The IDB can provide financing to the Caribbean Development Bank for use in some of its eligible member countries that are not members of the IDB. The IDB also has a private sector arm similar to the IFC at the World Bank. This part of the IDB is planned to expand in the near future.

The Eighth Replenishment of the IDB included a major focus on strengthening the environmental legal and regulatory framework of member countries and establishing efficient institutional mechanisms to address environmental matters. The Ninth Replenishment, which was the largest in the IDB's history, set a lending target of 25% to support climate change initiatives, sustainable energy and environmental sustainability.

d. European Bank for Reconstruction and Development

The European Bank for Reconstruction and Development (EBRD) was established in 1991, with headquarters in London. Unlike the World Bank and other regional development banks, the EBRD is by its Charter focused on issues beyond economic ones. The EBRD Establishing Agreement provides that members are committed to "the fundamental principles of multiparty democracy, the rule of law, respect for human rights and market economics." This is due in large part to its establishment in 1991, when western European countries saw the need to support a new private sector in a democratic environment in the formerly communist countries of Eastern Europe. The EBRD is owned by 66 countries and two intergovernmental institutions, the European Economic Community and the European Investment Bank. From the beginning, the EBRD included non-regional members. The United States is the single largest shareholder, followed by the UK, France, Germany, Italy, and Japan. The EBRD's 36 borrowing countries include several central Asian countries, which are also borrowers from the Asian Development Bank.

The EBRD aims to move member countries closer to a full market economy, and invests primarily in private enterprises. Like the other multilateral development banks, the EBRD promotes structural reforms, infrastructure development, and good governance. The Establishing Agreement states that one of the functions of the EBRD is "to promote in the full range of its activities environmentally sound and sustainable development." The EBRD's Environmental Policy, revised in 2003, calls for environmental appraisals for all EBRD-financed projects, which are to identify both negative environmental impacts and potential environmental benefits.

e.   North American Development Bank

In 1993, the United States and Mexico entered into an agreement for the border areas of the two countries to establish a Border Environment Commission and a North American Development Bank. As a subregional development bank, the NADB has a more narrow focus than the larger regional development banks. It concentrates exclusively on financing environmental infrastructure projects that are certified by the Border Environment Cooperation Commission (BECC), located in Ciudad Juarez, Mexico. The NADB and BECC share a board of directors and act interdependently, with BECC verifying the technical feasibility and environmental integrity of the projects seeking financing from the NADB, as well as ensuring community support for the project.

The NADB is governed and funded equally by the United States and Mexico. Eligible communities must be located within 100 kilometers (about 62 miles) north of the international boundary in the United States and within 300 kilometers (about 186 miles) south of the border in Mexico. The Bank provides financial assistance to both public and private sector entities. The primary focus has been on potable water supply, wastewater treatment and municipal solid waste management.

f.   The Asian Infrastructure Investment Bank (AIIB)

On 24 October 2014, twenty-one Asian States agreed to establish a new multilateral development bank that would focus on building infrastructure, such as roads and communication services, in poorer parts of Asia. On 29 June 2015, the AIIB was launched in Beijing, with 50 States signing the new Articles of Agreement. These included in addition to Asian countries and countries in the Middle East, many western European countries, including France, Germany, Italy, Netherlands, Portugal, Spain and the United Kingdom. All 50 States are regarded as Foundiing Members. The Countries have until December 2015 to sign the Agreement and until December 2016 to ratify it. The Agreement becomes effective when 10 members with 50% of the shares have ratified the agreement, which is expected before the end of 2015. The AIIB is headquartered in Beijing, China.

The Articles of Agreement provide that the AIIB will focus on infrastructure and "other productive sectors." (Article 1). The authorized capital is $100 billion, with $20 billion to be paid-in and $80 billion to be callable capital.

China led the effort to establish the AIIB. Her position has been that Asia suffers from a massive gap in the funding needed for infrastructure, which the Asian Development Bank and the World Bank cannot fill and which the new AIIB will fill. Neither Japan nor the United States signed the Agreement at its launch. The United States is concerned in particular about the implications of the new Bank for the World Bank and the Asian Development, which have been the major multilateral development banks in the Asia region.

The new AIIB will need to develop policies and practices regarding governance, debt, and procurement, and address whether there will be safeguard policies associated with its infrastructure investments in Asian countries. Infrastructure projects have traditionally raised important issues related to environmental, social and cultural protections. There will also be questions of how to ensure accountability to member States for the AIIB's projects. As discussed below in this chapter, safeguards and accountability have been important for other multilateral development banks.

NOTES AND QUESTIONS

1.   *Do we need another infrastructure development bank?* Why would China decide to fund a new multilateral bank rather than provide more funds to the Asian Development Bank or the World Bank? To what extent might China's and other countries' concerns about the pace of governance reforms in these institutions play a role? Note also that the President of the Asian Development Bank traditionally has been from Japan and that of the World Bank from the United States.

2.   *Links with the Asian Development Bank and the World Bank?* Both the Asian Development Bank and the World Bank have infrastructure projects in Asia. How will the three Banks interact? Could there be co-funding arrangements? Whose policies would apply?

3. ENVIRONMENTAL AND SOCIAL IMPACTS OF ACTIONS FUNDED BY MDBS

As described above, the World Bank and other MDBs finance a wide range of projects and policy reforms in support of economic development in developing countries. Many of these activities, however, have generated major adverse social and environmental impacts. These impacts have been most apparent, perhaps, in cases of large infrastructure projects such as dams, irrigation and drainage systems, and energy and transport development projects. Loans targeted towards policy reform can produce major social and environmental consequences, especially when applied to sectors such as forests, mining, agriculture, energy, trade and investment, and the like. Because policy loans may influence a wide range of activities across a sector or policy domain, they may produce impacts at an even larger scale than individual projects.

In the late 1980s and early 1990s, public concern over the negative impacts of MDB-funded projects and policy reforms reached an especially high pitch. Many perceived the MDBs to operate in a non-transparent manner, outside public view. Borrowing countries sometimes perceived that Bank officials believed they had the authority to dictate decisions largely on their own terms. Local communities and poor people affected by MDB-funded projects had little or no means even to learn about, much less influence, project decisions, even though those projects might affect them greatly. Some pressed the view that the institutions were doing more harm than good, and had outlived their usefulness. So, said some to the World Bank, "fifty years is enough."

In light of these concerns, the World Bank by the early 1990s had adopted a number of new *"safeguard policies"* designed to address potential social and environmental impacts of Bank-financed projects and programs. The environmental and social safeguard policies cover environmental assessment, natural habitats, forests, pesticides, indigenous peoples, cultural resources, involuntary resettlement, forests and safety of dams. Most have been revised one or more times.[1] As examples of the safeguard policies, the policy on environmental assessment calls for analyzing environmental impacts and alternatives, with the detail of the analysis depending upon how the project is classified. The policy on indigenous peoples provides for preparing an indigenous peoples development plan if such people will be affected by the project. The policy on natural habitats provides that the Bank does not support projects that, in its opinion, involve the significant conversion or degradation of critical habitat. The policy on involuntary resettlement calls upon the Bank to avoid involuntary resettlement where feasible or, if not, to assist displaced persons to improve or at least restore their livelihoods and standards of living. Several policies contain provision that call for meaningful consultations with locally affected people and communities, as a means to identify issues and promote informed and better decision-making in projects.

---

[1] A full list of current World Bank operational policies and procedures is contained at www.worldbank.org.

These safeguards are detailed in a series of operational policies and procedures (OPs and BPs), which are binding upon the Bank in the design, appraisal and implementation of Bank-funded projects. The safeguard policies mark important new ground in international law, and offer an avenue to advance the integration of economic, social and environmental policy dimensions in support of sustainable development, a basic goal of the international development agenda for many years.

In 2012, the World Bank began a review of these safeguard policies and the operational Policy on Piloting the Use of Borrower systems for Environmental and Social Safeguards. The Bank has proposed a new, significantly diluted set of draft safeguard policies, which largely shifts the responsibility for these issues to the borrowing country and relies primarily on the policies and procedures the borrower has in place. The Bank has engaged in several phases of consultations with interested stakeholders, including civil society. Nongovernmental organizations in particular have been concerned about the implications of this development for the well-being of people living in poverty and for sustainable development. In April 2014, 300 nongovernmental organizations signed a statement opposing the new draft policies. As of July 2015, the proposed policies were still in draft. One key controversy has been whether to continue to have any safeguard policy for indigenous peoples, with nearly all countries in Latin America firmly supporting the need for such a policy and several countries in Africa opposed on the grounds that their peoples are all indigenous. The latter countries want to be able to opt out of indigenous peoples provisions. The draft policies do not include a policy on supervision, unlike the existing policies.

NOTES AND QUESTIONS

1.   *Multiple policies, multiple sources of financing.* Each of the MDBs has its own environmental and social policies. How do you ensure that they are consistent with each other? What problems do you foresee from the borrower's point of view in complying with policies from different sources of funding?

2.   *Best practices.* If you were advising the new AIIB about best practices on safeguard policies for protecting the environment and ways to ensure accountability, how might you determine best practices and what might you recommend?

4.   PROMOTING ACCOUNTABILITY FOR COMPLYING WITH POLICIES AND PROCEDURES

In the early 1990s concern was widespread that the Bank was failing to comply with its existing social and environmental policies and procedures, and had systemic features that prevented their effective integration into Bank operations. Consider the following excerpt, which briefly summarizes the history behind the creation of the Inspection Panel:[2]

THE WORLD BANK'S NEW INSPECTION PANEL: WILL IT INCREASE THE BANK'S ACCOUNTABILITY?
David Hunter and Lori Udall
Center for International Environmental Law, Brief No. 1 (April 1994)

For the past decade, the World Bank has been the target of increasing criticism directed at systematic and pervasive problems in its loan portfolio. Of special concern is the lackluster environmental and social record of Bank projects and programs. Indeed, the Bank has financed a seemingly endless line of poorly designed, environmentally damaging development projects, including the Sardar Sarovar dam in western India, the Yacyretá water project on the Argentine-Brazil border, the Pak Mun dam in Thailand, the Polonoroeste project in the Brazilian Amazon, the Transmigration project and Kedung Ombo dam in Indonesia, and several forestry projects in Cote d'Ivoire and Gabon.

Numerous case studies by nongovernmental organizations (NGOs) and other researchers have also documented the lack of openness in the Bank's decision-making process that continues to undermine the institution's ability to promote environmentally responsible and socially progressive projects despite numerous reforms at the Bank, including establishment of an environment department, issuance of environmental and social policies and guidelines, and increased lending for programs that should benefit the environment and poverty-stricken areas.

In 1992, two Bank-sponsored studies brought even more attention to fundamental problems at the Bank. First, a high level, independent review of India's Sardar Sarovar projects uncovered the Bank's widespread failure to implement its resettlement and energy policies and loan agreements. The so-called Morse Commission concluded that the "problems besetting the Sardar Sarovar projects are more the rule than the exception to resettlement operations supported by the Bank" (Morse Commission 1992). India subsequently withdrew its request for additional funding for Sardar Sarovar, but the questions raised in the independent review about the Bank's appraisal process, its adherence to operational policies, and its lack of public accountability remained. The Morse Commission's well-documented investigation and clear analysis inspired the later efforts to create an inspection panel.

Shortly after the release of the Morse Commission report, an internal review of the Bank's loan portfolio (World Bank 1992) was leaked to the public. Now known as the Wapenhans report, the review criticized the

---

[2] *See also* Clark, Fox & Treakle, Demanding Accountability: Civil Society Claims and the World Bank Inspection Panel (2003); Accountability at the World Bank, The Inspection Panel at 15 Years, IBRD 2009.

quality of the Bank's portfolio and found that the Bank was not enforcing fully 78 percent of financial conditions in the loan agreements. Using the Bank's own criteria, the reviewers discovered that 37.5 percent of recently evaluated projects were unsatisfactory, up from 15 percent in 1981. The report linked the decline in project quality to a "pervasive" "culture of approval" for loans, whereby Bank staff members perceive the appraisal process as merely a "marketing device for securing loan approval," and pressure to lend overwhelms all other considerations.

5. THE WORLD BANK INSPECTION PANEL

As suggested by the above, the Inspection Panel was the result of controversy over Bank compliance with its policies and a combination of internal and external pressures. These pressures included both an internal review that criticized the effectiveness of World Bank operations and external concerns, including those from the U.S. Congress.

The 1993 Resolution established the Panel as an independent body that responds to complaints by people who believe that they are suffering, or may suffer, harm caused by a World Bank-financed project. In response to such a complaint, the Panel has authority to investigate whether the Bank is failing to comply with its operational policies and procedures in the design, appraisal and implementation of Bank-funded projects, resulting in harm to affected people. The Panel reports to the Board, and is independent of Management and Staff. The Resolution refers to the Panel as *"an independent Inspection Panel."*

The Panel process is centered on the notion of giving a voice to local people around the world who believe that they are being harmed by World Bank financed projects or programs, through the power of independent and factual investigation of submitted claims. Under the Panel's mandate, a Request for Inspection may be submitted by: two or more affected people; a local organization or other duly appointed representative, on behalf of the affected people; in exceptional circumstances, if no local representative is available, a foreign organization; or an Executive Director of the World Bank. In practice, a request usually comes from many people, in some cases more than a thousand individuals. This direct connection to the people affected by Bank-funded projects, and to the places they live, is crucial to the Panel process and to its ability to gather facts, determine instances of non-compliance with Bank policies and procedures, including those beyond the social and environmental safeguard policies, and identify impacts. Some of these features of the Inspection Panel are described in the excerpt below.

a.   The Inspection Panel's Structure

ACCOUNTABILITY AT THE WORLD BANK: THE INSPECTION PANEL 10 YEARS ON

Inspection Panel, 2003 [as edited with 2014 data]

PURPOSE AND SCOPE OF THE PANEL

The primary purpose of the Inspection Panel is to address the concerns of people who might be affected by Bank projects and to ensure that the Bank adheres to its operational policies and procedures in the design, preparation, and implementation of such projects. The approved procedure for the Panel embodies a fundamental innovation in the history of international financial institutions (IFIs). . . . The Panel represented the first time any IFI had provided a direct link between its governing body—in this case, the Board of Executive Directors—and the people whom its projects are intended to benefit. This was also the first time any IFI had provided a means of appeal—a safety net—in the event that its own standards might not have been met, thus possibly resulting in harm.

INDEPENDENCE OF THE INSPECTION PANEL

. . . The Board of Executive Directors believed that those objectives could be met only if the Panel was completely independent of Bank Management. They accordingly made it clear in the Resolution establishing the Panel that, even though funded by the Bank, the Panel would be completely independent from Bank Management. Therefore, the Panel reports directly to the Bank's Board; its reports go directly to the Board without being reviewed by any other party, including Bank Management, or by those who submit a Request for Inspection. The reports are published exactly as written. . .

COMPOSITION OF THE INSPECTION PANEL

[The Panel consists of three Panel members of different nationalities, who are selected for five year nonrenewable terms, and a small permanent Secretariat. The Bank's President, after consulting with the Executive Directors, nominates Panel members, who are then appointed for a period of 5 years by the Bank's Board.

The members of the Panel cannot work for the World Bank again after their service on the Panel. They cannot be removed from office except "for cause." . . . The Chair of the Panel works full-time, the other two members part-time, as the workload requires. (As of 2014, a second of the three Panel members also works full-time).

The Panel is supported by a small Secretariat that is functionally independent of Bank Management and is responsible solely to the Panel. The Panel can also call on its own external consultants to provide expert knowledge on any matters relevant to an investigation. In 1994, the

Panel adopted its own administrative procedures, which were designed (among other things) to promote efficiency and integrity of the Secretariat. (The procedures were modified in 2013.)]

---

b.   Inspection Panel's Authority

The Operating Procedures of the Inspection Panel specify that the Panel is authorized to accept Requests for Inspection "which claim that an actual or threatened material adverse effect on the affected party's rights or interests arises directly out of an action or omission of the Bank as a result of a failure by the Bank to follow its own operational policies and procedures during the design, appraisal and/or implementation of a Bank-financed project." The Panel has jurisdiction over projects and programmes that may also have financing from IFC or MIGA, so long as some World Bank or IDA financing is involved. The Panel also has jurisdiction over projects of the Global Environment Facility. Before submitting a request, some exhaustion of administrative remedies is required: steps should have been taken to bring the matter to the attention of the management, and a response received that was unsatisfactory to the requester. Operating Procedures, Article 1. The Panel is not authorized to deal with the following:

(a) complaints with respect to actions which are the responsibility of other parties . . . ;

(b) complaints against procurement decisions by Bank borrowers from suppliers of goods and services financed or expected to be financed by the Bank under a loan/credit agreement, or from losing tenderers for the supply of any such goods and services, which will continue to be addressed by Bank staff under existing procedures;

(c) requests filed after the Closing Date of the loan/credit financing the project . . . ; or

(d) requests related to a particular matter or matters over which the Panel has already made its recommendation after having received a prior Request, unless justified by new evidence. . . .

Operating Procedures, Article 2. The Panel registered all Requests unless a Request contravened one of the above provisions. In 2013, the Panel changed its operating procedures, so that Requests must be evaluated further beyond the above criteria, before the Panel will register them. For those who send the Request, it means that they are not sure whether it will become public even if it meets the criteria above, which reportedly has undermined confidence among affected people in the process.

c. Determining Whether a Request Is Eligible for an Investigation

Within 21 working days after a Request is registered, Bank management must provide a response providing evidence that it has complied or intends to comply with the Bank's policies and procedures. After receiving management's response, the panel has 21 working days in which to issue its report and recommendation as to whether the matter meets the criteria for an investigation. The Board of the Executive Directors decides on a non-objection basis whether to accept the Panel's recommendation. Before issuing its report, the Panel usually visits the country to meet with the Requesters and to visit the area of concern.

d. Panel Investigations

An investigation is a fact-finding process. If the Panel conducts an investigation, it generally engages one or more experts to assist with the specific issues. The Panel interviews relevant Bank staff, reviews all relevant Bank documents, visits the country and meets with affected people, government officials, and other interested persons, and reviews other relevant documents. After the Panel completes its Investigation Report, Management has 6 weeks to prepare its Response and Action Plan in response to any findings of noncompliance. The Board of Executive Directors then meets to consider both the Panel's report and Management's Response and Action Plan and makes decisions. All of the reports are made public shortly after the Board meeting.

e. Experience of the Inspection Panel

As of August 2014, the Panel had received 96 formal Requests for Investigation dealing with a wide variety of Bank-supported projects and programs, such as disposal of municipal wastes, land reform, extractive industries, including pipelines and mining, large infrastructure projects, including dams, and structural adjustment loans. The number of requests has risen in recent years. From March 2014 through July 2014, it received 5 Requests, only one of which had been registered under the revised Panel Operating Procedures as of August 2014. Two were under review, and two had been rejected as not meeting the Panel's new admissibility criteria for registration.

A forest project involving logging concessions in Cambodia illustrates the Panel's work. On January 28, 2005, the NGO Forum on Cambodia submitted a Request on behalf of a number of local, forest-dependent communities in Cambodia. They claimed that the communities were suffering harm, and would continue to suffer harm, as a result of failures by the Bank to comply with its social and environmental safeguard policies in the design and implementation of a Bank-financed project in the forest-sector of Cambodia.

Under the Project, the Bank committed to work with the Cambodian government to develop forest management and operational guidelines and control procedures, and to establish an effective forest crime monitoring and prevention capability. The local people complained, however, that the Bank violated its Forestry Policy, among others, by assisting and supporting concession companies with track-records of illegal and abusive logging. The NGO Forum on Cambodia argued that the Project failed to take the necessary steps to identify and protect the interest and rights of local communities and indigenous peoples in the forests targeted by the concession companies, and feared that the Project would lead to support for destructive logging in areas of great biological diversity, and of direct cultural and spiritual significance to the surrounding peoples.

The Panel found the Request to be eligible for Inspection and recommended it for full investigation, which the Board authorized on a no-objection basis. In its investigation, the Panel met with Requesters and local communities in Cambodia, government authorities, and other members of civil society including experts, NGOs, and representatives of the concession companies. The Panel also carried out fact-finding interviews with Bank staff in Washington, Bangkok and Phnom Penh. The Panel retained experts on forest issues, social and indigenous peoples issues, and environmental assessment and natural habitat issues, to assist in its investigation, including experts with extensive knowledge of Cambodia and the region.

The Panel submitted its final investigation report to the Board of Directors on March 30, 2006.[3] The Report included an overview of forests and society in Cambodia, stretching back into past years of conflict and, in the early 1990's, periods of heavy deforestation. The Report described the difficult choices facing decision-makers in Cambodia, noting the potential commercial values of timber and, on the other hand, the rights and interests in the forests of the rural poor and of indigenous peoples, many of whom lived in the heart of areas set for concession operations. The Report noted that for indigenous people the forests comprise their cultural and spiritual home, and described how they depend on and use forests in a great variety of ways. The Report also described the "world-class" ecological value of the forests, including rare bottomland forests having high biodiversity and home to internationally-listed endangered species.

The Panel noted the challenging context for work in the forest sector in Cambodia, and commended Bank Management, in principle, for engaging in this work. It found, however, that *"the Bank chose to give primary emphasis in the Project's design to the technical and financial aspects of concession reform at the expense of environmental and social*

---

[3]   The Final Investigation Report, the Management Action Plan, and other key documents are *available at* www.inspectionpanel.org.

aspects." The Panel found that the *"Project's design created a structure likely to lead to inadequate levels of local involvement, community consultations, and social and environmental assessments . . . ,"* which was not in compliance with Bank Forestry Policy (OP 4.36) and other Bank policies. The Panel found that while the Project *"did not explicitly support the significant conversion of natural habitats . . . the Project design and planning did not adequately recognize the existence of natural habitats, and particularly critical natural habitats."* This was not consistent with OP/BP 4.04 on Natural Habitats. The Panel found that the close association of the Project with when and how logging could occur (e.g., by providing advice and assistance to the concession approval process) had the potential for very significant impacts, and that the Bank's failure to designate the Project as *"Category A"* (linked to Projects having relatively higher levels of potential impacts) led to an inadequate environmental assessment of the Project and did not comply with OD 4.01 on Environmental Assessment.

With respect to the Project decision to defer identification of the affected population within the Project areas, and to develop an Indigenous Peoples Development Plan under OD 4.20 on Indigenous Peoples, the Panel found *"that a safeguard postponed is a safeguard denied, because by failing to identify beforehand the affected population, the Bank policies requiring consultation and participation of that population could not be properly followed."* The Panel noted failures of Management to identify and respond to, the claims and interests of local communities in resin trees and resin harvesting as a source of their livelihoods.

On the other hand, the Panel recognized that Management took a number of steps to attempt to address problems that arose in this complex and difficult situation. The Panel stated, for example, that *"overall Bank activity and discussions with the Government over the past decade, in combination with those of other important donors, may have ameliorated to some extent the damage to the forests and rural people in Cambodia by repeatedly raising the issue with Government at multiple levels."* The Panel also highlighted Management's letter to the Government of Cambodia in November 2005, noting flaws in the concession proposals and recommending appropriate action consistent with law to *"bring this unsatisfactory state of affairs to a quick conclusion."* It also noted the value for the Government to consider "expansion of community or commune-based forest protection and/or land titling for small holders."

The Management Response to the Panel Report, submitted to the Board of Directors on May 30, 2006, proposed both short-term and medium-term actions in response to the Panel's findings. Many elements of the action plan built upon the November 2005 letter, and appeared to suggest a new way forward in implementing environmental and social safeguards in forest-sector projects in Cambodia and other countries. The Action Plan highlighted, among other elements, the need to increase transparency and public participation in decision-making, greater emphasis on community and commune level planning and management of natural resources, the need for Indigenous Peoples Development Plans in such situations, and support for use and/or tenure rights of local communities. The Board of Directors approved the action plan and requested Management to report back in six months. As in many other such cases, the key question became how well these new commitments would be implemented, and how insights from this case would be taken on board in the future.

Another Panel case involved a Bank-financed urban transport project in Mumbai, India (the "MUTP" or "Project"), which illustrates a different set of issues. The Project, approved by the Bank in 2002 with IDA funding, was designed to expand road and rail transport infrastructure in Mumbai. It involved the demolition of homes and commercial shops and the displacement of over 100,000 people. It was the largest urban resettlement Project that the Bank had undertaken anywhere other than in China.

In 2004, the Panel received four successive requests from organizations and associations in Mumbai, complaining that the Bank had failed to meet, *inter alia*, its policy on Involuntary Resettlement Project. Among other things, the Requesters claimed that the Bank was failing to provide adequate income restoration for those displaced by the Project, failed to take into account the particular needs of shop-keepers being displaced, and was resettling people to sites with very poor environmental and living conditions.

After the Panel determined that the Requests (consolidated into one for purposes of economy and efficiency) were eligible for an investigation and the Board authorized it, the Panel carried out an intensive investigation in 2005. This included several visits to Mumbai, interviews with affected people at all levels of government, identification and review of relevant Bank and other documents, staff interviews, meetings with nongovernmental organizations, and input from experts on environmental assessment and social issues.

The Panel submitted its final Investigation Report to the Bank's Board of Directors on December 21, 2005. The Report found many significant instances of Bank non-compliance under OD 4.30 and other policies. These included: virtually no analysis of resettlement risks at the time of Project appraisal; inadequate institutional capacity for the resettlement; overlooking the particular needs of the shopkeepers in the resettlement; failures of planning and consultation; lack of attention to income restoration; and unsuitable living conditions at resettlement sites.

The Panel noted that certain actions were at the root of many of these problems, including a decision to disband what was originally a free-standing project on resettlement, and make the resettlement efforts a sub-component of the transport Project. This resulted in a lesser focus on resettlement and a failure to identify the different needs of shopkeepers affected by the widening of the road, and diverted efforts away from developing the necessary institutional capacity to achieve such a massive resettlement.

The Management Response to this Report was notable. Taking into consideration the Panel findings, Management suspended disbursements on the road and resettlement components of the MUTP. Its Response proposed that lifting of the suspension be subject to satisfactory completion of a number of specified actions to address problems identified. The proposed actions focused on remedying problems relating to planning, the shopkeepers, conditions at the resettlement site, and capacity within the implementing agency to achieve policy-consistent resettlement. The Board of Directors approved these actions and proposals at its meeting on March 28, 2006. The Board also asked Management to submit a progress report to the Board in six months, and the Panel also to report on progress to the Board.

The Mumbai case offers a study on how accountability mechanisms, such as the World Bank Inspection Panel, can achieve their intended purposes—to give voice to local people who believe that they are being harmed by a Bank-funded project, to use objective and independent fact-finding as a means to investigate the claims, to examine whether the Bank is meeting its policy commitments in practice, and to put this information before the decision-making body. The case also highlights the importance of an effective Response by Management to the Investigation Report as part of the overall process, as well as of the follow-up.

A number of observers and experts have written about the experiences of the Inspection Panel and lessons learned. Consider the following excerpt written early in the Panel's history:

DEMANDING ACCOUNTABILITY: CIVIL-SOCIETY CLAIMS AND THE WORLD BANK INSPECTION PANEL
Dana Clark, Jonathan Fox & Kay Treakle eds., 2003

The Inspection Panel has inserted a key political concept into the World Bank's governance model—that the institution must be accountable to the people directly affected by its lending. The Inspection Panel has given increased legitimacy to the claims of local people affected by the World Bank, and it serves as a forum through which their voices have been amplified within the institution. The panel represents the bank's formal acknowledgement of civil-society actors as stakeholders with rights and interests that are affected by the bank's decisions and operations. Thus, an important test of its effectiveness is whether the claims filed have had any impact on the projects they address. The Panel has also been a catalyst for broader change at the World Bank. In particular, it has heightened the debate about the bank's commitment to, and effectiveness in, promoting environmentally sustainable development, through the lens of its environmental and social safeguard policies. Another test of the panel's effectiveness, then, is its impact on the institution. . . .

. . . Through the Inspection Panel process, claimants have sought to receive adequate compensation for being forcibly displaced; to demand implementation of environmental protection and mitigation measures; to have their livelihoods restored; to receive support for social programs; to prevent threatened harm by stopping or delaying potentially destructive projects; and to hold the bank accountable for its role in causing their problems. . . .

The Panel does not have the power to issue an injunction, stop a project, or award financial compensation for harm suffered. Rather, the most that the panel can do is produce a public report with the impartial findings of its investigation. It is up to the board, after reviewing the panel's report of its investigation, to announce whether remedial measures will be undertaken. . . .

6. OTHER INTERNATIONAL ACCOUNTABILITY MECHANISMS

Since the creation of the World Bank Inspection Panel, other regional multilateral development banks, as well as the International Finance Corporation within the World Bank Group, have established their own international accountability and recourse mechanisms.

a. The Compliance Advisor/Ombudsman (CAO) of the International Finance Corporation

In 1999, the World Bank created the CAO with the mandate to act as an independent neutral party to resolve complaints by individuals, groups or communities affected by projects supported by the International Finance Corporation (IFC) and Multilateral Investment Guarantee Agency (MIGA). Unlike the Inspection Panel, the CAO is structurally linked to the President of the World Bank, not to the Board of Executive Directors. Under the CAO procedures, the complainants may be an individual, community or organization, such as an NGO, representing members of an affected community. The complaint may relate to actions by a company that is borrowing IFC funds or by an investor that is covered by a MIGA guarantee. Such companies and investors are expected to carry out projects in compliance with the environmental and social policies and procedures of IFC/MIGA. The IFC adopted a new set of environmental and social performance standards in 2006, and revised them in 2012.

In its role as Ombudsman, CAO tries to facilitate a collectively agreed solution to the complaint of the affected parties. As part of this process, CAO meets with the parties, examines files and conducts site visits, provides a report to the President of the World Bank Group and the parties on the nature of the complaint and possible ways to resolve it.

CAO also may determine whether a "compliance audit" is appropriate. A compliance audit consists of an independent assessment of whether IFC and MIGA have materially complied with the policies, guidelines and procedures for investing (IFC) or providing political risk insurance (MIGA).

CAO also acts as an advisor to the World Bank President and to IFC and MIGA Management, both in relation to specific projects and to broader questions of policies, procedures and resources.

b. **The Accountability Mechanism of the Asian Development Bank (AsDB)**

In 1995, the AsDB created its own inspection mechanism. By the year 2003, however, this mechanism had received only a small number of claims. In May 2003, the AsDB created a new accountability mechanism to replace the existing inspection function.

This new AsDB mechanism consists of two related functions: consultation and compliance review. The first function involves a process of consultation among stakeholders, focused on problem solving. If a satisfactory solution to the problems cannot be achieved, a complaint for consultation is ineligible, or the consultation process is at an advanced stage and there are compliance concerns, then a request may be made for compliance review.

The consultation phase is led by a facilitator who seeks to help reach agreement among concerned parties, which may include the complainant, the implementer of the project, the involved government or private sector sponsor, and the AsDB. The facilitator reports directly to the President of AsDB. The compliance review is carried out by an independent Compliance Review Panel. If an investigation is approved, the Panel conducts an investigation and makes recommendations to the AsDB Board of Directors to ensure project compliance with AsDB operational policies and procedures, including recommended remedial changes in project scope or implementation. Complaints may be filed by two or more people in the country of the AsDB-assisted project, by a local representative, a non-local representative in certain exceptional cases, or a member of the Board.

c. Others

Other regional development banks have also established accountability and recourse mechanisms in recent years. These include: the Independent Investigation Mechanisms of the Inter-American Development Bank, the Independent Review Mechanisms of the African Development Bank, and the Independent Recourse Mechanism of the European Bank of Reconstruction and Development. Other similar mechanisms have been developed at the national level in some countries, including the Examiner for Environmental Guidelines of the Japan Bank for International Cooperation; the Compliance Officer for Export Development Canada; and at one time, the Office of Accountability of the Overseas Private Investment Corporation (OPIC) of the United States, which no longer exists.

In addition, there are other international fact-finding and accountability mechanisms working on environment-related issues that are not associated with financial institutions. One important example, discussed in a previous chapter, is the Commission for Environmental Cooperation created under the North American Agreement on Environmental Cooperation, to which individuals and groups can complain about a failure to enforce environmental laws in the member country.

NOTES AND QUESTIONS

1. *Inspection panels and international law.* Some have characterized inspection panels as being a major development in international law in that they provide people affected by projects and programs access to the decision-making and adjudication processes of international organizations, where that access was traditionally reserved to States. *See, e.g.,* Ibrahim I.F. Shihata, The World Bank Inspection Panel 119 (1994). Do you draw the same conclusions from your brief introduction to this new institution? What is the value of giving voice to affected people? Assuming an Inspection Panel represents a new development in accountability in international law, as counsel to an NGO, how would you advise your organization to take advantage of the availability of such a panel and related mechanisms?

2. *When should the Affected People see the Investigation Report?* The Resolution establishing the World Bank Inspection Panel specifies that the Panel's Investigation Report, as well as the Management Response to the Report, shall be made publicly available within two weeks after the Board considers the Report. The Panel's Report, however, is completed and submitted to the Board well before the Board meeting, and Management is given six weeks to review the Report (not yet publicly available) and prepare

its Response. Consider the following excerpt from Clark, Fox & Treakle, *supra*, at 267:

> . . . there is a stark imbalance in access between the two adversarial parties—the claimants and management—once the panel has developed its final report to the board. At that point, management has the opportunity to react and provide recommendations to the board about how to resolve any identified policy violations. The claimants, in contrast, have no right to comment on what remedial measures would be appropriate to bring the project into compliance or rectify the harm that they have suffered. Thus, the board tends to adopt management-generated action plans, ignoring the experience, knowledge, and preferences of the people who have triggered the process in the first place.

Taking into consideration this critique, do you think that Inspection Panel Investigation Reports should be made available to requesters, and the public more generally, as soon as they are completed, before consideration by the Board of Executive Directors? Would the requirement that Management consult with the affected people in developing its response respond to the concerns expressed? If so, what would you advise Management that it had to provide to the affected people about the Report? What about the Management Response? Should it be made publicly available before the Board meeting? Are there strong reasons to argue for not releasing the reports until after the Board meeting?

7. WORLD BANK AND IFC LENDING

a. The World Bank's Country Systems Approach

Some borrowing countries and others have criticized the safeguard policies on the grounds that they are inflexible, do not respect the borrower countries policies sufficiently, increase transaction costs, and limit the impact of development assistance. Some argue that it is patronizing for an international institution to impose a set of safeguard policies upon a country, when it could rely on the country's own system to accomplish the same ends. This has led in part to the review of the safeguard policies considered earlier in the chapter.

Since 2004, the Bank has begun to work more directly with borrowing countries' institutions and systems. The Bank's use of country systems, as this approach is called, includes utilizing the country's legal and institutional framework, consisting of its national, sub-national, or sectoral implementing institutions and applicable laws, regulations, rules, and procedures. A pilot program launched in 2004, Operational Policy/Bank Procedure (OP/BP) 4.00, focused on using borrower countries' environmental and social safeguard systems. This operational policy is included as part of the safeguard policy review.

A major component of the use of country systems involves assessing the equivalency of borrower country fiduciary institutions. These assessments are made by Bank management. However, critics argue that the Bank's proposal would allow equivalency assessments to be made on future commitments—agreed improvements—rather than judgments based on a country's existing capacity and track record. The Center for International Environmental Law, in analyzing the new policy, stated: "This could allow a country to achieve 'equivalency' without actually having the necessary rules and regulations in place to ensure that even the relatively weak principles would be met."

One issue that arose was whether the use of country systems would affect the jurisdiction of the Inspection Panel, either at the project design and appraisal stage or in implementation. This issue was resolved in the Statement below. Note that in the letter the Inspection Panel's jurisdiction has not changed.

JOINT STATEMENT ON THE USE OF COUNTRY SYSTEMS
Edith Brown Weiss & Roberto Danino
(Chairperson, Inspection Panel; General Counsel, IBRD, respectively)
Source: Inspection Panel Annual Report
July 1, 2004 to June 30, 2005, The World Bank (2005)

We are in agreement that the country systems strategy would not change the role of the Inspection Panel as set forth in the 1993 Resolutions establishing the Panel. The Inspection Panel will continue to investigate whether Management is in compliance with its policies and procedures in the design, appraisal and implementation of projects and programs. This means that if a request were filed with the Inspection Panel in the context of the Mexico Decentralized Infrastructure Reform and Development Loan Project, the Inspection Panel could, with regard to the issues raised, examine Management's assessment of the equivalence of the relevant Bank policies and procedures with the country system (and any additional measures agreed upon to achieve equivalence) in materially achieving the objectives of Bank policies and procedures, as well as Management's supervision of the project. The operational framework for the specific project or program agreed upon with the borrower would be the frame of reference for the borrower's performance and the Bank's supervision.

NOTES AND QUESTIONS

1. *To whom do the policies apply?* World Bank safeguard policies set forth requirements that apply to Bank Management. The policies also may identify responsibilities of the Borrower. For example, OD 4.30 on involuntary resettlement sets forth various requirements upon the Bank, and also states that "*The borrower is responsible for preparing, implementing, and monitoring a resettlement plan, a resettlement policy framework, or a process*

framework . . . , as appropriate, that conform to this policy." The accountability mechanisms, however, assess compliance only by the Bank, and not by the Borrower. Why do you think that the mechanisms are limited in this respect? What effects might this limitation create in an investigation? How, if at all, is the performance of the Borrower to be judged?

2.   *What does equivalence mean?* OP 4.00, dated March 2005, is entitled "Piloting the Use of Borrower Systems to Address Environmental and Social Safeguard Issues in Bank-Supported Project." It provides in part:

> The Bank considers a borrower's environmental and social safeguard system to be equivalent to the Bank's if the borrower's system is designed to achieve the objectives and adhere to the applicable operational principles set out in Table A-1. . . . Before deciding on the use of borrower systems, the Bank also assesses the acceptability of the borrower's implementation practices, track record, and capacity. . . . The Bank is responsible for determining the equivalence and acceptability of borrower systems, and for appraising and supervising pilot projects that use these systems.

What problems do you foresee in making the determination of equivalence? Will it reduce transaction costs? What special problems might you encounter in supervising project implementation? Against what criteria would you supervise? Note that the Bank's policy on supervision still applies when country systems are used. The policy has been under review. The draft proposed safeguard policies do not include a policy on supervision.

3.   In April 2010, the World Bank's Inspection Panel received a Request for Inspection on a project involving coal power plants in South Africa, for which the World Bank approved a $3.75 billion loan. The purpose of the project was to help South Africa achieve a reliable supply of electricity. The World Bank approved the project under the country systems policy. The Request to the Inspection Panel alleged that the power plants would cause negative health and water use impacts and stated that relying on South African laws under the country systems approach was "inadequate to protect peoples' health and well-being." The Inspection Panel found, however, that the World Bank's assessment that the South African laws were equivalent to the World Bank's safeguard measures was "well-founded," and concluded that the application of the country systems was adequate, although the Inspection Panel Report found other problems. The project has subsequently encountered significant problems.

b.   Development Policy Lending

In August 2004, the World Bank replaced Adjustment Lending—one of its main lending instruments—with Development Policy Lending (OP/BP 8.60). The Development Policy Lending (DPL) framework covers lending that supports policy reforms, which as of July 2009 accounted for about 40 percent of Bank lending. DPL includes sectoral adjustment loans, structural adjustment loans and poverty reduction support credits.

The Bank's older policy lending programs were criticized for being too prescriptive and for setting unrealistic timeframes for reform. In contrast, DPL is more flexible, has more emphasis on the role of the private sector, and seeks to ensure broader participation than was the case with previous adjustment lending. The World Bank distinguishes policy lending from its other basic type of lending instrument—investment lending. Traditionally, policy loans were short-term, quick-disbursing, and preceded by an economic crisis. Investment lending has a longer-term focus and finances economic and development projects in a broad range of sectors. Most policy lending is now longer-term programmatic support for complex medium-term structural and institutional changes. Although DPL is more similar to investment lending, it has one crucial difference: social and environmental safeguards do not apply to DPL. OP/BP 8.60 describes Bank policy with regard to environmental considerations:

> 11. Environmental, Forests, and other Natural Resource Aspects. The Bank determines whether specific country policies supported by the operation are likely to cause significant effects on the country's environment, forests, and other natural resources. For country policies with likely significant effects, the Bank assesses in the Program Document the borrower's systems for reducing such adverse effects and enhancing positive effects, drawing on relevant country-level or sectoral environmental analysis. If there are significant gaps in the analysis or shortcomings in the borrower's systems, the Bank describes in the Program Document how such gaps or shortcomings would be addressed before or during program implementation, as appropriate.

Most recently, the World Bank has embarked upon what it terms Program-For-Results operations. These support government programs by strengthening institutions and building capacity. The instrument is intended to link the disbursement of funds directly to the delivery of defined results.

NOTES AND QUESTIONS

1.   Certain types of projects that have been treated as investment loans in some contexts appear as part of development policy lending in other cases. The World Bank has criteria for what qualifies as development policy lending. Do you foresee difficulties in applying the criteria?

2.   Is the provision in Article 11 of OP/BP 8.60 sufficient to ensure adequate environmental protection? How could you tell? What problems do you foresee in implementing the provision?

3.   Note the similarities with the country system approach for investments.

c. The IFC's Policy on Social and Environmental Sustainability

The International Finance Corporation (IFC), the private sector arm of the World Bank Group, adopted new environmental standards, effective as of April 30, 2006 and since updated in 2012. The Policy on Social and Environmental Sustainability (Sustainability Policy) defines IFC's role and responsibility in supporting project performance in partnership with clients. The Sustainability Policy strengthens and expands upon the older Social and Environmental Safeguards. The Sustainability Policy reviews projects proposed for direct financing against eight Performance Standards: social and environmental assessment and management system; labor and working conditions; pollution prevention and abatement; community health, safety and security; land acquisition and involuntary resettlement; biodiversity conservation and sustainable natural resource management; indigenous peoples; and cultural heritage. In 2010, the Independent Evaluation Group (IEG), an independent unit within the World Bank Group, published a report evaluating safeguard measures adopted in the World Bank, the IFC and the Multilateral Investment Guarantee Agency's (MIGA). The report made various recommendations to the three institutions to improve its safeguard measures. In 2012, the IFC's Sustainability Policy was updated in response to some of the concerns expressed by the IEG's evaluation report. Changes include adoption of free, prior, and informed consent (FPIC) from indigenous people in certain circumstances and disclosure requirement on the greenhouse gas emission from its direct investment portfolio. Clients are to meet these standards throughout the life of an investment by IFC.

In 2003, at the initiative of the IFC, ten of the world's largest banks adopted the Equator Principles, which are environmental and social guidelines for "ethical" financing of projects. The 80 banks in 34 countries (as of mid-2014) that are Equator Principles Financial Institutions (EPFIs) all voluntarily agree to follow the Equator Principles in finance deals greater than $10 million. The EPFIs account for more than 70 percent of the world's project financing.

The Equator Principles were significantly revised in July 2006 in order to ensure consistency with the new IFC Performance Standards, and to reflect lessons learned from the implementation of the original Equator Principles. The Equator Principles II were greatly expanded in scope, applying to all project financings with capital costs above $10 million, as compared to the previous threshold of $50 million. All industry sectors are now covered. They also now apply to project finance advisory activities and upgrades or expansions of existing projects.

In June 2013, the third version of Equator Principles ("Equator Principles III") went into effect. The Equator Principles III broadened the applicable scope by adding Project-Related-Corporate Loans and Bridge Loans in addition to Project Finance and Project Finance Advisory. As with the original Equator Principles and the Equator Principles II, the Equator Principles III state that the EPFIs will not provide loans to projects "where the client will not, or is unable to, comply with the Equator Principles." The Principles rely on the IFC's categorization of projects based on the nature and magnitude of a project's environmental and social impacts. For those projects likely to have significant adverse effects, Principle 2 requires that the borrower conduct an Environmental and Social Assessment that addresses relevant impacts and risks and "should propose measures to minimize, mitigate, and offset adverse impacts in a manner relevant and appropriate to the nature and scale of the proposed project." Principle 3 states that the Assessment "should, in the first instance, address compliance with relevant host country laws, regulations and permits that pertain to environmental and social issues" and will refer to the IFC Performance Standards and the World Bank Group EHS Guidelines.

For projects with potentially significant adverse impacts on affected communities, Principle 5 requires clients to conduct an "Informed Consultation and Participation process."[4] One of the significant changes from the Equator Principles II is that the Equator Principles III explicitly refer to indigenous people's rights and concerns. Specifically, Principle 5 states that "[p]rojects with adverse impacts on indigenous people will require their Free, Prior and Informed Consent (FPIC)." As in IFC Performance Standard 1, Equator Principle 6 requires the establishment of a grievance mechanism to facilitate resolution of affected communities' concerns.

The final significant change to the Equator Principles III is the new reporting requirement on GHG emission levels. The original Equator Principles made independent monitoring and reporting optional. The Equator Principles II required independent monitoring of all projects deemed to have significant adverse environmental and social impacts. Under Principle 10 of the Equator Principles III, EPFIs will also require clients to publicly report the GHG emission levels for projects emitting more than 100,000 tonnes of CO_2, and clients are encouraged to report the GHG emission levels for projects emitting more than 25,000 tons.

NOTES AND QUESTIONS

1.   *Consultation and prior informed consent?* What is the significance of the IFC Sustainability Policy and the Equator Principle III regarding "free,

---

[4] Informed Consultation and Participation is an "in-depth exchange of views and information and an organized and iterative consultation that leads the client to incorporate the views of Affected Communities, on issues that affect them directly (such as proposed mitigation measures, the sharing of development benefits and opportunities, and implementation issues), into their decision-making process."

prior, and informed consent (FPIC)" from indigenous people in certain circumstances?

2. *Equator Principles.* The Equator Principles are voluntary, and no banks had to join. Why have so many private banks signed onto the Equator Principles? Are the banks concerned about ensuring a level playing field among themselves for their investments? Is this an effective method of ensuring sustainable development?

3. *Transparency.* Some NGOs believe that the best way to determine whether the Sustainability Policy or Equator Principles are being applied is the number of projects declined by the IFC or the Equator Banks because they do not meet environmental standards. But the private banks contend that this could breach client confidentiality and, moreover, is not an accurate measure of such standards' effectiveness. Is there a better measure by which NGOs, local stakeholders, and banks can determine whether the standards are being correctly applied? What function is served by the new reporting requirement of the Equator Principles? Does it provide transparency?

4. *Financing for fossil fuels.* It has been estimated that in 2005, IFC was the world's largest multilateral financier of fossil fuel extraction. Meanwhile, the IFC devoted a mere 4 percent of its total energy lending to renewable energy sources. Some NGOs contend that the many transactions financed by the IFC and Equator Banks violate the IFC's safeguards policies and the Equator Principles, notably the Baku-Tbilisi-Ceyhan oil pipeline, which has been criticized as having a multitude of potential environmental problems. Complaints have been brought to the CAO at the IFC.

8. BRICS COUNTRIES' NEW DEVELOPMENT BANK

On July 15, 2014, in the Fortaleza Declaration, BRICS countries (Brazil, Russia, India, China and South Africa) announced the establishment of the New Development Bank (NDB). The bank is to serve similar functions as the existing financial institutions of the World Bank and the International Monetary Fund (IMF). The NDB will open with an initial subscribed capital of $50 billion and an initial authorized capital of $100 billion. The NDB will fund infrastructure and sustainable development projects in NDB member countries (with limited exceptions in non-member developing countries) through loans, guarantees and equity participation. It will also provide technical assistance for projects supported by the NDB.

Voting rights of member States would be equal to the number of a State's subscribed shares. As the initial subscribed capital of $50 billion is distributed equally among the five BRICS countries, each BRICS country will have an equal percentage of voting right. Other countries can become members of the NDB subject to approval by the Board of Governors (as described below), but the voting rights of BRICS founding members will not drop below 55 per cent regardless of how many countries join later. A non-founding member country cannot have more than seven percent of total voting power. All matters are decided by a simple majority of the votes cast.

The NDB will be based in Shanghai, China. There will be a first regional office in Johannesburg, South Africa. The first president of the NDB will be from India while the first chair of the Board of Governors will be from Russia and the first chair of the Board of Directors will be from Brazil.

Background

The NDB is aimed to lessen the influence of the World Bank and the IMF, both Bretton Woods institutions, whose presidents have been reserved to the United States and to Europe respectively. Developing countries have been frustrated with the existing institutions because of the unequal allocation of voting rights and rigid conditions attached to loans. In the IMF, the BRICS States account for more than 20 percent of global GDP but only have 10.3 percent of quota (voting rights) while European countries have 27.5 percent of quota even though their GDP only equals 18 percent of global GDP. In 2010, the IMF agreed to reform its structure by doubling the IMF's capital to about \$720 billion and transferring more than 6 percent of quota shares to developing countries. However, the reform has been put on hold pending approval by the United States Congress, which has not been forthcoming as of July 2015.

Structure of the NDB

The NDB will be governed by a Board of Governors, a Board of Directors, a President and Vice-Presidents. The Board of Governors is the highest governing body of the NDB. It will approve new member States of the NDB and elect the President and appoint Vice-Presidents. The Board will consist of one governor and one alternate appointed by each member country of the NDB, and annually select one of the governors as chairperson. There will be no compensation to the Board of Governors from the NDB.

The Board of Directors will be in charge of general operations of the NDB including decisions on loans and furnishing of technical assistance. Each of the BRICS founding members appoints one director and one alternate. The Board of Governors will establish a procedure by which additional Directors would be elected, but the total number of Directors may not exceed ten. Directors will serve a term of two years and may be re-elected. The Board of Directors will appoint a chairperson from among the Directors for a term of 4 years.

A President will be elected from one of the BRICS founding members on a rotational basis. At least one Vice-President will be appointed from each of the other BRICS founding members. Both the President and Vice-Presidents will serve for a non-renewable term of five years (except for the first Vice-Presidents serving six years).

Safeguard Measures

As of July 2015, no safeguard measures had been developed. There is no indication in the official documents whether the NDB is planning to develop safeguard measures. Article 21 (Operational Principles) of the Agreement on the New Development Bank ("Agreement") states that the NDB will apply "sound banking principles" but does not mention whether loans would be conditional on safeguard measures. The Agreement contains a few references to environment and sustainable development. Article 1 states that the purpose and functions of the NDB are to "mobilize resources for infrastructure and *sustainable development* projects" in BRICS and other developing countries. The preamble of the Annex provides that BRICS countries would contribute to "economic and social development *respectful of the global environment.*"

Contingent Reserve Arrangement

BRICS will create a separate $100 billion Contingent Reserve Arrangement (CRA), an emergency currency reserve fund for member countries to use during the time of payments crisis. Unlike the NDB with equal share of capitals by each BRICS founding country, China will contribute $41 billion to the CRA, while Brazil, Russia and India will contribute $18 billion each, and South Africa will contribute $5 billion. As a result of weighted voting based on countries' contribution, China will have the largest voting right.

NOTES AND QUESTIONS

1.   *Interactions with other MDBs.* How could the policies of a new BRICS Development Bank affect those of the other MDBs, especially the World Bank? What legal issues do you foresee?

2.   *The Borrowing States.* From the borrowing State's perspective, what issues do you foresee?

C. GLOBAL ENVIRONMENT FACILITY

1. STRUCTURE

The Global Environment Facility (GEF) is a partnership for international cooperation with 183 countries to protect the global environment and to promote environmental sustainable development. The GEF was established in 1991 as a $1 billion pilot program in the World Bank. After the 1992 Rio Earth Summit, it became a separate institution. Since 1991, the GEF has financed $12.5 billion in grants and leveraged $58 billion in co-financing for 3,690 projects in 165 developing countries.

The GEF provides "grants and concessional funding to cover the 'incremental' or additional costs associated with transforming a project with national benefits into one with global environmental benefits." The GEF provides grants for projects related to the following seven main areas: (1) Biodiversity; (2) Climate Change (Mitigation and Adaptation); (3) Chemicals or Persistent Organic Pollutants (POPs); (4) International Waters; (5) Land Degradation (primarily desertification and deforestation); (6) Sustainable Forest Management/REDD+ [5] ; and (7) Ozone Layer Depletion. The GEF also serves as the financial mechanisms for five major multilateral environmental agreements: the Convention on Biological Diversity (CBD); the United Nations Framework Convention on Climate Change (UNFCCC); the Stockholm Convention on Persistent Organic Pollutants (POPs); the UN Convention to Combat Desertification (UNCCD) and the Minamata Convention on Mercury. The GEF partners with the Montreal Protocol on Substances That Deplete the Ozone Layer and supports countries with economies in transition to phase out their use of ozone-depleting chemicals.

The GEF is primarily governed by the (1) GEF Council and (2) GEF Assembly. The GEF Council is the governing board of directors and has primary responsibility for developing, adopting and evaluating GEF programs. The Council has 32 GEF members: 16 from developing countries, 14 from developed countries, and two from countries with economies in transition. The GEF finances projects carried out by either the Implementing Agencies (UNDP, UNEP and World Bank) or the Executing Agencies (Asian, African, and Inter-American Development Banks, the European Bank for Reconstruction and Development, FAO, IFAD and UNIDO). Loans from multilateral development banks, such as the World Bank, may be coupled with grants provided by GEF. In May 2011, the GEF Council decided to expand its partnerships beyond the 10 existing Agencies and created the GEF Partners for the implementation of GEF projects in order to give States more choice of agencies with which to work. The newly accredited institutions will be referred to as GEF Project Agencies. In November 2013, the World Wildlife Fund, Inc. and the Conservation International were accredited as new GEF Project Agencies. In May 2014, GEF announced that the Development Bank of Southern Africa (DBSA) and the International Union for Conservation of Nature (IUCN) would become GEF Project Agencies. The Instrument for the Establishment of the Restructured Global Environmenal Facility. (March 2015) contains the text of the Instrument as amended through May 2014, decisions by the Implementing Agencies and Trustee, Replenishment Resolutions, and updated Commitments by participating States.

---

[5] Reducing Emissions from Deforestation and Forest Degradation (REDD) is an effort under the UN Framework Convention on Climate Change to create a financial value for the carbon stored in forests and thus, offering incentives for developing countries to reduce emissions from forested lands and to invest in low-carbon paths to sustainable development.

In order to implement GEF-financed projects, all the Implementing and Executing Agencies as well as institutions applying for accreditation as GEF Project Agencies must meet the minimum requirements of the *GEF Policy on Agency Minimum Standards on Environmental and Social Safeguards*. Those institutions must also meet the standards set forth in the *GEF Policy on Gender Mainstreaming*.

The GEF, like the multilateral development banks, has instituted mechanisms for accountability. GEF has its own Conflict Resolution Commissioner and requires implementing partners to have accountability systems or measures in place to receive complaints "to ensure enforcement of its environmental and social safeguard policies and related systems." (Minimum Standard I, Accountability and Grievance Systems (p.20, Policy noted above).

2. PROJECT FUNDING

Like the multilateral development banks, GEF funding is through contributions from donor countries. The GEF administers at least four different trust funds: the Global Environment Facility Trust Fund (GEF Trust Fund); the Least Developed Countries Trust Fund (LDCF); the Special Climate Change Trust Fund (SCCF); and the Nagoya Protocol Implementation Fund (NPIF). The World Bank serves in a fiduciary and administrative capacity as the trustee of the GEF Trust Fund. Resources for the GEF Trust Fund are replenished every four years by countries that wish to contribute to the GEF Trust Fund through a process called the "GEF Replenishment." Countries are eligible to receive GEF grants if they (1) have ratified the relevant treaty and meet eligibility criteria established by the relevant conference of the parties of the treaty (such as the CBD); (2) are eligible to borrow from the World Bank (IBRD and/or IDA); or (3) are eligible recipients of UNDP technical assistance through country programming. The GEF provides grants to four different types of projects: (1) Full-Sized Projects (FSPs) receiving more than US $2 million which must be approved by the GEF Council; (2) Medium-Sized Projects (MSPs) receiving up to US $2 million which can be approved through expedited procedures; (3) Enabling Activities (EAs), which help countries prepare inventories, strategies, action plans and reports for the conventions on biodiversity, climate change and persistent organic pollutants; and (4) Programmatic Approach (PA), which consists of several projects represented by a partnership between countries, the GEF and other stakeholders (private sector or the scientific community) for the purpose of securing a larger-scale and more sustainable impact on the global environment than a single FSP or MSP. Additionally, the Small Grants Programme (SGP), implemented by UNDP and executed by the United Nations Office for Project Services (UNOPS), offers grants up to $50,000 for community-based projects in the GEF focal areas.

Between 1991 and 2014, funding for the original four focal areas was as follows: $3.3 billion in grants matched by $9.8 billion in co-financing for biological diversity; $4.4 billion in grants matched by $30.7 billion in co-financing for climate change; $1.3 billion in grants matched by 7.7 billion in co-financing for international waters; and $189 million in grants matched by $207 million in co-financing to phase out ozone depleting substances. Two other focal areas were approved in 2002: land degradation and persistent organic pollutants.

3. EFFECTIVENESS OF GEF

GEF ANNUAL PERFORMANCE REPORT (2013)
GEF Evaluation Office (May 2013)

1.1 Background

1. The Annual Performance Report (APR), prepared by the GEF Independent Evaluation Office (IEO), provides a detailed overview of the performance of GEF activities and processes, key factors affecting performance, and the quality of Monitoring and Evaluation systems (M&E) within the GEF partnership. . . .

. . .

3. In total, APR 2013 projects account for $630.8 million in GEF funding and consist of projects for which terminal evaluation reports have been submitted to the GEF IEO from the period October 1, 2012 to December 31, 2013.

Conclusion 1: *Seventy nine percent of projects and 71% of funding in projects in the APR 2013 cohort have outcome ratings in the satisfactory range.*

Conclusion 7: *Around two thirds of completed GEF projects have satisfactory ratings on M&E design and/or M&E implementation. Ratings on M&E implementation for World Bank GEF projects have fallen considerably between the two most recent four year APR year cohorts.*

. . . 136. Some examples of best practices in M&E implementation among completed projects covered in APRs:

- GEF ID 845, *The Greater Berbak Sembilang Integrated Coastal Wetland Conservation Project,* implemented by the World Bank. M&E implementation for this project, which focused on strengthening conservation protections for threatened Indonesian wetlands, is notable for involving a large number of stakeholders, including forest rangers, local NGOs and local villagers in the assessment of biodiversity conditions and threats. To ensure consistent and high quality M&E, the project provided intensive training on wildlife and monitoring survey techniques to the M&E team. As noted in the project's terminal evaluation, local NGOs are likely to replicate the monitoring approach in nearby parks. Moreover, because the evaluation of project performance involved project counterparts and partners, it was "easy to discuss priorities and refocus project activities during implementation."

- GEF ID 2402, *Building Capacity for Participation in the Biosafety Clearing House (BCH),* implemented by UNEP. This project sought to strengthen the capacities of 112 countries to access and use the Biosafety Clearing House— an information repository and knowledge sharing platform established as part of the Cartagena Protocol on Biosafety. With such a large number of country stakeholders, effective implementation of M&E required efficient coordination of monitoring teams and dissemination of M&E findings. This was accomplished through the establishment of a network of regional advisors, on line open information management and knowledge sharing systems, and regional workshops where participants discussed project strengths and weaknesses, sustainability, and lessons learned.

Such meetings "provided important spaces for group reflection, enhancing adaptive management and learning." In addition, project experiences and learning were distilled into a project publication to help further knowledge dissemination and broader adoption of best practices.

In 2014, the nonprofit organization Transparency International released a report evaluating the transparency and accountability features of the Least Developed Countries Fund (LDCF) and Special Climate Change Fund (SCCF) within the Global Environment Facility. Although the report recognized several strong transparency and accountability features, the report highlighted a lack of sanctions against GEF Council members, and recommended making sanctions available to deter wrongdoing by GEF Council members. *See* Transparency International, Protecting Climate Finance: An Anti-Corruption Assessment of the Global Environment Facility's Least Developed Countries Fund & Special Climate Fund 14, 2014.

NOTES AND QUESTIONS

1.   If the World Bank is the implementing agency for GEF projects, the "safeguard policies" of the Bank apply. Because the GEF's safeguard measures derive from World Bank safeguard policies, they must meet the minimum requirements of the *GEF Policy on Agency Minimum Standards on*

Environmental and Social Safeguards. On at least two occasions the World Bank's Inspection Panel accepted complaints from people who believed they were or could be adversely affected by a GEF project (projects in Mexico and in Brazil).

2. What might be done to strengthen the role of GEF in financing sustainable development?

D. EXPORT CREDIT AGENCIES

Virtually all industrialized countries, and some developing countries, have created institutions that assist in financing exports and investment opportunities abroad. These are referred to as Export Credit Agencies (ECAs). They primarily operate by providing below-market-rate financing, guaranteeing loans, or insuring exports or foreign direct investment abroad. ECAs affect a very large amount of international trade and investment, already more than $50 billion per year in 2002.[6]

In the United States, the ECAs are the Export-Import Bank (Ex-Im Bank) and the Overseas Private Investment Corporation (OPIC). Both Ex-Im Bank and OPIC have internal policies directed at ensuring the environmental soundness of the activities. OPIC was a groundbreaker in this regard, for example, attempting to terminate insurance of a project in Indonesia on environmental grounds.

For many years, the United States tried unsuccessfully to convince other countries to adopt similar policies, for example at the Group of 7 Industrialized Countries (G-7) meeting in 1997. It initially had little success: the other countries seemed intent solely on promoting exports or foreign direct investment, without analyzing or otherwise taking into account the environmental and social implications of those activities.

1. THE OECD RECOMMENDATIONS

The Organizaton for Economic Co-operation and Development (OECD) discussed issues of environmental impacts and environmental soundness of projects in itsWorking Party on Export Credit and Export Guarantees (ECG. Building on earlier work of the ECG, the OECD adopted non-binding "Common Approaches" for ECAs with respect to the environmental impacts (defined broadly) of their activities in 2003. Excerpts from the OECD Recommendation follow:

---

[6]   For a listing of ECAs, *see* http://www.people.hbs.edu/besty/projfinportal/ecas.htm.

OECD RECOMMENDATION ON COMMON APPROACHES ON ENVIRONMENT AND OFFICIALLY SUPPORTED EXPORT CREDITS

1.1. THE COUNCIL . . .

Noting that OECD Ministers in 2001 have recognised that export credit policy can contribute positively to sustainable development and should be coherent with its objectives;

RECOMMENDS that Members, before taking decisions on officially supported export credits, apply the following common approaches for identifying and evaluating the environmental impacts of projects and exports of capital goods and services destined to projects (hereafter referred to as "projects"), including the impact on involuntary resettlement, indigenous peoples and cultural property (for the purpose of this Recommendation hereafter referred to as "environmental impacts").

1.2. I. GENERAL PRINCIPLES

i) Scope

1. This Recommendation applies to officially supported export credits for projects with a repayment term of two years or more.

ii) Objectives

2. The general objectives of this Recommendation are to:

- Promote coherence between policies regarding officially supported export credits and policies for the protection of the environment, including relevant international agreements and conventions, thereby contributing towards sustainable development.

- Develop common procedures and processes relating to the environmental review of projects benefiting from officially supported export credits, with a view to achieving equivalence among the measures taken by the Members and to reducing the potential for trade distortion.

- Promote good environmental practice and consistent processes for projects benefiting from officially supported export credits, with a view to achieving a high level of environmental protection.

- Enhance efficiency of official support procedures by ensuring that the administrative burden for applicants and export credit agencies is commensurate with the environment protection objectives of this Recommendation.

- Promote a level playing field for officially supported export credits.

3.   To achieve these objectives, Members seek to:

- Foster transparency, predictability and responsibility in decision-making, by encouraging disclosure of relevant environmental information with due regard to any legal stipulations, business confidentiality and other competitive concerns.

- Encourage the prevention and the mitigation of the adverse environmental impacts of projects.

- Enhance financial risk assessment of projects by taking into account their environmental aspects.

1.4. III. ENVIRONMENTAL REVIEW

7.   When undertaking an environmental review, Members should indicate to the appropriate parties involved in the project the type of environmental information they require in relation to the potential environmental impacts of the project, including, where appropriate, the need for an Environmental Impact Assessment (EIA). The information to be supplied should include:

- Potential environmental impacts (e.g. generation of significant air emissions, effluents, waste or noise, significant use of natural resources) including the impact on involuntary resettlement, indigenous peoples, and cultural property;

- The environmental standards, practices and processes that the parties involved in the project intend to apply;

- The results of any public consultations on the project with relevant stakeholders.

. . .

12.1 When undertaking environmental reviews, Members should benchmark projects against host country standards, against one or more relevant environmental standards and guidelines published by the World Bank Group, the European Bank for Reconstruction and Development, the Asian Development Bank, the African Development Bank and the Inter-American Development Bank and against the safeguard policies published by the World Bank Group. Members may also benchmark against any higher internationally recognised environmental standards, such as European Community standards.

12.2 Projects should, in all cases, comply with the standards of the host country and when the relevant international standards against which the project has been bench-marked are more stringent these standards would be applied.

12.3 If a Member finds it necessary to apply standards below the international standards against which the project has been benchmarked, it shall report and justify the standards applied on an annual ex-post basis in accordance with paragraph 19.

Countries have adopted the OECD Common Approaches to varying degrees.

In addition to ECAs' substantive environmental policies, an important issue is whether ECAs have accountability mechanisms similar to the World Bank Inspection Panel, described above. ECAs have been even slower to adopt these than they were to adopt environmental policies.

As in the case of IFIs, in the absence of an accountability mechanism people or communities affected by an ECA-supported project have no institutional forum in which to voice their concerns over projects that compromise their fundamental rights, destroy their livelihoods, or cause environmental destruction. An accountability mechanisms at an ECA can provide affected people with a tool to help ensure compliance by the ECA with its operating policies, and thus to safeguard their rights. An accountability mechanism can also facilitate a departure from a culture of approval, where ECA staff members are rewarded for the volume of funding they provide, toward a culture of results, where staff members are rewarded for concrete, measurable sustainable development results on the ground. Also, accountability mechanisms allow information to flow directly from affected individuals and communities to the highest levels at the ECA, usually directly involving its President (Executive Director) or Board of Directors.

OPIC created an accountability mechanism, the Office of Accountability, in 2004. The office conducted a compliance review to provide a forum to investigate and report on complaints regarding OPIC's compliance with its governing statutes, rules, policies, and procedures in the context of specific projects. It was also to review and try to resolve outstanding complaints of local communities relating to the impacts of OPIC-supported projects on such communities, with or without allegations of non-compliance on the part of OPIC. The Director of the office reported directly to the President and Chief Executive Officer of OPIC and had the ability to make reports to the OPIC Board of Directors. The office received and responded to a relatively small number of complaints and was dissolved in less than then years. Japan's ECA, the Japan Bank for International Cooperation (JBIC), and Export Development Canada (EDC) have also established accountability mechanisms. The vast majority of ECAs have not established an accountability mechanism.

E. SOVEREIGN WEALTH FUNDS

Sovereign wealth funds are funds held by governments, which are invested in various instruments. There are two kinds of sovereign wealth funds: those that are used to build up savings and those that are used to stabilize the volatility of the government's revenues and economy. Such funds have increased dramatically within the last decade and reportedly totaled over $5.76 trillion in 2013. This means that they potentially offer an important source of funding for sustainable development.

In 2008, the International Working Group of Sovereign Wealth Funds, which includes the major funds, agreed to a voluntary code of conduct, known as the Santiago Principles. The International Monetary Fund produced the initial draft of these principles. The 24 Santiago Principles provide for transparency, accountability and various measures tied to financial and economic soundness. They do not extend to other conditions for making investments.

F. DEBT RELIEF APPROACHES

Another means of financing environmental protection is via combining it with relief of the often substantial debt load carried by many developing countries. A debt-for-nature swap relieves foreign debt in exchange for a government's commitment to take certain pro-environment actions, e.g., to create a protected area or spend a certain amount of their local currency on conservation work. Nongovernmental organization created a way to use a country's commercial debt for bringing about environmental conservation in the country.

1. DEBT-FOR-NATURE SWAPS

DEBT-FOR-NATURE SWAPS, A NEW MEANS OF FUNDING CONSERVATION IN DEVELOPING NATIONS

Kathryn S. Fuller & Douglas F. Williamson
11 Intl. Envtl. Rep. (BNA) 301, 301–303 (May 11, 1988)

Developing nations owe more than one trillion dollars to lending institutions. The accelerating rate at which many banks are writing down portions of their loan portfolios—illustrated by the Bank of Boston's decision last December to write down 50 percent of its Latin American loans—shows fading confidence in the banking community that many of these loans will ever be repaid.

At the same time, deforestation in many tropical countries is occurring at an alarming rate. Developing countries, under pressure to meet domestic social needs as well as external financial obligations, may see no choice but to exploit their natural resource base at a pace that cannot be sustained. At the present rate of clearing, the forests of the tropics, which contain half of the animal and plant species on earth, could be destroyed in the next century. The result would be calamitous. In the tropics, rural people depend on these forests for food, fuel, building materials, medicines, fodder for livestock—indeed for many of their staples. In the developed world, too, people rely on the many agricultural, medicinal, and industrial products that originate in tropical forests.

In 1984, World Wildlife Fund's then vice-president for science, Dr. Thomas E. Lovejoy, proposed converting international debt into support for conservation. In an op-ed piece in the New York Times, Dr. Lovejoy drew a correlation between indebtedness and environmental degradation. In debtor nations, programs to manage natural resources were among the first slashed as governments struggled to reduce spending. As a consequence, these countries relied heavily on foreign donors to help support their biologically rich national parks. Development aid dollars, when made available, generally were channeled into export-oriented businesses that would yield foreign exchange to repay interest on the staggering debt. Because of pressing social needs, even under the best of circumstances debtor nations found it hard to address critical conservation needs. Why not, Lovejoy argued, use the debt crisis to help solve environmental problems? Why not convert tropical nations' debts directly into support for conservation—that is, swap debt for nature?

EXPLORING THE POSSIBILITIES

At first, the idea was greeted with skepticism. Why would a debtor government or a lender bank be interested in such a proposal? How could a private conservation group involve itself in something as complex as the international debt crisis?

Indeed, a number of questions needed answers. The governments of debtor nations needed to be assured that debt swaps neither would jeopardize their economy—by contributing to inflation if large amounts of local currency were printed to redeem debt—nor would they threaten sovereignty by transferring control of land and other national assets to foreigners. Banks in both the creditor and debtor nations had to be convinced that debt-for-nature programs were in their self-interest and presented no undue financial risks. The governments of creditor nations needed to confirm that debt-for-nature swaps were compatible with regulations governing the activities of nonprofit organizations. And conservation organizations needed to be convinced that debt-for-nature swaps would be a better use of their own resources than conventional projects.

In 1987, several factors combined to provide impetus to debt-for-nature swaps. Opportunities emerged as a growing number of debtors and lenders, frustrated by the failure of standard approaches to alleviating debt, became open to unconventional solutions. Many debtor nations instituted "debt-for-equity swaps" through which they redeemed portions of their debt in local currency by allowing debt-holders to take equity positions in commercial and industrial projects. At the same time, a growing number of lender banks began to conclude that sizable portions of their debt portfolios, especially in Latin America, were uncollectible. These banks began to write down or sell high-risk debts at substantial discounts, fueling increased activity in what is called the secondary-debt market.

World Wildlife Fund and other conservation organizations began to discuss with debtor nations ways in which debt could be converted to benefit local conservation programs. Rather than swap debt for commercial or industrial expansion, these groups proposed that countries rich in biological resources agree to swap a portion of their debt for conservation.

THE FIRST DEBT-FOR-NATURE SWAPS

In July 1987, Bolivia carried out the first debt-for-nature swap through an agreement between the Bolivian government and Conservation International. Conservation International purchased $650,000 of Bolivia's commercial debt through Citicorp Investment Bank for $100,000, that is, 15 cents on the dollar. In exchange for this debt, Bolivia's president agreed to set aside 3.7 million acres of tropical forest around the Beni Biosphere Reserve as a protected area and to establish a $250,000 fund in local currency for its management.

In October 1987, Ecuador announced its own $10 million debt-for-nature program. The concept behind the deal in Ecuador originated with Roque Sevilla, president of Fundacion Natura, Ecuador's leading private conservation organization. Under Ecuador's program, debt in a face amount of up to $10 million can be converted by the Central Bank into local currency bonds to be held by Fundacion Natura.

To date, World Wildlife Fund has purchased $1 million of Ecuadorean debt at 35 cents on the dollar with the help of both Citicorp and Bankers Trust Company. The interest on the nine-year bonds—33 percent in the first year—will be used to help manage Ecuador's new and existing parks, among them Cayambe-Coca Ecological Reserve, Podocarpus National Park, Pasochoa Nature Reserve, and the world famous Galapagos National Park. It will also be used to train national park personnel, strengthen local conservation institutions, and promote environmental education. Principal on the bonds, which is amortized over the life of the bonds, will provide an endowment for the Fundacion.

By issuing bonds rather than cash, Ecuador's Central Bank not only reduced the likelihood that the swap would have inflationary impacts locally but also provided a mechanism through which foreign donors could more than triple the value of their conservation investments. These donors could support the long-term development of a strong local conservation organization, while helping in a modest way to alleviate Ecuador's debt burden.

Because the bonds have a nine-year term, the planning and implementation of long-range programs can proceed without fear that project funding may be cut off next year.

Fundacion Natura actively sought contributions of the remaining $9 million of Ecuador's $10 million debt-for-nature program. This innovative program should substantially increase foreign investment in Ecuadorean conservation and provide much needed support not only to Fundacion Natura but also to other governmental and nongovernmental groups throughout Ecuador. . . . [The second exchange under the Ecuadorean program involving the remaining $9 million took place in April 1989. The Nature Conservancy ("TNC") and the Missouri Botanical Gardens joined WWF-US as purchasers of the debt at twelve cents on the dollar—Ens.] Also in 1987, Costa Rica announced a debt-for-nature program proposed by Alvaro Umana, Costa Rica's Minister of Natural Resources, Energy, and Mines. Under this initiative, the Central Bank of Costa Rica authorized up to $5.4 million in debt-for-nature swaps by autumn 1988. Contributions from a number of donors, including World Wildlife Fund, Conservation, International, and The Nature Conservancy have already resulted in the acquisition of the full face amount of debt at prices ranging between 15 to 17 cents on the dollar. As in the Ecuadorean program, the Central Bank has redeemed debt by issuing local currency bonds. Proceeds from the bonds are financing a wide range of conservation programs, including the acquisition by local Costa Rican groups of land to expand Guanacaste National Park and the Monteverde Cloud Forest Reserve, management of protected areas and their buffer zones, development of park facilities, and training of park personnel.

While the Fundacion de Parques Nacionales and the Fundacion Neotropica, two Costa Rican organizations, oversee payment of bond proceeds, a Costa Rican bank, the Banco Cooperativo, holds the bonds in trust. As a result of Costa Rica's quick success in securing the initial $5.4 million, the government plans to raise the ceiling on debt-for-nature swaps, perhaps up to $50 million. World Wildlife Fund has agreed to acquire up to $3 million of Costa Rican debt over a three-year period, and other prospective donors have also expressed interest in participating in further swaps.

HOW BENEFICIAL ARE DEBT-FOR-NATURE SWAPS?

A question often asked is what makes these swaps more desirable as a means of funding conservation than merely providing cash payments directly.

At a glance, it might appear that the amount of work necessary to conclude a sound debt-for-nature swap outweighs the potential gain. The deals are extremely complex. Each step requires specialized talents. Approval must be obtained from the debtor country's government and central bank. An agreement must be fashioned, and the debt acquired and converted into a local financial instrument. The host government must decide what exchange rate to apply in converting debt into local currency, what conditions of payment to use in exchange for the debt, and whom to designate as a local agent to control the funds and dispense the proceeds. Only then can a conservation program be implemented.

For the conservation organization in the creditor country, the choices also are difficult. Acquiring debt is a technically complex transaction. It is not possible to purchase debt as one might buy commercial bonds. The expansion of the secondary-debt market has opened many options, making it necessary to shop for debt that is available in the right denomination, acceptable to the debtor country government, and with a satisfactory schedule of maturation.

If the aim of conservation organizations in debt-for-nature swaps is to achieve maximum conservation benefit with their scarce funds, why would they take on so much trouble involving lawyers, bankers, tax analysts, and extensive staff commitments?

The answer is straightforward: Despite these administrative burdens, conservation still comes out ahead. Debt-for-nature swaps dramatically increase the impact of conservation dollars. At current exchange rates, one dollar face amount of acquired debt may yield many multiples over that in local currency. With the conversion of the debt into bonds, proceeds from the swap flow over a significant period of time. Good rates of return provide a strong incentive to foreign conservation donors to increase their contributions to countries that have approved debt-for-nature swaps.

In addition, debt-for-nature swaps promote and highlight the value of partnership between conservation organizations in the developed world and their counterparts in the developing world. It is of tremendous significance to conservation that the models in Ecuador and Costa Rica originated within those countries.

A third valuable aspect of these debt-for-nature swaps is the role they played in involving the business community in conservation. In the case of Ecuador and Costa Rica, for example, WWF was fortunate to receive pro bono legal services in negotiating the deal from the New York law firm of Shearman & Sterling and financial assistance in arranging the conversion and transfer of funds from Citibank, as well as several departments at Bankers Trust, the source bank for the debt.

THE FUTURE FOR DEBT-FOR-NATURE SWAPS

. . . Despite the complexity of these deals, debt swaps can be arranged successfully to meet the concerns of all parties. Bankers, government officials, and conservationists in debtor and creditor countries have managed to find the common ground necessary to conclude agreements. The possible inflationary impacts of swaps, for example, can be addressed not only through the use of bonds but also through the establishment of overall ceilings on debt-for-nature programs, although the amount of currency generated by debt swaps for conservation purposes is generally not large enough to have an appreciable impact on inflation.

Negotiators of debt-for-nature swaps may also face difficult questions when they work on setting up the delivery of conservation services. For example, should the money be channeled through one or two conservation groups in the debtor nation, or through a separately constituted trust? What criteria should be used to determine eligibility in the latter case?

These questions are important. Enormous sums of money suddenly made available may disrupt homegrown activities, among them a conservation movement deeply rooted in local needs and local culture. Experience has shown, however, that this can be avoided by listening to in-country partners, learning from them about their needs, and working with them to ensure that joint conservation efforts incorporate local views and experiences. The sovereignty concerns of debtor nations can thus be met through carefully constructed agreements.

Flexibility will be a key in any new debt-for-nature opportunities. Financial regulations vary from country to country. The particular value and structure of a country's debt may preclude debt-for-nature swaps from taking place, or necessitate innovative financial arrangements.

. . . The time frame for debt-for-nature swaps . . . is not open-ended. Debt-for-nature programs are responding to a specific situation that may not continue for very long. A solution to the debt burden may be negotiated by banks and debtor nations, or debt may be written down to a level that makes swaps impractical.

Conservation organizations are presently working with banks to ensure their continued involvement in debt-for-nature programs. Debt that otherwise might simply be written down by banks as a loss can be put to productive use through debt swaps. In particular, World Wildlife Fund and other groups are encouraging commercial banks to donate a portion of their debt for use in swaps. Most of the debt used in swaps to date has been purchased with funds provided by foundations and individual donors.

In February 1988, Fleet/Norstar Financial Group became the first financial institution to donate debt for a debt-for-nature swap. It donated through The Nature Conservancy $254,000 (face amount) in Costa Rican debt paper towards conservation efforts in the Braulio Carillo National Park.

Actions by the Treasury Department may help encourage further debt donations. Previously, a bank that donated debt for conservation could deduct only the fair market value of the debt—generally, the discounted price for which debt notes have been selling. Thus, banks had a greater financial incentive to sell their debt, claim the loss as a deduction, and then donate the proceeds to conservation.

In November 1987, the Treasury Department issued Revenue Ruling 87–124, which provides lenders a full-cost-basis deduction (one based on the face value of the debt rather than on its fair market value) for donations of developing country debt to fund charitable activities in the debtor nations. In April, the Treasury Department clarified the ruling, enhancing debt-for-nature swap possibilities even further. . . .

NOTES AND QUESTIONS

1.   Different types of debt-for-nature exchanges exist. The most common type is when a NGO purchases a lesser developed country's foreign debt on the secondary debt market and exchanges it for local currency or interest-bearing bonds to be managed by local environmental groups for designated conservation programs. A second type is similar to the first type, except that the lender bank donates the debt directly to the NGO rather than selling the debt in the secondary debt market. Another kind involves the sale of the debt to a corporate investor. Finally, the last kind provides continued funding for already established environmental programs in the debtor countries. To date, only the first two types have been used. Why is that?

2.   What are the requirements for establishing debt-for-nature swaps? What are the key concerns of the conservation donor, the lending institution, and the developing countries in formulating a debt-for-nature exchange? What are their long-term goals?

3.   The debt-for-equity swap was an innovative response to the international debt crisis. Spurred by the skyrocketing oil prices in the mid-1970s, developing countries borrowed heavily in order to finance oil imports and development projects. Commercial banks, induced by the higher rates and fees that they could demand from the developing countries over those they could obtain from domestic borrowers, exceeded their legal lending limit and overextended loans to the developing countries. These debtor countries struggled to make the interest payments of their staggering foreign debt and often could not make the principal payments. Finally, in 1982, Mexico declared that it would be unable to pay its debt. Many other countries, such as Bolivia, Brazil, Costa Rica, Peru, Ecuador, and the Dominican Republic followed suit by unilaterally suspending part or all of their interest payments. In order to minimize the risk of defaults by developing countries on their payments, banks began writing down or selling debts that they had little hope of collecting, thereby providing impetus to increased transactions in the secondary debt market. The debt-for-equity exchange emerged as a creative solution for alleviating the debt problem. In a debt-for-equity swap,

the creditor exchanges a country's foreign debt for equity interests in local firms or assets. The transaction, therefore, allowed creditors to earn returns on nonperforming assets. Debt-for-equity exchanges served as precursors to debt-for-nature exchanges.

4.   The Fuller and Williamson article points to the correlation made by Lovejoy between "indebtedness and environmental degradation." The requirement that international debt payments be made in hard currency further served to fuel the environmental degradation. In their efforts to raise the hard currency needed to service their foreign debt, some Latin American countries attempted to boost exports by clearing forests for timber and to create pasture lands for cattle grazing. A number of these countries switched from mixed farming to mainly cash crop agriculture. These practices resulted in soil erosion, diminishing water supplies, and the destruction of valuable wetlands, leading to extinction of plant and animal species.

5.   Aside from avoiding defaults on the risky loans made to the developing countries, what motivates commercial banks to participate in debt-for-nature swaps? What about multilateral development banks? Does Revenue Ruling 87–124, which provides two tax benefits to organizations that donate debt (a bad loan loss deduction and a charitable deduction), provide sufficient tax incentives for banks to donate debt? Would a tax credit constitute a better alternative? If so, how could it be reconciled with the absence of tax credits to aid United States farmers when they take environmental protection measures?

6.   If substantial administrative burdens accompany debt-for-nature transactions, why do NGOs promote them? How do NGOs choose the target areas for conservation, and how much input do the local environmental groups have in designing the type of conservation programs to be implemented? Does the national park model (which is more common in western countries) work in the context of Latin America? Is setting aside reserve areas enough? How do NGOs monitor and ensure proper implementation of the conservation programs in the developing countries? What happens when the funds created by the debt-for-nature swap run out? Would it be better for NGOs to concentrate their efforts on a fewer number of well-chosen projects to ensure the projects' perpetuity rather than attempting more numerous projects?

7.   If the debt relief provided by debt-for-nature swaps is so marginal in comparison to the total foreign debt of developing countries, what makes debt-for-nature exchanges an attractive option for developing countries? What concerns would make debt-for-nature swaps unattractive to developing countries? Would the benefits of the exchange outweigh the intrusions into the sovereignty and possible internal problems (i.e., inflation and increased domestic debt) of debtor countries?

8.   Should national governments take part in debt-for-nature swaps by adopting loan forgiveness policies in order to facilitate "real" debt relief for developing countries and encourage their continued participation in future

debt-for-nature exchanges? What political issues are implicated in subsidizing foreign debt, as compared to domestic debt?

9.   Taxes can play a major role in debt-for-nature swaps. Consider the following:

Conservation International, The Debt-for-Nature Exchange: A Tool for International Conservation

11, 17–19, 23–30, 37–40 (1989)

The United States tax code has been clarified to minimize some of the perceived disadvantages of debt donations, however. Revenue Ruling 87–124, issued in November, 1987, confirmed that U.S. financial institutions which donate debt to a U.S. non-profit 501(c)(3) organization may receive two tax benefits: 1) a bad loan loss deduction for any loss between the debt's original face value when the loan was made and its fair market value at the time of the donation, and 2) a charitable contribution deduction equal to the fair market value of the proceeds generated as a result of the exchange. These deductions effectively allow a donating bank to reduce its taxable income and, thus, its U.S. taxes.

10. Can debt-for-nature agreements be enforced at all? Given the weaker bargaining position that NGOs occupy in international law as private persons versus the superior position of countries as sovereign entities, how can the developing countries be influenced by the international community to adhere to debt-for-nature agreements? What factors must be considered in determining the best methodology for enforcement of the agreement? (Take into account the specific goal of the particular agreement along with the broad objectives of all the parties involved.) See also Laurie P. Greener (comment), *Debt-for-Nature Swaps in Latin American Countries: The Enforcement Dilemma*, 7 Conn. J. Intl. L. 123 (1991).

11. The language of debt-for-nature agreements is often vague and deliberately omits rigid enforcement terms. What is the rationale behind this? Should the agreements include provisions for foreseeable events/crises? What are they?

12. Why limit such exchanges to debt-for-nature? In a thought-provoking article, Sunstein and Catherine O'Neill propose a technology-for-nature swap. Catherine A. O'Neill & Cass R. Sunstein, *Economics and the Environment: Trading Debt and Technology for Nature*, 17 Colum. J. Envtl. L. 93 (1992). They state that such an exchange has considerable advantages over debt-for-nature kinds.

Its major advantage is that it promises to bring about large-scale, long-term reform and thus to create structures for encouraging not only lower cost economic development, but also the production of energy by means of creating minimal damage to the environment. In its ideal form, it will also advance progress in energy efficiency, an area that is vital to sustainable development. . . .

The proposed exchange raises some serious economic and ethical questions, and it is also fairly complex. For instance, developed countries may well be under an ethical obligation to transfer technology to developing countries for free or at significant reductions in price. This obligation might be justified by reference to general redistributive goals, environmental concerns, or the view that industrialized countries have profited from technological development producing environmental harms, that such countries benefit from environmental protection in developing countries, and that developing countries should not be placed under special economic disabilities because of environmental damage caused by others. These considerations suggest that at least a heavily discounted transfer of technology may be an ethical obligation of developed countries. . . .

A transfer of technology for nature requires the cooperation of several parties, all of whom wish to advance different agendas. The arrangement we propose should serve the interests of each party, and the resulting advances in combatting global environmental and developmental problems should benefit all concerned. . . .

Id. at 150.

Do you agree?

In another article, the author argues that environmental infrastructure development can be enhanced through debt-for-development exchanges. Nicholas Kublicki, *The Greening of Free Trade: NAFTA, Mexican Environmental Law, and Debt Exchanges for Mexican Environmental Infrastructure Development*, 19 Colum. J. Envtl. L. 59 (1994).

Such exchanges can be funded by official U.S. debt, donations of debt by institutional lenders, purchases of institutional debt on the secondary exchange through NGO fundraising, and USAID grants. Debt-for-EID [environmental infrastructure development] exchanges would allow creditors to recover a portion of their potentially uncollectible debt. At the same time, the mechanism would enable Mexico to develop its environmental infrastructure and reduce its massive foreign debt

Id. at 138–139.

What do you think of this approach?

13. The literature on debt-for-nature swaps is extensive. In addition to articles already cited, one could read: Congressional Research Service, Library of Congress, Debt-for-Nature Swaps in Developing Countries: An Overview of Recent Conservation (1988) (CRS Rep. No. 88–647 ENR); Danny Cassimon, Martin Prowse, & Dennis Essers, *The Pitfalls and Potential of Debt-for-Nature Swaps: A US-Indonesian Case Study*, 21 Global

Environmental Change 93 (2011); John M. Shandra, Michael Restivo, Eric Shircliff, & Bruce London, *Do Commercial Debt for Nature Swaps Matter for Forests? A Cross National Test of World Polity Theory*, 26 Sociological Forum 381 (2011); Jared E. Knicley, *Debt, Nature, and Indigenous Rights: Twenty-Five Years of Debt-for-Nature Evolution*, 36 Harv. Envtl. L. Rev. 79 (2012).

14. Political issues can affect the likelihood of a debt-for-nature swap or its long-term viability if one is entered into. Consider the following:

Conservation International, The Debt-for-Nature Exchange: A Tool for International Conservation

11, 17–19, 23–30, 37–40 (1989)

This growing recognition by host countries of the value of debt-for-nature exchanges has not been without some political backlash, however. For example, some initial press accounts in Bolivia of the first debt-for-nature exchange mischaracterized the exchange as a swap of debt for foreign ownership of land. Similar misconceptions regarding the debt-for-nature exchange mechanism have been voiced in Brazil where critics have charged that debt-for-nature exchanges may impinge on Brazil's national sovereignty in managing its natural resources. Such criticisms appear to be founded on serious misunderstandings of the purposes and uses to which the debt-for-nature exchange mechanism is put.

At least two positive consequences have followed from these politically charged reactions. First, the local beneficiaries of the proceeds of debt-for-nature exchanges (actual and potential) have been galvanized to present their case, in a public forum, for the commitment of government resources to a conservation agenda. Second, international conservation organizations have been reminded of the importance of developing these exchanges *in concert with* and *in response* to their local counterparts' needs. In short, debt-for-nature exchanges cannot be foisted upon unwilling participants. The process of negotiating and structuring a debt-for-nature exchange is a consensus building exercise.

In short, investments made via debt-for-nature exchanges probably are neither less nor more inherently vulnerable to political risks than any other conservation investment in a foreign country, unless the debt-for-nature exchange requires a long-term financial commitment of the host government. Then such exchanges run the risk that a new government or a change in the country's national agenda may cause a host government to breach its contractual agreement. Legal documentation may discourage such breaches and political risk insurance may minimize the financial costs of such a breach, but the best protected debt-for-nature exchanges are those that are supported by a local and international constituency that would protest loudly at any breach of the debt-for-nature agreement.

15. In 2002, government officials from the United States and Peru signed a debt-for-nature agreement to protect some of the most biologically rich tropical rainforests on Earth. For the first time, three leading conservation groups joined with the United States government to advance a debt-for-nature swap, The Nature Conservancy (TNC), Conservation International (CI), and World Wildlife Fund (WWF). The Peruvian debt swap was to generate funds for distribution to local Peruvian conservation groups engaged in a wide variety of conservation activities. Under the agreement, TNC, CI, and WWF each committed approximately $370,000 for a total of $1.1 million. The United States government allocated $5.5 million to cancel a portion of Peru's debt to the United States. In September 2008, the United States and Peru signed a second debt-for-nature swap agreement to generate more than $25 million in funds over 7 years.

The federal funding is authorized by the Tropical Forest Conservation Act (TFCA) of 1998, which was created to provide eligible developing countries the opportunity to reduce their concessional debts owed to the United States while at the same time generating funds for important activities to conserve important tropical forests. As a result of this swap, Peru will save about $14 million in debt payments over the next 16 years, and will provide the local currency equivalent of about $10.6 million toward conservation over the next 12 years.

In June 2009, the United States government signed a debt-for-nature agreement with Indonesia, generating nearly $30 million funds over the next eight years. The United States contributed around $20 million while the CI and the Indonesian Biodiversity Foundation (Yayasan Keanekaragaman Hayati or KEHATI) each committed $1 million to restructure the debt. Funds will help Indonesia protect forests and ecosystem on the island of Sumatra, home to many endangered species. In September 2011, the United States signed a second debt-for-nature swap agreement with Indonesia in partnership with World Wide Fund for Nature—Indonesia and the TNC. Under the second agreement, Indonesia's debt payments will be reduced by $28.5 million over the next eight years. The United States contributed $19.8 million while the WWF and the TNC contributed $3.6 million. This is the first debt-for-nature agreement that has a REDD+ initiative to reduce carbon emissions from deforestation and forest degradation.

As of July 2013, 19 agreements under the TFCA have been concluded with 14 countries, including Bangladesh, Belize, Botswana, Brazil, Columbia, Costa Rica, El Salvador, Guatemala, Indonesia, Jamaica, Panama, Paraguay, Peru and the Philippines. The most recent debt-for-nature agreement was signed by the Philippines in July 2013, generating $31.8 million funds for forest conservation. In total, these agreements will generate over $326 million for tropical forest conservation. *See* http://www.usaid.gov/biodiversity/TFCA/programs-by-country.

2. ENTERPRISE FOR THE AMERICAS INITIATIVE

In 1991, the United States launched the Enterprise for the Americas Initiative (EAI). Its intent was to reduce indebtedness to the United States for countries in Latin America and the Caribbean that satisfied certain political and economic eligibility criteria. If a country met the eligibility criteria, the United States and debtor countries enter into EAI agreements where the United States reduced a portion of original debt, and debtor countries agreed to pay the principal in dollars to the United States, while the new interest payments were paid in local currency to the local Enterprise for the Americas Fund ("Americas Fund"), which finances environmental projects in the debtor country. The Americas Fund was administered by at least one representative of the US government, at least one representative from a debtor country and other representatives of nongovernmental organizations active in the country. The dual advantages of debt reduction and environmental protection were a result of a joint effort by the United States Treasury Department and the Environmental Protection Agency. From 1991 to 1997, the United States entered into EAI agreements with eight countries (Argentina, Bolivia, Chile, Colombia, El Salvador, Jamaica, Peru and Uruguay), restructuring nearly $2 billion originally owed by those countries. The EAI generated more than $200 million in local currency for environmental projects. The EAI has been an important source of funding for environmental funds in Latin America and the Caribbean. Although the United States Congress no longer appropriates funds for the EAI, the subsequently enacted Tropical Forest Conservation Act (TFCA) was modeled after the EAI and has been contributing to tropical forest protection through debt-for-nature swaps. *See generally* Royal C. Gardner, *Taking the Principle of Just Compensation Abroad: Private Property Rights, National Sovereignty, and the Cost of Environmental Protection*, 65 U. Cin. L. Rev. 539 (1997).

NOTES AND QUESTIONS

Do you see elements here that are linked to debt-for-nature swaps?

G. OTHER FINANCING APPROACHES

1. *Innovative Financing.* At a follow-up Working Group of the Commission on Sustainable Development (CSD) in early 1994 charged with developing policy options/recommendations to the CSD, the Group encouraged further examination of tradeable permits; removing subsidies; reducing military spending; and the feasibility, legal modalities, and administrative aspects of such measures as international emission charges, internationally tradeable permits, taxes on air travel, and fees and arrangements to cover international environmental disasters, including those related to transportation of hazardous wastes and

materials. The exploration of using tradeable permits has subsequently been encouraged in other forums. Do you think these approaches have promise? What problems do you foresee?

2.   *Carbon taxes.* The European Union considered and ultimately adopted a carbon/energy tax approach based on the harmonization of excise taxes on energy consumption. Described as an effort to rely on market-based approaches (rather than "command-control" approaches), the tax was to be based on the energy value of fuels such as oil, coal, natural gas, kerosene, and electricity. Such a "green" tax, inspired by efforts to find longer-term sustainable development solutions rather than to generate revenues, would replace labor-based taxation approaches. What are the implications of the tax? Is it an appropriate application of the polluter-pays-principle?

The EU eventually issued Council Directive 2003/96/EC of 27 October 2003, restructuring the Community framework for the taxation of energy products and electricity. A 2005 EU study on energy taxation found that "Member States would benefit from common energy/carbon tax policies in the form of higher employment and welfare if they used tax revenues to reduce employers' social security contributions. A common EU carbon tax would be the most cost-efficient way of reaching the EU climate policy objectives. However, it would have a somewhat negative impact on competitiveness in some energy-intensive sectors. These effects would be alleviated only slightly by exempting energy-intensive sectors form energy taxation." *Available at* http://ec.europa.eu/taxation_customs/ resources/documents/taxation/gen_info/economic_analysis/economic_ studies/energy_tax_study.pdf.

3.   *Insurance.* Consider the possible role that insurance plays in financing environmentally sensitive activities. It can affect the calculation of risk of liability for environmental harm and therefore might be determinative in whether to undertake certain environmentally risky projects. In other words, the availability of insurance for environmental risk arguably could make it easier for environmentally dangerous projects to be undertaken. On the other hand, it can also improve the protection of the environment should damage occur (i.e., guaranty that various kinds of injury to the environment are covered). Can you think of any ways by which companies insuring environmentally sensitive activities (e.g., the building of a nuclear power plant or hydroelectric dam) might play an effective role in making projects less environmentally damaging? What effect could insurance have on the financing of environmental protection?

4.   *Tax subsidies.* What impact would tax subsidies given to individuals and corporations for pollution control facilities and equipment have on international trade? Would they be consistent with the WTO? Consider the 1974 OECD Recommendation on Polluter-Pays in Chapter 3.

H. MICROFINANCING AND BOTTOM-UP PRIVATE INITIATIVES

Increasingly financing for specific projects or programs for sustainable development comes from bottom-up microfinance organizations. The Grameen Bank in Bangladesh pioneered the approach. Microfinance institutions make very small loans to people who would not otherwise have access to more formal financial institutions. Sometimes this is complemented by technical assistance and the formation of support groups. There are also bottom-up informal institutions, such as Kiva (described below), which are singular private initiatives linking a funding organization in one country with a project in another, or crowdsourcing via the internet for a specific project. In addition, there are nonprofit organizations in industrialized countries that provide seed money for programs addressed to specific issues, such as education of youth, in developing countries, including in emerging market countries. EMpower, for example, provides seed money for projects targeted at youth and women in emerging market countries.

As of July 2015, there was no place where one could find out the totality of such efforts, though the impression is that they offer a significant source of small-scale financing for sustainable development. Bottom-up approaches to financing sustainable development are important, because they focus on poor and vulnerable people, who otherwise may have no source of funding. They enable individuals to begin small-scale enterprises, and have been especially helpful for women.

To understand this kind of financing, it is useful to look at the microfinance organization, Kiva, which operates through the internet. Kiva posts pictures and provides stories about poor people who need loans. A potential donor sends money to Kiva, which in turn sends it to a microlender, who in theory makes the loan to the person the donor has selected. In concept, there is a direct link between the donor and the borrower in this form of finance, and the donor receives the money back with no interest. In practice, this diagram may be somewhat fictional, because the links may not be direct and the donor might not hear about it if the borrower defaults, because the microlender may want to maintain its credit with the microfinance organization. Nonetheless, Kiva and other such initiatives tap an important source of financing, because they tap into the human desire to want to give to projects in which people can identify a human face and a specific need. The surge in crowd sourcing to fund a specific project or a specific need, which often are unrelated to development work, reflects this human desire.

Crowdsourcing is becoming another important form of financing for small scale development projects. Project creators propose an idea or a project and potential donors can choose ideas that appeal to them and select how much money to donate. Crowdsourcing generally only engages the project creators, donors, and a moderating platform. This allows those seeking funds to bypass traditional financial institutions or institutional funding structures. Backers or donors can choose how much to donate to the project and, rather than receive the money back, may be offered rewards in return for their pledge. Donations are generally processed once the minimum funding goal is reached. One important issue with this source of funding is that there is no guarantee that the funds will be used to implement the project or that the project will meet donor's expectations.

Accountability is an important issue with microfinance and more broadly with all bottom-up approaches to financing. Organizations engaged in bottom-up financings need to consider carefully how to provide for accountability of those who receive the financing or serve as microlenders.

Lastly, private foundations or wealthy individuals can be sources for very substantial funding of specific programs, such as controlling malaria in the health field. Such financing can provide very significant support for broad-based programs of sustainable development. It also raises several distinct issues, namely whether the financing reflects local community needs, whether adequate attention is paid to ensuring effective implementation at the local level, and whether there is provision for accountability.

CONCLUDING NOTES AND QUESTIONS

1. Returning to the two hypothetical problems posed at the beginning of the chapter, if you represented a community affected by the proposed project, how would you advise your clients to proceed?

2. How do you effectively institutionalize accountability in the various forms of financing discussed in this chapter? Accountable to whom? For what?

CHAPTER 18

ENVIRONMENTAL INSTITUTIONS AND GOVERNANCE

∎ ∎ ∎

Environmental law does not implement or enforce itself, either domestically or internationally. Protecting the environment and human health requires effective and efficient institutions and governance. Part I of this chapter describes the complicated international institutional architecture involved in environmental protection. Part II explores various issues related to environmental governance. Each part is relevant to three important questions: how can existing institutions be utilized to deal with transboundary and other international environmental problems; how can existing institutions be better coordinated and governed to deal with such problems more efficiently and effectively; and what would be the best overall governance structure to protect human health and the environment.

When considering the following materials, it may be useful to bear in mind an alternative model—the international trade regime described above in Chapter 11. To recapitulate, there is one trade regime at the global level and many regimes at regional and bilateral levels. The regime at the global level is the World Trade Organization (WTO). The legal framework of the WTO consists of an overarching WTO international agreement (the WTO Agreement) accompanied by a phalanx of subsidiary WTO agreements. The United States and all of its major trading partners are Parties to these agreements, each of which is legally binding and enforceable via the WTO dispute settlement process, which itself is governed by one of the subsidiary WTO agreements.

The primary trade discipline is non-discrimination, which in the trade context means two things: a country must offer goods from another country the same treatment that the first country offers to its own similar goods (National Treatment); and a country must offer goods from another country treatment as favorable as how it treats similar goods from any other country (Most-Favored Nation Treatment). There are two major structural exceptions to this, however. First, the WTO Agreement recognizes the legitimacy of sub-global arrangements in the form of customs unions and free trade areas. Thus the European Union (EU) and the North American Free Trade Agreement (NAFTA) are legally permissible under the WTO, and the members of the EU and NAFTA may offer each other better trade terms than they offer other WTO members.

There are many such customs unions and free trade areas, each with its own dispute-settlement system, and each of these takes precedence over the WTO agreements with respect to topics covered in them. Generally speaking, these agreements deal with the same issues and contain the same types of disciplines; but there are differences in detail. Indeed, as of July 2015, two major regional agreements are being negotiated (the Trans-Pacific Partnership involving the United States and 11 other States and the Transatlantic Trade and Investment Partnership between the European Union and the United States). The proliferation of regional and bilateral trade agreements threatens to undercut the unity provided by the global WTO regime. Second, the WTO Agreement allows special treatment of developing countries on a country-by-country basis. In considering this alternative model, it should be noted that the proliferation of regional and bilateral trade agreements threatens to undercut the unity provided by the global WTO system and is becoming an important issue for the international trade community.

As will be seen below, the international trade system differs markedly from the international environmental architecture. Are there lessons to be learned in the field of the environment from the international trade system, or vice versa? Are the two sufficiently analogous for solutions in one field to be transferred, with appropriate adaptations, to the other?

PROBLEM

Assume you are a national of State A concerned about unknown chemicals flowing across a border from an internationally funded project in State B. The chemicals enter State A via a waterway. You are concerned that the chemical is contaminating your land and your water supply, threatening the health of you and your family and decreasing the value of your land, as well as threatening the health of your community and the viability of an important wetland on and adjacent to your property. Assume that your government has objected to the government of State B, with no significant reduction in the flow of chemicals. To what international institutions might your government turn for a remedy?

Now assume that your own government decides not to take any further action to stop the flow of chemicals or ameliorate any damage it is causing. To what international institutions might you turn for a remedy or other assistance?

A. THE INTERNATIONAL INSTITUTIONAL FRAMEWORK

1. INTERNATIONAL ENVIRONMENTAL INSTITUTIONS

This section briefly introduces international organizations and provides an overview of some of the most important of those organizations active in the environmental field. It begins with a brisk taxonomy of international organizations, using examples with environmental mandates.

a. Background: The Nature and Functions of International Organizations

There are two main types of international organizations: intergovernmental organizations (IGOs) and international nongovernmental organizations (INGOs). Perhaps not surprisingly, there may be ambiguities about the precise classification of a particular organization. A prime example is the International Union for Conservation of Nature and Natural Resources (IUCN)—described briefly below—which has both States and non-State entities as members. There are hundreds of IGOs and INGOs. It should be noted that there also are national nongovernmental organizations (NNGOs) that are important to international environmental protection, but these are only minimally mentioned herein.

The principal subjects of this section are IGOs, which have a primary role in the formulation, promulgation, and monitoring of compliance with international environmental legal norms, and may often directly contribute to their implementation. In all these respects INGOs and some NNGOs may play an important, sometimes crucial, role.

These institutions can play many different, though often related, functions. Consider the following excerpt.

ENVIRONMENTAL PROTECTION: THE INTERNATIONAL DIMENSION

David A. Kay & Harold K. Jacobson
13–16 (1983)

The following is our attempt to develop a comprehensive typology for international action with respect to environmental problems.

1. *Problem Identification.* The first step in efforts to protect or improve the environment is to decide that a problem exists. Some problems, such as water and atmospheric pollution, are very visible: dying fish and smog are hard to ignore. Other

problems, just as serious or perhaps even more so, are much less apparent. For example, the danger of altering the ozone layer may be evident only after research about properties of the biosphere and may be understood by only a small number of specialists, only on the basis of uncertain projections of current trends. Probably more and more environmental problems will be of this nature. The application of science and technology to production, which is forcefully driven by increased population pressure and rising levels of consumption, appears to be raising increasing numbers of long-run dangers. We are constantly becoming aware of problems that earlier we did not know existed. Problem identification involves not only discovering the problem but also legitimately establishing that it is a problem. Data must be made widely available and must be accepted as valid. Serendipity undoubtedly plays an important role in assuring that environmental problems are recognized promptly; for any system to be effective in the recognition of problems it must involve substantial decentralization. On the other hand, before corrective action can be taken all parties whose support or action is necessary must accept the validity of the evidence that a genuine problem exists. Thus, establishing the legitimacy of problems could involve considerable centralized coordination.

2. *Monitoring and Evaluation.* Monitoring current conditions to determine changes in levels of selected variables is also an essential step. By monitoring we mean the organized, repetitious collection of base-line data. Once this data is gathered, it must be evaluated; it must be analyzed and interpreted. Effective monitoring requires the standardization of instruments and procedures. Data must be reported promptly for timely evaluation to occur. Legitimacy is again an issue in evaluation. For differing types of monitoring and evaluation, different degrees of decentralization/centralization could be envisaged.

3. *Data Gathering and Information Collection.* As opposed to the systematic, regular collection of data about a few variables that characterizes monitoring, this task involves much broader but less scheduled collection efforts that could include information about public policies as well as about physical phenomena. Monitoring involves a commitment to time-series data; data gathering and information collection could also involve cross-sectional data for a single point in time.

4. *Risk Estimation and Impact Assessment.* The concept of risk has become very important in national environmental policy. How dangerous is a particular activity or substance? Making such an analysis is an intellectually complicated task. Moreover, since

virtually all activities and substances involve some danger, it
almost inescapably involves determining at what level the risk
poses a serious threat to humankind. Policy-makers could be
given a series of contingency tables, but they are more likely to
want tables with clearly marked thresholds where corrective
action is indicated, even if these thresholds are established
arbitrarily. Given the intellectual difficulty of the task and the
requirement for value judgments, legitimacy is an extremely
important issue for risk estimation and impact assessment.

5. *Information Exchange and Dissemination.* Since states remain
the primary sources of effective action, often all that
international organizations need to or can do to protect the
environment is to make information available to national
governments so that they can take it into account in framing
national policies. Such information could involve data about
physical phenomena. It could also involve information about the
experiences with the application of public policies. Governments
may wish to emulate other states' successful policies, or to avoid
their mishaps and misfortunes. Information exchanges must be
properly focused and targeted to be effective, and they must
involve relevant subjects and reach individuals who have the
capacity for action. The format of the exchange must be timely;
to be judged effective it must occur before it is too late for action
to be taken.

6. *Facilitation and Coordination of National and International
Programs.* Sometimes one state's policies can be more effective if
they are put into effect in conjunction with another state's (or
states') similar or related action. For example, a decision by a
state to ban the export of a particular endangered species would
gain in effectiveness if potential importing states would
simultaneously ban the import of the same species. Given
asymmetries of technological capabilities and topographical
conditions, cooperation and sharing of facilities can enhance the
participating states' national capabilities. International
organizations provide frameworks for organizing such
collaboration, both among governments and among private
entities, such as scientific organizations. The key determinant of
effectiveness is the ability to involve the right participants, those
who will gain from collaboration and those who will have
something to contribute.

7. *Normative Pronouncements.* Often the coordination of policies
can be facilitated by a group of states or an international
organization adopting a normative pronouncement. This is
usually done in the form of a resolution that embodies a

declaration of principle. The Stockholm Conference adopted several declarations of principle, and other conferences and organizations have taken similar actions. Although declarations of principle do not have the same legally binding consequences as . . . treaties, they nonetheless often have a substantial effect on national policies, and they enjoy the substantial advantage of being easier to adopt. Officials in governments can point to such declarations and argue that their state should adhere to the norms that have been enunciated. States can be criticized for not adhering to the norms set forth in declarations of principle.

8. *Standard Setting and Rule Making.* Legally binding conventions and treaties are essential instruments of international action in almost all fields, and they certainly are important with respect to the protection of the environment. Some activities and substances may be so harmful to the environment that they must be outlawed. In other instances, states may be unwilling to enact domestic legislation that might increase the costs of manufacturing within their borders unless they are confident that their major commercial rivals will take similar action. Because of the prevailing concepts of state sovereignty, conventions and treaties that states can sign and ratify are the major legally binding instruments now available for attempting to ensure uniform action among states.

9. *Supervision of Norms, Standards and Rules.* For declarations, conventions, and treaties to be more than merely paper documents, measures must be taken to ensure the compliance of states. Many steps are involved in efforts to ensure compliance: examining the policies of states to gather evidence about the extent to which they are following or breaking the established rules; validating the evidence; and deciding upon action to be taken in the event of violations. In general, international organizations have been given little authority with respect to any of these tasks. Given the distribution of power in the world, it is inconceivable that any international organization could force the compliance of the most powerful states against their will, and there is little coercion even of weaker states. The techniques of international organization for the supervision of norms, standards, and rules are more likely to stress persuasion than coercion. Effectiveness in this sphere must be measured against the experience of voluntary systems rather than against that of hierarchically structured command systems, such as some of the governmental apparatus of national states.

10. *Direct Operational Activities.* This function involves international organizations conducting activities by themselves

rather than facilitating or coordinating the conduct of activities by states. International organizations might do all or part of several of the functions listed above. In addition, international organizations provide technical and financial assistance to states. These latter functions are their most important direct operational activities.

NOTES AND QUESTIONS

Can you think of any types of international actions to protect the environment not covered in Kay & Jacobson's typology? What about catalyzing political will and mobilizing financial resources?

b.   United Nations Organs with Environmental Functions[1]

Within the United Nations there is one entity that is primarily focused on environmental protection and a number of others for which this is one of many concerns. There have also been a number of environmental conferences, and UN organs have also sponsored numerous environmental treaties whose implementation in turn depends on treaty organs associated with such organs. These bodies are discussed below.

i.   Primarily Environmental Institutions—United Nations Environment Programme (UNEP)

UNEP is a standing quasi-autonomous subsidiary organ of the UN General Assembly, established as a result of the 1972 UN [Stockholm] Conference on the Human Environment (discussed below).[2] Actually, the Assembly did not, strictly speaking, establish UNEP as such, but rather it created[3] a number of organs that, together, constituted the complex subsidiary organ referred to as UNEP. These organs were a 58-member Governing Council of UNEP (a restricted representative organ); the Environment Secretariat (explicitly characterized as "small"), headed by the Executive Director of UNEP; the Environment Fund; and the Environment Coordination Board (with an undefined membership, but clearly meant to consist of representatives of all environmentally active UN System organs and organizations, under the chairmanship of the UNEP Executive Director). The primary functions of these organs (except

---

[1]   Portions of this section are adapted from P.C. Szasz, *Restructuring the International Organizational Framework (part A, The current structure)*, in Environmental Change and International Law, Chapter 11 (Edith Brown Weiss ed., 1992).

[2]   Indeed, the Action Plan for the Human Environment adopted by the Conference (A/CONF.48/14/Rev.1, Chapter II) did not call for the establishment of any UN organ, but principally for enhancing a number of organs and activities of various existing organs and organizations of the UN System, largely to be co-ordinated by the UN Secretary-General.

[3]   By A/RES/2997 (XXVII) of Dec. 15, 1972, on Institutional and Financial Arrangements for International Environmental Cooperation, which was reaffirmed by A/RES/31/ 112 of 16 December 1976, with the same title.

for the Fund) were to be to catalyze efforts to protect the environment, promote international environmental cooperation, and coordinate environmental programs within the UN system. In 1978 the Environment Coordination Board was created, with each UN agency appointing a Designated Official on Environmental Matters (DOEM) to work with and advise UNEP's Executive Director. In an evolutionary process, the Administrative Committee on Coordination (ACC) replaced the Environment Coordination Board and was subsequently replaced by the Chief Executive Board (CEB). CEB is an inter-agency coordination body for social, economic and other related matters that brings together every two years the executive heads of 29 participating entities. For a history of the establishment of UNEP, including its location in Nairobi, *see,* Nicholas Kimani, *From Stockholm to Nairobi,* 34 Envtl. Pol'y & L. 231 (2004).

In 2012 at the United Nations Conference on Sustainable Development (Rio+20) world leaders called for the strengthening and upgrading of UNEP, among other things, via the establishment of the universal membership of UNEP's Governing Council. Thereafter, in March 2013 pursuant to UN General Assembly resolution A/RES/67/251 the universal Governing Council was renamed as the United Nations Environment Assembly (UNEA). It has the mandate to "take strategic decisions, provide political guidance in the work of UNEP and promote a strong science-policy interface." In June 2014 UNEA held its first session composed of environmental ministers, government delegates, and representatives of major groups and stakeholders. Distinctions between UNEA and the former Governing Council are: (1) UNEA has universal UN membership; (2) it meets every two years; (3) at the end of each biannual meeting ministers decide on UNEA policies; [4] (4) UNEA's Bureau is composed of ten members—two from each UN geographic region; and (5) there are additional annual meetings where government representatives can meet with UNEP before seeking UNEA approval. Also, UNEA has a subsidiary inter-sessional body—the open-ended Committee of Permanent Representatives (CPR)—which provides policy advice, prepares the agenda and decisions to be adopted, and oversees policy implementation. The CPR has a subcommittee that reviews the medium-term strategy, program, and budget and has more participation by civil society than previously.

Considering the handicaps of its somewhat oblique establishment (due to a reluctance to create any new international institutions at that time), of its location for political reasons in remote Nairobi, far from the

---

[4] UNEA meetings allow the possibility of: (1) providing policy guidance and responses to environmental issues; (2) setting the global environmental agenda; (3) improving policies through discussion and exchange of ideas; (4) organizing discussions on environmental issues between concerned groups; and (5) assisting the development of partnerships to help achieve environmental goals. Our Planet (June 2014).

institutions it was supposed to coordinate, and of its always rather scanty funding, UNEP actually has become a remarkably effective centerpiece of the world organization's efforts to protect the environment. It has over the past four decades operated a strikingly varied and important set of programs, which include the stimulation of research, the collection and coordination of data, the promotion of new environmental laws at the national level, publications, education, the sponsorship of negotiations leading to the adoption of international treaties, and the establishment of numerous specialized environmental organs, as well as the issuing of guidelines and other types of "soft law." Some of UNEP's most important past activities, projects, and accomplishments are the following.[5]

(1) Ozone Layer. UNEP sponsored the negotiations leading first to the 1985 Vienna Convention for the Protection of the Ozone Layer and then to its 1987 Montreal Protocol, and provides the secretariat for the treaty organs (e.g., the Meetings of the Parties) established by either instrument; in the latter capacity it assisted in the Helsinki, London, and Copenhagen meetings at which important amendments to the protocol were negotiated and adopted.

(2) Climate. UNEP and WMO cosponsor the Intergovernmental Panel on Climate Change (IPCC) in which the scientific, technical, and political foundations were laid for the negotiation of the 1992 United Nations Framework Convention on Climate Change (UNFCCC), to create a regime to protect the global climate from greenhouse warming, as well as the 1997 Kyoto Protocol thereto and subsequent instruments.

(3) Hazardous Wastes. In 1987 the UNEP Governing Council adopted the Cairo Guidelines and Principles for the Environmentally Sound Management of Hazardous Wastes, and UNEP sponsored the negotiations that led to the adoption of the 1989 Basel Convention on the Control of Transboundary Movements of Hazardous Wastes and Their Disposal.

(4) Marine Environment. In 1974 UNEP initiated its Regional Seas Program,[6] which now covers some 11 distinct international seas, for each of which an action plan has been adopted by the States concerned (some

---

[5] Systematic information about UNEP activities can be obtained since 1982 from the Annual Reports of the Executive Director, and from the episodically published UNEP Profiles (which set out cumulative information). The Reports of the UNEP Governing Council to the General Assembly (always published as Supplement No. 25 to the Official Records of the General Assembly), merely report on the Council's biannual (and sometimes special) sessions, and are not particularly informative. UNEP also issues a very considerable number of miscellaneous publications of environmental information (e.g., its GEO series), maintains the International Register of reporting on or describing particular programs, projects, subsidiary or associated organs, and reproducing the texts of various legal instruments or expert committee reports. Information about selected technical assistance and other projects can be found in the annual *Evaluation Reports.* All of these are available on line.

[6] These are described in a series of publications entitled UNEP Regional Seas Reports and Studies.

143 in all the Programs), some eight of which are being implemented by a respective framework convention supplemented by one or more protocols.[7]

(5) Fresh Water. Under its Program for the Environmentally Sound Management of Inland Water (EMINWA), UNEP sponsored the 1987 Zambezi Action Plan, and assisted in the negotiation and preparation of such plans for Lake Chad and for the Aral Sea.

(6) Land Degradation. With the assistance of the Food and Agriculture Organization (FAO) and United Nations Educational, Scientific and Cultural Organization (UNESCO), UNEP prepared, and in 1982 the Governing Council, adopted a World Soils Policy.

(7) Forests. UNEP cooperated with a number of other UN agencies in developing FAO's 1985 Tropical Forest Action Plan, and assisted in formulating the environmental provisions of the 1985 International Tropical Timber Agreement.

(8) Biological Diversity. In 1987 UNEP initiated the preparation of a framework convention on the protection and preservation of biological diversity. It also acts as the secretariat of both the 1973 Washington Convention on International Trade in Endangered Species of Wild Fauna and Flora (CITES) and of the 1979 Bonn Convention on the Conservation of Migratory Species of Wild Animals (CMS).

(9) Monitoring and Information Systems. Under its "Earthwatch" program, UNEP has established the Global Environment Monitoring System (GEMS), in which 33 UN organs and specialized agencies, as well as 10 secretariats, IUCN and over 140 States, participate. It has also established INFOTERRA a decentralized international mechanism for the exchange of information, and with ILO and WHO operates the International Programme on Chemical Safety (IPCS).

(10) Toxic Chemicals. Each of UNEP's four sequential 10-year plans for developing environmental law (the Montevideo Programmes I, II, III and IV), mentioned immediately below, emphasized the need for progress in managing toxic chemicals. UNEP sponsored the negotiations of the Rotterdam Convention for the Application of the Prior Informed Consent Procedure for Certain Hazardous Chemicals and Pesticides in International Trade (PIC Convention), adopted in 1998, and the Stockholm Convention on Persistent Organic Pollutants, adopted in 2001. UNEP also participates in the International Forum on Chemical Safety and in the Strategic Approach to International Chemicals Management

---

[7] For example, the 1976 Barcelona Convention for the Protection of the Mediterranean Sea Against Pollution, supported by two simultaneously adopted Protocols for the Prevention of Pollution of the Mediterranean Sea by Dumping from Ships and Aircraft and concerning Cooperation in Combating Pollution of the Mediterranean Sea by Oil and Other Harmful Substances in Cases of Emergency; the 1980 Athens Protocol for the Protection of the Mediterranean Sea against Pollution from Land-Based Sources; and the 1982 Geneva Protocol concerning Mediterranean Specially Protected Areas.

(the latter was completed in February 2006 at the International Conference on Chemicals Management). UNEP also sponsored negotiations of the Minamata Convention on Mercury, adopted in 2013, a global treaty to protect human health and the environment against the adverse effects of mercury. As of August 2015 it is not in force.

(11) Environmental Planning. UNEP has taken a number of important initiatives for setting or resetting the UN System's environmental agenda, such as the formulation of The United Nations System-Wide Medium-Term Environment Programmes for 1984–1989[8] and 1990–1995; [9] the formulation of the 1982 Programme for the Development and Periodic Review of Environmental Law (Montevideo Programme I) and three subsequent 10-year Montevideo Programmes (II, III and IV); and the establishment of both the Intergovernmental Inter-sessional Preparatory Committee on the Environmental Perspective to the Year 2000 and Beyond and of the World Commission on Environment and Development (Brundtland Commission), the reports of which were endorsed by the General Assembly.[10]

(12) Environmental Rule of Law. Since 2002, UNEP has organized a series of meetings of judges, prosecutors and auditors to examine issues relating to environmental law. As part of this effort, UNEP in 2012 created a new program titled "Rule of Law in the Field of the Environment", with a nine-member International Advisory Council co-chaired by two Chief Justices. The Program has included the First Asia and Pacific Colloquium on Environmental Law in 2013, with judges from many countries in Asia and South Asia, a regional meeting on rule of law with the OAS in Jamaica in 2015, judicial meetings in Brazil, and other global and regional initiatives to promote environmental rule of law and build capacity for implementing it.

ii. Institutions to Integrate Environmental Policies with Other Policies

(a) High-Level Political Forum on Sustainable Development

During Rio+20, State leaders replaced the Commission on Sustainable Development (which had been created by the 1992 Earth Summit) with the High-Level Political Forum on sustainable development (HLPF). HLPF is the principal platform within the UN dealing with sustainable development and all follow-up from Rio+20; it will also convene a meeting of Heads of State and Government every four years

---

8   UNEP/GC/DEC/10/13 of May 31, 1982.

9   UNEP/GC/DEC/SS.I/3 of March 18, 1988. The plan is reproduced in document UNEP/GCSS.I/7/Add. 1, and *inter alia,* sets out, in over 400 paragraphs, the "Problems addressed," the "General objective," the detailed "Specific objectives," the "System-wide strategy" and the "Implementation of the strategy" on some 32 programmatic items grouped under 16 headings.

10   A/RES/42/186 and 187 of Dec. 11, 1987.

that will provide political declarations intended to become policy guidelines and expedite results. Its established functions include: "(a) provide political leadership and guidance on sustainable development; (b) follow up and review progress in implementing sustainable development commitments; (c) enhance the integration of economic, social and environmental dimensions of sustainable development and (d) address new and emerging sustainable development challenges."[11]

(b) Economic, Cultural and Social Council (ECOSOC)

As a result of the 2012 Rio+20 Conference, ECOSOC's mandate was enlarged with respect to environmental sustainability. See UNGA Resolution 68/1 (20 Sept. 2013), UN Doc. A/RES/68/1.

(c) International Law Commission (ILC)

The ILC is composed of 34 members elected by the UN General Assembly who serve in their personal capacity and are to be "persons of recognized competence in international law". The ILC has frequently considered environmental issues as part of its mandate of "the promotion of the progressive development of international law and its codification". As of August 2015, for example, the ILC is considering the topics of "Protection of the environment in relation to armed conflicts" and "Protection of the atmosphere". Earlier environment-related topics considered by the ILC include "Law of the non-navigational uses of international watercourses", "Law of transboundary aquifers", "Prevention of transboundary harm from hazardous activities", and "International liability for injurious consequences arising out of acts not prohibited by international law". Its reports are considered and sometimes adopted by the UN General Assembly.

iii. UN-Related Treaty Bodies

In relation to many of the new or more acute environmental concerns, such as long-range transboundary air pollution, threats to the ozone layer, or the need to protect some particularly threatened or fragile environment or species, specific treaties have been concluded under the auspices of some of the above-mentioned organs. Aside from establishing and defining relevant obligations for the State Parties, some of these treaties have created full-fledged though small international organizations, with their own political organs and secretariats, or sometimes merely political or expert treaty organs without their own secretariats. These mini-organizations and treaty organs in effect function within the United Nations system and thus constitute crucial parts of its machinery for dealing with environmental matters. For the

---

[11] http://sustainabledevelopment.un.org/index.php?menu=1556.

most part, the secretariat functions for servicing these organs have been assigned, sometimes on a permanent and sometimes on merely an interim or experimental basis, to some existing subsidiary UN organ, such as UNEP or a UN Regional Commission. These treaty bodies are discussed further in part B, below.

The treaty bodies often have very specific roles, such as the Compliance Committee under the Montreal Protocol on Ozone Depleting Chemicals. That committee has been quite successful, as described in Chapter 5, and it has been emulated in some subsequent environmental regimes. The Aarhus Convention on Access to Information, Public Participation in Decision-making and Access to Justice in Environmental Matters uses a different type of compliance committee, established pursuant to article 15 of the convention. Compliance matters may be brought by the Committee itself, a Party, the secretariat, and members of the public. The UN Economic Commission for Europe (ECE) Convention on the Protection and Use of Transboundary Watercourses and International Lakes (ECE Water Convention) also has such a committee, called the Implementation Committee. Created in 2012, the committee had received one submission as of January 1, 2015, from an NGO. Reports of the committee's meetings are publicly available on the Internet.

Information about various global multilateral environmental treaty regimes, together with who administers them and the location of their respective secretariats, is provided in part B of this chapter. Suffice it to say here that the architecture of those regimes is fragmented, with many different IGOs (e.g., FAO, International Atomic Energy Agency (IAEA), International Maritime Organization (IMO), ECE, UNEP, and UNESCO), an INGO (IUCN) and even sometimes the treaty bodies themselves (e.g., UN Convention on the Law of the Sea (UNCLOS) and UNFCCC) administering the individual treaties in many different cities (e.g., Bonn, Geneva, Hamburg, Kingston, London, Montreal, Nairobi, and Rome).

2. ENVIRONMENTAL CONFERENCES

Another type of IGO activity are conferences convened for the purpose of adopting environmental treaties and other related instruments or merely to give an international platform for the exploration of a particular theme. Although these conferences can be characterized as ad hoc high-level representative organs of the convening IGOs, it should be recognized that an international conference does not consist of merely the relatively short meeting denominated as such, but that almost always there are several other stages and manifestations, often involving both governmental and non-governmental actors. For example, there typically are one or more preparatory meetings to set the agenda and negotiate the documents to be considered at an international environmental conference;

and governments, IGOs, NGOs and others use the outcome documents from such conferences to set priorities, organize and coordinate activities, and allocate resources.

a.   General Environmental Conferences

There have been four general environmental conferences, all convened by the United Nations:

(1) 1972 Stockholm Conference. The 1972 United Nations Conference on the Human Environment served to awaken the international community to the importance of protecting the environment and was followed by a number of institutional arrangements for that purpose (in particular, UNEP). Its formal work was embodied in a declaration (known as the Stockholm Declaration) including 26 Principles, as well as in a more detailed Action Plan for the Human Environment.

(2) 1992 Rio Conference. The 1992 United Nations Conference on Environment and Development (also called UNCED or the Earth Summit), convened two decades after the Stockholm Conference as a follow-up thereto, addressed the more obviously divergent views of developed and developing countries towards environmental issues, and sought to bridge these by the concept of "sustainable development." To implement this concept it recommended the establishment of standing organs, such as the Commission on Sustainable Development and the High-Level Advisory Board on Sustainable Development. It issued the Rio Declaration on Environment and Development with 27 Principles; Agenda 21, consisting of 40 somewhat lengthy chapters; and a Non-Legally Binding Authoritative Statement of Principles for a Global Consensus on the Management, Conservation and Sustainable Development of all Types of Forests. The Conference also provided the forum for the opening for signature of the Convention on Biological Diversity and the UNFCCC, which had been negotiated and formulated separately from, but in parallel to, the preparations for the Conference.

(3) 2002 World Summit on Sustainable Development in Johannesburg. This conference completed the move to considering environmental protection in the context of sustainable development, which was begun at the Stockholm Conference (which discussed human rights and economic and social activities in its Declaration) and continued at UNCED. The WSSD finalized a Plan of Implementation that contained a few new commitments (including one on chemicals) and a new focus on the importance of "partnerships" between governments and all other sectors of society.

(4) 2012 United Nations Conference on Sustainable Development (Rio+20) in Rio de Janeiro. This conference sought to establish pathways for a safe, equitable, clean, green and prosperous world via two main themes: green economy and the international framework on sustainable

development. The outcomes, among others, were the political document *The Future We Want,* guidelines on green economy policies, a decision to strengthen UNEP, the establishment of the HLPF, and over 700 voluntary commitments and 196 partnerships to advance sustainable development.

b. Specific Environment-Related Conferences

Ever since the Stockholm Conference, the United Nations has convened a number of much more narrowly focused, environment-related conferences. Some of these have been essentially thematic, to focus attention on a particular problem; others have been charged with formulating treaties to formalize cooperative solutions to such problems. Following are some of the more important such meetings:

(1) The 1974 World Population Conference, Bucharest, adopted the World Population Plan of Action. It was followed by the 1984 International Conference on Population, which adopted the Mexico City Declaration on Population and Development, and the 1994 International Conference on Population and Development, Cairo, which adopted a 20-year Programme of Action (including a chapter on population and environment).

(2) The 1976 Conference on Human Settlements (Habitat), Vancouver, which adopted the Vancouver Declaration on Human Settlements leading to the establishment of the UN Centre for Human Settlements (Habitat) in Nairobi. Discussions among civil society representatives at that meeting led to the formation of Habitat for Humanity. It led to Habitat II in 1996, described below.

(3) The 1977 Conference on Desertification, Nairobi, produced the Plan of Action to Combat Desertification. After years of work on the subject within UNEP, the General Assembly in 1992 established the International Negotiating Committee for the Elaboration of an International Convention to Combat Desertification in Those Countries Experiencing Serious Drought and/or Desertification, particularly in Africa, which in 1994 adopted the eponymous Convention (UNCCD).

(4) The 1977 United Nations Water Conference, Mar del Plata (Argentina), approved the Mar del Plata Action Plan and several specific agreements. Many other conferences on fresh water have followed.

(5) The 1981 United Nations Conference on New and Renewable Sources of Energy, Nairobi, adopted the Nairobi Programme of Action for the Development and Utilization of New and Renewable Sources of Energy.

(6) The 1994 Global Conference on the Sustainable Development of Small Island Developing States, Bridgetown (Barbados), adopted the

Declaration of Barbados and the Programme of Action for the Sustainable Development of Small Island Developing States.

(7) The 1995 Conference on Straddling Fish Stocks and Highly Migratory Fish Stocks, New York, adopted the eponymous Convention.

(8) The 1995 World Summit on Social Development adopted the Copenhagen Declaration, paragraph 6 of which for the first time in a globally agreed UN document linked economic development, social development and environmental protection as essential and mutually supportive elements of sustainable development.

(9) The 1996 Second UN Conference on Human Settlements, Istanbul (Habitat II), adopted the Habitat Agenda and the Istanbul Declaration, which contained provisions related to environmental justice (withut using that term) and the commitment to eliminate lead from gasoline.

3.   IGOS THAT ARE NOT SPECIFICALLY ENVIRONMENTAL BUT NEVERTHELESS DEAL WITH ISSUES DIRECTLY RELATING TO THE ENVIRONMENT

a.   General

Several IGOs exist with mandates that are not expressly environmental but nevertheless address issues that relate directly to the environment. At the global level, these institutions include FAO, IAEA, ILO, IMO, and the International Renewable Energy Agency (IRENA). Most of these are referenced in section B of this chapter. Regional institutions also exist.

b.   International Financial Institutions

As discussed in Chapter 17, international finance institutions such as the World Bank also deal with environmental issues, as do regional financial institutions (e.g., the Inter-American Development Bank).

c.   Human Rights Bodies

Because of the growing importance of a rights-based approach to protecting the environment and human health, human rights institutions and other bodies are increasingly relevant to environmental protection. These entities are described in Chapter 15. Briefly, these institutions exist at global, regional, bilateral and national levels. The primary global ones are the UN Human Rights Council, committees associated with global human rights treaties, and so-called special procedures appointed by the Human Rights Council regarding specific human rights issues (e.g., the Special Rapporteur (formerly Independent Expert) on Human Rights and the Environment, and the Special Rapporteur on Human Rights and Toxic Substances).

At the regional level, each of Africa, the Americas and Europe have human rights instruments and dispute settlement institutions that allow, inter alia, individuals to bring complaints against States. The Association of Southeast Asian Nations (ASEAN) adopted a human rights instrument, though without an institutional structure such as the other three regions have. Regional institutions such as the Inter-American Commission on Human Rights also sometimes appoint special procedures to focus on specific human rights issues within their region (e.g., the Special Rapporteur on Indigenous Peoples appointed by that Commission).

National Human Rights Institutions (NHRIs) exist in most countries to coordinate human rights-related activities nationally. NHRIs meet annually to discuss good practices, etc.

4. INTERNATIONAL NON-GOVERNMENTAL ORGANIZATIONS

There are two areas of international intercourse where NGOs have made (and are making) a particularly significant impact: the protection of human rights and the protection of the environment. In each field these organizations, both INGOs and NNGOs, carry out important functions vis-à-vis IGOs and national governments. In both fields, but particularly regarding the environment, these functions include:

(1) Monitoring the condition of the environment, the impact on those conditions of particular anthropogenic events, and the environmental impact of particular protective measures undertaken by international, national and sub-national actors. The results of these studies are communicated to IGOs and national governments, as well as, through the media, to the public. NGO members also are often involved in crowd-sourcing (also referred to as "citizen science") regarding environmental conditions (e.g., River Watchers who conduct periodic sampling and upload the data to centralized collection bodies).

(2) Lobbying IGOs and governments, directly or through the generation of public pressure, for the establishment and implementation of regimes designed to protect the environment, whether in the form of treaties, statutes, regulations, guidelines, or other forms of international and national laws and regulations.

(3) Assisting IGO and governmental organs in formulating appropriate legal texts, and participating as observers in negotiating rules and treaties, such as the UNCITRAL Rules on Transparency in Treaty-Based Investor-State Arbitrations and the United Nations Convention on Transparency in Treaty-Based Investor-State Arbitrations (also known as the Mauritius Convention on Transparency).

(4) Providing information on factual matters to treaty-based compliance committees.

(5) In a few instances, participating in the administration of certain aspects of environmental regimes (e.g., the IUCN administers the Ramsar Convention on the Protection of Wetlands (Ramsar Convention)).

(6) In some cases, participating in international arbitrations involving environmental issues, such as the *Shrimp/Turtle* and *EC Biotech* cases in the World Trade Organization (discussed in Chapter 16), and the *Methanex* case under the North American Free Trade Agreement, and the *Suez Vivendi* case under an Argentinean bilateral investment agreement.

(7) Mobilizing international or domestic political pressure to take action.

There are a vast number of environmental NNGOs and many environmental INGOs, many of which have consultative status with ECOSOC and observer status with UNEP.

5.   SUMMARY AND CONCLUSIONS

The international institutional structure relevant to the protection of the environment in some ways resembles national regimes, but in many important ways differs from them. In both there are norm-creating legislative organs; in both there are executive ones charged with implementing these regimes, but the national ones are typically better equipped to do so effectively; and both have dispute settlement mechanisms, though the national ones are typically far more developed and effective, in particular because these, unlike most international ones (with the notable exceptions of the European Union (EU) and human rights bodies), have compulsory jurisdiction.

International regimes are more complex and decentralized than national ones. The reason of course is that there does not exist any world government, or even a regional one, with the possible exception of the EU for part of Europe. But a more fundamental reason probably is that the international community is far more diverse than any national one, which becomes obvious when one compares the actors (principally States) on the international scene, according to size, power, wealth, or stage of development. Consequently it is difficult to achieve agreement on any but the narrowest aspects of international governance (such as the establishment of a regime meant to protect against a very specific threat), which therefore is assigned somewhat haphazardly to numerous largely independently established IGOs, with essentially no hierarchical relationships. At most there are certain weak coordinating mechanisms within the groups into which many, but by no means all, international organizations are clustered. Because there is no central authority that could undertake to rearrange international organizations and organs into a more logical pattern, and because there is (and has been for some time) an aversion to the creation of any more significant new institutions, improvements can only be incremental. At present most of these consist of ad hoc additions, either to the functions of existing organizations or in a minor way to the international machinery by the creation of treaty organs or mini-IGOs.

This having been said, it should be noted that as far as environmental affairs are concerned, the world community has been able to formulate instruments and to create institutions essentially as fast as agreements can be reached on these—which of course is not always easy given the diversity in both the nature and the interests of the approximately 200 States now involved in the process. Naturally, these agreements often reflect a low common denominator—but this is a phenomenon also often observed in legislation produced in democratically governed States.

What the international system, to a considerable extent, lacks are simplicity, elegance, and the transparency that would go with these characteristics. Outsiders (and even sometimes insiders) may find it difficult to disentangle the multiplicity of institutions that may be dealing with a particular issue and to try to establish responsibility for failures. Nevertheless, once such understanding has been achieved—and this has been done by those operating many of the NGOs in this field and accounts for their ability to influence the process—it can be seen that international institutions respond to essentially the same stimuli as national ones, and that the abilities to secure and to present relevant facts persuasively, to identify the competent centers of power and to analyze their special interests and concerns, and above all to negotiate with those whose interests are different, are the elements essential to success in achieving improvements in both international and national environmental regimes.

As is explained in more detail below, the complex and fragmented international environmental legal architecture just described is confronted by numerous governance challenges. These challenges are multiplied because they must be dealt with in a kaleidoscopic world, i.e., a world in which there are many different actors in addition to States, in which the issues and coalitions are constantly changing, and in which bottom-up empowerment is central, though there may be powerful forces trying to control the configurations of the kaleidoscope.

NOTES AND QUESTIONS

What can we do? Consider the problem at the beginning of this part. What recourse or other assistance would be available from the institutions referred to above? In what order might you approach the relevant institutions?

B. ENVIRONMENTAL GOVERNANCE

1. WHAT IS ENVIRONMENTAL GOVERNANCE?

There is no agreed-upon definition of "governance" with respect to the environment. For purposes of this chapter, which takes a common-sense functional approach, the term "governance" refers to the means by which society, acting through multi-level interactions at the sub-national, national, regional and global levels by four main sets of actors, determines and acts on goals and priorities related to the management and protection of natural and cultural resources and the environmental aspects of human health. These actors are States, intergovernmental organizations (IGOs), civil society organizations (including non-governmental organizations (NGOs) and business enterprises), and individuals. "Governance" thus includes the rules, both formal and informal, that govern human behavior in environmental decision-making processes (including how transparent they are and who gets to participate in them), the decisions themselves, and the institutions involved in making, implementing and monitoring decisions. "Governance" also includes the financial management of institutions engaged in environmental governance and the coordination among environmental and other governance institutions.

Environmental governance should not be, and by and large is not, static. Rather it is a dynamic process that must adapt to changing environmental conditions, population increases or shifts, technological developments, scientific knowledge, public awareness and political realities. This chapter does not attempt to predict what governance challenges will result as these parameters change, for example as the climate is disrupted and changes. But it seems clear that climate change and other environmental factors, as well as technological developments and political changes, will have significant implications for environmental governance.

In sum, environmental governance occurs at many layers of governance, involves many actors, must constantly adapt to changing challenges, knowledge and circumstances, and is complex and in many ways fragmented.

NOTES AND QUESTIONS

While reading the following materials, students are encouraged to consider:

1. *What's coming?* What new governance challenges and opportunities will likely be created by climate change and geo-engineering, by population growth, and by technological developments such as changes in information technology and genetic engineering, nanotechnology and synthetic biology?

2.   *Are we up to the task?* Is the international community adequately considering these possible governance challenges now?

3.   *Who gets a say?* Would it be better if voting in environmental IGOs were based on population and/or on financial contributions to the IGO, instead of the now normal one-member, one-vote basis?

4.   *Who gets to pay?* Should contributions to environmental IGOs be on an assessed contribution, voluntary contribution, or some other basis?

5.   *Who gets to play?* Should environmental INGOs and NNGOs be given a greater role in shaping the work of IGOs? What might such increased roles be? Do you consider INGOs and NNGOs better representatives of the interests of normal citizens than the governmental representatives who determine the policies of IGOs? Why or why not? *See generally* Edith Brown Weiss, *The Changing Structure of International Law*, Georgetown Univeristy Law Center, May 23, 1996, reprinted in Geogetown Law—Res Ipsa Loquitur 52 (Spring 1997) and excerpted in Chapter 1.

6.   *Want to read more?* For discussions of governance in various environmental contexts, see: Rachel Gisselquist, *What does good governance mean?* United Nations University. http://unu.edu/publications/articles/what-does-good-governance-mean.html#info (2012); Rachel Gisselquist, *Good Governance as a Concept and Why This Matters for Policy Development.* Working Paper No. 2012/30 United Nations University (2012); Lawrence Busch, *Food Standards: the Cacophony of Governance*, Journal of Experimental Botany 62(10): 3247–3250 (2011); Lynda Cheshire & Geoffrey Lawrence, *Re-shaping the State: Global/local networks of association and the governing of agricultural production*, 3 in Higgins and Lawrence, eds., Agricultural Governance: Globalization and the New Politics of Regulation (2005); Jennifer Clapp & Doris Fuchs, eds., Corporate Power in Global Agrifood Governance, (2009); Peter Feindt, *The politics of biopatents in food and agriculture, 1950–2010: Value conflict, competing paradigms and contested institutionalisation in multi-level governance*, 31 Policy and Society 281–293 (2012); J.P. Voss, D. Bauknecht & R. Kemp, eds., Reflexive governance for sustainable development (2006); G. Jaffe, *Implementing the Cartagena Biosafety Protocol through national biosafety regulatory systems: an analysis of key unresolved issues*, 5 Journal of Public Affairs 299–311 (2005); G. Jaffe, Comparative Analysis of the National Biosafety Regulatory Systems In East Africa (2006) (IFPRI EPTD Discussion Paper 146, http://www.ifpri.org/publication/comparative-analysis-national-biosafety-regulatory-systems-east-africa).

2.   WHAT IS EFFECTIVE GOVERNANCE?

Just as there is no agreed definition of "governance", there also does not exist a commonly agreed definition of "effective governance" regarding the environment. As with the concept of "governance", this book takes a functional approach. Effective governance thus requires that States, IGOs and other international actors participate appropriately with respect to the governance of environmental legal regimes, that goverance be transparent and allow meaningful participation by the public, and that the governance institutions of those and other relevant legal regimes carry out their mandate, perform their functions and coordinate appropriately among themselves so that the environmental problem(s) in question are resolved. As explained further below, this must occur vertically among instruments and institutions at different levels dealing with the same set of substantive issues, horizontally among instruments and institutions at the same geographic level, and diagonally between geographic levels and across substantive areas.

Vertical governance refers to interactions among instruments and institutions at different geographic levels that deal with the same substantive issues. The need for effective vertical governance arises because it is quite common that the same or inter-related environmental problems are dealt with at different geographical levels. Sometimes this reflects operation of the principle of subsidiarity, i.e., the smallest, lowest or least centralized competent authority should deal with an issue. Sometimes this is a result of other environment-related political decisions and realities, or of political considerations unrelated to the environment or subsidiarity. Subsidiarity often makes sense with respect to environmental protection (and sustainable development) because it allocates decision-making and action to the level most knowledgeable about, and directly affected by, a policy or action. On the other hand, as the United States' experience with parklands demonstrates,[12] sometimes disparities in political interests at a lower level can overwhelm legitimate interests at a higher level.

Myriad instances of vertical governance exist with respect to protecting the environment. An example is the nested set of legal instruments and institutions relating to La Plata River basin, which contains the Uruguay River: Argentina and Uruguay are Parties to the bilateral Statute of the River Uruguay, the bilateral Treaty between Uruguay and Argentina concerning the Rio de la Plata and the Corresponding Maritime Boundary, the regional La Plata Basin Treaty, and the regional (but not yet in force) Guarani Aquifer Agreement regarding the aquifer that underlies La Plata basin (and part of the Amazon River basin, as well). Another example relates to the Danube River: Germany is a Party to the global United Nations Convention on the Non-Navigational Uses of International Watercourses (UN Watercourses Convention), the United Nations Economic Commission for Europe (ECE) Convention on the Protection and Use of Transboundary

---

[12] The United States' experience with Yosemite Valley is an example: initially the U.S. government gave the valley and surrounding lands to California for a state park, then Californian private interests exerted political pressure that resulted in damaging encroachments on the state park, and ultimately the US government repossessed the land and made it a national park.

Watercourses and International Lakes (ECE Water Convention), and the regional, basin-specific Convention on Cooperation for the Protection and Sustainable Use of the Danube (Danube Convention). Needless to say, Argentina, Uruguay and Germany also have domestic legislation relating to the water in these rivers, and Germany is subject to the European Union directive on water.

Because of the interdependence of environmental problems (addressed in Chapter 1) and the inter-relationship of environmental protection with other areas of international law (such as human rights and trade law, discussed in chapters 15 and 16, respectively), it is essential that horizontal coordination occur among instruments and institutions at the same geographic level, whether it be global, regional, national or sub-national. Thus efforts to protect biological diversity under the Convention on Biological Diversity (CBD) are related to, and should under some circumstances be coordinated with, activities pursuant to the Convention on International Trade in Endangered Species of Wild Fauna and Flora (CITES), the Ramsar Convention on the Protection of Wetlands (Ramsar Convention), various marine mammal and fisheries agreements such as the International Convention for the Conservation of Atlantic Tunas, and the World Trade Organization Agreement on Subsidies and Countervailing Measures (which affects fishing subsidies), each of which is directly related to biological diversity. Similarly, efforts to deal with the safety aspects of shipbreaking must consider the Hong Kong International Convention for the Safe and Environmentally Sound Recycling of Ships (Shipbreaking Convention), the Basel Convention on the International Transfer of Hazardous Substances (Basel Convention), and International Labour Organization (ILO) agreements. The governance structures of those agreements and the practices of their governing and administering bodies differ and affect how well such coordination can occur. Horizontal governance must deal with the political realities existing at the relevant level, of course, which can present opportunities or challenges.

Diagonal governance issues arise because instruments and institutions must interact across subject-matter areas that define vertical cooperation and between the geographic levels that define horizontal governance. For example, the Guiana Shield project (which involves Suriname, Guyana, French Guiana and the Brazilian state of Amapá) is a regional project addressing, inter alia, deforestation and REDD+ (discussed in Chapter 9). It thus deals with issues relating to climate change, biological diversity, forests and water. The project is cooperating with the regional Amazon Cooperation Treaty Organization (Brazil is a Party to the Amazon Cooperation Treaty) and expects to coordinate with the global secretariats of the CBD and UNFCCC. Similarly, environmental protection efforts regarding pollution of a community by lead or mercury or the local impacts of climate change may need to take into account human rights such as those regarding the right to life, the right to an adequate standard of living, and the right to enjoy culture.

3.   EFFICIENT GOVERNANCE

Protection of the environment also requires efficient governance. Financial and other resources available to protect the environment and human health are limited, at all levels of government and in all aspects of civil society. It is thus necessary either to achieve the most environmental protection possible from the available resources or to utilize the fewest resources possible to meet defined environmental objectives. Although in an ideal world the latter might be the more appropriate inquiry, in the authors' experience international political and financial realities typically result in inadequate funding for addressing international environmental problems, so that the former approach is needed.

Efficiency analyses must take into account the effects of a governance structure or practice on costs at all levels. For example, changes in practices of holding international meetings designed to save money at the global or regional level may have unintended cost consequences at the national level as governments have to staff those meetings in new ways. For a concrete instance, see the discussion of the co-ordination regarding the Basel, Rotterdam and Stockholm Conventions, below.

NOTES AND QUESTIONS

1.   *Unintended consequences.* How can inadvertent cost-raising effects be anticipated? Would it help accomplish this if national governments, civil society and other IGOs were consulted in advance?

2.   *Treaty promiscuity?* Why would a country enter into more than one agreement concerning the same thing? Isn't this overkill? Wouldn't it be confusing to the national authorities charged with ensuring compliance with the country's international agreements?

4.   OVERVIEW OF CURRENT GOVERNANCE SITUATION

Efforts to achieve effectiveness and efficiency in governance are complicated by the fact that the international environmental protection architecture is characterized by hundreds of separate international legal agreements and institutions at the global, regional, and bilateral levels,[13] together with thousands of binding and non-binding decisions issued by the governing bodies of those agreements, rather than by a single coherent international legal and institutional regime. This situation emerged as a result of many factors, including often that scientific

---

[13]   It is often said that there are over 500 multilateral environmental agreements (MEAs)—a number that includes MEAs at the regional level.

understanding of a particular problem crystallized before that regarding other related problems and that the political will to engage in trying to reach international solutions to different problems also developed at different times.

The governance picture is further complicated by hundreds of non-legally binding ("soft law") instruments, also at the global, regional, and bilateral levels,[14] as well as by presumably non-legally binding unilateral commitments such as those made by States in the context of the 2009 Copenhagen Accord on Climate Change and the 2009 Washington agreement on fissile materials. This situation is additionally complicated by conditions imposed by international financial institutions in carrying out their safeguard policies. Finally, still more complexity is added by the existence of voluntary standards such as those of the International Standard Organization (ISO) and the *Codex Alimentarius* Commission, the United Nations Compact on Corporate Responsibility, environment-related contractual provisions in supply chain contracts in the private sector (which cease to be voluntary once they are included in a loan agreement or purchase agreement), and industry- or enterprise-specific codes of conduct, as well as by the roles that civil society plays in catalyzing, promulgating and monitoring standards.

The discussion in this part focuses on horizontal governance among multilateral environmental agreements (MEAs) at the global level, though examples of vertical and diagonal governance issues and solutions are also provided at some points. For the sake of clarity, these global MEAs are referred to herein as "GMEAs", though students should be aware that this is not a common acronym.

This discussion describes the landscape in terms of governance characteristics of GMEAs, addresses the challenges arising from that landscape, examines measures undertaken to alleviate those challenges, and raises questions about future reform. Because serious efforts have been made to improve horizontal governance in the so-called "chemicals cluster" of GMEAs, the discussion herein often utilizes examples of horizontal governance challenges and measures from this cluster. This cluster consists of the Basel Convention on International Trade in Hazardous Wastes (Basel Convention), the Rotterdam Convention on Prior Informed Consent (Rotterdam Convention), the Stockholm Convention on Persistent Organic Pollutants (Stockholm Convention), and—probably in the future—the nascent Minamata Convention on Mercury.[15]

---

[14] For a list of more than 900 binding and non-binding international environmental instruments existing at the time of the 1992 United Nations Conference on Environment and Development, see Edith Brown Weiss, Daniel Magraw & Paul C. Szasz, International Environmental Law: Basic Instruments and References (1992).

[15] As of July 2015, the Minamata Convention has an interim secretariat that is reporting to the Chemicals division of UNEP. Some expect that when the Convention enters into force, the

It must be emphasized that this focus over-simplifies the range of issues that exist regarding environmental governance. For example, governance is complicated by the existence of regional and bilateral efforts that may parallel, complement or even conflict with approaches under GMEAs. An example of an important regional chemicals program is the European Union's regulation regarding Registration, Evaluation, Authorisation and Restriction of Chemicals (REACH). Space does not allow a full treatment of all of those issues.

NOTES AND QUESTIONS

1.   *Other clusters?* Students are encouraged to think about how governance issues play out among other possible clusters. These might include: a biological diversity cluster (e.g., Convention on Biological Diversity (CBD), Convention on International Trade in Endangered Species (CITES), Convention on Migratory Species (CMS), Ramsar Convention on Wetlands (Ramsar Convention) and World Heritage Convention (WHC)); a climate change cluster (e.g., UN Framework Convention on Climate Change (UNFCCC), the Kyoto Protocol to the UNFCCC, as amended, and the Vienna Convention on Chemicals that Deplete the Ozone Layer and its Montreal Protocol); or a water cluster (e.g., the UN Convention on Non-Navigational Uses of International Watercourses (UN Watercourses Convention) and the ECE Convention on the Protection and Use of Transboundary Watercourses and International Lakes (ECE Water Convention, which is in the process of being opened for universal membership)). Regarding the last-mentioned cluster, see, e.g., Stephen C. McCaffrey, *International Water Cooperation in the 21st Century: Recent Developments*, in the Law of International Watercourses, 23 RECIEL 4, 12–13 (2014).

2.   *Other levels?* What horizontal governance issues are likely to arise at regional and bilateral levels? Are these likely to differ in nature or scope from issues with respect to GMEAs? Are solutions to these issues likely to differ from those at the global level? Do normative, institutional or cultural differences exist that make horizontal governance at these levels different than horizontal governance at the global level?

3.   *Vertical, horizontal and diagonal governance: a directional mish-mash?* What vertical and diagonal governance issues are likely to arise at various levels? Will approaches used to deal with horizontal governance issues be effective? What additional challenges might exist, and how might they be overcome?

4.   *Too much governance?* Is the complexity of governance a bad thing? In which ways could it contribute to the solution or management of environmental problems? What are its drawbacks? This issue is raised again in the following section.

---

interim secretariat will be merged with the joint secretariat for the Basel, Rotterdam and Stockholm Conventions (the BRS secretariat), discussed further below.

5. *Is governance a hot topic*? Consider the following statement: Governance may not be an exciting topic to some, but it is terribly important for everyone. Do you agree?

5. THE CURRENT LANDSCAPE REGARDING GLOBAL MULTILATERAL ENVIRONMENTAL AGREEMENTS— FRAGMENTATION AND OVERLAP

a. Different Obligations and Parties

Each global multilateral environmental agreement (GMEA) is a separate international legal instrument. Because each GMEA was crafted to address a specific environmental threat or set of threats, GMEAs understandably contain different legal obligations. Among other things, GMEAs typically contain substantive obligations as well as requirements for periodic reporting. Just as do the substantive obligations, the reporting requirements vary among GMEAs regarding content and timing, though there is often some overlap or duplication. This has resulted in a proliferation of substantive and procedural obligations for Parties to GMEAs. This in turn has led to the situation where States, particularly developing countries, may have difficulty being aware of the full range of GMEA obligations to which they are subject.

Moreover, different GMEAs have different membership. For instance, as of November 1, 2014, in the chemicals cluster, the Basel Convention had 181 Parties, the Rotterdam Convention had 154 Parties, and the Stockholm Convention had 179 Parties; and the Minamata Convention had eight Parties. In the biological diversity cluster, the CBD had 194 Parties, CITES had 180 Parties, the CMS had 119 Parties, and the Ramsar Convention had 168 Parties. Table 18.1 provides a more complete sample of GMEAs and their respective number of Parties. The set of international legal obligations of a State arising under GMEAs thus often differs from those of other States because they are not Parties to the same GMEAs.

b. Different Administering Agencies and Separate Treaty Bodies and Secretariats Based at Different Locations

i. *Different Administering Agencies*

Several intergovernmental organizations administer GMEAs. For instance, the Basel and Stockholm Conventions are administered by the United Nations Environment Program (UNEP); UNEP and the Food and Agriculture Organization (FAO) have administrative roles with respect to the Rotterdam Convention; the International Plant Protection Convention is administered by FAO; the World Heritage Convention is administered by the United Nations Educational Scientific and Cultural Organization (UNESCO); the Convention on Assistance in Nuclear Accidents is administered by the International Atomic Energy Agency (IAEA); and the Convention on Marine Pollution (MARPOL) is administered by the International Maritime Organization (IMO). Two MEAs that were originally regional but now are open, or in the process of being opened, to universal membership—the Aarhus Convention on Access to Information, Public Participation in Decision-making and Access to Justice in Environmental Matters and the ECE Water Convention—are administered by the ECE. In addition, some GMEAs are administered directly by the United Nations and thus are relatively stand-alone: prime examples are the United Nations Convention on the Law of the Sea (UNCLOS, for which the the UN Office of Legal Affairs' Division of Ocean Affairs and Law of the Sea serves as secretariat) and the UNFCCC (which has its own secretariat). Finally, one GMEA—the Ramsar Convention—has no direct administrative ties to the United Nations or a United Nations Specialized Agency and rather is administered by the International Union for the Conservation of Nature and Natural Resources (IUCN), a hybrid INGO with both governmental and non-governmental members and commissions involving thousands of individuals around the world.

This situation can lead to difficulties. The sheer number of administering agencies involved causes inefficiencies in communicating. In addition, each administering agency has its own perspective and expertise based on its mandate; and these perspectives are not uniform and the expertise may not be complementary or conversely it may be duplicative. The result may be differing priorities and approaches, so that coordination among agencies can be time-consuming or worse. Moreover, the fairly universal tendency to protect or enlarge one's "turf" can lead to bureaucratic squabbling and inefficiencies among administering agencies.

ii. Separate Treaty Bodies and Secretariats Based at Different Locations

Each GMEA identified above establishes its own set of treaty bodies, typically consisting of a Conference of the Parties (COP), a secretariat, and one or more scientific committees and possibly a compliance mechanism. Each COP establishes rules and procedures with respect to its GMEA, and each COP issues scores or hundreds of decisions that are to be followed in implementing that GMEA. (The UN Watercourses Convention is unusual in that it does not establish any treaty bodies; whether the Parties will decide to establish such bodies, including a secretariat had not been determined as of July 2015.)

The secretariats of these GMEAs are located in several different countries that are widely dispersed geographically. For example, the joint secretariat of the Basel, Rotterdam and Stockholm Conventions (discussed below) is located in Geneva, Switzerland (before that, the

Rotterdam Convention secretariat consisted of two teams: an FAO team in Rome, Italy, and a UNEP team in Geneva); the Ramsar secretariat is located in Gland, Switzerland; the UNFCCC secretariat is located in Bonn, Germany; the CBD secretariat is located in Montreal, Canada; the World Heritage Convention secretariat is in Paris, France; and UNCLOS has its secretariat in New York City in the United States and major treaty bodies located in two other countries: the International Tribunal on the Law of the Sea is in Hamburg, Germany, and the International Seabed Authority is in Kingston, Jamaica.

To illustrate some aspects of the situation described above, Table 18.1 lists selected GMEAs by administrative agency, number of Parties, and location of secretariats.

Table 18.1   Proliferation and Fragmentation: Selected GMEAs

Administrative Body	MEA	Number of Parties as of 1 November 2014	Secretariat Location
United Nations Environment Programme (UNEP)	Vienna Convention for the Protection of the Ozone Layer	197	Nairobi, Kenya
	Basel Convention on Hazardous Waste	181	Geneva, Switzerland (administered by the joint Basel-Rotterdam-Stockholm (BRS) secretariat)
	Convention on Biological Diversity (CBD)	194	Montreal, Canada

Administrative Body	MEA	Number of Parties as of 1 November 2014	Secretariat Location
	Minamata Convention on Mercury	8	Geneva, Switzerland (at least temporarily administered by UNEP Chemicals; expected by some to join the joint BRS secretariat after the convention enters into force)
United Nations Educational, Scientific and Cultural Organization (UNESCO)	World Heritage Convention	191	Paris, France
	Convention on the Protection of the Underwater Cultural Heritage	48	Paris, France
International Union for the Conservation of Nature and Natural Resources (IUCN)	Ramsar Convention on Protection of Wetlands	168	Gland, Switzerland
Food and Agriculture Organization (FAO)	Convention on Plant Genetic Resources for Food and Agriculture	133	Rome, Italy
	International Plant Protection Convention	181	Rome, Italy

Administrative Body	MEA	Number of Parties as of 1 November 2014	Secretariat Location
International Maritime Organization (IMO)	International Convention for the Prevention of Pollution from Ships, 1973, as modified by the Protocol of 1978 relating thereto and by the Protocol of 1997 (MARPOL)	Annex I/II: 152 Annex III: 139 Annex IV: 132 Annex V: 145 Annex VI: 76	London, United Kingdom
	Hong Kong International Convention for the Safe and Environmentally Sound Recycling of Ships	3	
	London Dumping Convention	87	
	International Convention on Civil Liability for Oil Pollution Damage	35	
International Atomic Energy Agency (IEAE)	Convention on Assistance in the Case of a Nuclear Accident or Radiological Emergency	112	Vienna, Austria
	Convention on Early Notification of a Nuclear Accident	119	
	Joint Convention on the Safety of Spent Fuel Management and on the Safety of Radioactive Waste Management	69	

Administrative Body	MEA	Number of Parties as of 1 November 2014	Secretariat Location
	Vienna Convention on Civil Liability for Nuclear Damage	40	
Administered independently under the general auspices of the United Nations	United Nations Framework Convention on Climate Change (UNFCCC)	196	Bonn, Germany
	United Nations Convention on the Law of the Sea (UNCLOS)	166	New York, USA (secretariat in the UN Office of Legal Affairs)
			Kingston, Jamaica (International Seabed Authority)
			Hamburg, Germany (International Tribunal on the Law of the Sea)
	United Nations Convention on the Non-navigational Uses of International Watercourses	35	Unknown as of August, 2015

Administrative Body	MEA	Number of Parties as of 1 November 2014	Secretariat Location
UN Economic Commission for Europe	Aarhus Convention on Access to Information, Public Participation in Decision-making and Access to Justice in Environmental Matters	47	Geneva, Switzerland
	UNECE Convention on Protection and Use of Transboundary Watercourses and International Lakes	40 As of 31 January 2015, this convention is in the process of being opened to universal membership	

The size of GMEA secretariats varies greatly, with the result that the staff and other resources available differ significantly among secretariats. The UNFCCC secretariat has about 500 staff as of January 1, 2015, more personnel than the secretariats of the other GMEAs considered herein combined. Financial resources also vary greatly among GMEA regimes.

In addition, GMEAs typically have their own scientific and other committees. For example, the Rotterdam Convention has the Chemical Review Committee (CRC) to review chemicals and pesticide formulations and make recommendations to the COP for listing such chemicals in Annex III of the Convention. The Stockholm Convention has the Persistent Organic Pollutants Review Committee (POPRC) to review chemicals proposed for listing in the Annexes and specify the information required for new chemicals reviewing process.

GMEAs also sometimes have compliance committees, often modeled on the Montreal Protocol on Ozone Depleting Substances' compliance committee described in chapters 5 and 8. For instance, the Basel Convention has the Implementation and Compliance Committee (Compliance Committee) to assist Parties to comply with their obligation, and to facilitate, promote, monitor and secure implementation.

These committees have issued a large body of so-called technical guidelines and decision guidance documents. For example, the Compliance Committee of the Basel Convention establishes work programs regarding national reporting obligations, guidance on the development of inventories, strategies to promote legislative implementation, and other topics. The CRC of the Rotterdam Convention develops working procedures and policy guidance regarding proposals, documents for severely hazardous restricted chemicals and hazardous pesticide, among others. The POPRC of the Stockholm Convention publishes a list of codes of practice, proposals, guidance regarding new chemicals, evaluation, risk management, and treatment of confidential information.

GMEA treaty bodies, including COPs, secretariats and committees, typically hold periodic meetings, and sometimes ad hoc meetings. Unavoidably, meetings are sometimes scheduled at the same time as meetings of other treaty bodies. Moreover, the sheer number of meetings under GMEAs can be staggering, running to 100s per year.

c. Dispute Settlement

Each GMEA has its own dispute settlement regime, though the differences are not usually significant. Most of these regimes are quite weak, without any real obligations other than requiring Parties to consult and negotiate in good faith but lacking provisions for compulsory and binding International Court of Justice (ICJ) or arbitral dispute settlement.

Some GMEAs also allow a Party to institute conciliation proceedings in which the other Party or Parties are obligated to participate, but the outcome is a non-binding report of the conciliation commission with recommendations for solution of the issue. The term "conciliation" is not always used to describe these proceedings. For example, the "fact-finding" procedure in Article 33 of the UN Watercourses Convention is a type of conciliation proceeding. As of July 2015, none of these conciliation provisions have been formally utilized.

The Convention on Early Notification of a Nuclear Accident provides for mandatory jurisdiction in the ICJ, but States may make a reservation to this provision and important nuclear countries such as the United States and Russia did so, thus leaving them with only the weak provisions typical of GMEAs. UNCLOS is an exception, having quite robust dispute settlement provisions.

The Aarhus Convention on Access to Information, Public Participation in Decision-making and Access to Justice in Environmental Matters and the ECE Water Convention have committees whose memberships include members of the public and to which members of the public can bring complaints. These committees share characteristics with the Montreal Protocol-type compliance committee and more traditional dispute settlement.

d. Financing

Environmental governance can be viewed as requiring at least three types of financing. Operational financing is required for the IGOs that administer GMEAs and the treaty bodies created by the GMEAs. Coordination financing is necessary to support activities related to coordinating among treaty bodies and among administering agencies related to environmental governance. And program financing is required to finance the activities of treaty bodies related to carrying out their operational mandates, as those are defined in the relevant legal instrument(s).

Financing for sustainable development is covered in Chapter 17. Beyond what is in Notes 2 and 3 below, suffice it to say here that GMEAs, and other international environmental governance bodies, differ greatly in how they are funded, that this can affect their governance and effectiveness, and that there is no overarching mechanism to prioritize or allocate funding among GMEAs or MEAs generally.

NOTES AND QUESTIONS

1. *An environmental crazy quilt?* Can you make sense of the bewildering array of governance bodies and related obligations, dispute settlement regimes and financing mechanisms? Do you think the Parties to the relevant GMEAs can? To the extent your answer to the latter question is in the negative, what is the solution? A global super-body as proposed by Daniel Esty (see Concluding Note 3, below)? Or would that be too Orwellian (or potentially effective) to command governmental acceptance? Could you define environment for purposes of one central organization? Would a central organization give way to fragmentation over time?

2. *Safeguard policies and accountability mechanisms at international finance institutions.* As discussed in Chapter 17, the World Bank and some other multilateral development banks have both environmental and related safeguard policies and accountability mechanisms. Eighty private financial institutions have adopted safeguard policies in the form of the Equator Principles. The Equator Principles financial institutions cover over 70% of international project finance debt in developing countries. Most Export Credit Agencies (also discussed in Chapter 17) do not have either safeguard policies or accountability mechanisms, though the Organisation for Economic Co-operation and Development (OECD) has a series of agreements and recommendations relating to environmental and social impacts of projects relevant to members' export credit agencies.

3. *Global Environment Facility (GEF).* The GEF was established as a pilot project by the World Bank in 1991. It was restructured and became a separate and permanent institution in 1994, and further restructured in March 2015. The World Bank provides administrative services and serves as the Trustee of the GEF trust fund. The GEF focuses on five main areas:

(1) biological diversity; (2) climate change (including REDD+); (3) international waters; (4) land degradation, primarily desertification and deforestation; and (5) chemicals and waste. The GEF is the financing mechanism for several GMEAs, i.e., the CBD, Stockholm Convention, UNCCD, UNFCCC, and Minamata Convention on Mercury; and although not linked formally to the Montreal Protocol on Ozone Depletion, the GEF supports implementation of the protocol in countries with economies in transition. The GEF administers the Least Developed Countries Fund and Special Climate Change Fund established under the UNFCCC. The GEF also administers the Nagoya Protocol Implementation Fund (NPIF) that was established under the CBD. In addition, the GEF Secretariat hosts the Adaptation Fund Board Secretariat.

Among other activities related to governance, the GEF serves a coordinating function during its project proposal stage by requiring project proponents to describe what related activities are ongoing, which serves to identify related efforts and to reduce the likelihood of duplicative efforts. The GEF also has catalyzed many activities related to regional and basin water agreements.

e.   Monitoring, Assessment and Accountability

Good governance requires that adherence to norms, effectiveness and efficiency be assessed on an ongoing basis and that remedial steps be taken, or governance methodologies be modified, in accordance with those assessments. As indicated above, many GMEAs require periodic reporting that treaty bodies such as COPs and secretariats have mandates to review. There currently is no global mechanism for accomplishing this or conducting an overall assessment of reports submitted to GMEAs and MEAs.

NOTES AND QUESTIONS

1.   *The International Court of Justice (ICJ) and other international tribunals.* The ICJ and other international tribunals are part of the environmental governance regime, not only because they resolve some environmental disputes but also because their rulings clarify (some might say "crystallize") international law relating to the environment. A prime example is the ICJ's declaration in the *Pulp Mills* case that there is a general rule of international law that requires that a State conduct transboundary environmental impact assessments, described in Chapter 4 above. Sixty-six States have accepted as compulsory the jurisdiction of the ICJ under Article 36(2) of the Court's Statute (as of January 1, 2015) and an array of treaties contain ICJ clauses or provisions for binding arbitration. Does the mere availability of these possibilities tend to encourage compliance with international obligations?

2.   *OECD environmental performance reviews.* The OECD conducts periodic national environmental performance reviews of OECD members.

This useful exercise includes consideration, to some degree, of each country's compliance with its international commitments, including GMEAs.

3. *Sustainable development goals (SDGs)*. Following the 2012 Conference on Sustainable Development (Rio+20), the UN General Assembly appointed an Open Working Group on Sustainable Development Goals (OWG). The SDGs were called for in *The Future We Want*, the outcome document of Rio+20. After a wide-ranging process that included consultations with governments and civil society, and that drew on the Rio+20 outcome and the Secretary-General's High Level Panel of Eminent Persons on the Post-2015 Development Agenda, the OWG proposed a set SDGs and targets. The Secretary-General issued a report, *The Road to Dignity by 2030,* which presents a vision for UN Member States to consider leading up to the United Nations Special Summit on Sustainable Development, which will adopt the post-2015 development agenda, including the SDGs, in September 2015. The UN's post-2015 Development Agenda will presumably relate in a meaningful way to environmental protection and, at least indirectly, to environmental governance through, for example, provisions regarding environmental protection (in various goals) and rule of law (Goal 16) in the SDGs. *See* Draft outcome document of the United Nations summit for the adoption of the post-2015 development agenda, UN. Doc A/69/L.85 (Aug. 11, 2015); Transforming our world: the 2030 Agenda for Sustainable Development, *available at* https://sustainabledevelopment.un.org/post2015/transformingourworld.

f.   Overlap and Inconsistency Among GMEAs

Due the interdependence of environmental problems, a topic covered by one GMEA can also be covered under one or more other GMEAs. Indeed, different GMEAs sometimes have standards or regulations regarding the same, similar, or related problems. For instance, mercury is considered as "waste" that is governed by the Basel Convention, mercury compounds are categorized as a "pesticide" under the Rotterdam Convention, mercury is also related to "persistent organic pollutants" (POPs) under the Stockholm Convention, and mercury is the sole subject of the Minamata Convention on Mercury. More generally, a hazardous waste subject to the Basel Convention can, at the same time, be a hazardous chemical or pesticide subject to the Rotterdam Convention, a POP subject to the Stockholm Convention, or part of a ship subject to the Shipbreaking Convention. These hazardous wastes, chemicals, pesticides, and POPs can also be governed separately and simultaneously by other agreements, which involve soil, water, and air or that relate to the ozone layer, climate change, biological diversity, wild animals, wetlands, and plant resources, among others.

Not surprisingly, the fact that environmental threats are dealt with by different GMEAs can lead to inconsistent, and even conflicting, normative treatment or environmental impact. This does not appear to occur frequently, but it does happen. An important example of this involved actions under the Montreal Protocol promoting the production of HCFC 22, which is an effective substitute for some ozone-depleting chemicals but also is a powerful greenhouse gas (GHG potential of 1200) and has as a by-product HCHC 23, which is an even more powerful one (GHG potential of 12,000): the action to protect the ozone layer under the Montreal Protocol served to defeat the object and purpose of the UNFCCC and Kyoto Protocol. This is discussed further below.

6. GOVERNANCE CHALLENGES AND RESPONSES

a. Proliferation of International Environmental Obligations and Varying Membership of GMEAs

i. *Lack of Knowledge About What Substantive Obligations Apply to Which States*

As noted above, the proliferation of norms has resulted in a situation where States—particularly developing countries—and civil society have considerable difficulty knowing what obligations apply to particular States, as well as what those obligations require. These obligations include the norms contained in the texts of various GMEAs as well as the standards and directives included in the thousands of COP decisions regarding those GMEAs. This knowledge gap is exacerbated by the fact that membership in GMEAs is not consistent, so that different States are Parties to different GMEAs.

To alleviate this situation, the United Nations created the Multilateral Environmental Agreement Information and Knowledge Management (MEA IKM) Initiative, under the leadership of UNEP. This, in turn led to the creation of the web-based United Nations Information Portal on Multilateral Environmental Agreements, or InforMEA: http://www.informea.org/, which harvests information from COP decisions, MEA reports, press releases, national focal points and other sources and organizes that information by terms in a searchable form. The MEA IKM Initiative covers 17 GMEAs and 40 other MEAs.

ii. *Multiple and Duplicative Reporting Requirements*

The proliferation of reporting obligations causes unnecessary expense to State Parties to GMEAs because they have to submit multiple reports, sometimes containing the same information. InforMEA includes information on reporting obligations. Besides that and efforts in the context of the BRS (discussed below), as of July 2015, there has been little progress in alleviating the reporting situation, for example, by allowing consolidated reporting.

b. Overlap of Coverage of Environmental Problems and Inconsistency of Norms or Activities

The fact that more than one GMEA may deal with the same or a closely related environmental threat leads to legal and operational complexity. The shipbreaking example mentioned above demonstrates this.

The most troublesome problems arise in those few instances where there are inconsistencies between GMEAs, with the result that activities under one GMEA undercut the object and purpose of another. The HCFC 22 experience under the Montreal Protocol mentioned above is an extremely unfortunate example of what can transpire. In that case, remedial action was taken by changing the phase-out norms in the Montreal Protocol. As a result, it is estimated that the reduced emissions more than equal the amount of GHG emissions that would have been eliminated if the Kyoto Protocol had been fully implemented. But significant damage to the climate had already been done.

Beyond remedial action, there are three principles of international law that may help alleviate conflict. First, States are under an obligation under article 31.3(c) of the Vienna Convention on the Law of Treaties to take into account in interpreting international agreements "any relevant rules of international law applicable in the relations between the two parties"; how this applies in the context of multilateral treaties such as GMEAs is not clear. Second, the UN International Law Commission (ILC) considered the general question of the potential for conflict between two or more international agreements in the context of the increasing complexity and fragmentation of the international legal system. In its report, the ILC recommended the "harmonization principle" of interpretation: "when several norms bear on a single issue they should, to the extent possible, be interpreted so as to give rise to a single set of compatible obligations."[16] Third, the ICJ has held that new norms of international law must be taken into account even with respect to continuing activities governed by existing international agreements.[17] In discussing new norms relating to environmental protection and sustainable development, the ICJ said: "Such new norms have to be taken into consideration, and such new standards given proper weight, not only when States contemplate new activities but also when continuing with activities begun in the past."[18] This doctrine of "inter-temporal law" has been applied in at least two subsequent cases involving international rivers governed by basin agreements, once by the ICJ in the *Pulp Mills*

---

[16] Rep. of the Int'l Law Comm'n, 58th sess., May 1–June 9, July 3–Aug. 11, 2006, para. 251 § 1(4), U.N. Doc. A/61/10; GAOR 61st Sess., Supp. No. 10 (2006), http://daccess-dds-ny.un.org/doc/UNDOC/GEN/G06/636/20/PDF/G0663620.pdf?OpenElement.

[17] *See* Gabčíkovo-Nagymaros Project, *supra*, at 78, para. 140.

[18] *Id.*; *see also* Pulp Mills on the River Uruguay, *supra*, at para. 177.

case and once by the Court of Arbitration established pursuant to the Indus Waters Treaty of 1960 in the *Kishenganga* arbitration.

In at least some cases, these three approaches can help alleviate the potential for inconsistency between GMEA norms and the potential for discord between GMEAs and customary international law.

c.   Proliferation and Geographic Dispersal of Treaty Bodies

The proliferation of treaty bodies and their geographic dispersal raise several concerns. As far back as 1992, this was referred to as "treaty congestion." The situation has deteriorated since then. It is felt to lead system-wide to redundant staff and other expense, including the costs of coordinating, as well as decreased effectiveness and efficiency in other respects.

It has long been evident that the Basel, Rotterdam and Stockholm Conventions shared common interests. Several attempts have thus been made to increase synergies and reduce costs among the three regimes. An Ad Hoc Joint Working Group was established with the purpose to prepare "joint recommendations on enhanced cooperation and coordination"—all recommendations were submitted for adoption to each COP. The synergies decisions were then adopted in 2008–2009. Thereafter, the three conventions held simultaneous "extraordinary meetings" of the Conference of the Parties. The decisions from this extraordinary meeting addressed six themes: (1) joint activities, (2) joint managerial functions, (3) joint services, (4) synchronization of budget cycles, (5) joint audits, and (6) review arrangements. In 2011 the COP of each convention adopted almost identical decisions for cooperation and coordination, which approved an interim organization of the secretariats, cross-cutting and joint activities and detailed terms of reference for reviewing the synergies process and holding simultaneous extraordinary meetings for the 2013 COP. Thereafter, the Executive Secretaries of each convention prepared a proposal on how to organize the three conventions with details on staffing, numbers and structure. In 2013 extraordinary COP meetings were held and identical omnibus decisions on enhancing cooperation and coordination among the three conventions were adopted. Further review is to be conducted in 2017 on the synergies arrangements.

There is now a joint secretariat—referred to as the BRS secretariat—for the Basel, Rotterdam and Stockholm Conventions. The staffs have been merged, including mundane but nevertheless important details such as standardizing the format for email addresses. The BRS clustering process is intended to integrate the governance of the cross-border movement of hazardous wastes, prior informed consent (PIC) of hazardous chemicals, and elimination of POPs production. As of January 1, 2015, an interim secretariat exists for the Minamata Convention on Mercury, which is not in force as of that date. Some expect that this secretariat will be merged with the BRS secretariat once the Minamata Convention enters into force.

UNEP has also undertaken a synergies project involving the biological diversity cluster. This involves the CBD, CITES, CMS, Convention on Plant Genetic Resources for Food and Agriculture, International Plant Protection Convention, Ramsar Convention, and World Heritage Convention.

The development of synergies had also been pursued under the Ramsar Convention. Since 1996, the Ramsar Secretariat has been developing coordination and collaboration among conventions such as CBD, CMS, UNESCO World Heritage Convention, and UNFCCC, among others. For instance, the Ramsar Convention set out different Joint Work Plans (JWPs) with the CBD for 2011–2020 and with the CMS for 2012–14, as well as different Memorandums of Cooperation and Understanding with other conventions. Under the CBD-Ramsar JWP 2011–2020, the Parties and the secretariats have a "supporting and facilitating role" to promote and assist the implementation, which includes "recognizing the different resources" and "the comparative advantage" of each secretariat, "engaging with major groups and partners," and raising more effective activities that target "major stakeholders that influence policy and management outcomes for biodiversity;" the secretariats are to "jointly facilitat[e] preparation and issu[e] reports and information materials."[19]

GMEA secretariats and other institutions sometimes collaborate on specific operational issues. An example is the Green Customs Initiative (GCI). GCI partners are the secretariats of six GMEAs (Basel, Cartagena, Montreal, Rotterdam and Stockholm Conventions and CITES), Interpol, the Organisation for the Prohibition of Chemical Weapons, UNEP and the World Customs Organization. The GCI also works with other regional and international organizations.

Another issue relates to research efforts undertaken under the purview of a GMEA or that relate to the subject matter of a GMEA. Three concerns arise here. The first is that overarching issues might not be addressed because there is no overarching agency with responsibility for GMEAs and other MEAs. The second is that research may occur in silos due to a lack of coordination and communication, with resulting inefficiency and redundancy. The third is that sufficient resources may not be available to do adequate research. These may be addressed in part by the Green Growth Knowledge Project (GGKP), a collaborative effort started in 2012 jointly by the Green Growth Knowledge Institute, OECD, UNEP and the World Bank. Its mission is twofold: "first, to identify major knowledge gaps in green growth theory and practice, then address those gaps by promoting collaboration and coordinated research; and second, to

---

[19] http://www.ramsar.org/sites/default/files/documents/pdf/moc/CBD-Ramsar5thJWP_2011-2020.pdf.

use world-class knowledge management and communication tools to give practitioners and policymakers the policy analysis, guidance, information and data necessary to support a green economy transition." It is coordinated by UNEP in Geneva and as of July 2015 has partner organizations consisting of IGOs, governments, and NGOs working at global, regional, national and local levels. It is unclear how many of GGKP's activities will relate directly to GMEAs.

A different type of collaborative effort relates to climate change. The Intergovernmental Panel on Climate Change (IPCC) described in Chapter 9 is a joint project of UNEP and WMO and was endorsed by the UN General Assembly the same year it was created (1988). In addition, UNESCO established the Intersectoral Platform on Climate Change Mitigation and Adaption to promote an "interdisciplinary climate change knowledge base", enhancing climate science assessment, and climate change mitigation and adaption. The Platform also aims to develop close cooperation with relevant UN partners, such as the WMO, UNEP, and the UNESCO Climate Change Adaptation Forum. The UNESCO Forum is a collaborative process because it brings climate information generators, potential users, coastal managers, urban planners, community groups, and others together.

NOTES AND QUESTIONS

1.   *Pay to play?* States have jockeyed actively to attract secretariats to their territory, including by committing funds to establish secretariats. Could it be that the proliferation of treaty bodies has led to an overall increase in funding for GMEAs? If so, is that increase being used wisely?

2.   *More experimentation?* Has the proliferation of treaty bodies led to greater experimentation and thus greater effectiveness and efficiency?

3.   *Whither Minamata?* Why would not the Minamata Convention secretariat be immediately merged with the joint BRS secretariat? One answer might lie in the genesis of that Convention. Proposals to include mercury in the Stockholm Convention failed because of opposition from some countries. When those countries finally agreed to have a convention on mercury, in 2009, the only way forward was a convention on a single substance.

d. Myriad Meetings

GMEA treaty bodies typically hold periodic meetings, often annually, and they frequently hold ad hoc meetings. As indicated earlier, this sometimes results in the simultaneous scheduling of meetings, with the result that countries with relatively small staffs devoted to GMEAs cannot attend meetings. In addition, the number of COP, committee and other meetings under GMEAs is very large, running to 100s per year. This can effectively preclude the participation of countries that have limited staff assigned to the GMEAs, which are often developing countries. The fact that meetings are geographically dispersed exacerbates the cost of attending them all. These effects typically interfere more with developing countries' ability to participate more than with industrialized countries' ability to participate, but they even strain the resources of industrialized countries.

One effort to address this problem involved the Basel, Rotterdam and Stockholm Conventions as part of the BRS clustering process referred to above. In April and May 2013, the second simultaneous extraordinary meeting of the three COPs (the Basel, Rotterdam, and Stockholm Conventions) was held to enhance cooperation and collaboration. The participants, over eighty ministers and vice-ministers of Parties, called for an international panel on chemicals under the theme "Synergies and the implementation of the chemicals and wastes conventions at the national, regional, and global levels." The international panel is to integrate scientific expertise from industry, the private sector, and academic institutions in order to form the basis for a stronger interface between science and policy. The first joint meeting of the CRC of the Rotterdam Convention and the Stockholm Convention's POPRC was held in Rome on October 20, 2013. The synergies process is considered a continuing process for cost savings and implementation improvement.

It is not clear that the impacts of the joint COP were all positive. On the one hand, the time for the joint COP was two consecutive weeks, rather than the total of three weeks for the separate COPs, during which time the three COPs sometimes met together and sometimes separately. Thus there was a net savings of one week. The BRS staff, however, had to perform all the tasks formerly associated with preparing three COPs over three separate periods into one time period, without changing the nature or significantly decreasing the difficulty of those tasks, thus increasing the pressure on the BRS staff.

In terms of the personnel attending the joint COP from State Parties, the effects were also not necessarily all positive. On the one hand, some personnel could cover similar issues for more than one convention. On the other hand, because cross-cutting issues such as budget and compliance were covered throughout the two-week COP, some people who formerly would have stayed only for one week of the COP in which they were involved had to stay two weeks. This also applied to persons involved in some substantive issues. Whether the net savings to States were positive or negative thus is not clear. In addition, there is anecdotal evidence that some delegates felt that the two-week period did not allow sufficient time for substantive matters running across the mandates of the three conventions to be adequately discussed.

NOTES AND QUESTIONS

Fix that COP. What steps could be taken to alleviate the concerns just described about the joint BRS Conference of the Parties?

e.   Communications

Several aspects of communication are adversely affected by the proliferation of GMEAs, including by the proliferation and dispersal of treaty bodies.

Communicating at a distance increases some costs (e.g., mailing) and can cause other disadvantages such as difficulties arranging meetings across multiple time zones. To some extent these can be, and have been, reduced by judicious use of telecommunication technologies such as email, video conferencing, etc. The use of these technologies is unlikely replace entirely the creative spontaneity that can occur in face-to-face meetings, however.

GMEA treaty bodies developed incompatible knowledge management systems, e.g., data base structures. The result is that it was impossible to compare or consolidate data across GMEAs, even when the GMEAs deal with related matters. To address this, the MEA IKM Initiative mentioned above has developed voluntary standards for harmonizing the way GMEAs collect and store information and how they deal with national focal points. That system is now being used voluntarily, not only by the UNEP-administered GMEAs, but also by some other GMEAs such as the World Heritage Convention, the International Plant Protection Convention, and the ECE Water Convention; and it is on track as of July 2015 for use by the UNFCCC.

Inconsistent usage of common environmental terms can also lead to confusion, inability to compare and consolidate data, and inefficiencies. The MEA IKM Initiative undertook a collaborative thesaurus project involving UNEP, FAO, the European Environment Agency, the UNEP-World Conservation Monitoring Centre, the IUCN, and many GMEAs. This project arises out of the fact that GMEAs have their own terminology. The CBD, for example, uses roughly 1000 terms, whose meanings are not necessarily the same as identical terms used in other GMEAs or by collections such as the European environmental thesaurus, GEMET (the GEneral Multilingual Environmental Thesaurus).

It is not possible to harmonize the definitions of all terms because each MEA needs to use terms specifically as contained in the text of its legal instruments or as applied in that context. But it should be possible to standardize some definitions and the description of terminology among MEAs and to improve cross-references so that, for example, "prior informed consent" under the Rotterdam Convention is cross-referenced to "advance informed agreement" in the Cartagena Protocol on Bio-Safety.

The fact that many languages are used across the globe can also lead to inefficiencies and substantive misunderstandings. The GEMET is translated into 33 languages, including all the EU languages and the UN official languages. GMEA documents do not approach that number of official languages, nor will the MEA IKM Initiative's thesaurus.

f.   Multiple Administrative Agencies

The fact that GMEAs are administered under the purview of many different entities (e.g., FAO, IAEA, IMO, IUCN, UNEP, UNESCO and the United Nations—see Table 18.1) allows a particular GMEA to be administered by an agency whose mandate and expertise more closely fit the purpose and approach of the GMEA. This would not be the case if all GMEAs were administered under the purview of one organization. That fact also can give rise to bureaucratic barriers to substantive coordination and efforts to achieve efficiencies, however. Some of the efforts to remove these barriers are mentioned above with respect to the proliferation and geographic dispersal of treaty bodies.

g.   Different Rules Regarding Transparency and Public Participation

The multiplicity of environmental institutions has resulted in a multiplicity of rules and practices regarding the inter-related issues of transparency and public participation.

The differing rules and practices about transparency interfere with the ability of civil society, and even governments and other institutions, to know what is happening in environmental and other relevant institutions and to participate in their activities. Transparency issues relate primarily to access to documents and access to meetings. Different entities have different rules about whether the public has access to documents, including those prepared in the normal course of operating the entity concerned, documents before meetings (such as background papers, draft agenda and proposed resolutions) and documents prepared at meetings (such as discussion drafts and meeting reports). Similarly, rules and practices differ regarding whether the public has access to meetings. Needless to say, the nature and degree of transparency affect whether meaningful public participation is possible.

Apart from the rules and practices about transparency, three types of rules and practices are of greatest significance with respect to public participation: accreditation, submission of documents, and speaking privileges. Accreditation rules and practices determine which members of the public will be eligible to participate, e.g., to receive communications and enter the premises where meetings are being held. Rules and practices regarding submitting documents and making statements in meetings affect the types of communications members of the public will be allowed to engage in and thus their effectiveness, e.g., in what meetings and for how long members of the public will be allowed to speak. As with transparency, the fact that rules and practices regarding participation differ among institutions makes it difficult for the public, including environmental NGOs, businesses and other elements of civil society, to understand its rights and to give effect to them.

7. FUTURE REFORM?

As is evident from the preceding discussion, the environmental protection regime is atomized, without any overarching institution to make norms, settle disputes, and set priorities. This fragmented, multi-dimensional situation contrasts sharply with the multilateral trade regime. At the global level, the trade regime has a single institution (the World Trade Organization (WTO)), a single set of related agreements (i.e., the WTO Agreement and associated agreements), a single dispute settlement system (governed by the WTO Dispute Settlement Understanding), a single authoritative appellate body, and a single secretariat located in one place (Geneva). The WTO agreements also define the legal relationships relatively well between the global trade regime and trade agreements at the regional and bilateral levels, though issues of horizontal, vertical and diagonal governance do arise. The WTO was unified from its inception in 1994, though as pointed out above the proliferation of regional and bilateral trade regimes threatens to undercut that unity.

Another centralized model concerns intellectual property. The current regime represents the consolidation of a number of formerly separate regimes. The overarching institution is the World Intellectual Property Organization (WIPO), which administers 26 treaties and has 188 members. It is headquartered in Geneva, Switzerland, and has offices in Brazil, China, Japan, Russia, Singapore and the United States. WIPO was formally established in 1970 with entry into force of the Convention Establishing the World Intellectual Property Organization, as the successor to the United International Bureau for the Protection of Intellectual Property (BIRPI). BIRPI had been created in 1893 to administer the Berne Convention for the Protection of Literary and Artistic Works and the Paris Convention for the Protection of Industrial Property. WIPO also assumed jurisdiction over intellectual property treaties that were not under BIRPI's aegis, thus successfully merging the secretariats and implementation and oversight functions of these treaties. Uniquely, WIPO is self-funding: it generates financial resources necessary for its operation (rather than depending solely on contributions from Member States) through fees received in connection with the intellectual property application and registration systems that it administers, as well as a center for arbitration and mediation of IP-related disputes.

The question of whether there should be a single overarching institution for the environment was discussed in the run-up to the Rio+ 20 meeting in Rio de Janeiro in 2012. Various options were considered, including forming a new intergovernmental organization (often referred to as the World Environment Organization, or WEO) and converting the United Nations Trusteeship Council into the Environmental Council. The result was less dramatic: to enlarge somewhat the role of UNEP and to change its governing body from a limited-membership Governing Council to a universal-membership United Nations Environment Assembly (UNEA). The UNEA met for the first time in June 2014 in Nairobi, Kenya, and will meet every two years. The mandate, role and authority of UNEP fall far short of those of the WTO.

CONCLUDING NOTES AND QUESTIONS

1.   *The opening chemicals problem.* Consider the problem at the beginning of this chapter. What advocacy avenues and approaches might be available and advisable?

2.   *What works?* Based on the materials in this chapter, what seems to work in improving environmental governance?

3.   *A green WTO?* Should there be a World Environment Organization along the lines of the WTO (described very briefly at the beginning of this chapter and in greater detail in Chapter 16) or WIPO, that would embrace all or at least most of the existing environmental IGOs and IGO organs? What might be the arguments for and against? What legal steps would be necessary to accomplish this? For an analysis favoring such an organization, *see* Daniel C. Esty, Greening the GATT: Trade, Environment and the Future (1994). Consider the following quote from that book (at page 79, citation omitted):

> From the perspective of economic theory, the case for a strong and comprehensive Global Environmental Organization (GEO) is overwhelming. The presence of global environmental externalities, the public goods nature of environmental programs, and the intergenerational trade-offs inherent in environmental policy choices necessitate an overarching regulatory structure. Such a system is needed to limit self-serving (focused on local or national costs, not global consequences), irresponsible, and destructive behavior and to ensure that all of the relevant environmental actors participate in a unified regulatory program. Without global cooperation and collective action, there is a serious, ongoing risk of "market failure" in environmental protection, as some countries and some companies free ride on the pollution control efforts of others.

Are there good arguments to support the involvement of many institutions in the environmental field?

4. *More specifically tasked IGOs?* If you conclude that the comprehensive IGO suggested in Note 3 is too ambitious or unattractive for other reasons, would it be sensible to create one or more environmental IGOs that would deal with the following: All atmosphere related matters, such as ozone-layer protection; greenhouse gases; air pollution? All ocean and regional sea-related matters? All chemical-related matters? All UN System environmental activities? Whether or not such clusters are created, is UNEP or another organization best positioned to exercise leadership to improve coordination and governance? UNEP?

5. *Group exercise 1.* Divide the class into small groups and have each group devise a strategy with respect to the opening chemicals problem, involving the institutions and mechanisms described in this chapter. Compare the strategies when each group reports back to the class.

6. *Group exercise 2.* Divide the class into small groups and have each group debate within itself the issue of whether there should be a World Environment Organization, and then report back to the class.

CHAPTER 19

THE INTERNATIONAL LEGAL SYSTEM AND ENVIRONMENTAL PROTECTION

. . .

The possibilities and limitations of international environmental law and institutions as a means of helping resolve environmental problems can be understood only in the context of the international legal system considered as a whole. The fundamental characteristics of that system apply, of course, to the part of it that is environmental; and norms often apply across all of international law, so that their application to environmental issues must be consistent with their application to non-environmental issues. Discerning the precise meaning of international environmental norms—even those in treaties—may require recourse to other aspects of public or even private international law. In addition, the functioning of international environmental institutions, which are the subject of Chapter 18, is determined at least in part by the general international law principles relating to international organizations. It is thus clear that a competent international environmental lawyer must possess knowledge of the fundamentals of public international law. Similarly, the settlement (and avoidance) of international environmental disputes occurs within the overall context of public international law, as do efforts to secure compliance with international environmental norms. An international environmental lawyer must therefore also have knowledge of international dispute settlement and compliance generally.

This chapter is designed to provide an introduction to the fundamentals of international law and dispute settlement for those who have not yet studied them, utilizing examples relating to environmental issues. Because of the richness and bulk of these topics, which are covered in a course of three or more units in a typical United States law school, we have taken an approach somewhat different from that used in most other chapters of the course book (Chapter 18 being the main exception). The primary material in this chapter consists of text and Notes and Questions written specifically for this book, interspersed with selected excerpts of cases and other readings. Compliance with international environmental norms is dealt with in Chapter 5.

A. INTERNATIONAL LAW

1. OVERVIEW OF THE INTERNATIONAL LEGAL SYSTEM

The international legal system governs the interaction of nation-States, of which approximately 200 exist in the second decade of the twenty-first century. Though precursors of such a system can be found as far back as the reach of recorded history, for example, in respect to the city-states in Mesopotamia, states in classic Greece and the Hindu states of ancient India, the current system originated in seventeenth-century Europe.

After a relatively long static period, the international legal system has since the end of World War II seen rapid evolution. In particular, the system has been broadened to (1) include States all over the world, including many that only achieved independence after World War II; (2) regulate the rights and obligations of actors other than States, such as international organizations, transnational corporations, and even individuals; and (3) cover new fields of activities such as those in space, new concerns such as those for the protection of the environment, and even old ones that previously had been considered to be exclusively domestic, such as human rights. Finally, while through the end of the nineteenth century relations between and among States were for the most part direct, in recent years these increasingly take place within, or are mediated by, international intergovernmental organizations (IGOs) and are influenced by myriad non-governmental organizations (NGOs).

The international legal system can to some extent be analogized to the domestic legal system of a State, though in doing so one must be conscious of important differences. In particular, the international legal system, for most purposes, does not have a lawmaking authority to promulgate international norms of the type common to domestic legal systems, there is no overarching adjudicative body with compulsory and binding jurisdiction to settle disputes regarding alleged violations of international law, and there is no centralized enforcement authority to enforce international law. In general, it may be said that the international legal system is largely decentralized in character, in contrast to domestic legal systems. On the other hand, there are international laws or norms, as well as an international norm-making or legislative process, which are examined in section A below; there are processes for avoiding and, if necessary, resolving international disputes, examined in section B; and there are, albeit only rudimentary and generally very weak, devices to further compliance with international norms, examined in Chapters 4 and 5. These quasi-legislative, judicial and quasi-judicial, and quasi-executive functions are increasingly being carried out by IGOs, as is described in Chapter 18. In view of the differences between the two systems, it may seem surprising that the international legal system is, for the most part, quite effective. Extreme cases garner headlines but the myriad interactions between States every day continue to proceed normally, usually without notice.

Finally, it should be noted that it is somewhat of a misnomer to speak of *an* international legal system. Instead, it is necessary to recognize that there are a number of different systems, which have at best a partially hierarchical relationship. Thus there is a universal system, for the most part within or related to the United Nations (UN). This chapter largely concentrates on this system. However, there are also regional systems (such as those of Africa and the Americas, and several overlapping ones in Europe), sub-regional ones (such as those of Central America, the Caribbean, the Nordic States, southern African States, members of the Association of Southeast Asian Nations, etc.), and bilateral ones. There are also systems and corresponding IGOs that are primarily economic (e.g., the Organisation for Economic Co-operation and Development) or functional (e.g., the International Whaling Commission) or political (e.g., the League of Arab States) rather than geographically based.

2.   GENERAL CONSIDERATIONS

International law is the set of norms that governs the interaction between nation-States. As is described at greater length below, international law is largely though not exclusively made by States and reflects their will and consent. However, the obligations and rights set out in that law govern not only those States but also the establishment and functioning of international governmental (IGOs) and non-governmental organizations (NGOs) and, to a lesser extent and usually only mediatively through the States of their nationality, corporations, ships and individuals.

As pointed out above in connection with the international legal system, international law may be worldwide (also referred to as "global", "general" or "universal"), regional, subregional, restricted multilateral, or bilateral. Because the international system is hierarchical only to a most limited extent, it cannot be assumed that norms of a broader scope necessarily supersede or govern those of a lesser scope. It is for each State to see to it that new norms it consents to will not be inconsistent with a previous one by which it is bound and which it cannot change.

As is true of domestic or "municipal" law (as the internal law of States is called in international law), there are many different types of international law—but these generally do not correspond to the various forms of domestic law. The most important of these types are listed in Article 38(1) of the Statute of the International Court of Justice (ICJ or World Court). However, that listing was established roughly a century ago (for the predecessor of the ICJ, the Permanent Court of International Justice), and it is generally recognized that the list is no longer complete. Full agreement as to the components of an updated list does not currently exist.

The following types of law and related commitments are described and characterized below: (1) customary law; (2) international agreements, often referred to as "treaties" but which also have many other names such as "conventions" (hence the term "conventional law"); (3) general principles of law recognized by the world's organized legal systems; (4) international administrative law; (5) declarations of IGOs; (6) legally binding unilateral declarations; and (7) non-legally binding voluntary commitments and other forms of "soft law". There are various means of establishing or determining the existence of international law, some of which are also listed in Article 38(1) of the Statute ICJ. These means include the decisions of IGO organs; judicial and arbitral decisions; and the teachings of recognized publicists. These are discussed below in part A.9(c).

The diverse types of international law that have just been mentioned can be characterized in several overlapping ways:

(1) Some types of international law can be found in black-letter form, i.e., as written texts (in particular, treaties and many forms of soft law, such as decisions of IGO organs and certain rules, guidelines, etc. generated by them), while others have no precise, definitive statements (such as customary law and general principles). This distinction resembles that in domestic law between, on the one hand, statutes and regulations and, on the other, judge-made common law.

(2) Some legal obligations, particularly those originating in certain types of treaties, are merely reciprocal—i.e., they exist between pairs or specific groups of States (e.g., the Parties to bilateral agreements or to many multilateral agreements that basically establish networks of bilateral relationships, such as those concerning trade or diplomacy). Other legal obligations are characterized as *erga omnes,* i.e., they run from States bound by these obligations to all other States or rather to the world (or the regional) community as a whole. Although certain environmental norms, such as those relating to a particular river that flows along or through a boundary between two States, fall into the first category, those environmental obligations that relate to a global commons (such as the high seas or Antarctica) are *erga omnes.*

(3) Although the creation of international law depends on the will and sometimes on the continuing consent of States, it is increasingly recognized that certain norms—usually of customary law but also some deriving from important treaties like the UN Charter or even from general principles—may have or gradually acquire such a compelling and universal respect that States cannot be permitted to change or supersede

them by treaty or otherwise. These are called preemptory norms or *jus cogens*.[1] It should be noted that while by no means all *erga omnes* norms are also *jus cogens,* normally all *jus cogens* norms are likely to function *erga omnes*. The *Barcelona Traction* case provided an indicative list ("acts of aggression, and of genocide, as also from the principles and rules concerning basic rights of the human person including protection from slavery and racial discrimination"), 1970 ICJ Rep. 3, para. 34, but that was in 1970. In the absence of any definitive list of preemptory international norms, it is difficult to say whether any environment-related norms may at present be considered as falling into this category, but it seems likely that as this field matures and gains in generally recognized importance, certain of these norms will soon be characterized as *jus cogens*.

(4) Some types of international law, in particular customary law, treaties, and general principles of law, are binding on those States subject to them, and are therefore referred to as "hard law". Other statements—including political commitments—are at most hortatory or partially compelling. These are sometimes therefore characterized as "soft law". As is explained below, the characterization of even certain nonbinding statements as "law" arguably can be justified by the fact that States actually do largely conform to them and also because other States sometimes rely on such statements.

3.   CUSTOMARY LAW

Customary international law consists of the set of norms derived from the actual practice of States undertaken by these States in the belief that such practices are required by international law. To identify such norms it is therefore necessary to study how States (i.e., their official organs, which include executive, legislative, and judicial ones) actually behave. Although it is not necessary to document the practice of *all* States, a customary norm is one that can be shown to be generally followed (worldwide in respect to universal customary law, or regionally or sub-regionally in respect to geographically restricted customary law) out of a sense of legal obligation by the States concerned.

It can be seen that this is no easy task and not one that is likely to result in unambiguous formulations. Consequently, to the extent that a senior court (in particular the World Court) or some other tribunal determines the existence (or not) of some alleged customary norm, such determinations may constitute persuasive evidence for the existence of the norm. Similar effect may be attributed to a determination by a group of recognized legal scholars and other experts (such as the members of the International Law Commission (ILC), who serve in their individual

---

[1]   *See* Articles 53, 64, and 71 of the 1969 Vienna Convention on the Law of Treaties, May 23, 1969, 1155 U.N.T.S. 331, 8 I.L.M. 679 (1969).

capacities and are elected by the UN General Assembly) of the existence of a norm or sometimes to a statement of a senior IGO organ (such as the UN General Assembly). It should be emphasized that in order to establish the normative nature of a practice it is necessary to determine that it is based on a belief by the State organ(s) concerned that such is required by international law—i.e., that it is not merely a normal courtesy, a clearly advantageous act, or a means of seeking favor, creating good will, or escaping a threat. This requirement is called *opinio juris [sive necessitatis]. Opinio juris* often is not easy to establish strictly because the motivations for particular State actions are by no means always clear, though an action against a State's interest can be assumed to be motivated by a perception of legal obligation.

Though customary international law is therefore normally created by unconscious and inchoate processes that persuade States generally that they should behave in a particular way, there are devices—whether used deliberately or not—to induce States to consider that acting in a particular way is legally required. These include resolutions of senior IGO organs encouraging such behavior, particularly if these suggest that there is a legal requirement. The adoption of multilateral treaties may also have such an effect even before they have entered into force, either in anticipation or because States may consider that such treaties largely codify preexisting international law. Finally, the creation of soft law, though technically nonbinding, may still induce States to act in the indicated mode in the belief that such action is at least legally desirable.

As indicated above, in order for customary law to come into being, it is necessary that the norm in question be generally observed by States; but it is unnecessary, and in many instances impractical, to establish compliance by all the States concerned (whether of all countries in the world or those of a particular region or subregion). Once it comes into being, a customary law norm is binding on all States concerned. However, a State may, by persistently and from the beginning objecting to the norm (and not observing it) during the process of its formation, exempt itself from being bound by it. Of course, if there are too many such "persistent objectors," then the norm does not become binding as part of customary law.

An important customary norm, relevant but not peculiar to environmental law, is that every State may use its territory and carry out activities thereon as it wishes, but only to the extent that no harm is caused thereby to other States.[2] Historically the oldest source of general international law (as distinguished from the particular international law created by two parties to a bilateral international treaty), and the main

---

[2] *See, e.g.,* Principle 21 of the Stockholm Declaration of the 1972 UN Conference on the Human Environment, 11 I.L.M. 1416 (1972), and Principle 2 of the Rio Declaration of the 1992 UN Conference on Environment and Development, 31 I.L.M. 874 (1992).

source until as recently as the end of the Second World War, customary law is rapidly being superseded in importance by the massive quantities of blackletter law being created by the lawmaking multilateral treaties discussed immediately below. On the other hand, customary law remains highly relevant to international environmental protection, as is indicated by the World Court's increasing attention to the principle of sustainable development and its 2010 holding that a general rule of international law requires the preparation of a transboundary environmental impact assessment.

NOTES AND QUESTIONS

1. How does one determine whether (and when) a practice has become customary international law? The *North Sea Continental Shelf Cases,* 1969 I.C.J. Reports 3, involved the Federal Republic of Germany's claim against Denmark and the Netherlands for a boundary delimitation of the continental shelf. The ICJ was faced with the issue of what principles and rules of international law it should apply in delimiting the boundaries between these opposite and adjacent States. Denmark and the Netherlands argued that the "equidistance-special circumstances" principles in Article 6(2) of the 1958 Geneva Convention on the Continental Shelf applied. The concave nature of the coastline shared by the three countries—with Germany in the middle— meant that the application of this principle would render Germany a much smaller portion of the continental shelf than it would receive by the application of other delimitation rules. Accordingly, Germany opposed the application of this rule, partly on the ground that it was not then a Party to the Geneva Convention. It also opposed the Danish and Dutch contentions that the equidistance rule was customary international law at the time of the Convention, was "crystallized" as a rule of customary international law by the process of creating the Convention, or had come to be regarded as a rule of customary international law since the Convention. The following excerpt focuses on the latter question:

> 70. The Court must now proceed to the next stage in the argument put forward on behalf of Denmark and the Netherlands. This is to the effect that even if there was at the date of the Geneva Convention no rule of customary international law in favour of the equidistance principle, and no such rule was crystallized in Article 6 of the Convention, nevertheless such a rule has come into being since the Convention, partly because of its own impact, partly on the basis of subsequent State practice,—and that this rule, being now a rule of customary international law binding on all States, including therefore the Federal Republic, should be declared applicable to the delimitation of the boundaries between the Parties' respective continental shelf areas in the North Sea.

> 71. In so far as this contention is based on the view that Article 6 of the Convention has had the influence, and has produced the effect described, it clearly involves treating that Article as a norm-

creating provision which has constituted the foundation of, or has generated a rule which, while only conventional or contractual in its origin, has since passed into the general *corpus* of international law, and is now accepted as such by the *opinio juris,* so as to have become binding even for countries which have never, and do not, become parties to the Convention. There is no doubt that this process is a perfectly possible one and does from time to time occur: it constitutes indeed one of the recognized methods by which new rules of customary international law may be formed. At the same time this result is not lightly to be regarded as having been attained. . . .

72. The Court must now consider whether State practice in the matter of continental shelf delimitation has, subsequent to the Geneva Convention, been of such a kind as to satisfy this requirement. Leaving aside cases which, for various reasons, the Court does not consider to be reliable guides as precedents, such as delimitations effected between the present Parties themselves, or not relating to international boundaries, some 15 cases have been cited in the course of the present proceedings, occurring mostly since the signature of the 1958 Geneva Convention, in which continental shelf boundaries have been delimited according to the equidistance principle—in the majority of the cases by agreement, in a few others unilaterally—or else the delimitation was foreshadowed but has not yet been carried out. Amongst these 15 are the four North Sea delimitations, United Kingdom/Norway-Denmark-Netherlands, and Norway/Denmark already mentioned in paragraph 4 of this Judgment. But even if these various cases constituted more than a very small proportion of those potentially calling for delimitation in the world as a whole, the Court would not think it necessary to enumerate or evaluate them separately, since there are, a *priori,* several grounds which deprive them of weight as precedents in the present context.

. . .

76. To begin with, over half the States concerned, whether acting unilaterally or conjointly, were or shortly became parties to the Geneva Convention, and were therefore presumably, so far as they were concerned, acting actually or potentially in the application of the. Convention. From their action no inference could legitimately be drawn as to the existence of a rule of customary international law in favour of the equidistance principle. As regards those States, on the other hand, which were not, and have not become parties to the Convention, the basis of their action can only be problematical and must remain entirely speculative. Clearly, they were not applying the Convention. But from that no inference could justifiably be drawn that they believed themselves to be applying a mandatory rule of customary international law. There is not a shred

of evidence that they did and there is no lack of other reasons for using the equidistance method, so that acting, or agreeing to act in a certain way, does not of itself demonstrate anything of a juridical nature.

. . .

81. The Court accordingly concludes that if the Geneva Convention was not in its origins or inception declaratory of a mandatory rule of customary international law enjoining the use of the equidistance principle for the delimitation of continental shelf areas between adjacent States, neither has its subsequent effect been constitutive of such a rule; and that State practice up-to-date has equally been insufficient for the purpose.

Id. at paras. 70–81, 8 I.L.M. 340, at 373–77 (1969).

From a temporal perspective, what are the possible relationships between the creation of a rule of customary international law and the finalization of a treaty that expresses the same content as is contained in the customary norm? What types of state practice did the ICJ examine, and how much did it insist on before a norm could be created?

Judge Manfred Lachs, in dissent, wrote:

For in the world today an essential factor in the formation of a new rule of general international law is to be taken into account: namely that States with different political, economic and legal systems, States of all continents, participate in the process. No more can a general rule of international law be established by the fiat of one or of a few, or—as it was once claimed—by the consensus of European States only.

[The State Parties to the Convention on the Continental Shelf] include States of all continents, among them States of various political systems, with both new and old States representing the main legal systems of the world.

It may therefore be said that, from the viewpoints both of number and/or representativity, the participation in the Convention constitutes a solid basis for the formation of a general rule of law. It is upon that basis that further more extensive practice has developed.

[After concluding that the principles and rules in the Convention had been accepted by sufficient States to "be viewed as evidence of a practice widespread enough to satisfy the criteria for a general rule of law," Judge Lachs continued:] Can the practice summarized be considered as having been accepted as law, having regard to the subjective element *[opinio juris]* required? The process leading to this effect is necessarily complex. There are certain areas of State activity and international law which by their very character may only with great difficulty engender general law, but there are others, both old and new, which may do so with greater ease. Where continental shelf law is concerned, some States have at first probably accepted the rules in question, as States usually do, because they found them convenient and useful, the best possible solution for the problems involved. Others may also have been convinced that the instrument elaborated within the framework of the United Nations was intended to become and would in due course become general law. . . . Many States have followed suit under the conviction that it was law.

Thus at the successive stages in the development of the rule the motives which have prompted States to accept it have varied from case to case. It could not be otherwise. At all events, to postulate that all States, even those which initiate a given practice, believe themselves to be acting under a legal obligation is to resort to a fiction—and in fact to deny the possibility of developing such rules. For the path may indeed start from voluntary, unilateral acts relying on the confident expectation that they will find acquiescence or be emulated; alternatively, the starting-point may consist of a treaty to which more and more States accede and which is followed by unilateral acceptance. It is only at a later stage that, by the combined effect of individual or joint action, response and interaction in the field concerned, i.e., of that reciprocity so essential in international legal relations, there develops the chain-reaction productive of international consensus.

. . . In sum, the practice of States should be recognized as prima facie evidence that it is accepted as law. Such evidence may, of course, be controverted—even on the test of practice itself, if it shows "much uncertainty and contradiction." . . .

What did Judge Lachs mean by representative State practice? What types of factors are relevant to that determination?

2. In *The Paquete Habana*, 175 U.S. 677 (1900), the United States Supreme Court was posed the question of whether fishing vessels could be seized as prizes of war under international law. In determining the customary international rule to be applied, the Court undertook the following examination, demonstrating the methodology courts employ:

By an ancient usage among civilized nations, beginning centuries ago, and gradually ripening into a rule of international law, coast fishing vessels, pursuing their vocation of catching and bringing in fresh fish, have been recognized as exempt, with their cargoes and crews, from capture as prize of war.

This doctrine, however, has been earnestly contested at the bar; and no complete collection of the instances illustrating it is to be found, so far as we are aware, in a single published work, although many are referred to and discussed by the writers on international law. . . .

The earliest acts of any government on the subject, mentioned in the books, either emanated from, or were approved by, a King of England. In 1403 and 1406, Henry IV issued orders to his admirals and other officers [and] he took into his safe conduct . . . the fisherman of France . . . in regard to their fishery, while sailing . . . and lawfully fishing "without molestation", [and he ordered that fisherman should not be interfered with]. The treaty made October 2, 1521, between the Emperor Charles V and Francis I of France, through their ambassadors, recited that a great and fierce war had arisen between them . . . [and] agreed that the subjects of each sovereign, fishing in the sea, could . . . without incurring any attack . . . or hindrance . . . safely and freely take herrings and every other kind of fish, the existing war by land and sea notwithstanding. The herring fishery was [also] permitted, in time of war, by French and Dutch edicts in 1536.

The doctrine which exempts coast fishermen with their vessels and cargoes from capture as prize of war has been familiar to the United States from the time of the War of Independence. On June 5, 1779, Louis XVI, our ally in that war, addressed a letter to his admiral, [giving] orders to the commanders of all his ships not to disturb English fishermen, nor to arrest their vessels laden with fresh fish, even if not caught by those vessels; provided they had no offensive arms, and were not proved to have made any signals creating a suspicion of intelligence with the enemy. . . .

Among the standing orders made by Sir James Marriott, Judge of the English High Court of Admiralty, was one of April 11, 1780, by which it was "ordered that all causes of prize of fishing boats or vessels taken from the enemy may be consolidated . . . , if under 50 tons burthen, and not more than 6 in number." Marriott's Formulary, 4. But by the statements of his successor, and of both French and English writers, it appears that England, as well as France, during the American Revolutionary War, abstained from interfering with the coast fisheries. The Young Jacob and Johanna, 1 C. Rob. 20; 2 Ortlan, 53; Hall, § 148.

In the treaty of 1785 between the United States and Prussia, article 23 provided that, if war should arise between the contracting parties, "all women and children, scholars of every faculty, cultivators of the earth, artisans, manufacturers and fishermen, unarmed and inhabiting unfortified towns, villages or places, and in general all others whose occupations are for the common subsistence and benefit of mankind, shall be allowed to continue their respective employments, and shall not be molested in their persons." . . .

In the war with Mexico in 1846, the United States recognized the exemption of coast fishing boats from capture. In proof of this, counsel have referred to records of the Navy Department, which this court is clearly authorized to consult upon such a question.

International law is part of our law, and must be ascertained and administered by the courts of justice of appropriate jurisdiction, as often as questions of right depending upon it are duly presented for their determination. For this purpose, where there is no treaty, and no controlling executive or legislative act or judicial decision, resort must be had to the customs and usages of civilized nations; and, as evidence of these, to the works of jurists and commentators, who by years of labor, research and experience, have made themselves peculiarly well acquainted with the subjects of which they treat. Such works are resorted to by judicial tribunals, not for the speculations of their authors concerning what the law ought to be, but for trustworthy evidence of what the law really is.

Wheaton places, among the principal sources of international law, "Text-writers of authority, showing what is the approved usage of nations, or the general opinion respecting their mutual conduct, with the definitions and modifications introduced by general consent." As to these he forcibly observes: "Without wishing to exaggerate the importance of these writers, or to substitute, in any case, their authority for the principles of reason, it may be affirmed that they are generally impartial in their judgment. They are witnesses of the sentiments and usages of civilized nations, and the weight of their testimony increases every time that their authority is invoked by statesmen, and every year that passes without the rules laid down in their works being impugned by the avowal of contrary principles." Wheaton's International Law, (8th ed.) § 15. . . .

This review of the precedents and authorities on the subject appears to us abundantly to demonstrate that at the present day, by the general consent of the civilized nations of the world, and independently of any express treaty or other public act, it is an established rule of international law. . . .

This rule of international law is one which prize courts administering the law of nations are bound to take judicial notice of and to give effect to, in the absence of any treaty or other public act of their own government in relation to the matter. . . .

What kinds of State conduct did the Court look to for incidents of State practice? What did the Court consider to be evidence of the existence of norms? How did the Court deal with inconsistent State practice? What did the Court mean by the phrase, "in the absence of any . . . public act of their own government"? Why should that matter?

3.   Louis Sohn has written that unratified treaties may also be a source of customary international law. He states:

The [International Court of Justice] is thus willing to pay attention not only to a text that has codified a pre-existing customary law but also to one that has crystallized an "emergent rule of international law." It is sufficient for that purpose to have the rule in question adopted by an international conference by consensus or . . . without a dissenting vote. Later formalities, such as signing and ratification merely add icing to the cake. What is relevant is the fact that one can observe here the primordial creative force at work. It is generally recognized that international law has only one source— the common will of States. A new rule is created by its general acceptance by all the States concerned. The States themselves are the masters of the method by which they agree to express their common will. If they agree that a particular rule represents a satisfactory product of mutual accommodation, reasonableness and co-operation, they can agree in addition that they accept this rule as of that moment as binding upon them. Sometimes this second agreement is explicit, sometimes it is implicit, and its existence has to be deduced from the circumstances of the case. If most States, including almost all States having a special interest in the application of the rule, act in accordance with it, there is a clear presumption that the rule agreed upon at the conference, though the agreement has not yet been ratified, has become an accepted rule of customary international law.

Louis B. Sohn, *Unratified Treaties as a Source of Customary International Law*, in Realism in Law-Making: Essay on International Law in Honor of Wilem Riphagen (1986).

4. In *Nicaragua v. United States* (officially referred to as *Military and Paramilitary Activities in and against Nicaragua),* Merits, 1986 I.C.J. Rep. 14 (Judgment of June 27, 1986), the International Court of Justice determined, somewhat controversially, that certain multilateral treaties agreed to by the parties to the case (e.g., the United Nations Charter) in part reflected customary international legal principles that bound the parties. Thus, even though multilateral treaties were excluded (by the United States reservation contained in its Article 36(2) acceptance of the compulsory jurisdiction of the ICJ) from consideration by the ICJ in deciding the case, the Court held it could apply such derived customary international law to the facts of the case in arriving at a judgment. The Court stated:

[E]ven if two norms belonging to two sources of international law appear identical in content, and even if the States in question are bound by these rules both on the level of treaty-law and on that of customary international law, these norms retain a separate existence.

Id. at 95.

5. It has been said that "reciprocity is the foundation of international law." Do you agree?

4. TREATIES

a. General

Treaties are the other great, and increasingly predominant, form of binding international law. Unlike customary law, treaties are black-letter law—whose wording, but not necessarily meaning, is clearly established. Many different terms are used to describe agreements between States or IGOs that are governed by international law, for example, treaty, convention, agreement, covenant, protocol, constitution, statute, articles of agreement, executive agreement, memorandum of understanding, and so on. Generally speaking, that terminology does not have independent legal significance.

Originally treaties were usually bilateral instruments. There are many significant bilateral treaties that relate wholly or partially to environmental matters; for example, the many concluded between Canada and the United States relating to the boundary waters, including the Great Lakes and the St. Lawrence Seaway. Indeed, the first recorded treaty of any type is a water treaty between the two Mesopotamian city-states of Umma and Lagash regarding waters of the Euphrates River, bringing to an end a conflict over the waters of the Euphrates, which is usually dated ca. 3100 BCE and is inscribed on the Stella of the Vultures, housed in the Louvre.[3] Starting in the nineteenth century, and with increasing rapidity after World War II, a number of States, and often a significant fraction of all States (or of all States in a particular region), concluded multilateral treaties. Many of these treaties establish general environmental norms (such as those relating to the protection of the ozone layer or the prevention of marine pollution) or create international institutions with exclusively or at least significant environmental functions.

Because of the growing number of States (their number more than tripled from about 60 at the end of World War II to approximately 200 as of 2015) and the ever greater number, intensity, and complexity of their interactions on an increasing number of subjects, the number of treaties is constantly rising. As of 2015, there are well over 30,000, of which more than 1,500 are multilateral treaties with a significant number of Parties. The United States is a Party to more than 7,500 international agreements in force.

The law relating to treaties, their formulation, entry into force, effect, interpretation, revision, and termination is largely the subject of well-established customary norms. Many of these have been codified, and some have been revised, in a series of UN-sponsored treaties. The first and most important of these is the 1969 Vienna Convention on the Law of

---

[3] Stephen C. McCaffrey, The Law of International Watercourses 59–60 (2d ed. 2007). See Arthur Nussbaum, A Concise History of the Law of Nations 1-2 (1954).

Treaties (VCLT).[4] VCLT defines "convention" to cover all agreements between States set out in written form and governed by international law—no matter how designated. The most important rule regarding treaties is set out in Article 26 of the VCLT, which codifies preexisting customary law in requiring that the obligations under treaties must be carried out: *pacta sunt servanda*. Treaties may also be oral. While these are not technically covered by the VCLT, many, probably most, of the principles it embodies also apply to them.

b. Treaty-Making

Unlike the domestic legislative process, which when completed results in an instrument (e.g., a statute) that is automatically binding on all subjects of the State, the international process generally has two quite different phases: an international one, by which a treaty is formulated and adopted; and a domestic one, by which each interested and qualified State decides whether or not to become a Party to the treaty (and sometimes on what terms). Often the international phase precedes the domestic phase, but sometimes the two proceed concurrently. And sometimes, as typically is the case with executive agreements in the United States, the agreement takes effect upon signature. Normally a treaty does not enter into force until the requisite number of States (specified in the treaty in question) have expressed their consent to be bound by it,[5] and then only for those States that have done so.

i. The International Process

The formulation of bilateral treaties is basically a process of negotiation between the pair of States concerned. The nature and length of this process depends largely on the complexity and urgency of the subject and the substantive differences between the parties in relation thereto.

The formulation of multilateral agreements is more complicated, tending to increase in difficulty with the number of potential Parties. Nowadays, this process normally takes place within or under the auspices of an IGO—ideally the one whose membership and mandate best corresponds to the scope and subject of the proposed instrument. The process also tends to follow some general patterns and, in some IGOs, special procedural rules, although each process is unique. All steps in the

---

[4] 1155 U.N.I.T.S. 331; 8 I.L.M. 679 (1969).

[5] There are several processes whereby a State may definitively signal its consent to be bound by a treaty, which may be done by: a definitive signature, not requiring any subsequent expression of consent to be bound; a signature *ad referendum,* confirmed by ratification, adoption, or approval; accession without prior signature; and in some cases, notification of succession to a previous Party to a treaty. The domestic requirements for taking such steps are discussed below.

formulation process include, and in many instances principally consist of, negotiations.

Negotiations may start even before the first proposal concerning a treaty is publicly revealed and to some extent affect all the political decisions taken, including whether to initiate the process formally, the choice of fora, aspects of timing, and the decisions relating to the conclusion of the instrument. Negotiations may, in effect, even take place in expert organs (whose members are normally chosen by States even if they do not formally represent them) and in technical fora such as drafting committees. Moreover, the negotiations are not necessarily confined to the issue at hand, as State representatives may well engage in bargaining involving some of the thousands of other issues concurrently being considered in connection with the hundreds of items on the agendas of numerous international organs. In all this, the international legislative process fully mimics the corresponding domestic one. Moreover, negotiations may continue even after an instrument has been formally adopted, i.e., during the domestic phase and even after entry into force when changes to the treaty may be considered.

The methods of taking decisions in international bodies are diverse and somewhat complex. In a few international financial institutions (IFIs, such as the World Bank), votes are allocated to members roughly in accordance to their investments in or contributions to the organization. In most other IGO organs, each member (large or small, rich or poor, powerful or weak, democratic or authoritarian) is allocated one vote; substantive decisions normally require a two-thirds majority and procedural ones, a simple one. However, because that formula permits a large number of States with insignificant population and little economic or military strength to adopt decisions that are opposed by a number of powerful or otherwise significant States whose participation in a proposed treaty is essential for its proper functioning, the tendency has been to avoid formal votes at most stages of the treaty-making process. In particular, an attempt is made at all stages to achieve consensus, which normally requires achieving a sufficient measure of agreement so that no member vigorously opposes a decision. This search for consensus is likely to take longer than the resolution of issues by votes. And to some extent, it holds the process hostage to those who would impede it either to achieve a particular negotiating goal, out of fundamental opposition, merely capriciously, or sometimes in connection with some unrelated matter; through all this the process may be delayed—sometimes for years or even decades, and the resulting text is apt to be watered down to a low common denominator. On the other hand, a successful negotiation is likely to signal the willingness of most participants to become Parties to the adopted treaty (which may be a requirement for it to enter into force at all) and to implement it thereafter.

Usually at a late stage in the international phase of the treaty-making process the "Final Clauses" of the proposed treaty are formulated. These may include provisions regarding the making of reservations and other options to be available to prospective Parties (*see* below); which States or IGOs, such as the European Union, are eligible to become Parties; any preconditions for participation (e.g., the prior adoption of relevant legislation); the formal steps to be taken by prospective Parties (normally signature during a specified period—usually one year—at a specified place—usually the headquarters of the IGO), to be confirmed by ratification, approval or adoption, or accession without prior signature for States that missed the signature deadline; and conditions for entry into force (minimum number of Parties and usually a time delay of some months after a sufficient number have acted).

Though many of these conditions and provisions tend to be standard, at least for a particular type of treaty (e.g., environmental or human rights), those relating to entry into force may require some substantive decisions. Some multilateral treaties (e.g., human rights) are valuable even with a minimal number of participants. Others, such as those regulating a global commons, make sense only if substantially all important users of that commons participate; otherwise the Parties to the treaty restrain themselves to improve the commons, leaving more resources (e.g., fish or waste disposal sites) to be exploited by non-Parties that benefit as "free riders." Also, if a significant IGO is to be established by the treaty, then it is necessary that the Parties include States able and willing to bear most of the costs thereof.

ii.   *The Domestic Process*

Each State has its own domestic requirements and procedures for becoming a Party to a treaty. In some cases this decision is taken merely by the executive. In others, one or more branches of the legislature must agree. In certain federal States, the consent of the constituent states must be obtained in respect to obligations to be carried out by the latter. Substantively, a State must examine to what extent the proposed treaty is compatible with its own legal system—e.g., are there constitutional obstacles, are there laws or regulations that must be adopted or amended—and what steps need be taken to correct any deficiencies. It must also examine to what extent the proposed treaty is compatible with its other international legal obligations, perhaps flowing from earlier treaties or from customary law, and how any possible obstacles can be overcome.

All this may require the translation of the proposed treaty and perhaps any commentary thereto into the official language(s) of the country and the preparation of reports to the executive and legislature, explaining the treaty, analyzing its advantages, costs, and other disadvantages, proposing necessary legislative or regulatory texts, and so on. These requirements are likely to strain the capacities of even well-staffed bureaucracies. They may overwhelm those of smaller or less developed States, resulting in delays or often complete inaction based not on any opposition to an instrument but merely on an inability to cope rapidly with the requirements for bringing it into force domestically.

Some IGOs are equipped or are equipping themselves to assist members in processing treaties adopted under the auspices of the particular IGO. Such assistance in many instances need merely be technical to meet the requirements listed in the previous paragraph. In other instances, technical or even material assistance may be required to enable a State to comply substantively, e.g., to carry out monitoring of particular environment-relevant factors. This is discussed in Chapter 18.

iii. Options Available to Treaty Parties

In order to facilitate the participation of States in treaties—and thus their entry into force and the broadest possible coverage—a number of indulgences or options may be offered to them.

First, and especially in respect to certain environmental treaties, their substantive obligations may be adjusted to the capacities of specified groups of States, for example, by delaying the date by which they must comply with certain requirements. [6] This is also discussed further in Chapter 4 with respect to developing countries.

States may also, in becoming Parties to a treaty—though not normally later—indicate "reservations" designed to alter their obligations with respect to certain provisions of a treaty. For example, both the United States and the USSR made a reservation that they would not be bound by the mandatory dispute settlement article in the 1986 Convention on Early Notification of a Nuclear Accident. [7] The Final Clauses of a treaty often specify whether or not any reservations are "admissible" (i.e., permissible or recognizable), and, if so, which ones. If there is no such specification, the 1969 Vienna Convention on the Law of Treaties states that reservations not incompatible with the basic purpose of the treaty are admissible. The Vienna Convention also indicates how these are to be made and to what extent these change the respective treaty obligations of the reserving State and of other Parties, which may or may not object to the reservation. States may use reservations in order to enable them to become Parties to treaties of which they basically approve but some features of which are incompatible with provisions of their constitution or would face great resistance from domestic groups. For the same purpose, treaties may also offer Parties the opportunity to

---

[6]   E.g., Article 5 to the Montreal Protocol on Substances that Deplete the Ozone Layer, 1987, 26 I.L.M. 1550 (1987).

[7]   See Article 11 of the International Atomic Energy Agency (IAEA) Convention on Early Notification of a Nuclear Accident, 1986, 25 I.L.M. 1370 (1986).

exercise certain options built into the instrument (e.g., a choice of dispute settlement procedures such as in the UN Convention on the Law of the Sea) or of ancillary instruments (such as specialized protocols).

Related to reservations, but considerably narrower in scope, are statements referred to as understandings or declarations made by States when ratifying a treaty (or when agreeing to another type of instrument). These statements purport to explain how the State will interpret or apply some aspect of the treaty (or other instrument). Generally speaking, these are only admissible when there is ambiguity regarding the language to which they pertain, and even then the statement presumably must be consistent with the objects and purposes of the treaty.

Finally, some treaties may offer relatively easy withdrawal provisions, so that a State may feel reassured that its acceptance of certain obligations is not irrevocable if these prove to be too onerous or if relevant conditions should change. But it should be emphasized that in the absence of a termination or withdrawal provision, the grounds for successfully taking such actions are narrow and difficult to satisfy, as is evident in the discussion of the *Gabčíkovo* case in Chapter 12.

All the above-described devices are intended to facilitate the conclusion and entry into force of treaties by granting a certain measure of flexibility as to when, how, and to what extent States are to be bound by obligations under these instruments. The disadvantage is that they can result in a very uneven patchwork of international legal obligations. With respect to a particular treaty, some States may be Parties and others not (either not having become so, or having withdrawn); some States may have made reservations, to which others may or may not have objected; and various combinations of options may have been exercised with respect to provisions of the treaty or of ancillary instruments. In this respect, the international legislative process differs significantly from the domestic one, in which all subjects automatically have the same obligations. Governance issues arising from this situation are discussed in Chapter 18.

iv. Living Treaties

Historically, the relatively few multilateral treaties, once adopted, remained unchanged indefinitely. Often there was no urgency about changing them, and even if there was some reason to do so it was not an enterprise that could conveniently be undertaken. These treaties were adopted at ad hoc meetings of States rather than under the auspices of an IGO with a continuing interest in the subject, and they normally did not themselves establish any organs charged with their implementation and review. Eventually, once they became entirely obsolete, they might be superseded by a new instrument on the same subject.

In the modern fast-moving and changing world, with many treaties—particularly those in the environmental field—dealing with scientific and technical developments that either create new problems or promise novel solutions, this former rigid pattern is no longer appropriate. Nor is it necessary, because with respect to almost every significant multilateral treaty there exists a competent and concerned IGO that either participated in formulating the treaty or was established by it. However, if every change or addition requires a process comparable to that needed to formulate the treaty and to have it enter into force, then it would still be difficult to keep treaty law sufficiently up-to-date to respond to rapid developments in the real world, such as changes in scientific knowledge and environmental conditions. Consequently, a number of devices have been developed to shortcut either the international or the domestic phase of the treaty-making process, or both, so as to facilitate changing an existing instrument. To be effective, the legal basis for these devices must normally be written into the particular treaty or alternatively into a constitutional instrument of the IGO responsible for the amending process.

These devices often differentiate among (1) substantive amendments to the basic treaty, which normally require, at least in the domestic phase, the same steps and procedures as required for the treaty itself; (2) amendments to technical provisions, especially those set out in annexes, for which often both the international and the domestic phases of the legislative process are simplified; and (3) the adoption of additional technical protocols that also may have one or both phases streamlined.

With respect to the international phase, instead of establishing an ad hoc procedure as is usually required for a new treaty instrument, the consideration of amendments and of new protocols is often automatically assigned to standing expert and/or representative organs, assisted by a knowledgeable secretariat, which can formulate new texts expeditiously. Adoption can take place at a regularly or specially scheduled session of a general representative organ (e.g., a conference of the parties).

With respect to the domestic phase, various devices for facilitating entry into force can be used:

(1) Some amendments, particularly to the constitutional instruments of IGOs, require normal procedures with respect to signature, ratification, and so on and require such steps to be taken by a certain fraction (usually two-thirds) of the membership for entry into force; but such entry then applies automatically to all members, including those that have not acted.

(2) Some adopted amendments provide that they automatically enter into force for all states except those that by a given date indicate their intention to opt out—a decision that the states can then reverse at any time. It is usually also provided that if a certain fraction of the parties opts out, then the amendment fails.

(3) Some adopted amendments provide that they enter into force for States by a simple notification to the secretariat, which may enable many of the States to circumvent the domestic requirements regarding the ratification of treaties.

NOTES AND QUESTIONS

1. Reservations to multilateral treaties pose some particularly complex problems that the International Court of Justice addressed in a 1951 advisory opinion named *Reservations to the Convention on the Prevention and the Punishment of the Crime of Genocide.*[8] The UN General Assembly requested the opinion with respect to whether States making reservations to the convention became Parties thereto, when some of the States that had negotiated the convention objected to the reservations. The Court recalled the principle that a State could not be bound without its consent, and that no reservation could be made without a State Party's agreement. Thereafter, the Court concluded;

> [A] State which has made and maintained a reservation which has been objected to by one or more of the parties to the Convention but not by others, can be regarded as being a party to the Convention if the reservation is compatible with the object and purpose of the Convention, otherwise, that State cannot be regarded as being a party to the Convention. . . . [I]f a party to the Convention objects to a reservation which it considers to be incompatible with the object and purpose of the Convention, it can in fact consider that the reserving State is not a party to the Convention; if, on the other hand, a party accepts the reservation as being compatible with the object and purpose of the Convention, it can in fact consider that the reserving State is a party to the Convention.[9]

The United States Senate gave its advice and consent to the Genocide Convention in 1986; however, it was accompanied by two reservations, five understandings, and one declaration.[10] Understandings and declarations may also be made with respect to non-binding international instruments, as the United States did with respect to the Rio Declaration on Environment and Development.

2. The 1982 UN Convention on the Law of the Sea prohibits reservations. *See* Article 309. The United States refused to sign the convention because of its opposition to the part of the convention—Part XI— that deals with international seabed mining development. Twelve years after

---

[8] 1951 I.C.J. Reports 15.

[9] *Id.* at 29–30.

[10] *See* Leich, *Contemporary Practice of the United States Relating to International Law,* 80 Am. J. Intl. L. 61–2–(1986); *see also* Liesbeth Lijnzaad, Reservations to U.N.-Human Rights Treaties: Ratify and Ruin? (1995); 1969 Vienna Convention on the Law of Treaties, 1155 U.N.T.S. 336, *reprinted* in 63 Am. J. Intl. L. 875 (1969); and American Law Institute, Restatement (Third) of the Foreign Relations Law of the United States § 313, Reporter's Note 1 (1987). 33 I.L.M. 1309 (1994).

its completion, a separate agreement, 1994 Agreement Relating to the Implementation of Part XI of the United Nations Convention on the Law of the Sea of 10 December 1982 (Part XI Agreement),[11] was negotiated to allow States (primarily the United States) to join the 1982 Law of the Sea Convention without having to accept Part XI of the Convention. In spite of this, the United States has yet to ratify the Convention as of August 2015.

3.   Do you think international environmental conventions should permit reservations, understandings, and declarations? Does your answer depend on which States you want to be a Party? On the subject matter? On how many States will be Parties?

5.   GENERAL PRINCIPLES OF LAW

An apparently minor source of international law listed in Article 38(1)(c) of the ICJ Statute is "the general principles of law recognized by civilized nations." In this context, "civilized nations" means States that have an organized legal system.

It should be noted that the reference here is not to "general principles of international law," which are the rules of customary international law. Rather, what is referred to here are those common elements of all, or virtually all, domestic legal systems, which thus can be presumed also to pertain to the international domain. Though scholars have from time to time identified certain such principles, the World Court itself has relatively rarely said it is relying on them and when it does have recourse to them it is often in respect to procedural principles (e.g., no one can be a judge in one's own case) rather than in respect to substantive matters. They consist chiefly of fundamental principles that are universally recognized (e.g., estoppel or its equivalent), principles relating to the administration of justice, and other internal law principles that fill gaps in international law. All fifteen judges on the Court were trained in a domestic legal system before they became international lawyers, so these principles are likely to play a significant role in informing their thinking even if they are not referred to explicitly in the *ratio decidendi* of the judgment. It has been argued that the common practice of States to bar the import of a chemical unless the importer can demonstrate the safety of that chemical is such a principle, embodying the precautionary principle or approach discussed in Chapter 4.

NOTES AND QUESTIONS

For an early attempt to identify the consistency of national law concepts and principles in addressing environmental concerns—some of which today might qualify as "general principles of law"—*see* Robert E. Lutz, *The Laws of Environmental Management: A Comparative Study*, 24 Am. J. Comp. L. 447 (1976). Do you think the "polluter pays principle" can be considered a

---

[11]   33 I.L.M. 1309 (1994).

"general principle of law"? In the article cited, Lutz wrote that "[the polluter pays principle] has received wide acceptance among countries and international organizations" and cites the European Communities, Organisation for Economic and Co-operation and Development, Council of Europe, Australia, Canada, the United Kingdom, Federal Republic of Germany and Japan, as having adopted the principle.

6. INTERNATIONAL ADMINISTRATIVE LAW

International administrative law is the law that governs IGOs. It is not mentioned in the ICJ Statute but is nevertheless a form of international law. Its principal manifestations are the constitutional law of IGOs—i.e., the law governing and laid down in the treaties that create them—the procedural rules governing the business of international organs, the privileges and immunities of IGOs and their staffs, the rules governing the granting of assistance by IGOs to States, the rules governing the various types of activities carried out by IGOs within States (e.g., meetings; peacekeeping operations; humanitarian assistance; inspections and other types of monitoring), and the personnel and financial regime of IGOs. Much of that law is created by treaties, some by decisions of competent IGO organs, and some by the practices of these organizations, which largely are carried out by their secretariats. There are also a number of international courts (e.g., the World Court and the European Court of Justice) and administrative tribunals (the personnel courts of almost every IGO or group of IGOs, such as those of the UN and the International Labour Organization) that interpret and to some extent even create this type of law.

Because of the narrow subject matter of this area of international law, little of it is directly relevant to environmental matters. Only to the extent that the activities of IGOs active in relation to the environment, including the transparency of their operations and the conditions under which civil society may participate with respect to an IGO, are governed by international administrative law does that law have relevance to the subject of this volume. Regarding the participation of civil society, issues include: accreditation criteria and decision-making processes regarding which elements of civil society are allowed to participate; procedural and substantive rules regarding requests for information from civil society; rules regarding civil society's ability to be present at proceedings and meetings; rules regarding the ability of civil society to introduce documents into the record and distribute them; and rules regarding civil society's ability to make oral statements in meetings.

7. DECISIONS BY INTERGOVERNMENTAL ORGANIZATIONS

Except in respect of certain parts of international administrative law, the decisions of IGO organs, no matter how senior, are not binding on

States. The only exceptions are those IGOs in which States have empowered a particular organ to take decisions binding on them. This is rare, but when it is done it is normally accomplished through a treaty such as the constitutional instrument of an IGO. The prime example is Chapter VII of the UN Charter, which authorizes the UN Security Council to determine the existence of a threat to the peace, a breach of the peace, or an act of aggression and thereupon require all UN members (i.e., not only the offending State) to take specified economic, diplomatic, or even military actions to maintain or restore international peace and security.

The only instance in which the Security Council used this authority on an explicitly environmental matter as of August 2015 was in providing that Iraq is responsible and must pay compensation for the environmental harm that it caused during the Gulf War,[12] though there have been efforts to have the Security Council address climate change. More directly relevant to environmental protection are those instances in which States have empowered certain specified organs to make minor technical adjustments to a treaty or to issue binding regulations of a narrowly circumscribed nature. Even then, States usually reserve the right to opt out of such amendments or standards or to be bound only if they specifically opt in (see above). An important exception to this is the adjustment procedure contained in the Montreal Protocol on Substances that Deplete the Ozone layer, described in Chapter 8.

Most frequently, the decisions of IGO organs constitute, at most, recommendations to members of the organization. Such recommendations can relate to a treaty, such as to comply with its substantive or procedural obligations (e.g., to submit required reports). Recommendations to take certain substantive actions can also encourage behavior leading to the creation of customary law or the acceptance of soft law.

NOTES AND QUESTIONS

Consider the following excerpt from the *Texaco/Libya Arbitration Award* of Jan. 19, 1977, 17 I.L.M. 1 (1978):

> The general question of the legal validity of the Resolutions of the United Nations has been widely discussed by the writers. This Tribunal will recall first that, under Article 10 of the U.N. Charter, the General Assembly only issues "recommendations," which have long appeared to be texts having no binding force and carrying no obligations for the Member States.
>
> Refusal to recognize any legal validity of United Nations Resolutions must, however, be qualified according to the various

---

[12]   33 I.L.M. 1309 (1994).

texts enacted by the United Nations. These are very different and have varying legal value, but it is impossible to deny that the United Nations' activities have had a significant influence on the content of contemporary international law. In appraising the legal validity of the above-mentioned Resolutions, this Tribunal will take account of the criteria usually taken into consideration, *i.e.,* the examination of voting conditions and the analysis of the provisions concerned.

Suppose a UN General Assembly resolution declares that States are obligated to prohibit the import and sale of elephant ivory tusks from any African State. Even though all European States and African States and most North and South American States vote for this resolution, virtually all Asian and some developing countries from other regions vote against it, making the vote two-thirds for and one-third against. What is the international legal value of the resolution? Would it have mattered if the vote had been unanimous in favor of the resolution?[13]

8. UNILATERAL STATEMENTS

In a few cases, unilateral statements by State officials have been held to be legally binding on that State. For example, in the *Nuclear Weapons Cases*,[14] the ICJ held that unilateral statements by several French officials that France would no longer conduct nuclear weapons tests in the Pacific region bound France under international law. The legal foundation for these results is unclear, although it has been suggested that the pattern of behavior in those cases constructively constituted an international agreement of some type, perhaps because of reliance by other States (or the ICJ itself). The International Law Commission issued guiding principles regarding unilateral statements and legal obligations in 2006. See International Law Commission, *Guiding Principles Applicable to Unilateral Declarations of States Capable of Creating Legal Obligations*, 2006 Y.B. Int'l L. Comm'n, vol. 2, pt. 2, p. 160. These guiding principles are excerpted, and this topic is discussed further, in Chapter 4. As noted below, the use of so-called voluntary commitments appears to be increasing as of August 2015 (e.g., with respect to climate change), so this topic may become of increasing relevance

9. OTHER NORMS AND INSTRUMENTS

a. Soft Law

Hard international law (i.e., those types mentioned above, chiefly treaties and custom) is, by definition, legally binding, at least on some

---

[13] *See* Schachter, *Resolutions of the General Assembly as Evidence of Law*, 178 *Rec. des Cours* 114121 (1982-V); and S. Rosenne, Practice and Methods of International Law 111–17 (1984).

[14] New Zealand v. France, Australia v. France, 1974 ICJ Rep. 457.

international entities (States and IGOs), although not necessarily on all. By contrast, what some commentators refer to as "soft international law" is not binding, though perhaps superficially it may appear to be so. Nevertheless, the international entities concerned habitually comply with it, and it is this feature that arguably makes it appropriate to refer to it as "law."

Soft law manifests itself in various ways. One is in hortatory rather than obligatory language set out in otherwise binding instruments, such as when in a treaty in force certain actions to be taken are preceded by "should" rather than by "shall."[15] This needs to be differentiated from obligations that are by their very nature vague, such as to cooperate or consult or negotiate before taking certain actions, because the performance of such obligations must always be judged by the standard of good faith. Perhaps more frequent are obligations expressed as if they are binding (e.g., using the word "shall") but are set out in an instrument that is not binding, such as a resolution of a senior international organ (such as the World Charter for Nature promulgated by the UN General Assembly) or of a high-level conference (such as the Stockholm and Rio Declarations adopted at the 1972 Stockholm Conference on the Human Environment and the 1992 UN Conference on Environment and Development, respectively).

According to one view, such nonbinding precepts (rather than obligations) can be considered as soft law only if international entities, particularly States, habitually comply with them—or at least pretend to do so, thus in effect acknowledging their authority. Such behavior, even in the absence of a strict legal obligation, may be due to various factors, such as the existence of a control mechanism that notes and may report on noncompliance; it may also be due to a mere expectation of compliance expressed by other States and by the general public (including their own citizens) with respect to precepts that a government has helped to negotiate and include in an instrument adopted with the concurrence of— and possibly a political commitment by—its representatives in an international organ. Others use the term "soft law" to refer to any hortatory (or sometimes precatory) international statement.

Soft law is often generated as a compromise between those who desire a certain matter to be regulated definitively and those who, while not denying the merits of the substantive issue, do not wish (at least for a time) to be bound by a rigid and obligatory rule—perhaps because they cannot obtain the necessary domestic legislative approval. At other times a particular set of norms may not be considered ready to become a binding measure, though what is essentially voluntary compliance can be sought. Finally, certain matters may be considered to be too technical,

---

[15] *See, e.g.,* Article 3 of the Framework Convention on Climate Change (1992), *reprinted in* 31 I.L.M. 849 (1992).

trivial, or perhaps ephemeral for present inclusion in a treaty instrument. Consider the following excerpt from Edith Brown Weiss, In Fairness to Future Generations 103 (1989):

> [R]ecognition of a moral obligation does not in itself create legal obligations and rights. Rather it is a stage in the evolution of the public conscience. When this evolution has achieved a certain degree of maturity—the definition of which is impossible *in abstracto*—*legal* obligations and rights are formulated. This is the first condition for the legal protection by society.
>
> In international law, we must regard planetary obligations and planetary rights as in the formative stage. Concern for future generations exists, although there is limited awareness of the issues. The first step is for society to formulate planetary obligations and planetary rights, as by a solemn declaration of principles. Such declarations have been frequent since 1945 for other principles, and have assumed the crucial role of formulating social values. These declarations constitute only "soft law" instruments, which are not mandatory and may not be applied. But we can speak of pre-legal rules or emerging principles which can either prepare "hard law" rules (conclusion of treaties) or contribute to the creation of rules of customary international law.

Chapter 4 contains a further excerpt from Edith Brown Weiss analyzing scholarship regarding soft law: Edith Brown Weiss, *Voluntary Commitments as Emerging Instruments,* in International Environmental Law, 44 Environmental Policy and Law 83 (April 2014).

There is an ever-growing amount of soft law, most particularly in respect to the environment, expressed in the form of standards, guidelines, and rules formulated by expert organs and often promulgated by the executive head of a technical IGO or organ, such as UNEP. Examples of environment-related non-binding standards issued by non-governmental organizations include the environmental management standards issued by the International Standards Organization (ISO) and the standards regarding testing the safety of genetically engineered organisms issued by the Codex Alimentarius. While in principle the development of such norms mimics that of the process of formulating multilateral treaties, the process is apt to be a great deal quicker, more technical, and less political. Similarly, when such norms are to be amended or supplemented, this often can be done much more rapidly and simply than even a simplified treaty-amending procedure.

Inherently even less binding than soft law instruments that at least in form suggest an expectation of compliance are those that are merely presented as model legislation, regulations, or treaties—for example, those merely designed to assist States that wish to benefit from the technical expertise of an IGO without feeling under a legal obligation to do so. If formulated so as to be truly useful, such instruments may achieve a high level of acceptance, especially in technical fields in which many countries do not have the expertise to consider formulating standards of their own, while at the same time feeling the need to include appropriate provisions in their domestic legislation.

NOTES AND QUESTIONS

1.   *How can law be soft?* Is it accurate, or even helpful, to use the term "soft law"? How can something not legally binding be considered "law"? Does this usage provide fuel to those who doubt that even international obligations that are clearly legally binding are truly "law" as that term is used domestically (e.g., because there is not, generally speaking, any centralized law-making, judicial, or enforcement mechanism in the international system)? On the other hand, how else can one take account of the normative effect of some non-legally binding statements?

2.   Quite apart from the questions of terminology raised in Note 1, it is important to recognize the fact that non-legally binding statements and commitments often are complied with by States.

3.   Equally important is that non-legally binding statements sometimes are transformed into legally binding obligations, either by becoming customary international law or through incorporation in a treaty. Consider the following excerpt from Daniel Magraw, *International Pollution, Economic Development and Human Rights*, in International Law and Pollution 30, 49–50 (Daniel Barstow Magraw ed., 1991):

> One of the most striking developments in substantive international law since World War II has been the rapid transformation of aspirational goals to binding customary obligations in the international human rights area (i.e., as some describe it, from "soft" law to "hard" law). It is now widely acknowledged, for example, that many human rights norms are part of customary international law and that some of those have even risen to the status of *jus cogens,* that is, peremptory norms that cannot be abrogated by agreement. It has been strongly argued that the entire 1948 Universal Declaration of Human Rights, which unquestionably was aspirational when originally adopted, has become part of customary international law.

> Many reasons account for this transformation. Several human-rights or analogous norms, for example, prohibition of slavery and State responsibility for injuries to aliens (although the latter, in particular, retains a separate policy basis and jurisprudence), existed before World War II. The fundamental concept of human rights is widely accepted, at least in word (such as in national constitutions), if not in deed. Human rights have a powerful moral appeal. Moreover, perhaps because of the previously mentioned

factors, States are extremely reluctant to speak out against human rights (even if failing to do so is blatantly hypocritical, such as was the case when the General Assembly unanimously approved the Convention Against Torture). Nevertheless, the transformation of human rights aspirations to customary norms, in particular, is remarkable for several reasons: the time frame was relatively short, a substantial amount of contrary State practice occurred during the period, most of the consistent State practice was comprised of refraining from acting, and much of that refraining was already required by international agreements.

As you proceed through the materials in this book, consider whether international environmental law shares these characteristics and whether other circumstances favor or disfavor this process?

4.   An example of a successful attempt to harden soft law into treaty law is the transformation of the Guidelines for the Exchange of Information on Chemicals in International Trade (adopted by the United Nations Environment Programme Governing Council in 1987 and known as the UNEP PIC—prior informed consent—Guidelines) into a binding international agreement on prior informed consent. This instrument was adopted in 1998 as the Rotterdam Convention for the Application of the Prior Informed Consent Procedure for Certain Hazardous Chemicals and Pesticides in International Trade (PIC Convention), as is discussed in Chapter 10.

5.   One commentator (Günther Handl) has referred to soft law as "the Trojan Horse of international environmental law" because soft law often contains environmentally preferable language that would not have been agreed to as legally binding when it was adopted, yet it will, over time, become hard law, or at least sufficiently obligatory that environmental activists can argue it is legally binding.

6.   Are soft law obligations subject to sanctions for noncompliance? For further reading, see Gochalla-Wesierski, *A Framework for Understanding "Soft Law"*, 30 McGill Law. J. 37 (1984). For a discussion about the use of codes of conduct in regulating multinational enterprises, particularly with respect to their applicability to transfers of hazardous technologies and substances. *See* Robert E. Lutz & George D. Aron, *Codes of Conduct and Other International Instruments*, in Transferring Technologies and Substances: The International Legal Challenge, 129, 151–157 (G. Handl & R. Lutz eds., 1989).

7.   Hundreds of voluntary standards have been adopted by industries or individual companies or international standard-setting bodies such as the International Standards Organization referred to above. Under what circumstances, if any, do IGOs have a soft-law or hard-law obligation to insist that private organizations getting funding from them comply with such standards?

b.   Specific Voluntary Commitments

A type of non-binding commitment that is apparently becoming increasingly common consists of specific, country-by-country commitments made by States. In 2009, for example, States dealt with the financial crisis, the issue of non-weapons nuclear security and climate change by creating instruments that, although non-legally binding, contained a mechanism by which States could make specific commitments regarding their own behavior. See, e.g., the Copenhagen Accord, UNFCCC Conference of the Parties dec. 2/CP.15. (18 December 2009). Similarly, in 2014, China and the United States jointly announced national commitments to control their respective emissions of greenhouse gases. These are subject to the possibility of becoming legally binding, as discussed above, but presumably were not intended to be initially.

c.   Other Legal Statements

Although Article 38(1)(d) of the ICJ Statute specifically refers to "judicial decisions and the teachings of the most highly qualified publicists of the various nations," it characterizes these not as a type or source of law but merely as "subsidiary means for the determination of rules of law" (i.e., evidence of the existence of law). With respect to judicial decisions, this is in part because the international system lacks any hierarchy of courts (in which a senior one can effectively bind a junior one) and in part by deliberate decision that the doctrine of *stare decisis* does not apply. *See* Article 59 of the ICJ Statute.

These subsidiary means are, however, valuable in identifying, authenticating, and clearly expressing (e.g., in converting unwritten law into *lex scripta)* rules of customary international law or general principles of law, or in interpreting controverted texts in a treaty. At least in theory they are not independent sources of law, and thus there can be no legislative process in respect to them.

Importantly, however, although the traditional view is that the doctrine of *stare decisis* does not apply in the international legal system, tribunals and States do not always act as if that is the case. In practice, the situation is more nuanced.

First, some international legal (sub)systems provide for a type of *stare decisis*. The World Trade Organization is an example: first-level arbitral panels are expected to follow the jurisprudence of the WTO Appellate Body. For an example, see the *Shrimp/Turtle* case discussed in Chapter 16, in which the Appellate Body mandated a specific analytic process for panels when applying Article XX of the General Agreement on Tariffs and Trade.

Second, tribunals tend to be consistent with their own previous jurisprudence. Examples include the ICJ (e.g., the *Pulp Mills* case discussed in Chapter 4) and regional human rights tribunals (e.g., the Inter-American Court of Human Rights in the *Mayagna (Sumo) Awas Tingni Community v. Nicaragua* case discussed in Chapter 15).

Third, tribunals dealing with a particular subject matter often follow, or at least refer to, jurisprudence from other tribunals dealing with that subject matter, even when the source of jurisdiction and the legal rules are established by different instruments. Examples include arbitral tribunals considering claims by private investors against States under different bilateral investment treaties (e.g., *SGS v. Philippines Decision on Objections to Jurisdiction*, ICSID Case No. ARB/02/06 (2004), para. 97, distinguishing itself from the decision in *SGS v. Pakistan*), tribunals hearing State-to-State arbitrations (e.g., the *Indus Waters Kishenganga Arbitration,* discussed in Chapter 12, paras. 448–452, relying on, inter alia, the *Arbitration Regarding the Iron Rhine ("Ijzeren Rijn") Railway between the Kingdom of Belgium and the Kingdom of the Netherlands*, 24 May 2005, *PCA Award Series* (2007)), and regional human rights tribunals with different constitutive instruments (e.g., *Social and Economic Rights Center v. Nigeria*, African Comm'n on Human and Peoples' Rights, ACHPR/Comm/A044/1, Dec. re: Comm. No. 155/96 (2001), citing the European Court of Human Rights' jurisprudence).

Finally, tribunals tend to look to the jurisprudence of the ICJ for guidance when the ICJ has ruled on an issue. An example is the *Indus Waters Kishenganga Arbitration* discussed in Chapter 12, which relied on the ICJ's decisions in the *Gabčíkovo-Nagymaros Project* and *Pulp Mills* cases (discussed in Chapter 4).

Putting aside the situations such as the WTO where the tribunal's constitutive instrument effectively provides for *stare decisis*, tribunals do not normally explain the reason for acting in a *quasi-stare decisis* manner. Not surprisingly, international lawyers frequently cite authorities from various sources in their written and oral argumentation.

NOTES AND QUESTIONS

1. The case of *Filártiga v. Peña-Irala*, 630 F.2d 876 (2d Cir. 1980), 19 I.L.M. 966 (1980), indicates how a court might utilize "subsidiary means" to determine the applicable international legal rule. In that case, the court, applying the Alien Tort Statute, 28 U.S.C. § 1350, decided that torture committed by a state official against a person held in detention violated the law of nations. Consider this excerpt:

> [A]lthough there is no universal agreement as to the precise extent of the "human rights and fundamental freedoms" guaranteed to all by the Charter, there is at present no dissent from the view that the guaranties include, at a bare minimum, the right to be free from torture. This prohibition has become part of customary international law, as evidenced and defined by the Universal

Declaration of Human Rights. The General Assembly has declared that the Charter precepts embodied in this Universal Declaration "constitute basic principles of international law." G.A. Res. 2625 (XXV) (Oct. 24, 1970).

Particularly relevant is the Declaration on the Protection of All Persons from Being Subjected to Torture, General Assembly Resolution 3452. . . . This Declaration, like the Declaration of Human Rights before it, was adopted without dissent by the General Assembly.

These U.N. declarations are significant because they specify with great precision the obligations of member nations under the Charter. Since their adoption, "(m)embers can no longer contend that they do not know what human rights they promised in the Charter to promote." Moreover, a U.N. Declaration is, according to one authoritative definition, "a formal and solemn instrument, suitable for rare occasions when principles of great and lasting importance are being enunciated." Accordingly, it has been observed that the Universal Declaration of Human Rights "no longer fits into the dichotomy of 'binding treaty' against 'non-binding pronouncement,' but is rather an authoritative statement of the international community." Thus, a Declaration creates an expectation of adherence, and "insofar as the expectation is gradually justified by State practice, a declaration may by custom become recognized as laying down rules binding upon the States." Indeed, several commentators have concluded that the Universal Declaration has become, in toto, a part of binding, customary international law.

Turning to the act of torture, we have little difficulty discerning its universal renunciation in the modern usage and practice of nations. The international consensus surrounding torture has found expression in numerous international treaties and accords. E.g., American Convention on Human Rights Art. 5; International Covenant on Civil and Political Rights, U.N. General Assembly Res. 2200 (XXI)A (identical language); European Convention for the Protection of Human Rights and Fundamental Freedoms, Art. 3. The substance of these international agreements is reflected in modern municipal, i.e., national law as well. Although torture was once a routine concomitant of criminal interrogations in many nations, during the modern and hopefully more enlightened era it has been universally renounced. According to one survey, torture is prohibited, expressly or implicitly, by the constitutions of over fifty-five nations, including both the United States and Paraguay. Our State Department reports a general recognition of this principle.

On what grounds did the court reach its conclusion? How did it treat declarations of the General Assembly?

2. *In theory, theory and practice are the same. In practice, they are different.* As described above, tribunals often follow or distinguish the holdings of other tribunals, even though in theory there is no doctrine of *stare decisis* in international law. Why would tribunals do this? One can imagine interests such as achieving credibility for a particular decision, improving the likelihood of acceptance of and compliance with a decision once it has issued, and increasing coherence in the international legal system or in a discrete part of it. Can you think of other possible reasons?

9. RELATIONSHIP BETWEEN INTERNATIONAL AND DOMESTIC LAW

Broadly speaking, there are two alternative approaches to the relationship between international and domestic (or municipal) law:

1. the "monistic" approach, which considers that both systems of law constitute part of a single whole, in which international law is therefore necessarily hierarchically superior to domestic law. This is similar to a federal system in which federal law is, within its designated limits, superior to the law of the constituent entities of the federation. In such a system, even provisions of the national constitution must yield to international law binding on that State; and

2. the "dualist" approach, in which international and domestic law are considered to be basically separate. Usually the municipal rules ultimately determine the hierarchical relationship between the two.

International law itself relies on the monistic approach. Thus, for example, Article 37 of the 1969 Vienna Convention on the Law of Treaties provides that a State may not advance any provision of its domestic law (including its constitution) as an excuse for a failure to comply with a treaty obligation. However, States following the dualist system are in effect able to do so because ultimately States can rarely be compelled to act in a particular way. Fortunately, direct clashes between international and domestic law are relatively rare.

The United States clearly takes a dualist approach. The Supremacy Clause of the United States Constitution (Article VI, section 2), provides:

This Constitution, and the Laws of the United States which shall be made in Pursuance thereof; and all Treaties made, or which shall be made, under the Authority of the United States, shall be the supreme Law of the Land; and the Judges in every State shall be bound thereby, any Thing in the Constitution or Laws of any State to the Contrary notwithstanding.

Congress is given the power to—but not required to—"define and punish
. . . [o]ffenses against the Law of Nations" in Article I, section 8 of the
Constitution. The terminology here bears some examination. We would
now refer to the "Law of Nations" as international law.

The term "treaty" requires more explanation when discussing United
States law. Domestically, it is customary to distinguish between a
"treaty," which requires approval of two-thirds of the Senate present
(according to Art II, section 2 of the Constitution), and executive
agreements, which may be entered into by the President without such
approval. Article VI, quoted above, makes clear that "treaties" have
equivalent status with federal statutes. But what about executive
agreements?

For most purposes, executive agreements are treated like treaties,
but the situation is not entirely clear. In exploring the uncertainties, it is
helpful to distinguish among three types of executive agreements:
(1) "treaty executive agreements" entered into pursuant to a treaty;
(2) "congressional executive agreements" that have been approved by a
majority of each House of Congress (e.g., the North American Agreement
on Environmental Cooperation); and "sole executive agreements" that are
entered into by the President on his/her sole authority (e.g., the United
States-Mexico La Paz Agreement for Cooperation on Environmental
Programs and Transboundary Problems). Taking into account the United
States Constitution, decisions of the Supreme Court and other tribunals,
and the Restatement (Third) of the Foreign Relations Law of the United
States (1987) (a Restatement (Fourth) is being prepared as this book goes
to press), the current situation appears to be as follows:

1. The Constitution is superior to treaties. Thus the United
    States may not enter into a treaty violative of any part of
    the Constitution, and if it did so, the treaty may not be
    complied with to the extent it so violates, even if thereby the
    United States fails to comply with international law.

2. Treaties are at the same hierarchical level as federal laws; if
    they conflict, the later in time prevails—though, under a
    rule of interpretation applied by the courts, a later statute
    will only be allowed to cause a violation of an earlier treaty
    if the two cannot be reconciled and it is (utterly) clear that
    Congress intended that the treaty be violated.

3. Treaties are superior to federal regulations and to all state
    laws, including even their constitutions.

4. Customary international law has for the purpose of the
    above rules practically the same status as treaties.

5. The situation regarding (2) and (3) above is more
    complicated regarding executive agreements, depending on

whether they were entered into pursuant to a Senate-approved treaty, with the approval of both Houses of Congress, or on the sole authority of the President. Generally speaking, the first two are treated like treaties. The authority of the third (sole executive agreements) is not fully settled and probably depends, at least in large part, on the subject of the agreement and its relation to any specific allocations of power in the Constitution (e.g., to recognize ambassadors or regulate commerce with foreign nations).

It is not always clear whether an agreement needs to be a "treaty" or may be entered into as an "executive agreement". For an analysis of that question in the context of climate change, see David Wirth, *The International and Domestic Law of Climate Change: A Binding International Agreement Without the Senate or Congress?*, 39 Harv. Envtl. L. Rev. 515 (2015).

Another aspect of the relationship between international and municipal law relates to the customary international law rules regarding when it is permissible for a State to exercise jurisdiction, that is, to regulate behavior via legislation (called "jurisdiction to prescribe"), to adjudicate, or to enforce a law. For present purposes, it suffices to note that international law recognizes jurisdiction to prescribe based on the principle of territoriality (e.g., conduct within a State's territory or intended to have an effect within its territory); the principle of nationality (e.g., activities, relations or status of a state's nationals); the protective principle (e.g., offenses committed against the security of the State, such as counterfeiting); and the principle of universality (e.g., a universally condemned crime, such as piracy). A fifth principle—passive personality—is also gaining recognition. It would allow protection of a State's nationals from, for example, terrorism. *See generally* Restatement (Third) of the Foreign Relations Law of the United States §§ 402–416 (1987).

NOTES AND QUESTIONS

1. Recall the language of the Supreme Court in *The Paquette Habana* (*see* pp. 142–143) regarding the relationship of international law to United States law: "International law is part of our law. . . ."

2. Treaties and executive agreements may be either self-executing or non-self-executing. Self-executing instruments become immediately part of the domestic (municipal) law of the United States upon their international entry into force for the United States and may be used by courts for the rule of decision in cases before them. Non-self-executing agreements, on the other hand, require implementing legislation in order to execute them domestically. In some cases determining whether a treaty or an international agreement is self-executing or not can be a challenge. Does the following language from

People of Saipan v. United States Department of Interior, 502 F.2d 90 (9th Cir. 1974), suggest workable criteria for distinguishing between self- and non-self-executing international agreements?

> The extent to which an international agreement establishes affirmative and judicially enforceable obligations without implementing legislation must be determined in each case by reference to many contextual factors: the purposes of the treaty and the objectives of its creators, the existence of domestic procedures and institutions appropriate for direct implementation, the availability and feasibility of alternative enforcement methods, and the immediate and long-range social consequences of self- or non-self-execution. . . .

> The preponderance of features in this. . . . Agreement suggests the intention to establish direct, affirmative, and judicially enforceable rights. The issue involves the local economy and environment, not security; the concern with natural resources and the concern with political development are explicit in the agreement and are generally international concerns as well; the enforcement of these rights requires little legal or administrative innovation in the domestic fora; and the alternative forum . . . would present to the plaintiffs obstacles so great as to make their rights virtually unenforceable. . . .

B. AVOIDANCE AND SETTLEMENT OF DISPUTES

It is evident that in respect to the environment a number of types of disputes can arise between States. Disputes also arise with respect to other international entities, such as IGOs and NGOs. These may include accusations of causing specific harms through transboundary pollution and disputes about the measure of the resulting damages; accusations of damage to a global commons, such as the atmosphere or the high seas, or of the improper exploitation of a shared resource; questions involving the interpretation of environmental treaties or the degree of compliance by particular States with these treaties; and questions whether certain environmental principles not set out in treaties constitute customary law or merely nonbinding soft law. Some such disputes involve only the parties directly concerned. Others potentially involve all States in a particular region or pursuing a particular activity (e.g., fishing), or the world community as a whole. Finally, in the area of international human rights, disputes arise between individuals and groups, on the one hand, and States on the other, in which the individuals or group alleges that its human rights have been violated by the State.

International law requires that disputes between States be settled peacefully.[16] This means more than just avoiding the use of force, which is prohibited by UN Charter Article 2(4) and by customary international law. It also requires that every State must make good faith efforts toward resolving any international disputes to which it is a party.

No State, however, is under any obligation to consent to any particular method of settling disputes peacefully, unless on the basis of some applicable agreement. It is therefore said that States have a free choice of means in this respect. The effect, however, is that the obligation to settle disputes peacefully establishes an imperfect obligation because it is usually difficult to prove a clear violation, as long as each State asserts that it is eager to settle the impasse but merely considers inappropriate the particular method of dispute settlement proposed by the other side.

With respect to the environment, these principles are set out in a number of instruments including: (1) [UNEP] Principles of Conduct in the Field of the Environment for the Guidance of States in the Conservation and Harmonious Utilization of Natural Resources Shared by Two or More States, Principle 11;[17] (2) WCED Experts Group on Environmental Law: General Principles Concerning Natural Resources and Environmental Interferences, Article 22; [18] (3) Antarctic Treaty, Article XI; [19] and (4) Vienna Convention for the Protection of the Ozone Layer, Article 11.[20]

Article 33(1) of the UN Charter contains an essentially complete catalogue of the methods available for the peaceful settlement of international disputes. Each of these is described and discussed at some length in the *Handbook on the Peaceful Settlement of Disputes between States* that was prepared by the Secretary-General at the request of the General Assembly.[21] These several methods are analyzed, with particular reference to environmental disputes, under the subheadings below. In comparing and evaluating various methods for the peaceful settlement of disputes, it is useful to examine particularly the following features:

---

[16] UN Charter, Articles 2(3) and 33(1). *See* the Manila Declaration on the Peaceful Settlement of International Disputes, formulated by the UN General Assembly's Special Committee on the Charter of the United Nations and on Strengthening the Role of the Organization and approved by the Assembly by A/RES/37/10, of Nov. 15, 1982, to which the Declaration is annexed.

[17] Edith Brown Weiss, Daniel B. Magraw, & Paul C. Szasz, International Environmental Law: Basic Instruments and References (hereinafter "IEL") 183 (1991).

[18] *Id.* at 194.

[19] *Id.* at 518.

[20] *Id.* at 282.

[21] Report of the Special Committee on the Charter of the United Nations and on Strengthening the Role of the Organization, 46 GAOR Supp. No. 33 (A/46/33), Annex (1991), *reproduced in* UN doc. OLA/COD/2394 (UN, New York 1992), UN Publication Sales No. E.92.V.7, ISBN 92–1–133428–4. *See also* Dag Hammarskjold Library, Peaceful Settlement of Disputes between States: A Selective Bibliography (UN 1991), UN doc. ST/LIB/SER.B/ 39; UN Publication Sales No. E.91.I.49, ISBN 92–1–100464–0.

(1) Is the method useful in avoiding or deflecting incipient disputes?

(2) Does the method involve only the parties to the dispute, or does a neutral "third party" participate in some capacity?

(3) How structured is the method: is it entirely ad hoc or partly or wholly institutional?

(4) How easily can the method be frustrated by the intransigence of any of the parties? (In general, methods that involve third parties and particularly those that involve established institutions are more difficult to frustrate.)

(5) Is any resolution of the dispute binding on some or all of the parties?

(6) Is the resolution of the dispute enforceable in respect of any or all of the parties?

1. CONSULTATION AND EXCHANGE OF VIEWS

Consultations and exchanges of views are, as these terms indicate, informal methods normally pursued by two or more States or other entities, usually without the assistance or participation of any third party and usually without any defined structure. In some instances there are arrangements, usually provided for in a treaty, for regular consultations to take place, perhaps within a body set up for that purpose.

In effect, these methods are designed less for settling any dispute than for preventing disputes from arising, by reaching understandings before any actions are taken that could constitute the basis for a dispute.

There is no general obligation in international law to consult or to exchange views, but such obligations may arise from particular bilateral or multilateral treaties or be proposed in nonbinding declarations and other instruments. It should be noted that even where there is a duty to consult or to "take into account," there is no duty to agree or to conform one's behavior or attitude to that urged by another party. There is, however, an obligation to listen in good faith; for example, not to delay consultations until after a decision has in effect already been taken.

For environmentally relevant examples, *see:* (1) [UNEP] Principles of Conduct in the Field of the Environment for the Guidance of States in the Conservation and Harmonious Utilization of Natural Resources Shared by Two or More States, Principles 6(1) and 7;[22] (2) WCED Experts Group on Environmental Law: General Principles Concerning Natural Resources and Environmental Interferences, Article 17;[23] and

---

[22] IEL, *supra* note 17, at 183.
[23] *Id.* at 192.

(3) Convention on the Protection of the Environment, among Denmark, Finland, Norway, and Sweden, Article 11.[24]

2. NEGOTIATIONS

Negotiations in the international sphere means essentially the same as it does domestically: an attempt by the parties to communicate their positions and to identify and narrow their differences until complete agreement can be reached. Negotiation differs from mere consultations and exchanges of views because in these there is no implication of the need for a party to be prepared to change its position (which characterizes true negotiations). For this reason, an obligation to consult or to exchange views should not be construed as an obligation to negotiate.

Negotiation normally is a prerequisite for the other methods of settling disputes, sometimes as a formal requirement for embarking on methods such as arbitration or resort to a court, but more often just as the natural means of establishing: (1) whether a dispute exists; (2) what it is about; and (3) by what means it might be resolved. Negotiation, of course, is not only a means of dispute resolution, but also the basic method for reaching agreement on any question, such as establishing a new regime between the parties. Sometimes such an agreement can obviate the necessity of formally resolving an earlier dispute, which can then be set aside.

Negotiation normally permeates all other methods of settling disputes. That is, even while other methods (e.g., mediation, arbitration, or judicial proceedings) are being pursued, negotiations are likely to continue between the parties, which, if they show prospects of success, may lead to the suspension or termination of any formal proceedings. In turn, the likely outcome of these proceedings will influence the progress of the negotiations. In effect, there is a symbiotic relation between negotiations and other methods of disputes resolution.

A refusal to negotiate, except during the pendency of another agreed proceeding, is likely to be *prima facie* evidence of a violation of the general international duty of good faith and of the obligation to attempt to resolve disputes peacefully. However, there is no general duty to negotiate in certain situations, in particular in respect of matters essentially within a State's domestic jurisdiction. Frequently in the environmental field, however, there may be a disagreement about whether a particular matter (e.g., the damming of an international river or the release of pollutants into the stratosphere) can be considered as essentially domestic.

Negotiations can be entirely unstructured, consisting of only casual contacts or exchanges of communications. Indeed, parties may maintain

---

[24] *Id.* at 238.

different views as to the nature of such contacts, one asserting that negotiations are taking place while the other may (perhaps for domestic consumption) deny that and admit to only informal consultations. On the other hand, many negotiations are essentially formal, with teams of negotiators facing each other at scheduled sessions. Even then, however, much progress may be made in the course of informal contacts. Between States, negotiations normally take place on a diplomatic level, for example, between a foreign ministry on one side and a country's diplomatic mission on the other; more frequently, such contacts take place between diplomats accredited to a particular IGO, in particular one whose mandate is relevant to the issue at hand. On technical questions (such as many relating to the environment) the diplomats may be advised by scientists or other experts, or the negotiations may in part take place directly between experts. Because of the basically unstructured nature of negotiations, their venue often changes. Indeed, it is a well-established technique to shift negotiations that appear to be stuck to either a higher (e.g., Foreign Minister) or a lower (e.g., group of experts) level in the hope of thus making progress on at least some issues.

As a method of resolving disputes, negotiations can easily be frustrated either by the intransigence of one or more parties, or, even with their good will, by the inherent difficulty of the problem. Consequently, there is never any assurance about resolving a dispute by negotiations or about how long negotiations will require. Thus a party that insists on resolution of a dispute merely by negotiations and rejects all other methods is likely not to be acting in good faith.

Whether a resolution reached by negotiation is binding on the parties and whether it is enforceable depends on the method of resolution. If that takes the form of an international agreement—which may be a formal treaty or merely implicit in an official statement on behalf of each party that it will abide by the agreed resolution—then it becomes binding under the *pacta sunt servanda* rule applicable to all international agreements (*see* p. 145). Enforceability depends on other agreements between the parties, including their mutual participation in IGOs that have enforcement powers or as mutually agreed with regard to the matter at hand.

For some environmentally relevant examples, *see* (1) International Convention Relating to Intervention on the High Seas in Cases of Oil Pollution Casualties, Article VIII;[25] (2) [ECE] Convention on Long-Range Transboundary Air Pollution (LRTAP), Article 13;[26] and (3) USA-Canada Agreement on Air Quality, Article XIII.[27]

---

[25] 970 U.N.T.S. 911; 26 U.S.T. 765.

[26] IEL *supra* note 17, at 255.

[27] *Id.* at 268.

3.   ENQUIRY OR FACT-FINDING

Enquiry or fact-finding is a method of resolving or assisting in resolving disputes and perhaps in avoiding them altogether by establishing or agreeing on certain facts relevant to such disputes or potential disputes. The facts in question (e.g., the degree of pollution of a river or the number of fish in a lake) may be investigated unilaterally (e.g., by one of the parties), by some joint organ (such as a commission of scientists) of the parties or possibly also of some neutral States, or by an agreed IGO or even NGO. Some environmental treaties establish permanent or standby bodies for this purpose. Any technique of fact-finding may be used, including making use of the expertise and experience of the persons conducting the enquiry, contributions of other experts, research in the literature, experiments and measurements in the field, the testimony of witnesses, and so on.

After the body charged with the enquiry has established the facts, the parties have to decide whether to accept them, unless they have agreed in advance to accept the report of that body. To consider whether to do so, the diplomatic representatives of the parties may consider the expertise of the fact-finders, their methodology, or other matters. How much scope there is for this depends on the matter at hand. For example, to establish the flow or salinity of a river at a given time and place may not require complex studies, but there may be considerable disagreement about the time and place to be specified.

The UN General Assembly approved a Declaration on Fact-Finding by the United Nations in the Field of the Maintenance of International Peace and Security, in 1991.[28] Though probably few environmental disputes would fall directly within the purview of this declaration, it is not to be excluded that as these issues are taken more seriously by States some such disputes may escalate from threats of economic retaliation to those that actually endanger the peace.

As is true of other methods for the avoidance and resolution of international disputes, enquiry in most instances is likely to be more effective the more structured it is, and the more neutral third parties (e.g., a State or an organization) are involved. To the extent that fact-finding must take place within areas under the jurisdiction of any of the parties (e.g., to determine emissions from a particular facility), that State can, of course, completely or partially frustrate their work by refusing to cooperate with the fact-finders.

As fact-finding can rarely resolve a dispute by itself, the issue of the binding or enforceable nature of the outcome of the process rarely arises. Of course the parties may agree, in advance or afterward, that facts established in a particular way are binding on them in further

---

[28]   A/RES/46/59 of Dec. 9, 1991, Annex.

negotiations or that they may or must be taken into account by any arbitral or judicial tribunal to which the dispute is referred.

Some environmentally relevant examples are: (1) [UNEP] Principles of Conduct in the Field of the Environment for the Guidance of States in the Conservation and Harmonious Utilization of Natural Resources Shared by Two or More States, Principles 8 and 10;[29] (2) UN Convention on the Law of the Non-Navigational Uses of International Watercourses, Article 33; and (3) Convention on the Prohibition of Military and Other Hostile Use of Environmental Modification Techniques (ENMOD), Article V.1–2, Annex.[30]

4. GOOD OFFICES AND MEDIATION

Good offices and mediation are both methods by which a third (i.e., neutral) party—which may be a State or group of States, an IGO or an IGO official—assists parties to a dispute to negotiate a resolution. Though the two methods cannot be strictly distinguished, it is sometimes said that

(1) the exercise of good offices merely involves the encouragement of parties to negotiate and perhaps the facilitation of such negotiations by passing messages back and forth, when the parties are otherwise reluctant to engage in them at all or to pursue them seriously (perhaps because they have no diplomatic relations or do not even recognize each other); while

(2) mediators, by contrast, may also involve themselves in the substance of the dispute by introducing proposals of their own. This may be useful both because an impartial outsider may be in a position to sponsor proposals that did not occur to the parties involved or that a party may be reluctant to advance itself, or because these parties may seek to save face by accepting a neutrally sponsored proposal rather than one presented by an opponent.

A third party that is on reasonably good terms with all the parties to the dispute and not particularly close to just some of them may offer to exercise good offices or to mediate their dispute. Such an offer may be made publicly, though generally this is done only after first exploring privately whether such an offer would be welcome, unless an untested public offer is designed to force the hand of one or more parties to the dispute. Sometimes the intervention of a third party may be requested jointly by the parties to the dispute and sometimes unilaterally by one of them. In the latter case, there is a danger that other party(ies) will become suspicious and reject the initiative.

---

[29] IEL, *supra* note 17, at 182–183.
[30] *Id.* at 636, 637–638,.

Once all parties concerned agree to a particular good offices exercise or to mediation, or at least through silence indicate that they are willing to tolerate it, the third party can begin to function. Its efforts may be exercised largely in its own capital (e.g., through contacts with the respective diplomatic representatives there) or at the seat of an IGO at which all parties are represented; or special meetings may be called. The third party may succeed in getting all the parties to meet together or may instead meet in turn with the representatives of each party separately (so-called shuttle diplomacy or proximity talks, depending on how close the delegations of the parties are located), passing messages back and forth or seeking to establish whether particular proposals originating with one party, or with a mediator, are acceptable to the others.

The outcome of a successful good offices exercise or mediation is a negotiated agreement among the disputing parties. Sometimes such a resolution may be facilitated by having it merely announced by the mediator, while the parties at issue indicate their agreement either explicitly or by not objecting.

Because good offices and mediation merely facilitate negotiations, their ultimate effectiveness is essentially the same as for direct negotiations. However, because of the involvement of the third party, especially if it is able to exercise some leverage over all parties or at least the most obdurate one(s), such negotiations are somewhat less likely to be frustrated. Moreover, they are less likely to extend indefinitely, as unassisted negotiations may, because there the pace is usually set by the most reluctant party, while the pace of assisted negotiations is likely to be set or at least influenced by the third party.

Similarly, the binding nature and also the enforceability of a resolution reached by assisted negotiations may be enhanced if the third party in effect becomes, formally or informally, a guarantor of the agreement reached.

An interesting form of good offices is when each of two disputing States enters into an agreement with a third State—but not with each other—that resolves all or part of the dispute. An example consists of the agreements between Egypt and Sudan and Ethiopia and Sudan regarding the Nile River described in Chapter 12.

Other environmentally relevant examples include: (1) Vienna Convention on the Protection of the Ozone Layer, Article 11 (1, 2);[31] and (2) ILA: Helsinki Rules on the Uses of the Waters of International Rivers, Chapter 6 (Art. XXXII).[32]

---

[31] *Id.* at 282.

[32] *Id.* at 401.

5. CONCILIATION

Conciliation involves the establishment or choice, by the parties to a dispute, of an impartial body to resolve their dispute. In this sense, it is similar to arbitration (*see* section B.6, below). The most significant difference between conciliation and arbitration is that: a conciliation commission issues a nonbinding report, but an arbitral tribunal issues a binding award.

Any party to a conciliation proceeding may unilaterally declare, at any time, that it accepts or will accept the outcome as binding. However, if all the parties to such a proceeding agree in advance to accept a conciliation report as binding, they are in effect arbitrating, though they may not wish to admit this. Similarly, if the parties to a so-called arbitral proceeding agree in advance that the award is not to be binding on them, they are in effect merely conciliating. In some dispute settlement regimes, an unsuccessful effort at conciliation (e.g., an inability of the conciliators to prepare proposals acceptable to all the parties) is a prerequisite for subsequent arbitral or judicial proceedings.

Because of its binding character, arbitration is generally taken more seriously than conciliation by the parties. They (particularly the party whose case is weaker) are more likely to agree to conciliation than to arbitration, and having agreed to either procedure they often are less likely to try to frustrate conciliatory rather than an arbitral proceeding. Consequently the terms of an arbitration are likely to be more detailed and precise than those for a conciliation.

In other respects, the two procedures are in principle so similar that only arbitration will be discussed in detail (*see* immediately below, in which some features that distinguish conciliation are mentioned).

The Permanent Court of Arbitration adopted rules for environmental conciliation in 2002. Those rules and related procedures are discussed in the section on arbitration, below.

Some environmentally relevant examples of conciliation provisions are: (1) African Convention on the Conservation of Nature and Natural Resources, Article XVIII;[33] (2) Vienna Convention for the Protection of the Ozone Layer, Article 11 (3–5);[34] (3) ILA: Helsinki Rules on the Uses of the Waters of International Rivers, Article XXXIII and Annex; [35] and (4) United Nations Convention on the Law of the Sea, Article 284 and Annex V.

---

[33] *Id.* at 209–210.

[34] *Id.* at 282.

[35] *Id.* at 401, 402–403.

As of July 2015, no conciliation provision in a multilateral environmental agreement has been invoked, even though many such provisions exist.

6.   ARBITRATION

As already mentioned in connection with conciliation, arbitration involves the establishment or choice, by the parties, of an impartial body charged with resolving their dispute in a quasi-judicial proceeding. An arbitral tribunal issues a binding award. It may thus be considered as an ad hoc court established by the parties to the dispute.

a.   Agreement to Arbitrate

An agreement to engage in arbitration can be concluded before a dispute arises and is then normally included as a "compromissory clause" in an agreement. The agreement can either be generally concerned with the peaceful settlement of future disputes between the parties or regulate a substantive matter as to which the parties expect that disputes may arise. Many bilateral and multilateral agreements (*see* examples at end of this section) contain such clauses. Alternatively, such an agreement can be concluded with respect to a particular dispute that has already arisen, in which case it is normally called a *"compromis."* The relative advantages and disadvantages of these two approaches are discussed in section 7.b, below, with reference to international courts, but these considerations are also relevant here.

An agreement to arbitrate must specify how the arbitral tribunal is to be established (*see* section 6.b, below) and what its jurisdiction and procedures will be. Several observations provide perspective on various aspects of such agreements.

(1) It is important in respect of arbitration (which is designed to lead to a definitive settlement of the dispute) that the procedures for the establishment and operation of the tribunal be such that they cannot be frustrated by the obduracy of any party or parties. That is, if at least one party persists it should be able to cause the proceeding to move to a conclusion.

(2) In a compromissory clause *(see* above), the jurisdiction of the tribunal is described in terms of the types of disputes that may be submitted, and possibly some preliminary requirements for submission, such as prior negotiations. A *compromis,* on the other hand, must contain a sufficient description of the dispute being submitted and of the issues to be decided. In either case it is useful to provide that the tribunal has the power to decide any question concerning its own jurisdiction, unless there is some standing outside body to which such questions can be referred.

(3) An arbitral tribunal can be charged with establishing facts in dispute, to determine the law, and/or to act *ex aequo et bono* (i.e., on the basis of what is equitable and good). If the arbitral tribunal is to act according to legal rules, these may be specified explicitly or by reference to a governing legal system (e.g., a particular treaty regime), or they may be left to the tribunal to determine. In many cases the specification of the applicable legal regime may in effect resolve the contentious issue; and for just that reason the parties may find it difficult to agree on it.

(4) The procedures to be followed by the tribunal can be specified in great detail; but they generally need not be, either because the parties specify the application of one of the established international sets of arbitral rules (e.g., those of the UN Commission on International Trade Law (UNCITRAL) or the Permanent Court of Arbitration) or because the parties can leave it to that body itself to adopt most of these—except for those that are basic to its operations. Thus it is necessary to specify the voting rules if there is more than one arbitrator (normally a simple or qualified majority is preferable because a unanimity requirement enables any member—including one appointed by a party—to prevent any decision), the quorum (again only a majority should be required, in order to prevent possible sabotage), and the extent of the power of the tribunal to establish rules. In any event, whatever rules the parties specify in their agreement and whatever rules a tribunal may adopt, the parties typically jointly retain complete control over the proceeding and its procedures and thus can take any decisions thereon that all can agree to. Thus, for example, time limits may be set aside to enable the parties to engage in negotiations, for whatever period they wish. An exception is that parties may not change the UNCITRAL Transparency Rules in arbitrations to which they apply. http://www.uncitral.org/uncitral/en/uncitral_texts/arbitration/2014Transparency.html.

(5) The agreement may limit or constrain the tribunal in respect of its output. For example, it is customary to require that an award be reasoned and relate to every aspect of the dispute.

(6) Though implied by the use of the term "arbitration," it is useful for the agreement to specify the effect of the arbitral award, normally that it will be considered final and binding and will be complied with by all the parties. (In case of a conciliation, the agreement might specify that the parties will give serious or good faith consideration to or endeavor to follow the conciliation report or that it may be considered as a basis of any future litigation.)

b.   Establishment of an Arbitral Tribunal

An arbitral tribunal (like a conciliation commission) normally consists of an uneven number of members. If the tribunal consists of more than one person, an equal number of persons are appointed by each of the parties, subject to whatever constraints are provided for in the agreement—for example, that only so many may be their own nationals, that they should have particular expertise, or that they must be chosen from a list maintained by some institution. The rest of the arbitrators (one of whom will preside) are appointed by them jointly or are selected by the party-appointed members, which amounts to almost the same thing. If there are more than two parties and they cannot be divided into two sides, usually the only satisfactory disposition is that all the members must be appointed jointly.

To prevent any party from sabotaging the proceeding by simply not appointing its own members, it should either be provided that after a certain delay any party may petition a neutral "default" appointing authority to appoint such members or, more rarely, that the proceeding can go forward without such members. Similarly, if the parties or the tribunal member(s) they have appointed are unable to agree on the neutral members, then any party should be able to request the appointing authority to make the appointment(s). The appointing authority must be specified in the arbitral agreement. It can be either a named individual or a designated official (most frequently, in interstate proceedings, the President of the ICJ or the UN Secretary-General, or the executive head of a regional organization), or an institution (such as the International Chamber of Commerce (ICC)). It is best to make certain before the agreement is finalized that the designated appointing authority is prepared to accept the specified task, either because it is within its terms of reference or customary functions, or by specifically asking. Normally such an authority will carry out its designated functions in consultation with the parties. It should be understood that by acting the authority does not decide whether the body to be established will have jurisdiction over the dispute (often the noncooperating party will claim that the agreed arbitral procedure is for some reason inapplicable), since that is to be decided by the tribunal itself (*see* above).

Suitable provisions should be also made for replacing members of the tribunal whenever that proves necessary. Again, it should be kept in mind that no party should have the possibility of frustrating the proceeding through any means of noncooperation by itself or through persons it has appointed to the tribunal.

c.   The Proceeding

Basically it is for the parties to decide, either in their original agreement or at any time thereafter, how their tribunal is to carry out its task. To the extent they fail to do so, that body should be empowered, either explicitly or implicitly through normal custom, to make the necessary determinations.

There is one arbitral institution that has adopted rules specifically for environmental arbitration—the Permanent Court of Arbitration (PCA). The PCA adopted those rules in 2001 and, as mentioned above, adopted rules on conciliation a year later. The PCA also made its Financial Assistance Fund for developing countries available when developing countries seek to resolve a dispute relating to the environment or natural resources using one of the PCA's sets of environmental rules, or engages the services of the PCA in facilitating and administering resolution of such a dispute. The PCA also appointed more than 100 persons, including scientists, to the lists of the two PCA Environmental Panels, the Panel of Arbitrators and the Panel of Scientific Experts.

There also exist several ready-made sets of arbitral rules (such as those of the UN Commission on International Trade Law (UNCITRAL), which, for example, were designated with a few changes for use in the Iran-United States Claims Tribunal established in 1981); and it may suffice to incorporate by reference one of these "off-the-shelf" texts into an arbitral agreement. The rules for the Iran-United States Claims Tribunal, however, added to the UNCITRAL rules for their own purposes to clarify that amicus curiae briefs could be submitted under some circumstances. Many existing sets of ready-made rules, with the notable exception of the UNCITRAL Transparency Rules referred to above and the partial exception of the rules of the International Centre for Settlement of Investment Disputes, are notably lacking in transparency and opportunities for public participation.

Arbitral proceedings are normally quasi-judicial. This means, *inter alia,* (1) that the tribunal as a whole must be impartial, though not necessarily each of its members (i.e., the party-appointed ones); and (2) that each party must have a fair and equal opportunity to present its case, both as to the substantive issues and with respect to any preliminary or procedural questions that may arise.

In general, arbitral proceedings tend to follow a rather standard pattern:

(1)   almost always one or more rounds of written pleadings are provided for, submitted either alternately by the parties or simultaneously;

(2)   there generally also are oral proceedings, either just to hear the arguments of the parties or also for the presentation and questioning of witnesses;

(3)   other appropriate means of fact-finding may also be employed, such as visits to relevant sites, the appointment of masters, or the consultation of experts;

(4)   the proceedings are normally not open to the public and are conducted confidentially—a point usually considered

desirable by one or more of the parties but not necessarily by any concerned NGOs or other interested members of the public; and

(5) in due course an arbitral award is issued, generally in writing and supplied with reasons and indicating any dissenting views; the award is usually supplied only to the parties, and published only if they all agree.

Generally no challenges or appeals are possible in respect to an arbitral award. However, sometimes the arbitral agreement may provide, or the institution within which the proceeding takes place may foresee, certain limited challenges, such as charging corruption by a member of the tribunal or that the award does not fulfill certain substantive or formal requirements (e.g., that every point at issue must be decided and that reasons must be given). Such challenges are then submitted to another body and, if sustained, may lead to a reopening of the original proceeding or to an entirely new one. Enforcement actions in another jurisdiction may also expose an arbitral award to a limited range of challenges under the New York Convention on the Enforcement of Arbitral Awards.

d. Institutionalization

International arbitration may be arranged entirely ad hoc by the parties or may take place within the framework of an institution specified by the parties. It should be noted that even in respect of an entirely ad hoc proceeding, the general practice of relying on a default appointing authority to assist, if necessary, in the constitution of the tribunal may introduce an element of institutionalization if that authority is an official of a particular international organization (such as the UN Secretary-General or the ICJ President). If the proceeding is fully entrusted to an institution, it may be sufficient merely to specify so in the compromissory clause or the *compromis,* leaving all other decisions to the rules of that body.

e. Evaluation of Arbitration as a Dispute Settlement Method

Arbitration necessarily involves reliance on a type of third party, i.e., the tribunal, or in any event the independent members of these bodies. In addition, any default appointing authority is of course a neutral "third party," as is any institution under whose aegis the proceeding takes place.

As already pointed out, arbitration can be almost entirely ad hoc but certain standing institutions exist, and more are likely to be created to which parties to a dispute can agree to entrust all or many aspects of the proceeding. As of 2015, there was only one such institution with specifically environmental terms of reference, the Permanent Court of Arbitration, as noted above.

A well-designed arbitration clause can generally not be frustrated by a party (or a combination less than all parties).

Almost by definition, arbitral awards are generally binding on all parties and are final, in the sense that they cannot normally be appealed. Whether it is "enforceable" depends on the framework within which the proceeding is conducted or within which the parties are acting. Normally international obligations, whether arising through a treaty, through customary law, through a unilateral commitment, or through an arbitral or judicial decree, are not enforceable in the sense that their domestic equivalents are. However, parties acting within certain institutions may incur penalties if they violate its rules (such as compliance with arbitral awards) and, if such a violation threatens international peace and security, the UN Security Council may intervene.

Finally, it should be noted that the entire costs of the proceedings, both those incurred directly by the parties and those required for the tribunal, must be borne by the parties. Unless otherwise agreed, or unless the tribunal is authorized and does direct a different allocation, these latter expenditures, which may be considerable, are borne equally by the parties.

f. Environmentally Relevant Examples

(1) Paris Convention for the prevention of Marine Pollution from Land-Based Sources, Article 21 and Annex B.[36]

(2) ILA: Helsinki Rules on the Uses of the Waters of International Rivers, Articles xxxlv–xxxvi.[37]

(3) Bonn Convention for the Protection of the Rhine River Against Pollution, Article 15 and Annex B.[38]

(4) Trail Smelter Arbitration, extracts from:

   (a) Ottawa Convention for the Establishment of a Tribunal to Decide Questions of Indemnity Arising from the Operation of the Smelter at Trail, British Columbia (162 L.N.T.S. 73, 49 Stat. 3245);

   (b) Award of the Tribunal (3 UN R.I.A.A. 1911 (1941)); and

   (c) Supplementary Agreement to Decide Questions of Indemnity and Future Regime (151 U.N.T.S. 171, 3 U.S.T. 539).

(5) Convention on International Liability for Damage Caused by Space Objects, Articles XII, XTV–XX. [39] N.B.: These

---

[36] *Id.* at 366, 368–369.
[37] *Id.* at 401–402.
[38] *Id.* at 447–448.
[39] Done on March 29, 1972, 961 U.N.T.S. 187, 24 U.S.T. 2389, T.I.A.S. 7762.

provisions call for the establishment of a claims commission, which is a type of arbitral tribunal usually charged with deciding a whole series of disputes between the parties arising out of the same incident or legal situation.

(6) Indus Waters Treaty of 1960 (India-Pakistan).

7.   INTERNATIONAL COURTS

An international court is in many ways like a domestic one: it is a standing institution with incumbent judges charged with settling disputes properly submitted to it, for example, those that are within the competence of the institution and are brought within its jurisdiction. However, it does differ from its domestic counterparts in several important ways, which recall the arbitral origins of international judicial organs: (1) the jurisdiction of an international court normally requires the consent of all State parties to the dispute; (2) all parties are normally "represented" on the court; and (3) the court is likely to be more responsive to the desires of the parties as to certain aspects of the procedures to be followed, especially the timing of successive steps.

a. Locating a Competent Court

Only a very few international courts exist that have competence for disputes between States relating to the environment. The only such institutions on the worldwide level are the International Court of Justice (ICJ)—the so-called World Court—which is the principal judicial organ of the United Nations, and the International Tribunal on the Law of the Sea (ITLOS, discussed below).

All UN members are Parties to the Statute of the ICJ and thus can litigate with other such Parties about any question of international law. Because only States may be Parties, disputes involving international organizations or other non-State entities cannot be submitted to the ICJ directly. However, an alternative procedure, involving the Court's competence to give "advisory opinions," may be used to resolve such disputes (*see* below).

In 1997, 2010 and 2014, the full Court decided contentious cases with important environmental components, [40] it is considering two cases involving Costa Rica and Nicaragua involving environmental issues as of

---

[40] Gabčíkovo-Nagymaros Project (Hungary v. Slovakia), I.C.J. Reports 1997, in which the issue was whether Hungary was justified in cancelling a project to which it had agreed by treaty, on the asserted ground that it was likely to cause great environmental harm; Pulp Mills on the River Uruguay (Argentina v. Uruguay, discussed in Chapter 4), I.C.J. Reports 2010, in which Court addressed alleged pollution to a river and the need for transboundary environment impact assessment; Whaling in the Antarctic (Australia v. Japan: New Zealand intervening), I.C.J. Reports 2014, in which the Court addressed whether Japan's whaling program (purportedly to allow scientific research) violated the International Convention for the Regulation of Whaling. The full records of each case are available on the ICJ's web site: ICJ-CIJ.org.

August 2015,[41] and another case involving environmental issues was settled and therefore withdrawn.[42] A chamber of the Court decided another case with an environmental component.[43] In addition, the Court has given at least one advisory opinion (see below) in which environmental considerations figured importantly.[44] The many maritime boundary cases decided by the Court also are environmental in the sense of allocating natural resources. To respond to the question whether its classically trained and generally scientifically unversed judges would be factually competent in respect of this essentially modern subject, the Court in July 1993 established a seven-member standing Chamber for Environmental Matters. The Court may also resort to the use of expert assessors, which is foreseen in its Statute.[45]

The International Tribunal for the Law of the Sea (ITLOS), which is provided for in the 1982 United Nations Convention on the Law of the Sea (UNCLOS), is competent, inter alia, in respect of the convention's extensive environmental provisions if the parties to the dispute have selected ITLOS for dispute settlement. The tribunal was set up in 1996 and decided its first case (partially environmental) in 1997. The cases decided by the Commission on the Limits of the Continental Shelf (CLCS), also established by UNCLOS, are environmental in that they allocate natural resources.

Aside from the ICJ, ITLOS and CLCS, the only actually functioning international court with extensive competence including environmental matters is the Court of Justice of the European Union (EU). That court has jurisdiction not only in respect of the 28 Member States of the EU but also in respect of all the organs of the union as well as private individuals and entities. It has handed down a number of significant decisions relating to the environmental regime of the EU (and its predecessor, the European Communities). However, because of its geographically restricted competence and general atypical nature (the EU is characterized as a supranational entity rather than as an international one) it will not be considered further here.

---

[41] Certain Activities Carried Out by Nicaragua in the Border Area (Costa Rica v. Nicaragua), which included consideration of two wetlands listed under the Ramsar Convention on Wetlands of International Importance; and Construction of a Road in Costa Rica along the San Juan River (Nicaragua v. Costa Rica), which involves allegations of sedimentation of a river. The Court has joined the two cases, on which it is deliberating at this writing.

[42] Certain Phosphate Lands in Nauru (Nauru v. Australia), which revolved about the issue of the exhaustion of a natural resource.

[43] Case Concerning Delimitation of the Maritime Boundary in the Gulf of Maine Area (Canada v. United Sates), Judgment of 12 October 1984, in which the Court considered the argument that a boundary should not bisect a fishing ground because protecting and managing the fishing ground required a single national authority.

[44] Legality of the Threat or Use of Nuclear Weapons, Advisory Opinion of July 8, 1996, 1996 I.C.J.; 35 I.L.M. 869 and 1343 (1996).

[45] Article 30(2) of the ICJ Statute; see also Articles 9 and 21(2) of the Rules of Court.

Human rights cases involving environmental and health issues have been heard in human rights tribunals such as the Inter-American Court of Human Rights and the European Court of Human Rights. See part 9 below and Chapter 15. And some WTO cases have dealt with environmental issues, as discussed in Chapter 16.

No exclusively international environmental court exists, either on the worldwide or regional level. Though from time to time proposals have been made for the establishment of such courts to deal with the increasing number of environmental regimes and the potential disputes concerning them, there are no current projects actively under consideration at the political level.

In light of the above, the further discussion of international environmental litigation below will be restricted to the ICJ. The most relevant provisions of the UN Charter and of the ICJ Statute (which is an Annex to the Charter) are Charter Article 94 and Statute Articles 4(1) (first clause), 26, 31(1–3), 34(1–2), 36(1–3), 38, 41, 43(1–2, 5), 46, 50–51, 53, 55–57, 59–60, 61(1), 62.

b. Consent to Litigation

As pointed out above, for any international court, including the ICJ, to have jurisdiction in respect of a dispute, all the parties thereto must consent to submit it to the Court. As in respect of conciliation and arbitration, that consent can be given in two different ways: (1) an abstract submission, before any dispute has arisen, of all future disputes or of those in some defined categories (e.g., all environmental disputes or all disputes with reference to a particular environmental regime), or (2) the concrete submission of a particular existing dispute.

An abstract submission to an international court can be made either by a general bilateral or multilateral agreement relating to dispute settlement or by a particular treaty with respect to any disputes that might arise in respect thereto (i.e., in a "compromissory clause"). In respect of the ICJ, an abstract submission can also be made, under Article 36(2) of its Statute, by a declaration accepting the Court's jurisdiction in respect of all or of defined classes of disputes, but only on the basis of strict reciprocity in respect of other states making similar declarations. This, in effect, is the functional equivalent of a multilateral disputes settlement agreement.

The submission of an actual dispute is done by means of an ad hoc agreement between all the disputing parties, for example, by a *compromis.*

Although legally these two methods are equivalent, in practice there are important differences. While abstract consent to the submission of undefined future disputes may often be easier to secure than consent after a dispute has arisen (when relations among the parties may be embittered and one party may realize that it is likely to lose on a strictly legal basis), experience has shown that an ad hoc submission testifies to a real desire to have the dispute resolved and a willingness to abide by the court's judgment. In contrast, an advance consent that may have been given decades earlier by a politically different regime is in practice often disavowed by the current government, which may then refuse to cooperate with the proceeding and disregard its legally binding outcome.

c. Composition of the World Court

Because the ICJ already exists and its 15 judges have been elected, there is no need or opportunity to compose the Court (unlike an arbitral tribunal), with two exceptions. In a throw-back to its essentially arbitral origins, if any State party to a dispute before the ICJ does not have a judge of its nationality on the Court, it may appoint an ad hoc judge to sit for that case. (N.B.: in a national court, one might instead expect that if any judges on a standing panel are affiliated with one of the parties, they will recuse themselves.) Also, the parties jointly may request that the case not be heard by all the judges but by only a small chamber. For such a case including an environmental aspect, see *Case Concerning Delimitation of the Maritime Boundary in the Gulf of Maine Area* (Canada v. United Sates), I.C.J. Reports 1984. If that occurs, the parties may be consulted in composing the chamber; in the *Gulf of Maine* case, the parties specified the members of the chamber.

d. Procedures of the World Court

As a standing body, the ICJ has established procedures (e.g., as to the written and oral proceedings) set out in its Statute and the Rules of Court. Therefore the parties do not have to agree on any such points, though if they do the Court will do its best to accommodate them, in particular in respect of the timing of the various steps. This flexibility may enable the parties privately to negotiate in the shadow of the public litigation, and perhaps to resolve the dispute in a face-saving manner so as to obviate the need for a judgment, much as often happens in domestic courts. Thus the often lengthy proceedings in the World Court sometimes merely reflect the wishes of the parties rather than any inherent sluggishness of the Court.

The Court's proceedings are public (unlike most conciliation and arbitral ones). Memorials (briefs) are made public, though only on the day of the oral hearing; and oral hearings are open to the public and are webcast. Aside from the parties, no one can participate in the proceeding, i.e., neither other States (except in the event of rarely allowed formal interventions by a State necessarily affected by the outcome of the litigation), nor inter- or nongovernmental organizations, nor private entities. There is no possibility of submitting amicus briefs to the World

Court in contentious cases, though there is an informal procedure for doing so in advisory cases. Except to the extent that any of the State parties may invite some private entity (e.g., an environmental NGO) to join its legal team, there is thus no opportunity for participation by the public.

If any party defaults before the ICJ (e.g., it fails to appear, either altogether or from a given point of the proceeding), this does not result in a discontinuance of the proceeding. However, unlike in a domestic litigation where a defaulting party normally automatically loses, the ICJ under Article 53(2) of its Statute must in deciding the case "satisfy itself, not only that it has jurisdiction . . . , but also that the claim is well founded in fact and law."

Unlike many domestic courts, the ICJ cannot give binding injunctive relief to a party during the pendency of a proceeding. It can, however, under Article 41 of its Statute, "indicate, if it considers that circumstances so require, any provisional measures to be taken to preserve the respective rights of either party." Though not considered as binding, such suggested measures are automatically reported to the Security Council, which presumably can consider whether compliance therewith should be urged on or even required of the parties (if considered necessary to maintain peace and security).

As already mentioned, under Article 59 of the Court's Statute, its decisions have binding force only between the parties and in respect of the particular case—there is no *stare decisis* (though there is *res judicata*). However, like any court, the ICJ naturally strives for consistency in its jurisprudence, and therefore it frequently cites its earlier judgments and advisory opinions. Moreover, other international courts, arbitral tribunals, international organs, states, and legal scholars routinely cite pronouncements by the World Court as authoritative statements of international law. These *quasi-stare decisis* practices are described above.

e. Evaluation of ICJ Litigation as a Dispute Settlement Method

Litigation, in any court, by definition involves a "third party" and is necessarily highly structured, though, as indicated, the ICJ is usually responsive to procedural wishes of any party and particularly if all are in agreement. Technically, ICJ proceedings cannot be frustrated by an intransigent party, because the Court, if it finds that it has jurisdiction (which requires a finding that every party has in some way and at some time "consented"), will proceed to a judgment, even if a party defaults. It is, however, true that noncooperation by a party may make the Court's task of establishing the facts and the law more difficult and, though the resulting judgment is binding and enforceable, actually there is more likely to be noncompliance.

Under the UN Charter and the ICJ Statute, ICJ judgments are legally binding on the parties to the litigation. This requires no special advance agreement of the parties—indeed, if they should agree ahead of the litigation that they will not consider the judgment as binding the Court would probably decline to hear the case.

If a party to an ICJ litigation refuses to comply with the resulting judgment, the other party may refer the matter to the Security Council "which may, if it deems necessary, make recommendations or decide upon measures to give effect to the judgment."[46] The Council, of course, can orchestrate measures of enforcement by the world community in the form of economic or diplomatic sanctions or even military force if it considers that such measures are required to preserve peace and security,[47] which may sometimes, though probably rarely, be endangered by noncompliance with a judgment in an environmental dispute.

Finally, it should be noted that (in contrast to ad hoc conciliation or arbitration), the institutional costs of maintaining the ICJ, including any costs associated with a particular case before it, are borne by the regular budget of the United Nations.

f. The Advisory Competence of the World Court

In addition to its function in resolving interstate disputes, the ICJ also may give advisory opinions at the request of a restricted number of specified organs of IGOs within the UN system. That competence can be used in two significant ways. First, to advise the requesting organ as to legal questions—which in case of the UN General Assembly and Security Council can be "any legal question" but in the case of other organs would have to be one "arising within the scope of [its] activities." Thus the Court answered the query of the General Assembly as to the Legality of the Threat or Use of Nuclear Weapons, in which it took into account environmental considerations.[48] In the same way, the opinion of the Court could be secured as to the interpretation of environmental treaties, unless this was already an issue between State Parties to the treaty that they could submit to the Court under its contentious competence.

The second way to use the advisory competence of the ICJ is to resolve disputes involving a party or between parties that do not all have a right to participate in a contentious proceeding. What is required is that the dispute, with the consent of the parties thereto, be formulated as a

---

[46] UN Charter, Article 94(2).

[47] UN Charter, Chapter VII, in particular Articles 41 and 42.

[48] At the same time the ICJ declined to respond to a similar query from the World Health Assembly of the World Health Organization, on the ground that it did not arise within the scope of 'WHO's activities.

question (or series of questions) that is then addressed to the Court by an IGO organ competent to do so. The consent so required can in effect be given in the same ways as indicated in section B.7.b, above. However, as such submissions are not under the contentious competence of the Court, the responses of the Court are not automatically binding on the parties, unless they have agreed to make them so. Such disputes could, for example, relate to the respective competencies of two or more IGOs in respect of an environmental matter.

Environmentally relevant examples include: (1) Basel Convention on the Transboundary Movements of Hazardous Wastes and their Disposal, Article 20; [49] and (2) Convention on Early Notification of a Nuclear Accident, Article 11(2 (first sentence), 3–4).[50]

8.   RESORT TO REGIONAL OR OTHER INTERNATIONAL ORGANIZATIONS

A dispute may be taken up on submission by one or more parties or sometimes even *sua sponte* by an intergovernmental organization, whether created by a regional treaty or one that relates to a particular subject matter (e.g., the exploitation of a particular resource or species), when all the parties to the dispute are Parties to the treaty establishing the organization: the competent IGO organs can then either assist the parties in negotiating a solution or propose and perhaps even impose a solution on them.

Some treaties that establish IGOs require the members (i.e., the Parties to the treaty) to submit certain disputes to specified organs of the organization. Other treaties simply give an opportunity to the Parties to do so by mutual consent. If the submission is compulsory, then the consent thereto has, in effect, been given by becoming Party to the treaty that so provides.

Several types of IGO organs could consider interstate disputes. These include the standing organs of the IGO, or it may be one created ad hoc by a competent standing organ to deal with the particular submission. It may even be an essentially political one, such as a representative organ of the IGO. Alternatively, there may be a standing expert and/or quasi-judicial organ, or one may be created ad hoc. The body to consider the dispute may have competence to perform one or more of many of the third party functions discussed above: it may provide good offices, mediation, impartial fact-finding, conciliation, arbitration, or, in principle, even judicial settlement.

What procedures are applied to resolve disputes in this manner obviously depends on the nature and functions of the organ considering

---

[49]   IEL, *supra* note 17, at 616.
[50]   *Id.* at 586.

the dispute. In general the considerations recited above will apply to the corresponding methods relied on by an IGO. Of course, as such methods are by definition institutional, it will be less necessary to secure the agreement of the parties to every aspect of the creation and functioning of a fact-finding, conciliation, or arbitral organ.

The methods of resolving disputes through IGOs are quite varied, but the actual experience with such methods is relatively sparse. The following general observations are possible. First, because these methods involve a standing body, for example, the IGO, acting as a "third party," they may be generally more difficult to frustrate than ones that are purely created by the parties to the dispute. Second, whether the outcome is binding depends on the treaty pursuant to which the IGO is performing the dispute settlement function. And third, given that an IGO is involved, it may be able to enforce or at least to press for compliance—or provide assistance to enable compliance—by various measures taken within the IGO or that it can encourage or require the other members to take in respect of a recalcitrant state.

Following are some environmentally relevant examples: (1) Montreal Protocol on Substances That Deplete the Ozone Layer, interim procedures and institutional mechanisms adopted by the Parties at their second (London) Meeting;[51] (2) Convention on the Prohibition of Military or any Other Hostile Use of Environmental Modification Techniques (ENMOD), Article V and Annex;[52] and (3) the World Trade Organization's Understanding on Rules and Procedures Governing the Settlement of Disputes.[53]

9. DISPUTES INVOLVING HUMAN RIGHTS

It is now clear that environmental harm can violate the human rights of individuals and groups. As is discussed in Chapter 15, the global human rights system has developed mechanisms, including Special Procedures and treaty-based committees, which can under some circumstances receive complaints from individuals that a State has violated human rights. At this level, the findings of these bodies are not, strictly speaking, binding. However, the three major regional human rights systems—Africa, the Americas and Europe—include human rights courts that issue binding decisions, as well as human rights commissions with various powers. Because of the growing importance of the human rights implications of environmental degradation and natural resource management, these institutions should be borne in mind. See Chapter 15.

---

[51] *Id.* at 312–313.

[52] *Id.* at 636–638.

[53] 33 I.L.M. 1226 (1994).

NOTES AND QUESTIONS

1.   *Types of Norms.* In *Legal Treatment of Developing Countries: Differential, Contextual, and Absolute Norms*, 1 Colo. J. Intl. Envtl. L. & Pol. 69–70, 98–99 (1990), Daniel Magraw writes:

> International norms, including international environmental norms, take three general forms. One form is to provide what I call "differential" treatment to developing countries. The second form is what I call "contextual" treatment; i.e., the norm, without specifically mentioning developing countries, requires or allows consideration of characteristics that typically vary according to the economic developmental situation in a country. The third general form of norm is what I call "absolute" norms, i.e., norms that provide a common standard for all countries and that do not require or allow contextual treatment. These three types of norms have different advantages and disadvantages, and thus are appropriately used in different situations. . . .

> Although absolute norms predominate, the contemporary international legal system is replete with differential and contextual norms. Instances of each type occur in the evolving and interconnected areas of economic development, human rights, and environmental protection/resource management law. Indeed, there arguably is an existing, general customary obligation, stemming primarily from State practice in those three areas, to take the effect on sustainable development in developing countries into account—in order to foster, or at least avoid unduly interfering with, such development and in order to ensure that norms are not impossible to comply with—when fashioning international environmental norms. Similarly, it is arguable that developed countries have a customary law duty to assist developing countries meet international environmental norms relating to progressive realization of international human rights.

> The most important customary international environmental principles already contain a contextual element, although this is not always expressed. Customary environmental law does not contain any examples of differential treatment, with the possible exceptions of the principles discussed in the immediately preceding paragraph.

2.   *What type to use?* Under what circumstances are various forms of norms most useful in promoting compliance? What are the advantages and disadvantages of using different types of norms? Is it possible to apply a contextual or differential norm in a principled manner? Do any difficulties in that regard affect the likelihood of compliance with norms by developing countries? By developed countries?

3.   *Existing practice.* In analyzing the international environmental norms identified in this book, consider into which of the above categories they may fall. Further consider whether, in the case of developing counties,

differential or contextual treatment is warranted. Also consider what
approach is supported by Principle 7 on common but differentiated
responsibilities (CBDR; discussed in Chapter 4) of the 1992 Rio Declaration
on Environment and Development, which reads as follows:

> States shall cooperate in a spirit of global partnership to conserve,
> protect and restore the health and integrity of the Earth's
> ecosystem. In view of the different contributions to global
> environmental degradation, States have common but differentiated
> responsibilities. The developed countries acknowledge the
> responsibility that they bear in the international pursuit to
> sustainable development in view of the pressures their societies
> place on the global environment and of the technologies and
> financial resources they command.

INDEX

References are to Pages